The Sporting News
PRO FOOTBALL GUIDE

2000 EDITION

Editor/Pro Football Guide
CRAIG CARTER

Editorial Director, Books
Steve Meyerhoff

Contributors
Dave Sloan, Christen Sager, Terry Shea

CONTENTS

2000 Season..3
  National Football League directory 4
  Individual teams section
    (directories, results, schedules, rosters,
    historical data)..5
  Arizona Cardinals 5
  Atlanta Falcons..8
  Baltimore Ravens..11
  Buffalo Bills...14
  Carolina Panthers.......................................17
  Chicago Bears..20
  Cincinnati Bengals 23
  Cleveland Browns 26
  Dallas Cowboys 29
  Denver Broncos 32
  Detroit Lions..35
  Green Bay Packers.....................................38
  Indianapolis Colts 41
  Jacksonville Jaguars...................................44
  Kansas City Chiefs 47
  Miami Dolphins..50
  Minnesota Vikings......................................53
  New England Patriots.................................56
  New Orleans Saints....................................59
  New York Giants 62
  New York Jets..65
  Oakland Raiders...68
  Philadelphia Eagles 71
  Pittsburgh Steelers 74
  St. Louis Rams 77
  San Diego Chargers 80
  San Francisco 49ers 83
  Seattle Seahawks.......................................86
  Tampa Bay Buccaneers 89
  Tennessee Titans.......................................92
  Washington Redskins 95
  NFL schedule, week by week 98
  NFL college draft......................................103
  Playoff plan..107

1999 Review..**109**
  The top stories of the past year 110
  Final NFL standings 116
  Week-by-week review 117
    Regular season 117
    Wild-card playoff games 219
    Divisional playoff games 223
    Conference championship games.........227
    Super Bowl 34 229
    Pro Bowl 230
  Player participation 232
  Attendance 241
  Trades 243
1999 Statistics **245**
  Rushing 246
  Passing 250
  Receiving 254
  Scoring 258
  Interceptions 263
  Sacks 266
  Fumbles 270
  Field goals...276
  Punting 278
  Punt returns..280
  Kickoff returns 282
  Miscellaneous 285
History **299**
  Championship games 300
  Year-by-year standings 303
  Super Bowls..327
  Pro Bowls 329
  Records 331
  Statistical leaders....................................344
  Coaching records 352
  Hall of Fame..353
  The Sporting News awards 357
  Team by team 359

ON THE COVER: St. Louis Rams quarterback Kurt Warner. (Action photo by Bob Leverone/THE SPORTING NEWS, portrait by Albert Dickson/THE SPORTING NEWS.) Spine photo of Warren Sapp by Albert Dickson/THE SPORTING NEWS.

NFL week-by-week and postseason highlights written by Stacy Clardie, Evan A. Denbaum, Todd Fitzpatrick and Dave Sloan of THE SPORTING NEWS.

NFL statistics compiled by STATS, Inc., Lincolnwood, Ill.

Copyright © 2000 by The Sporting News, a division of Vulcan Print Media; 10176 Corporate Square Dr., Suite 200, St. Louis, MO 63132. All rights reserved. Printed in the U.S.A.

No part of the Pro Football Guide may be reproduced or transmitted in any form or by any means, electronic or mechanical, including photocopy, recording or any information storage and retrieval system now known or to be invented, without permission in writing from the publisher, except by a reviewer who wishes to quote brief passages in connection with a review written for inclusion in a magazine, newspaper or broadcast.

ISBN: 0-89204-635-X
                                                  10 9 8 7 6 5 4 3 2 1

2000 SEASON

NFL directory
Team information
Schedule
College draft
Expansion draft
Playoff plan

NFL DIRECTORY

2000 SEASON NFL directory

COMMISSIONER'S OFFICE

Address
280 Park Avenue
New York, NY 10017
Phone
212-450-2000
212-681-7573 (FAX)
Commissioner
Paul Tagliabue
Exec. v.p. for labor rel./chairman NFLMC
Harold Henderson
Executive v.p. & league counsel
Jeff Pash
Executive v.p. for business, properties and club services
Roger Goodell
Executive v.p. for new media/Internet and enterprises
Tom Spock
Sr. v.p. of comm. and gov't affairs
Joe Browne
Senior v.p. of broadcasting & network television
Dennis Lewin

Sr. v.p. of football operations
George Young
Vice president of public relations
Greg Aiello
Director of international public affairs
Pete Abitante
Director of media services
Leslie Hammond
Director of corporate communications
Chris Widmaier
Director of broadcasting services
Dick Maxwell
Senior director of security
Milt Ahlerich
Senior director of officiating
Jerry Seeman
Director of strategic development
Neil Glat
Director of game operations
Peter Hadhazy
Director of football development
Gene Washington

Vice president of special events
Jim Steeg
Director of special events operations
Don Renzulli
Director of special events planning
Sue Robichek
V.p.-law/enterprises, broadcast & finance
Frank Hawkins
Treasurer
Joe Siclare
Vice president-internal audit
Tom Sullivan
Controller
Peter Lops
V.p. of systems & info. processing
Mary Oliveti
Senior director of human resources & administration
John Buzzeo

OTHER ORGANIZATIONS

NFL MANAGEMENT COUNCIL

Address
280 Park Avenue
New York, NY 10017
Phone
212-450-2000
212-681-7590 (FAX)
Exec. v.p. for labor rel./chairman NFLMC
Harold Henderson
Sr. vice president and general counsel
Dennis Curran
Sr. vice president/labor relations
Peter Ruocco
V.p. of player & employee development
Lem Burnham
Sr. director of player personnel
Joel Bussert
Director of compliance
Mike Keenan
Director of player programs
Guy Troupe

PRO FOOTBALL WRITERS OF AMERICA

President
John Clayton, ESPN Magazine
First vice president
Adam Schefter, Denver Post
Second vice president
John McClain, Houston Chronicle
Secretary/treasurer
Howard Balzer

NFL FILMS, INC.

Address
330 Fellowship Road
Mt. Laurel, NJ 08054
Phone
856-778-1600
856-722-6779 (FAX)
President
Steve Sabol

PRO FOOTBALL HALL OF FAME

Address
2121 George Halas Drive, N.W.
Canton, OH 44708
Phone
330-456-8207
330-456-8175 (FAX)
Executive director
John W. Bankert
V.p./communications & exhibits
Joe Horrigan
V.p./operations and marketing
Dave Motts
V.p./merchandising & licensing
Judy Kuntz

NFL PLAYERS ASSOCIATION

Address
2021 L Street, N.W.
Washington, DC 20036
Phone
202-463-2200
202-835-9775 (FAX)
Executive director
Gene Upshaw
Assistant executive director
Doug Allen
Dir. P.R. and NFLPA retired players org.
Frank Woschitz
General counsel
Richard Berthelsen
Director of communications
Carl Francis
Director of player development
Stacey Robinson
Director of research department
Michael Duberstein
Asst. director of research department
Mark Levin
Manager/agent/coordinator
Athelia Doggette

NFL PROPERTIES

Address
280 Park Avenue
New York, NY 10017
Phone
212-450-2000
212-758-4239 (FAX)
V.p., development/special events
David Newman
V.p., corporate sponsorship
Jim Schwebel
V.p., marketing
Howard Handler
V.p., club marketing
Mark Holtzman
V.p., legal and business affairs
Gary Gertzog

NFL ALUMNI ASSOCIATION

Address
6550 N. Federal Highway
Suite 400
Ft. Lauderdale, FL 33308-1417
Phone
954-492-1220
954-492-8297 (FAX)
Executive director/CEO
Frank Krauser
Chairman of the board
Randy Minniear
Vice president/alumni relations
Martin Lerch
Director of communications
Remy Mackowski
Manager of player appearances
Amy Glanzman

– 4 –

ARIZONA CARDINALS
NFC EASTERN DIVISION

2000 SEASON

CLUB DIRECTORY

President
William V. Bidwill
Vice chairman
Thomas J. Guilfoil
Vice president
William V. Bidwill Jr.
Vice president and general counsel
Michael J. Bidwill
Vice president
Larry Wilson
Treasurer and chief financial officer
Charley Schlegel
Vice president/sales and marketing
Ron Minegar
General manager
Bob Ferguson
Assistant to the president
Rod Graves
Pro personnel assistant
Rod Newhouse
Player personnel administrator
Jay Nienkark
Senior scout
Bo Bolinger
National scouting coordinator
Jerry Hardaway
Scouts
Jim Carmody
Bob Mazie
Jim Stanley
Head trainer
John Omohundro
Assistant trainers
Jim Shearer
Jeff Herndon
Team physician (orthopedist)
Dr. Russell Chick
Team physician (internist)
Dr. Wayne Kuhl
Equipment manager
Mark Ahlemeier
Assistant equipment manager
Steve Christensen
Director of marketing
Joe Castor

Head coach
Vince Tobin

Assistant coaches
Jeff Fitzgerald (quality control)
John Garrett (quarterbacks)
Joe Greene (defensive line)
Hank Kuhlmann (special teams)
Don Lawrence (tight ends)
Larry Marmie (defensive backs)
Dave McGinnis (defensive coord.)
Glenn Pires (linebackers)
Vic Rapp (receivers)
Bob Rogucki (strength & cond.)
Johnny Roland (running backs)
Marc Trestman (offensive coord.)
George Warhop (offensive line)

Business manager
Steve Walsh
Ticket manager
Steve Bomar
Director of group sales
Scott Bull
Director of public relations
Paul Jensen
Media coordinator
Greg Gladysiewski
Publications/internet coordinator
Luke Sacks
Video director
Benny Greenberg
Director of community relations
Adele Harris
Director of player programs
Anthony Edwards

SCHEDULE

Sept. 3—	at N.Y. Giants	1:00
Sept. 10—	DALLAS	8:35
Sept. 17—	Open date	
Sept. 24—	GREEN BAY	4:05
Oct. 1—	at San Francisco	4:15
Oct. 8—	CLEVELAND	4:15
Oct. 15—	PHILADELPHIA	4:15
Oct. 22—	at Dallas	1:00
Oct. 29—	NEW ORLEANS	4:05
Nov. 5—	WASHINGTON	4:05
Nov. 12—	at Minnesota	1:00
Nov. 19—	at Philadelphia	1:00
Nov. 26—	N.Y. GIANTS	8:35
Dec. 3—	at Cincinnati	1:00
Dec. 10—	at Jacksonville	1:00
Dec. 17—	BALTIMORE	4:15
Dec. 24—	at Washington	1:00

All times are Eastern.
All games Sunday unless noted.

DRAFT CHOICES

Thomas Jones, RB, Virginia (first round/seventh pick overall).
Raynoch Thompson, LB, Tennessee (2/41).
Darwin Walker, DT, Tennessee (3/71).
David Barrett, DB, Arkansas (4/102).
Mao Tosi, DT, Idaho (5/136).
Jay Tant, TE, Northwestern (5/164).
Jabari Issa, DT, Washington (6/176).
Sekou Sanyika, LB, California (7/215).

1999 REVIEW

RESULTS

Sept.12—at Philadelphia	W	25-24
Sept.19—at Miami	L	16-19
Sept.27—SAN FRANCISCO	L	10-24
Oct. 3—at Dallas	L	7-35
Oct. 10—N.Y. GIANTS	W	14-3
Oct. 17—WASHINGTON	L	10-24
Oct. 24—Open date		
Oct. 31—NEW ENGLAND	L	3-27
Nov. 7—at N.Y. Jets	L	7-12
Nov. 14—DETROIT	W	23-19
Nov. 21—DALLAS	W	13-9
Nov. 28—at N.Y. Giants	W	34-24
Dec. 5—PHILADELPHIA	W	21-17
Dec. 12—at Washington	L	3-28
Dec. 19—BUFFALO	L	21-31
Dec. 26—at Atlanta	L	14-37
Jan. 2—at Green Bay	L	24-49

RECORDS/RANKINGS

1999 regular-season record: 6-10 (4th in NFC East); 5-3 in division; 6-6 in conference; 0-4 vs. AFC; 4-4 at home; 2-6 on road; 2-3 on turf; 4-7 on grass.
Team record last five years: 30-50 (.375, ranks T26th in league in that span).

1999 team rankings:

	No.	NFC	NFL
Total offense	*250.6	14	29
Rushing offense	*75.4	14	29
Passing offense	*175.2	13	27
Scoring offense	245	15	30
Total defense	*338.9	9	22
Rushing defense	*141.6	15	30
Passing defense	*197.3	3	10
Scoring defense	382	13	27
Takeaways	27	12	T22
Giveaways	40	T14	T30
Turnover differential	-13	14	30
Sacks	33	12	26
Sacks allowed	45	11	21

*Yards per game.

TEAM LEADERS

Scoring (kicking): Chris Jacke, 83 pts. (26/26 PATs, 19/27 FGs).
Scoring (touchdowns): Mario Bates, 54 pts. (9 rushing).
Passing: Jake Plummer, 2,111 yds. (381 att., 201 comp., 52.8%, 9 TDs, 24 int.).
Rushing: Adrian Murrell, 553 yds. (193 att., 2.9 avg., 0 TDs).
Receptions: Frank Sanders, 79 (954 yds., 12.1 avg., 1 TD).
Interceptions: Kwamie Lassiter, 2 (110 yds., 1 TD); Rob Fredrickson, 2 (57 yds., 1 TD); Tom Knight, 2 (16 yds., 0 TDs); Pat Tillman, 2 (7 yds., 0 TDs); Aeneas Williams, 2 (5 yds., 0 TDs).
Sacks: Simeon Rice, 16.5.
Punting: Scott Player, 42.0 avg. (94 punts, 3,948 yds., 0 blocked).
Punt returns: Mac Cody, 11.7 avg. (32 att., 373 yds., 0 TDs).
Kickoff returns: Mario Bates, 23.7 avg. (52 att., 1,231 yds., 0 TDs).

2000 SEASON
TRAINING CAMP ROSTER

ARIZONA CARDINALS

No.	QUARTERBACKS	Ht./Wt.	Born	NFL Exp.	College	How acq.	'99 Games GP/GS
17	Brown, Dave	6-6/225	2-25-70	9	Duke	FA/98	8/5
14	Greisen, Chris	6-3/225	7-2-76	2	Northwest Missouri State	D7/99	2/0
16	Plummer, Jake	6-2/199	12-19-74	4	Arizona State	D2/97	12/11
	RUNNING BACKS						
24	Bates, Mario	6-2/237	1-16-73	7	Arizona State	UFA/98	16/2
26	Jones, Thomas	5-10/205	8-19-78	R	Virginia	D1/00	—
34	Makovicka, Joel (FB)	5-11/246	10-6-75	2	Nebraska	D4/99	16/10
39	McKinley, Dennis (FB)	6-2/245	11-3-76	2	Mississippi State	D6c/99	16/0
32	Pittman, Michael	6-0/220	8-14-75	3	Fresno State	D4/98	10/2
	RECEIVERS						
89	Boston, David	6-2/210	8-19-78	2	Ohio State	D1a/99	16/8
83	Brown, Derek (TE)	6-6/271	3-31-70	9	Notre Dame	UFA/99	15/0
82	Cody, Mac	5-11/182	8-7-72	2	Memphis	W-StL/99	13/0
80	Hardy, Terry (TE)	6-4/271	5-31-76	3	Southern Mississippi	D5/98	16/16
19	Jenkins, MarTay	5-11/193	2-28-75	2	Nebraska-Omaha	W-Dal./99	3/0
86	Junkin, Trey (TE)	6-2/245	1-23-61	18	Louisiana Tech	W-Oak./96	16/0
18	McCullough, Andy	6-3/210	11-11-75	2	Tennessee	FA/99	2/0
85	Moore, Rob	6-3/202	9-27-68	11	Syracuse	T-NYJ/95	14/10
81	Sanders, Frank	6-2/204	2-17-73	6	Auburn	D2/95	16/16
87	Tant, Jay (TE)	6-3/252	12-4-77	R	Northwestern	D5b/00	—
	OFFENSIVE LINEMEN						
79	Clark, Jon (T)	6-7/346	4-11-73	5	Temple	FA/98	2/0
65	Clement, Anthony (T)	6-8/355	4-10-76	3	Southwestern Louisiana	D2b/98	16/14
64	Davidds-Garrido, Norberto (T)	6-5/315	6-11-72	5	Southern California	UFA/00	*16/0
62	Devlin, Mike (C)	6-2/325	11-16-69	7	Iowa	FA/96	16/0
67	Dishman, Chris (G)	6-3/338	2-27-74	4	Nebraska	D4/97	13/10
60	Gruttadauria, Mike (C)	6-3/297	12-6-72	5	Central Florida	UFA/00	*16/16
71	Holmes, Lester (G)	6-5/330	9-27-69	8	Jackson State	FA/98	13/13
73	Joyce, Matt	6-7/305	3-30-72	6	Richmond	FA/96	15/15
68	Scott, Yusuf (G)	6-3/332	11-30-76	2	Arizona	D5b/99	10/0
70	Shelton, L.J. (T)	6-6/343	3-21-76	2	Eastern Michigan	D1b/99	9/7
	DEFENSIVE LINEMEN						
95	Burke, Thomas (E)	6-3/261	10-12-76	2	Wisconsin	D3/99	16/3
76	Drake, Jerry (E)	6-5/312	7-9-69	5	Hastings (Neb.) College	FA/95	16/16
72	Issa, Jabari (T)	6-5/296	4-18-78	R	Washington	D6/00	—
96	Ottis, Brad (E)	6-5/293	8-2-72	6	Wayne State (Neb.)	FA/96	14/7
97	Rice, Simeon (E)	6-5/268	2-24-74	5	Illinois	D1/96	16/16
92	Rubio, Angel (T)	6-2/298	4-12-75	2	Southwest Missouri State	W-SF/99	2/0
94	Sears, Corey (T)	6-3/300	4-15-73	3	Mississippi State	W-StL/99	9/1
93	Smith, Mark (T)	6-4/294	8-28-74	4	Auburn	D7/97	2/0
98	Swann, Eric (T)	6-5/317	8-16-70	10	Wake Technical College (N.C.)	D1/91	9/0
91	Swinger, Rashod (T)	6-3/316	11-27-74	3	Rutgers	FA/97	15/14
78	Tosi, Mao (E)	6-5/291	12-12-76	R	Idaho	D5a/00	—
90	Wadsworth, Andre (E)	6-4/275	10-19-74	3	Florida State	D1/98	11/7
75	Walker, Darwin (T)	6-1/280	6-15-77	R	Tennessee	D3/00	—
	LINEBACKERS						
56	Bradley, Melvin	6-2/271	8-15-76	1	Arkansas	D6b/99	1/0
58	Folston, James	6-3/240	8-14-71	7	Northeast Louisiana	FA/99	6/0
59	Frederickson, Rob	6-4/235	5-13-71	7	Michigan State	UFA/99	16/16
53	Maddox, Mark	6-1/238	3-23-68	10	Northern Michigan	UFA/98	16/2
57	McKinnon, Ronald	6-0/240	9-20-73	5	North Alabama	FA/96	16/16
51	Rutledge, Johnny	6-3/242	1-4-77	2	Florida	D2/99	6/0
54	Sanyika, Sekou	6-4/237	3-17-78	R	California	D7/00	—
55	Thompson, Raynoch	6-3/220	11-21-77	R	Tennessee	D2/00	—
52	Walz, Zack	6-4/219	2-13-76	3	Dartmouth	D6/98	9/9
	DEFENSIVE BACKS						
36	Barrett, David (CB)	5-10/195	12-22-77	R	Arkansas	D4/00	—
28	Bennett, Tommy (S)	6-2/212	2-19-73	5	UCLA	FA/96	15/15
25	Chavous, Corey (CB)	6-1/200	1-15-76	3	Vanderbilt	D2a/98	15/4
22	Knight, Tom (CB)	6-0/197	12-29-74	4	Iowa	D1/97	16/11
42	Lassiter, Kwamie (S)	6-0/197	12-3-69	6	Kansas	FA/95	16/16
41	Lucas, Justin	5-10/187	7-15-76	2	Abilene Christian	FA/99	2/0
44	McCleskey, J.J. (CB)	5-8/180	4-10-70	7	Tennessee	W-NO/96	16/1
23	Rhinehart, Coby (CB)	5-10/186	2-7-77	2	Southern Methodist	D6a/99	16/0
40	Tillman, Pat (S)	5-11/192	11-6-76	3	Arizona State	D7b/98	16/1
35	Williams, Aeneas (CB)	5-11/200	1-29-68	10	Southern	D3/90	16/16
	SPECIALISTS						
15	Blanchard, Cary (K)	6-1/232	11-5-68	9	Oklahoma State	UFA/00	*10/0
10	Player, Scott (P)	6-1/221	12-17-69	3	Florida State	FA/98	16/0

*Not with Cardinals in 1999.
Other free agent veterans invited to camp: OL Ethan Brooks, DL Donald Broomfield, TE Chris Gedney, S Paris Johnson, WR Tywan Mitchell, DT Mike Moten, RB Clarence Williams.

Abbreviations: D1—draft pick, first round; SD-2—supplemental draft pick, second round; W—claimed on waivers; T—obtained in trade; PlanB—Plan B free-agent acquisition; FA—free-agent acquisition (other than Plan B); UFA—unconditional free agent acquisition; ED—expansion draft pick.

MISCELLANEOUS TEAM DATA

Stadium (capacity, surface):
Sun Devil Stadium (73,243, grass)
Business address:
P.O. Box 888
Phoenix, AZ 85001-0888
Business phone:
602-379-0101
Ticket information:
602-379-0102
Team colors:
Cardinal red, black and white
Flagship radio station:
KDUS, 1060 AM
Training site:
Northern Arizona University
Flagstaff, Ariz.
520-523-1818

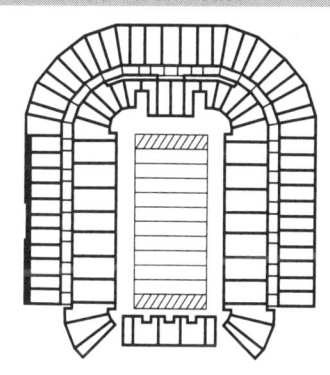

ARIZONA CARDINALS

TSN REPORT CARD

Coaching staff	B	Vince Tobin has kept the Cardinals playing hard throughout his four-year tenure and had them on the cusp of sustained success in 1998 before a litany of problems derailed the '99 season. Only a turnaround will suffice if Tobin is to live through his lame-duck contractual status and earn another deal from owner Bill Bidwill.
Quarterbacks	C+	Hip, finger and rib-cage injuries can be blamed for Jake Plummer's disastrous 1999 season. He won't be given the benefit of the doubt in his fourth NFL campaign. He needs to improve his decision-making and evolve into the play-making threat the team knows he can be—minus the myriad mistakes.
Running backs	B	The addition of Thomas Jones as an open-field threat could provide the immediate boost the team's flagging running game has needed. But Jones needs to prove it in the NFL. A return to health by hard-charging Michael Pittman would mean a formidable 1-2 punch. Mario Bates is solid as the team's goal-line back. The fullbacks need to play better.
Receivers	A-	Rob Moore, Frank Sanders and David Boston have the ability to produce big numbers but dropped too many balls last season. Boston needs to—and should be—more involved this season and provide the team the deep threat it envisioned when it drafted him No. 8 overall in 1999. Moore will benefit from a full training camp after a lengthy holdout in '99.
Offensive line	C-	The improvement of the entire offense hinges in large part on this group. Young tackles L.J. Shelton and Anthony Clement are talented but inexperienced and must continue to improve on the job. Rams signee Mike Gruttadauria should upgrade the center position. Neither Matt Joyce nor Lester Holmes have been overpowering at guard.
Defensive line	C	The Cardinals could have one of the best front fours in the NFL if everything fell right. But Simeon Rice and Mark Smith have been unhappy with their contracts and might be long-term holdouts. Eric Swann's knees haven't held up in two years. If none of these players are around for the opener—a definite possibility—Arizona will be in trouble up front.
Linebackers	C	The Cardinals have upgraded the athleticism and speed at the position the last two years but are still smallish overall. It's a big year for second-year pro Johnny Rutledge, who will battle rookie Raynoch Thompson and Zack Walz, recovering from an ACL tear last November, for the starting left-side position.
Secondary	B	The group overall is solid. Aeneas Williams is the rock that holds the corps of defensive backs together. Tom Knight at times last year seemed to finally put his injury history behind him and play to the potential that made him a first-round pick in 1997. He needs to put it all together for a season. The pressure's on Pat Tillman, who'll replace injured Tommy Bennett at strong safety.
Special teams	A-	Cary Blanchard should give Arizona a weapon outside 40 yards it lacked with Chris Jacke. Bates nearly broke several kickoff returns and has seemed to improve with experience.

ATLANTA FALCONS
NFC WESTERN DIVISION

2000 SEASON

CLUB DIRECTORY

President
Taylor Smith
Special assistant to president
Jerry Rhea
Executive v.p. of administration
Jim Hay
General manager
Harold Richardson
Vice president of football operations
Ron Hill
Vice president and chief financial officer
Kevin Anthony
Administrative assistant
John O. Knox
Vice president of marketing
Rob Jackson
Vice president of corporate development
Tommy Nobis
Marketing/sales assistants
Mark Fuhrman   Spencer Treadwell
Director of public relations
Aaron Salkin
Assistant director of public relations
Frank Kleha
Director of community relations
Carol Breeding
Coordinator of player programs
Billy "White Shoes" Johnson
Director of ticket operations
Jack Ragsdale
Controller
Wallace Norman
Accounting
Carolyn Cathey
Dir. of player personnel/college scouting
Reed Johnson
Admin. assistant/college scouting
LaDonna Jones
National scout
Mike Hagen
Scouts
Ken Blair   Melvin Bratton
Dick Corrick   Boyd Dowler
Elbert Dubenion   Bill Groman
Bob Harrison
Director of pro personnel
Chuck Connor
Pro personnel assistant
Les Sneed

Head coach/executive v.p. for football operations
Dan Reeves

Assistant coaches
Marvin Bass (asst. to head coach/player personnel)
Don Blackmon (linebackers)
Rich Brooks (assistant head coach/defensive coordinator)
Greg Brown (secondary)
Jack Burns (wide receivers)
Rocky Colburn (assistant strength & conditioning)
James Daniel (asst. offensive line)
Joe DeCamillis (special teams)
Thom Kaumeyer (def. quality control)
Bill Kollar (defensive line)
Al Miller (strength & conditioning)
Jerry Rhome (quarterbacks)
George Sefcik (off. coord./RBs)
Art Shell (offensive line)
Rennie Simmons (tight ends)
Ed West (off. quality control)

Admin. assistant/football operations
Kim Mauldin
Head trainer
Ron Medlin
Trainers
Harold King   Tom Reed
Equipment manager
Brian Boigner
Sr. equip. dir./gameday op. coord.
Horace Daniel
Video director
Tom Atcheson

SCHEDULE

Date	Opponent	Time
Sept. 3—	SAN FRANCISCO	1:00
Sept. 10—	at Denver	4:15
Sept. 17—	at Carolina	1:00
Sept. 24—	ST. LOUIS	1:00
Oct. 1—	at Philadelphia	8:35
Oct. 8—	N.Y. GIANTS	4:05
Oct. 15—	at St. Louis	1:00
Oct. 22—	NEW ORLEANS	1:00
Oct. 29—	CAROLINA	1:00
Nov. 5—	TAMPA BAY	1:00
Nov. 12—	at Detroit	1:00
Nov. 19—	at San Francisco	4:15
Nov. 26—	at Oakland	4:05
Dec. 3—	SEATTLE	1:00
Dec. 10—	Open date	
Dec. 17—	at New Orleans	1:00
Dec. 24—	KANSAS CITY	1:00

All times are Eastern.
All games Sunday unless noted.

DRAFT CHOICES

Travis Claridge, T, Southern California (second round/37th pick overall).
Mark Simoneau, LB, Kansas State (3/67).
Michael Thompson, T, Tennessee State (4/100).
Anthony Midget, DB, Virginia Tech (5/134).
Mareno Philyaw, WR, Troy State (6/172).
Darrick Vaughn, DB, Southwest Texas State (7/211).

1999 REVIEW

RESULTS

Sept.12—	MINNESOTA	L 14-17
Sept.20—	at Dallas	L 7-24
Sept.26—	at St. Louis	L 7-35
Oct. 3—	BALTIMORE (OT)	L 13-19
Oct. 10—	at New Orleans	W 20-17
Oct. 17—	ST. LOUIS	L 13-41
Oct. 25—	at Pittsburgh	L 9-13
Oct. 31—	CAROLINA	W 27-20
Nov. 7—	JACKSONVILLE	L 7-30
Nov. 14—	Open date	
Nov. 21—	at Tampa Bay	L 10-19
Nov. 28—	at Carolina	L 28-34
Dec. 5—	NEW ORLEANS	W 35-12
Dec. 12—	at San Francisco	L 7-26
Dec. 19—	at Tennessee	L 17-30
Dec. 26—	ARIZONA	W 37-14
Jan. 3—	SAN FRANCISCO	W 34-29

RECORDS/RANKINGS

1999 regular-season record: 5-11 (3rd in NFC West); 4-4 in division; 5-7 in conference; 0-4 vs. AFC; 4-4 at home; 1-7 on road; 5-7 on turf; 0-4 on grass.
Team record last five years: 38-42 (.475, ranks T16th in league in that span).

1999 team rankings:

	No.	NFC	NFL
Total offense	*283.9	12	27
Rushing offense	*74.8	15	30
Passing offense	*209.1	9	17
Scoring offense	285	10	23
Total defense	*326.4	5	16
Rushing defense	*129.5	14	29
Passing defense	*196.9	2	9
Scoring defense	380	11	25
Takeaways	18	15	31
Giveaways	35	T8	T23
Turnover differential	-17	15	31
Sacks	40	T6	T14
Sacks allowed	49	T12	T23

*Yards per game.

TEAM LEADERS

Scoring (kicking): Morten Andersen, 79 pts. (34/34 PATs, 15/21 FGs).
Scoring (touchdowns): Tim Dwight, 54 pts. (1 rushing, 7 receiving, 1 punt return).
Passing: Chris Chandler, 2,339 yds. (307 att., 174 comp., 56.7%, 16 TDs, 11 int.).
Rushing: Ken Oxendine, 452 yds. (141 att., 3.2 avg., 1 TD).
Receptions: Terance Mathis, 81 (1,016 yds., 12.5 avg., 6 TDs).
Interceptions: Ray Buchanan, 4 (81 yds., 1 TD).
Sacks: Chuck Smith, 10.0.
Punting: Dan Stryzinski, 39.5 avg. (80 punts, 3,163 yds., 0 blocked).
Punt returns: Tim Dwight, 11.0 avg. (20 att., 220 yds., 1 TD).
Kickoff returns: Tim Dwight, 21.5 avg. (44 att., 944 yds., 0 TDs).

2000 SEASON
TRAINING CAMP ROSTER

No.	QUARTERBACKS	Ht./Wt.	Born	NFL Exp.	College	How acq.	'99 Games GP/GS
12	Chandler, Chris	6-4/226	10-12-65	13	Washington	T/97	12/12
7	Graziani, Tony	6-2/215	12-23-73	4	Oregon	D7/97	11/3
13	Kanell, Danny	6-3/218	11-21-73	5	Florida State	FA/99	3/1
	RUNNING BACKS						
32	Anderson, Jamal	5-11/235	9-30-72	7	Utah	D7/94	2/2
44	Christian, Bob (FB)	5-11/232	11-14-68	9	Northwestern	FA/97	16/14
24	Hanspard, Byron	5-10/200	1-23-76	4	Texas Tech	D2b/97	12/4
26	Oliver, Winslow	5-7/200	3-3-73	5	New Mexico	FA/99	14/0
28	Oxendine, Ken	6-0/230	10-4-75	3	Virginia Tech	D7b/98	12/9
40	Paulk, Jeff (FB)	6-0/240	4-26-76	2	Arizona State	D3/99	1/0
	RECEIVERS						
15	Baker, Eugene	6-0/177	3-18-76	2	Kent	D5/99	3/1
83	Dwight, Tim	5-8/180	7-13-75	3	Iowa	D4b/98	12/8
86	Finneran, Brian	6-5/208	1-31-76	1	Villanova	FA/00	*3/0
87	German, Jammi	6-1/192	7-4-74	3	Miami (Fla.)	D3/98	14/0
82	Harris, Ronnie	5-11/180	6-4-70	7	Oregon	FA/98	13/0
84	Jefferson, Shawn	5-11/180	2-22-69	10	Central Florida	UFA/00	*16/16
89	Kelly, Reggie (TE)	6-3/255	2-22-77	2	Mississippi State	D2/99	16/2
85	Kozlowski, Brian (TE)	6-3/250	10-4-70	7	Connecticut	FA/97	16/3
16	Loud, Kamil	6-0/190	6-25-76	3	Cal Poly-SLO	W-Buf./00	*7/0
81	Mathis, Terance	5-10/185	6-7-67	11	New Mexico	UFA/94	16/16
49	Monroe, Rod (TE)	6-4/245	7-30-75	2	Cincinnati	FA/98	2/0
19	Philyaw, Mareno	6-2/208	12-19-77	R	Troy State	D6/00	—
88	Santiago, O.J. (TE)	6-7/265	4-4-74	4	Kent	D3/97	14/14
	OFFENSIVE LINEMEN						
71	Claridge, Travis (T)	6-5/308	3-23-78	R	Southern California	D2/00	—
68	Collins, Calvin (G)	6-2/310	1-5-74	4	Texas A&M	D6/97	14/8
64	Hallen, Bob (C)	6-4/292	3-9-75	3	Kent	D2/98	16/14
63	Pilgrim, Evan (G)	6-4/305	8-14-72	6	Brigham Young	FA/99	3/1
76	Portilla, Jose (T)	6-6/315	9-11-72	3	Arizona	FA/98	4/0
61	Redmon, Anthony (G)	6-5/308	4-9-71	7	Auburn	FA/00	*15/15
74	Salaam, Ephraim (T)	6-7/305	6-19-76	3	San Diego State	D7a/98	16/16
66	Thompson, Michael (T)	6-4/318	2-11-77	R	Tennessee State	D4/00	—
70	Whitfield, Bob (T)	6-5/318	10-18-71	9	Stanford	D1a/92	16/16
	DEFENSIVE LINEMEN						
75	Dronett, Shane (E)	6-6/300	1-12-71	9	Texas	FA/97	16/16
98	Hall, Travis (T)	6-5/297	8-3-72	6	Brigham Young	D6/95	16/15
95	Jasper, Ed (T)	6-2/295	1-18-73	4	Texas A&M	FA/99	13/0
97	Kerney, Patrick (E)	6-5/272	12-30-76	2	Virginia	D1/99	16/2
77	McDaniels, Pellom (E)	6-3/280	2-21-68	8	Oregon State	UFA/99	16/0
91	Smith, Brady (E)	6-5/270	6-5-73	5	Colorado State	UFA/00	*16/16
93	Swayda, Shawn (E)	6-5/294	9-4-74	3	Arizona State	FA/98	4/0
	LINEBACKERS						
56	Brooking, Keith	6-2/245	10-30-75	3	Georgia Tech	D1/98	13/13
52	Buckley, Marcus	6-3/240	2-3-71	8	Texas A&M	FA/00	*12/0
94	Crockett, Henri	6-2/238	10-28-74	4	Florida State	D4/97	16/14
54	Draft, Chris	5-11/230	2-26-76	2	Stanford	W-SF/00	*7/0
51	Kelly, Jeff	5-11/245	12-13-75	2	Kansas State	D6a/99	16/1
55	Marshall, Whit	6-2/242	1-6-73	2	Georgia	FA/99	15/0
53	Simoneau, Mark	6-0/233	1-16-77	R	Kansas State	D3/00	—
58	Tuggle, Jessie	5-11/232	4-4-65	14	Valdosta (Ga.) State	FA/87	14/14
	DEFENSIVE BACKS						
33	Ambrose, Ashley (CB)	5-10/185	9-17-70	9	Mississippi Valley State	UFA/00	*16/16
20	Booker, Michael (CB)	6-2/200	4-27-75	4	Nebraska	D1/97	13/1
23	Bradford, Ronnie (CB)	5-10/198	10-1-70	8	Colorado	UFA/97	16/16
27	Brown, Omar (S)	5-10/200	3-28-75	3	North Carolina	D4a/98	13/0
34	Buchanan, Ray (CB)	5-9/186	9-29-71	8	Louisville	UFA/97	16/16
25	Carter, Marty (S)	6-1/210	12-17-69	10	Middle Tennessee State	UFA/99	11/11
35	Carty, Johndale (S)	6-0/202	8-27-77	2	Utah State	D4/99	14/0
30	Gardner, Derrick (CB)	6-0/185	3-10-77	2	California	FA/99	7/0
22	McBurrows, Gerald (S)	5-11/210	10-7-73	6	Kansas	UFA/99	16/4
39	Midget, Anthony (CB)	5-11/193	2-22-78	R	Virginia Tech	D5/00	—
37	Vaughn, Darrick (CB)	5-11/190	10-2-78	R	Southwest Texas State	D7/00	—
21	Williams, Elijah (CB)	5-10/180	8-20-75	3	Florida	D6/98	15/2
	SPECIALISTS						
5	Andersen, Morten (K)	6-2/225	8-19-60	19	Michigan State	FA/95	16/0
4	Stryzinski, Dan (P)	6-2/205	5-15-65	11	Indiana	UFA/95	16/0

*Not with Falcons in 1999.
Other free agent veterans invited to camp: G Alex Bernstein, S Kerry Cooks, CB Reginald Doster, RB Gary Downs, DE Emil Ekiyor, DT Ben Huff, C Todd McClure, OT Ozell Powell, QB Wally Richardson, DE Sam Simmons, LB Brian Smith.

Abbreviations: D1—draft pick, first round; SD-2—supplemental draft pick, second round; W—claimed on waivers; T—obtained in trade; PlanB—Plan B free-agent acquisition; FA—free-agent acquisition (other than Plan B); UFA—unconditional free agent acquisition; ED—expansion draft pick.

ATLANTA FALCONS

MISCELLANEOUS TEAM DATA

Stadium (capacity, surface):
Georgia Dome
(71,228, artificial)

Business address:
4400 Falcon Parkway
Flowery Branch, GA 30542

Business phone:
770-945-1111; 770-965-3115 after mid-August 2000

Ticket information:
404-223-8444

Team colors:
Black, red, silver and white

Flagship radio station:
WGST, 920 AM

Training site:
4400 Falcon Parkway
Flowery Branch, GA 30542
770-945-1111; 770-965-3115 after mid-August 2000

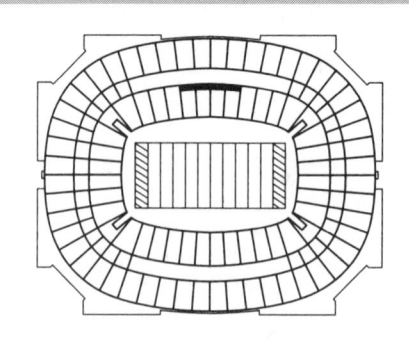

TSN REPORT CARD

Coaching staff	B -	On offense, there is good experience but a confusing hierarchy; there's no true coordinator, and as of early summer Dan Reeves had not decided who would take play-calling responsibility. One possibility is new quarterbacks coach Jerry Rhome. Defensive coordinator Rich Brooks and line coach Bill Kollar headline a strong defensive staff that has provided much-needed stability.
Quarterbacks	C +	There was much local sentiment for Reeves to draft Georgia Tech's Joe Hamilton in the seventh round. Instead, Reeves went with cornerback Darrick Vaughn and signed undrafted free agent quarterback Doug Johnson of Florida. Injuries and all, Chris Chandler ranks as one of the best bargains (two late draft picks) in team history. Reeves and Rhome are gambling that Danny Kanell will be a stronger backup than last year.
Running backs	B -	Reeves may make a late free-agent pickup here after other teams make salary cuts. Otherwise, depending on so many players returning from knee injuries is a huge gamble. Fullback Bob Christian is underrated—outside of the coaching staff. If he can return to his 1998 form, Jamal Anderson is one of the top three backs in the game. Byron Hanspard is the wild card of the group. Overall, there are too many ifs.
Receivers	B -	Chandler can bring out the best in a receiver with separation speed, and assuming Shawn Jefferson still has that kind of speed, he will be a key addition. If not, Tim Dwight will have to play a larger role. Terance Mathis is probably the most underrated player on the team. Rookie Mareno Philyaw has a size-speed combination worth watching for the future.
Offensive line	D +	Perhaps the biggest unknown on the team entering training camp is how this unit will shake out. At least one of the two rookies—probably Travis Claridge—has to make an immediate impact. Calvin Collins needs to re-adjust to center and Ephraim Salaam needs to show he won't relinquish the right tackle spot he has held for two years.
Defensive line	B	The ends are very young and fairly small, but Brady Smith stepped up with six sacks for New Orleans last year and Patrick Kerney showed glimpses of big-play ability last year. Pellom McDaniels is the only experienced backup behind the starting ends. Tackles Travis Hall and Shane Dronett should be in their most productive years.
Linebackers	B -	Losing top backup Craig Sauer hurts, but rookie Mark Simoneau and free agent Marcus Buckley will help fill the void. On the plus side all three starters return. Strongside linebacker Henri Crockett has shed a few pounds to help a sore knee as he enters his contract year. Jessie Tuggle is an ideal role model for such young players as Simoneau and Jeff Kelly, and at 35 he's still a punishing tackler. Keith Brooking could emerge with a big year.
Secondary	A	This should be the most improved area on the team. The Falcons tried to sign Ashley Ambrose last year and finally were successful this year, giving Atlanta its best combination at cornerback in at least 10 years. Free safety Marty Carter fulfilled expecations as a tackling force. A key will be Ronnie Bradford's transition from cornerback to free safety, where he will replace Eugene Robinson.
Special teams	B	For at least one more year, the Falcons can rest easy with kicker Morten Andersen and punter Dan Stryzinski. Both could be unrestricted free agents after 2000. Dwight's returns bring Falcons fans out of their seats and cause Falcons coaches to hold their breath out of concern for the 5-foot-8 dynamo's safety.

BALTIMORE RAVENS
AFC CENTRAL DIVISION

2000 SEASON

CLUB DIRECTORY

Owner/chief executive officer
Arthur B. Modell
President/chief operating officer
David O. Modell
Vice president of player personnel
Ozzie Newsome
Vice president/public relations
Kevin Byrne
Vice president of administration
Pat Moriarty
Vice president/chief financial officer
Luis Perez
V.p./business dev. and marketing
Dennis Mannion
Sr. dir./corp. & broadcast partnerships
Mark Burdett
Dir. of broadcasting & video production
Larry Rosen
Director of operations and information
Bob Eller
Director of publications
Francine Lubera
Director of ticket operations
Roy Sommerhof
Director of pro personnel
James Harris
Director of college scouting
Phil Savage
Scouting/pro personnel
Eric DeCosta
George Kokinis
Ron Marciniak
Terry McDonough
T.J. McCreight
Ellis Rainsberger
Art Perkins
Facilities manager
Chuck Cusick
Head trainer
Bill Tessendorf

Head coach
Brian Billick

Assistant coaches
Matt Cavanaugh (offensive coordinator)
Jim Colletto (offensive line)
Jack Del Rio (linebackers)
Jeff Friday (strength & conditioning)
Wade Harman (tight ends)
Donn Henderson (def. backs)
Milt Jackson (receivers)
Marvin Lewis (defensive coordinator)
Chip Morton (assistant strength & conditioning)
Russ Purnell (special teams)
Rex Ryan (defensive line)
Steve Shafer (defensive backs)
Matt Simon (running backs)
Mike Smith (defensive asst.)

Assistant trainer
Mark Smith
Team physicians
Dr. Andrew M. Tucker
Dr. Claude T. Moorman III
Dr. Andrew Pollak
Dr. Leigh Ann Curl
Equipment manager
Ed Carroll

SCHEDULE

Sept. 3—	at Pittsburgh	1:00
Sept. 10—	JACKSONVILLE	1:00
Sept. 17—	at Miami	8:35
Sept. 24—	CINCINNATI	1:00
Oct. 1—	at Cleveland	1:00
Oct. 8—	at Jacksonville	8:35
Oct. 15—	at Washington	1:00
Oct. 22—	TENNESSEE	1:00
Oct. 29—	PITTSBURGH	1:00
Nov. 5—	at Cincinnati	1:00
Nov. 12—	at Tennessee	1:00
Nov. 19—	DALLAS	4:15
Nov. 26—	CLEVELAND	1:00
Dec. 3—	Open date	
Dec. 10—	SAN DIEGO	1:00
Dec. 17—	at Arizona	4:15
Dec. 24—	N.Y. JETS	1:00

All times are Eastern.
All games Sunday unless noted.

DRAFT CHOICES

Jamal Lewis, RB, Tennessee (first round/fifth pick overall).
Travis Taylor, WR, Florida (1/10).
Chris Redman, QB, Louisville (3/75).
Richard Mercier, G, Miami, Fla. (5/148).
Adalius Thomas, DE, Southern Mississippi (6/186).
Cedric Woodard, DT, Texas (6/191).

1999 REVIEW

RESULTS

Sept.12—at St. Louis	L	10-27
Sept.19—PITTSBURGH	L	20-23
Sept.26—CLEVELAND	W	17-10
Oct. 3—at Atlanta (OT)	W	19-13
Oct. 10—at Tennessee	L	11-14
Oct. 17—Open date		
Oct. 21—KANSAS CITY	L	8-35
Oct. 31—BUFFALO	L	10-13
Nov. 7—at Cleveland	W	41-9
Nov. 14—at Jacksonville	L	3-6
Nov. 21—at Cincinnati	W	34-31
Nov. 28—JACKSONVILLE	L	23-30
Dec. 5—TENNESSEE	W	41-14
Dec. 12—at Pittsburgh	W	31-24
Dec. 19—NEW ORLEANS	W	31-8
Dec. 26—CINCINNATI	W	22-0
Jan. 2—at New England	L	3-20

RECORDS/RANKINGS

1999 regular-season record: 8-8 (3rd in AFC Central); 6-4 in division; 6-7 in conference; 2-1 vs. NFC; 4-4 at home; 4-4 on road; 3-1 on turf; 5-7 on grass.
Team record last five years: 29-50-1 (.369, ranks 28th in league in that span).

1999 team rankings:

	No.	AFC	NFL
Total offense	*298.6	13	24
Rushing offense	*109.6	10	16
Passing offense	*189.0	13	25
Scoring offense	324	8	14
Total defense	*263.9	2	2
Rushing defense	*76.9	1	2
Passing defense	*186.9	5	6
Scoring defense	277	3	6
Takeaways	31	T6	T14
Giveaways	31	T10	T13
Turnover differential	0	8	14
Sacks	49	4	6
Sacks allowed	56	T14	T28

*Yards per game.

TEAM LEADERS

Scoring (kicking): Matt Stover, 116 pts. (32/32 PATs, 28/33 FGs).
Scoring (touchdowns): Errict Rhett, 42 pts. (5 rushing, 2 receiving).
Passing: Tony Banks, 2,136 yds. (320 att., 169 comp., 52.8%, 17 TDs, 8 int.).
Rushing: Errict Rhett, 852 yds. (236 att., 3.6 avg., 5 TDs).
Receptions: Qadry Ismail, 68 (1,105 yds., 16.3 avg., 6 TDs).
Interceptions: Rod Woodson, 7 (195 yds., 2 TDs).
Sacks: Michael McCrary, 11.5.
Punting: Kyle Richardson, 42.3 avg. (103 punts, 4,355 yds., 1 blocked).
Punt returns: Jermaine Lewis, 7.9 avg. (57 att., 452 yds., 0 TDs).
Kickoff returns: Corey Harris, 22.2 avg. (38 att., 843 yds., 0 TDs).

2000 SEASON
TRAINING CAMP ROSTER

No.	QUARTERBACKS	Ht./Wt.	Born	NFL Exp.	College	How acq.	'99 Games GP/GS
12	Banks, Tony	6-4/225	4-5-73	5	Michigan State	T-StL/99	12/10
8	Dilfer, Trent	6-4/229	3-13-72	7	Fresno State	UFA/00	*10/10
7	Redman, Chris	6-3/223	7-7-77	R	Louisville	D3/00	—
	RUNNING BACKS						
30	Ayanbadejo, Obafemi (FB)	6-2/235	3-5-75	3	San Diego State	FA/99	14/0
29	Evans, Chuck (FB)	6-1/245	4-16-67	8	Clark Atlanta (Ga.)	UFA/99	16/10
34	Graham, Jay	5-11/215	7-14-75	4	Tennessee	D3/97	4/0
33	Holmes, Priest	5-9/205	10-7-73	4	Texas	FA/97	9/4
31	Lewis, Jamal	5-11/231	8-28-79	R	Tennessee	D1a/00	—
	RECEIVERS						
49	Collins, Ryan (TE)	6-6/259	11-1-75	2	St. Thomas (Minneapolis)	FA/99	4/3
86	Davis, Billy	6-1/205	7-6-72	6	Pittsburgh	FA/99	16/0
85	DeLong, Greg (TE)	6-4/255	4-3-73	6	North Carolina	UFA/99	16/7
87	Ismail, Qadry	6-0/200	11-8-70	8	Syracuse	FA/99	16/16
83	Johnson, Patrick	5-10/180	8-10-76	3	Oregon	D2/98	10/6
84	Lewis, Jermaine	5-7/175	10-16-74	5	Maryland	D5/96	15/6
11	Nash, Marcus	6-3/195	2-1-76	3	Tennessee	FA/99	3/1
2	Sharpe, Shannon (TE)	6-2/230	6-26-68	11	Savannah (Ga.) State	UFA/00	*5/5
80	Stokley, Brandon	5-11/197	6-23-76	2	Southwestern Louisiana	D4a/99	2/0
89	Taylor, Travis	6-1/200	3-30-78	R	Florida	D1b/00	—
82	Wainright, Frank (TE)	6-3/255	10-10-67	10	Northern Colorado	UFA/99	16/0
	OFFENSIVE LINEMEN						
76	Bobo, Orlando (G)	6-3/300	2-9-74	4	Northeast Louisiana	FA/00	*9/1
61	Denson, Damon (G)	6-4/310	2-8-75	4	Michigan	FA/00	*2/0
62	Flynn, Mike	6-3/295	6-15-74	3	Maine	FA/97	12/0
71	Folau, Spencer (T)	6-5/300	4-5-73	4	Idaho	FA/96	5/1
65	Mercier, Richard (G)	6-3/295	5-13-75	R	Miami (Fla.)	D5/00	—
60	Mitchell, Jeff (C)	6-4/300	1-29-74	4	Florida	D5/97	16/16
64	Mulitalo, Edwin	6-3/340	9-1-74	2	Arizona	D4b/99	10/8
75	Ogden, Jonathan	6-8/335	7-31-74	5	UCLA	D1a/96	16/16
70	Swayne, Harry (T)	6-5/295	2-2-65	14	Rutgers	UFA/99	6/6
77	Vickers, Kipp	6-2/298	8-27-69	8	Miami (Fla.)	UFA/00	*11/0
72	Williams, Sammy	6-5/318	12-14-74	3	Oklahoma	W-KC/99	1/0
	DEFENSIVE LINEMEN						
95	Adams, Sam (T)	6-3/297	6-13-73	7	Texas A&M	UFA/00	*13/13
90	Burnett, Rob (E)	6-4/270	8-27-67	11	Syracuse	D5/90	16/16
92	Chase, Martin (T)	6-2/310	12-19-74	3	Oklahoma	D5a/98	3/0
91	Dalton, Lional (T)	6-1/320	2-21-75	3	Eastern Michigan	FA/98	16/2
99	McCrary, Michael (E)	6-4/260	7-7-70	8	Wake Forest	UFA/97	16/16
98	Siragusa, Tony (T)	6-3/340	5-14-67	11	Pittsburgh	FA/97	14/14
96	Thomas, Adalius (E)	6-2/270	8-18-77	R	Southern Mississippi	D6a/00	—
93	Washington, Keith (E)	6-4/270	12-18-72	6	UNLV	FA/97	16/0
79	Webster, Larry	6-5/305	1-18-69	8	Maryland	FA/95	16/16
78	Woodard, Cedric (T)	6-2/290	9-5-77	R	Texas	D6b/00	—
	LINEBACKERS						
58	Boulware, Peter	6-4/255	12-18-74	4	Florida State	D1/97	16/11
51	Brown, Cornell	6-0/240	3-15-75	4	Virginia Tech	D6b/97	16/5
50	Jackson, Brad	6-0/230	1-11-75	2	Cincinnati	FA/98	13/0
52	Lewis, Ray	6-1/245	5-15-75	5	Miami (Fla.)	D1b/96	16/16
53	Peters, Tyrell	6-0/235	8-4-74	3	Oklahoma	FA/97	13/0
55	Sharper, Jamie	6-3/240	11-23-74	4	Virginia	D2a/97	16/16
56	Stallings, Dennis	6-0/240	5-25-74	4	Illinois	FA/00	*0/0
	DEFENSIVE BACKS						
35	Bailey, Robert (CB)	5-10/182	9-3-68	10	Miami (Florida)	UFA/00	*16/11
45	Harris, Corey (S)	5-11/200	10-25-69	9	Vanderbilt	FA/98	16/0
20	Herring, Kim (S)	6-0/200	9-10-75	4	Penn State	D2b/97	16/16
21	McAlister, Chris (CB)	6-1/206	6-14-77	2	Arizona	D1/99	16/12
22	Starks, Duane (CB)	5-10/170	5-23-74	3	Miami (Fla.)	D1/98	16/5
37	Thompson, Bennie (S)	6-0/220	2-10-63	11	Grambling State	FA/94	16/0
38	Trapp, James (CB)	6-0/190	12-28-69	8	Clemson	UFA/99	16/0
26	Woodson, Rod (CB)	6-0/205	3-10-65	14	Purdue	FA/98	16/16
	SPECIALISTS						
5	Richardson, Kyle (P)	6-2/210	3-2-73	4	Arkansas State	FA/98	16/0
3	Stover, Matt (K)	5-11/178	1-27-68	11	Louisiana Tech	PlanB/91	16/0

*Not with Ravens in 1999.

Other free agent veterans invited to camp: DT Marques Douglas, CB Clarence Love, OL Curtice MacFarlane, S Anthony Mitchell, WR Kendrick Nord, C Rod Payne, S Anthony Poindexter, DE Charles Preston.

Abbreviations: D1—draft pick, first round; SD-2—supplemental draft pick, second round; W—claimed on waivers; T—obtained in trade; PlanB—Plan B free-agent acquisition; FA—free-agent acquisition (other than Plan B); UFA—unconditional free agent acquisition; ED—expansion draft pick.

MISCELLANEOUS TEAM DATA

Stadium (capacity, surface):
PSINet Stadium
(69,354, grass)
Business address:
11001 Owings Mills Blvd.
Owings Mills, MD 21117
Business phone:
410-654-6200
Ticket information:
410-261-RAVE
Team colors:
Purple, black and metallic gold
Flagship radio stations:
WJFK 1300 AM & WLIF 101.9 FM
Training site:
Western Maryland College
Westminster, Md.
410-654-6200

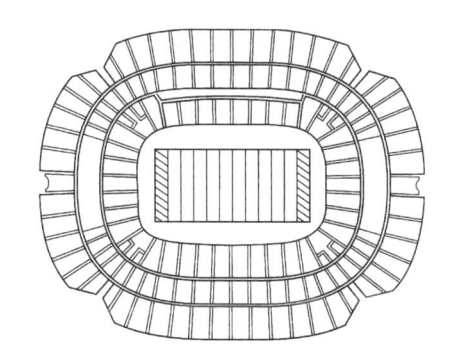

TSN REPORT CARD

Coaching staff	B	The group has a unique blend of youth and experience as well as assistants who were either former head coaches or coordinators. Head coach Brian Billick has learned to develop a better rapport with veteran players and it will pay off this season.
Quarterbacks	C +	As Tony Banks goes, so goes the Ravens offense. Trent Dilfer provides plenty of experience as a backup, but his days as a starter may be over. Rookie Chris Redman has potential, but he is still a few years away. Overall, though, not a bad group.
Running backs	C	The Ravens have hailed Jamal Lewis as their starter of the future, but he won't be able to wrestle the starting position away from Priest Holmes immediately. No. 3 Jay Graham better make his move soon or he could be seeking employment elsewhere. Chuck Evans is the starting fullback, but the team has no depth behind him.
Receivers	C +	If speed kills, the Ravens would win every game. But with the exception of Qadry Ismail, it's still a young group only in the second year of Billick's West Coast offense. Jermaine Lewis is on a mission after a poor performance last year and Patrick Johnson could have a breakthrough season. Rookie Travis Taylor, out of Florida, is the real deal.
Offensive line	C -	The Ravens are inexperienced at both guard positions and veteran right tackle Harry Swayne isn't getting any younger. If this group can hold together until midseason, it could be strong down the stretch. Center Jeff Mitchell is vastly underrated while left tackle Jonathan Ogden is pure stud.
Defensive line	A	If tackles Tony Siragusa and Sam Adams are physically in shape at the start of the regular season, then the line will be excellent again. Siragusa has the muscle while Adams has the quickness. Ends Michael McCrary and Rob Burnett complement each other as well. Both are Pro Bowl material.
Linebackers	A +	Middle linebacker Ray Lewis has to overcome all the obstacles from an offseason murder trial. He is the leader of the defense and the other players feed off his emotion. Strongside linebacker Peter Boulware, a two-time Pro Bowl pick, might have his best season this year while weakside linebacker Jamie Sharper is on the verge of stardom.
Secondary	C +	This unit is no longer the team's Achilles heel. The Ravens have great athletes on the corners and safety Rod Woodson gives them plenty experience to make the proper calls. The Ravens would like to add a thumper in the secondary, the missing ingredient from what may become a great defense. The team hasn't found the answer in Kim Herring at strong safety, but it might come in the form of Anthony Poindexter.
Special teams	C -	The kicking game is sound with punter Kyle Richardson and kicker Matt Stover. Long snapper Frank Wainwright is one of the best in the business. But the cover units have to be more aggressive and win the field-position battle. This is one area that needs drastic improvement from a year ago.

BUFFALO BILLS
AFC EASTERN DIVISION

2000 SEASON

CLUB DIRECTORY

President
 Ralph C. Wilson Jr.
Exec. vice president/general manager
 John Butler
Vice president/player personnel
 Dwight Adams
Vice president, communications
 Scott Berchtold
V.p., business dev. & marketing
 Russ Brandon
Vice president/operations
 Bill Munson
Vice president/administration
 Jim Overdorf
Corporate vice president
 Linda Bogdan
Treasurer
 Jeffrey C. Littmann
Director of administration/ticket sales
 Jerry Foran
Controller
 Frank Wojnicki
Director of marketing communications
 Marc Honan
Director of marketing partnerships
 Jeff Fernandez
Director of merchandising
 Christy Wilson Hofmann
Director of sales
 Pete Guelli
Media relations coordinator
 Mark Dalton
Ticket director
 June Foran
Video director
 Henry Kunttu
Director of stadium operations
 George Koch
Director of security
 Bill Bambach
Engineering and operations manager
 Joe Frandina
Director of pro personnel
 A.J. Smith

Head coach
Wade Phillips

Assistant coaches
 Max Bowman (asst. to head coach/tight ends)
 Bill Bradley (defensive backs)
 Ted Cottrell (def. coordinator)
 Chris Dickson (off. quality control)
 Charlie Joiner (receivers)
 Ronnie Jones (special teams)
 Rusty Jones (strength & cond.)
 Chuck Lester (linebackers)
 John Levra (defensive line)
 Carl Mauck (offensive line)
 Joe Pendry (off. coordinator)
 James Saxon (running backs)
 Turk Schonert (quarterbacks)

Scouts
 Brad Forsyth   Tom Gibbons
 Joe Haering   Doug Majeski
 Buddy Nix   Bob Ryan
 Chink Sengel   Bobby Williams
 Dave G. Smith   Dave W. Smith
Head trainer
 Bud Carpenter
Assistant trainers
 Corey Bennett
 Greg McMillen
Equipment manager
 Dave Hojnowski
Assistant equipment manager
 Woody Ribbeck

SCHEDULE

Sept. 3—	TENNESSEE	8:35
Sept. 10—	GREEN BAY	1:00
Sept. 17—	at N.Y. Jets	1:00
Sept. 24—	Open date	
Oct. 1—	INDIANAPOLIS	1:00
Oct. 8—	at Miami	1:00
Oct. 15—	SAN DIEGO	1:00
Oct. 22—	at Minnesota	1:00
Oct. 29—	N.Y. JETS	1:00
Nov. 5—	at New England	1:00
Nov. 12—	CHICAGO	1:00
Nov. 19—	at Kansas City	1:00
Nov. 26—	at Tampa Bay	1:00
Dec. 3—	MIAMI	1:00
Dec. 11—	at Indianapolis (Mon.)	9:00
Dec. 17—	NEW ENGLAND	1:00
Dec. 23—	at Seattle (Sat.)	8:35

All times are Eastern.
All games Sunday unless noted.

DRAFT CHOICES

Erik Flowers, DE, Arizona State (first round/26th pick overall).
Travares Tillman, S, Georgia Tech (2/58).
Corey Moore, LB, Virginia Tech (3/89).
Avion Black, WR, Tennessee State (4/121).
Sammy Morris, RB, Texas Tech (5/156).
Leif Larson, DT, Texas-El Paso (6/194).
Drew Haddad, WR, Buffalo (7/233).
DaShon Polk, LB, Arizona (7/251).

1999 REVIEW

RESULTS

Sept.12—at Indianapolis	L	14-31
Sept.19—N.Y. JETS	W	17-3
Sept.26—PHILADELPHIA	W	26-0
Oct. 4—at Miami	W	23-18
Oct. 10—PITTSBURGH	W	24-21
Oct. 17—OAKLAND	L	14-20
Oct. 24—at Seattle	L	16-26
Oct. 31—at Baltimore	W	13-10
Nov. 7—at Washington	W	34-17
Nov. 14—MIAMI	W	23-3
Nov. 21—at N.Y. Jets	L	7-17
Nov. 28—NEW ENGLAND	W	17-7
Dec. 5—Open date		
Dec. 12—N.Y. GIANTS	L	17-19
Dec. 19—at Arizona	W	31-21
Dec. 26—at New England (OT)	W	13-10
Jan. 2—INDIANAPOLIS	W	31-6
Jan. 8—at Tennessee*	L	16-22

*AFC wild-card game.

RECORDS/RANKINGS

1999 regular-season record: 11-5 (2nd in AFC East); 6-2 in division; 8-4 in conference; 3-1 vs. NFC; 6-2 at home; 5-3 on road; 6-5 on turf; 5-0 on grass.
Team record last five years: 47-33 (.588, ranks 7th in league in that span).

1999 team rankings:

	No.	AFC	NFL
Total offense	*333.3	4	11
Rushing offense	*127.5	5	8
Passing offense	*205.8	10	T19
Scoring offense	320	9	16
Total defense	*252.8	1	1
Rushing defense	*85.6	3	4
Passing defense	*167.2	1	1
Scoring defense	229	2	2
Takeaways	21	15	28
Giveaways	27	6	9
Turnover differential	-6	T13	T23
Sacks	37	13	T20
Sacks allowed	27	4	5

*Yards per game.

TEAM LEADERS

Scoring (kicking): Steve Christie, 108 pts. (33/33 PATs, 25/34 FGs).
Scoring (touchdowns): Eric Moulds, 42 pts. (7 receiving).
Passing: Doug Flutie, 3,171 yds. (478 att., 264 comp., 55.2%, 19 TDs, 16 int.).
Rushing: Jonathan Linton, 695 yds. (205 att., 3.4 avg., 5 TDs).
Receptions: Eric Moulds, 65 (994 yds., 15.3 avg., 7 TDs).
Interceptions: Kurt Schulz, 3 (26 yds., 0 TDs).
Sacks: Bruce Smith, 7.0.
Punting: Chris Mohr, 38.9 avg. (73 punts, 2,840 yds., 0 blocked).
Punt returns: Kevin Williams, 10.0 avg. (33 att., 331 yds., 0 TDs).
Kickoff returns: Kevin Williams, 20.0 avg. (42 att., 840 yds., 0 TDs).

2000 SEASON
TRAINING CAMP ROSTER

No.	QUARTERBACKS	Ht./Wt.	Born	NFL Exp.	College	How acq.	'99 Games GP/GS
7	Flutie, Doug	5-10/178	10-23-62	7	Boston College	FA/98	15/15
11	Johnson, Rob	6-4/212	3-18-73	6	Southern California	T-Jax./98	2/1
	RUNNING BACKS						
38	Bryson, Shawn	6-4/249	8-26-76	1	Tennessee	D3/99	0/0
31	Gordon, Lennox	6-0/201	4-9-78	2	New Mexico	FA/99	8/0
35	Linton, Jonathan (FB)	6-0/238	11-7-74	3	North Carolina	D5/98	16/2
45	Morris, Sammy	6-0/228	3-23-77	R	Texas Tech	D5/00	—
23	Smith, Antowain	6-2/225	3-14-72	4	Houston	D1/97	14/11
	RECEIVERS						
89	Black, Avion	5-11/181	4-24-77	R	Tennessee State	D4/00	—
84	Collins, Bobby (TE)	6-4/249	8-20-76	2	North Alabama	D4b/99	14/4
16	Haddad, Drew	5-11/184	8-15-78	R	Buffalo	D7a/00	—
88	Jackson, Sheldon (TE)	6-3/250	7-24-76	2	Nebraska	D7a/99	13/4
86	McDaniel, Jeremy	6-0/197	5-2-76	1	Arizona	FA/99	1/0
80	Moulds, Eric	6-0/204	7-17-73	5	Mississippi State	D1/96	14/14
81	Price, Peerless	5-11/180	10-27-76	2	Tennessee	D2/99	16/4
85	Riemersma, Jay (TE)	6-5/254	5-17-73	4	Michigan	D7b/96	14/11
	OFFENSIVE LINEMEN						
76	Albright, Ethan	6-5/278	5-1-71	7	North Carolina	FA/96	16/0
79	Brown, Ruben (G)	6-3/304	2-13-72	7	Pittsburgh	D1/95	14/14
63	Conaty, Billy	6-2/300	3-8-73	4	Virginia Tech	FA/97	7/1
70	Fina, John (T)	6-4/300	3-11-69	9	Arizona	D1/92	16/16
77	Hicks, Robert (T)	6-7/338	11-17-74	3	Mississippi State	D3/98	14/14
74	Nails, Jamie (T)	6-6/354	3-3-75	4	Florida A&M	D4/97	16/3
60	Ostroski, Jerry (C)	6-4/326	7-12-70	7	Tulsa	FA/93	15/15
72	Panos, Joe (G)	6-2/298	1-24-71	7	Wisconsin	FA/98	0/0
69	Spriggs, Marcus (T)	6-3/315	5-17-74	4	Houston	D6/97	11/2
	DEFENSIVE LINEMEN						
96	Flowers, Erik (E)	6-4/248	3-1-78	R	Arizona State	D1/00	—
90	Hansen, Phil (E)	6-5/278	5-20-68	10	North Dakota State	D2/91	14/14
97	Larson, Leif (T)	6-4/300	4-3-75	R	Texas-El Paso	D6/00	—
91	Price, Shawn (E)	6-4/290	3-28-70	8	Pacific	FA/96	15/1
92	Washington, Ted (NT)	6-5/330	4-13-68	10	Louisville	FA/95	16/16
75	Wiley, Marcellus (E)	6-4/275	11-30-74	4	Columbia	D2/97	16/1
93	Williams, Pat (T)	6-3/310	10-24-72	3	Texas A&M	FA/97	16/0
	LINEBACKERS						
56	Cowart, Sam	6-2/245	2-26-75	2	Florida State	D2/98	16/16
55	Foreman, Jay	6-1/240	12-16-76	2	Nebraska	D5/99	7/0
52	Holecek, John	6-2/242	5-7-72	6	Illinois	D5/95	14/14
54	Moore, Corey	5-11/213	3-20-77	R	Virginia Tech	D3/00	—
53	Newman, Keith	6-2/243	1-19-77	2	North Carolina	D4a/99	3/0
51	Polk, DaShon	6-1/221	3-13-77	R	Arizona	D7b/00	—
59	Rogers, Sam	6-3/245	5-30-70	7	Colorado	D2c/94	16/16
	DEFENSIVE BACKS						
29	Carpenter, Keion (S)	5-11/205	10-31-77	2	Virginia Tech	FA/99	10/0
25	Greer, Donovan	5-9/178	9-11-74	4	Texas A&M	FA/98	16/0
27	Irvin, Ken (CB)	5-10/186	7-11-72	6	Memphis	D4a/95	14/14
20	Jones, Henry (S)	6-0/197	12-29-67	10	Illinois	D1/91	16/16
22	Porter, Daryl (CB)	5-9/190	1-16-74	4	Boston College	FA/98	16/0
28	Tillman, Travares (S)	6-1/189	10-8-77	R	Georgia Tech	D2/00	—
26	Winfield, Antoine (CB)	5-8/180	6-24-77	2	Ohio State	D1/99	16/2
	SPECIALISTS						
2	Christie, Steve (K)	6-0/190	11-13-67	11	William & Mary	UFA/92	16/0
9	Mohr, Chris (P)	6-5/215	5-11-66	11	Alabama	FA/91	16/0

*Not with Bills in 1999.

Other free agent veterans invited to camp: G Victor Allotey, QB Mike Cawley, DT Bryce Fisher, S Raion Hill, G Corey Hulsey, TE John Jennings.

Abbreviations: D1—draft pick, first round; SD-2—supplemental draft pick, second round; W—claimed on waivers; T—obtained in trade; PlanB—Plan B free-agent acquisition; FA—free-agent acquisition (other than Plan B); UFA—unconditional free agent acquisition; ED—expansion draft pick.

MISCELLANEOUS TEAM DATA

Stadium (capacity, surface):
Ralph Wilson Stadium (75,339, artificial)
Business address:
One Bills Drive
Orchard Park, N.Y. 14127
Business phone:
716-648-1800
Ticket information:
716-BB-TICKS
Team colors:
Royal blue, scarlet and white
Flagship radio station:
WGRF, 96.9 FM; WEDG 103.3 FM
Training site:
St. John Fisher College
Rochester, N.Y.
716-648-1800

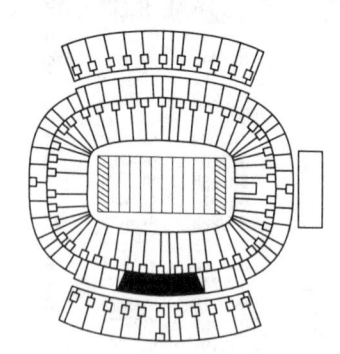

TSN REPORT CARD

Coaching staff	B +	Head coach Wade Phillips has guided the Bills to 21 wins in two years, and he isn't afraid to make tough decisions with personnel (starting Rob Johnson over Doug Flutie in playoffs, for example). Defensive coordinator Ted Cottrell has done a great job of getting players to execute assignments and minimize mistakes. He's also good at putting together game plans that confound opposing offenses. Offensive coordinator Joe Pendry got the most out of an injury-plagued unit last year. His ability to deal with the quarterback situation is commendable.
Quarterbacks	B	The Johnson-Flutie controversy still rages, but the team likes the fact it has two quality players. Johnson is younger, bigger, stronger and has more physical ability. He's also has a reputation of being fragile, which is why Flutie's great to have around. Flutie can be amazing and inconsistent. He frequently makes the offensive line look good by keeping drives alive with his legs. But he doesn't throw downfield as well or as accurately as Johnson.
Running backs	C +	Antowain Smith had a difficult year filled with injuries. Pendry seemed reluctant to give him the ball at times. The pressure's on Smith to return to the form that made him a 1,000-yard back in 1998. Jonathan Linton may have been the offense's savior last year. He stepped in for an injured Thurman Thomas and the offense didn't miss a beat. Shawn Bryson, who was out with a knee injury as a rookie, is pushing Smith and Linton. The Bills might miss the blocking of Pro Bowl fullback Sam Gash, who was released before the draft.
Receivers	B	Based on potential this could be the most explosive unit the Bills have had in years. Eric Moulds was slowed last year by a mid-season hamstring injury, but he should return to All-Pro form. Peerless Price got more playing time when Andre Reed fell out of favor late last season. It should pay huge dividends in 2000. Jay Riemersma was sixth among tight ends with 37 catches despite missing several games with a groin injury. Armed with a big contract, he could have a breakout year.
Offensive line	C +	The unit is much better than it was two years ago. Robert Hicks, who became a starter in his second year, looks like a future Pro Bowler. Jerry Ostroski's move from tackle to center solidified the line. Pro Bowl guard Ruben Brown and left tackle John Fina are the league's longest-running tandem. The only question mark is guard Joe Panos, who is coming off neck surgery.
Defensive line	A -	The move to a seven-man rotation worked wonders. Nose tackle Ted Washington is still a force in the middle. Backup Pat Williams was a revelation as he outplayed his mentor the last several weeks of 1999. Phil Hansen is a solid defensive end, but the pressure is on Marcellus Wiley, who replaces Bruce Smith at right end. Rookie Erik Flowers should contribute immediately. Will the pass rush suffer without Smith?
Linebackers	A	Sam Cowart and John Holecek are a super tandem inside. Cowart would have been in the Pro Bowl last year if there weren't so many great middle linebackers in the AFC. Strongside backer Sam Rogers is coming off an outstanding year. The big question mark is on the weak side, where second-year man Keith Newman will try to replace Gabe Northern, who wasn't re-signed. Rookie Corey Moore might be one of the draft-day steals of 2000.
Secondary	B	This unit doesn't make a lot of big plays, but it doesn't allow many either. The loss of top cornerback Thomas Smith and free safety Kurt Schulz are concerns. Antoine Winfield was drafted No. 1 last year as Smith's eventual replacement and is ready for prime time. Ken Irvin returns as the starter at left corner. Daryl Porter gets the nod at free safety, but rookie Travares Tillman is waiting in the wings. Entering his 10th season, Henry Jones remains one of league's best strong safeties.
Special teams	C -	As Home Run Throwback proved, kickoff coverage was a weak link last year. The return game is undergoing change, with reliable Kevin Williams being replaced by rookies Avion Black and Drew Haddad. Although kicker Steve Christie had a couple of bad games, he's still a clutch performer. Punter Chris Mohr makes up for lack of distance with great hang time that prevents big returns.

CAROLINA PANTHERS
NFC WESTERN DIVISION

2000 SEASON

CLUB DIRECTORY

Owner & founder
Jerry Richardson
President of Carolina Panthers
Mark Richardson
Director of football administration
Marty Hurney
Director of player personnel
Jack Bushofsky
President of Carolinas Stadium Corp.
Jon Richardson
Chief financial officer
Dave Olsen
General counsel
Richard Thigpen
Dir. of marketing & sponsorships
Charles Waddell
Director of ticket sales
Phil Youtsey
Director of communications
Charlie Dayton
Director of player relations
Donnie Shell
Director of facilities
Tom Fellows
Pro scout
Hal Hunter
Mark Koncz
Area scouts
Hal Athon
Joe Bushofsky
Jason Licht
Jeff Morrow
Tony Softli
Head groundskeeper
Billy Ball
Equipment manager
Jackie Miles
Video director
Mark Hobbs

Head coach
George Seifert

Assistant coaches
Don Breaux (tight ends)
Jacob Burney (defensive line)
Chick Harris (running backs)
Carlos Mainord (defensive backs)
John Marshall (assistant head coach/defensive coordinator)
Mike McCoy (offensive assistant)
Sam Mills (linebackers)
Bill Musgrave (off. coord./QBs)
Scott O'Brien (special teams)
Alvin Reynolds (def. qual. control)
Greg Roman (off. quality control)
Darrin Simmons (asst. strength & conditioning/special teams quality control)
Jerry Simmons (strength & conditioning)
Richard Williamson (assistant head coach/offense)
Tony Wise (offensive line)

Head trainer
John Kasik
Assistant trainers
Dan Ruiz
Al Shuford
Orthopedist
Dr. Don D'Alessandro

SCHEDULE

Sept. 3—	at Washington	1:00
Sept. 10—	at San Francisco	4:15
Sept. 17—	ATLANTA	1:00
Sept. 24—	Open date	
Oct. 1—	DALLAS	1:00
Oct. 8—	SEATTLE	4:15
Oct. 15—	at New Orleans	1:00
Oct. 22—	SAN FRANCISCO	1:00
Oct. 29—	at Atlanta	1:00
Nov. 5—	at St. Louis	8:35
Nov. 12—	NEW ORLEANS	1:00
Nov. 19—	at Minnesota	1:00
Nov. 27—	GREEN BAY (Mon.)	9:00
Dec. 3—	ST. LOUIS	1:00
Dec. 10—	at Kansas City	1:00
Dec. 17—	SAN DIEGO	1:00
Dec. 24—	at Oakland	4:15

All times are Eastern.
All games Sunday unless noted.

DRAFT CHOICES

Rashard Anderson, DB, Jackson State (first round/23rd pick overall).
Deon Grant, S, Tennessee (2/57).
Leander Jordan, G, Indiana, Pa. (3/82).
Alvin McKinley, DT, Mississippi State (4/120).
Gillis Wilson, DT, Southern (5/147).
Jeno James, T, Auburn (6/182).
Lester Towns, LB, Washington (7/221).

1999 REVIEW

RESULTS

Sept.12—at New Orleans	L	10-19
Sept.19—JACKSONVILLE	L	20-22
Sept.26—CINCINNATI	W	27-3
Oct. 3—at Washington	L	36-38
Oct. 10—Open date		
Oct. 17—at San Francisco	W	31-29
Oct. 24—DETROIT	L	9-24
Oct. 31—at Atlanta	L	20-27
Nov. 7—PHILADELPHIA	W	33-7
Nov. 14—at St. Louis	L	10-35
Nov. 21—at Cleveland	W	31-17
Nov. 28—ATLANTA	W	34-28
Dec. 5—ST. LOUIS	L	21-34
Dec. 12—at Green Bay	W	33-31
Dec. 18—SAN FRANCISCO	W	41-24
Dec. 26—at Pittsburgh	L	20-30
Jan. 2—NEW ORLEANS	W	45-13

RECORDS/RANKINGS

1999 regular-season record: 8-8 (2nd in NFC West); 4-4 in division; 6-6 in conference; 2-2 vs. AFC; 5-3 at home; 3-5 on road; 0-4 on turf; 8-4 on grass.
Team record last five years: 38-42 (.475, ranks T16th in league in that span).
1999 team rankings:

	No.	NFC	NFL
Total offense	*355.4	4	6
Rushing offense	*95.3	9	20
Passing offense	*260.1	2	2
Scoring offense	421	3	4
Total defense	*343.9	11	26
Rushing defense	*118.6	11	24
Passing defense	*225.3	10	23
Scoring defense	381	12	26
Takeaways	29	11	19
Giveaways	34	7	T21
Turnover differential	-5	T9	T19
Sacks	35	T10	T23
Sacks allowed	51	14	27

*Yards per game.

TEAM LEADERS

Scoring (kicking): John Kasay, 99 pts. (33/33 PATs, 22/25 FGs).
Scoring (touchdowns): Wesley Walls, 72 pts. (12 receiving); Patrick Jeffers, 72 pts. (12 receiving).
Passing: Steve Beuerlein, 4,436 yds. (571 att., 343 comp., 60.1%, 36 TDs, 15 int.).
Rushing: Tim Biakabutuka, 718 yds. (138 att., 5.2 avg., 6 TDs).
Receptions: Muhsin Muhammad, 96 (1,253 yds., 13.1 avg., 8 TDs).
Interceptions: Eric Davis, 5 (49 yds., 0 TDs).
Sacks: Kevin Greene, 12.0.
Punting: Ken Walter, 39.4 avg. (65 punts, 2,562 yds., 0 blocked).
Punt returns: Eric Metcalf, 7.0 avg. (34 att., 238 yds., 0 TDs).
Kickoff returns: Michael Bates, 24.8 avg. (52 att., 1,287 yds., 2 TDs).

– 17 –

2000 SEASON
TRAINING CAMP ROSTER

CAROLINA PANTHERS

No.	QUARTERBACKS	Ht./Wt.	Born	NFL Exp.	College	How acq.	'99 Games GP/GS
7	Beuerlein, Steve	6-3/220	3-7-65	14	Notre Dame	UFA/96	16/16
2	Craig, Dameyune	6-1/200	4-19-74	2	Auburn	FA/98	0/0
8	Lewis, Jeff	6-2/211	4-17-73	4	Northern Arizona	T-Den./99	2/0
	RUNNING BACKS						
24	Bates, Michael	5-10/189	12-19-69	8	Arizona	FA/96	16/0
21	Biakabutuka, Tshimanga	6-0/215	1-24-74	5	Michigan	D1/96	11/11
40	Floyd, William (FB)	6-1/242	2-17-72	7	Florida State	UFA/98	16/16
44	Hetherington, Chris (FB)	6-3/249	11-27-72	5	Yale	FA/99	14/0
23	Johnson, Anthony	6-0/225	10-25-67	11	Notre Dame	W-Chi./95	16/0
20	Means, Natrone	5-10/245	4-26-72	8	North Carolina	FA/00	*7/5
	RECEIVERS						
81	Hayes, Donald	6-4/208	7-13-75	3	Wisconsin	D4/98	13/1
83	Jeffers, Patrick	6-3/218	2-2-73	5	Virginia	FA/99	15/10
88	Kinchen, Brian (TE)	6-2/240	8-6-65	13	Louisiana State	UFA/99	16/0
86	Mangum, Kris (TE)	6-4/249	8-15-73	3	Mississippi	D7/97	11/0
87	Muhammad, Muhsin	6-2/217	5-5-73	5	Michigan State	D2/96	15/15
85	Walls, Wesley (TE)	6-5/250	2-26-66	12	Mississippi	UFA/96	16/16
	OFFENSIVE LINEMEN						
66	Campbell, Matt (G)	6-4/300	7-14-72	6	South Carolina	FA/95	10/10
64	Dexter, James	6-7/320	3-3-73	6	South Carolina	UFA/00	*8/5
65	Garcia, Frank (C)	6-2/302	1-28-72	6	Washington	D4/95	16/16
78	James, Jeno (G)	6-3/292	1-12-77	R	Auburn	D6/00	—
75	Jones, Clarence (T)	6-6/300	5-6-68	10	Maryland	UFA/99	16/16
76	Jordan, Leander (G)	6-3/333	9-15-77	R	Indiana (Pa.)	D3/00	—
63	Nesbit, Jamar (C)	6-4/330	12-17-76	2	South Carolina	FA/99	7/0
67	Stoltenberg, Bryan (C)	6-1/300	8-25-72	5	Colorado	FA/98	16/7
70	Terry, Chris (T)	6-5/295	8-8-75	2	Georgia	D2a/99	16/16
	DEFENSIVE LINEMEN						
74	Dingle, Antonio (T)	6-2/315	10-7-76	2	Virginia	W-GB/99	9/0
94	Gilbert, Sean (T)	6-5/318	4-10-70	8	Pittsburgh	FA/98	16/16
95	Maumau, Viliami (T)	6-2/302	4-3-75	1	Colorado	FA/99	1/0
98	McKinley, Alvin (T)	6-3/292	6-9-78	R	Mississippi State	D4/00	—
90	Morabito, Tim (T)	6-3/296	10-12-73	5	Boston College	W-Cin./97	16/16
97	Peter, Jason (E)	6-4/295	9-13-74	3	Nebraska	D1/98	9/9
93	Rucker, Michael (E)	6-5/258	2-28-75	2	Nebraska	D2b/99	16/0
91	Smith, Chuck (E)	6-2/262	12-21-69	9	Tennessee	UFA/00	*16/16
99	Wiley, Chuck	6-5/282	3-6-75	3	Louisiana State	D3a/98	16/16
96	Williams, Jay (E)	6-3/280	10-13-71	5	Wake Forest	UFA/00	*16/0
92	Wilson, Gillis (E)	6-2/282	10-15-77	R	Southern	D5/00	—
	LINEBACKERS						
50	Green, Lamont	6-3/230	7-10-76	1	Florida State	FA/99	1/0
54	Jones, Donta	6-2/235	8-27-72	6	Nebraska	UFA/99	16/0
53	Navies, Hannibal	6-2/240	7-19-77	2	Colorado	D4/99	9/0
56	Reid, Spencer	6-1/247	2-8-76	3	Brigham Young	T-Ind./00	*12/0
57	Towns, Lester	6-1/252	8-28-77	R	Washington	D7/00	—
95	Wells, Dean	6-3/248	7-20-70	8	Kentucky	UFA/99	16/10
58	Woodall, Lee	6-1/230	10-31-69	7	West Chester (Pa.) University	FA/00	*16/16
	DEFENSIVE BACKS						
46	Anderson, Rashard	6-2/204	6-14-77	R	Jackson State	D1/00	—
25	Davis, Eric (CB)	5-11/185	1-26-68	11	Jacksonville (Ala.) State	UFA/96	16/16
33	Evans, Doug (CB)	6-1/190	5-13-70	8	Louisiana Tech	UFA/98	16/16
27	Grant, Deon (S)	6-1/207	3-14-79	R	Tennessee	D2/00	—
36	Hitchcock, Jimmy (CB)	5-10/187	11-9-70	6	North Carolina	UFA/00	*16/16
30	Minter, Mike (S)	5-10/188	1-15-74	4	Nebraska	D2/97	16/16
39	Richardson, Damien (S)	6-1/210	4-3-76	3	Arizona State	D6/98	15/0
	SPECIALISTS						
3	Cunningham, Richie (K)	5-10/167	8-18-70	4	Southwestern Louisiana	FA/99	15/0
4	Kasay, John (K)	5-10/198	10-27-69	10	Georgia	UFA/95	13/0
13	Walter, Ken (P)	6-1/195	8-15-72	4	Kent	FA/97	16/0

*Not with Panthers in 1999.
Other free agent veterans invited to camp: OT Dan Best, DB Tony Booth, WR Dialleo Burks, DE Robert Daniel, WR Shawn Foreman, WR Karl Hankton, QB Matt Lytle, K Eric Meng, LB Kory Minor, WR Sirr Parker, WR Larry Ryans, C Clay Shiver, DE Rasheed Simmons, WR Jim Turner, DT Alton Weaver.

Abbreviations: D1—draft pick, first round; SD-2—supplemental draft pick, second round; W—claimed on waivers; T—obtained in trade; PlanB—Plan B free-agent acquisition; FA—free-agent acquisition (other than Plan B); UFA—unconditional free agent acquisition; ED—expansion draft pick.

MISCELLANEOUS TEAM DATA

Stadium (capacity, surface):
Ericsson Stadium
(73,248, grass)
Business address:
800 S. Mint St.
Charlotte, NC 28202-1502
Business phone:
704-358-7000
Ticket information:
704-358-7800
Team colors:
Blue, black and silver
Flagship radio station:
WRFX-99.7 FM
Training site:
Wofford College
Spartanburg, S.C.
704-358-7000

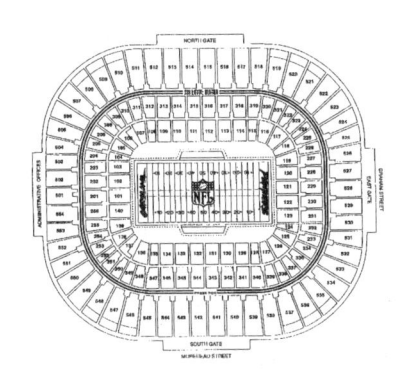

CAROLINA PANTHERS

TSN REPORT CARD

Coaching staff	B +	George Seifert took awhile to get to know his team last year, but his influence really became effective down the stretch. With a year under his belt, Seifert should be even more of a factor. He's assembled a solid staff and his strong history with new offensive coordinator Bill Musgrave should make for a good relationship. Defensive coordinator John Marshall has new weapons to work with and special teams coach Scott O'Brien and offensive line coach Tony Wise are among the best in the business.
Quarterbacks	B	Steve Beuerlein is coming off the best year of his career and he's very comfortable in the offensive system. He is surrounded by good receivers. But Beuerlein is 35 and has shown signs of wear and tear. Backups Jeff Lewis and Dameyune Craig are unproven, so it's critical that Beuerlein remains healthy.
Running backs	C	This area is a question mark because Tshimanga Biakabutuka and Natrone Means have long histories of injuries. When healthy, either one can be a very good back. The team is gambling that it can get a full season out of a combination between the two. Fullback William Floyd could factor into the offense more this year.
Receivers	A	With Muhsin Muhammad established as one of the league's top receivers and Wesley Walls as a top-notch tight end, this is the team's strongest area. Throw in receiver Patrick Jeffers, who came on strong late last year, and the passing game is in good hands. Donald Hayes should be more of a factor as a third receiver.
Offensive line	C	There still is not an abundance of talent here, but Wise gets the most out of his players. Right tackle Chris Terry had a good rookie year and is on his way to becoming the anchor of the offensive line. The acquisition of free agent guard/tackle James Dexter should give the line a lot more flexibility.
Defensive line	C +	What was a weak spot last year should be much improved. Defensive end Chuck Smith was signed as a free agent and should become the main pass rusher. More importantly, Smith's presence should have a positive effect on underachievers Sean Gilbert and Jason Peter.
Linebackers	C	The team released Mike Barrow and Kevin Greene and they'll be replaced by Lee Woodall and Donta Jones on the outside. Woodall lacks Greene's pass-rush ability, but is better all around. Jones isn't spectacular, but he won't be asked to do more than the basics. Dean Wells is solid in the middle.
Secondary	C	There have been major changes and that's a good thing because the pass defense was horrible at times last year. Jimmy Hitchcock was signed to challenge for a cornerback job and he'll probably push Doug Evans to nickel back. First-round pick Rashard Anderson probably will start at free safety because the team thinks he can help against big receivers. Mike Minter shifts from free to strong safety.
Special teams	B	Aside from the punt return unit, the special teams were very solid last year and that should continue. Michael Bates is a constant threat as a kick returner and John Kasay has been a very consistent kicker, but is recovering from major knee surgery. Punter Ken Walter was spotty last year, but has the ability to get better. The team needs to find a reliable punt returner.

CHICAGO BEARS
NFC CENTRAL DIVISION

2000 SEASON

CLUB DIRECTORY

Chairman emeritus
Edward W. McCaskey
Chairman of the board
Michael B. McCaskey
President/chief executive officer
Ted Phillips
Vice president
Timothy E. McCaskey
Secretary
Virginia H. McCaskey
Director/administration
Bill McGrane
Dir./marketing and communications
Ken Valdiserri
Director/community relations
John Bostrom
Manager of sales
Jack Trompeter
Director/public relations
Bryan Harlan
Assistant director/public relations
Scott Hagel
Ticket manager
George McCaskey
Vice president, player personnel
Mark Hatley
Director/pro personnel
Scott Campbell
Director/pro scouting
Rick Spielman
Pro scout
George Paton
Director/college scouting
Bill Rees
Regional scouts
Marty Barrett   Phil Emery
Shemy Schembechler Jeff Shiver
John Paul Young
Head trainer
Tim Bream
Assistant trainer
Eric Sugerman
Physical development coordinator
Russ Riederer

Head coach
Dick Jauron

Assistant coaches
Keith Armstrong (special teams)
Vance Bedford (defensive backs)
Greg Blache (defensive coord.)
Jim Bollman (tight ends)
Mike Borich (wide receivers)
Chuck Bullough (quality control assistant, defense)
Gary Crowton (offensive coord.)
Dale Lindsey (linebackers)
Steve Little (assistant strength & conditioning)
Earle Mosley (running backs)
Rex Norris (defensive line)
Russ Riederer (strength & cond.)
John Shoop (quarterbacks)
Eric Studesville (quality control assistant, offense)
Bob Wylie (offensive line)

Asst. physical development coordinator
Steve Little
Equipment manager
Tony Medlin
Assistant equipment manager
Carl Piekarski
Director of video services
Dean Pope
Assistant video director
Dave Hendrickson

SCHEDULE

Sept. 3—	at Minnesota	1:00
Sept. 10—	at Tampa Bay	1:00
Sept. 17—	N.Y. GIANTS	4:15
Sept. 24—	DETROIT	1:00
Oct. 1—	at Green Bay	4:15
Oct. 8—	NEW ORLEANS	1:00
Oct. 15—	MINNESOTA	8:35
Oct. 22—	at Philadelphia	1:00
Oct. 29—	Open date	
Nov. 5—	INDIANAPOLIS	1:00
Nov. 12—	at Buffalo	1:00
Nov. 19—	TAMPA BAY	1:00
Nov. 26—	at N.Y. Jets	1:00
Dec. 3—	GREEN BAY	8:35
Dec. 10—	NEW ENGLAND	1:00
Dec. 17—	at San Francisco	4:05
Dec. 24—	at Detroit	1:00

All times are Eastern.
All games Sunday unless noted.

DRAFT CHOICES

Brian Urlacher, LB, New Mexico (first round/ninth pick overall).
Mike Brown, S, Nebraska (2/39).
Dez White, WR, Georgia Tech (3/69).
Dustin Lyman, TE, Wake Forest (3/87).
Reggie Austin, DB, Wake Forest (4/125).
Frank Murphy, RB, Kansas State (6/170).
Paul Edinger, PK, Michigan State (6/174).
James Cotton, DE, Ohio State (7/223).
Mike Green, DB, Louisiana-Lafayette (7/254).

1999 REVIEW

RESULTS

Sept.12—	KANSAS CITY	W	20-17
Sept.19—	SEATTLE	L	13-14
Sept.26—	at Oakland	L	17-24
Oct. 3—	NEW ORLEANS	W	14-10
Oct. 10—	at Minnesota	W	24-22
Oct. 17—	PHILADELPHIA	L	16-20
Oct. 24—	at Tampa Bay	L	3-6
Oct. 31—	at Washington	L	22-48
Nov. 7—	at Green Bay	W	14-13
Nov. 14—	MINNESOTA (OT)	L	24-27
Nov. 21—	at San Diego (OT)	W	23-20
Nov. 25—	at Detroit	L	17-21
Dec. 5—	GREEN BAY	L	19-35
Dec. 12—	Open date		
Dec. 19—	DETROIT	W	28-10
Dec. 26—	at St. Louis	L	12-34
Jan. 2—	TAMPA BAY	L	6-20

RECORDS/RANKINGS

1999 regular-season record: 6-10 (5th in NFC Central); 3-5 in division; 4-8 in conference; 2-2 vs. AFC; 3-5 at home; 3-5 on road; 1-2 on turf; 5-8 on grass.
Team record last five years: 30-50 (.375, ranks T26th in league in that span).
1999 team rankings:

	No.	NFC	NFL
Total offense	*345.2	5	8
Rushing offense	*86.7	12	26
Passing offense	*258.5	3	3
Scoring offense	272	T11	T25
Total defense	*356.5	14	29
Rushing defense	*117.6	10	23
Passing defense	*238.9	13	29
Scoring defense	341	T6	T20
Takeaways	33	T6	T10
Giveaways	37	11	27
Turnover differential	-4	T7	T17
Sacks	37	T8	T20
Sacks allowed	38	6	T15

*Yards per game.

TEAM LEADERS

Scoring (kicking): Chris Boniol, 50 pts. (17/18 PATs, 11/18 FGs).
Scoring (touchdowns): Marcus Robinson, 54 pts. (9 receiving).
Passing: Shane Matthews, 1,645 yds. (275 att., 167 comp., 60.7%, 10 TDs, 6 int.).
Rushing: Curtis Enis, 916 yds. (287 att., 3.2 avg., 3 TDs).
Receptions: Marcus Robinson, 84 (1,400 yds., 16.7 avg., 9 TDs).
Interceptions: Chris Hudson, 3 (28 yds., 0 TDs).
Sacks: Clyde Simmons, 7.0.
Punting: Todd Sauerbrun, 40.9 avg. (85 punts, 3,478 yds., 0 blocked).
Punt returns: Glyn Milburn, 11.5 avg. (30 ret., 346 yds., 1 TDs).
Kickoff returns: Glyn Milburn, 23.4 avg. (61 att., 1,426 yds., 0 TDs).

– 20 –

2000 SEASON
TRAINING CAMP ROSTER

No.	QUARTERBACKS	Ht./Wt.	Born	NFL Exp.	College	How acq.	'99 Games GP/GS
8	McNown, Cade	6-1/213	1-12-77	2	UCLA	D1/99	15/6
9	Matthews, Shane	6-3/196	6-1-70	7	Florida	UFA/99	8/7
15	Miller, Jim	6-2/218	2-9-71	7	Michigan State	FA/98	5/3
	RUNNING BACKS						
20	Allen, James	5-10/215	3-28-75	3	Oklahoma	FA/97	12/3
44	Enis, Curtis	6-0/240	6-15-76	3	Penn State	D1/98	15/12
24	Milburn, Glyn	5-8/174	2-19-71	8	Stanford	T-GB/98	16/1
31	Murphy, Frank	6-0/206	2-11-77	R	Kansas State	D6a/00	—
	RECEIVERS						
84	Allred, John (TE)	6-4/249	9-9-74	4	Southern California	D2/97	16/5
87	Bates, D'Wayne	6-2/215	12-4-75	2	Northwestern	D3b/99	7/1
86	Booker, Marty	5-11/215	7-31-76	2	Northeastern Louisiana	D3c/99	9/4
83	Brooks, Macey	6-5/215	2-2-75	2	James Madison	FA/98	9/2
81	Engram, Bobby	5-10/192	1-7-73	5	Penn State	D2/96	16/14
82	Kennison, Eddie	6-0/195	1-20-73	5	Louisiana State	T-NO/00	*16/16
49	Lyman, Dustin (TE)	6-4/254	8-5-76	R	Wake Forest	D3b/00	—
85	Mayes, Alonzo (TE)	6-4/268	6-4-75	3	Oklahoma State	D4/98	16/9
88	Robinson, Marcus	6-3/215	2-27-75	4	South Carolina	D4b/99	16/11
16	Still, Bryan	5-11/174	6-3-74	5	Virginia Tech	FA/00	*7/1
89	Wetnight, Ryan (TE)	6-2/236	11-5-70	8	Stanford	FA/93	16/4
9	White, Dez	6-0/219	8-23-79	R	Georgia Tech	D3a/00	—
	OFFENSIVE LINEMEN						
78	Brockermeyer, Blake (T)	6-4/312	4-11-73	6	Texas	UFA/99	15/15
57	Kreutz, Olin (C)	6-2/295	6-9-77	3	Washington	D3/98	16/16
65	Mannelly, Patrick (T)	6-5/285	4-18-75	3	Duke	D6b/98	16/0
75	Perry, Todd (G)	6-5/308	11-28-70	8	Kentucky	D4a/93	16/16
64	Tucker, Rex	6-5/300	12-20-76	2	Texas A&M	D3a/99	2/1
58	Villarrial, Chris (C)	6-4/310	6-9-73	5	Indiana (Univ. of Pa.)	D5/96	15/15
60	Wiegmann, Casey (C)	6-3/295	7-20-73	5	Iowa	FA/97	16/0
71	Williams, James (T)	6-7/340	3-29-68	10	Cheyney (Pa.) State	FA/91	16/16
79	Wisne, Jerry (T)	6-6/308	7-28-76	2	Notre Dame	D5a/99	7/1
	DEFENSIVE LINEMEN						
70	Anderson, Ken (T)	6-3/310	10-4-75	2	Arkansas	FA/98	2/0
72	Cotton, James (E)	6-4/251	11-7-76	R	Ohio State	D7a/00	—
93	Daniels, Phillip (E)	6-5/284	3-4-73	5	Georgia	UFA/00	*16/16
95	Davis, Russell (E)	6-4/295	3-28-75	2	North Carolina	D2/99	11/8
99	Flanigan, Jim (T)	6-2/288	8-27-71	7	Notre Dame	D3/94	16/16
76	Mims, Chris (E)	6-5/300	9-29-70	9	Tennessee	FA/00	*9/0
98	Robinson, Bryan	6-4/295	6-22-74	4	Fresno State	W-StL/98	16/16
96	Simmons, Clyde (E)	6-5/292	8-4-64	15	Western Carolina	UFA/99	16/0
90	Tuinei, Van (E)	6-4/275	2-16-71	4	Arizona	W-Ind./99	16/8
97	Wells, Mike (T)	6-3/315	1-6-71	8	Iowa	UFA/98	16/16
	LINEBACKERS						
52	Burns, Keith	6-2/245	5-16-72	7	Oklahoma State	UFA/99	15/0
59	Colvin, Rosevelt	6-3/260	9-5-77	2	Purdue	D4b/99	11/0
94	Hallock, Ty	6-2/254	4-30-71	8	Michigan State	UFA/98	15/4
55	Harris, Sean	6-3/252	2-25-72	6	Arizona	D3/95	14/10
53	Holdman, Warrick	6-1/238	11-22-75	2	Texas A&M	D4a/99	16/5
92	Minter, Barry	6-2/245	1-28-70	8	Tulsa	T-Dal./93	16/16
91	Samuel, Khari	6-3/242	10-14-76	2	Massachusetts	D5b/99	13/1
54	Urlacher, Brian	6-3/249	5-25-78	R	New Mexico	D1/00	—
	DEFENSIVE BACKS						
36	Austin, Ray (S)	5-11/204	12-21-74	4	Tennessee	W-NYJ/98	15/0
39	Austin, Reggie (CB)	5-9/172	1-21-77	R	Wake Forest	D4/00	—
23	Azumah, Jerry (CB)	5-10/195	9-1-77	2	New Hampshire	D5c/99	16/2
30	Brown, Mike (S)	5-10/202	2-13-78	R	Nebraska	D2/00	—
21	Cousin, Terry (CB)	5-9/182	4-11-75	4	South Carolina	FA/97	16/9
43	Green, Mike (S)	6-0/176	12-6-76	R	Louisiana-Lafayette	D7b/00	—
27	Harris, Walt (CB)	5-11/195	8-10-74	5	Mississippi State	D1/96	15/15
26	Jones, Jermaine (CB)	5-8/183	7-25-76	2	Northwestern (La.) State	FA/99	2/0
37	Parrish, Tony (S)	5-10/206	11-23-75	3	Washington	D2/98	16/16
29	Smith, Frankie (S)	5-9/182	10-8-68	8	Baylor	UFA/98	15/0
25	Smith, Thomas (CB)	5-11/190	12-5-70	8	North Carolina	UFA/00	*16/16
33	Taylor, Cordell (CB)	6-0/190	12-22-73	3	Hampton (Va.)	FA/99	2/0
22	Wooden, Shawn (S)	5-11/205	10-23-73	5	Notre Dame	UFA/00	*15/6
	SPECIALISTS						
12	Bartholomew, Brent (P)	6-2/220	10-22-76	2	Ohio State	FA/00	*2/0
2	Edinger, Paul (K)	5-10/169	1-17-78	R	Michigan State	D6b/00	—
10	Holmes, Jaret (K)	6-0/203	3-3-76	2	Auburn	FA/99	3/0

*Not with Bears in 1999.
Other free agent veterans invited to camp: LB Brendon Ayanbadejo, LB Shawn Banks, RB Marlon Barnes, WR Corey Bridges, S Jim Cantelupe, CB Cedric Donaldson, FB Scott Dragos, QB Mark Hartsell, OT Jimmy Herndon, G/OT Keno Hills, RB Chad Levitt, WR Chad Mackey, CB Ray McElroy, OT Chad Overhauser, OT Dan Palmer, WR Sulecio Sanford, DE Chris Ward, CB John Williams.

Abbreviations: D1—draft pick, first round; SD-2—supplemental draft pick, second round; W—claimed on waivers; T—obtained in trade; PlanB—Plan B free-agent acquisition; FA—free-agent acquisition (other than Plan B); UFA—unconditional free agent acquisition; ED—expansion draft pick.

CHICAGO BEARS

MISCELLANEOUS TEAM DATA

Stadium (capacity, surface):
Soldier Field (66,944, grass)
Business address:
Halas Hall at Conway Park
1000 Football Drive
Lake Forest, IL 60045
Business phone:
847-295-6600
Ticket information:
847-615-2327
Team colors:
Navy blue, orange and white
Flagship radio station:
WMAQ, 670 AM
Training site:
University of Wisconsin-Platteville
Platteville, Wis.
608-342-1201

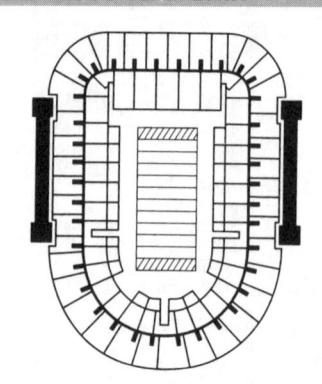

TSN REPORT CARD

Coaching staff	B+	The makeover started at the top, as the new staff gave the players a new attitude and installed systems they believed in. Restoring the psyche of the players was necessary and Dick Jauron's staff did it from the start.
Quarterbacks	B	Cade McNown opens as the starter, but he has not proved he can lead the team to wins. Jim Miller was re-signed and gives the Bears their most dangerous No. 2 since Steve Walsh in '94. Miller is good enough to edge out McNown with a strong showing in preseason games.
Running backs	D	Curtis Enis was the running game in '99, what there was of it, and he was generally ineffective coming of ACL surgery. He will be a 250-pound hammer this year but the Bears are moving away from a team that is willing or able to control the game on the ground.
Receivers	A-	Marcus Robinson is an emerging superstar and Bobby Engram is a superior all-around wideout. Marty Booker can score from anywhere and brings a physical element to the flanker-screen game. This group can be among the league's best if Eddie Kennison or rookie Dez White provide more of an outside deep threat.
Offensive line	B-	The pass protection is respectable but the run blocking is neither used much nor consistently effective. Olin Kreutz became a first-line center in his first season as a starter. The group should benefit from a year of experience with coach Bob Wylie's techniques.
Defensive line	C	The addition of right defensive end Phillip Daniels as a free agent will upgrade both the rush and run defense. He and left end Bryan Robinson are underrated all-around ends who can turn this line into one of the franchise's better groups in recent years.
Linebackers	C+	Ninth overall pick Brian Urlacher makes the group bigger and faster but no one has shown consistent big-play impact. Urlacher and weak-side backer Warrick Holdman infuse youth and bring real speed; they just need to do big things once they get where they're going.
Secondary	B	Signing cornerback Thomas Smith as a free agent was pivotal, and safeties Shawn Wooden and rookie Mike Brown should upgrade the deep middle. The enigma remains cornerback Walt Harris, who can flip between Pro Bowler and Mr. Irrelevant on the same series. This is a bad-hands group that could use some stick 'em.
Special teams	D-	Until new kickers and punters emerge, this is still potentially the game-killing area it was in '99. The coverage units must keep some veterans around if it is to improve at all. Glyn Milburn is one of the best kick returners in the league, but he's not much of a threat to score on his runbacks.

CINCINNATI BENGALS
AFC CENTRAL DIVISION

2000 SEASON

CLUB DIRECTORY

ADMINISTRATION
President
  Mike Brown
Executive vice president
  Katie Blackburn
Vice president
  John Sawyer
Business development
  Troy Blackburn
Business manager
  Bill Connelly
Chief financial officer
  Bill Scanlon
Controller
  Johanna Kappner
Managing director of Paul Brown Stadium
  Eric Brown
Director of technology
  Jo Ann Ralstin

SALES/TICKETING
Director of sales and community affairs
  Jeff Berding
Director of corporate sales and marketing
  Vince Cicero
Ticket manager
  Paul Kelly
Corporate sales executives
  Tony Kountz, Brian Sells
Corporate sales coordinator
  Jennifer Benjamin
Premium seating sales coordinator
  Stephanie Mileham
Group sales manager
  Kevin Lane
Merchandise manager
  Monty Montague
JungleVision producer
  Scott Simpson
Ticket office
  Tim Kelly, Bev Schmidt, Jason Williams

PUBLIC RELATIONS/INTERNET
Public relations director
  Jack Brennan
Assistant public relations director
  P.J. Combs
Internet editor/writer
  Geoff Hobson

Head coach
Bruce Coslet

Assistant coaches
  Paul Alexander (offensive line)
  Jim Anderson (running backs)
  Ken Anderson (offensive coord.)
  Louie Cioffi (def. staff assistant)
  Mark Duffner (linebackers)
  Ray Horton (defensive backs)
  Tim Krumrie (defensive line)
  Dick LeBeau (asst. HC/def. coord.)
  Steve Mooshagian (wide rec.)
  Al Roberts (special teams)
  Frank Verducci (tight ends)
  Kim Wood (strength & cond.)

PLAYER PERSONNEL
Senior vice president
  Pete Brown
Vice president
  Paul Brown
Director of pro/college personnel
  Jim Lippincott
Scouting
  Duke Tobin, Frank Smouse

FOOTBALL OPERATIONS
Athletic trainer
  Paul Sparling
Assistant athletic trainers
  Billy Brooks, Brian Dykhuizen
Equipment manager
  Rob Recker
Assistant equipment manager
  Jeff Brickner
Video director
  Travis Brammer
Assistant video director
  Andy Fineberg

SCHEDULE

Sept. 3—	Open date	
Sept. 10—	CLEVELAND	1:00
Sept. 17—	at Jacksonville	1:00
Sept. 24—	at Baltimore	1:00
Oct. 1—	MIAMI	4:05
Oct. 8—	TENNESSEE	1:00
Oct. 15—	at Pittsburgh	1:00
Oct. 22—	DENVER	1:00
Oct. 29—	at Cleveland	1:00
Nov. 5—	BALTIMORE	1:00
Nov. 12—	at Dallas	1:00
Nov. 19—	at New England	1:00
Nov. 26—	PITTSBURGH	1:00
Dec. 3—	ARIZONA	1:00
Dec. 10—	at Tennessee	1:00
Dec. 17—	JACKSONVILLE	1:00
Dec. 24—	at Philadelphia	1:00

All times are Eastern.
All games Sunday unless noted.

DRAFT CHOICES

Peter Warrick, WR, Florida State (first round/fourth pick overall).
Mark Roman, CB, Louisiana State (2/34).
Ron Dugans, WR, Florida State (3/66).
Curtis Keaton, RB, James Madison (4/97).
Robert Bean, DB, Mississippi State (5/133).
Neil Rackers, PK, Illinois (6/169).
Brad St. Louis, TE, Southwest Missouri State (7/210).

1999 REVIEW

RESULTS

Sept.12—at Tennessee	L	35-36
Sept.19—SAN DIEGO	L	7-34
Sept.26—at Carolina	L	3-27
Oct. 3—ST. LOUIS	L	10-38
Oct. 10—at Cleveland	W	18-17
Oct. 17—PITTSBURGH	L	3-17
Oct. 24—at Indianapolis	L	10-31
Oct. 31—JACKSONVILLE	L	10-41
Nov. 7—at Seattle	L	20-37
Nov. 14—TENNESSEE	L	14-24
Nov. 21—BALTIMORE	L	31-34
Nov. 28—at Pittsburgh	W	27-20
Dec. 5—SAN FRANCISCO	W	44-30
Dec. 12—CLEVELAND	W	44-28
Dec. 19—Open date		
Dec. 26—at Baltimore	L	0-22
Jan. 2—at Jacksonville	L	7-24

RECORDS/RANKINGS

1999 regular-season record: 4-12 (5th in AFC Central); 3-7 in division; 3-10 in conference; 1-2 vs. NFC; 2-6 at home; 2-6 on road; 3-8 on turf; 1-4 on grass.
Team record last five years: 29-51 (.363, ranks 29th in league in that span).
1999 team rankings:

	No.	AFC	NFL
Total offense	*329.8	8	15
Rushing offense	*128.2	4	T6
Passing offense	*201.6	12	23
Scoring offense	283	14	24
Total defense	*343.6	15	25
Rushing defense	*106.2	9	16
Passing defense	*237.4	16	28
Scoring defense	460	16	31
Takeaways	27	T11	T22
Giveaways	32	12	T16
Turnover differential	-5	T11	T19
Sacks	35	14	T23
Sacks allowed	49	T12	T27

*Yards per game.

TEAM LEADERS

Scoring (kicking): Doug Pelfrey, 81 pts. (27/27 PATs, 18/27 FGs).
Scoring (touchdowns): Darnay Scott, 42 pts. (7 receiving).
Passing: Jeff Blake, 2,670 yds. (389 att., 215 comp., 55.3%, 16 TDs, 12 int.).
Rushing: Corey Dillon, 1,200 yds. (263 att., 4.6 avg., 5 TDs).
Receptions: Darnay Scott, 68 (1,022 yds., 15.0 avg., 7 TDs).
Interceptions: Rodney Heath, 3 (72 yds., 1 TD).
Sacks: Michael Bankston, 6.0.
Punting: Will Brice, 41.3 avg. (60 punts, 2,475 yds., 2 blocked).
Punt returns: Craig Yeast, 20.9 avg. (10 att., 209 yds., 2 TDs).
Kickoff returns: Tremain Mack, 27.1 avg. (51 att., 1,382 yds., 1 TD).

– 23 –

2000 SEASON
TRAINING CAMP ROSTER

CINCINNATI BENGALS

No.	QUARTERBACKS	Ht./Wt.	Born	NFL Exp.	College	How acq.	'99 Games GP/GS
4	Covington, Scott	6-2/217	1-17-76	2	Miami (Fla.)	D7b/99	3/0
19	Mitchell, Scott	6-6/240	1-2-68	11	Utah	UFA/00	*2/2
11	Smith, Akili	6-3/220	8-21-75	2	Oregon	D1/99	7/4
	RUNNING BACKS						
35	Basnight, Michael	6-1/230	9-3-77	2	North Carolina A&T	FA/99	13/1
32	Carter, Ki-Jana	5-10/222	9-12-73	6	Penn State	D1/95	3/0
28	Dillon, Corey	6-1/225	10-24-75	4	Washington	D2/97	15/15
46	Groce, Clif (FB)	5-11/245	7-30-72	4	Texas A&M	FA/99	16/15
29	Keaton, Curtis	5-10/210	10-18-76	R	James Madison	D4/00	—
39	Shaw, Sedrick	6-0/214	11-16-73	4	Iowa	W-Cle./99	4/0
30	Williams, Nick (FB)	6-1/267	3-30-77	2	Miami (Fla.)	D5/99	11/0
	RECEIVERS						
89	Battaglia, Marco (TE)	6-3/252	1-25-73	5	Rutgers	D2/96	16/0
88	Bush, Steve (TE)	6-3/258	7-4-74	4	Arizona State	FA/97	13/0
8	Dugans, Ron	6-1/205	4-27-77	R	Florida State	D3/00	—
87	Griffin, Damon	5-9/186	6-14-76	2	Oregon	W-SF/99	13/0
85	Hundon, James	6-1/173	4-9-71	4	Portland State	FA/96	6/0
82	McGee, Tony (TE)	6-3/250	4-21-71	8	Michigan	D2/93	16/16
48	St. Louis, Brad (TE)	6-3/240	8-19-76	R	Southwest Missouri State	D7/00	—
86	Scott, Darnay	6-1/205	7-7-72	7	San Diego State	D2/94	16/16
80	Warrick, Peter	5-11/195	6-19-77	R	Florida State	D1/00	—
84	Yeast, Craig	5-7/160	11-20-76	2	Kentucky	D4/99	9/0
	OFFENSIVE LINEMEN						
71	Anderson, Willie (T)	6-5/340	7-11-75	5	Auburn	D1/96	14/14
74	Braham, Rich (C)	6-4/305	11-6-70	7	West Virginia	W-Ari./94	16/16
73	DeMarco, Brian (G)	6-7/323	4-9-72	6	Michigan State	UFA/99	7/7
63	Goff, Mike (G)	6-5/316	1-6-76	3	Iowa	D3b/98	12/1
62	Gutierrez, Brock (C)	6-3/304	9-25-73	4	Central Michigan	FA/98	16/0
60	Jones, Rod (T)	6-4/325	1-11-74	5	Kansas	D7/96	16/15
72	O'Dwyer, Matt (G)	6-5/300	9-1-72	6	Northwestern	UFA/99	16/16
79	Rehberg, Scott (T)	6-8/330	11-17-73	4	Central Michigan	FA/00	*15/13
75	Stephens, Jamain (T)	6-5/330	1-9-74	5	North Carolina A&T	W-Pit./99	7/2
	DEFENSIVE LINEMEN						
90	Bankston, Michael (E)	6-5/285	3-12-70	9	Sam Houston State	UFA/98	16/9
93	Barndt, Tom (T)	6-3/293	3-14-72	5	Pittsburgh	UFA/00	*16/13
96	Booker, Vaughn (E)	6-5/300	2-24-68	7	Cincinnati	UFA/00	*14/14
92	Copeland, John (E)	6-3/280	9-20-70	8	Alabama	D1/93	16/16
99	Gibson, Oliver (T)	6-2/290	3-15-72	6	Notre Dame	UFA/99	16/16
94	Langford, Jevon (E)	6-3/290	2-16-74	5	Oklahoma State	D4/96	12/7
97	Purvis, Andre (T)	6-4/310	7-14-73	4	North Carolina	D5/97	5/0
70	Steele, Glen (E)	6-4/295	10-4-74	3	Michigan	D4/98	16/1
	LINEBACKERS						
98	Curtis, Canute	6-2/256	8-4-74	4	West Virginia	FA/97	15/0
95	Foley, Steve	6-3/260	9-9-75	3	Northeast Louisiana	D3a/98	16/16
91	Granville, Billy	6-3/246	3-11-74	4	Duke	FA/97	16/0
50	Peterson, Ben	6-3/250	3-28-77	1	Pittsburg (Kan.) State	FA/99	3/0
57	Ross, Adrian	6-2/244	2-19-75	3	Colorado State	FA/98	16/10
56	Simmons, Brian	6-3/248	6-21-75	3	North Carolina	D1b/98	16/16
51	Spikes, Takeo	6-2/230	12-17-76	3	Auburn	D1a/98	16/16
55	Wilson, Reinard	6-2/261	12-17-73	4	Florida State	D1/97	15/0
	DEFENSIVE BACKS						
33	Armour, Jo Juan (S)	5-11/220	7-10-76	2	Miami (Ohio)	W-Jax./99	2/0
49	Bean, Robert (CB)	5-10/178	1-6-78	R	Mississippi State	D5/00	—
37	Blackmon, Roosevelt (CB)	6-1/185	9-10-74	3	Morris Brown (Ga.)	W-GB/98	5/3
21	Carter, Tom (CB)	6-0/190	9-5-72	8	Notre Dame	W-Chi./99	14/8
25	Fisher, Charles (CB)	6-0/185	2-2-76	2	West Virginia	D2/99	1/1
26	Hall, Cory (S)	6-0/205	12-5-76	2	Fresno State	D3/99	16/12
27	Hawkins, Artrell (CB)	5-10/190	11-24-75	3	Cincinnati	D2/98	14/13
22	Heath, Rodney (CB)	5-10/170	10-29-74	2	Minnesota	FA/99	16/9
20	Howard, Ty (CB)	5-10/185	11-30-73	4	Ohio State	W-Ari./99	12/3
34	Mack, Tremain (S)	6-0/193	11-21-74	4	Miami (Fla.)	D4/97	12/0
23	Myers, Greg (S)	6-1/202	9-30-72	5	Colorado State	D5/96	12/4
38	Roman, Mark (CB)	5-11/188	3-26-77	R	Louisiana State	D2/00	—
31	Williams, Darryl (S)	6-0/202	1-8-70	9	Miami (Fla.)	FA/00	*13/12
42	Wright, Lawrence (S)	6-1/211	9-6-73	3	Florida	FA/97	14/0
	SPECIALISTS						
6	Costello, Brad (P)	6-1/230	12-12-74	1	Boston University	FA/98	5/0
9	Pelfrey, Doug (K)	5-11/185	9-25-70	8	Kentucky	D8/93	16/0
5	Rackers, Neil (K)	6-0/200	8-16-76	R	Illinois	D6/00	—

*Not with Bengals in 1999.
Other free agent veterans invited to camp: HB Brandon Bennett, P Josh Boies, G Tony Coats, OT Mike Doughty, QB Eric Kresser, DT Chad Pegues, TE Damian Vaughn.

Abbreviations: D1—draft pick, first round; SD-2—supplemental draft pick, second round; W—claimed on waivers; T—obtained in trade; PlanB—Plan B free-agent acquisition; FA—free-agent acquisition (other than Plan B); UFA—unconditional free agent acquisition; ED—expansion draft pick.

MISCELLANEOUS TEAM DATA

Stadium (capacity, surface):
Paul Brown Stadium
(65,600, grass)
Business address:
One Paul Brown Stadium
Cincinnati, OH 45202-3492
Business phone:
513-621-3550
Ticket information:
513-621-8383
Team colors:
Black, orange and white
Flagship radio stations:
WCKY 1360 AM; WOFX 92.5 FM
Training site:
Georgetown College
Georgetown, Ky.
502-863-7088

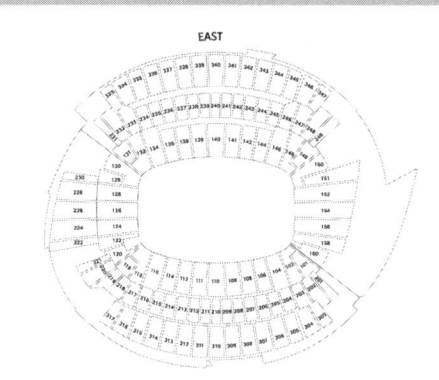

TSN REPORT CARD

Coaching staff	C -	Bruce Coslet is on the hot seat, and rightfully so. He owns a 21-36 record in three and a half years as head coach, but was spared the ax so that second-year quarterback Akili Smith wouldn't be forced to learn a new system. Coslet's first hire was Dick LeBeau, whose 3-4 defense didn't succeed so he switched to the 4-3. It's time to win or make a change.
Quarterbacks	B -	Smith is an awesome talent with raw skills that include a cannon arm and good mobility. He's also a tremendous leader with a commanding presence in the huddle. But he struggled in seven games as a rookie and needs more experience. Having solid weapons around him should lighten his load, but he'll still going through growing pains.
Running backs	C +	Hard-running Pro Bowl tailback Corey Dillon had an offseason of discontent, waiting impatiently for the monster contract he deserves. He's a critical figure in the team's success, but he's not the main man. Smith is. With Ki-Jana Carter injured again, others must step up. Brandon Bennett, Curtis Keaton, Michael Basnight and Sedrick Shaw have solid skills, but only Dillon is the complete package.
Receivers	A	Speed kills and the Bengals, loaded with their fastest set of receivers in more than decade, will spread the field in multiple sets in an attempt to fast break their way to the end zone. Rookie split end Peter Warrick, veteran flanker Darnay Scott and second-year man Craig Yeast all can score from anywhere. The addition of Warrick takes the Bengals from a predictable offense to a high-powered machine.
Offensive line	B +	Continuity is critical and the return of all five starters—C Rich Braham, LG Matt O'Dwyer, RG Brian DeMarco, LT Rod Jones and RT Willie Anderson—will allow the offense to make a smooth transition with Smith at quarterback. Jamain Stephens (OT), Mike Goff (G), Scott Rehberg (G) and Brock Gutierrez (C) are all capable backups, so there won't be much drop-off when an injury occurs.
Defensive line	B	The move to a 4-3 defense puts extra emphasis on the line, and an upgrade in talent and depth was dramatic with the offseason acquisitions of left end Vaughn Booker (Packers) and right tackle Tom Barndt (Chiefs). End John Copeland and tackle Oliver Gibson complete the front four. Backups Michael Bankston, Jevon Langford, Glen Steele and Reinard Wilson will rotate in to keep the starters fresh and to keep the pass rush coming.
Linebackers	A	Middle linebacker Brian Simmons and right linebacker Takeo Spikes are the heart and soul of the defense. As third-year players completely comfortable with the system, they're extremely productive and ready to dominate. Left linebacker Steve Foley needs to step up after leveling off in '99. This group made strides against the run last season. Now its goal is to be become an attacking, big-play unit that plays the pass better and applies more heat on the quarterback.
Secondary	D	If there's an Achilles heel, this is it. This unit has been burned by the bomb, but there's hope that will change because the pressure of the line and coverage by the linebackers should take some of the heat off the secondary. Veterans Tom Carter and Darryl Williams bring stability and leadership at left corner and free safety, but neither is real physical. The jury is still out on right corner Artrell Hawkins. He's a tough run defender, but struggled playing the ball in '99. Cory Hall offers a physical presence at strong safety. But cornerback play is the key. Rodney Heath is a capable backup to Carter. Rookies Mark Roman and Robert Bean need to come on strong and push Hawkins.
Special teams	C	The return game should be brilliant with Pro Bowl kickoff return specialist Tremain Mack and punt returner Yeast back to haunt opponents with their blinding speed and quickness. Add Warrick to the punt-return mix and that unit becomes so good it's scary. Punter Brad Costello is healthy again after being plagued by a torn right calf muscle that caused his net averge (28.7) to plummet in '99. Doug Pelfrey's nine missed field goals last season were so alarming that the team drafted Illinois kicker Neil Rackers in the sixth round.

CLEVELAND BROWNS
AFC CENTRAL DIVISION

2000 SEASON

CLUB DIRECTORY

Owner and chairman
Al Lerner
President and chief executive officer
Carmen Policy
V.p., director of football operations
Dwight Clark
V.p., chief administrative officer
Kofi Bonner
V.p. of finance and treasurer
Doug Jacobs
V.p., director of stadium operations and security
Lew Merletti
Asst. dir. of football operations and general counsel
Lal Heneghan
Director of player personnel
Joe Collins
College personnel coordinator
Phil Neri
Pro personnel coordinator
Keith Kidd
Director of operations
Bill Hampton
Executive director of marketing
Bruce Popko
Director of ticket operations
Mike Jennings
Manager of stadium operations
Diane Downing
Director, Cleveland Browns Foundation
Judge George White
Director of publicity/media relations
Todd Stewart
Director of publications/Internet
Dan Arthur
Coordinator of publicity/media relations
Ken Mather
Facilities manager
Greg Hipp

Head coach
Chris Palmer

Assistant coaches
Jerry Butler (wide receivers)
Keith Butler (linebackers)
Pete Carmichael Jr. (tight ends/offensive assistant)
Pete Carmichael Sr. (offensive coordinator)
Romeo Crennel (defensive coordinator/defensive line)
John Fabris (defensive/special teams assistant)
Jerry Holmes (defensive backs)
John Hufnagel (quarterbacks)
Tim Jorgensen (strength)
Joe Kim (assistant strength)
Mark Michaels (special teams)
Ray Perkins (running backs)
Mike Pitts (defensive assistant)
Tony Sparano (off. quality control)

Head athletic trainer
Mike Colello
Equipment manager
Bobby Monica
Video director
Pat Dolan
Head groundskeeper
Chris Powell

SCHEDULE

Sept. 3—	JACKSONVILLE	1:00
Sept. 10—	at Cincinnati	1:00
Sept. 17—	PITTSBURGH	1:00
Sept. 24—	at Oakland	4:15
Oct. 1—	BALTIMORE	1:00
Oct. 8—	at Arizona	4:15
Oct. 15—	at Denver	4:05
Oct. 22—	at Pittsburgh	1:00
Oct. 29—	CINCINNATI	1:00
Nov. 5—	N.Y. GIANTS	1:00
Nov. 12—	NEW ENGLAND	1:00
Nov. 19—	at Tennessee	1:00
Nov. 26—	at Baltimore	1:00
Dec. 3—	at Jacksonville	4:15
Dec. 10—	PHILADELPHIA	1:00
Dec. 17—	TENNESSEE	1:00
Dec. 24—	Open date	

All times are Eastern.
All games Sunday unless noted.

DRAFT CHOICES

Courtney Brown, DE, Penn State (first round/first pick overall).
Dennis Northcutt, WR, Arizona (2/32).
Travis Prentice, RB, Miami of O. (3/63).
JaJuan Dawson, WR, Tulane (3/79).
Lewis Sanders, CB, Maryland (4/95).
Aaron Shea, TE, Michigan (4/110).
Anthony Malbrough, DB, Texas Tech (5/130).
Lamar Chapman, DB, Kansas State (5/146).
Spergon Wynn, QB, SW Tex. St. (6/183).
Brad Bedell, G, Colorado (6/206).
Manuia Savea, G, Arizona (7/207).
Eric Chandler, DE, Jackson St. (7/209).
Rashidi Barnes, DB, Colorado (7/225).

1999 REVIEW

RESULTS

Sept.12—	PITTSBURGH	L	0-43
Sept.19—	at Tennessee	L	9-26
Sept.26—	at Baltimore	L	10-17
Oct. 3—	NEW ENGLAND	L	7-19
Oct. 10—	CINCINNATI	L	17-18
Oct. 17—	at Jacksonville	L	7-24
Oct. 24—	at St. Louis	L	3-34
Oct. 31—	at New Orleans	W	21-16
Nov. 7—	BALTIMORE	L	9-41
Nov. 14—	at Pittsburgh	W	16-15
Nov. 21—	CAROLINA	L	17-31
Nov. 28—	TENNESSEE	L	21-33
Dec. 5—	at San Diego	L	10-23
Dec. 12—	at Cincinnati	L	28-44
Dec. 19—	JACKSONVILLE	L	14-24
Dec. 26—	INDIANAPOLIS	L	28-29
Jan. 2—	Open date		

RECORDS/RANKINGS

1999 regular-season record: 2-14 (6th in AFC Central); 1-9 in division; 1-12 in conference; 1-2 vs. NFC; 0-8 at home; 2-6 on road; 2-2 on turf; 0-12 on grass.

1999 team rankings:

	No.	AFC	NFL
Total offense	*235.1	16	31
Rushing offense	*71.9	16	31
Passing offense	*163.3	16	29
Scoring offense	217	16	31
Total defense	*377.9	16	31
Rushing defense	*171.0	16	31
Passing defense	*206.9	8	11
Scoring defense	437	15	29
Takeaways	20	16	T29
Giveaways	31	T10	T13
Turnover differential	-11	16	28
Sacks	25	16	31
Sacks allowed	60	16	30

*Yards per game.

TEAM LEADERS

Scoring (kicking): Phil Dawson, 47 pts. (23/24 PATs, 8/12 FGs).
Scoring (touchdowns): Terry Kirby, 54 pts. (6 rushing, 3 receiving).
Passing: Tim Couch, 2,447 yds. (399 att., 223 comp., 55.9%, 15 TDs, 13 int.).
Rushing: Terry Kirby, 452 yds. (130 att., 3.5 avg., 6 TDs).
Receptions: Kevin Johnson, 66 (986 yds., 14.9 avg., 8 TDs).
Interceptions: Marquez Pope, 2 (15 yds., 0 TDs).
Sacks: John Thierry, 7.0.
Punting: Chris Gardocki, 43.8 avg. (106 punts, 4,645 yds., 0 blocked).
Punt returns: Kevin Johnson, 6.7 avg. (19 att., 128 yds., 0 TDs).
Kickoff returns: Ronnie Powell, 22.4 avg. (44 att., 986 yds., 0 TDs).

2000 SEASON
TRAINING CAMP ROSTER

No.	QUARTERBACKS	Ht./Wt.	Born	NFL Exp.	College	How acq.	'99 Games GP/GS
2	Couch, Tim	6-4/227	7-31-77	2	Kentucky	D1/99	15/14
11	Detmer, Ty	6-0/194	10-30-67	9	Brigham Young	T-SF/99	5/2
13	Wynn, Spergon	6-3/226	8-10-78	R	SW Texas State	D6a/00	—
	RUNNING BACKS						
44	Edwards, Marc (FB)	6-0/229	11-17-74	4	Notre Dame	T-SF/99	16/14
34	Hill, Madre	5-11/199	1-2-76	1	Arkansas	D7/99	5/0
42	Kirby, Terry	6-1/213	1-20-70	8	Virginia	UFA/99	16/10
41	Prentice, Travis	5-11/221	12-8-76	R	Miami (Ohio)	D3a/00	—
23	Rhett, Errict	5-11/211	12-11-70	7	Florida	UFA/00	*16/10
40	Saleh, Tarek (FB)	6-0/240	11-7-74	4	Wisconsin	ED/99(Car.)	16/0
	RECEIVERS						
83	Campbell, Mark (TE)	6-6/253	12-6-75	2	Michigan	FA/99	14/4
84	Chiaverini, Darrin	6-2/210	10-12-77	2	Colorado	D5/99	16/8
87	Davis, Zola	6-0/185	1-16-75	2	South Carolina	W-GB/99	6/1
88	Dawson, JaJuan	6-1/197	11-5-77	R	Tulane	D3b/00	—
81	Dunn, Damon	5-9/182	3-15-76	1	Stanford	FA/99	1/0
85	Johnson, Kevin	5-10/188	7-15-75	2	Syracuse	D2a/99	16/16
86	Northcutt, Dennis	5-10/167	12-22-77	R	Arizona	D2/00	—
89	Palmer, Randy (TE)	6-4/235	11-12-75	2	Texas A&M-Kingsville	W-Oak./99	3/0
82	Patten, David	5-9/193	8-19-74	4	Western Carolina	FA/00	*16/0
80	Powell, Ronnie	5-10/174	11-3-74	2	Northwestern (La.) State	FA/99	14/0
35	Shea, Aaron (TE)	6-3/244	12-5-76	R	Michigan	D4b/00	—
	OFFENSIVE LINEMEN						
63	Bedell, Brad	6-4/299	2-12-77	R	Colorado	D6b/00	—
77	Brown, Orlando (T)	6-7/350	12-20-70	8	South Carolina State	UFA/99	15/15
65	Bundren, Jim (C)	6-3/303	10-6-74	2	Clemson	ED/99(NYJ)	16/1
69	Chanoine, Roger (T)	6-4/295	8-11-76	1	Temple	FA/99	1/0
61	Lindsay, Everett	6-4/302	9-18-70	7	Mississippi	FA/00	*16/16
72	Oben, Roman (T)	6-4/305	10-9-72	5	Louisville	UFA/00	*16/16
71	Pyne, Jim (G)	6-2/297	11-23-71	7	Virginia Tech	ED/99(Det.)	16/16
68	Ruhman, Chris (T)	6-5/321	12-19-74	3	Texas A&M	FA/99	5/2
67	Savea, Manuia	6-2/306	2-22-75	R	Arizona	D7a/00	—
64	Wohlabaugh, Dave (C)	6-3/292	4-13-72	6	Syracuse	UFA/99	15/15
75	Zahursky, Steve (G)	6-6/305	9-2-76	2	Kent State	FA/99	9/7
	DEFENSIVE LINEMEN						
94	Alexander, Derrick (E)	6-4/286	11-13-73	6	Florida State	UFA/99	16/16
92	Brown, Courtney (E)	6-4/266	2-14-78	R	Penn State	D1/00	—
79	Chandler, Eric (E)	6-5/301	6-6-77	R	Jackson State	D7b/00	—
93	Colinet, Stalin (E)	6-6/288	7-19-74	4	Boston College	T-Min./99	14/10
62	Duff, Bill	6-3/285	2-24-74	2	Tennessee	FA/99	5/0
73	Holland, Darius (T)	6-5/320	11-10-73	6	Colorado	UFA/99	15/11
97	Kuehl, Ryan (T)	6-5/290	1-18-72	4	Virginia	FA/99	16/0
90	McKenzie, Keith (E)	6-3/266	10-17-73	5	Ball State	UFA/00	*16/2
98	Miller, Arnold (E)	6-3/239	1-3-75	2	Louisiana State	FA/99	9/0
78	Rogers, Tyrone (E)	6-5/240	10-11-76	1	Alabama State	FA/99	3/0
99	Roye, Orpheus	6-4/288	1-21-74	5	Florida State	UFA/00	*16/16
91	Spriggs, Marcus (T)	6-4/314	7-26-76	2	Troy (Ala.) State	D6a/99	10/0
96	Thompson, Mike (T)	6-4/296	12-22-71	4	Wisconsin	ED/99(Cin.)	10/0
	LINEBACKERS						
53	Abdullah, Rahim	6-5/233	3-22-76	2	Clemson	D2b/99	16/13
56	Jones, Lenoy	6-1/235	9-25-74	5	Texas Christian	ED/99(Ten.)	16/1
50	McCombs, Tony	6-2/256	8-24-74	3	Eastern Kentucky	FA/00	*0/0
95	Miller, Jamir	6-5/266	11-19-73	7	UCLA	UFA/99	15/15
55	Moore, Marty	6-1/245	3-19-71	7	Kentucky	UFA/00	*15/2
59	Ogle, Kendell	6-0/231	11-25-75	2	Maryland	D6b/99	2/0
58	Rainer, Wali	6-2/235	4-19-77	2	Virginia	D4/99	16/15
	DEFENSIVE BACKS						
28	Barnes, Rashidi	5-11/205	6-26-78	R	Colorado	D7c/00	—
27	Chapman, Lamar	6-0/176	11-6-76	R	Kansas State	D5b/00	—
43	Ellsworth, Percy (S)	6-2/225	10-19-74	5	Virginia	UFA/00	*14/14
24	Fuller, Corey	5-10/217	5-1-71	6	Florida State	UFA/00	16/16
31	Jackson, Raymond	5-10/189	2-17-73	5	Colorado State	ED/99(Buf.)	14/0
20	Little, Earl	6-0/191	3-10-73	3	Miami (Fla.)	W-NO/99	10/0
26	Malbrough, Anthony	5-8/178	12-9-76	R	Texas Tech	D5a/00	—
33	McCutcheon, Daylon (CB)	5-8/180	12-9-76	2	Southern California	D3a/99	16/15
22	McTyer, Tim	5-11/181	12-14-75	4	Brigham Young	ED/99(Phi.)	2/2
25	Sanders, Lewis (S)	6-0/200	6-22-78	R	Maryland	D4a/00	—
21	Smith, Marquis	6-2/213	1-13-75	2	California	D3b/99	16/2
	SPECIALISTS						
4	Dawson, Phil (K)	5-11/190	1-23-75	2	Texas	FA/99	15/0
17	Gardocki, Chris (P)	6-1/200	2-7-70	10	Clemson	UFA/99	16/0

– 27 –

*Not with Browns in 1999.
Other free agent veterans invited to camp: DL Geno Bell, LB Jason Kyle, OT Jeremy McKinney, LB Ryan Taylor.
Abbreviations: D1—draft pick, first round; SD-2—supplemental draft pick, second round; W—claimed on waivers; T—obtained in trade; PlanB—Plan B free-agent acquisition; FA—free-agent acquisition (other than Plan B); UFA—unconditional free agent acquisition; ED—expansion draft pick.

CLEVELAND BROWNS

MISCELLANEOUS TEAM DATA

Stadium (capacity, surface):
Cleveland Browns Stadium
(73,200, grass)
Business address:
76 Lou Groza Boulevard
Berea, Ohio 44017
Business phone:
440-891-5000
Ticket information:
440-891-5050
Team colors:
Brown, orange and white
Flagship radio stations:
WMJI, 105.7 FM
Training site:
76 Lou Groza Boulevard
Berea, Ohio
440-891-5000

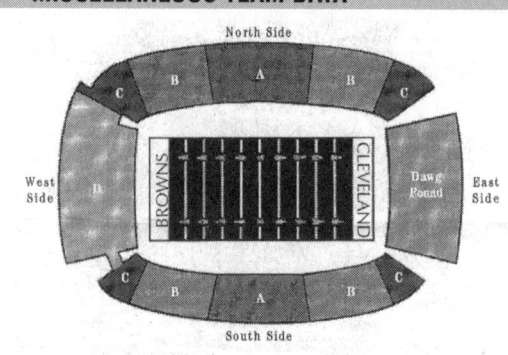

TSN REPORT CARD

Position	Grade	Comments
Coaching staff	B	Chris Palmer got a late start in assembling his staff last year. For example, he couldn't find an offensive coordinator, so he had to handle that job himself. It's an entirely different story this year, since he has the offensive coordinator he wants in Pete Carmichael and the defensive coordinator he wants in Romeo Crennel. All three coaches share the same philosophies, as all are from the Bill Parcells-Tom Coughlin tree. Look for better coaching decisions on game days.
Quarterbacks	B+	This is one of the Browns' few strengths. Tim Couch had one of the better rookie seasons in NFL history in 1999 and should only get better—especially if he can learn to get rid of the ball more quickly so as to avoid the sack, and to use the tight end more. When he went down with a season-ending ankle injury, Ty Detmer stepped in and did a solid job. He won't lose the game for the Browns.
Running backs	C	This position is much better off than it was a year ago. Errict Rhett, whose enthusiasm is contagious, will provide a solid presence as the feature back, which was sorely lacking in 1999. The Browns finally have Terry Kirby in right role, as a third-down pass catcher, and he's a good one. Rookie Travis Prentice is a big, strong, workmanlike back who can run between the tackles, something the Browns did not have last season.
Receivers	C	Kevin Johnson was not only the top rookie receivers in the league in 1999, but also one of the top players at any position. He and Couch form a nice combination. Darrin Chiaverini, also a '99 rookie, is a solid, productive, glue-fingered receiver who will not be easy to dislodge from a starting spot. Rookie Dennis Northcutt will try, though, and his quickness will help his cause. JaJuan Dawson seems more polished that originally thought. But both rookies will need time to develop. At tight end, the Browns will have to go with Mark Campbell and rookie Aaron Shea, both of whom are untested.
Offensive line	D	The Browns are hoping Roman Oben holds down the left tackle spot for forseeable future. Center Dave Wohlabaugh does not get the credit he deserves, and left guard Jim Pyne is solid and consistent. But there are tons of question marks involving the rest of the players here. Much of the problem has been caused by the uncertain availability of right tackle Orlando Brown because of an eye injury suffered late last year. If he returns, the chances of which are iffy at best, the grade could advance one letter.
Defensive line	B-	Last year, this group earned a solid F—it did not rush the passer or stop the run. The Browns attacked the problem in the offseason by taking defensive end Courtney Brown with the first pick in the draft and by signing ends Orpheus Roye and Keith McKenzie in free agency. This far outweighs the free-agent loss of John Thierry, the team's 1999 sack leader. Darius Holland is the best defensive tackle on the roster. The upgrade here has been so great that Derrick Alexander, who played relatively well as a starting end last year, is now a backup.
Linebackers	B	In middle man Wali Rainer, the team's leading tackler last year as a rookie, and weak-side backer Jamir Miller, arguably the best player on the team right now, the Browns are set. Marty Moore, signed in free agency from New England, can play inside or outside and is a much better backup than anyone the Browns had in 1999. The key to this position, if not the defense overall, is strong-side linebacker Rahim Abdullah. He was terribly inconsistent as a rookie last year and was too light to be effective against the run. The Browns are hoping an entire offseason in the weight room, along with another year of maturity, will do the trick.
Secondary	C-	This is an improvement, since the Browns rated a D-minus last year. Rookie right corner Daylon McCutcheon was solid, but beyond that, it was a mess. Corey Fuller, who was moved to free safety from left corner last year, has returned to corner. The Browns drafted three cornerbacks they think can help in Lewis Sanders, Anthony Malbrough and Lamar Chapman. Up-and-coming free safety Percy Ellsworth, signed in free agency, will give that position the ball-hawking ability it lacked last year. At strong safety the Browns are hoping Marquis Smith, who came on late last season a rookie, and Tim McTyer, returning from a broken forearm, can step it up.
Special teams	D	Other than Chris Gardocki's punting—and he was greatly overworked, reducing his effectiveness—there was nothing special about this group. Kicker Phil Dawson got few chances last year, so the Browns still don't know much about him other than he was only mildly successful on the few chances he did have. Thus, he will face a bevy of competition in training camp. The Browns also got no production from their returners, but they're hoping that with a more experienced Ronnie Powell coming back, along with getting some help from draftees Northcutt, Sanders and Chapman, they'll be much, much better in 2000.

DALLAS COWBOYS
NFC EASTERN DIVISION

2000 SEASON

CLUB DIRECTORY

President/general manager
Jerry Jones
Vice presidents
Charlotte Anderson
George Hays
Jerry Jones Jr.
Stephen Jones
Treasurer
Robert Nunez
Director of public relations
Rich Dalrymple
Assistant director of public relations
Brett Daniels
Ticket manager
Carol Padgett
Director of college and pro scouting
Larry Lacewell
Scouts
Tom Ciskowski
Jim Garrett
Tommy Hart
Jim Hess
Walter Juliff
Henry Sroka
Walt Yowarsky
Head athletic trainer
Jim Maurer
Assistant athletic trainers
Britt Brown
Bob Haas
Physicians
Robert Vandermeer
J.R. Zamorano
Equipment/practice fields manager
Mike McCord

Head coach
Dave Campo

Assistant coaches
Joe Avezzano (special teams)
Bill Bates (secondary)
Wes Chandler (wide receivers)
George Edwards (linebackers)
Buddy Geis (offensive nickel package)
Steve Hoffman (kickers/quality control)
Hudson Houck (offensive line)
Jim Jeffcoat (defensive ends)
Joe Juraszek (strength & cond.)
Les Miles (tight ends)
Andre Patterson (def. tackles)
Clancy Pendergrast (defensive nickel package)
Jack Reilly (off. coordinator)
Tommie Robinson (special teams assistant)
Clarence Shelmon (running backs)
Glenn Smith (offensive assistant)
Wade Wilson (quarterbacks)
Mike Zimmer (def. coordinator)

Video director
Robert Blackwell
Director of operations
Bruce Mays

SCHEDULE

Sept. 3—	PHILADELPHIA	4:05
Sept. 10—	at Arizona	8:35
Sept. 18—	at Washington (Mon.)	9:00
Sept. 24—	SAN FRANCISCO	1:00
Oct. 1—	at Carolina	1:00
Oct. 8—	Open date	
Oct. 15—	at N.Y. Giants	1:00
Oct. 22—	ARIZONA	1:00
Oct. 29—	JACKSONVILLE	4:15
Nov. 5—	at Philadelphia	1:00
Nov. 12—	CINCINNATI	1:00
Nov. 19—	at Baltimore	4:15
Nov. 23—	MINNESOTA (Thanks.)	4:05
Dec. 3—	at Tampa Bay	1:00
Dec. 10—	WASHINGTON	4:15
Dec. 17—	N.Y. GIANTS	8:35
Dec. 25—	at Tennessee (Mon.)	9:00

All times are Eastern.
All games Sunday unless noted.

DRAFT CHOICES

Dwayne Goodrich, DB, Tennessee (second round/49th pick overall).
Kareem Larrimore, DB, West Texas A&M (4/109).
Michael Wiley, WR, Ohio State (5/144).
Mario Edwards, DB, Florida State (6/180).
Orantes Grant, LB, Georgia (7/219).

1999 REVIEW

RESULTS

Sept.12—at Washington (OT)	W	41-35
Sept.20—ATLANTA	W	24-7
Sept.26—Open date		
Oct. 3—ARIZONA	W	35-7
Oct. 10—at Philadelphia	L	10-13
Oct. 18—at N.Y. Giants	L	10-13
Oct. 24—WASHINGTON	W	38-20
Oct. 31—at Indianapolis	L	24-34
Nov. 8—at Minnesota	L	17-27
Nov. 14—GREEN BAY	W	27-13
Nov. 21—at Arizona	L	9-13
Nov. 25—MIAMI	W	20-0
Dec. 5—at New England	L	6-13
Dec. 12—PHILADELPHIA	W	20-10
Dec. 19—N.Y. JETS	L	21-22
Dec. 24—at New Orleans	L	24-31
Jan. 2—N.Y. GIANTS	W	26-18
Jan. 9—at Minnesota*	L	10-27

*NFC wild-card game.

RECORDS/RANKINGS

1999 regular-season record: 8-8 (2nd in NFC East); 5-3 in division; 7-5 in conference; 1-3 vs. AFC; 7-1 at home; 1-7 on road; 7-6 on turf; 1-2 on grass.
Team record last five years: 46-34 (.575, ranks 8th in league in that span).
1999 team rankings:

	No.	NFC	NFL
Total offense	*323.6	8	16
Rushing offense	*128.2	3	T6
Passing offense	*195.4	12	24
Scoring offense	352	6	11
Total defense	*302.5	3	9
Rushing defense	*90.1	3	6
Passing defense	*212.4	4	13
Scoring defense	276	3	5
Takeaways	33	T6	T10
Giveaways	23	2	5
Turnover differential	10	T2	T6
Sacks	35	T10	T23
Sacks allowed	24	1	2

*Yards per game.

TEAM LEADERS

Scoring (kicking): Richie Cunningham, 67 pts. (31/31 PATs, 12/22 FGs).
Scoring (touchdowns): Emmitt Smith, 78 pts. (11 rushing, 2 receiving).
Passing: Troy Aikman, 2,964 yds. (442 att., 263 comp., 59.5%, 17 TDs, 12 int.).
Rushing: Emmitt Smith, 1,397 yds. (329 att., 4.2 avg., 11 TDs).
Receptions: Rocket Ismail, 80 (1,097 yds., 13.7 avg., 6 TDs).
Interceptions: Dexter Coakley, 4 (119 yds., 1 TD).
Sacks: Greg Ellis, 7.5.
Punting: Toby Gowin, 43.2 avg. (81 punts, 3,500 yds., 0 blocked).
Punt returns: Deion Sanders, 11.5 avg. (30 att., 344 yds., 1 TD).
Kickoff returns: Jason Tucker, 27.9 avg. (22 att., 613 yds., 0 TDs).

2000 SEASON
TRAINING CAMP ROSTER

DALLAS COWBOYS

No.	QUARTERBACKS	Ht./Wt.	Born	NFL Exp.	College	How acq.	'99 Games GP/GS
8	Aikman, Troy	6-4/220	11-21-66	12	UCLA	D1/89	14/14
7	Justin, Paul	6-4/211	5-19-68	6	Arizona State	UFA/00	*10/0
	RUNNING BACKS						
48	Johnston, Daryl (FB)	6-2/242	2-10-66	12	Syracuse	D2/89	1/0
39	Neufeld, Ryan (FB)	6-4/240	11-22-75	2	UCLA	FA/99	6/0
22	Smith, Emmitt	5-9/209	5-15-69	11	Florida	D1/90	15/15
44	Thomas, Robert (FB)	6-1/252	12-1-74	3	Henderson State (Ark.)	FA/98	16/7
42	Warren, Chris	6-2/227	1-24-68	11	Ferrum (Va.)	FA/98	16/1
	RECEIVERS						
18	Brazzell, Chris	6-2/193	5-22-76	2	Angelo State (Tex.)	W-NYJ/99	5/0
84	Galloway, Joey	5-11/188	11-20-71	6	Ohio State	T-Sea./00	*8/4
85	Harris, Jackie (TE)	6-4/250	1-4-68	11	Northeast Louisiana	UFA/00	*12/1
81	Ismail, Rocket	5-11/190	11-18-69	8	Notre Dame	UFA/99	16/14
89	LaFleur, David (TE)	6-7/272	1-29-74	4	Louisiana State	D1/97	16/16
86	Lucky, Mike (TE)	6-6/273	11-23-75	2	Arizona	D7a/99	14/4
83	McGarity, Wane	5-8/197	9-30-76	2	Texas	D4a/99	5/1
82	McKnight, James	6-1/198	6-17-72	7	Liberty (Va.)	T-Sea./99	0/0
2	Ogden, Jeff	6-0/190	2-22-75	3	Eastern Washington	FA/98	16/0
87	Tucker, Jason	6-1/182	6-24-76	2	Texas Christian	FA/99	15/4
12	Wiley, Michael	5-11/189	1-5-78	R	Ohio State	D5/00	—
	OFFENSIVE LINEMEN						
76	Adams, Flozell (T)	6-7/335	5-18-75	3	Michigan State	D2/98	16/16
73	Allen, Larry (G)	6-3/326	11-27-71	7	Sonoma State (Calif.)	D2/94	11/11
64	Diaz, Jorge (G)	6-4/315	11-15-73	5	Texas A&M-Kingsville	FA/00	*13/11
69	Fricke, Ben (G)	6-0/295	11-3-75	2	Houston	FA/99	3/0
66	Hutson, Tony (G)	6-3/317	3-13-74	4	Northeastern Oklahoma State	FA/96	2/2
77	Page, Solomon (T)	6-4/321	2-27-76	2	West Virginia	D2/99	14/6
53	Stepnoski, Mark (C)	6-2/265	1-20-67	12	Pittsburgh	UFA/99	15/15
79	Williams, Erik (T)	6-6/311	9-7-68	10	Central State (Ohio)	D3c/91	14/14
	DEFENSIVE LINEMEN						
96	Ekuban, Ebenezer (E)	6-3/265	5-29-76	2	North Carolina	D1/99	16/2
98	Ellis, Greg (E)	6-6/286	8-14-75	3	North Carolina	D1/98	13/13
95	Hennings, Chad (T)	6-6/291	10-20-65	9	Air Force	D11/88	16/16
78	Lett, Leon (T)	6-6/290	10-12-68	10	Emporia (Kan.) State	D7/91	8/1
94	Myers, Michael	6-2/288	1-20-76	3	Alabama	D4/98	6/0
75	Noble, Brandon (T)	6-2/285	4-10-74	2	Penn State	FA/99	16/0
90	Spellman, Alonzo	6-4/292	9-27-71	8	Ohio State	FA/99	16/6
93	Zellner, Peppi (E)	6-5/257	3-14-75	2	Fort Valley (Ga.) State	D4b/99	13/0
	LINEBACKERS						
55	Bordano, Chris	6-1/241	12-30-74	3	Southern Methodist	T-NO/00	*15/12
58	Bowden, Joe	5-11/235	2-25-70	9	Oklahoma	UFA/00	*15/15
52	Coakley, Dexter	5-10/228	10-20-72	4	Appalachian State	D3a/97	16/16
46	Grant, Orantes	6-0/225	3-18-78	R	Georgia	D7/00	—
54	Hambrick, Darren	6-2/227	8-30-75	3	South Carolina	D5a/98	16/12
59	Nguyen, Dat	5-11/231	9-25-75	2	Texas A&M	D3/99	16/0
56	Russ, Bernard	6-1/238	11-4-73	3	West Virginia	FA/00	*6/0
57	Wortham, Barron	5-11/245	11-1-69	7	Texas-El Paso	FA/00	*16/15
	DEFENSIVE BACKS						
29	Akins, Chris (S)	5-11/195	11-29-76	2	Arkansas-Pine Bluff	FA/99	9/0
27	Edwards, Mario (CB)	6-0/191	12-1-75	R	Florida State	D6/00	—
23	Goodrich, Dwayne (CB)	5-11/198	5-29-78	R	Tennessee	D2/00	—
38	Hawthorne, Duane (CB)	5-10/175	8-26-76	2	Northern Illinois	FA/99	13/0
20	Kaiser, Jason (S)	6-0/190	11-9-73	1	Culver-Stockton College (Mo.)	FA/99	0/0
41	Larrimore, Kareem (CB)	5-11/190	4-21-76	R	West Texas A&M	D4/00	—
47	McNeil, Ryan (CB)	6-2/192	10-4-70	8	Miami (Fla.)	UFA/99	*16/14
43	Reese, Izell (S)	6-2/190	5-7-74	3	Alabama-Birmingham	D6/98	8/4
21	Sanders, Deion (CB)	6-1/198	8-9-67	12	Florida State	FA/95	14/14
26	Smith, Kevin (CB)	5-11/190	4-7-70	9	Texas A&M	D1a/92	8/8
31	Teague, George (S)	6-1/196	2-18-71	8	Alabama	UFA/00	*14/14
25	Williams, Charlie (CB)	6-0/204	2-2-72	5	Bowling Green State	D3/95	16/8
28	Woodson, Darren (S)	6-1/219	4-25-69	9	Arizona State	D2b/92	15/15
	SPECIALISTS						
10	Cantrell, Barry (P)	6-1/195	11-2-76	1	Fordham	FA/00	*0/0

*Not with Cowboys in 1999.

Other free agent veterans invited to camp: WR Morris Anderson, RB Michael Black, C/G Chris Brymer, G Kelvin Garmon, DE Kendrick Gholston, WR Deon Mitchell, S Beau Morgan, LB Joe Phipps, TE Brian Roche, LB Brandon Tolbert, DE Dimitrius Underwood, DL Greg Wilkins.

Abbreviations: D1—draft pick, first round; SD-2—supplemental draft pick, second round; W—claimed on waivers; T—obtained in trade; PlanB—Plan B free-agent acquisition; FA—free-agent acquisition (other than Plan B); UFA—unconditional free agent acquisition; ED—expansion draft pick.

MISCELLANEOUS TEAM DATA

Stadium (capacity, surface):
Texas Stadium
(65,675, artificial)
Business address:
One Cowboys Parkway
Irving, TX 75063
Business phone:
972-556-9900
Ticket information:
972-785-5000
Team colors:
Blue, metallic silver blue and white
Flagship radio station:
KVIL, 103.7 FM
Training site:
Midwestern State University
Wichita Falls, Tex.
972-556-9900

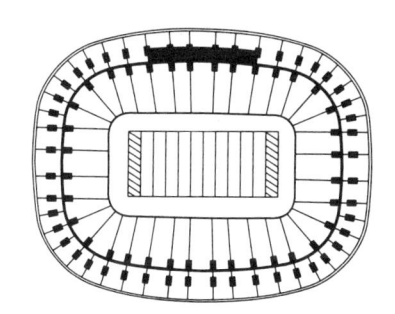

TSN REPORT CARD

Coaching staff	C +	There's a lot to prove with a first-time head coach (Dave Campo), a first-time NFL defensive coordinator (Mike Zimmer), a new offensive coordinator (Jack Reilly), a first-time NFL secondary coach (Bill Bates) and a first-time NFL wide receivers coach (Wes Chandler). But this staff has a lot of character and, best of all, a lot of fire.
Quarterbacks	B -	Troy Aikman still is one of the NFL bests, and his new offensive toys should make him even that much more dangerous. But the club might be hurting at the backup spot following the loss of Jason Garrett. Paul Justin, though in the league since 1991, has few NFL skins on the wall.
Running backs	B	Emmitt Smith proved last season he is fully capable of turning in 1,400-yard seasons, and that he still knows how to get into the end zone. He might not have the speed to consistently break long ones, but he'll average at least 4.2 yards a carry the hard way. Chris Warren is a capable backup, but there is little experience at fullback.
Receivers	B +	This undoubtedly is the Cowboys' most talented receiving corps since 1983. Certainly it's the fastest, likely in three decades. Both Joey Galloway and Rocket Ismail are legitimate NFL receivers, and the backups are more than just raw, developmental-type players.
Offensive line	A -	With the exception of proven backups, this line has the ability to dominate games. It has power, a nasty attitude and, really, no weak link. The only question is at right guard, where Solomon Page will likely become a full-time starter for the first time in his two-year career.
Defensive line	B -	This unit has the chance to become the most dominant on the team, but there is much to be proven. Like, can Greg Ellis return from a broken leg? Is Ebenezer Ekuban as good as his first-round draft status? Is Dimitrius Underwood serious about football? And can Leon Lett return to old form? If yes, watch out. If no, watch out below.
Linebackers	C	Another unproven group. There is projected talent with Dat Nguyen in the middle and either Darren Hambrick or veteran Joe Bowden on the outside. But Dexter Coakley is the only backer who previously has stood out. This is a team that has never won because of its linebacking talent anyway.
Secondary	C	Another who-really-knows position, especially at cornerback. Both veteran corners, Kevin Smith and Ryan McNeil, are coming off so-so seasons, and the youngsters, though talented, still have a lot to learn. The strength might be in the actual numbers and ability to play backup corners on the nickel.
Special teams	C	Kicking coach Steve Hoffman must once again spin his magic. He needs to come up with two new kickers, and even he's not sure of any of the candidates until they're exposed to NFL competition this summer. The return game should have enough talent to be dangerous. The depth at linebacker and cornerback should aid the coverage teams.

DENVER BRONCOS
AFC WESTERN DIVISION

2000 SEASON

CLUB DIRECTORY

President/chief executive officer
Pat Bowlen
General manager
Neal Dahlen
Vice president of business operations
Joe Ellis
Vice president of administration
John Beake
Chief financial officer
Allen Fears
Dir. of ticket operations/business dev.
Rick Nichols
Stadium operations manager
Gail Stuckey
Senior director of media relations
Jim Saccomano
Director of operations
Bill Harpole
Director of pro personnel
To be announced
Director of college scouting
Ted Sundquist
Director of special services
Fred Fleming
Director of player relations
Billy Thompson
Scouts
Bob Beers
Scott DiStefano
Jim Goodman
Cornell Green
Dan Rambo
Dale Strahm
Head trainer
Steve Antonopulos
Assistant trainers
Jim Keller
Corey Oshikoya
Physician
Richard Hawkins

Head coach
Mike Shanahan

Assistant coaches
Frank Bush (nickel package/secondary)
Larry Coyer (linebackers)
Rick Dennison (special teams)
Karl Dorrell (wide receivers)
George Dyer (defensive line)
Alex Gibbs (assistant head coach/offensive line)
Gary Kubiak (offensive coordinator/quarterbacks)
Pat McPherson (offensive assistant)
Ron Milus (defensive backs)
Brian Pariani (tight ends)
Greg Robinson (defensive coordinator)
Greg Saporta (assistant strength & conditioning)
John Teerlinck (pass rush specialist)
Terry Tumey (defensive assistant)
Bobby Turner (running backs)
Rich Tuten (strength & cond.)

Equipment manager
Doug West
Director/video operations
Kent Erickson

SCHEDULE

Date	Opponent	Time
Sept. 4—	at St. Louis (Mon.)	9:00
Sept. 10—	ATLANTA	4:15
Sept. 17—	at Oakland	4:05
Sept. 24—	KANSAS CITY	4:15
Oct. 1—	NEW ENGLAND	4:05
Oct. 8—	at San Diego	4:15
Oct. 15—	CLEVELAND	4:05
Oct. 22—	at Cincinnati	1:00
Oct. 29—	Open date	
Nov. 5—	at N.Y. Jets	4:15
Nov. 13—	OAKLAND (Mon.)	9:00
Nov. 19—	SAN DIEGO	4:05
Nov. 26—	at Seattle	4:15
Dec. 3—	at New Orleans	1:00
Dec. 10—	SEATTLE	4:05
Dec. 17—	at Kansas City	1:00
Dec. 23—	SAN FRANCISCO (Sat.)	4:15

All times are Eastern.
All games Sunday unless noted.

DRAFT CHOICES

Deltha O'Neal, DB, California (first round/15th pick overall).
Ian Gold, LB, Michigan (2/40).
Kenoy Kennedy, S, Arkansas (2/45).
Chris Cole, WR, Texas A&M (3/70).
Jerry Johnson, DT, Florida State (4/101).
Cooper Carlisle, T, Florida (4/112).
Muneer Moore, WR, Richmond (5/154).
Mike Anderson, RB, Utah (6/189).
Jarious Jackson, QB, Notre Dame (7/214).
Leroy Fields, WR, Jackson State (7/246).

1999 REVIEW

RESULTS

Sept.13—	MIAMI	L 21-38
Sept.19—	at Kansas City	L 10-26
Sept.26—	at Tampa Bay	L 10-13
Oct. 3—	N.Y. JETS	L 13-21
Oct. 10—	at Oakland	W 16-13
Oct. 17—	GREEN BAY	W 31-10
Oct. 24—	at New England	L 23-24
Oct. 31—	MINNESOTA	L 20-23
Nov. 7—	at San Diego	W 33-17
Nov. 14—	at Seattle	L 17-20
Nov. 22—	OAKLAND (OT)	W 27-21
Nov. 28—	Open date	
Dec. 5—	KANSAS CITY	L 10-16
Dec. 13—	at Jacksonville	L 24-27
Dec. 19—	SEATTLE (OT)	W 36-30
Dec. 25—	at Detroit	W 17-7
Jan. 2—	SAN DIEGO	L 6-12

RECORDS/RANKINGS

1999 regular-season record: 6-10 (5th in AFC West); 4-4 in division; 4-8 in conference; 2-2 vs. NFC; 3-5 at home; 3-5 on road; 1-1 on turf; 5-9 on grass.
Team record last five years: 53-27 (.663, ranks 2nd in league in that span).
1999 team rankings:

	No.	AFC	NFL
Total offense	*330.2	7	14
Rushing offense	*116.5	8	12
Passing offense	*213.7	7	15
Scoring offense	314	11	18
Total defense	*297.1	5	7
Rushing defense	*108.6	12	19
Passing defense	*188.5	7	8
Scoring defense	318	8	11
Takeaways	26	13	25
Giveaways	28	T7	T10
Turnover differential	-2	T9	T15
Sacks	50	3	T4
Sacks allowed	34	5	T8

*Yards per game.

TEAM LEADERS

Scoring (kicking): Jason Elam, 116 pts. (29/29 PATs, 29/36 FGs).
Scoring (touchdowns): Olandis Gary, 44 pts. (7 rushing, 1 2-pt. conv.).
Passing: Brian Griese, 3,032 yds. (452 att., 261 comp., 57.7%, 14 TDs, 14 int.).
Rushing: Olandis Gary, 1,159 yds. (276 att., 4.2 avg., 7 TDs).
Receptions: Rod Smith, 79 (1,020 yds., 12.9 avg., 4 TDs).
Interceptions: Tory James, 5 (59 yds., 0 TDs).
Sacks: Trevor Pryce, 13.0.
Punting: Tom Rouen, 46.5 avg. (84 punts, 3,908 yds., 0 blocked).
Punt returns: Chris Watson, 7.6 avg. (44 att., 334 yds., 1 TD).
Kickoff returns: Chris Watson, 23.7 avg. (48 att., 1,138 yds., 0 TDs).

2000 SEASON
TRAINING CAMP ROSTER

DENVER BRONCOS

No.	QUARTERBACKS	Ht./Wt.	Born	NFL Exp.	College	How acq.	'99 Games GP/GS
12	Frerotte, Gus	6-3/230	8-3-71	7	Tulsa	UFA/00	*9/6
14	Griese, Brian	6-3/215	3-18-75	3	Michigan	D3/98	14/13
17	Jackson, Jarious	6-0/228	5-3-77	R	Notre Dame	D7a/00	—
	RUNNING BACKS						
38	Anderson, Mike	6-0/235	9-21-73	R	Utah	D6/00	—
20	Avery, John	5-9/190	1-11-76	3	Mississippi	T-Mia./99	7/0
30	Davis, Terrell	5-11/210	10-28-72	6	Georgia	D6b/95	4/4
22	Gary, Olandis	5-11/218	5-18-75	2	Georgia	D4/99	12/12
29	Griffith, Howard (FB)	6-0/230	11-17-67	8	Illinois	UFA-Car./97	16/16
37	Lynn, Anthony (FB)	6-3/230	12-21-68	7	Texas Tech	FA/97	16/0
42	Smith, Detron (FB)	5-10/230	2-25-74	5	Texas A&M	D3a/96	16/0
	RECEIVERS						
89	Carswell, Dwayne (TE)	6-3/260	1-18-72	7	Liberty (Va.)	FA/94	16/11
86	Chamberlain, Byron (TE)	6-1/242	10-17-71	6	Wayne State (Neb.)	D7b/95	16/0
88	Clark, Desmond (TE)	6-3/255	4-20-77	2	Wake Forest	D6a/99	9/0
84	Cole, Chris	6-0/195	11-12-77	R	Texas A&M	D3/00	—
81	Cooper, Andre	6-2/210	6-21-75	2	Florida State	FA/98	10/1
85	Doering, Chris	6-4/195	5-19-73	4	Florida	FA/99	3/0
15	Fields, Leroy	6-3/205	12-2-75	R	Jackson State	D7b/00	—
87	McCaffrey, Ed	6-5/215	8-17-68	10	Stanford	UFA/95	15/15
83	McGriff, Travis	5-8/185	6-24-76	2	Florida	D3b/99	14/0
82	Miller, Billy	6-3/215	4-24-77	2	Southern California	D7a/99	10/0
19	Moore, Muneer	6-1/200	3-15-77	R	Richmond	D5/00	—
80	Smith, Rod	6-0/200	5-15-70	6	Missouri Southern	FA/94	15/15
	OFFENSIVE LINEMEN						
79	Banks, Chris (G)	6-1/300	4-4-73	3	Kansas	D7/96	16/1
65	Carlisle, Cooper (G)	6-5/300	8-11-77	R	Florida	D4b/00	—
	Diaz-Infante, David (G)	6-3/296	3-31-64	6	San Jose State	FA/00	*15/0
64	Friedman, Lennie (G)	6-3/300	10-13-76	2	Duke	D2b/99	0/0
	Johnson, Jason (C)	6-3/290	2-6-74	3	Kansas State	FA/00	*16/0
77	Jones, Tony (T)	6-5/291	5-24-66	13	Western Carolina	T-Bal./97	12/12
78	Lepsis, Matt (T)	6-4/290	1-13-74	4	Colorado	FA/97	16/16
66	Nalen, Tom (C)	6-2/286	5-13-71	7	Boston College	D7c/94	16/16
62	Neil, Dan (G)	6-2/281	10-21-73	4	Texas	D3/97	15/15
69	Schlereth, Mark (G)	6-3/287	1-25-66	12	Idaho	FA/95	15/16
70	Teague, Trey (T)	6-5/285	12-27-74	3	Tennessee	D7a/98	16/4
71	Tuten, Melvin (T)	6-6/305	11-11-71	4	Syracuse	FA/98	2/0
	DEFENSIVE LINEMEN						
92	Archambeau, Lester (E)	6-5/275	6-27-67	11	Stanford	UFA/00	*15/15
73	Brown, Cyron (E)	6-5/275	6-28-75	3	Western Illinois	FA/98	7/0
72	Davis, Nathan (T)	6-5/312	2-6-74	4	Indiana	FA/00	*4/0
96	Hasselbach, Harald (E)	6-6/285	9-22-67	7	Washington	FA/94	16/2
90	Johnson, Jerry (T)	6-0/292	7-11-77	R	Florida State	D4a/00	—
91	Kuberski, Bob (T)	6-4/300	4-5-71	6	Navy	UFA/00	*5/0
97	Lodish, Mike (T)	6-3/270	8-11-67	11	UCLA	UFA/95	13/2
95	Pittman, Kavika (E)	6-6/273	10-9-74	5	McNeese State	UFA/00	*16/16
93	Pryce, Trevor (T)	6-5/295	8-3-75	4	Clemson	D1/97	15/15
99	Reagor, Montae (E)	6-2/256	6-29-77	2	Texas Tech	D2a/99	9/0
98	Tanuvasa, Maa (T)	6-2/270	11-6-70	7	Hawaii	FA/95	16/16
94	Traylor, Keith (T)	6-2/304	9-3-69	9	Central Oklahoma	FA/97	15/15
	LINEBACKERS						
59	Cadrez, Glenn	6-3/240	1-2-70	9	Houston	FA/95	16/15
52	Gold, Ian	6-0/225	8-23-78	R	Michigan	D2a/00	—
	McDonald, Ricardo	6-2/248	11-8-69	9	Pittsburgh	UFA/00	*16/16
51	Mobley, John	6-1/236	10-10-73	5	Kutztown (Pa.) University	D1/96	2/2
53	Romanowski, Bill	6-4/245	4-2-66	13	Boston College	UFA/96	16/16
58	Russ, Steve	6-4/245	9-16-72	4	Air Force	D7a/95	8/0
54	Wayne, Nate	6-0/230	1-12-75	3	Mississippi	D7b/98	15/0
56	Wilson, Al	6-0/240	6-21-77	2	Tennessee	D1/99	16/12
	DEFENSIVE BACKS						
26	Brown, Eric (S)	6-0/210	3-20-75	3	Mississippi State	D2/98	10/10
48	Coghill, George (S)	6-0/210	3-30-70	4	Wake Forest	FA/97	13/5
39	Crockett, Ray (CB)	5-10/184	1-5-67	12	Baylor	UFA/94	16/16
32	Jenkins, Billy (S)	5-10/205	7-8-74	4	Howard	T-StL/00	*16/16
27	Kennedy, Kenoy (S)	6-1/203	11-15-77	R	Arkansas	D2b/00	—
28	Lincoln, Jeremy (CB)	5-10/182	4-7-69	9	Tennessee	UFA/00	*15/7
23	Moore, Jason (S)	5-10/191	1-15-76	2	San Diego State	FA/99	6/0
24	O'Neal, Deltha (CB)	5-10/196	1-30-77	R	California	D1/00	—
31	Pounds, Darryl (CB)	5-10/189	7-21-72	6	Nicholls State	UFA/00	*16/0
33	Spencer, Jimmy (CB)	5-9/180	3-29-69	9	Florida	FA/00	*14/7
35	Suttle, Jason (CB)	5-10/182	12-2-74	2	Wisconsin	FA/99	5/0
21	Watson, Chris (CB)	6-1/192	6-30-77	2	Eastern Illinois	D3a/99	14/1
	SPECIALISTS						
1	Elam, Jason (K)	5-11/200	3-8-70	8	Hawaii	D3b/93	16/0
16	Rouen, Tom (P)	6-3/225	6-9-68	8	Colorado	FA/93	16/0

– 33 –

DENVER BRONCOS

*Not with Broncos in 1999.
Other free agent veterans invited to camp: G Ian Beckles, CB DeAuntae Brown, QB Steve Buck, DE Jason Chorak, DE Willie Cohens, OT Allen DeGraffenreid, LB Chris Gizzi, CB William Hampton, OL Chris Harrison, TE Frank Hartley, S Chris Jones, C K.C. Jones, CB Toya Jones, FB Carlos King, G Glenn Roundtree, S Brad Trout, C Jason Watts.

Abbreviations: D1—draft pick, first round; SD-2—supplemental draft pick, second round; W—claimed on waivers; T—obtained in trade; PlanB—Plan B free-agent acquisition; FA—free-agent acquisition (other than Plan B); UFA—unconditional free agent acquisition; ED—expansion draft pick.

MISCELLANEOUS TEAM DATA

Stadium (capacity, surface):
Mile High Stadium
(76,078, grass)

Business address:
13655 Broncos Parkway
Englewood, CO 80112

Business phone:
303-649-9000

Ticket information:
303-433-7466

Team colors:
Orange, navy blue and white

Flagship radio station:
KOA, 850 AM

Training site:
University of Northern Colorado
Greeley, Colo.
303-623-5212

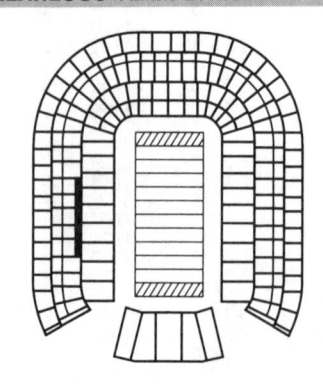

TSN REPORT CARD

Coaching staff	B +	In his second season without John Elway, this is coach Mike Shanahan's chance to prove he's not simply a good coach of great talent, but simply a great coach. He has rebuilt the Broncos' defense and fiddle with the offense. His success in 2000 will depend on his choice of quarterback and his ability to put some swagger back in his team.
Quarterbacks	C -	If Brian Griese is indeed the quarterback of the future, he'll have to prove it in the present. He has yet to show he's got an NFL-quality arm. He is tough and smart, but is he a team leader? He'd better be, or he'll be on the bench while journeyman Gus Frerotte takes over. Frerotte throws a beautiful pass, but is he ready for the complexities of Shanahan's offense? Bottom line: This position remains a huge question mark.
Running backs	B	If anyone can come back from a torn ACL in the knee, it's Terrell Davis. His offseason work ethic was unmatched. Still, he's bound to be a little tentative early on, which is why the Broncos are fortunate to have second-year workhorse Olandis Gary relief. He's not as talented as Davis, but he's a tough, downhill runner with great hands. At fullback, Denver will once again count on Howard Griffith, a great blocker and reliable short-pass receiver.
Receivers	B -	Ed McCaffrey and Rod Smith are quality starters, but what Denver lacks is depth and speed. Rookie wide receiver Chris Cole might have the wheels, but he's got to work on his hands. In the meantime, former practice squad player Billy Miller may be the dependable third receiver Denver needs. At tight end, look for the Broncos to combine the talents of Dwayne Carswell, Byron Chamberlain and Desmond Clark in an attempt to replace the departed Shannon Sharpe.
Offensive line	A -	This is a unit that does not need dramatic change. With tackle Tony Jones and guard Mark Schlereth anchoring the left side, Davis and Gary will have room to run. Tom Nalen is solid at center, while the Broncos hope tackle Matt Lepsis and guard Dan Neil work better together on the right. Overall, this is one of the best lines in football.
Defensive line	B -	With All-Pro tackle Trevor Pryce anchoring the middle, the defensive line has a chance to be excellent. But only if the men on the outside can provide a consistent pass rush and stuff the run better. Gone are popular veterans Neil Smith and Alfred Williams, replaced by free agents Kavika Pittman and Lester Archambeau. Those two have never been impact players, but along with Maa Tanuvasa they have a chance to plug some holes along the line.
Linebackers	A	If outside linebacker John Mobley returns to top form following knee surgery, Denver could have one of the finest best linebacking corps in football. Even if Mobley is not his old self, this group is still rock solid. Ageless Bill Romanowski, up-and-coming middle linebacker Al Wilson and steady Glenn Cadrez form a tough, nasty unit. Add in Michigan rookie Ian Gold to the mix and this group shines bright.
Secondary	C +	This unit must gel in a hurry or Denver could be in trouble. With Dale Carter suspended for a year, the Broncos had to scramble to replace him at cornerback. His successor will likely by former Charger Jimmy Spencer, who is not a great one-on-one defender, but has a knack for making big plays. Shanahan hopes first-round draft choice Deltha O'Neal is the answer for the future, but he might be a year away. At safety, the Broncos are counting on a healthy Eric Brown and former Ram Billy Jenkins to give them a solid one-two punch.
Special teams	C +	O'Neal is already being counted on to be a playmaking punt and kick returner. As long as he doesn't fumble, Denver should have a big-time threat. Jason Elam remains one of the league's best kickers, while punter Tom Rouen must get better at putting the ball inside the 20. The coverage teams must improve or Denver's going to continue to lose the field-position war.

DETROIT LIONS
NFC CENTRAL DIVISION

2000 SEASON

CLUB DIRECTORY

Chairman and president
William Clay Ford
Vice chairman
William Clay Ford Jr.
Exec. v.p. and chief operating officer
Chuck Schmidt
V.p. of marketing and sales
Steve Harms
Vice president of player personnel
Ron Hughes
V.p. of communications, sales and mktg.
Bill Keenist
V.p. of football administration
Larry Lee
V.p. of finance and chief financial officer
Tom Lesnau
V.p. of stadium dev. and salary cap
Tom Lewand
Secretary
David Hempstead
Director of pro personnel
Sheldon White
Director of college scouting
Scott McEwen
Pro and college scouts
Russ Bollinger   Chad Henry
Lance Newmark   Charlie Sanders
Hessley Hempstead (BLESTO)
Head athletic trainer
Jay Shoop
Physicians
Kyle Anderson   Keith Burch
David Collon
Equipment manger
Dan Jaroshewich
Video director
Steve Hermans
Groundskeeper
Charlie Coffin
Director of security
Allen Hughes
Director of broadcast services
Bryan Bender
Human resources director
Cheryl Carrier

Head coach
Bobby Ross

Assistant coaches
Brian Baker (defensive line)
Don Clemons (defensive assistant)
Sylvester Croom (off. coordinator)
Frank Falks (running backs)
Rob Graf (assistant strength and conditioning)
Bert Hill (strength & conditioning/assistant offensive line)
Stan Kwan (offense and special teams assistant)
John Misciagna (quality control-offense/administrative asst.)
Gary Moeller (assistant head coach/linebackers)
Denny Murphy (quality control-defense)
Larry Peccatiello (def. coordinator)
Chuck Priefer (special teams)
Golden Pat Ruel (offensive line)
Dick Selcer (defensive backs)
Danny Smith (tight ends)
Jerry Sullivan (wide receivers)
Jim Zorn (quarterbacks)

Director of ticket operations
Mark Graham
Dir. of ticket sales and customer service
Jennifer Manzo
Director of media relations
Steve Reaven
Dir. of com. rel. and Detroit Lions' charities
Tim Pendell

SCHEDULE

Sept. 3—	at New Orleans	1:00
Sept. 10—	WASHINGTON	4:15
Sept. 17—	TAMPA BAY	1:00
Sept. 24—	at Chicago	1:00
Oct. 1—	MINNESOTA	1:00
Oct. 8—	GREEN BAY	1:00
Oct. 15—	Open date	
Oct. 19—	at Tampa Bay (Thur.)	8:35
Oct. 29—	at Indianapolis	1:00
Nov. 5—	MIAMI	1:00
Nov. 12—	ATLANTA	1:00
Nov. 19—	at N.Y. Giants	1:00
Nov. 23—	NEW ENG. (Thanks.)	12:30
Nov. 30—	at Minnesota (Thur.)	8:35
Dec. 10—	at Green Bay	1:00
Dec. 17—	at N.Y. Jets	1:00
Dec. 24—	CHICAGO	1:00

All times are Eastern.
All games Sunday unless noted.

DRAFT CHOICES

Stockar McDougle, T, Oklahoma (first round/20th pick overall).
Barrett Green, LB, West Virginia (2/50).
Reuben Droughns, RB, Oregon (3/81).
Todd Franz, DB, Tulsa (5/145).
Quinton Reese, DE, Auburn (6/181).
Alfonso Boone, DT, Mount San Antonio J.C. (7/253).

1999 REVIEW

RESULTS

Sept.12—at Seattle	W	28-20
Sept.19—GREEN BAY	W	23-15
Sept.26—at Kansas City	L	21-31
Oct. 3—Open date		
Oct. 10—SAN DIEGO	L	10-20
Oct. 17—MINNESOTA	W	25-23
Oct. 24—at Carolina	W	24-9
Oct. 31—TAMPA BAY	W	20-3
Nov. 7—ST. LOUIS	W	31-27
Nov. 14—at Arizona	L	19-23
Nov. 21—at Green Bay	L	17-26
Nov. 25—CHICAGO	W	21-17
Dec. 5—WASHINGTON	W	33-17
Dec. 12—at Tampa Bay	L	16-23
Dec. 19—at Chicago	L	10-28
Dec. 25—DENVER	L	7-17
Jan. 2—at Minnesota	L	17-24
Jan. 8—at Washington*	L	13-27

*NFC wild-card game.

RECORDS/RANKINGS

1999 regular-season record: 8-8 (3rd in NFC Central); 4-4 in division; 7-5 in conference; 1-3 vs. AFC; 6-2 at home; 2-6 on road; 7-3 on turf; 1-5 on grass.
Team record last five years: 37-43 (.463, ranks T18th in league in that span).
1999 team rankings:

	No.	NFC	NFL
Total offense	*308.2	11	21
Rushing offense	*77.8	13	28
Passing offense	*230.4	8	9
Scoring offense	322	7	15
Total defense	*330.7	6	18
Rushing defense	*95.7	4	9
Passing defense	*235.0	12	27
Scoring defense	323	4	14
Takeaways	32	8	13
Giveaways	22	1	T2
Turnover differential	10	T2	T6
Sacks	50	2	T4
Sacks allowed	64	15	31

*Yards per game.

TEAM LEADERS

Scoring (kicking): Jason Hanson, 106 pts. (28/29 PATs, 26/32 FGs).
Scoring (touchdowns): Germane Crowell, 44 pts. (7 receiving, 1 2-pt. conv.).
Passing: Gus Frerotte, 2,117 yds. (288 att., 175 comp., 60.8%, 9 TDs, 7 int.).
Rushing: Greg Hill, 542 yds. (144 att., 3.8 avg., 2 TDs).
Receptions: Germane Crowell, 81 (1,338 yds., 16.5 avg., 7 TDs).
Interceptions: Ron Rice, 5 (82 yds., 0 TDs).
Sacks: Robert Porcher, 15.0.
Punting: John Jett, 42.3 avg. (86 punts, 3,637 yds., 0 blocked).
Punt returns: Iheanyi Uwaezuoke, 8.3 avg. (18 att., 150 yds., 0 TDs).
Kickoff returns: Terry Fair, 22.1 avg. (34 att., 752 yds., 0 TDs).

– 35 –

2000 SEASON
TRAINING CAMP ROSTER

DETROIT LIONS

No.	QUARTERBACKS	Ht./Wt.	Born	NFL Exp.	College	How acq.	'99 Games GP/GS
10	Batch, Charlie	6-2/220	12-5-74	3	Eastern Michigan	D2b/98	11/10
11	Stenstrom, Steve	6-2/202	12-23-71	6	Stanford	FA/00	*6/3
18	Tomczak, Mike	6-1/210	10-23-62	16	Ohio State	UFA/00	*16/5
	RUNNING BACKS						
21	Droughns, Reuben	5-11/207	8-21-78	R	Oregon	D3/00	—
33	Irvin, Sedrick	5-11/226	3-30-78	2	Michigan State	D4/99	14/0
26	Olivo, Brock (FB)	6-0/232	6-24-76	3	Missouri	FA/98	14/0
36	Reece, Travis (FB)	6-3/251	4-3-75	3	Michigan State	FA/98	4/0
30	Schlesinger, Cory (FB)	6-0/246	6-23-72	6	Nebraska	D6b/95	16/11
34	Stewart, James	6-1/226	12-27-71	6	Tennessee	UFA/00	*14/7
	RECEIVERS						
81	Chryplewicz, Pete (TE)	6-5/261	4-27-74	4	Notre Dame	D5a/97	11/1
82	Crowell, Germane	6-3/216	9-13-76	3	Virginia	D2a/98	16/15
84	Moore, Herman	6-4/224	10-20-69	10	Virginia	D1/91	8/4
87	Morton, Johnnie	6-0/190	10-7-71	7	Southern California	D1/94	16/12
89	Rasby, Walter (TE)	6-3/251	9-7-72	7	Wake Forest	UFA/98	16/6
86	Sloan, David (TE)	6-6/260	6-8-72	6	New Mexico	D3/95	16/15
83	Stablein, Brian	6-1/194	4-14-70	7	Ohio State	FA/98	16/2
	OFFENSIVE LINEMEN						
79	Beverly, Eric (C)	6-3/294	3-28-74	3	Miami (Ohio)	FA/97	16/2
65	Blaise, Kerlin (G)	6-5/323	12-25-74	3	Miami (Fla.)	FA/98	16/4
76	Brooks, Barrett (T)	6-4/326	5-5-72	6	Kansas State	UFA/99	16/12
77	Compton, Mike (C)	6-6/298	9-18-70	8	West Virginia	D3b/93	15/15
71	Gibson, Aaron (T)	6-4/380	9-27-77	2	Wisconsin	D1b/99	0/0
64	Hartings, Jeff (G)	6-3/295	9-7-72	5	Penn State	D1b/96	16/16
73	McDougle, Stockar (G)	6-6/350	1-11-77	R	Oklahoma	D1/00	—
75	Ramirez, Tony (T)	6-6/305	1-26-73	4	Northern Colorado	D6/97	12/3
72	Roberts, Ray (T)	6-6/320	6-3-69	9	Virginia	FA/96	14/14
74	Roque, Juan (T)	6-8/332	2-6-74	4	Arizona State	D2a/97	4/2
62	Semple, Tony (G)	6-5/303	12-20-70	7	Memphis State	D5/94	12/12
	DEFENSIVE LINEMEN						
70	Boone, Alfonso (T)	6-3/305	1-11-76	R	None.	D7/00	—
95	DeVries, Jared (E)	6-4/280	6-11-76	2	Iowa	D3/99	2/0
94	Elliss, Luther (T)	6-5/305	3-22-73	6	Utah	D1/95	15/14
98	Jones, James (T)	6-2/295	2-6-69	10	Northern Iowa	UFA/99	16/16
67	Kirschke, Travis (E)	6-3/287	9-6-74	4	UCLA	FA/97	15/7
91	Porcher, Robert (E)	6-3/282	7-30-69	9	South Carolina State	D1/92	15/14
92	Pringley, Mike (E)	6-4/277	5-22-76	2	North Carolina	D7/99	9/0
93	Pritchett, Kelvin (T)	6-3/319	10-24-69	10	Mississippi	UFA/99	16/2
66	Reese, Quinton (E)	6-4/252	8-26-77	R	Auburn	D6/00	—
97	Scroggins, Tracy (E)	6-3/273	9-11-69	9	Tulsa	D2a/92	14/11
60	Spicer, Paul (E)	6-4/269	8-18-75	2	Saginaw Valley State	FA/99	2/0
	LINEBACKERS						
55	Aldridge, Allen	6-1/254	5-30-72	7	Houston	UFA/98	16/14
57	Boyd, Stephen	6-0/242	8-22-72	6	Boston College	D5a/95	14/14
50	Claiborne, Chris	6-3/255	7-26-78	2	Southern California	D1a/99	15/13
51	Fields, Scott	6-2/220	4-22-73	3	Southern California	FA/99	2/0
54	Green, Barrett	6-0/217	10-29-77	R	West Virginia	D2/00	—
99	Jordan, Richard	6-1/256	12-1-74	4	Missouri Southern	D7c/97	9/0
52	Kowalkowski, Scott	6-2/220	8-23-68	10	Notre Dame	FA/94	16/3
58	Kriewaldt, Clint	6-1/236	3-16-76	2	Wisconsin-Stevens Point	D6/99	12/0
59	O'Neill, Kevin	6-2/249	4-14-75	3	Bowling Green State	FA/98	4/0
	DEFENSIVE BACKS						
24	Abrams, Kevin (CB)	5-8/170	2-28-74	4	Syracuse	D2b/97	1/0
44	Brown, Corwin (S)	6-1/205	4-25-70	8	Michigan	FA/99	13/1
39	Campbell, Lamar (CB)	5-11/183	8-29-76	3	Wisconsin	FA/98	15/2
31	Dixon, Andre (CB)	6-1/200	12-4-75	2	Northeastern	FA/99	4/0
23	Fair, Terry (CB)	5-9/183	7-20-76	3	Tennessee	D1/98	11/11
27	Franz, Todd	6-0/194	4-12-76	R	Tulsa	D5/00	—
28	Rice, Ron (S)	6-1/217	11-9-72	5	Eastern Michigan	FA/95	16/16
45	Schulz, Kurt (S)	6-1/208	12-12-68	9	Eastern Washington	UFA/00	*16/16
42	Stewart, Ryan (S)	6-1/206	9-30-73	5	Georgia Tech	FA/97	2/0
29	Supernaw, Kywin (S)	6-1/207	6-2-75	3	Indiana	FA/98	12/0
25	Talton, Ty (S)	5-11/201	5-10-76	2	Northern Iowa	FA/99	12/0
32	Westbrook, Bryant (CB)	6-0/198	12-19-74	4	Texas	D1/97	10/8
	SPECIALISTS						
4	Hanson, Jason (K)	5-11/182	6-17-70	9	Washington State	D2b/92	16/0
19	Jett, John (P)	6-0/197	11-11-68	8	East Carolina	UFA/97	16/0

*Not with Lions in 1999.
Other free agent veterans invited to camp: WR Tim Alexander, LB Delaunta Cameron, CB Chris Cummings, WR Henry Douglas, G Paul Janus, TE Tony Johnson, WR Andre Rone, LB Matt Russell, QB Cory Sauter, DT Henry Taylor.

Abbreviations: D1—draft pick, first round; SD-2—supplemental draft pick, second round; W—claimed on waivers; T—obtained in trade; PlanB—Plan B free-agent acquisition; FA—free-agent acquisition (other than Plan B); UFA—unconditional free agent acquisition; ED—expansion draft pick.

MISCELLANEOUS TEAM DATA

Stadium (capacity, surface):
Pontiac Silverdome
(80,311, artificial)
Business address:
1200 Featherstone Road
Pontiac, MI 48342
Business phone:
248-335-4131
Ticket information:
248-335-4151
Team colors:
Honolulu blue and silver
Flagship radio station:
WXYT, 1270 AM
Training site:
Saginaw Valley State University
Saginaw, Mich.
248-972-3700

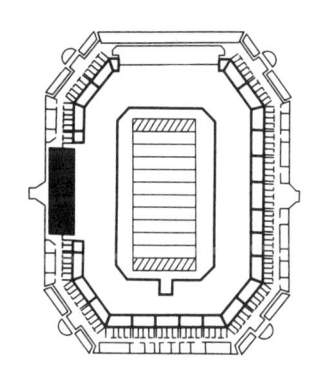

TSN REPORT CARD

Coaching staff	C	Didn't help that Barry Sanders opted for retirement before training camp, making coach Bobby Ross a victim of circumstances beyond his control with a team that wasn't very good. After starting out 6-2, mounting injuries did in the team's chances. The coaches did what they could with what they had.
Quarterbacks	B -	Charlie Batch has had more lows than highs in the two years since getting the keys to the Lions' offense. Every time he looks to accelerate, bothersome injuries have sidelined his efforts to competently lead the team. Without Batch healthy, the Lions are relegated to a combination of Mike Tomczak and Steve Stenstrom.
Running backs	C -	The jury is still out on the Lions' new running back-by-committee philosophy with James Stewart, Sedrick Irvin and Reuben Droughns. There's no doubt that there will always be fresh legs to carry the ball, but how well those legs churn out yardage is yet to be seen.
Receivers	A -	Depending on how well Herman Moore bounces back from a knee injury, the Lions could again terrify secondaries with a trio of fine pass-catchers, including Johnnie Morton and Germane Crowell, who caught a team-high 81 passes in '99. It's an extremely athletic group, with a keen sense for getting open.
Offensive line	D +	Rookie guard Stockar McDougle and tackle Aaron Gibson will be expected to learn fast and make immediate impacts on a unit which recently has had more patch work done than a used-tire store. There's a wealth of potential, but improvement is still needed in both run and pass blocking.
Defensive line	C +	Despite the lack of quality depth, this is the defense's most productive unit at stopping the run. Luther Elliss and James Jones are gap-stuffers who command most of the attention from offensive linemen. The pass-rush should continue to shine with the improvement of Robert Porcher and Tracy Scroggins on the outside.
Linebackers	B -	An athletic group, they all pursue with tremendous desire, shed blockers well and get to the ball carrier. Though Chris Claiborne took some lumps as a rookie last year, he isn't far from becoming a Pro Bowl player. Barrett Green gives the Lions the underneath coverage guy the nickel package has missed.
Secondary	C	Saying that this unit struggled last season is an understatement. As a group, they were absolutely pathetic, especially cornerback Bryant Westbrook, who made matters worse by playing with a hamstring injury. Another cornerback, Terry Fair, is returning from injury. The team signed safety Kurt Schulz away from Buffalo in the hope he might be able to add some punch to this listless bunch.
Special teams	B -	Detroit is very strong in the kicking department with Jason Hanson and punter John Jett. But the return game is a cause for concern. Injuries created havoc last season as 10 different players returned kickoffs and punts. Fair's health will be instrumental and re-signing Desmond Howard wouldn't hurt.

GREEN BAY PACKERS
NFC CENTRAL DIVISION

2000 SEASON

CLUB DIRECTORY

President/chief executive officer
Robert E. Harlan
Executive v.p./general manager
Ron Wolf
Executive assistant to the president
Phil Pionek
Senior v.p. of administration
John Jones
Vice president/general counsel
Lance Lopes
Corporate security officer
Jerry Parins
Director of administrative affairs
Mark Schiefelbein
Executive director/public relations
Lee Remmel
Associate director/public relations
Jeff Blumb
Asst. director of p.r./travel coordinator
Aaron Popkey
Director/marketing
Jeff Cieply
Executive director of player programs & community affairs
Gill Byrd
Director of family programs
Sherry Schuldes
Ticket director
Mark Wagner
Vice president of personnel
Ken Herock
Dir. of player finance/football ops.
Andrew Brandt
Pro personnel director
Reggie McKenzie
Scouting coordinator
Danny Mock
Scouts
John 'Red' Cochran   Lee Gissendaner
Brian Gutekunst   Shaun Herock
Alonzo Highsmith   Scot McCloughan
Sam Seale
Video director
Al Treml
Equipment manager
Gordon 'Red' Batty

Head coach
Mike Sherman

Assistant coaches
Larry Beightol (offensive line)
Darrell Bevell (offensive assistant/quality control)
Kippy Brown (running backs)
Billy Davis (defensive assistant/quality control)
Ed Donatell (defensive coordinator)
Jethro Franklin (defensive line)
Jeff Jagodzinski (tight ends)
Mark Lovat (strength and conditioning assistant)
Trent Miles (offensive assistant/quality control)
Frank Novak (special teams)
Bo Pelini (linebackers)
Tom Rossley (offensive coordinator)
Barry Rubin (strength & conditioning)
Ray Sherman (wide receivers)
Bob Slowik (defensive backs)
Lionel Washington (defensive backs assistant)

Assistant equipment manager
Tom Bakken   Brian Nehring
Head trainer
Pepper Burruss
Assistant trainers
Bryan Engel   Kurt Fielding
Building supervisor
Ted Eisenreich
Fields supervisor
Allen Johnson

SCHEDULE

Sept. 3—	N.Y. JETS	4:15
Sept. 10—	at Buffalo	1:00
Sept. 17—	PHILADELPHIA	1:00
Sept. 24—	at Arizona	4:05
Oct. 1—	CHICAGO	4:15
Oct. 8—	at Detroit	1:00
Oct. 15—	SAN FRANCISCO	4:15
Oct. 22—	Open date	
Oct. 29—	at Miami	1:00
Nov. 6—	MINNESOTA (Mon.)	9:00
Nov. 12—	at Tampa Bay	4:15
Nov. 19—	INDIANAPOLIS	1:00
Nov. 27—	at Carolina (Mon.)	9:00
Dec. 3—	at Chicago	8:35
Dec. 10—	DETROIT	1:00
Dec. 17—	at Minnesota	1:00
Dec. 24—	TAMPA BAY	1:00

All times are Eastern.
All games Sunday unless noted.

DRAFT CHOICES

Bubba Franks, TE, Miami, Fla. (first round/14th pick overall).
Chad Clifton, T, Tennessee (2/44).
Steve Warren, DT, Nebraska (3/74).
Na'il Diggs, LB, Ohio State (4/98).
Anthony Lucas, WR, Arkansas (4/114).
Gary Berry, DB, Ohio State (4/126).
Kabeer Gbaja-Biamila, DE, San Diego State (5/149).
Joey Jamison, KR, Tex. Southern (5/151).
Mark Tauscher, T, Wisconsin (7/224).
Ron Moore, DT, NW Oklahoma (7/229).
Charles Lee, WR, Central Fla. (7/242).
Eugene McCaslin, LB, Florida (7/249).
Rondell Mealey, RB, La. State (7/252).

1999 REVIEW

RESULTS

Sept.12—OAKLAND	W	28-24
Sept.19—at Detroit	L	15-23
Sept.26—MINNESOTA	W	23-20
Oct. 3—Open date		
Oct. 10—TAMPA BAY	W	26-23
Oct. 17—at Denver	L	10-31
Oct. 24—at San Diego	W	31-3
Nov. 1—SEATTLE	L	7-27
Nov. 7—CHICAGO	L	13-14
Nov. 14—at Dallas	L	13-27
Nov. 21—DETROIT	W	26-17
Nov. 29—at San Francisco	W	20-3
Dec. 5—at Chicago	W	35-19
Dec. 12—CAROLINA	L	31-33
Dec. 20—at Minnesota	L	20-24
Dec. 26—at Tampa Bay	L	10-29
Jan. 2—ARIZONA	W	49-24

RECORDS/RANKINGS

1999 regular-season record: 8-8 (4th in NFC Central); 4-4 in division; 6-6 in conference; 2-2 vs. AFC; 5-3 at home; 3-5 on road; 0-3 on turf; 8-5 on grass.
Team record last five years: 56-24 (.700, ranks 1st in league in that span).
1999 team rankings:

	No.	NFC	NFL
Total offense	*338.7	6	9
Rushing offense	*94.9	10	21
Passing offense	*243.8	6	7
Scoring offense	357	5	10
Total defense	*331.8	7	19
Rushing defense	*112.8	9	22
Passing defense	*219.1	7	T18
Scoring defense	341	T6	T20
Takeaways	41	2	3
Giveaways	36	10	26
Turnover differential	5	T5	T9
Sacks	30	15	29
Sacks allowed	36	5	T10

*Yards per game.

TEAM LEADERS

Scoring (kicking): Ryan Longwell, 113 pts. (38/38 PATs, 25/30 FGs).
Scoring (touchdowns): Dorsey Levens, 60 pts. (9 rushing, 1 receiving).
Passing: Brett Favre, 4,091 yds. (595 att., 341 comp., 57.3%, 22 TDs, 23 int.).
Rushing: Dorsey Levens, 1,034 yds. (279 att., 3.7 avg., 9 TDs).
Receptions: Antonio Freeman, 74 (1,074 yds., 14.5 avg., 6 TDs).
Interceptions: Mike McKenzie, 6 (4 yds., 0 TDs).
Sacks: Keith McKenzie, 8.0.
Punting: Louie Aguiar, 39.4 avg. (75 punts, 2,954 yds., 0 blocked).
Punt returns: Desmond Howard, 7.8 avg. (12 att., 93 yds., 0 TDs).
Kickoff returns: Basil Mitchell, 22.1 avg. (21 att., 464 yds., 1 TD).

2000 SEASON
TRAINING CAMP ROSTER

No.	QUARTERBACKS	Ht./Wt.	Born	NFL Exp.	College	How acq.	'99 Games GP/GS
2	Brooks, Aaron	6-4/205	3-24-76	2	Virginia	D4a/99	1/0
4	Favre, Brett	6-2/220	10-10-69	10	Southern Mississippi	T-Atl./92	16/16
11	Hasselbeck, Matt	6-4/220	9-25-75	2	Boston College	D6b/98	16/0
	RUNNING BACKS						
30	Green, Ahman	6-0/215	2-16-77	3	Nebraska	T-Sea./00	*14/0
33	Henderson, William (FB)	6-1/250	2-19-71	6	North Carolina	D3b/95	16/13
25	Levens, Dorsey	6-1/228	5-21-70	7	Georgia Tech	D5b/94	14/14
32	Mealey, Rondell	6-0/206	2-24-77	R	Louisiana State	D7e/00	—
28	Mitchell, Basil	5-10/200	9-7-75	2	Texas Christian	FA/99	16/2
22	Parker, De'Mond	5-10/188	12-24-76	2	Oklahoma	D5a/99	11/0
38	Snider, Matt (FB)	6-2/243	1-26-76	2	Richmond	W-Car./99	8/0
	RECEIVERS						
85	Bradford, Corey	6-1/205	12-8-75	3	Jackson State	D5/98	16/2
89	Chmura, Mark (TE)	6-5/255	2-22-69	9	Boston College	D6/92	2/2
81	Davis, Tyrone (TE)	6-4/255	6-30-72	5	Virginia	T-NYJ/97	16/13
80	Driver, Donald	6-0/175	2-2-75	2	Alcorn State	D7b/99	5/0
88	Franks, Bubba (TE)	6-6/252	1-6-78	R	Miami (Fla.)	D1/00	—
86	Freeman, Antonio	6-1/198	5-27-72	6	Virginia Tech	D3d/95	16/16
82	Hall, Lamont (TE)	6-4/260	11-16-74	2	Clemson	FA/99	14/0
41	Jamison, Joey	5-9/170	10-12-78	R	Texas Southern	D5b/00	—
17	Lee, Charles	6-2/202	11-19-77	R	Central Florida	D7c/00	—
87	Lucas, Anthony	6-3/192	11-20-76	R	Arkansas	D4b/00	—
84	Schroeder, Bill	6-3/205	1-9-71	5	Wisconsin-La Crosse	FA/96	16/16
83	Sinceno, Kaseem (TE)	6-4/259	3-26-76	3	Syracuse	T-Phi./00	*0/0
	OFFENSIVE LINEMEN						
70	Andruzzi, Joe (G)	6-3/310	8-23-75	4	Southern Connecticut State	FA/97	8/3
76	Clifton, Chad (T)	6-5/329	6-26-76	R	Tennessee	D2/00	—
61	Curry, Scott (T)	6-5/300	12-25-75	2	Montana	D6b/99	5/0
60	Davis, Rob (C)	6-3/285	12-10-68	5	Shippensburg (Pa.)	FA/97	16/0
72	Dotson, Earl (T)	6-4/310	12-17-70	8	Texas A&I	D3/93	15/15
58	Flanagan, Mike (C)	6-5/295	11-10-73	5	UCLA	D3a/96	15/0
75	Heimburger, Craig (G)	6-2/318	2-3-77	2	Missouri	D5b/99	2/0
63	McKenzie, Raleigh (G)	6-2/290	2-8-63	16	Tennessee	UFA/99	16/7
62	Rivera, Marco (G)	6-4/305	4-26-72	5	Penn State	D6/96	16/16
65	Tauscher, Mark (T)	6-3/314	6-17-77	R	Wisconsin	D7a/00	—
78	Verba, Ross (G)	6-4/308	10-31-73	4	Iowa	D2/97	11/10
68	Wahle, Mike (T)	6-6/306	3-29-77	3	Navy	SD-2/98	16/13
52	Winters, Frank (C)	6-3/305	1-23-64	14	Western Illinois	UFA/92	16/16
	DEFENSIVE LINEMEN						
96	Bowens, David (E)	6-2/255	7-3-77	2	Western Illinois	T-Den./00	*16/0
71	Dotson, Santana (T)	6-5/290	12-19-69	9	Baylor	UFA/96	12/12
94	Gbaja-Biamila, Kabeer (E)	6-4/244	9-24-77	R	San Diego State	D5a/00	—
90	Holliday, Vonnie (E)	6-5/300	12-11-75	3	North Carolina	D1/98	16/16
97	Hunt, Cletidus (E)	6-4/295	1-2-76	2	Kentucky State	D3b/99	11/1
98	Lyon, Billy (T)	6-5/300	12-10-73	3	Marshall	FA/97	16/4
67	Maryland, Russell (T)	6-1/300	3-22-69	10	Miami (Fla.)	FA/00	*16/16
73	Moore, Ron (T)	6-2/316	8-10-77	R	Northwestern Oklahoma State	D7b/00	—
99	Smith, Jermaine (T)	6-3/298	2-3-72	3	Georgia	D4/97	10/0
91	Thierry, John (E)	6-4/260	9-4-71	7	Alcorn State	UFA/00	*16/10
95	Warren, Steve (T)	6-1/307	1-22-78	R	Nebraska	D3/00	—
	LINEBACKERS						
59	Diggs, Na'il	6-4/226	7-8-78	R	Ohio State	D4a/00	—
50	Harris, Anthony	6-1/240	1-25-73	5	Auburn	FA/00	*4/0
55	Harris, Bernardo	6-2/250	10-15-71	6	North Carolina	FA/95	16/15
53	Koonce, George	6-1/245	10-15-68	9	East Carolina	FA/92	15/15
56	Mays, Kivuusama	6-3/248	1-7-75	3	North Carolina	W-Min./99	14/0
45	McCaslin, Eugene	6-1/221	7-12-77	R	Florida	D7d/00	—
56	Morton, Mike	6-4/235	3-28-72	6	North Carolina	UFA/00	*16/0
57	Nelson, Jim	6-1/238	4-16-75	2	Penn State	W-SF/98	16/0
54	Waddy, Jude	6-2/220	9-12-75	3	William and Mary	FA/98	14/8
51	Williams, Brian	6-1/245	12-17-72	6	Southern California	D3c/95	7/7
	DEFENSIVE BACKS						
47	Bell, Tyrone (CB)	6-2/210	10-20-74	1	North Alabama	FA/99	1/0
21	Berry, Gary (S)	5-11/199	10-24-77	R	Ohio State	D4c/00	—
36	Butler, LeRoy (S)	6-0/203	7-19-68	11	Florida State	D2/90	16/16
24	Edwards, Antuan (CB)	6-1/205	5-26-77	2	Clemson	D1/99	16/1
27	McBride, Tod (S)	6-1/208	1-26-76	2	UCLA	W-Sea./99	15/0
43	McGarrahan, Scott (S)	6-1/198	2-12-74	3	New Mexico	D6a/97	13/0
34	McKenzie, Mike (CB)	6-0/190	4-26-76	2	Memphis	D3a/99	16/16
42	Sharper, Darren (S)	6-2/210	11-3-75	4	William & Mary	D2/97	16/16
37	Williams, Tyrone (CB)	5-11/195	5-31-73	5	Nebraska	D3b/96	16/16

— 39 —

GREEN BAY PACKERS

No.	SPECIALISTS	Ht./Wt.	Born	Exp.	College	How acq.	GP/GS
9	Bidwell, Josh (P)	6-3/225	3-13-76	1	Oregon	D4b/99	0/0
	Hutton, Tom (P)	6-1/193	7-8-72	5	Tennessee	UFA/00	*14/0
8	Longwell, Ryan (K)	6-0/197	8-16-74	4	California	W-SF/97	16/0

*Not with Packers in 1999.

Other free agent veterans invited to camp: WR Tyrone Goodson, TE Lawrence Hart, LB Kevin Johnson, CB Steve Johnson, C Mike Newell.

Abbreviations: D1—draft pick, first round; SD-2—supplemental draft pick, second round; W—claimed on waivers; T—obtained in trade; PlanB—Plan B free-agent acquisition; FA—free-agent acquisition (other than Plan B); UFA—unconditional free agent acquisition; ED—expansion draft pick.

MISCELLANEOUS TEAM DATA

Stadium (capacity, surface):
Lambeau Field
(60,890, grass)
Business address:
P.O. Box 10628
Green Bay, WI 54307-0628
Business phone:
920-496-5700
Ticket information:
920-496-5719
Team colors:
Dark green, gold and white
Flagship radio station:
WTMJ, 620 AM
Training site:
St. Norbert College
West De Pere, Wis.
920-496-5700

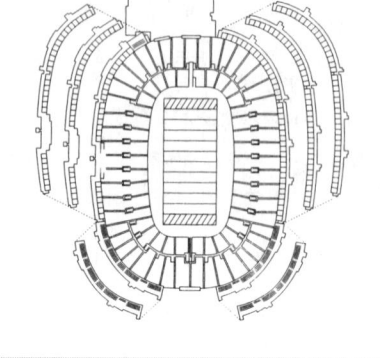

TSN REPORT CARD

Coaching staff	C	There is some experience on this staff, but the head coach and the two coordinators haven't done it before and will be under tremendous pressure on a team with a high standard for excellence. Mike Sherman has to assume control early in training camp and not let any players slide.
Quarterbacks	B	It should be evident this season which direction Brett Favre's career is heading. He turns 31 in October, and another season with more than 20 interceptions would signal a deep-seated problem. There's no question he still has the ability to dominate, but doing it game after game is another matter.
Running backs	B	Dorsey Levens' per carry average slipped to 3.7 last year and it could be a sign he's slowing down. The addition of Ahman Green should give the running game a shot in the arm given his blazing speed. Both players have to solve fumbling problems from last year.
Receivers	C	If Antonio Freeman plays like he did in '99, the club made a mistake giving him the contract it did. He must report to camp in peak condition and run more routes over the middle. Overall, the rest of the group is very average unless Corey Bradford has a breakout season. Rookie tight end Bubba Franks must have an immediate impact.
Offensive line	B +	As long as Mike Wahle pans out at left tackle, this should be a very solid group. There will be more punch in the running game with Ross Verba at left guard and Earl Dotson no longer suffering from a herniated disk in his back. Depth is excellent although some of the backups are inexperienced.
Defensive line	C -	There are a ton of question marks here. Vonnie Holliday hasn't proven he's a big-time pass rusher and John Thierry has had one-half of a good season in six years. Santana Dotson didn't play up to his big contract last year, although a shoulder injury held him back. There isn't a dominant player in the group.
Linebackers	C -	If Brian Williams doesn't come back healthy, the defense is in trouble. He's the best all-around defensive player on the roster and should have a big year in this system. The strong-side position is a huge question mark and could be a thorn in the team's side all year.
Secondary	B -	A lot has been made of the importance of Darren Sharper making improvement, but Tyrone Williams' performance might be more critical. He was supposed to be the stopper last year and didn't fill that role. Strong safety LeRoy Butler has to get himself in peak condition so he can fight off the aging process.
Special teams	D	No area of the team needs more improvement. The punting game isn't settled, the coverage units were ineffective and the return game was a flop. There is some good, young talent to fill those units and a new coach, but there's a lot still to be done.

INDIANAPOLIS COLTS
AFC EASTERN DIVISION

2000 SEASON

CLUB DIRECTORY

Owner and CEO
James Irsay
President
Bill Polian
Vice chairman and COO
Michael G. Chernoff
Senior vice president
Bob Terpening
Sr. vice president of administration
Pete Ward
Vice president of finance
Kurt Humphrey
Controller
Herm Stonitsch
Vice president of public relations
Craig Kelley
Assistant director of public relations
Ryan Robinson
Vice president of ticket operations
Larry Hall
Director of football operations
Dom Anile
Director of college scouting
George Boone
Director of player development
Steve Champlin
Director of pro scouting
Chris Polian
Director of pro player personnel
Clyde Powers
College scouts
Mike Butler
Ralph Hawkins
David Caldwell
Tom Gamble
Bo Guarani
Byron Lusby
Paul Roell
Tom Telesco
Todd Vasvari
Head trainer
Hunter Smith

Head coach
Jim Mora

Assistant coaches
Bruce Arians (quarterbacks)
George Catavolos (asst. head coach/defensive backs)
Vic Fangio (def. coordinator)
Todd Grantham (defensive line)
Richard Howell (asst. strength & conditioning)
Gene Huey (running backs)
Tony Marciano (tight ends)
Tom Moore (off. coordinator)
Howard Mudd (offensive line)
Mike Murphy (linebackers)
Jay Norvell (wide receivers)
John Pagano (def. assistant)
Kevin Spencer (special teams)
Jon Torine (strength & conditioning)

Assistant trainers
Dave Hammer
Dave Walston
Orthopedic surgeon
Arthur C. Rettig, M.D.
Physician
Doug Robertson, M.D.
Video director
Marty Heckscher
Equipment manager
Jon Scott
Assistant equipment manager
Mike Mays

SCHEDULE

Sept. 3—	at Kansas City	1:00
Sept. 10—	OAKLAND	1:00
Sept. 17—	Open date	
Sept. 25—	JACKSONVILLE (Mon.)	9:00
Oct. 1—	at Buffalo	1:00
Oct. 8—	at New England	1:00
Oct. 15—	at Seattle	4:05
Oct. 22—	NEW ENGLAND	1:00
Oct. 29—	DETROIT	1:00
Nov. 5—	at Chicago	1:00
Nov. 12—	N.Y. JETS	8:35
Nov. 19—	at Green Bay	1:00
Nov. 26—	MIAMI	1:00
Dec. 3—	at N.Y. Jets	4:15
Dec. 11—	BUFFALO (Mon.)	9:00
Dec. 17—	at Miami	4:15
Dec. 24—	MINNESOTA	4:15

All times are Eastern.
All games Sunday unless noted.

DRAFT CHOICES

Rob Morris, LB, Brigham Young (first round/28th pick overall).
Marcus Washington, DE, Auburn (2/59).
David Macklin, DB, Penn State (3/91).
Josh Williams, DT, Michigan (4/122).
Matt Johnson, C, Brigham Young (5/138).
Rob Renes, DT, Michigan (7/235).
Rodregis Brooks, DB, Alabama-Birmingham (7/238).

1999 REVIEW

RESULTS

Sept.12—BUFFALO	W	31-14
Sept.19—at New England	L	28-31
Sept.26—at San Diego	W	27-19
Oct. 3—Open date		
Oct. 10—MIAMI	L	31-34
Oct. 17—at N.Y. Jets	W	16-13
Oct. 24—CINCINNATI	W	31-10
Oct. 31—DALLAS	W	34-24
Nov. 7—KANSAS CITY	W	25-17
Nov. 14—at N.Y. Giants	W	27-19
Nov. 21—at Philadelphia	W	44-17
Nov. 28—N.Y. JETS	W	13-6
Dec. 5—at Miami	W	37-34
Dec. 12—NEW ENGLAND	W	20-15
Dec. 19—WASHINGTON	W	24-21
Dec. 26—at Cleveland	W	29-28
Jan. 2—at Buffalo	L	6-31
Jan. 16—TENNESSEE*	L	16-19

*AFC divisional playoff game.

RECORDS/RANKINGS

1999 regular-season record: 13-3 (1st in AFC East); 5-3 in division; 9-3 in conference; 4-0 vs. NFC; 7-1 at home; 6-2 on road; 10-2 on turf; 3-1 on grass.
Team record last five years: 37-43 (.463, ranks T18th in league in that span).
1999 team rankings:

	No.	AFC	NFL
Total offense	*357.9	1	4
Rushing offense	*103.8	11	19
Passing offense	*254.1	1	4
Scoring offense	423	1	3
Total defense	*326.3	11	15
Rushing defense	*107.2	11	18
Passing defense	*219.1	12	T18
Scoring defense	333	13	17
Takeaways	23	14	27
Giveaways	28	T7	T10
Turnover differential	-5	T11	T19
Sacks	41	T7	T12
Sacks allowed	14	1	1

*Yards per game.

TEAM LEADERS

Scoring (kicking): Mike Vanderjagt, 145 pts. (43/43 PATs, 34/38 FGs).
Scoring (touchdowns): Edgerrin James, 102 pts. (13 rushing, 4 receiving).
Passing: Peyton Manning, 4,135 yds. (533 att., 331 comp., 62.1%, 26 TDs, 15 int.).
Rushing: Edgerrin James, 1,553 yds. (369 att., 4.2 avg., 13 TDs).
Receptions: Marvin Harrison, 115 (1,663 yds., 14.5 avg., 12 TDs).
Interceptions: Tyrone Poole, 3 (85 yds., 0 TDs).
Sacks: Chad Bratzke, 12.0.
Punting: Hunter Smith, 42.5 avg. (58 punts, 2,467 yds., 2 blocked).
Punt returns: Terrence Wilkins, 9.5 avg. (41 att., 388 yds., 1 TD).
Kickoff returns: Terrence Wilkins, 22.2 avg. (51 att., 1,134 yds., 1 TD).

– 41 –

2000 SEASON
TRAINING CAMP ROSTER

INDIANAPOLIS COLTS

No.	QUARTERBACKS	Ht./Wt.	Born	NFL Exp.	College	How acq.	'99 Games GP/GS
7	Gonzalez, Pete	6-1/217	7-4-74	3	Pittsburgh	FA/00	*1/0
13	Holcomb, Kelly	6-2/212	7-9-73	4	Middle Tennessee State	FA/96	0/0
18	Manning, Peyton	6-5/230	3-24-76	3	Tennessee	D1/98	16/16
	RUNNING BACKS						
32	James, Edgerrin	6-0/216	8-1-78	2	Miami (Fla.)	D1/99	16/16
23	Lane, Fred	5-10/205	9-6-75	4	Lane (Tenn.)	T-Car./00	*15/5
39	Shields, Paul	6-1/238	1-31-76	2	Arizona	FA/99	13/3
	RECEIVERS						
83	Banta, Bradford (TE)	6-6/255	12-14-70	7	Southern California	D4/94	16/0
85	Dilger, Ken (TE)	6-5/255	2-2-71	6	Illinois	D2/95	15/15
84	Green, E.G.	5-11/190	6-28-75	3	Florida State	D3/98	11/4
88	Harrison, Marvin	6-0/181	8-25-72	5	Syracuse	D1/96	16/16
15	Jones, Isaac	6-0/190	12-7-75	2	Purdue	FA/99	1/1
86	Pathon, Jerome	6-0/187	12-16-75	3	Washington	D2/98	10/2
16	Plummer, Chad	6-3/218	11-30-75	2	Cincinnati	FA/99	1/0
81	Pollard, Marcus (TE)	6-4/252	2-8-72	6	Bradley	FA/95	16/12
80	Wilkins, Terrence	5-8/179	7-29-75	2	Virginia	FA/99	16/11
	OFFENSIVE LINEMEN						
78	Glenn, Tarik (T)	6-5/335	5-25-76	4	California	D1/97	16/16
74	Jackson, Waverly (G)	6-2/315	12-19-72	3	Virginia Tech	FA/98	16/16
68	Johnson, Matt (G)	6-4/332	9-24-73	R	Brigham Young	D5b/00	—
76	McKinney, Steve (G)	6-4/302	10-15-75	3	Texas A&M	D4/98	15/14
73	Meadows, Adam (T)	6-5/295	1-25-74	4	Georgia	D2/97	16/16
50	Moore, Larry (C)	6-2/212	6-1-75	3	Brigham Young	FA/98	16/16
63	Saturday, Jeff	6-2/295	6-18-75	2	North Carolina	FA/99	11/2
	DEFENSIVE LINEMEN						
92	Bratzke, Chad (E)	6-5/275	9-15-71	7	Eastern Kentucky	UFA/99	16/16
64	Chester, Larry (T)	6-2/310	10-17-75	3	Temple	FA/98	16/8
79	Holsey, Bernard	6-2/285	12-10-73	5	Duke	UFA/00	*16/0
62	Johnson, Ellis (T)	6-2/288	10-30-73	6	Florida	D1/95	16/16
61	McCoy, Tony (T)	6-1/285	6-10-69	9	Florida	D4b/92	10/0
91	Nwkorie, Chukie (E)	6-2/286	7-10-75	2	Purdue	FA/99	1/0
60	Renes, Rob (T)	6-1/308	3-28-77	R	Michigan	D7a/00	—
99	Scioli, Brad (E)	6-3/277	9-6-76	2	Penn State	D5/99	10/0
90	Thomas, Mark (E)	6-5/265	5-6-69	9	North Carolina State	W-Chi./98	15/2
95	Whittington, Bernard (E)	6-5/280	8-20-71	7	Indiana	FA/94	15/15
96	Williams, Josh (T)	6-3/284	8-9-76	R	Michigan	D4/00	—
	LINEBACKERS						
97	Bennett, Cornelius	6-3/240	8-25-65	14	Alabama	FA/99	16/16
94	Morris, Rob	6-2/250	1-18-75	R	Brigham Young	D1/00	—
52	Peterson, Mike	6-2/235	6-17-76	2	Florida	D2/99	16/13
55	Thomas, Ratcliff	6-0/240	1-2-74	3	Maryland	FA/98	16/0
53	Washington, Marcus	6-3/247	10-17-77	R	Auburn	D2/00	—
	DEFENSIVE BACKS						
47	Austin, Billy	5-10/195	3-8-75	2	New Mexico	FA/98	16/0
29	Belser, Jason	5-9/196	5-28-70	9	Oklahoma	D8a/92	16/16
26	Blevins, Tony	6-0/165	1-29-75	3	Kansas	W-SF/98	15/0
42	Brooks, Rodregis (CB)	5-10/181	8-30-78	R	Alabama-Birmingham	D7b/00	—
20	Burris, Jeff	6-0/190	6-7-72	7	Notre Dame	UFA/98	16/16
37	Cota, Chad	6-1/195	8-8-71	6	Oregon	UFA/99	15/15
28	Macklin, David	5-9/195	7-14-78	R	Penn State	D3/00	—
21	Miranda, Paul	5-10/184	5-2-76	2	Central Florida	D4/99	5/0
31	Muhammad, Mustafah	5-10/180	10-19-73	2	Fresno State	FA/99	11/1
38	Poole, Tyrone	5-8/188	2-3-72	6	Fort Valley (Ga.) State	T-Car./98	15/14
	SPECIALISTS						
7	Kight, Danny (K)	6-0/214	8-18-71	2	Augusta State	FA/99	12/0
17	Smith, Hunter (P)	6-2/212	8-9-77	2	Notre Dame	D7a/99	16/0
12	Vanderjagt, Mike (K)	6-5/210	3-24-70	3	West Virginia	FA/98	16/0

*Not with Colts in 1999.

Other free agent veterans invited to camp: C Phillip Armour, OL Joel Davis, RB Jim Finn, WR Darran Hall, TE Josh Keur, LB Paul LaCoste, DB Craig Miller, QB Gus Ornstein, OL Tim Ridder, OT Paul Snellings, LB Nate Stimson, DB Scott Thomas, DB Damon Troy.

Abbreviations: D1—draft pick, first round; SD-2—supplemental draft pick, second round; W—claimed on waivers; T—obtained in trade; PlanB—Plan B free-agent acquisition; FA—free-agent acquisition (other than Plan B); UFA—unconditional free agent acquisition; ED—expansion draft pick.

MISCELLANEOUS TEAM DATA

Stadium (capacity, surface):
RCA Dome (56,500, artificial)
Business address:
P.O. Box 535000
Indianapolis, IN 46253
Business phone:
317-297-2658
Ticket information:
317-297-7000
Team colors:
Royal blue and white
Flagship radio stations:
WNDE, 1260 AM
WFBQ, 94.5 FM
Training site:
Rose Hulman Technical Institute
Terre Haute, Ind.
317-297-2658

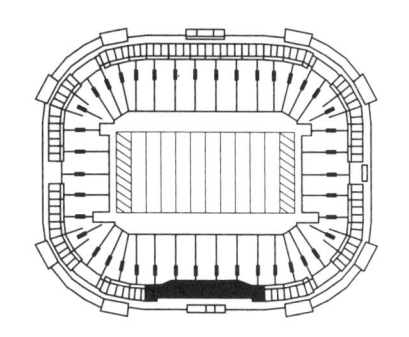

INDIANAPOLIS COLTS

TSN REPORT CARD

Coaching staff	B+	Jim Mora has put together an elite staff and delegated authority. His no-nonsense approach, which begins on the practice field, is evident on game day and is a major reason the Colts seldom beat themselves with foolish penalties or botched assignments.
Quarterbacks	A-	In two years and 32 regular-season games, Peyton Manning has established himself as a current and future star. After enduring a rookie season that was as erratic as it was efficient, he took a quantum leap in '99 and was voted to his first Pro Bowl. Manning is a workaholic, so slippage is unlikely. What's missing is a proven backup.
Running backs	A-	Edgerrin James did the impossible as a rookie: He made Colts fans forget Marshall Faulk. His objective now is to maintain the excellence that produced a league-best 1,553 yards and 13 rushing touchdowns. James complemented his running with 62 receptions, but he spent the offseason honing his receiving skills. The team upgraded the position when it traded for Fred Lane, but there still is no proven blocking fullback on the roster.
Receivers	B+	Marvin Harrison's stock has never been higher. He's coming off a 115-catch, 1,663-yard season that resulted in his first Pro Bowl. Terrence Wilkins and tight ends Ken Dilger and Marcus Pollard are quality options. The key to the unit, though, is whether E.G. Green or Jerome Pathon can remain healthy and become productive No. 2 receivers.
Offensive line	B	It's hard to knock productivity. In 1999, the unit yielded the fewest sacks (14) in the league while paving the way for James to lead the NFL is rushing. The last time that was accomplished was in 1983. The run blocking needs to be more assertive, but Manning can't complain about his protection (36 sacks in 1,140 dropbacks over the last two years).
Defensive line	C+	E Chad Bratzke and T Ellis Johnson represent a top-notch tandem on the right side of the line. They combined for 19.5 sacks last season and neither has reached his prime. The effectiveness of the unit hinges on solidifying the left side. The early leaders to start are newcomer Bernard Holsey at end and Bernard Whittington at tackle.
Linebackers	C	The spotlight will be shared by Cornelius Bennett, the strong-side starter who is entering his 14th season, and Rob Morris, the inside starter who is entering his first. Bennett spent his second straight offseason rehabbing an injury to his left knee. The defense needs him to be 100 percent, and it needs Morris to provide a nasty edge.
Secondary	C	Cornerbacks Tyrone Poole and Jeff Burris, free safety Jason Belser and strong safety Chad Cota have a combined 300 NFL starts, so experience isn't a concern. But the group must increase the number of impact plays. The Colts have intercepted just 18 passes over the last two seasons.
Special teams	B-	Kicker Mike Vanderjagt has converted 61-of-69 field-goal attempts in two years and closed last season by nailing a club-record 26 straight. Hunter Smith should be more consistent in his second year as the punter. The return game is in reliable hands with Wilkins, but the coverage teams need to be improved.

JACKSONVILLE JAGUARS
AFC CENTRAL DIVISION

2000 SEASON

CLUB DIRECTORY

Chairman & CEO
Wayne Weaver
Senior vice president/football operations
Michael Huyghue
Senior v.p./marketing
Dan Connell
Vice president/chief financial officer
Bill Prescott
V.p., administration/general counsel
Paul Vance
Exec. director of communications
Dan Edwards
Director of player personnel
Rick Reiprish
Director of pro scouting
Fran Foley
Director of college scouting
Rick Mueller
Director of finance
Kim Dodson
Director of facilities
Jeff Cannon
Director of football administration
Skip Richardson
Director of information technology
Bruce Swindell
Director of corporate sponsorship
Macky Weaver
Director of special events
Roddy White
Director of player programs
Quentin Williams
Director of broadcasting
Jennifer Kumik
Director of ticket sales
Steve Swetoha
Head athletic trainer
Mike Ryan

Head coach
Tom Coughlin

Assistant coaches
John Bonamego (assistant special teams)
Dom Capers (def. coordinator)
Perry Fewell (secondary)
Greg Finnegan (asst. strength & conditioning)
Frank Gansz (special teams coordinator)
Fred Hoaglin (tight ends)
Jerald Ingram (running backs)
Mike Maser (offensive line)
John McNulty (wide receivers)
Jerry Palmieri (strength & conditioning)
John Pease (defensive line)
Bob Petrino (quarterbacks)
Lucious Selmon (outside linebackers)
Steve Szabo (inside linebackers)

Video director
Mike Perkins
Equipment manager
Drew Hampton

SCHEDULE

Sept. 3	at Cleveland	1:00
Sept. 10	at Baltimore	1:00
Sept. 17	CINCINNATI	1:00
Sept. 25	at Indianapolis (Mon.)	9:00
Oct. 1	PITTSBURGH	1:00
Oct. 8	BALTIMORE	8:35
Oct. 16	at Tennessee (Mon.)	9:00
Oct. 22	WASHINGTON	4:15
Oct. 29	at Dallas	4:15
Nov. 5	Open date	
Nov. 12	SEATTLE	1:00
Nov. 19	at Pittsburgh	8:35
Nov. 26	TENNESSEE	4:15
Dec. 3	CLEVELAND	4:15
Dec. 10	ARIZONA	1:00
Dec. 17	at Cincinnati	1:00
Dec. 23	at N.Y. Giants (Sat.)	12:30

All times are Eastern.
All games Sunday unless noted.

DRAFT CHOICES

R. Jay Soward, WR, Southern California (first round/29th pick overall).
Brad Meester, C, Northern Iowa (2/60).
T.J. Slaughter, LB, Southern Mississippi (3/92).
Joey Chustz, T, Louisiana Tech (4/123).
Kiwaukee Thomas, DB, Georgia Southern (5/159).
Emanuel Smith, WR, Arkansas (6/196).
Erik Olson, DB, Colorado State (7/236).
Rob Meier, DE, Washington St. (7/241).
Shyrone Stith, RB, Virginia Tech (7/243).
Danny Clark, LB, Illinois (7/245).
Mark Baniewicz, T, Syracuse (7/247).

1999 REVIEW

RESULTS

Sept.12	SAN FRANCISCO	W	41-3
Sept.19	at Carolina	W	22-20
Sept.26	TENNESSEE	L	19-20
Oct. 3	at Pittsburgh	W	17-3
Oct. 11	at N.Y. Jets	W	16-6
Oct. 17	CLEVELAND	W	24-7
Oct. 24	Open date		
Oct. 31	at Cincinnati	W	41-10
Nov. 7	at Atlanta	W	30-7
Nov. 14	BALTIMORE	W	6-3
Nov. 21	NEW ORLEANS	W	41-23
Nov. 28	at Baltimore	W	30-23
Dec. 2	PITTSBURGH	W	20-6
Dec. 13	DENVER	W	27-24
Dec. 19	at Cleveland	W	24-14
Dec. 26	at Tennessee	L	14-41
Jan. 2	CINCINNATI	W	24-7
Jan. 15	MIAMI*	W	62-7
Jan. 23	TENNESSEE†	L	14-33

*AFC divisional playoff game.
†AFC championship game.

RECORDS/RANKINGS

1999 regular-season record: 14-2 (1st in AFC Central); 8-2 in division; 10-2 in conference; 4-0 vs. NFC; 7-1 at home; 7-1 on road; 4-0 on turf; 10-2 on grass.
Team record last five years: 49-31 (.613, ranks 6th in league in that span).

1999 team rankings:

	No.	AFC	NFL
Total offense	*349.1	3	7
Rushing offense	*130.7	1	2
Passing offense	*218.4	4	12
Scoring offense	396	2	6
Total defense	*270.9	3	4
Rushing defense	*90.3	4	7
Passing defense	*180.6	2	3
Scoring defense	217	1	1
Takeaways	30	8	T17
Giveaways	18	1	1
Turnover differential	12	4	T4
Sacks	57	1	T1
Sacks allowed	36	6	T10

*Yards per game.

TEAM LEADERS

Scoring (kicking): Mike Hollis, 130 pts. (37/37 PATs, 31/38 FGs).
Scoring (touchdowns): James Stewart, 78 pts. (13 rushing).
Passing: Mark Brunell, 3,060 yds. (441 att., 259 comp., 58.7%, 14 TDs, 9 int.).
Rushing: James Stewart, 931 yds. (249 att., 3.7 avg., 13 TDs).
Receptions: Jimmy Smith, 116 (1,636 yds., 14.1 avg., 6 TDs).
Interceptions: Aaron Beasley, 6 (206 yds., 2 TDs).
Sacks: Tony Brackens, 12.0.
Punting: Bryan Barker, 41.8 avg. (78 punts, 3,260 yds., 0 blocked).
Punt returns: Reggie Barlow, 10.9 avg. (38 att., 414 yds., 1 TD).
Kickoff returns: Reggie Barlow, 20.8 avg. (19 att., 396 yds., 0 TDs).

2000 SEASON
TRAINING CAMP ROSTER

No.	QUARTERBACKS	Ht./Wt.	Born	NFL Exp.	College	How acq.	'99 Games GP/GS
8	Brunell, Mark	6-1/216	9-17-70	8	Washington	T-GB/95	15/15
10	Martin, Jamie	6-2/206	2-8-70	6	Weber State	UFA/00	*0/0
12	Quinn, Jonathon	6-6/240	2-27-75	3	Middle Tennessee State	D3/98	0/0
	RUNNING BACKS						
22	Banks, Tavian	5-10/208	2-17-74	3	Iowa	D4a/98	8/1
24	Howard, Chris	5-10/226	5-5-75	3	Michigan	FA/98	12/0
34	Mack, Stacey (FB)	6-1/237	6-26-75	2	Temple	FA/99	12/0
31	Shelton, Daimon (FB)	6-0/254	9-15-72	4	Cal State Sacramento	D6/97	16/9
33	Stith, Shyrone	5-7/203	4-2-78	R	Virginia Tech	D7c/00	—
28	Taylor, Fred	6-1/227	6-27-76	3	Florida	D1a/98	10/9
	RECEIVERS						
84	Barlow, Reggie	6-0/186	1-22-73	5	Alabama State	D4/96	14/2
80	Brady, Kyle (TE)	6-6/274	1-14-72	6	Penn State	TFA/99	13/12
85	Griffith, Rich (TE)	6-5/260	7-31-69	7	Arizona	FA/95	16/0
83	Jackson, Lenzie	6-0/187	6-17-77	2	Arizona State	FA/99	4/0
88	Jones, Damon (TE)	6-5/266	9-18-74	4	Southern Illinois	D5/97	15/8
87	McCardell, Keenan	6-1/185	1-6-70	9	UNLV	UFA/96	16/15
19	Smith, Emanuel	6-1/219	2-3-76	R	Arkansas	D6/00	—
82	Smith, Jimmy	6-1/200	2-9-69	8	Jackson State	FA/95	16/16
81	Soward, R.Jay	5-11/177	1-16-78	R	Southern California	D1/00	—
86	Whitted, Alvis	6-0/186	9-4-74	3	North Carolina State	D7a/98	14/1
	OFFENSIVE LINEMEN						
69	Baniewicz, Mark (T)	6-6/303	3-24-77	R	Syracuse	D7e/00	—
71	Boselli, Tony (T)	6-7/319	4-17-72	6	Southern California	D1a/95	16/16
76	Chustz, Joey (T)	6-7/304	1-18-77	R	Louisiana Tech	D4/00	—
78	Fordham, Todd (G)	6-5/303	10-9-73	4	Florida State	FA/97	0/0
67	Ingram, Stephen (G)	6-4/315	5-8-71	5	Maryland	FA/99	6/0
63	Meester, Brad (G)	6-3/298	3-23-77	R	Northern Iowa	D2/00	—
65	Neujahr, Quentin (C)	6-4/294	1-30-71	6	Kansas State	FA/98	16/0
72	Searcy, Leon (T)	6-4/315	12-21-69	9	Miami (Fla.)	FA/96	16/16
66	Wade, John (C)	6-5/294	1-25-75	3	Marshall	D5/98	16/16
77	Wiegert, Zach (G)	6-5/310	8-16-72	6	Nebraska	FA/99	16/12
	DEFENSIVE LINEMEN						
90	Brackens, Tony (E)	6-4/257	12-26-74	5	Texas	D2a/96	16/15
75	Curry, Eric (E)	6-6/277	2-3-70	8	Alabama	FA/98	5/0
93	Landolt, Kevin (T)	6-4/298	10-25-75	2	West Virginia	D4/99	1/0
61	Leroy, Emarlos (T)	6-1/310	7-31-75	2	Georgia	D6/99	13/0
92	Meier, Rob (E)	6-5/282	8-29-77	R	Washington State	D7b/00	—
91	Payne, Seth (T)	6-4/289	2-12-75	4	Cornell	D4/97	16/16
99	Smeenge, Joel (E)	6-6/265	4-1-68	11	Western Michigan	UFA/95	15/7
94	Smith, Larry (T)	6-5/282	12-4-74	2	Florida State	D2/99	15/0
96	Walker, Gary (T)	6-2/293	2-28-73	6	Auburn	UFA/99	16/16
97	Wynn, Renaldo (E)	6-3/280	9-3-74	4	Notre Dame	D1/97	12/10
	LINEBACKERS						
52	Boyer, Brant	6-1/232	6-27-71	7	Arizona	ED22/95	15/0
54	Burnett, Chester	5-10/238	4-15-75	1	Arizona	FA/99	0/0
55	Clark, Danny	6-2/230	5-9-77	R	Illinois	D7d/00	—
51	Hardy, Kevin	6-4/247	7-24-73	5	Illinois	D1/96	16/16
51	Marts, Lonnie	6-2/246	11-10-68	11	Tulane	FA/99	16/16
56	Nickerson, Hardy	6-2/236	9-1-65	14	California	UFA/00	*16/16
95	Paup, Bryce	6-5/250	2-29-68	11	Northern Iowa	UFA/98	15/14
53	Slaughter, T.J.	6-0/247	2-20-77	R	Southern Mississippi	D3/00	—
50	Storz, Erik	6-2/240	6-24-75	2	Boston College	FA/98	7/0
57	Terry, Corey	6-3/246	3-6-76	2	Tennessee	FA/99	8/0
	DEFENSIVE BACKS						
21	Beasley, Aaron (CB)	6-0/195	7-7-73	5	West Virginia	D3/96	16/16
25	Bryant, Fernando (CB)	5-10/174	3-26-77	2	Alabama	D1/99	16/16
23	Chamblin, Corey (CB)	5-10/188	5-29-77	2	Tennessee Tech	FA/99	11/0
29	Craft, Jason (CB)	5-10/178	2-13-76	2	Colorado State	D5/99	16/0
20	Darius, Donovin (S)	6-1/212	8-12-75	3	Syracuse	D1b/98	16/16
37	Lake, Carnell (S)	6-1/207	7-15-67	12	UCLA	UFA/99	16/16
32	Logan, Mike (S)	6-0/211	9-15-74	4	West Virginia	D2/97	2/0
38	McElmurry, Blaine (S)	6-0/192	10-23-73	2	Montana	FA/98	16/0
45	Olson, Erik (S)	6-1/215	1-4-77	R	Colorado State	D7a/00	—
26	Stewart, Rayna (S)	5-10/198	6-18-73	5	Northern Arizona	FA/99	14/0
41	Thomas, Kiwaukee (CB)	5-11/186	6-19-77	R	Georgia Southern	D5/00	—
	SPECIALISTS						
4	Barker, Bryan (P)	6-2/199	6-28-64	11	Santa Clara	UFA/95	16/0
1	Hollis, Mike (K)	5-7/178	5-22-72	6	Idaho	FA/95	16/0
2	Lindsey, Steve (K)	6-1/176	11-25-74	2	Mississippi	FA/99	16/0

– 45 –

*Not with Jaguars in 1999.

Other free agent veterans invited to camp: WR James Battle, FB Trevor Bollers, G Anthony Cesario, RB Leroy Collins, C/G David Kempfert, CB Zebbie Lethridge, S Kevin Peoples, QB Roderick Robinson, LB Brandon Southward, DE Rahmaan Streater, WR Gunnard Twyner, DE Chris White, G Donnie Young.

Abbreviations: D1—draft pick, first round; SD-2—supplemental draft pick, second round; W—claimed on waivers; T—obtained in trade; PlanB—Plan B free-agent acquisition; FA—free-agent acquisition (other than Plan B); UFA—unconditional free agent acquisition; ED—expansion draft pick.

MISCELLANEOUS TEAM DATA

Stadium (capacity, surface):
ALLTEL Stadium (73,000, grass)
Business address:
One ALLTEL Stadium Place
Jacksonville, FL 32202
Business phone:
904-633-6000
Ticket information:
904-633-2000
Team colors:
Teal, black and gold
Flagship radio station:
WOKV, 690 AM
Training site:
ALLTEL Stadium
Jacksonville, Fla.
904-633-6000

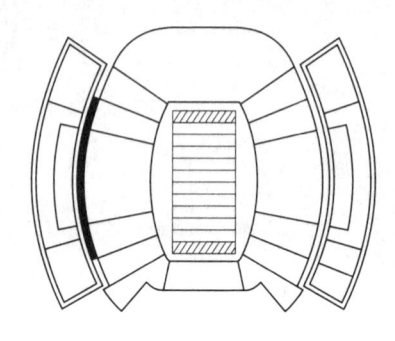

TSN REPORT CARD

Coaching staff	A	Tom Coughlin has built an outstanding team and does a good job making it all work. As an offensive coordinator, he tends to lean too much to the conservative side, which probably costs his team some points. Defensive coordinator Dom Capers may be the best in the league at what he does. New special teams coach Frank Gansz will liven up those units.
Quarterbacks	B	Mark Brunell has to have a very good year for the Jaguars to get to the Super Bowl. He has all the tools, but he needs to stay healthy. The backup situation isn't so good. Jamie Martin, who is two seasons removed from an ACL knee injury, will battle Jonathon Quinn, who didn't play a down last year. The Jaguars better hope Brunell stays healthy.
Running backs	B	Fred Taylor, when healthy, is the best runner in the league. But he has missed time in both of his first two seasons with minor aches. He has to stay on the field. Keep an eye on backup Stacey Mack, a bruising 235-pounder who offers a nice change of pace. Fullback Daimon Shelton is a good lead blocker.
Receivers	A -	Jimmy Smith is one of the best in the NFL, leading the league last season in catches. But he will be 30 when the season starts, so you have to wonder when he will start to slow down. The same can be said for Keenan McCardell, who remains one of the best route runners in the league. Rookie R. Jay Soward will add some much-needed speed and, it's hoped, fill the need for a No. 3 receiver.
Offensive line	B -	The tackle tandem of Tony Boselli and Leon Searcy is one of the best in the NFL. But Boselli is coming off ACL surgery and that may slow him at the start of the season. The inside three remain a concern. Zach Wiegert will start at one guard, but he needs to be more consistent. Center John Wade has to be stronger at the point. The other guard spot is wide open.
Defensive line	B -	The 1999 line was the best in team history, and it should be even better this season. End Tony Brackens, provided he doesn't sit out the year in a contract dispute, is the key to the unit. He made his first Pro Bowl appearance last year and has to remain a disruptive force. Tackle Gary Walker is the key player inside, but watch out for second-year player Larry Smith.
Linebackers	A	The signing of veteran middle linebacker Hardy Nickerson, a five-time Pro Bowler, makes this the best group of linebackers in the team's short history. With Nickerson, Lonnie Marts and Kevin Hardy, the Jaguars have three very good players. Hardy is the best of the group, and may be the best all-round linebacker in the NFL.
Secondary	B	Starting cornerbacks Aaron Beasley and Fernando Bryant both had good seasons in 1999 and should play to a higher level in 2000. Bryant, now in his second season, may be on his way to the Pro Bowl. The safety duo of Carnell Lake and Donovin Darius is a good one, but Lake could be slowing down in his 12th season. The nickel package has to play better than it did in last season.
Special teams	B	The kicking game is in good shape with punter Bryan Barker and kicker Mike Hollis. Kickoff specialist Steve Lindsey led the NFL in touchbacks. The return game will get a boost from Soward, but the coverage teams have to be better.

KANSAS CITY CHIEFS
AFC WESTERN DIVISION

2000 SEASON

CLUB DIRECTORY

Founder
Lamar Hunt
Chairman of the board
Jack Steadman
President/g.m./chief executive officer
Carl Peterson
Executive vice president/assistant g.m.
Dennis Thum
Senior vice president
Dennis Watley
Secretary/legal
Jim Seigfreid
Treasurer and director/finance
Dale Young
Vice president/sales and marketing
Wallace Bennett
Director/operations
Steve Schneider
Director/development
Ken Blume
Director/corporate sponsorship sales
Anita Bailey
Director/advance sales & hospitality
Gary Spani
Director/public relations
Bob Moore
Assistant director/public relations
Peter Moris
Director of player personnel
Terry Bradway
Director of pro personnel
John Schneider
Director of college scouting
Chuck Cook
Scouts
Frank Acevedo   Scott Campbell
Jeff Ireland   Quintin Smith
Trainer
Dave Kendall
Assistant trainer
Bud Epps

Head coach
Gunther Cunningham

Assistant coaches
Tom Clements (quarterbacks)
Jeff Fish (assistant strength & conditioning)
Jim Hosler (offensive assistant/ quality control)
Jeff Hurd (strength & cond.)
Bob Karmelowicz (defensive line)
Al Lavan (running backs)
Richard Mann (wide receivers)
Jimmy Raye (off. coordinator)
Keith Rowen (tight ends)
Kurt Schottenheimer (def. coord.)
Willie Shaw (assistant head coach/defensive backs)
Mike Solari (offensive line)
Mike Stock (special teams)
Joe Vitt (linebackers)
Darvin Wallis (defensive assistant/quality control)

Physicians
Cris Barnthouse
Joseph Brewer
Jon Browne
Mike Monaco
Equipment manager
Mike Davidson

SCHEDULE

Sept. 3—	INDIANAPOLIS	1:00
Sept. 10—	at Tennessee	1:00
Sept. 17—	SAN DIEGO	1:00
Sept. 24—	at Denver	4:15
Oct. 2—	SEATTLE (Mon.)	9:00
Oct. 8—	Open date	
Oct. 15—	OAKLAND	1:00
Oct. 22—	ST. LOUIS	1:00
Oct. 29—	at Seattle	4:15
Nov. 5—	at Oakland	4:15
Nov. 12—	at San Francisco	4:05
Nov. 19—	BUFFALO	1:00
Nov. 26—	at San Diego	4:15
Dec. 4—	at New England (Mon.)	9:00
Dec. 10—	CAROLINA	1:00
Dec. 17—	DENVER	1:00
Dec. 24—	at Atlanta	1:00

All times are Eastern.
All games Sunday unless noted.

DRAFT CHOICES

Sylvester Morris, WR, Jackson State (first round/21st pick overall).
William Bartee, DB, Oklahoma (2/54).
Gregory Wesley, DB, Arkansas-Pine Bluff (3/85).
Frank Moreau, RB, Louisville (4/115).
Dante Hall, RB, Texas A&M (5/153).
Pat Dennis, DB, Louisiana-Monroe (5/162).
Darnell Alford, T, Boston College (6/188).
Desmond Kitchings, WR, Furman (7/208).

1999 REVIEW

RESULTS

Sept.12—at Chicago	L	17-20
Sept.19—DENVER	W	26-10
Sept.26—DETROIT	W	31-21
Oct. 3—at San Diego	L	14-21
Oct. 10—NEW ENGLAND	W	16-14
Oct. 17—Open date		
Oct. 21—at Baltimore	W	35-8
Oct. 31—SAN DIEGO	W	34-0
Nov. 7—at Indianapolis	L	17-25
Nov. 14—at Tampa Bay	L	10-17
Nov. 21—SEATTLE	L	19-31
Nov. 28—at Oakland	W	37-34
Dec. 5—at Denver	W	16-10
Dec. 12—MINNESOTA	W	31-28
Dec. 18—PITTSBURGH	W	35-19
Dec. 26—at Seattle	L	14-23
Jan. 2—OAKLAND (OT)	L	38-41

RECORDS/RANKINGS

1999 regular-season record: 9-7 (2nd in AFC West); 4-4 in division; 7-5 in conference; 2-2 vs. NFC; 6-2 at home; 3-5 on road; 0-2 on turf; 9-5 on grass.
Team record last five years: 51-29 (.638, ranks T4th in league in that span).

1999 team rankings:	No.	AFC	NFL
Total offense	*332.6	5	12
Rushing offense	*130.1	3	4
Passing offense	*202.4	11	22
Scoring offense	390	T4	T8
Total defense	*314.9	10	14
Rushing defense	*97.3	7	11
Passing defense	*217.6	10	16
Scoring defense	322	10	13
Takeaways	45	1	2
Giveaways	24	4	6
Turnover differential	21	1	1
Sacks	40	9	T14
Sacks allowed	26	3	4

*Yards per game.

TEAM LEADERS

Scoring (kicking): Pete Stoyanovich, 108 pts. (45/45 PATs, 21/28 FGs).
Scoring (touchdowns): Tony Gonzalez, 66 pts. (11 receiving).
Passing: Elvis Grbac, 3,389 yds. (499 att., 294 comp., 58.9%, 22 TDs, 15 int.).
Rushing: Donnell Bennett, 627 yds. (161 att., 3.9 avg., 8 TDs).
Receptions: Tony Gonzalez, 76 (849 yds., 11.2 avg., 11 TDs).
Interceptions: James Hasty, 7 (98 yds., 2 TDs).
Sacks: Derrick Thomas, 7.0.
Punting: Daniel Pope, 41.8 avg. (101 punts, 4,218 yds., 2 blocked).
Punt returns: Tamarick Vanover, 12.3 avg. (51 att., 627 yds., 2 TDs).
Kickoff returns: Tamarick Vanover, 20.1 avg. (44 att., 886 yds., 0 TDs).

– 47 –

2000 SEASON
TRAINING CAMP ROSTER

KANSAS CITY CHIEFS

No.	QUARTERBACKS	Ht./Wt.	Born	NFL Exp.	College	How acq.	'99 Games GP/GS
15	Collins, Todd	6-4/228	11-5-71	6	Michigan	W-Buf./98	0/0
18	Grbac, Elvis	6-5/237	8-13-70	8	Michigan	UFA/97	16/16
1	Moon, Warren	6-3/218	11-18-56	17	Washington	FA/99	1/0
	RUNNING BACKS						
38	Anders, Kimble	5-11/226	9-10-66	10	Houston	FA/91	2/2
30	Bennett, Donnell (FB)	6-0/245	9-14-72	7	Miami (Fla.)	D2/94	15/1
34	Cloud, Mike	5-10/205	7-1-75	2	Boston College	D2/99	11/0
20	Hall, Dante	5-8/188	9-1-78	R	Texas A&M	D5a/00	—
46	Moreau, Frank	6-0/224	9-9-76	R	Louisville	D4/00	—
49	Richardson, Tony (FB)	6-1/235	12-17-71	6	Auburn	FA/95	16/15
22	Shehee, Rashaan	5-10/210	6-20-75	3	Washington	D3/98	9/5
	RECEIVERS						
82	Alexander, Derrick	6-2/210	11-6-71	7	Michigan	UFA/98	16/15
11	Dar Dar, Kirby	5-9/186	3-27-72	3	Syracuse	FA/99	0/0
83	Gammon, Kendall (TE)	6-4/260	10-23-68	9	Pittsburg (Kan.) State	UFA/00	*16/0
88	Gonzalez, Tony (TE)	6-4/251	2-27-76	4	California	D1/97	15/15
85	Jacoby, Mitch (TE)	6-4/260	12-8-73	4	Northern Illinois	T-StL/99	5/0
17	Kitchings, Desmond	5-9/175	7-19-78	R	Furman	D7/00	—
81	Lockett, Kevin	6-0/187	9-8-74	4	Kansas State	D2/97	16/1
84	Morris, Sylvester	6-3/208	10-6-77	R	Jackson State	D1/00	—
80	Parker, Larry	6-1/200	7-14-76	2	Southern California	D4/99	10/0
89	Rison, Andre	6-1/199	3-18-67	12	Michigan State	FA/97	15/14
	OFFENSIVE LINEMEN						
72	Alford, Darnell (T)	6-4/334	6-11-77	R	Boston College	D6/00	—
69	Blackshear, Jeff (G)	6-6/323	3-29-69	8	Northeast Louisiana	FA/00	*16/16
54	Graham, Aaron (C)	6-4/301	5-22-73	5	Nebraska	UFA/00	*16/16
61	Grunhard, Tim (C)	6-2/311	5-17-68	11	Notre Dame	D2/90	16/16
66	Riley, Victor (T)	6-5/334	11-4-74	3	Auburn	D1/98	16/16
68	Shields, Will (G)	6-3/321	9-15-71	8	Nebraska	D3/93	16/16
65	Smith, Jeff (C)	6-3/322	5-25-73	5	Tennessee	D7b/96	15/2
70	Spears, Marcus (T)	6-4/320	9-28-71	7	Northwestern (La.) State	FA/97	10/2
77	Stai, Brenden (G)	6-4/310	3-30-72	6	Nebraska	FA/00	*16/16
79	Szott, Dave (G)	6-4/289	12-12-67	11	Penn State	D7/90	14/14
76	Tait, John (T)	6-6/306	1-26-75	2	Brigham Young	D1/99	12/3
	DEFENSIVE LINEMEN						
93	Browning, John (E)	6-4/305	9-30-73	5	West Virginia	D3/96	0/0
99	Clemons, Duane (E)	6-5/272	5-23-74	5	California	UFA/00	*16/9
98	Hicks, Eric (E)	6-6/278	6-17-76	3	Maryland	FA/98	16/16
90	Martin, Steve (T)	6-4/303	5-31-74	5	Missouri	UFA/00	*16/15
75	McGlockton, Chester (T)	6-4/328	9-16-69	9	Clemson	FA/98	16/16
91	O'Neal, Leslie (E)	6-4/281	5-7-64	15	Oklahoma State	FA/98	16/10
95	Ransom, Derrick (T)	6-3/307	9-13-76	3	Cincinnati	D6/98	10/0
92	Williams, Dan (E)	6-4/293	12-15-69	7	Toledo	FA/97	14/9
96	Word, Mark (E)	6-4/270	11-23-75	2	Jacksonville State	FA/99	5/0
	LINEBACKERS						
51	Bush, Lew	6-2/245	12-2-69	7	Washington State	FA/00	*16/14
59	Edwards, Donnie	6-2/235	4-6-73	5	UCLA	D4/96	16/16
55	George, Ron	6-2/247	3-20-70	8	Stanford	FA/98	16/0
57	Maslowski, Mike	6-1/246	7-11-74	2	Wisconsin-La Crosse	FA/99	15/0
53	Patton, Marvcus	6-2/243	5-1-67	11	UCLA	UFA/99	16/16
56	Stills, Gary	6-2/235	7-11-74	2	West Virginia	D3a/99	2/0
	DEFENSIVE BACKS						
35	Atkins, Larry (S)	6-3/230	7-21-75	2	UCLA	D3b/99	9/0
24	Bartee, William (CB)	6-1/190	6-25-77	R	Oklahoma	D2/00	—
41	Dennis, Pat (CB)	6-0/202	6-3-78	R	Louisiana-Monroe	D5b/00	—
26	Dishman, Cris (CB)	6-0/196	8-13-65	13	Purdue	FA/99	16/16
23	Gray, Carlton (CB)	6-0/198	6-26-71	8	UCLA	FA/99	16/0
40	Hasty, James (CB)	6-0/213	5-23-65	13	Washington State	UFA/95	15/15
29	Serwanga, Wasswa (CB)	5-11/190	7-23-76	2	UCLA	FA/00	*9/0
27	Walker, Bracey (S)	6-0/204	6-11-70	7	North Carolina	FA/98	16/1
44	Warfield, Eric (CB)	6-0/195	3-3-76	3	Nebraska	D7a/98	16/1
25	Wesley, Greg (S)	6-2/214	3-19-76	R	Arkansas-Pine Bluff	D3/00	—
21	Woods, Jerome (S)	6-2/202	3-17-73	5	Memphis	D1/96	15/15
	SPECIALISTS						
13	Pope, Daniel (P)	5-10/203	3-28-75	2	Alabama	FA/99	16/0
5	Sauerbrun, Todd (P)	5-10/204	1-4-73	6	West Virginia	UFA/00	*16/0
10	Stoyanovich, Pete (K)	5-11/194	4-28-67	12	Indiana	T-Mia./96	16/0

*Not with Chiefs in 1999.

Other free agent veterans invited to camp: WR Scott Cloman, QB Marcus Crandell, Chris Gall, P Nick Gallery, C Grant Garrett, CB Ray Jackson, FB Vershan Jackson, G Eric King, FB Charles Kirby, G Brad Kubik, QB Bill Lindquist, G Rob Murphy, TE Melvin Pearsall, RB Brian Shay, LB Tim Terry, C Brian Waters, QB Ted White, G Donald Willis.

Abbreviations: D1—draft pick, first round; SD-2—supplemental draft pick, second round; W—claimed on waivers; T—obtained in trade; PlanB—Plan B free-agent acquisition; FA—free-agent acquisition (other than Plan B); UFA—unconditional free agent acquisition; ED—expansion draft pick.

MISCELLANEOUS TEAM DATA

Stadium (capacity, surface):
Arrowhead Stadium
(79,451, grass)
Business address:
One Arrowhead Drive
Kansas City, MO 64129
Business phone:
816-920-9300
Ticket information:
816-920-9400
Team colors:
Red, gold and white
Flagship radio station:
KYYS, 99.7 FM
Training site:
U. of Wisconsin-River Falls
River Falls, Wis.
715-425-4580

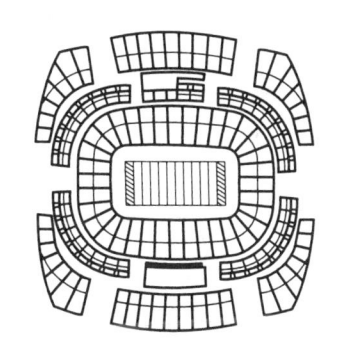

TSN REPORT CARD

Category	Grade	Comments
Coaching staff	B	Of the six rookie head coaches in the NFL last season, Gunther Cunningham was the only one to produce a winning record, at 9-7. That still wasn't good enough to get the Chiefs into the playoffs, and Cunningham will be under pressure this season. The hiring of former Oakland defensive coordinator Willie Shaw as secondary coach was a coup.
Quarterbacks	B	Elvis Grbac proved he could stay healthy and be effective last season when he took all but three snaps. Most importantly, Grbac's dependability won the confidence of his teammates, who now view him as a leader after watching him miss large chunks of his first two seasons with the Chiefs because of injuries.
Running backs	C	The Chiefs haven't had a 1,000-yard rusher since 1991, but their running back-by committee system led the NFL with 521 rushing attempts and ranked fourth in rushing. Seven different players led the Chiefs in single-game rushing, which either says they have an abundance of depth or don't have one bonafide back. Truth is, it's a little bit of both. Barring a late move before training camp, the Chiefs plan to give second-year man Mike Cloud the first chance as the feature back in 2000.
Receivers	B	The passing game revolves around Tony Gonzalez, who fulfilled his enormous potential last season by emerging as the NFL's most prolific pass-catching tight end. Alexander had four 100-yard games but continues to be an enigma. While he has the flair for making the impossible catch, he's been known to drop the easy ball, too. And he tends to disappear in critical situations. Kevin Lockett split time with Andre Rison and excelled as a sure-handed receiver who could convert third downs. Rison was a non-factor last season and could lose his roster spot to No. 1 draft pick Sylvester Morris.
Offensive line	B -	The core of the line, center Tim Grunhard and right guard Will Shields, have started alongside each other for 111 straight games, while left guard Dave Szott's streak of 77 starts was snapped in 1998. But neither guard may be flanking Grunhard when camp opens. Szott is in the last year of his contract and wants to be traded to an East Coast team for family reasons and is talking about retirement. Shields is an unrestricted free agent and the Chiefs designated him as their franchise player, causing a lengthy negotiating impasse. As insurance, the Chiefs signed Brenden Stai and Jeff Blackshear. Both tackles are youngsters. Right tackle Victor Riley has been starting since the second game of his rookie 1998 year and left tackle John Tait, the No. 1 pick in 1999, appeared in 12 games last season after missing all of preseason in a nasty holdout.
Defensive line	A -	Another monster season is expected from tackle Chester McGlockton. The team moved Dan Williams from end to tackle late last season, but he was hampered all season by nagging thigh, knee and ankle injuries, a by-product of sitting out all of 1998 in a contract dispute. The Chiefs like to rotate in fresh linemen, and Williams' history of injuries should give free agent Steve Martin plenty of opportunities as the replacement for Tom Barndt, who left for Cincinnati. The starting ends are solid in Duane Clemons and Eric Hicks, but it gets a little thin beyond that.
Linebackers	A	Donnie Edwards is considered the best all-round athlete on the team, and he proved it after he was moved from middle linebacker, where he was productive but undersized, to the weakside, where he became a dynamic playmaker in the team's 4-3 scheme. Given freedom to roam, Edwards led the Chiefs in tackles with 143 and led NFL linebackers with five interceptions. Free-agent signee Lew Bush will open the season on the strong side, but he likely will be replaced in nickel situations by second-year man Gary Stills, who was active for only two games as a rookie. Veteran Ron George is a steady backup at both outside spots. Middle linebacker Marvcus Patton provides dependability and consistency.
Secondary	B	Starting cornerbacks James Hasty and Cris Dishman exemplify the aggressive, bump-and-run press coverage the Chiefs love to play. However, both are 35 years old. Hasty played through painful Achilles, leg and knee injuries in 1999 and earned his second Pro Bowl berth. Dishman, in his first year with the Chiefs, was the corner targeted by quarterbacks, and the referees picked on him as well. Dishman intercepted five passes, but his aggressive tactics drew a team-leading 13 penalties for 173 yards. Third-year man Eric Warfield, who served as the nickel back last season, will challenge Dishman for the left cornerback job. Second-year man Larry Atkins will be on the spot at strong safety after three-year starter Reggie Tongue signed with Seattle. Atkins lacks Tongue's ball-hawking ability, but he brings linebacker's size to the position. Atkins will benefit from playing alongside free safety Jerome Woods, a three-year starter and a ferocious tackler.
Special teams	C	The Chiefs have corrected a horrid kicking game that cost them a division title and a playoff berth last year. Former Chicago kicker Todd Sauerbrun was signed for the dual role of kickoff specialist and punter, two areas in which the Chiefs constantly handed over favorable field position last season with short kickoffs and shaky punting. Sauerbrun fills three roster spots because he can also serve as holder for Pete Stoyanovich. Stoyanovich is coming off his second-worst season as a pro and is entering the final year of his contract. Leaving the kickoff duties to Sauerbrun will enable Stoyanovich to focus exclusively on placements, and that should help his performance. A host of unproven candidates will compete for the kick-return duties.

MIAMI DOLPHINS
AFC EASTERN DIVISION

2000 SEASON

CLUB DIRECTORY

Owner/chairman of the board
H. Wayne Huizenga
President/chief operating officer
Eddie J. Jones
Sr. vice president/business operations
Bryan Wiedmeier
Sr. vice president/finance and admin.
Jill R. Strafaci
Sr. vice president/ticket sales
Bill Galante
Director of football operations
Bob Ackles
Director of pro personnel
Tom Heckert
Director of college scouting
Tom Braatz
Vice president/media relations
Harvey Greene
Director of media relations
Neal Gulkis
Vice president/sales and marketing
Jim Ross
Director of publications & internet
Scott Stone
Sr. dir./community & alumni relations
Fudge Browne
Scouts
Mike Cartwright
Tom Heckert, Jr.
Ron Labadie
Jeff Smith
Jere Stripling
Head trainer
Kevin O'Neill
Trainers
Troy Maurer
Ryan Vermillion

Head coach
Dave Wannstedt

Assistant coaches
Jim Bates (defensive coordinator)
Doug Blevins (kicking)
Paul Boudreau (offensive line)
Clarence Brooks (defensive line)
Joel Collier (running backs)
Robert Ford (wide receivers)
Chan Gailey (off. coordinator)
John Gamble (strength & conditioning)
Judd Garrett (offensive assistant)
Pat Jones (tight ends)
Bill Lewis (defensive nickel package)
Robert Nunn (def. assistant)
Mel Phillips (secondary)
Brad Roll (assistant strength and conditioning)
Randy Shannon (linebackers)
Mike Shula (quarterbacks)
Mike Westhoff (special teams)

Physician
Daniel Kanell
John Uribe
Equipment manager
Tony Egues
Video director
Dave Hack

SCHEDULE

Sept. 3—	SEATTLE	4:15
Sept. 10—	at Minnesota	1:00
Sept. 17—	BALTIMORE	8:35
Sept. 24—	NEW ENGLAND	1:00
Oct. 1—	at Cincinnati	4:05
Oct. 8—	BUFFALO	1:00
Oct. 15—	Open date	
Oct. 23—	at N.Y. Jets (Mon.)	9:00
Oct. 29—	GREEN BAY	1:00
Nov. 5—	at Detroit	1:00
Nov. 12—	at San Diego	4:05
Nov. 19—	N.Y. JETS	4:05
Nov. 26—	at Indianapolis	1:00
Dec. 3—	at Buffalo	1:00
Dec. 10—	TAMPA BAY	1:00
Dec. 17—	INDIANAPOLIS	4:15
Dec. 24—	at New England	1:00

All times are Eastern.
All games Sunday unless noted.

DRAFT CHOICES

Todd Wade, T, Mississippi (second round/53rd pick overall).
Ben Kelly, DB, Colorado (3/84).
Deon Dyer, FB, North Carolina (4/117).
Arturo Freeman, DB, South Carolina (5/152).
Earnest Grant, DT, Arkansas-Pine Bluff (6/167).
Jeff Harris, DB, Georgia (7/232).

1999 REVIEW

RESULTS

Sept.13—at Denver	W	38-21
Sept.19—ARIZONA	W	19-16
Sept.26—Open date		
Oct. 4—BUFFALO	L	18-23
Oct. 10—at Indianapolis	W	34-31
Oct. 17—at New England	W	31-30
Oct. 24—PHILADELPHIA	W	16-13
Oct. 31—at Oakland	W	16-9
Nov. 7—TENNESSEE	W	17-0
Nov. 14—at Buffalo	L	3-23
Nov. 21—NEW ENGLAND	W	27-17
Nov. 25—at Dallas	L	0-20
Dec. 5—INDIANAPOLIS	L	34-37
Dec. 12—at N.Y. Jets	L	20-28
Dec. 19—SAN DIEGO	W	12-9
Dec. 27—N.Y. JETS	L	31-38
Jan. 2—at Washington	L	10-21
Jan. 9—at Seattle*	W	20-17
Jan. 15—at Jacksonville†	L	7-62

*AFC wild-card game.
†AFC divisional playoff game.

RECORDS/RANKINGS

1999 regular-season record: 9-7 (3rd in AFC East); 3-5 in division; 7-5 in conference; 2-2 vs. NFC; 5-3 at home; 4-4 on road; 1-3 on turf; 8-4 on grass.
Team record last five years: 45-35 (.563, ranks T9th in league in that span).
1999 team rankings:

	No.	AFC	NFL
Total offense	*308.6	10	20
Rushing offense	*90.8	12	22
Passing offense	*217.8	T5	T13
Scoring offense	326	7	13
Total defense	*275.3	4	5
Rushing defense	*92.6	5	8
Passing defense	*183.0	4	5
Scoring defense	336	14	19
Takeaways	28	T9	T20
Giveaways	34	15	T21
Turnover differential	-6	T13	T23
Sacks	39	T10	T17
Sacks allowed	37	T7	T12

*Yards per game.

TEAM LEADERS

Scoring (kicking): Olindo Mare, 144 pts. (27/27 PATs, 39/46 FGs).
Scoring (touchdowns): Oronde Gadsden, 36 pts. (6 receiving).
Passing: Dan Marino, 2,448 yds. (369 att., 204 comp., 55.3%, 12 TDs, 17 int.).
Rushing: J.J. Johnson, 558 yds. (164 att., 3.4 avg., 4 TDs).
Receptions: Tony Martin, 67 (1,037 yds., 15.5 avg., 5 TDs).
Interceptions: Sam Madison, 7 (164 yds., 1 TD).
Sacks: Rich Owens, 8.5.
Punting: Tom Hutton, 40.8 avg. (73 punts, 2,978 yds., 0 blocked).
Punt returns: Nate Jacquet, 12.5 avg. (28 att., 351 yds., 0 TDs).
Kickoff returns: Brock Marion, 24.6 avg. (62 att., 1,524 yds., 0 TDs).

2000 SEASON
TRAINING CAMP ROSTER

MIAMI DOLPHINS

No.	QUARTERBACKS	Ht./Wt.	Born	NFL Exp.	College	How acq.	'99 Games GP/GS
16	Druckenmiller, Jim	6-5/234	9-19-72	4	Virginia Tech	T-SF/99	0/0
9	Fiedler, Jay	6-2/220	12-29-71	5	Dartmouth	UFA/00	*7/1
11	Huard, Damon	6-3/215	7-9-73	4	Washington	FA/97	16/5
	Quinn, Mike	6-4/217	4-15-74	4	Stephen F. Austin	FA/00	*0/0
	RUNNING BACKS						
21	Denson, Autry	5-10/193	12-8-76	2	Notre Dame	FA/99	6/1
33	Dyer, Deon (FB)	6-0/264	10-2-77	R	North Carolina	D4/00	—
32	Johnson, J.J.	6-1/230	4-20-74	2	Mississippi State	D2a/99	13/4
44	Konrad, Rob (FB)	6-3/255	11-12-76	2	Syracuse	D2b/99	15/9
26	Smith, Lamar	5-11/225	11-29-70	7	Houston	FA/00	*13/2
34	Thomas, Thurman	5-10/200	5-16-66	13	Oklahoma State	FA/00	*5/3
	RECEIVERS						
84	Emanuel, Bert	5-10/175	10-28-70	7	UCLA, then Rice	FA/00	*11/10
86	Gadsden, Oronde	6-2/215	8-20-71	3	Winston-Salem	FA/98	16/7
83	Goodwin, Hunter (TE)	6-5/270	10-10-72	5	Texas A&M	FA/99	15/5
87	Green, Yatil	6-2/205	11-25-73	4	Miami (Fla.)	D1/97	8/1
88	Jacquet, Nate	6-0/185	9-2-75	4	San Diego State	W-Ind./98	13/0
80	Martin, Tony	6-1/175	9-5-65	11	Mesa State College (Colo.)	FA/99	16/13
81	McDuffie, O.J.	5-10/194	12-2-69	8	Penn State	D1/93	12/10
82	McKenzie, Kevin	5-9/187	9-20-75	1	Washington State	W-Phi./99	1/0
89	Perry, Ed (TE)	6-4/265	9-1-74	4	James Madison	D6d/97	16/1
85	Thomas, Lamar	6-1/170	2-12-70	8	Miami (Fla.)	FA/96	0/0
	OFFENSIVE LINEMEN						
60	Bock, John (G)	6-3/295	2-1-71	6	Indiana State	FA/96	7/0
76	Brown, James (T)	6-6/325	11-30-70	8	Virginia State	T-NYJ/96	15/14
63	Dixon, Mark (G)	6-4/300	11-6-70	3	Virginia	FA/98	13/13
65	Donnalley, Kevin (G)	6-5/310	6-10-68	10	North Carolina	UFA/00	16/9
66	Irwin, Heath (G)	6-4/300	6-27-73	5	Colorado	UFA/00	*15/13
61	Ruddy, Tim (C)	6-3/300	4-27-72	7	Notre Dame	D2b/94	16/16
68	Sheldon, Mike (T)	6-4/305	6-8-73	3	Grand Valley State (Mich.)	FA/96	9/0
74	Smith, Brent (T)	6-5/315	11-21-73	4	Mississippi State	D3d/97	13/4
71	Wade, Todd (T)	6-8/319	10-30-76	R	Mississippi	D2/00	—
78	Webb, Richmond (T)	6-6/315	1-11-67	11	Texas A&M	D1/90	15/14
	DEFENSIVE LINEMEN						
93	Armstrong, Trace (E)	6-4/270	10-5-65	12	Florida	T-Chi./95	16/2
95	Bowens, Tim (T)	6-4/315	2-7-73	7	Mississippi	D1/94	16/15
91	Bromell, Lorenzo (E)	6-6/270	9-23-75	3	Clemson	D4/98	15/1
92	Gardener, Daryl (T)	6-6/315	2-25-73	5	Baylor	D1/96	16/15
97	Grant, Earnest (T)	6-5/297	5-17-76	R	Arkansas-Pine Bluff	D6/00	—
79	Mixon, Kenny (E)	6-4/282	5-31-75	3	Louisiana State	D2b/98	11/2
96	Owens, Rich (E)	6-6/275	5-22-72	6	Lehigh	UFA/99	16/14
98	Simpson, Antoine (T)	6-2/310	12-2-76	2	Houston	FA/99	4/0
99	Taylor, Jason (E)	6-6/260	9-1-74	4	Akron	D3a/97	15/15
	LINEBACKERS						
58	Galyon, Scott	6-2/245	3-23-74	5	Tennessee	UFA/00	*16/0
53	Izzo, Larry	5-10/228	9-26-74	5	Rice	FA/96	16/0
52	Jones, Robert	6-3/245	9-27-69	9	East Carolina	FA/98	16/15
59	Rodgers, Derrick	6-1/230	10-14-71	4	Arizona State	D3b/97	16/15
56	Russell, Twan	6-1/220	4-25-74	4	Miami (Fla.)	FA/00	*9/0
54	Thomas, Zach	5-11/235	9-1-73	5	Texas Tech	D5c/96	16/16
	DEFENSIVE BACKS						
27	Freeman, Arturo (S)	6-0/196	10-27-76	R	South Carolina	D5/00	—
30	Harris, Jeff (CB)	5-11/178	7-19-77	R	Georgia	D7/00	—
28	Hill, Ray (CB)	6-0/195	8-7-75	3	Michigan State	W-Buf./98	16/0
38	Jackson, Calvin (S)	5-9/195	10-28-72	6	Auburn	FA/94	16/10
25	Jeffries, Greg (CB)	5-9/195	10-16-71	8	Virginia	UFA/99	16/0
35	Kelly, Ben (CB)	5-10/191	9-15-78	R	Colorado	D3/00	—
29	Madison, Sam (CB)	5-11/185	4-23-74	4	Louisville	D2/97	16/16
31	Marion, Brock (S)	5-11/205	6-11-70	8	Nevada	UFA/98	16/16
23	Surtain, Patrick (CB)	5-11/190	6-19-76	3	Southern Mississippi	D2a/98	16/6
45	Walker, Brian (S)	6-1/200	5-31-72	5	Washington State	UFA/00	*5/0
24	Wilson, Jerry (CB)	5-10/187	7-17-73	6	Southern	FA/96	16/1
	SPECIALISTS						
5	Hanson, Chris (P)	6-1/214	10-25-76	1	Marshall	FA/00	*1/0
10	Mare, Olindo (K)	5-10/190	6-6-73	4	Syracuse	FA/97	16/0
1	Turk, Matt (P)	6-5/235	6-16-68	6	Wisconsin-Whitewater	T-Was./00	*14/0

*Not with Dolphins in 1999.
Other free agent veterans invited to camp: G Ben Adams, RB Curtis Alexander, WR Robert Baker, WR Todd Doxzon, RB Brian Edwards, DT Jermaine Haley, WR Tony Hamler, OT Willie Jones, FB Frank Leatherwood, TE Hayward Clay, G O'Lester Pope, C Grey Ruegamer, S Kelvin Sigler, S Orlando Steinauer, WR Corey Thomas, OT Joe Wong.

Abbreviations: D1—draft pick, first round; SD-2—supplemental draft pick, second round; W—claimed on waivers; T—obtained in trade; PlanB—Plan B free-agent acquisition; FA—free-agent acquisition (other than Plan B); UFA—unconditional free agent acquisition; ED—expansion draft pick.

MIAMI DOLPHINS

MISCELLANEOUS TEAM DATA

Stadium (capacity, surface):
Pro Player Stadium
(75,192, grass)
Business address:
7500 S.W. 30th St.
Davie, FL 33314
Business phone:
954-452-7000
Ticket information:
305-620-2578
Team colors:
Aqua, coral, blue and white
Flagship radio station:
WQAM, 560 AM
Training site:
Nova Southeastern University
Davie, Fla.
954-452-7000

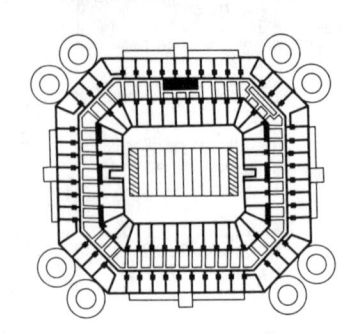

TSN REPORT CARD

Coaching staff	B	Dave Wannstedt was criticized in Chicago not for his ability with the Xs and Os but for his personnel decisions. If the way he filled out his coaching staff is any indication, Wannstedt should do a lot better in Miami. Former Cowboys coach Chan Gailey will operate a much more diverse offense than has been seen in these parts in a long time, and Jim Bates will only tweak a defense that was among the best in the NFL last year.
Quarterbacks	C	Damon Huard was an impressive 5-1 as Dan Marino's replacement last year, but he knows he needs to be better over a 16-game season. Jay Fiedler has started just one game in his career, but he's a better athlete than people think. Jim Druckenmiller is a darkhorse to win the job but has the strongest arm.
Running backs	C	J.J. Johnson will get the first crack at the job, and if he remains healthy he is a good one. Thurman Thomas was brought in to be a third-down specialist, while Lamar Smith was brought in to challenge Johnson. Rob Konrad had an up-and-down rookie season, but the coaches are looking for big things in 2000.
Receivers	B -	This group is very deep but has questions. O.J. McDuffie is coming off toe surgery. Tony Martin had two shoulder surgeries. Oronde Gadsden was in a contract dispute. Bert Emanuel was brought in after two subpar seasons in Tampa. This group needs to be above average to make the quarterbacks better.
Offensive line	C -	The coaches want to run the ball, which is nothing new to the Dolphins. The line returns intact except for right guard Heath Irwin. Richmond Webb is a solid pass protector on the left side, but James Brown will be pushed by rookie Todd Wade at right tackle.
Defensive line	A -	This might be the most complete group in the league and they are all playing for contracts. Jason Taylor needs a big year after a disappointing '99, while Rich Owens just needs to be as good as he was last year. Daryl Gardener and Tim Bowens are premier run stoppers.
Linebackers	B +	Zach Thomas will lead the team in tackles again because of his work ethic and desire. The outside linebackers, Derrick Rodgers and Robert Jones, will have to make more impact plays. If they do, then the Dolphins defense will be even scarier. If not, then Scott Galyon will see a lot of playing time.
Secondary	B	Sam Madison is one of the best young corners in the game, but it's doubtful he will get as many interceptions in 2000 because teams will look elsewhere. That's where Patrick Surtain, in his first year as a full-time starter, needs to step up. Brock Marion and Calvin Jackson are solid if not spectacular defenders.
Special teams	A	Olindo Mare is the best kicker in the AFC, but the Dolphins hope he's not as busy as he was a year ago. Matt Turk, acquired from Washington, should improve the punting game, and the coverage teams should really benefit from his high, directional kicks. Marion set team records in kickoffs last year, but he could be challenged by rookie Ben Kelly, who set records at Colorado.

MINNESOTA VIKINGS
NFC CENTRAL DIVISION

2000 SEASON

CLUB DIRECTORY

Owner
Red McCombs
President
Gary Woods
Head coach & v.p. of football operations
Dennis Green
Executive v.p. of business operations
Mike Kelly
Vice president of player personnel
Frank Gilliam
National scout
Jerry Reichow
Director of pro personnel
Paul Wiggin
Director of football administration
Rob Brzezinski
Player personnel coordinator
Scott Studwell
Vice president of finance
Steve Poppen
Vice president of sales & marketing
Terri Huml
Director of research & development
Mike Eayrs
Director of public relations
Bob Hagan
Director of ticket sales
Phil Huebner
Director of operations
Breck Spinner
Equipment manager
Dennis Ryan
Coordinator of medical services
Fred Zamberletti
Head athletic trainer
Chuck Barta

Head coach
Dennis Green

Assistant coaches
Charlie Baggett (wide receivers)
Dean Dalton (quality control)
John Fontes (outside linebackers)
Carl Hargrave (running backs)
Chuck Knox (defensive asst.)
Daryl Lawrence (asst. strength & conditioning)
Sherman Lewis (off. coordinator)
Richard Solomon (defensive backs/asst. head coach)
Emmitt Thomas (defensive coordinator)
John Tice (tight ends)
Mike Tice (offensive line)
Fred vonAppen (defensive line)
Trent Walters (inside linebackers)
Steve Wetzel (strength & conditioning)
Alex Wood (quarterbacks)
Gary Zauner (special teams)

SCHEDULE

Sept. 3—	CHICAGO	1:00
Sept. 10—	MIAMI	1:00
Sept. 17—	at New England	4:15
Sept. 24—	Open date	
Oct. 1—	at Detroit	1:00
Oct. 9—	TAMPA BAY (Mon.)	9:00
Oct. 15—	at Chicago	8:35
Oct. 22—	BUFFALO	1:00
Oct. 29—	at Tampa Bay	1:00
Nov. 6—	at Green Bay (Mon.)	9:00
Nov. 12—	ARIZONA	1:00
Nov. 19—	CAROLINA	1:00
Nov. 23—	at Dallas (Thanks.)	4:05
Nov. 30—	DETROIT (Thur.)	8:35
Dec. 10—	at St. Louis	1:00
Dec. 17—	GREEN BAY	1:00
Dec. 24—	at Indianapolis	4:15

All times are Eastern.
All games Sunday unless noted.

DRAFT CHOICES

Chris Hovan, DT, Boston College (first round/25th pick overall).
Fred Robbins, DT, Wake Forest (2/55).
Michael Boireau, DE, Miami, Fla. (2/56).
Doug Chapman, RB, Marshall (3/88).
Antonio Wilson, LB, Texas A&M-Commerce (4/106).
Tyrone Carter, DB, Minnesota (4/118).
Troy Walters, WR, Stanford (5/165).
Mike Malano, C, San Diego St. (7/240).
Giles Cole, TE, Texas A&M-Kingsville (7/244).
Lewis Kelly, G, South Carolina State (7/248).

1999 REVIEW

RESULTS

Sept.12—at Atlanta	W	17-14
Sept.19—OAKLAND	L	17-22
Sept.26—at Green Bay	L	20-23
Oct. 3—TAMPA BAY	W	21-14
Oct. 10—CHICAGO	L	22-24
Oct. 17—at Detroit	L	23-25
Oct. 24—SAN FRANCISCO	W	40-16
Oct. 31—at Denver	W	23-20
Nov. 8—DALLAS	W	27-17
Nov. 14—at Chicago (OT)	W	27-24
Nov. 21—Open date		
Nov. 28—SAN DIEGO	W	35-27
Dec. 6—at Tampa Bay	L	17-24
Dec. 12—at Kansas City	L	28-31
Dec. 20—GREEN BAY	W	24-20
Dec. 26—at N.Y. Giants	W	34-17
Jan. 2—DETROIT	W	24-17
Jan. 9—DALLAS*	W	27-10
Jan. 16—at St. Louis†	L	37-49

*NFC wild-card game.
†NFC divisional playoff game.

RECORDS/RANKINGS

1999 regular-season record: 10-6 (2nd in NFC Central); 4-4 in division; 8-4 in conference; 2-2 vs. AFC; 6-2 at home; 4-4 on road; 8-3 on turf; 2-3 on grass.
Team record last five years: 51-29 (.638, ranks T4th in league in that span).

1999 team rankings:	No.	NFC	NFL
Total offense	*362.1	3	3
Rushing offense	*112.8	5	14
Passing offense	*249.3	4	5
Scoring offense	399	4	5
Total defense	*349.8	12	27
Rushing defense	*101.1	6	14
Passing defense	*248.8	14	30
Scoring defense	335	5	18
Takeaways	30	10	T17
Giveaways	40	T14	T30
Turnover differential	-10	12	27
Sacks	46	3	7
Sacks allowed	43	10	20

*Yards per game.

TEAM LEADERS

Scoring (kicking): Gary Anderson, 103 pts. (46/46 PATs, 19/30 FGs).
Scoring (touchdowns): Cris Carter, 78 pts. (13 receiving).
Passing: Jeff George, 2,816 yds. (329 att., 191 comp., 58.1%, 23 TDs, 12 int.).
Rushing: Robert Smith, 1,015 yds. (221 att., 4.6 avg., 2 TDs).
Receptions: Randy Moss, 80 (1,413 yds., 17.7 avg., 11 TDs).
Interceptions: Robert Griffith, 3 (0 yds., 0 TDs).
Sacks: John Randle, 10.0.
Punting: Mitch Berger, 45.4 avg. (61 punts, 2,769 yds., 0 blocked).
Punt returns: Randy Moss, 9.5 avg. (17 att., 162 yds., 1 TD).
Kickoff returns: Robert Tate, 25.1 avg. (25 att., 627 yds., 1 TD).

– 53 –

2000 SEASON
TRAINING CAMP ROSTER

No.	QUARTERBACKS	Ht./Wt.	Born	NFL Exp.	College	How acq.	'99 Games GP/GS
6	Brister, Bubby	6-3/205	8-15-62	13	Northeast Louisiana	FA/00	*2/0
11	Culpepper, Daunte	6-4/250	1-28-77	2	Central Florida	D1a/99	1/0
7	Cunningham, Randall	6-4/213	3-27-63	15	UNLV	FA/97	6/6
	RUNNING BACKS						
35	Chapman, Doug	5-10/215	8-22-77	R	Marshall	D3/00	—
40	Kleinsasser, Jim (FB)	6-3/272	1-31-77	2	North Dakota	D2/99	13/7
33	Morrow, Harold (FB)	5-11/224	2-24-73	5	Auburn	W-Dal./96	16/0
22	Palmer, David	5-8/172	11-19-72	7	Alabama	D2a/94	8/2
26	Smith, Robert	6-2/210	3-4-72	8	Ohio State	D1/93	13/12
21	Williams, Moe	6-1/205	7-26-74	5	Kentucky	D3/96	14/0
	RECEIVERS						
80	Carter, Cris	6-3/220	11-25-65	14	Ohio State	W-Phi./90	16/16
47	Cole, Giles (TE)	6-6/230	2-4-76	R	Texas A&M-Kingsville	D7b/00	—
87	Crumpler, Carlester (TE)	6-6/253	9-5-71	7	East Carolina	UFA/99	11/1
86	Fann, Chad (TE)	6-3/250	6-7-70	7	Florida A&M	FA/00	*16/3
89	Hatchette, Matthew	6-2/201	5-1-74	4	Langston University (Okla.)	D7b/97	13/0
85	Jordan, Andrew (TE)	6-6/272	6-21-72	7	Western Carolina	FA/99	11/1
84	Moss, Randy	6-4/198	2-13-77	3	Marshall	D1/98	16/16
83	Thomas, Chris	6-2/190	7-16-71	5	Cal Poly-SLO	UFA/00	*8/0
81	Walsh, Chris	6-1/199	12-12-68	8	Stanford	FA/94	16/1
82	Walters, Troy	5-7/171	12-15-76	R	Stanford	D5/00	—
	OFFENSIVE LINEMEN						
74	Badger, Brad (G)	6-4/298	1-11-75	4	Stanford	FA/00	*14/4
78	Birk, Matt (C)	6-4/304	7-23-76	3	Harvard	D6/98	15/0
71	Dixon, David (G)	6-5/346	1-5-69	7	Arizona State	FA/94	16/16
61	Kelly, Lewis (G)	6-4/272	4-21-77	R	South Carolina State	D7c/00	—
63	Lacina, Corbin (G)	6-4/302	11-2-70	7	Augustana (S.D.)	FA/99	14/0
69	Malano, Mike	6-2/307	10-16-76	R	San Diego State	D7a/00	—
73	Steussie, Todd (T)	6-6/308	12-1-70	7	California	D1b/94	16/16
77	Stringer, Korey (T)	6-4/339	5-8-74	6	Ohio State	D1b/95	16/16
	DEFENSIVE LINEMEN						
96	Ball, Jerry (T)	6-1/330	12-15-64	14	Southern Methodist	T-Cle./99	16/13
92	Boireau, Michael (E)	6-4/274	7-24-78	R	Miami (Fla.)	D2b/00	—
91	Burrough, John (E)	6-5/276	5-17-72	6	Wyoming	UFA/99	10/3
99	Hovan, Chris (T)	6-2/305	5-12-78	R	Boston College	D1/00	—
93	Randle, John (T)	6-1/287	12-12-67	11	Texas A&I	FA/90	16/16
98	Robbins, Fred (T)	6-4/312	3-25-77	R	Wake Forest	D2a/00	—
97	Sawyer, Talance (E)	6-2/272	6-14-76	1	UNLV	D6a/99	2/0
90	Smith, Fernando (E)	6-6/287	8-2-71	7	Jackson State	UFA/00	*15/0
94	Williams, Tony (T)	6-1/292	7-9-75	4	Memphis	D5/97	16/12
	LINEBACKERS						
50	Dalton, Antico	6-1/241	12-31-75	1	Hampton (Va.)	D6b/99	2/0
53	Hall, Lemanski	6-0/235	11-24-70	6	Alabama	UFA/00	*10/0
55	Johnson, Olrick	6-0/244	8-20-77	2	Florida A&M	FA/99	8/0
58	McDaniel, Ed	5-11/229	2-23-69	9	Clemson	D5/92	16/16
57	Rudd, Dwayne	6-2/233	2-3-76	4	Alabama	D1/97	16/16
59	Sauer, Craig	6-1/235	12-13-72	5	Minnesota	UFA/00	*16/3
54	Wilson, Antonio	6-2/244	12-29-77	R	Texas A&M-Commerce	D4a/00	—
52	Wong, Kailee	6-2/247	5-23-76	3	Stanford	D2/98	13/8
	DEFENSIVE BACKS						
30	Banks, Antonio (CB)	5-10/195	3-12-73	3	Virginia Tech	D4/97	6/1
32	Bass, Anthony	6-1/200	3-27-75	3	Bethune-Cookman	FA/98	14/3
37	Carter, Tyrone	5-8/190	3-31-76	R	Minnesota	D4b/00	—
24	Griffith, Robert (S)	5-11/198	11-30-70	7	San Diego State	FA/94	16/16
31	Morgan, Don (S)	5-11/200	9-18-75	2	Nevada-Reno	FA/99	2/0
29	Rogers, Chris (S)	5-10/192	1-3-77	2	Howard	FA/99	10/4
28	Tate, Robert (CB)	5-10/192	10-19-73	4	Cincinnati	D6/97	16/1
27	Thibodeaux, Keith (CB)	5-11/189	5-16-74	3	Northwestern (La.) State	FA/99	11/0
42	Thomas, Orlando (S)	6-1/211	10-21-72	6	Southwestern Louisiana	D2a/95	13/12
20	Wright, Kenny (CB)	6-1/196	9-14-77	2	Northwestern (La.) State	D4a/99	16/12
	SPECIALISTS						
1	Anderson, Gary (K)	5-11/170	7-16-59	19	Syracuse	UFA/98	16/0
17	Berger, Mitch (P)	6-4/221	6-24-72	5	Colorado	FA/96	16/0

*Not with Vikings in 1999.

Other free agent veterans invited to camp: OT Chad Abernathy, QB Todd Bouman, CB Paul Bradford, TE Matt Cercone, DE Keith Council, WR Darryl Daniel, OL Seth Dittman, S Torrian Gray, OT Jay Humphrey, CB Carlos Jones, CB Carl Kidd, OL Chris Liwienski, S Anthony Marshall, RB Carl McCullough, LB Mike Parker, WR Gregory Spann, C Cory Withrow.

Abbreviations: D1—draft pick, first round; SD-2—supplemental draft pick, second round; W—claimed on waivers; T—obtained in trade; PlanB—Plan B free-agent acquisition; FA—free-agent acquisition (other than Plan B); UFA—unconditional free agent acquisition; ED—expansion draft pick.

MISCELLANEOUS TEAM DATA

Stadium (capacity, surface):
Metrodome (64,121, artificial)
Business address:
9520 Viking Drive
Eden Prairie, MN 55344
Business phone:
612-828-6500
Ticket information:
612-333-8828
Team colors:
Purple, gold and white
Flagship radio station:
WCCO, 830 AM
Training site:
Minnesota State University-Mankato
Mankato, Minn.
612-828-6500

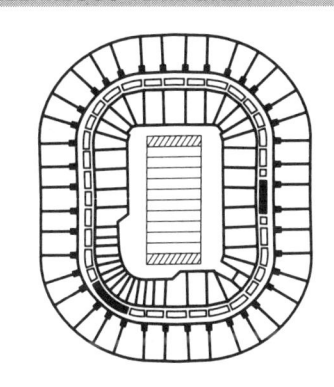

TSN REPORT CARD

Coaching staff	B	Dennis Green is clearly in the upper tier of NFL coaches, but his playoff record is only 3-7 and he has led the Vikings to just one NFC title game appearance. And given the major changes in his coaching staff—both coordinators, Sherm Lewis on offense and Emmitt Thomas on defense, are new—he'll have to develop a rapport before the season starts.
Quarterbacks	C	Daunte Culpepper faces a daunting task. After taking just three snaps as a rookie, he will have to play beyond his years as a sophomore in order to lead this veteran team to the playoffs. Every opponent will do their best to rattle Culpepper's nerves, so nothing will come easy. Just in case he isn't ready, Green signed veteran journeyman Bubby Brister to be the backup.
Running backs	A -	Keeping Robert Smith healthy will be critical to the early success of the Vikings. And given his performance late in the 1999 season, Smith seems poised to excel and showcase his well-rounded abilities. The development of fullback Jimmy Kleinsasser can only make Smith's goals even more attainable.
Receivers	A +	No NFL team has a better group. If Cris Carter doesn't hurt you, Randy Moss will, and vice versa. Throw Matthew Hatchette into the mix, and you've got another major headache. Carter may be pushing 35, but he shows no signs of aging, and Moss appears focused on another eye-opening season. The coaching staff is confident Hatchette can pick up any slack left by the departure of Jake Reed.
Offensive line	C +	The loss of two Pro Bowl linemen (Randall McDaniel and Jeff Christy) can never be viewed as a positive, but at the very least the Vikings helped themselves by bulking up at the two positions, left guard and center. Also, the addition of Brad Badger, a starter in Washington, gives the unit some much-needed depth.
Defensive line	C	John Randle barely reached double-digits in sacks last season, and this season could be even harder unless others on the defensive line step up and make consistent contributions. The end positions are of particular concern, especially on the right side where two unproven players are currently battling it out.
Linebackers	A -	The most talented unit on the defense got even better after a little tinkering during the offseason. The starting lineup was changed, and reserve Craig Sauer was added to serve as a dependable backup and potential starter in the event of an injury. Ed McDaniel (166) and Dwayne Rudd (152) ranked 1-2 on the team in tackles.
Secondary	C -	A case could be made for an even lower grade, given that Robert Griffith is the only proven performer in recent memory. As badly as this unit finished last season, it didn't get much help during the offseason. Kenny Wright and Robert Tate must continue to grow up fast.
Special teams	B +	Despite Morten Anderson's struggles last year, this unit remains one of the best in the NFL. Punter Mitch Berger does a good job of helping the Vikings establish good field position, and aces such as Moe Williams and Harold Morrow stifle opposing returners. The team could use more consistency from its own return game, though.

NEW ENGLAND PATRIOTS
AFC EASTERN DIVISION

2000 SEASON

CLUB DIRECTORY

President and chief executive officer
Robert K. Kraft
Executive vice president
Jonathan A. Kraft
Senior v.p. & chief operating officer
Andy Wasynczuk
Assistant director of player personnel
Scott Pioli
Vice president, finance
James Hausmann
Vice president of marketing
Lou Imbriano
V.p., player dev. and com. relations
Donald Lowery
Director of pro scouting
Dave Uyrus
Director of media relations
Stacey James
Director of football operations
Ken Deininger
Controller
Jim Nolan
Director of ticket operations
Mike Nichols
Corporate sales executive
Jon Levy
General manager of Foxboro Stadium
Dan Murphy
Building services superintendent
Bernie Reinhart
Head trainer
Ron O'Neil
Equipment manager
Don Brocher

Head coach
Bill Belichick

Assistant coaches
Jeff Davidson (asst. off. line)
Ivan Fears (wide receivers)
Eric Mangini (defensive backs)
Randy Melvin (defensive line)
Markus Paul (assistant strength and conditioning)
Dick Rehbein (quarterbacks)
Rob Ryan (linebackers)
Dante Scarnecchia (assistant head coach/offensive line)
Brad Seely (special teams)
DeWayne Walker (def. assistant)
Charlie Weis (off. coordinator/ running backs)
Mike Woicik (strength and conditioning)

SCHEDULE

Sept. 3—	TAMPA BAY	1:00
Sept. 11—	at N.Y. Jets (Mon.)	9:00
Sept. 17—	MINNESOTA	4:15
Sept. 24—	at Miami	1:00
Oct. 1—	at Denver	4:05
Oct. 8—	INDIANAPOLIS	1:00
Oct. 15—	N.Y. JETS	4:05
Oct. 22—	at Indianapolis	1:00
Oct. 29—	Open date	
Nov. 5—	BUFFALO	1:00
Nov. 12—	at Cleveland	1:00
Nov. 19—	CINCINNATI	1:00
Nov. 23—	at Detroit (Thanks.)	12:30
Dec. 4—	KANSAS CITY (Mon.)	9:00
Dec. 10—	at Chicago	1:00
Dec. 17—	at Buffalo	1:00
Dec. 24—	MIAMI	1:00

All times are Eastern.
All games Sunday unless noted.

DRAFT CHOICES

Adrian Klemm, T, Hawaii (second round/46th pick overall).
J.R. Redmond, RB, Arizona State (3/76).
Greg Robinson-Randall, T, Michigan State (4/127).
Dave Stachelski, TE, Boise State (5/141).
Jeff Marriott, DT, Missouri (5/161).
Antwan Harris, DB, Virginia (6/187).
Tom Brady, QB, Michigan (6/199).
David Nugent, DT, Purdue (6/201).
Casey Tisdale, DE, New Mexico (7/226).
Patrick Pass, RB, Georgia (7/239).

1999 REVIEW

RESULTS

Sept.12—at N.Y. Jets	W	30-28
Sept.19—INDIANAPOLIS	W	31-28
Sept.26—N.Y. GIANTS	W	16-14
Oct. 3—at Cleveland	W	19-7
Oct. 10—at Kansas City	L	14-16
Oct. 17—MIAMI	L	30-31
Oct. 24—DENVER	W	24-23
Oct. 31—at Arizona	W	27-3
Nov. 7—Open date		
Nov. 15—N.Y. JETS	L	17-24
Nov. 21—at Miami	L	17-27
Nov. 28—at Buffalo	L	7-17
Dec. 5—DALLAS	W	13-6
Dec. 12—at Indianapolis	L	15-20
Dec. 19—at Philadelphia	L	9-24
Dec. 26—BUFFALO (OT)	L	10-13
Jan. 2—BALTIMORE	W	20-3

RECORDS/RANKINGS

1999 regular-season record: 8-8 (5th in AFC East); 2-6 in division; 5-7 in conference; 3-1 vs. NFC; 5-3 at home; 3-5 on road; 1-3 on turf; 7-5 on grass.
Team record last five years: 44-36 (.550, ranks T11th in league in that span).
1999 team rankings:

	No.	AFC	NFL
Total offense	*316.4	9	18
Rushing offense	*89.1	13	23
Passing offense	*227.3	2	10
Scoring offense	299	13	T20
Total defense	*300.5	6	8
Rushing defense	*112.2	13	21
Passing defense	*188.3	6	7
Scoring defense	284	4	7
Takeaways	31	T6	T14
Giveaways	33	T13	T19
Turnover differential	-2	T9	T15
Sacks	42	6	11
Sacks allowed	56	T14	T28

*Yards per game.

TEAM LEADERS

Scoring (kicking): Adam Vinatieri, 107 pts. (29/30 PATs, 26/33 FGs).
Scoring (touchdowns): Terry Allen, 54 pts. (8 rushing, 1 receiving).
Passing: Drew Bledsoe, 3,985 yds. (539 att., 305 comp., 56.6%, 19 TDs, 21 int.).
Rushing: Terry Allen, 896 yds. (254 att., 3.5 avg., 8 TDs).
Receptions: Terry Glenn, 69 (1,147 yds., 16.6 avg., 4 TDs).
Interceptions: Lawyer Milloy, 4 (17 yds., 0 TDs).
Sacks: Willie McGinest, 9.0.
Punting: Lee Johnson, 41.5 avg. (90 punts, 3,735 yds., 0 blocked).
Punt returns: Troy Brown, 10.7 avg. (38 att., 405 yds., 0 TDs).
Kickoff returns: Kevin Faulk, 24.2 avg. (39 att., 943 yds., 0 TDs).

2000 SEASON
TRAINING CAMP ROSTER

NEW ENGLAND PATRIOTS

No.	Player	Ht./Wt.	Born	NFL Exp.	College	How acq.	'99 Games GP/GS
	QUARTERBACKS						
7	Bishop, Michael	6-2/217	5-15-76	2	Kansas State	D7a/99	0/0
11	Bledsoe, Drew	6-5/233	2-14-72	8	Washington State	D1/93	16/16
12	Brady, Tom	6-4/211	8-3-77	R	Michigan	D6b/00	—
17	Friesz, John	6-4/223	5-19-67	11	Idaho	UFA/99	1/0
	RUNNING BACKS						
30	Carter, Tony (FB)	6-0/232	8-23-72	7	Minnesota	UFA/98	16/14
47	Edwards, Robert	5-11/218	10-2-74	2	Georgia	D1a/98	0/0
33	Faulk, Kevin	5-8/197	6-15-76	2	Louisiana State	D2/99	11/2
37	Floyd, Chris (FB)	6-2/235	6-23-75	3	Michigan	D3a/98	13/0
28	Harris, Raymont	6-0/230	12-23-70	5	Ohio State	FA/00	*0/0
35	Pass, Patrick	5-10/208	12-31-77	R	Georgia	D7b/00	—
21	Redmond, J.R.	5-11/216	9-28-77	R	Arizona State	D3/00	—
44	Shaw, Harold (FB)	6-0/228	9-3-74	3	Southern Mississippi	D6/98	8/0
	RECEIVERS						
18	Bailey, Aaron	5-10/185	10-24-71	6	Louisville	FA/00	*0/0
86	Bjornson, Eric (TE)	6-4/236	12-15-71	6	Washington	UFA/00	*16/6
82	Brisby, Vincent	6-3/193	1-25-71	8	Northeast Louisiana	D2c/93	12/1
80	Brown, Troy	5-10/190	7-2-71	8	Marshall	D8/93	13/1
88	Glenn, Terry	5-11/185	7-23-74	5	Ohio State	D1/96	14/13
85	Morey, Sean	5-11/190	2-26-76	1	Brown	D7b/99	2/0
83	Rutledge, Rod (TE)	6-5/262	8-12-75	3	Alabama	D2b/98	16/2
81	Simmons, Tony	6-1/206	12-8-74	3	Wisconsin	D2a/98	15/1
84	Stachelski, Dave (TE)	6-3/250	3-1-77	R	Boise State	D5a/00	—
	OFFENSIVE LINEMEN						
67	Andersen, Jason (C)	6-6/295	9-3-75	3	Brigham Young	D7/98	9/0
66	Ellis, Ed (T)	6-7/330	10-13-75	4	Buffalo	D4/97	1/1
70	Klemm, Adrian (T)	6-3/308	5-21-77	R	Hawaii	D2/00	—
68	Lane, Max (G)	6-6/320	2-22-71	7	Navy	D6/94	16/6
77	Robinson-Randall, Greg (T)	6-5/339	6-23-78	R	Michigan State	D4/00	—
71	Rucci, Todd (G)	6-5/296	7-14-70	8	Penn State	D2b/93	16/15
63	Scott, Lance (C)	6-3/295	2-15-72	6	Utah	FA/00	*0/0
76	Williams, Grant (T)	6-7/323	5-10-74	5	Louisiana Tech	UFA/00	*16/16
65	Woody, Damien (C)	6-3/319	11-3-77	2	Boston College	D1a/99	16/16
	DEFENSIVE LINEMEN						
90	Eaton, Chad (T)	6-5/300	4-6-72	4	Washington State	D7/95	16/16
93	Marriott, Jeff (T)	6-4/301	3-3-77	R	Missouri	D5b/00	—
55	McGinest, Willie (E)	6-5/265	12-11-71	7	Southern California	D1/94	16/16
98	Mitchell, Brandon (E)	6-3/289	6-19-75	4	Texas A&M	D2/97	16/16
92	Nugent, David	6-4/303	10-27-75	R	Purdue	D6c/00	—
94	Spires, Greg (E)	6-1/265	8-12-74	3	Florida State	D3b/98	11/0
95	Thomas, Henry (T)	6-2/277	1-12-65	14	Louisiana Tech	FA/97	16/16
99	Tisdale, Casey (E)	6-4/258	6-18-76	R	New Mexico	D7a/00	—
	LINEBACKERS						
54	Bruschi, Tedy	6-1/245	6-9-73	5	Arizona	D3/96	14/14
52	Johnson, Ted	6-4/250	12-4-72	6	Colorado	D2/95	5/5
59	Katzenmoyer, Andy	6-3/255	12-2-77	2	Ohio State	D1b/99	16/11
53	Slade, Chris	6-5/245	1-30-71	8	Virginia	D2/93	16/16
	DEFENSIVE BACKS						
42	Carter, Chris (S)	6-2/209	9-27-74	4	Texas	D3b/97	15/15
41	George, Tony (S)	5-11/200	8-10-75	2	Florida	D3/99	16/1
23	Harris, Antwan (CB)	5-9/186	5-29-77	R	Virginia	D6a/00	—
34	Jones, Tebucky (CB)	6-2/219	10-6-74	3	Syracuse	D1b/98	11/2
43	Langham, Antonio (CB)	6-0/184	7-31-72	7	Alabama	FA/00	*13/2
24	Law, Ty (CB)	5-11/200	2-10-74	6	Michigan	D1/95	13/13
36	Milloy, Lawyer (S)	6-0/208	11-14-73	5	Washington	D2/96	16/16
31	Serwanga, Kato (CB)	6-0/198	7-23-76	2	California	FA/98	16/3
25	Whigham, Larry (S)	6-2/205	6-23-72	7	Northeast Louisiana	FA/94	16/0
	SPECIALISTS						
10	Johnson, Lee (P)	6-2/200	11-27-61	16	Brigham Young	FA/99	16/0
4	Vinatieri, Adam (K)	6-0/200	12-28-72	5	South Dakota State	FA/96	16/0

*Not with Patriots in 1999.
Other free agent veterans invited to camp: RB Derrick Cullors, OT/G Derrick Fletcher, WR Tony Gaiter, S Cory Gilliard, DT Garrett Johnson, DB Kelly Malveaux, LB Marc Megna, LB John Munch, DT Noel Scarlett, TE Robert Tardio, TE Kerry Taylor.
Abbreviations: D1—draft pick, first round; SD-2—supplemental draft pick, second round; W—claimed on waivers; T—obtained in trade; PlanB—Plan B free-agent acquisition; FA—free-agent acquisition (other than Plan B); UFA—unconditional free agent acquisition; ED—expansion draft pick.

NEW ENGLAND PATRIOTS

MISCELLANEOUS TEAM DATA

Stadium (capacity, surface):
Foxboro Stadium
(60,292, grass)
Business address:
60 Washington St.
Foxboro, MA 02035
Business phone:
508-543-8200
Ticket information:
508-543-1776
Team colors:
Silver, red, white and blue
Flagship radio station:
WBCN, 104.1 FM
Training site:
Bryant College
Smithfield, R.I.
508-543-8200

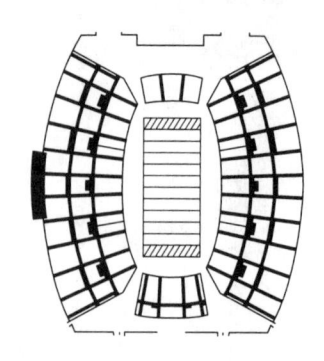

TSN REPORT CARD

Category	Grade	Comments
Coaching staff	B -	This grade probably should be "incomplete." Bill Belichick hasn't been a head coach since 1995, when he concluded a five-year stint with a 37-45 record in Cleveland. He has the technical knowledge, but can he effectively lead a 53-man roster? Offensive coordinator Charlie Weis is somewhat unproven, as he never had full play-calling powers with the Jets.
Quarterbacks	B +	The grade here is admittedly influenced by past deeds. Even though Drew Bledsoe has his faults and is coming off his worst season as a pro, there are about 25 NFL teams that would be thrilled to have him. The arm strength, touch and accuracy remain. He's still The Franchise.
Running backs	C	Raymont Harris was out of football last year and was ineffective with the Packers in 1998. It's hard to imagine the Patriots will get much out of him. The Pats hope they got a steal in third-round J.R. Redmond, but calling him an everydown NFL back may be a stretch. Kevin Faulk certainly doesn't fit that description.
Receivers	B -	Troy Brown is this unit's hardest-working and most productive player. Which is too bad, because Terry Glenn should be that guy. Tony Simmons must prove himself this year while Vincent Brisby should once again hang around in a backup role. Look for second-year player Sean Morey to also get a look. The tight end spot is a real concern.
Offensive line	D	New England had the league's 23rd-ranked rushing attack and allowed 55 sacks last season. The scary part? Given the player turnover, it's hard to imagine the unit being much better in 2000. But while the unit will be inexperienced, it will at least have room for growth. The old line had none.
Defensive line	C	This was an average (at best) unit in 1999, and while Belichick should make it better, don't expect any miracles. Players like Chad Eaton and Willie McGinest should be buoyed by the new system, but a major talent infusion is still needed.
Linebackers	B	If healthy, the Pats have the personnel do to some different things here. Ted Johnson's health is the key to the whole picture. Andy Katzenmoyer is on the rise while Chris Slade is on the decline. Tedy Bruschi is a steady, solid presence.
Secondary	B	There's a lot of money in Ty Law and Lawyer Milloy and a lot of question marks at free safety and right cornerback. Antonio Langham should help the situation at the latter, but what the Pats really need is for Tebucky Jones to finally become a factor. Belichick also needs to find a proven safety to play next to Milloy.
Special teams	B	The Pats are all set in terms of specialists. Brown is a great punt returner, Faulk shows promise as a kick returner and Adam Vinatieri and Lee Johnson are proven kickers. The coverage teams, however, have struggled in the past and Vinatieri missed a few key kicks in '99.

NEW ORLEANS SAINTS
NFC WESTERN DIVISION

2000 SEASON

CLUB DIRECTORY

Owner
Tom Benson

FOOTBALL OPERATIONS
General manager of football operations
Randy Mueller
Director of football administration
Mickey Loomis
Assistant g.m of football operations
Charles Bailey
Director of player personnel
Rick Mueller
College scouting coordinator
Rick Thompson
Scouting supervisor
Pat Mondock
Pro scouts
Mike Baugh   Bill Quinter
Area scouts
Matt Boockmeier, Cornell Gowdy, Tim Heffelfinger, James Jefferson, Mark Sadowski
Combine scout
Andy Weidel
Player personnel assistant
Grant Neill
Football operations assistant
Barrett Wiley
Dir. of player dev. and community relations
Ricky Porter
Equipment manager
Dan Simmons
Assistant equipment manager
Glennon "Silky" Powell
Equipment assistant
Nolan Castex
Asst. athletic trainer/dir. of rehabilitation
Kevin Mangum
Assistant athletic trainer
Aaron Miller
Video director
Joe Malota
Assistant video director
Bob Lee
Director of media & public relations
Greg Bensel
Media & public relations assistant
Justin Macione
Director of photography
Michael C. Hebert

Head coach
Jim Haslett

Assistant coaches
Hubbard Alexander (wide receivers)
Dave Atkins (running backs)
Joe Baker (secondary/special teams assistant)
John Bunting (linebackers)
Frank Cignetti Jr. (quarterbacks)
Sam Clancy (defensive line)
Al Everest (special teams)
Rock Gullickson (strength & cond.)
Jack Henry (offensive line)
Mike McCarthy (off. coordinator)
Evan Marcus (asst. strength & conditioning)
Winston Moss (defensive assistant)
Bob Palcic (tight ends)
Phil Pettey (offensive assistant)
Rick Venturi (asst. head coach/ secondary)
Ron Zook (defensive coordinator)

Administrative assistant/coaching
Omar Khan

ADMINISTRATION
Director of administration
Arnold D Fielkow
Chief financial officer
Dennis Lauscha
Dir. of marketing & business development
Wayne Hodes
Sr. dir. of broadcasting and special projects
Greg Suit
Director of ticket operations
James Nagaoka
Director of ticket sales
Mike Stanfield

SCHEDULE

Sept. 3— DETROIT   1:00
Sept. 10— at San Diego   4:15
Sept. 17— at Seattle   4:15
Sept. 24— PHILADELPHIA   1:00
Oct. 1— Open date
Oct. 8— at Chicago   1:00
Oct. 15— CAROLINA   1:00
Oct. 22— at Atlanta   1:00
Oct. 29— at Arizona   4:05
Nov. 5— SAN FRANCISCO   1:00
Nov. 12— at Carolina   1:00
Nov. 19— OAKLAND   1:00
Nov. 26— at St. Louis   1:00
Dec. 3— DENVER   1:00
Dec. 10— at San Francisco 4:15
Dec. 17— ATLANTA   1:00
Dec. 24— ST. LOUIS   1:00
All times are Eastern.
All games Sunday unless noted.

DRAFT CHOICES

Darren Howard, DE, Kansas State (second round/33rd pick overall).
Terrelle Smith, RB, Arizona State (4/96).
Tutan Reyes, T, Mississippi (5/131).
Austin Wheatley, TE, Iowa (5/158).
Chad Morton, RB, Southern California (5/166).
Marc Bulger, QB, West Virginia (6/168).
Michael Hawthorne, DB, Purdue (6/195).
Sherrod Gideon, WR, Southern Mississippi (6/200).
Kevin Houser, TE, Ohio State (7/228).

1999 REVIEW

RESULTS

Sept.12—CAROLINA   W 19-10
Sept.19—at San Francisco L 21-28
Sept.26—Open date
Oct. 3—at Chicago   L 10-14
Oct. 10—ATLANTA   L 17-20
Oct. 17—TENNESSEE   L 21-24
Oct. 24—at N.Y. Giants   L 3-31
Oct. 31—CLEVELAND   L 16-21
Nov. 7—TAMPA BAY   L 16-31
Nov. 14—SAN FRANCISCO   W 24-6
Nov. 21—at Jacksonville L 23-41
Nov. 28—at St. Louis   L 12-43
Dec. 5—at Atlanta   L 12-35
Dec. 12—ST. LOUIS   L 14-30
Dec. 19—at Baltimore   L 8-31
Dec. 24—DALLAS   W 31-24
Jan. 2—at Carolina   L 13-45

RECORDS/RANKINGS

1999 regular-season record: 3-13 (5th in NFC West); 2-6 in division; 3-9 in conference; 0-4 vs. AFC; 3-5 at home; 0-8 on road; 3-8 on turf; 0-5 on grass.
Team record last five years: 25-55 (.313, ranks 30th in league in that span).
1999 team rankings:

	No.	NFC	NFL
Total offense	*311.4	10	19
Rushing offense	*105.6	8	18
Passing offense	*205.8	10	T19
Scoring offense	260	14	29
Total defense	*332.4	8	20
Rushing defense	*110.9	8	20
Passing defense	*221.5	9	21
Scoring defense	434	14	28
Takeaways	34	5	9
Giveaways	39	T12	T28
Turnover differential	-5	T9	T19
Sacks	45	4	8
Sacks allowed	41	7	17

*Yards per game.

TEAM LEADERS

Scoring (kicking): Doug Brien, 92 pts. (20/21 PATs, 24/29 FGs).
Scoring (touchdowns): Keith Poole, 36 pts. (6 receiving).
Passing: Billy Joe Tolliver, 1,916 yds. (268 att., 139 comp., 51.9%, 7 TDs, 16 int.).
Rushing: Ricky Williams, 884 yds. (253 att., 3.5 avg., 2 TDs).
Receptions: Eddie Kennison, 61 (835 yds., 13.7 avg., 4 TDs).
Interceptions: Ashley Ambrose, 6 (27 yds., 0 TDs).
Sacks: La'Roi Glover, 8.5.
Punting: Tommy Barnhardt, 39.8 avg. (82 punts, 3,262 yds., 0 blocked).
Punt returns: Eddie Kennison, 7.4 avg. (35 att., 258 yds., 0 TDs).
Kickoff returns: Dino Philyaw, 22.0 avg. (53 att., 1,165 yds., 0 TDs).

2000 SEASON
TRAINING CAMP ROSTER

NEW ORLEANS SAINTS

No.	QUARTERBACKS	Ht./Wt.	Born	NFL Exp.	College	How acq.	'99 Games GP/GS
18	Blake, Jeff	6-0/210	12-4-70	9	East Carolina	UFA/00	*14/12
14	Bulger, Marc	6-2/206	4-5-77	R	West Virginia	D6a/00	—
12	Delhomme, Jake	6-2/205	1-10-75	2	Southwestern La.	FA/97	2/2
11	Tolliver, Billy Joe	6-1/217	2-7-66	11	Texas Tech	UFA/98	10/7
	RUNNING BACKS						
32	Craver, Aaron (FB)	6-0/232	12-18-68	10	Fresno State	UFA/98	13/10
47	Houser, Kevin (FB)	6-2/250	8-23-72	R	Ohio State	D7/00	—
30	Morton, Chad	5-8/186	4-4-77	R	Southern California	D5c/00	—
33	Perry, Wilmont	6-1/235	2-24-75	3	Livingstone (N.C.)	D5/98	7/3
37	Philyaw, Dino	5-10/205	10-30-70	4	Oregon	FA/99	13/0
40	Powell, Marvin (FB)	6-2/235	6-6-76	2	Southern California	FA/99	9/0
41	Smith, Terrelle (FB)	6-0/246	3-12-78	R	Arizona State	D4/00	—
34	Williams, Ricky	5-10/236	5-21-77	2	Texas	D1/99	12/12
	RECEIVERS						
85	Cleeland, Cam (TE)	6-4/272	4-15-75	3	Washington	D2/98	11/8
80	Franklin, P.J.	5-10/180	9-28-77	1	Tulane	FA/99	3/0
15	Gideon, Sherrod	5-11/176	2-21-77	R	Southern Mississippi	D6c/00	—
82	Glover, Andrew (TE)	6-6/252	8-12-67	10	Grambling State	UFA/00	*16/13
87	Horn, Joe	6-1/206	1-16-72	5	None	UFA/00	*16/1
88	Jackson, Willie	6-1/212	8-16-71	6	Florida	UFA/00	*16/2
83	Poole, Keith	6-0/193	6-18-74	4	Arizona State	D4b/97	15/15
86	Reed, Jake	6-3/216	9-28-67	10	Grambling State	UFA/00	*16/8
46	Wheatley, Austin (TE)	6-5/254	11-16-77	R	Iowa	D5b/00	—
16	Wilson, Robert	5-11/176	6-23-74	2	Florida A&M	FA/00	*2/0
	OFFENSIVE LINEMEN						
69	Ackerman, Tom (C)	6-3/298	9-6-72	5	Eastern Washington	D5b/96	16/8
62	Fontenot, Jerry (C)	6-3/300	11-21-66	12	Texas A&M	UFA/97	16/16
79	Halapin, Mike (T)	6-5/310	7-1-73	4	Pittsburgh	FA/99	9/3
65	Naeole, Chris (G)	6-3/313	12-25-74	4	Colorado	D1/97	15/15
72	Reyes, Tutan (T)	6-3/299	10-28-77	R	Mississippi	D5a/00	—
77	Roaf, Willie (T)	6-5/312	4-18-70	8	Louisiana Tech	D1/93	16/16
78	Terrell, Daryl (T)	6-5/296	1-25-75	2	Southern Mississippi	FA/98	12/1
68	Turley, Kyle (T)	6-5/300	9-24-75	3	San Diego State	D1/98	16/16
63	Williams, Wally (G)	6-2/321	2-19-71	8	Florida A&M	UFA/99	6/6
	DEFENSIVE LINEMEN						
97	Glover, La'Roi (T)	6-2/285	7-4-74	5	San Diego State	W-Oak./97	16/16
96	Hamiter, Uhuru (E)	6-4/280	3-14-73	3	Delaware State	W-Phi./98	5/0
99	Hand, Norman (T)	6-3/310	9-4-72	6	Mississippi	UFA/00	*14/14
93	Howard, Darren (E)	6-3/281	11-19-76	R	Kansas State	D2/00	—
94	Johnson, Joe (E)	6-4/270	7-11-72	7	Louisville	D1/94	0/0
64	Newkirk, Robert (T)	6-3/290	3-6-77	1	Michigan State	FA/99	5/0
90	Tomich, Jared (E)	6-2/272	4-24-74	4	Nebraska	D2b/97	8/6
98	Whitehead, Willie (E)	6-3/285	1-26-73	2	Auburn	FA/99	16/3
92	Wilson, Troy (E)	6-4/257	11-22-70	5	Pittsburg (Kan.) State	W-SF/98	16/4
	LINEBACKERS						
51	Clarke, Phil	6-0/241	1-9-77	2	Pittsburgh	FA/99	8/3
56	Clemons, Charlie	6-2/250	7-4-72	4	Georgia	FA/00	*16/0
55	Fields, Mark	6-2/244	11-9-72	6	Washington State	D1/95	14/14
59	Mitchell, Keith	6-2/245	7-24-74	4	Texas A&M	FA/97	16/16
54	Williams, K.D.	6-0/235	4-21-73	2	Henderson State (Ark.)	FA/00	*9/8
	DEFENSIVE BACKS						
26	Harris, Corey (CB)	5-10/191	11-28-76	1	North Alabama	FA/99	3/0
36	Hawthorne, Michael (CB)	6-3/196	1-26-75	R	Purdue	D6b/00	—
21	Israel, Steve (CB)	5-11/197	3-16-69	9	Pittsburgh	UFA/00	*13/13
27	Kelly, Rob (S)	6-0/199	6-21-74	4	Ohio State	D2a/97	16/7
29	Knight, Sammy (S)	6-0/205	9-10-75	4	Southern California	FA/97	16/16
35	Mathis, Kevin (CB)	5-9/181	4-9-74	4	East Texas State	T-Dal./00	*8/4
25	Molden, Alex (CB)	5-10/190	8-4-73	5	Oregon	D1/96	13/0
28	Oldham, Chris	5-9/200	10-26-68	10	Oregon	UFA/00	*15/0
23	Thomas, Fred (CB)	5-9/172	9-11-73	5	Tennessee-Martin	UFA/00	*1/0
24	Weary, Fred (CB)	5-10/181	4-12-74	3	Florida	D4a/98	16/11
	SPECIALISTS						
10	Brien, Doug (K)	6-0/180	11-24-70	7	California	FA/95	16/0
4	Gowin, Toby (P)	5-10/167	3-30-75	4	North Texas	FA/00	*16/0

*Not with Saints in 1999.

Other free agent veterans invited to camp: TE Cuncho Brown, C Justin Burroughs, DT Winfield Garnett, CB Shannon Garrett, G Robert Hunt, S Eric Johnson, C Jason McEndoo, LB Ron Merkerson, S Darren Perry, OT Marcus Price, WR Anthony Rodgers, DE Bobby Setzer, LB Donnie Spragan, WR L.C. Stevens, WR Ryan Thelwell, DT Kevin Thomas, LB Joe Tuipala, S Gerald Vaughn, LB Philip Ward, G Brent Warren, K Matt Wieland.

Abbreviations: D1—draft pick, first round; SD-2—supplemental draft pick, second round; W—claimed on waivers; T—obtained in trade; PlanB—Plan B free-agent acquisition; FA—free-agent acquisition (other than Plan B); UFA—unconditional free agent acquisition; ED—expansion draft pick.

MISCELLANEOUS TEAM DATA

Stadium (capacity, surface):
Louisiana Superdome
(70,200, artificial)
Business address:
5800 Airline Drive
Metairie, LA 70003
Business phone:
504-733-0255
Ticket information:
504-731-1700
Team colors:
Old gold, black and white
Flagship radio station:
WWL-870 AM
Training site:
Nicholls State University
Thibodaux, La.
504-448-4282

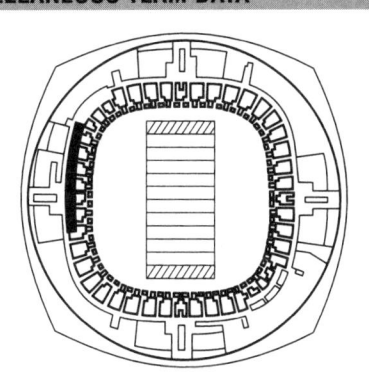

NEW ORLEANS SAINTS

TSN REPORT CARD

Coaching staff	B	By all accounts, Jim Haslett and his hard-working assistants are a decided upgrade over Mike Ditka's woefully disorganized, overmatched group. The jury is out on Haslett's game-day ability, and his coordinators are equally unproven, but they have done wonders for the morale and attitude within the Saints' long-suffering locker room.
Quarterbacks	B -	Streaky Jeff Blake is mobile and throws the best deep ball in the league. His success or failure will depend on his ability to direct the team's ball-control West Coast passing attack. If Blake goes down the Saints are in trouble. Defenses don't fear backups Billy Joe Tolliver and Jake Delhomme.
Running backs	B	Injuries and poor schemes strangled Ricky Williams' production as a rookie. Running behind a veteran line and bone-crushing fullback Terrelle Smith, he should be a completely different back this year. Smith is raw but has great potential. Besides slippery rookie Chad Morton, Williams' backups lack speed and special qualities.
Receivers	C +	Cam Cleeland and Andrew Glover form one of the best tight end tandems in the league. The Saints are gambling on a pair of players who couldn't start for other teams to be their 1-2 punch. Joe Horn, no better than the fourth option in Kansas City, is the new No. 1. Jake Reed, after being run out of Minnesota, is the other starter. Keith Poole has deceptive deep speed. Backups Willie Jackson and Ryan Thelwell have been inconsistent.
Offensive line	B	For a unit with three first-round draft picks and one of the league's highest-paid free agents, this unit has underachieved in recent years. Willie Roaf and Kyle Turley are dominant tackles, but the Saints need center Wally Williams to return to health and guard Chris Naole to emerge. Depth is a major question.
Defensive line	A -	La'Roi Glover and Norman Hand form one of the best tackle tandems in football. Left end is solid with promising rookie Darren Howard and brawler Jared Tomich. If right end Joe Johnson returns to Pro Bowl form after a serious knee injury, the front four could be dominant. Defensive tackle depth is a concern.
Linebackers	C +	In Mark Fields, Charlie Clemons and Keith Mitchell, the Saints boast three special athletes versatile enough to rush the passer or drop into coverage. If healthy, Fields could have a monster year. Mitchell made great strides in 1999. K.D. Williams is the only experienced backup.
Secondary	D	Question mark city. Can Steve Israel stay healthy? Can Alex Molden regain his confidence? Will a nickel back emerge? Without a bona fide shutdown corner, this group will have to play over its head to survive in a division loaded with prime-time receivers.
Special teams	C	Aside from Doug Brien's kicking, these units were horrendous in 1999. Brien is coming off a strong year but must adjust to a new snapper and holder. Punter-kickoff specialist Toby Gowin should thrive in the Superdome. Morton should spice up returns. The coverage units should be upgraded because of speed.

NEW YORK GIANTS
NFC EASTERN DIVISION

2000 SEASON

CLUB DIRECTORY

President/co-CEO
Wellington T. Mara
Chairman/co-CEO
Preston Robert Tisch
Exec. v.p./general counsel
John K. Mara
Vice president/general manager
Ernie Accorsi
Treasurer
Jonathan Tisch
Assistant general manager
Rick Donohue
Assistant to the general manager
Harry Hulmes
V.P. and chief financial officer
John Pasquali
Controller
Christine Procops
Vice president/player personnel
Tom Boisture
Director/player personnel
Marv Sunderland
Director of administration
Jim Phelan
Vice president, marketing
Rusty Hawley
Director/promotion
Francis X. Mara
Ticket manager
John Gorman
Director/pro personnel
Dave Gettleman
Director/research and development
Raymond J. Walsh Jr.
Director/college scouting
Jerry Shay
Vice president of communications
Pat Hanlon
Director of corporate sponsorships
Bill Smith
Head trainer
Ronnie Barnes
Assistant trainers
Byron Hansen   Steve Kennelly

Head coach
Jim Fassel

Assistant coaches
Dave Brazil (def. quality control)
John Dunn (strength & cond.)
John Fox (defensive coordinator)
Mike Gillhamer (offensive assistant)
Johnnie Lynn (defensive backs)
Larry Mac Duff (special teams)
Denny Marcin (defensive line)
Jim McNally (offensive line)
Tom Olivadotti (linebackers)
Sean Payton (quarterbacks)
Mike Pope (tight ends)
Jimmy Robinson (wide receivers)
Jim Skipper (offensive coord./RBs)
Craig Stoddard (assistant strength & conditioning)

Director of player development
Greg Gabriel
Scouts
Rosey Brown   John Crea
Jeremiah Davis   Ken Kavanaugh
Jerry Reese   Steve Verderosa
Team physician
Russell Warren
Locker room manager
Ed Wagner
Equipment manager
Ed Wagner Jr.
Video director
John Mancuso

SCHEDULE

Sept. 3—	ARIZONA	1:00
Sept. 10—	at Philadelphia	1:00
Sept. 17—	at Chicago	4:15
Sept. 24—	WASHINGTON	8:35
Oct. 1—	at Tennessee	1:00
Oct. 8—	at Atlanta	4:05
Oct. 15—	DALLAS	1:00
Oct. 22—	Open date	
Oct. 29—	PHILADELPHIA	4:05
Nov. 5—	at Cleveland	1:00
Nov. 12—	ST. LOUIS	4:15
Nov. 19—	DETROIT	1:00
Nov. 26—	at Arizona	8:35
Dec. 3—	at Washington	1:00
Dec. 10—	PITTSBURGH	1:00
Dec. 17—	at Dallas	8:35
Dec. 23—	JACKSONVILLE (Sat.)	12:30

All times are Eastern.
All games Sunday unless noted.

DRAFT CHOICES

Ron Dayne, RB, Wisconsin (first round/11th pick overall).
Cornelius Griffin, DT, Alabama (2/42).
Ronald Dixon, WR, Lambuth (Tenn.) (3/73).
Brandon Short, LB, Penn State (4/105).
Ralph Brown, DB, Nebraska (5/140).
Dhani Jones, LB, Michigan (6/177).
Jeremiah Parker, DE, California (7/217).

1999 REVIEW

RESULTS

Sept. 12—at Tampa Bay	W	17-13
Sept. 19—WASHINGTON	L	21-50
Sept. 26—at New England	L	14-16
Oct. 3—PHILADELPHIA	W	16-15
Oct. 10—at Arizona	L	3-14
Oct. 18—DALLAS	W	13-10
Oct. 24—NEW ORLEANS	W	31-3
Oct. 31—at Philadelphia (OT)	W	23-17
Nov. 7—Open date		
Nov. 14—INDIANAPOLIS	L	19-27
Nov. 21—at Washington	L	13-23
Nov. 28—ARIZONA	L	24-34
Dec. 5—N.Y. JETS	W	41-28
Dec. 12—at Buffalo	W	19-17
Dec. 19—at St. Louis	L	10-31
Dec. 26—MINNESOTA	L	17-34
Jan. 2—at Dallas	L	18-26

RECORDS/RANKINGS

1999 regular-season record: 7-9 (3rd in NFC East); 3-5 in division; 5-7 in conference; 2-2 vs. AFC; 4-4 at home; 3-5 on road; 6-6 on turf; 1-3 on grass.
Team record last five years: 36-43-1 (.456, ranks 20th in league in that span).

1999 team rankings:

	No.	NFC	NFL
Total offense	*320.4	9	17
Rushing offense	*88.0	11	T24
Passing offense	*232.4	7	8
Scoring offense	299	8	T20
Total defense	*311.3	4	13
Rushing defense	*97.5	5	13
Passing defense	*213.8	5	14
Scoring defense	358	9	23
Takeaways	24	13	26
Giveaways	32	T5	T16
Turnover differential	-8	11	T25
Sacks	32	T13	T27
Sacks allowed	42	T8	T18

*Yards per game.

TEAM LEADERS

Scoring (kicking): Cary Blanchard, 73 pts. (19/19 PATs, 18/21 FGs).
Scoring (touchdowns): Amani Toomer, 36 pts. (6 receiving).
Passing: Kerry Collins, 2,318 yds. (331 att., 190 comp., 57.4%, 8 TDs, 11 int.).
Rushing: Joe Montgomery, 348 yds. (115 att., 3.0 avg., 3 TDs).
Receptions: Amani Toomer, 79 (1,183 yds., 15.0 avg., 6 TDs).
Interceptions: Percy Ellsworth, 6 (80 yds., 0 TDs).
Sacks: Jessie Armstead, 9.0.
Punting: Brad Maynard, 41.0 avg. (89 punts, 3,651 yds., 0 blocked).
Punt returns: Tiki Barber, 11.5 avg. (44 att., 506 yds., 1 TD).
Kickoff returns: Bashir Levingston, 24.2 avg. (22 att., 532 yds., 0 TDs).

– 62 –

2000 SEASON
TRAINING CAMP ROSTER

No.	QUARTERBACKS	Ht./Wt.	Born	NFL Exp.	College	How acq.	'99 Games GP/GS
18	Cherry, Mike	6-3/225	12-15-73	4	Murray State	D6/97	0/0
5	Collins, Kerry	6-5/250	12-30-72	6	Penn State	UFA/99	10/7
17	Garrett, Jason	6-2/200	3-28-66	8	Princeton	UFA/00	*9/2
	RUNNING BACKS						
21	Barber, Tiki	5-10/200	4-7-75	4	Virginia	D2/97	16/1
44	Bennett, Sean	6-1/230	11-9-75	2	Northwestern	D4/99	9/2
34	Comella, Greg (FB)	6-1/248	7-29-75	3	Stanford	FA/98	16/3
27	Dayne, Ron	5-10/253	3-14-78	R	Wisconsin	D1/00	—
33	Montgomery, Joe	5-10/230	6-8-76	2	Ohio State	D2/99	7/5
30	Way, Charles (FB)	6-0/247	12-27-72	6	Virginia	D6b/95	11/8
	RECEIVERS						
80	Alford, Brian	6-1/190	6-7-75	3	Purdue	D3/98	2/0
89	Campbell, Dan (TE)	6-5/265	4-13-76	2	Texas A&M	D3/99	12/1
87	Cross, Howard (TE)	6-5/285	8-8-67	12	Alabama	D6/89	16/15
86	Dixon, Ronald	6-0/176	5-28-76	R	Lambuth (Tenn.)	D3/00	—
88	Hilliard, Ike	5-11/198	4-5-76	4	Florida	D1/97	16/16
84	Jurevicius, Joe	6-5/230	12-23-74	3	Penn State	D2/98	16/1
83	Mitchell, Pete (TE)	6-2/248	10-9-71	6	Boston College	FA/99	15/6
85	Thomas, Mark (TE)	6-4/258	5-26-75	2	North Carolina State	FA/99	2/0
81	Toomer, Amani	6-3/205	9-8-74	5	Michigan	D2/96	16/16
	OFFENSIVE LINEMEN						
76	Brown, Lomas (T)	6-4/290	3-30-63	16	Florida	FA/00	*10/10
69	Engler, Derek (C)	6-5/300	7-11-74	4	Wisconsin	FA/97	10/4
62	Parker, Glenn (G)	6-5/311	4-22-66	10	Arizona	UFA/00	*12/11
77	Petitgout, Luke (T)	6-6/315	6-16-76	2	Notre Dame	D1/99	15/8
78	Rosenthal, Mike (G)	6-7/315	6-10-77	2	Notre Dame	D5/99	9/7
65	Stone, Ron (G)	6-5/320	7-20-71	8	Boston College	FA/96	16/16
66	Whittle, Jason (G)	6-4/305	3-7-75	3	Southwest Missouri State	FA/98	16/1
52	Zeigler, Dusty (C)	6-5/303	9-27-73	5	Notre Dame	UFA/00	*15/15
	DEFENSIVE LINEMEN						
97	Griffin, Cornelius (T)	6-3/294	12-3-76	R	Alabama	D2/00	—
93	Hale, Ryan (T)	6-4/295	7-10-75	2	Arkansas	D7a/99	8/0
75	Hamilton, Keith (T)	6-6/295	5-25-71	9	Pittsburgh	D4/92	16/16
94	Jones, Cedric (E)	6-4/275	4-30-74	5	Oklahoma	D1/96	16/16
79	Parker, Jeremiah (E)	6-5/275	11-15-77	R	California	D7/00	—
99	Peter, Christian (T)	6-3/300	10-5-72	4	Nebraska	FA/97	16/10
92	Strahan, Michael (E)	6-5/275	11-21-71	8	Texas Southern	D2/93	16/16
96	Williams, George (T)	6-3/298	12-8-75	3	North Carolina State	FA/98	16/0
	LINEBACKERS						
98	Armstead, Jessie	6-1/240	10-26-70	8	Miami (Fla.)	D8/93	16/16
58	Barrow, Mike	6-2/236	4-19-70	8	Miami (Fla.)	FA/00	*16/16
57	Childress, O.J.	6-1/245	12-6-75	2	Clemson	D7b/99	4/0
55	Jones, Dhani	6-1/235	2-22-78	R	Michigan	D6/00	—
51	Monty, Pete	6-2/250	7-3-74	4	Wisconsin	D4/97	16/3
91	Phillips, Ryan	6-4/252	2-7-74	4	Idaho	D3a/97	16/16
53	Short, Brandon	6-3/253	7-11-77	R	Penn State	D4/00	—
90	Widmer, Corey	6-3/255	12-25-68	9	Montana State	D7/92	15/13
	DEFENSIVE BACKS						
22	Brown, Ralph (CB)	5-10/178	9-9-78	R	Nebraska	D5/00	—
20	Garnes, Sam (S)	6-3/225	7-12-74	4	Cincinnati	D5/97	16/16
41	Hamilton, Conrad (CB)	5-10/195	11-5-74	5	Eastern New Mexico	D7/96	3/2
24	Levingston, Bashir (CB)	5-9/180	10-2-76	2	Eastern Washington	FA/99	12/0
26	McDaniel, Emmanuel (CB)	5-9/180	7-27-72	3	East Carolina	W-Mia./99	7/2
31	Sehorn, Jason (CB)	6-2/215	4-15-71	7	Southern California	D2b/94	10/10
28	Stephens, Reggie (CB)	5-9/200	2-21-75	1	Rutgers	FA/99	1/0
23	Thomas, Dave (CB)	6-3/218	8-25-68	8	Tennessee	UFA/00	*15/0
35	Weathers, Andre (CB)	6-0/190	8-6-76	2	Michigan	D6b/99	9/0
37	West, Lyle (S)	6-0/215	12-20-76	2	San Jose State	D6a/99	6/0
36	Williams, Shaun (S)	6-2/215	10-10-76	3	UCLA	D1/98	11/0
	SPECIALISTS						
3	Daluiso, Brad (K)	6-1/180	12-31-67	10	UCLA	FA/93	6/0
9	Maynard, Brad (P)	6-1/190	2-9-74	4	Ball State	D3b/97	16/0

*Not with Giants in 1999.

Other free agent veterans invited to camp: FB Brian Aikins, DE Jomo Cousins, DE Lavell Ellis, DE Frank Ferrara, DT Carl Hansen, G Scott Kiernan, G Mark Nori, S Tawambi Settles, LB Vernon Strickland, WR Anthony Tucker, TE Adam Young.

Abbreviations: D1—draft pick, first round; SD-2—supplemental draft pick, second round; W—claimed on waivers; T—obtained in trade; PlanB—Plan B free-agent acquisition; FA—free-agent acquisition (other than Plan B); UFA—unconditional free agent acquisition; ED—expansion draft pick.

NEW YORK GIANTS

MISCELLANEOUS TEAM DATA

Stadium (capacity, surface):
Giants Stadium
(79,593, grass)
Business address:
East Rutherford, NJ 07073
Business phone:
201-935-8111
Ticket information:
201-935-8222
Team colors:
Blue, white and red
Flagship radio station:
WNEW, 102.7 FM
Training site:
University at Albany
Albany, N.Y.
201-935-8111

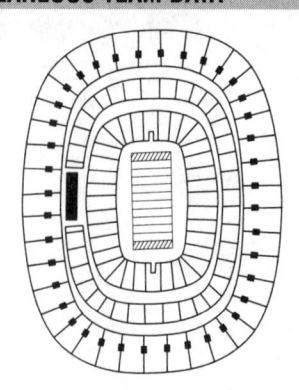

TSN REPORT CARD

Coaching staff	B -	This is Jim Fassel's moment of truth. Was he a one-season wonder, or the victim of shaky talent and devastating injuries the past two years? The jury still is out. If he doesn't make the playoffs, Fassel will be, too. His staff is solid, led by aggressive coordinators Sean Payton and John Fox.
Quarterbacks	B -	Kerry Collins put up eye-popping numbers in his seven starts last season, but it is impossible to ignore his year-long problem with throwing interceptions, and that he was only 2-5 as a starter. He has shown enough to warrant optimism, but it's cautious optimism. Jason Garrett is a great fit as the new backup, but soon the team will need young blood at the position.
Running backs	C	Injuries ruined the backfield last season, and now the team is relying on first-round draft pick Ron Dayne to turn things around. It could happen, and if it doesn't Joe Montgomery is waiting in the wings. If one or the other doesn't become a reliable, between-the-tackles ballcarrier, the offense could be in for another strange, unbalanced season. Tiki Barber has developed into an ideal third-down back. The fullback situation remains up in the air because of Charles Way's lingering knee problems.
Receivers	B +	The team's long-time weakness has become a strength, but the unit still lacks a classic, breakaway speed threat. Maybe Brian Alford can do it, or maybe third-round draft pick Ron Dixon can. Still, Amani Toomer and Ike Hilliard were a highly productive starting pair last season, and tight end Pete Mitchell provided an entirely new dimension for the offense.
Offensive line	C -	This has been a weakness for years, and now is a huge question mark with four new starters, including three who are new to the team. If warhorses Lomas Brown and Glenn Parker have something left as the left side combo, there is hope. But even then, the team needs 1999 first-round pick Luke Petitgout to fit in at right tackle as he never did at left guard. The only returning starter is Ron Stone, a solid player but no superstar.
Defensive line	B -	On paper, the starting foursome is very talented, but three-time Pro Bowler Michael Strahan must prove that last season was not the real him. The potential weak spot on the line is Christian Peter, but if second-round pick Cornelius Griffin develops quickly, he could turn into a supplement at one tackle spot and give opponents a different look than Peter.
Linebackers	B	Three-time Pro Bowler Jessie Armstead and his old friend from Miami, Mike Barrow, give the linebacking corps an entirely new look. The speed is back. But it won't be an elite group until a third man steps up, perhaps Pete Monty or rookie Brandon Short. Ryan Phillips was solid but not special on the strong side, a long-time problem area, last season.
Secondary	C +	The secondary was solid at this time last year, but now is full of potential disasters. It is essential players such as Jason Sehorn, Sam Garnes and Shaun Williams stay healthy, and that either Dave Thomas or Conrad Hamilton emerges as a reliable left cornerback. There is a stable or promising young cornerbacks, and the team needs one or two to develop for defending the inevitable multiple-receiver sets.
Special teams	B -	Bashir Levingston, Barber, Dixon and even Sean Bennett give the team some promising return men, and the kickers, Brad Daluiso and Brad Maynard, are among the league's most solid pairs. The key is coverage on kickoffs and punts, always an adventure when you are perhaps the slowest team in the league. Injuries ate away at the return units last season. If the team stays healthy and does not have to dip into its reserve pool, the special teams should be better.

NEW YORK JETS
AFC EASTERN DIVISION

2000 SEASON

CLUB DIRECTORY

Owner
Woody Johnson
President
Steve Gutman
Chief football operations officer
Bill Parcells
Director of player personnel
Dick Haley
Director of pro player development and contract negotiations
Mike Tannenbaum
Director of player development
Carl Banks
Treasurer & chief financial officer
Mike Gerstle
Exec. director of business operations
Bob Parente
Director of public relations
Frank Ramos
Assistant director of public relations
Douglas Miller
Director of operations
Mike Kensil
Scouting coordinator
John Griffin
Personnel scouts
Trent Baalke, Joey Clinkscales, Michael Davis, Jessie Kaye, Bob Schmitz, Gary Smith, Lionel Vitale
Controller
Mike Minarczyk
Sr. dir. of marketing & business dev.
Marc Riccio
Sr. mgr., Internet & special projects
Ken Ilchuk
Director of ticket operations
John Buschhorn
Director of team travel
Kevin Coyle
Head athletic trainer
David Price
Assistant athletic trainer
John Mellody
Equipment manager
Bill Hampton

Head coach
Al Groh

Assistant coaches
Todd Bowles (secondary)
Maurice Carthon (assistant head coach/running backs)
Mike Groh (QC/offensive assistant)
Todd Haley (wide receivers)
Ray Hamilton (defensive line)
Dan Henning (off. coordinator/QBs)
Pat Hodgson (offensive assistant/ planning and research)
John Lott (strength & condit.)
Bill Muir (offensive line)
Mike Nolan (def. coordinator)
William Roberts (asst. off. line)
Dan Rocco (quality control/LBs)
Bob Sutton (linebackers)
Mike Sweatman (special teams)
Ken Whisenhunt (tight ends)

Equipment director
Clay Hampton
Assistant equipment director
Gus Granneman
Video director
John Seiter
Groundskeeper
Bob Hansen
Chairman of medical department
Dr. Elliot Pellman
Team orthopedist
Dr. Elliott Hershman
Associate team orthopedist
Kenneth Montgomery

SCHEDULE

Sept. 3—	at Green Bay	4:15
Sept. 11—	NEW ENGLAND (Mon.)	9:00
Sept. 17—	BUFFALO	1:00
Sept. 24—	at Tampa Bay	4:15
Oct. 1—	Open date	
Oct. 8—	PITTSBURGH	1:00
Oct. 15—	at New England	4:05
Oct. 23—	MIAMI (Mon.)	9:00
Oct. 29—	at Buffalo	1:00
Nov. 5—	DENVER	4:15
Nov. 12—	at Indianapolis	8:35
Nov. 19—	at Miami	4:05
Nov. 26—	CHICAGO	1:00
Dec. 3—	INDIANAPOLIS	4:15
Dec. 10—	at Oakland	8:35
Dec. 17—	DETROIT	1:00
Dec. 24—	at Baltimore	1:00

All times are Eastern.
All games Sunday unless noted.

DRAFT CHOICES

Shaun Ellis, DE, Tennessee (first round/12th pick overall).
John Abraham, LB, S. Carolina (1/13).
Chad Pennington, QB, Marshall (1/18).
Anthony Becht, TE, West Virginia (1/27).
Laveranues Coles, WR, Florida State (3/78).
Windrell Hayes, WR, Southern California (5/143).
Tony Scott, DB, N. Carolina State (6/179).
Richard Seals, DT, Utah (7/218).

1999 REVIEW

RESULTS

Sept.12—	NEW ENGLAND	L	28-30
Sept.19—	at Buffalo	L	3-17
Sept.26—	WASHINGTON	L	20-27
Oct. 3—	at Denver	W	21-13
Oct. 11—	JACKSONVILLE	L	6-16
Oct. 17—	INDIANAPOLIS	L	13-16
Oct. 24—	at Oakland	L	23-24
Oct. 31—	Open date		
Nov. 7—	ARIZONA	W	12-7
Nov. 15—	at New England	W	24-17
Nov. 21—	BUFFALO	W	17-7
Nov. 28—	at Indianapolis	L	6-13
Dec. 5—	at N.Y. Giants	L	28-41
Dec. 12—	MIAMI	W	28-20
Dec. 19—	at Dallas	W	22-21
Dec. 27—	at Miami	W	38-31
Jan. 2—	SEATTLE	W	19-9

RECORDS/RANKINGS

1999 regular-season record: 8-8 (4th in AFC East); 4-4 in division; 6-6 in conference; 2-2 vs. NFC; 4-4 at home; 4-4 on road; 5-7 on turf; 3-1 on grass.
Team record last five years: 33-47 (.413, ranks 25th in league in that span).

1999 team rankings:

	No.	AFC	NFL
Total offense	*297.0	14	25
Rushing offense	*122.6	7	11
Passing offense	*174.4	15	28
Scoring offense	308	12	19
Total defense	*336.2	13	21
Rushing defense	*106.4	10	17
Passing defense	*229.8	14	24
Scoring defense	309	6	9
Takeaways	35	4	8
Giveaways	22	T2	T2
Turnover differential	13	3	3
Sacks	26	15	30
Sacks allowed	37	T7	T12

*Yards per game.

TEAM LEADERS

Scoring (kicking): John Hall, 108 pts. (27/29 PATs, 27/33 FGs).
Scoring (touchdowns): Keyshawn Johnson, 48 pts. (8 receiving).
Passing: Ray Lucas, 1,678 yds. (272 att., 161 comp., 59.2%, 14 TDs, 6 int.).
Rushing: Curtis Martin, 1,464 yds. (367 att., 4.0 avg., 5 TDs).
Receptions: Keyshawn Johnson, 89 (1,170 yds., 13.1 avg., 8 TDs).
Interceptions: Marcus Coleman, 6 (165 yds., 1 TD).
Sacks: Mo Lewis, 5.5.
Punting: Tom Tupa, 45.2 avg. (81 punts, 3,659 yds., 0 blocked).
Punt returns: Dedric Ward, 7.6 avg. (38 att., 288 yds., 0 TDs).
Kickoff returns: Dwight Stone, 24.6 avg. (28 att., 689 yds., 0 TDs).

– 65 –

2000 SEASON
TRAINING CAMP ROSTER

NEW YORK JETS

No.	QUARTERBACKS	Ht./Wt.	Born	NFL Exp.	College	How acq.	'99 Games GP/GS
6	Lucas, Ray	6-3/214	8-6-72	4	Rutgers	W-NE/97	9/9
10	Pennington, Chad	6-3/229	6-26-76	R	Marshall	D1c/00	—
16	Testaverde, Vinny	6-5/235	11-13-63	14	Miami (Fla.)	FA/98	1/1
	RUNNING BACKS						
20	Anderson, Richie	6-2/230	9-13-71	8	Penn State	D6/93	16/9
25	Farmer, Robert	5-11/217	3-4-74	2	Notre Dame	FA/97	13/0
32	Johnson, Leon	6-0/218	7-13-74	4	North Carolina	D4b/97	1/0
28	Martin, Curtis	5-11/210	5-1-73	6	Pittsburgh	FA/98	16/16
34	Parmalee, Bernie	5-11/210	9-16-67	9	Ball State	FA/99	16/0
33	Sowell, Jerald (FB)	6-0/245	1-21-74	4	Tulane	W-GB/97	16/0
82	Spence, Blake (FB)	6-4/249	6-20-75	3	Oregon	D5c/98	10/0
	RECEIVERS						
84	Baxter, Fred (TE)	6-3/265	6-14-71	8	Auburn	D5a/93	14/8
88	Becht, Anthony (TE)	6-5/267	8-8-77	R	West Virginia	D1d/00	—
80	Chrebet, Wayne	5-10/188	8-14-73	6	Hofstra	FA/95	11/11
87	Coles, Laveranues	5-11/188	12-29-77	R	Florida State	D3/00	—
86	Hayes, Windrell	5-11/204	12-14-76	R	Southern California	D5/00	—
83	Stone, Dwight	6-0/195	1-28-64	14	Middle Tennessee State	UFA/99	16/0
89	Ward, Dedric	5-9/184	9-29-74	4	Northern Iowa	D3/97	16/10
	OFFENSIVE LINEMEN						
69	Fabini, Jason (T)	6-7/312	8-25-74	3	Cincinnati	D4/98	9/9
67	Gisler, Mike (C)	6-4/300	8-26-69	8	Houston	UFA/98	16/0
71	Jenkins, Kerry (G)	6-5/305	9-6-73	3	Troy (Ala.) State	FA/97	16/16
63	Machado, J.P. (G)	6-4/300	1-6-76	2	Illinois	D6b/99	5/0
68	Mawae, Kevin (C)	6-4/305	1-23-71	7	Louisiana State	UFA/98	16/16
75	Rafferty, Ian (T)	6-5/300	9-2-76	2	North Carolina State	FA/99	5/0
77	Thomas, Randy (G)	6-4/301	1-19-76	2	Mississippi State	D2/99	16/16
74	Young, Ryan (T)	6-5/320	6-28-76	2	Kansas State	D7a/99	15/7
	DEFENSIVE LINEMEN						
97	Boose, Dorian (E)	6-5/292	1-29-74	3	Washington State	D2/98	12/0
98	Burton, Shane (T)	6-6/305	1-18-74	5	Tennessee	UFA/00	*15/0
92	Ellis, Shaun (E)	6-5/280	6-24-77	R	Tennessee	D1a/00	—
72	Ferguson, Jason (T)	6-3/305	11-28-74	4	Georgia	D7b/97	9/9
93	Logan, Ernie (T)	6-3/290	5-18-68	9	East Carolina	UFA/97	14/7
95	Lyle, Rick (E)	6-5/290	2-26-71	7	Missouri	UFA/97	16/16
99	Ogbogu, Eric (E)	6-4/285	7-18-75	3	Maryland	D6a/98	14/0
61	Seals, Richard (T)	6-2/316	3-18-76	R	Utah	D7/00	—
91	Wiltz, Jason (T)	6-4/300	11-23-76	2	Nebraska	D4/99	12/1
	LINEBACKERS						
94	Abraham, John	6-4/250	5-6-78	R	South Carolina	D1b/00	—
51	Cox, Bryan	6-4/250	2-17-68	10	Western Illinois	FA/98	12/11
53	Dailey, Casey	6-3/249	6-11-75	3	Northwestern	D5a/98	6/0
58	Farrior, James	6-2/244	1-6-75	4	Virginia	D1/97	16/4
54	Gordon, Dwayne	6-1/245	11-2-69	8	New Hampshire	UFA/97	16/4
55	Jones, Marvin	6-2/250	6-28-72	8	Florida State	D1/93	16/16
57	Lewis, Mo	6-3/258	10-21-69	10	Georgia	D3/91	16/16
56	Phifer, Roman	6-2/248	3-5-68	10	UCLA	UFA/99	16/12
50	Syvrud, J.J.	6-3/255	5-10-77	2	Jamestown College	D7b/99	1/0
	DEFENSIVE BACKS						
42	Coleman, Marcus (CB)	6-2/210	5-24-74	5	Texas Tech	D5/96	16/10
36	Crutchfield, Buddy (CB)	6-0/196	3-7-76	3	North Carolina Central	FA/98	4/0
47	Frost, Scott (S)	6-3/219	1-4-75	3	Nebraska	D3a/98	14/0
31	Glenn, Aaron (CB)	5-9/185	7-16-72	7	Texas A&M	D1/94	16/16
21	Green, Victor (S)	5-11/210	12-8-69	8	Akron	FA/93	16/16
30	Hayes, Chris (S)	6-0/206	5-7-72	4	Washington State	T-GB/96	15/0
35	Lee, Del (CB)	5-10/187	1-19-76	2	McNeese State	FA/99	4/0
24	Mickens, Ray (CB)	5-8/184	1-4-73	5	Texas A&M	D3/96	15/5
27	Scott, Tony (CB)	5-10/193	10-3-76	R	North Carolina State	D6/00	—
45	Smith, Otis (CB)	5-11/195	10-22-65	11	Missouri	UFA/97	1/1
26	Stoutmire, Omar (S)	5-11/198	7-9-74	4	Fresno State	FA/99	12/5
23	Williams, Kevin (CB)	6-0/190	8-4-75	3	Oklahoma State	D3b/98	4/0
	SPECIALISTS						
9	Hall, John (K)	6-3/228	3-17-74	4	Wisconsin	FA/97	16/0
7	Tupa, Tom (P)	6-4/225	2-6-66	12	Ohio State	UFA/99	16/0

*Not with Jets in 1999.

Other free agent veterans invited to camp: WR Fred Coleman, QB Jim Kubiak, LB Courtney Ledyard, OT Greg Lotyez, G David Loverne, C Dennis O'Sullivan, FB Jermaine Wiggins.

Abbreviations: D1—draft pick, first round; SD-2—supplemental draft pick, second round; W—claimed on waivers; T—obtained in trade; PlanB—Plan B free-agent acquisition; FA—free-agent acquisition (other than Plan B); UFA—unconditional free agent acquisition; ED—expansion draft pick.

– 66 –

MISCELLANEOUS TEAM DATA

Stadium (capacity, surface):
Giants Stadium
(79,466, grass)
Business address:
1000 Fulton Avenue
Hempstead, NY 11550
Business phone:
516-560-8100
Ticket information:
516-560-8200
Team colors:
Green and white
Flagship radio station:
To be announced
Training site:
Hofstra University
Hempstead, N.Y.
516-560-8100

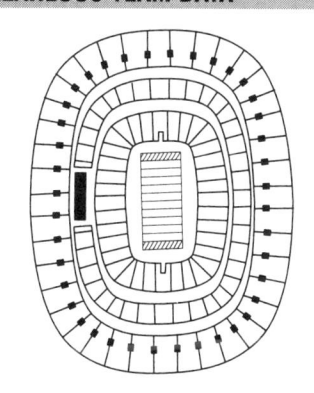

NEW YORK JETS

TSN REPORT CARD

Coaching staff	C +	A year ago, the staff received an A, but it lost a future Hall of Fame coach (Bill Parcells) and a great defensive coordinator (Bill Belichick). Al Groh has many positive qualities, but he's an unknown as a head coach. New defensive coordinator Mike Nolan is on the hot seat after a tough time in Washington. New offensive coordinator Dan Henning is a solid, meat-and-potatoes coach, but not terribly innovative.
Quarterbacks	A -	The Jets are fortunate; they have two quarterbacks who can win—Vinny Testaverde and Ray Lucas. All eyes will be on Testaverde, who will attempt to rebound from Achilles surgery. But at 36, there are no guarantees. Lucas proved last season he can lead the team. The quarterback of the future is first-round pick Chad Pennington, who will carry the clipboard in 2000.
Running backs	A -	As long as Curtis Martin stays healthy and doesn't run out of gas, the Jets will be in good shape. Martin is one of the top five backs in the NFL, and the Jets will be relying on him a lot more now that wide receiver Keyshawn Johnson is gone. Backups Leon Johnson and Bernie Parmalee are OK. The Jets lack a bruising, change-of-pace back.
Receivers	C -	After trading Johnson to the Bucs, the Jets are left with only one proven target—Wayne Chrebet, who will miss Johnson more than he's willing to admit. The Jets' goal was to sign another veteran, preferably taller than six feet, to take pressure off Chrebet. Dedric Ward and rookie Laveranues Coles bring the speed dimension. Rookie tight end Anthony Becht will start very soon.
Offensive line	B	This unit proved last season that it can slug it out in the running game. The Jets are strong in the middle with Pro Bowl center Kevin Mawae and right guard Randy Thomas, but there are questions at the tackle. Can Jason Fabini make the switch to left tackle, replacing the retired Jumbo Elliott? Is right tackle Ryan Young ready for prime time? Left guard Kerry Jenkins will be pushed by David Loverne.
Defensive line	C	The line produced only nine sacks last season; 19 NFL players had more. But the outlook is brighter. Rookie end Shaun Ellis has the potential to be an impact player. Veteran nose tackle Jason Ferguson is almost there. After that, there's a big dropoff. The Jets are hoping Eric Ogbogu will emerge as the starter at right end.
Linebackers	B +	This is one of the better groups in the league. Not a lot of flash, but a bunch of strong, hard-nosed football players. Mo Lewis is the leader, followed by Marvin Jones and Bryan Cox. Will James Farrior ever step up? Rookie John Abraham, a pass-rushing specialist, has Jevon Kearse-like speed off the corner.
Secondary	B	Cornerbacks Marcus Coleman and Aaron Glenn and strong safety Victor Green form a strong trio, but there's a big question mark at free safety. So what else is new? Omar Stoutmire will get the first crack, but don't be surprised if the position changes hands a couple of times. Ray Mickens is a solid nickel back.
Special teams	B	The Jets are a punt returner away from having a potentially dominant special teams unit. Everything else is above average, from Pro Bowl punter Tom Tupa to kicker John Hall to dynamic coverage teams.

OAKLAND RAIDERS
AFC WESTERN DIVISION

2000 SEASON

CLUB DIRECTORY

Owner
Al Davis
Executive assistant
Al LoCasale
Chief executive
Amy Trask
Senior assistant
Bruce Allen
Senior administrator
Morris Bradshaw
Senior executive
John Herrera
Special projects
Jim Otto
Public relations director
Mike Taylor
Public relations
Craig Long
Broadcast/multi-media
Billy Zagger
Finance/technology
Tom Blanda
Finance
Marc Badain
Ron LaVelle
Business affairs
Scott Fink, Wendy Gottlieb, Dawn Roberts
Legal affairs
Roxanne Kosarzycki
General counsel
Jeff Birren
Ticket manager
Peter Eiges
Admin. assistant to the head coach
Mark Arteaga
Head trainer
H. Rod Martin
Assistant trainers
Mark Mayer
Scott Touchet
Player personnel
Angelo Coia, Chet Franklin, Bruce Kebric, Jon Kingdon, Mike Lombardi, Mickey Marvin, David McCloughan, Kent McCloughan

Head coach
Jon Gruden

Assistant coaches
Fred Biletnikoff (wide receivers)
Chuck Bresnahan (def. coord.)
Willie Brown (squad development)
Bill Callahan (offensive coordinator/offensive line)
Bob Casullo (special teams)
Jim Erkenbeck (tight ends)
Garrett Giemont (strength & conditioning)
Ron Linn (defensive backs)
Woodrow Lowe (def. assistant)
Don Martin (quality control-def.)
John Morton (offensive assistant)
Skip Peete (running backs)
Robin Ross (linebackers)
David Shaw (quality control-off.)
Gary Stevens (quarterbacks)
Mike Waufle (defensive line)

Building and grounds
Ken Irons
Equipment managers
Bob Romanski
Rich Romanski
Equipment assistant
Kevyn Bazzy
Video director
Dave Nash
Video operations
Jim Otten
Computer operations
John Otten

SCHEDULE

Date	Opponent	Time
Sept. 3—	SAN DIEGO	4:15
Sept. 10—	at Indianapolis	1:00
Sept. 17—	DENVER	4:05
Sept. 24—	CLEVELAND	4:15
Oct. 1—	Open date	
Oct. 8—	at San Francisco	4:15
Oct. 15—	at Kansas City	1:00
Oct. 22—	SEATTLE	4:05
Oct. 29—	at San Diego	8:35
Nov. 5—	KANSAS CITY	4:15
Nov. 13—	at Denver (Mon.)	9:00
Nov. 19—	at New Orleans	1:00
Nov. 26—	ATLANTA	4:05
Dec. 3—	at Pittsburgh	1:00
Dec. 10—	N.Y. JETS	8:35
Dec. 16—	at Seattle (Sat.)	4:05
Dec. 24—	CAROLINA	4:15

All times are Eastern.
All games Sunday unless noted.

DRAFT CHOICES

Sebastian Janikowski, PK, Florida State (first round/17th pick overall).
Jerry Porter, WR, West Virginia (2/47).
Junior Ioane, DT, Arizona State (4/107).
Shane Lechler, P, Texas A&M (5/142).
Mondriel Fulcher, TE, Miami, Fla. (7/227).
Cliffton Black, DB, Southwest Texas State (7/231).

1999 REVIEW

RESULTS

Sept.12—at Green Bay		L 24-28
Sept.19—at Minnesota		W 22-17
Sept.26—CHICAGO		W 24-17
Oct. 3—at Seattle		L 21-22
Oct. 10—DENVER		L 13-16
Oct. 17—at Buffalo		W 20-14
Oct. 24—N.Y. JETS		W 24-23
Oct. 31—MIAMI		L 9-16
Nov. 7—Open date		
Nov. 14—SAN DIEGO		W 28-9
Nov. 22—at Denver (OT)		L 21-27
Nov. 28—KANSAS CITY		L 34-37
Dec. 5—SEATTLE		W 30-21
Dec. 9—at Tennessee		L 14-21
Dec. 19—TAMPA BAY		W 45-0
Dec. 26—at San Diego		L 20-23
Jan. 2—at Kansas City (OT)		W 41-38

RECORDS/RANKINGS

1999 regular-season record: 8-8 (4th in AFC West); 3-5 in division; 5-7 in conference; 3-1 vs. NFC; 5-3 at home; 3-5 on road; 2-1 on turf; 6-7 on grass.
Team record last five years: 35-45 (.438, ranks T21st in league in that span).
1999 team rankings:

	No.	AFC	NFL
Total offense	*355.8	2	5
Rushing offense	*130.3	2	3
Passing offense	*225.6	3	11
Scoring offense	390	T4	T8
Total defense	*305.0	7	10
Rushing defense	*97.4	8	12
Passing defense	*207.6	9	12
Scoring defense	329	12	16
Takeaways	33	5	T10
Giveaways	29	9	12
Turnover differential	4	5	11
Sacks	44	5	9
Sacks allowed	49	T12	T23

*Yards per game.

TEAM LEADERS

Scoring (kicking): Michael Husted, 90 pts. (30/30 PATs, 20/31 FGs).
Scoring (touchdowns): Tyrone Wheatley, 66 pts. (8 rushing, 3 receiving).
Passing: Rich Gannon, 3,840 yds. (515 att., 304 comp., 59.0%, 24 TDs, 14 int.).
Rushing: Tyrone Wheatley, 936 yds. (242 att., 3.9 avg., 8 TDs).
Receptions: Tim Brown, 90 (1,344 yds., 14.9 avg., 6 TDs).
Interceptions: Darrien Gordon, 3 (44 yds., 0 TDs); Eric Turner, 3 (43 yds., 0 TDs); Eric Allen, 3 (33 yds., 0 TDs).
Sacks: Lance Johnstone, 10.0.
Punting: Leo Araguz, 40.1 avg. (76 punts, 3,045 yds., 1 blocked).
Punt returns: Darrien Gordon, 9.5 avg. (42 att., 397 yds., 0 TDs).
Kickoff returns: Napoleon Kaufman, 19.8 avg. (42 att., 831 yds., 0 TDs).

2000 SEASON
TRAINING CAMP ROSTER

No.	QUARTERBACKS	Ht./Wt.	Born	NFL Exp.	College	How acq.	'99 Games GP/GS
12	Gannon, Rich	6-3/210	12-20-65	13	Delaware	UFA/99	16/16
14	Hoying, Bobby	6-3/220	9-20-72	5	Ohio State	T-Phi./99	2/0
8	Whelihan, Craig	6-5/220	4-15-71	4	Pacific (Calif.)	FA/00	*0/0
	RUNNING BACKS						
32	Crockett, Zack	6-2/240	12-2-72	6	Florida State	UFA/99	13/1
28	Jordan, Randy	5-11/215	6-6-70	7	North Carolina	UFA/99	16/0
26	Kaufman, Napoleon	5-9/185	6-7-73	6	Washington	D1/95	16/5
40	Ritchie, Jon	6-1/250	9-4-74	3	Stanford	D3/98	16/14
47	Wheatley, Tyrone	6-0/235	1-19-72	6	Michigan	FA/99	16/9
34	Williams, Jermaine	6-0/235	7-3-72	3	Houston	FA/98	15/0
	RECEIVERS						
87	Brigham, Jeremy (TE)	6-6/255	3-22-75	3	Washington	D5a/98	16/2
81	Brown, Tim	6-0/195	7-22-66	13	Notre Dame	D1/88	16/16
	Drayton, Troy (TE)	6-3/270	6-29-70	7	Penn State	FA/00	*14/13
83	Dudley, Rickey (TE)	6-6/255	7-15-72	5	Ohio State	D1/96	16/16
88	Dunn, David	6-3/210	6-10-72	6	Fresno State	FA/00	*6/0
48	Fulcher, Mondriel (TE)	6-3/250	10-15-76	R	Miami (Fla.)	D7a/00	—
82	Jett, James	5-10/170	12-28-70	8	West Virginia	FA/93	16/11
85	Mickens, Terry	6-1/200	2-21-71	7	Florida A&M	UFA/98	16/3
86	Porter, Jerry	6-2/220	7-14-78	R	West Virginia	D2/00	—
19	Shannon, Larry	6-4/210	2-2-75	1	East Carolina	FA/00	*2/0
84	Shedd, Kenny	5-10/165	2-14-71	6	Northern Iowa	FA/96	12/0
89	Williams, Rodney	6-0/190	8-15-73	3	Arizona	FA/98	5/0
	OFFENSIVE LINEMEN						
73	Ashmore, Darryl (G)	6-7/310	11-1-69	8	Northwestern	FA/98	16/2
79	Collins, Mo (T)	6-4/325	9-22-76	3	Florida	D1b/98	13/12
64	DiNapoli, Gennaro (G)	6-3/300	5-25-75	3	Virginia Tech	D4/98	11/9
72	Kennedy, Lincoln (T)	6-6/335	2-12-71	8	Washington	T-Atl./96	15/15
77	Myles, Toby (T)	6-5/320	7-23-75	2	Jackson State	FA/00	*8/0
71	Parks, Nathan (G)	6-5/305	10-24-74	1	Stanford	FA/99	2/0
63	Robbins, Barret (C)	6-3/320	8-26-73	6	Texas Christian	D2/95	16/16
65	Sims, Barry (G)	6-5/295	12-1-74	2	Utah	FA/99	16/10
74	Stinchcomb, Matt (T)	6-6/310	6-3-77	2	Georgia	D1/99	0/0
62	Treu, Adam (C)	6-5/300	6-24-74	4	Nebraska	D3/97	16/0
76	Wisniewski, Steve (G)	6-4/305	4-7-67	12	Penn State	D2/89	16/16
	DEFENSIVE LINEMEN						
94	Bryant, Tony (E)	6-6/275	9-3-76	2	Florida State	D2/99	10/0
57	Coleman, Roderick (E)	6-2/265	8-16-76	2	East Carolina	D5b/99	3/0
92	Ioane, Junior (T)	6-4/320	7-21-77	R	Arizona State	D4/00	—
90	Jackson, Grady (T)	6-2/325	1-21-73	4	Knoxville (Tenn.) College	D6b/97	15/0
51	Johnstone, Lance (E)	6-4/250	6-11-73	5	Temple	D2/96	16/16
97	Lee, Shawn (T)	6-2/300	10-24-66	12	North Alabama	UFA/00	*0/0
98	Osborne, Chuck (T)	6-2/290	11-2-73	5	Arizona	FA/98	16/0
95	Robbins, Austin (T)	6-6/290	3-1-71	7	North Carolina	UFA/00	*14/3
96	Russell, Darrell (T)	6-5/325	5-27-76	4	Southern California	D1/97	16/16
91	Upshaw, Regan (E)	6-4/260	8-12-75	5	California	UFA/00	*7/0
	LINEBACKERS						
50	Barton, Eric	6-2/245	9-29-77	2	Maryland	D5a/99	16/3
54	Biekert, Greg	6-2/255	3-14-69	8	Colorado	D7/93	16/16
41	Brooks, Bobby	6-2/235	3-3-76	1	Fresno State	FA/99	1/0
53	Smith, Travian	6-4/240	8-26-75	3	Oklahoma	D5b/98	16/1
56	Sword, Sam	6-1/245	12-9-74	2	Michigan	FA/99	10/5
	DEFENSIVE BACKS						
21	Allen, Eric	5-10/185	11-22-65	13	Arizona State	T-NO/98	16/16
43	Black, Cliffton (S)	6-0/195	4-11-77	R	Southwest Texas State	D7b/00	—
27	Branch, Calvin (S)	5-11/195	5-8-74	4	Colorado State	D6/97	16/1
30	Cherry, Je'Rod (S)	6-1/205	5-30-73	5	California	UFA/00	*16/0
33	Dorsett, Anthony (S)	5-11/200	9-14-73	5	Pittsburgh	UFA/00	*16/1
23	Gordon, Darrien (CB)	5-11/190	11-14-70	8	Stanford	FA/99	16/2
44	Harris, Johnnie (S)	6-2/210	8-21-72	2	Mississippi State	FA/99	4/0
20	James, Tory (CB)	6-2/185	5-18-73	5	Louisiana State	UFA/00	*16/4
22	Mincy, Charles (S)	6-0/200	12-16-69	10	Washington	FA/99	16/6
	Pope, Marquez (CB)	5-11/193	10-29-70	9	Fresno State	FA/00	*16/15
42	Ray, Marcus (S)	5-11/215	8-14-76	2	Michigan	FA/99	8/0
38	Walker, Marquis (CB)	5-10/175	7-6-72	5	Southeast Missouri State	FA/98	16/0
24	Woodson, Charles	6-1/205	10-7-76	3	Michigan	D1a/98	16/16
	SPECIALISTS						
2	Araguz, Leo (P)	5-11/190	1-18-70	5	Stephen F. Austin State	FA/96	16/0
5	Husted, Michael (K)	6-0/195	6-16-70	8	Virginia	FA/99	13/0
11	Janikowski, Sebastian (K)	6-1/255	3-2-78	R	Florida State	D1/00	—
9	Lechler, Shane (P)	6-2/230	8-7-76	R	Texas A&M	D5/00	—
6	Nedney, Joe (K)	6-5/220	3-22-73	5	San Jose State	FA/99	4/0

OAKLAND RAIDERS

– 69 –

*Not with Raiders in 1999.
Other free agent veterans invited to camp: G Jeremy Akers, LB Elijah Alexander, LB Bobby Brooks, TE John Burke, WR Rico Cannon, LB Jimmy Clements, WR Horace Copeland, CB Donnell Day, QB Scott Dreisbach, DE Jamal Duff, TE Chris Fontenot, OT Sale Isala, G/OT Tim Kohn, RB Jerald Moore, WR Creig Spann, OT Barry Stokes, DE Josh Taves, WR Gerald Williams, S Sean Woodson.
Abbreviations: D1—draft pick, first round; SD-2—supplemental draft pick, second round; W—claimed on waivers; T—obtained in trade; PlanB—Plan B free-agent acquisition; FA—free-agent acquisition (other than Plan B); UFA—unconditional free agent acquisition; ED—expansion draft pick.

MISCELLANEOUS TEAM DATA

Stadium (capacity, surface):
Network Associates Coliseum
(63,026, grass)
Business address:
1220 Harbor Bay Parkway
Alameda, CA 94502
Business phone:
510-864-5000
Ticket information:
800-949-2626
Team colors:
Silver and black
Flagship radio station:
The Ticket, 1050 AM
Training site:
Napa, Calif.
707-256-1000

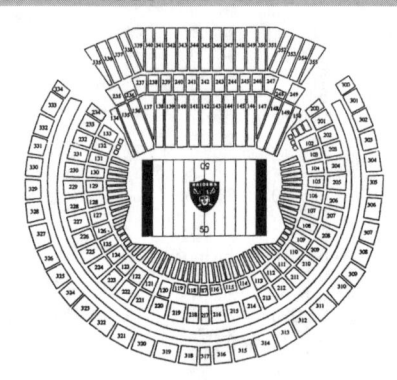

TSN REPORT CARD

Coaching staff	B-		Coach Jon Gruden has weeded out players who were either unproductive or divisive forces. Bill Callahan showed he is capable of forming a cohesive offensive line and helping design the offensive game plans. Chuck Bresnahan is in his first year as a defensive coordinator. Special teams coach Bob Casullo is in his first year at the pro level.
Quarterbacks	A-		Rich Gannon showed last season that he is durable and well-suited for Gruden's complex West Coast-style offense. He handles pressure well, especially on the road, is adept at running the ball. He makes his offensive line better with his improvisational skills. Bobby Hoying is a capable backup. Scott Dreisbach looks like a future starter.
Running backs	A-		Tyrone Wheatley and Napoleon Kaufman give Oakland one of the league's top 1-2 punches and complement each other well. Jon Ritchie is an effective blocker and developed into one of the league's best pass catchers last season. Zack Crockett and Randy Jordan are dependable backs in short-yardage and goal-line situations.
Receivers	C		Tim Brown remains one of the league's premier go-to receivers and is coming off one of his best all-around seasons. James Jett is a dangerous deep threat but lacks the desired consistency of a No. 2 man. Terry Mickens is the only other receiver who caught any passes last season. David Dunn, Larry Shannon and rookie Jerry Porter should provide much-needed production and depth. Newcomer Troy Drayton will back up Rickey Dudley at tight end.
Offensive line	B		Mo Collins, Steve Wisniewski, Barret Robbins, Barry Sims and Lincoln Kennedy keyed an offense that ranked fifth last season and protected Gannon well enough for him to have a Pro Bowl season. Matt Stinchcomb should crack the starting lineup this season. Darryl Ashmore and Adam Treu are solid backups.
Defensive line	B		Darrell Russell is one of the best tackles in the league. End Lance Johnstone led the team in sacks last season and should have an even better season this year in the final year of his contract. Grady Jackson replaces veteran Russell Maryland, alongside Russell, and should be a dominant force. Tony Bryant and Regan Upshaw should solidify left end. Shawn Lee and Chuck Osborne are productive backups.
Linebackers	C		Greg Biekert is the lone returning starter at linebacker. Eric Barton started the final three games on the weak side last season, but he still has plenty to learn. Elijah Alexander and Travian Smith are the leading candidates for the starting spot at strong side. Sam Sword is being groomed to replace Biekert.
Secondary	B		Charles Woodson is perhaps the league's top cornerback and teams with Eric Allen to give Oakland one of the best tandems. Tory James is good enough to start and should push Allen for a spot. Until then, James will split time with Darrien Gordon in obvious passing situations. Marquez Pope and Anthony Dorsett will battle at strong safety. Charles Mincy is the likely candidate to replace Eric Turner at free safety. Je'Rod Cherry will provide adequate depth.
Special teams	B-		Kicker Sebastian Janikowski and punter Shane Lechler were drafted with the intent of solving Oakland's kicking woes and helping it improve in the never-ending battle for field position. Gordon is one of the game's best punt returners ever. Casullo's special teams sparkled during his tenures at Syracuse, Georgia Tech and Michigan State.

PHILADELPHIA EAGLES
NFC EASTERN DIVISION

2000 SEASON

CLUB DIRECTORY

Owner/chief executive officer
Jeffrey Lurie
Executive v.p./chief operating officer
Joe Banner
Director of football operations
Tom Modrak
Senior v.p./chief of business operations
Len Komoroski
Chief financial officer
Don Smolenski
Vice president, corporate sales
Dave Rowan
Executive dir. of Eagles Youth Partnership
Sarah Helfman
Director of pro scouting
Mike McCartney
Director of college scouting
John Goeller
Director of administration
Vicki Chatley
Director of public relations
Ron Howard
Assistant director of public relations
Derek Boyko
Public relations assistant
Rich Burg
Dir. of player and community relations
Harold Carmichael
Ticket manager
Leo Carlin
Director of sales
Jason Gonella
Director of facility development
Dan McGregor
Director of merchandising
Steve Strawbridge
Director of advertising and promotions
Kim Babiak
Office manager/travel coordinator
Tracey Bucher
Director of security
Anthony Buchanico

Head coach
Andy Reid

Assistant coaches
Tommy Brasher (defensive line)
Juan Castillo (offensive line)
Brad Childress (quarterbacks)
Dave Culley (wide receivers)
Rod Dowhower (off. coordinator)
Leslie Frazier (defensive backs)
John Harbaugh (special teams)
Jim Johnson (def. coordinator)
Tom Melvin (offensive assistant/quality control)
Ron Rivera (linebackers)
Pat Shurmur (tight ends/assistant offensive line)
Steve Spagnuolo (defensive assistant/quality control)
Ted Williams (running backs)
Mike Wolf (strength & cond.)

Director of penthouse operations
Christiana Noyalas
Director of broadcasting
Rob Alberino
Head athletic trainer
Rick Burkholder
Assistant trainers
Scottie Patton   Chris Peduzzi
Video director
Mike Dougherty
Equipment manager
John Hatfield

SCHEDULE

Sept. 3—	at Dallas	4:05
Sept. 10—	N.Y. GIANTS	1:00
Sept. 17—	at Green Bay	1:00
Sept. 24—	at New Orleans	1:00
Oct. 1—	ATLANTA	8:35
Oct. 8—	WASHINGTON	1:00
Oct. 15—	at Arizona	4:15
Oct. 22—	CHICAGO	1:00
Oct. 29—	at N.Y. Giants	4:05
Nov. 5—	DALLAS	1:00
Nov. 12—	at Pittsburgh	1:00
Nov. 19—	ARIZONA	1:00
Nov. 26—	at Washington	1:00
Dec. 3—	TENNESSEE	1:00
Dec. 10—	at Cleveland	1:00
Dec. 17—	Open date	
Dec. 24—	CINCINNATI	1:00

All times are Eastern.
All games Sunday unless noted.

DRAFT CHOICES

Corey Simon, DT, Florida State (first round/sixth pick overall).
Todd Pinkston, WR, Southern Mississippi (2/36).
Bobby Williams, G, Arkansas (2/61).
Gari Scott, WR, Michigan State (4/99).
Thomas Hamner, RB, Minnesota (6/171).
John Frank, DE, Utah (6/178).
John Romero, C, California (6/192).

1999 REVIEW

RESULTS

Sept.12—ARIZONA	L	24-25
Sept.19—TAMPA BAY	L	5-19
Sept.26—at Buffalo	L	0-26
Oct. 3—at N.Y. Giants	L	15-16
Oct. 10—DALLAS	W	13-10
Oct. 17—at Chicago	W	20-16
Oct. 24—at Miami	L	13-16
Oct. 31—N.Y. GIANTS (OT)	L	17-23
Nov. 7—at Carolina	L	7-33
Nov. 14—WASHINGTON	W	35-28
Nov. 21—INDIANAPOLIS	L	17-44
Nov. 28—at Washington (OT)	L	17-20
Dec. 5—at Arizona	L	17-21
Dec. 12—at Dallas	L	10-20
Dec. 19—NEW ENGLAND	W	24-9
Dec. 26—Open date		
Jan. 2—ST. LOUIS	W	38-31

RECORDS/RANKINGS

1999 regular-season record: 5-11 (5th in NFC East); 2-6 in division; 4-8 in conference; 1-3 vs. AFC; 4-4 at home; 1-7 on road; 4-7 on turf; 1-4 on grass.
Team record last five years: 34-45-1 (.431, ranks 23rd in league in that span).
1999 team rankings:

	No.	NFC	NFL
Total offense	*239.4	15	30
Rushing offense	*109.1	7	17
Passing offense	*130.3	15	31
Scoring offense	272	T11	T25
Total defense	*341.4	10	24
Rushing defense	*125.1	13	28
Passing defense	*216.3	6	15
Scoring defense	357	8	22
Takeaways	46	1	1
Giveaways	39	T12	T28
Turnover differential	7	4	8
Sacks	37	T8	T20
Sacks allowed	49	T12	T23

*Yards per game.

TEAM LEADERS

Scoring (kicking): Norm Johnson, 79 pts. (25/25 PATs, 18/25 FGs).
Scoring (touchdowns): Duce Staley, 36 pts. (4 rushing, 2 receiving).
Passing: Doug Pederson, 1,276 yds. (227 att., 119 comp., 52.4%, 7 TDs, 9 int.).
Rushing: Duce Staley, 1,273 yds. (325 att., 3.9 avg., 4 TDs).
Receptions: Torrance Small, 49 (655 yds., 13.4 avg., 4 TDs).
Interceptions: Troy Vincent, 7 (91 yds., 0 TDs).
Sacks: Mike Mamula, 8.5.
Punting: Sean Landeta, 42.3 avg. (107 punts, 4,524 yds., 1 blocked).
Punt returns: Allen Rossum, 8.9 avg. (28 att., 250 yds., 0 TDs).
Kickoff returns: Allen Rossum, 24.9 avg. (54 att., 1,347 yds., 1 TD).

2000 SEASON
TRAINING CAMP ROSTER

PHILADELPHIA EAGLES

No.	QUARTERBACKS	Ht./Wt.	Born	NFL Exp.	College	How acq.	'99 Games GP/GS
10	Detmer, Koy	6-1/195	7-5-73	4	Colorado	D7a/97	1/1
5	McNabb, Donovan	6-2/226	11-25-76	2	Syracuse	D1/99	12/6
14	Pederson, Doug	6-3/216	1-31-68	8	Northeast Louisiana	UFA/99	16/9
	RUNNING BACKS						
30	Hamner, Thomas	6-0/197	12-25-76	R	Minnesota	D6a/00	—
38	Martin, Cecil (FB)	6-0/235	7-8-75	2	Wisconsin	D6a/99	12/5
36	Pritchett, Stanley	6-1/240	12-22-73	5	South Carolina	UFA/00	*14/7
22	Staley, Duce	5-11/220	2-27-75	4	South Carolina	D3/97	16/16
35	Watson, Edwin	6-0/225	9-29-76	3	Purdue	FA/99	6/0
	RECEIVERS						
88	Bartrum, Mike (TE)	6-4/245	6-23-70	7	Marshall	FA/00	*16/0
84	Broughton, Luther (TE)	6-2/248	11-30-74	4	Furman	T-Car./99	16/3
85	Brown, Na	6-0/187	2-22-77	2	North Carolina	D4c/99	12/5
82	Douglas, Dameane	6-0/195	3-15-76	2	California	W-Oak/99	14/0
18	Jells, Dietrich	5-10/185	4-11-72	5	Pittsburgh	T-NE/98	14/3
81	Johnson, Charles	6-0/200	1-3-72	7	Colorado	UFA/99	11/11
89	Lewis, Chad (TE)	6-6/252	10-5-71	3	Brigham Young	W-StL/99	12/4
17	Pinkston, Todd	6-2/170	4-23-77	R	Southern Mississippi	D2a/00	—
16	Scott, Gari	6-0/191	6-2-78	R	Michigan State	D4/00	—
80	Small, Torrance	6-3/209	9-4-70	9	Alcorn State	UFA/99	15/15
19	Smith, Troy	6-2/193	7-30-77	2	East Carolina	D6b/99	1/0
83	Thomason, Jeff (TE)	6-5/255	12-30-69	8	Oregon	T-GB/00	*14/2
86	Van Dyke, Alex	6-0/205	7-24-74	5	Nevada	FA/99	2/0
87	Weaver, Jed (TE)	6-4/246	8-11-76	2	Oregon	D7a/99	16/10
	OFFENSIVE LINEMEN						
74	Brzezinski, Doug (G)	6-4/305	3-11-76	2	Boston College	D3/99	16/16
71	Mayberry, Jermane (G)	6-4/325	8-29-73	5	Texas A&M-Kingsville	D1/96	13/5
65	Miller, Bubba (C)	6-1/305	1-24-73	5	Tennessee	FA/96	14/0
77	Palelei, Lonnie (G)	6-3/310	10-15-70	7	Purdue, then UNLV	UFA/99	16/12
63	Romero, John (C)	6-3/326	10-3-76	R	California	D6c/00	—
69	Runyan, Jon (T)	6-7/330	11-27-73	5	Michigan	UFA/00	*16/16
67	Schau, Ryan (G)	6-6/300	12-30-75	2	Illinois	FA/99	1/0
72	Thomas, Tra (T)	6-7/349	11-20-74	3	Florida State	D1/98	16/15
76	Welbourn, John (T)	6-5/318	3-30-76	2	California	D4a/99	1/1
66	Williams, Bobby (G)	6-3/320	9-25-76	R	Arkansas	D2b/00	—
	DEFENSIVE LINEMEN						
93	Davis, Pernell (T)	6-2/320	5-19-76	2	Alabama-Birmingham	D7b/99	2/0
91	Frank, John (E)	6-4/280	7-1-74	R	Utah	D6b/00	—
96	Grasmanis, Paul (T)	6-2/298	8-2-74	5	Notre Dame	UFA/00	*5/0
94	Gregg, Kelly (T)	6-0/285	11-1-76	1	Oklahoma	FA/99	3/0
79	Jefferson, Greg (E)	6-3/280	8-31-71	6	Central Florida	D3a/95	16/16
90	Simon, Corey (T)	6-2/293	3-2-77	R	Florida State	D1/00	—
78	Thomas, Hollis (T)	6-0/306	1-10-74	5	Northern Illinois	FA/96	16/16
50	Wallace, Al (E)	6-5/258	3-25-74	3	Maryland	FA/97	0/0
97	Wheeler, Mark (T)	6-3/285	4-1-70	9	Texas A&M	UFA/99	13/0
98	Whiting, Brandon (T)	6-3/278	7-30-76	3	California	D4a/98	13/2
95	Williams, Tyrone (E)	6-4/292	10-22-72	2	Wyoming	FA/99	4/0
	LINEBACKERS						
55	Brandenburg, Dan	6-2/255	2-16-73	4	Indiana State	UFA/00	*14/0
56	Caldwell, Mike	6-2/237	8-31-71	8	Middle Tennessee State	FA/98	14/2
57	Darling, James	6-0/250	12-29-74	4	Washington State	D2/97	15/10
53	Douglas, Hugh	6-2/280	8-23-71	6	Central State (Ohio)	T-NYJ/98	4/2
51	Emmons, Carlos	6-5/250	9-3-73	5	Arkansas State	UFA/00	*16/16
52	Gardner, Barry	6-0/248	12-13-76	2	Northwestern	D2/99	16/5
59	Mamula, Mike	6-4/252	8-14-73	6	Boston College	D1/95	16/13
58	Reese, Ike	6-2/222	10-16-73	3	Michigan State	D5/98	16/0
54	Trotter, Jeremiah	6-0/261	1-20-77	3	Stephen F. Austin (Tex.)	D3a/98	16/16
	DEFENSIVE BACKS						
32	Bostic, Jason (CB)	5-9/181	6-30-76	1	Georgia Tech	FA/99	1/0
42	Cook, Rashard (S)	5-11/197	4-18-77	2	Southern California	W-Chi./99	13/0
20	Dawkins, Brian (S)	5-11/200	10-13-73	5	Clemson	D2b/96	16/16
31	Harris, Al (CB)	6-1/185	12-7-74	3	Texas A&M-Kingsville	W-TB/98	16/6
43	Moore, Damon (S)	5-11/215	9-15-76	2	Ohio State	D4b/99	16/1
25	Rossum, Allen (CB)	5-8/178	10-22-75	3	Notre Dame	D3/98	16/0
21	Taylor, Bobby (CB)	6-3/216	12-28-73	6	Notre Dame	D2a/95	15/14
23	Vincent, Troy (CB)	6-1/200	6-8-71	9	Wisconsin	FA/96	14/14
	SPECIALISTS						
2	Akers, David (K)	5-10/180	12-9-74	2	Louisville	FA/99	16/0
6	Brice, Will (P)	6-4/220	10-24-74	3	Virginia	FA/00	*11/0
7	Landeta, Sean (P)	6-0/215	1-6-62	16	Towson State	UFA/99	16/0

– 72 –

*Not with Eagles in 1999.
Other free agent veterans invited to camp: RB Darnell Autry, OT Robert Barr, OT Jon Blackman, C/G Eugene Chung, CB Eric Edwards, S Lemar Marshall, QB Ron Powlus, FB Jamie Reader, OT Oliver Ross, TE Eric Stocz, CB Mark Tate.
Abbreviations: D1—draft pick, first round; SD-2—supplemental draft pick, second round; W—claimed on waivers; T—obtained in trade; PlanB—Plan B free-agent acquisition; FA—free-agent acquisition (other than Plan B); UFA—unconditional free agent acquisition; ED—expansion draft pick.

MISCELLANEOUS TEAM DATA

Stadium (capacity, surface):
Veterans Stadium
(65,352, artificial)
Business address:
3501 South Broad Street
Philadelphia, PA 19148
Business phone:
215-463-2500
Ticket information:
215-463-5500
Team colors:
Midnight green, silver and white
Flagship radio station:
WYSP, 94.1 FM
Training site:
Lehigh University
Bethlehem, Pa.
610-758-6868

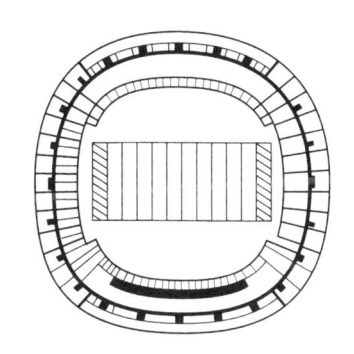

TSN REPORT CARD

Coaching staff	C +	Head coach Andy Reid made his share of rookie mistakes, but seems to have learned from some of them. His game-day decisions this year bear watching, however. Defensive coordinator Jim Johnson seems to get the most from his players. However, he needs to show he can do more than just blitz. The rising young star of the staff is special teams coordinator John Harbaugh.
Quarterbacks	C	The jury remains out on talented but untested Donovan McNabb. The second-year player shows great confidence and leadership for someone so young, but he still must produce on the field. The backups are journeyman Doug Pederson and undersized Koy Detmer. Pederson was a complete flop as a starter last year. Detmer won his only start and could win the No. 2 spot.
Running backs	B	In a quiet and unassuming manner Duce Staley has become one of the top backs in the league. He can run, catch, block and play with injuries. You can't ask for much more. Stanley Pritchett, Staley's old college teammate, should win the fullback job from second-year man Cecil Martin. That's a good starting duo. There just isn't much in reserve.
Receivers	C -	There still isn't a true go-to-guy at either wide receiver or tight end. Charles Johnson is the best of a deep, but average, group of wideouts. And every tight end on the roster has been cut at least once in his career, except for second-year man Jed Weaver, and he may be by the time you read this.
Offensive line	B -	Tra Thomas and Jon Runyan give the Eagles their best set of tackles since Stan Walters and Jerry Sisemore started on the Super Bowl team of 20 years ago. The interior of the line could be good, but it's very young and inexperienced. Guards Doug Brzezinski and Bobby Williams and center Bubba Miller have a combined one year of starting experience.
Defensive line	B -	Ends Mike Mamula and Hugh Douglas can get to the quarterback, but they have to prove they will not be a liability against the run. Rookie Corey Simon should help stuff the run in the middle and create some inside pressure. But keep in mind he's still a rookie. There is very little proven depth in reserve.
Linebackers	B	Jeremiah Trotter is a star-in-waiting in the middle. Carlos Emmons gives the team a true strongside player for the first time since Seth Joyner. Barry Gardner is unproven and untested on the weakside, but he has some ability. There is excellent depth with James Darling, Mike Caldwell and Ike Reese.
Secondary	A -	Cornerback Troy Vincent and free safety Brian Dawkins both went to the Pro Bowl last season, despite the team's last-place finish. That's an impressive half of a secondary. Vincent's counterpart, Bobby Taylor, and nickel back Al Harris are also very solid. The one uncertain is strong safety, but second-year man Rashard Cook may be the answer.
Special teams	B -	With all those linebackers, the coverage teams should be even better than last year. And they were good last year. If rookie Gari Scott can handle punt returns, Allen Rossum will be fine with kickoffs. Punter Sean Landeta is still going strong, and young kicker David Akers is better than most realize.

PITTSBURGH STEELERS
AFC CENTRAL DIVISION

2000 SEASON

CLUB DIRECTORY

President
Daniel M. Rooney
Vice president/general counsel
Arthur J. Rooney II
Administration advisor
Charles H. Noll
Director of business
Mark Hart
Business coordinator
Dan Ferens
Accounts coordinator
Jim Ellenberger
Office ticket coordinator
Geraldine Glenn
Director of football operations
Kevin Colbert
Player relations
Anthony Griggs
Communications coordinator
Ron Wahl
Public relations/media manager
Dave Lockett
Pro scouting personnel
Doug Whaley
College scouting coordinator
Bill Baker
College scouts
Mark Gorscak
Phil Kreidler
Doug Kretz
Bob Lane
Bruce McNorton
Dan Rooney
Director of marketing
Tony Quatrini
Trainers
John Norwig
Ryan Grove

Head coach
Bill Cowher

Assistant coaches
Mike Archer (linebackers)
Bob Bratkowski (wide receivers)
Irv Eatman (offensive line)
Kevin Gilbride (off. coordinator)
Jay Hayes (special teams)
Dick Hoak (running backs)
Tim Lewis (defensive coordinator)
John Mitchell (defensive line)
Mike Mularkey (tight ends)
Willy Robinson (defensive backs)
Kent Stephenson (offensive line)

Physicians
James P. Bradley
Richard Rydze
Abraham J. Twerski
Anthony P. Yates
Equipment manager
Rodgers Freyvogel
Field manager
Rich Baker
Video coordinator
Bob McCartney
Video assistant
Andy Lizanich
Photographer
Mike Fabus

SCHEDULE

Sept. 3—	BALTIMORE	1:00
Sept. 10—	Open date	
Sept. 17—	at Cleveland	1:00
Sept. 24—	TENNESSEE	1:00
Oct. 1—	at Jacksonville	1:00
Oct. 8—	at N.Y. Jets	1:00
Oct. 15—	CINCINNATI	1:00
Oct. 22—	CLEVELAND	1:00
Oct. 29—	at Baltimore	1:00
Nov. 5—	at Tennessee	1:00
Nov. 12—	PHILADELPHIA	1:00
Nov. 19—	JACKSONVILLE	8:35
Nov. 26—	at Cincinnati	1:00
Dec. 3—	OAKLAND	1:00
Dec. 10—	at N.Y. Giants	1:00
Dec. 16—	WASHINGTON (Sat.)	12:30
Dec. 24—	at San Diego	4:05

All times are Eastern.
All games Sunday unless noted.

DRAFT CHOICES

Plaxico Burress, WR, Michigan State (first round/eighth pick overall).
Marvel Smith, T, Arizona State (2/38).
Kendrick Clancy, DT, Mississippi (3/72).
Hank Poteat, DB, Pittsburgh (3/77).
Danny Farmer, WR, UCLA (4/103).
Clark Haggans, LB, Colorado State (5/137).
Tee Martin, QB, Tennessee (5/163).
Chris Combs, DT, Duke (6/173).
Jason Gavadza, TE, Kent (6/204).

1999 REVIEW

RESULTS

Sept.12	—at Cleveland	W	43-0
Sept.19	—at Baltimore	W	23-20
Sept.26	—SEATTLE	L	10-29
Oct. 3	—JACKSONVILLE	L	3-17
Oct. 10	—at Buffalo	L	21-24
Oct. 17	—at Cincinnati	W	17-3
Oct. 25	—ATLANTA	W	13-9
Oct. 31	—Open date		
Nov. 7	—at San Francisco	W	27-6
Nov. 14	—CLEVELAND	L	15-16
Nov. 21	—at Tennessee	L	10-16
Nov. 28	—CINCINNATI	L	20-27
Dec. 2	—at Jacksonville	L	6-20
Dec. 12	—BALTIMORE	L	24-31
Dec. 18	—at Kansas City	L	19-35
Dec. 26	—CAROLINA	W	30-20
Jan. 2	—TENNESSEE	L	36-47

RECORDS/RANKINGS

1999 regular-season record: 6-10 (4th in AFC Central); 3-7 in division; 3-10 in conference; 3-0 vs. NFC; 2-6 at home; 4-4 on road; 3-7 on turf; 3-3 on grass.
Team record last five years: 45-35 (.563, ranks T9th in league in that span).
1999 team rankings:

	No.	AFC	NFL
Total offense	*304.6	11	22
Rushing offense	*124.4	6	10
Passing offense	*180.2	14	26
Scoring offense	317	10	17
Total defense	*305.3	8	11
Rushing defense	*122.4	15	26
Passing defense	*182.9	3	4
Scoring defense	320	9	12
Takeaways	28	T9	T20
Giveaways	25	5	T7
Turnover differential	3	T6	T12
Sacks	39	T10	T17
Sacks allowed	37	T7	T12

*Yards per game.

TEAM LEADERS

Scoring (kicking): Kris Brown, 105 pts. (30/31 PATs, 25/29 FGs).
Scoring (touchdowns): Richard Huntley, 48 pts. (5 rushing, 3 receiving).
Passing: Mike Tomczak, 1,625 yds. (258 att., 139 comp., 53.9%, 12 TDs, 8 int.).
Rushing: Jerome Bettis, 1,091 yds. (299 att., 3.6 avg., 7 TDs).
Receptions: Troy Edwards, 61 (714 yds., 11.7 avg., 5 TDs).
Interceptions: Scott Shields, 4 (75 yds., 0 TDs); Dewayne Washington, 4 (1 yds., 0 TDs).
Sacks: Jason Gildon, 8.5.
Punting: Josh Miller, 45.2 avg. (84 punts, 3,795 yds., 0 blocked).
Punt returns: Troy Edwards, 9.4 avg. (25 att., 234 yds., 0 TDs).
Kickoff returns: Amos Zereoue, 24.1 avg. (7 att., 169 yds., 0 TDs).

– 74 –

2000 SEASON
TRAINING CAMP ROSTER

PITTSBURGH STEELERS

No.	QUARTERBACKS	Ht./Wt.	Born	NFL Exp.	College	How acq.	'99 Games GP/GS
11	Graham, Kent	6-5/245	11-1-68	9	Ohio State	UFA/00	*9/9
17	Martin, Tee	6-1/221	7-25-78	R	Tennessee	D5b/00	—
10	Stewart, Kordell	6-1/211	10-16-72	6	Colorado	D2/95	16/12
	RUNNING BACKS						
36	Bettis, Jerome	5-11/250	2-16-72	8	Notre Dame	T-StL/96	16/16
45	Fuamatu-Ma'afala, Chris	5-11/252	3-4-77	3	Utah	D6a/98	10/0
33	Huntley, Richard	5-11/225	9-18-72	4	Winston-Salem (N.C.) State	FA/98	16/2
38	Witman, Jon (FB)	6-1/240	6-1-72	5	Penn State	D3b/96	16/11
21	Zereoue, Amos	5-8/202	10-8-76	2	West Virginia	D3c/99	8/0
	RECEIVERS						
89	Blackwell, Will	6-0/190	7-6-75	4	San Diego State	D2/97	11/1
87	Bruener, Mark (TE)	6-4/261	9-16-72	6	Washington	D1/95	14/14
88	Burress, Plaxico	6-5/229	8-12-77	R	Michigan State	D1/00	—
80	Cushing, Matt (TE)	6-3/258	7-2-75	2	Illinois	FA/98	7/1
81	Edwards, Troy	5-9/192	4-7-77	2	Louisiana Tech	D1/99	16/6
16	Farmer, Danny	6-3/217	5-21-77	R	UCLA	D4/00	—
48	Gavadza, Jason (TE)	6-3/247	1-31-76	R	Kent	D6b/00	—
83	Johnson, Malcolm	6-5/215	8-27-77	2	Notre Dame	D5b/99	6/0
82	Shaw, Bobby	6-0/186	4-23-75	3	California	FA/98	15/1
84	Tuman, Jerame (TE)	6-3/250	3-24-76	2	Michigan	D5a/99	7/0
86	Ward, Hines	6-0/197	3-8-76	3	Georgia	D3b/98	16/14
	OFFENSIVE LINEMEN						
60	Brown, Anthony (T)	6-5/315	11-6-72	6	Utah	UFA/99	16/11
78	Conrad, Chris (T)	6-6/310	5-27-75	3	Fresno State	D3a/98	11/3
63	Dawson, Dermontti (C)	6-2/292	6-17-65	13	Kentucky	D2/88	7/7
62	Duffy, Roger (G)	6-3/299	7-16-67	11	Penn State	UFA/98	16/11
66	Faneca, Alan (G)	6-4/315	12-7-76	3	Louisiana State	D1/98	15/14
71	Farris, Kris (T)	6-8/322	3-26-77	2	UCLA	D3b/99	0/0
72	Gandy, Wayne (T)	6-5/310	2-10-71	7	Auburn	UFA/99	16/16
61	Myslinski, Tom (G)	6-3/293	12-7-68	8	Tennessee	UFA/00	*10/2
67	Pourdanesh, Shar	6-6/312	7-19-70	5	Nevada-Reno	T-Was./99	4/2
54	Schneck, Mike (C)	6-0/242	8-4-77	2	Wisconsin	FA/99	16/0
77	Smith, Marvel (T)	6-5/320	8-6-78	R	Arizona State	D2/00	—
79	Tharpe, Larry (T)	6-4/305	11-19-70	8	Tennessee State	UFA/00	*0/0
65	Tylski, Rich (G)	6-5/308	2-27-71	5	Utah State	UFA/00	*10/8
	DEFENSIVE LINEMEN						
98	Brown, Ernie	6-3/295	3-14-71	2	Syracuse	FA/99	3/0
96	Clancy, Kendrick (T)	6-1/280	9-17-78	R	Mississippi	D3a/00	—
73	Combs, Chris (E)	6-4/284	12-15-76	R	Duke	D6a/00	—
53	Haggans, Clark (E)	6-3/250	1-10-77	R	Colorado State	D5a/00	—
76	Henry, Kevin (E)	6-4/285	10-23-68	8	Mississippi State	D4/93	16/13
91	Smith, Aaron (E)	6-5/281	4-9-76	2	Northern Colorado	D4/99	6/0
94	Staat, Jeremy (E)	6-5/300	10-10-76	3	Arizona State	D2/98	16/2
93	Steed, Joel (NT)	6-2/308	2-17-69	9	Colorado	D3/92	14/14
95	Sullivan, Chris	6-4/285	3-14-73	5	Boston College	UFA/00	*16/0
69	von Oelhoffen, Kimo	6-4/305	1-30-71	7	Boise State	UFA/00	*16/5
	LINEBACKERS						
57	Fiala, John	6-2/235	11-25-73	3	Washington	FA/98	16/0
92	Gildon, Jason	6-3/255	7-31-72	7	Oklahoma State	D3a/94	16/16
50	Holmes, Earl	6-2/250	4-28-73	5	Florida A&M	D4a/96	16/16
97	Kelsay, Chad	6-2/252	4-9-77	2	Nebraska	D7b/99	6/0
99	Kirkland, Levon	6-1/270	2-17-69	9	Clemson	D2/92	16/16
55	Porter, Joey	6-2/240	3-22-77	2	Colorado State	D3a/99	16/0
56	Vrabel, Mike	6-4/250	8-14-75	4	Ohio State	D3b/97	10/0
	DEFENSIVE BACKS						
	Alexander, Brent (S)	5-11/196	7-10-71	7	Tennessee State	FA/00	*16/16
29	Brown, Lance	6-2/203	2-2-72	4	Indiana	FA/98	16/0
41	Flowers, Lee (S)	6-0/211	1-14-73	6	Georgia Tech	D5a/95	15/15
22	Poteat, Hank (CB)	5-10/190	8-30-77	R	Pittsburgh	D3b/00	—
30	Scott, Chad	6-1/192	9-6-74	4	Maryland	D1/97	13/12
47	Shields, Scott (S)	6-4/228	3-29-76	2	Weber State	D2/99	16/1
23	Simmons, Jason (CB)	5-8/186	3-30-76	3	Arizona State	D5/98	16/0
26	Townsend, Deshea (CB)	5-10/175	9-8-75	3	Alabama	D4a/98	16/4
20	Washington, Dewayne (CB)	6-0/193	12-27-72	7	North Carolina State	UFA/98	16/16
	SPECIALISTS						
3	Brown, Kris (K)	5-10/204	12-23-76	2	Nebraska	D7c/99	16/0
4	Miller, Josh (P)	6-3/219	7-14-70	5	Arizona	FA/96	16/0

*Not with Steelers in 1999.
Other free agent veterans invited to camp: S Nakia Codie, TE Corey Geason, LB Reggie Lowe, WR Shawn McWashington, G Tony Orlandini, QB Anthony Wright.

PITTSBURGH STEELERS

Abbreviations: D1—draft pick, first round; SD-2—supplemental draft pick, second round; W—claimed on waivers; T—obtained in trade; PlanB—Plan B free-agent acquisition; FA—free-agent acquisition (other than Plan B); UFA—unconditional free agent acquisition; ED—expansion draft pick.

MISCELLANEOUS TEAM DATA

Stadium (capacity, surface):
Three Rivers Stadium
(59,600, artificial)
Business address:
3400 South Water St.
Pittsburgh, PA 15203-2349
Business phone:
412-323-0300
Ticket information:
412-323-1200
Team colors:
Black and gold
Flagship radio station:
WDVE, 102.7 FM
Training site:
St. Vincent College
Latrobe, Pa.
412-539-8515

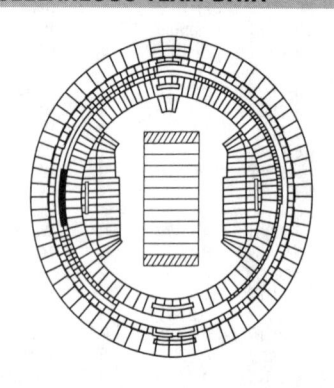

TSN REPORT CARD

Coaching staff	B	Bill Cowher is on the hot seat after forcing the ouster of personnel man Tom Donahoe, and his every move will be scrutinized. Another losing season and he likely will be fired. Cowher has to become more disciplined and more demanding. He cannot afford to tolerate the lackluster attitude that permeated the ranks in 1999. New defensive coordinator Tim Lewis has to find ways so the defense doesn't run out of gas late in the year.
Quarterbacks	C	The team brought in Kent Graham to back up Kordell Stewart, and if the Steelers have to turn to the former Giants quarterback they are in trouble. Graham is not very mobile and the offensive line isn't good enough to give him the time he would need to throw. Stewart has a bigger chore in front of him—regaining the confidence of the fans and his teammates after two bad seasons. If he doesn't, his psyche won't be able to handle the pressure.
Running backs	B -	Jerome Bettis has not been as productive the past two seasons, which has coincided with the poor performance of the offensive line. But he will see even less playing time this season with Richard Huntley, who is a better pass receiver for offensive coordinator Kevin Gilbride's spread offense and more of a threat to break a big run. The team re-signed Huntley during the offseason and, depending on who you believe, told him he would be the team's feature back.
Receivers	C +	This is an underachieving but young group that has lots of potential but still not lots of speed. The drafting of Plaxico Burress with the top pick will make last year's No. 1 pick, Troy Edwards, that much better. It will also make Hines Ward the No. 3 receiver, which is where he is better served. The Steelers think Edwards is better as a No. 2 man because he is not a deep threat but is very dangerous running with the ball after a catch. If last year's No. 5 pick, Malcolm Johnson, continues to develop, the team has the makings of a tall and physically imposing group of receivers. Tight end Mark Bruener is not used much to catch passes.
Offensive line	C	For all their maneuvering, the Steelers still have a problem at right tackle. For the third year in a row, they go to training camp looking for a new starter at that position. The waiving of Justin Strzelczyk hurts because he was a proven veteran, but back-to-back offseason injuries were too much for the team to take. Kris Farris, who missed all of last season, will come in as the starter. But don't be surprised if rookie Marvel Smith, who is more comfortable at left tackle, forces the team to shift veteran Wayne Gandy to right tackle.
Defensive line	C -	The free-agent loss of end Orpheus Roye hurts because he was the team's best lineman. And if Joel Steed is unable to play on his bad knees, which appears to be the case, the team will be losing a Pro Bowl nose tackle. That's why the Steelers went out and signed Kimo von Oelhoffen from the Bengals. But right defensive end Kevin Henry needs to play like he did in 1997, and free-agent newcomer Chris Sullivan has to be able to rush the passer from the left side, something the Steelers have been unable to do.
Linebackers	B	This is probably the team's strongest unit, but it did wear down in 1999. The Steelers are excited about their new right outside linebacker, Joey Porter, who was a training camp sensation last season and looks a lot like a young Greg Lloyd. But if the team doesn't get more inspired play from Levon Kirkland, it could be a long season. Earl Holmes is solid as the other inside linebacker, but he is only as good as Kirkland allows him to be. Kirkland has to make sure he keeps his weight in check and does not allow it to slow him down.
Secondary	C +	There are good corners in Chad Scott and Dewayne Washington and a solid, hard-hitting strong safety in Lee Flowers. Still, the secondary has been susceptible to too many big plays that have led to too many losses. Flowers and free safety Travis Davis did a poor job reacting to deep passes last year and it cost the Steelers on almost every occasion. That has to stop.
Special teams	B -	The problem areas are not the punter and the kicker (Josh Miller and Kris Brown, respectively, are fine), but the return teams. The Steelers have not returned a kickoff for a touchdown in almost two years and their average starting drive was among the worst in the league in '99. Edwards is a good punt returner, but his hands and decision-making were suspect. The drafting of cornerback Hank Poteat on the third round could help the return teams because he was among the nation's leaders on punt and kick returns.

ST. LOUIS RAMS
NFC WESTERN DIVISION

2000 SEASON

CLUB DIRECTORY

Chairman
Georgia Frontiere
Vice chairman
Stan Kroenke
President
John Shaw
President/football operations
Jay Zygmunt
Sr. v.p./administration, gen. counsel
Bob Wallace
General manager
Charley Armey
Vice president/football operations
Kevin Warren
Director of pro scouting
Mike Ackerley
Director of scouting
Lawrence McCutcheon
Vice president/finance
Adrian Barr-Bracy
Treasurer
Jeff Brewer
Director of operations
John Oswald
Vice president/marketing and sales
Phil Thomas
Vice president of ticket operations
Michael T. Naughton
Director of public relations
Rick Smith
Assistant director of public relations
Duane Lewis
Scouts
Ryan Grigson   Kevin McCabe
David Razzano   Pete Russell
Harley Sewell
Head trainer
Jim Anderson
Assistant trainers
Ron DuBuque
Dake Walden

Head coach
Mike Martz

Assistant coaches
Steve Brown (secondary)
Sam Clark (offensive assistant)
Chris Clausen (strength & cond.)
Peter Giunta (defensive coord.)
Carl Hairston (defensive line)
Mike Haluchak (linebackers)
Jim Hanifan (offensive line)
Bobby Jackson (running backs)
Dana LeDuc (strength & cond.)
John Matsko (asst. head coach/offensive line)
Wilbert Montgomery (tight ends)
John Ramsdell (quarterbacks)
Larry Pasquale (special teams)
Al Saunders (wide receivers)
Howard Tippett (def. assistant)
Ken Zampese (off. assistant)

Physicians
Dr. Bernard Garfinkel Dr. James Loomis
Dr. Robert Shively   Dr. Rick Wright
Equipment manager
Todd Hewitt
Assistant equipment manager
Jim Lake
Video director
Larry Clerico
Assistant video director
Scott Nyberg

SCHEDULE

Sept. 4—	DENVER (Mon.)	9:00
Sept. 10—	at Seattle	4:15
Sept. 17—	SAN FRANCISCO	1:00
Sept. 24—	at Atlanta	1:00
Oct. 1—	SAN DIEGO	1:00
Oct. 8—	Open date	
Oct. 15—	ATLANTA	1:00
Oct. 22—	at Kansas City	1:00
Oct. 29—	at San Francisco	4:05
Nov. 5—	CAROLINA	8:35
Nov. 12—	at N.Y. Giants	4:15
Nov. 20—	WASHINGTON (Mon.)	9:00
Nov. 26—	NEW ORLEANS	1:00
Dec. 3—	at Carolina	1:00
Dec. 10—	MINNESOTA	1:00
Dec. 18—	at Tampa Bay (Mon.)	9:00
Dec. 24—	at New Orleans	1:00

All times are Eastern.
All games Sunday unless noted.

DRAFT CHOICES

Trung Canidate, RB, Arizona (first round/31st pick overall).
Jacoby Shepherd, DB, Oklahoma State (2/62).
John St. Clair, C, Virginia (3/94).
Kaulana Noa, G, Hawaii (4/104).
Brian Young, DL, Texas-El Paso (5/139).
Matt Bowen, DB, Iowa (6/198).
Andrew Kline, G, San Diego St. (7/220).

1999 REVIEW

RESULTS

Sept.12—BALTIMORE	W	27-10	
Sept.19—Open date			
Sept.26—ATLANTA	W	35-7	
Oct. 3—at Cincinnati	W	38-10	
Oct. 10—SAN FRANCISCO	W	42-20	
Oct. 17—at Atlanta	W	41-13	
Oct. 24—CLEVELAND	W	34-3	
Oct. 31—at Tennessee	L	21-24	
Nov. 7—at Detroit	L	27-31	
Nov. 14—CAROLINA	W	35-10	
Nov. 21—at San Francisco	W	23-7	
Nov. 28—NEW ORLEANS	W	43-12	
Dec. 5—at Carolina	W	34-21	
Dec. 12—at New Orleans	W	30-14	
Dec. 19—N.Y. GIANTS	W	31-10	
Dec. 26—CHICAGO	W	34-12	
Jan. 2—at Philadelphia	L	31-38	
Jan. 16—MINNESOTA*	W	49-37	
Jan. 23—TAMPA BAY†	W	11-6	
Jan. 30—TENNESSEE‡	W	23-16	

*NFC divisional playoff game.
†NFC conference game.
‡Super Bowl 34.

RECORDS/RANKINGS

1999 regular-season record: 13-3 (1st in NFC West); 8-0 in division; 10-2 in conference; 3-1 vs. AFC; 8-0 at home; 5-3 on road; 11-2 on turf; 2-1 on grass.
Team record last five years: 35-45 (.438, ranks T21st in league in that span).
1999 team rankings:

	No.	NFC	NFL
Total offense	*400.8	1	1
Rushing offense	*128.7	2	5
Passing offense	*272.1	1	1
Scoring offense	526	1	1
Total defense	*293.6	2	6
Rushing defense	*74.3	1	1
Passing defense	*219.3	8	20
Scoring defense	242	2	4
Takeaways	36	4	T6
Giveaways	31	4	T13
Turnover differential	5	T5	T9
Sacks	57	1	T1
Sacks allowed	33	3	7

*Yards per game.

TEAM LEADERS

Scoring (kicking): Jeff Wilkins, 124 pts. (64/64 PATs, 20/28 FGs).
Scoring (touchdowns): Marshall Faulk, 74 pts. (7 rushing, 5 receiving, 1 2-pt. conv.); Isaac Bruce, 74 pts. (12 receiving, 1 2-pt. conv.).
Passing: Kurt Warner, 4,353 yds. (499 att., 325 comp., 65.1%, 41 TDs, 13 int.).
Rushing: Marshall Faulk, 1,381 yds. (253 att., 5.5 avg., 7 TDs).
Receptions: Isaac Bruce, 77 (1,165 yds., 15.1 avg., 12 TDs).
Interceptions: Todd Lyght, 6 (112 yds., 1 TD).
Sacks: Kevin Carter, 17.0.
Punting: Rick Tuten, 42.5 avg. (32 punts, 1,359 yds., 0 blocked).
Punt returns: Az-Zahir Hakim, 10.5 avg. (44 att., 461 yds., 1 TD).
Kickoff returns: Tony Horne, 29.7 avg. (30 att., 892 yds., 2 TDs).

2000 SEASON
TRAINING CAMP ROSTER

ST. LOUIS RAMS

No.	QUARTERBACKS	Ht./Wt.	Born	NFL Exp.	College	How acq.	'99 Games GP/GS
9	Germaine, Joe	6-0/203	8-11-75	2	Ohio State	D4/99	3/0
10	Green, Trent	6-3/215	7-9-70	7	Indiana	UFA/99	0/0
13	Warner, Kurt	6-2/220	6-22-71	3	Northern Iowa	FA/98	16/16
	RUNNING BACKS						
24	Canidate, Trung	5-11/192	3-3-77	R	Arizona	D1/00	—
28	Faulk, Marshall	5-10/211	2-26-73	7	San Diego State	T-Ind./99	16/16
42	Hodgins, James	5-11/230	4-30-77	2	San Jose State	FA/99	15/0
25	Holcombe, Robert	5-11/220	12-11-75	3	Illinois	D2/98	15/7
31	Loville, Derek	5-10/210	7-4-68	10	Oregon	T-Den./00	*10/0
33	Watson, Justin	6-0/225	1-1-75	2	San Diego State	FA/99	8/0
	RECEIVERS						
80	Bruce, Isaac	6-0/188	11-10-72	7	Memphis State	D2/94	16/16
84	Conwell, Ernie (TE)	6-1/265	8-17-72	5	Washington	D2b/96	3/0
81	Hakim, Az-Zahir	5-10/178	6-3-77	3	San Diego State	D4a/98	15/0
88	Holt, Torry	6-0/190	6-5-76	2	North Carolina State	D1/99	16/15
82	Horne, Tony	5-9/173	3-21-76	3	Clemson	FA/98	12/0
87	Proehl, Ricky	6-0/190	3-7-68	11	Wake Forest	UFA/98	15/2
45	Robinson, Jeff (TE)	6-4/275	2-20-70	8	Idaho	UFA/97	16/9
86	Williams, Roland (TE)	6-5/269	4-27-75	3	Syracuse	D4b/98	16/15
	OFFENSIVE LINEMEN						
72	Kline, Andrew (G)	6-2/303	10-5-76	R	San Diego State	D7/00	—
67	McCollum, Andy (G)	6-4/295	6-2-70	7	Toledo	UFA/99	16/2
71	Noa, Kaulana (T)	6-3/307	12-29-76	R	Hawaii	D4/00	—
61	Nutten, Tom (G)	6-5/300	6-8-71	4	Western Michigan	FA/98	14/14
76	Pace, Orlando (T)	6-7/320	11-4-75	4	Ohio State	D1/97	16/16
73	Spikes, Cameron (G)	6-2/310	11-6-76	2	Texas A&M	D5/99	5/0
70	St. Clair, John (C)	6-4/293	7-15-77	R	Virginia	D3/00	—
62	Timmerman, Adam (G)	6-4/300	8-14-71	6	South Dakota State	UFA/99	16/16
50	Tucker, Ryan (C)	6-5/305	6-12-75	4	Texas Christian	D4/97	16/0
	DEFENSIVE LINEMEN						
99	Agnew, Ray (T)	6-3/285	12-9-67	11	North Carolina State	UFA/98	16/16
92	Barnes, Lionel (E)	6-4/264	4-19-76	2	Northeast Louisiana	D6/99	3/0
93	Carter, Kevin (E)	6-5/280	9-21-73	6	Florida	D1/95	16/16
75	Farr, D'Marco (T)	6-1/280	6-9-71	7	Washington	FA/94	16/16
95	Hobgood-Chittick, Nate (T)	6-3/290	11-30-74	3	North Carolina	FA/99	10/1
94	Hyder, Gaylon (T)	6-5/290	10-18-74	2	Texas Christian	FA/99	4/0
96	Moran, Sean (E)	6-3/275	6-5-73	5	Colorado State	UFA/00	*16/0
98	Wistrom, Grant (E)	6-4/267	7-3-76	3	Nebraska	D1/98	16/16
66	Young, Brian (E)	6-2/278	7-8-77	R	Texas-El Paso	D5/00	—
90	Zgonina, Jeff (T)	6-2/300	5-24-70	8	Purdue	UFA/99	16/0
	LINEBACKERS						
54	Collins, Todd	6-2/248	5-27-70	8	Carson-Newman (Tenn.)	UFA/99	16/13
59	Fletcher, London	5-10/241	5-19-75	3	John Carroll	FA/98	16/16
52	Jones, Mike	6-1/240	4-15-69	10	Missouri	UFA/97	16/16
57	Little, Leonard	6-3/237	10-19-74	3	Tennessee	D3/98	6/0
53	Miller, Keith	6-1/238	7-9-76	R	California	FA/00	—
91	Pelshak, Troy	6-2/242	3-6-77	2	North Carolina A&T		9/0
	DEFENSIVE BACKS						
20	Allen, Taje (CB)	5-10/185	11-6-73	4	Texas	D5/97	16/2
32	Bly, Dre' (CB)	5-9/185	5-22-77	2	North Carolina	D2/99	16/2
39	Bowen, Matt (S)	6-1/202	11-12-76	R	Iowa	D6/00	—
23	Bush, Devin (S)	6-0/210	7-3-73	6	Florida State	UFA/99	16/7
38	Coady, Rich (S)	6-0/203	1-26-76	2	Texas A&M	D3/99	16/0
26	Crosby, Clifton (CB)	5-9/172	9-17-74	1	Maryland	FA/99	1/0
41	Lyght, Todd (CB)	6-0/190	2-9-69	10	Notre Dame	D1/91	16/16
35	Lyle, Keith (S)	6-2/210	4-17-72	7	Virginia	D3/94	9/9
21	McCleon, Dexter (CB)	5-10/195	10-9-73	4	Clemson	D2/97	15/15
22	Shepherd, Jacoby (CB)	6-1/195	8-31-79	R	Oklahoma State	D2/00	—
	SPECIALISTS						
11	Tuten, Rick (P)	6-2/221	1-5-65	12	Florida State	UFA/98	8/0
14	Wilkins, Jeff (K)	6-2/205	4-19-72	7	Youngstown State	FA/97	16/0

*Not with Rams in 1999.
Other free agent veterans invited to camp: WR Darrius Blevins, CB Darwin Brown, LB Matt Chatham, K Jeff Hall, WR Siaha Burley, LB Bryan Jones, RB James Kidd, TE Derek Lewis, DT Barry Mitchell, RB Damon Washington.
Abbreviations: D1—draft pick, first round; SD-2—supplemental draft pick, second round; W—claimed on waivers; T—obtained in trade; PlanB—Plan B free-agent acquisition; FA—free-agent acquisition (other than Plan B); UFA—unconditional free agent acquisition; ED—expansion draft pick.

MISCELLANEOUS TEAM DATA

Stadium (capacity, surface):
Trans World Dome (66,000, artificial)
Business address:
1 Rams Way
St. Louis, MO 63045
Business phone:
314-982-7267
Ticket information:
314-425-8830
Team colors:
Rams navy blue, Rams gold
Flagship radio station:
KLOU, 103.3 FM; KATZ, 1600 AM
Training site:
Western Illinois University
Macomb, Ill.
314-982-7267

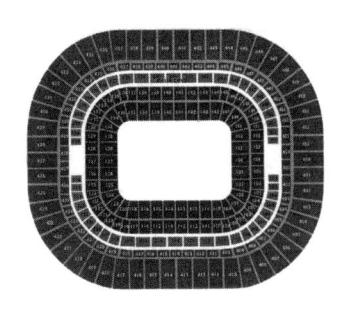

ST. LOUIS RAMS

TSN REPORT CARD

Coaching staff	B	The same qualities that characterized Mike Martz as an offensive coordinator—confidence and a willingness to take chances—will drive him as a head coach. How he responds to the pressure of being the head man, and the pressure of taking over a Super Bowl championship team, remains to be seen. The addition of running backs coach Bobby Jackson and special teams coach Larry Pasquale are pluses.
Quarterbacks	A	Kurt Warner is coming off one of the best seasons ever logged by an NFL quarterback. Judging by his off-season work habits, he seems determined to show he's no one-year wonder. Even if he is, the Rams have one of the best insurance policies in the NFL in Trent Green, who is good enough to start for several clubs.
Running backs	B +	After setting a league record for yards from scrimmage (2,429) last season, Marshall Faulk deserves consideration as one of the best all-purpose backs in NFL history. A few more productive seasons will cement the argument, and Faulk has plenty of tread left on his tires. At fullback, Robert Holcombe has yet to show the kind of consistency to be considered an elite player at his position.
Receivers	A	There isn't a better quartet in the league than Isaac Bruce, Torry Holt, Az-Zahir Hakim and Ricky Proehl. Bruce, Holt and Hakim are shifty playmakers who excel after the catch. Proehl has developed into a clutch third-down receiver, adept at getting the necessary yards to keep the chains moving.
Offensive line	B -	The Rams have an anchor on the left in tackle Orlando Pace, and an anchor on the right in guard Adam Timmerman. Left guard Tom Nutten played like a Pro Bowler in the postseason. But there will be a new center (Andy McCollum) and a new right tackle (Ryan Tucker) in the starting lineup, and depth is a concern.
Defensive line	B +	Kevin Carter and Grant Wistrom emerged as the best young defensive end tandem in the league a year ago. Carter has become a disruptive sack master, and Wistrom never takes a play off. Tackles D'Marco Farr and Ray Agnew are a tad undersized, but Farr has one of the quickest first steps in the game. Agnew is a steady, resourceful influence.
Linebackers	B	This group overachieved a year ago—can it do so again? Long before "The Tackle" in the Super Bowl, outside backer Mike Jones was enjoying a career year. Speedy London Fletcher quickly established himself as one of the better middle linebackers in the game. Leonard Little could press Todd Collins for playing time.
Secondary	B	Todd Lyght may fall short of "shutdown corner" status, but the 10-year veteran plays at a high level. Dexter McCleon is developing into a solid NFL corner, and nickel back Dre' Bly has uncanny ball instincts and plays with aggressiveness. Devin Bush finally gets his chance to start at strong safety. Free safety Keith Lyle is one of the best in the business.
Special teams	B	Tony Horne is one of the most dangerous kickoff return men in the game. Who knows how many kickoffs he would have returned for touchdowns last season were it not for a four-game drug suspension? Hakim is an above average punt returner who is also capable of taking it the distance. Veterans Jeff Wilkins (kicker) and Rick Tuten (punter) are coming off injury-plagued '99 seasons.

SAN DIEGO CHARGERS
AFC WESTERN DIVISION

2000 SEASON

CLUB DIRECTORY

Chairman of the board
Alex G. Spanos
President/vice chairman
Dean A. Spanos
Executive vice president
Michael A. Spanos
General manager
Bobby Beathard
Vice president/finance
Jeremiah T. Murphy
Chief financial & administrative officer
Jeanne Bonk
Director/player personnel
Billy Devaney
Director/pro personnel
Greg Gaines
Coordinator/football operations
Ed McGuire
Business manager
John Hinek
Director/ticket operations
Mike Dougherty
Director/public relations
Bill Johnston
Director/sales and marketing
To be announced
Director/security
Dick Lewis
Trainer
James Collins
Equipment manager
Bob Wick
Director/video operations
Brian Duddy

Head coach
Mike Riley

Assistant coaches
DelVaughn Alexander (offensive assistant)
Mark Banker (defensive coverage)
Joe Bugel (offensive line)
Geep Chryst (offensive coordinator)
Paul Chryst (tight ends)
John Hastings (strength & conditioning)
Mike Johnson (quarterbacks)
Andrew McClave (def. assistant)
Wayne Nunnely (defensive line)
Joe Pascale (defensive coordinator)
Rod Perry (defensive backs)
Bruce Read (special teams)
Mike Sanford (wide receivers)
Mike Schleelein (strength & conditioning assistant)
Jim Vechiarella (linebackers)
Ollie Wilson (running backs)

SCHEDULE

Sept. 3—	at Oakland	4:15
Sept. 10—	NEW ORLEANS	4:15
Sept. 17—	at Kansas City	1:00
Sept. 24—	SEATTLE	4:15
Oct. 1—	at St. Louis	1:00
Oct. 8—	DENVER	4:15
Oct. 15—	at Buffalo	1:00
Oct. 22—	Open date	
Oct. 29—	OAKLAND	8:35
Nov. 5—	at Seattle	4:15
Nov. 12—	MIAMI	4:05
Nov. 19—	at Denver	4:05
Nov. 26—	KANSAS CITY	4:15
Dec. 3—	SAN FRANCISCO	4:05
Dec. 10—	at Baltimore	1:00
Dec. 17—	at Carolina	1:00
Dec. 24—	PITTSBURGH	4:05

All times are Eastern.
All games Sunday unless noted.

DRAFT CHOICES

Rogers Beckett, S, Marshall (second round/43rd pick overall).
Damion McIntosh, T, Kansas St. (3/83).
Trevor Gaylor, WR, Miami of Ohio (4/111).
Leonardo Carson, DE, Auburn (4/113).
Shannon Taylor, LB, Virginia (6/184).
Damen Wheeler, DB, Colorado (6/203).
JaJuan Seider, QB, Florida A&M (6/205).
Jason Thomas, G, Hampton (7/222).

1999 REVIEW

RESULTS

Sept.12—	Open date		
Sept.19—	at Cincinnati	W	34-7
Sept.26—	INDIANAPOLIS	L	19-27
Oct. 3—	KANSAS CITY	W	21-14
Oct. 10—	at Detroit	W	20-10
Oct. 17—	SEATTLE	W	13-10
Oct. 24—	GREEN BAY	L	3-31
Oct. 31—	at Kansas City	L	0-34
Nov. 7—	DENVER	L	17-33
Nov. 14—	at Oakland	L	9-28
Nov. 21—	CHICAGO (OT)	L	20-23
Nov. 28—	at Minnesota	L	27-35
Dec. 5—	CLEVELAND	W	23-10
Dec. 12—	at Seattle	W	19-16
Dec. 19—	at Miami	L	9-12
Dec. 26—	OAKLAND	W	23-20
Jan. 2—	at Denver	W	12-6

RECORDS/RANKINGS

1999 regular-season record: 8-8 (3rd in AFC West); 5-3 in division; 7-5 in conference; 1-3 vs. NFC; 4-4 at home; 4-4 on road; 3-1 on turf; 5-7 on grass.
Team record last five years: 34-46 (.425, ranks 24th in league in that span).
1999 team rankings:

	No.	AFC	NFL
Total offense	*286.8	15	26
Rushing offense	*77.9	15	27
Passing offense	*208.9	9	18
Scoring offense	269	15	28
Total defense	*306.6	9	12
Rushing defense	*82.6	2	3
Passing defense	*224.0	13	22
Scoring defense	316	7	10
Takeaways	27	T11	T22
Giveaways	35	16	T23
Turnover differential	-8	15	T25
Sacks	41	T7	T12
Sacks allowed	46	11	22

*Yards per game.

TEAM LEADERS

Scoring (kicking): John Carney, 115 pts. (22/23 PATs, 31/36 FGs).
Scoring (touchdowns): Natrone Means, 30 pts. (4 rushing, 1 receiving).
Passing: Jim Harbaugh, 2,761 yds. (434 att., 249 comp., 57.4%, 10 TDs, 14 int.).
Rushing: Jermaine Fazande, 365 yds. (91 att., 4.0 avg., 2 TDs).
Receptions: Jeff Graham, 57 (968 yds., 17.0 avg., 2 TDs).
Interceptions: Darryll Lewis, 4 (9 yds., 0 TDs); Jimmy Spencer, 4 (1 yds., 0 TDs).
Sacks: Raylee Johnson, 10.5.
Punting: Darren Bennett, 43.9 avg. (89 punts, 3,910 yds., 0 blocked).
Punt returns: Chris Penn, 7.0 avg. (21 att., 148 yds., 0 TDs).
Kickoff returns: Kenny Bynum, 21.1 avg. (37 att., 781 yds., 0 TDs).

2000 SEASON
TRAINING CAMP ROSTER

SAN DIEGO CHARGERS

No.	QUARTERBACKS	Ht./Wt.	Born	NFL Exp.	College	How acq.	'99 Games GP/GS
4	Harbaugh, Jim	6-3/215	12-23-63	14	Michigan	T-Bal./99	14/12
16	Leaf, Ryan	6-5/235	5-15-76	3	Washington State	D1/98	0/0
13	Moreno, Moses	6-1/205	9-5-75	3	Colorado State	FA/99	1/0
7	Seider, Ja Juan	6-1/230	4-16-77	R	Florida A&M	D6c/00	—
	RUNNING BACKS						
43	Bynum, Kenny	5-11/191	5-29-74	4	South Carolina State	D5a/97	16/5
32	Chancey, Robert	6-0/252	9-7-72	4	None	FA/00	*3/0
35	Fazande, Jermaine	6-2/255	1-14-75	2	Oklahoma	D2/99	7/3
41	Fletcher, Terrell	5-8/196	9-14-73	6	Wisconsin	D2b/95	15/2
33	Harris, Derrick (FB)	6-0/252	9-18-72	5	Miami (Fla.)	FA/00	*1/0
44	McCrary, Fred (FB)	6-0/235	9-19-72	4	Mississippi State	FA/99	16/14
34	Stephens, Tremayne	5-11/206	4-16-76	3	North Carolina State	W-Ind./99	11/2
	RECEIVERS						
80	Conway, Curtis	6-1/196	1-13-71	8	Southern California	UFA/00	9/8
84	Davis, Reggie (TE)	6-3/233	9-3-76	2	Washington	FA/99	16/3
19	Gaylor, Trevor	6-3/195	11-3-77	R	Miami (Ohio)	D4a/00	—
81	Graham, Jeff	6-2/206	2-14-69	10	Ohio State	FA/99	16/11
83	Heiden, Steve (TE)	6-5/270	9-21-76	2	South Dakota State	D3/99	11/0
82	Jones, Charlie	5-8/175	12-1-72	5	Fresno State	D4/96	8/1
88	Jones, Freddie (TE)	6-5/270	9-16-74	4	North Carolina	D2/97	16/16
85	Reed, Robert	6-1/203	1-14-75	2	Lambuth (Tenn.)	FA/99	3/0
86	Ricks, Mikhael	6-5/237	11-14-74	3	Stephen F. Austin State	D2/98	16/15
15	Williams, Stepfret	6-0/175	6-14-73	4	Northeast Louisiana	FA/00	*0/0
	OFFENSIVE LINEMEN						
50	Binn, David (C)	6-3/245	2-6-72	7	California	FA/94	16/0
60	Brown, Wilbert (G)	6-2/310	5-9-77	2	Houston	FA/99	5/0
67	Fortin, Roman (C)	6-5/297	2-26-67	11	San Diego State	FA/98	16/16
71	Graham, DeMingo (G)	6-3/310	9-10-73	2	Hofstra	FA/98	16/10
65	Jackson, John (T)	6-6/297	1-4-65	13	Eastern Kentucky	UFA/98	15/15
64	Jacox, Kendyl (C)	6-2/330	6-10-75	3	Kansas State	FA/98	10/5
77	McIntosh, Damion (T)	6-4/325	3-25-77	R	Kansas State	D3/00	—
66	Nelson, Reggie (G)	6-4/310	6-23-76	2	McNeese State	D5b/99	2/0
70	Parker, Vaughn (T)	6-3/300	6-5-71	7	UCLA	D2b/94	15/15
68	Patton, Joe (G)	6-4/310	1-5-72	6	Alabama A&M	UFA/00	*0/0
74	Roundtree, Raleigh (G)	6-4/295	8-31-75	4	South Carolina State	D4/97	15/5
63	Thomas, Jason (G)	6-3/300	6-10-77	R	Hampton (Va.)	D7/00	—
	DEFENSIVE LINEMEN						
96	Carson, Leonardo (T)	6-2/285	2-11-77	R	Auburn	D4b/00	—
	Fontenot, Al (E)	6-4/287	9-17-70	8	Baylor	FA/99	15/15
92	Harden, Cedric (E)	6-6/260	10-19-74	2	Florida A&M	D5/98	5/0
99	Johnson, Raylee (E)	6-3/272	6-1-70	8	Arkansas	D4a/93	16/16
93	Mickell, Darren (E)	6-5/285	8-3-70	8	Florida	FA/00	*1/0
98	Mohring, Michael (T)	6-5/295	3-22-74	4	Pittsburgh	FA/97	16/1
97	Parrella, John (T)	6-3/300	11-22-69	8	Nebraska	FA/94	16/16
76	Williams, Jamal (T)	6-3/305	4-28-76	3	Oklahoma State	SD-2/98	16/2
	LINEBACKERS						
51	Dixon, Gerald	6-3/250	6-20-69	8	South Carolina	UFA/98	14/1
53	Hamilton, Michael	6-2/245	12-3-73	4	North Carolina A&T	D3/97	14/2
54	Hill, Eric	6-2/265	11-14-66	12	Louisiana State	FA/99	12/10
52	Reeves, John	6-3/236	2-23-75	2	Purdue	FA/99	5/0
56	Ruff, Orlando	6-3/247	9-28-76	2	Furman	FA/99	14/0
55	Seau, Junior	6-3/250	1-19-69	11	Southern California	D1/90	14/14
94	Taylor, Shannon	6-3/247	2-16-75	R	Virginia	D6a/00	—
	DEFENSIVE BACKS						
45	Beckett, Rogers (S)	6-3/205	1-31-77	R	Marshall	D2/00	—
24	Brown, Fakhir (S)	5-11/192	9-21-77	2	Grambling State	FA/99	9/3
38	Dumas, Mike (S)	6-0/202	3-18-69	9	Indiana	FA/97	14/14
37	Harrison, Rodney (S)	6-1/207	12-15-72	7	Western Illinois	D5b/94	6/6
42	Jackson, Greg (S)	6-1/217	8-20-66	12	Louisiana State	UFA/97	14/9
23	Jenkins, DeRon (CB)	5-11/192	11-14-73	5	Tennessee	UFA/00	*16/15
26	Lewis, Darryll (CB)	5-9/188	12-16-68	10	Arizona	FA/99	13/8
31	Perry, Jason (S)	6-0/200	8-1-76	2	North Carolina State	D4/99	16/5
25	Rusk, Reggie (CB)	5-10/190	12-19-72	4	Kentucky	FA/98	9/0
21	Turner, Scott (CB)	5-10/180	2-26-72	6	Illinois	W-Was./98	15/0
28	Vance, Eric (S)	6-2/218	7-14-75	3	Vanderbilt	FA/00	*6/0
22	Wheeler, Damen (CB)	5-9/170	9-3-77	R	Colorado	D6b/00	—
	SPECIALISTS						
2	Bennett, Darren (P)	6-5/235	1-9-65	6	None	FA/94	16/0
3	Carney, John (K)	5-11/170	4-20-64	12	Notre Dame	FA/90	16/0
6	Cortez, Jose (K)	5-11/205	5-27-75	1	Oregon State	FA/00	*1/0

– 81 –

*Not with Chargers in 1999.

Other free agent veterans invited to camp: G Rick Austin, QB Sherdrick Bonner, CB Tony Darden, DE Adrian Dingle, CB Dwight Henry, LB Richard Hogans, TE Wendell Davis, WR Reggie Jones, WR Calvin Schexnayder, OT Pete Swanson, WR Kevin Swayne, DT Pene Talamaivao.

Abbreviations: D1—draft pick, first round; SD-2—supplemental draft pick, second round; W—claimed on waivers; T—obtained in trade; PlanB—Plan B free-agent acquisition; FA—free-agent acquisition (other than Plan B); UFA—unconditional free agent acquisition; ED—expansion draft pick.

MISCELLANEOUS TEAM DATA

Stadium (capacity, surface):
Qualcomm Stadium
(71,000, grass)
Business address:
P.O. Box 609609
San Diego, CA 92160-9609
Business phone:
858-874-4500
Ticket information:
619-280-2121
Team colors:
Navy blue, white and gold
Flagship radio station:
KFMB, 760 AM/STAR 100.7 FM
Training site:
UC San Diego
La Jolla, Calif.
858-455-1976

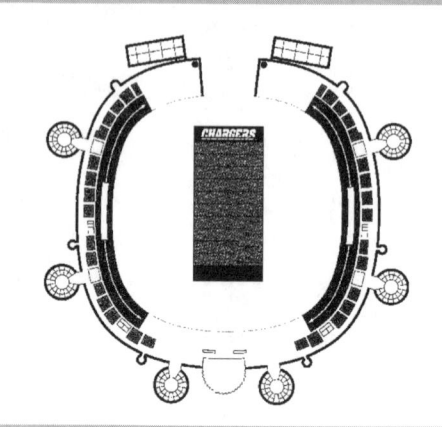

TSN REPORT CARD

Coaching staff	B+	Mike Riley has half the battle won. His players love him. On top of it, he's very bright and well-organized. Riley never seems to have a bad day. Win or lose, he always seems the same. He's also fortunate to have a good blend of veteran and young minds on his staff and they all seem to get along. Defensive coordinator Joe Pascale is a miracle worker, a head coaching candidate waiting to happen.
Quarterbacks	C-	Incumbent Jim Harbaugh had trouble throwing the ball 50 yards in minicamp. He's 36 years old and still game, but he may be ready for retirement. He also hasn't completed a 16-game season since 1991. Third-year pro Moses Moreno is the favorite to take his place, but Moreno is very green and remains a definite wait-and-see, which is not a good sign heading into a season. Ryan Leaf? Nobody knows and many people don't care.
Running backs	C-	Now that Natrone Means has been released, youth will be served. Jermaine Fazande and Robert Chancey will be the big backs Nos. 1 and 2, and both are inexperienced. Fazande is the favorite based on his 183-yard rushing performance in the season finale against Denver. Chancey seems more the fullback type and may see duty there, what with Fred McCrary the only real fullback on the roster. The versatile Terrell Fletcher will be the third-down back.
Receivers	B	Only veteran Jeff Graham played well a year ago and even he had his bad moments. Help is on the way. With the arrival of free-agent speedster Curtis Conway from Chicago, the Chargers have their first real deep threat since Tony Martin. Graham and Conway should make a nice tandem. Rookie Trevor Gaylor is 6-3, can flat run and already has impressed the staff. Robert Reed is a marvelous athlete, but that No. 4 spot appears up for grabs.
Offensive line	D	If this team is going anywhere, the line must improve. Especially its run blocking, which was dismal in '99, when the backs averaged 3.0 yards per rush. Left tackle John Jackson is aging and left guard Kendyl Jacox has had weight and injury problems. Every man is a veteran, so there is no excuse for another subpar performance, especially with famed offensive line guru Joe Bugel coaching them.
Defensive line	B	The line was not overwhelming in the pass rushing department, although end Raylee Johnson is coming off a breakout season in which he totaled 10.5 sacks. The loss of Norman Hand to free agency hurts depth at tackle, although Jamal Williams and John Parrella are more than capable. Al Fontenot was a surprise at the other end position. There isn't much depth, but these guys play hard.
Linebackers	B	All three starters—Junior Seau and Gerald Dixon on the outside and Eric Hill in the middle—are in their 30's. Seau remains a great player, perhaps the best all-around linebacker of his generation. The team will miss outside man Lew Bush, who has left for Kansas City, but Dixon, while not the run-stopper Bush was, is a better pass rusher. Hill is just a solid, no-nonsense veteran.
Secondary	B	It should be better. Disappointing corner Terrance Shaw was released after DeRon Jenkins was brought in as a free agent from Baltimore. Rookie Fakhir Brown was the favorite to win the job on the other side but he tore the labrum in his right shoulder in an April auto accident. He's expected to be ready by training camp and will battle veteran playmaker Darryll Lewis. Impact strong safety Rodney Harrison seems to have recovered from shoulder surgery, which is the biggest plus of this offseason.
Special teams	B	The search for a return specialist failed. So it will either be Reed or Charlie Jones returning punts and Kenny Bynum returning kickoffs. Bynum is average at best, Reed has great potential, Jones is so-so. The kick coverage improved dramatically last year after a horrible 1998. Kicker John Carney and punter Darren Bennett are two of the very best. David Binn is an expert long snapper.

– 82 –

SAN FRANCISCO 49ERS
NFC WESTERN DIVISION

2000 SEASON

CLUB DIRECTORY

Chairman/owner
Denise DeBartolo-York
Vice president
John York
V.p./general manager
Bill Walsh
V.p./director of football administration
John McVay
V.p./business operations and CFO
Keith Lenhart
Director of player personnel
Terry Donahue
Pro personnel director
Bill McPherson
Controller
Melrene Frear
Dir. of communications & marketing
Rodney Knox
Director of public relations
Kirk Reynolds
Public relations assistants
Tom Hastings
Kristin Johnson
Darla Maeda
Chad Steele
Scouts
Jim Abrams   John Brunner
Brian Gardner   Jeremy Green
Jim Gruden   Oscar Lofton
Head trainer
Lindsy McLean
Assistant trainers
Todd Lazenby
Jeff Tanaka
Physicians
Michael Dillingham, M.D.
James Klint, M.D.
Stadium operations director
Murlan "Mo" Fowell

Head coach
Steve Mariucci

Assistant coaches
Jerry Attaway (physical development coordinator)
Mike Barnes (strength development coordinator)
Joe Barry (def. quality control)
Tom Batta (tight ends)
Chris Beake (defensive assistant)
Dwaine Board (defensive line)
Bruce DeHaven (special teams)
Greg Knapp (quarterbacks)
Brett Maxie (defensive assistant/secondary)
Jim Mora (defensive coordinator)
Marty Mornhinweg (offensive coordinator)
Patrick Morris (offensive line)
Tom Rathman (running backs)
Richard Smith (linebackers)
George Stewart (wide receivers)
Andy Sugarman (off. assistant)

Equipment manager
Kevin "Tique" Lartigue
Equipment assistants
Mike McBride
Nick Pettit
Steve Urbaniak

SCHEDULE

Sept. 3—	at Atlanta	1:00
Sept. 10—	CAROLINA	4:15
Sept. 17—	at St. Louis	1:00
Sept. 24—	at Dallas	1:00
Oct. 1—	ARIZONA	4:15
Oct. 8—	OAKLAND	4:15
Oct. 15—	at Green Bay	4:15
Oct. 22—	at Carolina	1:00
Oct. 29—	ST. LOUIS	4:05
Nov. 5—	at New Orleans	1:00
Nov. 12—	KANSAS CITY	4:05
Nov. 19—	ATLANTA	4:15
Nov. 26—	Open date	
Dec. 3—	at San Diego	4:05
Dec. 10—	NEW ORLEANS	4:15
Dec. 17—	CHICAGO	4:05
Dec. 23—	at Denver (Sat.)	4:15

All times are Eastern.
All games Sunday unless noted.

DRAFT CHOICES

Julian Peterson, LB, Michigan State (first round/16th pick overall).
Ahmed Plummer, DB, Ohio State (1/24).
John Engelberger, DE, Va. Tech (2/35).
Jason Webster, DB, Texas A&M (2/48).
Giovanni Carmazzi, QB, Hofstra (3/65).
Jeff Ulbrich, LB, Hawaii (3/86).
John Keith, S, Furman (4/108).
Paul Smith, RB, Texas-El Paso (5/132).
John Milem, DE, Lenoir-Rhyne (5/150).
Tim Rattay, QB, Louisiana Tech (7/212).
Brian Jennings, TE, Arizona St. (7/230).

1999 REVIEW

RESULTS

Sept.12—	at Jacksonville	L	3-41
Sept.19—	NEW ORLEANS	W	28-21
Sept.27—	at Arizona	W	24-10
Oct. 3—	TENNESSEE	W	24-22
Oct. 10—	at St. Louis	L	20-42
Oct. 17—	CAROLINA	L	29-31
Oct. 24—	at Minnesota	L	16-40
Oct. 31—	Open date		
Nov. 7—	PITTSBURGH	L	6-27
Nov. 14—	at New Orleans	L	6-24
Nov. 21—	ST. LOUIS	L	7-23
Nov. 29—	GREEN BAY	L	3-20
Dec. 5—	at Cincinnati	L	30-44
Dec. 12—	ATLANTA	W	26-7
Dec. 18—	at Carolina	L	24-41
Dec. 26—	WASHINGTON (OT)	L	20-26
Jan. 3—	at Atlanta	L	29-34

RECORDS/RANKINGS

1999 regular-season record: 4-12 (4th in NFC West); 2-6 in division; 3-9 in conference; 1-3 vs. AFC; 3-5 at home; 1-7 on road; 0-5 on turf; 4-7 on grass.
Team record last five years: 52-28 (.650, ranks 3rd in league in that span).

1999 team rankings:

	No.	NFC	NFL
Total offense	*336.3	7	10
Rushing offense	*130.9	1	1
Passing offense	*205.3	11	21
Scoring offense	295	9	22
Total defense	*355.4	13	28
Rushing defense	*101.2	7	15
Passing defense	*254.3	15	31
Scoring defense	453	15	30
Takeaways	20	14	T29
Giveaways	32	T5	T16
Turnover differential	-12	13	29
Sacks	32	T13	T27
Sacks allowed	34	4	T8

*Yards per game.

TEAM LEADERS

Scoring (kicking): Wade Richey, 93 pts. (30/31 PATs, 21/23 FGs).
Scoring (touchdowns): Charlie Garner, 36 pts. (4 rushing, 2 receiving).
Passing: Jeff Garcia, 2,544 yds. (375 att., 225 comp., 60.0%, 11 TDs, 11 int.).
Rushing: Charlie Garner, 1,229 yds. (241 att., 5.1 avg., 4 TDs).
Receptions: Jerry Rice, 67 (830 yds., 12.4 avg., 5 TDs).
Interceptions: Lance Schulters, 6 (127 yds., 1 TD).
Sacks: Bryant Young, 11.0.
Punting: Chad Stanley, 39.7 avg. (69 punts, 2,737 yds., 2 blocked).
Punt returns: R.W. McQuarters, 5.0 avg. (18 att., 90 yds., 0 TDs).
Kickoff returns: R.W. McQuarters, 21.8 avg. (26 att., 568 yds., 0 TDs).

2000 SEASON
TRAINING CAMP ROSTER

SAN FRANCISCO 49ERS

No.	QUARTERBACKS	Ht./Wt.	Born	NFL Exp.	College	How acq.	'99 Games GP/GS
19	Carmazzi, Giovanni	6-3/224	4-14-77	R	Hofstra	D3a/00	—
5	Garcia, Jeff	6-1/195	2-24-70	2	San Jose State	FA/99	13/10
13	Rattay, Tim	6-0/215	3-15-77	R	Louisiana Tech	D7a/00	—
8	Young, Steve	6-2/215	10-11-61	16	Brigham Young	T-TB/87	3/3
	RUNNING BACKS						
40	Beasley, Fred (FB)	6-0/235	9-18-74	2	Auburn	D6/98	13/11
25	Garner, Charlie	5-9/187	2-13-72	7	Tennessee	FA/99	16/15
20	Hearst, Garrison	5-11/215	1-4-71	8	Georgia	FA/97	0/0
22	Jackson, Terry	6-0/218	1-10-76	2	Florida	D5a/99	16/0
32	Jervey, Travis	6-0/222	5-5-72	6	The Citadel	UFA/99	8/0
27	Smith, Paul	5-11/234	1-31-78	R	Texas-El Paso	D5a/00	—
	RECEIVERS						
82	Bell, Shonn (TE)	6-5/257	10-25-74	2	Clinch Valley (Va.)	FA/98	2/0
85	Clark, Greg (TE)	6-4/251	4-7-72	4	Stanford	D3/97	12/11
86	Jennings, Brian (TE)	6-5/238	10-14-76	R	Arizona State	D7/00	—
81	Owens, Terrell	6-3/217	12-7-73	5	Tennessee-Chattanooga	D3/96	14/14
80	Rice, Jerry	6-2/196	10-13-62	16	Mississippi Valley State	D1/85	16/16
83	Stokes, J.J.	6-4/217	10-6-72	6	UCLA	D1/95	16/7
89	Streets, Tai	6-1/193	4-20-77	2	Michigan	D6/99	2/0
45	Swift, Justin (TE)	6-3/265	8-14-75	1	Kansas State	FA/00	*1/0
	OFFENSIVE LINEMEN						
65	Brown, Ray (G)	6-5/318	12-12-62	15	Arkansas State	FA/96	16/16
67	Dalman, Chris (C)	6-3/297	3-15-70	8	Stanford	D6/93	15/15
63	Deese, Derrick (T)	6-3/289	5-17-70	9	Southern California	FA/92	16/16
79	Dercher, Dan (T)	6-5/293	6-26-76	2	Kansas	FA/99	9/0
74	Fiore, Dave (T)	6-4/290	8-10-74	5	Hofstra	FA/97	16/16
66	Hopson, Tyrone (G)	6-2/305	5-28-76	2	Eastern Kentucky	D5b/99	1/0
60	Lynch, Ben (C)	6-4/295	11-18-72	2	California	FA/99	16/1
62	Newberry, Jeremy (G)	6-5/315	3-23-76	3	California	D2/98	16/16
69	Ostrowski, Phil (G)	6-4/291	9-23-75	3	Penn State	D5/98	15/0
	DEFENSIVE LINEMEN						
90	Bryant, Junior (T)	6-4/278	1-16-71	6	Notre Dame	FA/93	16/16
95	Engelberger, John (E)	6-4/260	10-18-76	R	Virginia Tech	D2a/00	—
92	McGrew, Reggie (T)	6-1/301	12-16-76	2	Florida	D1/99	0/0
93	Milem, John (E)	6-7/290	6-9-75	R	Lenoir-Rhyne	D5b/00	—
91	Okeafor, Chike (E)	6-4/248	3-27-76	2	Purdue	D3/99	12/0
96	Posey, Jeff (E)	6-4/240	8-14-75	3	Southern Mississippi	FA/98	16/6
98	Wilkins, Gabe (E)	6-5/305	9-1-71	7	Gardner-Webb (N.C.)	D4/94	16/15
97	Young, Bryant (T)	6-3/291	1-27-72	7	Notre Dame	D1/94	16/16
	LINEBACKERS						
51	Norton, Ken	6-2/254	9-29-66	13	UCLA	UFA/94	16/16
58	Peterson, Julian	6-3/235	7-28-78	R	Michigan State	D1a/00	—
55	Tubbs, Winfred	6-4/254	9-24-70	8	Texas	D3/94	16/15
53	Ulbrich, Jeff	6-0/249	2-17-77	R	Hawaii	D3b/00	—
56	Wesley, Joe	6-1/229	11-10-76	2	Louisiana State	FA/99	8/0
	DEFENSIVE BACKS						
31	Bronson, Zack (S)	6-1/195	1-28-74	4	McNeese State	FA/97	15/2
28	Keith, John (S)	6-0/207	2-4-77	R	Furman	D4/00	—
35	McDonald, Ramos (CB)	5-11/194	4-30-76	3	New Mexico	W-Min/99	14/12
21	McQuarters, R.W. (CB)	5-9/198	12-21-76	3	Oklahoma State	D1/98	11/4
24	Montgomery, Monty (CB)	5-11/197	12-8-73	4	Houston	FA/99	7/2
29	Plummer, Ahmed (CB)	5-11/191	3-26-76	R	Ohio State	D1b/00	—
23	Prioleau, Pierson (CB)	5-10/191	8-6-77	2	Virginia Tech	D4b/99	14/5
30	Schulters, Lance (S)	6-2/195	5-27-75	3	Hofstra	D4/98	13/13
36	Webster, Jason (CB)	5-9/180	9-8-77	R	Texas A&M	D2b/00	—
	SPECIALISTS						
7	Richey, Wade (K)	6-4/200	5-19-76	3	Louisiana State	FA/98	16/0
4	Stanley, Chad (P)	6-3/205	1-29-76	2	Stephen F. Austin	FA/99	16/0

*Not with 49ers in 1999.

Other free agent veterans invited to camp: OT Dwayne Ledford, CB Anthony Parker, OT Jason Tenner.

Abbreviations: D1—draft pick, first round; SD-2—supplemental draft pick, second round; W—claimed on waivers; T—obtained in trade; PlanB—Plan B free-agent acquisition; FA—free-agent acquisition (other than Plan B); UFA—unconditional free agent acquisition; ED—expansion draft pick.

MISCELLANEOUS TEAM DATA

Stadium (capacity, surface):
3Com Park at Candlestick Point
(70,270, grass)
Business address:
4949 Centennial Blvd.
Santa Clara, CA 95054-1229
Business phone:
408-562-4949
Ticket information:
415-656-4900
Team colors:
Forty Niners gold and cardinal
Flagship radio station:
KGO, 810 AM
Training site:
University of Pacific
Stockton, Calif.
209-932-4949

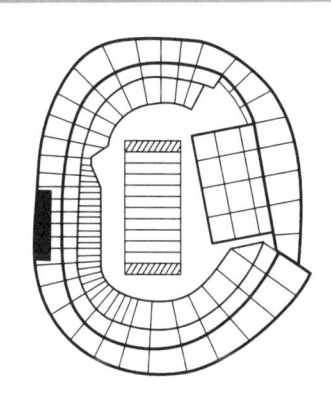

SAN FRANCISCO 49ERS

TSN REPORT CARD

Coaching staff	C +	Steve Mariucci didn't get credit for his 13-3 rookie effort three years ago or blame for his 4-12 record last season. But after finally getting some input on personnel decisions, this is finally his team. The former college coach's energetic "rah-rah" style should work with a young squad, and his history as a quarterback guru will be key.
Quarterbacks	C	Jeff Garcia blames himself for most of the 49ers' offensive woes (non-cohesive line, inactive receivers, inability to develop a running game), but he is brimming with confidence in his second NFL season as he takes a lion's share of the snaps in camp. Last year he caved under pressure after being thrown into the fire.
Running backs	B +	Charlie Garner rescued the team's running attack—not to mention his own career—subbing for Garrison Hearst last year. If Hearst comes back to split time with Garner, worries about Garner's every-down toughness will be appeased. Both are explosive in the open field and the 49ers offense knows how to free them up.
Receivers	B +	No trio of players was as underused in the NFL last year, but with a more experienced quarterback running the show, these weapons can again hurt defenses. As the losses piled on, youngsters Terrell Owens and J.J. Stokes grew disinterested, and Jerry Rice became the unexpected go-to guy during an inconsistent season that hinted at his age.
Offensive line	C	This unit took the biggest strides in '99, growing more cohesive with each week. All five starters return after playing 15 games together and paving the way for the No. 2 rushing offense in the NFL. An unspectacular group that could have used help from the draft will at least play relatively mistake-free after an entire year together.
Defensive line	C -	An absolute absence of an outside pass rush was the 49ers' downfall last year, with all of the pressure coming from the tackles, including one of the league's top defensive players, Bryant Young. The team needs major contributions from younger, faster defensive ends like Jeff Posey, Chike Okeafor and John Engelberger.
Linebackers	C +	The 49ers hope to allow both outside linebackers the freedom to take chances and make things happen. First-round draft pick Julian Peterson will be the team's top pass rushing option when he's not busy covering the tight end. And veteran Ken Norton will again be in on almost every tackle. Inside, Winfred Tubbs needs to pick up the intensity.
Secondary	D +	Three new cornerbacks will be in the mix as the 49ers desperately try to shore up the too-short, too-soft unit that lost too many loose-ball battles and allowed too many deep passes. With opponents trying to exploit the cornerbacks once again, free safety Lance Schulters will continue to make plays on the ball like he did in making the Pro Bowl last year.
Special teams	C -	A large number of speedy defensive rookies should impact last year's horrible kick coverage, but the punter position has not been upgraded. Kicker Wade Richey was the team's MVP in his second year, adding accuracy to the clutch performances he gave in his '98 rookie season. A solid kick returner has yet to be found.

SEATTLE SEAHAWKS
AFC WESTERN DIVISION

2000 SEASON

CLUB DIRECTORY

Owner
Paul Allen
Vice chairman
Bert Kolde
President
Bob Whitsitt
Senior vice president
Mike Reinfeldt
Vice president/football operations
Ted Thompson
V.p./ticket sales & services
Duane McLean
V.p./communications
Gary Wright
Public relations director
Dave Pearson
Community outreach director
Sandy Gregory
Player relations director
Nesby Glasgow
Assistant to the general manager
Gary Reynolds
Admin. assistant/football operations
Bill Nayes
Director of player personnel
John Schneider
College scouting director
Scott McCloughan
Pro scouting director
Will Lewis
Eastern supervisor
To be announced
Western supervisor
To be announced
Scouts
Bucky Brooks   Derrick Jensen
Mike Murphy   John Peterson
Head trainer
Paul Federici
Assistant trainers
James Oglesby Jr.
Sam Ramsden
Ken Smith

Executive v.p. of football ops. /g.m. and head coach
Mike Holmgren

Assistant coaches
Larry Brooks (defensive line)
Jerry Colquitt (off. qual. control)
Nolan Cromwell (wide receivers)
Ken Flajole (linebackers)
Gil Haskell (offensive coordinator)
Johnny Holland (asst. special teams/asst. strength & cond.)
Kent Johnston (strength and conditioning)
Jim Lind (tight ends)
Clayton Lopez (def. qual. control)
Tom Lovat (asst. head coach/offensive line)
Stump Mitchell (running backs)
Dick Roach (defensive backs)
Pete Rodriguez (special teams)
Mike Sheppard (quarterbacks)
Steve Sidwell (def. coordinator)
Rod Springer (assistant strength and conditioning)

Equipment manager
Erik Kennedy
Assistant equipment managers
Jeff Bower
Brad Melland
Video director
Thom Fermstad

SCHEDULE

Sept. 3—	at Miami	4:15
Sept. 10—	ST. LOUIS	4:15
Sept. 17—	NEW ORLEANS	4:15
Sept. 24—	at San Diego	4:15
Oct. 2—	at Kansas City (Mon.)	9:00
Oct. 8—	at Carolina	4:15
Oct. 15—	INDIANAPOLIS	4:05
Oct. 22—	at Oakland	4:05
Oct. 29—	KANSAS CITY	4:15
Nov. 5—	SAN DIEGO	4:15
Nov. 12—	at Jacksonville	1:00
Nov. 19—	Open date	
Nov. 26—	DENVER	4:15
Dec. 3—	at Atlanta	1:00
Dec. 10—	at Denver	4:05
Dec. 16—	OAKLAND (Sat.)	4:05
Dec. 23—	BUFFALO (Sat.)	8:35

All times are Eastern.
All games Sunday unless noted.

DRAFT CHOICES

Shaun Alexander, RB, Alabama (first round/19th pick overall).
Chris McIntosh, T, Wisconsin (1/22).
Ike Charlton, DB, Virginia Tech (2/52).
Darrell Jackson, WR, Florida (3/80).
Marcus Bell, LB, Arizona (4/116).
Isaiah Kacyvenski, LB, Harvard (4/119).
James Williams, WR, Marshall (6/175).
Tim Watson, DT, Rowan (N.J.) (6/185).
John Hilliard, DT, Mississippi State (6/190).

1999 REVIEW

RESULTS

Sept.12—	DETROIT	L	20-28
Sept.19—	at Chicago	W	14-13
Sept.26—	at Pittsburgh	W	29-10
Oct. 3—	OAKLAND	W	22-21
Oct. 10—	Open date		
Oct. 17—	at San Diego	L	10-13
Oct. 24—	BUFFALO	W	26-16
Nov. 1—	at Green Bay	W	27-7
Nov. 7—	CINCINNATI	W	37-20
Nov. 14—	DENVER	W	20-17
Nov. 21—	at Kansas City	W	31-19
Nov. 28—	TAMPA BAY	L	3-16
Dec. 5—	at Oakland	L	21-30
Dec. 12—	SAN DIEGO	L	16-19
Dec. 19—	at Denver (OT)	L	30-36
Dec. 26—	KANSAS CITY	W	23-14
Jan. 2—	at N.Y. Jets	L	9-19
Jan. 9—	MIAMI*	L	17-20

*AFC wild-card game.

RECORDS/RANKINGS

1999 regular-season record: 9-7 (1st in AFC West); 4-4 in division; 7-5 in conference; 2-2 vs. NFC; 5-3 at home; 4-4 on road; 6-4 on turf; 3-3 on grass.
Team record last five years: 40-40 (.500, ranks 14th in league in that span).
1999 team rankings:

	No.	AFC	NFL
Total offense	*300.3	12	23
Rushing offense	*88.0	14	T24
Passing offense	*212.3	8	16
Scoring offense	338	6	12
Total defense	*339.1	14	23
Rushing defense	*120.9	14	25
Passing defense	*218.3	11	17
Scoring defense	298	5	8
Takeaways	36	3	T6
Giveaways	33	T13	T19
Turnover differential	3	T6	T12
Sacks	38	12	19
Sacks allowed	38	10	T15

*Yards per game.

TEAM LEADERS

Scoring (kicking): Todd Peterson, 134 pts. (32/32 PATs, 34/40 FGs).
Scoring (touchdowns): Derrick Mayes, 60 pts. (10 receiving).
Passing: Jon Kitna, 3,346 yds. (495 att., 270 comp., 54.5%, 23 TDs, 16 int.).
Rushing: Ricky Watters, 1,210 yds. (325 att., 3.7 avg., 5 TDs).
Receptions: Sean Dawkins, 58 (992 yds., 17.1 avg., 7 TDs).
Interceptions: Shawn Springs, 5 (77 yds., 0 TDs); Willie Williams, 5 (43 yds., 1 TD).
Sacks: Phillip Daniels, 9.0.
Punting: Jeff Feagles, 40.8 avg. (84 punts, 3,425 yds., 0 blocked).
Punt returns: Charlie Rogers, 14.5 avg. (22 att., 318 yds., 1 TD).
Kickoff returns: Ahman Green, 22.7 avg. (36 att., 818 yds., 0 TDs).

2000 SEASON
TRAINING CAMP ROSTER

No.	QUARTERBACKS	Ht./Wt.	Born	NFL Exp.	College	How acq.	'99 Games GP/GS
13	Foley, Glenn	6-2/220	10-10-70	7	Boston College	T-NYJ/99	3/1
11	Huard, Brock	6-4/228	4-15-76	2	Washington	D3a/99	0/0
7	Kitna, Jon	6-2/217	9-21-72	4	Central Washington	FA/96	15/15
	RUNNING BACKS						
37	Alexander, Shaun	5-11/218	8-30-77	R	Alabama	D1a/00	—
34	Brown, Reggie (FB)	6-0/244	6-26-73	5	Fresno State	D3b/96	16/8
31	Rogers, Charlie	5-9/179	6-19-76	2	Georgia Tech	D5b/99	12/0
38	Strong, Mack (FB)	6-0/235	9-11-71	7	Georgia	FA/93	14/1
32	Watters, Ricky	6-1/217	4-7-69	10	Notre Dame	UFA/98	16/16
	RECEIVERS						
83	Bailey, Karsten	5-10/201	4-26-77	2	Auburn	D3b/99	2/0
19	Bownes, Fabien	5-11/192	2-29-72	4	Western Illinois	W-Chi./99	15/0
81	Dawkins, Sean	6-4/218	2-3-71	8	California	UFA/99	16/13
86	Fauria, Christian (TE)	6-4/245	9-22-71	6	Colorado	D2/95	16/16
82	Jackson, Darrell	6-0/197	12-6-78	R	Florida	D3/00	—
88	May, Deems (TE)	6-4/263	3-6-69	9	North Carolina	UFA/97	15/0
87	Mayes, Derrick	6-0/205	1-28-74	5	Notre Dame	T-GB/99	16/15
89	Mili, Itula (TE)	6-4/265	4-20-73	4	Brigham Young	D6/97	16/1
85	Pritchard, Mike	5-10/193	10-26-69	10	Colorado	FA/96	14/5
15	Williams, James	5-10/180	3-6-78	R	Marshall	D6a/00	—
	OFFENSIVE LINEMEN						
63	Beede, Frank (G)	6-4/296	5-1-73	5	Panhandle State (Okla.)	FA/96	10/0
60	Bloedorn, Greg (C)	6-6/278	11-15-72	4	Cornell	FA/98	9/0
62	Gray, Chris (G)	6-4/305	6-19-70	8	Auburn	UFA/98	16/10
71	Jones, Walter (T)	6-5/300	1-19-74	4	Florida State	D1b/97	16/16
66	Kendall, Pete (G)	6-5/292	7-9-73	5	Boston College	D1/96	16/16
75	McIntosh, Chris (T)	6-6/315	2-20-77	R	Wisconsin	D1b/00	—
61	Tobeck, Robbie (C)	6-4/298	3-6-70	7	Washington State	UFA/00	*15/15
74	Weiner, Todd (T)	6-4/300	9-16-75	3	Kansas State	D2/98	11/1
	DEFENSIVE LINEMEN						
90	Cochran, Antonio (E)	6-4/297	6-21-76	2	Georgia	D4/99	4/0
95	Hilliard, John (T)	6-2/285	4-16-76	R	Mississippi State	D6c/00	—
78	Keneley, Matt (T)	6-5/284	12-1-73	2	Southern California	FA/00	*7/0
96	Kennedy, Cortez (T)	6-3/306	8-23-68	11	Miami (Fla.)	D1a/90	16/16
92	King, Lamar (E)	6-3/294	8-10-75	2	Saginaw Valley State (Mich.)	D1/99	14/0
99	LaBounty, Matt (E)	6-4/275	1-3-69	8	Oregon	T-GB/96	16/1
97	Parker, Riddick (T)	6-3/274	11-20-72	4	North Carolina	FA/96	16/3
70	Sinclair, Michael (E)	6-4/275	1-31-68	10	Eastern New Mexico	D6/91	15/15
91	Watson, Tim (T)	6-4/290	12-23-74	R	Rowan College (N.J.)	D6b/00	—
	LINEBACKERS						
55	Bell, Marcus	6-1/237	7-19-77	R	Arizona	D4a/00	—
94	Brown, Chad	6-2/240	7-12-70	8	Colorado	UFA/97	15/15
58	Kacyvenski, Isaiah	6-1/250	10-3-77	R	Harvard	D4b/00	—
59	Kopp, Jeff	6-4/244	7-8-71	6	Southern California	UFA/00	*6/0
56	Logan, James	6-2/225	12-6-72	6	Memphis State	W-Cin./95	16/2
50	Myles, DeShone	6-2/235	10-31-74	3	Nevada	D4/98	5/0
51	Simmons, Anthony	6-0/230	6-20-76	3	Clemson	D1/98	16/16
	DEFENSIVE BACKS						
20	Bellamy, Jay (S)	5-11/199	7-8-72	6	Rutgers	FA/94	16/16
26	Canty, Chris (CB)	5-9/185	3-30-76	4	Kansas State	W-Chi./99	14/1
23	Charlton, Ike (CB)	5-11/205	10-6-77	R	Virginia Tech	D2/00	—
43	Eloms, Joey (CB)	5-10/183	4-4-76	3	Indiana	FA/99	4/0
28	Joseph, Kerry (S)	6-2/205	10-4-73	4	McNeese State	FA/98	16/4
24	Springs, Shawn (CB)	6-0/195	3-11-75	4	Ohio State	D1a/97	16/16
25	Tongue, Reggie (S)	6-0/206	4-11-73	5	Oregon State	UFA/00	*16/16
21	Vinson, Fred (CB)	5-11/180	4-2-77	2	Vanderbilt	T-GB/00	*16/1
27	Williams, Willie (CB)	5-9/180	12-26-70	8	Western Carolina	UFA/97	15/14
	SPECIALISTS						
10	Feagles, Jeff (P)	6-1/207	8-7-66	13	Miami (Fla.)	UFA/98	16/0
2	Peterson, Todd (K)	5-10/177	2-4-70	6	Georgia	FA/95	16/0

*Not with Seahawks in 1999.
Other free agent veterans invited to camp: DE Kendrick Burton, TE Rufus French, TE James Hill, G Marcus Jenkins, DT Ed Kehl, P Brian Moorman, WR Reginald Swinton, RB Cory Walker, OT Floyd Wedderburn, DE Lamanzer Williams.
Abbreviations: D1—draft pick, first round; SD-2—supplemental draft pick, second round; W—claimed on waivers; T—obtained in trade; PlanB—Plan B free-agent acquisition; FA—free-agent acquisition (other than Plan B); UFA—unconditional free agent acquisition; ED—expansion draft pick.

SEATTLE SEAHAWKS

MISCELLANEOUS TEAM DATA

Stadium (capacity, surface):
Husky Stadium (72,500, artificial)
Business address:
11220 N.E. 53rd Street
Kirkland, WA 98033
Business phone:
425-827-9777
Ticket information:
800-635-4295
Team colors:
Blue, green and silver
Flagship radio station:
KIRO, 710 AM
Training site:
Eastern Washington University
Cheney, Wash.
206-827-9777

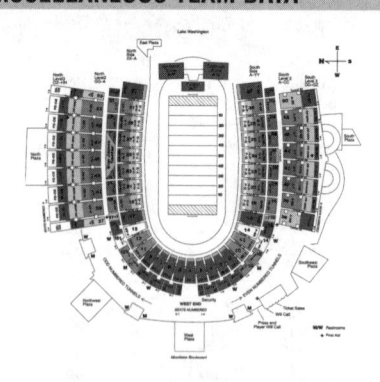

TSN REPORT CARD

Coaching staff	B	The addition of Steve Sidwell to coordinate a defense that allowed too many yards in 1999 is a huge plus. The return of Gil Haskell as offensive coordinator more than offsets the loss of Mike Sherman to the Packers. But even more important will be Mike Holmgren's ability to coax the best effort from a group that has underachieved.
Quarterbacks	C	After being better than expected in the first half of the '99 season, Jon Kitna performed as you might expect a first-year starter in a complex scheme to play over the final six weeks. He must be more consistent, not to mention better, if he is to have a long-term future with this team.
Running backs	B -	The still-productive Ricky Watters ran hard but eventually ran down last season. The addition of first-round draft choice Shaun Alexander will supply Watters with some needed rest, as well as added incentive when he is on the field.
Receivers	C +	Derrick Mayes and Sean Dawkins found a way to combine for 120 catches and 17 touchdowns in their first season with the Seahawks. They will have to find a way to be even more productive if they're going to make everyone forget Joey Galloway.
Offensive line	D +	The weakest link of last year's playoff team took a serious hit when the versatile Robbie Tobeck was lost for six to eight months after tearing a tendon in his left knee in May. His loss creates another season of question marks on the right side of the line. The real plus here is the continuing ascension of LT Walter Jones.
Defensive line	B -	Even with the losses of right end Phillip Daniels and left tackle Sam Adams in free agency, this remains the strength of a defense that wasn't stout enough last year. Lamar King must step up as Daniels' replacement and left end Michael Sinclair must return to his Pro Bowl form.
Linebackers	C +	Chad Brown's do-everything ability should benefit from Sidwell's presence, and unpredictability. The move of Anthony Simmons outside was needed, and overdo. But the Seahawks will open this season just as they closed the '99 season—without a proven middle linebacker and with concerns about a lack of depth.
Secondary	C +	The arrival of strong safety Reggie Tongue in free agency supplies some needed toughness. But the best thing about this group remains left corner Shawn Springs, who shut down some of the game's top receivers last year. Now the Seahawks need better play from right corner Willie Williams and a next-level performance from free safety Jay Bellamy.
Special teams	B +	It didn't take long for Pete Rodriguez to work his magic, transforming special teams units that ranked as the league's worst in 1997 into consistent units that ranked first last year. The honor roll includes the additions of punter Jeff Feagles and punt returner Charlie Rogers, and the continued steadiness of kicker Todd Peterson.

TAMPA BAY BUCCANEERS
NFC CENTRAL DIVISION

2000 SEASON

CLUB DIRECTORY

Owner
Malcolm Glazer
Executive vice president
Bryan Glazer
Executive vice president
Joel Glazer
Executive vice president
Edward Glazer
General manager
Rich McKay
Chief financial officer
Tom Alas
Director of player personnel
Jerry Angelo
Director of college scouting
Tim Ruskell
Director of football administration
John Idzik
Executive director of the Glazer Foundation
Veronica (Roni) Costello
Director of communications
Reggie Roberts
Director of marketing
George Woods
Special events manager
Maury Wilks
Director of premium seating
Jim Overton
Director of community relations
Stephanie Waller
Dir. of ticketing and customer relations
Mike Newquist
Director of player programs
Kevin Winston
Luxury suite manager
Cheryll Pritcher
Group sales
Bill Butler
Coordinator of pro personnel
Mark Dominik
Pro scout
Lloyd Richards Jr.
College scouts
Mike Ackerley, Joe DiMarzo Jr., Dennis Hickey, Ruston Webster, Mike Yowarsky
Communications manager
Carter Toole

Head coach
Tony Dungy

Assistant coaches
Mark Asanovich (strength & conditioning)
Wendell Avery (off. assistant)
Clyde Christensen (quarterbacks)
Herman Edwards (assistant head coach/defensive backs)
Chris Foerster (offensive line)
Monte Kiffin (def. coordinator)
Joe Marciano (special teams)
Rod Marinelli (defensive line)
Tony Nathan (running backs)
Kevin O'Dea (defensive assistant)
Lovie Smith (linebackers)
Les Steckel (off. coordinator)
Ricky Thomas (tight ends)
Charlie Williams (wide receivers)

Communications coordinator
Zack Bolno
Internet manager
Scott Smith
Trainer
Todd Toriscelli
Assistant trainers
Keith Abrams   Jim Whalen
Video director
Dave Levy
Assistant video director
Pat Brazil
Equipment manager
Darin Kerns
Assistant equipment manager
Mark Meschede

SCHEDULE

Sept. 3— at New England	1:00
Sept. 10— CHICAGO	1:00
Sept. 17— at Detroit	1:00
Sept. 24— N.Y. JETS	4:15
Oct. 1— at Washington	4:15
Oct. 9— at Minnesota (Mon.)	9:00
Oct. 15— Open date	
Oct. 19— DETROIT (Thur.)	8:35
Oct. 29— MINNESOTA	1:00
Nov. 5— at Atlanta	1:00
Nov. 12— GREEN BAY	4:15
Nov. 19— at Chicago	1:00
Nov. 26— BUFFALO	1:00
Dec. 3— DALLAS	1:00
Dec. 10— at Miami	1:00
Dec. 18— ST. LOUIS (Mon.)	9:00
Dec. 24— at Green Bay	1:00

All times are Eastern.
All games Sunday unless noted.

DRAFT CHOICES

Cosey Coleman, G, Tennessee (second round/51st pick overall).
Nate Webster, LB, Miami, Fla. (3/90).
James Whalen, TE, Kentucky (5/157).
David Gibson, DB, Southern California (6/193).
Joe Hamilton, QB, Georgia Tech (7/234).

1999 REVIEW

RESULTS

Sept. 12—N.Y. GIANTS	L	13-17
Sept. 19—at Philadelphia	W	19-5
Sept. 26—DENVER	W	13-10
Oct. 3—at Minnesota	L	14-21
Oct. 10—at Green Bay	L	23-26
Oct. 17—Open date		
Oct. 24—CHICAGO	W	6-3
Oct. 31—at Detroit	L	3-20
Nov. 7—at New Orleans	W	31-16
Nov. 14—KANSAS CITY	W	17-10
Nov. 21—ATLANTA	W	19-10
Nov. 28—at Seattle	W	16-3
Dec. 6—MINNESOTA	W	24-17
Dec. 12—DETROIT	W	23-16
Dec. 19—at Oakland	L	0-45
Dec. 26—GREEN BAY	W	29-10
Jan. 2—at Chicago	W	20-6
Jan. 15—WASHINGTON*	W	14-13
Jan. 23—at St. Louis†	L	6-11

*NFC divisional playoff game.
†NFC conference championship game.

RECORDS/RANKINGS

1999 regular-season record: 11-5 (1st in NFC Central); 5-3 in division; 8-4 in conference; 3-1 vs. AFC; 7-1 at home; 4-4 on road; 3-2 on turf; 8-3 on grass.
Team record last five years: 42-38 (.525), ranks 13th in league in that span).
1999 team rankings:

	No.	NFC	NFL
Total offense	*265.9	13	28
Rushing offense	*111.0	6	15
Passing offense	*154.9	14	30
Scoring offense	270	13	27
Total defense	*267.5	1	3
Rushing defense	*87.9	2	5
Passing defense	*179.6	1	2
Scoring defense	235	1	3
Takeaways	31	9	T14
Giveaways	35	T8	T23
Turnover differential	-4	T7	T17
Sacks	43	5	10
Sacks allowed	42	T8	T18

*Yards per game.

TEAM LEADERS

Scoring (kicking): Martin Gramatica, 106 pts. (25/25 PATs, 27/32 FGs).
Scoring (touchdowns): Mike Alstott, 54 pts. (7 rushing, 2 receiving).
Passing: Trent Dilfer, 1,619 yds. (244 att., 146 comp., 59.8%, 11 TDs, 11 int.).
Rushing: Mike Alstott, 949 yds. (242 att., 3.9 avg., 7 TDs).
Receptions: Jacquez Green, 56 (791 yds., 14.1 avg., 3 TDs).
Interceptions: Donnie Abraham, 7 (115 yds., 2 TDs).
Sacks: Warren Sapp, 12.5.
Punting: Mark Royals, 43.1 avg. (90 punts, 3,882 yds., 0 blocked).
Punt returns: Jacquez Green, 8.9 avg. (23 att., 204 yds., 0 TDs).
Kickoff returns: Reidel Anthony, 20.7 avg. (21 att., 434 yds., 0 TDs).

– 89 –

2000 SEASON
TRAINING CAMP ROSTER

TAMPA BAY BUCCANEERS

No.	QUARTERBACKS	Ht./Wt.	Born	NFL Exp.	College	How acq.	'99 Games GP/GS
14	Hamilton, Joe	5-10/190	3-13-77	R	Georgia Tech	D7/00	—
10	King, Shaun	6-0/225	5-29-77	2	Tulane	D2/99	6/5
15	Zeier, Eric	6-1/214	9-6-72	6	Georgia	T-Bal./99	2/1
	RUNNING BACKS						
27	Abdullah, Rabih	6-1/227	4-27-75	3	Lehigh	FA/98	15/1
40	Alstott, Mike (FB)	6-1/248	12-21-73	5	Purdue	D2/96	16/16
28	Dunn, Warrick	5-8/180	1-5-75	4	Florida State	D1a/97	15/15
37	Ellison, Jerry	5-10/204	12-20-71	6	Tennessee-Chattanooga	UFA/00	*12/0
43	McLeod, Kevin (FB)	6-0/252	10-17-74	2	Auburn	FA/98	7/0
	RECEIVERS						
85	Anthony, Reidel	5-11/180	10-20-76	4	Florida	D1b/97	13/7
81	Green, Jacquez	5-9/168	1-15-76	3	Florida	D2a/98	16/10
82	Hape, Patrick (TE)	6-4/262	6-6-74	4	Alabama	D5/97	15/1
19	Johnson, Keyshawn	6-4/212	7-22-72	5	Southern California	T-NYJ/00	*16/16
84	McDonald, Darnell	6-3/199	5-26-76	2	Kansas State	D7c/99	8/0
83	Moore, Dave (TE)	6-2/258	11-11-69	8	Pittsburgh	FA/92	16/16
88	Murphy, Yo	5-10/178	5-11-71	2	Idaho	FA/00	8/0
45	Purnell, Lovett (TE)	6-3/245	4-7-72	5	West Virginia	FA/00	*2/0
87	Whalen, James (TE)	6-2/228	12-11-77	R	Kentucky	D5/00	—
86	Williams, Karl	5-10/177	4-10-71	5	Texas A&M-Kingsville	FA/96	13/4
	OFFENSIVE LINEMEN						
62	Christy, Jeff (C)	6-2/285	2-3-69	8	Pittsburgh	UFA/00	*16/16
60	Coleman, Cosey (G)	6-4/322	10-27-78	R	Tennessee	D2/00	—
65	Dogins, Kevin (C)	6-1/301	12-7-72	4	Texas A&M-Kingsville	FA/96	11/5
74	Gruber, Paul (T)	6-5/292	2-24-65	13	Wisconsin	D1/88	16/16
79	Hegamin, George (T)	6-7/331	2-14-73	7	North Carolina State	FA/99	1/0
64	McDaniel, Randall (G)	6-3/287	12-19-64	12	Arizona State	FA/00	*16/16
73	Middleton, Frank (G)	6-3/334	10-25-74	4	Arizona	D3a/97	16/16
70	Odom, Jason (T)	6-5/312	3-31-74	5	Florida	D4a/96	3/3
69	Pierson, Pete (T)	6-5/315	2-4-71	6	Washington	D5/94	15/0
68	Unutoa, Morris (C)	6-1/284	3-10-71	5	Brigham Young	FA/99	12/0
75	Washington, Todd (C)	6-3/324	7-19-76	3	Virginia Tech	D4/98	6/0
71	Wunsch, Jerry (T)	6-6/339	1-21-74	4	Wisconsin	D2/97	16/13
	DEFENSIVE LINEMEN						
72	Ahanotu, Chidi (E)	6-2/285	10-11-70	8	California	D6/93	16/15
98	Cannida, James (T)	6-2/291	1-3-75	3	Nevada-Reno	D6a/98	2/1
77	Culpepper, Brad (T)	6-1/270	5-8-69	9	Florida	W-Min./94	16/16
97	Jackson, Tyoka (E)	6-2/280	11-22-71	6	Penn State	FA/96	6/0
78	Jones, Marcus (E)	6-6/278	8-15-73	5	North Carolina	D1b/96	16/4
92	McFarland, Anthony (T)	6-0/300	12-18-77	2	Louisiana State	D1/99	14/0
95	McLaughlin, John (E)	6-4/247	11-13-75	2	California	D5/99	12/0
99	Sapp, Warren (T)	6-2/303	12-19-72	6	Miami (Fla.)	D1a/95	15/15
94	White, Steve (E)	6-2/271	10-25-73	5	Tennessee	FA/96	13/13
	LINEBACKERS						
55	Brooks, Derrick	6-0/235	4-18-73	6	Florida State	D1b/95	16/16
59	Duncan, Jamie	6-0/242	7-20-75	3	Vanderbilt	D3/98	16/0
50	Gooch, Jeff	5-11/225	10-31-74	5	Austin Peay State	FA/96	15/0
57	Palmer, Mitch	6-4/259	9-2-73	3	Colorado State	FA/98	4/0
53	Quarles, Shelton	6-1/230	9-11-71	4	Vanderbilt	FA/97	16/14
51	Singleton, Alshermond	6-2/228	8-7-75	4	Temple	D4/97	15/0
52	Webster, Nate	5-11/225	11-29-77	R	Miami (Fla.)	D3/00	—
	DEFENSIVE BACKS						
21	Abraham, Donnie (CB)	5-10/192	10-8-73	5	East Tennessee State	D3/96	16/16
20	Barber, Ronde (CB)	5-10/184	4-7-75	4	Virginia	D3b/97	16/15
46	Gibson, David (S)	6-1/210	11-5-77	R	Southern California	D6/00	—
34	Jackson, Dexter (S)	6-0/196	7-28-77	2	Florida State	D4/99	12/0
25	Kelly, Brian (CB)	5-11/193	1-14-76	3	Southern California	D2b/98	16/3
47	Lynch, John (S)	6-2/220	9-25-71	8	Stanford	D3/93	16/16
24	Robinson, Damien (S)	6-2/214	12-22-73	4	Iowa	FA/97	16/16
30	Smith, Shevin (S)	5-11/204	6-17-75	3	Florida State	D6b/98	16/0
31	Young, Floyd (CB)	6-0/179	11-23-75	4	Texas A&M-Kingsville	FA/97	6/0
	SPECIALISTS						
7	Gramatica, Martin (K)	5-8/170	11-27-75	2	Kansas State	D3/99	16/0
3	Royals, Mark (P)	6-5/215	6-22-64	12	Appalachian State	FA/97	16/0

*Not with Buccaneers in 1999.

Other free agent veterans invited to camp: G Ken Blackman, OT DeMarcus Curry, C Eric De Groh, TE Jason Freeman, LB Bobbie Howard, LB Antony Jordan, FB Jim Kitts, TE Henry Lusk, CB Deshone Mallard, QB Scott Milanovich, WR Drew O'Connor, P John Shay, FB Jameion Spencer, RB Aaron Stecker, LB Shawn Stuckey, LB Kinnon Tatum.

Abbreviations: D1—draft pick, first round; SD-2—supplemental draft pick, second round; W—claimed on waivers; T—obtained in trade; PlanB—Plan B free-agent acquisition; FA—free-agent acquisition (other than Plan B); UFA—unconditional free agent acquisition; ED—expansion draft pick.

MISCELLANEOUS TEAM DATA

Stadium (capacity, surface):
Raymond James Stadium (65,394, grass)
Business address:
One Buccaneer Place
Tampa, FL 33607
Business phone:
813-870-2700
Ticket information:
813-879-2827
Team colors:
Buccaneer red, pewter, black and orange
Flagship radio station:
WQYK, 99.5 FM
Training site:
University of Tampa
Tampa, Fla.
813-253-6215

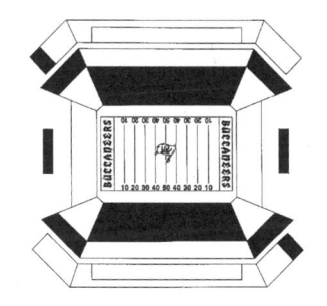

TSN REPORT CARD

Coaching staff	B +	Tony Dungy's easy-going style is perfect for today's athlete, and he has surrounded himself with some of the most underrated coaches in the game. Defensive coordinator Monte Kiffin and defensive backs coach Herman Edwards are among the best at what they do. Les Steckel is flexible enough to produce what's needed out of the Bucs offense.
Quarterbacks	C	Shaun King is not an outstanding athlete but he finds a way to make the right play, to make the big play and to win. He doesn't get rattled and that will help him during what figures to be a season laced with pressures. The team needs to get a veteran behind him who has won and won big. Eric Zeier isn't going to get this team to the Super Bowl.
Running backs	B	Mike Alstott and Warrick Dunn are one of the most formidable duos in the league. Both are durable and both can hurt you either as ball carriers or pass rushers. The downside is that Alstott fumbles too much and doesn't block very well. If he could do the latter, the team could make more use of Dunn near the goal line, where its increased use of Alstott makes the offense rather predictable.
Receivers	B	Keyshawn Johnson may be the best all-around receiver in the game. He creates matchup problems, makes big plays and blocks. The team has speed threats in Jacquez Green and Reidel Anthony but neither has proven to be strong in traffic. Tight end Dave Moore is underrated, especially in the red zone. Karl Williams and up-and-comers Drew O'Connor, Darnell McDonald and James Whalen add depth to the receiving corps.
Offensive line	C +	Newcomers Jeff Christy (center) and Randall McDaniel (left guard) will make this unit better, but it still may not be good enough to get to the Super Bowl. Left tackle is a potential problem area, no matter who plays there, and depth is a problem as well. The reserves are either too young or too old to make an impact if thrust into regular duty.
Defensive line	A	This is the best defensive front in the league. The ends don't produce a lot of sacks, but with Warren Sapp leading the way at tackle, the unit produces all the necessary quarterback pressure, enough to allow linebackers and defensive backs to stay back in coverage and blitz only occasionally. Marcus Jones and Anthony McFarland are reserves good enough to start for several NFL teams.
Linebackers	B +	This unit may not be as dominant as it was without Hardy Nickerson. However, the players are all outstanding athletes. They're all fast and smart, and that fits in well with what the Bucs ask them to do, which is pursue the ball. Derrick Brooks was arguably the best outside backer in the game last year and he's only getting better as he gets smarter and more experienced.
Secondary	A	This is one of the hardest-hitting and perhaps one of the most underrated units in the league. Safeties John Lynch and Damien Robinson will flat-out pop you and Donnie Abraham is one of the best cover corners in the game. Ronde Barber is a little small but he's effective. The team was second against the pass last year.
Special teams	B -	Kicker Martin Gramatica is accurate from better than 50 yards and capable of hitting a 60-yard field goal, but his kickoffs come up a little short. Mark Royals can do anything you ask of a punter. The return game is a little weak and needs to add some fearless elements.

TENNESSEE TITANS
AFC CENTRAL DIVISION

2000 SEASON

CLUB DIRECTORY

Owner
K.S. "Bud" Adams Jr.
President/chief operating officer
Jeff Diamond
Executive v.p./general manager
Floyd Reese
Executive assistant to owner
Thomas S. Smith
Vice president/legal counsel
Steve Underwood
Vice president/finance
Jackie Curley
Exec. v.p./broadcasting and marketing
Don MacLachlan
Director of player personnel
Rich Snead
Director/sales operations
Stuart Spears
Dir. of media relations and services
Tony Wyllie
Vice president for community affairs
Bob Hyde
Director/ticket operations
Marty Collins
Director/security
Steve Berk
Director/player programs
Al Smith
Asst. dir. of media rel. and services
Robbie Bohren
Head trainer
Brad Brown
Scouts
Ray Biggs   C.O. Brocato
Dub Fesperman   Chris Landry
Director of college scouting
Glenn Cumbee
Equipment manager
Paul Noska

Head coach
Jeff Fisher

Assistant coaches
Jerry Gray (defensive backs)
Mike Heimerdinger (offensive coordinator)
George Henshaw (asst. head coach/offense)
Craig Johnson (off. assistant)
Alan Lowry (special teams)
Mike Munchak (offensive line)
Jim Schwartz (linebackers)
Sherman Smith (running backs)
Ronnie Vinklarek (def. assistant)
Steve Walters (wide receivers)
Jim Washburn (defensive line)
Steve Watterson (strength & rehabilitation)
Gregg Williams (defensive coordinator)

Videotape coordinator
Ken Sparacino
Team physicians
Elrod Burton
Craig Rutland
John Williams

SCHEDULE

Sept. 3—	at Buffalo	8:35
Sept. 10—	KANSAS CITY	1:00
Sept. 17—	Open date	
Sept. 24—	at Pittsburgh	1:00
Oct. 1—	N.Y. GIANTS	1:00
Oct. 8—	at Cincinnati	1:00
Oct. 16—	JACKSONVILLE (Mon.)	9:00
Oct. 22—	at Baltimore	1:00
Oct. 30—	at Washington (Mon.)	9:00
Nov. 5—	PITTSBURGH	1:00
Nov. 12—	BALTIMORE	1:00
Nov. 19—	CLEVELAND	1:00
Nov. 26—	at Jacksonville	4:15
Dec. 3—	at Philadelphia	1:00
Dec. 10—	CINCINNATI	1:00
Dec. 17—	at Cleveland	1:00
Dec. 25—	DALLAS (Mon.)	9:00

All times are Eastern.
All games Sunday unless noted.

DRAFT CHOICES

Keith Bulluck, LB, Syracuse (first round/30th pick overall).
Erron Kinney, TE, Florida (3/68).
Byron Frisch, DE, Brigham Young (3/93).
Bobby Myers, S, Wisconsin (4/124).
Peter Sirmon, LB, Oregon (4/128).
Aric Morris, DB, Michigan State (5/135).
Frank Chamberlin, LB, Boston College (5/160).
Robaire Smith, DE, Michigan St. (6/197).
Mike Green, RB, Houston (7/213).
Wes Shivers, G, Mississippi St. (7/237).

1999 REVIEW

RESULTS

Sept.12—CINCINNATI	W	36-35
Sept.19—CLEVELAND	W	26-9
Sept.26—at Jacksonville	W	20-19
Oct. 3—at San Francisco	L	22-24
Oct. 10—BALTIMORE	W	14-11
Oct. 17—at New Orleans	W	24-21
Oct. 24—Open date		
Oct. 31—ST. LOUIS	W	24-21
Nov. 7—at Miami	L	0-17
Nov. 14—at Cincinnati	W	24-14
Nov. 21—PITTSBURGH	W	16-10
Nov. 28—at Cleveland	W	33-21
Dec. 5—at Baltimore	L	14-41
Dec. 9—OAKLAND	W	21-14
Dec. 19—ATLANTA	W	30-17
Dec. 26—JACKSONVILLE	W	41-14
Jan. 2—at Pittsburgh	W	47-36
Jan. 8—BUFFALO*	W	22-16
Jan. 16—at Indianapolis†	W	19-16
Jan. 23—at Jacksonville‡	W	33-14
Jan. 30—St. Louis§	L	16-23

*AFC wild-card game.
†AFC divisional playoff game.
‡AFC conference championship game.
§Super Bowl 34.

RECORDS/RANKINGS

1999 regular-season record: 13-3 (2nd in AFC Central); 9-1 in division; 10-2 in conference; 3-1 vs. NFC; 8-0 at home; 5-3 on road; 3-0 on turf; 10-3 on grass.
Team record last five years: 44-36 (.550, ranks T11th in league in that span).
1999 team rankings:

	No.	AFC	NFL
Total offense	*331.0	6	13
Rushing offense	*113.2	9	13
Passing offense	*217.8	T5	T13
Scoring offense	392	3	7
Total defense	*327.8	12	17
Rushing defense	*96.9	6	10
Passing defense	*230.9	15	25
Scoring defense	324	11	15
Takeaways	40	2	4
Giveaways	22	T2	T2
Turnover differential	18	2	2
Sacks	54	2	3
Sacks allowed	25	2	3

*Yards per game.

TEAM LEADERS

Scoring (kicking): Al Del Greco, 106 pts. (43/43 PATs, 21/25 FGs).
Scoring (touchdowns): Eddie George, 78 pts. (9 rushing, 4 receiving).
Passing: Steve McNair, 2,179 yds. (331 att., 187 comp., 56.5%, 12 TDs, 8 int.).
Rushing: Eddie George, 1,304 yds. (320 att., 4.1 avg., 9 TDs).
Receptions: Kevin Dyson, 54 (658 yds., 12.2 avg., 4 TDs).
Interceptions: Samari Rolle, 4 (65 yds., 0 TDs).
Sacks: Jevon Kearse, 14.5.
Punting: Craig Hentrich, 42.5 avg. (90 punts, 3,824 yds., 0 blocked).
Punt returns: Derrick Mason, 8.7 avg. (26 att., 225 yds., 1 TD).
Kickoff returns: Derrick Mason, 19.6 avg. (41 att., 805 yds., 0 TDs).

– 92 –

2000 SEASON
TRAINING CAMP ROSTER

TENNESSEE TITANS

No.	QUARTERBACKS	Ht./Wt.	Born	NFL Exp.	College	How acq.	'99 Games GP/GS
13	Daft, Kevin	6-1/202	11-19-75	2	California-Davis	D5/99	0/0
9	McNair, Steve	6-2/225	2-14-73	6	Alcorn State	D1/95	11/11
14	O'Donnell, Neil	6-3/228	7-3-66	11	Maryland	UFA/99	8/5
	RUNNING BACKS						
27	George, Eddie	6-3/240	9-24-73	5	Ohio State	D1/96	16/16
26	George, Spencer	5-9/200	10-28-73	3	Rice	FA/97	8/0
22	Green, Mike	6-0/249	9-2-76	R	Houston	D7a/00	—
41	Neal, Lorenzo (FB)	5-11/240	12-27-70	8	Fresno State	UFA/99	16/14
20	Thomas, Rodney	5-10/210	3-30-73	6	Texas A&M	D3b/95	16/0
	RECEIVERS						
84	Brown, Larry (TE)	6-4/280	9-1-76	2	Georgia	FA/99	9/0
83	Byrd, Isaac	6-1/188	11-16-74	4	Kansas	FA/97	12/6
87	Dyson, Kevin	6-1/201	6-23-75	3	Utah	D1/98	16/16
86	Kent, Joey	6-1/191	4-23-74	4	Tennessee	D2/97	8/0
88	Kinney, Erron (TE)	6-5/272	7-28-77	R	Florida	D3a/00	—
85	Mason, Derrick	5-10/188	1-17-74	4	Michigan State	D4a/97	13/0
80	Roan, Michael (TE)	6-3/250	8-29-72	6	Wisconsin	D4/95	11/1
81	Sanders, Chris	6-1/188	5-8-72	6	Ohio State	D3a/95	16/0
82	Thigpen, Yancey	6-1/203	8-15-69	9	Winston-Salem (N.C.) State	FA/98	10/10
89	Wycheck, Frank (TE)	6-3/250	10-14-71	8	Maryland	W-Was./95	16/16
	OFFENSIVE LINEMEN						
72	Hopkins, Brad (T)	6-3/305	9-5-70	8	Illinois	D1/93	16/16
60	Long, Kevin (C)	6-5/295	5-2-75	3	Florida State	D7b/98	16/12
76	Mathews, Jason (T)	6-5/304	2-9-71	7	Texas A&M	FA/98	5/0
74	Matthews, Bruce (G)	6-5/305	8-8-61	18	Southern California	D1/83	16/16
71	Miller, Fred (T)	6-7/315	2-6-73	5	Baylor	UFA/00	*16/16
75	Olson, Benji (G)	6-3/315	6-5-75	3	Washington	D5/98	16/16
69	Piller, Zach (G)	6-5/330	5-2-76	2	Florida	D3/99	8/0
73	Sanderson, Scott (G)	6-6/295	7-25-74	4	Washington State	D3b/97	3/3
68	Shivers, Wes (T)	6-5/318	3-8-77	R	Mississippi State	D7b/00	—
	DEFENSIVE LINEMEN						
91	Evans, Josh (T)	6-2/288	9-6-72	6	Alabama-Birmingham	FA/95	11/10
97	Fisk, Jason (T)	6-3/295	9-4-72	6	Stanford	UFA/99	16/16
92	Ford, Henry (T)	6-3/295	10-30-71	7	Arkansas	D1/94	12/9
93	Frisch, Byron (E)	6-5/267	12-17-76	R	Brigham Young	D3b/00	—
99	Holmes, Kenny (E)	6-4/270	10-24-73	4	Miami (Fla.)	D1/97	14/7
96	Jones, Mike (T)	6-4/280	8-25-69	10	North Carolina State	UFA/99	11/3
90	Kearse, Jevon (E)	6-4/265	9-3-76	2	Florida	D1/99	16/16
95	Salave'a, Joe (T)	6-3/290	3-23-75	3	Arizona	D4/98	10/0
98	Smith, Robaire (E)	6-4/271	11-15-77	R	Michigan State	D6/00	—
78	Thornton, John (T)	6-2/295	10-2-76	2	West Virginia	D2/99	16/3
	LINEBACKERS						
53	Bulluck, Keith	6-3/232	4-4-77	R	Syracuse	D1/00	—
57	Chamberlin, Frank	6-1/250	1-2-78	R	Boston College	D5b/00	—
51	Favors, Greg	6-1/244	9-30-74	3	Mississippi State	W-KC/99	15/0
54	Glover, Phil	5-11/241	12-17-75	2	Utah	D7/99	1/0
56	Godfrey, Randall	6-2/245	4-6-73	5	Georgia	UFA/00	*16/16
50	Killens, Terry	6-1/235	3-24-74	5	Penn State	D3/96	16/1
55	Robinson, Eddie	6-1/243	4-13-70	9	Alabama State	FA/98	16/16
59	Sirmon, Peter	6-2/246	2-18-77	R	Oregon	D4b/00	—
	DEFENSIVE BACKS						
23	Bishop, Blaine (S)	5-9/203	7-24-70	8	Ball State	D8/93	15/15
38	McCullough, George (CB)	5-10/187	2-18-75	3	Baylor	D5/97	5/0
30	Mitchell, Donald (CB)	5-9/185	12-14-76	2	Southern Methodist	D4b/99	16/0
28	Morris, Aric (S)	5-10/208	7-22-77	R	Michigan State	D5a/00	—
32	Myers, Bobby (S)	6-1/189	10-11-76	R	Wisconsin	D4a/00	—
35	Phenix, Perry (S)	5-11/210	11-14-74	3	Southern Mississippi	FA/98	16/1
31	Robertson, Marcus (S)	5-11/205	10-2-69	10	Iowa State	D4b/91	15/15
21	Rolle, Samari (CB)	6-0/175	8-10-76	3	Florida State	D2/98	16/16
37	Sidney, Dainon (CB)	6-0/188	5-30-75	3	Alabama-Birmingham	D3/98	16/2
25	Walker, Denard (CB)	6-1/190	8-9-73	4	Louisiana State	D3a/97	15/14
	SPECIALISTS						
3	Del Greco, Al (K)	5-10/202	3-2-62	17	Auburn	FA/91	16/0
15	Hentrich, Craig (P)	6-3/205	5-18-71	7	Notre Dame	UFA/98	16/0

*Not with Titans in 1999.
Other free agent veterans invited to camp: C Craig Page, DT Rod Walker, S Brad Ware.
Abbreviations: D1—draft pick, first round; SD-2—supplemental draft pick, second round; W—claimed on waivers; T—obtained in trade; PlanB—Plan B free-agent acquisition; FA—free-agent acquisition (other than Plan B); UFA—unconditional free agent acquisition; ED—expansion draft pick.

TENNESSEE TITANS

MISCELLANEOUS TEAM DATA

Stadium (capacity, surface):
Adelphia Coliseum
(67,000, grass)
Business address:
460 Great Circle Road
Nashville, TN 37228
Business phone:
615-565-4000
Ticket information:
615-341-SNAP
Team colors:
Navy, red, Titan blue and white
Flagship radio station:
WGFX, 104.5 FM
Training site:
460 Great Circle Road
Nashville, TN 37228
615-565-4000

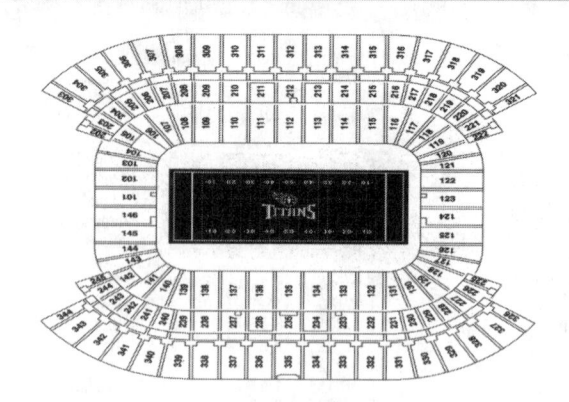

TSN REPORT CARD

Coaching staff	A -	This is a quality group that got the most of out of last season's team. This year's challenge is to stay at the front of the pack. The role of new offensive coordinator Mike Heimerdinger will be worth watching. He trained under Mike Shanahan, is no-nonsense and figures to demand more from those with the ball.
Quarterbacks	B +	Steve McNair and Neil O'Donnell give the Titans as good a 1-2 duo as any team in the league. McNair still needs to refine his downfield reads to complete his package, but he is certainly poised for a huge season. O'Donnell has been the ultimate professional since arriving in Nashville. No. 3 man Kevin Daft played well in NFL Europe.
Running backs	A	Eddie George is tough, consistent and motivated. Enough said. Depth is a concern, but fullback Lorenzo Neal is certainly an underused player in this offense. Rodney Thomas faces a stiff challenge for the No. 2 spot behind George.
Receivers	C	There's talent here, yes, but they have yet to mesh into the offense. There's no doubt they need more opportunities in an offense built around the run, but they need to do more with the ball once it is in their hands.
Offensive line	B +	The line rebounded from last year's early struggles in the run game when Bruce Matthews moved back to guard. Fred Miller is the key as he replaces Jon Runyan at right tackle. Overall this is a powerful group that works well together.
Defensive line	B	Jevon Kearse can dominate and Jason Fisk is underappreciated by most around the league. It's a solid group overall, good against the run, but it likely will need to overcome the loss of tackle Josh Evans due to NFL suspension. Evans' absence means John Thornton gets his chance.
Linebackers	B +	There will be more than a few new faces here, led by free-agent signee Randall Godfrey and first-round pick Keith Bulluck. Look for the linebackers to attack a lot more in 2000.
Secondary	B	The secondary surrendered some big plays to some middle-of-the-road quarterbacks last season, and being in a division that likes throw and drafted a host of wide receivers this year, improvement is necessary. The Titans need to tighten up at the corners and keep safety Marcus Robertson healthy.
Special teams	B	There are no worries at kicker or punter, but consistency is needed in the return game from Derrick Mason. The coverage units still take too many penalties.

WASHINGTON REDSKINS
NFC EASTERN DIVISION

2000 SEASON

CLUB DIRECTORY

Chairman and chief executive officer
Daniel M. Snyder
President
Steve Baldacci
House counsel
Bob Gordon
Assistant general manager
Bobby Mitchell
Vice president of finance
Greg Dillon
Director of player personnel
Vinny Cerrato
Senior vice president of operations
Michael Dillow
Contract negotiator
Joe Mendes
Director of player programs
John Jefferson
Director of college scouting
Mike Faulkner
Scouts
To be announced
NFC pro coordinator
Melvin Bratton
AFC pro coordinator
To be announced
Director of public relations
To be announced
Publications/Internet director
Terence J. (Casey) Husband
Community relations manager
Marie Reynolds
Director of leadership council
Alex Hahn
Director of administration
Barry Asimos
Video director
Rob Porteus
Assistant video director
Mike Bracken

Head coach
Norv Turner

Assistant coaches
Jason Arapoff (conditioning dir.)
Rubin Carter (co-defensive line)
Foge Fazio (linebackers)
Pat Flaherty (tight ends)
Russ Grimm (offensive line)
LeCharls McDaniel (special teams)
Ron Meeks (defensive backs)
Kirk Olivadotti (off. assistant)
Rich Olson (quarterbacks)
Ray Rhodes (defensive coord.)
Dan Riley (strength)
Terry Robiskie (wide receivers)
Mike Trgovac (defensive line)
Jason Verduzco (def. assistant)
Kirby Wilson (running backs)

Ticket manager
Jeff Ritter
Head trainer
Bubba Tyer
Assistant trainers
Al Bellamy, Kevin Bastin
Equipment manager
Jay Brunetti
Asst. equipment manager
Jeff Parsons

SCHEDULE

Sept. 3—	CAROLINA	1:00
Sept. 10—	at Detroit	4:15
Sept. 18—	DALLAS (Mon.)	9:00
Sept. 24—	at N.Y. Giants	8:35
Oct. 1—	TAMPA BAY	4:15
Oct. 8—	at Philadelphia	1:00
Oct. 15—	BALTIMORE	1:00
Oct. 22—	at Jacksonville	4:15
Oct. 30—	TENNESSEE (Mon.)	9:00
Nov. 5—	at Arizona	4:05
Nov. 12—	Open date	
Nov. 20—	at St. Louis (Mon.)	9:00
Nov. 26—	PHILADELPHIA	1:00
Dec. 3—	N.Y. GIANTS	1:00
Dec. 10—	at Dallas	4:15
Dec. 16—	at Pittsburgh (Sat.)	12:30
Dec. 24—	ARIZONA	1:00

All times are Eastern.
All games Sunday unless noted.

DRAFT CHOICES

LaVar Arrington, LB, Penn State (first round/second pick overall).
Chris Samuels, T, Alabama (1/3).
Lloyd Harrison, DB, North Carolina State (3/64).
Michael Moore, G, Troy State (4/129).
Quincy Sanders, DB, UNLV (5/155).
Todd Husak, QB, Stanford (6/202).
Delbert Cowsette, DT, Maryland (7/216).
Ethan Howell, WR, Oklahoma State (7/250).

1999 REVIEW

RESULTS

Sept.12—DALLAS (OT)		L	35-41
Sept.19—at N.Y. Giants		W	50-21
Sept.26—at N.Y. Jets		W	27-20
Oct. 3—CAROLINA		W	38-36
Oct. 10—Open date			
Oct. 17—at Arizona		W	24-10
Oct. 24—at Dallas		L	20-38
Oct. 31—CHICAGO		W	48-22
Nov. 7—BUFFALO		L	17-34
Nov. 14—at Philadelphia		L	28-35
Nov. 21—N.Y. GIANTS		W	23-13
Nov. 28—PHILADELPHIA (OT)	W	20-17
Dec. 5—at Detroit		L	17-33
Dec. 12—ARIZONA		W	28-3
Dec. 19—at Indianapolis		L	21-24
Dec. 26—at San Francisco (OT)	W	26-20
Jan. 2—MIAMI		W	21-10
Jan. 8—DETROIT*		W	27-13
Jan. 15—at Tampa Bay†		L	13-14

*NFC wild-card game.
†NFC divisional playoff game.

RECORDS/RANKINGS

1999 regular-season record: 10-6 (1st in NFC East); 5-3 in division; 8-4 in conference; 2-2 vs. AFC; 6-2 at home; 4-4 on road; 2-4 on turf; 8-2 on grass.
Team record last five years: 39-40-1 (.494, ranks 15th in league in that span).
1999 team rankings:

	No.	NFC	NFL
Total offense	*372.8	2	2
Rushing offense	*127.4	4	9
Passing offense	*245.4	5	6
Scoring offense	443	2	2
Total defense	*356.6	15	30
Rushing defense	*123.3	12	27
Passing defense	*233.3	11	26
Scoring defense	377	10	24
Takeaways	37	3	5
Giveaways	25	3	T7
Turnover differential	12	1	T4
Sacks	40	T6	T14
Sacks allowed	31	2	6

*Yards per game.

TEAM LEADERS

Scoring (kicking): Brett Conway, 115 pts. (49/50 PATs, 22/32 FGs).
Scoring (touchdowns): Stephen Davis, 104 pts. (17 rushing, 1 2-pt. conv.).
Passing: Brad Johnson, 4,005 yds. (519 att., 316 comp., 60.9%, 24 TDs, 13 int.).
Rushing: Stephen Davis, 1,405 yds. (290 att., 4.8 avg., 17 TDs).
Receptions: Michael Westbrook, 65 (1,191 yds., 18.3 avg., 9 TDs).
Interceptions: Matt Stevens, 6 (61 yds., 0 TDs).
Sacks: Dan Wilkinson, 8.0.
Punting: Matt Turk, 41.4 avg. (62 punts, 2,564 yds., 0 blocked).
Punt returns: : Brian Mitchell, 8.3 avg. (40 att., 332 yds., 0 TDs).
Kickoff returns: Brian Mitchell, 20.8 avg. (43 att., 893 yds., 0 TDs).

2000 SEASON
TRAINING CAMP ROSTER

WASHINGTON REDSKINS

No.	QUARTERBACKS	Ht./Wt.	Born	NFL Exp.	College	How acq.	'99 Games GP/GS
3	George, Jeff	6-4/215	12-8-67	10	Illinois	UFA/00	*12/10
8	Husak, Todd	6-3/216	7-6-78	R	Stanford	D6/00	—
14	Johnson, Brad	6-5/224	9-13-68	9	Florida State	T-Min./99	16/16
	RUNNING BACKS						
47	Bowie, Larry (FB)	6-0/249	3-21-73	5	Georgia	FA/96	2/0
37	Centers, Larry	6-0/225	6-1-68	11	Stephen F. Austin State	FA/99	16/12
48	Davis, Stephen	6-0/234	3-1-74	5	Auburn	D4/96	14/14
20	Hicks, Skip	6-0/230	10-13-74	3	UCLA	D3/98	10/2
30	Mitchell, Brian	5-10/221	8-18-68	11	Southwestern Louisiana	D5/90	16/0
22	Murrell, Adrian	5-11/210	10-16-70	7	West Virginia	UFA/00	*16/12
45	Sellers, Mike (FB)	6-3/260	7-21-75	3	None	FA/98	16/2
	RECEIVERS						
80	Alexander, Stephen (TE)	6-4/246	11-7-75	3	Oklahoma	D2/98	15/15
83	Connell, Albert	6-0/179	5-13-74	4	Texas A&M	D4/97	15/14
86	Fryar, Irving	6-0/198	9-28-62	17	Nebraska	FA/99	16/1
89	Howell, Ethan	5-11/178	10-14-77	R	Oklahoma State	D7b/00	—
88	Jenkins, James (TE)	6-2/249	8-17-67	10	Rutgers	FA/91	16/4
84	Thompson, Derrius	6-2/215	7-5-77	2	Baylor	FA/99	1/0
87	Thrash, James	6-0/200	4-28-75	4	Missouri Southern	FA/97	16/0
82	Westbrook, Michael	6-3/220	7-7-72	6	Colorado	D1/95	16/16
85	Zelenka, Joe (TE)	6-3/280	3-9-76	2	Wake Forest	T-SF/00	*13/0
	OFFENSIVE LINEMEN						
64	Heck, Andy (T)	6-6/298	1-1-67	12	Notre Dame	FA/99	16/16
76	Jansen, Jon (T)	6-6/302	1-28-76	2	Michigan	D2/99	16/16
77	Johnson, Tre' (G)	6-2/326	8-30-71	7	Temple	D2/94	16/16
66	Moore, Michael (G)	6-3/320	11-1-76	R	Troy State	D4/00	—
52	Raymer, Cory (C)	6-2/289	3-3-73	6	Wisconsin	D2/95	16/16
60	Samuels, Chris (T)	6-5/325	7-28-77	R	Alabama	D1b/00	—
63	Sims, Keith (G)	6-3/318	6-17-67	11	Iowa State	FA/98	12/12
	DEFENSIVE LINEMEN						
79	Brown, Doug (T)	6-7/290	9-29-74	3	Simon Fraser (B.C.)	FA/98	10/0
99	Coleman, Marco (E)	6-3/267	12-18-69	9	Georgia Tech	UFA/99	16/16
75	Cook, Anthony (E)	6-3/295	5-30-72	6	South Carolina State	UFA/99	16/7
91	Cowsette, Delbert (T)	6-1/274	9-3-77	R	Maryland	D7a/00	—
72	Kalu, Ndukwe (E)	6-3/246	8-3-75	4	Rice	FA/98	12/0
90	Lang, Kenard (E)	6-4/277	1-31-75	4	Miami (Fla.)	D1/97	16/9
78	Smith, Bruce (E)	6-4/279	6-18-63	15	Virginia Tech	FA/00	*16/16
94	Stubblefield, Dana (T)	6-2/315	11-14-70	8	Kansas	UFA/98	16/16
95	Wilkinson, Dan (T)	6-5/313	3-13-73	7	Ohio State	T-Cin./98	16/16
	LINEBACKERS						
56	Arrington, LaVar	6-3/250	6-20-78	R	Penn State	D1a/00	—
59	Barber, Shawn	6-2/224	1-14-75	3	Richmond	D4/98	16/16
54	Jones, Greg	6-4/238	5-22-74	4	Colorado	D2/97	15/15
53	Mason, Eddie	6-0/236	1-9-72	4	North Carolina	FA/99	14/0
55	Mitchell, Kevin	6-1/254	1-1-71	6	Syracuse	UFA/00	*16/1
	Peterson, Anthony	6-1/232	1-23-72	8	Notre Dame	UFA/00	*12/0
50	Smith, Derek M.	6-2/239	1-18-75	4	Arizona State	D3/97	16/16
	DEFENSIVE BACKS						
24	Bailey, Champ (CB)	6-1/184	6-22-78	2	Georgia	D1/99	16/16
26	Buckley, Curtis (CB)	6-0/182	9-25-70	8	East Texas State	FA/99	7/0
27	Carrier, Mark (S)	6-1/190	4-28-68	10	Southern California	UFA/00	*15/15
25	Denton, Tim	5-11/182	2-2-73	3	Sam Houston State	FA/98	16/0
28	Green, Darrell (CB)	5-8/184	2-15-60	18	Texas A&I	D1/83	16/16
22	Harrison, Lloyd (CB)	5-10/190	6-21-77	R	North Carolina State	D3/00	—
35	Sanders, Quincy (S)	6-1/204	4-8-77	R	UNLV	D5/00	—
29	Shade, Sam (S)	6-1/201	6-14-73	6	Alabama	UFA/99	16/16
	SPECIALISTS						
	Barnhardt, Tommy (P)	6-2/228	6-11-63	13	North Carolina	FA/00	*16/0
5	Conway, Brett (K)	6-2/192	3-8-75	4	Penn State	FA/98	16/0

*Not with Redskins in 1999.

Other free agent veterans invited to camp: RB Chad Dukes, C Mark Fischer, DE Derrick Ham, LB Tyrus McCloud, WR Rondel Menendez, RB Norman Miller, TE Kevin Pesak, TE Todd Pollack, C Juan Porter, OT Derek G. Smith, DT Barron Tanner, CB David Terrell, P Rodney Williams, RB Ray Zellars.

Abbreviations: D1—draft pick, first round; SD-2—supplemental draft pick, second round; W—claimed on waivers; T—obtained in trade; PlanB—Plan B free-agent acquisition; FA—free-agent acquisition (other than Plan B); UFA—unconditional free agent acquisition; ED—expansion draft pick.

— 96 —

MISCELLANEOUS TEAM DATA

Stadium (capacity, surface):
FedEx Field (80,116, grass)
Business address:
P.O. Box 17247
Dulles International Airport
Washington, D.C. 20041
Business phone:
703-478-8900
Ticket information:
301-276-6050
Team colors:
Burgundy and gold
Flagship radio station:
WJFK, 106.7 FM
Training site:
To be announced
301-687-7975

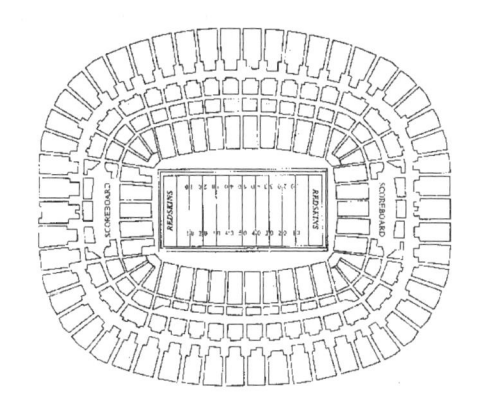

TSN REPORT CARD

Coaching staff	B	Norv Turner knows how to design an offense, to get receivers open and to give running backs open spaces. Ray Rhodes and his defensive staff should be able to revitalize a unit that has struggled for too many seasons. Turner's biggest challenge will be handling a potentially volatile quarterback situation.
Quarterbacks	A	It is difficult to imagine there is a team in the league with more quality at this position. Brad Johnson was the reason the Redskins reached the playoffs last season. The same can be said for Jeff George in Minnesota. The only problem will be if egos clash and get in the way of the team's success.
Running backs	A	Stephen Davis could be on the verge of a brilliant career, and the addition of Adrian Murrell has added depth. Murrell should be able to keep the inside power running game going if Davis goes down this year. Larry Centers provides reliable hands on the field and reliable leadership in the locker room. Skip Hicks is running out of time to prove he belongs on the roster.
Receivers	B -	Michael Westbrook is capable and finally proved he can be tough and durable. He needs to build on his solid 1999 season. Albert Connell should be on the verge of a breakout season. Tight end Stephen Alexander can be a bigger part of the offense if he has better luck with injuries this season.
Offensive line	B	The tackles are young and gifted. The guards are experienced and tough. The center is solid. There are two keys, though. Rookie Chris Samuels has to grow up quickly at left tackle, and veteran Tre' Johnson has to stay healthy for an entire season at left guard.
Defensive line	C	There is no lack of big, experienced bodies here. But that hasn't translated into domination at the line of scrimmage in recent seasons. The talent is available, and if the new system permits them more freedom to be playmakers, this group should be effective.
Linebackers	C +	They'll be asked to do less, but do it better this season. That should help Derek Smith and Shawn Barber make more plays. The depth is decent. LaVar Arrington could make this a standout group, but he has to learn the pro game quickly.
Secondary	B	The cornerbacks can cover and the safeties can hit. There's depth at the nickel and dime spots, and Deion Sanders could make this group even better. With all the experience here, it's going to be tough for opposing offenses to fool anyone.
Special teams	C -	Inconsistency has been a killer for these units, so they are getting a makeover for 2000. Young players who take their jobs seriously and understand the importance of their roles have to be found.

SCHEDULE

PRESEASON
(All times Eastern)

WEEK 1

SATURDAY, JULY 29

Atlanta at Indianapolis	8:00
New Orleans at N.Y. Jets	8:00

SUNDAY, JULY 30

Philadelphia at Cleveland	8:00
Pittsburgh at Dallas	8:00

MONDAY, JULY 31

New England vs. San Francisco at Canton, Ohio	8:00

WEEK 2

FRIDAY, AUGUST 4

New England at Detroit	7:00
Cincinnati at Buffalo	7:30
Washington at Tampa Bay	7:30
Jacksonville at Carolina	8:00
N.Y. Jets at Green Bay	8:00

SATURDAY, AUGUST 5

Miami at Pittsburgh	7:30
Chicago at N.Y. Giants	8:00
Indianapolis at Seattle	8:00
Kansas City at Tennessee	8:00
New Orleans at Minnesota	8:00
Oakland at St. Louis	8:00
Philadelphia at Baltimore	8:00
San Diego at San Francisco	9:00
Atlanta vs. Dallas at Tokyo	10:00
Denver at Arizona	10:00

WEEK 3

THURSDAY, AUGUST 10

Tampa Bay at Miami	7:00
Carolina at Pittsburgh	7:30

FRIDAY, AUGUST 11

Cincinnati at Atlanta	7:30
New England at Washington	8:00
N.Y. Giants at Jacksonville	8:00

SATURDAY, AUGUST 12

Cleveland at Chicago	8:00
N.Y. Jets at Baltimore	8:00
Buffalo at Detroit	8:35
Minnesota at San Diego	9:00
Seattle at Arizona	10:00
New Orleans at Indianapolis	TBA

SUNDAY, AUGUST 13

Green Bay at Denver	4:00

Oakland at Dallas	7:00
San Francisco at Kansas City	8:30

MONDAY, AUGUST 14

St. Louis at Tennessee	8:00

WEEK 4

FRIDAY, AUGUST 18

San Diego at Atlanta	7:30
Tennessee at Philadelphia	7:30
Baltimore at Carolina	8:00
N.Y. Giants at N.Y. Jets	8:00
Arizona at Minnesota	8:35
Detroit at Oakland	9:00

SATURDAY, AUGUST 19

Chicago at Cincinnati	7:30
Washington at Cleveland	7:30
Indianapolis vs. Pittsburgh at Mexico City	8:00
Buffalo at St. Louis	8:00
Jacksonville at Kansas City	8:30
Dallas at Denver	9:00
San Francisco at Seattle	11:00

SUNDAY, AUGUST 20

Tampa Bay at New England	4:00

MONDAY, AUGUST 21

Green Bay at Miami	8:00

WEEK 5

THURSDAY, AUGUST 24

Atlanta at Jacksonville	7:30
Buffalo at Philadelphia	8:00
Carolina at New England	8:00
Minnesota at Indianapolis	8:00
St. Louis at Dallas	8:35
Seattle at Oakland	9:00

FRIDAY, AUGUST 25

Detroit at Cincinnati	7:30
Kansas City at Tampa Bay	7:30
Baltimore at N.Y. Giants	8:00
Miami at New Orleans	8:00
Pittsburgh at Washington	8:00
Tennessee at Chicago	8:00
Denver at San Francisco	9:00
Arizona at San Diego	10:00

SATURDAY, AUGUST 26

Cleveland at Green Bay	5:00

REGULAR SEASON
(All times Eastern)

WEEK 1

SUNDAY, SEPTEMBER 3

Arizona at N.Y. Giants	1:00
Baltimore at Pittsburgh	1:00
Carolina at Washington	1:00
Chicago at Minnesota	1:00
Detroit at New Orleans	1:00
Indianapolis at Kansas City	1:00
Jacksonville at Cleveland	1:00
N.Y. Jets at Green Bay	4:15
Philadelphia at Dallas	4:05
San Diego at Oakland	4:15
San Francisco at Atlanta	1:00
Seattle at Miami	4:15

Tampa Bay at New England	1:00
Tennessee at Buffalo	8:35

MONDAY, SEPTEMBER 4

Denver at St. Louis	9:00

Open date: Cincinnati

WEEK 2

SUNDAY, SEPTEMBER 10

Atlanta at Denver	4:15
Carolina at San Francisco	4:15
Chicago at Tampa Bay	1:00
Cleveland at Cincinnati	1:00
Green Bay at Buffalo	1:00
Jacksonville at Baltimore	1:00
Kansas City at Tennessee	1:00
Miami at Minnesota	1:00
New Orleans at San Diego	4:15
N.Y. Giants at Philadelphia	1:00
Oakland at Indianapolis	1:00
St. Louis at Seattle	4:15
Washington at Detroit	4:15
Dallas at Arizona	8:35

MONDAY, SEPTEMBER 11

New England at N.Y. Jets	9:00

Open date: Pittsburgh

WEEK 3

SUNDAY, SEPTEMBER 17

Atlanta at Carolina	1:00
Buffalo at N.Y. Jets	1:00
Cincinnati at Jacksonville	1:00
Denver at Oakland	4:05
Minnesota at New England	4:15
New Orleans at Seattle	4:15
N.Y. Giants at Chicago	4:15
Philadelphia at Green Bay	1:00
Pittsburgh at Cleveland	1:00
San Diego at Kansas City	1:00
San Francisco at St. Louis	1:00
Tampa Bay at Detroit	1:00
Baltimore at Miami	8:35

MONDAY, SEPTEMBER 18

Dallas at Washington	9:00

Open date: Arizona, Indianapolis, Tennessee

WEEK 4

SUNDAY, SEPTEMBER 24

Cincinnati at Baltimore	1:00
Cleveland at Oakland	4:15
Detroit at Chicago	1:00
Green Bay at Arizona	4:05
Kansas City at Denver	4:15
New England at Miami	1:00
N.Y. Jets at Tampa Bay	4:15
Philadelphia at New Orleans	1:00
St. Louis at Atlanta	1:00
San Francisco at Dallas	1:00
Seattle at San Diego	4:15
Tennessee at Pittsburgh	1:00
Washington at N.Y. Giants	8:35

MONDAY, SEPTEMBER 25

Jacksonville at Indianapolis	9:00

Open date: Buffalo, Carolina, Minnesota

WEEK 5

SUNDAY, OCTOBER 1

Arizona at San Francisco	4:15
Baltimore at Cleveland	1:00
Chicago at Green Bay	4:15
Dallas at Carolina	1:00
Indianapolis at Buffalo	1:00
Miami at Cincinnati	4:05
Minnesota at Detroit	1:00
New England at Denver	4:05
N.Y. Giants at Tennessee	1:00
Pittsburgh at Jacksonville	1:00
San Diego at St. Louis	1:00
Tampa Bay at Washington	4:15
Atlanta at Philadelphia	8:35

MONDAY, OCTOBER 2

Seattle at Kansas City	9:00

Open date: New Orleans, N.Y. Jets, Oakland

WEEK 6

SUNDAY, OCTOBER 8

Buffalo at Miami	1:00
Cleveland at Arizona	4:15
Denver at San Diego	4:15
Green Bay at Detroit	1:00
Indianapolis at New England	1:00
New Orleans at Chicago	1:00
N.Y. Giants at Atlanta	4:05
Oakland at San Francisco	4:15
Pittsburgh at N.Y. Jets	1:00
Seattle at Carolina	4:15
Tennessee at Cincinnati	1:00
Washington at Philadelphia	1:00
Baltimore at Jacksonville	8:35

MONDAY, OCTOBER 9

Tampa Bay at Minnesota	9:00

Open date: Dallas, Kansas City, St. Louis

WEEK 7

SUNDAY, OCTOBER 15

Atlanta at St. Louis	1:00
Baltimore at Washington	1:00
Carolina at New Orleans	1:00
Cincinnati at Pittsburgh	1:00
Cleveland at Denver	4:05
Dallas at N.Y. Giants	1:00
Indianapolis at Seattle	4:05
N.Y. Jets at New England	4:05
Oakland at Kansas City	1:00
Philadelphia at Arizona	4:15
San Diego at Buffalo	1:00
San Francisco at Green Bay	4:15
Minnesota at Chicago	8:35

MONDAY, OCTOBER 16

Jacksonville at Tennessee	9:00

Open date: Detroit, Miami, Tampa Bay

WEEK 8

THURSDAY, OCTOBER 19

Detroit at Tampa Bay	8:35

SUNDAY, OCTOBER 22

Arizona at Dallas	1:00
Buffalo at Minnesota	1:00
Chicago at Philadelphia	1:00
Cleveland at Pittsburgh	1:00
Denver at Cincinnati	1:00
New England at Indianapolis	1:00
New Orleans at Atlanta	1:00
St. Louis at Kansas City	1:00
San Francisco at Carolina	1:00
Seattle at Oakland	4:05
Tennessee at Baltimore	1:00
Washington at Jacksonville	4:15

2000 SEASON Schedule

MONDAY, OCTOBER 23

Miami at N.Y. Jets	9:00

Open date: Green Bay, N.Y. Giants, San Diego

WEEK 9

SUNDAY, OCTOBER 29

Carolina at Atlanta	1:00
Cincinnati at Cleveland	1:00
Detroit at Indianapolis	1:00
Green Bay at Miami	1:00
Jacksonville at Dallas	4:15
Kansas City at Seattle	4:15
Minnesota at Tampa Bay	1:00
New Orleans at Arizona	4:05
N.Y. Jets at Buffalo	1:00
Philadelphia at N.Y. Giants	4:05
Pittsburgh at Baltimore	1:00
St. Louis at San Francisco	4:05
Oakland at San Diego	8:35

MONDAY, OCTOBER 30

Tennessee at Washington	9:00

Open date: Chicago, Denver, New England

WEEK 10

SUNDAY, NOVEMBER 5

Baltimore at Cincinnati	1:00
Buffalo at New England	1:00
Dallas at Philadelphia	1:00
Denver at N.Y. Jets	4:15
Indianapolis at Chicago	1:00
Kansas City at Oakland	4:15
Miami at Detroit	1:00
N.Y. Giants at Cleveland	1:00
Pittsburgh at Tennessee	1:00
San Diego at Seattle	4:15
San Francisco at New Orleans	1:00
Tampa Bay at Atlanta	1:00
Washington at Arizona	4:05
Carolina at St. Louis	8:35

MONDAY, NOVEMBER 6

Minnesota at Green Bay	9:00

Open date: Jacksonville

WEEK 11

SUNDAY, NOVEMBER 12

Arizona at Minnesota	1:00
Atlanta at Detroit	1:00
Baltimore at Tennessee	1:00
Chicago at Buffalo	1:00
Cincinnati at Dallas	1:00
Green Bay at Tampa Bay	4:15
Kansas City at San Francisco	4:05
Miami at San Diego	4:05
New England at Cleveland	1:00
New Orleans at Carolina	1:00
Philadelphia at Pittsburgh	1:00
St. Louis at N.Y. Giants	4:15
Seattle at Jacksonville	1:00
N.Y. Jets at Indianapolis	8:35

MONDAY, NOVEMBER 13

Oakland at Denver	9:00

Open date: Washington

WEEK 12

SUNDAY, NOVEMBER 19

Arizona at Philadelphia	1:00
Atlanta at San Francisco	4:15
Buffalo at Kansas City	1:00
Carolina at Minnesota	1:00
Cincinnati at New England	1:00
Cleveland at Tennessee	1:00
Dallas at Baltimore	4:15
Detroit at N.Y. Giants	1:00
Indianapolis at Green Bay	1:00
N.Y. Jets at Miami	4:05
Oakland at New Orleans	1:00
San Diego at Denver	4:05
Tampa Bay at Chicago	1:00
Jacksonville at Pittsburgh	8:35

MONDAY, NOVEMBER 20

Washington at St. Louis	9:00

Open date: Seattle

WEEK 13

THURSDAY, NOVEMBER 23

Minnesota at Dallas	4:05
New England at Detroit	12:30

SUNDAY, NOVEMBER 26

Atlanta at Oakland	4:05
Buffalo at Tampa Bay	1:00
Chicago at N.Y. Jets	1:00
Cleveland at Baltimore	1:00
Denver at Seattle	4:15
Kansas City at San Diego	4:15
Miami at Indianapolis	1:00
New Orleans at St. Louis	1:00
Philadelphia at Washington	1:00
Pittsburgh at Cincinnati	1:00
Tennessee at Jacksonville	4:15
N.Y. Giants at Arizona	8:35

MONDAY, NOVEMBER 27

Green Bay at Carolina	9:00

Open date: San Francisco

WEEK 14

THURSDAY, NOVEMBER 30

Detroit at Minnesota	8:35

SUNDAY, DECEMBER 3

Arizona at Cincinnati	1:00
Cleveland at Jacksonville	4:15
Dallas at Tampa Bay	1:00
Denver at New Orleans	1:00
Indianapolis at N.Y. Jets	4:15
Miami at Buffalo	1:00
N.Y. Giants at Washington	1:00
Oakland at Pittsburgh	1:00
St. Louis at Carolina	1:00
San Francisco at San Diego	4:05
Seattle at Atlanta	1:00
Tennessee at Philadelphia	1:00
Green Bay at Chicago	8:35

MONDAY, DECEMBER 4

Kansas City at New England	9:00

Open date: Baltimore

WEEK 15

SUNDAY, DECEMBER 10

Arizona at Jacksonville	1:00
Carolina at Kansas City	1:00
Cincinnati at Tennessee	1:00
Detroit at Green Bay	1:00
Minnesota at St. Louis	1:00
New England at Chicago	1:00
New Orleans at San Francisco	4:15
Philadelphia at Cleveland	1:00
Pittsburgh at N.Y. Giants	1:00
San Diego at Baltimore	1:00
Seattle at Denver	4:05

Tampa Bay at Miami	1:00
Washington at Dallas	4:15
N.Y. Jets at Oakland	8:35

MONDAY, DECEMBER 11

Buffalo at Indianapolis	9:00

Open date: Atlanta

WEEK 16

SATURDAY, DECEMBER 16

Washington at Pittsburgh	12:30
Oakland at Seattle	4:05

SUNDAY, DECEMBER 17

Atlanta at New Orleans	1:00
Baltimore at Arizona	4:15
Chicago at San Francisco	4:05
Denver at Kansas City	1:00
Detroit at N.Y. Jets	1:00
Green Bay at Minnesota	1:00
Indianapolis at Miami	4:15
Jacksonville at Cincinnati	1:00
New England at Buffalo	1:00
San Diego at Carolina	1:00
Tennessee at Cleveland	1:00
N.Y. Giants at Dallas	8:35

MONDAY, DECEMBER 18

St. Louis at Tampa Bay	9:00

Open date: Philadelphia

WEEK 17

SATURDAY, DECEMBER 23

Jacksonville at N.Y. Giants	12:30
San Francisco at Denver	4:15
Buffalo at Seattle	8:35

SUNDAY, DECEMBER 24

Arizona at Washington	1:00
Carolina at Oakland	4:15
Chicago at Detroit	1:00
Cincinnati at Philadelphia	1:00
Kansas City at Atlanta	1:00
Miami at New England	1:00
Minnesota at Indianapolis	4:15
N.Y. Jets at Baltimore	1:00
Pittsburgh at San Diego	4:05
St. Louis at New Orleans	1:00
Tampa Bay at Green Bay	1:00

MONDAY, DECEMBER 25

Dallas at Tennessee	9:00

Open date: Cleveland

1999 SEASON Schedule

NATIONALLY TELEVISED GAMES

(All times Eastern)

PRESEASON

Mon.	July	31—	New England vs. San Francisco at Canton, Ohio (8:00, ABC)
Sat.	Aug.	5—	Atlanta vs. Dallas at Tokyo (10:00, ESPN)
Fri.	Aug.	11—	N.Y. Giants at Jacksonville (8:00, CBS)
Sat.	Aug.	12—	Buffalo at Detroit (8:35, ESPN)
Sun.	Aug.	13—	Green Bay at Denver (4:00, FOX)
Mon.	Aug.	14—	St. Louis at Tennessee (8:00, ABC)
Fri.	Aug.	18—	Arizona at Minnesota (8:35, ESPN)
Sat.	Aug.	19—	Indianapolis vs. Pittsburgh at Mexico City (8:00, CBS)
Sun.	Aug.	20—	Tampa Bay at New England (4:00, FOX)
Mon.	Aug.	21—	Green Bay at Miami (8:00, ABC)
Thur.	Aug.	24—	St. Louis at Dallas (8:35, ESPN)

REGULAR SEASON

Sun.	Sept.	3—	N.Y. Jets at Green Bay (4:15, CBS)
			Tennessee at Buffalo (8:35, ESPN)
Mon.	Sept.	4—	Denver at St. Louis (9:00, ABC)
Sun.	Sept.	10—	St. Louis at Seattle (4:15, CBS)
			Dallas at Arizona (8:35, ESPN)
Mon.	Sept.	11—	New England at N.Y. Jets (9:00, ABC)
Sun.	Sept.	17—	Minnesota at New England (4:15, FOX)
			Baltimore at Miami (8:35, ESPN)
Mon.	Sept.	18—	Dallas at Washington (9:00, ABC)
Sun.	Sept.	24—	N.Y. Jets at Tampa Bay (4:15, CBS)
			Washington at N.Y. Giants (8:35, ESPN)
Mon.	Sept.	25—	Jacksonville at Indianapolis (9:00, ABC)
Sun.	Oct.	1—	Tampa Bay at Washington (4:15, FOX)
			Atlanta at Philadelphia (8:35, ESPN)
Mon.	Oct.	2—	Seattle at Kansas City (9:00, ABC)
Sun.	Oct.	8—	Oakland at San Francisco (4:15, CBS)
			Baltimore at Jacksonville (8:35, ESPN)
Mon.	Oct.	9—	Tampa Bay at Minnesota (9:00, ABC)
Sun.	Oct.	15—	San Francisco at Green Bay (4:15, FOX)
			Minnesota at Chicago (8:35, ESPN)
Mon.	Oct.	16—	Jacksonville at Tennessee (9:00, ABC)
Thur.	Oct.	19—	Detroit at Tampa Bay (8:35, ESPN)
Sun.	Oct.	22—	Washington at Jacksonville (4:15, FOX)
Mon.	Oct.	23—	Miami at N.Y. Jets (9:00, ABC)
Sun.	Oct.	29—	Jacksonville at Dallas (4:15, CBS)
			Oakland at San Diego (8:35, ESPN)
Mon.	Oct.	30—	Tennessee at Washington (9:00, ABC)
Sun.	Nov.	5—	Denver at N.Y. Jets (4:15, CBS)
			Carolina at St. Louis (8:35, ESPN)
Mon.	Nov.	6—	Minnesota at Green Bay (9:00, ABC)
Sun.	Nov.	12—	Green Bay at Tampa Bay (4:15, FOX)
			N.Y. Jets at Indianapolis (8:35, ESPN)
Mon.	Nov.	13—	Oakland at Denver (9:00, ABC)
Sun.	Nov.	19—	Dallas at Baltimore (4:15, FOX)
			Jacksonville at Pittsburgh (8:35, ESPN)
Mon.	Nov.	20—	Washington at St. Louis (9:00, ABC)
Thur.	Nov.	23—	Minnesota at Dallas (4:05, FOX)
			New England at Detroit (12:30, CBS)
Sun.	Nov.	26—	Tennessee at Jacksonville (4:15, CBS)
			N.Y. Giants at Arizona (8:35, ESPN)
Mon.	Nov.	27—	Green Bay at Carolina (9:00, ABC)
Thur.	Nov.	30—	Detroit at Minnesota (8:35, ESPN)
Sun.	Dec.	3—	Indianapolis at N.Y. Jets (4:15, CBS)
			Green Bay at Chicago (8:35, ESPN)
Mon.	Dec.	4—	Kansas City at New England (9:00, ABC)
Sun.	Dec.	10—	Washington at Dallas (4:15, FOX)
			N.Y. Jets at Oakland (8:35, ESPN)
Mon.	Dec.	11—	Buffalo at Indianapolis (9:00, ABC)
Sat.	Dec.	16—	Washington at Pittsburgh (12:30, FOX)
			Oakland at Seattle (4:05, CBS)
Sun.	Dec.	17—	Indianapolis at Miami (4:15, CBS)
			N.Y. Giants at Dallas (8:35, ESPN)
Mon.	Dec.	18—	St. Louis at Tampa Bay (9:00, ABC)
Sat.	Dec.	23—	Jacksonville at N.Y. Giants (12:30, CBS)
			San Francisco at Denver (4:15, FOX)
			Buffalo at Seattle (8:35, ESPN)
Sun.	Dec.	24—	Minnesota at Indianapolis (4:15, FOX)
Mon.	Dec.	25—	Dallas at Tennessee (9:00, ABC)

POSTSEASON

Sat.	Dec.	30—	AFC, NFC wild-card playoffs (ABC)
Sun.	Dec.	31—	AFC, NFC wild-card playoffs (CBS, FOX)
Sat.	Jan.	6—	AFC, NFC divisional playoffs (CBS, FOX)
Sun.	Jan.	7—	AFC, NFC divisional playoffs (CBS, FOX)
Sun.	Jan.	14—	AFC, NFC championship games (CBS, FOX)
Sun.	Jan.	28—	Super Bowl at Raymond James Stadium, Tampa (CBS)
Sun.	Feb.	4—	Pro Bowl at Honolulu (ABC)

INTERCONFERENCE GAMES

(All times Eastern)

Day	Date	Game	Time
Sun.	Sept. 3	N.Y. Jets at Green Bay	4:15
		Tampa Bay at New England	1:00
Mon.	Sept. 4	Denver at St. Louis	9:00
Sun.	Sept. 10	Atlanta at Denver	4:15
		Green Bay at Buffalo	1:00
		Miami at Minnesota	1:00
		New Orleans at San Diego	4:15
		St. Louis at Seattle	4:15
Sun.	Sept. 17	Minnesota at New England	4:15
		New Orleans at Seattle	4:15
Sun.	Sept. 24	N.Y. Jets at Tampa Bay	4:15
Sun.	Oct. 1	N.Y. Giants at Tennessee	1:00
		San Diego at St. Louis	1:00
Sun.	Oct. 8	Cleveland at Arizona	4:15
		Oakland at San Francisco	4:15
		Seattle at Carolina	4:15
Sun.	Oct. 15	Baltimore at Washington	1:00
Sun.	Oct. 22	Buffalo at Minnesota	1:00
		St. Louis at Kansas City	1:00
		Washington at Jacksonville	4:15
Sun.	Oct. 29	Detroit at Indianapolis	1:00
		Green Bay at Miami	1:00
		Jacksonville at Dallas	4:15
Mon.	Oct. 30	Tennessee at Washington	9:00
Sun.	Nov. 5	Indianapolis at Chicago	1:00
		Miami at Detroit	1:00
		N.Y. Giants at Cleveland	1:00
Sun.	Nov. 12	Chicago at Buffalo	1:00
		Cincinnati at Dallas	1:00
		Kansas City at San Francisco	4:05
		Philadelphia at Pittsburgh	1:00
Sun.	Nov. 19	Dallas at Baltimore	4:15
		Indianapolis at Green Bay	1:00
		Oakland at New Orleans	1:00
Thanks.	Nov. 23	New England at Detroit	12:30
Sun.	Nov. 26	Atlanta at Oakland	4:05
		Buffalo at Tampa Bay	1:00
		Chicago at N.Y. Jets	1:00
Sun.	Dec. 3	Arizona at Cincinnati	1:00
		Denver at New Orleans	1:00
		San Francisco at San Diego	4:05
		Seattle at Atlanta	1:00
		Tennessee at Philadelphia	1:00
Sun.	Dec. 10	Arizona at Jacksonville	1:00
		Carolina at Kansas City	1:00
		New England at Chicago	1:00
		Philadelphia at Cleveland	1:00
		Pittsburgh at N.Y. Giants	1:00
		Tampa Bay at Miami	1:00
Sat.	Dec. 16	Washington at Pittsburgh	12:30
Sun.	Dec. 17	Baltimore at Arizona	4:15
		Detroit at N.Y. Jets	1:00
		San Diego at Carolina	1:00
Sat.	Dec. 23	Jacksonville at N.Y. Giants	12:30
		San Francisco at Denver	4:15
Sun.	Dec. 24	Carolina at Oakland	4:15
		Cincinnati at Philadelphia	1:00
		Kansas City at Atlanta	1:00
		Minnesota at Indianapolis	4:15
Mon.	Dec. 25	Dallas at Tennessee	9:00

2000 STRENGTH OF SCHEDULE

(Teams are ranked from most difficult to easiest schedules, based on 2000 opponents' combined 1999 records)

	Team	Opp. Wins	Opp. Losses	Opp. Pct.
1.	Buffalo (25)	150	106	.586
2.	Miami (14)	146	110	.570
3.	Indianapolis (11)	144	112	.563
4.	N.Y. Jets (T2)	143	113	.559
5.	Minnesota (T7)	142	114	.555
6.	New England (6)	138	118	.539
	Seattle (15)	138	118	.539
8.	Kansas City (16)	137	119	.535
9.	Tampa Bay (T2)	136	120	.531
10.	Green Bay (T7)	134	122	.523
11.	Chicago (22)	133	123	.520
	Detroit (10)	133	123	.520
	Washington (27)	133	123	.520
14.	Cleveland (31)	130	126	.508
15.	Cincinnati (30)	128	128	.500
	Dallas (12)	128	128	.500
	Pittsburgh (17)	128	128	.500
18.	Baltimore (T23)	127	129	.496
19.	San Diego (9)	126	130	.492
20.	N.Y. Giants (26)	125	131	.488
21.	Carolina (20)	120	136	.469
22.	Atlanta (T18)	119	137	.465
	Jacksonville (21)	119	137	.465
24.	Tennessee (T23)	118	138	.461
25.	San Francisco (T18)	117	139	.457
26.	New Orleans (13)	116	140	.453
27.	Denver (T4)	115	141	.449
28.	Arizona (T4)	113	143	.441
	Oakland (1)	113	143	.441
30.	St. Louis (29)	110	146	.430
31.	Philadelphia (28)	109	147	.426

NOTE: Number in parentheses is 1999 rank.

COLLEGE DRAFT

ROUND-BY-ROUND SELECTIONS, APRIL 15-16, 2000

FIRST ROUND

Team	Player selected	Pos.	College	Draft pick origination
1. Cleveland	Courtney Brown	DE	Penn State	
2. Washington	LaVar Arrington	LB	Penn State	From New Orleans
3. Washington	Chris Samuels	T	Alabama	From San Francisco
4. Cincinnati	Peter Warrick	WR	Florida State	
5. Baltimore	Jamal Lewis	RB	Tennessee	From Atlanta
6. Philadelphia	Corey Simon	DT	Florida State	
7. Arizona	Thomas Jones	RB	Virginia	
8. Pittsburgh	Plaxico Burress	WR	Michigan State	
9. Chicago	Brian Urlacher	LB	New Mexico	
10. Baltimore	Travis Taylor	WR	Florida	From Denver
11. N.Y. Giants	Ron Dayne	RB	Wisconsin	
12. N.Y. Jets	Shaun Ellis	DE	Tennessee	From Carolina through Was. and S.F.
13. N.Y. Jets	John Abraham	LB	South Carolina	From San Diego through Tampa Bay
14. Green Bay	Bubba Franks	TE	Miami, Fla.	
15. Denver	Deltha O'Neal	DB	California	From Baltimore
16. San Francisco	Julian Peterson	LB	Michigan State	From New England through N.Y. Jets
17. Oakland	Sebastian Janikowski	PK	Florida State	
18. N.Y. Jets	Chad Pennington	QB	Marshall	
19. Seattle	Shaun Alexander	RB	Alabama	From Dallas
20. Detroit	Stockar McDougle	T	Oklahoma	
21. Kansas City	Sylvester Morris	WR	Jackson State	
22. Seattle	Chris McIntosh	T	Wisconsin	
23. Carolina	Rashard Anderson	DB	Jackson State	From Miami
24. San Francisco	Ahmed Plummer	DB	Ohio State	From Washington
25. Minnesota	Chris Hovan	DT	Boston College	
26. Buffalo	Erik Flowers	DE	Arizona State	
27. N.Y. Jets	Anthony Becht	TE	West Virginia	From Tampa Bay
28. Indianapolis	Rob Morris	LB	Brigham Young	
29. Jacksonville	R. Jay Soward	WR	Southern California	
30. Tennessee	Keith Bulluck	LB	Syracuse	
31. St. Louis	Trung Canidate	RB	Arizona	

SECOND ROUND

Team	Player selected	Pos.	College	Draft pick origination
32. Cleveland	Dennis Northcutt	WR	Arizona	
33. New Orleans	Darren Howard	DE	Kansas State	
34. Cincinnati	Mark Roman	CB	Louisiana State	
35. San Francisco	John Engelberger	DE	Virginia Tech	
36. Philadelphia	Todd Pinkston	WR	Southern Mississippi	
37. Atlanta	Travis Claridge	T	Southern California	
38. Pittsburgh	Marvel Smith	T	Arizona State	
39. Chicago	Mike Brown	S	Nebraska	
40. Denver	Ian Gold	LB	Michigan	
41. Arizona	Raynoch Thompson	LB	Tennessee	
42. N.Y. Giants	Cornelius Griffin	DT	Alabama	
43. San Diego	Rogers Beckett	S	Marshall	
44. Green Bay	Chad Clifton	T	Tennessee	
45. Denver	Kenoy Kennedy	S	Arkansas	From Baltimore
46. New England	Adrian Klemm	T	Hawaii	
47. Oakland	Jerry Porter	WR	West Virginia	
48. San Francisco	Jason Webster	DB	Texas A&M	From N.Y. Jets
49. Dallas	Dwayne Goodrich	DB	Tennessee	
50. Detroit	Barrett Green	LB	West Virginia	
51. Tampa Bay	Cosey Coleman	G	Tennessee	From Carolina
52. Seattle	Ike Charlton	DB	Virginia Tech	
53. Miami	Todd Wade	T	Mississippi	
54. Kansas City	William Bartee	DB	Oklahoma	
55. Minnesota	Fred Robbins	DT	Wake Forest	
56. Minnesota	Michael Boireau	DE	Miami, Fla.	From Washington
57. Carolina	Deon Grant	S	Tennessee	From Tampa Bay
58. Buffalo	Travares Tillman	S	Georgia Tech	
59. Indianapolis	Marcus Washington	DE	Auburn	
60. Jacksonville	Brad Meester	C	Northern Iowa	
61. Philadelphia	Bobby Williams	G	Arkansas	From Tennessee
62. St. Louis	Jacoby Shepherd	DB	Oklahoma State	

2000 SEASON *College draft*

2000 SEASON College draft

THIRD ROUND

	Team	Player selected	Pos.	College	Draft pick origination
63.	Cleveland	Travis Prentice	RB	Miami of Ohio	
64.	Washington	Lloyd Harrison	DB	North Carolina State	From New Orleans
65.	San Francisco	Giovanni Carmazzi	QB	Hofstra	
66.	Cincinnati	Ron Dugans	WR	Florida State	
67.	Atlanta	Mark Simoneau	LB	Kansas State	
68.	Tennessee	Erron Kinney	TE	Florida	From Philadelphia
69.	Chicago	Dez White	WR	Georgia Tech	
70.	Denver	Chris Cole	WR	Texas A&M	
71.	Arizona	Darwin Walker	DT	Tennessee	
72.	Pittsburgh	Kendrick Clancy	DT	Mississippi	
73.	N.Y. Giants	Ronald Dixon	WR	Lambuth (Tenn.)	
74.	Green Bay	Steve Warren	DT	Nebraska	
75.	Baltimore	Chris Redman	QB	Louisville	
76.	New England	J.R. Redmond	RB	Arizona State	
77.	Pittsburgh	Hank Poteat	DB	Pittsburgh	From Oakland
78.	N.Y. Jets	Laveranues Coles	WR	Florida State	
79.	Cleveland†	JaJuan Dawson	WR	Tulane	
80.	Seattle	Darrell Jackson	WR	Florida	From Dallas
81.	Detroit	Reuben Droughns	RB	Oregon	
82.	Carolina	Leander Jordan	G	Indiana, Pa.	
83.	San Diego	Damion McIntosh	T	Kansas State	
84.	Miami	Ben Kelly	DB	Colorado	
85.	Kansas City	Gregory Wesley	DB	Arkansas-Pine Bluff	
86.	San Francisco	Jeff Ulbrich	LB	Hawaii	From Seattle
87.	Chicago	Dustin Lyman	TE	Wake Forest	From Washington
88.	Minnesota	Doug Chapman	RB	Marshall	
89.	Buffalo	Corey Moore	LB	Virginia Tech	
90.	Tampa Bay	Nate Webster	LB	Miami, Fla.	
91.	Indianapolis	David Macklin	DB	Penn State	
92.	Jacksonville	T.J. Slaughter	LB	Southern Mississippi	
93.	Tennessee	Byron Frisch	DE	Brigham Young	
94.	St. Louis	John St. Clair	C	Virginia	

FOURTH ROUND

	Team	Player selected	Pos.	College	Draft pick origination
95.	Cleveland	Lewis Sanders	CB	Maryland	
96.	New Orleans	Terrelle Smith	RB	Arizona State	
97.	Cincinnati	Curtis Keaton	RB	James Madison	
98.	Green Bay	Na'il Diggs	LB	Ohio State	From San Francisco
99.	Philadelphia	Gari Scott	WR	Michigan State	
100.	Atlanta	Michael Thompson	T	Tennessee State	
101.	Denver	Jerry Johnson	DT	Florida State	
102.	Arizona	David Barrett	DB	Arkansas	
103.	Pittsburgh	Danny Farmer	WR	UCLA	
104.	St. Louis	Kaulana Noa	G	Hawaii	From Chicago
105.	N.Y. Giants	Brandon Short	LB	Penn State	
106.	Minnesota	Antonio Wilson	LB	Texas A&M-Commerce	From Baltimore
107.	Oakland	Junior Ioane	DT	Arizona State	
108.	San Francisco	John Keith	S	Furman	From N.Y. Jets through Green Bay
109.	Dallas	Kareem Larrimore	DB	West Texas A&M	
110.	Cleveland†	Aaron Shea	TE	Michigan	
111.	San Diego	Trevor Gaylor	WR	Miami of Ohio	From Detroit through Philadelphia
112.	Denver	Cooper Carlisle	T	Florida	From Carolina
113.	San Diego	Leonardo Carson	DE	Auburn	
114.	Green Bay	Anthony Lucas	WR	Arkansas	
115.	Kansas City	Frank Moreau	RB	Louisville	
116.	Seattle	Marcus Bell	LB	Arizona	
117.	Miami	Deon Dyer	FB	North Carolina	
118.	Minnesota	Tyrone Carter	DB	Minnesota	
119.	Seattle	Isaiah Kacyvenski	LB	Harvard	From Washington through San Francisco
120.	Carolina	Alvin McKinley	DT	Mississippi State	From Tampa Bay
121.	Buffalo	Avion Black	WR	Tennessee State	
122.	Indianapolis	Josh Williams	DT	Michigan	
123.	Jacksonville	Joey Chustz	T	Louisiana Tech	
124.	Tennessee	Bobby Myers	S	Wisconsin	
125.	Chicago	Reggie Austin	DB	Wake Forest	From St. Louis
126.	Green Bay*	Gary Berry	DB	Ohio State	
127.	New England*	Greg Robinson-Randall	T	Michigan State	
128.	Tennessee*	Peter Sirmon	LB	Oregon	
129.	Washington*	Michael Moore	G	Troy State	

FIFTH ROUND

Team	Player selected	Pos.	College	Draft pick origination
130. Cleveland	Anthony Malbrough	DB	Texas Tech	
131. New Orleans	Tutan Reyes	T	Mississippi	
132. San Francisco	Paul Smith	RB	Texas-El Paso	From San Francisco through Green Bay
133. Cincinnati	Robert Bean	DB	Mississippi State	
134. Atlanta	Anthony Midget	DB	Virginia Tech	
135. Tennessee	Aric Morris	DB	Michigan State	From Philadelphia
136. Arizona	Mao Tosi	DT	Idaho	
137. Pittsburgh	Clark Haggans	LB	Colorado State	
138. Indianapolis	Matt Johnson	C	Brigham Young	From Chicago through New Orleans
139. St. Louis	Brian Young	DL	Texas-El Paso	From Denver
140. N.Y. Giants	Ralph Brown	DB	Nebraska	
141. New England	Dave Stachelski	TE	Boise State	
142. Oakland	Shane Lechler	P	Texas A&M	
143. N.Y. Jets	Windrell Hayes	WR	Southern California	
144. Dallas	Michael Wiley	WR	Ohio State	
145. Detroit	Todd Franz	DB	Tulsa	
146. Cleveland†	Lamar Chapman	DB	Kansas State	
147. Carolina	Gillis Wilson	DT	Southern	
148. Baltimore	Richard Mercier	G	Miami, Fla.	From San Diego
149. Green Bay	Kabeer Gbaja-Biamila	DE	San Diego State	
150. San Francisco	John Milem	DE	Lenoir-Rhyne	From Baltimore through Det., St.L. and Chi.
151. Green Bay	Joey Jamison	KR	Texas Southern	From Seattle
152. Miami	Arturo Freeman	DB	South Carolina	
153. Kansas City	Dante Hall	RB	Texas A&M	
154. Denver	Muneer Moore	WR	Richmond	From Washington through S.F. and and Sea.
155. Washington	Quincy Sanders	DB	UNLV	From Minnesota
156. Buffalo	Sammy Morris	RB	Texas Tech	
157. Tampa Bay	James Whalen	TE	Kentucky	
158. New Orleans	Austin Wheatley	TE	Iowa	From Indianapolis
159. Jacksonville	Kiwaukee Thomas	DB	Georgia Southern	
160. Tennessee	Frank Chamberlin	LB	Boston College	
161. New England	Jeff Marriott	DT	Missouri	From St. Louis
162. Kansas City*	Pat Dennis	DB	Louisiana-Monroe	
163. Pittsburgh*	Tee Martin	QB	Tennessee	
164. Arizona*	Jay Tant	TE	Northwestern	
165. Minnesota*	Troy Walters	WR	Stanford	
166. New Orleans*	Chad Morton	RB	Southern California	

SIXTH ROUND

Team	Player selected	Pos.	College	Draft pick origination
167. Miami	Earnest Grant	DT	Arkansas-Pine Bluff	From Cleveland
168. New Orleans	Marc Bulger	QB	West Virginia	
169. Cincinnati	Neil Rackers	PK	Illinois	
170. Chicago	Frank Murphy	RB	Kansas State	From San Francisco
171. Philadelphia	Thomas Hamner	RB	Minnesota	
172. Atlanta	Mareno Philyaw	WR	Troy State	
173. Pittsburgh	Chris Combs	DT	Duke	
174. Chicago	Paul Edinger	PK	Michigan State	
175. Seattle	James Williams	WR	Marshall	From Denver
176. Arizona	Jabari Issa	DT	Washington	
177. N.Y. Giants	Dhani Jones	LB	Michigan	
178. Philadelphia	John Frank	DE	Utah	From Oakland
179. N.Y. Jets	Tony Scott	DB	North Carolina State	
180. Dallas	Mario Edwards	DB	Florida State	
181. Detroit	Quinton Reese	DE	Auburn	
182. Carolina	Jeno James	T	Auburn	
183. Cleveland†	Spergon Wynn	QB	Southwest Texas State	
184. San Diego	Shannon Taylor	LB	Virginia	
185. Seattle	Tim Watson	DT	Rowan (N.J.)	From Green Bay
186. Baltimore	Adalius Thomas	DE	Southern Mississippi	
187. New England	Antwan Harris	DB	Virginia	
188. Kansas City	Darnell Alford	T	Boston College	From Miami
189. Denver	Mike Anderson	RB	Utah	From Kansas City through St. Louis
190. Seattle	John Hilliard	DT	Mississippi State	
191. Baltimore	Cedric Woodard	DT	Texas	From Minnesota
192. Philadelphia	John Romero	C	California	From Washington
193. Tampa Bay	David Gibson	DB	Southern California	
194. Buffalo	Leif Larson	DT	Texas-El Paso	
195. New Orleans	Michael Hawthorne	DB	Purdue	From Indianapolis

2000 SEASON College draft

Team	Player selected	Pos.	College	Draft pick origination
196. Jacksonville	Emanuel Smith	WR	Arkansas	
197. Tennessee	Robaire Smith	DE	Michigan State	
198. St. Louis	Matt Bowen	DB	Iowa	
199. New England*	Tom Brady	QB	Michigan	
200. New Orleans*	Sherrod Gideon	WR	Southern Mississippi	
201. New England*	David Nugent	DT	Purdue	
202. Washington*	Todd Husak	QB	Stanford	
203. San Diego*	Damen Wheeler	DB	Colorado	
204. Pittsburgh*	Jason Gavadza	TE	Kent	
205. San Diego*	JaJuan Seider	QB	Florida A&M	
206. Cleveland†	Brad Bedell	G	Colorado	

SEVENTH ROUND

Team	Player selected	Pos.	College	Draft pick origination
207. Cleveland	Manuia Savea	G	Arizona	
208. Kansas City	Desmond Kitchings	WR	Furman	From New Orleans
209. Cleveland	Eric Chandler	DE	Jackson State	From San Francisco through Chicago
210. Cincinnati	Brad St. Louis	TE	Southwest Missouri State	
211. Atlanta	Darrick Vaughn	DB	Southwest Texas State	
212. San Francisco	Tim Rattay	QB	Louisiana Tech	From Philadelphia through New England
213. Tennessee	Mike Green	RB	Houston	From Chicago
214. Denver	Jarious Jackson	QB	Notre Dame	
215. Arizona	Sekou Sanyika	LB	California	
216. Washington	Delbert Cowsette	DT	Maryland	From Pittsburgh
217. N.Y. Giants	Jeremiah Parker	DE	California	
218. N.Y. Jets	Richard Seals	DT	Utah	
219. Dallas	Orantes Grant	LB	Georgia	
220. St. Louis	Andrew Kline	G	San Diego State	From Detroit
221. Carolina	Lester Towns	LB	Washington	
222. San Diego	Jason Thomas	G	Hampton	
223. Chicago	James Cotton	DE	Ohio State	From Cleveland†
224. Green Bay	Mark Tauscher	T	Wisconsin	
225. Cleveland	Rashidi Barnes	DB	Colorado	From Baltimore through St.L. and Chi.
226. New England	Casey Tisdale	DE	New Mexico	
227. Oakland	Mondriel Fulcher	TE	Miami, Fla.	
228. New Orleans	Kevin Houser	TE	Ohio State	From Kansas City
229. Green Bay	Ron Moore	DT	Northwestern Oklahoma	From Seattle
230. San Francisco	Brian Jennings	TE	Arizona State	From Miami
231. Oakland	Cliffton Black	DB	Southwest Texas State	From Washington through Den. and Sea.
232. Miami	Jeff Harris	DB	Georgia	From Minnesota through Cle. and Chi.
233. Buffalo	Drew Haddad	WR	Buffalo	
234. Tampa Bay	Joe Hamilton	QB	Georgia Tech	
235. Indianapolis	Rob Renes	DT	Michigan	
236. Jacksonville	Erik Olson	DB	Colorado State	
237. Tennessee	Wes Shivers	G	Mississippi State	
238. Indianapolis	Rodregis Brooks	DB	Alabama-Birmingham	From St. Louis through Oakland
239. New England*	Patrick Pass	RB	Georgia	
240. Minnesota*	Mike Malano	C	San Diego State	
241. Jacksonville*	Rob Meier	DE	Washington State	
242. Green Bay*	Charles Lee	WR	Central Florida	
243. Jacksonville*	Shyrone Stith	RB	Virginia Tech	
244. Minnesota*	Giles Cole	TE	Texas A&M-Kingsville	
245. Jacksonville*	Danny Clark	LB	Illinois	
246. Denver*	Leroy Fields	WR	Jackson State	
247. Jacksonville*	Mark Baniewicz	T	Syracuse	
248. Minnesota*	Lewis Kelly	G	South Carolina State	
249. Green Bay*	Eugene McCaslin	LB	Florida	
250. Washington*	Ethan Howell	WR	Oklahoma State	
251. Buffalo*	DaShon Polk	LB	Arizona	
252. Green Bay*	Rondell Mealey	RB	Louisiana State	
253. Detroit*	Alfonso Boone	DT	Mount San Antonio J.C.	
254. Chicago	Mike Green	DB	Louisiana-Lafayette	From Cleveland†

*Pick awarded to team as compensation for loss of a free agent. †Supplemental pick awarded to Browns.

PLAYOFF PLAN

TIEBREAKING PROCEDURES

DIVISION TIES

TWO CLUBS
1. Head-to-head (best won-lost-tied percentage in games between the clubs).
2. Best won-lost-tied percentage in games played within the division.
3. Best won-lost-tied percentage in games played within the conference.
4. Best won-lost-tied percentage in common games, if applicable.
5. Best net points in division games.
6. Best net points in all games.
7. Strength of schedule.
8. Best net touchdowns in all games.
9. Coin toss.

THREE OR MORE CLUBS
(Note: If two clubs remain tied after other clubs are eliminated during any step, tie-breaker reverts to step 1 of two-club format.)
1. Head-to-head (best won-lost-tied percentage in games among the clubs).
2. Best won-lost-tied percentage in games played within the division.
3. Best won-lost-tied percentage in games played within the conference.
4. Best won-lost-tied percentage in common games.
5. Best net points in division games.
6. Best net points in all games.
7. Strength of schedule.
8. Best net touchdowns in all games.
9. Coin toss.

WILD-CARD TIES

If necessary to break ties to determine the three wild-card clubs from each conference, the following steps will be taken:
1. If all the tied clubs are from the same division, apply division tie-breaker.
2. If the tied clubs are from different divisions, apply the steps listed below.
3. When the first wild-card team has been identified, the procedure is repeated to name the second wild card (i.e., eliminate all but the highest-ranked club in each division prior to proceeding to step 2), and repeated a third time, if necessary, to identify the third wild card. In situations where three or more teams from the same division are involved in the procedure, the original seeding of the teams remains the same for subsequent applications of the tie-breaker if the top-ranked team in that division qualifies for a wild-card berth.

TWO CLUBS
1. Head-to-head, if applicable.
2. Best won-lost-tied percentage in games played within the conference.
3. Best won-lost-tied percentage in common games, minimum of four.
4. Best average net points in conference games.
5. Best net points in all games.
6. Strength of schedule.
7. Best net touchdowns in all games.
8. Coin toss.

THREE OR MORE CLUBS
(Note: If two clubs remain tied after other clubs are eliminated, tie-breaker reverts to step 1 of two-club format.)
1. Apply division tie-breaker to eliminate all but highest-ranked club in each division prior to proceeding to step 1. The original seeding within a division upon application of the division tie-breaker remains the same for all subsequent applications of the procedure that are necessary to identify the three wild-card participants.
2. Head-to-head sweep (applicable only if one club has defeated each of the others or one club has lost to each of the others).
3. Best won-lost-tied percentage in games played within the conference.
4. Best won-lost-tied percentage in common games, minimum of four.
5. Best average net points in conference games.
6. Best net points in all games.
7. Strength of schedule.
8. Best net touchdowns in all games.
9. Coin toss.

1999 REVIEW

Year in review
Final standings
Weeks 1 through 17
Wild-card games
Divisional playoffs
Conference championships
Super Bowl 34
Pro Bowl
Player participation
Attendance
Trades

YEAR IN REVIEW
THE TOP STORIES OF THE PAST YEAR

Sanders (left) and Marino both bid farewell to the NFL, with Sanders' surprising announcement coming one month before the season began and Marino's not-so-surprising announcement coming after its conclusion. (Left photo by Robert Seale/THE SPORTING NEWS. Right photo by Bob Leverone/THE SPORTING NEWS.)

By STEVE MEYERHOFF

It was a year that defied predictions, a year of improbability and even impossibility. It was a year in which the have-nots became the haves, winners became losers and losers became winners, a year of unexpected retirements and untimely injuries.

It was a year of change.

In came the St. Louis Rams, Tennessee Titans, Indianapolis Colts and Cleveland Browns—the revised edition. Out went the Denver Broncos, Atlanta Falcons, Green Bay Packers and Dallas Cowboys. In came Kurt Warner, Edgerrin James and Tim Couch. Out went Barry Sanders, Dan Marino, Terrell Davis and Steve Young.

Out forever went Walter Payton, Tom Landry and Derrick Thomas.

Yes, it's safe to call 1999 a season of change.

THE BEGINNING, THE END

The season began, ironically, the same way it ended—with one of the game's brightest stars announcing his retirement. When Lions running back Barry Sanders jolted the football world with the August news that he was burned out on football and ready to call it a career, he set a wild tone for one of the most bizarre NFL campaigns in history.

The 1999 season was supposed to be a coronation for Sanders. With only 1,457 yards separating him from all-time leading rusher Walter Payton, he figured to ascend to the NFL rushing throne. Numerous other records were either already his (consecutive 1,000-yard seasons, consecutive 100-yard games) or within grasp, including the career mark for rushing touchdowns.

But Sanders didn't even make it to the starting gate. Saying he was tired and in need of a rest, the Lions' running back, at the tender age of 31, astonished everybody by walking away from the game.

Many speculated he was tired of losing in Detroit. Others called it a play for more money, or a trade. Many predicted he would be back during the season.

Many were wrong.

Six months later, after the season officially had concluded, Dolphins quarterback Dan Marino made a more predictable exit, ending his 17-year career with record-setting numbers: 61,361 passing yards, 420 touchdown passes, 4,967 completions. The man who recorded phenomenal single-season passing highs of 5,084 yards and 48 TDs in 1984 stepped down as the most prolific passer in NFL history and a sure-bet Hall of Famer. But one lesser number will haunt him forever— zero, the number of Super Bowl championships he brought to Miami.

The 38-year-old Marino called it a career with his famed quick release and analytic mind still sharp, but his knees betrayed him. After the Dolphins dropped a 62-7 divisional playoff battle to Jacksonville, rumors circulated that Marino might quarterback a new team—perhaps the Vikings—in 2000. But he decided to go out the way he will always be remembered: as a Dolphin.

ACHES AND PAINS

The Rams' rise was helped by key injuries to the teams everybody expected to contend in 1999. And the transition started immediately, with a Week 1 shocker that transformed the New York Jets from contenders to pretenders.

With Vinny Testaverde calling the signals, New York contended in 1998, eventually losing to the Broncos in the AFC championship game. But the 1999 season opener provided a doubled whammy to their hopes for a second Super Bowl championship—the Jets lost to New England and Testaverde ruptured his Achilles' tendon, an injury that would sideline him for the season. With Rick Mirer thrust into a starting role, the Jets struggled until unheralded Ray Lucas took over and brought them home with an 8-8 record.

The Falcons, coming off the franchise's first Super Bowl appearance, had equally high hopes. But they played the bulk of the season without their most vital offensive weapon, running back Jamal Anderson. Anderson's difficult campaign began with a training camp holdout and ended in the team's second regular-season game, a loss to Dallas. Anderson

When Testaverde went down in Week 1, the Jets went down with him. (Photo by John Dunn for THE SPORTING NEWS.)

went down with a torn anterior cruciate ligament and his absence, coupled with the loss of quarterback Chris Chandler to a hamstring injury in the season opener, devastated the Falcons. They struggled to a 1-6 start en route to a 5-11 season.

The most devastating injury crumbled the hopes of the defending two-time Super Bowl-champion Broncos. With their offense already in transition after the retirement of quarterback John Elway, running back Terrell Davis suffered a partial tear of his medial collateral ligament in the fourth game and underwent surgery on October 13. He missed the rest of the season. Denver, without its biggest offensive guns, opened 0-4 and struggled home 6-10.

THE RISE OF THE RAMS

Ironically, it was an injury that opened the door for the Rams' sudden rise to prominence. It occurred August 28, during the team's third preseason game. Quarterback Trent Green, a free-agent acquisition who was being handed

The Rams' remarkable turnaround was spearheaded by league MVP Warner (left) and Pro Bowler Bruce, who combined for the winning touchdown in the waning moments of Super Bowl 34. (Photos by Bob Leverone/THE SPORTING NEWS.)

the keys to a high-powered offense, went down with a season-ending knee injury, courtesy of a hit from behind by San Diego strong safety Rodney Harrison.

With Green performing flawlessly, the Rams offense, with a healthy Isaac Bruce, newcomer Marshall Faulk, rookie Torry Holt and an emerging Az-Zahir Hakim under the guidance of coach Dick Vermeil and offensive coordinator Mike Martz, looked like a well-oiled machine. Without him, the quarterback depth chart read like an unedited novel: Joe Germaine, Paul Justin and Kurt Warner.

The improbable and soon-to-be much-told story of a grocery store clerk- turned-MVP and Super Bowl champion started with that shocking preseason injury to Green.

Warner looked good in a preseason-closing 17-6 win at Detroit. But "good" turned to "great" in Week 1 of the regular season, Warner's first NFL start: 309 passing yards, three touchdowns in a 27-10 win over the Ravens. Game 2: 275 yards, 17-of-25 passing and three more touchdowns in a 35-7 rout of Atlanta. Game 3: 17-of-22, 310 yards, three touchdowns in a 38-10 win over the Bengals. Game 4: 323 yards, 20-of-23 passing, five TDs in a 42-20 pounding of the 49ers.

And so it continued until Game 7, when the Tennessee Titans—a team the Rams would meet again in January—ended a six-game St. Louis win streak, 24-21. By season's end, the Rams were an NFC-best 13-3, an improvement from 4-12 in 1998, and owned home-field advantage throughout the NFC playoffs.

Warner's regular-season numbers were staggering for any quarterback, but especially one who had attempted just 11 passes in one NFL game prior to 1999: 4,353 yards, 41 touchdown passes, a 65.1 percent completion percentage and a whopping quarterback rating of 109.2. The league MVP became only the second player to throw for 40 TDs in a season.

With Faulk, Bruce, Holt and company performing their big-play magic week after week, the speedy Rams marched into the playoffs, knocked out the Vikings, 49-37, in a divisional offensive showdown and then slipped past the Tampa Bay Buccaneers, 11-6, in the NFC championship game on a late touchdown pass from Warner to Ricky Proehl.

That set up a Super Bowl battle against the Titans, who powered their way to a regular-season 13-3 record behind the running of Eddie George (1,304 yards) but had to qualify for the playoffs as a wild card behind the 14-2 Jacksonville Jaguars. The Titans' path to the franchise's first Super Bowl required a stunning 22-16 wild-card victory over the Buffalo Bills that was decided on a controversial final-play cross-field lateral on a kickoff return and a 19-16 second-round win over 1999 rushing champion James (1,553 yards) and his Eastern Division-champion Indianapolis Colts.

In a Super Bowl many considered one of the most exciting ever played, a last-play tackle by Rams linebacker Mike Jones stopped Titans receiver Kevin Dyson on the 1-yard line, saving a 23-16 win and the first Super Bowl championship in Rams history. It also was the first for Vermeil, who retired two days after the victory and turned the coaching reins over to Martz.

THE BROWNS ARE BACK

While new-found enthusiasm was gushing in St. Louis, an old, contagious enthusiasm was spilling through the streets of Cleveland, thanks to the rebirth of the Browns.

After suffering through three years without pro football, Cleveland fans, some of the most fervent in the game, welcomed the first expansion franchise with a football legacy. While the new Browns were young, fresh and short on depth and talent, they arrived with a long, winning history (four NFL championships and 11 title-game appearances from 1950-69) and promise for the future. They also began play in a new lakefront stadium and came equipped with a franchise quarterback (Couch), the first overall pick of the NFL draft.

The unusual revival took root in 1995 when longtime Browns owner Art Modell moved his

Carruth was one of many players to run afoul of the law during the 1999 season. (Photo by Bob Leverone/THE SPORTING NEWS.)

team to Baltimore and renamed them the Ravens. Cleveland fans mourned, pondered their situation and then fought frantically for a new team.

The result, the new Browns, finished with an NFL-worst 2-14 record in their debut season.

PLAYERS IN TROUBLE

While the NFL was choreographing one of the most interesting seasons in recent memory, it also was struggling with a severe image problem. Having struggled with drugs and assorted off-field problems in past years, the league found its name being bandied around courtrooms for more deadly and serious crimes allegedly perpetrated by several of its star players.

First came the news that Rae Carruth, a wide receiver for the Carolina Panthers, was being charged with three others of plotting a November 16, 1999, drive-by shooting that killed his pregnant girlfriend, Cherica Adams. She died December 14, after doctors had saved her baby. Carruth, who originally fled

Thomas' accident and subsequent death shocked all NFL fans, but especially those in Kansas City, where he broke in as a rookie in 1989. (Photo by Albert Dickson/THE SPORTING NEWS.)

from authorities and was subsequently released by the Panthers, was arrested pending his spring 2000 trial.

On the heels of the Carruth matter came news that Baltimore Ravens linebacker Ray Lewis was being charged with murder along with two friends in the January 31 stabbing death of two men during a brawl following a Super Bowl party outside a nightclub in Atlanta. The trial for Lewis, a three-time All-Pro, also began in spring 2000.

The NFL was shocked one more time when three-time Green Bay Pro Bowl tight end Mark Chmura was arrested and charged with sexually assaulting his 17-year-old baby sitter at an April 9, 2000, post-prom party thrown by a friend. If convicted, Chmura faced up to 10 years in prison and a $10,000 fine.

SAD FAREWELLS

While reeling from its sudden image problem, the NFL lost three of its greatest ambassadors—two of whom died tragically within days of each other.

Walter Payton, the former Chicago Bears star they called Sweetness, died November 1 of cancer, the result of his fight with a rare liver condition. Payton, the consummate professional, retired in 1987 as the NFL's all-time leading rusher. Not only was Payton a hard-nosed, scratch-for-every-yard type running back, he was the hard-working, fun-loving role model who combined grace, power and speed in his rock-hard, 5-foot-11 frame.

Three months later, Kansas City linebacker Derrick Thomas and former Dallas coach Tom Landry died four days apart.

News that Thomas, 33, one of the league's most dominant defensive players of the 1990s, had been paralyzed from the chest down in a January 23 automobile accident was bad enough. But on February 8, when Thomas appeared to be in good spirits and ready to tackle a different kind of life, word swept the nation that he had died suddenly from a blood clot in his lung while rehabbing at a Miami hospital.

Chiefs fans went into mourning over their longtime star, who was known as much for his humanitarian efforts around the Kansas City area as his vicious assaults on quarterbacks. As a player, Thomas was the guy opposing offenses went to the greatest lengths to avoid. A 1989 first-round draft pick after an All-American career at Alabama, he played in nine consecutive Pro Bowls and recorded 126 1/2 career sacks, including an NFL-record seven in one memorable 1990 game against Seattle.

The accident occurred as Thomas and two friends were heading to St. Louis to watch the NFC championship game between the Rams and Buccaneers. Driving fast on snow-slickened roads en route to the Kansas City airport, Thomas turned over the vehicle and was thrown from the wreck. One friend was killed and the other, who was wearing a seatbelt, escaped unhurt.

As the football world was trying to recover from the death of Thomas, the 75-year-old

Landry died of leukemia on February 12. Known affectionately as the stoic man in the fedora, Landry had coached the Dallas Cowboys for 29 seasons and won 270 games (third on the all-time list), 13 division titles, five NFC championships and two Super Bowls.

Landry, who played defensive back for the Giants in the 1950s and later coached alongside the legendary Vince Lombardi when both were assistants in New York, will be remembered for the defensive genius he used to turn the expansion Cowboys into "America's Team." He introduced the flex defense featuring Randy White, Harvey Martin and Ed "Too Tall" Jones, reintroduced the shotgun offensive wrinkle to the NFL and he choreographed an efficient offense featuring quarterback Roger Staubach passing to Drew Pearson, Bob Hayes, Golden Richards and Billy Joe DuPree, and the running exploits of Hall of Famer Tony Dorsett.

He also will be remembered for the class and respect he brought to the field, and the Christian work he performed away from it.

FINAL STANDINGS

AMERICAN FOOTBALL CONFERENCE

EASTERN DIVISION

	W	L	T	Pct.	Pts.	Opp.	Home	Away	Vs. AFC	Vs. NFC	Vs. AFC East
Indianapolis*	13	3	0	.813	423	333	7-1	6-2	9-3	4-0	5-3
Buffalo†	11	5	0	.688	320	229	6-2	5-3	8-4	3-1	6-2
Miami†	9	7	0	.563	326	336	5-3	4-4	7-5	2-2	3-5
N.Y. Jets	8	8	0	.500	308	309	4-4	4-4	6-6	2-2	4-4
New England	8	8	0	.500	299	284	5-3	3-5	5-7	3-1	2-6

CENTRAL DIVISION

	W	L	T	Pct.	Pts.	Opp.	Home	Away	Vs. AFC	Vs. NFC	Vs. AFC Central
Jacksonville*	14	2	0	.875	396	217	7-1	7-1	10-2	4-0	8-2
Tennessee†	13	3	0	.813	392	324	8-0	5-3	10-2	3-1	9-1
Baltimore	8	8	0	.500	324	277	4-4	4-4	6-7	2-1	6-4
Pittsburgh	6	10	0	.375	317	320	2-6	4-4	3-10	3-0	3-7
Cincinnati	4	12	0	.250	283	460	2-6	2-6	3-10	1-2	3-7
Cleveland	2	14	0	.125	217	437	0-8	2-6	1-12	1-2	1-9

WESTERN DIVISION

	W	L	T	Pct.	Pts.	Opp.	Home	Away	Vs. AFC	Vs. NFC	Vs. AFC West
Seattle*	9	7	0	.563	338	298	5-3	4-4	7-5	2-2	4-4
Kansas City	9	7	0	.563	390	322	6-2	3-5	7-5	2-2	4-4
San Diego	8	8	0	.500	269	316	4-4	4-4	7-5	1-3	5-3
Oakland	8	8	0	.500	390	329	5-3	3-5	5-7	3-1	3-5
Denver	6	10	0	.375	314	318	3-5	3-5	4-8	2-2	4-4

*Division champion. †Wild-card team.

NATIONAL FOOTBALL CONFERENCE

EASTERN DIVISION

	W	L	T	Pct.	Pts.	Opp.	Home	Away	Vs. AFC	Vs. NFC	Vs. NFC East
Washington*	10	6	0	.625	443	377	6-2	4-4	2-2	8-4	5-3
Dallas†	8	8	0	.500	352	276	7-1	1-7	1-3	7-5	5-3
N.Y. Giants	7	9	0	.438	299	358	4-4	3-5	2-2	5-7	3-5
Arizona	6	10	0	.375	245	382	4-4	2-6	0-4	6-6	5-3
Philadelphia	5	11	0	.313	272	357	4-4	1-7	1-3	4-8	2-6

CENTRAL DIVISION

	W	L	T	Pct.	Pts.	Opp.	Home	Away	Vs. AFC	Vs. NFC	Vs. NFC Central
Tampa Bay*	11	5	0	.688	270	235	7-1	4-4	3-1	8-4	5-3
Minnesota†	10	6	0	.625	399	335	6-2	4-4	2-2	8-4	4-4
Detroit†	8	8	0	.500	322	323	6-2	2-6	1-3	7-5	4-4
Green Bay	8	8	0	.500	357	341	5-3	3-5	2-2	6-6	4-4
Chicago	6	10	0	.375	272	341	3-5	3-5	2-2	4-8	3-5

WESTERN DIVISION

	W	L	T	Pct.	Pts.	Opp.	Home	Away	Vs. AFC	Vs. NFC	Vs. NFC West
St. Louis*	13	3	0	.813	526	242	8-0	5-3	3-1	10-2	8-0
Carolina	8	8	0	.500	421	381	5-3	3-5	2-2	6-6	4-4
Atlanta	5	11	0	.313	285	380	4-4	1-7	0-4	5-7	4-4
San Francisco	4	12	0	.250	295	453	3-5	1-7	1-3	3-9	2-6
New Orleans	3	13	0	.188	260	434	3-5	0-8	0-4	3-9	2-6

*Division champion. †Wild-card team.

AFC PLAYOFFS

AFC wild card: Miami 20, Seattle 17
Tennessee 22, Buffalo 16
AFC semifinals: Tennessee 19, Indianapolis 16
Jacksonville 62, Miami 7
AFC championship: Tennessee 33, Jacksonville 14

NFC PLAYOFFS

NFC wild card: Minnesota 27, Dallas 10
Washington 27, Detroit 13
NFC semifinals: St. Louis 49, Minnesota 37
Tampa Bay 14, Washington 13
NFC championship: St. Louis 11, Tampa Bay 6

SUPER BOWL

St. Louis 23, Tennessee 16

WEEK 1

RESULTS

Arizona 25, PHILADELPHIA 24
CHICAGO 20, Kansas City 17
Dallas 41, WASHINGTON 35 (OT)
Detroit 28, SEATTLE 20
GREEN BAY 28, Oakland 24
INDIANAPOLIS 31, Buffalo 14
JACKSONVILLE 41, San Francisco 3
Minnesota 17, ATLANTA 14
New England 30, N.Y. JETS 28
NEW ORLEANS 19, Carolina 10
N.Y. Giants 17, TAMPA BAY 13
Pittsburgh 43, CLEVELAND 0
ST. LOUIS 27, Baltimore 10
TENNESSEE 36, Cincinnati 35
Miami 38, DENVER 21
Open date: San Diego

STANDINGS

AFC EAST
	W	L	T	Pct.
Indianapolis	1	0	0	1.000
Miami	1	0	0	1.000
New England	1	0	0	1.000
N.Y. Jets	0	1	0	.000
Buffalo	0	1	0	.000

AFC CENTRAL
	W	L	T	Pct.
Jacksonville	1	0	0	1.000
Pittsburgh	1	0	0	1.000
Tennessee	1	0	0	1.000
Baltimore	0	1	0	.000
Cincinnati	0	1	0	.000
Cleveland	0	1	0	.000

AFC WEST
	W	L	T	Pct.
San Diego	0	0	0	.000
Denver	0	1	0	.000
Kansas City	0	1	0	.000
Oakland	0	1	0	.000
Seattle	0	1	0	.000

NFC EAST
	W	L	T	Pct.
Arizona	1	0	0	1.000
Dallas	1	0	0	1.000
N.Y. Giants	1	0	0	1.000
Philadelphia	0	1	0	.000
Washington	0	1	0	.000

NFC CENTRAL
	W	L	T	Pct.
Chicago	1	0	0	1.000
Detroit	1	0	0	1.000
Green Bay	1	0	0	1.000
Minnesota	1	0	0	1.000
Tampa Bay	0	1	0	.000

NFC WEST
	W	L	T	Pct.
New Orleans	1	0	0	1.000
St. Louis	1	0	0	1.000
Atlanta	0	1	0	.000
Carolina	0	1	0	.000
San Francisco	0	1	0	.000

HIGHLIGHTS

Hero of the week: Brett Favre guided the Packers 82 yards in 11 plays in the final 1:51—without a timeout—and found tight end Jeff Thomason for a touchdown to lead the Packers to a 28-24 win over Oakland. On the previous possession, Favre, who was playing with an injured right thumb, marched Green Bay 76 yards in eight plays and hit Corey Bradford on an eight-yard score to cut Oakland's lead to 24-21.

Goat of the week: The usually reliable Morten Andersen missed two fourth-quarter field goals in the Falcons' 17-14 loss to the Vikings. He missed from 35 yards out (wide right) and then 39 yards (wide left) with 3:38 left in the game. On attempts from 30-39 yards, Andersen was a combined 14-of-14 over the last two seasons.

Sub of the week: Rookie Andre Weathers, who was playing in the Giants' dime package only because veteran corners Jason Sehorn (hamstring) and Conrad Hamilton (knee) were sidelined, intercepted a pass from Tampa Bay quarterback Trent Dilfer and returned it eight yards for the go-ahead touchdown in New York's 17-13 win over the Bucs.

Comeback of the week: Dallas matched its biggest comeback ever by battling back from a 35-14 fourth-quarter deficit to beat the Redskins 41-35 in overtime. Troy Aikman connected with Rocket Ismail on a 76-yard touchdown for the game-winner. After Michael Irvin hauled in his second touchdown from Troy Aikman with 1:46 left in regulation, kicker Richie Cunningham's extra-point kick hit off the left upright before going through to force overtime. Washington had a chance to win on the last play of regulation, but holder Matt Turk fumbled the snap on what would have been a 41-yard field goal attempt by Brett Conway.

Blowout of the week: A pregame that included fireworks, a marching band and comedian Drew Carey leading the crowd in a "Cleveland rocks" chant wasn't enough to get the expansion Browns fired up in their home opener. The Steelers built a 20-0 halftime lead and cruised to a 43-0 win. Richard Huntley had three touchdowns to lead the Steelers, who led in time of possession by a whopping 47:49 to 12:11.

Nail-biter of the week: Al Del Greco kicked a 33-yard field goal with eight seconds left to give the Titans a 36-35 comeback win over the Bengals. Eddie George scored on a 17-yard swing pass with 4:30 left, and then the Titans moved 34 yards in seven plays to set up Del Greco's game-winner. Steve McNair finished with 341 yards and four touchdowns, including a 1-yard run.

Hit of the week: The Saints sacked Carolina quarterback Steve Beuerlein seven times, including one by Austin Robbins in the third quarter that forced a fumble that led to a go-ahead field goal. Carolina turned the ball over three times, including a fumble on the opening kickoff that the Saints returned for a touchdown. New Orleans' Fred Weary delivered a jarring hit to Michael Bates at the 22-yard line, and Tyronne Drakeford picked up the ball at the 20 and ran for the score.

Oddity of the week: Confusion among parking attendants prevented thousands of fans from seeing the Cowboys-Redskins overtime thriller. Traffic in the Jack Kent Cooke Stadium lot was tied up for hours, and many fans didn't even make it into the stadium. There were hundreds who still were trying to park at halftime. Thousands of fans left in overtime, hoping to avoid traffic. They were lucky—police said traffic was backed up three hours after the game.

Top rusher: In his NFL debut, running back Edgerrin James rushed for 112 yards on 26 carries in the Colts' 31-14 win over Buffalo. James also had a 1-yard touchdown run in the first quarter.

Top passer: Aikman passed for 362 yards and five touchdowns in the Cowboys' comeback win at Washington. It was the first five-touchdown performance of his 11-year NFL career.

Top receiver: Keyshawn Johnson had eight catches for 194 yards and a touchdown in the Jets' 30-28 loss to the Patriots.

Notes: Ricky Williams, the 1998 Heisman Trophy winner, gained 40 yards on 10 carries in his NFL debut against Carolina but re-injured the ankle that kept him out of the Saints' final three preseason games. ... The Jets suffered a severe blow when quarterback Vinny Testaverde ruptured his left Achilles' tendon in the second quarter of the team's opener against New England. Testaverde fell to the turf untouched after making a quick cut to the ball when Curtis Martin fumbled in the second quarter. Testaverde would miss the rest of the season. ... Arizona snapped a seven-game losing streak in season openers. ... Kurt Warner, a former Arena League quarterback, received the game ball after throwing for 316 yards and three touchdowns to lead the Rams to a 27-10 win over the Ravens in his first NFL start.

Quote of the week: Packers coach Ray Rhodes, on Favre's comeback. "The game came down to No. 4, two minutes, making plays. He's amazing. I thought it was a great drive; a picture-perfect drive."

GAME SUMMARIES

TITANS 36, BENGALS 35
Sunday, September 12

Cincinnati .... 7 14   8   6—35
Tennessee .... 14 12   0 10—36

First Quarter
Ten.—McNair 1 run (Del Greco kick), 1:55.
Cin.—Dillon 1 run (Pelfrey kick), 9:31.
Ten.—Dyson 13 pass from McNair (Del Greco kick), 14:55.

Second Quarter
Ten.—Safety, out of end zone, forced by team, 0:53.
Ten.—FG, Del Greco 50, 4:58.
Ten.—Dyson 47 pass from McNair (Del Greco kick), 9:28.
Cin.—Carter 2 run (Jackson pass from Blake), 13:05.
Cin.—McGee 3 pass from Blake (run failed), 14:54.

Third Quarter
Cin.—Jackson 17 pass from Blake (Milne pass from Blake), 4:23.

Fourth Quarter
Cin.—FG, Pelfrey 33, 4:45.
Cin.—FG, Pelfrey 38, 7:04.
Ten.—E. George 17 pass from McNair (Del Greco kick), 10:30.
Ten.—FG, Del Greco 33, 14:52.
A—65,272.

	Cincinnati	Tennessee
First downs	28	22
Rushes-yards	42-201	18-69
Passing	197	334
Punt returns	0-0	3-62
Kickoff returns	6-118	6-87
Interception returns	1-5	2-34
Comp.-att.-int.	20-34-2	21-32-1
Sacked-yards lost	1-0	2-7
Punts	4-47	2-47
Fumbles-lost	2-0	4-3
Penalties-yards	9-79	8-62
Time of possession	36:45	23:15

INDIVIDUAL STATISTICS
RUSHING—Cincinnati, Dillon 21-66, Blake 11-90, Carter 6-15, Milne 3-30, Smith 1-0. Tennessee, E. George 12-42, McNair 6-27.
PASSING—Cincinnati, Blake 18-31-2-182, Smith 1-2-0-11, Covington 1-1-0-4. Tennessee, McNair 21-32-1-341.
RECEIVING—Cincinnati, Scott 7-80, Jackson 5-60, Pickens 3-21, McGee 2-14, Dillon 2-11, Carter 1-11. Tennessee, Dyson 9-162, Thigpen 4-74, Wycheck 3-51, E. George 3-37, Sanders 2-17.
MISSED FIELD GOAL ATTEMPTS—None.

INTERCEPTIONS—Cincinnati, Hawkins 1-5. Tennessee, Walker 1-27, Sidney 1-7.
KICKOFF RETURNS—Cincinnati, Jackson 3-68, Yeast 3-50. Tennessee, S. George 4-63, Kent 2-24.
PUNT RETURNS—Tennessee, Rolle 1-23, Thigpen 1-21, S. George 1-18.
SACKS—Cincinnati, Simmons 1, Spikes 1. Tennessee, Wortham 0.5, Robertson 0.5.

STEELERS 43, BROWNS 0
Sunday, September 12

Pittsburgh .... 7 13   6 17—43
Cleveland 0   0   0   0— 0

First Quarter
Pit.—Stewart 1 run (K. Brown kick), 9:44.

Second Quarter
Pit.—FG, K. Brown 19, 5:04.
Pit.—Huntley 5 pass from Stewart (K. Brown kick), 10:11.
Pit.—FG, K. Brown 28, 14:54.

Third Quarter
Pit.—Huntley 3 run (kick blocked), 9:32.

Fourth Quarter
Pit.—FG, K. Brown 19, 3:50.
Pit.—Huntley 21 pass from Tomczak (K. Brown kick), 4:12.
Pit.—Ward 1 pass from Tomczak (K. Brown kick), 8:52.
Attendance—73,138.

	Pittsburgh	Cleveland
First downs	32	2
Rushes-yards	55-213	9-9
Passing	247	31
Punt returns	3-17	0-0
Kickoff returns	0-0	8-119
Interception returns	2-21	0-0
Comp.-att.-int.	24-32-0	6-16-2
Sacked-yards lost	1-12	3-21
Punts	1-35	6-48
Fumbles-lost	0-0	2-2
Penalties-yards	4-26	4-23
Time of possession	47:49	12:11

INDIVIDUAL STATISTICS
RUSHING—Pittsburgh, Bettis 18-89, Zereoue 16-42, Huntley 10-41, Stewart 6-33, Witman 3-11, Gonzalez 2-(minus 3). Cleveland, Kirby 5-10, Shaw 2-(minus 5), Edwards 1-1, Detmer 1-(minus 1).
PASSING—Pittsburgh, Stewart 15-23-0-173, Tomczak 8-8-0-78, Gonzalez 1-1-0-8. Cleveland, Detmer 6-13-1-52, Couch 0-3-1-0.
RECEIVING—Pittsburgh, Huntley 5-67, Edwards 4-45, Ward 3-51, Hawkins 3-27, Shaw 3-26, Blackwell 2-18, Witman 2-9, Zereoue 1-14, Bettis 1-2. Cleveland, Shepherd 2-32, Johnson 2-13, Edwards 1-5, Kirby 1-2.
MISSED FIELD GOAL ATTEMPTS—None.
INTERCEPTIONS—Pittsburgh, Shields 1-12, Oldham 1-9.
KICKOFF RETURNS—Cleveland, Powell 4-71, Chiaverini 2-35, Saleh 1-14, I. Smith 1-(minus 1).
PUNT RETURNS—Pittsburgh, Edwards 3-17.
SACKS—Pittsburgh, Gildon 1, Oldham 1, Porter 1. Cleveland, Alexander 1.

CARDINALS 25, EAGLES 24
Sunday, September 12

Arizona 0   6   6 13—25
Philadelphia 21   3   0   0—24

First Quarter
Phi.—Staley 24 run (N. Johnson kick), 7:07.
Phi.—Staley 3 pass from Pederson (N. Johnson kick), 12:41.
Phi.—Broughton 15 pass from Pederson (N. Johnson kick), 14:44.

Second Quarter
Ariz.—FG, Jacke 31, 6:49.
Ariz.—FG, Jacke 25, 9:45.
Phi.—FG, N. Johnson 25, 15:00.

Third Quarter
Ariz.—Bates 1 run (pass failed), 5:58.

Fourth Quarter
Ariz.—FG, Jacke 32, 0:07.
Ariz.—Moore 20 pass from Plummer (Jacke kick), 10:57.
Ariz.—FG, Jacke 31, 15:00.
Attendance—64,113.

— 118 —

	Arizona	Philadelphia
First downs	23	13
Rushes-yards	36-78	26-138
Passing	266	75
Punt returns	4-16	1-2
Kickoff returns	4-105	6-128
Interception returns	2-40	3-89
Comp.-att.-int.	25-48-3	12-26-2
Sacked-yards lost	1-8	3-16
Punts	5-34	7-43
Fumbles-lost	2-1	2-2
Penalties-yards	8-40	7-54
Time of possession	34:51	25:09

INDIVIDUAL STATISTICS

RUSHING—Arizona, Murrell 24-53, Plummer 6-25, Bates 4-6, Boston 1-1, Makovicka 1-(minus 7). Philadelphia, Staley 21-111, Pederson 2-21.

PASSING—Arizona, Plummer 25-48-3-274. Philadelphia, Pederson 12-26-2-91.

RECEIVING—Arizona, Sanders 5-50, Hardy 5-49, Murrell 5-47, Moore 4-79, Boston 3-19, Pittman 2-26, Makovicka 1-4. Philadelphia, Broughton 3-29, C. Johnson 3-24, Staley 3-19, Jells 2-9, Finneran 1-10.

MISSED FIELD GOAL ATTEMPTS—None.

INTERCEPTIONS—Arizona, Lassiter 1-32, Williams 1-8. Philadelphia, Darling 1-33, Harris 1-33, Dawkins 1-23.

KICKOFF RETURNS—Arizona, Bates 3-83, Pittman 1-22. Philadelphia, Rossum 4-95, Bieniemy 1-19, Broughton 1-14.

PUNT RETURNS—Arizona, Pittman 4-16. Philadelphia, Rossum 1-2.

SACKS—Arizona, Rice 2, Drake 1. Philadelphia, H. Douglas 1.

VIKINGS 17, FALCONS 14

Sunday, September 12

| Minnesota | 0 | 17 | 0 | 0 | —17 |
| Atlanta | 0 | 7 | 0 | 7 | —14 |

Second Quarter
Min.—Carter 2 pass from Cunningham (Anderson kick), 1:58.
Min.—FG, Anderson 36, 4:37.
Min.—Hoard 1 run (Anderson kick), 13:12.
Atl.—Calloway 23 pass from Chandler (Andersen kick), 14:17.

Fourth Quarter
Atl.—Christian 1 run (Andersen kick), 1:42.
Attendance—69,555.

	Minnesota	Atlanta
First downs	19	22
Rushes-yards	32-115	23-81
Passing	184	278
Punt returns	1-(-1)	0-0
Kickoff returns	3-94	3-67
Interception returns	0-0	0-0
Comp.-att.-int.	22-33-0	18-31-0
Sacked-yards lost	0-0	2-12
Punts	3-40	2-44
Fumbles-lost	0-0	3-3
Penalties-yards	9-81	4-84
Time of possession	33:14	26:46

INDIVIDUAL STATISTICS

RUSHING—Minnesota, Smith 16-47, Hoard 12-50, Cunningham 3-12, Moss 1-6. Atlanta, Anderson 16-50, Chandler 3-21, Hanspard 3-9, Christian 1-1.

PASSING—Minnesota, Cunningham 22-33-0-184. Atlanta, Chandler 17-30-0-258, Graziani 1-1-0-32.

RECEIVING—Minnesota, Carter 7-70, Glover 3-37, Moss 3-24, Smith 3-6, Hoard 2-24, Reed 2-13, Walsh 1-6, Crumpler 1-4. Atlanta, Calloway 5-84, Mathis 4-40, Harris 3-63, Santiago 2-53, Anderson 2-34, Christian 1-14, Kozlowski 1-2.

MISSED FIELD GOAL ATTEMPTS—Minnesota, Anderson 26, 30. Atlanta, Andersen 35, 39.

INTERCEPTIONS—None.

KICKOFF RETURNS—Minnesota, Palmer 3-94. Atlanta, Dwight 3-67.

PUNT RETURNS—Minnesota, Palmer 1-(minus 1).

SACKS—Minnesota, Rudd 1, Clemons 1.

BEARS 20, CHIEFS 17

Sunday, September 12

| Kansas City | 3 | 0 | 7 | 7 | —17 |
| Chicago | 7 | 13 | 0 | 0 | —20 |

First Quarter
K.C.—FG, Stoyanovich 27, 5:46.
Chi.—Enis 10 pass from Matthews (Gowins kick), 10:28.

Second Quarter
Chi.—FG, Gowins 21, 2:15.
Chi.—FG, Gowins 24, 11:11.
Chi.—Allred 1 pass from Matthews (Gowins kick), 14:09.

Third Quarter
K.C.—Alexander 86 pass from Grbac (Stoyanovich kick), 9:59.

Fourth Quarter
K.C.—Edwards 79 fumble return (Stoyanovich), 2:36.
Attendance—58,381.

	Kansas City	Chicago
First downs	17	22
Rushes-yards	17-71	28-81
Passing	278	307
Punt returns	2-7	0-0
Kickoff returns	4-71	4-92
Interception returns	0-0	1-41
Comp.-att.-int.	20-42-1	31-47-0
Sacked-yards lost	1-5	1-15
Punts	4-45	5-37
Fumbles-lost	1-0	2-2
Penalties-yards	7-40	6-44
Time of possession	25:06	34:54

INDIVIDUAL STATISTICS

RUSHING—Kansas City, Anders 10-39, Shehee 4-13, Richardson 3-19. Chicago, Enis 22-64, Matthews 3-(minus 3), Milburn 2-11, Engram 1-9.

PASSING—Kansas City, Grbac 20-42-1-283. Chicago, Matthews 25-38-0-245, McNown 6-9-0-77.

RECEIVING—Kansas City, Alexander 6-154, Richardson 4-24, Johnson 3-41, Shehee 2-20, Anders 2-14, Rison 1-12, Horn 1-10, Lockett 1-8. Chicago, Conway 9-88, Engram 6-53, Enis 5-69, M. Robinson 4-47, Brooks 2-28, Wetnight 2-25, Milburn 1-8, Hallock 1-3, Allred 1-1.

MISSED FIELD GOAL ATTEMPTS—Kansas City, Stoyanovich 38.

INTERCEPTIONS—Chicago, Parrish 1-41.

KICKOFF RETURNS—Kansas City, Vanover 4-71. Chicago, Milburn 4-92.

PUNT RETURNS—Kansas City, Vanover 2-7.

SACKS—Kansas City. Chicago, Davis 1.

GIANTS 17, BUCCANEERS 13

Sunday, September 12

| N.Y. Giants | 7 | 0 | 7 | 3 | —17 |
| Tampa Bay | 0 | 10 | 3 | 0 | —13 |

First Quarter
NYG—Peter 38 fumble return (Daluiso kick), 3:23.

Second Quarter
T.B.—FG, Gramatica 23, 0:45.
T.B.—Moore 1 pass from Dilfer (Gramatica kick), 14:44.

Third Quarter
NYG—Weathers 8 interception return (Daluiso kick), 11:29.
T.B.—FG, Gramatica 36, 14:45.

Fourth Quarter
NYG—FG, Daluiso 36, 2:50.
Attendance—65,026.

	N.Y. Giants	Tampa Bay
First downs	4	15
Rushes-yards	24-27	27-77
Passing	80	177
Punt returns	4-25	3-30
Kickoff returns	2-23	2-44
Interception returns	4-62	0-0
Comp.-att.-int.	12-24-0	18-42-4
Sacked-yards lost	2-11	2-11
Punts	12-44	8-46
Fumbles-lost	0-0	2-1
Penalties-yards	9-59	3-20
Time of possession	27:01	32:59

INDIVIDUAL STATISTICS

RUSHING—New York, Bennett 13-24, Way 6-2, Graham 5-1. Tampa Bay, Dunn 15-46, Alstott 9-12, Green 1-15, Dilfer 1-4, Abdullah 1-0.

PASSING—New York, Graham 12-24-0-91. Tampa Bay, Dilfer 15-31-3-174, Zeier 3-11-1-14.

1999 REVIEW Week 1

RECEIVING—New York, Toomer 4-36, Mitchell 3-25, Hilliard 2-18, Bennett 1-7, Jurevicius 1-4, Way 1-1. Tampa Bay, Emanuel 3-53, Green 3-27, Dunn 3-26, Moore 2-27, Alstott 2-25, Williams 2-14, Anthony 2-10, McDonald 1-6.
MISSED FIELD GOAL ATTEMPTS—None.
INTERCEPTIONS—New York, Ellsworth 2-26, Sparks 1-28, Weathers 1-8.
KICKOFF RETURNS—New York, Levingston 1-16, Patten 1-7. Tampa Bay, Green 2-44.
PUNT RETURNS—New York, Barber 4-25. Tampa Bay, Green 3-30.
SACKS—New York, Widmer 1, Armstead 1. Tampa Bay, Sapp 1, White 1.

PATRIOTS 30, JETS 28

Sunday, September 12

New England	3	7	17	3—30
N.Y. Jets	7	9	6	6—28

First Quarter
N.E.—FG, Vinatieri 33, 5:56.
NYJ—Anderson 27 pass from Testaverde (Hall kick), 12:44.
Second Quarter
N.E.—Simmons 58 pass from Bledsoe (Vinatieri kick), 5:38.
NYJ—K. Johnson 25 pass from Tupa (Hall kick), 8:05.
NYJ—Safety, L. Johnson tackled by team in end zone, 14:54.
Third Quarter
N.E.—McGinest recovered ball in end zone (Vinatieri kick), 1:24.
N.E.—Allen 22 run (Vinatieri kick), 3:25.
N.E.—FG, Vinatieri 21, 8:54.
NYJ—Baxter 7 pass from Tupa (pass failed), 11:07.
Fourth Quarter
NYJ—Cox 27 interception return (pass failed), 5:26.
N.E.—FG, Vinatieri 23, 14:57.
Attendance—78,227.

	New England	N.Y. Jets
First downs	16	19
Rushes-yards	27-70	24-111
Passing	326	257
Punt returns	2-33	3-23
Kickoff returns	3-69	6-146
Interception returns	3-0	1-27
Comp.-att.-int.	21-30-1	20-36-3
Sacked-yards lost	2-14	4-32
Punts	4-48	3-41
Fumbles-lost	2-1	3-1
Penalties-yards	6-43	6-40
Time of possession	28:50	31:10

INDIVIDUAL STATISTICS
RUSHING—New England, Allen 15-54, Faulk 10-17, L. Johnson 1-0, Bledsoe 1-(minus 1). New York, Martin 19-85, Tupa 2-8, Anderson 1-16, L. Johnson 1-2, K. Johnson 1-0.
PASSING—New England, Bledsoe 21-30-1-340. New York, Testaverde 10-15-1-96, Mirer 4-11-2-28, Tupa 6-10-0-165.
RECEIVING—New England, Glenn 7-113, Jefferson 4-67, Coates 3-51, Brown 2-33, Simmons 1-58, Rutledge 1-9, Faulk 1-8, Warren 1-6, Allen 1-(minus 5). New York, K. Johnson 8-194, Ward 5-41, Martin 4-17, Anderson 1-27, Baxter 1-7, E. Green 1-3.
MISSED FIELD GOAL ATTEMPTS—None.
INTERCEPTIONS—New England, Milloy 1-0, Israel 1-0, Slade 1-0. New York, Cox 1-27.
KICKOFF RETURNS—New England, Faulk 3-69. New York, Glenn 3-96, L. Johnson 2-31, Williams 1-19.
PUNT RETURNS—New England, Brown 2-33. New York, Ward 2-17, L. Johnson 1-6.
SACKS—New England, McGinest 2, Israel 1, Bruschi 0.5, Thomas 0.5. New York, Phifer 1, Wiltz 1.

COLTS 31, BILLS 14

Sunday, September 12

Buffalo	0	6	8	0—14
Indianapolis	7	7	7	10—31

First Quarter
Ind.—James 1 run (Vanderjagt kick), 11:25.
Second Quarter
Buf.—FG, Christie 36, 1:25.
Ind.—Harrison 5 pass from Manning (Vanderjagt kick), 11:45.
Buf.—FG, Christie 29, 14:42.

Third Quarter
Ind.—Harrison 24 pass from Manning (Vanderjagt kick), 7:37.
Buf.—Reed 6 pass from Flutie (Linton run), 12:39.
Fourth Quarter
Ind.—FG, Vanderjagt 35, 2:22.
Ind.—Blevins 74 interception return (Vanderjagt kick), 11:40.
Attendance—56,238.

	Buffalo	Indianapolis
First downs	18	19
Rushes-yards	15-47	29-109
Passing	274	284
Punt returns	1-27	0-0
Kickoff returns	6-156	3-51
Interception returns	2-3	2-102
Comp.-att.-int.	22-42-2	21-33-2
Sacked-yards lost	5-26	0-0
Punts	6-34	3-44
Fumbles-lost	1-1	1-1
Penalties-yards	12-90	8-75
Time of possession	26:23	33:37

INDIVIDUAL STATISTICS
RUSHING—Buffalo, A. Smith 6-7, Linton 5-16, Flutie 4-24. Indianapolis, James 26-112, Manning 3-(minus 3).
PASSING—Buffalo, Flutie 22-42-2-300. Indianapolis, Manning 21-33-2-284.
RECEIVING—Buffalo, Moulds 10-147, Reed 4-39, P. Price 3-51, Linton 3-42, Gash 1-12, A. Smith 1-9. Indianapolis, Harrison 8-121, Green 5-124, James 4-14, Dilger 2-19, Pathon 2-6.
MISSED FIELD GOAL ATTEMPTS—Indianapolis, Vanderjagt 45.
INTERCEPTIONS—Buffalo, Winfield 1-3, Martin 1-0. Indianapolis, Blevins 1-74, Burris 1-28.
KICKOFF RETURNS—Buffalo, K. Williams 6-156. Indianapolis, Elias 2-37, Greene 1-14.
PUNT RETURNS—Buffalo, K. Williams 1-27.
SACKS—Indianapolis, Bratzke 3, Royal 1, Berry 1.

SAINTS 19, PANTHERS 10

Sunday, September 12

Carolina	0	10	0	0—10
New Orleans	7	3	9	0—19

First Quarter
N.O.—Drakeford 20 fumble return (Brien kick), 0:12.
Second Quarter
N.O.—FG, Brien 46, 2:08.
Car.—Walls 5 pass from Beuerlein (Kasay kick), 5:38.
Car.—FG, Kasay 52, 13:21.
Third Quarter
N.O.—FG, Brien 21, 8:46.
N.O.—Poole 67 pass from Hobert (kick failed), 10:46.
Attendance—58,166.

	Carolina	New Orleans
First downs	12	13
Rushes-yards	16-85	41-147
Passing	161	108
Punt returns	6-22	5-20
Kickoff returns	5-87	2-51
Interception returns	0-0	1-18
Comp.-att.-int.	16-32-1	11-22-0
Sacked-yards lost	7-46	4-24
Punts	8-44	10-36
Fumbles-lost	2-2	1-0
Penalties-yards	6-40	4-26
Time of possession	26:56	33:04

INDIVIDUAL STATISTICS
RUSHING—Carolina, Biakabutuka 8-45, Lane 6-30, Beuerlein 1-8, Floyd 1-2. New Orleans, L. Smith 13-66, R. Williams 10-40, Davis 9-18, Craver 5-16, Hobert 4-7.
PASSING—Carolina, Beuerlein 16-32-1-207. New Orleans, Hobert 11-22-0-132.
RECEIVING—Carolina, Carruth 5-63, Muhammad 4-64, Walls 3-37, Lane 2-36, Biakabutuka 1-5, Bates 1-2. New Orleans, Craver 4-23, Poole 3-89, Kennison 2-11, Hastings 1-12, L. Smith 1-(minus 3).
MISSED FIELD GOAL ATTEMPTS—Carolina, Kasay 53.
INTERCEPTIONS—New Orleans, Kei. Mitchell 1-18.

KICKOFF RETURNS—Carolina, Bates 4-73, Kinchen 1-14. New Orleans, Philyaw 2-51.
PUNT RETURNS—Carolina, Metcalf 6-22. New Orleans, Kennison 5-20.
SACKS—Carolina, Peter 2, Greene 1, Richardson 1. New Orleans, B. Smith 2, Glover 1.5, Martin 1.5, Robbins 1, Knight 0.5, Whitehead 0.5.

JAGUARS 41, 49ERS 3

Sunday, September 12

San Francisco	3	0	0	0—	3
Jacksonville	3	3	18	17—	41

First Quarter
S.F.—FG, Richey 42, 7:22.
Jac.—FG, Hollis 41, 9:56.

Second Quarter
Jac.—FG, Hollis 32, 13:11.

Third Quarter
Jac.—FG, Hollis 50, 5:39.
Jac.—Craft 23 fumble return (Brunell run), 5:52
Jac.—Jones 4 pass from Brunell (Hollis kick), 13:23.

Fourth Quarter
Jac.—FG, Hollis 42, 0:14.
Jac.—Stewart 1 run (Hollis kick), 5:47.
Jac.—Beasley 90 interception return (Hollis kick), 12:07.
Attendance—68,678.

	San Fran.	Jacksonville
First downs	11	18
Rushes-yards	20-93	34-97
Passing	112	247
Punt returns	1-(-2)	5-54
Kickoff returns	7-116	0-0
Interception returns	0-0	3-90
Comp.-att.-int.	14-35-3	22-31-0
Sacked-yards lost	4-29	2-18
Punts	8-47	5-43
Fumbles-lost	3-2	0-0
Penalties-yards	2-10	6-57
Time of possession	24:45	35:15

INDIVIDUAL STATISTICS
RUSHING—San Francisco, Garner 11-61, S. Young 6-24, Phillips 3-8. Jacksonville, Taylor 24-74, Stewart 4-15, Brunell 2-12, Banks 2-(minus 2), Fiedler 2-(minus 2).
PASSING—San Francisco, S. Young 9-26-2-96, Garcia 5-9-1-45. Jacksonville, Brunell 22-30-0-265, Fiedler 0-1-0-0.
RECEIVING—San Francisco, Owens 5-76, Rice 2-17, Vardell 2-17, Garner 1-14, Phillips 1-5, Stokes 1-5, Harris 1-4, Jackson 1-3. Jacksonville, McCardell 8-78, J. Smith 6-139, Barlow 2-41, Brady 2-13, Taylor 2-(minus 7), Jones 1-4, Wiegert 1-(minus 3).
MISSED FIELD GOAL ATTEMPTS—None.
INTERCEPTIONS—Jacksonville, Beasley 2-90, Darius 1-0.
KICKOFF RETURNS—San Francisco, McQuarters 6-98, Phillips 1-18.
PUNT RETURNS—San Francisco, McQuarters 1-(minus 2). Jacksonville, Barlow 5-54.
SACKS—San Francisco, Bryant 1, Posey 1. Jacksonville, Hardy 1, Brackens 1, Walker 1, Smeenge 0.5, Curry 0.5.

PACKERS 28, RAIDERS 24

Sunday, September 12

Oakland	3	7	7	7—	24
Green Bay	7	0	7	14—	28

First Quarter
G.B.—Schroeder 4 pass from Favre (Longwell kick), 9:16.
Oak.—FG, Husted 41, 12:03.

Second Quarter
Oak.—Jordan 1 run (Husted kick), 4:06.

Third Quarter
G.B.—Freeman 12 pass from Favre (Longwell kick), 8:18.
Oak.—Wheatley 5 run (Husted kick), 12:32.

Fourth Quarter
Oak.—Jordan 1 run (Husted kick), 4:08.
G.B.—Bradford 8 pass from Favre (Longwell kick), 7:40.
G.B.—Thomason 1 pass from Favre (Longwell kick), 14:49.
Attendance—59,872.

	Oakland	Green Bay
First downs	20	25
Rushes-yards	32-153	20-91
Passing	210	318
Punt returns	2-3	2-20
Kickoff returns	4-72	3-53
Interception returns	3-44	1-0
Comp.-att.-int.	16-31-1	28-47-3
Sacked-yards lost	4-17	3-15
Punts	5-42	4-39
Fumbles-lost	2-0	1-1
Penalties-yards	6-55	7-47
Time of possession	30:19	29:41

INDIVIDUAL STATISTICS
RUSHING—Oakland, Wheatley 15-52, Kaufman 11-87, Jordan 3-3, Ritchie 2-5, Gannon 1-6. Green Bay, Levens 18-78, Favre 2-13.
PASSING—Oakland, Gannon 16-31-1-227. Green Bay, Favre 28-47-3-333.
RECEIVING—Oakland, Brown 4-51, Jett 3-88, Jordan 3-49, Ritchie 2-19, Wheatley 2-10, Kaufman 1-6, Brigham 1-4. Green Bay, Freeman 7-111, Levens 6-46, Chmura 4-44, Schroeder 4-42, T. Davis 2-50, Bradford 2-27, Henderson 2-12, Thomason 1-1.
MISSED FIELD GOAL ATTEMPTS—Oakland, Husted 47, 48.
INTERCEPTIONS—Oakland, Biekert 1-21, K. Williams 1-14, Gordon 1-9. Green Bay, M. McKenzie 1-0.
KICKOFF RETURNS—Oakland, Jordan 2-38, Kaufman 1-28, Treu 1-6. Green Bay, Mitchell 2-33, Howard 1-20.
PUNT RETURNS—Oakland, Gordon 2-3. Green Bay, Howard 2-20.
SACKS—Oakland, Harvey 1, Jackson 1, Russell 0.5, Harris 0.5. Green Bay, B. Williams 1, S. Dotson 1, Booker 1, K. McKenzie 1.

COWBOYS 41, REDSKINS 35

Sunday, September 12

Dallas	7	7	0	21	6—41
Washington	3	10	22	0	0—35

First Quarter
Dal.—LaFleur 15 pass from Aikman (Cunningham kick), 9:02.
Was.—FG, Conway 25, 11:23.

Second Quarter
Dal.—LaFleur 14 pass from Aikman (Cunningham kick), 0:05.
Was.—Westbrook 41 pass from B. Johnson (Conway kick), 2:22.
Was.—FG, Conway 42, 10:48.

Third Quarter
Was.—Davis 3 run (Davis run), 7:02.
Was.—Davis 7 run (Conway kick), 12:01.
Was.—Connell 50 pass from B. Johnson (Conway kick), 13:56.

Fourth Quarter
Dal.—E. Smith 1 run (Cunningham kick), 4:17.
Dal.—Irvin 37 pass from Aikman (Cunningham kick), 11:09.
Dal.—Irvin 12 pass from Aikman (Cunningham kick), 13:14.

Overtime
Dal.—Ismail 76 pass from Aikman, 2:13.
Attendance—79,237.

	Dallas	Washington
First downs	30	25
Rushes-yards	34-186	30-135
Passing	355	369
Punt returns	0-0	4-48
Kickoff returns	6-131	4-78
Interception returns	0-0	3-4
Comp.-att.-int.	28-49-3	20-34-0
Sacked-yards lost	1-7	2-13
Punts	4-42	5-39
Fumbles-lost	1-0	3-2
Penalties-yards	9-99	8-45
Time of possession	33:54	28:19

INDIVIDUAL STATISTICS
RUSHING—Dallas, E. Smith 23-109, Warren 8-58, Aikman 2-4, Ismail 1-15. Washington, Davis 24-109, Mitchell 3-12, Connell 1-8, Hicks 1-4, Centers 1-2.
PASSING—Dallas, Aikman 28-49-3-362. Washington, B. Johnson 20-33-0-382, Conway 0-1-0-0.
RECEIVING—Dallas, Ismail 8-149, Irvin 5-122, LaFleur 4-41, E. Smith 4-(minus 5), Mills 3-24, Bjornson 1-13, Ogden 1-8, Warren 1-4, Johnston 1-4. Washington, Centers 6-42, Westbrook 5-159, Connell 4-137, Fryar 3-34, Davis 1-5, Alexander 1-5.

1999 REVIEW Week 1

MISSED FIELD GOAL ATTEMPTS—None.
INTERCEPTIONS—Washington, Bailey 1-4, Pounds 1-0, Stevens 1-0.
KICKOFF RETURNS—Dallas, Ogden 6-131. Washington, Mitchell 4-78.
PUNT RETURNS—Washington, Mitchell 4-48.
SACKS—Dallas, Ellis 2. Washington, Coleman 1.

RAMS 27, RAVENS 10

Sunday, September 12

Baltimore	0	3	7	0—10
St. Louis	3	14	0	10—27

First Quarter
St.L.—FG, Wilkins 36, 6:04.
Second Quarter
St.L.—R. Williams 6 pass from Warner (Wilkins kick), 1:32.
Bal.—FG, Stover 25, 9:00.
St.L.—Bruce 2 pass from Warner (Wilkins kick), 14:27.
Third Quarter
Bal.—Stokley 28 pass from S. Mitchell (Stover kick), 14:45.
Fourth Quarter
St.L.—FG, Wilkins 51, 6:04.
St.L.—Holt 20 pass from Warner (Wilkins kick), 12:20.
Attendance—62,100.

	Baltimore	St. Louis
First downs	13	23
Rushes-yards	15-60	25-59
Passing	163	280
Punt returns	0-0	4-51
Kickoff returns	5-113	3-60
Interception returns	2-81	2-36
Comp.-att.-int.	17-40-2	28-44-2
Sacked-yards lost	5-25	3-25
Punts	6-48	4-37
Fumbles-lost	1-0	1-1
Penalties-yards	11-106	7-65
Time of possession	22:35	37:25

INDIVIDUAL STATISTICS
RUSHING—Baltimore, Holmes 12-52, Evans 3-8. St. Louis, Faulk 19-54, Holcombe 4-1, Watson 1-5, Warner 1-(minus 1).
PASSING—Baltimore, S. Mitchell 17-40-2-188. St. Louis, Warner 28-44-2-309.
RECEIVING—Baltimore, Armour 4-76, Ismail 4-46, Evans 4-27, Holmes 2-3, Stokley 1-28, DeLong 1-5, Pierce 1-3. St. Louis, Bruce 8-92, Faulk 7-72, Hakim 5-63, Holt 3-36, Proehl 2-24, R. Williams 2-17, Lewis 1-12.
MISSED FIELD GOAL ATTEMPTS—Baltimore, Stover 54, 54.
INTERCEPTIONS—Baltimore, R. Lewis 1-60, McAlister 1-21. St. Louis, Lyght 1-0, Lyle 1-0.
KICKOFF RETURNS—Baltimore, Harris 5-113. St. Louis, Horne 3-60.
PUNT RETURNS—St. Louis, Hakim 4-51.
SACKS—Baltimore, R. Lewis 1, Burnett 1, Jenkins 1. St. Louis, Carter 2, Lyght 1, Farr 1, Wistrom 1.

LIONS 28, SEAHAWKS 20

Sunday, September 12

Detroit	3	22	0	3—28
Seattle	0	7	7	6—20

First Quarter
Det.—FG, Hanson 51, 2:54.
Second Quarter
Det.—Crowell 16 pass from Batch (Hanson kick), 0:05.
Det.—Sloan 5 pass from Batch (kick failed), 4:34.
Det.—Safety, D. May snapped ball out of end zone, 5:32.
Sea.—W. Williams 40 interception return (Peterson kick), 5:46.
Det.—Crowell 41 pass from Batch (Hanson kick), 10:27.
Third Quarter
Sea.—Dawkins 26 pass from Kitna (Peterson kick), 11:31.
Fourth Quarter
Sea.—Dawkins 3 pass from Kitna (pass failed), 7:49.
Det.—FG, Hanson 49, 12:50.
Attendance—66,238.

	Detroit	Seattle
First downs	19	16
Rushes-yards	36-167	16-31
Passing	202	174
Punt returns	3-11	3-6
Kickoff returns	5-92	6-105
Interception returns	0-0	1-40
Comp.-att.-int.	16-26-1	20-30-0
Sacked-yards lost	5-14	6-28
Punts	7-40	6-48
Fumbles-lost	1-0	4-2
Penalties-yards	11-123	5-34
Time of possession	34:45	25:15

INDIVIDUAL STATISTICS
RUSHING—Detroit, Rivers 16-96, Schlesinger 10-50, Hill 7-24, Batch 3-(minus 3). Seattle, Watters 13-21, Kitna 1-7, R. Brown 1-3, Feagles 1-0.
PASSING—Detroit, Batch 16-26-1-216. Seattle, Kitna 20-30-0-202.
RECEIVING—Detroit, Crowell 7-141, Rivers 4-39, Sloan 3-31, Schlesinger 1-5, Irvin 1-0. Seattle, Dawkins 7-85, R. Brown 5-25, Watters 4-29, Mayes 3-54, Bownes 1-9.
MISSED FIELD GOAL ATTEMPTS—Seattle, Peterson 32.
INTERCEPTIONS—Seattle, W. Williams 1-40.
KICKOFF RETURNS—Detroit, Olivo 4-75, Fair 1-17. Seattle, Green 6-105.
PUNT RETURNS—Detroit, Fair 3-11. Seattle, Rogers 3-6.
SACKS—Detroit, Porcher 3, Aldridge 1, Elliss 1, Stewart 1. Seattle, C. Brown 1.5, Smith 1, Daniels 1, Sinclair 1, Kennedy 0.5.

DOLPHINS 38, BRONCOS 21

Monday, September 13

Miami	0	17	7	14—38
Denver	7	0	7	7—21

First Quarter
Den.—McCaffrey 61 pass from Griese (Elam kick), 3:45.
Second Quarter
Mia.—Abdul-Jabbar 1 run (Mare kick), 6:06.
Mia.—Konrad 12 pass from Marino (Mare kick), 11:58.
Mia.—FG, Mare 37, 14:59.
Third Quarter
Mia.—Johnson 1 run (Mare kick), 4:58.
Den.—McCaffrey 11 pass from Griese (Elam kick), 11:18.
Fourth Quarter
Mia.—McDuffie 4 pass from Marino (Mare kick), 5:29.
Mia.—Taylor 4 fumble return (Mare kick), 11:04.
Den.—McCaffrey 4 pass from Griese (Elam kick), 14:26.
Attendance—75,623.

	Miami	Denver
First downs	22	25
Rushes-yards	33-111	26-113
Passing	215	242
Punt returns	1-0	1-3
Kickoff returns	2-55	4-105
Interception returns	0-0	0-0
Comp.-att.-int.	15-23-0	24-40-0
Sacked-yards lost	0-0	2-28
Punts	4-44	3-38
Fumbles-lost	1-0	2-1
Penalties-yards	8-60	4-30
Time of possession	28:49	31:11

INDIVIDUAL STATISTICS
RUSHING—Miami, Abdul-Jabbar 16-60, Johnson 14-45, Konrad 2-7, Marino 1-(minus 1). Denver, Davis 19-61, Loville 5-48, Griese 2-4.
PASSING—Miami, Marino 15-23-0-215. Denver, Griese 24-40-0-270.
RECEIVING—Miami, Martin 4-101, McDuffie 4-54, Konrad 3-26, Drayton 2-21, Abdul-Jabbar 1-7, Green 1-6. Denver, Sharpe 7-47, McCaffrey 6-105, Chamberlain 4-52, Doering 3-22, Griffith 2-21, Loville 1-15, Davis 1-8.
MISSED FIELD GOAL ATTEMPTS—Denver, Elam 44, 41.
INTERCEPTIONS—None.
KICKOFF RETURNS—Miami, Avery 2-55. Denver, Watson 3-94, D. Smith 1-11.
PUNT RETURNS—Miami, Buckley 1-0. Denver, Watson 1-3.
SACKS—Miami, Thomas 1, Owens 1.

1999 REVIEW Week 1

WEEK 2

RESULTS

BUFFALO 17, N.Y. Jets 3
DETROIT 23, Green Bay 15
Jacksonville 22, CAROLINA 20
KANSAS CITY 26, Denver 10
MIAMI 19, Arizona 16
NEW ENGLAND 31, Indianapolis 28
Oakland 22, MINNESOTA 17
Pittsburgh 23, BALTIMORE 20
San Diego 34, CINCINNATI 7
SAN FRANCISCO 28, New Orleans 21
Seattle 14, CHICAGO 13
Tampa Bay 19, PHILADELPHIA 5
TENNESSEE 26, Cleveland 9
Washington 50, N.Y. GIANTS 21
DALLAS 24, Atlanta 7
 Open date: St. Louis

STANDINGS

AFC EAST
	W	L	T	Pct.
Miami	2	0	0	1.000
New England	2	0	0	1.000
Buffalo	1	1	0	.500
Indianapolis	1	1	0	.500
N.Y. Jets	0	2	0	.000

AFC CENTRAL
	W	L	T	Pct.
Jacksonville	2	0	0	1.000
Pittsburgh	2	0	0	1.000
Tennessee	2	0	0	1.000
Baltimore	0	2	0	.000
Cincinnati	0	2	0	.000
Cleveland	0	2	0	.000

AFC WEST
	W	L	T	Pct.
San Diego	1	0	0	1.000
Kansas City	1	1	0	.500
Oakland	1	1	0	.500
Seattle	1	1	0	.500
Denver	0	2	0	.000

NFC EAST
	W	L	T	Pct.
Dallas	2	0	0	1.000
Arizona	1	1	0	.500
N.Y. Giants	1	1	0	.500
Washington	1	1	0	.500
Philadelphia	0	2	0	.000

NFC CENTRAL
	W	L	T	Pct.
Detroit	2	0	0	1.000
Chicago	1	1	0	.500
Green Bay	1	1	0	.500
Minnesota	1	1	0	.500
Tampa Bay	1	1	0	.500

NFC WEST
	W	L	T	Pct.
St. Louis	1	0	0	1.000
New Orleans	1	1	0	.500
San Francisco	1	1	0	.500
Atlanta	0	2	0	.000
Carolina	0	2	0	.000

HIGHLIGHTS

Hero of the week: Second-year safety Lance Schulters picked off a Billy Joe Hobert pass and returned it 64 yards for a touchdown with 1:31 left to give San Francisco a 29-21 victory over the visiting New Orleans Saints. The 49ers, who were pounded at Jacksonville a week earlier, thus avoided their first 0-2 start since 1982.

Goat of the week: In his first return to Kansas City after signing as a free agent with the Broncos, cornerback Dale Carter got beat twice on deep patterns by Derrick Alexander (for gains of 30 and 49 yards) and nullified a 15-yard sack of Elvis Grbac when he was called for illegal contact on the Chiefs' last touchdown drive. Denver lost the game 26-10.

Sub of the week: Neil O'Donnell, filling in for an injured Steve McNair, completed 31-of-40 passes for 310 yards in the Titans' 26-9 win over Browns. He also threw a four-yard touchdown pass to Yancey Thigpen. McNair had reinjured his back during practice the previous Friday and underwent surgery hours before the game.

Comeback of the week: Adam Vinatieri's 26-yard field goal with 35 seconds left capped a 31-28 win for New England over the visiting Indianapolis Colts. Two Colts fumbles aided the Patriots, who trailed 28-7 at halftime. Tight end Marcus Pollard fumbled in the fourth quarter, and eight plays later Drew Bledsoe found Ben Coates for a touchdown to cut the lead to 28-21. The Patriots' Brandon Mitchell then recovered an Edgerrin James fumble at the Colts' 37 with 2:32 to play to set up Vinatieri's game-winner.

Blowout of the week: The Redskins dominated the first quarter in a 50-21 rout of the Giants. In the first 15 minutes Washington had more first downs (12) than the Giants did offensive plays (eight). Stephen Davis had three rushing touchdowns in the opening quarter and Brad Johnson completed all eight of his passes for 106 yards. Johnson finished the game 20-for-28 for 231 yards with three touchdowns and no interceptions. Davis racked up 126 yards on 23 carries.

Nail-biter of the week: Rookie Kris Brown kicked a 36-yard field goal as time expired to give the Steelers a 23-20 win over Baltimore. Ravens quarterback Stoney Case, who took over in the third quarter for Scott Mitchell, moved the Ravens 72 yards in six plays, tying the game on a 19-yard touchdown pass to Qadry Ismail. Will Blackwell returned the ensuing kickoff 37 yards to midfield and Kordell Stewart completed two passes to set up Brown's game-winner, the rookie's third field goal of the game.

Hit of the week: San Diego linebacker Junior Seau delivered a crushing blow, knocking Cincinnati quarterback Jeff Blake out of the game with a sprained shoulder with a second-quarter hit. Blake fumbled on the play and linebacker Gerald Dixon returned the ball 27 yards for a touchdown, a key play in San Diego's 34-7 win.

Oddity of the week: The 49ers-Saints game had some bizarre plays. The teams combined to botch two snaps on punts, a dropped pitch, and a trick play in which Saints holder Tommy Barnhardt lined up at quarterback. 49ers quarterback Steve Young completed a handoff lying on his back.

Top rusher: Dorsey Levens rushed 29 times for 153 yards in Green Bay's 22-15 loss to Detroit.

Top passer: Randall Cunningham threw for 364 yards and two touchdowns but also threw two interceptions in the Vikings' 22-17 loss to Oakland.

Top receiver: Derrick Mayes had seven catches for 137 yards, including a go-ahead 34-yard touchdown, in Seattle's 14-13 victory over the Bears.

Notes: The 50 points were the most the Giants allowed in New York since 1964, when the Browns won 52-20 at Yankee Stadium. ... Seattle coach Mike Holmgren earned his 11th straight coaching victory over the Bears, the other wins coming when he coached in the NFC Central with the Packers. ... Tampa Bay had nine sacks in a 19-5 win at Philadelphia, tying a franchise record set 20 years earlier. Warren Sapp had a career-high three sacks. ... Prior to beating Cincinnati, the Chargers had not won a road opener since their 1994 Super Bowl season.

Quote of the week: Sapp, on Eagles quarterback Donovan McNabb, who made his NFL debut in the second half when starter Doug Pederson sprained his right shoulder: "It's always special when you get a new quarterback. It's new meat, you know?"

GAME SUMMARIES

CHIEFS 26, BRONCOS 10
Sunday, September 19

Denver	0	3	0	7	—10
Kansas City	0	6	10	10	—26

Second Quarter
Den.—FG, Elam 50, 3:26.
K.C.—FG, Stoyanovich 19, 12:06.
K.C.—FG, Stoyanovich 42, 15:00.

Third Quarter
K.C.—Richardson 1 run (Stoyanovich kick), 5:44.
K.C.—FG, Stoyanovich 44, 8:46.

Fourth Quarter
Den.—Davis 1 run (Elam kick), 0:02.
K.C.—Morris 5 run (Stoyanovich kick), 5:35.
K.C.—FG, Stoyanovich 27, 12:46.
Attendance—78,683.

	Denver	Kansas City
First downs	20	17
Rushes-yards	26-88	41-188
Passing	156	177
Punt returns	3-6	2-10
Kickoff returns	5-113	3-63
Interception returns	1-0	2-5
Comp.-att.-int.	20-31-2	15-20-1
Sacked-yards lost	2-16	1-2
Punts	4-40	4-40
Fumbles-lost	4-2	1-0
Penalties-yards	8-50	10-84
Time of possession	26:32	33:28

INDIVIDUAL STATISTICS
RUSHING—Denver, Davis 21-79, Griese 2-0, D. Smith 1-7, Griffith 1-2, Brister 1-0. Kansas City, Anders 22-142, Morris 11-32, Richardson 4-7, Shehee 3-7, Grbac 1-0.
PASSING—Denver, Griese 11-16-1-107, Brister 9-15-1-65. Kansas City, Grbac 15-20-1-179.
RECEIVING—Denver, Sharpe 6-52, McCaffrey 4-44, Griffith 4-20, Davis 2-18, D. Smith 2-16, Chamberlain 1-17, Loville 1-5. Kansas City, Alexander 6-117, Shehee 3-7, Gonzalez 2-27, Rison 2-24, Lockett 1-5, Richardson 1-(minus 1).
MISSED FIELD GOAL ATTEMPTS—None.
INTERCEPTIONS—Denver, Pryce 1-0. Kansas City, Woods 1-5, Warfield 1-0.
KICKOFF RETURNS—Denver, Watson 5-113. Kansas City, Vanover 2-52, Parten 1-11.
PUNT RETURNS—Denver, Watson 3-6. Kansas City, Vanover 2-10.
SACKS—Denver, Bowens 1. Kansas City, Thomas 1, O'Neal 1.

TITANS 26, BROWNS 9
Sunday, September 19

Cleveland	0	3	6	0	— 9
Tennessee	2	14	3	7	—26

First Quarter
Ten.—Safety, T. Couch sacked by E. Robinson in end zone, 10:14.

Second Quarter
Ten.—E. George 1 run (Del Greco kick), 2:01.
Cle.—FG, Dawson 41, 8:10.
Ten.—E. George 1 run (Del Greco kick), 12:39.

Third Quarter
Ten.—FG, Del Greco 35, 8:21.
Cle.—Johnson 39 pass from Couch (sack), 12:09.

Fourth Quarter
Ten.—Thigpen 14 pass from O'Donnell (Del Greco kick), 5:08.
Attendance—65,904.

	Cleveland	Tennessee
First downs	12	24
Rushes-yards	16-83	34-102
Passing	90	310
Punt returns	1-3	4-29
Kickoff returns	5-122	3-76
Interception returns	0-0	0-0
Comp.-att.-int.	12-24-0	31-40-0
Sacked-yards lost	7-44	0-0
Punts	5-48	4-40
Fumbles-lost	2-1	1-0
Penalties-yards	2-7	7-70
Time of possession	18:40	41:20

INDIVIDUAL STATISTICS
RUSHING—Cleveland, Kirby 10-40, Couch 5-40, Shaw 1-3. Tennessee, E. George 31-97, O'Donnell 2-(minus 1), Thomas 1-6.
PASSING—Cleveland, Couch 12-24-0-134. Tennessee, O'Donnell 31-40-0-310.
RECEIVING—Cleveland, Johnson 4-62, Campbell 2-28, Kirby 2-27, Shaw 2-8, Shepherd 1-7, I. Smith 1-2. Tennessee, Wycheck 9-80, Thigpen 6-84, Dyson 5-52, E. George 4-27, Sanders 2-21, Harris 2-16, Thomas 2-15, Roan 1-9.
MISSED FIELD GOAL ATTEMPTS—Tennessee, Del Greco 44.
INTERCEPTIONS—None.
KICKOFF RETURNS—Cleveland, Powell 5-122. Tennessee, Preston 3-76.
PUNT RETURNS—Cleveland, Johnson 1-3. Tennessee, Preston 4-29.
SACKS—Tennessee, Kearse 3, Thornton 1.5, Robinson 1, Bowden 1, Frederick 0.5.

SEAHAWKS 14, BEARS 13
Sunday, September 19

Seattle	0	0	0	14	—14
Chicago	0	10	3	0	—13

Second Quarter
Chi.—Enis 2 run (Gowins kick), 4:40.
Chi.—FG, Gowins 29, 11:33.

Third Quarter
Chi.—FG, Gowins 43, 12:53.

Fourth Quarter
Sea.—Mayes 34 pass from Foley (Peterson kick), 1:56.
Sea.—Bownes 49 pass from Foley (Peterson kick), 7:09.
Attendance—66,944.

	Seattle	Chicago
First downs	19	20
Rushes-yards	28-94	30-115
Passing	249	196
Punt returns	2-45	2-54
Kickoff returns	3-67	3-68
Interception returns	0-0	0-0
Comp.-att.-int.	18-30-0	23-44-0
Sacked-yards lost	6-34	3-20
Punts	6-35	5-48
Fumbles-lost	3-3	1-1
Penalties-yards	8-70	13-89
Time of possession	28:03	31:57

INDIVIDUAL STATISTICS
RUSHING—Seattle, Watters 23-99, Foley 3-(minus 1), R. Brown 1-2, Feagles 1-(minus 6). Chicago, Enis 25-94, Milburn 2-20, Bennett 1-4, Matthews 1-(minus 1), Conway 1-(minus 2).
PASSING—Seattle, Foley 18-30-0-283. Chicago, Matthews 22-42-0-212, McNown 1-2-0-4.
RECEIVING—Seattle, Mayes 7-137, Watters 3-34, R. Brown 3-26, Bownes 2-54, Pritchard 1-21, Dawkins 1-7, Mili 1-4. Chicago, M. Robinson 3-42, Engram 3-33, Enis 3-29, Conway 3-26, Wetnight 3-17, Milburn 2-18, Allred 2-17, Hallock 2-8, Brooks 1-15, Mayes 1-11.
MISSED FIELD GOAL ATTEMPTS—Chicago, Gowins 50, 48.
INTERCEPTIONS—None.
KICKOFF RETURNS—Seattle, Green 1-24, Joseph 1-24, Rogers 1-19. Chicago, Milburn 2-66, Wiegmann 1-2.
PUNT RETURNS—Seattle, Rogers 2-45. Chicago, Milburn 2-54.
SACKS—Seattle, Kennedy 1, Adams 1, Hanks 1. Chicago, B. Robinson 2, Burton 1, Holdman 1, Simmons 1, Wells 0.5, Tuinei 0.5.

BILLS 17, JETS 3
Sunday, September 19

N.Y. Jets	0	0	3	0	— 3
Buffalo	0	7	7	3	—17

Second Quarter
Buf.—A. Smith 1 run (Christie kick), 14:21.
Third Quarter
Buf.—Flutie 24 run (Christie kick), 5:36.
NYJ—FG, Hall 31, 8:45.
Fourth Quarter
Buf.—FG, Christie 35, 12:55.
Attendance—68,839.

	N.Y. Jets	Buffalo
First downs	11	23
Rushes-yards	18-74	47-224
Passing	116	160
Punt returns	1-6	4-42
Kickoff returns	4-73	1-28
Interception returns	0-0	0-0
Comp.-att.-int.	13-28-0	15-25-0
Sacked-yards lost	2-5	0-0
Punts	6-49	3-43
Fumbles-lost	0-0	2-1
Penalties-yards	9-67	8-50
Time of possession	23:36	36:24

INDIVIDUAL STATISTICS

RUSHING—New York, Martin 9-45, Mirer 3-16, Sowell 3-5, Anderson 2-9, Ward 1-(minus 1). Buffalo, A. Smith 30-113, Linton 10-44, Flutie 7-67.

PASSING—New York, Mirer 13-28-0-121. Buffalo, Flutie 15-25-0-160.

RECEIVING—New York, K. Johnson 3-47, Anderson 3-40, Spence 2-13, Early 1-13, Martin 1-4, Baxter 1-2, Ward 1-1, Parmalee 1-1. Buffalo, Reed 4-35, K. Williams 3-40, Moulds 3-38, Gash 3-18, Riemersma 2-29.

MISSED FIELD GOAL ATTEMPTS—Buffalo, Christie 44, 45.

INTERCEPTIONS—None.

KICKOFF RETURNS—New York, Glenn 3-58, Williams 1-15. Buffalo, K. Williams 1-28.

PUNT RETURNS—New York, Sawyer 1-6. Buffalo, K. Williams 4-42.

SACKS—Buffalo, Rogers 0.5, Perry 0.5, Washington 0.5, Wiley 0.5.

49ERS 28, SAINTS 21

Sunday, September 19

New Orleans 0   14   7   0—21
San Francisco 7   7   0   14—28

First Quarter
S.F.—Owens 5 pass from S. Young (Richey kick), 8:52.
Second Quarter
N.O.—Kennison 2 pass from Hobert (Barnhardt kick), 1:21.
N.O.—Poole 58 pass from Hobert (Barnhardt kick), 5:09.
S.F.—Vardell 1 run (Richey kick), 9:01.
Third Quarter
N.O.—Dawsey 12 pass from Hobert (Barnhardt kick), 5:14.
Fourth Quarter
S.F.—Owens 4 pass from S. Young (Richey kick), 12:57.
S.F.—Schulters 64 interception return (Richey kick), 13:29.
Attendance—67,685.

	New Orleans	San Francisco
First downs	17	21
Rushes-yards	30-101	23-88
Passing	223	223
Punt returns	1-0	2-0
Kickoff returns	4-89	4-91
Interception returns	1-16	2-64
Comp.-att.-int.	20-37-2	23-35-1
Sacked-yards lost	0-0	5-35
Punts	4-40	4-39
Fumbles-lost	3-1	1-0
Penalties-yards	8-79	3-28
Time of possession	30:45	29:15

INDIVIDUAL STATISTICS

RUSHING—New Orleans, R. Williams 22-80, Craver 3-4, L. Smith 2-11, Hobert 2-2, Barnhardt 1-4. San Francisco, Garner 12-72, Vardell 5-1, S. Young 3-13, Phillips 2-2, Stanley 1-0.

PASSING—New Orleans, Hobert 20-37-2-223. San Francisco, S. Young 23-35-1-258.

RECEIVING—New Orleans, Kennison 5-46, Dawsey 3-34, Craver 3-14, R. Williams 3-5, Poole 2-69, Cleeland 2-32, Hastings 2-23. San Francisco, Garner 5-88, Phillips 5-61, Owens 5-49, Rice 5-47, Stokes 2-12, Vardell 1-1.

MISSED FIELD GOAL ATTEMPTS—None.

INTERCEPTIONS—New Orleans, Ambrose 1-16. San Francisco, Schulters 1-64, McMillian 1-0.

KICKOFF RETURNS—New Orleans, Davis 3-74, Philyaw 1-15. San Francisco, McQuarters 4-91.

PUNT RETURNS—New Orleans, Kennison 1-0. San Francisco, McQuarters 2-0.

SACKS—New Orleans, Wilson 1.5, Fields 1, Martin 1, Hewitt 1, Kei. Mitchell 0.5.

RAIDERS 22, VIKINGS 17

Sunday, September 19

Oakland 0   6   16   0—22
Minnesota 7   3   0   7—17

First Quarter
Min.—Crumpler 31 pass from Cunningham (Anderson kick), 9:57.
Second Quarter
Oak.—FG, Husted 36, 3:26.
Min.—FG, Anderson 36, 6:44.
Oak.—FG, Husted 37, 14:24.
Third Quarter
Oak.—Jett 9 pass from Gannon (Husted kick), 6:05.
Oak.—FG, Husted 42, 7:59.
Oak.—Gannon 5 run (pass failed), 13:52.
Fourth Quarter
Min.—Reed 28 pass from Cunningham (Anderson kick), 0:54.
Attendance—64,080.

	Oakland	Minnesota
First downs	22	19
Rushes-yards	33-162	15-34
Passing	240	320
Punt returns	1-11	1-11
Kickoff returns	1-19	5-106
Interception returns	2-2	0-0
Comp.-att.-int.	21-33-0	23-39-2
Sacked-yards lost	1-8	6-44
Punts	6-38	3-55
Fumbles-lost	2-1	2-1
Penalties-yards	9-78	7-42
Time of possession	33:17	26:43

INDIVIDUAL STATISTICS

RUSHING—Oakland, Wheatley 18-83, Kaufman 9-31, Gannon 5-48, Jordan 1-0. Minnesota, Smith 11-24, Hoard 2-(minus 1), Moss 1-11, Cunningham 1-0.

PASSING—Oakland, Gannon 21-33-0-248. Minnesota, Cunningham 23-39-2-364.

RECEIVING—Oakland, Brown 9-86, Dudley 2-49, Jett 2-40, Brigham 2-39, Jordan 2-12, Mickens 1-12, Ritchie 1-5, Kaufman 1-3, Wheatley 1-2. Minnesota, Reed 5-100, Carter 5-70, Moss 4-86, Glover 4-60, Crumpler 1-31, Smith 1-6, Kleinsasser 1-9, Palmer 1-3, Hoard 1-2.

MISSED FIELD GOAL ATTEMPTS—Minnesota, Anderson 50, 42.

INTERCEPTIONS—Oakland, Maryland 1-2, Turner 1-0.

KICKOFF RETURNS—Oakland, Jordan 1-19. Minnesota, Palmer 5-106.

PUNT RETURNS—Oakland, Gordon 1-11. Minnesota, Palmer 1-11.

SACKS—Oakland, K. Williams 1, Harvey 1, Bryant 1, Johnstone 1, Russell 1, Maryland 0.5, Osborne 0.5. Minnesota, Team.

STEELERS 23, RAVENS 20

Sunday, September 19

Pittsburgh 7   7   3   6—23
Baltimore 7   3   0   10—20

First Quarter
Pit.—Stewart 8 run (K. Brown kick), 4:03.
Bal.—Rhett 2 run (Stover kick), 13:21.
Second Quarter
Pit.—Huntley 17 run (K. Brown kick), 13:14.
Bal.—FG, Stover 45, 13:45.
Third Quarter
Pit.—FG, K. Brown 32, 10:44.
Fourth Quarter
Bal.—FG, Stover 28, 7:05.
Pit.—FG, K. Brown 28, 12:21.
Bal.—Ismail 19 pass from Case (Stover kick), 13:38.
Pit.—FG, K. Brown 36, 15:00.
Attendance—68,965.

	Pittsburgh	Baltimore
First downs	19	16
Rushes-yards	36-149	29-125
Passing	121	167
Punt returns	2-6	6-56
Kickoff returns	5-117	5-139
Interception returns	2-1	0-0
Comp.-att.-int.	18-27-0	14-31-2
Sacked-yards lost	3-17	2-11
Punts	9-46	7-40
Fumbles-lost	2-0	1-1
Penalties-yards	7-37	9-67
Time of possession	34:07	25:53

INDIVIDUAL STATISTICS

RUSHING—Pittsburgh, Bettis 16-46, Huntley 10-49, Stewart 8-51, Ward 1-3, Witman 1-0. Baltimore, Rhett 22-101, Evans 4-13, Case 1-8, Holmes 1-2, S. Mitchell 1-1.

PASSING—Pittsburgh, Stewart 18-27-0-138. Baltimore, S. Mitchell 7-16-2-48, Case 7-15-0-130.

RECEIVING—Pittsburgh, Hawkins 6-54, Edwards 5-38, Ward 2-31, Huntley 2-10, Bruener 2-4, Witman 1-1. Baltimore, Ismail 4-53, J. Lewis 3-48, Armour 2-43, Pierce 2-19, Purnell 2-10, DeLong 1-5.

MISSED FIELD GOAL ATTEMPTS—None.

INTERCEPTIONS—Pittsburgh, Washington 2-1.

KICKOFF RETURNS—Pittsburgh, Blackwell 3-83, Edwards 2-34. Baltimore, Harris 4-120, Ismail 1-19.

PUNT RETURNS—Pittsburgh, Edwards 2-6. Baltimore, J. Lewis 6-56.

SACKS—Pittsburgh, Emmons 1, Gildon 1. Baltimore, Boulware 1, McCrary 1, Trapp 1.

REDSKINS 50, GIANTS 21

Sunday, September 19

Washington	21	12	10	7—50
N.Y. Giants	0	14	0	7—21

First Quarter
Was.—Davis 1 run (Conway kick), 5:35.
Was.—Davis 1 run (Conway kick), 10:21.
Was.—Davis 19 run (Conway kick), 13:24.

Second Quarter
NYG—Way 7 run (Daluiso kick), 3:50.
Was.—Barber 70 interception return (kick blocked), 11:45.
NYG—Johnson 11 run (Daluiso kick), 12:44.
Was.—Alexander 1 pass from B. Johnson (run failed), 14:54.

Third Quarter
Was.—FG, Conway 48, 4:56.
Was.—Westbrook 15 pass from B. Johnson (Conway kick), 6:34.

Fourth Quarter
Was.—Alexander 27 pass from B. Johnson (Conway kick), 3:47.
NYG—Hilliard 7 pass from Graham (Daluiso kick), 7:48.
Attendance—73,170.

	Washington	N.Y. Giants
First downs	28	18
Rushes-yards	41-164	17-83
Passing	231	290
Punt returns	3-39	2-8
Kickoff returns	2-29	9-198
Interception returns	2-88	0-0
Comp.-att.-int.	20-28-0	23-38-2
Sacked-yards lost	0-0	2-22
Punts	3-42	5-47
Fumbles-lost	2-0	3-2
Penalties-yards	5-40	8-106
Time of possession	33:13	26:47

INDIVIDUAL STATISTICS

RUSHING—Washington, Davis 23-126, Hicks 8-22, Mitchell 3-13, Weldon 3-(minus 2), B. Johnson 2-11, Centers 1-(minus 2), Westbrook 1-(minus 4). New York, Johnson 8-18, Bennett 4-45, Way 3-15, Graham 2-5.

PASSING—Washington, B. Johnson 20-28-0-231. New York, Graham 20-31-1-268, Collins 3-7-1-44.

RECEIVING—Washington, Alexander 5-86, Westbrook 4-59, Centers 4-39, Connell 4-29, Fryar 1-10, Davis 1-5, Sellers 1-3. New York, Hilliard 8-114, Toomer 5-105, Jurevicius 3-36, Mitchell 2-28, Bennett 2-14, Johnson 1-8, Barber 1-4, Patten 1-3.

MISSED FIELD GOAL ATTEMPTS—None.

INTERCEPTIONS—Washington, Barber 1-70, Stevens 1-18.

KICKOFF RETURNS—Washington, Mitchell 1-29, Centers 1-0. New York, Patten 6-151, Barber 2-47, Galyon 1-0.

PUNT RETURNS—Washington, Mitchell 3-39. New York, Barber 2-8.

SACKS—Washington, Lang 1, Pounds 1.

DOLPHINS 19, CARDINALS 16

Sunday, September 19

Arizona	0	13	3	0—16
Miami	3	10	6	0—19

First Quarter
Mia.—FG, Mare 39, 9:07.

Second Quarter
Mia.—FG, Mare 51, 0:51.
Ariz.—FG, Jacke 36, 8:06.
Ariz.—FG, Jacke 44, 9:16.
Ariz.—Fredrickson 34 interception return (Jacke kick), 9:40.
Mia.—Drayton 10 pass from Marino (Mare kick), 14:35.

Third Quarter
Ariz.—FG, Jacke 38, 5:48.
Mia.—FG, Mare 48, 9:49.
Mia.—FG, Mare 44, 10:34.
Attendance—73,618.

	Arizona	Miami
First downs	13	14
Rushes-yards	28-64	31-83
Passing	120	221
Punt returns	4-63	4-27
Kickoff returns	4-72	5-119
Interception returns	2-57	4-31
Comp.-att.-int.	12-28-4	21-35-2
Sacked-yards lost	2-18	0-0
Punts	5-40	4-43
Fumbles-lost	0-0	3-2
Penalties-yards	2-15	9-81
Time of possession	28:08	31:52

INDIVIDUAL STATISTICS

RUSHING—Arizona, Murrell 20-59, Pittman 5-(minus 1), Plummer 2-4, Boston 1-2. Miami, Collins 15-45, Abdul-Jabbar 9-33, Johnson 3-4, Konrad 3-3, Marino 1-(minus 2).

PASSING—Arizona, Plummer 11-27-4-112, Pittman 1-1-0-26. Miami, Marino 21-35-2-221.

RECEIVING—Arizona, Sanders 7-76, Moore 2-48, Murrell 2-9, Boston 1-5. Miami, Drayton 5-50, McDuffie 4-85, Abdul-Jabbar 3-18, Martin 2-32, Konrad 2-12, Gadsden 2-11, Green 1-7, Johnson 1-5, Goodwin 1-1.

MISSED FIELD GOAL ATTEMPTS—Arizona, Jacke 32. Miami, Mare 42.

INTERCEPTIONS—Arizona, Fredrickson 1-34, Wadsworth 1-23. Miami, Madison 2-29, Marion 1-2, Thomas 1-0.

KICKOFF RETURNS—Arizona, Bates 3-63, Pittman 1-9. Miami, Marion 5-119.

PUNT RETURNS—Arizona, Boston 4-63. Miami, Buckley 3-18, McDuffie 1-9.

SACKS—Miami, Wilson 1, Armstrong 1.

BUCCANEERS 19, EAGLES 5

Sunday, September 19

Tampa Bay	7	6	6	0—19
Philadelphia	5	0	0	0— 5

First Quarter
T.B.—Emanuel 19 pass from Dilfer (Gramatica kick), 5:40.
Phi.—FG, N. Johnson 39, 9:31.
Phi.—Safety, out of end zone, 11:03.

Second Quarter
T.B.—FG, Gramatica 51, 6:08.
T.B.—FG, Gramatica 24, 9:55.

Third Quarter
T.B.—Alstott 17 pass from Dilfer (run failed), 8:35.
Attendance—64,285.

	Tampa Bay	Philadelphia
First downs	16	9
Rushes-yards	44-156	20-84
Passing	64	66
Punt returns	3-17	2-9
Kickoff returns	2-53	4-64
Interception returns	1-4	2-63

	Tampa Bay	Philadelphia
Comp.-att.-int.	7-14-2	16-30-1
Sacked-yards lost	2-25	9-60
Punts	5-41	9-41
Fumbles-lost	1-0	2-0
Penalties-yards	6-55	3-45
Time of possession	32:50	27:10

INDIVIDUAL STATISTICS

RUSHING—Tampa Bay, Dunn 24-82, Alstott 15-64, Dilfer 4-10, Mayberry 1-0. Philadelphia, Staley 13-42, McNabb 5-38, Pederson 1-2, Turner 1-2.

PASSING—Tampa Bay, Dilfer 7-14-2-89. Philadelphia, Pederson 12-19-1-100, McNabb 4-11-0-26.

RECEIVING—Tampa Bay, Alstott 3-33, Moore 2-23, Emanuel 1-19, Green 1-14. Philadelphia, Turner 6-32, C. Johnson 3-38, D. Douglas 3-15, Staley 2-22, Broughton 2-19.

MISSED FIELD GOAL ATTEMPTS—Philadelphia, N. Johnson 26, 50.

INTERCEPTIONS—Tampa Bay, Lynch 1-4. Philadelphia, Dawkins 1-37, Vincent 1-26.

KICKOFF RETURNS—Tampa Bay, Green 2-53. Philadelphia, Rossum 3-48, Bieniemy 1-16.

PUNT RETURNS—Tampa Bay, Green 3-17. Philadelphia, Rossum 2-9.

SACKS—Tampa Bay, Sapp 3.5, Ahanotu 2, Jones 2, Culpepper 1.5. Philadelphia, Vincent 1, H. Douglas 1.

CHARGERS 34, BENGALS 7

Sunday, September 19

San Diego	13	15	3	3—34
Cincinnati	7	0	0	0— 7

First Quarter
Cin.—McGee 12 pass from Blake (Pelfrey kick), 2:56.
S.D.—FG, Carney 27, 5:32.
S.D.—FG, Carney 23, 11:53.
S.D.—Means 12 pass from Harbaugh (Carney kick), 13:21.

Second Quarter
S.D.—J. Graham 29 pass from Harbaugh (Carney kick), 12:52.
S.D.—Dixon 27 fumble return (Ricks pass from Harbaugh), 14:06.

Third Quarter
S.D.—FG, Carney 21, 10:15.

Fourth Quarter
S.D.—FG, Carney 42, 0:10.
Attendance—47,660.

	San Diego	Cincinnati
First downs	14	10
Rushes-yards	35-91	17-47
Passing	175	125
Punt returns	3-25	4-28
Kickoff returns	2-39	7-202
Interception returns	1-1	0-0
Comp.-att.-int.	18-30-0	17-33-1
Sacked-yards lost	4-31	3-43
Punts	7-47	8-40
Fumbles-lost	2-0	7-4
Penalties-yards	6-47	6-40
Time of possession	38:30	21:30

INDIVIDUAL STATISTICS

RUSHING—San Diego, Means 27-79, Fletcher 3-9, Bynum 3-4, Harbaugh 1-0, Kramer 1-(minus 1). Cincinnati, Dillon 12-37, Blake 3-6, Smith 2-4.

PASSING—San Diego, Harbaugh 15-26-0-164, Kramer 3-4-0-42. Cincinnati, Smith 10-17-1-100, Blake 7-16-0-68.

RECEIVING—San Diego, Ricks 4-91, Still 4-32, J. Graham 2-45, Means 2-14, Pupunu 2-7, Fletcher 2-6, McCrary 1-5, F. Jones 1-3. Cincinnati, Scott 6-88, McGee 2-32, Williams 2-13, Carter 2-13, Pickens 2-10, Groce 2-3, Jackson 1-5.

MISSED FIELD GOAL ATTEMPTS—None.

INTERCEPTIONS—San Diego, Dimry 1-1.

KICKOFF RETURNS—San Diego, Fletcher 2-39. Cincinnati, Griffin 5-124, Jackson 2-78.

PUNT RETURNS—San Diego, Penn 3-25. Cincinnati, Griffin 4-28.

SACKS—San Diego, Seau 1, Johnson 1, Mohring 1. Cincinnati, Copeland 1.5, Gibson 1, Curtis 1, Bell 0.5.

LIONS 23, PACKERS 15

Sunday, September 19

Green Bay	3	3	0	9—15
Detroit	0	14	0	9—23

First Quarter
G.B.—FG, Longwell 45, 8:13.

Second Quarter
Det.—Morton 45 pass from Batch (Hanson kick), 0:07.
Det.—Sloan 74 pass from Batch (Hanson kick), 5:11.
G.B.—FG, Longwell 24, 14:50.

Fourth Quarter
G.B.—Safety, J. Jett forced out of end zone by B. Harris, 0:03.
G.B.—Levens 2 run (Longwell kick), 2:35.
Det.—Batch 1 run (sack), 4:03.
Det.—FG, Hanson 48, 12:14.
Attendance—76,202.

	Green Bay	Detroit
First downs	21	9
Rushes-yards	31-154	32-82
Passing	283	196
Punt returns	3-26	5-59
Kickoff returns	2-36	3-133
Interception returns	2-0	1-31
Comp.-att.-int.	20-41-1	9-16-2
Sacked-yards lost	1-5	4-23
Punts	6-39	5-41
Fumbles-lost	2-2	3-0
Penalties-yards	5-25	6-52
Time of possession	33:43	26:17

INDIVIDUAL STATISTICS

RUSHING—Green Bay, Levens 29-153, Favre 2-1. Detroit, Rivers 17-54, Schlesinger 7-10, Batch 3-9, Hill 3-8, Irvin 1-1, Jett 1-0.

PASSING—Green Bay, Favre 20-41-1-288. Detroit, Batch 9-16-2-219.

RECEIVING—Green Bay, Freeman 6-85, Schroeder 4-87, Levens 4-53, Bradford 3-25, T. Davis 2-27, Chmura 1-11. Detroit, Morton 4-118, Sloan 1-74, Stablein 1-13, Rivers 1-11, Crowell 1-3, Hill 1-0.

MISSED FIELD GOAL ATTEMPTS—None.

INTERCEPTIONS—Green Bay, B. Williams 1-0, Butler 1-0. Detroit, Bailey 1-31.

KICKOFF RETURNS—Green Bay, Howard 2-36. Detroit, Olivo 2-42, Fair 1-91.

PUNT RETURNS—Green Bay, Howard 3-26. Detroit, Fair 5-59.

SACKS—Green Bay, K. McKenzie 2, Booker 1, Butler 1. Detroit, Aldridge 1.

JAGUARS 22, PANTHERS 20

Sunday, September 19

Jacksonville	3	3	6	10—22
Carolina	0	14	0	6—20

First Quarter
Jac.—FG, Hollis 36, 9:18.

Second Quarter
Jac.—FG, Hollis 40, 2:10.
Car.—Walls 10 pass from Beuerlein (Kasay kick), 11:54.
Car.—Muhammad 60 pass from Beuerlein (Kasay kick), 13:32.

Third Quarter
Jac.—Stewart 1 run (pass failed), 7:29.

Fourth Quarter
Jac.—FG, Hollis 31, 4:38.
Jac.—Stewart 44 run (Hollis kick), 13:12.
Car.—Walls 1 pass from Beuerlein (pass failed), 14:29.
Attendance—64,261.

	Jacksonville	Carolina
First downs	27	16
Rushes-yards	46-214	18-87
Passing	200	196
Punt returns	2-2	1-15
Kickoff returns	2-43	3-83
Interception returns	1-0	0-0
Comp.-att.-int.	20-32-0	16-26-1
Sacked-yards lost	2-14	4-20
Punts	3-48	5-45
Fumbles-lost	1-1	0-0
Penalties-yards	5-35	5-37
Time of possession	38:09	21:51

INDIVIDUAL STATISTICS

RUSHING—Jacksonville, Stewart 27-124, Banks 8-43, Brunell 6-20, Taylor 5-27. Carolina, Lane 8-32, Biakabutuka 6-47, Floyd 2-5, Johnson 1-2, Beuerlein 1-1.

PASSING—Jacksonville, Brunell 20-32-0-214. Carolina, Beuerlein 16-26-1-216.
RECEIVING—Jacksonville, J. Smith 10-115, Brady 3-22, McCardell 2-22, Jones 1-31, Stewart 1-11, Banks 1-6, Shelton 1-6, Barlow 1-1. Carolina, Walls 5-53, Muhammad 4-103, Carruth 2-27, Floyd 2-13, Lane 1-18, Biakabutuka 1-2, Johnson 1-0.
MISSED FIELD GOAL ATTEMPTS—Jacksonville, Hollis 49.
INTERCEPTIONS—Jacksonville, Bryant 1-0.
KICKOFF RETURNS—Jacksonville, Logan 1-25, Banks 1-18. Carolina, Bates 2-64, Lane 1-19.
PUNT RETURNS—Jacksonville, Barlow 2-2. Carolina, Metcalf 1-15.
SACKS—Jacksonville, Walker 2, Hardy 1.5, Wynn 0.5. Carolina, E. Jones 1, Team 1.

PATRIOTS 31, COLTS 28

Sunday, September 19

Indianapolis	14	14	0	0	—28
New England	0	7	7	17	—31

First Quarter
Ind.—Harrison 42 pass from Manning (Vanderjagt kick), 9:09.
Ind.—Harrison 10 pass from Manning (Vanderjagt kick), 14:23.

Second Quarter
Ind.—James 1 run (Vanderjagt kick), 2:21.
N.E.—Jefferson 11 pass from Bledsoe (Vinatieri kick), 7:16.
Ind.—Harrison 8 pass from Manning (Vanderjagt kick), 14:12.

Third Quarter
N.E.—Allen 8 pass from Bledsoe (Vinatieri kick), 10:25.

Fourth Quarter
N.E.—Coates 3 pass from Bledsoe (Vinatieri kick), 5:17.
N.E.—Coates 10 pass from Bledsoe (Vinatieri kick), 11:57.
N.E.—FG, Vinatieri 26, 14:25.
Attendance—59,640.

	Indianapolis	New England
First downs	23	26
Rushes-yards	33-121	27-108
Passing	223	292
Punt returns	3-38	2-5
Kickoff returns	6-120	5-82
Interception returns	0-0	2-13
Comp.-att.-int.	18-30-2	27-45-0
Sacked-yards lost	0-0	1-7
Punts	5-39	6-49
Fumbles-lost	2-2	1-1
Penalties-yards	7-59	15-135127
Time of possession	30:57	29:03

INDIVIDUAL STATISTICS
RUSHING—Indianapolis, James 32-118, Manning 1-3. New England, Allen 15-74, Faulk 5-9, Warren 4-18, Bledsoe 3-7.
PASSING—Indianapolis, Manning 18-30-2-223. New England, Bledsoe 27-45-0-299.
RECEIVING—Indianapolis, Harrison 7-105, Green 5-61, Pollard 4-44, James 1-9, Greene 1-4. New England, Glenn 7-122, Coates 4-34, T. Carter

4-24, Jefferson 3-34, Brown 2-37, Simmons 2-16, Allen 2-8, Warren 1-16, Rutledge 1-7, Faulk 1-1.
MISSED FIELD GOAL ATTEMPTS—None.
INTERCEPTIONS—New England, C. Carter 2-13.
KICKOFF RETURNS—Indianapolis, Wilkins 5-97, Pathon 1-23. New England, Faulk 4-64, Jones 1-18.
PUNT RETURNS—Indianapolis, Wilkins 3-38. New England, Brown 2-5.
SACKS—Indianapolis, Whittington 1.

COWBOYS 24, FALCONS 7

Monday, September 20

Atlanta	0	0	0	7	— 7
Dallas	10	0	7	7	—24

First Quarter
Dal.—FG, Cunningham 23, 5:07.
Dal.—E. Smith 2 run (Cunningham kick), 14:29.

Third Quarter
Dal.—E. Smith 7 run (Cunningham kick), 3:36.

Fourth Quarter
Atl.—Dwight 45 pass from Kanell (Andersen kick), 11:00.
Dal.—Ellis 87 interception return (Cunningham kick), 14:14.
Attendance—63,663.

	Atlanta	Dallas
First downs	13	17
Rushes-yards	23-85	37-134
Passing	231	98
Punt returns	1-4	3-16
Kickoff returns	4-55	0-0
Interception returns	2-28	3-154
Comp.-att.-int.	16-38-3	10-22-2
Sacked-yards lost	5-31	2-11
Punts	7-41	6-37
Fumbles-lost	1-1	0-0
Penalties-yards	11-82	9-69
Time of possession	27:12	32:48

INDIVIDUAL STATISTICS
RUSHING—Atlanta, Hanspard 19-76, Anderson 3-9, Mathis 1-0. Dallas, E. Smith 29-109, Warren 6-15, Tucker 1-8, Aikman 1-2.
PASSING—Atlanta, Kanell 9-22-2-172, Graziani 7-16-1-90. Dallas, Aikman 10-22-2-109.
RECEIVING—Atlanta, Mathis 4-73, Calloway 3-52, Harris 3-46, Santiago 2-17, Dwight 1-45, Kozlowski 1-14, Christian 1-8, Hanspard 1-7. Dallas, Ogden 2-18, Irvin 2-13, Ismail 1-38, Bjornson 1-18, LaFleur 1-9, Mills 1-8, Warren 1-4, E. Smith 1-1.
MISSED FIELD GOAL ATTEMPTS—Atlanta, Andersen 49. Dallas, Cunningham 47.
INTERCEPTIONS—Atlanta, Buchanan 1-28, Robinson 1-0. Dallas, Ellis 1-87, Coakley 1-43, Reese 1-24.
KICKOFF RETURNS—Atlanta, Dwight 3-50, Harris 1-5.
PUNT RETURNS—Atlanta, Dwight 1-4. Dallas, McGarity 3-16.
SACKS—Atlanta, Smith 1, Crockett 0.5, Dronett 0.5. Dallas, Hennings 2, Woodson 1, Coakley 1, Zellner 1.

WEEK 3

RESULTS

BALTIMORE 17, Cleveland 10
BUFFALO 26, Philadelphia 0
CAROLINA 27, Cincinnati 3
GREEN BAY 23, Minnesota 20
Indianapolis 27, SAN DIEGO 19
KANSAS CITY 31, Detroit 21
NEW ENGLAND 16, N.Y. Giants 14
OAKLAND 24, Chicago 17
ST. LOUIS 35, Atlanta 7
Seattle 29, PITTSBURGH 10
TAMPA BAY 13, Denver 10
Tennessee 20, JACKSONVILLE 19
Washington 27, N.Y. JETS 20
San Francisco 24, ARIZONA 10
Open date: Dallas, Miami, New Orleans

STANDINGS

AFC EAST
	W	L	T	Pct.
New England	3	0	0	1.000
Miami	2	0	0	1.000
Buffalo	2	1	0	.667
Indianapolis	2	1	0	.667
N.Y. Jets	0	3	0	.000

AFC CENTRAL
	W	L	T	Pct.
Tennessee	3	0	0	1.000
Jacksonville	2	1	0	.667
Pittsburgh	2	1	0	.667
Baltimore	1	2	0	.333
Cincinnati	0	3	0	.000
Cleveland	0	3	0	.000

AFC WEST
	W	L	T	Pct.
Kansas City	2	1	0	.667
Oakland	2	1	0	.667
Seattle	2	1	0	.667
San Diego	1	1	0	.500
Denver	0	3	0	.000

NFC EAST
	W	L	T	Pct.
Dallas	2	0	0	1.000
Washington	2	1	0	.667
Arizona	1	2	0	.333
N.Y. Giants	1	2	0	.667
Philadelphia	0	3	0	.000

NFC CENTRAL
	W	L	T	Pct.
Detroit	2	1	0	.667
Green Bay	2	1	0	.667
Tampa Bay	2	1	0	.667
Chicago	1	2	0	.333
Minnesota	1	2	0	.333

NFC WEST
	W	L	T	Pct.
St. Louis	2	0	0	1.000
San Francisco	2	1	0	.667
New Orleans	1	1	0	.500
Carolina	1	2	0	.333
Atlanta	0	3	0	.000

HIGHLIGHTS

Hero of the week: Tennessee cornerback Samari Rolle intercepted a pass from Jacksonville quarterback Mark Brunell in the end zone with 57 seconds left in the game, sealing the Titans' 20-19 win over their AFC Central Division rival. It was the first interception of Rolle's NFL career.

Goat of the week: Jets cornerback Ray Mickens was called for pass interference twice on an 80-yard drive by Washington that ended with a four-yard go-ahead touchdown run by Stephen Davis. The first penalty cost the Jets 35 yards when Mickens bumped wide receiver Michael Westbrook, and the second nullified a stop on third down when he held Albert Connell. The Redskins won the game, 27-20, behind three TD runs by Davis.

Sub of the week: Tight end Michael Roan, who was playing because starter Jackie Harris was injured, caught a 12-yard pass from Neil O'Donnell early in the fourth quarter for what proved to be the game-winning touchdown in the Titans' victory over Jacksonville. It was the first NFL touchdown for Roan, who caught just 33 passes in his first four seasons and just one in 1999 before the game-winner.

Comeback of the week: Brett Favre pulled off his 12th fourth-quarter comeback and second of the season when he hit Corey Bradford with a 23-yard touchdown pass with 12 seconds left to give the Packers a 23-20 win over the Vikings. Bradford's catch capped a 77-yard drive in which Favre completed six of seven passes. Favre, who finished 24-of-39 for 304 yards, collapsed onto a sideline bench shortly after throwing the final pass and had to be helped off the field by the Packers' medical staff.

Blowout of the week: Kurt Warner produced touchdowns on the Rams' first four possessions in a 35-7 rout of the Falcons. St. Louis opened the game with a 17-play, 80-yard drive that ended on a Robert Holcombe 1-yard touchdown run. Warner then threw touchdown passes to rookie Torry Holt (38 yards), Isaac Bruce (46) and Marshall Faulk (17). The Rams had the ball for all but 1:49 and three plays of the first quarter while outgaining the Falcons 131-3. They went into halftime up 28-0 after converting eight of nine third-down plays and outgaining Atlanta 311-67.

Nail-biter of the week: In a game that had 26 penalties for 206 yards, Tyrone Wheatley scored on an eight-yard run with 6:45 left as the Raiders beat the Bears, 24-17. Wheatley, making his first start for the Raiders, had eight carries for 41 yards, most of them on the game-winning drive. Chicago quarterback Shane Matthews connected with Curtis Enis for a 16-yard touchdown to give the Bears a 17-14 lead in the third quarter, but Oakland tied it early in the fourth on a 47-yard Michael Husted field goal.

Hit of the week: Redskins defensive end Kenard Lang had three of Washington's six sacks and forced a fumble that set up the game's final touchdown in a 27-20 win over the Jets.

Oddity of the week: Referee Phil Luckett, who was involved in separate controversies involving the Steelers and Seahawks in 1998, was chosen by the NFL as the referee for the Seattle-Pittsburgh game. Luckett made a disputed coin flip call in the Steelers' Thanksgiving Day game at Detroit in '98, and his crew awarded Vinny Testaverde a touchdown when the Jets quarterback clearly did not score in a one-point victory over Seattle later that season.

Top rusher: Tshimanga Biakabutuka rushed for 132 yards on only eight carries in Carolina's 27-3 victory over Cincinnati.

Top passer: Peyton Manning connected on 29-of-54 passes for 404 yards and two touchdowns and added a 12-yard run for a score in the Colts' 27-19 win over the Chargers.

Top receiver: Indianapolis' Marvin Harrison, who tied a franchise record with 13 catches, had a career-high 196 yards and a touchdown.

Notes: Manning joined Johnny Unitas as the only Colt with a 400-yard passing game. Unitas threw for 401 yards in a 1967 game against Atlanta. ... Biakabutuka was a one-man wrecking crew against Cincinnati. On the first play from scrimmage, he shed a few tackles and raced down the sideline for a

62-yard score. Later, he broke the club record for longest run from scrimmage with a 67-yard TD run. ... Buffalo receiver Andre Reed caught three passes against Philadelphia to bring his career total to 900. Reed is third on the NFL's career list behind Jerry Rice (1,146) and Art Monk (940). ... Carolina tight end Wesley Walls had one reception, giving him 177 with the Panthers and moving him past Mark Carrier atop the team's list for career receptions leaders. ... Prior to their 13-10 victory over Denver, the Bucs had never won a game against a defending Super Bowl champion, losing 10 consecutive times. **Quote of the week:** Favre, on his winning TD pass: "Those touchdown passes. I've dreamed about them a million times since I was a kid. Of course, Corey Bradford wasn't in them."

GAME SUMMARIES

COLTS 27, CHARGERS 19

Sunday, September 26

Indianapolis	10	0	3	14	—27
San Diego	0	16	3	0	—19

First Quarter
Ind.—FG, Vanderjagt 35, 9:10.
Ind.—Harrison 33 pass from Manning (Vanderjagt kick), 13:41.
Second Quarter
S.D.—Means 1 run (Carney kick), 3:22.
S.D.—Lewis 0 blocked punt return (Carney kick), 4:31.
S.D.—Safety, Manning out of end zone, 12:15.
Third Quarter
S.D.—FG, Carney 50, 6:34.
Ind.—FG, Vanderjagt 42, 10:47.
Fourth Quarter
Ind.—Manning 12 run (Vanderjagt kick), 3:19.
Ind.—Wilkins 26 pass from Manning (Vanderjagt kick), 12:26.
Attendance—56,942.

	Indianapolis	San Diego
First downs	26	16
Rushes-yards	22-64	25-95
Passing	404	179
Punt returns	4-31	0-0
Kickoff returns	4-91	7-103
Interception returns	1-38	1-1
Comp.-att.-int.	29-54-1	15-37-1
Sacked-yards lost	0-0	3-9
Punts	3-28	8-38
Fumbles-lost	2-0	0-0
Penalties-yards	8-60	5-45
Time of possession	31:33	28:27

INDIVIDUAL STATISTICS
RUSHING—Indianapolis, James 17-46, Manning 4-14, Harrison 1-4. San Diego, Means 19-59, Harbaugh 4-22, Fletcher 2-14.
PASSING—Indianapolis, Manning 29-54-1-404. San Diego, Harbaugh 15-37-1-188.
RECEIVING—Indianapolis, Harrison 13-196, Pathon 4-55, James 3-36, Dilger 3-36, Green 3-29, Wilkins 2-37, Pollard 1-15. San Diego, F. Jones 5-45, J. Graham 4-48, Still 2-24, Means 2-16, Davis 1-46, Ricks 1-9.
MISSED FIELD GOAL ATTEMPTS—Indianapolis, Vanderjagt 36, 55.
INTERCEPTIONS—Indianapolis, Poole 1-38. San Diego, Spencer 1-1.
KICKOFF RETURNS—Indianapolis, Pathon 3-68, Wilkins 1-23. San Diego, Bynum 5-78, Fletcher 1-17, Still 1-8.
PUNT RETURNS—Indianapolis, Wilkins 4-31.
SACKS—Indianapolis, King 1.5, Burris 1, E. Johnson 0.5.

PATRIOTS 16, GIANTS 14

Sunday, September 26

N.Y. Giants	7	0	0	7	—14
New England	0	7	6	3	—16

First Quarter
NYG—Johnson 6 pass from Graham (Daluiso kick), 7:12.
Second Quarter
N.E.—Allen 1 run (Vinatieri kick), 6:39.
Third Quarter
N.E.—FG, Vinatieri 38, 6:05.
N.E.—FG, Vinatieri 19, 13:28.
Fourth Quarter
N.E.—FG, Vinatieri 41, 11:48.
NYG—Barber 1 pass from Graham (Daluiso kick), 13:46.
Attendance—59,169.

	N.Y. Giants	New England
First downs	19	17
Rushes-yards	26-57	29-67
Passing	201	223
Punt returns	0-0	2-18
Kickoff returns	5-124	3-43
Interception returns	0-0	0-0
Comp.-att.-int.	23-36-0	20-28-0
Sacked-yards lost	1-15	1-10
Punts	5-36	4-41
Fumbles-lost	0-0	0-0
Penalties-yards	2-10	3-25
Time of possession	29:19	30:41

INDIVIDUAL STATISTICS
RUSHING—New York, Johnson 10-18, Way 8-23, Graham 6-12, Barber 1-3, Bennett 1-1. New England, Allen 20-50, Warren 4-7, Bledsoe 3-0, T. Carter 2-10.
PASSING—New York, Graham 23-36-0-216. New England, Bledsoe 20-28-0-233.
RECEIVING—New York, Toomer 7-69, Barber 5-46, Hilliard 4-47, Mitchell 3-30, Johnson 2-7, Way 1-11, Cross 1-6. New England, Glenn 5-95, Brown 4-50, Jefferson 4-35, Coates 3-33, T. Carter 2-8, Warren 1-12, Allen 1-0.
MISSED FIELD GOAL ATTEMPTS—New York, Daluiso 41.
INTERCEPTIONS—None.
KICKOFF RETURNS—New York, Patten 3-74, Barber 2-50. New England, Jones 2-43, Coates 1-0.
PUNT RETURNS—New England, Brown 2-18.
SACKS—New York, K. Hamilton 1. New England, Slade 1.

RAIDERS 24, BEARS 17

Sunday, September 26

Chicago	7	3	7	0	—17
Oakland	7	7	0	10	—24

First Quarter
Oak.—Brown 20 pass from Gannon (Husted kick), 10:53.
Chi.—Conway 11 pass from Matthews (Jaeger kick), 11:54.
Second Quarter
Chi.—FG, Jaeger 52, 13:10.
Oak.—Dudley 13 pass from Gannon (Husted kick), 14:51.
Third Quarter
Chi.—Enis 16 pass from Matthews (Jaeger kick), 6:03.
Fourth Quarter
Oak.—FG, Husted 47, 1:47.
Oak.—Wheatley 8 run (Husted kick), 8:15.
Attendance—50,458.

	Chicago	Oakland
First downs	11	22
Rushes-yards	16-34	26-109
Passing	198	283
Punt returns	0-0	3-20
Kickoff returns	5-172	4-82
Interception returns	0-0	1-28
Comp.-att.-int.	23-35-1	26-35-0
Sacked-yards lost	3-18	4-12
Punts	4-48	3-38
Fumbles-lost	3-2	5-5
Penalties-yards	17-121	9-85
Time of possession	25:31	34:29

INDIVIDUAL STATISTICS
RUSHING—Chicago, Enis 15-35, Matthews 1-(minus 1). Oakland, Kaufman 10-18, Wheatley 8-41, Gannon 5-47, Jordan 2-4, Ritchie 1-(minus 1).

PASSING—Chicago, Matthews 20-30-1-178, McNown 3-5-0-38. Oakland, Gannon 26-35-0-295.
RECEIVING—Chicago, Enis 4-37, Conway 4-33, Brooks 3-51, Engram 3-42, Wetnight 3-9, M. Robinson 2-29, Milburn 2-9, Allred 1-3, Hallock 1-3. Oakland, Brown 9-121, Ritchie 4-41, Dudley 3-35, Jett 2-29, Kaufman 2-22, Brigham 2-15, Wheatley 2-14, Mickens 1-15, Jordan 1-3.
MISSED FIELD GOAL ATTEMPTS—Chicago, Jaeger 48, 46.
INTERCEPTIONS—Oakland, Gordon 1-28.
KICKOFF RETURNS—Chicago, Milburn 4-157, Bennett 1-15. Oakland, Jordan 2-47, Kaufman 2-35.
PUNT RETURNS—Oakland, Gordon 3-20.
SACKS—Chicago, Simmons 3, Burton 1. Oakland, Johnstone 2, Bryant 1.

TITANS 20, JAGUARS 19

Sunday, September 26

Tennessee.	0	0	7	13—20
Jacksonville	3	0	14	2—19

First Quarter
Jac.—FG, Hollis 42, 11:35.

Third Quarter
Ten.—E. George 8 pass from O'Donnell (Del Greco kick), 2:12.
Jac.—J. Smith 11 pass from Brunell (Hollis kick), 13:42.
Jac.—Beasley 35 interception return (Hollis kick), 14:38.

Fourth Quarter
Ten.—FG, Del Greco 44, 3:34.
Ten.—FG, Del Greco 48, 6:29.
Ten.—Roan 12 pass from O'Donnell (Del Greco kick), 11:34.
Jac.—Safety, C. Hentrich forced out of end zone by team, 15:00.
Attendance—61,502.

	Tennessee	Jacksonville
First downs	15	22
Rushes-yards	27-40	33-137
Passing	191	232
Punt returns	4-30	3-14
Kickoff returns	2-43	4-50
Interception returns	3-62	1-35
Comp.-att.-int.	17-32-1	22-42-3
Sacked-yards lost	2-13	0-0
Punts	6-37	5-46
Fumbles-lost	2-1	2-1
Penalties-yards	9-71	9-79
Time of possession	27:54	32:06

INDIVIDUAL STATISTICS
RUSHING—Tennessee, E. George 18-57, O'Donnell 6-1, Thomas 2-(minus 7), Hentrich 1-(minus 11). Jacksonville, J. Stewart 25-98, Brunell 6-33, Barker 1-6, Banks 1-0.
PASSING—Tennessee, O'Donnell 17-32-1-204. Jacksonville, Brunell 22-42-3-232.
RECEIVING—Tennessee, Dyson 6-79, E. George 4-36, Wycheck 3-34, Thigpen 2-42, Roan 1-12, Thomas 1-1. Jacksonville, J. Smith 10-129, McCardell 4-55, Jones 2-15, Brady 2-12, J. Stewart 2-1, Shelton 1-13, Banks 1-7.
MISSED FIELD GOAL ATTEMPTS—None.
INTERCEPTIONS—Tennessee, Dorsett 1-43, Holmes 1-19, Rolle 1-0. Jacksonville, Beasley 1-35.
KICKOFF RETURNS—Tennessee, Preston 2-43. Jacksonville, Banks 2-36, Barlow 1-14, Whitted 1-0.
PUNT RETURNS—Tennessee, Preston 4-30. Jacksonville, Barlow 3-14.
SACKS—Jacksonville, L. Smith 1, Team 1.

CHIEFS 31, LIONS 21

Sunday, September 26

Detroit	0	7	6	8—21
Kansas City	7	10	7	7—31

First Quarter
K.C.—Gonzalez 15 pass from Grbac (Stoyanovich kick), 13:30.

Second Quarter
Det.—Irvin 16 run (Hanson kick), 5:46.
K.C.—Shehee 6 run (Stoyanovich kick), 10:42.
K.C.—FG, Stoyanovich 51, 14:59.

Third Quarter
K.C.—Horn 25 pass from Grbac (Stoyanovich kick), 10:00.
Det.—Rasby 3 pass from Batch (pass failed), 13:36.

Fourth Quarter
K.C.—Bennett 7 run (Stoyanovich kick), 4:22.
Det.—Rivers 31 pass from Batch (Stablein pass from Batch), 12:49.
Attendance—78,384.

	Detroit	Kansas City
First downs	18	21
Rushes-yards	22-118	35-155
Passing	193	228
Punt returns	3-24	7-104
Kickoff returns	6-91	1-24
Interception returns	0-0	2-25
Comp.-att.-int.	16-34-2	20-29-0
Sacked-yards lost	4-20	1-7
Punts	8-51	8-44
Fumbles-lost	0-0	0-0
Penalties-yards	7-52	6-70
Time of possession	28:53	31:07

INDIVIDUAL STATISTICS
RUSHING—Detroit, Rivers 13-66, Batch 4-12, Irvin 3-20, Crowell 1-20, Schlesinger 1-0. Kansas City, Bennett 12-73, Shehee 11-46, Morris 7-16, Richardson 3-14, Grbac 2-6.
PASSING—Detroit, Batch 16-34-2-213. Kansas City, Grbac 20-29-0-235.
RECEIVING—Detroit, Sloan 4-31, Rivers 3-46, Schlesinger 3-33, Crowell 2-48, Morton 2-31, Irvin 1-21, Rasby 1-3. Kansas City, Gonzalez 7-72, Lockett 4-36, Alexander 3-69, Shehee 3-15, Horn 2-35, Rison 1-8.
MISSED FIELD GOAL ATTEMPTS—None.
INTERCEPTIONS—Kansas City, Dishman 1-25, Hasty 1-0.
KICKOFF RETURNS—Detroit, Fair 3-55, Olivo 2-36, Irvin 1-0. Kansas City, Vanover 1-24.
PUNT RETURNS—Detroit, Uwaezuoke 3-24. Kansas City, Vanover 7-104.
SACKS—Detroit, Elliss 1. Kansas City, D. Williams 2, Edwards 1, Patton 1.

PACKERS 23, VIKINGS 20

Sunday, September 26

Minnesota.	7	3	3	7—20
Green Bay.	0	10	3	10—23

First Quarter
Min.—Hoard 2 run (Anderson kick), 10:34.

Second Quarter
G.B.—FG, Longwell 28, 0:53.
G.B.—Edwards 26 interception return (Longwell kick), 7:23.
Min.—FG, Anderson 34, 14:10.

Third Quarter
Min.—FG, Anderson 22, 5:43.
G.B.—FG, Longwell 35, 11:55.

Fourth Quarter
G.B.—FG, Longwell 34, 10:35.
Min.—Moss 10 pass from Cunningham (Anderson kick), 13:04.
G.B.—Bradford 23 pass from Favre (Longwell kick), 14:48.
Attendance—59,868.

	Minnesota	Green Bay
First downs	21	20
Rushes-yards	29-97	22-71
Passing	231	289
Punt returns	0-0	0-0
Kickoff returns	5-125	4-80
Interception returns	0-0	2-26
Comp.-att.-int.	18-32-2	24-39-0
Sacked-yards lost	2-13	2-15
Punts	3-59	3-44
Fumbles-lost	0-0	0-0
Penalties-yards	5-30	5-47
Time of possession	30:54	29:06

INDIVIDUAL STATISTICS
RUSHING—Minnesota, Smith 21-85, Hoard 4-1, M. Williams 2-10, Cunningham 2-1. Green Bay, Levens 18-49, Favre 3-13, Henderson 1-9.
PASSING—Minnesota, Cunningham 18-32-2-244. Green Bay, Favre 24-39-0-304.
RECEIVING—Minnesota, Reed 6-108, Carter 4-85, Smith 3-19, Glover 2-13, Moss 2-13, Palmer 1-6. Green Bay, Levens 9-84, Schroeder 5-85, Bradford 4-72, Freeman 4-56, Henderson 2-7.
MISSED FIELD GOAL ATTEMPTS—None.
INTERCEPTIONS—Green Bay, Edwards 2-26.
KICKOFF RETURNS—Minnesota, Palmer 4-105, M. Williams 1-20. Green Bay, Mitchell 2-41, Howard 2-39.

PUNT RETURNS—None.
SACKS—Minnesota, Clemons 2. Green Bay, Lyon 1, Booker 1.

SEAHAWKS 29, STEELERS 10

Sunday, September 26

Seattle	17	9	0	3	—29
Pittsburgh	0	0	0	10	—10

First Quarter
Sea.—Hanks 23 interception return (Peterson kick), 1:08.
Sea.—Rogers 94 punt return (Peterson kick), 3:20.
Sea.—FG, Peterson 45, 8:07.

Second Quarter
Sea.—FG, Peterson 51, 5:07.
Sea.—FG, Peterson 41, 11:46.
Sea.—FG, Peterson 26, 14:58.

Fourth Quarter
Pit.—FG, K. Brown 33, 2:57.
Sea.—FG, Peterson 38, 10:36.
Pit.—Edwards 16 pass from Tomczak (K. Brown kick), 13:25.
Attendance—57,881.

	Seattle	Pittsburgh
First downs	16	15
Rushes-yards	34-90	19-65
Passing	251	207
Punt returns	2-106	1-39
Kickoff returns	1-22	6-98
Interception returns	5-81	0-0
Comp.-att.-int.	18-29-0	21-41-5
Sacked-yards lost	1-14	2-13
Punts	4-39	5-56
Fumbles-lost	3-2	1-0
Penalties-yards	7-50	5-43
Time of possession	32:47	27:13

INDIVIDUAL STATISTICS
RUSHING—Seattle, Watters 29-98, Kitna 3-(minus 3), R. Brown 1-9, Bownes 1-(minus 14). Pittsburgh, Bettis 11-39, Huntley 5-19, Stewart 2-3, Tomczak 1-4.
PASSING—Seattle, Kitna 18-29-0-265. Pittsburgh, Tomczak 14-27-2-159, Stewart 7-14-3-61.
RECEIVING—Seattle, Pritchard 6-90, Dawkins 5-105, Mayes 3-28, Fauria 2-30, Watters 2-12. Pittsburgh, Edwards 6-72, Hawkins 5-63, Bruener 3-25, Huntley 2-30, Ward 2-18, Bettis 2-9, Zereoue 1-3.
MISSED FIELD GOAL ATTEMPTS—Seattle, Peterson 30.
INTERCEPTIONS—Seattle, Springs 1-42, Hanks 1-23, D. Williams 1-9, Bellamy 1-7, W. Williams 1-0.
KICKOFF RETURNS—Seattle, Green 1-22. Pittsburgh, Blackwell 5-89, Lyons 1-9.
PUNT RETURNS—Seattle, Rogers 2-106. Pittsburgh, Blackwell 1-39.
SACKS—Seattle, Kennedy 1, Daniels 1. Pittsburgh, Roye 1.

RAVENS 17, BROWNS 10

Sunday, September 26

Cleveland	0	0	3	7	—10
Baltimore	3	7	7	0	—17

First Quarter
Bal.—FG, Stover 44, 12:46.

Second Quarter
Bal.—Case 1 run (Stover kick), 4:29.

Third Quarter
Cle.—FG, Dawson 49, 1:41.
Bal.—Case 1 run (Stover kick), 9:30.

Fourth Quarter
Cle.—Johnson 11 pass from Couch (Dawson kick), 0:57.
Attendance—68,803.

	Cleveland	Baltimore
First downs	11	16
Rushes-yards	24-100	37-184
Passing	89	150
Punt returns	4-30	6-63
Kickoff returns	3-56	3-77
Interception returns	3-15	1-0
Comp.-att.-int.	13-32-1	12-25-3
Sacked-yards lost	4-34	4-15
Punts	10-45	8-42
Fumbles-lost	2-2	1-0
Penalties-yards	2-20	8-65
Time of possession	27:08	32:52

INDIVIDUAL STATISTICS
RUSHING—Cleveland, Kirby 18-51, Couch 6-49. Baltimore, Rhett 22-113, Case 11-57, Evans 3-13, J. Lewis 1-1.
PASSING—Cleveland, Couch 13-32-1-123. Baltimore, Case 12-25-3-165.
RECEIVING—Cleveland, Kirby 7-75, Edwards 3-16, Johnson 2-18, Shepherd 1-14. Baltimore, Rhett 3-27, J. Lewis 3-23, Ismail 2-49, Evans 2-37, Armour 1-16, Pierce 1-13.
MISSED FIELD GOAL ATTEMPTS—None.
INTERCEPTIONS—Cleveland, McCutcheon 1-12, L. Jones 1-3, Abdullah 1-0. Baltimore, McAlister 1-0.
KICKOFF RETURNS—Cleveland, Powell 2-44, G. Jones 1-12. Baltimore, Harris 2-64, Ismail 1-13.
PUNT RETURNS—Cleveland, Johnson 2-21, Gibson 2-9. Baltimore, J. Lewis 6-63.
SACKS—Cleveland, Holland 1, McCormack 1, Alexander 1, Ball 1. Baltimore, Boulware 2, R. Lewis 1, McCrary 1.

BUCCANEERS 13, BRONCOS 10

Sunday, September 26

Denver	7	0	0	3	—10
Tampa Bay	7	6	0	0	—13

First Quarter
T.B.—Alstott 28 run (Gramatica kick), 5:38.
Den.—McCaffrey 12 pass from Griese (Elam kick), 10:31.

Second Quarter
T.B.—FG, Gramatica 38, 2:05.
T.B.—FG, Gramatica 35, 15:00.

Fourth Quarter
Den.—FG, Elam 44, 0:56.
Attendance—65,297.

	Denver	Tampa Bay
First downs	8	17
Rushes-yards	20-53	42-165
Passing	120	78
Punt returns	5-40	4-40
Kickoff returns	3-62	3-51
Interception returns	0-0	1-18
Comp.-att.-int.	14-28-1	15-19-0
Sacked-yards lost	2-12	7-57
Punts	7-47	6-45
Fumbles-lost	2-0	2-2
Penalties-yards	8-62	2-14
Time of possession	23:01	36:59

INDIVIDUAL STATISTICS
RUSHING—Denver, Davis 19-53, Griese 1-0. Tampa Bay, Alstott 25-131, Dilfer 8-17, Dunn 8-15, Anthony 1-2.
PASSING—Denver, Griese 14-28-1-132. Tampa Bay, Dilfer 15-18-0-135, Royals 0-1-0-0.
RECEIVING—Denver, Sharpe 5-39, McCaffrey 3-26, R. Smith 2-24, Griffith 2-5, Cooper 1-21, Carswell 1-17. Tampa Bay, Dunn 9-82, Anthony 2-18, Emanuel 1-14, Williams 1-9, Green 1-7, Alstott 1-5.
MISSED FIELD GOAL ATTEMPTS—None.
INTERCEPTIONS—Tampa Bay, Nickerson 1-18.
KICKOFF RETURNS—Denver, Watson 3-62. Tampa Bay, Green 3-51.
PUNT RETURNS—Denver, Watson 5-40. Tampa Bay, Green 4-40.
SACKS—Denver, Pryce 3, N. Smith 2, Cadrez 1, Braxton 1. Tampa Bay, Lynch 1, Ahanotu 1.

RAMS 35, FALCONS 7

Sunday, September 26

Atlanta	0	0	7	0	— 7
St. Louis	7	21	7	0	—35

First Quarter
St.L.—Holcombe 1 run (Wilkins kick), 10:13.

Second Quarter
St.L.—Holt 38 pass from Warner (Wilkins kick), 0:07.
St.L.—Bruce 46 pass from Warner (Wilkins kick), 0:36.
St.L.—Faulk 17 pass from Warner (Wilkins kick), 8:25.

— 132 —

Third Quarter
Atl.—Kozlowski 1 pass from Graziani (Andersen kick), 7:28.
St.L.—Warner 5 run (Wilkins kick), 13:06.
Attendance—63,253.

	Atlanta	St. Louis
First downs	12	19
Rushes-yards	22-68	34-167
Passing	165	275
Punt returns	1-20	1-6
Kickoff returns	6-146	2-42
Interception returns	0-0	1-18
Comp.-att.-int.	19-31-1	17-25-0
Sacked-yards lost	2-15	0-0
Punts	4-39	3-37
Fumbles-lost	1-0	0-0
Penalties-yards	3-25	3-26
Time of possession	27:33	32:27

INDIVIDUAL STATISTICS
RUSHING—Atlanta, Hanspard 17-50, Oxendine 2-6, Graziani 1-9, Christian 1-3, Chandler 1-0. St. Louis, Faulk 17-105, Holcombe 8-24, Watson 6-20, Warner 2-7, Bruce 1-11.

PASSING—Atlanta, Graziani 14-22-0-152, Chandler 5-9-1-28. St. Louis, Warner 17-25-0-275.

RECEIVING—Atlanta, Christian 5-37, Mathis 4-51, Santiago 4-29, Hanspard 2-40, Calloway 2-21, Kozlowski 2-2. St. Louis, Faulk 5-67, Bruce 3-68, Holt 2-47, Holcombe 2-42, R. Williams 2-17, Hakim 2-17, Robinson 1-3.

MISSED FIELD GOAL ATTEMPTS—None.

INTERCEPTIONS—St. Louis, Lyght 1-18.

KICKOFF RETURNS—Atlanta, Oliver 6-146. St. Louis, Horne 2-42.

PUNT RETURNS—Atlanta, Oliver 1-20. St. Louis, Hakim 1-6.

SACKS—St. Louis, Lyght 1, Carter 1.

PANTHERS 27, BENGALS 3
Sunday, September 26

Cincinnati	0	0	3	0—	3
Carolina	10	3	7	7—27	

First Quarter
Car.—Biakabutuka 62 run (Kasay kick), 3:44.
Car.—FG, Kasay 48, 10:18.
Second Quarter
Car.—FG, Kasay 21, 15:00.
Third Quarter
Cin.—FG, Pelfrey 39, 9:03.
Car.—Biakabutuka 67 run (Kasay kick), 10:13.
Fourth Quarter
Car.—Walls 4 pass from Beuerlein (Kasay kick), 3:57.
Attendance—61,269.

	Cincinnati	Carolina
First downs	20	13
Rushes-yards	28-129	18-146
Passing	243	197
Punt returns	1-2	3-14
Kickoff returns	4-50	2-51
Interception returns	0-0	1-27
Comp.-att.-int.	24-43-1	17-23-0
Sacked-yards lost	3-8	1-7
Punts	4-38	3-43
Fumbles-lost	1-0	3-2
Penalties-yards	8-50	3-20
Time of possession	37:24	22:36

INDIVIDUAL STATISTICS
RUSHING—Cincinnati, Dillon 20-113, Blake 4-9, Williams 3-4, Groce 1-3. Carolina, Biakabutuka 8-132, Lane 5-5, Beuerlein 3-0, Floyd 2-9.

PASSING—Cincinnati, Blake 24-43-1-251. Carolina, Beuerlein 17-23-0-204.

RECEIVING—Cincinnati, Scott 7-78, Pickens 5-58, Jackson 3-33, Dillon 3-24, Groce 3-20, McGee 1-24, Battaglia 1-7, Griffin 1-7. Carolina, Muhammad 8-117, Carruth 3-35, Lane 2-19, Jeffers 1-17, Floyd 1-8, Biakabutuka 1-4, Walls 1-4.

MISSED FIELD GOAL ATTEMPTS—Cincinnati, Pelfrey 47, 37, 30.

INTERCEPTIONS—Carolina, Richardson 1-27.

KICKOFF RETURNS—Cincinnati, Griffin 3-32, Williams 1-18. Carolina, Bates 2-51.

PUNT RETURNS—Cincinnati, Griffin 1-2. Carolina, Metcalf 2-11, Johnson 1-3.

SACKS—Cincinnati, Ross 1. Carolina, Barrow 1, Edwards 1, Rucker 1.

BILLS 26, EAGLES 0
Sunday, September 26

Philadelphia	0	0	0	0—	0
Buffalo	9	10	7	0—26	

First Quarter
Buf.—FG, Christie 24, 5:19.
Buf.—FG, Christie 29, 11:07.
Buf.—FG, Christie 19, 13:33.
Second Quarter
Buf.—Riemersma 15 pass from Flutie (Christie kick), 13:06.
Buf.—FG, Christie 36, 15:00.
Third Quarter
Buf.—A. Smith 4 run (Christie kick), 10:14.
Attendance—70,872.

	Philadelphia	Buffalo
First downs	11	25
Rushes-yards	12-22	40-191
Passing	147	186
Punt returns	0-0	6-66
Kickoff returns	5-108	0-0
Interception returns	1-0	0-0
Comp.-att.-int.	20-37-0	20-29-1
Sacked-yards lost	2-24	1-9
Punts	9-49	4-34
Fumbles-lost	3-2	2-0
Penalties-yards	7-50	4-20
Time of possession	22:38	37:22

INDIVIDUAL STATISTICS
RUSHING—Philadelphia, Staley 10-6, McNabb 1-10, Pederson 1-6. Buffalo, A. Smith 16-64, Linton 15-57, Flutie 5-32, Johnson 1-25, K. Williams 1-13, Moulds 1-1, Van Pelt 1-(minus 1).

PASSING—Philadelphia, Pederson 14-26-0-137, McNabb 6-11-0-34. Buffalo, Flutie 18-26-1-175, Johnson 1-2-0-11, Van Pelt 1-1-0-9.

RECEIVING—Philadelphia, C. Johnson 4-45, Staley 4-19, Bostic 4-2, Broughton 3-52, Weaver 2-22, Small 1-12, Finneran 1-11, D. Douglas 1-8. Buffalo, Linton 4-31, Reed 3-41, Moulds 3-37, Gash 3-25, Riemersma 2-22, K. Williams 2-14, Loud 1-11, P. Price 1-9, Jackson 1-5.

MISSED FIELD GOAL ATTEMPTS—Philadelphia, N. Johnson 50. Buffalo, Christie 49.

INTERCEPTIONS—Philadelphia, Dawkins 1-0.

KICKOFF RETURNS—Philadelphia, Rossum 3-56, Bieniemy 2-52.

PUNT RETURNS—Buffalo, K. Williams 5-50, P. Price 1-16.

SACKS—Philadelphia, Trotter 1. Buffalo, Northern 1, B. Smith 1.

REDSKINS 27, JETS 20
Sunday, September 26

Washington	0	10	3	14—27	
N.Y. Jets	7	0	7	6—20	

First Quarter
NYJ—Ward 35 pass from Mirer (Hall kick), 7:18.
Second Quarter
Was.—FG, Conway 26, 8:38.
Was.—Davis 1 run (Conway kick), 13:49.
Third Quarter
Was.—FG, Conway 50, 5:16.
NYJ—Martin 3 run (Hall kick), 13:14.
Fourth Quarter
NYJ—FG, Hall 37, 6:50.
Was.—Davis 4 run (Conway kick), 10:49.
Was.—Davis 7 run (Conway kick), 12:39.
NYJ—FG, Hall 34, 13:15.
Attendance—78,161.

	Washington	N.Y. Jets
First downs	21	19
Rushes-yards	29-96	31-142
Passing	237	195
Punt returns	5-47	4-17
Kickoff returns	2-37	6-148
Interception returns	1-0	0-0
Comp.-att.-int.	17-28-0	17-31-1
Sacked-yards lost	1-4	6-32
Punts	6-44	6-48
Fumbles-lost	0-0	2-1

1999 REVIEW Week 3

	Washington	N.Y. Jets
Penalties-yards	5-35	8-86
Time of possession	28:22	31:38

INDIVIDUAL STATISTICS

RUSHING—Washington, Davis 24-93, B. Johnson 3-1, Mitchell 2-2. New York, Martin 20-85, Parmalee 10-51, Mirer 1-6.

PASSING—Washington, B. Johnson 17-28-0-241. New York, Mirer 17-31-1-227.

RECEIVING—Washington, Connell 5-75, Westbrook 4-84, Alexander 4-62, Mitchell 2-15, Davis 1-8, Centers 1-(minus 3). New York, Anderson 5-71, Ward 3-73, K. Johnson 3-27, Early 2-39, Martin 2-1, Parmalee 1-14, E. Green 1-2.

MISSED FIELD GOAL ATTEMPTS—None.

INTERCEPTIONS—Washington, Green 1-0.

KICKOFF RETURNS—Washington, Mitchell 2-37. New York, Williams 3-111, Glenn 3-37.

PUNT RETURNS—Washington, Mitchell 5-47. New York, Ward 4-17.

SACKS—Washington, Lang 3, Stubblefield 1, Kalu 1, Wilkinson 1. New York, Pleasant 1.

49ERS 24, CARDINALS 10

Monday, September 27

San Francisco	14	3	0	7—24
Arizona	0	0	10	0—10

First Quarter
S.F.—Rice 13 pass from S. Young (Richey kick), 8:19.
S.F.—Garner 11 run (Richey kick), 9:13.

Second Quarter
S.F.—FG, Richey 33, 5:59.

Third Quarter
Ariz.—Bates 1 run (Jacke kick), 5:15.
Ariz.—FG, Jacke 43, 13:51.

Fourth Quarter
S.F.—Phillips 68 run (Richey kick), 13:18.
Attendance—72,100.

	San Fran.	Arizona
First downs	18	20
Rushes-yards	36-210	29-101
Passing	112	149
Punt returns	3-14	5-34
Kickoff returns	2-49	2-33
Interception returns	2-36	1-0
Comp.-att.-int.	18-29-1	16-31-2
Sacked-yards lost	1-10	5-27
Punts	7-45	6-42
Fumbles-lost	1-0	4-2
Penalties-yards	8-72	4-41
Time of possession	31:37	28:23

INDIVIDUAL STATISTICS

RUSHING—San Francisco, Garner 21-75, Phillips 9-102, Garcia 3-9, S. Young 2-19, Vardell 1-5. Arizona, Murrell 16-42, Pittman 6-35, Plummer 5-20, Makovicka 1-3, Bates 1-1.

PASSING—San Francisco, S. Young 13-23-1-92, Garcia 5-6-0-30. Arizona, Plummer 16-31-2-176.

RECEIVING—San Francisco, Owens 4-59, Rice 3-28, Phillips 3-15, Garner 3-0, Vardell 2-9, Stokes 2-4, Harris 1-7. Arizona, Sanders 7-74, Hardy 4-31, McCullough 2-43, Pittman 1-11, Murrell 1-10, McWilliams 1-7.

MISSED FIELD GOAL ATTEMPTS—None.

INTERCEPTIONS—San Francisco, McDonald 1-18, Schulters 1-18. Arizona, Drake 1-0.

KICKOFF RETURNS—San Francisco, McQuarters 2-49. Arizona, Bates 2-33.

PUNT RETURNS—San Francisco, McQuarters 3-14. Arizona, Boston 3-(minus 1), Knight 2-35.

SACKS—San Francisco, Haley 2, Buckner 1, Walker 1, B. Young 1. Arizona, Rice 1.

WEEK 4

RESULTS

Baltimore 19, ATLANTA 13 (OT)
CHICAGO 14, New Orleans 10
DALLAS 35, Arizona 7
Jacksonville 17, PITTSBURGH 3
MINNESOTA 21, Tampa Bay 14
New England 19, CLEVELAND 7
N.Y. GIANTS 16, Philadelphia 15
N.Y. Jets 21, DENVER 13
St. Louis 38, CINCINNATI 10
SAN DIEGO 21, Kansas City 14
SAN FRANCISCO 24, Tennessee 22
SEATTLE 22, Oakland 21
WASHINGTON 38, Carolina 36
Buffalo 23, MIAMI 18
Open date: Detroit, Green Bay, Indianapolis

STANDINGS

AFC EAST
	W	L	T	Pct.
New England	4	0	0	1.000
Buffalo	3	1	0	.750
Indianapolis	2	1	0	.667
Miami	2	1	0	.667
N.Y. Jets	1	3	0	.250

AFC CENTRAL
	W	L	T	Pct.
Jacksonville	3	1	0	.750
Tennessee	3	1	0	.750
Baltimore	2	2	0	.500
Pittsburgh	2	2	0	.500
Cincinnati	0	4	0	.000
Cleveland	0	4	0	.000

AFC WEST
	W	L	T	Pct.
Seattle	3	1	0	.750
Oakland	2	2	0	.500
San Diego	2	1	0	.667
Kansas City	2	2	0	.500
Denver	0	4	0	.000

NFC EAST
	W	L	T	Pct.
Dallas	3	0	0	1.000
Washington	3	1	0	.750
N.Y. Giants	2	2	0	.500
Arizona	1	3	0	.250
Philadelphia	0	4	0	.000

NFC CENTRAL
	W	L	T	Pct.
Detroit	2	1	0	.667
Green Bay	2	1	0	.667
Chicago	2	2	0	.500
Minnesota	2	2	0	.500
Tampa Bay	2	2	0	.500

NFC WEST
	W	L	T	Pct.
St. Louis	3	0	0	1.000
San Francisco	3	1	0	.750
Carolina	1	3	0	.250
New Orleans	1	2	0	.333
Atlanta	0	4	0	.000

HIGHLIGHTS

Hero of the week: Shane Matthews and Curtis Conway hooked up for two touchdowns in the final two minutes to lead the Bears to a 14-10 win over Mike Ditka's Saints. Matthews completed seven-of-eight passes for 52 yards, including a 22-yard touchdown to Conway, on the drive that pulled the Bears within three with 1:57 to play. On the game's decisive drive, Matthews hit Conway for 14 yards on third-and-6 for a first down at the Saints' 36. Then, with 19 seconds left, Matthews found Conway again for 30 yards before he was pushed out at the 6. Instead of going for the tying field goal, Matthews hit Conway on a six-yard pass for the game-winning score.

Goat of the week: After Ravens receiver Patrick Johnson beat Atlanta cornerback Ray Buchanan for a 52-yard touchdown in the third quarter, Johnson began to taunt Buchanan, dancing around the fallen Falcons defender. Buchanan, incensed, responded by getting to his feet and body-slamming Johnson, followed by an open-handed punch to Johnson's back. Buchanan was ejected. His replacement, Ronnie Bradford, then allowed the game-winning touchdown in overtime when he was beaten on a 54-yard pass from Stoney Case to second-string receiver Justin Armour.

Sub of the week: Kerry Collins replaced Kent Graham in the third quarter, and while he didn't light up the scoreboard, he did manage to lead the Giants on a game-winning drive in the fourth quarter capped by a 23-yard field goal by Brad Daluiso. The Eagles took a 15-13 lead early in the fourth quarter, but Collins kept his poise and made some good throws in driving the Giants from their 27-yard line to the Eagles' 5 before settling for the field goal.

Comeback of the week: The Seahawks overcame a 21-9 deficit by scoring 13 straight points to beat the Raiders 22-21. Darryl Williams intercepted a Rich Gannon pass at the Seattle 25 and the Seahawks drove 48 yards. Todd Peterson kicked a 45-yard field goal that proved to be the game-winner with 10:07 left. The Seahawks had a 75-yard touchdown drive, capped by a Jon Kitna 21-yard touchdown pass to Derrick Mayes, to cut Oakland's lead to 21-16. Rookie Charlie Rogers had a 68-yard punt return to set up Peterson's second field goal, a 29-yarder with 1:58 left, making it 21-19 in the third quarter.

Blowout of the week: The Cowboys exploded out of the gate in their 35-7 victory over Arizona, avenging at least a little a 20-7 playoff loss the year before. George Teague intercepted Jake Plummer's first pass and returned it 32 yards for a touchdown. Dallas led 21-7 at the half and opened the second half with a 12-play, 73-yard drive that chewed up 7:01. Everyone got into the scoring act for the Cowboys. Michael Irvin hauled in an 18-yard touchdown after besting nemesis Aeneas Williams; Rocket Ismail scored from 63 yards; Emmitt Smith scored from the 1; and end Greg Ellis scooped up a Plummer fumble and went 98 yards for a score.

Nail-biter of the week: Washington's Brett Conway kicked a 31-yard field goal with six seconds left to lift the Redskins to a 38-36 win over Carolina. After the Panthers had taken a 36-35 lead on a Steve Beuerlein-to-Wesley Walls six-yard TD, Carolina's Brian Kinchen recovered a fumbled punt return by Brian Mitchell at Washington's 19. But officials reviewed the play and ruled Mitchell's knee was down before the fumble. The Redskins then began the game-winning drive that culminated in Conway's field goal.

Hit of the week: San Francisco linebacker Lee Woodall shot through a convoy of blockers to haul down Titans running back Eddie George, running wide on a pitch right, to stop a 2-point conversion that would have tied the game with 1:48 left. The 49ers held on for a 24-22 win.

Oddity of the week: Pittsburgh quarterback Kordell Stewart surrendered back-to-back safeties in the fourth quarter in the Steelers' 17-3 loss to Jacksonville. He fumbled out of the end zone for the first safety, then was sacked by Joel Sweenge with under a minute to play.

Top rusher: Carolina running back Tshimanga Biakabutuka had another big week. One week after rushing for 132 yards on eight carries, Biakabutuka rushed for 142 yards on 12 carries against the

1999 REVIEW Week 4

– 135 –

Redskins. He had 123 yards on five carries in the first period alone.

Top passer: Drew Bledsoe completed 28-of-42 passes for 389 yards to lead New England to a 19-7 win over the Browns.

Top receiver: Terry Glenn caught a club-record 13 passes for 214 yards and a touchdown in the Patriots' win.

Notes: With four touchdowns in St. Louis' 38-10 win at Cincinnati, Az-Zahir Hakim became the fourth Rams player to score four TDs in one game. Bob Shaw was the first to do it, in 1949; Elroy Hirsch did it in 1951 and Harold Jackson joined the club in 1973. ... The Chiefs had 13 holding penalties in their 21-14 loss to the Chargers. ... Glenn broke the Patriots club record of 12 receptions set by Ben Coates on November 27, 1994, vs. Indianapolis. ... Cleveland's Tim Couch and Kevin Johnson became the first pair of rookies in the 1990s to hook up for touchdowns three weeks in a row.

Quote of the week: Bengals cornerback Artrell Hawkins, on Rams quarterback Kurt Warner, who connected on 17-of-21 passes for 310 yards in St. Louis' 38-10 win: "We were hoping he wouldn't be as accurate as he was, but he's hot. For a guy who played Arena Football, he's a full-fledged NFL quarterback."

GAME SUMMARIES

PATRIOTS 19, BROWNS 7

Sunday, October 3

New England	0	6	7	6—19
Cleveland	7	0	0	0— 7

First Quarter
Cle.—Johnson 64 pass from Couch (Dawson kick), 10:29.
Second Quarter
N.E.—FG, Vinatieri 22, 4:39.
N.E.—FG, Vinatieri 21, 14:34.
Third Quarter
N.E.—Allen 3 run (Vinatieri kick), 5:37.
Fourth Quarter
N.E.—Glenn 54 pass from Bledsoe (pass failed), 0:09.
Attendance—72,368.

	New England	Cleveland
First downs	23	12
Rushes-yards	35-90	20-70
Passing	361	180
Punt returns	6-33	4-12
Kickoff returns	1-16	5-101
Interception returns	0-0	0-0
Comp.-att.-int.	29-43-0	12-27-0
Sacked-yards lost	5-45	4-21
Punts	6-44	9-43
Fumbles-lost	3-2	1-1
Penalties-yards	7-59	4-30
Time of possession	36:51	23:09

INDIVIDUAL STATISTICS
RUSHING—New England, Allen 21-68, Warren 8-16, Bledsoe 3-(minus 1), Floyd 2-7, C. Carter 1-4. Cleveland, Kirby 17-65, Couch 3-18, G. Jones 1-2, Powell 0-(minus 14).
PASSING—New England, Bledsoe 29-43-0-393. Cleveland, Couch 12-27-0-195.
RECEIVING—New England, Glenn 13-214, Brown 4-59, Simmons 4-29, Brisby 2-27, Jefferson 1-32, Floyd 1-11, Warren 1-8, Allen 1-5, T. Carter 1-4. Cleveland, Johnson 6-131, Kirby 3-33, Chiaverini 2-23, Shepherd 1-8.
MISSED FIELD GOAL ATTEMPTS—New England, Vinatieri 42. Cleveland, Dawson 38.

INTERCEPTIONS—None.
KICKOFF RETURNS—New England, Brown 1-16. Cleveland, Dunn 3-64, Powell 2-37.
PUNT RETURNS—New England, Brown 6-33. Cleveland, Johnson 4-12.
SACKS—New England, Milloy 1, Bruschi 1, McGinest 1, Mitchell 1. Cleveland, J. Miller 2, McCormack 1, Thierry 1, Team 1.

RAMS 38, BENGALS 10

Sunday, October 3

St. Louis	7	14	14	3—38
Cincinnati	3	0	0	7—10

First Quarter
Cin.—FG, Pelfrey 36, 6:55.
St.L.—Hakim 9 pass from Warner (Wilkins kick), 9:25.
Second Quarter
St.L.—Holcombe 1 run (Wilkins kick), 3:22.
St.L.—Hakim 51 pass from Warner (Wilkins kick), 11:55.
Third Quarter
St.L.—Hakim 84 punt return (Wilkins kick), 2:01.
St.L.—Hakim 18 pass from Warner (Wilkins kick), 12:28.
Fourth Quarter
St.L.—FG, Wilkins 19, 4:18.
Cin.—Smith 1 run (Pelfrey kick), 12:34.
Attendance—45,481.

	St. Louis	Cincinnati
First downs	18	18
Rushes-yards	28-73	26-92
Passing	326	165
Punt returns	5-147	2-21
Kickoff returns	2-40	4-126
Interception returns	1-10	0-0
Comp.-att.-int.	18-22-0	19-41-1
Sacked-yards lost	2-11	3-26
Punts	4-54	8-40
Fumbles-lost	3-2	0-0
Penalties-yards	5-34	5-25
Time of possession	29:07	30:53

INDIVIDUAL STATISTICS
RUSHING—St. Louis, Faulk 11-23, Holcombe 7-20, Watson 6-13, Hodgins 2-3, Holt 1-14, Warner 1-0. Cincinnati, Dillon 15-39, Basnight 6-27, Smith 3-12, Blake 2-14.
PASSING—St. Louis, Warner 17-21-0-310, Justin 1-1-0-27. Cincinnati, Blake 12-23-0-114, Smith 7-18-1-77.
RECEIVING—St. Louis, Bruce 6-152, Holt 4-58, Hakim 3-78, Faulk 3-17, Proehl 1-27, Holcombe 1-5. Cincinnati, Scott 6-61, Griffin 3-34, Battaglia 3-30, Pickens 2-30, McGee 1-15, Jackson 1-13, Basnight 1-6, Groce 1-2, Dillon 1-0.
MISSED FIELD GOAL ATTEMPTS—Cincinnati, Pelfrey 33.
INTERCEPTIONS—St. Louis, Lyle 1-10.
KICKOFF RETURNS—St. Louis, Horne 2-40. Cincinnati, Griffin 3-93, Jackson 1-33.
PUNT RETURNS—St. Louis, Hakim 5-147. Cincinnati, Griffin 2-21.
SACKS—St. Louis, Fletcher 1, Jenkins 1, Wistrom 1. Cincinnati, Copeland 1, Wilson 1.

SEAHAWKS 22, RAIDERS 21

Sunday, October 3

Oakland	7	7	7	0—21
Seattle	3	6	10	3—22

First Quarter
Oak.—Wheatley 7 run (Husted kick), 3:55.
Sea.—FG, Peterson 28, 11:24.
Second Quarter
Oak.—Brown 6 pass from Gannon (Husted kick), 3:52.
Sea.—Mayes 29 pass from Kitna (pass failed), 14:01.
Third Quarter
Oak.—Dudley 3 pass from Gannon (Husted kick), 3:36.
Sea.—R. Brown 21 pass from Kitna (Peterson kick), 8:14.
Sea.—FG, Peterson 29, 13:02.
Fourth Quarter
Sea.—FG, Peterson 45, 4:53.
Attendance—66,400.

	Oakland	Seattle
First downs	21	15
Rushes-yards	32-166	26-75
Passing	217	201
Punt returns	2-4	2-75
Kickoff returns	6-107	4-86
Interception returns	1-24	1-7
Comp.-att.-int.	19-34-1	15-30-1
Sacked-yards lost	2-3	2-12
Punts	5-35	4-47
Fumbles-lost	0-0	2-0
Penalties-yards	9-88	5-40
Time of possession	32:20	27:40

INDIVIDUAL STATISTICS

RUSHING—Oakland, Wheatley 20-100, Kaufman 7-42, Crockett 3-11, Gannon 2-13. Seattle, Watters 24-71, R. Brown 1-4, Kitna 1-0.

PASSING—Oakland, Gannon 19-34-1-220. Seattle, Kitna 15-30-1-213.

RECEIVING—Oakland, Kaufman 5-41, Brown 4-56, Dudley 4-40, Jett 2-17, Mickens 1-30, Ritchie 1-19, Jordan 1-9, Wheatley 1-8. Seattle, Watters 5-55, Pritchard 3-59, Mayes 2-36, Fauria 2-17, R. Brown 1-21, Dawkins 1-17, Mili 1-8.

MISSED FIELD GOAL ATTEMPTS—Oakland, Husted 61.

INTERCEPTIONS—Oakland, Turner 1-24. Seattle, D. Williams 1-7.

KICKOFF RETURNS—Oakland, Kaufman 3-41, Jordan 2-50, Branch 1-16. Seattle, Green 3-66, Joseph 1-20.

PUNT RETURNS—Oakland, Gordon 2-4. Seattle, Rogers 2-75.

SACKS—Oakland, Harris 1, Jackson 1. Seattle, Sinclair 1, Parker 1.

49ERS 24, TITANS 22

Sunday, October 3

Tennessee	3	7	3	9 — 22
San Francisco	0	14	0	10 — 24

First Quarter
Ten.—FG, Del Greco 21, 11:29.

Second Quarter
Ten.—E. George 54 pass from O'Donnell (Del Greco kick), 5:28.
S.F.—Garcia 1 run (Richey kick), 10:56.
S.F.—Garner 21 pass from Garcia (Richey kick), 13:04.

Third Quarter
Ten.—FG, Del Greco 22, 12:17.

Fourth Quarter
S.F.—FG, Richey 39, 4:10.
S.F.—Owens 22 pass from Garcia (Richey kick), 8:05.
Ten.—FG, Del Greco 28, 11:22.
Ten.—Thigpen 32 pass from O'Donnell (run failed), 13:12.
Attendance—67,447.

	Tennessee	San Francisco
First downs	17	17
Rushes-yards	21-55	26-86
Passing	337	243
Punt returns	2-8	2-37
Kickoff returns	4-81	5-91
Interception returns	0-0	1-8
Comp.-att.-int.	20-40-1	21-33-0
Sacked-yards lost	3-18	1-0
Punts	5-41	6-33
Fumbles-lost	0-0	0-0
Penalties-yards	4-30	8-67
Time of possession	27:33	32:27

INDIVIDUAL STATISTICS

RUSHING—Tennessee, E. George 15-26, Thomas 5-28, O'Donnell 1-1. San Francisco, Garner 12-69, Garcia 8-8, Phillips 4-5, Beasley 2-4.

PASSING—Tennessee, O'Donnell 20-40-1-355. San Francisco, Garcia 21-33-0-243.

RECEIVING—Tennessee, Thigpen 6-143, Wycheck 5-50, E. George 3-81, Roan 3-24, Dyson 2-25, Sanders 1-32. San Francisco, Rice 6-56, Garner 4-47, Owens 3-33, Clark 3-29, Cline 2-39, Beasley 2-27, Stokes 1-12.

MISSED FIELD GOAL ATTEMPTS—None.

INTERCEPTIONS—San Francisco, Tubbs 1-8.

KICKOFF RETURNS—Tennessee, Mason 4-81. San Francisco, Phillips 2-42, Prioleau 2-41, McQuarters 1-8.

PUNT RETURNS—Tennessee, Mason 2-8. San Francisco, McQuarters 2-37.

SACKS—Tennessee, Ford 1. San Francisco, Bryant 2, Woodall 1.

BEARS 14, SAINTS 10

Sunday, October 3

New Orleans	0	7	3	0 — 10
Chicago	0	0	0	14 — 14

Second Quarter
N.O.—Hobert 2 run (Brien kick), 10:28.

Third Quarter
N.O.—FG, Brien 30, 11:37.

Fourth Quarter
Chi.—Conway 22 pass from Matthews (Jaeger kick), 13:12.
Chi.—Conway 6 pass from Matthews (Jaeger kick), 14:53.
Attendance—66,944.

	New Orleans	Chicago
First downs	17	20
Rushes-yards	35-138	28-116
Passing	132	212
Punt returns	4-34	3-18
Kickoff returns	3-27	2-36
Interception returns	2-5	0-0
Comp.-att.-int.	15-28-0	25-43-2
Sacked-yards lost	4-46	3-12
Punts	7-35	5-44
Fumbles-lost	3-1	4-3
Penalties-yards	6-41	5-35
Time of possession	31:10	28:50

INDIVIDUAL STATISTICS

RUSHING—New Orleans, R. Williams 21-84, L. Smith 10-20, Tolliver 2-32, Hobert 1-2, Craver 1-0. Chicago, Enis 23-87, Matthews 3-23, Allen 1-4, McNown 1-2.

PASSING—New Orleans, Tolliver 7-15-0-102, Hobert 8-13-0-76. Chicago, Matthews 25-39-2-224, McNown 0-4-0-0.

RECEIVING—New Orleans, Kennison 4-55, Craver 3-12, Poole 2-45, Hastings 2-15, L. Smith 1-16, Cleeland 1-13, Slutzker 1-12, R. Williams 1-10. Chicago, Conway 8-103, Wetnight 6-47, Engram 4-33, Bennett 3-27, M. Robinson 1-5, Brooks 1-4, Mayes 1-3, Enis 1-2.

MISSED FIELD GOAL ATTEMPTS—Chicago, Jaeger 32.

INTERCEPTIONS—New Orleans, Ambrose 2-5.

KICKOFF RETURNS—New Orleans, Philyaw 1-13, Davis 1-11, Craver 1-3. Chicago, Milburn 2-36.

PUNT RETURNS—New Orleans, Kennison 4-34. Chicago, Milburn 3-18.

SACKS—New Orleans, Fields 1, Glover 1, Robbins 1. Chicago, Davis 1, Holdman 1, Burton 1, Cousin 0.5, Simmons 0.5.

CHARGERS 21, CHIEFS 14

Sunday, October 3

Kansas City	14	0	0	0 — 14
San Diego	0	14	7	0 — 21

First Quarter
K.C.—Horn 31 pass from Grbac (Stoyanovich kick), 5:18.
K.C.—Gonzalez 12 pass from Grbac (Stoyanovich kick), 13:20.

Second Quarter
S.D.—Means 4 run (Carney kick), 7:40.
S.D.—Bynum 18 pass from Kramer (Carney kick), 13:19.

Third Quarter
S.D.—Penn 11 pass from Kramer (Carney kick), 4:03.
Attendance—58,099.

	Kansas City	San Diego
First downs	19	8
Rushes-yards	38-121	17-40
Passing	193	92
Punt returns	3-67	3-18
Kickoff returns	3-66	3-42
Interception returns	2-0	4-24
Comp.-att.-int.	19-40-4	14-29-2
Sacked-yards lost	1-7	2-18
Punts	5-45	9-40
Fumbles-lost	2-0	1-0
Penalties-yards	13-113	6-54
Time of possession	36:59	23:01

INDIVIDUAL STATISTICS

RUSHING—Kansas City, Shehee 22-86, Bennett 10-31, Richardson 3-3, Grbac 1-1, Alexander 1-0, Pope 1-0. San Diego, Means 14-26, Fletcher 1-7, Ricks 1-7, Bynum 1-0.

PASSING—Kansas City, Grbac 19-40-4-200. San Diego, Kramer 8-20-1-72, Harbaugh 6-9-1-38.
RECEIVING—Kansas City, Gonzalez 7-68, Lockett 4-33, Horn 2-41, Rison 2-25, Richardson 2-6, Alexander 1-14, Shehee 1-13. San Diego, F. Jones 4-48, Fletcher 3-7, McCrary 2-15, Means 2-5, Bynum 1-18, Penn 1-11, Pupunu 1-6.
MISSED FIELD GOAL ATTEMPTS—Kansas City, Stoyanovich 47.
INTERCEPTIONS—Kansas City, Patton 1-0, Edwards 1-0. San Diego, Lewis 2-0, Dumas 1-24, Harrison 1-0.
KICKOFF RETURNS—Kansas City, Vanover 3-66. San Diego, Fletcher 3-42.
PUNT RETURNS—Kansas City, Vanover 3-67. San Diego, Penn 3-18.
SACKS—Kansas City, Patton 2. San Diego, Johnson 1.

REDSKINS 38, PANTHERS 36

Sunday, October 3

Carolina	21	3	3	9	36
Washington	0	28	7	3	38

First Quarter
Car.—Biakabutuka 60 run (Kasay kick), 3:22.
Car.—Biakabutuka 1 run (Kasay kick), 5:08.
Car.—Biakabutuka 45 run (Kasay kick), 8:59.

Second Quarter
Was.—Davis 1 run (Conway kick), 1:34.
Car.—FG, Kasay 43, 4:48.
Was.—Westbrook 17 pass from B. Johnson (Conway kick), 6:30.
Was.—Westbrook 11 pass from B. Johnson (Conway kick), 10:27.
Was.—Connell 62 pass from B. Johnson (Conway kick), 12:27.

Third Quarter
Was.—Connell 32 pass from B. Johnson (Conway kick), 4:39.
Car.—FG, Kasay 43, 14:00.

Fourth Quarter
Car.—FG, Kasay 42, 3:23.
Car.—Walls 6 pass from Beuerlein (pass failed), 7:03.
Was.—FG, Conway 31, 14:54.
Attendance—76,831.

	Carolina	Washington
First downs	23	22
Rushes-yards	19-155	31-110
Passing	328	308
Punt returns	2-22	4-19
Kickoff returns	5-70	7-131
Interception returns	0-0	1-12
Comp.-att.-int.	23-47-1	20-33-0
Sacked-yards lost	2-6	3-29
Punts	5-41	6-43
Fumbles-lost	0-0	1-1
Penalties-yards	6-80	8-60
Time of possession	28:26	31:34

INDIVIDUAL STATISTICS
RUSHING—Carolina, Biakabutuka 12-142, Lane 4-9, Floyd 2-0, Carruth 1-4. Washington, Davis 21-72, Mitchell 5-15, B. Johnson 4-11, Westbrook 1-12.
PASSING—Carolina, Beuerlein 23-47-1-334. Washington, B. Johnson 20-33-0-337.
RECEIVING—Carolina, Muhammad 8-151, Jeffers 5-57, Carruth 3-62, Walls 2-19, Johnson 2-9, Metcalf 1-19, Biakabutuka 1-12, Lane 1-5. Washington, Westbrook 8-140, Connell 5-134, Centers 4-35, Fryar 2-23, Alexander 1-5.
MISSED FIELD GOAL ATTEMPTS—Carolina, Kasay 52.
INTERCEPTIONS—Washington, Pounds 1-12.
KICKOFF RETURNS—Carolina, Bates 4-53, Lane 1-17. Washington, Mitchell 7-131.
PUNT RETURNS—Carolina, Metcalf 2-22. Washington, Mitchell 4-19.
SACKS—Carolina, Barrow 1, Edwards 1, Rucker 1. Washington, Wilkinson 1, Kalu 1.

JETS 21, BRONCOS 13

Sunday, October 3

N.Y. Jets	7	0	0	14	21
Denver	10	3	0	0	13

First Quarter
Den.—FG, Elam 26, 3:36.
NYJ—K. Johnson 26 pass from Mirer (Hall kick), 5:10.
Den.—Davis 1 run (Elam kick), 6:48.

Second Quarter
Den.—FG, Elam 51, 14:42.

Fourth Quarter
NYJ—Martin 2 run (Hall kick), 4:08.
NYJ—Ward 16 pass from Mirer (Hall kick), 9:03.
Attendance—74,181.

	N.Y. Jets	Denver
First downs	23	17
Rushes-yards	35-110	29-108
Passing	224	218
Punt returns	2-23	3-6
Kickoff returns	4-90	2-98
Interception returns	5-55	2-11
Comp.-att.-int.	17-28-2	18-36-5
Sacked-yards lost	4-18	1-16
Punts	5-41	3-50
Fumbles-lost	0-0	2-1
Penalties-yards	4-43	7-82
Time of possession	33:18	26:42

INDIVIDUAL STATISTICS
RUSHING—New York, Martin 31-95, Mirer 2-(minus 2), Parmalee 1-18, K. Johnson 1-(minus 1). Denver, Loville 16-57, Davis 8-18, Griese 4-16, Brister 1-17.
PASSING—New York, Mirer 17-28-2-242. Denver, Griese 15-31-3-212, Brister 3-5-2-22.
RECEIVING—New York, K. Johnson 8-98, Ward 4-84, Martin 3-28, Parmalee 1-23, Anderson 1-9. Denver, Sharpe 5-86, R. Smith 3-90, McCaffrey 3-17, Loville 3-15, Griffith 3-13, Chamberlain 1-13.
MISSED FIELD GOAL ATTEMPTS—New York, Hall 43.
INTERCEPTIONS—New York, V. Green 2-36, Coleman 2-7, Glenn 1-12. Denver, Crockett 1-10, Romanowski 1-1.
KICKOFF RETURNS—New York, Glenn 3-69, Williams 1-21. Denver, Watson 2-98.
PUNT RETURNS—New York, Ward 2-23. Denver, Watson 3-6.
SACKS—New York, Mickens 1. Denver, Pryce 1, Cadrez 1, Crockett 1, E. Brown 0.5, Tanuvasa 0.5.

COWBOYS 35, CARDINALS 7

Sunday, October 3

Arizona	0	7	0	0	7
Dallas	14	7	7	7	35

First Quarter
Dal.—Teague 32 interception return (Cunningham kick), 1:32.
Dal.—Irvin 18 pass from Aikman (Cunningham kick), 11:41.

Second Quarter
Dal.—Ismail 63 pass from Aikman (Cunningham kick), 2:59.
Ariz.—Makovicka 2 pass from Plummer (Jacke kick), 14:49.

Third Quarter
Dal.—E. Smith 1 run (Cunningham kick), 7:01.

Fourth Quarter
Dal.—Ellis 98 fumble return (Cunningham kick), 4:47.
Attendance—64,169.

	Arizona	Dallas
First downs	12	17
Rushes-yards	21-71	39-117
Passing	137	192
Punt returns	4-59	6-32
Kickoff returns	4-79	2-34
Interception returns	0-0	4-61
Comp.-att.-int.	20-39-4	15-21-0
Sacked-yards lost	1-4	0-0
Punts	8-45	6-44
Fumbles-lost	1-1	2-1
Penalties-yards	6-50	10-84
Time of possession	26:13	33:47

INDIVIDUAL STATISTICS
RUSHING—Arizona, Murrell 14-44, Pittman 4-9, Plummer 3-18. Dallas, E. Smith 22-77, Warren 11-27, Ismail 2-14, Aikman 2-1, Garrett 2-(minus 2).
PASSING—Arizona, Plummer 16-33-3-111, Da. Brown 4-6-1-30. Dallas, Aikman 15-21-0-192.
RECEIVING—Arizona, Hardy 5-17, Pittman 4-42, Murrell 3-11, Sanders 2-42, Boston 2-11, Cody 1-11, McWilliams 1-3, Makovicka 1-2, McCullough 1-2. Dallas, Ismail 4-101, Irvin 2-24, Mills 2-23, Thomas 2-19, Warren 2-10, Ogden 1-10, Lester 1-3, Lucky 1-2.
MISSED FIELD GOAL ATTEMPTS—Dallas, Cunningham 24.

– 138 –

INTERCEPTIONS—Dallas, Teague 1-32, Hambrick 1-25, Nguyen 1-6, Hawthorne 1-(minus 2).
KICKOFF RETURNS—Arizona, Bates 3-64, Cody 1-15. Dallas, Ogden 2-34.
PUNT RETURNS—Arizona, Cody 4-59. Dallas, Sanders 6-32.
SACKS—Dallas, Ellis 1.

VIKINGS 21, BUCCANEERS 14

Sunday, October 3

Tampa Bay	0	7	0	7—14
Minnesota	21	0	0	0—21

First Quarter
Min.—Moss 61 pass from Cunningham (Anderson kick), 4:13.
Min.—Moss 27 pass from Cunningham (Anderson kick), 8:10.
Min.—Glover 12 pass from Cunningham (Anderson kick), 14:38.

Second Quarter
T.B.—Moore 26 pass from Dilfer (Gramatica kick), 5:38.

Fourth Quarter
T.B.—Anthony 26 pass from Dilfer (Gramatica kick), 7:26.
Attendance—64,106.

	Tampa Bay	Minnesota
First downs	22	20
Rushes-yards	24-84	23-68
Passing	283	296
Punt returns	4-36	2-9
Kickoff returns	4-95	1-17
Interception returns	1-0	1-0
Comp.-att.-int.	25-39-1	26-35-1
Sacked-yards lost	3-18	0-0
Punts	5-41	5-51
Fumbles-lost	1-1	0-0
Penalties-yards	10-74	5-50
Time of possession	30:36	29:24

INDIVIDUAL STATISTICS
RUSHING—Tampa Bay, Dunn 16-49, Alstott 6-32, Dilfer 2-3. Minnesota, Smith 19-59, M. Williams 2-1, Palmer 1-5, Cunningham 1-3.
PASSING—Tampa Bay, Dilfer 25-39-1-301. Minnesota, Cunningham 26-34-1-296, George 0-1-0-0.
RECEIVING—Tampa Bay, Anthony 7-94, Moore 4-58, Dunn 4-52, Green 4-49, Williams 3-26, Alstott 3-22. Minnesota, Carter 6-41, Smith 6-21, Moss 4-120, Glover 2-37, Reed 2-37, Palmer 2-16, Kleinsasser 1-9, M. Williams 1-12, Tate 1-3.
MISSED FIELD GOAL ATTEMPTS—Minnesota, Anderson 37.
INTERCEPTIONS—Tampa Bay, Abraham 1-0. Minnesota, Miller 1-0.
KICKOFF RETURNS—Tampa Bay, Murphy 2-58, Green 2-37. Minnesota, M. Williams 1-17.
PUNT RETURNS—Tampa Bay, Williams 2-19, Green 2-17. Minnesota, Palmer 2-9.
SACKS—Minnesota, Randle 2, T. Williams 1.

RAVENS 19, FALCONS 13

Sunday, October 3

Baltimore	0	3	7	3	6—19
Atlanta	0	6	7	0	0—13

Second Quarter
Bal.—FG, Stover 38, 8:00.
Atl.—FG, Andersen 41, 13:42.
Atl.—FG, Andersen 35, 15:00.

Third Quarter
Atl.—German 30 pass from Kanell (Andersen kick), 11:28.
Bal.—Johnson 52 pass from Case (Stover kick), 13:27.

Fourth Quarter
Bal.—FG, Stover 26, 4:46.

Overtime
Bal.—Armour 54 pass from Case, 2:29.
Attendance—50,712.

	Baltimore	Atlanta
First downs	17	20
Rushes-yards	34-144	26-52
Passing	163	239
Punt returns	1-6	2-12
Kickoff returns	3-69	4-60
Interception returns	0-0	0-0
Comp.-att.-int.	13-27-0	24-45-0
Sacked-yards lost	5-29	3-18
Punts	7-37	6-43
Fumbles-lost	1-0	3-3
Penalties-yards	5-38	6-40
Time of possession	30:13	32:16

INDIVIDUAL STATISTICS
RUSHING—Baltimore, Rhett 27-136, Case 5-3, Evans 1-4, J. Lewis 1-1. Atlanta, Hanspard 14-20, Oxendine 11-27, Christian 1-5.
PASSING—Baltimore, Case 13-27-0-192. Atlanta, Kanell 15-32-0-184, Graziani 9-13-0-73.
RECEIVING—Baltimore, Ismail 6-65, J. Lewis 2-6, Armour 1-54, Johnson 1-52, Davis 1-8, Pierce 1-4, DeLong 1-3. Atlanta, Mathis 7-66, Calloway 4-53, Christian 4-33, German 3-48, Oxendine 2-24, Hanspard 2-14, Harris 1-10, Santiago 1-9.
MISSED FIELD GOAL ATTEMPTS—Baltimore, Stover 38. Atlanta, Andersen 33.
INTERCEPTIONS—None.
KICKOFF RETURNS—Baltimore, Harris 3-69. Atlanta, Oliver 4-60.
PUNT RETURNS—Baltimore, J. Lewis 1-6. Atlanta, Oliver 2-12.
SACKS—Baltimore, Boulware 2, Smith 1. Atlanta, Brooking 2, Tuggle 1, Dronett 1, Kerney 1.

GIANTS 16, EAGLES 15

Sunday, October 3

Philadelphia	9	0	3	3—15
N.Y. Giants	7	3	3	3—16

First Quarter
NYG—Hilliard 9 pass from Graham (Daluiso kick), 5:53.
Phi.—Safety, P. Sparks tackled by C. Johnson in end zone, 11:51.
Phi.—Taylor 18 interception return (N. Johnson kick), 15:00.

Second Quarter
NYG—FG, Daluiso 35, 14:54.

Third Quarter
NYG—FG, Daluiso 25, 7:11.
Phi.—FG, N. Johnson 26, 11:49.

Fourth Quarter
Phi.—FG, N. Johnson 32, 2:23.
NYG—FG, Daluiso 23, 7:17.
Attendance—73,274.

	Philadelphia	N.Y. Giants
First downs	10	24
Rushes-yards	26-84	38-128
Passing	90	233
Punt returns	1-8	5-58
Kickoff returns	3-71	3-57
Interception returns	3-19	2-11
Comp.-att.-int.	9-22-2	21-41-3
Sacked-yards lost	5-23	2-24
Punts	7-50	3-35
Fumbles-lost	1-1	6-2
Penalties-yards	6-35	5-51
Time of possession	24:55	35:05

INDIVIDUAL STATISTICS
RUSHING—Philadelphia, Staley 21-62, Pederson 2-3, McNabb 1-13, Bostic 1-5, C. Martin 1-1. New York, Brown 27-87, Way 5-19, Graham 3-23, Collins 2-(minus 2), Johnson 1-1.
PASSING—Philadelphia, Pederson 6-15-2-75, McNabb 3-7-0-38. New York, Graham 15-29-3-171, Collins 6-12-0-86.
RECEIVING—Philadelphia, C. Johnson 3-38, Small 2-15, Broughton 1-32, Jells 1-13, Weaver 1-9, Bostic 1-6. New York, Toomer 8-123, Hilliard 4-64, Mitchell 2-20, Way 2-14, Barber 2-6, Jurevicius 1-26, Cross 1-3, Brown 1-1.
MISSED FIELD GOAL ATTEMPTS—None.
INTERCEPTIONS—Philadelphia, Taylor 1-18, Vincent 1-1, Trotter 1-0. New York, Ellsworth 1-15, Sehorn 1-(minus 4).
KICKOFF RETURNS—Philadelphia, Rossum 3-71. New York, Patten 3-57.
PUNT RETURNS—Philadelphia, Rossum 1-8. New York, Barber 5-58.
SACKS—Philadelphia, B. Johnson 1, Reese 1. New York, Strahan 3, Armstead 2.

JAGUARS 17, STEELERS 3

Sunday, October 3

Jacksonville	0	7	3	7—17
Pittsburgh	0	3	0	0— 3

Second Quarter
Jac.—McCardell 7 pass from Brunell (Hollis kick), 0:45.
Pit.—FG, K. Brown 48, 15:00.

Third Quarter
Jac.—FG, Hollis 27, 8:42.

Fourth Quarter
Jac.—FG, Hollis 41, 9:20.
Jac.—Safety, K. Stewart hit, fumbled out of end zone, 10:13.
Jac.—Safety, K. Stewart sacked by J. Smeenge in end zone, 14:06.
Attendance—57,308.

	Jacksonville	Pittsburgh
First downs	13	14
Rushes-yards	35-124	31-117
Passing	80	99
Punt returns	4-47	2-36
Kickoff returns	2-66	2-72
Interception returns	1-0	1-1
Comp.-att.-int.	10-25-1	15-32-1
Sacked-yards lost	1-5	4-27
Punts	8-42	6-44
Fumbles-lost	0-0	4-1
Penalties-yards	5-32	7-65
Time of possession	28:47	31:13

INDIVIDUAL STATISTICS

RUSHING—Jacksonville, J. Stewart 21-73, Taylor 8-28, Brunell 5-21, Banks 1-2. Pittsburgh, Bettis 20-58, Stewart 6-41, Huntley 5-18.

PASSING—Jacksonville, Brunell 10-25-1-85. Pittsburgh, Stewart 15-32-1-126.

RECEIVING—Jacksonville, McCardell 3-24, Brady 2-20, J. Smith 2-18, Shelton 1-13, J. Stewart 1-7, Banks 1-3. Pittsburgh, Bettis 4-27, Edwards 2-22, Ward 2-19, Blackwell 2-18, Hawkins 1-19, Lyons 1-13, Bruener 1-5, Witman 1-4, Huntley 1-(minus 1).

MISSED FIELD GOAL ATTEMPTS—None.

INTERCEPTIONS—Jacksonville, Thomas 1-0. Pittsburgh, Davis 1-1.

KICKOFF RETURNS—Jacksonville, Barlow 1-56, McCardell 1-10. Pittsburgh, Edwards 2-72.

PUNT RETURNS—Jacksonville, Barlow 4-47. Pittsburgh, Edwards 2-36.

SACKS—Jacksonville, Brackens 2.5, Smeenge 1, Beasley 0.5. Pittsburgh, Gildon 1.

BILLS 23, DOLPHINS 18

Monday, October 4

Buffalo	3	10	0	10—23
Miami	6	3	0	9—18

First Quarter
Buf.—FG, Christie 26, 4:14.
Mia.—FG, Mare 30, 8:14.
Mia.—FG, Mare 44, 13:03.

Second Quarter
Buf.—FG, Christie 52, 2:02.
Buf.—Northern 59 fumble return (Christie kick), 10:29.
Mia.—FG, Mare 26, 15:00.

Fourth Quarter
Mia.—FG, Mare 26, 1:37.
Buf.—Moulds 6 pass from Flutie (Christie kick), 4:58.
Buf.—FG, Christie 31, 8:04.
Mia.—McDuffie 9 pass from Marino (run failed), 9:47.
Attendance—74,073.

	Buffalo	Miami
First downs	11	18
Rushes-yards	27-73	24-59
Passing	177	233
Punt returns	1-14	2-8
Kickoff returns	5-86	6-200
Interception returns	2-35	0-0
Comp.-att.-int.	12-25-0	22-44-2
Sacked-yards lost	1-9	2-18
Punts	7-38	5-39
Fumbles-lost	1-1	3-1
Penalties-yards	8-74	7-50
Time of possession	28:00	32:00

INDIVIDUAL STATISTICS

RUSHING—Buffalo, A. Smith 12-36, Flutie 9-29, Linton 6-8. Miami, Collins 16-47, Johnson 4-11, Abdul-Jabbar 3-2, Pritchett 1-(minus 1).

PASSING—Buffalo, Flutie 12-25-0-186. Miami, Marino 22-44-2-251.

RECEIVING—Buffalo, Riemersma 4-85, Moulds 4-60, K. Williams 2-26, Linton 2-15. Miami, McDuffie 7-64, Konrad 3-48, Gadsden 3-46, Drayton 3-29, Martin 2-38, Collins 2-5, Pritchett 1-18, Johnson 1-3.

MISSED FIELD GOAL ATTEMPTS—None.

INTERCEPTIONS—Buffalo, Holecek 1-35, Schulz 1-0.

KICKOFF RETURNS—Buffalo, K. Williams 5-86. Miami, Marion 4-157, Wilson 2-43.

PUNT RETURNS—Buffalo, K. Williams 1-14. Miami, Buckley 2-8.

SACKS—Buffalo, Holecek 1, Hansen 1. Miami, Jackson 1.

1999 REVIEW Week 4

WEEK 5

RESULTS

ARIZONA 14, N.Y. Giants 3
Atlanta 20, NEW ORLEANS 17
BUFFALO 24, Pittsburgh 21
Chicago 24, MINNESOTA 22
Cincinnati 18, CLEVELAND 17
Denver 16, OAKLAND 13
GREEN BAY 26, Tampa Bay 23
KANSAS CITY 16, New England 14
Miami 34, INDIANAPOLIS 31
PHILADELPHIA 13, Dallas 10
ST. LOUIS 42, San Francisco 20
San Diego 20, DETROIT 10
TENNESSEE 14, Baltimore 11
Jacksonville 16, N.Y. JETS 6
    Open date: Carolina, Seattle, Washington

STANDINGS

AFC EAST
	W	L	T	Pct.
Buffalo	4	1	0	.800
New England	4	1	0	.800
Miami	3	1	0	.750
Indianapolis	2	2	0	.500
N.Y. Jets	1	4	0	.200

AFC CENTRAL
	W	L	T	Pct.
Jacksonville	4	1	0	.800
Tennessee	4	1	0	.800
Baltimore	2	3	0	.400
Pittsburgh	2	3	0	.400
Cincinnati	1	4	0	.200
Cleveland	0	5	0	.000

AFC WEST
	W	L	T	Pct.
San Diego	3	1	0	.750
Seattle	3	1	0	.750
Kansas City	3	2	0	.600
Oakland	2	3	0	.400
Denver	1	4	0	.200

NFC EAST
	W	L	T	Pct.
Dallas	3	1	0	.750
Washington	3	1	0	.750
Arizona	2	3	0	.400
N.Y. Giants	2	3	0	.400
Philadelphia	1	4	0	.200

NFC CENTRAL
	W	L	T	Pct.
Green Bay	3	1	0	.750
Chicago	3	2	0	.600
Detroit	2	2	0	.500
Minnesota	2	3	0	.400
Tampa Bay	2	3	0	.400

NFC WEST
	W	L	T	Pct.
St. Louis	4	0	0	1.000
San Francisco	3	2	0	.600
Carolina	1	3	0	.250
New Orleans	1	3	0	.250
Atlanta	1	4	0	.200

HIGHLIGHTS

Hero of the week: Cincinnati rookie quarterback Akili Smith threw a two-yard touchdown pass to Carl Pickens with five seconds left to give the Bengals an 18-17 win over cross-state rival Cleveland. On the decisive drive, Smith, making his first NFL start, found Darnay Scott for a nine-yard gain on fourth-and-four from the Browns' 29. After a pass interference call gave the Bengals first-and-goal at the 2, Smith connected with Pickens on third-and-goal for the go-ahead score.

Goat of the week: Patriots kicker Adam Vinatieri hit the right upright on a 32-yard field-goal attempt with four seconds left, costing previously unbeaten New England a chance for a 5-0 start. The Chiefs held on for a 16-14 win.

Sub of the week: Erik Kramer didn't post great numbers (20-of-34 for 208 yards and one interception) filling in for the injured Jim Harbaugh, but he was good enough to lead the Chargers to a 20-10 win over Detroit. Kramer, a former Lion, completed four of five passes for 68 yards on an 11-play, 80-yard drive in the second quarter that resulted in the game-tying touchdown.

Comeback of the week: Trailing 17-9 in the third quarter, the Miami Dolphins rallied for 25 points in the fourth quarter to beat the Colts, 34-31. The Dolphins trailed, 31-27, with 1:22 to play when Dan Marino appeared to fumble. Referee Gerry Austin, however, reversed the on-field ruling after checking instant replay, giving Marino another chance. On fourth-and-10, the future Hall of Fame quarterback connected with Oronde Gadsden on a 48-yard completion to the Colts' 2-yard line. Two plays later, Gadsden pulled down a floater from Marino in the end zone with 27 seconds left.

Blowout of the week: While most of the Week 5 games were close, the San Francisco-St. Louis game was decidedly not. Before a sold-out crowd at the Trans World Dome, the Rams smoked the 49ers, 42-20. Kurt Warner had five touchdown passes, including four to Isaac Bruce, and finished 20-for-23 for 323 yards. The Rams took a 21-3 lead in the first quarter on three Warner-to-Bruce TD passes, including a 45-yarder. San Francisco closed to 28-20 in the third quarter, but Tony Horne responded by returning a kickoff 97 yards for a touchdown. Bruce finished the game with five receptions for 134 yards.

Nail-biter of the week: Mike Alstott capped a four-play, 65-yard drive to give Tampa Bay a 23-19 lead over the Packers with 1:45 left, but the Bucs didn't hold the lead for long. Actually, only 40 seconds. Brett Favre marched Green Bay down the field on the ensuing drive, completing a 42-yard fade to Bill Schroeder to move the Packers to the Bucs' 31. Four plays later, with 1:05 left on the clock, Favre found Antonio Freeman for a 21-yard go-ahead touchdown. Trent Dilfer had 55 seconds to mount a Tampa Bay comeback, but he was intercepted by Darren Sharper with 13 seconds left to seal the Packers' victory.

Hit of the week: With less than four minutes left and clinging to a 10-6 lead, the Cowboys tried to run the clock against Philadelphia. Dallas needed two yards for a first down to keep possession, but Emmitt Smith was stuffed on consecutive running plays. The Eagles ended up scoring the game-winning touchdown on their next drive.

Oddity of the week: Kicker Phil Dawson scored Cleveland's first rushing touchdown of the season. With the Browns trailing 6-0 early in the second quarter, Dawson lined up for a 21-yard field goal attempt against Cincinnati. Holder Chris Gardocki, however, took the snap and flipped it to Dawson, who ran four yards for the score.

Top rusher: Corey Dillon exploded for 168 yards on 28 carries in the Bengals' 18-17 win.

Top passer: Favre completed 22-of-40 passes for 390 yards and two touchdowns against the Bucs.

Top receiver: Bill Schroeder caught seven of Favre's passes for 158 yards.

Notes: Warner became the first quarterback in NFL history to throw at least three touchdown passes in each of his first four games of a season. ... The Rams ended a 17-game losing streak against the 49ers that stretched back to 1990. ... Tennessee set an NFL record for penalty yardage in a 14-11 win over Baltimore. The Titans were penalized 15 times for 212 yards. ... The Packers had two receivers top the 100-yard mark (Schroeder's 158 and Freeman's 152) in the same game for the first time in five years. ... Buffalo's Andre Reed had six catches for 68 yards against Pittsburgh to pass Art Monk and move into fifth place on the NFL's career yards receiving list with 12,742.

Quote of the week: Tampa Bay quarterback Dilfer, after Favre completed the 16th fourth-quarter comeback of his career: "We got Favred. I don't know what else you can say. He's the best."

GAME SUMMARIES

BILLS 24, STEELERS 21

Sunday, October 10

Pittsburgh	7	7	0	7	—21
Buffalo	7	10	7	0	—24

First Quarter
Pit.—Ward 12 pass from Stewart (K. Brown kick), 5:20.
Buf.—Gash 2 pass from Flutie (Christie kick), 13:13.

Second Quarter
Buf.—Moulds 49 pass from Flutie (Christie kick), 0:47.
Buf.—FG, Christie 29, 10:29.
Pit.—Edwards 17 pass from Stewart (K. Brown kick), 14:09.

Third Quarter
Buf.—Riemersma 8 pass from Flutie (Christie kick), 14:28.

Fourth Quarter
Pit.—Bettis 1 run (K. Brown kick), 12:16.
Attendance—71,038.

	Pittsburgh	Buffalo
First downs	17	24
Rushes-yards	23-48	33-111
Passing	207	254
Punt returns	1-5	2-12
Kickoff returns	3-55	4-75
Interception returns	0-0	1-24
Comp.-att.-int.	21-29-1	21-32-0
Sacked-yards lost	2-9	2-7
Punts	6-40	4-41
Fumbles-lost	0-0	1-1
Penalties-yards	2-20	4-40
Time of possession	27:20	32:40

INDIVIDUAL STATISTICS
RUSHING—Pittsburgh, Bettis 13-24, Huntley 5-16, Stewart 3-11, Witman 1-2, Ward 1-(minus 5). Buffalo, Linton 15-45, A. Smith 11-27, Flutie 7-39.
PASSING—Pittsburgh, Stewart 21-29-1-216. Buffalo, Flutie 21-32-0-261.
RECEIVING—Pittsburgh, Ward 6-67, Edwards 4-50, Huntley 3-32, Lyons 2-31, Hawkins 2-11, Bettis 2-10, Blackwell 1-10, Bruener 1-5. Buffalo, Moulds 6-122, Reed 6-68, Riemersma 4-35, Gash 3-14, Linton 1-15, Jackson 1-7.
MISSED FIELD GOAL ATTEMPTS—Buffalo, Christie 36.
INTERCEPTIONS—Buffalo, Rogers 1-24.
KICKOFF RETURNS—Pittsburgh, Blackwell 3-55. Buffalo, K. Williams 3-69, Collins 1-6.
PUNT RETURNS—Pittsburgh, Edwards 1-5. Buffalo, K. Williams 2-12.
SACKS—Pittsburgh, Flowers 1, Steed 1. Buffalo, S. Price 1, Northern 1.

CHIEFS 16, PATRIOTS 14

Sunday, October 10

New England	7	0	0	7	—14
Kansas City	3	0	10	3	—16

First Quarter
K.C.—FG, Stoyanovich 22, 8:58.
N.E.—Glenn 49 pass from Bledsoe (Vinatieri kick), 13:03.

Third Quarter
K.C.—Bennett 1 run (Stoyanovich kick), 8:06.
K.C.—FG, Stoyanovich 41, 14:37.

Fourth Quarter
K.C.—FG, Stoyanovich 23, 10:08.
N.E.—Jefferson 8 pass from Bledsoe (Vinatieri kick), 12:17.
Attendance—78,636.

	New England	Kansas City
First downs	18	20
Rushes-yards	19-62	43-140
Passing	316	189
Punt returns	1-(-1)	2-9
Kickoff returns	5-112	3-57
Interception returns	1-0	2-15
Comp.-att.-int.	23-45-2	18-26-1
Sacked-yards lost	3-18	1-9
Punts	3-46	5-31
Fumbles-lost	5-2	2-1
Penalties-yards	7-35	4-24
Time of possession	24:23	35:37

INDIVIDUAL STATISTICS
RUSHING—New England, Allen 11-53, Faulk 3-2, Warren 2-5, Bledsoe 2-1, Floyd 1-1. Kansas City, Bennett 15-52, Morris 15-45, Shehee 5-28, Richardson 5-15, Grbac 3-0.
PASSING—New England, Bledsoe 23-45-2-334. Kansas City, Grbac 18-26-1-198.
RECEIVING—New England, Simmons 7-107, Glenn 5-92, Allen 3-39, Jefferson 2-35, Warren 2-25, Coates 1-18, Rutledge 1-8, Floyd 1-5, T. Carter 1-5. Kansas City, Horn 4-75, Lockett 4-40, Bennett 4-12, Gonzalez 3-40, Alexander 2-25, Rison 1-6.
MISSED FIELD GOAL ATTEMPTS—New England, Vinatieri 48, 32.
INTERCEPTIONS—New England, Milloy 1-0. Kansas City, Edwards 1-15, Hasty 1-0.
KICKOFF RETURNS—New England, Faulk 3-68, Brown 1-28, Warren 1-16. Kansas City, Vanover 3-57.
PUNT RETURNS—New England, Faulk 1-(minus 1). Kansas City, Vanover 2-9.
SACKS—New England, Eaton 1. Kansas City, Thomas 1, O'Neal 1, Ransom 1.

RAMS 42, 49ERS 20

Sunday, October 10

San Francisco	3	14	3	0	—20
St. Louis	21	7	7	7	—42

First Quarter
St.L.—Bruce 13 pass from Warner (Wilkins kick), 7:18.
St.L.—Bruce 5 pass from Warner (Wilkins kick), 10:34.
S.F.—FG, Richey 42, 13:26.
St.L.—Bruce 45 pass from Warner (Wilkins kick), 13:48.

Second Quarter
S.F.—Phillips 2 run (Richey kick), 2:36.
St.L.—Robinson 22 pass from Warner (Wilkins kick), 10:51.
S.F.—Bryant recovered ball in end zone (Richey kick), 13:01.

Third Quarter
S.F.—FG, Richey 43, 13:18.
St.L.—Horne 97 kickoff return (Wilkins kick), 13:35.

Fourth Quarter
St.L.—Bruce 42 pass from Warner (Wilkins kick), 3:49.
Attendance—65,872.

	San Fran.	St. Louis
First downs	21	20
Rushes-yards	21-72	28-109
Passing	233	316
Punt returns	0-0	2-0
Kickoff returns	5-123	4-199
Interception returns	1-0	3-51
Comp.-att.-int.	22-36-3	20-23-1
Sacked-yards lost	0-0	1-7
Punts	4-39	2-31
Fumbles-lost	0-0	3-1
Penalties-yards	7-70	11-73
Time of possession	29:11	30:49

INDIVIDUAL STATISTICS
RUSHING—San Francisco, Garner 13-52, Phillips 4-9, Beasley 2-4, Garcia 1-5, Rice 1-2. St. Louis, Watson 11-46, Faulk 7-6, Holcombe 6-47, Justin 2-(minus 2), Warner 1-10, Hodgins 1-2.
PASSING—San Francisco, Garcia 22-36-3-233. St. Louis, Warner 20-23-1-323.
RECEIVING—San Francisco, Owens 6-60, Garner 5-57, Stokes 4-54, Rice 4-42, Phillips 2-11, Beasley 1-9. St. Louis, Bruce 5-134, Faulk 4-38, Holt 3-67, Robinson 2-31, Hakim 2-22, Holcombe 2-15, Hodgins 1-10, Proehl 1-6.
MISSED FIELD GOAL ATTEMPTS—None.

INTERCEPTIONS—San Francisco, Schulters 1-0. St. Louis, Allen 1-40, M. Jones 1-11, Bly 1-0.
KICKOFF RETURNS—San Francisco, McQuarters 3-68, Phillips 2-55. St. Louis, Horne 4-199.
PUNT RETURNS—St. Louis, Hakim 2-0.
SACKS—San Francisco, McDonald 1.

DOLPHINS 34, COLTS 31

Sunday, October 10

Miami	3	6	0	25	—34
Indianapolis	3	7	7	14	—31

First Quarter
Ind.—FG, Vanderjagt 41, 3:41.
Mia.—FG, Mare 37, 13:19.

Second Quarter
Mia.—FG, Mare 27, 5:15.
Ind.—Harrison 33 pass from Manning (Vanderjagt kick), 10:21.
Mia.—FG, Mare 21, 14:36.

Third Quarter
Ind.—Pollard 9 pass from Manning (Vanderjagt kick), 6:26.

Fourth Quarter
Mia.—Martin 28 pass from Marino (pass failed), 1:52.
Ind.—Wilkins 97 kickoff return (Vanderjagt kick), 2:08.
Mia.—Collins 25 run (Mare kick), 5:15.
Ind.—Pollard 32 pass from Manning (Vanderjagt kick), 6:46.
Mia.—FG, Mare 43, 11:40.
Mia.—Safety, P. Manning tackled by S. Madison in end zone, 13:06.
Mia.—Gadsden 2 pass from Marino (Mare kick), 14:33.
 Attendance—56,810.

	Miami	Indianapolis
First downs	20	18
Rushes-yards	28-76	24-68
Passing	393	264
Punt returns	2-28	2-14
Kickoff returns	7-143	6-183
Interception returns	1-0	0-0
Comp.-att.-int.	25-38-0	17-24-1
Sacked-yards lost	0-0	2-10
Punts	3-43	2-37
Fumbles-lost	2-0	2-1
Penalties-yards	6-62	4-30
Time of possession	34:07	25:53

INDIVIDUAL STATISTICS
RUSHING—Miami, Collins 21-76, Johnson 3-6, Pritchett 1-1, Konrad 1-0, Marino 1-(minus 1), Martin 1-(minus 6). Indianapolis, James 22-81, Manning 2-(minus 13).
PASSING—Miami, Marino 25-38-0-393. Indianapolis, Manning 17-24-1-274.
RECEIVING—Miami, Martin 10-166, Gadsden 4-123, McDuffie 4-42, Konrad 4-33, Pritchett 2-18, Drayton 1-11. Indianapolis, Wilkins 4-81, Pollard 4-64, Harrison 3-91, Dilger 2-22, James 2-1, Pathon 1-12, Shields 1-3.
MISSED FIELD GOAL ATTEMPTS—None.
INTERCEPTIONS—Miami, Buckley 1-0.
KICKOFF RETURNS—Miami, Marion 5-119, McDuffie 1-17, Wilson 1-7. Indianapolis, Wilkins 4-153, Elias 2-30.
PUNT RETURNS—Miami, McDuffie 2-28. Indianapolis, Wilkins 2-14.
SACKS—Miami, Owens 1, Armstrong 1.

EAGLES 13, COWBOYS 10

Sunday, October 10

Dallas	3	7	0	0	—10
Philadelphia	0	0	0	13	—13

First Quarter
Dal.—FG, Cunningham 42, 7:53.

Second Quarter
Dal.—E. Smith 9 pass from Aikman (Cunningham kick), 3:25.

Fourth Quarter
Phi.—FG, N. Johnson 48, 3:12.
Phi.—FG, N. Johnson 31, 9:18.
Phi.—C. Johnson 28 pass from Pederson (N. Johnson kick), 13:53.
 Attendance—66,669.

	Dallas	Philadelphia
First downs	19	12
Rushes-yards	32-130	27-105
Passing	170	139
Punt returns	5-55	1-13
Kickoff returns	4-97	3-60
Interception returns	1-0	2-13
Comp.-att.-int.	21-39-2	11-30-1
Sacked-yards lost	1-7	2-6
Punts	6-38	8-45
Fumbles-lost	2-1	0-0
Penalties-yards	6-65	7-82
Time of possession	36:11	23:49

INDIVIDUAL STATISTICS
RUSHING—Dallas, E. Smith 30-114, Ismail 1-17, Aikman 1-(minus 1). Philadelphia, Staley 22-110, Pederson 4-(minus 9), Bostic 1-4.
PASSING—Dallas, Aikman 21-39-2-177. Philadelphia, Pederson 11-29-1-145, Small 0-1-0-0.
RECEIVING—Dallas, Ismail 7-88, E. Smith 5-31, LaFleur 3-22, Mills 2-16, Warren 2-6, Irvin 1-8, Tucker 1-6. Philadelphia, Staley 4-19, Small 3-48, C. Johnson 2-64, Broughton 1-11, Weaver 1-3.
MISSED FIELD GOAL ATTEMPTS—Dallas, Cunningham 50.
INTERCEPTIONS—Dallas, Reese 1-0. Philadelphia, Taylor 1-13, Vincent 1-0.
KICKOFF RETURNS—Dallas, Ogden 3-74, Sanders 1-23. Philadelphia, Rossum 2-41, Bieniemy 1-19.
PUNT RETURNS—Dallas, Sanders 5-55. Philadelphia, Rossum 1-13.
SACKS—Dallas, Hennings 1, Ellis 1. Philadelphia, Mamula 1.

FALCONS 20, SAINTS 17

Sunday, October 10

Atlanta	7	0	7	6	—20
New Orleans	0	17	0	0	—17

First Quarter
Atl.—Mathis 22 pass from Graziani (Andersen kick), 6:43.

Second Quarter
N.O.—FG, Brien 42, 1:48.
N.O.—Kennison 90 pass from Hobert (Brien kick), 5:13.
N.O.—Bech 23 pass from Tolliver (Brien kick), 14:14.

Third Quarter
Atl.—Christian 1 run (Andersen kick), 4:01.

Fourth Quarter
Atl.—FG, Andersen 36, 0:43.
Atl.—FG, Andersen 44, 6:31.
 Attendance—57,289.

	Atlanta	New Orleans
First downs	12	18
Rushes-yards	33-104	24-71
Passing	147	319
Punt returns	2-(-5)	1-5
Kickoff returns	4-69	5-107
Interception returns	2-11	0-0
Comp.-att.-int.	11-20-0	22-40-2
Sacked-yards lost	3-15	3-19
Punts	6-40	4-36
Fumbles-lost	3-2	3-0
Penalties-yards	9-68	7-64
Time of possession	29:39	30:21

INDIVIDUAL STATISTICS
RUSHING—Atlanta, Oxendine 20-57, Hanspard 10-32, Graziani 2-14, Christian 1-1. New Orleans, R. Williams 19-53, Tolliver 3-9, L. Smith 2-9.
PASSING—Atlanta, Graziani 11-20-0-162. New Orleans, Tolliver 13-26-2-185, Hobert 9-14-0-153.
RECEIVING—Atlanta, Mathis 5-67, Oxendine 2-4, German 1-62, R. Kelly 1-16, Calloway 1-9, Christian 1-4. New Orleans, Cleeland 5-69, Kennison 4-138, Poole 3-50, R. Williams 3-16, Bech 2-37, Slutzker 2-14, L. Smith 2-9, Hastings 1-5.
MISSED FIELD GOAL ATTEMPTS—New Orleans, Brien 28, 49.
INTERCEPTIONS—Atlanta, Booker 1-10, Buchanan 1-1.
KICKOFF RETURNS—Atlanta, Dwight 4-69. New Orleans, Davis 5-107.
PUNT RETURNS—Atlanta, Dwight 2-(minus 5). New Orleans, Kennison 1-5.
SACKS—Atlanta, Kerney 1, Hall 1, McBurrows 1. New Orleans, B. Smith 2, Martin 1.

BEARS 24, VIKINGS 22
Sunday, October 10

Chicago	7	7	7	3—24
Minnesota	3	9	3	7—22

First Quarter
Chi.—S. Harris recovered fumble in end zone (Jaeger kick), 5:42.
Min.—FG, Anderson 26, 11:56.

Second Quarter
Min.—FG, Anderson 40, 0:08.
Min.—FG, Anderson 23, 8:40.
Chi.—Conway 30 pass from Matthews (Jaeger kick), 13:47.
Min.—FG, Anderson 26, 15:00.

Third Quarter
Chi.—M. Robinson 3 pass from Matthews (Jaeger kick), 7:13.
Min.—FG, Anderson 34, 12:29.

Fourth Quarter
Chi.—FG, Jaeger 41, 2:39.
Min.—Walsh 18 pass from Cunningham (Anderson kick), 14:58.
Attendance—64,107.

	Chicago	Minnesota
First downs	23	26
Rushes-yards	33-101	20-166
Passing	278	279
Punt returns	2-7	1-0
Kickoff returns	3-63	4-62
Interception returns	3-69	0-0
Comp.-att.-int.	28-42-0	25-47-3
Sacked-yards lost	1-3	4-30
Punts	5-37	3-47
Fumbles-lost	0-0	2-2
Penalties-yards	3-23	5-40
Time of possession	33:34	26:26

INDIVIDUAL STATISTICS
RUSHING—Chicago, Enis 27-66, McNown 2-17, Bennett 1-15, Matthews 1-6, Allen 1-1, Milburn 1-(minus 4). Minnesota, Smith 12-107, Hoard 5-17, Cunningham 3-42.
PASSING—Chicago, Matthews 19-28-0-184, McNown 9-14-0-97. Minnesota, Cunningham 25-47-3-309.
RECEIVING—Chicago, M. Robinson 8-90, Conway 5-60, Enis 3-32, Engram 3-17, Wetnight 2-26, Allred 2-16, Milburn 2-15, Mayes 1-12, Bennett 1-7, Brooks 1-6. Minnesota, Moss 8-122, Carter 5-62, Glover 5-48, Kleinsasser 2-(minus 13), Hoard 1-29, Reed 1-23, Hatchette 1-22, Walsh 1-18, Smith 1-(minus 2).
MISSED FIELD GOAL ATTEMPTS—Chicago, Jaeger 49, 48, 37.
INTERCEPTIONS—Chicago, Carter 1-36, Minter 1-32, Cousin 1-1.
KICKOFF RETURNS—Chicago, Milburn 3-63. Minnesota, Tate 3-62, Kleinsasser 1-0.
PUNT RETURNS—Chicago, Milburn 2-7. Minnesota, Moss 1-0.
SACKS—Chicago, Flanigan 2, Minter 1, Smith 1. Minnesota, Rudd 1.

CARDINALS 14, GIANTS 3
Sunday, October 10

N.Y. Giants	0	0	0	3— 3
Arizona	0	14	0	0—14

Second Quarter
Ariz.—Plummer 1 run (Jacke kick), 0:02.
Ariz.—Boston 11 pass from Plummer (Jacke kick), 14:27.

Fourth Quarter
NYG—FG, Daluiso 31, 4:47.
Attendance—49,015.

	N.Y. Giants	Arizona
First downs	15	13
Rushes-yards	28-107	27-31
Passing	178	175
Punt returns	7-86	4-52
Kickoff returns	3-65	1-51
Interception returns	0-0	1-1
Comp.-att.-int.	24-38-1	17-27-0
Sacked-yards lost	3-24	4-22
Punts	6-47	9-47
Fumbles-lost	2-1	1-0
Penalties-yards	8-52	3-14
Time of possession	31:51	28:09

INDIVIDUAL STATISTICS
RUSHING—New York, Brown 18-67, Way 5-10, Collins 4-23, Barber 1-7. Arizona, Murrell 14-8, Pittman 8-20, Plummer 3-3, Bates 1-0, Makovicka 1-0.
PASSING—New York, Collins 24-38-1-202. Arizona, Plummer 13-19-0-156, Da. Brown 4-8-0-41.
RECEIVING—New York, Hilliard 5-78, Toomer 5-34, Mitchell 4-30, Barber 4-23, Way 3-17, Patten 1-10, Cross 1-9, Brown 1-1. Arizona, Boston 8-101, Sanders 5-37, Hardy 2-31, Pittman 1-21, Murrell 1-7.
MISSED FIELD GOAL ATTEMPTS—New York, Daluiso 42. Arizona, Jacke 53, 34.
INTERCEPTIONS—Arizona, Tillman 1-1.
KICKOFF RETURNS—New York, Patten 2-40, Barber 1-25. Arizona, Bates 1-51.
PUNT RETURNS—New York, Barber 6-72, Toomer 1-14. Arizona, Cody 4-52.
SACKS—New York, Armstead 1.5, Jones 1, Strahan 1, K. Hamilton 0.5. Arizona, Rice 2, Burke 1.

BRONCOS 16, RAIDERS 13
Sunday, October 10

Denver	3	10	0	3—16
Oakland	0	0	10	3—13

First Quarter
Den.—FG, Elam 48, 8:49.

Second Quarter
Den.—FG, Elam 47, 11:04.
Den.—R. Smith 3 pass from Griese (Elam kick), 14:44.

Third Quarter
Oak.—D. Walker 21 pass from Gannon (Husted kick), 6:00.
Oak.—FG, Husted 47, 11:25.

Fourth Quarter
Oak.—FG, Husted 19, 0:03.
Den.—FG, Elam 26, 4:42.
Attendance—55,704.

	Denver	Oakland
First downs	16	17
Rushes-yards	28-81	24-55
Passing	221	210
Punt returns	3-4	5-129
Kickoff returns	2-51	5-97
Interception returns	2-61	1-2
Comp.-att.-int.	17-30-1	25-36-2
Sacked-yards lost	2-13	6-38
Punts	5-54	4-46
Fumbles-lost	2-1	1-0
Penalties-yards	3-17	3-30
Time of possession	27:19	32:41

INDIVIDUAL STATISTICS
RUSHING—Denver, Gary 20-64, Griese 7-16, Lynn 1-1. Oakland, Wheatley 11-30, Crockett 6-11, Gannon 4-8, Kaufman 3-6.
PASSING—Denver, Griese 17-29-1-234, R. Smith 0-1-0-0. Oakland, Gannon 25-36-2-248.
RECEIVING—Denver, R. Smith 7-79, McCaffrey 5-88, Chamberlain 3-40, Griffith 1-17, Gary 1-10. Oakland, Brown 6-51, Ritchie 4-47, Crockett 4-22, Dudley 2-25, Mickens 2-22, Wheatley 2-15, D. Walker 1-21, Jett 1-19, Kaufman 1-17, Brigham 1-12, Gannon 1-(minus 3).
MISSED FIELD GOAL ATTEMPTS—None.
INTERCEPTIONS—Denver, James 1-45, Romanowski 1-16. Oakland, Allen 1-2.
KICKOFF RETURNS—Denver, Watson 2-51. Oakland, Kaufman 2-50, Jordan 2-27, Branch 1-20.
PUNT RETURNS—Denver, Watson 3-4. Oakland, Gordon 5-129.
SACKS—Denver, Williams 2, Wilson 1, Cadrez 1, Pryce 1, Hasselbach 0.5, Traylor 0.5. Oakland, Russell 1, Johnstone 1.

TITANS 14, RAVENS 11
Sunday, October 10

Baltimore	3	3	5	0—11
Tennessee	7	0	7	0—14

First Quarter
Bal.—FG, Stover 44, 8:07.
Ten.—Neal 1 run (Del Greco kick), 13:14.

Second Quarter
Bal.—FG, Stover 46, 6:27.

1999 REVIEW Week 5

— 144 —

Third Quarter
Bal.—FG, Stover 50, 4:18.
Ten.—Thigpen 27 pass from O'Donnell (Del Greco kick), 7:37.
Bal.—Safety, J. Lewis tackled by R.Thomas in end zone, 11:27.
   Attendance—65,486.

	Baltimore	Tennessee
First downs	16	16
Rushes-yards	26-68	24-56
Passing	178	216
Punt returns	4-20	4-26
Kickoff returns	4-73	3-52
Interception returns	0-0	0-0
Comp.-att.-int.	15-37-0	24-35-0
Sacked-yards lost	3-29	0-0
Punts	8-47	9-44
Fumbles-lost	1-1	0-0
Penalties-yards	9-81	15-212
Time of possession	28:59	31:01

INDIVIDUAL STATISTICS
RUSHING—Baltimore, Rhett 21-59, Case 3-2, Evans 2-7. Tennessee, E. George 20-55, Thomas 2-1, Neal 1-1, O'Donnell 1-(minus 1).
PASSING—Baltimore, Case 15-37-0-207. Tennessee, O'Donnell 24-35-0-216.
RECEIVING—Baltimore, J. Lewis 4-58, Johnson 4-57, Ismail 3-47, Armour 2-35, Evans 2-10. Tennessee, Thigpen 5-99, E. George 5-23, Dyson 4-34, Wycheck 4-19, Byrd 3-22, Neal 1-8, Roan 1-7, Mason 1-4.
MISSED FIELD GOAL ATTEMPTS—None.
INTERCEPTIONS—None.
KICKOFF RETURNS—Baltimore, Harris 3-54, J. Lewis 1-19. Tennessee, Mason 2-38, Neal 1-14.
PUNT RETURNS—Baltimore, J. Lewis 4-20. Tennessee, Mason 4-26.
SACKS—Tennessee, Rolle 2, Thornton 1.

CHARGERS 20, LIONS 10
Sunday, October 10

San Diego	0	10	3	7—20
Detroit	7	3	0	0—10

First Quarter
Det.—Crowell 41 pass from Batch (Hanson kick), 9:40.
Second Quarter
S.D.—FG, Carney 33, 1:38.
Det.—FG, Hanson 23, 8:07.
S.D.—Stephens 3 run (Carney kick), 14:18.
Third Quarter
S.D.—FG, Carney 24, 5:12.
Fourth Quarter
S.D.—Lewis 42 fumble return (Carney kick), 7:08.
   Attendance—61,481.

	San Diego	Detroit
First downs	15	14
Rushes-yards	24-64	24-37
Passing	192	192
Punt returns	2-13	2-33
Kickoff returns	1-26	5-112
Interception returns	1-4	1-8
Comp.-att.-int.	20-34-1	21-38-1
Sacked-yards lost	2-16	6-38
Punts	5-51	5-38
Fumbles-lost	1-1	3-2
Penalties-yards	4-20	1-5
Time of possession	30:25	29:35

INDIVIDUAL STATISTICS
RUSHING—San Diego, Fletcher 11-24, Bynum 9-37, Stephens 3-4, Kramer 1-(minus 1). Detroit, Rivers 13-30, Batch 5-20, Hill 3-(minus 3), Schlesinger 2-(minus 5), Irvin 1-(minus 5).
PASSING—San Diego, Kramer 20-34-1-208. Detroit, Batch 21-38-1-230.
RECEIVING—San Diego, Penn 7-79, McCrary 4-17, Fletcher 3-51, Still 2-40, Bynum 2-12, F. Jones 2-9. Detroit, Rivers 9-63, Crowell 6-99, Morton 6-68.
MISSED FIELD GOAL ATTEMPTS—San Diego, Carney 47.
INTERCEPTIONS—San Diego, Simien 1-4. Detroit, Bailey 1-8.
KICKOFF RETURNS—San Diego, Bynum 1-26. Detroit, Fair 5-112.
PUNT RETURNS—San Diego, Penn 2-13. Detroit, Uwaezuoke 1-20, Fair 1-13.
SACKS—San Diego, Seau 2, Harrison 1, Hand 1, Fontenot 1, Johnson 0.5, Harden 0.5. Detroit, Aldridge 1, Pringley 0.5, Kirschke 0.5.

BENGALS 18, BROWNS 17
Sunday, October 10

Cincinnati	6	6	0	6—18
Cleveland	0	14	0	3—17

First Quarter
Cin.—FG, Pelfrey 27, 4:03.
Cin.—FG, Pelfrey 26, 13:09.
Second Quarter
Cle.—Dawson 4 run (Dawson kick), 1:14.
Cle.—Kirby 1 run (Dawson kick), 2:56.
Cin.—Pickens 5 pass from Smith (pass failed), 13:52.
Fourth Quarter
Cle.—FG, Dawson 33, 0:51.
Cin.—Pickens 2 pass from Smith (run failed), 14:55.
   Attendance—73,048.

	Cincinnati	Cleveland
First downs	25	13
Rushes-yards	35-212	23-80
Passing	204	144
Punt returns	4-32	4-43
Kickoff returns	4-88	5-104
Interception returns	1-0	0-0
Comp.-att.-int.	25-42-0	15-27-1
Sacked-yards lost	4-17	3-20
Punts	7-41	8-43
Fumbles-lost	1-1	2-0
Penalties-yards	4-70	8-81
Time of possession	36:49	23:11

INDIVIDUAL STATISTICS
RUSHING—Cincinnati, Dillon 28-168, Basnight 4-35, Smith 3-9. Cleveland, Kirby 15-57, G. Jones 6-14, Couch 1-5, Dawson 1-4.
PASSING—Cincinnati, Smith 25-42-0-221. Cleveland, Couch 15-27-1-164.
RECEIVING—Cincinnati, Scott 8-110, Pickens 7-38, McGee 3-33, Groce 3-25, Griffin 2-10, Bush 1-4, Dillon 1-1. Cleveland, Johnson 5-73, Kirby 4-30, Shepherd 3-22, Edwards 2-29, Chiaverini 1-10.
MISSED FIELD GOAL ATTEMPTS—None.
INTERCEPTIONS—Cincinnati, Blackmon 1-0.
KICKOFF RETURNS—Cincinnati, Mack 4-88. Cleveland, Powell 4-104, Dunn 1-0.
PUNT RETURNS—Cincinnati, Griffin 4-32. Cleveland, Johnson 4-43.
SACKS—Cincinnati, Simmons 1, Copeland 1, Wilson 1. Cleveland, J. Miller 2, McNeil 1, Holland 1.

PACKERS 26, BUCCANEERS 23
Sunday, October 10

Tampa Bay	0	13	0	10—23
Green Bay	10	3	3	10—26

First Quarter
G.B.—Freeman 19 pass from Favre (Longwell kick), 3:01.
G.B.—FG, Longwell 42, 7:23.
Second Quarter
T.B.—Dunn 16 pass from Dilfer (Gramatica kick), 0:07.
T.B.—FG, Gramatica 41, 4:17.
T.B.—FG, Gramatica 36, 11:27.
G.B.—FG, Longwell 49, 14:03.
Third Quarter
G.B.—FG, Longwell 38, 8:08.
Fourth Quarter
T.B.—FG, Gramatica 36, 0:32.
G.B.—FG, Longwell 43, 9:03.
T.B.—Alstott 22 run (Gramatica kick), 13:15.
G.B.—Freeman 21 pass from Favre (Longwell kick), 13:55.
   Attendance—59,868.

	Tampa Bay	Green Bay
First downs	21	18
Rushes-yards	32-173	23-98
Passing	100	352
Punt returns	2-48	1-4
Kickoff returns	6-119	6-119
Interception returns	0-0	3-5
Comp.-att.-int.	16-26-3	22-40-0
Sacked-yards lost	2-10	5-38

1999 REVIEW Week 5

– 145 –

	Tampa Bay	Green Bay
Punts	3-44	4-35
Fumbles-lost	1-1	3-1
Penalties-yards	3-40	9-88
Time of possession	29:53	30:07

INDIVIDUAL STATISTICS

RUSHING—Tampa Bay, Alstott 14-87, Dunn 14-39, Dilfer 4-47. Green Bay, Levens 22-99, Favre 1-(minus 1).

PASSING—Tampa Bay, Dilfer 16-26-3-110. Green Bay, Favre 22-40-0-390.

RECEIVING—Tampa Bay, Dunn 6-41, Anthony 3-23, Alstott 2-16, Emanuel 2-8, Green 1-12, Williams 1-7, Moore 1-3. Green Bay, Schroeder 7-158, Freeman 7-152, Levens 5-57, Henderson 2-4, Bradford 1-19.

MISSED FIELD GOAL ATTEMPTS—Green Bay, Longwell 45.

INTERCEPTIONS—Green Bay, Sharper 1-3, Smith 1-2, T. Williams 1-0.

KICKOFF RETURNS—Tampa Bay, Anthony 6-119. Green Bay, Howard 6-119.

PUNT RETURNS—Tampa Bay, Williams 2-48. Green Bay, Howard 1-4.

SACKS—Tampa Bay, Ahanotu 2, Sapp 2, Jones 1. Green Bay, B. Williams 1, K. McKenzie 1.

JAGUARS 16, JETS 6

Monday, October 11

Jacksonville	7	3	3	3—16
N.Y. Jets	0	3	0	3— 6

First Quarter
Jac.—J. Stewart 3 run (Hollis kick), 8:24.

Second Quarter
Jac.—FG, Hollis 32, 9:21.
NYJ—FG, Hall 33, 13:17.

Third Quarter
Jac.—FG, Hollis 44, 4:46.

Fourth Quarter
NYJ—FG, Hall 42, 6:07.
Jac.—FG, Hollis 21, 13:14.
Attendance—78,216.

	Jacksonville	N.Y. Jets
First downs	16	13
Rushes-yards	34-125	24-89
Passing	197	141
Punt returns	4-25	3-19
Kickoff returns	3-61	3-81
Interception returns	2-55	0-0
Comp.-att.-int.	21-35-0	19-38-2
Sacked-yards lost	2-18	4-23
Punts	7-46	7-45
Fumbles-lost	2-1	1-0
Penalties-yards	7-67	2-15
Time of possession	32:33	27:27

INDIVIDUAL STATISTICS

RUSHING—Jacksonville, J. Stewart 26-96, Banks 3-14, Howard 3-9, Brunell 2-6. New York, Martin 18-59, Parmalee 4-16, Mirer 2-14.

PASSING—Jacksonville, Brunell 21-35-0-215. New York, Mirer 19-38-2-164.

RECEIVING—Jacksonville, Brady 5-42, McCardell 4-60, Banks 3-26, J. Smith 3-21, Shelton 2-14, J. Stewart 2-11, Barlow 1-31, Jones 1-10. New York, K. Johnson 8-94, Anderson 4-14, Martin 3-15, Ward 2-16, Early 1-17, Parmalee 1-8.

MISSED FIELD GOAL ATTEMPTS—None.

INTERCEPTIONS—Jacksonville, Darius 1-29, McElmurry 1-26.

KICKOFF RETURNS—Jacksonville, Barlow 3-61. New York, Farmer 2-38, Stone 1-43.

PUNT RETURNS—Jacksonville, Barlow 4-25. New York, Sawyer 3-19.

SACKS—Jacksonville, Brackens 1.5, Hardy 1, Walker 1, Payne 0.5. New York, Lewis 2.

WEEK 6

RESULTS

Carolina 31, SAN FRANCISCO 29
DENVER 31, Green Bay 10
DETROIT 25, Minnesota 23
Indianapolis 16, N.Y. JETS 13
JACKSONVILLE 24, Cleveland 7
Miami 31, NEW ENGLAND 30
Oakland 20, BUFFALO 14
Philadelphia 20, CHICAGO 16
Pittsburgh 17, CINCINNATI 3
St. Louis 41, ATLANTA 13
SAN DIEGO 13, Seattle 10
Tennessee 24, NEW ORLEANS 21
Washington 24, ARIZONA 10
N.Y. GIANTS 13, Dallas 10
Open date: Baltimore, Kansas City, Tampa Bay

STANDINGS

AFC EAST
	W	L	T	Pct.
Miami	4	1	0	.800
Buffalo	4	2	0	.667
New England	4	2	0	.667
Indianapolis	3	2	0	.600
N.Y. Jets	1	5	0	.167

AFC CENTRAL
	W	L	T	Pct.
Jacksonville	5	1	0	.833
Tennessee	5	1	0	.833
Pittsburgh	3	3	0	.500
Baltimore	2	3	0	.400
Cincinnati	1	5	0	.167
Cleveland	0	6	0	.000

AFC WEST
	W	L	T	Pct.
San Diego	4	1	0	.800
Kansas City	3	2	0	.600
Seattle	3	2	0	.600
Oakland	3	3	0	.500
Denver	2	4	0	.333

NFC EAST
	W	L	T	Pct.
Washington	4	1	0	.800
Dallas	3	2	0	.600
N.Y. Giants	3	3	0	.500
Arizona	2	4	0	.333
Philadelphia	2	4	0	.333

NFC CENTRAL
	W	L	T	Pct.
Detroit	3	2	0	.600
Green Bay	3	2	0	.600
Chicago	3	3	0	.500
Tampa Bay	2	3	0	.400
Minnesota	2	4	0	.333

NFC WEST
	W	L	T	Pct.
St. Louis	5	0	0	1.000
San Francisco	3	3	0	.500
Carolina	2	3	0	.400
New Orleans	1	4	0	.200
Atlanta	1	5	0	.167

HIGHLIGHTS

Hero of the week: After missing earlier from 42 yards, John Carney hit two field goals in the game's final three minutes—the second as time expired—to give the Chargers a 13-10 win over Seattle and sole possession of first place in the AFC West.

Goat of the week: New Orleans quarterback Billy Joe Tolliver passed for 354 yards and two touchdowns, but his blunders late in the second half allowed the Titans to come from behind and beat the Saints 24-21. Interceptions by defensive tackle Jason Fisk and cornerback Donald Mitchell were the difference in the Saints' latest defeat.

Sub of the week: With the Dolphins down 7-0, backup quarterback Damon Huard was forced to replace ailing Dan Marino. Huard threw for a touchdown on his first pass, but the receiver was the Patriots' Ty Law, who returned it 27 yards for a New England touchdown. Huard, who had only six NFL completions before the game, bounced back, completing 24 of 42 passes for 240 yards and two touchdowns. His five-yard strike with 23 seconds remaining to fullback Stanley Pritchett capped an improbable 31-30 comeback victory.

Comeback of the week: Jeff George led the Vikings on a ferocious comeback, turning a 19-0 halftime deficit into a 23-22 lead with under two minutes left. But with seven seconds on the clock, Lions kicker Jason Hanson ended the drama with his league-best sixth field goal, putting the Lions ahead for good 25-23. The Vikings thought they had life when an apparent 43-yard, game-winning field goal by Hanson was wiped-out by a delay of game penalty. But Hanson's second attempt was also good.

Blowout of the week: The Rams remained the NFL's only unbeaten team (5-0), mauling the Falcons 41-13 on the strength of running back Marshall Faulk's 213 total yards. Even the defense and special teams put points on the board for St. Louis. End Grant Wistrom had a 92-yard interception return, and Tony Horne returned a kickoff 101 yards.

Nail-biter of the week: With under eight minutes remaining, the Giants' Tiki Barber returned a punt 85 yards for a touchdown, and a 10-3 New York lead. The Cowboys, however, answered with a two-yard touchdown run by Emmitt Smith. Overtime seemed inevitable, but Barber struck again, catching a 56-yard pass that set up Brad Daluiso's decisive 21-yard field goal. On the kickoff that followed, Dallas lateraled its way to an apparent game-winning touchdown. But the play—and win—was negated by an illegal forward pass.

Hit of the week: Despite losing on a last-minute touchdown, the Patriots' defense pounded Huard throughout the Miami-New England game. By the final buzzer the Pats had nine sacks, the most ever allowed by the Dolphins in a single game.

Oddity of the week: Backup quarterbacks invaded the NFL in Week 6, ousting starters for a multitude of reasons. The Jaguars' Jay Fiedler, the Redskins' Gus Frerotte, the Cardinals' Dave Brown, the Falcons' Tony Graziani and the Dolphins' Damon Huard all replaced injured incumbents. The Jets' Ray Lucas and the Vikings' Jeff George started as coaches' decisions.

Top rusher: Faulk had 181 rushing yards on 18 carries against Atlanta. Combined with his 32 yards receiving, he averaged more than a first down each time he touched the ball.

Top passer: Tolliver, in his first start for the injured Billy Joe Hobert, completed 28 of 45 passes for 354 yards. But it still wasn't enough to hold off the surging Titans, who overcame a second-half deficit for the fourth time this season.

Top receiver: Marcus Robinson caught four passes for 136 yards in the Bears' 20-16 loss against Philadelphia, including an 80-yard touchdown bomb from rookie Cade McNown.

Notes: Marino lasted only two offensive series before muscle spasms in his neck and shoulder forced him to the sideline, but he stayed in the game long enough to become the first 60,000-yard passer in NFL history. ... Miami's Olindo Mare kicked at least four field goals for the fourth consecutive game, an NFL first. ... The Rams scored 40 or more points in consecutive games for the first time since 1958. ... McNown completed 17 of 33 passes for 255 yards in his first start in place of injured Shane Matthews, but his Bears still lost 20-16. It was the first time the Eagles have ever won in Chicago, breaking a 60-year, 0-14 streak. ... The Broncos outgained the Packers 514-133 in their 31-10 victory at Mile High Stadium. ... Seattle failed to score a rushing touchdown for the fifth consecutive game. ... Rookie Champ Bailey intercepted three passes, including one for a touchdown, in the Redskins' 24-10 victory over the Cardinals. Bailey, 21, became the youngest player in history to intercept three passes in one game. ... The Colts' 16-13 win over the Jets marked the third fourth-quarter comeback in Peyton Manning's 21-game professional career.

Quote of the week: Saints coach Mike Ditka, on his team blowing a fourth-quarter lead for the fourth consecutive game: "They're trying. There's nothing wrong with their psyche. They're probably not very happy right now. I'm not very happy. If that was the problem, I'd get a hold of Sigmund Freud or somebody and we'd straighten that out."

GAME SUMMARIES

DOLPHINS 31, PATRIOTS 30
Sunday, October 17

Miami	3	16	0	12	—31
New England	14	10	3	3	—30

First Quarter
N.E.—Katzenmoyer 57 interception return (Vinatieri kick), 2:54.
N.E.—Law 27 interception return (Vinatieri kick), 6:56.
Mia.—FG, Mare 20, 13:56.

Second Quarter
Mia.—FG, Mare 33, 3:31.
Mia.—Martin 69 pass from Huard (Mare kick), 7:12.
N.E.—FG, Vinatieri 41, 8:20.
Mia.—FG, Mare 45, 13:34.
N.E.—Simmons 29 pass from Bledsoe (Vinatieri kick), 14:37.
Mia.—FG, Mare 45, 14:58.

Third Quarter
N.E.—FG, Vinatieri 39, 2:37.

Fourth Quarter
Mia.—FG, Mare 41, 1:35.
N.E.—FG, Vinatieri 34, 5:55.
Mia.—FG, Mare 53, 12:15.
Mia.—Pritchett 5 pass from Huard (pass failed), 14:37.
Attendance—60,006.

	Miami	New England
First downs	22	14
Rushes-yards	32-122	14-46
Passing	195	213
Punt returns	4-86	3-17
Kickoff returns	6-160	6-144
Interception returns	1-0	2-84
Comp.-att.-int.	25-45-2	17-36-1
Sacked-yards lost	9-53	2-12
Punts	5-40	6-42
Fumbles-lost	0-0	1-1
Penalties-yards	13-99	6-45
Time of possession	40:07	19:53

INDIVIDUAL STATISTICS
RUSHING—Miami, Collins 20-59, Huard 6-54, Pritchett 3-8, Johnson 2-(minus 2), Konrad 1-3. New England, Allen 10-19, Faulk 2-3, Warren 1-18, Bledsoe 1-6.
PASSING—Miami, Huard 24-42-1-240, Marino 1-3-1-8. New England, Bledsoe 17-36-1-225.
RECEIVING—Miami, Martin 7-118, Pritchett 6-33, Drayton 4-49, McDuffie 3-20, Johnson 2-16, Collins 1-5, Gadsden 1-4, Konrad 1-3. New England, Jefferson 4-65, Brisby 3-68, Simmons 3-49, Warren 3-17, Allen 2-18, Coates 2-8.
MISSED FIELD GOAL ATTEMPTS—None.
INTERCEPTIONS—Miami, Surtain 1-0. New England, Katzenmoyer 1-57, Law 1-27.
KICKOFF RETURNS—Miami, Marion 5-141, Johnson 1-19. New England, Faulk 5-143, Sullivan 1-1.
PUNT RETURNS—Miami, Jacquet 4-86. New England, Faulk 3-17.
SACKS—Miami, Bromell 2. New England, Katzenmoyer 2, Slade 2, McGinest 2, C. Carter 1, Law 0.5, Mitchell 0.5, Eaton 0.5, Spires 0.5.

COLTS 16, JETS 13
Sunday, October 17

Indianapolis	0	7	3	6	—16
N.Y. Jets	6	7	0	0	—13

First Quarter
NYJ—FG, Hall 45, 11:26.
NYJ—FG, Hall 39, 13:27.

Second Quarter
NYJ—Anderson 18 pass from Lucas (Hall kick), 5:45.
Ind.—Wilkins 22 pass from Manning (Vanderjagt kick), 8:38.

Third Quarter
Ind.—FG, Vanderjagt 31, 10:01.

Fourth Quarter
Ind.—FG, Vanderjagt 18, 2:54.
Ind.—FG, Vanderjagt 27, 14:46.
Attendance—78,112.

	Indianapolis	N.Y. Jets
First downs	19	16
Rushes-yards	28-108	29-160
Passing	210	125
Punt returns	1-11	3-42
Kickoff returns	4-65	5-161
Interception returns	1-55	1-24
Comp.-att.-int.	21-35-1	16-30-1
Sacked-yards lost	0-0	1-12
Punts	4-42	4-44
Fumbles-lost	2-0	1-0
Penalties-yards	1-5	6-51
Time of possession	30:24	29:36

INDIVIDUAL STATISTICS
RUSHING—Indianapolis, James 26-111, Manning 2-(minus 3). New York, Martin 23-128, Lucas 3-18, Parmalee 3-14.
PASSING—Indianapolis, Manning 21-35-1-210. New York, Lucas 16-30-1-137.
RECEIVING—Indianapolis, Harrison 6-40, Dilger 4-59, Pathon 4-42, James 4-20, Wilkins 2-40, Shields 1-9. New York, Chrebet 5-51, K. Johnson 5-45, Anderson 1-18, Early 1-9, Martin 1-8, Ward 1-5, Baxter 1-3, Parmalee 1-(minus 2).
MISSED FIELD GOAL ATTEMPTS—New York, Hall 43.
INTERCEPTIONS—Indianapolis, Burris 1-55. New York, V. Green 1-24.
KICKOFF RETURNS—Indianapolis, Wilkins 2-33, Pathon 2-32. New York, Stone 4-135, Farmer 1-26.
PUNT RETURNS—Indianapolis, Wilkins 1-11. New York, Ward 3-42.
SACKS—Indianapolis, E. Johnson 1.

RAIDERS 20, BILLS 14
Sunday, October 17

Oakland	10	3	7	0	—20
Buffalo	7	0	0	7	—14

First Quarter
Oak.—Wheatley 3 run (Husted kick), 3:25.
Buf.—A. Smith 52 run (Christie kick), 5:44.
Oak.—FG, Husted 25, 11:31.

Second Quarter
Oak.—FG, Husted 32, 4:46.

Third Quarter
Oak.—Wheatley 11 run (Husted kick), 4:43.

Fourth Quarter
Buf.—Moulds 12 pass from Flutie (Christie kick), 1:31.
Attendance—71,113.

	Oakland	Buffalo
First downs	23	14
Rushes-yards	48-195	13-109
Passing	148	201
Punt returns	2-19	3-31
Kickoff returns	3-50	4-66
Interception returns	3-57	0-0
Comp.-att.-int.	15-22-0	19-41-3
Sacked-yards lost	2-7	1-9
Punts	6-42	5-46
Fumbles-lost	0-0	0-0
Penalties-yards	9-60	6-46
Time of possession	39:35	20:25

INDIVIDUAL STATISTICS

RUSHING—Oakland, Wheatley 25-97, Kaufman 12-72, Crockett 7-4, Gannon 4-22. Buffalo, A. Smith 5-57, Linton 5-29, Flutie 3-23.

PASSING—Oakland, Gannon 15-22-0-155. Buffalo, Flutie 19-41-3-210.

RECEIVING—Oakland, Jett 4-37, Brown 3-47, Wheatley 2-21, Ritchie 2-20, D. Walker 2-17, Mickens 1-12, Kaufman 1-1. Buffalo, Linton 5-20, K. Williams 4-63, Moulds 3-54, P. Price 2-30, Riemersma 2-26, Reed 2-23, Hicks 1-(minus 6).

MISSED FIELD GOAL ATTEMPTS—Oakland, Husted 32.

INTERCEPTIONS—Oakland, Allen 1-31, Turner 1-19, Gordon 1-7.

KICKOFF RETURNS—Oakland, Kaufman 2-50, Ashmore 1-0. Buffalo, K. Williams 4-66.

PUNT RETURNS—Oakland, Gordon 2-19. Buffalo, K. Williams 3-31.

SACKS—Oakland, Russell 1. Buffalo, Hansen 1, Wiley 1.

JAGUARS 24, BROWNS 7

Sunday, October 17

Cleveland	0	7	0	0— 7
Jacksonville	3	3	8	10—24

First Quarter
Jac.—FG, Hollis 20, 12:07.

Second Quarter
Cle.—Kirby 9 pass from Couch (Dawson kick), 2:39.
Jac.—FG, Hollis 36, 14:09.

Third Quarter
Jac.—Brady 8 pass from Fiedler (Brady pass from Fiedler), 13:13.

Fourth Quarter
Jac.—J. Stewart 2 run (Hollis kick), 9:06.
Jac.—FG, Hollis 24, 14:16.
Attendance—62,047.

	Cleveland	Jacksonville
First downs	16	21
Rushes-yards	28-113	33-103
Passing	130	222
Punt returns	4-18	2-21
Kickoff returns	4-82	1-12
Interception returns	0-0	0-0
Comp.-att.-int.	18-23-0	24-33-0
Sacked-yards lost	4-31	0-0
Punts	7-35	4-44
Fumbles-lost	2-1	0-0
Penalties-yards	6-55	7-55
Time of possession	27:36	32:24

INDIVIDUAL STATISTICS

RUSHING—Cleveland, Kirby 22-71, Couch 2-36, Edwards 2-5, Salaam 1-2, G. Jones 1-(minus 1). Jacksonville, J. Stewart 23-58, Fiedler 3-27, Howard 3-7, Brunell 2-8, Shelton 1-2, Banks 1-1.

PASSING—Cleveland, Couch 18-23-0-161. Jacksonville, Brunell 12-19-0-109, Fiedler 12-14-0-113.

RECEIVING—Cleveland, Chiaverini 5-45, Johnson 3-38, Edwards 3-35, Kirby 3-21, I. Smith 3-18, Dunn 1-4. Jacksonville, McCardell 7-76, J. Smith 6-62, Banks 5-40, J. Stewart 3-18, Brady 2-21, Shelton 1-11.

MISSED FIELD GOAL ATTEMPTS—None.

INTERCEPTIONS—None.

KICKOFF RETURNS—Cleveland, Powell 4-82. Jacksonville, Banks 1-12.

PUNT RETURNS—Cleveland, Johnson 4-18. Jacksonville, Barlow 2-21.

SACKS—Jacksonville, Hardy 1, Smeenge 1, Walker 1, Roberson 1.

EAGLES 20, BEARS 16

Sunday, October 17

Philadelphia	7	13	0	0—20
Chicago	3	3	7	3—16

First Quarter
Chi.—FG, Boniol 46, 7:41.
Phi.—Jells 57 pass from Pederson (N. Johnson kick), 9:26.

Second Quarter
Phi.—FG, N. Johnson 28, 0:42.
Chi.—FG, Boniol 40, 5:04.
Phi.—Broughton 3 pass from Pederson (N. Johnson kick), 9:37.
Phi.—FG, N. Johnson 27, 12:21.

Third Quarter
Chi.—M. Robinson 80 pass from McNown (Boniol kick), 2:19.

Fourth Quarter
Chi.—FG, Boniol 41, 7:20.
Attendance—66,944.

	Philadelphia	Chicago
First downs	19	17
Rushes-yards	26-99	29-113
Passing	217	239
Punt returns	2-17	2-13
Kickoff returns	5-141	5-121
Interception returns	2-63	0-0
Comp.-att.-int.	22-39-0	17-33-2
Sacked-yards lost	1-11	4-16
Punts	7-32	6-39
Fumbles-lost	3-2	1-0
Penalties-yards	6-53	9-85
Time of possession	28:24	31:36

INDIVIDUAL STATISTICS

RUSHING—Philadelphia, Staley 23-101, Pederson 2-(minus 2), C. Martin 1-0. Chicago, Enis 24-86, McNown 4-23, Milburn 1-4.

PASSING—Philadelphia, Pederson 22-38-0-228, Small 0-1-0-0. Chicago, McNown 17-33-2-255.

RECEIVING—Philadelphia, Small 6-50, Staley 4-37, C. Johnson 4-30, Jells 2-69, Broughton 2-18, C. Martin 2-1, Brown 1-12, Weaver 1-11. Chicago, Engram 6-59, M. Robinson 4-136, Bennett 3-22, Wetnight 2-19, Mayes 1-16, Allred 1-3.

MISSED FIELD GOAL ATTEMPTS—Chicago, Boniol 32.

INTERCEPTIONS—Philadelphia, Vincent 1-35, Moore 1-28.

KICKOFF RETURNS—Philadelphia, Rossum 3-122, Whiting 1-14, Broughton 1-5. Chicago, Milburn 5-121.

PUNT RETURNS—Philadelphia, Rossum 2-17. Chicago, Milburn 2-13.

SACKS—Philadelphia, Trotter 1, Jefferson 1, S. Martin 1, H. Thomas 1. Chicago, Flanigan 1.

STEELERS 17, BENGALS 3

Sunday, October 17

Pittsburgh	7	7	0	3—17
Cincinnati	3	0	0	0— 3

First Quarter
Pit.—Bettis 1 run (K. Brown kick), 8:43.
Cin.—FG, Pelfrey 37, 13:19.

Second Quarter
Pit.—Bettis 5 run (K. Brown kick), 8:25.

Fourth Quarter
Pit.—FG, K. Brown 43, 5:38.
Attendance—59,669.

	Pittsburgh	Cincinnati
First downs	18	14
Rushes-yards	37-130	20-84
Passing	125	177
Punt returns	4-30	6-50
Kickoff returns	2-36	3-49
Interception returns	2-2	0-0
Comp.-att.-int.	17-29-0	19-38-2
Sacked-yards lost	2-9	4-30
Punts	7-43	6-37
Fumbles-lost	0-0	2-1
Penalties-yards	7-41	8-60
Time of possession	31:48	28:12

INDIVIDUAL STATISTICS

RUSHING—Pittsburgh, Bettis 26-111, Stewart 7-1, Huntley 4-18. Cincinnati, Dillon 16-78, Smith 3-7, Basnight 1-(minus 1).

PASSING—Pittsburgh, Stewart 17-29-0-134. Cincinnati, Smith 19-38-2-207.
RECEIVING—Pittsburgh, Edwards 4-58, Blackwell 3-24, Ward 3-18, Hawkins 3-17, Huntley 2-8, Witman 1-5, Bettis 1-4. Cincinnati, Pickens 4-54, Griffin 4-46, Jackson 3-39, Dillon 2-24, Battaglia 2-15, Groce 2-11, Scott 1-11, McGee 1-7.
MISSED FIELD GOAL ATTEMPTS—Cincinnati, Pelfrey 41.
INTERCEPTIONS—Pittsburgh, Roye 1-2, Washington 1-0.
KICKOFF RETURNS—Pittsburgh, Blackwell 1-21, Edwards 1-15. Cincinnati, Williams 2-21, Mack 1-28.
PUNT RETURNS—Pittsburgh, Edwards 3-22, Hawkins 1-8. Cincinnati, Griffin 6-50.
SACKS—Pittsburgh, Roye 1, Emmons 1, Gildon 1, Oldham 1. Cincinnati, Bankston 1, von Oelhoffen 1.

BRONCOS 31, PACKERS 10

Sunday, October 17

Green Bay	0	3	7	0	—10
Denver	3	0	21	7	—31

First Quarter
Den.—FG, Elam 20, 11:34.
Second Quarter
G.B.—FG, Longwell 50, 13:18.
Third Quarter
Den.—McCaffrey 10 pass from Griese (Elam kick), 3:43.
G.B.—Levens 1 run (Longwell kick), 8:13.
Den.—McCaffrey 78 pass from Griese (Elam kick), 8:39.
Den.—Gary 1 run (Elam kick), 13:44.
Fourth Quarter
Den.—Griese 2 run (Elam kick), 3:54.
Attendance—73,352.

	Green Bay	Denver
First downs	5	28
Rushes-yards	11-21	51-151
Passing	112	363
Punt returns	2-11	6-44
Kickoff returns	6-113	2-30
Interception returns	1-60	3-31
Comp.-att.-int.	7-23-3	19-31-1
Sacked-yards lost	1-8	0-0
Punts	7-51	4-51
Fumbles-lost	1-0	4-0
Penalties-yards	9-51	9-64
Time of possession	14:46	45:14

INDIVIDUAL STATISTICS
RUSHING—Green Bay, Levens 10-12, Favre 1-9. Denver, Gary 37-124, Griffith 7-25, Griese 5-(minus 2), Avery 2-6.
PASSING—Green Bay, Favre 7-23-3-120. Denver, Griese 19-31-1-363.
RECEIVING—Green Bay, Schroeder 3-41, Bradford 1-54, T. Davis 1-16, Freeman 1-9, Levens 1-0. Denver, McCaffrey 5-116, R. Smith 4-57, Chamberlain 3-123, Gary 2-26, Carswell 2-17, Avery 1-11, Griffith 1-8, Clark 1-5.
MISSED FIELD GOAL ATTEMPTS—Denver, Elam 53.
INTERCEPTIONS—Green Bay, B. Williams 1-60. Denver, Carter 1-14, E. Brown 1-13, Crockett 1-4.
KICKOFF RETURNS—Green Bay, Howard 4-78, Mitchell 1-19, Parker 1-16. Denver, Avery 2-30.
PUNT RETURNS—Green Bay, Howard 2-11. Denver, McGriff 6-44.
SACKS—Denver, Williams 1.

TITANS 24, SAINTS 21

Sunday, October 17

Tennessee	0	0	7	17	—24
New Orleans	3	7	3	8	—21

First Quarter
N.O.—FG, Brien 24, 14:51.
Second Quarter
N.O.—Slutzker 10 pass from Tolliver (Brien kick), 10:33.
Third Quarter
Ten.—Neal 4 pass from O'Donnell (Del Greco kick), 7:02.
N.O.—FG, Brien 42, 13:04.
Fourth Quarter
Ten.—Dyson 11 pass from O'Donnell (Del Greco kick), 4:52.
Ten.—FG, Del Greco 19, 12:02.
Ten.—Mitchell 42 interception return (Del Greco kick), 12:20.
N.O.—L. Smith 4 pass from Tolliver (Bech pass from Tolliver), 14:15.
Attendance—51,875.

	Tennessee	New Orleans
First downs	15	22
Rushes-yards	35-165	21-55
Passing	113	354
Punt returns	1-6	4-40
Kickoff returns	4-61	5-119
Interception returns	2-59	2-8
Comp.-att.-int.	12-25-2	28-45-2
Sacked-yards lost	1-11	0-0
Punts	5-48	5-38
Fumbles-lost	1-1	4-2
Penalties-yards	8-75	13-103
Time of possession	30:00	30:00

INDIVIDUAL STATISTICS
RUSHING—Tennessee, E. George 28-155, O'Donnell 5-4, Dyson 1-3, Thomas 1-3. New Orleans, R. Williams 17-35, L. Smith 2-16, Tolliver 2-4.
PASSING—Tennessee, O'Donnell 12-25-2-124. New Orleans, Tolliver 28-45-2-354.
RECEIVING—Tennessee, Dyson 3-41, Neal 3-15, Sanders 2-16, Mason 1-31, E. George 1-12, Wycheck 1-5, Byrd 1-4. New Orleans, Kennison 7-94, Cleeland 7-84, Slutzker 4-63, Craver 4-22, Poole 2-25, L. Smith 2-9, Hastings 1-42, Bech 1-15.
MISSED FIELD GOAL ATTEMPTS—Tennessee, Del Greco 42.
INTERCEPTIONS—Tennessee, Mitchell 1-42, Fisk 1-17. New Orleans, Ambrose 1-6, Molden 1-2.
KICKOFF RETURNS—Tennessee, Mason 4-61. New Orleans, Philyaw 5-119.
PUNT RETURNS—Tennessee, Mason 1-6. New Orleans, Kennison 4-40.
SACKS—New Orleans, Wilson 1.

RAMS 41, FALCONS 13

Sunday, October 17

St. Louis	14	14	6	7	—41
Atlanta	0	10	0	3	—13

First Quarter
St.L.—Bruce 4 pass from Warner (Wilkins kick), 5:40.
St.L.—Faulk 6 run (Wilkins kick), 12:57.
Second Quarter
Atl.—Christian 13 pass from Chandler (Andersen kick), 3:41.
St.L.—Horne 101 kickoff return (Wilkins kick), 4:01.
St.L.—Wistrom 91 interception return (Wilkins kick), 13:18.
Atl.—FG, Andersen 19, 14:28.
Third Quarter
St.L.—FG, Wilkins 22, 2:18.
St.L.—FG, Wilkins 49, 7:34.
Fourth Quarter
St.L.—Holcombe 1 run (Wilkins kick), 4:34.
Atl.—FG, Andersen 25, 10:35.
Attendance—51,973.

	St. Louis	Atlanta
First downs	17	16
Rushes-yards	28-189	19-41
Passing	94	275
Punt returns	1-(-3)	2-13
Kickoff returns	4-126	7-157
Interception returns	2-105	0-0
Comp.-att.-int.	13-20-0	20-36-2
Sacked-yards lost	2-17	3-19
Punts	3-33	5-40
Fumbles-lost	2-1	1-1
Penalties-yards	8-45	10-88
Time of possession	28:48	31:12

INDIVIDUAL STATISTICS
RUSHING—St. Louis, Faulk 18-181, Holcombe 5-2, Lee 3-3, Warner 2-3. Atlanta, Oxendine 8-32, Hanspard 5-3, Christian 3-(minus 2), Chandler 2-(minus 1), Dwight 1-9.
PASSING—St. Louis, Warner 13-20-0-111. Atlanta, Chandler 10-18-1-168, Graziani 10-18-1-126.

RECEIVING—St. Louis, Bruce 6-48, Faulk 3-32, R. Williams 2-17, Holcombe 2-14. Atlanta, Mathis 7-75, R. Kelly 3-70, Christian 3-31, Dwight 2-56, Oxendine 2-20, Calloway 2-19, Hanspard 1-23.
MISSED FIELD GOAL ATTEMPTS—None.
INTERCEPTIONS—St. Louis, Wistrom 1-91, Jenkins 1-14.
KICKOFF RETURNS—St. Louis, Horne 2-127, Fletcher 1-0, Proehl 1-(minus 1). Atlanta, Dwight 7-157.
PUNT RETURNS—St. Louis, Hakim 1-(minus 3). Atlanta, Dwight 1-17, Oliver 1-(minus 4).
SACKS—St. Louis, Clemons 1, Zgonina 1, Agnew 0.5, Wistrom 0.5. Atlanta, Sauer 1, Archambeau 1.

PANTHERS 31, 49ERS 29
Sunday, October 17

Carolina	0	24	7	0	—31
San Francisco	6	10	0	13	—29

First Quarter
S.F.—FG, Richey 38, 5:41.
S.F.—FG, Richey 34, 9:23.
Second Quarter
Car.—FG, Kasay 19, 0:56.
S.F.—FG, Richey 40, 4:07.
Car.—Jeffers 7 pass from Beuerlein (Kasay kick), 7:55.
S.F.—Walker 27 interception return (Richey kick), 10:46.
Car.—Muhammad 22 pass from Beuerlein (Kasay kick), 11:50.
Car.—Walls 25 pass from Beuerlein (Kasay kick), 13:04.
Third Quarter
Car.—Jeffers 33 pass from Beuerlein (Kasay kick), 8:12.
Fourth Quarter
S.F.—McMillian 41 fumble return (Richey kick), 6:01.
S.F.—Rice 11 pass from Garcia (pass failed), 13:32.
Attendance—68,151.

	Carolina	San Francisco
First downs	18	23
Rushes-yards	27-101	24-124
Passing	282	209
Punt returns	0-0	4-14
Kickoff returns	4-127	4-85
Interception returns	0-0	3-52
Comp.-att.-int.	23-36-3	22-45-0
Sacked-yards lost	2-18	3-27
Punts	6-36	5-37
Fumbles-lost	1-1	4-3
Penalties-yards	6-57	3-25
Time of possession	32:11	27:49

INDIVIDUAL STATISTICS
RUSHING—Carolina, Biakabutuka 20-83, Lane 4-11, Floyd 2-3, Beuerlein 1-4. San Francisco, Garner 16-85, Garcia 4-24, Phillips 3-18, Beasley 1-(minus 3).
PASSING—Carolina, Beuerlein 23-36-3-300. San Francisco, Garcia 22-45-0-236.
RECEIVING—Carolina, Muhammad 6-96, Jeffers 6-93, Walls 5-70, Metcalf 3-19, Carruth 1-13, Floyd 1-9, Biakabutuka 1-0. San Francisco, Rice 5-59, Clark 5-43, Beasley 4-46, Stokes 3-53, Garner 3-24, Fann 1-6, Harris 1-5.
MISSED FIELD GOAL ATTEMPTS—None.
INTERCEPTIONS—San Francisco, Walker 1-27, McQuarters 1-25, Schulters 1-0.
KICKOFF RETURNS—Carolina, Bates 2-112, Kinchen 2-15. San Francisco, Phillips 3-53, Prioleau 1-32.
PUNT RETURNS—San Francisco, McQuarters 3-14, Givens 1-0.
SACKS—Carolina, Greene 1, Barrow 0.5, Wells 0.5, Gilbert 0.5, E. Jones 0.5. San Francisco, McDonald 1, Bryant 1.

LIONS 25, VIKINGS 23
Sunday, October 17

Minnesota	0	0	14	9	—23
Detroit	10	9	0	6	—25

First Quarter
Det.—Fair 41 interception return (Hanson kick), 7:43.
Det.—FG, Hanson 20, 13:57.
Second Quarter
Det.—FG, Hanson 49, 4:54.
Det.—FG, Hanson 29, 8:25.
Det.—FG, Hanson 30, 14:25.

Third Quarter
Min.—Carter 17 pass from George (Anderson kick), 2:56.
Min.—Moss 36 pass from George (Anderson kick), 5:44.
Fourth Quarter
Min.—Hoard 2 run (pass failed), 1:30.
Det.—FG, Hanson 47, 7:54.
Min.—FG, Anderson 26, 13:20.
Det.—FG, Hanson 48, 14:53.
Attendance—76,516.

	Minnesota	Detroit
First downs	17	19
Rushes-yards	19-60	24-118
Passing	267	189
Punt returns	2-18	2-15
Kickoff returns	8-143	5-106
Interception returns	0-0	2-43
Comp.-att.-int.	20-27-2	24-40-0
Sacked-yards lost	5-25	4-21
Punts	2-45	3-26
Fumbles-lost	3-3	0-0
Penalties-yards	3-61	7-50
Time of possession	24:44	35:16

INDIVIDUAL STATISTICS
RUSHING—Minnesota, Hoard 13-45, Smith 4-14, M. Williams 2-1. Detroit, Hill 11-67, Rivers 11-45, Frerotte 1-4, Crowell 1-2.
PASSING—Minnesota, Cunningham 10-15-1-78, George 10-12-1-214. Detroit, Frerotte 15-24-0-140, Batch 9-16-0-70.
RECEIVING—Minnesota, Moss 10-125, Carter 4-45, Reed 3-66, Glover 2-42, Mills 1-14. Detroit, Morton 8-74, Crowell 8-61, Sloan 3-30, Stablein 2-24, Hill 2-15, Rivers 1-6.
MISSED FIELD GOAL ATTEMPTS—Detroit, Hanson 49.
INTERCEPTIONS—Detroit, Fair 2-43.
KICKOFF RETURNS—Minnesota, Palmer 7-143, Jordan 1-0. Detroit, Fair 5-106.
PUNT RETURNS—Minnesota, Palmer 2-18. Detroit, Irvin 2-15.
SACKS—Minnesota, Griffith 1, Clemons 1, Randle 1, T. Williams 1. Detroit, Jones 1.5, Pringley 1, Scroggins 1, Kirschke 0.5, Team 1.

CHARGERS 13, SEAHAWKS 10
Sunday, October 17

Seattle	0	3	7	0	—10
San Diego	0	7	0	6	—13

Second Quarter
Sea.—FG, Peterson 40, 10:47.
S.D.—Means 5 run (Carney kick), 14:18.
Third Quarter
Sea.—Mili 1 pass from Kitna (Peterson kick), 9:23.
Fourth Quarter
S.D.—FG, Carney 28, 12:06.
S.D.—FG, Carney 41, 15:00.
Attendance—60,000.

	Seattle	San Diego
First downs	15	19
Rushes-yards	27-61	21-49
Passing	140	281
Punt returns	2-3	4-30
Kickoff returns	3-86	3-66
Interception returns	4-35	1-4
Comp.-att.-int.	17-29-1	27-45-4
Sacked-yards lost	3-11	2-15
Punts	8-41	5-47
Fumbles-lost	1-0	1-0
Penalties-yards	6-49	10-56
Time of possession	28:04	31:56

INDIVIDUAL STATISTICS
RUSHING—Seattle, Watters 21-54, R. Brown 4-7, Kitna 1-0, Strong 1-0. San Diego, Means 17-35, Bynum 2-16, Fletcher 2-(minus 2).
PASSING—Seattle, Kitna 17-29-1-151. San Diego, Kramer 27-44-4-296, Ricks 0-1-0-0.
RECEIVING—Seattle, Fauria 4-60, Mayes 4-32, Pritchard 3-24, Watters 2-12, R. Brown 2-9, Dawkins 1-13, Mili 1-1. San Diego, J. Graham 6-92, Fletcher 6-57, F. Jones 5-74, Stephens 3-22, Ricks 2-22, Means 2-7, Penn 1-16, McCrary 1-5, Pupunu 1-1.
MISSED FIELD GOAL ATTEMPTS—Seattle, Peterson 48. San Diego, Carney 42.

INTERCEPTIONS—Seattle, Walker 1-21, Kennedy 1-7, Canty 1-7, W. Williams 1-0. San Diego, Lewis 1-4.
KICKOFF RETURNS—Seattle, Green 3-86. San Diego, Bynum 3-66.
PUNT RETURNS—Seattle, Rogers 2-3. San Diego, Penn 3-30, Turner 1-0.
SACKS—Seattle, Parker 1, LaBounty 1. San Diego, Hand 1, Dumas 1, Simien 1.

INTERCEPTIONS—Washington, Bailey 3-51. Arizona, McCleskey 1-2, McKinnon 1-0.
KICKOFF RETURNS—Washington, Mitchell 3-59. Arizona, Bates 3-55.
PUNT RETURNS—Washington, Mitchell 2-(minus 5), Pounds 1-0. Arizona, McCleskey 1-0.
SACKS—Washington, Barber 1, Wilkinson 1. Arizona, Wadsworth 1.

REDSKINS 24, CARDINALS 10

Sunday, October 17

Washington	0	10	7	7	—24
Arizona	3	0	0	7	—10

First Quarter
Ariz.—FG, Jacke 44, 11:45.
Second Quarter
Was.—FG, Conway 36, 7:10.
Was.—Bailey 59 interception return (Conway kick), 11:27.
Third Quarter
Was.—Alexander 1 pass from B. Johnson (Conway kick), 13:40.
Fourth Quarter
Ariz.—Moore 10 pass from Da. Brown (Jacke kick), 8:01.
Was.—Hicks 14 run (Conway kick), 12:57.
Attendance—55,893.

	Washington	Arizona
First downs	24	15
Rushes-yards	34-167	20-67
Passing	243	207
Punt returns	3-(-5)	1-0
Kickoff returns	3-59	3-55
Interception returns	3-51	2-2
Comp.-att.-int.	24-40-2	20-43-3
Sacked-yards lost	1-5	2-9
Punts	6-40	7-44
Fumbles-lost	2-1	0-0
Penalties-yards	8-54	4-30
Time of possession	34:22	25:38

INDIVIDUAL STATISTICS
RUSHING—Washington, Davis 18-91, Hicks 9-45, Centers 3-18, B. Johnson 2-2, Mitchell 1-9, Westbrook 1-2. Arizona, Murrell 15-51, Pittman 2-15, Da. Brown 1-6, Makovicka 1-3, Boston 1-(minus 8).
PASSING—Washington, B. Johnson 24-40-2-248. Arizona, Plummer 12-23-2-99, Da. Brown 8-20-1-117.
RECEIVING—Washington, Connell 8-110, Centers 5-34, Westbrook 3-25, Fryar 2-20, Alexander 2-18, Sellers 1-17, Hicks 1-13, Mitchell 1-9, Davis 1-2. Arizona, Murrell 7-20, Sanders 3-68, Boston 3-44, Pittman 2-33, Makovicka 2-18, Cody 1-16, Moore 1-10, Hardy 1-7.
MISSED FIELD GOAL ATTEMPTS—Washington, Conway 52. Arizona, Jacke 42.

GIANTS 13, COWBOYS 10

Monday, October 18

Dallas	3	0	0	7	—10
N.Y. Giants	0	3	0	10	—13

First Quarter
Dal.—FG, Cunningham 38, 10:00.
Second Quarter
NYG—FG, Daluiso 27, 12:02.
Fourth Quarter
NYG—Barber 85 punt return (Daluiso kick), 7:10.
Dal.—E. Smith 2 run (Cunningham kick), 13:03.
NYG—FG, Daluiso 21, 14:59.
Attendance—78,204.

	Dallas	N.Y. Giants
First downs	14	13
Rushes-yards	25-24	30-75
Passing	250	153
Punt returns	1-10	5-123
Kickoff returns	3-48	2-35
Interception returns	0-0	1-3
Comp.-att.-int.	20-33-1	15-21-0
Sacked-yards lost	3-16	5-30
Punts	5-48	8-36
Fumbles-lost	1-0	2-0
Penalties-yards	10-59	9-75
Time of possession	31:19	28:41

INDIVIDUAL STATISTICS
RUSHING—Dallas, E. Smith 22-26, Warren 1-5, Aikman 1-0, Ismail 1-(minus 7). New York, Barber 10-35, Brown 10-23, Graham 7-10, Way 3-7.
PASSING—Dallas, Aikman 20-33-1-266. New York, Graham 15-21-0-183.
RECEIVING—Dallas, Mills 6-76, Ismail 4-74, Warren 3-40, McGarity 3-36, Tucker 2-25, LaFleur 2-15. New York, Barber 5-73, Toomer 5-44, Hilliard 2-41, Mitchell 2-14, Jurevicius 1-11.
MISSED FIELD GOAL ATTEMPTS—Dallas, Cunningham 48, 41.
INTERCEPTIONS—New York, Garnes 1-3.
KICKOFF RETURNS—Dallas, Mathis 2-36, Sanders 1-12. New York, Patten 2-35.
PUNT RETURNS—Dallas, Sanders 1-10. New York, Barber 5-123.
SACKS—Dallas, Hennings 1, Ellis 1, Hambrick 1, Spellman 1, Pittman 1. New York, Strahan 1, Harris 1, Widmer 1.

WEEK 7

RESULTS

Kansas City 35, BALTIMORE 8
DALLAS 38, Washington 20
Detroit 24, CAROLINA 9
Green Bay 31, SAN DIEGO 3
INDIANAPOLIS 31, Cincinnati 10
MIAMI 16, Philadelphia 13
MINNESOTA 40, San Francisco 16
NEW ENGLAND 24, Denver 23
N.Y. GIANTS 31, New Orleans 3
OAKLAND 24, N.Y. Jets 23
ST. LOUIS 34, Cleveland 3
SEATTLE 26, Buffalo 16
TAMPA BAY 6, Chicago 3
PITTSBURGH 13, Atlanta 9
Open date: Arizona, Jacksonville, Tennessee

STANDINGS

AFC EAST
	W	L	T	Pct.
Miami	5	1	0	.833
New England	5	2	0	.714
Indianapolis	4	2	0	.667
Buffalo	4	3	0	.571
N.Y. Jets	1	6	0	.143

AFC CENTRAL
	W	L	T	Pct.
Jacksonville	5	1	0	.833
Tennessee	5	1	0	.833
Pittsburgh	4	3	0	.571
Baltimore	2	4	0	.333
Cincinnati	1	6	0	.143
Cleveland	0	7	0	.000

AFC WEST
	W	L	T	Pct.
Kansas City	4	2	0	.667
San Diego	4	2	0	.667
Seattle	4	2	0	.667
Oakland	4	3	0	.571
Denver	2	5	0	.286

NFC EAST
	W	L	T	Pct.
Dallas	4	2	0	.667
Washington	4	2	0	.667
N.Y. Giants	4	3	0	.571
Arizona	2	4	0	.333
Philadelphia	2	5	0	.286

NFC CENTRAL
	W	L	T	Pct.
Detroit	4	2	0	.667
Green Bay	4	2	0	.667
Tampa Bay	3	3	0	.500
Chicago	3	4	0	.429
Minnesota	3	4	0	.429

NFC WEST
	W	L	T	Pct.
St. Louis	6	0	0	1.000
San Francisco	3	4	0	.429
Carolina	2	4	0	.333
New Orleans	1	5	0	.167
Atlanta	1	6	0	.143

HIGHLIGHTS

Hero of the week: The Detroit defense was terrific in the Lions' 24-9 victory over Carolina. Twelve times the Panthers ran a play from the 5-yard line or closer, and 12 times they were stopped—or pushed backwards. Carolina's net yardage for those dozen plays was minus-30.
Goat of the week: Chargers quarterback Erik Kramer threw two ugly interceptions in four failed trips into the Packers' red zone in a 31-3 home loss. With his team trailing 14-3 but poised on the Packers' 10 with 11 seconds left in the first half, Kramer wasted five seconds on an incomplete pass, and then froze on the final play—getting tackled on the 7-yard line rather than taking a shot at the end zone or setting up a field goal. Kramer was pulled in favor of Jim Harbaugh after his third interception.
Sub of the week: The backup duo of Jeff George and Leroy Hoard combined for four touchdowns in the Vikings' 40-16 win over the 49ers. George started because of Randall Cunningham's ineffective play, and Hoard replaced Robert Smith, who was out with an injury.
Comeback of the week: Even with a sore wrist, Rich Gannon threw three touchdown passes in the final 16 minutes to lead the Raiders to a 24-23 win over the Jets. His five-yard toss to James Jett with 17 seconds remaining capped the comeback, in which Oakland overcame a 17-point second-half deficit.
Blowout of the week: George's three touchdown passes and Hoard's 105 yards rushing paced the Vikings in their blowout win over San Francisco. The 49ers were decimated by injuries, and replacement quarterback Jeff Garcia struggled in situations in which Steve Young usually thrives.
Nail-biter of the week: The Patriots, who had lost 11 straight games against Denver, nearly lost another before holding on for a 24-23 win. New England led, 24-13, after three quarters when Brian Griese made things interesting, driving the Broncos 85 yards in 12 plays before capping the drive with a seven-yard quarterback sneak. Griese then completed six passes in the next series, which ended with a 30-yard field goal by Jason Elam with 6:10 left. Pats cornerback Ty Law halted a third Broncos drive with a hard hit on Ed McCaffrey, setting the stage for Elam, whose 59-yard attempt with 1:37 left fell short.
Hit of the week: Steelers linebackers Earl Holmes and Levon Kirkland stopped Falcons running back Ken Oxendine on fourth-and-goal from the 2-yard line with under two minutes left, preserving a 13-9 Pittsburgh win on Monday night. The stand was especially meaningful because the 1974 Steelers team, known for its stingy defense, was honored at Three Rivers Stadium before the game.
Oddity of the week: The Patriots actually beat the Broncos, something that had not happened since September 29, 1980.
Top rusher: Marshall Faulk's toughest battle Sunday wasn't with the Browns' defense, but with the effects of food poisoning that kept him hospitalized the night before the game. Faulk fought through the flu-like symptoms and beat up the 0-7 Browns for 133 yards on 16 carries. He had one touchdown, and put the Rams in position for two more with runs to the 1-yard line.
Top passer: Gannon completed 26 passes in 51 tries for 352 yards and two touchdowns in Oakland's 24-23 win over the Jets.
Top receiver: Tim Brown caught 11 of Gannon's passes for a career-best 190 yards and scored one TD. Brown was the Raiders' go-to receiver all day, setting up the game-winning score with a 36-yard catch to the Jets' 5-yard line with 39 seconds remaining.
Notes: The Browns' only bright spot in a 34-3 trouncing by the Rams was a 40-yard run by Tim Couch, which broke a franchise record for the longest run by a quarterback. ... The crowd of 68,274 at San Diego's Qualcomm Stadium was the largest during the regular season in Chargers' history. ... Kansas City moved to 4-0 in Thursday night games with a 35-8 win against the Ravens. ... Jon Kitna completed 17 of 30 passes for 276 yards with no interceptions and Todd Peterson kicked four field goals in the Seahawks' 26-16 victory over

Buffalo. ... For the first time in 19 years, the 49ers were riding a three-game losing streak. ... Kent Graham made a strong bid to keep the Giants' starting quarterback job, rushing for a touchdown and completing 19 of 29 passes for 239 yards in a 31-3 victory over New Orleans. ... Rookie kicker Martin "Automatica" Gramatica accounted for all six of the Buccaneers' points with two field goals, but it was enough to outscore the Bears' anemic offense, 6-3. ... NFL receptions leader Marvin Harrison caught eight passes for 156 yards in helping the Colts beat the Bengals 31-10.

Quote of the week: Dolphins linebacker Zach Thomas, on his team's 16-13 squeaker over the Eagles, the Dolphins' third straight win by less than three points: "My family doesn't have a history of going bald. But after all these close games, I'm afraid my hair is going to start thinning out. Our games will do it to you."

GAME SUMMARIES

CHIEFS 35, RAVENS 8
Thursday, October 21

Kansas City	0	7	7	21	35
Baltimore	0	0	0	8	8

Second Quarter
K.C.—Gonzalez 11 pass from Grbac (Stoyanovich kick), 2:59.
Third Quarter
K.C.—Hasty 56 interception return (Stoyanovich kick), 9:50.
Fourth Quarter
K.C.—Gonzalez 22 pass from Grbac (Stoyanovich kick), 2:23.
K.C.—Tongue 38 interception return (Stoyanovich kick), 4:25.
Bal.—Rhett 2 run (Evans run), 10:55.
K.C.—Morris 1 run (Stoyanovich kick), 12:30.
Attendance—68,771.

	Kansas City	Baltimore
First downs	12	18
Rushes-yards	35-112	27-105
Passing	106	172
Punt returns	4-28	3-23
Kickoff returns	2-29	6-88
Interception returns	3-108	0-0
Comp.-att.-int.	9-16-0	23-51-3
Sacked-yards lost	1-6	0-0
Punts	8-45	7-41
Fumbles-lost	0-0	0-0
Penalties-yards	9-113	9-81
Time of possession	26:12	33:48

INDIVIDUAL STATISTICS
RUSHING—Kansas City, Morris 16-70, Bennett 12-40, Shehee 5-(minus 5), Grbac 2-7. Baltimore, Rhett 19-59, Case 5-38, Banks 2-6, J. Lewis 1-2.
PASSING—Kansas City, Grbac 9-16-0-112. Baltimore, Case 15-37-3-103, Banks 8-14-0-69.
RECEIVING—Kansas City, Gonzalez 4-54, Lockett 2-31, Horn 1-17, Johnson 1-6, Richardson 1-4. Baltimore, Armour 6-70, Evans 4-13, Ismail 3-25, Pierce 2-35, Ofodile 2-13, Rhett 2-7, DeLong 2-5, J. Lewis 2-4.
MISSED FIELD GOAL ATTEMPTS—Kansas City, Stoyanovich 42. Baltimore, Stover 37.
INTERCEPTIONS—Kansas City, Hasty 2-59, Edwards 1-11.
KICKOFF RETURNS—Kansas City, Vanover 1-29, Lockett 1-0. Baltimore, Harris 5-72, Ismail 1-16.
PUNT RETURNS—Kansas City, Vanover 4-28. Baltimore, J. Lewis 3-23.
SACKS—Baltimore, Boulware 1.

COWBOYS 38, REDSKINS 20
Sunday, October 24

Washington	0	10	10	0	20
Dallas	10	7	7	14	38

First Quarter
Dal.—Ismail 13 pass from Aikman (Cunningham kick), 7:52.
Dal.—FG, Cunningham 32, 12:25.
Second Quarter
Dal.—E. Smith 1 run (Cunningham kick), 6:01.
Was.—Sellers 33 pass from B. Johnson (Conway kick), 8:08.
Was.—FG, Conway 36, 14:06.
Third Quarter
Was.—FG, Conway 24, 4:25.
Dal.—LaFleur 4 pass from Aikman (Cunningham kick), 10:19.
Was.—Connell 44 pass from B. Johnson (Conway kick), 12:44.
Fourth Quarter
Dal.—Aikman 1 run (Cunningham kick), 4:10.
Dal.—Sanders 70 punt return (Cunningham kick), 5:57.
Attendance—64,377.

	Washington	Dallas
First downs	14	23
Rushes-yards	16-61	34-108
Passing	211	244
Punt returns	3-42	4-81
Kickoff returns	6-116	5-112
Interception returns	0-0	0-0
Comp.-att.-int.	23-35-0	20-32-0
Sacked-yards lost	1-7	0-0
Punts	6-38	4-53
Fumbles-lost	1-0	1-1
Penalties-yards	8-70	9-97
Time of possession	25:28	34:32

INDIVIDUAL STATISTICS
RUSHING—Washington, Davis 14-62, Centers 1-0, B. Johnson 1-(minus 1). Dallas, E. Smith 24-80, Warren 8-8, Ismail 1-19, Aikman 1-1.
PASSING—Washington, B. Johnson 23-35-0-218. Dallas, Aikman 20-32-0-244.
RECEIVING—Washington, Davis 5-20, Westbrook 3-38, Alexander 3-24, Centers 3-20, Mitchell 3-17, Connell 2-52, Sellers 2-39, Fryar 2-8. Dallas, Ismail 6-76, LaFleur 4-34, Mills 3-24, Warren 2-21, Tucker 1-52, Ogden 1-25, Lester 1-6, Lucky 1-5, E. Smith 1-1.
MISSED FIELD GOAL ATTEMPTS—None.
INTERCEPTIONS—None.
KICKOFF RETURNS—Washington, Mitchell 6-116. Dallas, Mathis 4-99, Ogden 1-13.
PUNT RETURNS—Washington, Mitchell 3-42. Dallas, Sanders 3-78, Ogden 1-3.
SACKS—Dallas, Noble 1.

COLTS 31, BENGALS 10
Sunday, October 24

Cincinnati	0	3	0	7	10
Indianapolis	7	17	0	7	31

First Quarter
Ind.—Harrison 56 pass from Manning (Vanderjagt kick), 3:28.
Second Quarter
Ind.—James 1 run (Vanderjagt kick), 5:27.
Ind.—James 2 run (Vanderjagt kick), 10:19.
Ind.—FG, Vanderjagt 22, 13:07.
Cin.—FG, Pelfrey 32, 14:45.
Fourth Quarter
Ind.—Dilger 10 pass from Manning (Vanderjagt kick), 5:43.
Cin.—Scott 10 pass from Blake (Pelfrey kick), 9:47.
Attendance—55,996.

	Cincinnati	Indianapolis
First downs	12	18
Rushes-yards	26-105	28-57
Passing	149	278
Punt returns	4-53	4-28
Kickoff returns	6-157	3-44
Interception returns	1-5	0-0
Comp.-att.-int.	17-31-0	17-33-1
Sacked-yards lost	5-25	1-6
Punts	8-35	5-40
Fumbles-lost	0-0	0-0
Penalties-yards	10-99	6-45
Time of possession	28:09	31:51

INDIVIDUAL STATISTICS

RUSHING—Cincinnati, Basnight 11-26, Dillon 6-7, Smith 4-42, Williams 4-18, Blake 1-12. Indianapolis, James 26-52, Manning 2-5.

PASSING—Cincinnati, Smith 12-24-0-122, Blake 5-7-0-52. Indianapolis, Manning 17-33-1-284.

RECEIVING—Cincinnati, Scott 5-49, Pickens 3-46, Jackson 2-27, Williams 2-21, Battaglia 2-15, Griffin 1-7, Dillon 1-6, Groce 1-3. Indianapolis, Harrison 8-156, Wilkins 3-54, Dilger 3-25, Pollard 2-16, James 1-33.

MISSED FIELD GOAL ATTEMPTS—Indianapolis, Vanderjagt 37.

INTERCEPTIONS—Cincinnati, Bell 1-5.

KICKOFF RETURNS—Cincinnati, Mack 6-157. Indianapolis, Muhammad 2-41, Shields 1-3.

PUNT RETURNS—Cincinnati, Griffin 4-53. Indianapolis, Wilkins 4-28.

SACKS—Cincinnati, Bankston 1. Indianapolis, Bratzke 2, E. Johnson 2, Peterson 1.

VIKINGS 40, 49ERS 16

Sunday, October 24

San Francisco	3	10	3	0	—16
Minnesota	7	17	7	9	—40

First Quarter
Min.—Hoard 1 run (Anderson kick), 4:30.
S.F.—FG, Richey 22, 12:05.

Second Quarter
S.F.—Walker 71 fumble return (Richey kick), 0:18.
Min.—Hatchette 80 pass from George (Anderson kick), 0:35.
S.F.—FG, Richey 31, 7:22.
Min.—Jordan 7 pass from George (Anderson kick), 13:54.
Min.—FG, Anderson 33, 15:00.

Third Quarter
S.F.—FG, Richey 26, 6:58.
Min.—M. Williams 9 run (Anderson kick), 12:06.

Fourth Quarter
Min.—Carter 2 pass from George (Anderson kick), 2:55.
Min.—Safety, San Francisco called for offensive holding in end zone, 7:40.
Attendance—64,109.

	San Fran.	Minnesota
First downs	14	25
Rushes-yards	21-82	31-155
Passing	178	240
Punt returns	0-0	3-12
Kickoff returns	5-102	2-66
Interception returns	1-14	2-6
Comp.-att.-int.	18-35-2	15-28-1
Sacked-yards lost	3-23	1-10
Punts	4-34	2-61
Fumbles-lost	2-0	2-1
Penalties-yards	15-104	4-30
Time of possession	29:59	30:01

INDIVIDUAL STATISTICS

RUSHING—San Francisco, Garner 10-27, Garcia 5-35, Beasley 5-20, Phillips 1-0. Minnesota, Hoard 17-105, M. Williams 6-25, Culpepper 3-6, Palmer 2-7, Morrow 2-1, Moss 1-11.

PASSING—San Francisco, Garcia 14-31-2-188, Stenstrom 4-4-0-13. Minnesota, George 15-28-1-250.

RECEIVING—San Francisco, Rice 5-45, Phillips 3-49, Clark 3-27, Stokes 2-27, Garner 2-13, Harris 1-33, Beasley 1-4, Cline 1-3. Minnesota, Carter 7-84, Reed 3-42, Hatchette 2-88, Moss 1-24, Jordan 1-7, Glover 1-5.

MISSED FIELD GOAL ATTEMPTS—Minnesota, Anderson 47.

INTERCEPTIONS—San Francisco, Schulters 1-14. Minnesota, Thomas 1-5, Randle 1-1.

KICKOFF RETURNS—San Francisco, Phillips 5-102. Minnesota, Palmer 2-66.

PUNT RETURNS—Minnesota, Palmer 3-12.

SACKS—San Francisco, B. Young 1. Minnesota, E. McDaniel 2, Hitchcock 1.

PATRIOTS 24, BRONCOS 23

Sunday, October 24

Denver	0	10	3	10	—23
New England	10	7	7	0	—24

First Quarter
N.E.—Faulk 15 run (Vinatieri kick), 7:33.
N.E.—FG, Vinatieri 28, 12:23.

Second Quarter
Den.—FG, Elam 40, 3:49.
Den.—R. Smith 28 pass from Griese (Elam kick), 7:08.
N.E.—Allen 1 run (Vinatieri kick), 14:34.

Third Quarter
Den.—FG, Elam 28, 3:27.
N.E.—Allen 1 run (Vinatieri kick), 6:35.

Fourth Quarter
Den.—Griese 7 run (Elam kick), 0:45.
Den.—FG, Elam 30, 8:50.
Attendance—60,011.

	Denver	New England
First downs	23	15
Rushes-yards	27-133	28-133
Passing	309	192
Punt returns	3-25	4-70
Kickoff returns	5-107	6-140
Interception returns	0-0	0-0
Comp.-att.-int.	25-38-0	13-22-0
Sacked-yards lost	3-7	4-22
Punts	5-53	7-46
Fumbles-lost	1-0	0-0
Penalties-yards	10-70	5-34
Time of possession	31:39	28:21

INDIVIDUAL STATISTICS

RUSHING—Denver, Gary 19-90, Griese 3-23, Avery 2-13, Griffith 2-7, Rouen 1-0. New England, Allen 17-106, Faulk 5-24, Bledsoe 3-(minus 2), Warren 2-(minus 1), T. Carter 1-6.

PASSING—Denver, Griese 25-38-0-316. New England, Bledsoe 13-22-0-214.

RECEIVING—Denver, McCaffrey 5-111, Chamberlain 4-46, Gary 4-39, R. Smith 3-44, Carswell 3-31, Avery 3-13, Cooper 2-21, B. Miller 1-11. New England, Coates 3-40, Glenn 2-80, T. Carter 2-31, Warren 2-21, Jefferson 2-11, Brisby 1-27, Faulk 1-4.

MISSED FIELD GOAL ATTEMPTS—Denver, Elam 59.

INTERCEPTIONS—None.

KICKOFF RETURNS—Denver, Avery 5-107. New England, Faulk 6-140.

PUNT RETURNS—Denver, Coghill 3-25. New England, Faulk 4-70.

SACKS—Denver, E. Brown 1, Hasselbach 1, Bowens 1, N. Smith 1. New England, Slade 2, Eaton 1.

LIONS 24, PANTHERS 9

Sunday, October 24

Detroit	0	10	14	0	—24
Carolina	3	3	3	0	— 9

First Quarter
Car.—FG, Kasay 21, 8:11.

Second Quarter
Det.—Irvin 1 run (Hanson kick), 5:27.
Det.—FG, Hanson 29, 10:13.
Car.—FG, Kasay 30, 14:40.

Third Quarter
Car.—FG, Kasay 23, 3:41.
Det.—Sloan 22 pass from Batch (Hanson kick), 7:52.
Det.—Stablein 3 pass from Batch (Hanson kick), 11:47.
Attendance—64,322.

	Detroit	Carolina
First downs	20	22
Rushes-yards	27-90	21-61
Passing	210	259
Punt returns	0-0	1-(-1)
Kickoff returns	4-130	3-50
Interception returns	1-0	1-4
Comp.-att.-int.	16-27-1	26-47-1
Sacked-yards lost	0-0	4-40
Punts	3-38	4-44
Fumbles-lost	2-1	2-1
Penalties-yards	3-21	9-55
Time of possession	26:40	33:20

INDIVIDUAL STATISTICS

RUSHING—Detroit, Hill 16-70, Batch 5-13, Irvin 5-9, Rivers 1-(minus 2). Carolina, Biakabutuka 9-10, Lane 6-20, Floyd 3-(minus 2), Beuerlein 2-16, Metcalf 1-17.

PASSING—Detroit, Batch 16-27-1-210. Carolina, Beuerlein 26-47-1-299.

1999 REVIEW Week 7

– 155 –

RECEIVING—Detroit, Morton 5-66, Crowell 3-45, Sloan 2-39, Irvin 2-28, Stablein 2-7, Schlesinger 1-20, Hill 1-5. Carolina, Walls 7-83, Jeffers 5-60, Muhammad 4-62, Johnson 4-41, Biakabutuka 2-35, Lane 2-3, Kinchen 1-8, Hayes 1-7.
MISSED FIELD GOAL ATTEMPTS—None.
INTERCEPTIONS—Detroit, Carrier 1-0. Carolina, Gilbert 1-4.
KICKOFF RETURNS—Detroit, Fair 4-130. Carolina, Bates 3-50.
PUNT RETURNS—Carolina, Metcalf 1-(minus 1).
SACKS—Detroit, Porcher 1.5, Rice 1, Jones 1, Claiborne 0.5.

GIANTS 31, SAINTS 3

Sunday, October 24

New Orleans	3	0	0	0—	3
N.Y. Giants	7	17	7	0—	31

First Quarter
NYG—Graham 6 run (Blanchard kick), 11:16.
N.O.—FG, Brien 25, 15:00.

Second Quarter
NYG—FG, Blanchard 41, 4:12.
NYG—Toomer 27 pass from Graham (Blanchard kick), 13:57.
NYG—Jurevicius 53 pass from Graham (Blanchard kick), 15:00.

Third Quarter
NYG—Montgomery 12 run (Blanchard kick), 10:53.
Attendance—77,982.

	New Orleans	N.Y. Giants
First downs	12	19
Rushes-yards	27-107	37-106
Passing	163	215
Punt returns	3-31	3-25
Kickoff returns	5-112	1-32
Interception returns	1-0	3-44
Comp.-att.-int.	14-35-3	19-29-1
Sacked-yards lost	2-13	4-24
Punts	6-39	6-40
Fumbles-lost	1-0	2-1
Penalties-yards	5-40	7-49
Time of possession	27:49	32:11

INDIVIDUAL STATISTICS
RUSHING—New Orleans, R. Williams 24-111, Powell 1-1, Wuerffel 1-0, L. Smith 1-(minus 5). New York, Johnson 18-36, Montgomery 14-28, Graham 3-9, Hilliard 1-24, Barber 1-9.
PASSING—New Orleans, Tolliver 14-33-3-176, L. Smith 0-1-0-0, Wuerffel 0-1-0-0. New York, Graham 19-29-1-239.
RECEIVING—New Orleans, Kennison 5-62, Craver 3-51, Wilcox 2-30, Dawsey 2-18, Hastings 1-24, R. Williams 1-(minus 9). New York, Mitchell 5-69, Toomer 3-59, Hilliard 3-17, Jurevicius 2-63, Johnson 2-16, Way 2-6, Barber 1-7, Cross 1-2.
MISSED FIELD GOAL ATTEMPTS—None.
INTERCEPTIONS—New Orleans, Kei. Mitchell 1-0. New York, Armstead 1-31, Ellsworth 1-13, Phillips 1-0.
KICKOFF RETURNS—New Orleans, Philyaw 3-57, Davis 2-55. New York, Levingston 1-32.
PUNT RETURNS—New Orleans, Kennison 3-31. New York, Barber 3-25.
SACKS—New Orleans, Wilson 2, Glover 1, Whitehead 0.5, B. Smith 0.5. New York, Jones 1, K. Hamilton 0.5, Strahan 0.5.

BUCCANEERS 6, BEARS 3

Sunday, October 24

Chicago	0	0	0	3—	3
Tampa Bay	3	3	0	0—	6

First Quarter
T.B.—FG, Gramatica 49, 4:13.

Second Quarter
T.B.—FG, Gramatica 34, 11:58.

Fourth Quarter
Chi.—FG, Boniol 28, 12:36.
Attendance—65,283.

	Chicago	Tampa Bay
First downs	15	11
Rushes-yards	24-86	28-124
Passing	186	101
Punt returns	6-34	3-40
Kickoff returns	3-80	2-40
Interception returns	0-0	2-13

	Chicago	Tampa Bay
Comp.-att.-int.	19-45-2	16-27-0
Sacked-yards lost	2-13	2-20
Punts	8-40	7-41
Fumbles-lost	1-0	1-0
Penalties-yards	6-55	4-30
Time of possession	29:03	30:57

INDIVIDUAL STATISTICS
RUSHING—Chicago, Enis 20-69, McNown 3-10, Brooks 1-7. Tampa Bay, Alstott 14-72, Dunn 9-21, Dilfer 5-31.
PASSING—Chicago, McNown 9-23-1-82, Miller 10-22-1-117. Tampa Bay, Dilfer 16-27-0-121.
RECEIVING—Chicago, M. Robinson 5-80, Engram 4-64, Brooks 3-23, Wetnight 3-20, Enis 3-10, Allred 1-2. Tampa Bay, Anthony 5-47, Dunn 5-27, McDonald 3-17, Green 1-14, Williams 1-9, Moore 1-7.
MISSED FIELD GOAL ATTEMPTS—Chicago, Boniol 44. Tampa Bay, Gramatica 43, 39.
INTERCEPTIONS—Tampa Bay, Brooks 2-13.
KICKOFF RETURNS—Chicago, Milburn 3-80. Tampa Bay, Murphy 1-21, Alstott 1-19.
PUNT RETURNS—Chicago, Milburn 6-34. Tampa Bay, Green 2-40, Williams 1-0.
SACKS—Chicago, B. Robinson 1, Wells 0.5, McDonald 0.5. Tampa Bay, Culpepper 1, Sapp 1.

DOLPHINS 16, EAGLES 13

Sunday, October 24

Philadelphia	0	3	7	3—	13
Miami	10	3	0	3—	16

First Quarter
Mia.—FG, Mare 37, 8:55.
Mia.—Johnson 18 run (Mare kick), 13:56.

Second Quarter
Phi.—FG, Akers 53, 3:50.
Mia.—FG, Mare 37, 8:34.

Third Quarter
Phi.—Dawkins 67 interception return (N. Johnson kick), 11:13.

Fourth Quarter
Mia.—FG, Mare 53, 0:05.
Phi.—FG, N. Johnson 44, 8:52.
Attendance—73,975.

	Philadelphia	Miami
First downs	11	15
Rushes-yards	22-93	39-149
Passing	82	134
Punt returns	2-54	4-49
Kickoff returns	0-0	3-75
Interception returns	1-67	1-5
Comp.-att.-int.	13-25-1	15-21-1
Sacked-yards lost	4-26	1-8
Punts	5-48	4-43
Fumbles-lost	1-1	1-1
Penalties-yards	3-19	7-54
Time of possession	23:55	36:05

INDIVIDUAL STATISTICS
RUSHING—Philadelphia, Staley 19-73, Pederson 3-20. Miami, Collins 26-97, Huard 6-12, Johnson 5-35, Pritchett 2-5.
PASSING—Philadelphia, Pederson 13-25-1-108. Miami, Huard 15-21-1-142.
RECEIVING—Philadelphia, C. Johnson 4-59, Weaver 4-27, Staley 2-1, Small 1-10, Jells 1-8, Turner 1-3. Miami, McDuffie 4-41, Drayton 4-38, Martin 3-26, Gadsden 1-17, Goodwin 1-14, Collins 1-6, Pritchett 1-0.
MISSED FIELD GOAL ATTEMPTS—Philadelphia, N. Johnson 42.
INTERCEPTIONS—Philadelphia, Dawkins 1-67. Miami, Rodgers 1-5.
KICKOFF RETURNS—Miami, Marion 3-75.
PUNT RETURNS—Philadelphia, Rossum 2-54. Miami, Jacquet 3-43, Preston 1-6.
SACKS—Philadelphia, Jefferson 1. Miami, Bromell 1.5, Marion 1, Taylor 1, Armstrong 0.5.

RAMS 34, BROWNS 3

Sunday, October 24

Cleveland	3	0	0	0—	3
St. Louis	14	7	3	10—	34

First Quarter
St.L.—R. Williams 1 pass from Warner (Wilkins kick), 6:26.
St.L.—Bruce 4 pass from Warner (Wilkins kick), 8:11.
Cle.—FG, Dawson 47, 14:43.

Second Quarter
St.L.—R. Williams 1 pass from Warner (Wilkins kick), 4:01.

Third Quarter
St.L.—FG, Wilkins 28, 11:47.

Fourth Quarter
St.L.—Faulk 33 run (Wilkins kick), 0:10.
St.L.—FG, Wilkins 36, 10:54.
Attendance—65,866.

	Cleveland	St. Louis
First downs	13	27
Rushes-yards	15-94	29-211
Passing	178	225
Punt returns	1-13	3-15
Kickoff returns	5-140	2-48
Interception returns	0-0	2-26
Comp.-att.-int.	22-40-2	27-34-0
Sacked-yards lost	1-7	2-3
Punts	5-49	3-52
Fumbles-lost	1-1	1-0
Penalties-yards	6-30	4-29
Time of possession	23:14	36:46

INDIVIDUAL STATISTICS
RUSHING—Cleveland, Abdul-Jabbar 6-27, Kirby 6-12, Couch 2-50, Shepherd 1-5. St. Louis, Faulk 16-133, Watson 9-69, Germaine 2-(minus 2), Bruce 1-6, Holt 1-5.
PASSING—Cleveland, Couch 22-40-2-185. St. Louis, Warner 23-29-0-203, Justin 4-5-0-25.
RECEIVING—Cleveland, Shepherd 6-85, Kirby 6-18, Johnson 3-35, I. Smith 3-31, Abdul-Jabbar 2-8, Edwards 2-8. St. Louis, Faulk 9-67, R. Williams 5-50, Proehl 5-29, Bruce 4-44, Holt 2-24, Hodgins 2-14.
MISSED FIELD GOAL ATTEMPTS—None.
INTERCEPTIONS—St. Louis, Lyght 1-15, Coady 1-11.
KICKOFF RETURNS—Cleveland, Powell 4-120, Dunn 1-20. St. Louis, Carpenter 2-48.
PUNT RETURNS—Cleveland, Dunn 1-13. St. Louis, Holt 3-15.
SACKS—Cleveland, A. Miller 1, Barker 1. St. Louis, McCleon 0.5, Zgonina 0.5.

PACKERS 31, CHARGERS 3
Sunday, October 24

Green Bay	7	7	14	3—31
San Diego	0	3	0	0— 3

First Quarter
G.B.—Henderson 7 pass from Favre (Longwell kick), 14:39.

Second Quarter
G.B.—Levens 6 run (Longwell kick), 1:41.
S.D.—FG, Carney 28, 10:59.

Third Quarter
G.B.—Schroeder 6 pass from Favre (Longwell kick), 3:12.
G.B.—Freeman 3 pass from Favre (Longwell kick), 14:57.

Fourth Quarter
G.B.—FG, Longwell 46, 13:06.
Attendance—68,274.

	Green Bay	San Diego
First downs	19	21
Rushes-yards	28-129	27-76
Passing	166	227
Punt returns	0-0	3-19
Kickoff returns	2-65	6-146
Interception returns	6-0	1-0
Comp.-att.-int.	12-25-1	25-54-6
Sacked-yards lost	1-7	3-12
Punts	4-40	3-35
Fumbles-lost	1-1	2-0
Penalties-yards	5-45	6-73
Time of possession	25:50	34:10

INDIVIDUAL STATISTICS
RUSHING—Green Bay, Levens 21-77, Parker 4-35, Hasselbeck 2-12, Mitchell 1-5. San Diego, Means 12-28, Bynum 6-30, Stephens 4-10, Kramer 3-3, Ricks 1-4, Fletcher 1-1.

PASSING—Green Bay, Favre 12-22-1-173, Hasselbeck 0-3-0-0. San Diego, Kramer 18-36-3-161, Harbaugh 7-18-3-78.
RECEIVING—Green Bay, Freeman 5-82, Schroeder 4-45, Levens 1-25, T. Davis 1-14, Henderson 1-7. San Diego, F. Jones 7-87, Ricks 6-42, Fletcher 3-32, J. Graham 2-39, Penn 2-23, Stephens 2-7, Bynum 1-8, Davis 1-2, McCrary 1-(minus 1).
MISSED FIELD GOAL ATTEMPTS—None.
INTERCEPTIONS—Green Bay, T. Williams 2-0, Edwards 1-0, M. McKenzie 1-0, Sharper 1-0, Vinson 1-0. San Diego, Spencer 1-0.
KICKOFF RETURNS—Green Bay, Parker 1-36, Mitchell 1-29. San Diego, Stephens 3-78, Bynum 3-68.
PUNT RETURNS—San Diego, Penn 3-19.
SACKS—Green Bay, K. McKenzie 1, Holliday 1, Lyon 0.5, Smith 0.5. San Diego, Dixon 1.

RAIDERS 24, JETS 23
Sunday, October 24

N.Y. Jets	0	10	10	3—23
Oakland	3	0	7	14—24

First Quarter
Oak.—FG, Husted 25, 6:41.

Second Quarter
NYJ—FG, Hall 32, 1:31.
NYJ—Mirer 9 run (Hall kick), 5:09.

Third Quarter
NYJ—E. Green 2 pass from Mirer (Hall kick), 5:11.
NYJ—FG, Hall 37, 11:32.
Oak.—Brown 45 pass from Gannon (Husted kick), 14:31.

Fourth Quarter
Oak.—Crockett 3 run (Husted kick), 6:37.
NYJ—FG, Hall 43, 13:05.
Oak.—Jett 5 pass from Gannon (Husted kick), 14:34.
Attendance—47,326.

	N.Y. Jets	Oakland
First downs	14	24
Rushes-yards	34-177	23-117
Passing	147	344
Punt returns	1-0	3-9
Kickoff returns	5-112	4-103
Interception returns	1-6	2-0
Comp.-att.-int.	13-22-2	26-51-1
Sacked-yards lost	2-11	2-8
Punts	5-46	4-38
Fumbles-lost	1-0	3-3
Penalties-yards	7-70	2-20
Time of possession	30:37	29:23

INDIVIDUAL STATISTICS
RUSHING—New York, Martin 26-123, Mirer 6-14, Stone 1-36, Anderson 1-4. Oakland, Wheatley 8-18, Kaufman 7-33, Gannon 5-60, Crockett 3-6.
PASSING—New York, Mirer 13-22-2-158. Oakland, Gannon 26-51-1-352.
RECEIVING—New York, K. Johnson 5-72, Chrebet 2-49, Martin 2-14, E. Green 2-7, Anderson 1-9, Parmalee 1-7. Oakland, Brown 11-190, Jett 4-58, Mickens 4-42, Dudley 2-36, Ritchie 2-9, Brigham 1-9, Jordan 1-9, Wheatley 1-(minus 1).
MISSED FIELD GOAL ATTEMPTS—None.
INTERCEPTIONS—New York, Glenn 1-6. Oakland, Allen 1-0, M. Walker 1-0.
KICKOFF RETURNS—New York, Stone 3-74, Farmer 1-20, Glenn 1-18. Oakland, Kaufman 3-77, Jordan 1-26.
PUNT RETURNS—New York, Ward 1-0. Oakland, Gordon 3-9.
SACKS—New York, Lewis 1, Stoutmire 1. Oakland, Bryant 2.

SEAHAWKS 26, BILLS 16
Sunday, October 24

Buffalo	0	3	6	7—16
Seattle	13	10	0	3—26

First Quarter
Sea.—Mayes 7 pass from Kitna (Peterson kick), 2:30.
Sea.—FG, Peterson 40, 9:13.
Sea.—FG, Peterson 21, 13:21.

Second Quarter
Sea.—Mayes 43 pass from Kitna (Peterson kick), 7:24.
Sea.—FG, Peterson 42, 14:43.
Buf.—FG, Christie 50, 15:00.

– 157 –

Third Quarter
Buf.—P. Price 18 pass from Flutie (conversion failed), 13:01.
Fourth Quarter
Sea.—FG, Peterson 34, 4:58.
Buf.—Riemersma 1 pass from Flutie (Christie kick), 7:28.
Attendance—66,301.

	Buffalo	Seattle
First downs	25	18
Rushes-yards	24-103	32-110
Passing	249	275
Punt returns	0-0	1-5
Kickoff returns	7-100	2-69
Interception returns	0-0	2-10
Comp.-att.-int.	24-50-2	17-30-0
Sacked-yards lost	4-45	1-1
Punts	6-37	5-32
Fumbles-lost	1-1	0-0
Penalties-yards	6-35	6-40
Time of possession	30:49	29:11

INDIVIDUAL STATISTICS

RUSHING—Buffalo, A. Smith 10-34, Linton 8-23, Flutie 5-48, Hicks 1-(minus 2). Seattle, Watters 22-75, Kitna 6-4, Green 3-29, R. Brown 1-2.

PASSING—Buffalo, Flutie 24-50-2-294. Seattle, Kitna 17-30-0-276.

RECEIVING—Buffalo, P. Price 5-106, Loud 5-55, K. Williams 4-52, Reed 4-31, Gash 2-16, Linton 2-11, Collins 1-22, Riemersma 1-1. Seattle, Mayes 6-105, Dawkins 4-91, Fauria 3-42, R. Brown 3-37, Watters 1-1.

MISSED FIELD GOAL ATTEMPTS—None.

INTERCEPTIONS—Seattle, Joseph 1-13, Bellamy 1-(minus 3).

KICKOFF RETURNS—Buffalo, K. Williams 5-74, Loud 2-26. Seattle, Green 1-54, Springs 1-15.

PUNT RETURNS—Seattle, Rogers 1-5.

SACKS—Buffalo, Northern 1. Seattle, Daniels 2, Adams 1, Sinclair 1.

STEELERS 13, FALCONS 9
Monday, October 25

Atlanta	0	0	0	9—	9
Pittsburgh	7	6	0	0—	13

First Quarter
Pit.—Huntley 13 pass from Stewart (K. Brown kick), 13:24.
Second Quarter
Pit.—FG, K. Brown 51, 9:59.
Pit.—FG, K. Brown 25, 15:00.
Fourth Quarter
Atl.—Mathis 5 pass from Chandler (Andersen kick), 8:18.
Atl.—Safety, J.Miller stepped out of end zone, 13:40.
Attendance—58,141.

	Atlanta	Pittsburgh
First downs	20	14
Rushes-yards	25-49	35-111
Passing	187	115
Punt returns	2-15	2-1
Kickoff returns	4-71	1-9
Interception returns	0-0	1-16
Comp.-att.-int.	20-34-1	13-21-0
Sacked-yards lost	7-46	1-12
Punts	6-37	6-46
Fumbles-lost	1-0	1-1
Penalties-yards	3-15	9-91
Time of possession	33:08	26:52

INDIVIDUAL STATISTICS

RUSHING—Atlanta, Oxendine 14-30, Hanspard 4-6, Christian 3-0, Dwight 2-8, Chandler 2-5. Pittsburgh, Bettis 23-80, Stewart 10-37, Huntley 1-3, Miller 1-(minus 9).

PASSING—Atlanta, Chandler 20-34-1-233. Pittsburgh, Stewart 13-21-0-127.

RECEIVING—Atlanta, Mathis 12-166, Christian 4-13, Dwight 3-44, Calloway 1-10. Pittsburgh, Blackwell 3-46, Ward 3-28, Hawkins 3-27, Bettis 2-14, Huntley 2-12.

MISSED FIELD GOAL ATTEMPTS—Atlanta, Andersen 47.

INTERCEPTIONS—Pittsburgh, Scott 1-16.

KICKOFF RETURNS—Atlanta, Dwight 3-61, Kozlowski 1-10. Pittsburgh, Edwards 1-9.

PUNT RETURNS—Atlanta, Dwight 2-15. Pittsburgh, Hawkins 2-1.

SACKS—Atlanta, Smith 1. Pittsburgh, Steed 2, Gildon 1.5, Emmons 1, Kirkland 1, Vrabel 1, Roye 0.5.

WEEK 8

RESULTS

ATLANTA 27, Carolina 20
Buffalo 13, BALTIMORE 10
Cleveland 21, NEW ORLEANS 16
DETROIT 20, Tampa Bay 3
INDIANAPOLIS 34, Dallas 24
Jacksonville 41, CINCINNATI 10
KANSAS CITY 34, San Diego 0
Miami 16, OAKLAND 9
Minnesota 23, DENVER 20
New England 27, ARIZONA 3
N.Y. Giants 23, PHILADELPHIA 17 (OT)
TENNESSEE 24, St. Louis 21
WASHINGTON 48, Chicago 22
Seattle 27, GREEN BAY 7
Open date: N.Y. Jets, Pittsburgh, San Francisco

STANDINGS

AFC EAST
	W	L	T	Pct.
Miami	6	1	0	.857
New England	6	2	0	.750
Indianapolis	5	2	0	.714
Buffalo	5	3	0	.625
N.Y. Jets	1	6	0	.143

AFC CENTRAL
	W	L	T	Pct.
Jacksonville	6	1	0	.857
Tennessee	6	1	0	.857
Pittsburgh	4	3	0	.571
Baltimore	2	5	0	.286
Cincinnati	1	7	0	.125
Cleveland	1	7	0	.125

AFC WEST
	W	L	T	Pct.
Kansas City	5	2	0	.714
Seattle	5	2	0	.714
San Diego	4	3	0	.571
Oakland	4	4	0	.500
Denver	2	6	0	.250

NFC EAST
	W	L	T	Pct.
Washington	5	2	0	.714
N.Y. Giants	5	3	0	.625
Dallas	4	3	0	.571
Arizona	2	5	0	.286
Philadelphia	2	6	0	.250

NFC CENTRAL
	W	L	T	Pct.
Detroit	5	2	0	.714
Green Bay	4	3	0	.571
Minnesota	4	4	0	.500
Tampa Bay	3	4	0	.429
Chicago	3	5	0	.375

NFC WEST
	W	L	T	Pct.
St. Louis	6	1	0	.857
San Francisco	3	4	0	.429
Carolina	2	5	0	.286
Atlanta	2	6	0	.250
New Orleans	1	6	0	.143

HIGHLIGHTS

Hero of the week: Facing fourth-and-15 with under four minutes left and his team trailing Baltimore 10-6, Bills quarterback Doug Flutie got a first down the only way he could—running the ball himself. Then he found Jonathan Linton in the end zone for the game-winning touchdown with 1:36 left, capping Buffalo's 13-10 victory over the Ravens.

Goat of the week: The Bucs stuffed so many blunders into a single crucial sequence in their 20-3 loss to Detroit that it is difficult to decide exactly who's to blame. Late in the third quarter, with Tampa Bay trailing 17-3, Warrick Dunn took a handoff from quarterback Eric Zeier and seemed to sprint just far enough for a 12-yard score before sliding to a stop in the end zone. The Bucs tried to kick the point-after, but couldn't get their line set. Rather than take a timeout, Dungy chose to absorb a delay-of-game penalty. But before Tampa Bay could snap the ball, which would have protected the previous play from review, Lions coach Bobby Ross challenged the TD ruling. After the head official took another look, Dunn was ruled down at the 1-yard line. Despite the confusion and controversy, the Buccaneers were only a few feet from scoring a touchdown. But two plays later Alstott fumbled away the football and the Bucs never got close to the goal line again.

Sub of the week: Giants defensive tackle Christian Peter, who replaced the injured Robert Harris, slapped down a 33-yard field goal by Norm Johnson with 6:30 left in the game, keeping the Eagles from increasing their 17-10 lead. Then, after the Giants scored a touchdown to send the game into overtime, Peter deflected a pass from Doug Pederson, and the ball hung in the air until Michael Strahan could cradle it and return it 44 yards for a score, clinching New York's 23-17 win.

Comeback of the week: After spotting the Titans 21 first-quarter points with uncharacteristically sloppy play, the Rams made a run at preserving their perfect record. The defense did its part, and quarterback Kurt Warner hit Marshall Faulk for a 57-yard touchdown and Isaac Bruce for a 3-yard score in the third quarter. Trailing 24-14 in the fourth, the Rams marched the length of the field and Warner put his third TD on the board with 2:14 remaining. Lorenzo Styles recovered the onside kick that followed, and Warner got St. Louis down to the 20. But the Rams were out of timeouts, and Jeff Wilkins' 38-yard game-tying field goal attempt sailed wide right with 22 seconds left.

Blowout of the week: The Chiefs whipped the Chargers, 34-0, in what should have been a close battle between co-leaders in the AFC West. Instead, San Diego mustered just one first down and 28 yards in a first half that ended with Kansas City up 20-0. Reggie Tongue's seven-yard fumble return for a TD in the first period got the Chiefs off and rolling.

Nail-biter of the week: The Giants trailed the Eagles, 17-3, after three quarters before quarterback Kent Graham led New York on a 16-play, 83-yard scoring drive to cut the deficit to 17-10. Then, with the ball at the Philly 3-yard line on the Eagles' next possession, Duce Staley tried to take it up the middle to gain some breathing room, but free safety Brandon Sanders stood him up and defensive tackle Keith Hamilton ripped the ball free. Graham subsequently threw a seven-yard touchdown pass to Pete Mitchell to tie the game. New York's first overtime drive stalled quickly, but Peter's deflection and Strahan's TD run-back ended the game in dramatic fashion.

Hit of the week: Devastating hits paved the way in a second-half rally by the Colts, who scored on five consecutive possessions to turn a 17-6 deficit into a 34-24 win over Dallas. Jeff Burris blasted Troy Aikman on a corner blitz in the fourth quarter, with the helmet-to-helmet blow forcing Aikman out of the game. Earlier, defensive end Chad Bratzke sacked Aikman, forcing a fumble that led to a touchdown.

Oddity of the week: The Saints gave up a Hail Mary touchdown pass for the second straight week. One week after being burned by the Giants at the end of the first half, the Saints this time were burned at the end of the game, as Tim Couch and fellow rookie Kevin Johnson hooked up on a 56-yard score to give Browns their first win of the season, 21-16.

Top rusher: Ricky Williams rushed a team-record 40

times for 179 yards in the Saints' loss to the Browns.
Top passer: Kurt Warner completed 29 of 46 passes for 328 yards and three touchdowns in the Rams' loss at Tennessee.
Top receiver: Marcus Robinson caught nine passes for 161 yards and two touchdowns in the Bears' 48-22 loss at Washington.
Notes: Flutie upped his personal record against NFC Central teams to 7-0. ... Mike Holmgren's return to Green Bay was a successful one as the Seahawks pounded the Packers, 27-7, on Monday night. It was only the Packers' second loss in their last 35 games at Lambeau Field. ... Williams' rushing total after seven games—582 yards—was 125 yards more than last year's leading Saints rusher, Lamar Smith, had all season. ... Carl Pickens caught his 500th career pass in Cincinnati's 41-10 loss to Jacksonville. It was the 85th consecutive game in which Pickens caught at least one pass. ... The Raiders failed to score a touchdown for the first time since 1981 in their 16-9 loss to Miami. ... Patriots quarterback Drew Bledsoe tied his career high with four touchdown passes in New England's 27-3 romp over Arizona. His QB rating for the game was 146.8. ... The Redskins' top-rated offense had 376 total yards and 45 points before Chicago scored its first points.
Quote of the week: Panthers quarterback Steve Beuerlein, reflecting on a turnover-filled, 27-20 loss to the lowly Falcons, one week after a 15-point setback to the Lions: "We laid two eggs in a row. We better be worried. We better be concerned about the direction we're heading."

GAME SUMMARIES

FALCONS 27, PANTHERS 20
Sunday, October 31

Carolina		3	3	7 7—20
Atlanta		7	6	7 7—27

First Quarter
Car.—FG, Kasay 31, 9:35.
Atl.—Dwight 35 pass from Chandler (Andersen kick), 12:25.
Second Quarter
Atl.—FG, Andersen 39, 6:38.
Atl.—FG, Andersen 24, 11:22.
Car.—FG, Kasay 51, 14:49.
Third Quarter
Atl.—Oxendine 1 run (Andersen kick), 9:16.
Car.—Bates 100 kickoff return (Kasay kick), 9:35.
Fourth Quarter
Atl.—Dwight 4 pass from Chandler (Andersen kick), 0:17.
Car.—Beuerlein 1 run (Kasay kick), 11:53.
Attendance—52,594.

	Carolina	Atlanta
First downs	19	20
Rushes-yards	18-63	32-107
Passing	227	176
Punt returns	4-8	1-11
Kickoff returns	5-180	5-101
Interception returns	0-0	3-52
Comp.-att.-int.	21-35-3	14-21-0
Sacked-yards lost	6-29	3-25
Punts	2-36	6-39
Fumbles-lost	2-2	0-0
Penalties-yards	9-48	9-75
Time of possession	28:42	31:18

INDIVIDUAL STATISTICS
RUSHING—Carolina, Lane 15-55, Beuerlein 3-8. Atlanta, Oxendine 17-64, Hanspard 14-44, Chandler 1-(minus 1).
PASSING—Carolina, Beuerlein 21-35-3-256. Atlanta, Chandler 14-21-0-201.
RECEIVING—Carolina, Muhammad 5-62, Lane 4-17, Walls 3-48, Metcalf 3-32, Johnson 3-31, Hayes 2-60, Mangum 1-6. Atlanta, Mathis 4-53, Dwight 3-61, Christian 3-40, Oxendine 2-38, Calloway 1-11, Hanspard 1-(minus 2).
MISSED FIELD GOAL ATTEMPTS—None.
INTERCEPTIONS—Atlanta, McBurrows 1-41, Robinson 1-7, Carter 1-4.
KICKOFF RETURNS—Carolina, Bates 5-180. Atlanta, Dwight 4-100, German 1-1.
PUNT RETURNS—Carolina, Metcalf 4-8. Atlanta, Dwight 1-11.
SACKS—Carolina, Gilbert 1, Greene 1, E. Jones 1. Atlanta, Smith 3, Dronett 2, Archambeau 1.

TITANS 24, RAMS 21
Sunday, October 31

St. Louis	0	0	14	7—21
Tennessee	21	0	3	0—24

First Quarter
Ten.—Neal 1 pass from McNair (Del Greco kick), 6:32.
Ten.—E. George 17 pass from McNair (Del Greco kick), 12:19.
Ten.—McNair 10 run (Del Greco kick), 13:36.
Third Quarter
St.L.—Faulk 57 pass from Warner (Wilkins kick), 0:27.
St.L.—Bruce 3 pass from Warner (Wilkins kick), 7:05.
Ten.—FG, Del Greco 27, 10:42.
Fourth Quarter
St.L.—Lee 15 pass from Warner (Wilkins kick), 12:46.
Attendance—66,415.

	St. Louis	Tennessee
First downs	23	17
Rushes-yards	19-128	31-103
Passing	287	178
Punt returns	7-68	2-10
Kickoff returns	5-144	2-33
Interception returns	0-0	0-0
Comp.-att.-int.	29-46-0	13-29-0
Sacked-yards lost	6-41	1-8
Punts	7-47	9-46
Fumbles-lost	5-3	1-0
Penalties-yards	15-97	8-85
Time of possession	31:43	28:17

INDIVIDUAL STATISTICS
RUSHING—St. Louis, Faulk 16-90, Warner 2-22, Hakim 1-16. Tennessee, E. George 17-68, McNair 12-36, Thomas 2-(minus 1).
PASSING—St. Louis, Warner 29-46-0-328. Tennessee, McNair 13-29-0-186.
RECEIVING—St. Louis, Faulk 6-94, Bruce 6-53, Hakim 5-62, Holt 5-55, Proehl 4-45, Lee 1-15, R. Williams 1-4, Hodgins 1-0. Tennessee, Harris 3-44, E. George 3-35, Thigpen 2-49, Wycheck 2-38, Dyson 2-19, Neal 1-1.
MISSED FIELD GOAL ATTEMPTS—St. Louis, Wilkins 54, 38.
INTERCEPTIONS—None.
KICKOFF RETURNS—St. Louis, Carpenter 5-144. Tennessee, Mason 2-33.
PUNT RETURNS—St. Louis, Hakim 7-68. Tennessee, Mason 2-10.
SACKS—St. Louis, Carter 1. Tennessee, Evans 1.5, Kearse 1, Bowden 1, Robinson 1, Ford 0.5, Team 1.

BILLS 13, RAVENS 10
Sunday, October 31

Buffalo	0	3	0	10—13
Baltimore	10	0	0	0—10

First Quarter
Bal.—Armour 7 pass from Banks (Stover kick), 10:00.
Bal.—FG, Stover 37, 14:54.
Second Quarter
Buf.—FG, Christie 25, 14:23.
Fourth Quarter
Buf.—FG, Christie 40, 8:39.
Buf.—Linton 5 pass from Flutie (Christie kick), 13:25.
Attendance—68,673.

	Buffalo	Baltimore
First downs	19	12
Rushes-yards	29-111	27-82
Passing	138	118
Punt returns	1-12	2-8
Kickoff returns	3-60	3-49
Interception returns	1-26	3-19
Comp.-att.-int.	18-40-3	13-34-1
Sacked-yards lost	3-17	3-11
Punts	6-39	7-48
Fumbles-lost	1-0	1-1
Penalties-yards	7-50	10-113
Time of possession	32:05	27:55

INDIVIDUAL STATISTICS

RUSHING—Buffalo, Linton 14-56, Flutie 8-50, A. Smith 6-5, Mohr 1-0. Baltimore, Rhett 24-73, Evans 2-6, Banks 1-3.

PASSING—Buffalo, Flutie 18-40-3-155. Baltimore, Banks 13-34-1-129.

RECEIVING—Buffalo, Reed 7-76, K. Williams 4-35, P. Price 3-26, Linton 2-10, Riemersma 1-7, Gash 1-1. Baltimore, Ismail 5-54, Armour 3-35, Evans 3-26, Rhett 1-8, J. Lewis 1-6.

MISSED FIELD GOAL ATTEMPTS—Baltimore, Stover 51.

INTERCEPTIONS—Buffalo, Schulz 1-26. Baltimore, McAlister 1-7, Starks 1-7, Woodson 1-5.

KICKOFF RETURNS—Buffalo, K. Williams 3-60. Baltimore, Harris 3-49.

PUNT RETURNS—Buffalo, K. Williams 1-12. Baltimore, J. Lewis 2-8.

SACKS—Buffalo, Cowart 1, Wiley 1, S. Price 1. Baltimore, R. Lewis 1, McCrary 1, Burnett 1.

REDSKINS 48, BEARS 22

Sunday, October 31

Chicago	0	0	14	8—22
Washington	14	17	14	3—48

First Quarter
Was.—Davis 76 run (Conway kick), 0:25.
Was.—Wilkinson 88 interception return (Conway kick), 5:43.

Second Quarter
Was.—FG, Conway 50, 1:28.
Was.—B. Johnson 1 run (Conway kick), 8:35.
Was.—Westbrook 13 pass from B. Johnson (Conway kick), 14:25.

Third Quarter
Was.—Davis 2 run (Conway kick), 1:30.
Was.—Centers 22 pass from B. Johnson (Conway kick), 8:23.
Chi.—M. Robinson 30 pass from McNown (Boniol kick), 12:02.
Chi.—M. Robinson 52 pass from McNown (Boniol kick), 13:21.

Fourth Quarter
Was.—FG, Conway 51, 0:05.
Chi.—Wetnight 3 pass from McNown (McNown run), 13:48.
Attendance—77,621.

	Chicago	Washington
First downs	22	18
Rushes-yards	26-74	24-164
Passing	371	212
Punt returns	1-39	2-10
Kickoff returns	8-133	1-14
Interception returns	1-15	4-120
Comp.-att.-int.	36-63-4	17-33-1
Sacked-yards lost	3-14	0-0
Punts	5-44	3-44
Fumbles-lost	2-1	2-1
Penalties-yards	9-85	3-15
Time of possession	35:56	24:04

INDIVIDUAL STATISTICS

RUSHING—Chicago, Enis 19-56, McNown 2-10, Bennett 2-6, Engram 1-2, Matthews 1-0, Milburn 1-0. Washington, Davis 12-143, Hicks 7-22, Mitchell 2-(minus 1), Peete 2-(minus 1), B. Johnson 1-1.

PASSING—Chicago, McNown 23-40-3-272, Matthews 13-23-1-113. Washington, B. Johnson 15-25-0-204, Peete 2-8-1-8.

RECEIVING—Chicago, M. Robinson 9-161, Engram 7-65, Milburn 6-59, Enis 6-39, Brooks 2-23, Bennett 2-10, Wetnight 2-9, Bates 1-11, Allred 1-8. Washington, Westbrook 5-85, Centers 3-32, Connell 2-46, Davis 2-26, Hicks 2-8, Fryar 1-6, Mitchell 1-5, Alexander 1-4.

MISSED FIELD GOAL ATTEMPTS—Washington, Conway 53.

INTERCEPTIONS—Chicago, Burns 1-15. Washington, Stevens 2-25, Wilkinson 1-88, Shade 1-7.

KICKOFF RETURNS—Chicago, Milburn 7-130, Hallock 1-3. Washington, Mitchell 1-14.

PUNT RETURNS—Chicago, Milburn 1-39. Washington, Mitchell 2-10.

SACKS—Washington, Coleman 1.5, Wilkinson 1, Francis 0.5.

CHIEFS 34, CHARGERS 0

Sunday, October 31

San Diego	0	0	0	0— 0
Kansas City	10	10	14	0—34

First Quarter
K.C.—FG, Stoyanovich 43, 4:49.
K.C.—Tongue 7 fumble return (Stoyanovich kick), 7:10.

Second Quarter
K.C.—FG, Stoyanovich 39, 5:01.
K.C.—Horn 9 pass from Grbac (Stoyanovich kick), 12:25.

Third Quarter
K.C.—Alexander 81 pass from Grbac (Stoyanovich kick), 11:33.
K.C.—Bennett 7 run (Stoyanovich kick), 12:02.
Attendance—78,473.

	San Diego	Kansas City
First downs	10	10
Rushes-yards	20-72	39-97
Passing	141	186
Punt returns	2-21	4-16
Kickoff returns	7-141	1-24
Interception returns	0-0	2-27
Comp.-att.-int.	20-37-2	11-15-0
Sacked-yards lost	5-42	1-8
Punts	8-40	7-40
Fumbles-lost	2-2	1-0
Penalties-yards	12-74	3-15
Time of possession	29:10	30:50

INDIVIDUAL STATISTICS

RUSHING—San Diego, Bynum 12-55, Harbaugh 3-8, Fletcher 3-7, Stephens 2-2. Kansas City, Bennett 14-38, Morris 11-25, Cloud 7-21, Richardson 6-14, Grbac 1-(minus 1).

PASSING—San Diego, Harbaugh 18-34-1-174, Kramer 2-3-1-9. Kansas City, Grbac 11-15-0-194.

RECEIVING—San Diego, F. Jones 4-57, McCrary 4-25, Bynum 3-26, J. Graham 3-26, Fletcher 2-19, C. Jones 2-5, Penn 1-16, Ricks 1-9. Kansas City, Horn 3-26, Alexander 2-113, Lockett 2-40, Cloud 1-6, Jacoby 1-6, Gonzalez 1-4, Morris 1-(minus 1).

MISSED FIELD GOAL ATTEMPTS—None.

INTERCEPTIONS—Kansas City, Thomas 1-20, Dishman 1-7.

KICKOFF RETURNS—San Diego, Stephens 5-105, Bynum 2-36. Kansas City, L. Parker 1-24.

PUNT RETURNS—San Diego, Penn 2-21. Kansas City, L. Parker 4-16.

SACKS—San Diego, Parrella 1. Kansas City, Hicks 2, Thomas 1, Patton 1, Tongue 1.

JAGUARS 41, BENGALS 10

Sunday, October 31

Jacksonville	14	13	7	7—41
Cincinnati	0	0	3	7—10

First Quarter
Jac.—Taylor 1 run (Hollis kick), 4:22.
Jac.—McCardell 23 pass from Brunell (Hollis kick), 8:30.

Second Quarter
Jac.—FG, Hollis 43, 0:14.
Jac.—J. Smith 3 pass from Brunell (Hollis kick), 9:06.
Jac.—FG, Hollis 21, 13:14.

Third Quarter
Cin.—FG, Pelfrey 29, 7:40.
Jac.—J. Stewart 1 run (Hollis kick), 13:19.

Fourth Quarter
Jac.—J. Stewart 1 run (Hollis kick), 8:23.
Cin.—Jackson 15 pass from Blake (Pelfrey kick), 15:00.
Attendance—49,138.

	Jacksonville	Cincinnati
First downs	23	14
Rushes-yards	34-183	23-93
Passing	194	207
Punt returns	2-14	1-10
Kickoff returns	2-41	6-149
Interception returns	2-39	0-0

1999 REVIEW Week 8

	Jacksonville	Cincinnati
Comp.-att.-int.	17-28-0	20-36-2
Sacked-yards lost	2-20	4-21
Punts	2-45	4-40
Fumbles-lost	0-0	1-1
Penalties-yards	2-16	4-24
Time of possession	30:01	29:59

INDIVIDUAL STATISTICS

RUSHING—Jacksonville, Taylor 15-128, J. Stewart 10-32, Banks 6-12, Brunell 2-11, Fiedler 1-0. Cincinnati, Dillon 14-32, Basnight 4-11, Smith 3-40, Blake 2-10.

PASSING—Jacksonville, Brunell 11-19-0-145, Fiedler 6-9-0-69. Cincinnati, Blake 13-23-0-155, Smith 6-12-2-67, Pickens 1-1-0-6.

RECEIVING—Jacksonville, J. Smith 8-89, Banks 2-50, Brady 2-29, McCardell 1-23, Barlow 1-11, Jones 1-11, Taylor 1-3, J. Stewart 1-(minus 2). Cincinnati, Basnight 3-47, Yeast 3-20, Pickens 2-31, Dillon 2-25, Jackson 2-22, McGee 2-18, Scott 2-11, Battaglia 1-23, Williams 1-16, Groce 1-9, Smith 1-6.

MISSED FIELD GOAL ATTEMPTS—None.

INTERCEPTIONS—Jacksonville, Beasley 1-39, Darius 1-0.

KICKOFF RETURNS—Jacksonville, Barlow 2-41. Cincinnati, Mack 6-149.

PUNT RETURNS—Jacksonville, Barlow 2-14. Cincinnati, Yeast 1-10.

SACKS—Jacksonville, Beasley 1, Hardy 1, Brackens 1, Smeenge 1. Cincinnati, von Oelhoffen 1, Foley 0.5, Bell 0.5.

DOLPHINS 16, RAIDERS 9

Sunday, October 31

Miami	3	7	3	3—16
Oakland	3	0	6	0— 9

First Quarter
Oak.—FG, Husted 49, 3:06.
Mia.—FG, Mare 21, 10:07.

Second Quarter
Mia.—Collins 1 run (Mare kick), 8:26.

Third Quarter
Oak.—FG, Husted 34, 4:04.
Mia.—FG, Mare 34, 8:54.
Oak.—FG, Husted 47, 11:46.

Fourth Quarter
Mia.—FG, Mare 44, 11:39.
Attendance—61,556.

	Miami	Oakland
First downs	19	13
Rushes-yards	42-141	19-80
Passing	184	107
Punt returns	4-73	3-42
Kickoff returns	3-72	3-57
Interception returns	1-(-15)	0-0
Comp.-att.-int.	16-32-0	9-31-1
Sacked-yards lost	5-37	5-33
Punts	6-41	8-44
Fumbles-lost	0-0	1-1
Penalties-yards	7-48	2-25
Time of possession	37:29	22:31

INDIVIDUAL STATISTICS

RUSHING—Miami, Johnson 21-86, Collins 15-49, Huard 6-6. Oakland, Kaufman 8-39, Wheatley 8-16, Jordan 3-25.

PASSING—Miami, Huard 16-32-0-221. Oakland, Gannon 7-28-1-130, Hoying 2-3-0-10.

RECEIVING—Miami, Gadsden 3-70, Martin 3-34, Pritchett 3-19, McDuffie 2-54, Collins 2-16, Johnson 1-17, Konrad 1-11, Huard 1-0. Oakland, Brown 7-113, J. Williams 1-20, Jett 1-7.

MISSED FIELD GOAL ATTEMPTS—Miami, Mare 46.

INTERCEPTIONS—Miami, Buckley 1-(minus 15).

KICKOFF RETURNS—Miami, Marion 3-72. Oakland, Kaufman 3-57.

PUNT RETURNS—Miami, Jacquet 3-64, McDuffie 1-9. Oakland, Gordon 3-42.

SACKS—Miami, Armstrong 2, Taylor 1, Bromell 1, Gardener 1. Oakland, Russell 3, Harris 1, Jackson 0.5, Bryant 0.5.

VIKINGS 23, BRONCOS 20

Sunday, October 31

Minnesota	0	13	0	10—23
Denver	12	0	0	8—20

First Quarter
Den.—Loville 36 run (Elam kick), 2:48.
Den.—Safety, J. George sacked by T. Pryce in end zone, 4:23.
Den.—FG, Elam 19, 9:01.

Second Quarter
Min.—Thomas 27 interception return (Anderson kick), 7:54.
Min.—Carter 37 pass from George (pass failed), 11:32.

Fourth Quarter
Min.—Carter 16 pass from George (Anderson kick), 2:15.
Den.—Chamberlain 1 pass from Griese (Gary run), 9:51.
Min.—FG, Anderson 23, 14:59.
Attendance—75,021.

	Minnesota	Denver
First downs	15	24
Rushes-yards	24-97	30-135
Passing	205	256
Punt returns	3-44	3-42
Kickoff returns	4-75	5-94
Interception returns	1-27	0-0
Comp.-att.-int.	17-29-0	24-40-1
Sacked-yards lost	2-13	4-18
Punts	6-44	4-54
Fumbles-lost	1-0	2-2
Penalties-yards	9-78	7-39
Time of possession	28:06	31:54

INDIVIDUAL STATISTICS

RUSHING—Minnesota, Hoard 18-84, M. Williams 4-9, Tate 1-4, George 1-0. Denver, Gary 19-79, Griese 7-10, Loville 3-45, Lynn 1-1.

PASSING—Minnesota, George 17-29-0-218. Denver, Griese 24-40-1-274.

RECEIVING—Minnesota, Carter 8-144, Moss 3-39, Reed 3-18, Glover 2-11, Hoard 1-6. Denver, R. Smith 7-117, Chamberlain 5-42, Cooper 4-38, Carswell 3-31, McCaffrey 2-18, McGriff 1-15, Griffith 1-9, B. Miller 1-4.

MISSED FIELD GOAL ATTEMPTS—Denver, Elam 37.

INTERCEPTIONS—Minnesota, Thomas 1-27.

KICKOFF RETURNS—Minnesota, Palmer 4-75. Denver, Watson 4-94, D. Smith 1-0.

PUNT RETURNS—Minnesota, Palmer 3-44. Denver, Watson 3-42.

SACKS—Minnesota, Doleman 2, T. Williams 1, Phillips 1. Denver, Pryce 1, Williams 1.

COLTS 34, COWBOYS 24

Sunday, October 31

Dallas	10	7	7	0—24
Indianapolis	3	3	15	13—34

First Quarter
Dal.—E. Smith 2 run (Cunningham kick), 2:02.
Dal.—FG, Cunningham 24, 8:26.
Ind.—FG, Vanderjagt 43, 12:58.

Second Quarter
Dal.—Warren 4 run (Cunningham kick), 4:34.
Ind.—FG, Vanderjagt 30, 13:45.

Third Quarter
Ind.—Wilkins recovered fumble in end zone (Harrison pass from Manning), 6:25.
Ind.—James 1 run (Vanderjagt kick), 6:59.
Dal.—E. Smith 4 run (Cunningham kick), 11:34.

Fourth Quarter
Ind.—Harrison 40 pass from Manning (Vanderjagt kick), 0:05.
Ind.—FG, Vanderjagt 33, 4:17.
Ind.—FG, Vanderjagt 27, 10:24.
Attendance—56,860.

	Dallas	Indianapolis
First downs	18	23
Rushes-yards	26-103	28-119
Passing	129	300
Punt returns	1-76	3-12
Kickoff returns	4-114	5-121
Interception returns	0-0	0-0
Comp.-att.-int.	19-25-0	22-34-0
Sacked-yards lost	5-30	1-13
Punts	4-44	4-36
Fumbles-lost	2-1	4-0
Penalties-yards	6-50	8-35
Time of possession	27:29	32:31

INDIVIDUAL STATISTICS

RUSHING—Dallas, E. Smith 22-93, Warren 3-9, Aikman 1-1. Indianapolis, James 27-117, Wilkins 1-2.

PASSING—Dallas, Aikman 19-24-0-159, Garrett 0-1-0-0. Indianapolis, Manning 22-34-0-313.

RECEIVING—Dallas, Mills 4-37, Ismail 4-31, Warren 3-20, E. Smith 3-6, LaFleur 2-31, Ogden 2-25, Thomas 1-9. Indianapolis, James 7-92, Harrison 6-85, Wilkins 5-60, Dilger 2-22, Pathon 1-38, Pollard 1-16.

MISSED FIELD GOAL ATTEMPTS—None.

INTERCEPTIONS—None.

KICKOFF RETURNS—Dallas, Tucker 4-114. Indianapolis, Wilkins 5-121.

PUNT RETURNS—Dallas, Sanders 1-76. Indianapolis, Wilkins 3-12.

SACKS—Dallas, Nguyen 1. Indianapolis, Bratzke 2, Burris 1, Bennett 1, Blevins 1.

GIANTS 23, EAGLES 17

Sunday, October 31

N.Y. Giants	3	0	0	14	6—23
Philadelphia	3	14	0	0	0—17

First Quarter
Phi.—FG, N. Johnson 28, 8:20.
NYG—FG, Blanchard 28, 15:00.

Second Quarter
Phi.—Staley 21 run (N. Johnson kick), 9:30.
Phi.—Small 84 pass from Pederson (N. Johnson kick), 12:28.

Fourth Quarter
NYG—Johnson 2 run (Blanchard kick), 1:53.
NYG—Mitchell 7 pass from Graham (Blanchard kick), 13:00.

Overtime
NYG—Strahan 44 interception return, 4:24.
Attendance—66,481.

	N.Y. Giants	Philadelphia
First downs	20	15
Rushes-yards	25-91	31-112
Passing	207	248
Punt returns	2-10	4-38
Kickoff returns	4-105	4-93
Interception returns	2-48	0-0
Comp.-att.-int.	26-41-0	19-30-2
Sacked-yards lost	5-33	3-8
Punts	8-42	5-42
Fumbles-lost	0-0	2-1
Penalties-yards	5-40	3-15
Time of possession	34:42	29:42

INDIVIDUAL STATISTICS

RUSHING—New York, Johnson 14-31, Graham 5-40, Way 5-16, Barber 1-4. Philadelphia, Staley 26-97, Turner 2-7, Pederson 2-6, Bostic 1-2.

PASSING—New York, Graham 26-41-0-240. Philadelphia, Pederson 18-28-2-256, McNabb 1-2-0-0.

RECEIVING—New York, Mitchell 6-41, Barber 4-43, Johnson 4-35, Hilliard 3-33, Cross 3-31, Way 3-21, Toomer 1-25, Jurevicius 1-12, Graham 1-(minus 1). Philadelphia, C. Johnson 8-84, Small 4-119, Staley 3-32, Broughton 2-8, Jells 1-8, Turner 1-5.

MISSED FIELD GOAL ATTEMPTS—New York, Blanchard 34. Philadelphia, N. Johnson 33, Akers 59.

INTERCEPTIONS—New York, Strahan 1-44, Armstead 1-4.

KICKOFF RETURNS—New York, Levingston 3-79, Patten 1-26. Philadelphia, Bieniemy 3-72, Rossum 1-21.

PUNT RETURNS—New York, Barber 2-10. Philadelphia, Rossum 4-38.

SACKS—New York, Garnes 1, Armstead 1, K. Hamilton 1. Philadelphia, W. Thomas 1, Dawkins 1, Jefferson 1, S. Martin 1, Reese 1.

BROWNS 21, SAINTS 16

Sunday, October 31

Cleveland	0	7	7	7—21	
New Orleans	7	3	3	3—16	

First Quarter
N.O.—Poole 5 pass from Hobert (Brien kick), 11:01.

Second Quarter
Cle.—Edwards 27 pass from Couch (Dawson kick), 7:23.
N.O.—FG, Brien 49, 14:52.

Third Quarter
Cle.—Johnson 24 pass from Couch (Dawson kick), 6:07.
N.O.—FG, Brien 22, 13:45.

Fourth Quarter
N.O.—FG, Brien 46, 14:39.
Cle.—Johnson 56 pass from Couch (Dawson kick), 15:00.
Attendance—48,817.

	Cleveland	New Orleans
First downs	9	25
Rushes-yards	21-62	50-231
Passing	181	120
Punt returns	2-8	5-52
Kickoff returns	5-123	2-28
Interception returns	2-16	0-0
Comp.-att.-int.	11-19-0	13-29-2
Sacked-yards lost	2-12	0-0
Punts	7-44	2-46
Fumbles-lost	1-1	3-3
Penalties-yards	8-64	6-38
Time of possession	19:10	40:50

INDIVIDUAL STATISTICS

RUSHING—Cleveland, Abdul-Jabbar 13-39, Kirby 6-18, Couch 2-5. New Orleans, R. Williams 40-179, Tolliver 4-24, L. Smith 4-17, Hobert 1-9, Craver 1-2.

PASSING—Cleveland, Couch 11-19-0-193. New Orleans, Tolliver 9-20-1-92, Hobert 4-9-1-28.

RECEIVING—Cleveland, Johnson 4-96, Shepherd 4-52, Edwards 2-37, Kirby 1-8. New Orleans, Poole 5-23, R. Williams 3-8, Craver 2-32, Kennison 2-27, L. Smith 1-11, Dawsey 1-11, Cleeland 1-8.

MISSED FIELD GOAL ATTEMPTS—Cleveland, Dawson 46. New Orleans, Brien 47.

INTERCEPTIONS—Cleveland, Barker 1-14, Pope 1-2.

KICKOFF RETURNS—Cleveland, Powell 2-58, Little 2-40, Johnson 1-25. New Orleans, Davis 2-28.

PUNT RETURNS—Cleveland, Dunn 2-8. New Orleans, Kennison 5-52.

SACKS—New Orleans, Tomich 1, Martin 0.5, Wilson 0.5.

PATRIOTS 27, CARDINALS 3

Sunday, October 31

New England	14	6	0	7—27
Arizona	0	0	3	0— 3

First Quarter
N.E.—Warren 3 pass from Bledsoe (Vinatieri kick), 6:04.
N.E.—Jefferson 64 pass from Bledsoe (Vinatieri kick), 13:47.

Second Quarter
N.E.—Jefferson 35 pass from Bledsoe (kick blocked), 10:15.

Third Quarter
Ariz.—FG, Jacke 24, 5:03.

Fourth Quarter
N.E.—Glenn 36 pass from Bledsoe (Vinatieri kick), 0:40.
Attendance—55,830.

	New England	Arizona
First downs	17	8
Rushes-yards	43-142	19-76
Passing	244	90
Punt returns	2-4	3-49
Kickoff returns	1-14	5-139
Interception returns	2-(-5)	0-0
Comp.-att.-int.	14-22-0	13-39-2
Sacked-yards lost	5-32	3-21
Punts	10-38	9-43
Fumbles-lost	3-0	0-0
Penalties-yards	4-36	5-30
Time of possession	36:04	23:56

INDIVIDUAL STATISTICS

RUSHING—New England, Allen 21-88, Faulk 17-42, T. Carter 2-6, Friesz 2-(minus 2), Ellison 1-8. Arizona, Murrell 13-47, Pittman 4-29, Makovicka 2-0.

PASSING—New England, Bledsoe 14-22-0-276. Arizona, Da. Brown 12-33-2-107, Greisen 1-6-0-7.

RECEIVING—New England, Glenn 4-63, Jefferson 3-113, Brisby 2-41, T. Carter 2-8, Allen 1-38, Rutledge 1-10, Warren 1-3. Arizona, Sanders 4-34, Murrell 3-29, Moore 2-27, Boston 2-14, McKinley 1-4, Hardy 1-3.

MISSED FIELD GOAL ATTEMPTS—None.

INTERCEPTIONS—New England, Serwanga 1-2, Law 1-(minus 7).

KICKOFF RETURNS—New England, Faulk 1-14. Arizona, Bates 5-139.

PUNT RETURNS—New England, Faulk 2-4. Arizona, Cody 3-49.

SACKS—New England, Thomas 1, Mitchell 1, McGinest 0.5, Slade 0.5. Arizona, Rice 2, Swinger 1, Walz 1, Ottis 1.

LIONS 20, BUCCANEERS 3

Sunday, October 31

Tampa Bay	0	3	0	0—	3
Detroit	0	10	7	3—	20

Second Quarter
Det.—FG, Hanson 47, 2:01.
T.B.—FG, Gramatica 49, 6:58.
Det.—Irvin 2 run (Hanson kick), 11:08.

Third Quarter
Det.—Aldridge 21 fumble return (Hanson kick), 0:59.

Fourth Quarter
Det.—FG, Hanson 50, 3:26.
Attendance—63,135.

	Tampa Bay	Detroit
First downs	18	13
Rushes-yards	22-72	24-147
Passing	220	109
Punt returns	2-22	1-17
Kickoff returns	3-36	2-37
Interception returns	0-0	0-0
Comp.-att.-int.	29-44-0	10-19-0
Sacked-yards lost	5-36	3-19
Punts	4-41	6-40
Fumbles-lost	2-2	0-0
Penalties-yards	4-22	8-53
Time of possession	34:31	25:29

INDIVIDUAL STATISTICS

RUSHING—Tampa Bay, Alstott 10-32, Dunn 9-33, Zeier 3-7. Detroit, Hill 16-123, Batch 5-15, Irvin 2-5, Schlesinger 1-4.

PASSING—Tampa Bay, Zeier 29-44-0-256. Detroit, Batch 10-19-0-128.

RECEIVING—Tampa Bay, Dunn 11-77, Green 7-96, Murphy 4-28, Anthony 2-14, Hape 2-6, Alstott 1-16, McDonald 1-11, Abdullah 1-8. Detroit, Morton 3-54, Sloan 2-36, Irvin 2-19, Schlesinger 1-9, Crowell 1-8, Stablein 1-2.

MISSED FIELD GOAL ATTEMPTS—Tampa Bay, Gramatica 36.

INTERCEPTIONS—None.

KICKOFF RETURNS—Tampa Bay, Murphy 3-36. Detroit, Fair 1-23, Olivo 1-14.

PUNT RETURNS—Tampa Bay, Green 2-22. Detroit, Uwaezuoke 1-17.

SACKS—Tampa Bay, Jones 1, T. Jackson 1, Robinson 0.5, Singleton 0.5. Detroit, Scroggins 2, Elliss 1.5, Claiborne 1, Porcher 0.5.

SEAHAWKS 27, PACKERS 7

Monday, November 1

Seattle	7	7	7	6—	27
Green Bay	0	7	0	0—	7

First Quarter
Sea.—Springs 61 blocked field goal return (Peterson kick), 10:15.

Second Quarter
G.B.—Bradford 74 pass from Favre (Longwell kick), 4:43.
Sea.—Mayes 10 pass from Kitna (Peterson kick), 9:12.

Third Quarter
Sea.—Dawkins 2 pass from Kitna (Peterson kick), 4:30.

Fourth Quarter
Sea.—FG, Peterson 19, 5:49.
Sea.—FG, Peterson 29, 8:24.
Attendance—59,869.

	Seattle	Green Bay
First downs	12	17
Rushes-yards	36-132	29-125
Passing	90	182
Punt returns	3-5	3-26
Kickoff returns	2-24	6-91
Interception returns	4-18	0-0
Comp.-att.-int.	12-19-0	16-41-4
Sacked-yards lost	2-19	4-30
Punts	8-40	6-40
Fumbles-lost	5-2	6-3
Penalties-yards	6-67	10-103
Time of possession	31:08	28:52

INDIVIDUAL STATISTICS

RUSHING—Seattle, Watters 31-125, Kitna 3-3, R. Brown 2-4. Green Bay, Levens 24-104, Favre 3-16, Mitchell 2-5.

PASSING—Seattle, Kitna 12-19-0-109. Green Bay, Favre 14-35-4-180, Hasselbeck 2-6-0-32.

RECEIVING—Seattle, Mayes 4-36, Dawkins 3-23, Fauria 2-11, Watters 1-21, Pritchard 1-11, Mili 1-7. Green Bay, Bradford 3-106, Henderson 3-30, Levens 3-22, Schroeder 3-21, Freeman 2-10, Hall 1-13, T. Davis 1-10.

MISSED FIELD GOAL ATTEMPTS—Green Bay, Longwell 50.

INTERCEPTIONS—Seattle, Springs 2-8, Hanks 1-7, W. Williams 1-3.

KICKOFF RETURNS—Seattle, Green 2-24. Green Bay, Howard 3-58, Parker 2-(minus 1), Mitchell 1-34.

PUNT RETURNS—Seattle, Rogers 3-5. Green Bay, Howard 3-26.

SACKS—Seattle, Kennedy 3, Team 1. Green Bay, Holliday 2.

WEEK 9

RESULTS

Baltimore 41, CLEVELAND 9
Buffalo 34, WASHINGTON 17
CAROLINA 33, Philadelphia 7
Chicago 14, GREEN BAY 13
Denver 33, SAN DIEGO 17
DETROIT 31, St. Louis 27
INDIANAPOLIS 25, Kansas City 17
Jacksonville 30, ATLANTA 7
MIAMI 17, Tennessee 0
N.Y. JETS 12, Arizona 7
Pittsburgh 27, SAN FRANCISCO 6
SEATTLE 37, Cincinnati 20
Tampa Bay 31, NEW ORLEANS 16
MINNESOTA 27, Dallas 17
Open date: N.Y. Giants, New England, Oakland

STANDINGS

AFC EAST

	W	L	T	Pct.
Miami	7	1	0	.875
Indianapolis	6	2	0	.750
New England	6	2	0	.750
Buffalo	6	3	0	.667
N.Y. Jets	2	6	0	.250

AFC CENTRAL

	W	L	T	Pct.
Jacksonville	7	1	0	.875
Tennessee	6	2	0	.750
Pittsburgh	5	3	0	.625
Baltimore	3	5	0	.375
Cincinnati	1	8	0	.111
Cleveland	1	8	0	.111

AFC WEST

	W	L	T	Pct.
Seattle	6	2	0	.750
Kansas City	5	3	0	.625
Oakland	4	4	0	.500
San Diego	4	4	0	.500
Denver	3	6	0	.333

NFC EAST

	W	L	T	Pct.
N.Y. Giants	5	3	0	.625
Washington	5	3	0	.625
Dallas	4	4	0	.500
Arizona	2	6	0	.250
Philadelphia	2	7	0	.222

NFC CENTRAL

	W	L	T	Pct.
Detroit	6	2	0	.750
Minnesota	5	4	0	.556
Green Bay	4	4	0	.500
Tampa Bay	4	4	0	.500
Chicago	4	5	0	.444

NFC WEST

	W	L	T	Pct.
St. Louis	6	2	0	.750
Carolina	3	5	0	.375
San Francisco	3	5	0	.375
Atlanta	2	7	0	.222
New Orleans	1	7	0	.125

HIGHLIGHTS

Hero of the week: Bryan Robinson blocked a 28-yard field goal attempt on the last play of the game to preserve Chicago's 14-13 victory over the Packers, the Bears' first win over Green Bay in 11 games and their first at Lambeau Field since 1992. Bears players, all wearing "No. 34" patches in remembrance of the great Walter Payton, who died six days earlier, stormed the field to celebrate the win.

Goat of the week: Ravens owner Art Modell, who chose not to return to the scene of the crime when his club visited Cleveland for the first time since Modell moved the then-Cleveland Browns to Baltimore in 1995. Browns fans, denied an opportunity to boo the despised Modell in person, were disappointed. But maybe not as disappointed as in the game itself, a 41-9 Ravens romp.

Sub of the week: Buccaneers quarterback Trent Dilfer, starting in place of the ailing and ineffective Eric Zeier, threw three touchdowns—including a 62-yarder to Jacquez Green in the first quarter—to lead Tampa Bay to a 31-16 win over New Orleans. The Saints lost their league-high seventh straight game.

Comeback of the week: Trailing 7-3 at halftime, the Jets scored nine unanswered points to beat the Cardinals 12-7. Curtis Martin spearheaded the New York attack, carrying the ball seven times for 36 yards on a drive that ended on a 33-yard John Hall field goal in the third period. Midway through the fourth quarter, Keyshawn Johnson broke away from linebacker Rob Fredrickson to catch a slant pass from Rick Mirer to score the game-winning points from 43 yards out.

Blowout of the week: The Ravens-Browns game was never close. Errict Rhett rushed 17 times for 117 yards and two touchdowns to complement a Baltimore defense which sacked Tim Couch four times and held him to 57 passing yards. The beleaguered Couch was benched after three quarters.

Nail-biter of the week: Trailing 27-24 with 1:17 left and facing fourth-and-26 at their own 21-yard line, the Lions stunned the Rams when Gus Frerotte and Germane Crowell hooked up for a 57-yard completion to the St. Louis 22, setting up Frerotte's game-winning 12-yard touchdown pass to Johnnie Morton three plays later. The Lions' final touchdown marked the seventh lead change in a see-saw game.

Hit of the week: Kevin Hardy, Carnell Lake and Brant Boyer each had two sacks as Jacksonville racked up a team-record nine sacks in a 30-7 victory over Atlanta.

Oddity of the week: Ronde Barber tried to disguise a short-hopped interception in the Buccaneers' end zone by quickly getting up and continuing the play, but his subterfuge didn't fool Saints coach Mike Ditka, who saw the ball bounce on a stadium replay and challenged the interception call. Inexplicably, the ruling was upheld. Officials later explained that the 90 seconds allowed for a review wasn't enough to discover the error, and by the time anyone in the replay booth saw the crucial end zone angle of the play, it was too late to overturn.

Top rusher: Charlie Garner carried the ball 20 times for a career-high 166 yards, but the injury-riddled 49ers couldn't score a touchdown and lost, 27-6, to the Steelers.

Top passer: Kurt Warner completed 25 of 42 passes for 305 yards and three touchdowns in the Rams' loss at Detroit.

Top receiver: Crowell caught eight passes for 163 yards and one touchdown in the Lions' win.

Notes: The Ravens set team records for the most points scored and fewest points allowed in their win over the Browns. ... Brett Favre started his 117th consecutive game for the Packers, breaking the record for consecutive quarterback starts held by Ron Jaworski, who started 116 for the Eagles from 1977-84. ... Fredrickson was credited with 22 tackles in the Cardinals' loss to the Jets, a modern-era single-game club record. ... The Panthers defense forced five turnovers that were converted into 20 points in their 33-7 victory over the Eagles. ... Although eight different San Francisco players caught passes against Pittsburgh, Jerry Rice caught only two, for two yards. ... Curtis Martin set a Jets

– 165 –

record with 38 carries (131 yards). ... Peyton Manning threw a touchdown pass in his 21st straight game. ... The Bills scored on five of their first six possessions in their 34-17 win at Washington. ... Emmitt Smith moved into third place on the NFL's all-time rushing list (behind Walter Payton and Barry Sanders) with a 140-yard performance in a 27-17 loss at Minnesota on Monday night. Smith also made history by scoring two touchdowns in an 18-second span of the second quarter, the fastest any player has scored two touchdowns in NFL history.

Quote of the week: The Bears' Robinson, on his game-saving field goal block: "I think Walter Payton picked me up because I can't jump that high. I just got my hand on that leather, and it felt so good . ... It's for you, Walter."

GAME SUMMARIES

JETS 12, CARDINALS 7
Sunday, November 7

Arizona	0	7	0	0— 7
N.Y. Jets	3	0	3	6—12

First Quarter
NYJ—FG, Hall 44, 8:22.
Second Quarter
Ariz.—Pittman 4 run (Jacke kick), 9:43.
Third Quarter
NYJ—FG, Hall 33, 11:53.
Fourth Quarter
NYJ—K. Johnson 43 pass from Mirer (pass failed), 9:31.
Attendance—77,857.

	Arizona	N.Y. Jets
First downs	10	15
Rushes-yards	18-55	46-184
Passing	151	111
Punt returns	2-3	6-44
Kickoff returns	3-70	2-46
Interception returns	0-0	0-0
Comp.-att.-int.	16-26-0	12-18-0
Sacked-yards lost	6-48	3-11
Punts	10-34	6-47
Fumbles-lost	4-1	2-0
Penalties-yards	4-25	3-25
Time of possession	23:48	36:12

INDIVIDUAL STATISTICS
RUSHING—Arizona, Pittman 9-41, Murrell 7-10, Da. Brown 1-3, Makovicka 1-1. New York, Martin 38-131, Mirer 7-41, K. Johnson 1-12.
PASSING—Arizona, Da. Brown 16-26-0-199. New York, Mirer 12-18-0-122.
RECEIVING—Arizona, Sanders 5-44, Moore 3-98, Murrell 3-19, McWilliams 2-12, Pittman 2-11, Makovicka 1-15. New York, Martin 4-2, K. Johnson 2-51, Chrebet 2-19, Baxter 1-24, Ward 1-11, Parmalee 1-8, Anderson 1-7.
MISSED FIELD GOAL ATTEMPTS—New York, Hall 29, 45.
INTERCEPTIONS—None.
KICKOFF RETURNS—Arizona, Bates 3-70. New York, Stone 2-46.
PUNT RETURNS—Arizona, Knight 1-3, Cody 1-0. New York, Ward 6-44.
SACKS—Arizona, Rice 2, Fredrickson 1. New York, Logan 2, Lewis 1, Lyle 1, Phifer 1, Farrior 1.

COLTS 25, CHIEFS 17
Sunday, November 7

Kansas City	3	7	7	0—17
Indianapolis	3	10	3	9—25

First Quarter
Ind.—FG, Vanderjagt 47, 8:02.
K.C.—FG, Stoyanovich 38, 14:44.
Second Quarter
Ind.—FG, Vanderjagt 34, 2:18.
K.C.—Bennett 23 run (Stoyanovich kick), 6:09.
Ind.—James 30 pass from Manning (Vanderjagt kick), 9:15.
Third Quarter
K.C.—Lockett 18 pass from Grbac (Stoyanovich kick), 6:03.
Ind.—FG, Vanderjagt 29, 11:00.
Fourth Quarter
Ind.—Manning 7 run (pass failed), 4:11.
Ind.—FG, Vanderjagt 37, 13:50.
Attendance—56,689.

	Kansas City	Indianapolis
First downs	19	21
Rushes-yards	29-108	23-119
Passing	211	256
Punt returns	1-35	3-27
Kickoff returns	6-131	4-95
Interception returns	1-37	0-0
Comp.-att.-int.	19-34-0	21-33-1
Sacked-yards lost	1-5	3-34
Punts	5-43	2-53
Fumbles-lost	1-1	1-1
Penalties-yards	10-75	5-28
Time of possession	31:15	28:45

INDIVIDUAL STATISTICS
RUSHING—Kansas City, Morris 13-37, Bennett 12-64, Richardson 3-5, Grbac 1-2. Indianapolis, James 20-109, Manning 3-10.
PASSING—Kansas City, Grbac 18-31-0-196, Moon 1-3-0-20. Indianapolis, Manning 21-33-1-290.
RECEIVING—Kansas City, Lockett 3-54, Alexander 3-42, Gonzalez 3-37, Johnson 3-33, Horn 2-20, Morris 2-13, Bennett 2-6, Rison 1-11. Indianapolis, Harrison 7-93, James 7-90, Wilkins 3-26, Pollard 2-30, Dilger 1-30, Shields 1-21.
MISSED FIELD GOAL ATTEMPTS—Kansas City, Stoyanovich 47.
INTERCEPTIONS—Kansas City, McGlockton 1-30.
KICKOFF RETURNS—Kansas City, Horn 6-131. Indianapolis, Wilkins 4-95.
PUNT RETURNS—Kansas City, L. Parker 1-35. Indianapolis, Wilkins 3-27.
SACKS—Kansas City, Tongue 1, Edwards 1, Thomas 1. Indianapolis, Poole 1.

JAGUARS 30, FALCONS 7
Sunday, November 7

Jacksonville	7	10	10	3—30
Atlanta	0	7	0	0— 7

First Quarter
Jac.—J. Smith 44 pass from Brunell (Hollis kick), 7:56.
Second Quarter
Jac.—Jones 9 pass from Brunell (Hollis kick), 0:46.
Jac.—FG, Hollis 27, 6:24.
Atl.—Dwight 17 pass from Chandler (Andersen kick), 14:31.
Third Quarter
Jac.—FG, Hollis 24, 6:50.
Jac.—McCardell 2 pass from Brunell (Hollis kick), 13:19.
Fourth Quarter
Jac.—FG, Hollis 34, 10:31.
Attendance—68,466.

	Jacksonville	Atlanta
First downs	20	10
Rushes-yards	34-152	11-42
Passing	215	140
Punt returns	3-9	2-27
Kickoff returns	2-25	6-142
Interception returns	3-18	0-0
Comp.-att.-int.	19-34-0	17-30-3
Sacked-yards lost	3-23	9-63
Punts	4-42	6-37
Fumbles-lost	1-0	2-1
Penalties-yards	5-40	5-34
Time of possession	34:24	25:36

INDIVIDUAL STATISTICS
RUSHING—Jacksonville, Taylor 27-124, J. Stewart 2-11, Brunell 2-7, Fiedler 2-(minus 2), Banks 1-12. Atlanta, Oxendine 5-11, Hanspard 4-11, Christian 1-10, Oliver 1-10.
PASSING—Jacksonville, Brunell 14-27-0-203, Fiedler 5-7-0-35. Atlanta, Chandler 14-25-2-163, Graziani 3-5-1-40.

RECEIVING—Jacksonville, McCardell 9-62, J. Smith 4-77, Taylor 2-54, Barlow 1-20, Brady 1-11, Jones 1-9, Banks 1-5. Atlanta, Kozlowski 3-49, Oxendine 3-39, Mathis 3-28, Dwight 2-47, Christian 2-8, Hanspard 2-7, German 1-23, Santiago 1-2.
MISSED FIELD GOAL ATTEMPTS—Jacksonville, Hollis 48.
INTERCEPTIONS—Jacksonville, Marts 1-10, Darius 1-8, Brackens 1-0.
KICKOFF RETURNS—Jacksonville, Barlow 1-13, Banks 1-12. Atlanta, Dwight 6-142.
PUNT RETURNS—Jacksonville, Barlow 3-9. Atlanta, Dwight 2-27.
SACKS—Jacksonville, Hardy 2, Boyer 2, Lake 2, Walker 1, Paup 1, Wynn 1. Atlanta, Tuggle 2, Archambeau 1.

LIONS 31, RAMS 27

Sunday, November 7

St. Louis	2	10	0	15	27
Detroit	0	10	11	10	31

First Quarter
St.L.—Safety, G. Hill tackled by L. Fletcher in end zone, 8:02.
Second Quarter
Det.—Crowell 4 pass from Batch (Hanson kick), 0:41.
St.L.—Robinson 6 pass from Warner (Wilkins kick), 3:28.
Det.—FG, Hanson 29, 8:09.
St.L.—FG, Wilkins 34, 14:19.
Third Quarter
Det.—Schlesinger 3 pass from Frerotte (Crowell pass from Frerotte), 5:40.
Det.—FG, Hanson 43, 10:11.
Fourth Quarter
St.L.—Hakim 75 pass from Warner (Wilkins kick), 4:54.
Det.—FG, Hanson 44, 8:50.
St.L.—Tucker 2 pass from Warner (Bruce pass from Warner), 12:18.
Det.—Morton 12 pass from Frerotte (Hanson kick), 14:32.
Attendance—73,224.

	St. Louis	Detroit
First downs	20	17
Rushes-yards	16-57	21-24
Passing	275	311
Punt returns	3-34	4-27
Kickoff returns	8-184	5-99
Interception returns	0-0	2-26
Comp.-att.-int.	25-43-2	22-36-0
Sacked-yards lost	4-30	6-46
Punts	8-37	6-41
Fumbles-lost	3-0	3-0
Penalties-yards	7-54	9-95
Time of possession	30:00	30:00

INDIVIDUAL STATISTICS
RUSHING—St. Louis, Faulk 11-15, Warner 3-26, Holcombe 2-16. Detroit, Hill 11-3, Frerotte 5-8, Irvin 4-10, Batch 1-3.
PASSING—St. Louis, Warner 25-42-2-305, Faulk 0-1-0-0. Detroit, Batch 10-20-0-148, Frerotte 12-16-0-209.
RECEIVING—St. Louis, Faulk 10-78, Proehl 4-36, Holt 3-31, Hakim 2-94, Bruce 2-34, R. Williams 1-15, Lee 1-9, Robinson 1-6, Tucker 1-2. Detroit, Crowell 8-163, Irvin 4-65, Morton 4-59, Stablein 2-48, Chryplewicz 2-18, Schlesinger 1-3, Sloan 1-1.
MISSED FIELD GOAL ATTEMPTS—None.
INTERCEPTIONS—Detroit, Rice 1-20, Fair 1-6.
KICKOFF RETURNS—St. Louis, Carpenter 6-149, Hakim 2-35. Detroit, Fair 1-26, Morton 1-22, Irvin 1-21, Talton 1-17, Schlesinger 1-13.
PUNT RETURNS—St. Louis, Hakim 3-34. Detroit, Uwaezuoke 3-18, Fair 1-9.
SACKS—St. Louis, Carter 3, Farr 2, Wistrom 1. Detroit, Jones 1.5, Porcher 1, Scroggins 1, Elliss 0.5.

PANTHERS 33, EAGLES 7

Sunday, November 7

Philadelphia	0	0	0	7	7
Carolina	3	20	3	7	33

First Quarter
Car.—FG, Kasay 38, 2:34.
Second Quarter
Car.—Muhammad 4 pass from Beuerlein (Kasay kick), 2:00.
Car.—Muhammad 12 pass from Beuerlein (Kasay kick), 11:56.
Car.—FG, Kasay 28, 13:03.
Car.—FG, Kasay 33, 14:54.

Third Quarter
Car.—FG, Kasay 22, 7:25.
Fourth Quarter
Car.—Jeffers 21 pass from Beuerlein (Kasay kick), 0:28.
Phi.—Staley 14 run (N. Johnson kick), 12:23.
Attendance—62,569.

	Philadelphia	Carolina
First downs	17	24
Rushes-yards	23-168	38-111
Passing	81	270
Punt returns	2-1	4-37
Kickoff returns	7-101	2-24
Interception returns	0-0	1-0
Comp.-att.-int.	11-29-1	21-35-0
Sacked-yards lost	3-15	2-11
Punts	5-43	3-37
Fumbles-lost	4-4	0-0
Penalties-yards	11-93	7-74
Time of possession	23:22	36:38

INDIVIDUAL STATISTICS
RUSHING—Philadelphia, Staley 17-140, McNabb 3-21, Bostic 2-8, Pederson 1-(minus 1). Carolina, Lane 20-74, Johnson 7-4, Floyd 4-8, Bates 2-14, Hetherington 2-7, Bono 2-(minus 2), Beuerlein 1-6.
PASSING—Philadelphia, McNabb 8-20-1-68, Pederson 3-9-0-28. Carolina, Beuerlein 21-34-0-281, Bono 0-1-0-0.
RECEIVING—Philadelphia, Small 4-39, C. Johnson 3-32, Staley 2-11, Weaver 1-8, Broughton 1-6. Carolina, Muhammad 8-88, Walls 5-70, Metcalf 2-48, Jeffers 2-30, Lane 2-20, Floyd 1-14, Johnson 1-11.
MISSED FIELD GOAL ATTEMPTS—None.
INTERCEPTIONS—Carolina, Evans 1-0.
KICKOFF RETURNS—Philadelphia, Rossum 5-88, Bieniemy 1-12, Smith 1-1. Carolina, Bates 2-24.
PUNT RETURNS—Philadelphia, Rossum 2-1. Carolina, Metcalf 4-37.
SACKS—Philadelphia, Trotter 0.5, Mamula 0.5, W. Thomas 0.5, Whiting 0.5. Carolina, Greene 2, Gilbert 1.

BILLS 34, REDSKINS 17

Sunday, November 7

Buffalo	3	14	14	3	34
Washington	7	3	0	7	17

First Quarter
Was.—Davis 8 run (Conway kick), 4:05.
Buf.—FG, Christie 23, 11:12.
Second Quarter
Buf.—Collins 6 pass from Flutie (Christie kick), 6:15.
Was.—FG, Conway 41, 9:36.
Buf.—A. Smith 1 run (Christie kick), 14:42.
Third Quarter
Buf.—A. Smith 10 run (Christie kick), 8:10.
Buf.—Moulds 14 pass from Flutie (Christie kick), 14:10.
Fourth Quarter
Was.—Connell 19 pass from B. Johnson (Conway kick), 7:33.
Buf.—FG, Christie 20, 10:59.
Attendance—78,721.

	Buffalo	Washington
First downs	24	16
Rushes-yards	49-204	13-57
Passing	209	222
Punt returns	0-0	0-0
Kickoff returns	1-21	7-149
Interception returns	1-0	0-0
Comp.-att.-int.	16-22-0	19-37-1
Sacked-yards lost	1-2	2-10
Punts	2-29	2-31
Fumbles-lost	0-0	1-1
Penalties-yards	6-79	2-15
Time of possession	41:00	19:00

INDIVIDUAL STATISTICS
RUSHING—Buffalo, Linton 24-96, A. Smith 20-68, Flutie 5-40. Washington, Davis 9-33, Mitchell 2-12, Westbrook 2-12.
PASSING—Buffalo, Flutie 16-22-0-211. Washington, B. Johnson 19-37-1-232.
RECEIVING—Buffalo, Moulds 5-61, Riemersma 4-86, Reed 4-51, Linton 2-7, Collins 1-6. Washington, Connell 4-84, Westbrook 4-72, Mitchell 4-39, Centers 3-1, Davis 2-27, Alexander 2-9.

MISSED FIELD GOAL ATTEMPTS—Washington, Conway 55.
INTERCEPTIONS—Buffalo, Schulz 1-0.
KICKOFF RETURNS—Buffalo, K. Williams 1-21. Washington, Mitchell 3-86, Sellers 2-25, Thrash 1-28, Jenkins 1-10.
PUNT RETURNS—None.
SACKS—Buffalo, P. Williams 1, Cummings 1. Washington, Stevens 1.

RAVENS 41, BROWNS 9

Sunday, November 7

Baltimore	7	10	7	17—	41
Cleveland	3	0	0	6—	9

First Quarter
Bal.—Rhett 11 run (Stover kick), 6:55.
Cle.—FG, Dawson 25, 14:42.
Second Quarter
Bal.—Ismail 28 pass from Banks (Stover kick), 6:51.
Bal.—FG, Stover 28, 14:57.
Third Quarter
Bal.—Rhett 52 run (Stover kick), 12:10.
Fourth Quarter
Bal.—FG, Stover 44, 6:35.
Bal.—Woodson 66 interception return (Stover kick), 8:01.
Cle.—Kirby 5 pass from Detmer (kick blocked), 9:47.
Bal.—Case 20 run (Stover kick), 12:22.
Attendance—72,898.

	Baltimore	Cleveland
First downs	20	10
Rushes-yards	38-203	20-51
Passing	112	114
Punt returns	7-49	1-4
Kickoff returns	2-27	8-173
Interception returns	2-66	0-0
Comp.-att.-int.	14-25-0	16-36-2
Sacked-yards lost	2-17	3-24
Punts	4-41	8-46
Fumbles-lost	1-1	3-0
Penalties-yards	4-29	4-25
Time of possession	33:52	26:08

INDIVIDUAL STATISTICS
RUSHING—Baltimore, Rhett 17-117, Holmes 10-40, Banks 4-23, Case 4-17, Evans 3-6. Cleveland, Abdul-Jabbar 9-23, Kirby 6-19, Couch 4-2, Detmer 1-7.
PASSING—Baltimore, Banks 14-25-0-129. Cleveland, Couch 9-21-1-57, Detmer 7-15-1-81.
RECEIVING—Baltimore, Armour 5-38, Rhett 4-21, Ismail 2-43, Pierce 2-17, Johnson 1-10. Cleveland, Kirby 5-52, Johnson 3-43, Shepherd 3-23, Edwards 2-9, I. Smith 2-9, Abdul-Jabbar 1-2.
MISSED FIELD GOAL ATTEMPTS—None.
INTERCEPTIONS—Baltimore, Woodson 1-66, Starks 1-0.
KICKOFF RETURNS—Baltimore, Harris 1-20, Pierce 1-7. Cleveland, Dunn 4-96, Powell 3-67, Campbell 1-10.
PUNT RETURNS—Baltimore, J. Lewis 7-49. Cleveland, Dunn 1-4.
SACKS—Baltimore, Sharper 1, Burnett 1, McCrary 1. Cleveland, McCutcheon 1, Thierry 1.

BEARS 14, PACKERS 13

Sunday, November 7

Chicago	7	0	7	0—	14
Green Bay	3	7	0	3—	13

First Quarter
G.B.—FG, Longwell 37, 10:14.
Chi.—Milburn 49 run (Boniol kick), 12:44.
Second Quarter
G.B.—T. Davis 7 pass from Favre (Longwell kick), 14:30.
Third Quarter
Chi.—Engram 6 pass from Miller (Boniol kick), 14:31.
Fourth Quarter
G.B.—FG, Longwell 26, 3:54.
Attendance—59,867.

	Chicago	Green Bay
First downs	19	21
Rushes-yards	29-160	30-81
Passing	151	259
Punt returns	2-26	1-6
Kickoff returns	4-58	3-33
Interception returns	1-0	3-9
Comp.-att.-int.	18-34-3	27-40-1
Sacked-yards lost	1-6	2-8
Punts	4-39	5-40
Fumbles-lost	3-1	1-0
Penalties-yards	3-24	4-30
Time of possession	29:28	30:32

INDIVIDUAL STATISTICS
RUSHING—Chicago, Enis 20-88, Allen 4-17, Milburn 3-54, Bennett 1-1, McNown 1-0. Green Bay, Levens 26-79, Favre 3-4, Freeman 1-(minus 2).
PASSING—Chicago, Miller 16-29-3-142, McNown 2-5-0-15. Green Bay, Favre 27-40-1-267.
RECEIVING—Chicago, Engram 6-48, M. Robinson 4-66, Milburn 2-1, Brooks 1-10, Enis 1-8, Bates 1-8, Allred 1-6, Bennett 1-5, Wetnight 1-5. Green Bay, Freeman 8-71, Schroeder 4-25, Levens 4-25, Bradford 3-53, Henderson 3-25, T. Davis 3-24, Thomason 2-12.
MISSED FIELD GOAL ATTEMPTS—Chicago, Boniol 34. Green Bay, Longwell 28.
INTERCEPTIONS—Chicago, Hudson 1-0. Green Bay, Sharper 1-9, M. McKenzie 1-0, Edwards 1-0.
KICKOFF RETURNS—Chicago, Milburn 3-58, Tuinei 1-0. Green Bay, Howard 1-14, Parker 1-12, Henderson 1-7.
PUNT RETURNS—Chicago, Milburn 2-26. Green Bay, Howard 1-6.
SACKS—Chicago, W. Harris 1, Flanigan 1. Green Bay, Lyon 1.

BUCCANEERS 31, SAINTS 16

Sunday, November 7

Tampa Bay	7	10	7	7—	31
New Orleans	3	3	0	10—	16

First Quarter
N.O.—FG, Brien 29, 9:25.
T.B.—Green 62 pass from Dilfer (Gramatica kick), 10:59.
Second Quarter
T.B.—FG, Gramatica 35, 5:11.
T.B.—J. Davis 1 pass from Dilfer (Gramatica kick), 10:33.
N.O.—FG, Brien 39, 14:30.
Third Quarter
T.B.—McDonald 10 pass from Dilfer (Gramatica kick), 7:12.
Fourth Quarter
N.O.—FG, Brien 37, 4:15.
N.O.—Poole 1 pass from Tolliver (Brien kick), 14:12.
T.B.—Alstott 25 run (Gramatica kick), 14:45.
Attendance—47,129.

	Tampa Bay	New Orleans
First downs	18	21
Rushes-yards	40-156	23-98
Passing	225	205
Punt returns	0-0	1-10
Kickoff returns	5-116	6-96
Interception returns	2-55	0-0
Comp.-att.-int.	15-20-0	18-37-2
Sacked-yards lost	1-2	1-6
Punts	2-47	3-39
Fumbles-lost	2-2	1-1
Penalties-yards	9-70	5-40
Time of possession	33:51	26:09

INDIVIDUAL STATISTICS
RUSHING—Tampa Bay, Alstott 25-117, Dunn 12-42, Dilfer 2-2, Green 1-(minus 5). New Orleans, R. Williams 14-41, Tolliver 5-28, L. Smith 2-22, Kennison 1-4, Craver 1-3.
PASSING—Tampa Bay, Dilfer 15-20-0-227. New Orleans, Tolliver 18-37-2-211.
RECEIVING—Tampa Bay, Green 4-89, Dunn 3-54, McDonald 3-47, Anthony 2-14, Alstott 1-15, Moore 1-7, J. Davis 1-1. New Orleans, L. Smith 4-27, R. Williams 4-22, Poole 3-23, Hastings 2-45, Kennison 2-42, Cleeland 2-39, Bech 1-13.
MISSED FIELD GOAL ATTEMPTS—Tampa Bay, Gramatica 51.
INTERCEPTIONS—Tampa Bay, Brooks 1-38, Barber 1-17.
KICKOFF RETURNS—Tampa Bay, Murphy 4-113, Moore 1-3. New Orleans, Davis 3-78, Perry 2-6, Bech 1-12.
PUNT RETURNS—New Orleans, Kennison 1-10.
SACKS—Tampa Bay, Culpepper 0.5, Ahanotu 0.5. New Orleans, Tomich 1.

DOLPHINS 17, TITANS 0

Sunday, November 7

Tennessee	0	0	0	0—	0
Miami	0	14	0	3—	17

Second Quarter
Mia.—Pritchett 6 pass from Huard (Mare kick), 1:17.
Mia.—Martin 43 pass from Huard (Mare kick), 7:33.

Fourth Quarter
Mia.—FG, Mare 46, 0:05.
Attendance—74,109.

	Tennessee	Miami
First downs	14	14
Rushes-yards	23-103	27-52
Passing	190	185
Punt returns	2-23	3-17
Kickoff returns	3-77	0-0
Interception returns	0-0	3-101
Comp.-att.-int.	22-42-3	15-25-0
Sacked-yards lost	4-15	4-25
Punts	6-39	7-44
Fumbles-lost	0-0	3-1
Penalties-yards	2-19	5-40
Time of possession	31:58	28:02

INDIVIDUAL STATISTICS
RUSHING—Tennessee, E. George 14-65, McNair 7-33, Thomas 2-5. Miami, Collins 14-41, Johnson 11-9, Huard 2-2.
PASSING—Tennessee, McNair 22-42-3-205. Miami, Huard 15-25-0-210.
RECEIVING—Tennessee, Thigpen 5-60, Harris 5-32, Dyson 3-32, Wycheck 3-15, E. George 2-20, Thomas 2-4, Sanders 1-40, Neal 1-2. Miami, Martin 5-95, McDuffie 4-41, Gadsden 2-47, Pritchett 2-15, Konrad 1-8, Johnson 1-4.
MISSED FIELD GOAL ATTEMPTS—Tennessee, Del Greco 33. Miami, Mare 43.
INTERCEPTIONS—Miami, Madison 3-101.
KICKOFF RETURNS—Tennessee, Mason 3-77.
PUNT RETURNS—Tennessee, Mason 2-23. Miami, Jacquet 2-17, McDuffie 1-0.
SACKS—Tennessee, Ford 2.5, Bowden 0.5, Kearse 0.5, Holmes 0.5. Miami, Owens 1, Wilson 1, Armstrong 1, Gardener 0.5, Bowens 0.5.

BRONCOS 33, CHARGERS 17

Sunday, November 7

Denver	3	10	7	13—	33
San Diego	0	3	7	7—	17

First Quarter
Den.—FG, Elam 44, 6:10.

Second Quarter
Den.—Romanowski recovered fumble in end zone (Elam kick), 1:40.
S.D.—FG, Carney 46, 9:09.
Den.—FG, Elam 55, 15:00.

Third Quarter
Den.—Gary 23 run (Elam kick), 6:32.
S.D.—F. Jones 7 pass from Harbaugh (Carney kick), 11:50.

Fourth Quarter
Den.—FG, Elam 41, 1:34.
S.D.—C. Jones 44 pass from Harbaugh (Carney kick), 5:43.
Den.—FG, Elam 24, 10:42.
Den.—Gary 5 run (Elam kick), 13:04.
Attendance—61,204.

	Denver	San Diego
First downs	17	19
Rushes-yards	31-114	19-59
Passing	127	214
Punt returns	3-12	2-6
Kickoff returns	4-106	7-119
Interception returns	2-17	0-0
Comp.-att.-int.	14-24-0	25-39-2
Sacked-yards lost	5-39	4-21
Punts	4-40	3-44
Fumbles-lost	2-0	4-2
Penalties-yards	8-61	6-55
Time of possession	29:28	30:32

INDIVIDUAL STATISTICS
RUSHING—Denver, Gary 30-108, Griffith 1-6. San Diego, Bynum 11-24, Stephens 3-13, Fletcher 3-8, Harbaugh 2-14.
PASSING—Denver, C. Miller 14-24-0-166. San Diego, Harbaugh 25-39-2-235.
RECEIVING—Denver, R. Smith 5-70, B. Miller 2-36, Griffith 2-23, Cooper 2-18, Gary 2-11, Carswell 1-8. San Diego, Ricks 5-41, F. Jones 4-65, McCrary 4-4, Stephens 3-38, Bynum 3-10, C. Jones 2-53, Penn 2-13, J. Graham 2-11.
MISSED FIELD GOAL ATTEMPTS—None.
INTERCEPTIONS—Denver, Romanowski 1-17, James 1-0.
KICKOFF RETURNS—Denver, Watson 4-106. San Diego, Stephens 4-53, Bynum 3-66.
PUNT RETURNS—Denver, Watson 3-12. San Diego, Penn 2-6.
SACKS—Denver, Tanuvasa 2, Pryce 1, Wayne 1. San Diego, Dumas 1, Fontenot 1, Parrella 1, Dixon 1, Team 1.

STEELERS 27, 49ERS 6

Sunday, November 7

Pittsburgh	14	3	3	7—	27
San Francisco	3	3	0	0—	6

First Quarter
Pit.—Bettis 1 run (K. Brown kick), 7:31.
S.F.—FG, Richey 19, 9:51.
Pit.—Ward 13 pass from Stewart (K. Brown kick), 12:08.

Second Quarter
Pit.—FG, K. Brown 28, 0:09.
S.F.—FG, Richey 20, 8:07.

Third Quarter
Pit.—FG, K. Brown 38, 11:19.

Fourth Quarter
Pit.—Bettis 22 run (K. Brown kick), 11:45.
Attendance—68,657.

	Pittsburgh	San Francisco
First downs	14	16
Rushes-yards	31-141	34-223
Passing	130	90
Punt returns	1-12	4-5
Kickoff returns	1-20	6-145
Interception returns	1-25	0-0
Comp.-att.-int.	15-26-0	12-33-1
Sacked-yards lost	1-9	1-3
Punts	5-42	3-45
Fumbles-lost	0-0	2-1
Penalties-yards	6-33	11-95
Time of possession	28:33	31:27

INDIVIDUAL STATISTICS
RUSHING—Pittsburgh, Bettis 18-53, Huntley 7-83, Stewart 3-8, Tomczak 3-(minus 3). San Francisco, Garner 20-166, Beasley 5-25, Garcia 4-25, Phillips 4-0, Stenstrom 1-7.
PASSING—Pittsburgh, Stewart 15-26-0-139. San Francisco, Garcia 7-18-0-39, Stenstrom 5-15-1-54.
RECEIVING—Pittsburgh, Edwards 6-76, Ward 4-31, Hawkins 2-26, Blackwell 2-6, Bruener 1-5. San Francisco, Garner 3-33, Owens 2-15, Rice 2-2, Phillips 1-11, Stokes 1-11, Beasley 1-9, Stenstrom 1-9, Cline 1-3.
MISSED FIELD GOAL ATTEMPTS—Pittsburgh, K. Brown 31. San Francisco, Richey 49.
INTERCEPTIONS—Pittsburgh, Shields 1-25.
KICKOFF RETURNS—Pittsburgh, Edwards 1-20. San Francisco, Phillips 6-145.
PUNT RETURNS—Pittsburgh, Hawkins 1-12. San Francisco, McQuarters 4-5.
SACKS—Pittsburgh, Oldham 1. San Francisco, Tubbs 0.5, Woodall 0.5.

SEAHAWKS 37, BENGALS 20

Sunday, November 7

Cincinnati	10	0	3	7—	20
Seattle	14	14	3	6—	37

First Quarter
Sea.—Watters 19 run (Peterson kick), 2:54.
Cin.—FG, Pelfrey 50, 4:58.
Sea.—Watters 8 pass from Kitna (Peterson kick), 8:24.
Cin.—Pickens 75 pass from Blake (Pelfrey kick), 12:58.

1999 REVIEW Week 9

Second Quarter
Sea.—Pritchard 20 pass from Kitna (Peterson kick), 4:12.
Sea.—Mayes 10 pass from Kitna (Peterson kick), 10:01.
Third Quarter
Sea.—FG, Peterson 29, 4:15.
Cin.—FG, Pelfrey 34, 9:22.
Fourth Quarter
Sea.—FG, Peterson 45, 2:35.
Cin.—Blake 1 run (Pelfrey kick), 11:07.
Sea.—FG, Peterson 35, 13:30.
Attendance—66,303.

	Cincinnati	Seattle
First downs	19	26
Rushes-yards	23-103	37-173
Passing	294	187
Punt returns	1-8	2-9
Kickoff returns	7-132	4-95
Interception returns	2-7	2-5
Comp.-att.-int.	20-38-2	14-24-2
Sacked-yards lost	1-8	2-15
Punts	3-39	2-37
Fumbles-lost	1-0	1-0
Penalties-yards	16-107	8-71
Time of possession	30:27	29:33

INDIVIDUAL STATISTICS
RUSHING—Cincinnati, Dillon 16-81, Blake 5-34, Basnight 1-1, Yeast 1-(minus 13). Seattle, Watters 27-133, Green 9-40, Kitna 1-0.
PASSING—Cincinnati, Blake 18-35-2-287, Covington 2-3-0-15. Seattle, Kitna 14-24-2-202.
RECEIVING—Cincinnati, McGee 5-77, Pickens 4-104, Jackson 4-75, Battaglia 3-24, Williams 2-15, Basnight 2-7. Seattle, Mayes 5-61, Pritchard 3-61, Dawkins 3-52, Fauria 1-14, Watters 1-8, Jordan 1-6.
MISSED FIELD GOAL ATTEMPTS—None.
INTERCEPTIONS—Cincinnati, Spikes 1-7, Hall 1-0. Seattle, Kennedy 1-5, Smith 1-0.
KICKOFF RETURNS—Cincinnati, Mack 7-132. Seattle, Green 4-95.
PUNT RETURNS—Cincinnati, Jackson 1-8. Seattle, Jordan 2-9.
SACKS—Cincinnati, Bell 1, Simmons 1. Seattle, Daniels 1.

VIKINGS 27, COWBOYS 17
Monday, November 8

Dallas 0   17   0   0—17
Minnesota 0   7   6 14—27

Second Quarter
Dal.—FG, Cunningham 39, 3:39.
Dal.—E. Smith 63 run (Cunningham kick), 8:39.
Dal.—E. Smith 24 run (Cunningham kick), 8:57.
Min.—Moss 4 pass from George (Anderson kick), 13:07.
Third Quarter
Min.—FG, Anderson 31, 4:31.
Min.—FG, Anderson 40, 10:20.
Fourth Quarter
Min.—Carter 4 pass from George (Anderson kick), 1:22.
Min.—Moss 47 pass from George (Anderson kick), 9:50.
Attendance—64,111.

	Dallas	Minnesota
First downs	14	17
Rushes-yards	24-205	32-118
Passing	119	190
Punt returns	4-31	4-58
Kickoff returns	6-115	4-87
Interception returns	1-4	1-0
Comp.-att.-int.	17-35-1	17-30-1
Sacked-yards lost	2-14	4-28
Punts	6-47	6-45
Fumbles-lost	3-1	1-1
Penalties-yards	8-55	12-95
Time of possession	27:22	32:38

INDIVIDUAL STATISTICS
RUSHING—Dallas, E. Smith 13-140, Warren 7-52, Garrett 2-11, Ismail 1-2, Aikman 1-0. Minnesota, Hoard 21-87, M. Williams 6-20, George 5-11.
PASSING—Dallas, Aikman 14-24-0-129, Garrett 3-11-1-4. Minnesota, George 17-30-1-218.
RECEIVING—Dallas, Ismail 7-63, Warren 5-29, Mills 3-31, E. Smith 1-9, Tucker 1-1. Minnesota, Carter 9-116, Moss 6-91, Jordan 1-9, Glover 1-2.
MISSED FIELD GOAL ATTEMPTS—Dallas, Cunningham 42, 37. Minnesota, Anderson 49.
INTERCEPTIONS—Dallas, Reese 1-4. Minnesota, Hitchcock 1-0.
KICKOFF RETURNS—Dallas, Mathis 6-115. Minnesota, Palmer 2-32, Tate 1-29, M. Williams 1-26.
PUNT RETURNS—Dallas, Ogden 3-25, Sanders 1-6. Minnesota, Moss 4-58.
SACKS—Dallas, Ellis 2, Noble 1, Pittman 1. Minnesota, Ball 1, Randle 1.

1999 REVIEW Week 9

WEEK 10

RESULTS

ARIZONA 23, Detroit 19
BUFFALO 23, Miami 3
Cleveland 16, PITTSBURGH 15
DALLAS 27, Green Bay 13
Indianapolis 27, N.Y. GIANTS 19
JACKSONVILLE 6, Baltimore 3
Minnesota 27, CHICAGO 24 (OT)
NEW ORLEANS 24, San Francisco 6
OAKLAND 28, San Diego 9
PHILADELPHIA 35, Washington 28
ST. LOUIS 35, Carolina 10
SEATTLE 20, Denver 17
TAMPA BAY 17, Kansas City 10
Tennessee 24, CINCINNATI 14
N.Y. Jets 24, NEW ENGLAND 17
Open date: Atlanta

STANDINGS

AFC EAST
	W	L	T	Pct.
Indianapolis	7	2	0	.778
Miami	7	2	0	.778
Buffalo	7	3	0	.700
New England	6	3	0	.667
N.Y. Jets	3	6	0	.333

AFC CENTRAL
	W	L	T	Pct.
Jacksonville	8	1	0	.889
Tennessee	7	2	0	.778
Pittsburgh	5	4	0	.556
Baltimore	3	6	0	.333
Cleveland	2	8	0	.200
Cincinnati	1	9	0	.100

AFC WEST
	W	L	T	Pct.
Seattle	7	2	0	.778
Kansas City	5	4	0	.556
Oakland	5	4	0	.556
San Diego	4	5	0	.444
Denver	3	7	0	.300

NFC EAST
	W	L	T	Pct.
Dallas	5	4	0	.556
N.Y. Giants	5	4	0	.556
Washington	5	4	0	.556
Arizona	3	6	0	.333
Philadelphia	3	7	0	.300

NFC CENTRAL
	W	L	T	Pct.
Detroit	6	3	0	.667
Minnesota	6	4	0	.600
Tampa Bay	5	4	0	.556
Green Bay	4	5	0	.444
Chicago	4	6	0	.400

NFC WEST
	W	L	T	Pct.
St. Louis	7	2	0	.778
Carolina	3	6	0	.333
San Francisco	3	6	0	.333
Atlanta	2	7	0	.222
New Orleans	2	7	0	.222

HIGHLIGHTS

Hero of the week: Rookie Tim Couch completed 18 of 28 passes for 199 yards and two touchdowns and then led his team on a five-play, 58-yard drive to set up Phil Dawson's 39-yard game-winning field goal with no time left as Cleveland upset Pittsburgh 16-15. The victory was especially notable because it avenged a 43-0 rout the Browns suffered at the hands of the Steelers in Cleveland in Week 1.

Goat of the week: Bears kicker Chris Boniol barely missed a 41-yard field goal in overtime against the Vikings, but miss it he did, costing his team the game. The Vikings won, 27-24, when Gary Anderson hit a 38-yard field goal on Minnesota's next possession.

Sub of the week: Jets quarterback Ray Lucas, subbing for Rick Mirer, completed 18-of-31 passes for 153 yards in his second NFL start in leading New York to a 24-17 win at New England on Monday night. Lucas' supporting cast of running back Curtis Martin, tight end Wayne Chrebet and wide receiver Keyshawn Johnson helped to take some of the pressure off him with their solid play.

Comeback of the week: The Packers trailed at Dallas, 20-3, with 10:40 left when Brett Favre threw a 28-yard touchdown pass to Antonio Freeman and then directed another drive that resulted in a 31-yard field goal by Ryan Longwell, trimming the Cowboys' lead to 20-13 with under two minutes left. The Packers then recovered the onside kick and Favre drove the team to the Dallas 25 with 21 seconds remaining. George Teague ended the Green Bay march by picking off a Favre pass and returning it 95 yards for a touchdown, clinching a 27-13 Cowboys win.

Blowout of the week: A rested Raiders team coming off its bye week had no trouble with the Chargers, winning 28-9 and outgaining San Diego 417 total yards to 225. Veteran quarterback Rich Gannon, who used the week off to get healthy, served up short strikes all over the field, completing 18 of 24 passes for 254 yards and four touchdowns.

Nail-biter of the week: Anderson was set to kick a 20-yard field goal on the last play of regulation and hand the Vikings their sixth win. Instead, he sent the ball a mile wide of the upright because holder Mitch Berger couldn't cleanly handle the snap. The Vikings won the toss in overtime, but Walt Harris picked off a Jeff George pass on Minnesota's first play, giving Chicago possession at the Vikings 29. After three plays, it was the Bears' chance to try a game-winning field goal. But Boniol, given a chance to redeem his lackluster season with one kick, missed from 41 yards out, and the Vikings had another chance. George got a 22-yard gift when Bears cornerback Terry Cousins was called for pass interference on Cris Carter, setting up Anderson for a second field goal attempt to end the game. This time Anderson didn't miss, putting a 38-yarder between the posts to give the Vikings the victory.

Hit of the week: The Jaguars led Baltimore, 6-3, when defensive end Gary Walker broke through the Ravens' line, drilling quarterback Tony Banks on fourth-and-three on the final play of the game to preserve the Jacksonville win. The Jaguars, playing without running back Fred Taylor, relied on their formidable defense to keep the score low and make plays. Walker did.

Oddity of the week: When Cardinals running back Michael Pittman's fourth-quarter fumble was returned 35 yards by Detroit's Terry Fair for a touchdown with 5:26 left in the game, Arizona was on the ropes. Fair's touchdown cut the Cardinals' lead to 23-19, and it appeared likely that the Lions would reduce the deficit to three points on the ensuing PAT. Coach Bobby Ross, however, eschewed the point-after, opting instead for a two-point try. The Lions failed to convert, and Ross' decision was severely second-guessed after the Lions drove into field goal range with seconds to play but were forced to go for a touchdown because they trailed by four points. The Lions' final possession ended with three straight incompletions at the Arizona 10-yard line.

Top rusher: Pittman, in his first professional start, carried the ball 23 times for 133 yards and a TD.

Top passer: Jim Miller completed 34-of-48 passes

for 442 yards and three touchdowns in the Bears' overtime loss to Minnesota.

Top receiver: Randy Moss caught a season-high 12 passes for 204 yards for the Vikings against Chicago.

Notes: The Saints had lost 14 of 16 games to San Francisco prior to their 24-6 victory. ... In Buffalo's 23-3 win over Miami, Steve Christie became the 16th player in NFL history to kick 200 field goals with one team. He had three against the Dolphins. ... Chiefs safety Reggie Tongue forced three fumbles and his team caused six turnovers, but Kansas City still lost to the Buccaneers, 17-10. ... The Rams' sixth consecutive home win, 35-10 over Carolina, was the team's longest home winning streak since the 1984-85 season. ... The Jaguars had four sacks against the Ravens to increase their league leading total to 39. ... Joey Galloway's returned from a contract holdout to catch four passes for 88 yards in Seattle's 20-17 win over Denver. ... San Diego was riding a four-game losing streak, outscored by a combined score of 126-29. ... Redskins quarterback Brad Johnson threw a career-high three interceptions and fumbled twice in Washington's 35-28 loss at Philadelphia. ... Miller became the first Bears quarterback to throw for 400 yards since Bill Wade threw for 466 yards in 1962.

Quote of the week: Cleveland defensive tackle John Jurkovic, on the Browns' upset of the Steelers and the damage it did to Pittsburgh's playoff hopes: "This had to tear the living hearts out of the Pittsburgh Steelers. Too bad for them."

GAME SUMMARIES

RAMS 35, PANTHERS 10
Sunday, November 14

Carolina		7	3	0	0—10
St. Louis		14	7	7	7—35

First Quarter
Car.—Walls 14 pass from Beuerlein (Kasay kick), 5:22.
St.L.—Bruce 22 pass from Warner (Wilkins kick), 7:58.
St.L.—Lyght 57 interception return (Wilkins kick), 14:45.
Second Quarter
St.L.—R. Williams 19 pass from Warner (Wilkins kick), 9:29.
Car.—FG, Kasay 24, 14:16.
Third Quarter
St.L.—M. Jones 37 fumble return (Wilkins kick), 3:35.
Fourth Quarter
St.L.—Faulk 18 run (Wilkins kick), 13:49.
Attendance—65,965.

	Carolina	St. Louis
First downs	18	16
Rushes-yards	23-117	20-79
Passing	260	283
Punt returns	3-9	4-35
Kickoff returns	6-156	3-65
Interception returns	1-2	2-57
Comp.-att.-int.	24-39-2	19-29-1
Sacked-yards lost	6-26	0-0
Punts	5-37	5-39
Fumbles-lost	1-1	1-1
Penalties-yards	10-89	5-35
Time of possession	34:45	25:15

INDIVIDUAL STATISTICS
RUSHING—Carolina, Lane 13-54, Floyd 5-14, Beuerlein 3-20, Johnson 2-29. St. Louis, Faulk 16-73, Holcombe 2-4, Warner 1-2, Hakim 1-0.
PASSING—Carolina, Beuerlein 24-39-2-286. St. Louis, Warner 19-29-1-283.
RECEIVING—Carolina, Muhammad 9-125, Walls 5-54, Jeffers 3-43, Floyd 3-31, Lane 3-9, Hayes 1-24. St. Louis, Bruce 5-69, R. Williams 3-38, Faulk 2-64, Holcombe 2-45, Proehl 2-18, Holt 2-16, Robinson 1-30, Hakim 1-5, Lee 1-(minus 2).
MISSED FIELD GOAL ATTEMPTS—None.
INTERCEPTIONS—Carolina, Davis 1-2. St. Louis, Lyght 1-57, Bly 1-0.
KICKOFF RETURNS—Carolina, Bates 6-156. St. Louis, Carpenter 3-65.
PUNT RETURNS—Carolina, Metcalf 3-9. St. Louis, Hakim 4-35.
SACKS—St. Louis, Carter 2.5, Fletcher 1, J. Williams 1, Agnew 1, Farr 0.5.

COLTS 27, GIANTS 19
Sunday, November 14

Indianapolis		7	0	17	3—27
N.Y. Giants		0	6	0	13—19

First Quarter
Ind.—Harrison 19 pass from Manning (Vanderjagt kick), 14:12.
Second Quarter
NYG—FG, Blanchard 33, 2:51.
NYG—FG, Blanchard 42, 12:15.
Third Quarter
Ind.—Harrison 57 pass from Manning (Vanderjagt kick), 5:54.
Ind.—FG, Vanderjagt 40, 10:36.
Ind.—Wilkins 39 punt return (Vanderjagt kick), 12:16.
Fourth Quarter
NYG—Toomer 33 pass from Graham (pass failed), 0:43.
Ind.—FG, Vanderjagt 35, 3:23.
NYG—Mitchell 7 pass from Graham (Blanchard kick), 8:10.
Attendance—78,081.

	Indianapolis	N.Y. Giants
First downs	13	26
Rushes-yards	19-105	24-147
Passing	237	237
Punt returns	2-56	3-67
Kickoff returns	4-84	5-105
Interception returns	2-4	1-4
Comp.-att.-int.	20-35-1	27-50-2
Sacked-yards lost	0-0	3-16
Punts	5-38	5-38
Fumbles-lost	0-0	2-2
Penalties-yards	9-79	7-76
Time of possession	27:55	32:05

INDIVIDUAL STATISTICS
RUSHING—Indianapolis, James 16-108, Manning 3-(minus 3). New York, Barber 9-57, Johnson 5-36, Way 5-23, Graham 3-30, Bennett 1-3, Hilliard 1-(minus 2).
PASSING—Indianapolis, Manning 20-35-1-237. New York, Graham 27-50-2-253.
RECEIVING—Indianapolis, Harrison 6-109, James 5-72, Dilger 3-26, Pollard 3-17, Pathon 2-10, Wilkins 1-3. New York, Mitchell 9-62, Hilliard 6-78, Toomer 5-71, Barber 4-15, Johnson 2-9, Jurevicius 1-18.
MISSED FIELD GOAL ATTEMPTS—None.
INTERCEPTIONS—Indianapolis, Wooten 1-4, Randolph 1-0. New York, Garnes 1-4.
KICKOFF RETURNS—Indianapolis, Wilkins 3-69, Elias 1-15. New York, Levingston 3-70, Patten 2-35.
PUNT RETURNS—Indianapolis, Wilkins 2-56. New York, Barber 3-67.
SACKS—Indianapolis, E. Johnson 2, Bennett 1.

BILLS 23, DOLPHINS 3
Sunday, November 14

Miami		0	3	0	0— 3
Buffalo		9	7	7	0—23

First Quarter
Buf.—FG, Christie 31, 3:31.
Buf.—FG, Christie 48, 8:16.
Buf.—FG, Christie 47, 11:15.
Second Quarter
Buf.—Linton 4 run (Christie kick), 3:57.
Mia.—FG, Mare 30, 14:15.
Third Quarter
Buf.—Moulds 53 pass from Flutie (Christie kick), 10:49.
Attendance—72,810.

	Miami	Buffalo
First downs	6	18
Rushes-yards	19-60	48-177
Passing	41	157
Punt returns	1-25	6-67
Kickoff returns	6-119	2-30
Interception returns	0-0	1-10
Comp.-att.-int.	9-25-1	10-20-0
Sacked-yards lost	3-24	0-0
Punts	8-40	4-38
Fumbles-lost	0-0	0-0
Penalties-yards	5-41	11-75
Time of possession	21:37	38:23

INDIVIDUAL STATISTICS

RUSHING—Miami, Johnson 12-50, Collins 4-0, Huard 2-9, Konrad 1-1. Buffalo, A. Smith 29-126, Linton 7-28, Flutie 7-8, Gordon 5-15.

PASSING—Miami, Huard 9-25-1-65. Buffalo, Flutie 10-20-0-157.

RECEIVING—Miami, Johnson 3-11, Martin 2-27, McDuffie 2-21, Pritchett 1-4, Konrad 1-2. Buffalo, Riemersma 2-35, Reed 2-23, K. Williams 2-15, Moulds 1-53, Gash 1-12, Linton 1-10, P. Price 1-9.

MISSED FIELD GOAL ATTEMPTS—Buffalo, Christie 35.

INTERCEPTIONS—Buffalo, Winfield 1-10.

KICKOFF RETURNS—Miami, Marion 5-112, Johnson 1-7. Buffalo, K. Williams 2-30.

PUNT RETURNS—Miami, Jacquet 1-25. Buffalo, K. Williams 6-67.

SACKS—Buffalo, B. Smith 2, Hansen 1.

VIKINGS 27, BEARS 24

Sunday, November 14

| Minnesota | 7 | 7 | 3 | 3—27 |
| Chicago | 14 | 3 | 0 | 7 0—24 |

First Quarter
Chi.—M. Robinson 77 pass from Miller (Boniol kick), 5:17.
Min.—Carter 21 pass from George (Anderson kick), 8:19.
Chi.—Booker 57 pass from Miller (Boniol kick), 10:56.

Second Quarter
Min.—Carter 7 pass from George (Anderson kick), 9:02.
Chi.—FG, Boniol 34, 13:53.

Third Quarter
Min.—FG, Anderson 38, 10:05.

Fourth Quarter
Min.—Carter 1 pass from George (Anderson kick), 8:54.
Chi.—Booker 25 pass from Miller (Boniol kick), 14:11.

Overtime
Min.—FG, Anderson 38, 5:58.
Attendance—66,944.

	Minnesota	Chicago
First downs	23	21
Rushes-yards	28-110	22-49
Passing	349	407
Punt returns	0-0	2-39
Kickoff returns	4-54	5-105
Interception returns	1-0	1-(-1)
Comp.-att.-int.	25-44-1	34-48-1
Sacked-yards lost	3-25	3-15
Punts	5-42	6-34
Fumbles-lost	2-2	3-1
Penalties-yards	6-62	11-102
Time of possession	33:53	32:05

INDIVIDUAL STATISTICS

RUSHING—Minnesota, Smith 20-83, Hoard 7-28, George 1-(minus 1). Chicago, Enis 19-54, Milburn 2-(minus 7), Allen 1-2.

PASSING—Minnesota, George 25-44-1-374. Chicago, Miller 34-48-1-422.

RECEIVING—Minnesota, Moss 12-204, Carter 9-141, Mills 2-16, Jordan 1-11, Glover 1-2. Chicago, M. Robinson 7-148, Booker 7-134, Engram 6-42, Wetnight 4-27, Enis 4-26, Bennett 2-36, Milburn 2-6, Allen 1-2, Hallock 1-1.

MISSED FIELD GOAL ATTEMPTS—Minnesota, Anderson 20. Chicago, Boniol 41.

INTERCEPTIONS—Minnesota, Hitchcock 1-0. Chicago, W. Harris 1-(minus 1).

KICKOFF RETURNS—Minnesota, M. Williams 3-35, Tate 1-19. Chicago, Milburn 5-105.

PUNT RETURNS—Chicago, Milburn 2-39.

SACKS—Minnesota, Clemons 2, Griffith 1. Chicago, Tuinei 1, Hudson 1, Team 1.

SAINTS 24, 49ERS 6

Sunday, November 14

| San Francisco | 3 | 3 | 0 | 0— 6 |
| New Orleans | 7 | 7 | 7 | 3—24 |

First Quarter
N.O.—Tolliver 2 run (Brien kick), 5:23.
S.F.—FG, Richey 52, 13:27.

Second Quarter
N.O.—Tolliver 2 run (Brien kick), 5:29.
S.F.—FG, Richey 22, 14:25.

Third Quarter
N.O.—Hastings 11 pass from Tolliver (Brien kick), 7:30.

Fourth Quarter
N.O.—FG, Brien 28, 7:22.
Attendance—52,198.

	San Fran.	New Orleans
First downs	16	21
Rushes-yards	19-94	39-143
Passing	140	222
Punt returns	2-18	1-3
Kickoff returns	4-94	3-53
Interception returns	0-0	1-24
Comp.-att.-int.	18-32-1	12-15-0
Sacked-yards lost	2-17	2-20
Punts	4-35	2-47
Fumbles-lost	1-0	0-0
Penalties-yards	11-86	11-103
Time of possession	27:37	32:23

INDIVIDUAL STATISTICS

RUSHING—San Francisco, Garner 12-60, Beasley 6-26, Stenstrom 1-8. New Orleans, R. Williams 30-99, Tolliver 6-36, L. Smith 3-8.

PASSING—San Francisco, Stenstrom 18-32-1-157. New Orleans, Tolliver 12-15-0-242.

RECEIVING—San Francisco, Owens 5-56, Stokes 4-35, Rice 4-31, Beasley 2-19, Garner 2-8, Clark 1-8. New Orleans, R. Williams 3-57, Kennison 3-41, Poole 2-74, Hastings 2-53, Slutzker 1-11, L. Smith 1-6.

MISSED FIELD GOAL ATTEMPTS—None.

INTERCEPTIONS—New Orleans, Clay 1-24.

KICKOFF RETURNS—San Francisco, McQuarters 4-94. New Orleans, Davis 3-53.

PUNT RETURNS—San Francisco, McQuarters 2-18. New Orleans, Kennison 1-3.

SACKS—San Francisco, B. Young 2. New Orleans, Tomich 1, Wilson 1.

BROWNS 16, STEELERS 15

Sunday, November 14

| Cleveland | 7 | 0 | 0 | 9—16 |
| Pittsburgh | 3 | 0 | 9 | 3—15 |

First Quarter
Cle.—Johnson 35 pass from Couch (Dawson kick), 2:35.
Pit.—FG, K. Brown 41, 7:26.

Third Quarter
Pit.—FG, K. Brown 32, 5:03.
Pit.—Huntley 5 run (run failed), 6:42.

Fourth Quarter
Pit.—FG, K. Brown 47, 4:50.
Cle.—Edwards 5 pass from Couch (run failed), 9:48.
Cle.—FG, Dawson 39, 15:00.
Attendance—58,213.

	Cleveland	Pittsburgh
First downs	14	17
Rushes-yards	21-74	37-168
Passing	161	130
Punt returns	1-5	6-87
Kickoff returns	5-91	3-43
Interception returns	2-21	1-15
Comp.-att.-int.	18-28-1	15-32-2
Sacked-yards lost	6-38	1-7
Punts	8-43	6-40
Fumbles-lost	1-1	0-0
Penalties-yards	6-64	9-95
Time of possession	26:45	33:15

1999 REVIEW Week 10

— 173 —

INDIVIDUAL STATISTICS

RUSHING—Cleveland, Abdul-Jabbar 18-56, Couch 2-15, Kirby 1-3. Pittsburgh, Bettis 26-99, Stewart 6-52, Huntley 4-12, Witman 1-5.

PASSING—Cleveland, Couch 18-28-1-199. Pittsburgh, Stewart 15-32-2-137.

RECEIVING—Cleveland, Johnson 5-73, Edwards 4-22, Chiaverini 3-44, Shepherd 2-31, Kirby 2-10, Campbell 1-12, Abdul-Jabbar 1-7. Pittsburgh, Ward 4-39, Hawkins 3-29, Edwards 2-29, Bruener 2-20, Bettis 1-7, Huntley 1-7, Blackwell 1-4, Witman 1-2.

MISSED FIELD GOAL ATTEMPTS—None.

INTERCEPTIONS—Cleveland, Pope 1-13, Thierry 1-8. Pittsburgh, Shields 1-15.

KICKOFF RETURNS—Cleveland, Powell 3-46, Kirby 2-45. Pittsburgh, Edwards 3-43.

PUNT RETURNS—Cleveland, Johnson 1-5. Pittsburgh, Edwards 4-73, Hawkins 2-14.

SACKS—Cleveland, J. Miller 1. Pittsburgh, Gildon 2, Flowers 1, Emmons 1, Roye 1, Vrabel 1.

BUCCANEERS 17, CHIEFS 10

Sunday, November 14

Kansas City	3	0	0	7—10
Tampa Bay	0	10	7	0—17

First Quarter
K.C.—FG, Stoyanovich 20, 3:01.

Second Quarter
T.B.—Moore 35 pass from Dilfer (Gramatica kick), 6:11.
T.B.—FG, Gramatica 25, 14:32.

Third Quarter
T.B.—Green 52 pass from Dilfer (Gramatica kick), 12:22.

Fourth Quarter
K.C.—Horn 50 pass from Grbac (Stoyanovich kick), 4:20.
Attendance—64,927.

	Kansas City	Tampa Bay
First downs	11	14
Rushes-yards	22-87	37-100
Passing	184	270
Punt returns	3-22	4-13
Kickoff returns	4-74	3-50
Interception returns	1-0	1-0
Comp.-att.-int.	23-38-1	17-27-1
Sacked-yards lost	2-18	0-0
Punts	9-37	6-44
Fumbles-lost	3-2	5-5
Penalties-yards	6-30	1-5
Time of possession	27:13	32:47

INDIVIDUAL STATISTICS

RUSHING—Kansas City, Shehee 10-54, Bennett 9-23, Richardson 2-7, Grbac 1-3. Tampa Bay, Dunn 18-66, Alstott 16-33, Dilfer 3-1.

PASSING—Kansas City, Grbac 23-38-1-202. Tampa Bay, Dilfer 17-27-1-270.

RECEIVING—Kansas City, Alexander 7-41, Gonzalez 6-62, Horn 3-63, Shehee 3-8, Lockett 2-26, Richardson 2-2. Tampa Bay, Green 7-164, Moore 3-56, Anthony 3-28, Dunn 2-11, Alstott 1-7, Hape 1-4.

MISSED FIELD GOAL ATTEMPTS—Kansas City, Stoyanovich 42.

INTERCEPTIONS—Kansas City, Hasty 1-0. Tampa Bay, Nickerson 1-0.

KICKOFF RETURNS—Kansas City, Vanover 4-74. Tampa Bay, Murphy 3-50.

PUNT RETURNS—Kansas City, Vanover 3-22. Tampa Bay, Green 4-13.

SACKS—Tampa Bay, Abraham 1, Sapp 1.

RAIDERS 28, CHARGERS 9

Sunday, November 14

San Diego	0	0	3	6— 9
Oakland	14	0	7	7—28

First Quarter
Oak.—Wheatley 26 pass from Gannon (Husted kick), 4:47.
Oak.—Dudley 2 pass from Gannon (Husted kick), 14:21.

Third Quarter
S.D.—FG, Carney 39, 6:16.
Oak.—Wheatley 7 pass from Gannon (Husted kick), 11:53.

Fourth Quarter
Oak.—Dudley 12 pass from Gannon (Husted kick), 9:02.
S.D.—F. Jones 11 pass from Harbaugh (pass failed), 14:16.
Attendance—43,353.

	San Diego	Oakland
First downs	12	25
Rushes-yards	16-33	43-173
Passing	192	244
Punt returns	1-3	3-32
Kickoff returns	5-110	2-49
Interception returns	0-0	0-0
Comp.-att.-int.	18-32-0	18-24-0
Sacked-yards lost	2-12	1-10
Punts	5-49	3-36
Fumbles-lost	0-0	1-0
Penalties-yards	9-62	6-38
Time of possession	22:52	37:08

INDIVIDUAL STATISTICS

RUSHING—San Diego, Fazande 13-29, Stephens 1-9, Harbaugh 1-3, C. Jones 1-(minus 8). Oakland, Wheatley 22-59, Kaufman 12-65, Gannon 7-43, Brown 1-4, Crockett 1-2.

PASSING—San Diego, Harbaugh 18-32-0-204. Oakland, Gannon 18-24-0-254.

RECEIVING—San Diego, F. Jones 5-65, J. Graham 3-66, C. Jones 3-17, Stephens 2-14, McCrary 2-14, Ricks 2-12, Bynum 1-16. Oakland, Brown 7-117, Jett 3-52, Ritchie 3-19, Wheatley 2-33, Dudley 2-14, Woodson 1-19.

MISSED FIELD GOAL ATTEMPTS—Oakland, Husted 32.

INTERCEPTIONS—None.

KICKOFF RETURNS—San Diego, Stephens 3-55, Bynum 2-55. Oakland, Kaufman 1-32, Branch 1-17.

PUNT RETURNS—San Diego, Penn 1-3. Oakland, Gordon 3-32.

SACKS—San Diego, Parrella 1. Oakland, Russell 2.

CARDINALS 23, LIONS 19

Sunday, November 14

Detroit	7	0	6	6—19
Arizona	3	13	7	0—23

First Quarter
Det.—Sloan 7 pass from Frerotte (Hanson kick), 4:16.
Ariz.—FG, Jacke 35, 7:01.

Second Quarter
Ariz.—Bates 3 run (Jacke kick), 1:42.
Ariz.—FG, Jacke 35, 9:49.
Ariz.—FG, Jacke 49, 15:00.

Third Quarter
Ariz.—Pittman 58 run (Jacke kick), 3:49.
Det.—Crowell 77 pass from Frerotte (pass failed), 4:09.

Fourth Quarter
Det.—Fair 35 fumble return (pass failed), 9:34.
Attendance—49,600.

	Detroit	Arizona
First downs	17	17
Rushes-yards	14-42	32-159
Passing	331	184
Punt returns	4-28	5-55
Kickoff returns	5-77	4-79
Interception returns	0-0	0-0
Comp.-att.-int.	24-39-0	16-30-0
Sacked-yards lost	5-44	3-25
Punts	7-44	5-45
Fumbles-lost	2-1	3-1
Penalties-yards	10-102	6-46
Time of possession	27:16	32:44

INDIVIDUAL STATISTICS

RUSHING—Detroit, Hill 10-25, Irvin 4-17. Arizona, Pittman 23-133, Da. Brown 6-19, Murrell 2-4, Bates 1-3.

PASSING—Detroit, Frerotte 24-39-0-375. Arizona, Da. Brown 16-30-0-209.

RECEIVING—Detroit, Sloan 7-88, Crowell 5-142, Morton 4-110, Irvin 3-18, Schlesinger 3-9, Uwaezuoke 1-5, Hill 1-3. Arizona, Sanders 5-86, Boston 4-53, Moore 3-24, Pittman 2-44, McWilliams 1-3, Murrell 1-(minus 1).

MISSED FIELD GOAL ATTEMPTS—Detroit, Hanson 57. Arizona, Jacke 53, 54.

INTERCEPTIONS—None.

KICKOFF RETURNS—Detroit, Fair 5-77. Arizona, Bates 3-64, Tillman 1-15.

PUNT RETURNS—Detroit, Uwaezuoke 3-23, Fair 1-5. Arizona, Cody 5-55.

SACKS—Detroit, Kowalkowski 1, Porcher 1, Bailey 1. Arizona, Swann 2, McKinnon 1, Burke 1, Rice 1.

JAGUARS 6, RAVENS 3

Sunday, November 14

Baltimore	0	3	0	0—3
Jacksonville	0	3	3	0—6

Second Quarter
Jac.—FG, Hollis 28, 4:44.
Bal.—FG, Stover 23, 14:58.

Third Quarter
Jac.—FG, Hollis 28, 13:08.
Attendance—67,391.

	Baltimore	Jacksonville
First downs	13	9
Rushes-yards	24-88	26-47
Passing	154	85
Punt returns	4-14	6-73
Kickoff returns	1-12	2-24
Interception returns	0-0	0-0
Comp.-att.-int.	17-33-0	20-29-0
Sacked-yards lost	4-22	6-33
Punts	9-38	9-43
Fumbles-lost	3-1	1-0
Penalties-yards	6-30	4-30
Time of possession	27:09	32:51

INDIVIDUAL STATISTICS
RUSHING—Baltimore, Rhett 19-50, Banks 3-22, Case 2-16. Jacksonville, J. Stewart 18-25, Taylor 7-12, Brunell 1-10.
PASSING—Baltimore, Banks 10-21-0-73, Case 7-12-0-103. Jacksonville, Brunell 20-29-0-118.
RECEIVING—Baltimore, Ismail 3-33, J. Lewis 3-13, Armour 2-44, Evans 2-33, Rhett 2-20, Davis 1-11, Ofodile 1-9, Pierce 1-7, DeLong 1-4, Ayanbadejo 1-2. Jacksonville, J. Smith 7-52, McCardell 4-18, Brady 2-17, Jones 2-9, J. Stewart 2-6, Barlow 1-7, Shelton 1-6, Taylor 1-3.
MISSED FIELD GOAL ATTEMPTS—Jacksonville, Hollis 41.
INTERCEPTIONS—None.
KICKOFF RETURNS—Baltimore, Washington 1-12. Jacksonville, Barlow 1-24, Shelton 1-0.
PUNT RETURNS—Baltimore, J. Lewis 4-14. Jacksonville, Barlow 6-73.
SACKS—Baltimore, Sharper 2, Boulware 1.5, Burnett 1, McCrary 1, R. Lewis 0.5. Jacksonville, Marts 1, Walker 1, Smeenge 1, Brackens 1.

TITANS 24, BENGALS 14

Sunday, November 14

Tennessee	14	0	10	0—24
Cincinnati	0	0	7	7—14

First Quarter
Ten.—E. George 23 run (Del Greco kick), 4:36.
Ten.—McNair 1 run (Del Greco kick), 14:46.

Third Quarter
Cin.—Mack 99 kickoff return (Pelfrey kick), 0:18.
Ten.—E. George 14 run (Del Greco kick), 7:55.
Ten.—FG, Del Greco 26, 12:34.

Fourth Quarter
Cin.—Scott 24 pass from Blake (Pelfrey kick), 12:22.
Attendance—46,017.

	Tennessee	Cincinnati
First downs	16	15
Rushes-yards	37-149	19-67
Passing	98	197
Punt returns	2-5	3-4
Kickoff returns	2-62	5-204
Interception returns	0-0	0-0
Comp.-att.-int.	12-25-0	18-32-0
Sacked-yards lost	1-5	7-39
Punts	7-43	5-37
Fumbles-lost	2-1	4-4
Penalties-yards	9-62	8-66
Time of possession	33:09	26:51

INDIVIDUAL STATISTICS
RUSHING—Tennessee, E. George 29-123, McNair 5-14, Thomas 2-12, Hentrich 1-0. Cincinnati, Dillon 14-33, Blake 5-34.
PASSING—Tennessee, McNair 12-25-0-103. Cincinnati, Blake 18-32-0-236.
RECEIVING—Tennessee, Dyson 4-39, Harris 3-21, Thigpen 2-30, Wycheck 2-1, Byrd 1-12. Cincinnati, Scott 5-85, Pickens 4-28, Dillon 3-37, McGee 2-49, Groce 2-20, Jackson 2-17.

MISSED FIELD GOAL ATTEMPTS—Cincinnati, Pelfrey 32.
INTERCEPTIONS—None.
KICKOFF RETURNS—Tennessee, Mason 2-62. Cincinnati, Mack 4-187, Griffin 1-17.
PUNT RETURNS—Tennessee, Mason 2-5. Cincinnati, Yeast 2-6, Jackson 1-(minus 2).
SACKS—Tennessee, Kearse 2, Robinson 1.5, Bishop 1, Fisk 1, Holmes 1, Ford 0.5. Cincinnati, Bankston 1.

EAGLES 35, REDSKINS 28

Sunday, November 14

Washington	14	7	0	7—28
Philadelphia	10	3	11	11—35

First Quarter
Was.—Davis 2 run (Conway kick), 1:32.
Phi.—FG, N. Johnson 49, 5:49.
Was.—Connell 54 pass from B. Johnson (Conway kick), 9:16.
Phi.—Rossum 89 kickoff return (N. Johnson kick), 9:31.

Second Quarter
Was.—Davis 1 run (Conway kick), 2:00.
Phi.—FG, N. Johnson 29, 14:37.

Third Quarter
Phi.—FG, N. Johnson 20, 6:19.
Phi.—Staley 20 run (McNabb run), 14:52.

Fourth Quarter
Phi.—FG, N. Johnson 30, 3:27.
Was.—Westbrook 43 pass from B. Johnson (Conway kick), 4:15.
Phi.—Bieniemy 11 run (Weaver pass from McNabb), 11:43.
Attendance—66,591.

	Washington	Philadelphia
First downs	22	16
Rushes-yards	27-130	42-198
Passing	294	38
Punt returns	2-20	1-0
Kickoff returns	7-86	5-222
Interception returns	0-0	3-58
Comp.-att.-int.	18-33-3	8-21-0
Sacked-yards lost	4-19	3-22
Punts	2-47	4-37
Fumbles-lost	4-3	1-1
Penalties-yards	5-44	5-51
Time of possession	26:14	33:46

INDIVIDUAL STATISTICS
RUSHING—Washington, Davis 25-122, Westbrook 1-9, B. Johnson 1-(minus 1). Philadelphia, Staley 28-122, McNabb 9-49, Bieniemy 5-27.
PASSING—Washington, B. Johnson 18-33-3-313. Philadelphia, McNabb 8-21-0-60.
RECEIVING—Washington, Connell 6-88, Westbrook 4-152, Alexander 3-23, Mitchell 2-9, Sellers 1-32, Davis 1-8, Centers 1-1. Philadelphia, Small 4-30, Staley 1-11, Weaver 1-11, Turner 1-6, Broughton 1-2.
MISSED FIELD GOAL ATTEMPTS—Washington, Conway 50. Philadelphia, N. Johnson 32.
INTERCEPTIONS—Philadelphia, Vincent 1-29, Harris 1-17, Caldwell 1-12.
KICKOFF RETURNS—Washington, Mitchell 5-65, Thrash 1-21, Milstead 1-0. Philadelphia, Rossum 5-222.
PUNT RETURNS—Washington, Mitchell 2-20. Philadelphia, C. Johnson 1-0.
SACKS—Washington, Lang 1, Bailey 1, Wilkinson 1. Philadelphia, Caldwell 1, Mamula 1, Jefferson 0.5, Whiting 0.5, Team 1.

SEAHAWKS 20, BRONCOS 17

Sunday, November 14

Denver	0	0	17	0—17
Seattle	3	7	0	10—20

First Quarter
Sea.—FG, Peterson 35, 6:33.

Second Quarter
Sea.—Mayes 10 pass from Kitna (Peterson kick), 2:08.

Third Quarter
Den.—FG, Elam 25, 3:17.
Den.—McCaffrey 23 pass from C. Miller (Elam kick), 9:31.
Den.—Griffith 1 pass from C. Miller (Elam kick), 14:10.

1999 REVIEW Week 10

Fourth Quarter
Sea.—FG, Peterson 43, 0:40.
Sea.—Dawkins 20 pass from Kitna (Peterson kick), 7:41.
   Attendance—66,314.

	Denver	Seattle
First downs	18	14
Rushes-yards	31-87	21-41
Passing	236	230
Punt returns	1-2	1-13
Kickoff returns	5-86	4-113
Interception returns	1-2	1-29
Comp.-att.-int.	20-30-1	16-31-1
Sacked-yards lost	1-3	1-5
Punts	5-40	4-38
Fumbles-lost	0-0	2-1
Penalties-yards	6-55	9-105
Time of possession	36:03	23:57

INDIVIDUAL STATISTICS
RUSHING—Denver, Gary 26-65, C. Miller 4-20, Avery 1-2. Seattle, Watters 17-29, Green 2-13, Kitna 2-(minus 1).
PASSING—Denver, C. Miller 20-30-1-239. Seattle, Kitna 16-31-1-235.
RECEIVING—Denver, R. Smith 7-63, McCaffrey 6-125, Gary 3-20, Griffith 2-21, Carswell 1-8, Chamberlain 1-2. Seattle, Dawkins 5-91, Galloway 4-88, Mayes 4-39, Watters 1-6, Fauria 1-6, R. Brown 1-5.
MISSED FIELD GOAL ATTEMPTS—None.
INTERCEPTIONS—Denver, James 1-2. Seattle, Joseph 1-29.
KICKOFF RETURNS—Denver, Watson 5-86. Seattle, Green 4-113.
PUNT RETURNS—Denver, Watson 1-2. Seattle, Rogers 1-13.
SACKS—Denver, Wayne 1. Seattle, C. Brown 1.

COWBOYS 27, PACKERS 13
Sunday, November 14

Green Bay	0	3	0	10	—13
Dallas	7	3	7	10	—27

First Quarter
Dal.—LaFleur 6 pass from Garrett (Cunningham kick), 7:03.
Second Quarter
G.B.—FG, Longwell 38, 13:53.
Dal.—FG, Cunningham 44, 15:00.
Third Quarter
Dal.—Ismail 37 pass from Garrett (Cunningham kick), 9:32.
Fourth Quarter
Dal.—FG, Cunningham 47, 4:20.
G.B.—Freeman 28 pass from Favre (Longwell kick), 8:07.
G.B.—FG, Longwell 31, 13:39.
Dal.—Teague 95 interception return (Cunningham kick), 14:56.
   Attendance—64,634.

	Green Bay	Dallas
First downs	20	19
Rushes-yards	17-40	34-149
Passing	244	190
Punt returns	2-0	3-57
Kickoff returns	4-64	2-39
Interception returns	0-0	2-111
Comp.-att.-int.	26-50-2	13-23-0
Sacked-yards lost	3-16	2-9
Punts	6-42	4-45
Fumbles-lost	1-0	2-2
Penalties-yards	8-52	10-135
Time of possession	29:26	30:34

INDIVIDUAL STATISTICS
RUSHING—Green Bay, Levens 15-31, Favre 2-9. Dallas, Warren 19-85, Chancey 14-57, Ismail 1-7.
PASSING—Green Bay, Favre 26-50-2-260. Dallas, Garrett 13-23-0-199.
RECEIVING—Green Bay, Levens 8-40, Freeman 6-110, Schroeder 4-61, Bradford 3-35, T. Davis 3-9, Henderson 2-5. Dallas, Ismail 6-86, Mills 2-49, LaFleur 2-16, Bjornson 1-32, Tucker 1-11, Warren 1-5.
MISSED FIELD GOAL ATTEMPTS—Green Bay, Longwell 44. Dallas, Cunningham 22.
INTERCEPTIONS—Dallas, Teague 1-95, K. Smith 1-16.
KICKOFF RETURNS—Green Bay, Mitchell 2-38, R. McKenzie 1-13, Parker 1-13. Dallas, Tucker 2-39.
PUNT RETURNS—Green Bay, Mitchell 2-0. Dallas, Tucker 2-41, Sanders 1-16.
SACKS—Green Bay, Waddy 1, Sharper 1. Dallas, Pittman 1, Spellman 1, Hennings 1.

JETS 24, PATRIOTS 17
Monday, November 15

N.Y. Jets	0	21	0	3	—24
New England	0	3	0	14	—17

Second Quarter
NYJ—K. Johnson 1 pass from Lucas (Hall kick), 6:13.
N.E.—FG, Vinatieri 22, 13:14.
NYJ—Martin 36 run (Hall kick), 13:51.
NYJ—Baxter 11 pass from Lucas (Hall kick), 14:40.
Fourth Quarter
NYJ—FG, Hall 26, 2:31.
N.E.—Faulk 13 pass from Bledsoe (Vinatieri kick), 4:53.
N.E.—Brown 31 pass from Bledsoe (Vinatieri kick), 8:02.
   Attendance—59,077.

	N.Y. Jets	New England
First downs	19	16
Rushes-yards	43-188	20-79
Passing	153	150
Punt returns	1-8	3-17
Kickoff returns	4-83	5-198
Interception returns	3-41	2-17
Comp.-att.-int.	18-31-2	15-36-3
Sacked-yards lost	0-0	3-20
Punts	7-46	4-39
Fumbles-lost	3-0	0-0
Penalties-yards	9-93	5-45
Time of possession	37:38	22:22

INDIVIDUAL STATISTICS
RUSHING—New York, Martin 31-149, Lucas 6-15, Anderson 4-21, K. Johnson 1-3, Parmalee 1-0. New England, Allen 14-36, Bledsoe 3-25, Faulk 2-7, Warren 1-11.
PASSING—New York, Lucas 18-31-2-153. New England, Bledsoe 15-36-3-170.
RECEIVING—New York, Chrebet 7-70, K. Johnson 6-57, Baxter 2-10, Martin 2-8, Anderson 1-8. New England, Glenn 4-58, Brown 2-41, Faulk 2-21, Coates 2-14, Rutledge 1-13, Jefferson 1-11, Simmons 1-7, Allen 1-5, Warren 1-0.
MISSED FIELD GOAL ATTEMPTS—None.
INTERCEPTIONS—New York, Coleman 2-26, M. Jones 1-15. New England, Milloy 1-17, C. Carter 1-0.
KICKOFF RETURNS—New York, Glenn 4-83. New England, Faulk 4-170, Jones 1-28.
PUNT RETURNS—New York, Ward 1-8. New England, Brown 3-17.
SACKS—New York, Pleasant 1, Phifer 1, M. Jones 1.

WEEK 11

RESULTS

ARIZONA 13, Dallas 9
Baltimore 34, CINCINNATI 31
Carolina 31, CLEVELAND 17
Chicago 23, SAN DIEGO 20 (OT)
GREEN BAY 26, Detroit 17
Indianapolis 44, PHILADELPHIA 17
JACKSONVILLE 41, New Orleans 23
MIAMI 27, New England 17
N.Y. JETS 17, Buffalo 7
St. Louis 23, SAN FRANCISCO 7
Seattle 31, KANSAS CITY 19
TAMPA BAY 19, Atlanta 10
TENNESSEE 16, Pittsburgh 10
WASHINGTON 23, N.Y. Giants 13
DENVER 27, Oakland 21 (OT)
 Open date: Minnesota

STANDINGS

AFC EAST
	W	L	T	Pct.
Indianapolis	8	2	0	.800
Miami	8	2	0	.800
Buffalo	7	4	0	.636
New England	6	4	0	.600
N.Y. Jets	4	6	0	.400

AFC CENTRAL
	W	L	T	Pct.
Jacksonville	9	1	0	.900
Tennessee	8	2	0	.800
Pittsburgh	5	5	0	.500
Baltimore	4	6	0	.400
Cleveland	2	9	0	.182
Cincinnati	1	10	0	.091

AFC WEST
	W	L	T	Pct.
Seattle	8	2	0	.800
Kansas City	5	5	0	.500
Oakland	5	5	0	.500
San Diego	4	6	0	.400
Denver	4	7	0	.363

NFC EAST
	W	L	T	Pct.
Washington	6	4	0	.600
Dallas	5	5	0	.500
N.Y. Giants	5	5	0	.500
Arizona	4	6	0	.400
Philadelphia	3	8	0	.273

NFC CENTRAL
	W	L	T	Pct.
Detroit	6	4	0	.600
Minnesota	6	4	0	.600
Tampa Bay	6	4	0	.600
Green Bay	5	5	0	.500
Chicago	5	6	0	.455

NFC WEST
	W	L	T	Pct.
St. Louis	8	2	0	.800
Carolina	4	6	0	.400
San Francisco	3	7	0	.300
Atlanta	2	8	0	.200
New Orleans	2	8	0	.200

HIGHLIGHTS

Hero of the week: Bucs cornerback Donnie Abraham intercepted two fourth-quarter passes, returning one 47 yards for a TD in the final minute to seal Tampa Bay's 19-10 win over the Falcons.

Goat of the week: San Francisco receiver Jerry Rice caught three passes for only 23 yards in the 49ers' 23-7 loss to St. Louis. He also dropped two others, helping the Rams complete their first season sweep over San Francisco since 1980.

Sub of the week: Reserve defensive lineman Eric Ogbogu recovered a fumble by Bills quarterback Doug Flutie in the end zone, giving the Jets a 14-0 second-quarter lead. The Jets went on to a 17-7 victory, their third in a row.

Comeback of the week: Baltimore trailed Cincinnati 14-0 in the first quarter and 14-10 at halftime before storming back to win 34-31. With the score tied at 31, Tony Banks completed 6-of-8 passes to get the Ravens in position for the victory. Matt Stover kicked a 50-yard field goal as time ran out to complete the comeback.

Blowout of the week: Indianapolis routed Philadelphia, 44-17, after building a 17-0 lead after the first quarter and a 30-3 lead at halftime. Peyton Manning threw for 235 yards and three touchdowns in three quarters, and rookie Edgerrin James rushed for 152 yards and two touchdowns.

Nail-biter of the week: The Chargers trailed, 20-17, with less than two minutes remaining when quarterback Jim Harbaugh drove them 67 yards in nine plays. With one second left, John Carney kicked a 28-yarder to send the game to overtime. Nearly five minutes into overtime, Chris Boniol kicked a 36-yarder to give the Bears a 23-20 victory. A week earlier Boniol had missed a 41-yard field goal that would have beaten Minnesota in overtime.

Hit of the week: Denver's Trevor Pryce sacked Oakland's Rich Gannon, forcing a fumble that Pryce recovered at the Oakland 24, setting up a 24-yard touchdown run by Olandis Gary with 12:20 left in overtime. The touchdown gave the Broncos a 27-21 Monday night victory.

Oddity of the week: Perennial Pro Bowl linebacker Junior Seau lined up as a tight end on San Diego's first drive and caught his first NFL pass, a 2-yarder. Even though he was drilled by Chicago linebacker Rico McDonald on the play, Seau nonetheless got up and spiked the ball.

Top rusher: Stephen Davis rushed for a career-high 183 yards and a touchdown on 33 carries to help Washington beat the Giants, 23-13. Davis' big day gave him his first career 1,000-yard season.

Top passer: Jim Miller was 25-of-38 for 357 yards and a touchdown in the Bears' 23-20 overtime victory against San Diego.

Top receiver: Jimmy Smith caught nine passes for 220 yards and scored one touchdown in the Jaguars' 41-23 win over the Falcons.

Notes: Redskins defensive end Marco Coleman had a big day, first knocking Giants quarterback Kent Graham from the game on a second-quarter sack, and later grabbing a fumble by Graham's replacement, Kerry Collins, and running 42 yards for a touchdown in a 23-13 Redskins win.... When Saints quarterback Billy Joe Tolliver scored on a 1-yard sneak in the first quarter, it was the first touchdown the Jaguars had given up in the opening quarter all season.... Saints safety Willie Clay's interception against Jacksonville was the first time quarterback Mark Brunell had a pass picked off in 148 attempts.... Rookie Martin Gramatica kicked field goals of 24, 26, 50 and 53 yards in Tampa Bay's win over Atlanta.... Tackle Eric Swann, coming off reconstructive knee surgery, had both of the Cardinals' sacks against Dallas.... Terrell Owens (120 yards) became the 49ers' first 100-yard receiver in '99.... Miami's Olindo Mare kicked two field goals against New England, giving him 20 consecutive games with at least one field goal. The streak tied Garo Yepremian's team record.... Tennessee won its fourth straight game against the Steelers, a franchise first.... Panthers quarterback Steve Beuerlein threw the 100th touchdown pass of his career in the third quarter of Carolina's 31-17 victo-

1999 REVIEW Week 11

– 177 –

ry over Cleveland. . . . When Eric Warfield intercepted a Jon Kitna pass in the first quarter, it marked the ninth consecutive game in which the Chiefs intercepted a pass. . . . Jets kicker John Hall lined up for a 54-yard field goal, then took a direct snap and punted the ball 34 yards against the Bills. . . . Green Bay won its ninth game in a row against Detroit at Lambeau Field. . . . Tampa Bay's Karl Williams became the NFL's all-time leader in punt return average (13.6 yards) in the second quarter against Atlanta, passing Darrien Gordon. Although the return was for just one yard, it was the 75th of Williams' career, the number it takes to qualify for the all-time rankings.

Quote of the week: Outside linebacker Jamir Miller was not happy after Cleveland's loss to Carolina despite leading the Browns with 11 tackles: "Missed tackles? Yeah, that (ticks) me off," he said. "That's a lack of concentration. That's want-to. You've got to have want-to to make tackles. We weren't truly ready to play."

GAME SUMMARIES

BUCCANEERS 19, FALCONS 10

Sunday, November 21

Atlanta	10	0	0	0	—10
Tampa Bay	0	6	0	13	—19

First Quarter
Atl.—Dwight 8 run (Andersen kick), 7:50.
Atl.—FG, Andersen 28, 14:07.
Second Quarter
T.B.—FG, Gramatica 24, 5:47.
T.B.—FG, Gramatica 26, 14:52.
Fourth Quarter
T.B.—FG, Gramatica 50, 9:28.
T.B.—FG, Gramatica 53, 14:02.
T.B.—Abraham 47 interception return (Gramatica kick), 14:33.
Attendance—65,158.

	Atlanta	Tampa Bay
First downs	9	12
Rushes-yards	24-77	27-119
Passing	92	120
Punt returns	3-31	2-7
Kickoff returns	6-118	3-54
Interception returns	1-0	2-47
Comp.-att.-int.	14-25-2	15-31-1
Sacked-yards lost	2-17	3-22
Punts	6-41	5-43
Fumbles-lost	0-0	0-0
Penalties-yards	4-29	2-20
Time of possession	29:33	30:27

INDIVIDUAL STATISTICS
RUSHING—Atlanta, Oxendine 14-48, Hanspard 4-3, Christian 3-14, Chandler 2-4, Dwight 1-8. Tampa Bay, Alstott 12-48, Dunn 11-44, Dilfer 3-29, Green 1-(minus 2).
PASSING—Atlanta, Chandler 14-25-2-109. Tampa Bay, Dilfer 15-31-1-142.
RECEIVING—Atlanta, Oliver 4-33, Dwight 4-20, Christian 3-36, German 1-10, Mathis 1-6, Oxendine 1-4. Tampa Bay, Green 5-75, Emanuel 3-30, Williams 2-14, Alstott 2-9, Dunn 2-8, J. Davis 1-6.
MISSED FIELD GOAL ATTEMPTS—None.
INTERCEPTIONS—Atlanta, Robinson 1-0. Tampa Bay, Abraham 2-47.
KICKOFF RETURNS—Atlanta, Dwight 5-102, Oliver 1-16. Tampa Bay, Murphy 2-29, Dunn 1-25.
PUNT RETURNS—Atlanta, Dwight 3-31. Tampa Bay, Williams 2-7.
SACKS—Atlanta, Dronett 1.5, Kerney 1, Hall 0.5. Tampa Bay, Brooks 1, Sapp 1.

TITANS 16, STEELERS 10

Sunday, November 21

Pittsburgh	7	0	0	3	—10
Tennessee	14	0	2	0	—16

First Quarter
Ten.—McNair 2 run (Del Greco kick), 5:32.
Pit.—Edwards 15 pass from Stewart (K. Brown kick), 9:13.
Ten.—McNair 3 run (Del Greco kick), 15:00.
Third Quarter
Ten.—Safety, Stewart called for intentional grounding in end zone, 7:10.
Fourth Quarter
Pit.—FG, K. Brown 24, 8:05.
Attendance—66,619.

	Pittsburgh	Tennessee
First downs	14	17
Rushes-yards	20-106	32-112
Passing	161	149
Punt returns	4-4	2-14
Kickoff returns	3-38	4-66
Interception returns	1-0	1-(-2)
Comp.-att.-int.	18-30-1	14-26-1
Sacked-yards lost	5-16	0-0
Punts	4-53	6-41
Fumbles-lost	0-0	0-0
Penalties-yards	11-73	4-30
Time of possession	28:51	31:09

INDIVIDUAL STATISTICS
RUSHING—Pittsburgh, Bettis 14-88, Stewart 3-14, Huntley 3-4. Tennessee, E. George 21-83, McNair 10-20, Thomas 1-9.
PASSING—Pittsburgh, Stewart 18-30-1-177. Tennessee, McNair 14-26-1-149.
RECEIVING—Pittsburgh, Blackwell 4-41, Shaw 3-38, Ward 3-20, Huntley 2-28, Edwards 2-24, Hawkins 2-12, Lyons 1-7, Witman 1-7. Tennessee, Wycheck 5-25, Harris 3-16, Dyson 2-27, Sanders 1-46, Kent 1-25, E. George 1-9, Neal 1-1.
MISSED FIELD GOAL ATTEMPTS—Pittsburgh, K. Brown 44.
INTERCEPTIONS—Pittsburgh, Washington 1-0. Tennessee, Holmes 1-(minus 2).
KICKOFF RETURNS—Pittsburgh, Blackwell 2-34, Edwards 1-4. Tennessee, Mason 4-66.
PUNT RETURNS—Pittsburgh, Hawkins 4-4. Tennessee, Mason 2-14.
SACKS—Tennessee, Holmes 1, Robinson 1, Bowden 1, Jones 1, Kearse 1.

SEAHAWKS 31, CHIEFS 19

Sunday, November 21

Seattle	0	14	10	7	—31
Kansas City	3	10	0	6	—19

First Quarter
K.C.—FG, Stoyanovich 29, 8:53.
Second Quarter
Sea.—Watters 2 run (Peterson kick), 4:41.
K.C.—Bennett 1 run (Stoyanovich kick), 9:57.
Sea.—Watters 22 pass from Kitna (Peterson kick), 13:14.
K.C.—FG, Stoyanovich 29, 14:58.
Third Quarter
Sea.—FG, Peterson 38, 5:43.
Sea.—Dawkins 45 pass from Kitna (Peterson kick), 11:47.
Fourth Quarter
K.C.—Bennett 4 run (pass failed), 8:11.
Sea.—Watters 5 run (Peterson kick), 12:17.
Attendance—78,714.

	Seattle	Kansas City
First downs	20	22
Rushes-yards	32-133	25-76
Passing	235	295
Punt returns	3-38	3-20
Kickoff returns	5-96	6-135
Interception returns	1-0	1-0
Comp.-att.-int.	14-33-1	30-49-1
Sacked-yards lost	0-0	2-25
Punts	5-45	7-41
Fumbles-lost	3-1	1-1
Penalties-yards	5-29	8-60
Time of possession	28:01	31:59

INDIVIDUAL STATISTICS

RUSHING—Seattle, Watters 24-107, Kitna 7-15, Green 1-12. Kansas City, Bennett 17-60, Shehee 5-9, Richardson 2-4, Cloud 1-3.

PASSING—Seattle, Kitna 14-33-1-235. Kansas City, Grbac 30-49-1-320.

RECEIVING—Seattle, Dawkins 5-114, Watters 4-67, Fauria 2-20, Galloway 1-18, Pritchard 1-12, R. Brown 1-4. Kansas City, Alexander 8-101, Gonzalez 8-62, Shehee 6-73, Rison 4-42, Horn 2-10, Richardson 1-29, Lockett 1-3.

MISSED FIELD GOAL ATTEMPTS—None.

INTERCEPTIONS—Seattle, Canty 1-0. Kansas City, Warfield 1-0.

KICKOFF RETURNS—Seattle, Green 3-83, Bownes 1-7, Joseph 1-6. Kansas City, Vanover 5-111, Bennett 1-24.

PUNT RETURNS—Seattle, Jordan 3-38. Kansas City, Vanover 3-20.

SACKS—Seattle, Sinclair 1, King 1.

PACKERS 26, LIONS 17

Sunday, November 21

Detroit	7	10	0	0	—17
Green Bay	0	12	11	3	—26

First Quarter
Det.—Irvin 2 run (Hanson kick), 7:01.

Second Quarter
G.B.—FG, Longwell 23, 1:37.
G.B.—FG, Longwell 33, 7:22.
Det.—Crowell 14 pass from Frerotte (Hanson kick), 10:56.
G.B.—Levens 1 run (pass failed), 13:47.
Det.—FG, Hanson 46, 15:00.

Third Quarter
G.B.—Bradford 17 pass from Favre (Bradford pass from Favre), 7:40.
G.B.—FG, Longwell 45, 11:46.

Fourth Quarter
G.B.—FG, Longwell 31, 2:08.
Attendance—59,869.

	Detroit	Green Bay
First downs	20	24
Rushes-yards	23-110	27-64
Passing	225	307
Punt returns	2-14	2-20
Kickoff returns	7-88	2-33
Interception returns	0-0	2-21
Comp.-att.-int.	20-39-2	26-40-0
Sacked-yards lost	0-0	1-2
Punts	5-45	4-34
Fumbles-lost	0-0	0-0
Penalties-yards	8-119	10-90
Time of possession	26:00	34:00

INDIVIDUAL STATISTICS

RUSHING—Detroit, Hill 10-32, Irvin 8-62, Schlesinger 3-5, Frerotte 1-7, Crowell 1-4. Green Bay, Levens 23-47, Parker 2-17, Henderson 1-1, Favre 1-(minus 1).

PASSING—Detroit, Frerotte 20-39-2-225. Green Bay, Favre 26-40-0-309.

RECEIVING—Detroit, Crowell 8-112, Morton 5-64, Sloan 4-30, Irvin 3-19. Green Bay, Levens 10-99, Bradford 6-94, Schroeder 4-69, Henderson 4-28, Thomason 1-12, T. Davis 1-7.

MISSED FIELD GOAL ATTEMPTS—None.

INTERCEPTIONS—Green Bay, Vinson 1-21, Nelson 1-0.

KICKOFF RETURNS—Detroit, Fair 4-49, Schlesinger 1-20, Olivo 1-19, Irvin 1-0. Green Bay, Parker 1-17, Henderson 1-16.

PUNT RETURNS—Detroit, Uwaezuoke 2-14. Green Bay, Edwards 2-20.

SACKS—Detroit, Bailey 1.

PANTHERS 31, BROWNS 17

Sunday, November 21

Carolina	3	14	7	7	—31
Cleveland	0	3	0	14	—17

First Quarter
Car.—FG, Kasay 44, 2:56.

Second Quarter
Cle.—FG, Dawson 23, 0:03.
Car.—Floyd 1 run (Kasay kick), 4:09.
Car.—Walls 8 pass from Beuerlein (Kasay kick), 14:42.

Third Quarter
Car.—Kinchen 1 pass from Beuerlein (Kasay kick), 6:47.

Fourth Quarter
Car.—Floyd 1 run (Kasay kick), 1:46.
Cle.—Kirby 2 run (Dawson kick), 9:39.
Cle.—Chiaverini 12 pass from Couch (Dawson kick), 14:50.
Attendance—72,818.

	Carolina	Cleveland
First downs	22	22
Rushes-yards	31-129	18-60
Passing	201	257
Punt returns	3-26	0-0
Kickoff returns	3-66	6-115
Interception returns	2-16	0-0
Comp.-att.-int.	23-30-0	29-46-2
Sacked-yards lost	2-9	1-2
Punts	3-30	3-51
Fumbles-lost	1-1	1-0
Penalties-yards	4-23	4-20
Time of possession	32:53	27:07

INDIVIDUAL STATISTICS

RUSHING—Carolina, Biakabutuka 17-93, Floyd 6-8, Lane 3-12, Lewis 2-3, Johnson 1-6, Beuerlein 1-4, Metcalf 1-3. Cleveland, Abdul-Jabbar 7-11, Kirby 6-22, Couch 5-27.

PASSING—Carolina, Beuerlein 21-27-0-199, Lewis 2-3-0-11. Cleveland, Couch 29-46-2-259.

RECEIVING—Carolina, Muhammad 7-72, Walls 4-39, Biakabutuka 3-42, Jeffers 3-34, Johnson 2-11, Floyd 2-10, Kinchen 2-2. Cleveland, Kirby 9-79, Chiaverini 8-72, Johnson 5-55, I. Smith 2-26, Edwards 2-4, Abdul-Jabbar 2-2, Campbell 1-21.

MISSED FIELD GOAL ATTEMPTS—Cleveland, Dawson 38.

INTERCEPTIONS—Carolina, Davis 1-16, Alexander 1-0.

KICKOFF RETURNS—Carolina, Metcalf 1-31, Bates 1-28, Mangum 1-7. Cleveland, Powell 3-66, Kirby 2-43, I. Smith 1-6.

PUNT RETURNS—Carolina, Metcalf 3-26.

SACKS—Carolina, Minter 1. Cleveland, Thierry 1, Barker 1.

DOLPHINS 27, PATRIOTS 17

Sunday, November 21

New England	7	3	7	0	—17
Miami	3	7	14	3	—27

First Quarter
N.E.—Allen 6 run (Vinatieri kick), 7:35.
Mia.—FG, Mare 19, 12:00.

Second Quarter
N.E.—FG, Vinatieri 27, 0:52.
Mia.—Gadsden 4 pass from Huard (Mare kick), 6:36.

Third Quarter
Mia.—Gadsden 3 pass from Huard (Mare kick), 6:05.
Mia.—Johnson 1 run (Mare kick), 11:41.
N.E.—Jefferson 68 pass from Bledsoe (Vinatieri kick), 12:10.

Fourth Quarter
Mia.—FG, Mare 23, 11:49.
Attendance—74,295.

	New England	Miami
First downs	14	19
Rushes-yards	19-102	36-117
Passing	168	112
Punt returns	3-16	3-8
Kickoff returns	6-116	3-76
Interception returns	0-0	5-72
Comp.-att.-int.	15-34-5	18-34-0
Sacked-yards lost	5-33	2-19
Punts	6-38	7-43
Fumbles-lost	1-0	2-2
Penalties-yards	5-50	5-30
Time of possession	27:42	32:18

INDIVIDUAL STATISTICS

RUSHING—New England, Allen 13-42, Faulk 5-61, Bledsoe 1-(minus 1). Miami, Johnson 31-106, Huard 3-13, Zolak 2-(minus 2).

PASSING—New England, Bledsoe 15-34-5-201. Miami, Huard 18-30-0-131, Zolak 0-4-0-0.

RECEIVING—New England, Glenn 3-39, Brown 3-26, Jefferson 2-86, Coates 2-27, Faulk 2-6, Allen 1-8, Brisby 1-7, T. Carter 1-2. Miami, Martin 4-44, Gadsden 4-36, Drayton 4-25, Pritchett 2-13, Konrad 2-2, Johnson 1-6, McDuffie 1-5.

MISSED FIELD GOAL ATTEMPTS—None.

1999 REVIEW Week 11

— 179 —

INTERCEPTIONS—Miami, Marion 1-28, Buckley 1-18, Madison 1-13, Wilson 1-13, Taylor 1-0.
KICKOFF RETURNS—New England, Faulk 6-115. Miami, Marion 3-76.
PUNT RETURNS—New England, Brown 3-16. Miami, Jacquet 3-8.
SACKS—New England, McGinest 1, Whigham 1. Miami, Owens 1.5, Buckley 1, Wilson 1, Taylor 0.5, Gardener 0.5, Bowens 0.5.

CARDINALS 13, COWBOYS 9

Sunday, November 21

Dallas	7	0	0	2—	9
Arizona	0	3	7	3—	13

First Quarter
Dal.—LaFleur 11 pass from Garrett (Cunningham kick), 14:02.
Second Quarter
Ariz.—FG, Jacke 24, 14:45.
Third Quarter
Ariz.—Moore 21 pass from Da. Brown (Jacke kick), 1:50.
Fourth Quarter
Ariz.—FG, Jacke 38, 3:30.
Dal.—Safety, S. Player forced out of end zone, 13:11.
Attendance—72,015.

	Dallas	Arizona
First downs	15	13
Rushes-yards	34-156	30-102
Passing	102	105
Punt returns	3-16	3-35
Kickoff returns	5-94	2-54
Interception returns	2-2	0-0
Comp.-att.-int.	16-29-0	13-29-2
Sacked-yards lost	2-9	2-10
Punts	6-46	5-42
Fumbles-lost	1-0	1-0
Penalties-yards	6-47	5-40
Time of possession	33:03	26:57

INDIVIDUAL STATISTICS
RUSHING—Dallas, E. Smith 29-127, Warren 2-10, Garrett 2-3, Ismail 1-16. Arizona, Murrell 17-72, Bates 6-20, Da. Brown 4-17, Boston 1-7, Tillman 1-4, Player 1-(minus 18).
PASSING—Dallas, Garrett 16-29-0-111. Arizona, Da. Brown 13-29-2-115.
RECEIVING—Dallas, Ismail 5-43, Mills 3-26, Warren 3-10, Thomas 2-8, LaFleur 1-11, Bjornson 1-7, E. Smith 1-6. Arizona, Boston 3-47, Sanders 3-17, Murrell 3-9, Moore 1-21, Hardy 1-9, Makovicka 1-9, McWilliams 1-3.
MISSED FIELD GOAL ATTEMPTS—Dallas, Cunningham 48.
INTERCEPTIONS—Dallas, Sanders 1-2, Hawthorne 1-0.
KICKOFF RETURNS—Dallas, Tucker 3-54, Sanders 1-31, Noble 1-9. Arizona, Bates 2-54.
PUNT RETURNS—Dallas, Tucker 2-11, Sanders 1-5. Arizona, Cody 3-35.
SACKS—Dallas, Coakley 1, Ellis 1. Arizona, Swann 2.

JETS 17, BILLS 7

Sunday, November 21

Buffalo	0	0	7	0—	7
N.Y. Jets	0	14	3	0—	17

Second Quarter
NYJ—Lucas 9 run (Hall kick), 0:13.
NYJ—Ogbogu recovered fumble in end zone (Hall kick), 5:19.
Third Quarter
NYJ—FG, Hall 36, 7:47.
Buf.—P. Price 2 pass from Flutie (Christie kick), 11:31.
Attendance—79,285.

	Buffalo	N.Y. Jets
First downs	14	14
Rushes-yards	17-60	34-96
Passing	205	112
Punt returns	2-18	4-37
Kickoff returns	3-100	2-56
Interception returns	0-0	2-37
Comp.-att.-int.	22-40-2	16-21-0
Sacked-yards lost	2-15	5-30
Punts	6-44	7-42
Fumbles-lost	2-1	0-0
Penalties-yards	2-15	6-50
Time of possession	26:03	33:57

INDIVIDUAL STATISTICS
RUSHING—Buffalo, Linton 12-28, Flutie 3-26, A. Smith 2-6. New York, Martin 23-64, Lucas 8-24, Parmalee 2-8, Anderson 1-0.
PASSING—Buffalo, Flutie 22-40-2-220. New York, Lucas 16-20-0-142, K. Johnson 0-1-0-0.
RECEIVING—Buffalo, Moulds 8-77, Reed 4-34, P. Price 3-12, Riemersma 2-41, K. Williams 2-30, Linton 2-14, Collins 1-12. New York, Martin 7-42, K. Johnson 4-42, Chrebet 3-37, Anderson 2-21.
MISSED FIELD GOAL ATTEMPTS—Buffalo, Christie 40, 45.
INTERCEPTIONS—New York, V. Green 1-32, Wiltz 1-5.
KICKOFF RETURNS—Buffalo, K. Williams 3-100. New York, Stone 2-56.
PUNT RETURNS—Buffalo, K. Williams 2-18. New York, Ward 4-37.
SACKS—Buffalo, Hansen 1.5, Cowart 1, Wiley 1, Moran 0.5, P. Williams 0.5, B. Smith 0.5. New York, Mickens 1, Phifer 1.

BEARS 23, CHARGERS 20

Sunday, November 21

Chicago	0	3	14	3	3—23
San Diego	7	3	0	10	0—20

First Quarter
S.D.—Davis 2 pass from Harbaugh (Carney kick), 9:07.
Second Quarter
Chi.—FG, Boniol 29, 5:14.
S.D.—FG, Carney 28, 12:13.
Third Quarter
Chi.—M. Robinson 38 pass from Miller (Boniol kick), 9:34.
Chi.—Enis 3 run (Boniol kick), 12:30.
Fourth Quarter
Chi.—FG, Boniol 26, 9:38.
S.D.—Stephens 13 pass from Harbaugh (Carney kick), 10:57.
S.D.—FG, Carney 28, 14:59.
Overtime
Chi.—FG, Boniol 36, 4:58.
Attendance—56,055.

	Chicago	San Diego
First downs	19	20
Rushes-yards	28-75	27-84
Passing	355	264
Punt returns	2-44	1-2
Kickoff returns	6-104	5-81
Interception returns	1-37	0-0
Comp.-att.-int.	25-39-0	29-46-1
Sacked-yards lost	1-2	1-9
Punts	6-31	6-44
Fumbles-lost	2-1	0-0
Penalties-yards	8-56	5-40
Time of possession	32:01	32:57

INDIVIDUAL STATISTICS
RUSHING—Chicago, Enis 19-41, Allen 5-21, Miller 2-9, Booker 1-8, Milburn 1-(minus 4). San Diego, Fazande 18-50, Stephens 5-22, Harbaugh 2-5, Bynum 1-5, Fletcher 1-2.
PASSING—Chicago, Miller 25-38-0-357, McNown 0-1-0-0. San Diego, Harbaugh 29-46-1-273.
RECEIVING—Chicago, Engram 8-121, M. Robinson 6-163, Conway 4-24, Enis 3-27, Mayes 2-13, Wetnight 1-6, Booker 1-3. San Diego, Stephens 7-49, Davis 6-26, J. Graham 5-83, F. Jones 4-36, Ricks 2-19, McCrary 2-13, Penn 1-43, Fletcher 1-2, Seau 1-2.
MISSED FIELD GOAL ATTEMPTS—Chicago, Boniol 33. San Diego, Carney 38.
INTERCEPTIONS—Chicago, Burton 1-37.
KICKOFF RETURNS—Chicago, Milburn 5-97, Hallock 1-7. San Diego, Stephens 3-44, Bynum 2-37.
PUNT RETURNS—Chicago, Milburn 2-44. San Diego, Penn 1-2.
SACKS—Chicago, Minter 1. San Diego, Dixon 1.

RAMS 23, 49ERS 7

Sunday, November 21

St. Louis	3	10	10	0—	23
San Francisco	0	7	0	0—	7

First Quarter
St.L.—FG, Wilkins 40, 10:13.
Second Quarter
S.F.—Beasley 1 run (Richey kick), 6:47.
St.L.—Bruce 5 pass from Warner (Wilkins kick), 11:58.
St.L.—FG, Wilkins 20, 15:00.

Third Quarter
St.L.—M. Jones 44 interception return (Wilkins kick), 5:19.
St.L.—FG, Wilkins 49, 12:37.
Attendance—68,193.

	St. Louis	San Francisco
First downs	21	14
Rushes-yards	30-164	25-106
Passing	181	145
Punt returns	4-58	0-0
Kickoff returns	1-0	5-103
Interception returns	3-44	1-31
Comp.-att.-int.	22-40-1	15-27-3
Sacked-yards lost	3-20	7-52
Punts	5-38	5-39
Fumbles-lost	0-0	5-2
Penalties-yards	7-58	3-15
Time of possession	31:30	28:30

INDIVIDUAL STATISTICS
RUSHING—St. Louis, Faulk 21-126, Holcombe 5-16, Warner 2-12, Holt 1-6, Bruce 1-4. San Francisco, Garner 16-77, Beasley 4-16, Garcia 4-13, Stenstrom 1-0.
PASSING—St. Louis, Warner 22-40-1-201. San Francisco, Garcia 8-15-2-89, Stenstrom 7-12-1-108.
RECEIVING—St. Louis, Bruce 11-93, Faulk 4-43, Holt 3-25, Hakim 2-32, Thomas 1-6, R. Williams 1-2. San Francisco, Owens 6-120, Beasley 3-25, Rice 3-23, Clark 2-22, Stokes 1-7.
MISSED FIELD GOAL ATTEMPTS—St. Louis, Wilkins 43.
INTERCEPTIONS—St. Louis, M. Jones 1-44, Bush 1-0, McCleon 1-0. San Francisco, Schulters 1-31.
KICKOFF RETURNS—St. Louis, Hodgins 1-0. San Francisco, McQuarters 4-92, Harris 1-11.
PUNT RETURNS—St. Louis, Hakim 4-58.
SACKS—St. Louis, Carter 2, Farr 1, Fletcher 1, Wistrom 1, Agnew 1, Zgonina 1. San Francisco, Tubbs 1, B. Young 1, Okeafor 1.

REDSKINS 23, GIANTS 13
Sunday, November 21

N.Y. Giants	0	6	0	7—13
Washington	7	3	3	10—23

First Quarter
Was.—Davis 1 run (Conway kick), 7:57.
Second Quarter
NYG—FG, Blanchard 44, 4:03.
Was.—FG, Conway 24, 7:58.
NYG—FG, Blanchard 44, 15:00.
Third Quarter
Was.—FG, Conway 21, 13:46.
Fourth Quarter
Was.—Coleman 42 fumble return (Conway kick), 0:09.
NYG—Way 1 run (Blanchard kick), 4:34.
Was.—FG, Conway 37, 14:39.
Attendance—78,641.

	N.Y. Giants	Washington
First downs	21	22
Rushes-yards	24-72	41-205
Passing	229	158
Punt returns	0-0	3-33
Kickoff returns	5-126	2-31
Interception returns	1-26	3-25
Comp.-att.-int.	16-31-3	17-29-1
Sacked-yards lost	4-28	0-0
Punts	5-44	3-46
Fumbles-lost	4-2	1-1
Penalties-yards	7-97	8-64
Time of possession	25:15	34:45

INDIVIDUAL STATISTICS
RUSHING—New York, Barber 10-44, Way 8-26, Collins 4-(minus 3), Johnson 2-5. Washington, Davis 33-183, Hicks 5-14, B. Johnson 3-8.
PASSING—New York, Collins 13-21-1-221, Graham 3-10-2-36. Washington, B. Johnson 17-29-1-158.
RECEIVING—New York, Hilliard 4-101, Barber 4-46, Patten 3-51, Mitchell 3-30, Toomer 1-18, Jurevicius 1-11. Washington, Centers 6-69, Fryar 3-10, Davis 3-5, Jenkins 1-30, Thrash 1-25, Connell 1-16, Mitchell 1-2, Westbrook 1-1.
MISSED FIELD GOAL ATTEMPTS—Washington, Conway 38, 50, 27.

INTERCEPTIONS—New York, Ellsworth 1-26. Washington, Green 1-25, Smith 1-0, Shade 1-0.
KICKOFF RETURNS—New York, Levingston 2-59, Patten 2-53, Comella 1-14. Washington, Mitchell 1-17, Thrash 1-14.
PUNT RETURNS—Washington, Mitchell 3-33.
SACKS—Washington, Shade 1, Coleman 1, Kalu 1, Stubblefield 1.

COLTS 44, EAGLES 17
Sunday, November 21

Indianapolis	17	13	14	0—44
Philadelphia	0	3	0	14—17

First Quarter
Ind.—FG, Vanderjagt 45, 4:14.
Ind.—James 1 run (Vanderjagt kick), 12:20.
Ind.—James 62 run (Vanderjagt kick), 14:48.
Second Quarter
Ind.—FG, Vanderjagt 29, 1:39.
Ind.—Harrison 5 pass from Manning (Vanderjagt kick), 3:33.
Phi.—FG, Akers 48, 13:33.
Ind.—FG, Vanderjagt 34, 15:00.
Third Quarter
Ind.—Wilkins 80 pass from Manning (Vanderjagt kick), 2:05.
Ind.—James 17 pass from Manning (Vanderjagt kick), 8:09.
Fourth Quarter
Phi.—Lewis 6 pass from McNabb (Akers kick), 6:33.
Phi.—Whiting 22 interception return (Akers kick), 8:59.
Attendance—65,521.

	Indianapolis	Philadelphia
First downs	22	13
Rushes-yards	36-200	20-94
Passing	255	120
Punt returns	4-18	1-8
Kickoff returns	2-39	8-192
Interception returns	2-41	1-22
Comp.-att.-int.	20-31-1	19-36-2
Sacked-yards lost	1-8	4-45
Punts	4-47	7-40
Fumbles-lost	2-2	5-3
Penalties-yards	6-38	9-67
Time of possession	33:47	26:13

INDIVIDUAL STATISTICS
RUSHING—Indianapolis, James 22-152, Elias 12-34, Manning 2-14. Philadelphia, Staley 16-78, McNabb 3-13, Bieniemy 1-3.
PASSING—Indianapolis, Manning 16-26-0-235, Walsh 4-5-1-28. Philadelphia, McNabb 19-36-2-165.
RECEIVING—Indianapolis, Harrison 5-60, James 5-47, Wilkins 4-111, Pollard 2-25, Elias 2-8, Jones 1-8, Shields 1-4. Philadelphia, Small 6-59, Broughton 4-65, Staley 2-17, Lewis 2-16, Brown 2-9, C. Martin 2-(minus 2), Bieniemy 1-1.
MISSED FIELD GOAL ATTEMPTS—None.
INTERCEPTIONS—Indianapolis, Blevins 1-41, R. Thomas 1-0. Philadelphia, Whiting 1-22.
KICKOFF RETURNS—Indianapolis, Wilkins 2-39. Philadelphia, Rossum 8-192.
PUNT RETURNS—Indianapolis, Wilkins 4-18. Philadelphia, Rossum 1-8.
SACKS—Indianapolis, Belser 1, Bennett 1, M. Thomas 1, Chester 1. Philadelphia, Mamula 1.

RAVENS 34, BENGALS 31
Sunday, November 21

Baltimore	0	10	21	3—34
Cincinnati	14	0	7	10—31

First Quarter
Cin.—Pickens 7 pass from Blake (Pelfrey kick), 7:48.
Cin.—Scott 23 pass from Blake (Pelfrey kick), 10:20.
Second Quarter
Bal.—FG, Stover 25, 1:25.
Bal.—DeLong 2 pass from Banks (Stover kick), 14:06.
Third Quarter
Bal.—Rhett 2 run (Stover kick), 6:42.
Bal.—Johnson 25 pass from Banks (Stover kick), 9:27.
Bal.—Starks 43 interception return (Stover kick), 10:22.
Cin.—Scott 15 pass from Blake (Pelfrey kick), 12:17.

Fourth Quarter
Cin.—Yeast 86 punt return (Pelfrey kick), 5:51.
Cin.—FG, Pelfrey 19, 13:10.
Bal.—FG, Stover 50, 15:00.
  Attendance—43,279.

	Baltimore	Cincinnati
First downs	19	20
Rushes-yards	26-56	22-102
Passing	225	246
Punt returns	4-29	2-86
Kickoff returns	6-124	5-128
Interception returns	2-43	1-0
Comp.-att.-int.	24-40-1	20-39-2
Sacked-yards lost	7-49	1-0
Punts	7-47	5-50
Fumbles-lost	2-1	2-1
Penalties-yards	7-48	15-127
Time of possession	33:51	26:09

INDIVIDUAL STATISTICS
RUSHING—Baltimore, Rhett 23-36, Banks 2-17, J. Lewis 1-3. Cincinnati, Dillon 15-74, Blake 4-27, Groce 2-1, Basnight 1-0.
PASSING—Baltimore, Banks 24-40-1-274. Cincinnati, Blake 20-39-2-246.
RECEIVING—Baltimore, Johnson 6-73, DeLong 4-23, Evans 3-32, Ismail 3-26, Rhett 3-22, Davis 2-86, J. Lewis 1-5, Pierce 1-4, Ofodile 1-3. Cincinnati, Scott 5-67, Groce 5-26, Jackson 4-47, Pickens 2-54, McGee 2-18, Basnight 1-19, Dillon 1-15.
MISSED FIELD GOAL ATTEMPTS—Cincinnati, Pelfrey 39.
INTERCEPTIONS—Baltimore, Starks 1-43, Woodson 1-0. Cincinnati, Spikes 1-0.
KICKOFF RETURNS—Baltimore, J. Lewis 6-124. Cincinnati, Mack 4-105, Griffin 1-23.
PUNT RETURNS—Baltimore, J. Lewis 4-29. Cincinnati, Yeast 2-86.
SACKS—Baltimore, R. Lewis 1. Cincinnati, Foley 3, Spikes 1, Bankston 1, Gibson 1, Wilson 1.

JAGUARS 41, SAINTS 23
Sunday, November 21

New Orleans	7	10	0	6—23
Jacksonville	14	3	14	10—41

First Quarter
Jac.—Barlow 74 punt return (Hollis kick), 1:51.
N.O.—Tolliver 1 run (Brien kick), 9:32.
Jac.—Jones 7 pass from Brunell (Hollis kick), 13:30.
Second Quarter
N.O.—R. Williams 19 run (Brien kick), 1:55.
N.O.—FG, Brien 52, 13:12.
Jac.—FG, Hollis 45, 15:00.
Third Quarter
Jac.—J. Stewart 4 run (Hollis kick), 2:34.
Jac.—J. Smith 46 pass from Brunell (Hollis kick), 5:30.
Fourth Quarter
Jac.—FG, Hollis 32, 4:32.
Jac.—J. Stewart 1 run (Hollis kick), 7:30.
N.O.—R. Williams 1 run (pass failed), 10:37.
  Attendance—69,772.

	New Orleans	Jacksonville
First downs	21	29
Rushes-yards	29-106	27-139
Passing	233	355
Punt returns	1-4	3-83
Kickoff returns	6-122	5-100
Interception returns	1-0	1-0
Comp.-att.-int.	18-27-1	21-32-1
Sacked-yards lost	2-18	3-17
Punts	4-43	2-26
Fumbles-lost	2-0	0-0
Penalties-yards	8-43	4-50
Time of possession	32:08	27:52

INDIVIDUAL STATISTICS
RUSHING—New Orleans, R. Williams 19-94, L. Smith 3-(minus 12), Hobert 2-16, Craver 2-6, Kennison 1-1, Tolliver 1-1, Davis 1-0. Jacksonville, J. Stewart 16-87, Mack 6-27, Brunell 3-27, Fiedler 2-(minus 2).
PASSING—New Orleans, Tolliver 10-14-0-159, Hobert 8-13-1-92. Jacksonville, Brunell 19-30-1-351, Fiedler 2-2-0-21.
RECEIVING—New Orleans, Hastings 5-58, Slutzker 3-64, Poole 3-44, Kennison 2-38, R. Williams 2-27, Dawsey 1-13, L. Smith 1-4, Wilcox 1-3. Jacksonville, J. Smith 9-220, J. Stewart 5-53, Barlow 2-30, Jones 2-20, McCardell 2-19, Brady 1-30.
MISSED FIELD GOAL ATTEMPTS—New Orleans, Brien 39.
INTERCEPTIONS—New Orleans, Clay 1-0. Jacksonville, Bryant 1-0.
KICKOFF RETURNS—New Orleans, Philyaw 5-113, Gammon 1-9. Jacksonville, Barlow 3-68, Mack 1-23, McCardell 1-9.
PUNT RETURNS—New Orleans, Kennison 1-4. Jacksonville, Barlow 2-80, McCardell 1-3.
SACKS—New Orleans, Whitehead 2, Glover 1. Jacksonville, Boyer 1, L. Smith 1.

BRONCOS 27, RAIDERS 21
Monday, November 22

Oakland	0	7	11	3 0—21
Denver	10	5	0	6 6—27

First Quarter
Den.—Griffith 1 run (Elam kick), 7:00.
Den.—FG, Elam 30, 13:47.
Second Quarter
Den.—Safety, D. Smith blocked a punt out of the end zone, 5:27.
Den.—FG, Elam 24, 8:23.
Oak.—Ritchie 20 pass from Gannon (Husted kick), 10:16.
Third Quarter
Oak.—Dudley 12 pass from Gannon (Jett pass from Gannon), 0:56.
Oak.—FG, Husted 33, 13:47.
Fourth Quarter
Den.—FG, Elam 38, 10:56.
Oak.—FG, Husted 44, 13:43.
Den.—FG, Elam 53, 14:53.
Overtime
Den.—Gary 24 run, 2:40.
  Attendance—70,012.

	Oakland	Denver
First downs	16	17
Rushes-yards	29-79	30-120
Passing	205	171
Punt returns	3-40	2-6
Kickoff returns	5-93	7-153
Interception returns	0-0	1-34
Comp.-att.-int.	17-34-1	18-41-0
Sacked-yards lost	5-17	2-11
Punts	7-26	9-38
Fumbles-lost	2-2	4-2
Penalties-yards	7-90	9-60
Time of possession	31:59	30:41

INDIVIDUAL STATISTICS
RUSHING—Oakland, Wheatley 16-53, Kaufman 11-22, Gannon 2-4. Denver, Gary 22-95, C. Miller 4-20, Griffith 2-4, Griese 2-1.
PASSING—Oakland, Gannon 17-34-1-222. Denver, C. Miller 12-27-0-122, Griese 6-14-0-60.
RECEIVING—Oakland, Dudley 4-72, Ritchie 4-41, Brown 3-46, Jett 2-13, D. Walker 2-12, Brigham 1-29, Mickens 1-9. Denver, McCaffrey 7-82, R. Smith 7-66, Chamberlain 1-11, McGriff 1-9, B. Miller 1-8, Gary 1-6.
MISSED FIELD GOAL ATTEMPTS—Oakland, Husted 37.
INTERCEPTIONS—Denver, Carter 1-34.
KICKOFF RETURNS—Oakland, Kaufman 3-84, Branch 1-9, Mincy 1-0. Denver, Watson 6-153, B. Miller 1-0.
PUNT RETURNS—Oakland, Gordon 3-40. Denver, McGriff 1-6, Watson 1-0.
SACKS—Oakland, Johnstone 1, Maryland 1. Denver, Cadrez 3, Tanuvasa 1, Pryce 1.

WEEK 12

RESULTS

DETROIT 21, Chicago 17
DALLAS 20, Miami 0
Arizona 34, N.Y. GIANTS 24
BUFFALO 17, New England 7
CAROLINA 34, Atlanta 28
Cincinnati 27, PITTSBURGH 20
INDIANAPOLIS 13, N.Y. Jets 6
Jacksonville 30, BALTIMORE 23
Kansas City 37, OAKLAND 34
MINNESOTA 35, San Diego 27
ST. LOUIS 43, New Orleans 12
Tampa Bay 16, SEATTLE 3
Tennessee 33, CLEVELAND 21
WASHINGTON 20, Philadelphia 17 (OT)
Green Bay 20, SAN FRANCISCO 3
Open date: Denver

STANDINGS

AFC EAST
	W	L	T	Pct.
Indianapolis	9	2	0	.818
Miami	8	3	0	.727
Buffalo	8	4	0	.667
New England	6	5	0	.545
N.Y. Jets	4	7	0	.364

AFC CENTRAL
	W	L	T	Pct.
Jacksonville	10	1	0	.909
Tennessee	9	2	0	.818
Pittsburgh	5	6	0	.455
Baltimore	4	7	0	.364
Cincinnati	2	10	0	.167
Cleveland	2	10	0	.167

AFC WEST
	W	L	T	Pct.
Seattle	8	3	0	.727
Kansas City	6	5	0	.545
Oakland	5	6	0	.455
Denver	4	7	0	.364
San Diego	4	7	0	.364

NFC EAST
	W	L	T	Pct.
Washington	7	4	0	.636
Dallas	6	5	0	.545
Arizona	5	6	0	.455
N.Y. Giants	5	6	0	.455
Philadelphia	3	9	0	.250

NFC CENTRAL
	W	L	T	Pct.
Detroit	7	4	0	.636
Minnesota	7	4	0	.636
Tampa Bay	7	4	0	.636
Green Bay	6	5	0	.545
Chicago	5	7	0	.417

NFC WEST
	W	L	T	Pct.
St. Louis	9	2	0	.818
Carolina	5	6	0	.455
San Francisco	3	9	0	.250
Atlanta	2	9	0	.182
New Orleans	2	9	0	.182

HIGHLIGHTS

Hero of the week: Cincinnati cornerback Rodney Heath intercepted two passes—returning one 58 yards for a touchdown and returning the other nine yards to set up another TD—in the Bengals' 27-20 win over the Steelers. Heath also broke up a fourth-and-6 pass in the final minute to preserve the victory.

Goat of the week: Miami quarterback Dan Marino, playing at Dallas on Thanksgiving Day in his first start in more than a month because of a pinched nerve in his neck, completed just 15-of-36 passes for 178 yards and threw five interceptions in a 20-0 nationally televised loss to the Cowboys. It was the most interceptions Marino threw in a game since 1988.

Sub of the week: Jake Plummer replaced Dave Brown at quarterback for the Cardinals in the second half against the Giants and threw two touchdown passes to lead Arizona to a 34-24 victory. Plummer began the season as the team's starting quarterback, but he had missed the previous four weeks because of a broken finger.

Comeback of the week: Kansas City trailed Oakland, 34-20, early in the fourth quarter before the Chiefs rallied to tie the score and then take the lead with a game-winning drive in the final three minutes. Quarterback Elvis Grbac drove the Chiefs to the Raiders' 27-yard line, setting up a 44-yard field goal by Pete Stoyanovich as time expired to give his team a 37-34 victory.

Blowout of the week: New Orleans trailed St. Louis by just three points late in the third quarter, but the Rams scored 28 points in the game's last 19 minutes to cruise to a 43-12 victory. St. Louis quarterback Kurt Warner was 10-for-12 for 153 yards in the second half with an amazing 146.5 passer rating.

Nail-biter of the week: The Redskins began the fourth quarter with a 17-3 lead over Philadelphia before the Eagles rallied for two 91-yard touchdown drives to tie the score. Then, Washington's Brett Conway missed a 28-yard field goal attempt as time expired, forcing overtime. Luckily for Conway, he got a chance to redeem himself by kicking a 27-yarder in overtime to give the Redskins a 20-17 victory.

Hit of the week: The Falcons rallied from a 34-14 deficit to pull within six points of the Panthers, and then got the ball at the Carolina 20-yard line with 2:59 left when Travis Hall recovered a fumble. But Kevin Greene sacked Atlanta quarterback Chris Chandler and knocked the ball loose, and Carolina's Esera Tuaolo pounced on it to end the threat.

Oddity of the week: New Orleans' Willie Whitehead became the first player to be fined by the NFL for using the forbidden throat slash gesture. Whitehead made the gesture after sacking Warner in the first quarter of the Rams' 43-12 rout. Just a few days before the game, the NFL sent a letter to all 31 teams banning the drawing of a finger across the throat, calling it "an unacceptable act of violence." Whitehead was fined $5,000 for the incident.

Top rusher: Corey Dillon carried 23 times for 120 yards in the Bengals' 27-20 victory over the Steelers.

Top passer: Jim Harbaugh was 25-of-39 for 404 yards and one touchdown in the Chargers' 35-27 loss to the Vikings.

Top receiver: Jeff Graham contributed to Harbaugh's big game by catching six passes for 141 yards in San Diego's loss to Minnesota.

Notes: Atlanta kicker Morten Andersen scored for the 248th consecutive game, extending his NFL record. ... The Rams won their sixth division game in a season for the first time. The NFL went to the division format in 1967. ... Jimmy Smith (132 yards) and Keenan McCardell (102) became the first wide receivers to post 100-yard games against Baltimore in 1999. ... The Cardinals' victory was only their second in 16 games at Giants Stadium. ... Curtis Martin went over the 1,000-yard rushing mark for the fifth consecutive season. He joined Barry Sanders, Eric Dickerson and Tony Dorsett as the only players to do it their first five years in the league. ... After their 37-34 victory over the Raiders, the Chiefs owned a winning record against every original AFL team. ... Tampa Bay won for the first time in five meetings against Seattle. Both teams joined the league in 1976. ... Seattle's Joey Galloway had one catch for 18 yards, giving him at least one catch in each of his first 66 NFL games. ... Titans guard Bruce Matthews played in his 259th game, tying Jackie Slater for the most games played by an NFL offensive lineman.

Quote of the week: After the Rams routed the Saints, a New Orleans reporter asked coach Mike Ditka if he still was the right man for the job. Ditka, without raising his voice, said, "I don't know. Did I do anything wrong out there? What did I do wrong? Did I drop a ball? Did I miss the field goal? Did I miss the tackles? I'm not sure. Did I throw the interception? I'm not sure what you're asking. If you're asking me because things are going bad if I don't think I'm the right guy for the job, yeah, I think I'm the right guy for this job. Was I the right guy for the job when we drove down there with seven minutes to go in the third quarter, and we could have tied it up, 15-15? There's the answer to your question. Players play football."

GAME SUMMARIES

COWBOYS 20, DOLPHINS 0

Thursday, November 25

Miami	0	0	0	0	0
Dallas	0	0	7	13	20

Third Quarter
Dal.—Coakley 46 interception return (Cunningham kick), 7:52.
Fourth Quarter
Dal.—FG, Cunningham 36, 3:13.
Dal.—Ismail 65 pass from Aikman (Cunningham kick), 8:36.
Dal.—FG, Cunningham 23, 13:03.
Attendance—64,328.

	Miami	Dallas
First downs	16	15
Rushes-yards	20-69	34-101
Passing	204	223
Punt returns	3-28	1-(-5)
Kickoff returns	5-92	1-21
Interception returns	0-0	5-58
Comp.-att.-int.	18-40-5	16-29-0
Sacked-yards lost	2-16	1-9
Punts	4-38	6-43
Fumbles-lost	0-0	1-1
Penalties-yards	5-42	13-103
Time of possession	25:21	34:39

INDIVIDUAL STATISTICS
RUSHING—Miami, Johnson 19-63, Huard 1-6. Dallas, E. Smith 31-103, Aikman 2-(minus 1), Mills 1-(minus 1).
PASSING—Miami, Marino 14-35-5-176, Huard 4-5-0-44. Dallas, Aikman 16-29-0-232.
RECEIVING—Miami, Pritchett 5-59, Green 3-47, Gadsden 3-39, Martin 2-45, Drayton 2-20, Konrad 2-7, Johnson 1-3. Dallas, Ismail 5-125, Tucker 2-35, Lucky 2-15, Thomas 2-12, LaFleur 1-13, Mills 1-11, Bjornson 1-10, Warren 1-8, McGarity 1-3.
MISSED FIELD GOAL ATTEMPTS—Miami, Mare 52, 47, 47.
INTERCEPTIONS—Dallas, Coakley 2-58, Sanders 2-0, Hawthorne 1-0.
KICKOFF RETURNS—Miami, Marion 5-92. Dallas, Tucker 1-21.
PUNT RETURNS—Miami, Jacquet 3-28. Dallas, Sanders 1-(minus 5).
SACKS—Miami, Owens 1. Dallas, Noble 1, Spellman 1.

LIONS 21, BEARS 17

Thursday, November 25

Chicago	0	7	3	7	17
Detroit	7	14	0	0	21

First Quarter
Det.—Crowell 45 pass from Frerotte (Hanson kick), 3:47.
Second Quarter
Det.—Hill 29 run (Hanson kick), 12:15.

Det.—Morton 2 pass from Frerotte (Hanson kick), 13:15.
Chi.—Mayes 3 pass from Miller (Boniol kick), 14:30.
Third Quarter
Chi.—FG, Boniol 27, 7:31.
Fourth Quarter
Chi.—Booker 23 pass from Miller (Boniol kick), 0:07.
Attendance—77,905.

	Chicago	Detroit
First downs	12	20
Rushes-yards	12-52	29-84
Passing	184	293
Punt returns	2-14	5-34
Kickoff returns	4-96	4-66
Interception returns	0-0	1-29
Comp.-att.-int.	25-39-1	29-42-0
Sacked-yards lost	2-20	2-16
Punts	9-44	7-39
Fumbles-lost	1-0	1-1
Penalties-yards	3-25	6-40
Time of possession	21:44	38:16

INDIVIDUAL STATISTICS
RUSHING—Chicago, Enis 6-10, Allen 2-1, Milburn 1-30, McNown 1-9, Bennett 1-2, Miller 1-0. Detroit, Hill 19-68, Schlesinger 4-8, Frerotte 4-5, Irvin 2-3.
PASSING—Chicago, Miller 25-37-1-204, McNown 0-2-0-0. Detroit, Frerotte 29-42-0-309.
RECEIVING—Chicago, Conway 5-31, M. Robinson 4-61, Engram 4-41, Enis 4-7, Booker 2-27, Wetnight 2-15, Bennett 2-9, Milburn 1-10, Mayes 1-3. Detroit, Crowell 7-91, Morton 5-59, Sloan 3-34, Hill 3-32, Schlesinger 3-27, Irvin 3-20, Moore 2-26, Rasby 2-16, Stablein 1-4.
MISSED FIELD GOAL ATTEMPTS—Detroit, Hanson 53.
INTERCEPTIONS—Detroit, Kowalkowski 1-29.
KICKOFF RETURNS—Chicago, Milburn 4-96. Detroit, Fair 4-66.
PUNT RETURNS—Chicago, Milburn 2-14. Detroit, Uwaezuoke 5-34.
SACKS—Chicago, Minter 1, Colvin 1. Detroit, Jones 1, Bailey 0.5, Porcher 0.5.

VIKINGS 35, CHARGERS 27

Sunday, November 28

San Diego	7	0	17	3	27
Minnesota	0	28	7	0	35

First Quarter
S.D.—Stephens 1 run (Carney kick), 6:26.
Second Quarter
Min.—Moss 34 pass from George (Anderson kick), 0:05.
Min.—Reed 5 pass from George (Anderson kick), 5:47.
Min.—Carter 4 pass from George (Anderson kick), 9:05.
Min.—Hoard 4 run (Anderson kick), 11:16.
Third Quarter
S.D.—Bynum 80 pass from Harbaugh (Carney kick), 0:20.
S.D.—Stephens 1 run (Carney kick), 4:27.
S.D.—FG, Carney 40, 7:20.
Min.—Carter 34 pass from George (Anderson kick), 10:50.
Fourth Quarter
S.D.—FG, Carney 40, 3:19.
Attendance—64,232.

	San Diego	Minnesota
First downs	19	27
Rushes-yards	20-62	29-129
Passing	396	356
Punt returns	0-0	0-0
Kickoff returns	5-119	6-122
Interception returns	2-68	1-0
Comp.-att.-int.	25-39-1	28-43-2
Sacked-yards lost	1-8	1-7
Punts	4-43	5-39
Fumbles-lost	2-2	0-0
Penalties-yards	1-5	5-35
Time of possession	24:46	35:14

INDIVIDUAL STATISTICS
RUSHING—San Diego, Bynum 8-26, Stephens 6-1, Harbaugh 3-20, Fazande 3-15. Minnesota, Smith 20-104, Hoard 6-28, George 3-(minus 3).
PASSING—San Diego, Harbaugh 25-39-1-404. Minnesota, George 28-43-2-363.

RECEIVING—San Diego, J. Graham 6-141, Ricks 5-64, McCrary 4-21, Fletcher 3-11, Bynum 2-90, Davis 2-32, Penn 1-32, F. Jones 1-7, Seau 1-6. Minnesota, Carter 11-136, Moss 7-127, Reed 4-46, Hoard 3-24, Glover 1-14, Kleinsasser 1-11, Smith 1-5.

MISSED FIELD GOAL ATTEMPTS—None.

INTERCEPTIONS—San Diego, Dumas 1-68, Dimry 1-0. Minnesota, Griffith 1-0.

KICKOFF RETURNS—San Diego, Bynum 5-119. Minnesota, Tate 5-103, M. Williams 1-19.

PUNT RETURNS—None.

SACKS—San Diego, Johnson 1. Minnesota, Doleman 1.

RAMS 43, SAINTS 12

Sunday, November 28

New Orleans	3	9	0	0	—12
St. Louis	7	8	7	21	—43

First Quarter
St.L.—Holt 25 pass from Warner (Wilkins kick), 1:02.
N.O.—FG, Brien 51, 8:23.

Second Quarter
N.O.—FG, Brien 42, 0:04.
N.O.—FG, Brien 45, 5:52.
St.L.—Faulk 1 run (Faulk run), 7:45.
N.O.—FG, Brien 35, 14:53.

Third Quarter
St.L.—Faulk 6 run (Wilkins kick), 11:52.

Fourth Quarter
St.L.—Holcombe 3 run (Wilkins kick), 2:45.
St.L.—Holt 20 pass from Warner (Wilkins kick), 8:24.
St.L.—Hodgins 1 run (Wilkins kick), 13:46.
Attendance—65,864.

	New Orleans	St. Louis
First downs	20	24
Rushes-yards	28-102	27-129
Passing	263	195
Punt returns	3-15	2-25
Kickoff returns	7-171	5-163
Interception returns	0-0	2-14
Comp.-att.-int.	25-47-2	15-27-0
Sacked-yards lost	2-10	2-18
Punts	4-44	5-45
Fumbles-lost	1-0	0-0
Penalties-yards	8-80	7-50
Time of possession	33:44	26:16

INDIVIDUAL STATISTICS

RUSHING—New Orleans, L. Smith 18-54, Perry 6-19, Hobert 2-11, Kennison 1-15, Davis 1-3. St. Louis, Faulk 18-102, Holcombe 4-24, Hodgins 3-3, Warner 2-0.

PASSING—New Orleans, Hobert 23-41-2-254, Wuerffel 2-6-0-19. St. Louis, Warner 15-27-0-213.

RECEIVING—New Orleans, Hastings 9-113, Cleeland 5-62, Kennison 5-33, L. Smith 4-36, Poole 1-18, Perry 1-11. St. Louis, Holt 5-87, Bruce 5-81, Hakim 2-22, Faulk 2-13, Holcombe 1-10.

MISSED FIELD GOAL ATTEMPTS—New Orleans, Brien 24.

INTERCEPTIONS—St. Louis, McCleon 1-14, Clemons 1-0.

KICKOFF RETURNS—New Orleans, Philyaw 7-171. St. Louis, Horne 4-160, McCollum 1-3.

PUNT RETURNS—New Orleans, Kennison 3-15. St. Louis, Hakim 2-25.

SACKS—New Orleans, Kei. Mitchell 1, Whitehead 1. St. Louis, Farr 2.

BILLS 17, PATRIOTS 7

Sunday, November 28

New England	0	0	0	7	— 7
Buffalo	3	7	7	0	—17

First Quarter
Buf.—FG, Christie 28, 13:28.

Second Quarter
Buf.—Moulds 54 pass from Flutie (Christie kick), 13:59.

Third Quarter
Buf.—Gash 31 pass from Flutie (Christie kick), 4:39.

Fourth Quarter
N.E.—Glenn 45 pass from Bledsoe (Vinatieri kick), 12:19.
Attendance—72,111.

	New England	Buffalo
First downs	17	13
Rushes-yards	25-93	34-92
Passing	174	202
Punt returns	3-34	1-6
Kickoff returns	4-71	1-26
Interception returns	0-0	1-1
Comp.-att.-int.	18-34-1	9-16-0
Sacked-yards lost	6-31	1-5
Punts	6-35	5-41
Fumbles-lost	2-1	2-1
Penalties-yards	8-101	6-39
Time of possession	30:46	29:14

INDIVIDUAL STATISTICS

RUSHING—New England, Allen 13-47, Faulk 7-22, Bledsoe 2-6, Warren 2-5, L. Johnson 1-13. Buffalo, Linton 17-67, A. Smith 9-21, Flutie 4-(minus 7), Gordon 3-18, P. Price 1-(minus 7).

PASSING—New England, Bledsoe 18-34-1-205. Buffalo, Flutie 9-16-0-207.

RECEIVING—New England, Glenn 3-69, Jefferson 3-36, Warren 3-34, Faulk 2-15, Coates 2-14, T. Carter 2-9, Brown 1-11, Simmons 1-10, Rutledge 1-7. Buffalo, Linton 3-37, Moulds 1-54, Collins 1-45, Gash 1-31, A. Smith 1-23, Reed 1-10, P. Price 1-7.

MISSED FIELD GOAL ATTEMPTS—None.

INTERCEPTIONS—Buffalo, Irvin 1-1.

KICKOFF RETURNS—New England, Faulk 3-62, Warren 1-9. Buffalo, K. Williams 1-26.

PUNT RETURNS—New England, Brown 3-34. Buffalo, K. Williams 1-6.

SACKS—New England, McGinest 1. Buffalo, Washington 2, Perry 1, Hansen 1, Northern 0.5, Rogers 0.5, Wiley 0.5, Moran 0.5.

BENGALS 27, STEELERS 20

Sunday, November 28

Cincinnati	14	10	3	0	—27
Pittsburgh	3	10	7	0	—20

First Quarter
Cin.—Scott 76 pass from Blake (Pelfrey kick), 1:27.
Cin.—Blake 4 run (Pelfrey kick), 6:56.
Pit.—FG, K. Brown 35, 13:39.

Second Quarter
Cin.—Heath 58 interception return (Pelfrey kick), 1:30.
Cin.—FG, Pelfrey 29, 4:27.
Pit.—FG, K. Brown 33, 9:17.
Pit.—Shaw 15 pass from Tomczak (K. Brown kick), 13:07.

Third Quarter
Pit.—Ward 34 pass from Tomczak (K. Brown kick), 1:28.
Cin.—FG, Pelfrey 29, 5:16.
Attendance—50,907.

	Cincinnati	Pittsburgh
First downs	18	20
Rushes-yards	34-182	31-111
Passing	233	280
Punt returns	1-10	1-10
Kickoff returns	5-76	5-113
Interception returns	2-67	1-22
Comp.-att.-int.	15-28-1	24-46-2
Sacked-yards lost	3-8	2-20
Punts	5-38	4-47
Fumbles-lost	2-0	1-1
Penalties-yards	5-35	6-45
Time of possession	27:25	32:35

INDIVIDUAL STATISTICS

RUSHING—Cincinnati, Dillon 23-120, Blake 10-27, Basnight 1-35. Pittsburgh, Bettis 22-81, Huntley 5-12, Tomczak 2-10, Fuamatu-Ma'afala 1-4, Zereoue 1-4.

PASSING—Cincinnati, Blake 15-28-1-241. Pittsburgh, Tomczak 19-35-0-264, Stewart 5-11-2-36.

RECEIVING—Cincinnati, Scott 4-123, Williams 3-27, Dillon 3-20, Pickens 2-41, Basnight 2-22, Jackson 1-8. Pittsburgh, Ward 7-89, Edwards 7-86, Shaw 3-36, Bruener 2-51, Blackwell 2-19, Lyons 1-7, Bettis 1-6, Huntley 1-6.

MISSED FIELD GOAL ATTEMPTS—Cincinnati, Pelfrey 25.

INTERCEPTIONS—Cincinnati, Heath 2-67. Pittsburgh, Emmons 1-22.

KICKOFF RETURNS—Cincinnati, Mack 3-69, Griffin 2-7. Pittsburgh, Huntley 3-73, Zereoue 2-40.

PUNT RETURNS—Cincinnati, Yeast 1-10. Pittsburgh, Hawkins 1-10.
SACKS—Cincinnati, Bankston 1, Copeland 0.5, Gibson 0.5. Pittsburgh, Roye 2, Flowers 1.

COLTS 13, JETS 6
Sunday, November 28

N.Y. Jets	6	0	0	0—	6
Indianapolis	7	3	0	3—	13

First Quarter
NYJ—FG, Hall 33, 4:14.
NYJ—FG, Hall 30, 8:08.
Ind.—Pollard 2 pass from Manning (Vanderjagt kick), 14:28.
Second Quarter
Ind.—FG, Vanderjagt 22, 14:59.
Fourth Quarter
Ind.—FG, Vanderjagt 37, 6:00.
Attendance—56,689.

	N.Y. Jets	Indianapolis
First downs	14	23
Rushes-yards	26-126	27-100
Passing	88	187
Punt returns	1-1	4-37
Kickoff returns	3-73	3-80
Interception returns	2-2	0-0
Comp.-att.-int.	12-23-0	23-31-2
Sacked-yards lost	2-14	2-11
Punts	5-46	2-51
Fumbles-lost	0-0	1-1
Penalties-yards	10-72	3-24
Time of possession	28:02	31:58

INDIVIDUAL STATISTICS
RUSHING—New York, Martin 19-83, Lucas 3-28, Anderson 2-12, Parmalee 2-3. Indianapolis, James 24-74, Manning 3-26.
PASSING—New York, Lucas 12-22-0-102, Sowell 0-1-0-0. Indianapolis, Manning 23-31-2-198.
RECEIVING—New York, K. Johnson 4-56, Chrebet 3-21, Martin 3-12, Anderson 2-13. Indianapolis, James 7-53, Harrison 5-58, Wilkins 5-39, Green 2-29, Pollard 2-12, Dilger 2-7.
MISSED FIELD GOAL ATTEMPTS—None.
INTERCEPTIONS—New York, Mickens 1-2, Wiltz 1-0.
KICKOFF RETURNS—New York, Stone 2-51, Glenn 1-22. Indianapolis, Wilkins 3-80.
PUNT RETURNS—New York, Ward 1-1. Indianapolis, Wilkins 4-37.
SACKS—New York, Logan 1, Ogbogu 1. Indianapolis, Peterson 1, E. Johnson 1.

JAGUARS 30, RAVENS 23
Sunday, November 28

Jacksonville	0	7	0	23—	30
Baltimore	10	3	3	7—	23

First Quarter
Bal.—Rhett 20 pass from Banks (Stover kick), 6:53.
Bal.—FG, Stover 46, 11:42.
Second Quarter
Jac.—J. Smith 8 pass from Brunell (Hollis kick), 4:22.
Bal.—FG, Stover 31, 14:00.
Third Quarter
Bal.—FG, Stover 33, 14:56.
Fourth Quarter
Jac.—McCardell 1 pass from Brunell (Hollis kick), 4:00.
Jac.—Brackens 21 interception return (McCardell pass from Brunell), 4:16.
Bal.—Evans 3 pass from Banks (Stover kick), 8:34.
Jac.—J. Stewart 4 run (J. Smith pass from Brunell), 13:21.
Attendance—68,428.

	Jacksonville	Baltimore
First downs	24	14
Rushes-yards	25-60	22-81
Passing	328	199
Punt returns	1-7	3-35
Kickoff returns	6-112	4-145
Interception returns	1-21	2-20
Comp.-att.-int.	27-47-2	17-34-1
Sacked-yards lost	3-10	3-15

	Jacksonville	Baltimore
Punts	6-43	5-38
Fumbles-lost	1-1	4-2
Penalties-yards	8-41	6-39
Time of possession	32:35	27:25

INDIVIDUAL STATISTICS
RUSHING—Jacksonville, J. Stewart 20-46, Brunell 4-5, Whitted 1-9. Baltimore, Rhett 13-30, Evans 8-47, Ismail 1-4.
PASSING—Jacksonville, Brunell 27-47-2-338. Baltimore, Banks 17-34-1-214.
RECEIVING—Jacksonville, J. Smith 10-132, McCardell 8-102, Brady 4-65, J. Stewart 3-10, Jones 1-18, Barlow 1-11. Baltimore, Ismail 5-76, Rhett 3-32, Evans 3-3, Armour 2-27, DeLong 2-11, J. Lewis 1-46, Johnson 1-19.
MISSED FIELD GOAL ATTEMPTS—None.
INTERCEPTIONS—Jacksonville, Brackens 1-21. Baltimore, R. Lewis 1-18, Woodson 1-2.
KICKOFF RETURNS—Jacksonville, Mack 4-73, Barlow 2-39. Baltimore, Harris 3-130, J. Lewis 1-15.
PUNT RETURNS—Jacksonville, Barlow 1-7. Baltimore, J. Lewis 3-35.
SACKS—Jacksonville, Brackens 1, Hardy 1, Walker 1. Baltimore, Boulware 1.5, Harris 1, Smith 0.5.

REDSKINS 20, EAGLES 17
Sunday, November 28

Philadelphia	0	3	0	14	0—17
Washington	3	7	7	0	3—20

First Quarter
Was.—FG, Conway 43, 8:09.
Second Quarter
Was.—Sellers 6 pass from B. Johnson (Conway kick), 6:58.
Phi.—FG, N. Johnson 34, 12:01.
Third Quarter
Was.—Davis 1 run (Conway kick), 3:28.
Fourth Quarter
Phi.—Broughton 3 pass from McNabb (N. Johnson kick), 3:13.
Phi.—Broughton 26 pass from McNabb (N. Johnson kick), 13:08.
Overtime
Was.—FG, Conway 27, 4:34.
Attendance—74,741.

	Philadelphia	Washington
First downs	16	23
Rushes-yards	28-143	32-94
Passing	156	218
Punt returns	1-3	2-19
Kickoff returns	4-89	5-147
Interception returns	1-0	0-0
Comp.-att.-int.	16-28-0	25-36-1
Sacked-yards lost	2-16	0-0
Punts	4-39	3-35
Fumbles-lost	0-0	2-0
Penalties-yards	5-59	3-24
Time of possession	29:56	34:38

INDIVIDUAL STATISTICS
RUSHING—Philadelphia, Staley 19-44, McNabb 8-71, Bieniemy 1-28. Washington, Davis 24-61, Mitchell 3-24, B. Johnson 3-1, Centers 2-8.
PASSING—Philadelphia, McNabb 16-28-0-172. Washington, B. Johnson 25-36-1-218.
RECEIVING—Philadelphia, Staley 4-39, Broughton 3-38, C. Martin 3-9, Small 2-35, Brown 2-15, Bieniemy 1-27, D. Douglas 1-9. Washington, Centers 9-71, Connell 6-69, Westbrook 4-51, Fryar 2-11, Mitchell 1-9, Sellers 1-6, Alexander 1-4, Davis 1-(minus 3).
MISSED FIELD GOAL ATTEMPTS—Philadelphia, N. Johnson 47. Washington, Conway 28.
INTERCEPTIONS—Philadelphia, Taylor 1-0.
KICKOFF RETURNS—Philadelphia, Rossum 3-68, Whiting 1-21. Washington, Thrash 2-72, Mitchell 2-68, Sellers 1-7.
PUNT RETURNS—Philadelphia, Rossum 1-3. Washington, Mitchell 2-19.
SACKS—Washington, Stubblefield 1, Smith 0.5, Cook 0.5.

BUCCANEERS 16, SEAHAWKS 3
Sunday, November 28

Tampa Bay	0	6	0	10—	16
Seattle	3	0	0	0—	3

1999 REVIEW Week 12

– 186 –

First Quarter
Sea.—FG, Peterson 25, 4:20.
Second Quarter
T.B.—FG, Gramatica 42, 0:09.
T.B.—FG, Gramatica 40, 13:48.
Fourth Quarter
T.B.—Hape 2 pass from King (Gramatica kick), 2:39.
T.B.—FG, Gramatica 37, 6:00.
Attendance—66,314.

	Tampa Bay	Seattle
First downs	9	15
Rushes-yards	37-105	22-89
Passing	51	170
Punt returns	1-3	3-38
Kickoff returns	2-58	4-55
Interception returns	5-86	0-0
Comp.-att.-int.	8-18-0	19-44-5
Sacked-yards lost	5-31	3-27
Punts	9-40	7-38
Fumbles-lost	1-0	2-1
Penalties-yards	2-15	5-50
Time of possession	31:56	28:04

INDIVIDUAL STATISTICS
RUSHING—Tampa Bay, Alstott 17-49, Dunn 15-57, King 3-(minus 1), Dilfer 2-0. Seattle, Watters 17-64, Kitna 2-16, Green 2-5, R. Brown 1-4.
PASSING—Tampa Bay, Dilfer 5-11-0-50, King 3-7-0-32. Seattle, Kitna 19-44-5-197.
RECEIVING—Tampa Bay, Moore 2-31, Anthony 2-10, Alstott 1-24, Dunn 1-9, Green 1-6, Hape 1-2. Seattle, R. Brown 5-24, Dawkins 4-87, Mayes 3-35, Fauria 3-15, Watters 2-7, Galloway 1-18, Pritchard 1-11.
MISSED FIELD GOAL ATTEMPTS—None.
INTERCEPTIONS—Tampa Bay, Barber 1-43, Kelly 1-26, Brooks 1-10, Singleton 1-7, Abraham 1-0.
KICKOFF RETURNS—Tampa Bay, Anthony 2-58. Seattle, Green 2-36, Joseph 1-12, Fauria 1-7.
PUNT RETURNS—Tampa Bay, Williams 1-3. Seattle, Rogers 3-38.
SACKS—Tampa Bay, Brooks 1, Sapp 1, McFarland 1. Seattle, C. Brown 1, Daniels 1, Hanks 1, LaBounty 1, King 1.

TITANS 33, BROWNS 21

Sunday, November 28

Tennessee	7	6	13	7	—33
Cleveland	0	14	0	7	—21

First Quarter
Ten.—E. George 14 run (Del Greco kick), 4:42.
Second Quarter
Cle.—Couch 4 run (Dawson kick), 3:08.
Cle.—Kirby 78 pass from Couch (Dawson kick), 5:34.
Ten.—FG, Del Greco 27, 11:28.
Ten.—FG, Del Greco 31, 14:55.
Third Quarter
Ten.—McNair 1 run (Del Greco kick), 5:02.
Ten.—Mason 65 punt return (run failed), 13:23.
Fourth Quarter
Ten.—E. George 5 run (Del Greco kick), 11:31.
Cle.—K. Johnson 6 pass from Couch (Dawson kick), 14:45.
Attendance—72,008.

	Tennessee	Cleveland
First downs	22	18
Rushes-yards	33-158	24-81
Passing	179	227
Punt returns	5-98	2-9
Kickoff returns	3-65	7-112
Interception returns	0-0	0-0
Comp.-att.-int.	18-36-0	19-35-0
Sacked-yards lost	0-0	7-34
Punts	4-48	6-39
Fumbles-lost	1-1	5-2
Penalties-yards	4-18	5-30
Time of possession	32:36	27:24

INDIVIDUAL STATISTICS
RUSHING—Tennessee, E. George 26-113, McNair 7-45. Cleveland, Abdul-Jabbar 15-35, Couch 5-29, Kirby 4-17.
PASSING—Tennessee, McNair 18-36-0-179. Cleveland, Couch 19-35-0-261.
RECEIVING—Tennessee, Dyson 4-42, Harris 3-44, Mason 3-28, Wycheck 3-27, E. George 3-21, Kent 2-17. Cleveland, Johnson 5-84, Chiaverini 5-57, Kirby 4-87, Campbell 2-25, Edwards 1-4, I. Smith 1-3, Abdul-Jabbar 1-1.
MISSED FIELD GOAL ATTEMPTS—Tennessee, Del Greco 37.
INTERCEPTIONS—None.
KICKOFF RETURNS—Tennessee, Mason 3-65. Cleveland, Hill 2-41, Saleh 2-24, Kirby 1-20, Powell 1-19, Campbell 1-8.
PUNT RETURNS—Tennessee, Mason 5-98. Cleveland, Johnson 2-9.
SACKS—Tennessee, Rolle 1, Bishop 1, Fisk 1, Evans 1, Holmes 1, Kearse 1, Team 1.

CARDINALS 34, GIANTS 24

Sunday, November 28

Arizona	3	3	7	21	—34
N.Y. Giants	0	10	0	14	—24

First Quarter
Ariz.—FG, Jacke 39, 9:06.
Second Quarter
NYG—Collins 1 run (Blanchard kick), 8:36.
Ariz.—FG, Jacke 20, 13:09.
NYG—FG, Blanchard 24, 14:58.
Third Quarter
Ariz.—Moore 2 pass from Plummer (Jacke kick), 3:10.
Fourth Quarter
Ariz.—McWilliams 9 pass from Plummer (Jacke kick), 0:05.
NYG—Bennett 1 run (Blanchard kick), 6:09.
Ariz.—Bates 2 run (Jacke kick), 10:44.
Ariz.—Swann 42 interception return (Jacke kick), 13:03.
NYG—Barber 34 pass from Collins (Blanchard kick), 14:18.
Attendance—77,809.

	Arizona	N.Y. Giants
First downs	23	20
Rushes-yards	34-69	20-52
Passing	222	282
Punt returns	4-39	3-8
Kickoff returns	4-55	7-124
Interception returns	3-62	0-0
Comp.-att.-int.	23-35-0	22-45-3
Sacked-yards lost	4-29	2-16
Punts	4-37	6-42
Fumbles-lost	4-1	2-1
Penalties-yards	2-22	6-50
Time of possession	35:17	24:43

INDIVIDUAL STATISTICS
RUSHING—Arizona, Bates 16-37, Murrell 15-28, Plummer 2-0, Da. Brown 1-4. New York, Barber 10-37, Bennett 5-16, Johnson 3-(minus 2), Collins 1-1, Way 1-0.
PASSING—Arizona, Plummer 12-18-0-125, Da. Brown 11-17-0-126. New York, Collins 22-45-3-298.
RECEIVING—Arizona, Moore 7-102, Sanders 6-73, Murrell 5-50, Boston 1-9, McWilliams 1-9, Cody 1-5, Hardy 1-2, Makovicka 1-1. New York, Toomer 6-87, Mitchell 5-47, Hilliard 4-72, Barber 3-64, Patten 2-21, Bennett 1-6, Comella 1-1.
MISSED FIELD GOAL ATTEMPTS—Arizona, Jacke 44.
INTERCEPTIONS—Arizona, Swann 1-42, Fredrickson 1-23, Williams 1-(minus 3).
KICKOFF RETURNS—Arizona, Bates 2-42, Lassiter 1-13, Tillman 1-0. New York, Patten 6-105, Barber 1-19.
PUNT RETURNS—Arizona, Cody 4-39. New York, Barber 3-8.
SACKS—Arizona, Rice 2. New York, Jones 2, Armstead 1, Galyon 1.

CHIEFS 37, RAIDERS 34

Sunday, November 28

Kansas City	0	10	10	17	—37
Oakland	3	10	21	0	—34

First Quarter
Oak.—FG, Husted 33, 10:51.
Second Quarter
K.C.—Bennett 2 run (Stoyanovich kick), 2:30.
Oak.—FG, Husted 30, 6:22.
K.C.—FG, Stoyanovich 47, 10:09.
Oak.—Dudley 16 pass from Gannon (Husted kick), 13:41.

– 187 –

Third Quarter
K.C.—FG, Stoyanovich 37, 4:40.
K.C.—Dishman 47 interception return (Stoyanovich kick), 6:04.
Oak.—Gannon 6 run (Husted kick), 9:45.
Oak.—Dudley 3 pass from Gannon (Husted kick), 10:54.
Oak.—Woodson 15 interception return (Husted kick), 14:57.

Fourth Quarter
K.C.—Gonzalez 73 pass from Grbac (Stoyanovich kick), 1:22.
K.C.—Dishman 40 fumble return (Stoyanovich kick), 8:36.
K.C.—FG, Stoyanovich 44, 15:00.
Attendance—48,632.

	Kansas City	Oakland
First downs	16	18
Rushes-yards	27-103	25-108
Passing	190	207
Punt returns	5-34	2-7
Kickoff returns	6-110	7-141
Interception returns	2-52	2-51
Comp.-att.-int.	18-27-2	19-29-2
Sacked-yards lost	5-36	5-25
Punts	5-38	5-43
Fumbles-lost	1-1	3-1
Penalties-yards	8-55	6-37
Time of possession	30:23	29:37

INDIVIDUAL STATISTICS
RUSHING—Kansas City, Cloud 11-58, Bennett 9-27, Richardson 3-15, Morris 3-4, Grbac 1-(minus 1). Oakland, Wheatley 11-48, Kaufman 7-22, Gannon 4-30, Crockett 2-5, Ritchie 1-3.
PASSING—Kansas City, Grbac 18-27-2-226. Oakland, Gannon 19-29-2-232.
RECEIVING—Kansas City, Richardson 5-37, Gonzalez 3-90, Alexander 3-26, Bennett 3-23, Lockett 1-20, Rison 1-12, Horn 1-11, Cloud 1-7. Oakland, Brown 5-83, Ritchie 5-48, Dudley 4-62, D. Walker 2-21, Wheatley 1-7, Crockett 1-6, Jett 1-5.
MISSED FIELD GOAL ATTEMPTS—Oakland, Husted 44.
INTERCEPTIONS—Kansas City, Dishman 1-47, Hasty 1-5. Oakland, Biekert 1-36, Woodson 1-15.
KICKOFF RETURNS—Kansas City, Vanover 5-98, Bennett 1-12. Oakland, Kaufman 7-141.
PUNT RETURNS—Kansas City, Vanover 5-34. Oakland, Gordon 2-7.
SACKS—Kansas City, Edwards 1, Patton 1, Barndt 1, D. Williams 1, McGlockton 1. Oakland, Biekert 1, Sword 1, Johnstone 1, Harris 1, M. Walker 1.

PANTHERS 34, FALCONS 28

Sunday, November 28

Atlanta	0	14	0	14—28
Carolina	3	17	7	7—34

First Quarter
Car.—FG, Kasay 30, 12:19.

Second Quarter
Car.—FG, Kasay 24, 5:18.
Atl.—Oxendine 5 pass from Chandler (Andersen kick), 10:47.
Car.—Hayes 56 pass from Beuerlein (Kasay kick), 12:12.
Atl.—Christian 12 pass from Chandler (Andersen kick), 14:04.
Car.—Jeffers 1 pass from Beuerlein (Kasay kick), 14:56.

Third Quarter
Car.—Biakabutuka 11 run (Kasay kick), 10:04.

Fourth Quarter
Car.—Walls 11 pass from Beuerlein (Kasay kick), 2:13.
Atl.—Kozlowski 15 pass from Chandler (Andersen kick), 6:26.
Atl.—Mathis 18 pass from Chandler (Andersen kick), 11:48.
Attendance—55,507.

	Atlanta	Carolina
First downs	22	25
Rushes-yards	15-64	38-126
Passing	279	252
Punt returns	2-15	1-30
Kickoff returns	7-113	4-58
Interception returns	0-0	0-0
Comp.-att.-int.	24-42-0	18-27-0
Sacked-yards lost	4-36	2-10
Punts	6-39	4-41
Fumbles-lost	1-1	2-1
Penalties-yards	14-137	8-54
Time of possession	23:57	36:03

INDIVIDUAL STATISTICS
RUSHING—Atlanta, Oxendine 11-36, Chandler 1-11, Christian 1-11, Dwight 1-3, Oliver 1-3. Carolina, Biakabutuka 31-94, Floyd 3-23, Johnson 2-10, Beuerlein 2-(minus 1).
PASSING—Atlanta, Chandler 24-42-0-315. Carolina, Beuerlein 18-27-0-262.
RECEIVING—Atlanta, Mathis 9-98, Dwight 5-102, Kozlowski 3-29, Calloway 2-33, Christian 2-19, R. Kelly 1-22, Santiago 1-7, Oxendine 1-5. Carolina, Hayes 5-133, Walls 3-33, Jeffers 3-31, Biakabutuka 3-25, Floyd 2-24, Kinchen 1-9, Metcalf 1-7.
MISSED FIELD GOAL ATTEMPTS—Carolina, Kasay 47.
INTERCEPTIONS—None.
KICKOFF RETURNS—Atlanta, Dwight 6-115, Marshall 1-(minus 2). Carolina, Bates 2-33, Mangum 1-13, Metcalf 1-12.
PUNT RETURNS—Atlanta, Dwight 2-15. Carolina, Metcalf 1-30.
SACKS—Atlanta, Smith 1, Dronett 1. Carolina, Greene 2.5, Tuaolo 1, Barrow 0.5.

PACKERS 20, 49ERS 3

Monday, November 29

Green Bay	0	10	7	3—20
San Francisco	0	3	0	0— 3

Second Quarter
S.F.—FG, Richey 35, 0:09.
G.B.—Bradford 13 pass from Favre (Longwell kick), 3:10.
G.B.—FG, Longwell 23, 14:33.

Third Quarter
G.B.—T. Davis 10 pass from Favre (Longwell kick), 11:18.

Fourth Quarter
G.B.—FG, Longwell 22, 3:24.
Attendance—68,304.

	Green Bay	San Francisco
First downs	19	14
Rushes-yards	21-69	23-137
Passing	239	185
Punt returns	3-53	3-7
Kickoff returns	1-22	5-111
Interception returns	1-0	0-0
Comp.-att.-int.	25-36-0	19-35-1
Sacked-yards lost	1-7	2-10
Punts	6-39	6-36
Fumbles-lost	0-0	2-1
Penalties-yards	4-22	8-105
Time of possession	30:26	29:34

INDIVIDUAL STATISTICS
RUSHING—Green Bay, Levens 12-46, Parker 5-19, Hasselbeck 3-3, Mitchell 1-1. San Francisco, Garner 15-90, Beasley 8-47.
PASSING—Green Bay, Favre 25-36-0-246. San Francisco, Stenstrom 19-35-1-195.
RECEIVING—Green Bay, Freeman 7-73, Levens 5-41, Schroeder 4-58, T. Davis 3-20, Bradford 2-25, Crawford 1-14, Thomason 1-7, Henderson 1-6, Parker 1-2. San Francisco, Garner 6-36, Rice 4-63, Clark 3-44, Beasley 3-26, Owens 2-21, Stokes 1-5.
MISSED FIELD GOAL ATTEMPTS—Green Bay, Longwell 30.
INTERCEPTIONS—Green Bay, Butler 1-0.
KICKOFF RETURNS—Green Bay, Mitchell 1-22. San Francisco, Jervey 2-67, McQuarters 2-29, Harris 1-15.
PUNT RETURNS—Green Bay, Edwards 3-53. San Francisco, Harris 2-3, McQuarters 1-4.
SACKS—Green Bay, Holliday 1, Team 1. San Francisco, Tubbs 1.

WEEK 13

RESULTS

JACKSONVILLE 20, Pittsburgh 6
ARIZONA 21, Philadelphia 17
ATLANTA 35, New Orleans 12
BALTIMORE 41, Tennessee 14
CINCINNATI 44, San Francisco 30
DETROIT 33, Washington 17
Green Bay 35, CHICAGO 19
Indianapolis 37, MIAMI 34
Kansas City 16, DENVER 10
NEW ENGLAND 13, Dallas 6
N.Y. GIANTS 41, N.Y. Jets 28
OAKLAND 30, Seattle 21
St. Louis 34, CAROLINA 21
SAN DIEGO 23, Cleveland 10
TAMPA BAY 24, Minnesota 17
Open date: Buffalo

STANDINGS

AFC EAST
	W	L	T	Pct.
Indianapolis	10	2	0	.833
Buffalo	8	4	0	.667
Miami	8	4	0	.667
New England	7	5	0	.583
N.Y. Jets	4	8	0	.333

AFC CENTRAL
	W	L	T	Pct.
Jacksonville	11	1	0	.917
Tennessee	9	3	0	.750
Baltimore	5	7	0	.417
Pittsburgh	5	7	0	.417
Cincinnati	3	10	0	.231
Cleveland	2	11	0	.154

AFC WEST
	W	L	T	Pct.
Seattle	8	4	0	.667
Kansas City	7	5	0	.583
Oakland	6	6	0	.500
San Diego	5	7	0	.417
Denver	4	8	0	.333

NFC EAST
	W	L	T	Pct.
Washington	7	5	0	.583
Arizona	6	6	0	.500
Dallas	6	6	0	.500
N.Y. Giants	6	6	0	.500
Philadelphia	3	10	0	.231

NFC CENTRAL
	W	L	T	Pct.
Detroit	8	4	0	.667
Tampa Bay	8	4	0	.667
Green Bay	7	5	0	.583
Minnesota	7	5	0	.583
Chicago	5	8	0	.385

NFC WEST
	W	L	T	Pct.
St. Louis	10	2	0	.833
Carolina	5	7	0	.417
Atlanta	3	9	0	.250
San Francisco	3	9	0	.250
New Orleans	2	10	0	.167

HIGHLIGHTS

Hero of the week: Falcons defensive back Ray Buchanan, penalized nine times in the first 11 games of the season, jokingly presented the officials with roses before the game against New Orleans. It must have worked, because he intercepted two passes (returning one 52 yards for a touchdown), made six tackles and broke up three passes in Atlanta's 35-12 win over the Saints.

Goat of the week: Ricky Watters rushed for only 51 yards on 14 carries and fumbled twice in Seattle's 30-21 loss to Oakland. Both fumbles gave the Raiders good field position, and they helped Oakland hold off a Seahawks rally that pulled them to within three points in the third quarter.

Sub of the week: One day after being signed to replace injured kick returner Terry Fair, Detroit's Desmond Howard showed why he's such a valuable player. With the Lions and Redskins tied 10-10 in the second quarter, he returned a punt 68 yards for a touchdown that pushed the Lions ahead for good. Detroit went on to win, 33-17.

Comeback of the week: Philadelphia led Arizona, 17-7, late in the fourth quarter before quarterback Jake Plummer rallied the Cardinals to two touchdowns in the final five minutes for a 21-17 win. For the first touchdown, Plummer drove his team 80 yards in 16 plays and threw a 3-yard touchdown pass to David Boston with 4:31 remaining. A few minutes later, Frank Sanders' diving catch of Plummer's 38-yard pass just inches from the goal line set up the second touchdown—a 1-yard sneak by Plummer with 57 seconds left.

Blowout of the week: The Ravens, who had struggled offensively all season, shocked the Tennessee Titans 41-14 at PSINet Stadium in Baltimore. Quarterback Tony Banks had a career day, throwing for 332 yards and four touchdowns. Baltimore's defense sacked elusive Titans quarterback Steve McNair five times. The Ravens outscored Tennessee 24-0 in the second half.

Nail-biter of the week: The Colts never trailed and led by as many as 14 points before quarterback Dan Marino and the Dolphins clawed back to tie the score 34-34 with just 36 seconds remaining. With the game seemingly headed for overtime, quarterback Peyton Manning drove the Colts 33 yards in 30 seconds to set up Mike Vanderjagt's 53-yard field goal attempt. Vanderjagt's kick was good, giving the Colts a 37-34 victory.

Hit of the week: In the fourth quarter of Detroit's win over Washington, Lions tackle James Jones slammed into Redskins quarterback Brad Johnson, forcing a fumble that Luther Elliss returned 11 yards for a touchdown. The score secured the Lions' victory and briefly moved them into sole possession of first place in the NFC Central.

Oddity of the week: Washington receiver Michael Westbrook accused an NFL official of nepotism after the Redskins were called for a season-high 14 penalties in their loss to the Lions. Westbrook pointed out that the line judge for the game, Byron Boston, was the father of Arizona rookie receiver David Boston. Arizona and Washington were fighting for a playoff spot in the NFC East. Westbrook said Byron Boston called two penalties against Redskins right tackle Jon Jansen that weren't evident on the game film.

Top rusher: James Stewart ran for 145 yards and one touchdown in leading Jacksonville to a 20-6 victory over Pittsburgh.

Top passer: San Francisco's Jeff Garcia completed 33-of-49 passes for 437 yards in the 49ers' 44-30 loss to the Bengals.

Top receiver: Amani Toomer caught six passes for 181 yards and three touchdowns in the Giants' 41-28 victory over the Jets.

Notes: Emmitt Smith hit the 1,000-yard rushing mark for the ninth time in as many seasons. Only Barry Sanders (10) had more successive 1,000-yard seasons. ... Kerry Collins became the first Giants quarterback to have a 300-yard game since Phil Simms in 1993. ... Kwamie Lassiter's 78-yard interception return for a touchdown was the Cardinals' longest interception return since 1979. ... Tim Brown became the fourth player in NFL history to record seven consecutive 1,000-yard receiving seasons. San Francisco's Jerry Rice had 11 from 1986-96. San Diego's Lance Alworth had seven from 1963-69. Minnesota's Cris Carter had seven from 1993-99. ... Tennessee guard Bruce Matthews played his 260th NFL game, breaking the record he shared with former Rams great Jackie Slater. ... The Lions' 33-17 victory ended the Redskins' streak of 16 consecutive victories (18 overall) in the series, dating to 1965.

Quote of the week: Packers rookie running back De'Mond Parker, making his first start because Dorsey Levens was sidelined with cracked ribs, endured howling wind, cold rain and snow at Chicago's Soldier Field to rush for 113 yards and two fourth-quarter touchdowns in Green Bay's 35-19 victory over the Bears: "I didn't have butterflies. I was just cold."

GAME SUMMARIES

JAGUARS 20, STEELERS 6
Thursday, December 2

Pittsburgh	3	0	3	0	6
Jacksonville	0	6	7	7	20

First Quarter
Pit.—FG, K. Brown 40, 6:09.

Second Quarter
Jac.—FG, Hollis 25, 13:00.
Jac.—FG, Hollis 32, 15:00.

Third Quarter
Pit.—FG, K. Brown 38, 5:18.
Jac.—J. Smith 27 pass from Brunell (Hollis kick), 8:55.

Fourth Quarter
Jac.—J. Stewart 1 run (Hollis kick), 6:54.
Attendance—68,806.

	Pittsburgh	Jacksonville
First downs	15	24
Rushes-yards	15-63	34-168
Passing	172	298
Punt returns	1-0	1-12
Kickoff returns	4-66	3-41
Interception returns	0-0	0-0
Comp.-att.-int.	19-39-0	25-37-0
Sacked-yards lost	3-22	2-10
Punts	6-53	5-30
Fumbles-lost	2-0	3-1
Penalties-yards	9-78	9-98
Time of possession	23:54	36:06

INDIVIDUAL STATISTICS
RUSHING—Pittsburgh, Bettis 12-23, Huntley 2-37, Tomczak 1-3. Jacksonville, J. Stewart 30-145, Brunell 3-10, Mack 1-13.
PASSING—Pittsburgh, Tomczak 19-39-0-194. Jacksonville, Brunell 25-37-0-308.
RECEIVING—Pittsburgh, Shaw 4-52, Ward 4-35, Bruener 3-27, Stewart 3-21, Edwards 2-29, Bettis 1-14, Witman 1-9, Lyons 1-7. Jacksonville, J. Smith 10-124, McCardell 5-113, Barlow 4-31, Shelton 3-9, Jones 1-24, Howard 1-8, J. Stewart 1-(minus 1).
MISSED FIELD GOAL ATTEMPTS—None.
INTERCEPTIONS—None.
KICKOFF RETURNS—Pittsburgh, Huntley 2-35, Lyons 1-16, Zereoue 1-15. Jacksonville, Barlow 2-25, Mack 1-16.
PUNT RETURNS—Pittsburgh, Edwards 1-0. Jacksonville, Barlow 1-12.
SACKS—Pittsburgh, Emmons 2. Jacksonville, Brackens 1, Hardy 1, L. Smith 1.

GIANTS 41, JETS 28
Sunday, December 5

N.Y. Jets	0	7	0	21	28
N.Y. Giants	17	10	7	7	41

First Quarter
NYG—FG, Blanchard 41, 4:02.
NYG—Montgomery 4 run (Blanchard kick), 6:37.
NYG—Toomer 61 pass from Collins (Blanchard kick), 9:32.

Second Quarter
NYJ—K. Johnson 13 pass from Lucas (Hall kick), 4:52.
NYG—Collins 1 run (Blanchard kick), 9:51.
NYG—FG, Blanchard 31, 14:50.

Third Quarter
NYG—Toomer 9 pass from Collins (Blanchard kick), 8:59.

Fourth Quarter
NYJ—E. Green 10 pass from Lucas (Hall kick), 0:13.
NYJ—Chrebet 10 pass from Lucas (Hall kick), 10:46.
NYG—Toomer 80 pass from Collins (Blanchard kick), 11:14.
NYJ—Chrebet 5 pass from Lucas (Hall kick), 14:55.
Attendance—78,200.

	N.Y. Jets	N.Y. Giants
First downs	18	25
Rushes-yards	12-15	45-152
Passing	276	338
Punt returns	1-6	6-95
Kickoff returns	7-126	4-71
Interception returns	0-0	0-0
Comp.-att.-int.	31-48-0	17-29-0
Sacked-yards lost	2-8	1-3
Punts	6-48	3-31
Fumbles-lost	4-0	3-1
Penalties-yards	4-50	3-67
Time of possession	24:10	35:50

INDIVIDUAL STATISTICS
RUSHING—New York, Martin 6-4, Lucas 5-20, Stone 1-(minus 9). New York, Montgomery 38-111, Barber 4-9, Patten 1-27, Bennett 1-4, Collins 1-1.
PASSING—New York, Lucas 31-48-0-284. New York, Collins 17-29-0-341.
RECEIVING—New York, K. Johnson 10-98, Chrebet 7-84, Martin 6-24, Parmalee 5-52, E. Green 2-17, Anderson 1-9. New York, Toomer 6-181, Hilliard 6-121, Mitchell 4-46, Barber 1-(minus 7).
MISSED FIELD GOAL ATTEMPTS—None.
INTERCEPTIONS—None.
KICKOFF RETURNS—New York, Stone 6-100, Glenn 1-26. New York, Levingston 2-48, Barber 1-19, Patten 1-4.
PUNT RETURNS—New York, Ward 1-6. New York, Barber 6-95.
SACKS—New York, Lewis 1. New York, Armstead 1, Jones 1.

RAMS 34, PANTHERS 21
Sunday, December 5

St. Louis	14	7	0	13	34
Carolina	0	7	7	7	21

First Quarter
St.L.—R. Williams 14 pass from Warner (Wilkins kick), 4:48.
St.L.—Hakim 48 pass from Warner (Wilkins kick), 9:19.

Second Quarter
St.L.—Hakim 49 pass from Warner (Wilkins kick), 10:33.
Car.—Walls 15 pass from Beuerlein (Kasay kick), 14:19.

Third Quarter
Car.—Hayes 36 pass from Beuerlein (Kasay kick), 9:47.

Fourth Quarter
St.L.—FG, Wilkins 44, 0:04.
Car.—Jeffers 71 pass from Beuerlein (Kasay kick), 0:29.
St.L.—Bly 53 interception return (Wilkins kick), 5:12.
St.L.—FG, Wilkins 29, 11:21.
Attendance—62,285.

	St. Louis	Carolina
First downs	22	14
Rushes-yards	32-124	16-55
Passing	356	252
Punt returns	2-0	0-0
Kickoff returns	3-55	6-141
Interception returns	3-58	2-10
Comp.-att.-int.	23-32-2	21-43-3
Sacked-yards lost	2-7	3-14
Punts	1-13	4-37
Fumbles-lost	1-1	2-0
Penalties-yards	5-50	6-85
Time of possession	34:10	25:50

INDIVIDUAL STATISTICS

RUSHING—St. Louis, Faulk 22-118, Holcombe 8-10, Warner 1-(minus 1), Hakim 1-(minus 3). Carolina, Biakabutuka 11-42, Floyd 2-1, Beuerlein 1-12, Lane 1-2, Bates 1-(minus 2).

PASSING—St. Louis, Warner 22-31-2-351, Justin 1-1-0-12. Carolina, Beuerlein 21-43-3-266.

RECEIVING—St. Louis, Bruce 6-111, Faulk 6-79, Hakim 4-122, Proehl 4-31, R. Williams 2-16, Holt 1-4. Carolina, Jeffers 7-107, Muhammad 4-46, Walls 4-45, Biakabutuka 3-17, Hayes 1-36, Metcalf 1-8, Floyd 1-7.

MISSED FIELD GOAL ATTEMPTS—St. Louis, Wilkins 51.

INTERCEPTIONS—St. Louis, Bly 1-53, M. Jones 1-5, Lyght 1-0. Carolina, Davis 1-10, Minter 1-0.

KICKOFF RETURNS—St. Louis, Horne 2-42, Fletcher 1-13. Carolina, Bates 5-125, Hetherington 1-16.

PUNT RETURNS—St. Louis, Hakim 2-0.

SACKS—St. Louis, Carter 1.5, McCleon 1, Hobgood-Chittick 0.5. Carolina, Rucker 1, Greene 1.

CARDINALS 21, EAGLES 17

Sunday, December 5

Philadelphia	0	14	3	0—17
Arizona	7	0	0	14—21

First Quarter
Ariz.—Lassiter 78 interception return (Jacke kick), 9:36.

Second Quarter
Phi.—Lewis 11 pass from McNabb (N. Johnson kick), 7:04.
Phi.—D. Douglas 29 pass from McNabb (N. Johnson kick), 14:17.

Third Quarter
Phi.—FG, N. Johnson 29, 9:29.

Fourth Quarter
Ariz.—Boston 4 pass from Plummer (Jacke kick), 10:29.
Ariz.—Plummer 1 run (Jacke kick), 14:03.
Attendance—46,550.

	Philadelphia	Arizona
First downs	18	16
Rushes-yards	37-146	19-54
Passing	148	173
Punt returns	2-18	2-14
Kickoff returns	4-81	3-85
Interception returns	1-28	1-78
Comp.-att.-int.	19-31-1	20-38-1
Sacked-yards lost	1-9	1-6
Punts	5-42	4-51
Fumbles-lost	1-1	4-1
Penalties-yards	9-64	1-5
Time of possession	37:56	22:04

INDIVIDUAL STATISTICS

RUSHING—Philadelphia, Staley 25-72, McNabb 9-67, Bieniemy 2-5, C. Martin 1-2. Arizona, Murrell 8-24, Plummer 7-22, Bates 4-8.

PASSING—Philadelphia, McNabb 19-31-1-157. Arizona, Plummer 20-37-1-179, Sanders 0-1-0-0.

RECEIVING—Philadelphia, Staley 5-42, Brown 4-29, D. Douglas 3-47, Small 3-24, Lewis 1-11, C. Martin 1-5, Broughton 1-5, McNabb 1-(minus 6). Arizona, Sanders 6-72, Murrell 5-39, Boston 3-28, Cody 2-19, McWilliams 2-16, Hardy 1-4, Bates 1-1.

MISSED FIELD GOAL ATTEMPTS—None.

INTERCEPTIONS—Philadelphia, Taylor 1-28. Arizona, Lassiter 1-78.

KICKOFF RETURNS—Philadelphia, Rossum 3-61, Bieniemy 1-20. Arizona, Bates 3-85.

PUNT RETURNS—Philadelphia, Rossum 2-18. Arizona, Cody 2-14.

SACKS—Philadelphia, Reese 1. Arizona, Rice 1.

RAIDERS 30, SEAHAWKS 21

Sunday, December 5

Seattle	0	7	7	7—21
Oakland	3	14	7	6—30

First Quarter
Oak.—FG, Husted 18, 7:36.

Second Quarter
Oak.—Brown 14 pass from Gannon (Husted kick), 3:19.
Oak.—Brown 5 pass from Gannon (Husted kick), 8:24.
Sea.—Watters 8 run (Peterson kick), 14:29.

Third Quarter
Sea.—Galloway 31 pass from Kitna (Peterson kick), 4:06.
Oak.—Crockett 1 run (Husted kick), 11:29.

Fourth Quarter
Oak.—FG, Husted 41, 0:43.
Sea.—Dawkins 3 pass from Kitna (Peterson kick), 4:05.
Oak.—FG, Husted 23, 13:07.
Attendance—44,716.

	Seattle	Oakland
First downs	20	24
Rushes-yards	19-90	41-162
Passing	234	253
Punt returns	0-0	1-(-1)
Kickoff returns	7-160	4-63
Interception returns	1-40	2-37
Comp.-att.-int.	22-39-2	19-24-1
Sacked-yards lost	1-11	0-0
Punts	1-43	0-0
Fumbles-lost	2-2	0-0
Penalties-yards	1-14	1-5
Time of possession	24:05	35:55

INDIVIDUAL STATISTICS

RUSHING—Seattle, Watters 14-51, Kitna 3-15, Green 1-21, R. Brown 1-3. Oakland, Wheatley 21-80, Kaufman 10-76, Crockett 6-4, Gannon 3-(minus 3), Ritchie 1-5.

PASSING—Seattle, Kitna 22-39-2-245. Oakland, Gannon 19-24-1-253.

RECEIVING—Seattle, Mayes 5-56, Watters 5-53, Galloway 4-68, R. Brown 3-11, Pritchard 2-26, Dawkins 2-24, Fauria 1-7. Oakland, Brown 6-75, Dudley 4-54, Jett 3-56, Ritchie 3-27, Mickens 2-33, Kaufman 1-8.

MISSED FIELD GOAL ATTEMPTS—Oakland, Husted 51.

INTERCEPTIONS—Seattle, Joseph 1-40. Oakland, Mincy 1-21, Newman 1-16.

KICKOFF RETURNS—Seattle, Green 3-65, Jordan 3-62, Bownes 1-33. Oakland, Kaufman 3-48, Branch 1-15.

PUNT RETURNS—Oakland, Gordon 1-(minus 1).

SACKS—Oakland, Russell 1.

LIONS 33, REDSKINS 17

Sunday, December 5

Washington	3	7	7	0—17
Detroit	0	20	0	13—33

First Quarter
Was.—FG, Conway 42, 8:38.

Second Quarter
Det.—FG, Hanson 50, 8:58.
Was.—Thrash 95 kickoff return (Conway kick), 9:14.
Det.—Moore 23 pass from Frerotte (Hanson kick), 11:37.
Det.—Howard 68 punt return (Hanson kick), 13:26.
Det.—FG, Hanson 45, 14:55.

Third Quarter
Was.—Westbrook 39 pass from B. Johnson (Conway kick), 2:39.

Fourth Quarter
Det.—FG, Hanson 37, 0:04.
Det.—FG, Hanson 52, 6:37.
Det.—Elliss 11 fumble return (Hanson kick), 6:51.
Attendance—77,693.

	Washington	Detroit
First downs	16	12
Rushes-yards	21-116	15-31
Passing	217	261
Punt returns	2-25	3-86
Kickoff returns	6-169	4-89
Interception returns	0-0	2-23
Comp.-att.-int.	26-43-2	21-32-0
Sacked-yards lost	5-32	5-19
Punts	6-38	6-40
Fumbles-lost	6-2	0-0
Penalties-yards	14-122	9-65
Time of possession	32:54	27:06

INDIVIDUAL STATISTICS

RUSHING—Washington, Davis 12-51, Mitchell 6-60, Westbrook 1-4, Centers 1-2, B. Johnson 1-(minus 1). Detroit, Hill 11-16, Schlesinger 2-10, Crowell 1-4, Frerotte 1-1.

PASSING—Washington, B. Johnson 26-43-2-249. Detroit, Frerotte 21-32-0-280.

RECEIVING—Washington, Centers 7-47, Westbrook 5-108, Davis 5-8, Mitchell 4-41, Connell 3-35, Sellers 1-8, Thrash 1-2. Detroit, Crowell 5-122, Morton 5-44, Moore 4-47, Sloan 3-44, Olivo 2-10, Hill 1-8, Schlesinger 1-5.

1999 REVIEW Week 13

– 191 –

MISSED FIELD GOAL ATTEMPTS—Detroit, Hanson 46.
INTERCEPTIONS—Detroit, Boyd 1-18, Rice 1-5.
KICKOFF RETURNS—Washington, Mitchell 3-60, Thrash 2-109, Bowie 1-0. Detroit, Howard 4-89.
PUNT RETURNS—Washington, Mitchell 2-25. Detroit, Howard 3-86.
SACKS—Washington, Coleman 2, Cook 1.5, Kalu 0.5, Wilkinson 0.5, Jones 0.5. Detroit, Scroggins 2, Owens 1, Jones 1, Porcher 1.

CHARGERS 23, BROWNS 10

Sunday, December 5

Cleveland	3	7	0	0	—10
San Diego	3	10	3	7	—23

First Quarter
Cle.—FG, Dawson 33, 5:30.
S.D.—FG, Carney 44, 13:52.

Second Quarter
S.D.—FG, Carney 19, 6:59.
S.D.—Bynum 1 run (Carney kick), 12:49.
Cle.—Johnson 19 pass from Couch (Dawson kick), 14:54.

Third Quarter
S.D.—FG, Carney 30, 7:19.

Fourth Quarter
S.D.—Fazande 2 run (Carney kick), 8:32.
Attendance—53,147.

	Cleveland	San Diego
First downs	13	20
Rushes-yards	16-55	44-145
Passing	147	132
Punt returns	1-7	4-60
Kickoff returns	6-117	3-43
Interception returns	0-0	2-5
Comp.-att.-int.	18-30-2	16-23-0
Sacked-yards lost	6-37	4-29
Punts	5-45	3-36
Fumbles-lost	1-0	2-1
Penalties-yards	13-94	7-56
Time of possession	23:20	36:40

INDIVIDUAL STATISTICS
RUSHING—Cleveland, Abdul-Jabbar 10-29, Kirby 4-21, Couch 1-4, Edwards 1-1. San Diego, Bynum 17-60, Fazande 12-42, Fletcher 9-28, Harbaugh 6-15.
PASSING—Cleveland, Couch 18-29-2-184, Johnson 0-1-0-0. San Diego, Harbaugh 16-23-0-161.
RECEIVING—Cleveland, Kirby 5-43, Johnson 5-41, Chiaverini 4-46, Abdul-Jabbar 1-21, I. Smith 1-16, Campbell 1-12, Edwards 1-5. San Diego, J. Graham 5-82, F. Jones 4-42, McCrary 4-18, Ricks 2-18, Reed 1-1.
MISSED FIELD GOAL ATTEMPTS—Cleveland, Dawson 45.
INTERCEPTIONS—San Diego, Lewis 1-5, Spencer 1-0.
KICKOFF RETURNS—Cleveland, Powell 4-81, Hill 2-36. San Diego, Bynum 1-29, Reed 1-10, McCrary 1-4.
PUNT RETURNS—Cleveland, Johnson 1-7. San Diego, Reed 3-49, Penn 1-11.
SACKS—Cleveland, Thierry 3, Rainer 1. San Diego, Johnson 3, Fontenot 1, Bush 1, Mohring 1.

BENGALS 44, 49ERS 30

Sunday, December 5

San Francisco	0	10	14	6	—30
Cincinnati	10	17	10	7	—44

First Quarter
Cin.—Dillon 10 run (Pelfrey kick), 9:35.
Cin.—FG, Pelfrey 29, 12:26.

Second Quarter
S.F.—Garner 6 run (Richey kick), 2:21.
Cin.—Pickens 11 pass from Blake (Pelfrey kick), 6:00.
S.F.—FG, Richey 47, 11:00.
Cin.—Scott 58 pass from Blake (Pelfrey kick), 12:51.
Cin.—FG, Pelfrey 24, 15:00.

Third Quarter
S.F.—Rice 7 pass from Garcia (Richey kick), 5:11.
Cin.—FG, Pelfrey 27, 8:32.
S.F.—Rice 55 pass from Garcia (Richey kick), 10:11.
Cin.—Dillon 12 pass from Blake (Pelfrey kick), 12:15.

Fourth Quarter
S.F.—Stokes 11 pass from Garcia (kick failed), 0:49.
Cin.—Pickens 13 pass from Blake (Pelfrey kick), 5:37.
Attendance—53,463.

	San Fran.	Cincinnati
First downs	29	27
Rushes-yards	23-105	28-151
Passing	437	325
Punt returns	2-5	0-0
Kickoff returns	6-81	6-189
Interception returns	0-0	1-12
Comp.-att.-int.	33-49-1	21-30-0
Sacked-yards lost	0-0	2-9
Punts	1-43	3-31
Fumbles-lost	4-2	1-0
Penalties-yards	9-82	2-10
Time of possession	31:31	28:29

INDIVIDUAL STATISTICS
RUSHING—San Francisco, Garner 18-91, Beasley 4-2, Garcia 1-12. Cincinnati, Dillon 25-133, Blake 3-18.
PASSING—San Francisco, Garcia 33-49-1-437. Cincinnati, Blake 21-30-0-334.
RECEIVING—San Francisco, Rice 9-157, Owens 9-145, Garner 5-52, Stokes 4-38, Clark 3-24, Beasley 2-19, Fann 1-2. Cincinnati, Pickens 7-107, Dillon 5-77, Scott 3-80, Groce 2-12, Battaglia 1-30, McGee 1-12, Jackson 1-11, Basnight 1-5.
MISSED FIELD GOAL ATTEMPTS—None.
INTERCEPTIONS—Cincinnati, Copeland 1-12.
KICKOFF RETURNS—San Francisco, Jervey 4-71, Peterson 2-10. Cincinnati, Mack 6-189.
PUNT RETURNS—San Francisco, Harris 2-5.
SACKS—San Francisco, B. Young 2.

FALCONS 35, SAINTS 12

Sunday, December 5

New Orleans	3	3	0	6	—12
Atlanta	7	14	14	0	—35

First Quarter
N.O.—FG, Brien 24, 5:29.
Atl.—Mathis 8 pass from Chandler (Andersen kick), 13:08.

Second Quarter
Atl.—Chandler 1 run (Andersen kick), 5:07.
N.O.—FG, Brien 34, 10:05.
Atl.—Dwight 48 pass from Chandler (Andersen kick), 11:11.

Third Quarter
Atl.—Christian 1 run (Andersen kick), 8:38.
Atl.—Buchanan 52 interception return (Andersen kick), 12:17.

Fourth Quarter
N.O.—Wuerffel 29 run (run failed), 4:36.
Attendance—62,568.

	New Orleans	Atlanta
First downs	21	21
Rushes-yards	26-149	28-128
Passing	91	233
Punt returns	1-4	2-10
Kickoff returns	6-120	3-81
Interception returns	3-0	2-52
Comp.-att.-int.	17-37-2	15-25-3
Sacked-yards lost	7-48	0-0
Punts	5-39	3-42
Fumbles-lost	0-0	0-0
Penalties-yards	7-52	11-116
Time of possession	30:35	29:25

INDIVIDUAL STATISTICS
RUSHING—New Orleans, Perry 16-93, Davis 7-7, Philyaw 2-20, Wuerffel 1-29. Atlanta, Oxendine 19-85, Christian 6-44, Graziani 2-(minus 2), Chandler 1-1.
PASSING—New Orleans, Wuerffel 15-30-2-127, Hobert 2-7-0-12. Atlanta, Chandler 15-25-3-233.
RECEIVING—New Orleans, Hastings 5-46, Kennison 4-23, Davis 4-20, L. Smith 1-21, Dawsey 1-15, Poole 1-8, Perry 1-6. Atlanta, Mathis 3-46, Dwight 2-80, Oliver 2-21, Oxendine 2-15, Still 2-14, R. Kelly 2-9, Kozlowski 1-26, Calloway 1-22.
MISSED FIELD GOAL ATTEMPTS—None.
INTERCEPTIONS—New Orleans, Fields 1-0, Ambrose 1-0, Clay 1-0. Atlanta, Buchanan 2-52.

KICKOFF RETURNS—New Orleans, Philyaw 5-100, Dawsey 1-20. Atlanta, Dwight 3-81.
PUNT RETURNS—New Orleans, Kennison 1-4. Atlanta, Dwight 1-5, Oliver 1-5.
SACKS—Atlanta, Archambeau 3, Hall 2, Tuggle 1, Smith 1.

COLTS 37, DOLPHINS 34

Sunday, December 5

Indianapolis	17	7	7	6	—37
Miami	3	7	14	10	—34

First Quarter
Ind.—FG, Vanderjagt 44, 6:50.
Mia.—FG, Mare 31, 11:58.
Ind.—James 41 run (Vanderjagt kick), 14:18.
Ind.—Cota 25 fumble return (Vanderjagt kick), 14:41.

Second Quarter
Mia.—Gadsden 24 pass from Marino (Mare kick), 9:44.
Ind.—James 1 run (Vanderjagt kick), 14:03.

Third Quarter
Mia.—Madison 21 interception return (Mare kick), 0:49.
Ind.—Wilkins 5 pass from Manning (Vanderjagt kick), 5:32.
Mia.—Martin 33 pass from Marino (Mare kick), 11:07.

Fourth Quarter
Mia.—Pritchett 1 pass from Marino (Mare kick), 1:53.
Ind.—FG, Vanderjagt 48, 10:36.
Mia.—FG, Mare 32, 14:24.
Ind.—FG, Vanderjagt 53, 15:00.
Attendance—74,096.

	Indianapolis	Miami
First downs	21	22
Rushes-yards	25-129	22-69
Passing	241	299
Punt returns	3-41	1-13
Kickoff returns	5-105	5-122
Interception returns	1-36	2-49
Comp.-att.-int.	23-29-2	24-38-1
Sacked-yards lost	2-19	2-14
Punts	4-37	4-44
Fumbles-lost	1-0	2-2
Penalties-yards	7-89	7-64
Time of possession	31:32	28:28

INDIVIDUAL STATISTICS
RUSHING—Indianapolis, James 23-130, Manning 2-(minus 1). Miami, Johnson 21-62, Pritchett 1-7.
PASSING—Indianapolis, Manning 23-29-2-260. Miami, Marino 24-38-1-313.
RECEIVING—Indianapolis, Harrison 8-125, Dilger 5-80, Pollard 3-20, James 3-1, Wilkins 2-25, Green 2-9. Miami, Martin 6-109, Gadsden 6-103, Green 5-64, Johnson 3-26, Pritchett 3-2, Drayton 1-9.
MISSED FIELD GOAL ATTEMPTS—None.
INTERCEPTIONS—Indianapolis, Poole 1-36. Miami, Surtain 1-28, Madison 1-21.
KICKOFF RETURNS—Indianapolis, Wilkins 5-105. Miami, Marion 4-96, Jacquet 1-26.
PUNT RETURNS—Indianapolis, Wilkins 3-41. Miami, Jacquet 1-13.
SACKS—Indianapolis, M. Thomas 1, Bennett 1. Miami, Owens 1, Armstrong 1.

RAVENS 41, TITANS 14

Sunday, December 5

Tennessee	3	11	0	0	—14
Baltimore	7	10	7	17	—41

First Quarter
Ten.—FG, Del Greco 39, 8:50.
Bal.—Johnson 76 pass from Banks (Stover kick), 11:48.

Second Quarter
Bal.—J. Lewis 6 pass from Banks (Stover kick), 3:18.
Ten.—E. George 3 run (Harris pass from McNair), 7:37.
Bal.—FG, Stover 21, 10:38.
Ten.—FG, Del Greco 33, 14:52.

Third Quarter
Bal.—Armour 1 pass from Banks (Stover kick), 5:42.

Fourth Quarter
Bal.—FG, Stover 27, 5:46.
Bal.—J. Lewis 39 pass from Banks (Stover kick), 8:58.
Bal.—Woodson 47 interception return (Stover kick), 10:48.
Attendance—67,854.

	Tennessee	Baltimore
First downs	20	17
Rushes-yards	14-65	22-116
Passing	288	331
Punt returns	1-4	4-55
Kickoff returns	7-109	3-32
Interception returns	0-0	2-47
Comp.-att.-int.	31-53-2	18-31-0
Sacked-yards lost	5-27	1-1
Punts	6-46	3-41
Fumbles-lost	0-0	1-1
Penalties-yards	6-91	9-68
Time of possession	32:19	27:41

INDIVIDUAL STATISTICS
RUSHING—Tennessee, E. George 8-32, McNair 6-33. Baltimore, Holmes 9-100, Evans 5-5, Rhett 4-7, Case 3-(minus 4), Banks 1-8.
PASSING—Tennessee, McNair 28-48-2-288, O'Donnell 3-5-0-27. Baltimore, Banks 18-31-0-332.
RECEIVING—Tennessee, Wycheck 10-87, E. George 5-44, Harris 4-52, Sanders 4-50, Thomas 3-26, Byrd 2-32, Mason 2-18, Dyson 1-6. Baltimore, Ismail 5-113, J. Lewis 5-72, Armour 3-28, Johnson 1-76, Holmes 1-13, Evans 1-13, Davis 1-9, Rhett 1-8.
MISSED FIELD GOAL ATTEMPTS—None.
INTERCEPTIONS—Baltimore, Woodson 1-47, McAlister 1-0.
KICKOFF RETURNS—Tennessee, Mason 6-108, Neal 1-1. Baltimore, McAlister 1-12, DeLong 1-11, Harris 1-9.
PUNT RETURNS—Tennessee, Sidney 1-4. Baltimore, J. Lewis 4-55.
SACKS—Tennessee, Kearse 1. Baltimore, McCrary 3.5, R. Lewis 0.5, Siragusa 0.5, Burnett 0.5.

CHIEFS 16, BRONCOS 10

Sunday, December 5

Kansas City	0	10	0	6	—16
Denver	3	7	0	0	—10

First Quarter
Den.—FG, Elam 39, 6:32.

Second Quarter
K.C.—Gonzalez 10 pass from Grbac (Stoyanovich kick), 4:45.
Den.—Gary 3 run (Elam kick), 12:49.
K.C.—FG, Stoyanovich 43, 14:24.

Fourth Quarter
K.C.—Vanover 80 punt return (pass failed), 10:07.
Attendance—73,855.

	Kansas City	Denver
First downs	17	14
Rushes-yards	38-177	18-83
Passing	175	208
Punt returns	7-131	4-39
Kickoff returns	3-55	4-82
Interception returns	1-14	1-0
Comp.-att.-int.	20-34-1	20-36-1
Sacked-yards lost	1-8	2-19
Punts	9-49	9-53
Fumbles-lost	2-0	0-0
Penalties-yards	11-106	7-52
Time of possession	33:37	26:23

INDIVIDUAL STATISTICS
RUSHING—Kansas City, Bennett 13-66, Richardson 12-80, Morris 6-14, Cloud 4-13, Grbac 2-(minus 2), Horn 1-6. Denver, Gary 14-61, Griffith 2-19, Loville 1-2, Griese 1-1.
PASSING—Kansas City, Grbac 20-34-1-183. Denver, Griese 20-36-1-227.
RECEIVING—Kansas City, Gonzalez 5-35, Rison 3-30, Alexander 3-29, Lockett 3-25, Horn 2-36, Richardson 2-16, Morris 2-12. Denver, R. Smith 8-106, Griffith 4-26, McCaffrey 3-66, Gary 2-15, Loville 2-9, Carswell 1-5.
MISSED FIELD GOAL ATTEMPTS—None.
INTERCEPTIONS—Kansas City, Dishman 1-14. Denver, Coghill 1-0.
KICKOFF RETURNS—Kansas City, Vanover 3-55. Denver, Watson 4-82.
PUNT RETURNS—Kansas City, Vanover 7-131. Denver, Watson 4-39.
SACKS—Kansas City, Hasty 1, O'Neal 1. Denver, N. Smith 1.

PACKERS 35, BEARS 19

Sunday, December 5

Green Bay	0	21	0	14	—35
Chicago	7	6	6	0	—19

First Quarter
Chi.—Minter 34 interception return (Boniol kick), 9:01.

Second Quarter
Chi.—FG, Boniol 24, 3:14.
G.B.—Schroeder 6 pass from Favre (Longwell kick), 7:53.
G.B.—Henderson 2 run (Longwell kick), 11:17.
G.B.—K. McKenzie 45 fumble return (Longwell kick), 13:51.
Chi.—FG, Boniol 23, 14:53.

Third Quarter
Chi.—Enis 1 run (pass failed), 14:41.

Fourth Quarter
G.B.—Parker 12 run (Longwell kick), 5:58.
G.B.—Parker 21 run (Longwell kick), 11:52.
Attendance—66,944.

	Green Bay	Chicago
First downs	19	17
Rushes-yards	35-188	24-91
Passing	139	206
Punt returns	3-4	0-0
Kickoff returns	6-87	5-144
Interception returns	1-0	2-34
Comp.-att.-int.	17-24-2	21-39-1
Sacked-yards lost	2-16	3-20
Punts	6-29	4-40
Fumbles-lost	2-1	3-1
Penalties-yards	3-25	4-35
Time of possession	32:42	27:18

INDIVIDUAL STATISTICS
RUSHING—Green Bay, Parker 19-113, Mitchell 11-47, Henderson 4-18, Favre 1-10. Chicago, Enis 19-80, Matthews 3-7, McNown 1-6, Sauerbrun 1-(minus 2).
PASSING—Green Bay, Favre 17-24-2-155. Chicago, Matthews 20-36-1-223, McNown 1-3-0-3.
RECEIVING—Green Bay, Freeman 6-97, Schroeder 4-25, Henderson 2-13, Parker 2-6, Hall 1-9, T. Davis 1-5, Mitchell 1-0. Chicago, Enis 7-48, Conway 5-57, M. Robinson 3-25, Engram 2-60, Milburn 2-25, Hallock 1-7, Booker 1-4.
MISSED FIELD GOAL ATTEMPTS—Chicago, Boniol 51.
INTERCEPTIONS—Green Bay, M. McKenzie 1-0. Chicago, Minter 1-34, Hudson 1-0.
KICKOFF RETURNS—Green Bay, Mitchell 4-36, Parker 2-51. Chicago, Milburn 5-144.
PUNT RETURNS—Green Bay, Edwards 3-4.
SACKS—Green Bay, K. McKenzie 2, Holliday 1. Chicago, Flanigan 1, Simmons 1.

PATRIOTS 13, COWBOYS 6

Sunday, December 5

Dallas	3	0	0	3	— 6
New England	3	3	0	7	—13

First Quarter
N.E.—FG, Vinatieri 41, 4:46.
Dal.—FG, Cunningham 20, 12:11.

Second Quarter
N.E.—FG, Vinatieri 23, 8:11.

Fourth Quarter
N.E.—Allen 3 run (Vinatieri kick), 8:21.
Dal.—FG, Cunningham 34, 12:10.
Attendance—58,444.

	Dallas	New England
First downs	12	18
Rushes-yards	23-63	36-108
Passing	140	176
Punt returns	1-15	3-32
Kickoff returns	4-103	2-50
Interception returns	2-18	0-0
Comp.-att.-int.	20-30-0	14-25-2
Sacked-yards lost	3-20	1-0
Punts	4-44	4-41
Fumbles-lost	2-0	0-0
Penalties-yards	6-35	2-20
Time of possession	30:31	29:29

INDIVIDUAL STATISTICS
RUSHING—Dallas, E. Smith 19-75, Aikman 2-(minus 1), Warren 1-(minus 3), Ismail 1-(minus 8). New England, Allen 18-53, Faulk 9-36, Bledsoe 7-10, Warren 1-7, Floyd 1-2.
PASSING—Dallas, Aikman 20-30-0-160. New England, Bledsoe 14-25-2-176.
RECEIVING—Dallas, Ismail 8-58, McGarity 3-31, E. Smith 3-10, LaFleur 2-21, Ogden 2-21, Tucker 1-22, Warren 1-(minus 3). New England, Brown 4-40, Faulk 3-43, Glenn 3-27, Jefferson 2-46, Warren 1-13, Brisby 1-7.
MISSED FIELD GOAL ATTEMPTS—Dallas, Cunningham 43.
INTERCEPTIONS—Dallas, Coakley 1-18, Woodson 1-0.
KICKOFF RETURNS—Dallas, Mathis 4-103. New England, Faulk 2-50.
PUNT RETURNS—Dallas, Sanders 1-15. New England, Brown 3-32.
SACKS—Dallas, Ellis 1. New England, Collons 1, Whigham 1, McGinest 1.

BUCCANEERS 24, VIKINGS 17

Monday, December 6

Minnesota	0	14	0	3	—17
Tampa Bay	7	3	7	7	—24

First Quarter
T.B.—Abraham 55 interception return (Gramatica kick), 1:29.

Second Quarter
T.B.—FG, Gramatica 20, 0:48.
Min.—Hoard 1 run (Anderson kick), 9:08.
Min.—Carter 1 pass from George (Anderson kick), 14:33.

Third Quarter
T.B.—Green 29 pass from King (Gramatica kick), 7:46.

Fourth Quarter
T.B.—Moore 1 pass from King (Gramatica kick), 3:14.
Min.—FG, Anderson 34, 9:10.
Attendance—65,741.

	Minnesota	Tampa Bay
First downs	21	13
Rushes-yards	25-92	27-103
Passing	247	87
Punt returns	4-21	2-0
Kickoff returns	5-102	4-78
Interception returns	1-0	2-55
Comp.-att.-int.	26-45-2	11-19-1
Sacked-yards lost	3-24	2-6
Punts	3-36	4-45
Fumbles-lost	2-2	3-2
Penalties-yards	8-50	6-35
Time of possession	32:52	27:08

INDIVIDUAL STATISTICS
RUSHING—Minnesota, Smith 20-77, Hoard 3-9, George 2-6. Tampa Bay, Alstott 23-95, King 4-8.
PASSING—Minnesota, George 26-45-2-271. Tampa Bay, King 11-19-1-93.
RECEIVING—Minnesota, Reed 6-63, Hoard 6-61, Carter 6-42, Smith 5-68, Moss 2-32, Glover 1-5. Tampa Bay, Green 5-70, Emanuel 2-12, Williams 1-5, Abdullah 1-3, Alstott 1-2, Moore 1-1.
MISSED FIELD GOAL ATTEMPTS—Minnesota, Anderson 46.
INTERCEPTIONS—Minnesota, Griffith 1-0. Tampa Bay, Abraham 2-55.
KICKOFF RETURNS—Minnesota, Murphy 4-80, M. Williams 1-22. Tampa Bay, Anthony 3-63, Williams 1-15.
PUNT RETURNS—Minnesota, Murphy 4-21. Tampa Bay, Williams 2-0.
SACKS—Minnesota, Doleman 2. Tampa Bay, Culpepper 2, Barber 1.

WEEK 14

RESULTS

TENNESSEE 21, Oakland 14
Baltimore 31, PITTSBURGH 24
Carolina 33, GREEN BAY 31
CINCINNATI 44, Cleveland 28
DALLAS 20, Philadelphia 10
INDIANAPOLIS 20, New England 15
KANSAS CITY 31, Minnesota 28
N.Y. Giants 19, BUFFALO 17
N.Y. JETS 28, Miami 20
St. Louis 30, NEW ORLEANS 14
San Diego 19, SEATTLE 16
SAN FRANCISCO 26, Atlanta 7
TAMPA BAY 23, Detroit 16
WASHINGTON 28, Arizona 3
JACKSONVILLE 27, Denver 24
Open date: Chicago

STANDINGS

AFC EAST
	W	L	T	Pct.
Indianapolis	11	2	0	.846
Buffalo	8	5	0	.615
Miami	8	5	0	.615
New England	7	6	0	.538
N.Y. Jets	5	8	0	.385

AFC CENTRAL
	W	L	T	Pct.
Jacksonville	12	1	0	.923
Tennessee	10	3	0	.769
Baltimore	6	7	0	.462
Pittsburgh	5	8	0	.385
Cincinnati	4	10	0	.286
Cleveland	2	12	0	.143

AFC WEST
	W	L	T	Pct.
Kansas City	8	5	0	.615
Seattle	8	5	0	.615
Oakland	6	7	0	.462
San Diego	6	7	0	.462
Denver	4	9	0	.308

NFC EAST
	W	L	T	Pct.
Washington	8	5	0	.615
Dallas	7	6	0	.538
N.Y. Giants	7	6	0	.538
Arizona	6	7	0	.462
Philadelphia	3	11	0	.214

NFC CENTRAL
	W	L	T	Pct.
Tampa Bay	9	4	0	.692
Detroit	8	5	0	.615
Green Bay	7	6	0	.538
Minnesota	7	6	0	.538
Chicago	5	8	0	.385

NFC WEST
	W	L	T	Pct.
St. Louis	11	2	0	.846
Carolina	6	7	0	.462
San Francisco	4	9	0	.308
Atlanta	3	10	0	.231
New Orleans	2	11	0	.154

HIGHLIGHTS

Hero of the week: Veteran Cary Blanchard kicked four field goals, including the game-winner from 48 yards with 40 seconds left, in the Giants' 19-17 victory over Buffalo. Blanchard, signed after Brad Daluiso was lost for the season in Week 6, was responsible for more than half of New York's points.

Goat of the week: Seattle kicker Todd Peterson missed three fourth-quarter field goals, including one with 1:15 remaining, as San Diego held on to beat the Seahawks, 19-16. Peterson, usually reliable, made his first three attempts of the game and set a franchise record when he made his 16th consecutive field goal. But then he was short on attempts from 48 and 52 yards before his final miss, a 38-yarder that hit the left upright.

Sub of the week: When Jacksonville running back James Stewart sprained his foot in the third quarter against Denver, Fred Taylor came to the rescue. Taylor, who began the season as the Jaguars' starting running back, rushed for 74 yards on nine carries, including a 38-yard touchdown run with 2:35 remaining. Taylor had not played since Week 10 because of a lingering hamstring injury.

Comeback of the week: Jacksonville trailed Denver, 14-0, in the second quarter before reeling off 17 unanswered points to take a 17-14 halftime lead. The Jaguars escaped with a 27-24 victory thanks to two rushing TDs by Stewart and one by Taylor.

Blowout of the week: The Redskins held a players-only meeting on the Saturday night before the game to re-affirm their commitment during the team's stretch run. It worked, because they pummeled Arizona, 28-3, the following afternoon. Running back Stephen Davis rushed for career highs of 189 yards on 37 carries, and quarterback Brad Johnson passed for 191 yards and two touchdowns.

Nail-biter of the week: Carolina rushed for only 13 yards against the Packers, but it was the final five yards that mattered most. With the Panthers trailing 31-27 late in the fourth quarter at Lambeau Field, Steve Beuerlein led his team on a 63-yard drive. He capped it off with a five-yard quarterback draw with no time remaining, giving Carolina a 33-31 victory.

Hit of the week: Chiefs linebacker Derrick Thomas sacked Minnesota's Jeff George with 8:01 remaining, forcing a fumble that was picked up by defensive end Eric Hicks and returned 44 yards for a touchdown. The touchdown ended the Vikings' 21-point rally and gave the Chiefs a 28-21 lead. Kansas City went on to win the game, 31-28, on Pete Stoyanovich's 38-yard field goal with three seconds remaining.

Oddity of the week: The Jets' John Hall missed two extra points against Miami. It was the first time an NFL kicker botched two extra points in the same game since Kansas City's Lin Elliott did so in 1995. Despite Hall's misses, the Jets beat Miami, 28-20.

Top rusher: Tennessee's Eddie George carried 28 times for 199 yards and two touchdowns in the Titans' 21-14 victory over Oakland.

Top passer: Drew Bledsoe completed 31-of-44 passes for 379 yards and one touchdown in New England's 20-15 loss to the Colts.

Top receiver: Qadry Ismail caught six passes for 258 yards, including three touchdowns, in the Ravens' 31-24 victory over Pittsburgh.

Notes: Olindo Mare's field goals of 24 and 33 yards against the Jets gave him 33 field goals for the season, setting a new Dolphins franchise record. The old record was held by Pete Stoyanovich. ... Troy Aikman's touchdown pass to tight end David LaFleur was the 153rd of his career, tying him with Roger Staubach for second place (behind Danny White, with 155) on the Cowboys' career list. ... The Ravens' 31-24 victory over the Steelers was the first for a Baltimore team in Pittsburgh since 1968. ... Eddie George passed the 5,000-yard mark in career rushing, making him only the ninth NFL player to reach that plateau in his first four seasons. ... The Bengals' 44-28 win over the Browns marked their final game at Cinergy Field. The Bengals were 133-101, including playoffs, in 20 years at the stadium. They will move a few blocks away to Paul Brown Stadium in 2000. ... With 75 rushing yards, Seattle's Ricky Watters went over the 1,000-yard mark for the

1999 REVIEW Week 14

– 195 –

fifth consecutive season. ... When Tampa Bay defensive lineman Brad Culpepper sacked Detroit quarterback Gus Frerotte for a safety, it was the Buccaneers' first safety since 1989. ... The 49ers held the ball for 40 minutes, 43 seconds compared to the Falcons' 19 minutes, 17 seconds. Not surprisingly, San Francisco routed Atlanta, 26-7. ... Washington quarterback Brad Johnson's two touchdown passes gave him a career-high 21. ... Buffalo's Andre Reed became the fifth player in NFL history with more than 13,000 career receiving yards. ... Indianapolis' Peyton Manning became the third quarterback in league history to pass for 7,000 yards in his first two seasons, joining Drew Bledsoe and Dan Marino. ... Brett Favre's 25th 300-yard passing game pushed him over 30,000-yard mark in career passing yardage. He became the 23rd NFL quarterback to hit the 30,000-yard level.

Quote of the week: Redskins guard Tre Johnson, following his team's 28-3 blowout victory over Arizona, stressed the importance of continuing to grind it out the rest of the season: "I don't want to kill it for the kids, but Santa Claus is not going to bring us the playoffs. We got to go out there and snatch it. We got to go out there, put the mask on and go rob."

GAME SUMMARIES

TITANS 21, RAIDERS 14
Thursday, December 9

Oakland 0   0   7   7—14
Tennessee 0   0   7 14—21

Third Quarter
Ten.—McNair 1 run (Del Greco kick), 6:14.
Oak.—Crockett 1 run (Husted kick), 12:24.
Fourth Quarter
Ten.—E. George 8 run (Del Greco kick), 2:19.
Ten.—E. George 19 run (Del Greco kick), 6:59.
Oak.—Dudley 2 pass from Gannon (Husted kick), 11:01.
Attendance—66,357.

	Oakland	Tennessee
First downs	21	17
Rushes-yards	22-111	33-204
Passing	253	103
Punt returns	1-0	1-4
Kickoff returns	3-36	3-69
Interception returns	1-0	1-2
Comp.-att.-int.	20-28-1	12-20-1
Sacked-yards lost	4-20	2-11
Punts	2-38	4-31
Fumbles-lost	2-2	0-0
Penalties-yards	8-44	6-55
Time of possession	29:09	30:51

INDIVIDUAL STATISTICS
RUSHING—Oakland, Wheatley 11-49, Kaufman 7-51, Crockett 3-8, Gannon 1-3. Tennessee, E. George 28-199, McNair 4-5, Neal 1-0.
PASSING—Oakland, Gannon 20-28-1-273. Tennessee, McNair 12-20-1-114.
RECEIVING—Oakland, Dudley 4-44, Kaufman 3-62, Jett 3-44, Ritchie 3-42, Brown 3-30, Wheatley 2-26, Mickens 2-25. Tennessee, E. George 6-50, Wychek 3-36, Roan 1-13, Byrd 1-11, Dyson 1-4.
MISSED FIELD GOAL ATTEMPTS—Oakland, Husted 32, 45.
INTERCEPTIONS—Oakland, Johnstone 1-0. Tennessee, Jackson 1-2.
KICKOFF RETURNS—Oakland, Kaufman 3-36. Tennessee, Mason 3-69.
PUNT RETURNS—Oakland, Gordon 1-0. Tennessee, Mason 1-4.
SACKS—Oakland, Johnstone 1, Jackson 1. Tennessee, Robinson 2, Kearse 2.

BENGALS 44, BROWNS 28
Sunday, December 12

Cleveland 7   8   6   7—28
Cincinnati .... 10 20 14   0—44

First Quarter
Cin.—FG, Pelfrey 28, 7:03.
Cin.—Yeast 81 punt return (Pelfrey kick), 12:42.
Cle.—Abdul-Jabbar 8 pass from Couch (Dawson kick), 15:00.
Second Quarter
Cin.—Groce 1 run (Pelfrey kick), 2:49.
Cin.—Dillon 2 run (pass failed), 12:26.
Cle.—Kirby 1 run (Couch run), 14:15.
Cin.—Dillon 2 run (Pelfrey kick), 14:45.
Third Quarter
Cin.—Dillon 11 run (Pelfrey kick), 1:46.
Cle.—I. Smith 16 pass from Couch (pass failed), 9:58.
Cin.—Scott 52 pass from Blake (Pelfrey kick), 11:45.
Fourth Quarter
Cle.—Chiaverini 19 pass from Detmer (Dawson kick), 14:11.
Attendance—59,972.

	Cleveland	Cincinnati
First downs	19	25
Rushes-yards	11-11	53-279
Passing	312	180
Punt returns	0-0	3-91
Kickoff returns	8-128	5-91
Interception returns	0-0	2-4
Comp.-att.-int.	22-41-2	12-23-0
Sacked-yards lost	3-16	0-0
Punts	5-45	3-36
Fumbles-lost	2-2	5-1
Penalties-yards	7-79	9-84
Time of possession	22:41	37:19

INDIVIDUAL STATISTICS
RUSHING—Cleveland, Abdul-Jabbar 5-10, Kirby 3-5, Detmer 1-2, Edwards 1-0, Johnson 1-(minus 6). Cincinnati, Dillon 28-192, Basnight 12-44, Blake 4-28, Groce 3-14, Williams 3-8, Covington 2-(minus 4), Yeast 1-(minus 3).
PASSING—Cleveland, Couch 16-28-2-239, Detmer 6-13-0-89. Cincinnati, Blake 11-22-0-176, Covington 1-1-0-4.
RECEIVING—Cleveland, Johnson 7-135, Chiaverini 4-48, I. Smith 3-33, Campbell 2-33, Kirby 2-24, Abdul-Jabbar 2-7, Powell 1-45, Edwards 1-3. Cincinnati, Pickens 3-46, McGee 3-27, Scott 2-75, Dillon 2-20, Griffin 1-8, Basnight 1-4.
MISSED FIELD GOAL ATTEMPTS—None.
INTERCEPTIONS—Cincinnati, Copeland 1-4, Myers 1-0.
KICKOFF RETURNS—Cleveland, Powell 3-69, Hill 2-28, Saleh 1-11, Campbell 1-10, I. Smith 1-10. Cincinnati, Williams 3-32, Mack 1-55, Dillon 1-4.
PUNT RETURNS—Cincinnati, Yeast 3-91.
SACKS—Cincinnati, von Oelhoffen 1.5, Spikes 1, Bankston 0.5.

PANTHERS 33, PACKERS 31
Sunday, December 12

Carolina 3   7 14   9—33
Green Bay 7   7   7 10—31

First Quarter
Car.—FG, Kasay 20, 9:37.
G.B.—K. McKenzie 18 interception return (Longwell kick), 13:22.
Second Quarter
Car.—Jeffers 35 pass from Beuerlein (Kasay kick), 9:33.
G.B.—Freeman 19 pass from Favre (Longwell kick), 13:12.
Third Quarter
Car.—Jeffers 38 pass from Beuerlein (Kasay kick), 0:21.
G.B.—Driver 8 pass from Favre (Longwell kick), 6:37.
Car.—Kinchen 26 pass from Beuerlein (Kasay kick), 10:33.
Fourth Quarter
G.B.—FG, Longwell 40, 3:55.
Car.—FG, Kasay 37, 7:12.
G.B.—Henderson 1 run (Longwell kick), 11:00.
Car.—Beuerlein 5 run (run failed), 15:00.
Attendance—59,869.

	Carolina	Green Bay
First downs	21	26
Rushes-yards	13-13	24-79
Passing	373	283
Punt returns	1-0	1-6
Kickoff returns	6-135	6-126
Interception returns	1-16	1-18
Comp.-att.-int.	29-42-1	26-38-1
Sacked-yards lost	0-0	2-19
Punts	1-47	3-36
Fumbles-lost	3-3	2-1
Penalties-yards	9-64	10-81
Time of possession	26:59	33:01

INDIVIDUAL STATISTICS

RUSHING—Carolina, Biakabutuka 8-6, Beuerlein 4-8, Lane 1-(minus 1). Green Bay, Mitchell 12-49, Parker 6-0, Favre 5-29, Henderson 1-1.

PASSING—Carolina, Beuerlein 29-42-1-373. Green Bay, Favre 26-38-1-302.

RECEIVING—Carolina, Jeffers 8-147, Muhammad 8-51, Walls 6-96, Biakabutuka 3-26, Floyd 2-24, Kinchen 1-26, Lane 1-3. Green Bay, Schroeder 6-84, Henderson 5-58, Freeman 4-46, Mitchell 4-39, Driver 3-31, T. Davis 2-22, Bradford 1-15, Parker 1-7.

MISSED FIELD GOAL ATTEMPTS—None.

INTERCEPTIONS—Carolina, Davis 1-16. Green Bay, K. McKenzie 1-18.

KICKOFF RETURNS—Carolina, Bates 5-113, Lane 1-22. Green Bay, Parker 5-108, Mitchell 1-18.

PUNT RETURNS—Carolina, Metcalf 1-0. Green Bay, Edwards 1-6.

SACKS—Carolina, Greene 2.

COLTS 20, PATRIOTS 15

Sunday, December 12

New England	3	3	3	6—15
Indianapolis	7	7	6	0—20

First Quarter
Ind.—Pollard 5 pass from Manning (Vanderjagt kick), 5:28.
N.E.—FG, Vinatieri 28, 10:37.

Second Quarter
N.E.—FG, Vinatieri 28, 9:21.
Ind.—James 2 pass from Manning (Vanderjagt kick), 12:03.

Third Quarter
Ind.—FG, Vanderjagt 28, 4:11.
Ind.—FG, Vanderjagt 31, 10:46.
N.E.—FG, Vinatieri 26, 14:05.

Fourth Quarter
N.E.—Jefferson 10 pass from Bledsoe (pass failed), 11:53.
Attendance—56,975.

	New England	Indianapolis
First downs	23	15
Rushes-yards	20-57	25-109
Passing	344	178
Punt returns	4-69	1-10
Kickoff returns	5-109	4-56
Interception returns	0-0	1-11
Comp.-att.-int.	31-44-1	15-27-0
Sacked-yards lost	5-35	1-8
Punts	5-44	5-47
Fumbles-lost	2-0	2-1
Penalties-yards	11-85	4-26
Time of possession	32:08	27:52

INDIVIDUAL STATISTICS

RUSHING—New England, Allen 12-23, Bledsoe 4-18, Warren 2-12, Faulk 2-4. Indianapolis, James 20-101, Manning 5-8.

PASSING—New England, Bledsoe 31-44-1-379. Indianapolis, Manning 15-27-0-186.

RECEIVING—New England, Glenn 9-148, Jefferson 7-76, Warren 4-39, Coates 4-34, Brown 3-53, Brisby 2-25, T. Carter 2-4. Indianapolis, Harrison 6-118, Pollard 3-32, Wilkins 3-18, James 2-8, Dilger 1-10.

MISSED FIELD GOAL ATTEMPTS—None.

INTERCEPTIONS—Indianapolis, Poole 1-11.

KICKOFF RETURNS—New England, Faulk 2-48, Simmons 2-37, Jones 1-24. Indianapolis, Wilkins 3-54, Belser 1-2.

PUNT RETURNS—New England, Brown 4-69. Indianapolis, Wilkins 1-10.

SACKS—New England, Sullivan 1. Indianapolis, Bratzke 2, E. Johnson 1, Peterson 1, M. Thomas 1.

GIANTS 19, BILLS 17

Sunday, December 12

N.Y. Giants	3	10	3	3—19
Buffalo	3	7	0	7—17

First Quarter
Buf.—FG, Christie 50, 5:44.
NYG—FG, Blanchard 42, 10:35.

Second Quarter
NYG—FG, Blanchard 21, 2:51.
Buf.—Thomas 23 pass from Flutie (Christie kick), 13:09.
NYG—Toomer 14 pass from Collins (Blanchard kick), 14:57.

Third Quarter
NYG—FG, Blanchard 21, 10:32.

Fourth Quarter
Buf.—Linton 2 run (Christie kick), 5:26.
NYG—FG, Blanchard 48, 14:20.
Attendance—72,527.

	N.Y. Giants	Buffalo
First downs	20	13
Rushes-yards	28-94	28-76
Passing	240	161
Punt returns	1-(-2)	3-30
Kickoff returns	4-101	5-94
Interception returns	1-34	1-52
Comp.-att.-int.	23-44-1	15-32-1
Sacked-yards lost	0-0	3-23
Punts	5-47	4-45
Fumbles-lost	1-1	1-1
Penalties-yards	6-40	6-63
Time of possession	31:11	28:49

INDIVIDUAL STATISTICS

RUSHING—New York, Montgomery 20-77, Barber 4-6, Collins 2-7, Toomer 1-4, Comella 1-0. Buffalo, Linton 8-17, Thomas 8-15, Flutie 6-25, A. Smith 6-19.

PASSING—New York, Collins 23-44-1-240. Buffalo, Flutie 15-32-1-184.

RECEIVING—New York, Barber 8-90, Hilliard 6-62, Mitchell 5-41, Toomer 3-35, Jurevicius 1-12. Buffalo, Moulds 3-55, Reed 3-40, Thomas 2-35, Collins 2-20, P. Price 2-16, K. Williams 2-10, Gash 1-8.

MISSED FIELD GOAL ATTEMPTS—Buffalo, Christie 39, 48.

INTERCEPTIONS—New York, Levingston 1-34. Buffalo, Wiley 1-52.

KICKOFF RETURNS—New York, Levingston 3-74, Barber 1-27. Buffalo, Porter 2-41, P. Price 1-27, K. Williams 1-13, Gash 1-13.

PUNT RETURNS—New York, Barber 1-(minus 2). Buffalo, K. Williams 3-30.

SACKS—New York, Strahan 1, Armstead 1, Jones 1.

COWBOYS 20, EAGLES 10

Sunday, December 12

Philadelphia	3	0	0	7—10
Dallas	7	6	7	0—20

First Quarter
Phi.—FG, N. Johnson 44, 6:01.
Dal.—Warren 4 run (Murray kick), 10:11.

Second Quarter
Dal.—FG, Murray 30, 8:10.
Dal.—FG, Murray 34, 15:00.

Third Quarter
Dal.—LaFleur 8 pass from Aikman (Murray kick), 8:50.

Fourth Quarter
Phi.—Brown 25 pass from Pederson (N. Johnson kick), 8:19.
Attendance—64,086.

	Philadelphia	Dallas
First downs	14	22
Rushes-yards	24-90	31-112
Passing	143	225
Punt returns	2-10	5-23
Kickoff returns	3-48	2-55
Interception returns	0-0	1-19
Comp.-att.-int.	15-29-1	22-40-0
Sacked-yards lost	3-14	1-17
Punts	8-43	6-40
Fumbles-lost	3-2	2-1
Penalties-yards	6-68	9-55
Time of possession	25:55	34:05

1999 REVIEW Week 14

INDIVIDUAL STATISTICS

RUSHING—Philadelphia, Staley 18-78, McNabb 3-24, Pederson 2-(minus 18), Watson 1-6. Dallas, Warren 25-92, Aikman 4-6, Ismail 1-12, E. Smith 1-2.

PASSING—Philadelphia, McNabb 7-17-1-49, Pederson 8-12-0-108. Dallas, Aikman 22-40-0-242.

RECEIVING—Philadelphia, Small 4-54, Brown 3-37, Staley 3-11, Jells 2-29, Lewis 1-19, Broughton 1-4, C. Martin 1-3. Dallas, Ismail 4-52, Warren 4-46, LaFleur 4-44, Tucker 3-37, Bjornson 2-25, Sanders 2-14, Thomas 2-12, Brazzell 1-12.

MISSED FIELD GOAL ATTEMPTS—Dallas, Murray 49, 33.

INTERCEPTIONS—Dallas, Hambrick 1-19.

KICKOFF RETURNS—Philadelphia, Rossum 3-48. Dallas, Mathis 2-55.

PUNT RETURNS—Philadelphia, Rossum 2-10. Dallas, Sanders 5-23.

SACKS—Philadelphia, Mamula 1. Dallas, Ekuban 2, Spellman 1.

REDSKINS 28, CARDINALS 3

Sunday, December 12

Arizona	3	0	0	0— 3
Washington	7	14	0	7—28

First Quarter
Was.—Davis 50 run (Conway kick), 4:08.
Ariz.—FG, Jacke 31, 11:48.

Second Quarter
Was.—Fryar 7 pass from B. Johnson (Conway kick), 2:07.
Was.—Westbrook 25 pass from B. Johnson (Conway kick), 14:49.

Fourth Quarter
Was.—Hicks 11 run (Conway kick), 12:21.
Attendance—75,851.

	Arizona	Washington
First downs	9	25
Rushes-yards	14-53	46-226
Passing	120	180
Punt returns	2-8	3-18
Kickoff returns	5-141	2-37
Interception returns	2-1	3-16
Comp.-att.-int.	15-32-3	17-31-2
Sacked-yards lost	5-27	2-11
Punts	5-40	5-41
Fumbles-lost	3-1	1-0
Penalties-yards	5-42	12-97
Time of possession	21:14	38:46

INDIVIDUAL STATISTICS

RUSHING—Arizona, Murrell 8-41, Pittman 3-8, Plummer 2-6, Boston 1-(minus 2). Washington, Davis 37-189, Mitchell 3-19, Centers 2-10, Hicks 2-10, B. Johnson 2-(minus 2).

PASSING—Arizona, Plummer 15-32-3-147. Washington, B. Johnson 17-31-2-191.

RECEIVING—Arizona, Murrell 4-44, Moore 4-24, Makovicka 3-21, Pittman 2-8, Boston 1-43, Hardy 1-7. Washington, Westbrook 4-52, Centers 4-38, Connell 3-54, Fryar 3-19, Mitchell 2-14, Alexander 1-14.

MISSED FIELD GOAL ATTEMPTS—None.

INTERCEPTIONS—Arizona, Chavous 1-1, Knight 1-0. Washington, Green 1-8, Stevens 1-8, Bailey 1-0.

KICKOFF RETURNS—Arizona, Bates 3-114, Tillman 1-18, Dishman 1-9. Washington, Thrash 2-29.

PUNT RETURNS—Arizona, Cody 2-8. Washington, Mitchell 3-18.

SACKS—Arizona, Fredrickson 1, Burke 0.5, Rice 0.5. Washington, Coleman 1, Stubblefield 1, Cook 1, Smith 0.5, McMillian 0.5, Wilkinson 0.5, Shade 0.5.

RAMS 30, SAINTS 14

Sunday, December 12

St. Louis	7	17	3	3—30
New Orleans	6	8	0	0—14

First Quarter
N.O.—FG, Brien 29, 4:19.
St.L.—Holcombe 1 pass from Warner (Wilkins kick), 9:21.
N.O.—FG, Brien 26, 13:31.

Second Quarter
N.O.—Cleeland 2 pass from Tolliver (Kennison pass from Tolliver), 5:51.
St.L.—FG, Wilkins 40, 7:36.
St.L.—Faulk 4 run (Wilkins kick), 11:32.
St.L.—Faulk 30 pass from Warner (Wilkins kick), 14:09.

Third Quarter
St.L.—FG, Wilkins 30, 9:20.

Fourth Quarter
St.L.—FG, Wilkins 38, 12:31.
Attendance—46,838.

	St. Louis	New Orleans
First downs	23	13
Rushes-yards	34-156	18-66
Passing	336	144
Punt returns	3-2	0-0
Kickoff returns	4-47	7-215
Interception returns	3-25	1-27
Comp.-att.-int.	21-31-1	12-28-3
Sacked-yards lost	1-10	6-44
Punts	0-0	4-44
Fumbles-lost	2-1	0-0
Penalties-yards	9-54	4-35
Time of possession	36:24	23:36

INDIVIDUAL STATISTICS

RUSHING—St. Louis, Faulk 29-154, Warner 2-4, Justin 2-(minus 2), Holcombe 1-0. New Orleans, Perry 14-54, Tolliver 1-6, Hastings 1-4, Davis 1-2, Philyaw 1-0.

PASSING—St. Louis, Warner 21-31-1-346. New Orleans, Tolliver 12-28-3-188.

RECEIVING—St. Louis, Holt 6-113, Faulk 5-56, Bruce 4-102, R. Williams 2-26, Proehl 2-23, Hakim 1-25, Holcombe 1-1. New Orleans, Poole 3-83, Hastings 2-45, Kennison 2-19, L. Smith 2-15, Davis 1-20, Perry 1-4, Cleeland 1-2.

MISSED FIELD GOAL ATTEMPTS—St. Louis, Wilkins 41, 40.

INTERCEPTIONS—St. Louis, Lyght 1-22, McCleon 1-3, Allen 1-0. New Orleans, Weary 1-27.

KICKOFF RETURNS—St. Louis, Horne 3-43, Hodgins 1-4. New Orleans, Philyaw 7-215.

PUNT RETURNS—St. Louis, Hakim 3-2.

SACKS—St. Louis, J. Williams 2, Zgonina 2, Wistrom 1, Clemons 1. New Orleans, Whitehead 1.

RAVENS 31, STEELERS 24

Sunday, December 12

Baltimore	7	3	21	0—31
Pittsburgh	10	0	7	7—24

First Quarter
Pit.—Ward 21 pass from Bettis (K. Brown kick), 2:32.
Bal.—Holmes 64 run (Stover kick), 3:48.
Pit.—FG, K. Brown 31, 10:49.

Second Quarter
Bal.—FG, Stover 19, 1:05.

Third Quarter
Bal.—Ismail 54 pass from Banks (Stover kick), 2:13.
Pit.—Edwards 6 pass from Tomczak (K. Brown kick), 5:30.
Bal.—Ismail 59 pass from Banks (Stover kick), 6:32.
Bal.—Ismail 76 pass from Banks (Stover kick), 11:41.

Fourth Quarter
Pit.—Stewart 11 pass from Tomczak (K. Brown kick), 12:15.
Attendance—46,715.

	Baltimore	Pittsburgh
First downs	12	21
Rushes-yards	25-132	22-109
Passing	247	243
Punt returns	2-0	5-50
Kickoff returns	3-46	6-147
Interception returns	0-0	0-0
Comp.-att.-int.	8-26-0	24-43-0
Sacked-yards lost	4-21	5-27
Punts	7-45	7-43
Fumbles-lost	5-0	3-1
Penalties-yards	9-73	12-73
Time of possession	25:46	34:14

INDIVIDUAL STATISTICS

RUSHING—Baltimore, Holmes 18-130, Banks 6-0, Evans 1-2. Pittsburgh, Bettis 13-39, Huntley 8-68, Tomczak 1-2.

PASSING—Baltimore, Banks 8-26-0-268. Pittsburgh, Tomczak 22-41-0-249, Bettis 1-1-0-21, Stewart 1-1-0-0.

RECEIVING—Baltimore, Ismail 6-258, Davis 1-7, Evans 1-3. Pittsburgh, Edwards 6-64, Stewart 4-71, Shaw 4-30, Bettis 4-11, Ward 3-43, Bruener 2-33, Johnson 1-18.

MISSED FIELD GOAL ATTEMPTS—Pittsburgh, K. Brown 46.
INTERCEPTIONS—None.
KICKOFF RETURNS—Baltimore, Harris 3-46. Pittsburgh, Huntley 4-110, Edwards 2-37.
PUNT RETURNS—Baltimore, Woodson 2-0. Pittsburgh, Edwards 5-50.
SACKS—Baltimore, Burnett 2, Siragusa 1, Webster 1. Pittsburgh, Flowers 1, Henry 1, L. Brown 1, Shields 1.

CHARGERS 19, SEAHAWKS 16

Sunday, December 12

San Diego	10	3	0	6—19
Seattle	3	6	7	0—16

First Quarter
S.D.—Means 1 run (Carney kick), 3:58.
Sea.—FG, Peterson 28, 8:29.
S.D.—FG, Carney 33, 13:19.

Second Quarter
Sea.—FG, Peterson 40, 1:42.
S.D.—FG, Carney 42, 8:39.
Sea.—FG, Peterson 33, 14:31.

Third Quarter
Sea.—Mayes 14 pass from Kitna (Peterson kick), 3:40.

Fourth Quarter
S.D.—FG, Carney 28, 2:56.
S.D.—FG, Carney 41, 11:41.
Attendance—66,318.

	San Diego	Seattle
First downs	22	20
Rushes-yards	39-107	21-76
Passing	222	271
Punt returns	0-0	1-14
Kickoff returns	5-84	6-163
Interception returns	1-0	1-21
Comp.-att.-int.	20-35-1	25-40-1
Sacked-yards lost	1-7	3-14
Punts	5-43	3-49
Fumbles-lost	0-0	1-1
Penalties-yards	9-55	5-47
Time of possession	32:00	28:00

INDIVIDUAL STATISTICS
RUSHING—San Diego, Bynum 15-24, Means 14-42, Fletcher 6-16, Harbaugh 3-23, Fazande 1-2. Seattle, Watters 20-75, Kitna 1-1.
PASSING—San Diego, Harbaugh 20-35-1-229. Seattle, Kitna 25-40-1-285.
RECEIVING—San Diego, J. Graham 9-114, Fletcher 5-57, F. Jones 2-30, Bynum 1-11, Means 1-9, Ricks 1-7, McCrary 1-1. Seattle, Galloway 6-85, Mayes 5-58, Dawkins 4-59, Fauria 4-35, Pritchard 2-21, Watters 2-17, Bownes 1-5, Strong 1-5.
MISSED FIELD GOAL ATTEMPTS—Seattle, Peterson 48, 52, 38.
INTERCEPTIONS—San Diego, Spencer 1-0. Seattle, D. Williams 1-21.
KICKOFF RETURNS—San Diego, Reed 4-62, Bynum 1-22. Seattle, Rogers 5-154, Joseph 1-9.
PUNT RETURNS—Seattle, Galloway 1-14.
SACKS—San Diego, Johnson 1, Dixon 1, Fontenot 1. Seattle, Kennedy 1.

JETS 28, DOLPHINS 20

Sunday, December 12

Miami	6	0	7	7—20
N.Y. Jets	0	6	0	22—28

First Quarter
Mia.—FG, Mare 24, 12:12.
Mia.—FG, Mare 33, 13:51.

Second Quarter
NYJ—FG, Hall 28, 7:25.
NYJ—FG, Hall 31, 14:09.

Third Quarter
Mia.—Pritchett 1 run (Mare kick), 8:08.

Fourth Quarter
NYJ—K. Johnson 26 pass from Lucas (Hall kick), 0:06.
NYJ—K. Johnson 24 pass from Lucas (kick failed), 5:26.
NYJ—FG, Hall 46, 12:09.
NYJ—Stoutmire 67 interception return (kick failed), 13:16.
Mia.—Gadsden 8 pass from Huard (Mare kick), 14:43.
Attendance—78,246.

	Miami	N.Y. Jets
First downs	20	18
Rushes-yards	20-69	28-95
Passing	250	225
Punt returns	2-30	4-30
Kickoff returns	7-143	4-99
Interception returns	0-0	2-69
Comp.-att.-int.	24-46-2	22-38-0
Sacked-yards lost	2-17	1-5
Punts	6-36	4-36
Fumbles-lost	0-0	2-1
Penalties-yards	6-43	2-20
Time of possession	28:08	31:52

INDIVIDUAL STATISTICS
RUSHING—Miami, Pritchett 18-64, Denson 2-5. New York, Martin 24-75, Lucas 4-20.
PASSING—Miami, Marino 18-39-2-192, Huard 6-7-0-75. New York, Lucas 22-38-0-230.
RECEIVING—Miami, Pritchett 6-45, Green 4-73, Gadsden 4-57, Drayton 4-33, Konrad 3-29, Martin 2-12, Jacquet 1-18. New York, K. Johnson 11-144, Chrebet 3-42, Ward 2-13, Martin 1-8, Anderson 1-8, E. Green 1-8, Baxter 1-6, Early 1-5, Parmalee 1-(minus 4).
MISSED FIELD GOAL ATTEMPTS—New York, Hall 47.
INTERCEPTIONS—New York, Stoutmire 1-67, Glenn 1-2.
KICKOFF RETURNS—Miami, Marion 7-143. New York, Stone 2-61, Glenn 2-38.
PUNT RETURNS—Miami, Jacquet 1-35, Buckley 1-(minus 5). New York, Ward 4-30.
SACKS—Miami, Owens 0.5, Bowens 0.5. New York, Farrior 1, Lewis 0.5, Phifer 0.5.

BUCCANEERS 23, LIONS 16

Sunday, December 12

Detroit	10	0	3	3—16
Tampa Bay	0	7	2	14—23

First Quarter
Det.—FG, Hanson 37, 5:45.
Det.—Hill 10 run (Hanson kick), 14:08.

Second Quarter
T.B.—McLeod 3 pass from King (Gramatica kick), 13:26.

Third Quarter
T.B.—Safety, G. Frerotte sacked by B. Culpepper in end zone, 1:52.
Det.—FG, Hanson 25, 9:32.

Fourth Quarter
Det.—FG, Hanson 27, 0:49.
T.B.—Alstott 1 run (Gramatica kick), 5:34.
T.B.—Alstott 22 pass from King (Gramatica kick), 10:42.
Attendance—65,536.

	Detroit	Tampa Bay
First downs	16	17
Rushes-yards	20-55	19-41
Passing	210	271
Punt returns	2-20	2-10
Kickoff returns	3-37	6-107
Interception returns	1-0	1-28
Comp.-att.-int.	23-44-1	23-37-1
Sacked-yards lost	4-31	3-26
Punts	5-38	6-45
Fumbles-lost	1-0	1-1
Penalties-yards	8-61	7-58
Time of possession	30:41	29:19

INDIVIDUAL STATISTICS
RUSHING—Detroit, Hill 10-25, Schlesinger 7-25, Frerotte 2-4, Olivo 1-1. Tampa Bay, Alstott 8-28, Dunn 8-6, King 3-7.
PASSING—Detroit, Frerotte 23-44-1-241. Tampa Bay, King 23-37-1-297.
RECEIVING—Detroit, Morton 7-107, Crowell 4-47, Schlesinger 3-19, Hill 3-9, Moore 2-22, Olivo 2-14, Sloan 1-14, Stablein 1-9. Tampa Bay, Dunn 6-115, Emanuel 4-46, Williams 4-31, Alstott 3-39, Green 3-22, Anthony 1-30, Moore 1-11, McLeod 1-3.
MISSED FIELD GOAL ATTEMPTS—None.
INTERCEPTIONS—Detroit, Carrier 1-0. Tampa Bay, Lynch 1-28.
KICKOFF RETURNS—Detroit, Howard 2-31, Talton 1-6. Tampa Bay, Anthony 5-107, Green 1-0.
PUNT RETURNS—Detroit, Howard 2-20. Tampa Bay, Green 1-5, Williams 1-5.
SACKS—Detroit, Porcher 3. Tampa Bay, Culpepper 1.5, Sapp 1.5, Jones 1.

49ERS 26, FALCONS 7

Sunday, December 12

Atlanta	0	0	7	0—	7
San Francisco	7	12	0	7—	26

First Quarter
S.F.—Garner 8 run (Richey kick), 14:03.

Second Quarter
S.F.—Beasley 2 run (Richey kick), 12:17.
S.F.—Safety, C. Chandler sacked by B. Young in end zone, 13:08.
S.F.—FG, Richey 23, 14:20.

Third Quarter
Atl.—Oliver 58 punt return (Andersen kick), 9:19.

Fourth Quarter
S.F.—Beasley 1 run (Richey kick), 1:52.
Attendance—67,465.

	Atlanta	San Francisco
First downs	7	21
Rushes-yards	12-38	44-181
Passing	67	153
Punt returns	3-83	1-(-1)
Kickoff returns	5-62	2-52
Interception returns	0-0	1-0
Comp.-att.-int.	9-27-1	17-26-0
Sacked-yards lost	5-39	2-16
Punts	8-38	6-39
Fumbles-lost	1-1	0-0
Penalties-yards	6-65	7-87
Time of possession	19:17	40:43

INDIVIDUAL STATISTICS

RUSHING—Atlanta, Oxendine 7-15, Oliver 2-7, Christian 2-5, Chandler 1-11. San Francisco, Garner 26-107, Beasley 8-26, Jackson 5-24, Garcia 3-18, Jervey 2-6.

PASSING—Atlanta, Chandler 8-18-1-95, Graziani 1-9-0-11. San Francisco, Garcia 16-24-0-160, Stenstrom 1-2-0-9.

RECEIVING—Atlanta, Mathis 4-58, German 2-24, Oxendine 1-13, Monroe 1-8, Christian 1-3. San Francisco, Garner 5-62, Clark 4-46, Beasley 3-14, Owens 2-21, Rice 2-17, Harris 1-9.

MISSED FIELD GOAL ATTEMPTS—San Francisco, Richey 39.

INTERCEPTIONS—San Francisco, T. McDonald 1-0.

KICKOFF RETURNS—Atlanta, Oliver 4-53, E. Williams 1-9. San Francisco, Preston 2-52.

PUNT RETURNS—Atlanta, Oliver 3-83. San Francisco, Preston 1-(minus 1).

SACKS—Atlanta, Smith 1, Crockett 1. San Francisco, B. Young 2.5, Norton 1, Haley 1, Posey 0.5.

CHIEFS 31, VIKINGS 28

Sunday, December 12

Minnesota	0	14	7	7—	28
Kansas City	14	7	0	10—	31

First Quarter
K.C.—Bennett 2 run (Stoyanovich kick), 6:18.
K.C.—Gonzalez 13 pass from Grbac (Stoyanovich kick), 11:51.

Second Quarter
K.C.—Gonzalez 9 pass from Grbac (Stoyanovich kick), 0:13.
Min.—Tate 76 kickoff return (Anderson kick), 0:28.
Min.—Hatchette 8 pass from George (Anderson kick), 14:20.

Third Quarter
Min.—Moss 12 pass from George (Anderson kick), 10:26.

Fourth Quarter
K.C.—Hicks 44 fumble return (Stoyanovich kick), 6:59.
Min.—Moss 64 punt return (Anderson kick), 13:22.
K.C.—FG, Stoyanovich 38, 14:57.
Attendance—78,932.

	Minnesota	Kansas City
First downs	21	22
Rushes-yards	35-175	40-173
Passing	151	207
Punt returns	4-72	2-26
Kickoff returns	6-177	5-82
Interception returns	0-0	0-0
Comp.-att.-int.	13-23-0	19-29-0
Sacked-yards lost	4-39	2-8
Punts	4-43	5-39
Fumbles-lost	4-4	3-2
Penalties-yards	8-91	7-40
Time of possession	30:05	29:55

INDIVIDUAL STATISTICS

RUSHING—Minnesota, Smith 21-118, Hoard 11-35, George 2-7, Moss 1-15. Kansas City, Bennett 13-55, Richardson 11-57, Cloud 8-26, Morris 4-33, Grbac 2-2.

PASSING—Minnesota, George 13-23-0-190. Kansas City, Grbac 19-29-0-215.

RECEIVING—Minnesota, Moss 5-76, Reed 3-41, Hatchette 2-30, Smith 2-21, Carter 1-22. Kansas City, Gonzalez 6-63, Horn 4-65, Lockett 3-36, Alexander 3-21, Rison 2-21, Richardson 1-9.

MISSED FIELD GOAL ATTEMPTS—Minnesota, Anderson 45. Kansas City, Stoyanovich 45.

INTERCEPTIONS—None.

KICKOFF RETURNS—Minnesota, Tate 6-177. Kansas City, Vanover 3-49, Cloud 1-18, Bennett 1-15.

PUNT RETURNS—Minnesota, Moss 4-72. Kansas City, Vanover 2-26.

SACKS—Minnesota, Doleman 1, Randle 1. Kansas City, Thomas 1, D. Williams 1, O'Neal 1.

JAGUARS 27, BRONCOS 24

Monday, December 13

Denver	7	7	3	7—	24
Jacksonville	0	17	0	10—	27

First Quarter
Den.—R. Smith 22 pass from Griese (Elam kick), 6:59.

Second Quarter
Den.—Gary 1 run (Elam kick), 1:20.
Jac.—J. Stewart 5 run (Hollis kick), 8:45.
Jac.—FG, Hollis 49, 12:26.
Jac.—J. Stewart 1 run (Hollis kick), 14:31.

Third Quarter
Den.—FG, Elam 40, 12:16.

Fourth Quarter
Jac.—Taylor 38 run (Hollis kick), 12:25.
Den.—Chamberlain 57 pass from Griese (Elam kick), 13:17.
Jac.—FG, Hollis 23, 15:00.
Attendance—71,357.

	Denver	Jacksonville
First downs	18	18
Rushes-yards	27-90	32-161
Passing	275	104
Punt returns	5-15	2-33
Kickoff returns	4-85	4-73
Interception returns	0-0	2-11
Comp.-att.-int.	21-33-2	11-25-0
Sacked-yards lost	1-0	3-11
Punts	6-42	7-41
Fumbles-lost	4-0	4-0
Penalties-yards	9-83	3-20
Time of possession	32:25	27:35

INDIVIDUAL STATISTICS

RUSHING—Denver, Gary 20-67, Griese 3-13, Loville 3-9, Griffith 1-1. Jacksonville, J. Stewart 18-79, Taylor 9-74, Brunell 5-8.

PASSING—Denver, Griese 21-33-2-275. Jacksonville, Brunell 11-25-0-115.

RECEIVING—Denver, R. Smith 6-92, McCaffrey 6-61, Chamberlain 3-75, Carswell 3-22, Griffith 2-20, Gary 1-5. Jacksonville, J. Smith 5-55, Barlow 2-19, McCardell 2-13, Jones 1-21, Shelton 1-7.

MISSED FIELD GOAL ATTEMPTS—None.

INTERCEPTIONS—Jacksonville, Beasley 1-6, Boyer 1-5.

KICKOFF RETURNS—Denver, B. Miller 2-49, Watson 2-36. Jacksonville, Barlow 3-55, Whitted 1-18.

PUNT RETURNS—Denver, Watson 5-15. Jacksonville, Barlow 2-33.

SACKS—Denver, Pryce 3. Jacksonville, Brackens 1.

WEEK 15

RESULTS

KANSAS CITY 35, Pittsburgh 19
CAROLINA 41, San Francisco 24
BALTIMORE 31, New Orleans 8
Buffalo 31, ARIZONA 21
CHICAGO 28, Detroit 10
DENVER 36, Seattle 30 (OT)
INDIANAPOLIS 24, Washington 21
Jacksonville 24, CLEVELAND 14
MIAMI 12, San Diego 9
N.Y. Jets 22, DALLAS 21
OAKLAND 45, Tampa Bay 0
PHILADELPHIA 24, New England 9
ST. LOUIS 31, N.Y. Giants 10
TENNESSEE 30, Atlanta 17
MINNESOTA 24, Green Bay 20
Open date: Cincinnati

STANDINGS

AFC EAST
	W	L	T	Pct.
Indianapolis	12	2	0	.857
Buffalo	9	5	0	.643
Miami	9	5	0	.643
New England	7	7	0	.500
N.Y. Jets	6	8	0	.429

AFC CENTRAL
	W	L	T	Pct.
Jacksonville	13	1	0	.929
Tennessee	11	3	0	.786
Baltimore	7	7	0	.500
Pittsburgh	5	9	0	.357
Cincinnati	4	10	0	.286
Cleveland	2	13	0	.133

AFC WEST
	W	L	T	Pct.
Kansas City	9	5	0	.643
Seattle	8	6	0	.571
Oakland	7	7	0	.500
San Diego	6	8	0	.429
Denver	5	9	0	.357

NFC EAST
	W	L	T	Pct.
Washington	8	6	0	.571
Dallas	7	7	0	.500
N.Y. Giants	7	7	0	.500
Arizona	6	8	0	.429
Philadelphia	4	11	0	.267

NFC CENTRAL
	W	L	T	Pct.
Tampa Bay	9	5	0	.643
Detroit	8	6	0	.571
Minnesota	8	6	0	.571
Green Bay	7	7	0	.500
Chicago	6	8	0	.429

NFC WEST
	W	L	T	Pct.
St. Louis	12	2	0	.857
Carolina	7	7	0	.500
San Francisco	4	10	0	.286
Atlanta	3	11	0	.214
New Orleans	2	12	0	.143

HIGHLIGHTS

Hero of the week: Carolina quarterback Steve Beuerlein had one of the best games of his career, completing 27-of-38 passes for 368 yards, four touchdowns and no interceptions. He helped the Panthers score at least 30 points for the seventh time this season as they beat San Francisco, 41-24.

Goat of the week: Patriots quarterback Drew Bledsoe threw four interceptions and no TDs against the Eagles. He also was sacked six times as New England lost to Philadelphia, 24-9. Bledsoe increased his interception total to 15 in his last six games.

Sub of the week: Eagles quarterback Koy Detmer, filling in for injured starter Donovan McNabb and backup Doug Pederson, threw a career-high three touchdown passes in the victory over New England. Detmer completed 10-of-29 passes for 181 yards, and his TD passes covered 50, 44 and 11 yards.

Comeback of the week: Dallas led the Jets, 21-13, early in the third quarter, but quarterback Ray Lucas led New York on a 62-yard scoring drive a few minutes later. The Jets' two-point conversion failed, and they trailed 21-19 until late in the fourth quarter. With 1:39 remaining, John Hall booted a 37-yard field goal to give the Jets a 22-21 victory.

Blowout of the week: Oakland shocked Tampa Bay, 45-0, handing the Bucs their worst loss ever. It also was the Raiders' biggest margin of victory since they joined the NFL in 1970. The Buccaneers' vaunted defense allowed 400 total yards, and the offense, led by rookie quarterback Shaun King, never came close to scoring. Oakland running backs Napoleon Kaufman and Tyrone Wheatley both rushed for more than 100 yards. Meanwhile, Tampa Bay's Warrick Dunn and Mike Alstott managed only 17 yards combined.

Nail-biter of the week: Miami's Olindo Mare and San Diego's John Carney both made their first three field goal attempts on Sunday. But it was their respective fourth attempts that made the difference. Mare kicked a 31-yarder with 3:22 left to give the Dolphins a 12-9 lead. But Carney's 36-yard attempt with 10 seconds remaining bounced off the left upright, giving Miami the victory. Mare's four field goals improved his season total to 37, tying the all-time record set by Carolina's John Kasay in 1996.

Hit of the week: In the third minute of overtime, Denver cornerback Ray Crockett sacked Seattle's Jon Kitna on an undetected blitz to force a fumble, and linebacker Glenn Cadrez scooped up the ball and ran 37 yards for the game-winning touchdown. The Broncos' 36-30 victory continued their dominance against Seattle at Mile High Stadium, where the Seahawks have not won since 1995 and have won just once in their last 11 games.

Oddity of the week: In one of the most disturbing incidents of the season, 6-7, 350-pound Cleveland offensive tackle Orlando Brown became enraged when referee Jeff Triplette threw his penalty flag—weighted with BBs—toward the line of scrimmage and accidentally struck Brown in the right eye. After staggering toward the bench, Brown suddenly turned and stormed back onto the field. He gestured toward his eye as he approached Triplette, then flattened him with a two-handed shove to the chest. As Triplette was lying on the ground, Brown had to be restrained by teammates.

Top rusher: Olandis Gary gained a career-high 183 yards on 22 carries in Denver's 36-30 overtime victory against Seattle.

Top passer: Steve Beuerlein was 27-of-38 for 368 yards, four touchdowns and no interceptions in Carolina's 41-24 win over San Francisco.

Top receiver: Marcus Robinson caught 11 passes for 170 yards and three touchdowns as the Bears defeated the Lions, 28-10.

Notes: Marvin Harrison's nine-catch, 117-yard game for Indianapolis was his eighth 100-yard game, breaking Raymond Berry's 1960 club record. ... The Jaguars' six sacks raised their season total to a team-record 54. ... Tennessee defensive end Jevon Kearse had two sacks against Atlanta and raised his season total to 13.5, breaking the NFL record for sacks by a rookie set by Simeon Rice in 1996. ... With three field goals and three PATs, Titans kicker Al Del Greco became the NFL's No. 9 all-time scorer (1,446), passing Jim Turner (1,439). ... Rams running back

1999 REVIEW Week 15

– 201 –

Marshall Faulk's 165 combined yards gave him 2,065 for the season and made him only the second player in NFL history to achieve that feat for two different teams. The other was Eric Dickerson, who coincidentally also played for the Rams and Colts. ... Raiders wide receiver Tim Brown scored his 75th career touchdown, one shy of Fred Biletnikoff's club record. ... The Seahawks lost their fourth game in a row, marking the first time in Mike Holmgren's 14 years as either an NFL assistant or head coach that his team had lost four consecutive games. ... Emmitt Smith's second-quarter touchdown against the Jets was memorable for three reasons: it was the 146th touchdown of his career, moving him past Marcus Allen for No. 2 on the career list, behind Jerry Rice; it made him the leading scorer in Cowboys' history, surpassing Rafael Septien; and it moved him past former Cowboy Tony Dorsett for No. 8 on the NFL's all-time combined net yardage list.

Quote of the week: Orlando Brown's teammate, Cleveland defensive end Derrick Alexander, dismissed any notions that Brown needs anger counseling: "If that's the case, then all of us need help on Sunday because we're out there trying to kill each other."

GAME SUMMARIES

CHIEFS 35, STEELERS 19
Saturday, December 18

Pittsburgh	10	3	0	6	—19
Kansas City	7	14	7	7	—35

First Quarter
Pit.—Edwards 12 pass from Tomczak (K. Brown kick), 3:50.
K.C.—Gonzalez 15 pass from Grbac (Stoyanovich kick), 6:17.
Pit.—FG, K. Brown 42, 9:53.
Second Quarter
K.C.—Edwards 28 interception return (Stoyanovich kick), 4:44.
K.C.—Gonzalez 2 pass from Grbac (Stoyanovich kick), 10:43.
Pit.—FG, K. Brown 47, 14:57.
Third Quarter
K.C.—Alexander 82 run (Stoyanovich kick), 13:31.
Fourth Quarter
K.C.—Morris 10 run (Stoyanovich kick), 13:04.
Pit.—Shaw 11 pass from Tomczak (pass failed), 14:26.
Attendance—78,697.

	Pittsburgh	Kansas City
First downs	21	16
Rushes-yards	28-107	32-218
Passing	269	145
Punt returns	6-51	2-33
Kickoff returns	6-99	4-46
Interception returns	0-0	4-59
Comp.-att.-int.	23-46-4	12-22-0
Sacked-yards lost	2-9	1-4
Punts	5-41	7-42
Fumbles-lost	1-0	1-0
Penalties-yards	10-65	8-60
Time of possession	33:45	26:15

INDIVIDUAL STATISTICS
RUSHING—Pittsburgh, Bettis 19-63, Huntley 6-37, Tomczak 2-2, Stewart 1-5. Kansas City, Morris 17-71, Richardson 11-57, Alexander 1-82, Horn 1-9, Cloud 1-0, Grbac 1-(minus 1).
PASSING—Pittsburgh, Tomczak 23-46-4-278. Kansas City, Grbac 12-22-0-149.
RECEIVING—Pittsburgh, Edwards 5-58, Ward 4-41, Shaw 3-69, Huntley 3-33, Witman 2-25, Stewart 2-21, Lyons 2-16, Bettis 1-9, Bruener 1-5. Kansas City, Gonzalez 6-93, Alexander 2-20, Horn 1-23, Cloud 1-12, Morris 1-4, Richardson 1-(minus 3).

MISSED FIELD GOAL ATTEMPTS—Pittsburgh, K. Brown 49.
INTERCEPTIONS—Kansas City, Edwards 2-32, Tongue 1-27, Warfield 1-0.
KICKOFF RETURNS—Pittsburgh, Huntley 3-67, Lyons 1-17, Fuamatu-Ma'afala 1-9, Vrabel 1-6. Kansas City, Vanover 1-25, Johnson 1-11, Cloud 1-10, Manusky 1-0.
PUNT RETURNS—Pittsburgh, Shaw 3-36, Edwards 3-15. Kansas City, Horn 1-18, Vanover 1-15.
SACKS—Pittsburgh, Gildon 1. Kansas City, Patton 1, Thomas 1.

PANTHERS 41, 49ERS 24
Saturday, December 18

San Francisco	10	0	7	7	—24
Carolina	17	7	10	7	—41

First Quarter
Car.—Muhammad 8 pass from Beuerlein (Cunningham kick), 2:59.
S.F.—FG, Richey 37, 5:45.
Car.—Muhammad 14 pass from Beuerlein (Cunningham kick), 9:52.
Car.—FG, Cunningham 21, 13:08.
S.F.—Rice 48 pass from Garcia (Richey kick), 14:36.
Second Quarter
Car.—Floyd 1 run (Cunningham kick), 2:45.
Third Quarter
S.F.—Beasley 44 run (Richey kick), 4:42.
Car.—Jeffers 55 pass from Beuerlein (Cunningham kick), 6:27.
Car.—FG, Cunningham 43, 12:16.
Fourth Quarter
S.F.—Garner 17 pass from Garcia (Richey kick), 0:05.
Car.—Muhammad 7 pass from Beuerlein (Cunningham kick), 7:30.
Attendance—62,373.

	San Fran.	Carolina
First downs	18	25
Rushes-yards	18-100	26-90
Passing	297	362
Punt returns	1-1	0-0
Kickoff returns	6-128	3-18
Interception returns	0-0	1-5
Comp.-att.-int.	29-46-1	27-38-0
Sacked-yards lost	2-6	1-6
Punts	3-26	2-28
Fumbles-lost	2-0	0-0
Penalties-yards	7-55	6-40
Time of possession	27:40	32:20

INDIVIDUAL STATISTICS
RUSHING—San Francisco, Garner 14-39, Garcia 2-6, Beasley 1-44, Rice 1-11. Carolina, Lane 10-66, Johnson 9-10, Beuerlein 2-20, Floyd 2-3, Lewis 2-(minus 2), Jeffers 1-(minus 7).
PASSING—San Francisco, Garcia 29-46-1-303. Carolina, Beuerlein 27-38-0-368.
RECEIVING—San Francisco, Garner 9-62, Beasley 6-66, Owens 5-66, Clark 5-40, Rice 2-56, Harris 1-8, Stokes 1-5. Carolina, Muhammad 11-126, Jeffers 8-138, Walls 3-57, Lane 3-33, Hayes 1-10, Floyd 1-4.
MISSED FIELD GOAL ATTEMPTS—None.
INTERCEPTIONS—Carolina, Davis 1-5.
KICKOFF RETURNS—San Francisco, Preston 6-128. Carolina, Metcalf 2-13, Bates 1-5.
PUNT RETURNS—San Francisco, Preston 1-1.
SACKS—San Francisco, Wilkins 1. Carolina, Barrow 1, Peter 1.

JAGUARS 24, BROWNS 14
Sunday, December 19

Jacksonville	0	14	3	7	—24
Cleveland	0	7	7	0	—14

Second Quarter
Jac.—Jones 3 pass from Brunell (Hollis kick), 1:31.
Jac.—Brunell 9 run (Hollis kick), 6:47.
Cle.—Kirby 1 run (Dawson kick), 12:51.
Third Quarter
Jac.—FG, Hollis 41, 5:24.
Cle.—Chiaverini 10 pass from Detmer (Dawson kick), 13:40.
Fourth Quarter
Jac.—Taylor 41 run (Hollis kick), 4:50.
Attendance—72,038.

– 202 –

	Jacksonville	Cleveland
First downs	20	19
Rushes-yards	33-181	20-72
Passing	261	197
Punt returns	3-43	1-4
Kickoff returns	2-19	4-82
Interception returns	0-0	1-0
Comp.-att.-int.	21-33-1	24-41-0
Sacked-yards lost	1-6	6-44
Punts	3-43	8-43
Fumbles-lost	1-1	1-1
Penalties-yards	4-57	5-40
Time of possession	31:44	28:16

INDIVIDUAL STATISTICS

RUSHING—Jacksonville, Taylor 26-136, Howard 4-29, Brunell 3-16. Cleveland, Abdul-Jabbar 13-36, Kirby 4-14, Detmer 2-22, Couch 1-0.

PASSING—Jacksonville, Brunell 21-33-1-267. Cleveland, Detmer 13-24-0-153, Couch 10-16-0-86, Kirby 1-1-0-2.

RECEIVING—Jacksonville, J. Smith 8-134, McCardell 8-96, Jones 2-16, Taylor 2-13, Shelton 1-8. Cleveland, Chiaverini 10-108, Johnson 4-54, I. Smith 4-36, Edwards 2-10, Kirby 2-4, Davis 1-25, Abdul-Jabbar 1-4.

MISSED FIELD GOAL ATTEMPTS—Jacksonville, Hollis 49, 48.

INTERCEPTIONS—Cleveland, Little 1-0.

KICKOFF RETURNS—Jacksonville, Jackson 1-13, Whitted 1-6. Cleveland, Kirby 2-50, Hill 2-32.

PUNT RETURNS—Jacksonville, McCardell 3-43. Cleveland, Johnson 1-4.

SACKS—Jacksonville, Marts 1, Lake 1, Boyer 1, Walker 1, Brackens 1, Smeenge 1. Cleveland, Thierry 1.

TITANS 30, FALCONS 17

Sunday, December 19

Atlanta	7	7	3	0	—17
Tennessee	14	6	0	10	—30

First Quarter
Ten.—Sanders 48 pass from McNair (Del Greco kick), 3:11.
Atl.—German 16 pass from Kanell (Andersen kick), 8:54.
Ten.—Byrd 61 pass from Wycheck (Del Greco kick), 14:18.

Second Quarter
Ten.—FG, Del Greco 38, 4:06.
Atl.—German 6 pass from Kanell (Andersen kick), 13:32.
Ten.—FG, Del Greco 27, 14:47.

Third Quarter
Atl.—FG, Andersen 32, 7:21.

Fourth Quarter
Ten.—McNair 3 run (Del Greco kick), 0:41.
Ten.—FG, Del Greco 43, 8:32.
Attendance—66,196.

	Atlanta	Tennessee
First downs	23	14
Rushes-yards	18-65	28-131
Passing	282	268
Punt returns	4-36	2-15
Kickoff returns	7-92	4-69
Interception returns	0-0	3-7
Comp.-att.-int.	24-43-3	16-30-0
Sacked-yards lost	3-28	2-9
Punts	4-42	7-44
Fumbles-lost	3-3	2-0
Penalties-yards	5-46	14-90
Time of possession	29:13	30:47

INDIVIDUAL STATISTICS

RUSHING—Atlanta, Oxendine 12-41, Christian 3-20, Oliver 3-4. Tennessee, E. George 19-55, McNair 9-76.

PASSING—Atlanta, Kanell 18-29-2-237, Graziani 6-14-1-73. Tennessee, McNair 15-29-0-216, Wycheck 1-1-0-61.

RECEIVING—Atlanta, Christian 6-55, Mathis 5-79, Baker 5-66, Harris 3-45, German 3-35, Santiago 1-20, Oxendine 1-10. Tennessee, Sanders 5-100, E. George 4-26, Byrd 2-84, Wycheck 2-29, Thomas 1-26, Mason 1-8, Dyson 1-4.

MISSED FIELD GOAL ATTEMPTS—None.

INTERCEPTIONS—Tennessee, Sidney 2-5, Robertson 1-3.

KICKOFF RETURNS—Atlanta, Oliver 4-55, E. Williams 2-28, Kozlowski 1-9. Tennessee, Mason 4-69.

PUNT RETURNS—Atlanta, Oliver 4-36. Tennessee, Mason 2-15.

SACKS—Atlanta, Dronett 1, Hall 1. Tennessee, Kearse 2, Thornton 1.

RAVENS 31, SAINTS 8

Sunday, December 19

New Orleans	0	0	0	8	— 8
Baltimore	3	14	0	14	—31

First Quarter
Bal.—FG, Stover 36, 11:56.

Second Quarter
Bal.—Holmes 34 pass from Banks (Stover kick), 0:48.
Bal.—Armour 6 pass from Banks (Stover kick), 14:36.

Fourth Quarter
Bal.—Ismail 47 pass from Banks (Stover kick), 0:46.
N.O.—Poole 20 pass from Tolliver (Cleeland pass from Tolliver), 4:30.
Bal.—Harris 24 interception return (Stover kick), 13:11.
Attendance—67,597.

	New Orleans	Baltimore
First downs	8	15
Rushes-yards	16-11	24-61
Passing	237	274
Punt returns	1-3	7-34
Kickoff returns	6-111	2-41
Interception returns	4-18	4-74
Comp.-att.-int.	21-49-4	24-39-4
Sacked-yards lost	2-15	5-24
Punts	11-37	9-36
Fumbles-lost	2-0	0-0
Penalties-yards	6-48	7-60
Time of possession	28:30	31:30

INDIVIDUAL STATISTICS

RUSHING—New Orleans, Perry 11-11, Tolliver 2-2, Davis 1-2, Franklin 1-0, Philyaw 1-(minus 4). Baltimore, Rhett 11-21, Holmes 10-28, Evans 1-7, Banks 1-6, Case 1-(minus 1).

PASSING—New Orleans, Tolliver 16-35-3-207, Wuerffel 5-11-1-45, Hobert 0-3-0-0. Baltimore, Banks 24-36-3-298, Case 0-3-1-0.

RECEIVING—New Orleans, Kennison 5-67, Poole 4-51, Dawsey 3-73, Hastings 3-9, Philyaw 2-23, Davis 2-13, Cleeland 1-11, Perry 1-5. Baltimore, Ismail 7-115, Armour 4-50, Rhett 4-22, Holmes 3-44, Johnson 3-43, Collins 1-21, Evans 1-7, DeLong 1-(minus 4).

MISSED FIELD GOAL ATTEMPTS—None.

INTERCEPTIONS—New Orleans, Kelly 1-6, Kei. Mitchell 1-4, Ambrose 1-0, Knight 1-0. Baltimore, Woodson 1-31, Harris 1-24, R. Lewis 1-19, Starks 1-0.

KICKOFF RETURNS—New Orleans, Philyaw 6-111. Baltimore, Harris 2-41.

PUNT RETURNS—New Orleans, Kennison 1-3. Baltimore, J. Lewis 7-34.

SACKS—New Orleans, Glover 2, Fields 1, Whitehead 1. Baltimore, Smith 1, Burnett 0.5, McCrary 0.5.

RAMS 31, GIANTS 10

Sunday, December 19

N.Y. Giants	0	0	3	7	—10
St. Louis	3	7	7	14	—31

First Quarter
St.L.—FG, Wilkins 47, 11:36.

Second Quarter
St.L.—Hakim 3 pass from Warner (Wilkins kick), 1:29.

Third Quarter
NYG—FG, Blanchard 23, 4:52.
St.L.—Bush 45 interception return (Wilkins kick), 9:35.

Fourth Quarter
St.L.—Hakim 65 pass from Warner (Wilkins kick), 1:02.
St.L.—M. Jones 22 interception return (Wilkins kick), 7:50.
NYG—Hilliard 7 pass from Collins (Blanchard kick), 10:12.
Attendance—66,065.

	N.Y. Giants	St. Louis
First downs	20	19
Rushes-yards	19-67	27-100
Passing	261	312
Punt returns	1-2	2-12
Kickoff returns	5-117	2-31
Interception returns	0-0	2-67
Comp.-att.-int.	21-37-2	18-32-0
Sacked-yards lost	2-12	1-7
Punts	5-40	3-41

1999 REVIEW Week 15

	N.Y. Giants	St. Louis
Fumbles-lost	0-0	2-1
Penalties-yards	6-50	8-88
Time of possession	28:13	31:47

INDIVIDUAL STATISTICS

RUSHING—New York, Montgomery 12-41, Barber 5-33, Collins 1-(minus 1), Hilliard 1-(minus 6). St. Louis, Faulk 16-68, Holcombe 8-20, Warner 2-10, Hodgins 1-2.

PASSING—New York, Collins 21-37-2-273. St. Louis, Warner 18-32-0-319.

RECEIVING—New York, Toomer 9-162, Hilliard 5-51, Barber 3-43, Mitchell 2-16, Comella 2-1. St. Louis, Faulk 6-97, Holt 5-70, Hakim 3-79, Bruce 2-39, Proehl 1-30, R. Williams 1-4.

MISSED FIELD GOAL ATTEMPTS—New York, Blanchard 42. St. Louis, Wilkins 50.

INTERCEPTIONS—St. Louis, Bush 1-45, M. Jones 1-22.

KICKOFF RETURNS—New York, Levingston 2-52, Barber 2-42, Patten 1-23. St. Louis, Horne 2-31.

PUNT RETURNS—New York, Barber 1-2. St. Louis, Hakim 2-12.

SACKS—New York, Jones 1. St. Louis, Wistrom 1, Carter 1.

DOLPHINS 12, CHARGERS 9

Sunday, December 19

San Diego	0	3	0	6—	9
Miami	3	3	0	6—	12

First Quarter
Mia.—FG, Mare 32, 7:41.

Second Quarter
S.D.—FG, Carney 23, 0:03.
Mia.—FG, Mare 21, 9:32.

Fourth Quarter
S.D.—FG, Carney 22, 0:03.
S.D.—FG, Carney 31, 4:49.
Mia.—FG, Mare 30, 8:54.
Mia.—FG, Mare 31, 11:38.
Attendance—73,765.

	San Diego	Miami
First downs	13	11
Rushes-yards	21-26	23-53
Passing	160	231
Punt returns	4-23	5-23
Kickoff returns	2-39	4-98
Interception returns	0-0	0-0
Comp.-att.-int.	20-40-0	22-36-0
Sacked-yards lost	5-18	2-10
Punts	9-46	7-38
Fumbles-lost	3-1	3-2
Penalties-yards	4-40	11-106
Time of possession	29:19	30:41

INDIVIDUAL STATISTICS

RUSHING—San Diego, Means 9-8, Fletcher 5-12, Bynum 5-0, Harbaugh 2-6. Miami, Pritchett 15-38, Denson 5-13, Marino 2-(minus 2), Jacquet 1-4.

PASSING—San Diego, Harbaugh 20-40-0-178. Miami, Marino 22-36-0-241.

RECEIVING—San Diego, Fletcher 9-66, Ricks 3-29, F. Jones 2-10, McCrary 2-4, Davis 1-26, Penn 1-24, Bynum 1-13, J. Graham 1-6. Miami, Martin 8-86, Gadsden 4-83, Pritchett 3-22, Goodwin 2-17, Drayton 2-14, McDuffie 1-10, Green 1-7, Denson 1-2.

MISSED FIELD GOAL ATTEMPTS—San Diego, Carney 36.

INTERCEPTIONS—None.

KICKOFF RETURNS—San Diego, Bynum 2-39. Miami, Marion 4-98.

PUNT RETURNS—San Diego, C. Jones 4-23. Miami, Jacquet 4-19, McDuffie 1-4.

SACKS—San Diego, Parrella 1, Hand 1. Miami, Gardener 2, Owens 2, Bromell 0.5, Armstrong 0.5.

BRONCOS 36, SEAHAWKS 30

Sunday, December 19

Seattle	7	7	3	13	0—30
Denver	14	3	6	7	6—36

First Quarter
Den.—Watson 81 punt return (Elam kick), 2:09.
Sea.—Pritchard 16 pass from Kitna (Peterson kick), 4:17.
Den.—R. Smith 14 pass from Griese (Elam kick), 9:06.

Second Quarter
Den.—FG, Elam 28, 8:12.
Sea.—Watters 1 run (Peterson kick), 10:53.

Third Quarter
Den.—FG, Elam 46, 5:59.
Sea.—FG, Peterson 40, 9:19.
Den.—FG, Elam 33, 14:59.

Fourth Quarter
Sea.—FG, Peterson 32, 11:19.
Den.—Carswell 9 pass from Griese (Elam kick), 13:13.
Sea.—Mayes 36 pass from Kitna (Peterson kick), 14:06.
Sea.—FG, Peterson 45, 14:51.

Overtime
Den.—Cadrez 37 fumble return, 2:43.
Attendance—65,987.

	Seattle	Denver
First downs	19	26
Rushes-yards	17-114	33-260
Passing	250	170
Punt returns	1-6	5-110
Kickoff returns	7-171	7-133
Interception returns	2-0	0-0
Comp.-att.-int.	22-42-0	20-39-2
Sacked-yards lost	3-28	2-10
Punts	6-43	3-49
Fumbles-lost	2-2	1-0
Penalties-yards	12-118	8-62
Time of possession	28:12	34:31

INDIVIDUAL STATISTICS

RUSHING—Seattle, Watters 16-115, Galloway 1-(minus 1). Denver, Gary 22-183, Loville 7-25, Griese 4-52.

PASSING—Seattle, Kitna 22-42-0-278. Denver, Griese 20-39-2-180.

RECEIVING—Seattle, Dawkins 5-88, Mayes 4-70, Galloway 3-34, Watters 3-20, R. Brown 3-20, Pritchard 2-27, Fauria 1-11, Mili 1-8. Denver, R. Smith 7-82, McCaffrey 3-40, Carswell 2-19, Gary 2-16, Loville 2-7, D. Smith 2-7, Griffith 1-8, Chamberlain 1-1.

MISSED FIELD GOAL ATTEMPTS—Denver, Elam 64, 45.

INTERCEPTIONS—Seattle, W. Williams 1-0, Springs 1-0.

KICKOFF RETURNS—Seattle, Rogers 5-102, Joseph 1-61, Fauria 1-8. Denver, Watson 5-93, B. Miller 1-30, Loville 1-10.

PUNT RETURNS—Seattle, Rogers 1-6. Denver, Watson 5-110.

SACKS—Seattle, Daniels 2. Denver, Crockett 1, Tanuvasa 1, Pryce 1.

JETS 22, COWBOYS 21

Sunday, December 19

N.Y. Jets	6	7	6	3—	22
Dallas	0	14	7	0—	21

First Quarter
NYJ—FG, Hall 47, 3:19.
NYJ—FG, Hall 33, 8:50.

Second Quarter
Dal.—E. Smith 14 pass from Aikman (Murray kick), 2:16.
NYJ—Anderson 1 pass from Lucas (Hall kick), 7:18.
Dal.—Bjornson 20 run (Murray kick), 10:44.

Third Quarter
Dal.—Ismail 27 run (Murray kick), 3:42.
NYJ—Spence 2 pass from Lucas (run failed), 6:44.

Fourth Quarter
NYJ—FG, Hall 37, 13:25.
Attendance—64,271.

	N.Y. Jets	Dallas
First downs	19	16
Rushes-yards	35-126	31-195
Passing	229	152
Punt returns	3-18	2-26
Kickoff returns	4-100	5-110
Interception returns	2-30	1-10
Comp.-att.-int.	20-35-1	12-28-2
Sacked-yards lost	0-0	1-6
Punts	4-48	7-40
Fumbles-lost	1-1	0-0
Penalties-yards	3-20	8-92
Time of possession	30:41	29:19

INDIVIDUAL STATISTICS
RUSHING—New York, Martin 26-113, Lucas 5-10, Anderson 2-5, Parmalee 1-6, K. Johnson 1-(minus 8). Dallas, E. Smith 19-110, Warren 5-20, Thomas 4-22, Ismail 2-23, Bjornson 1-20.
PASSING—New York, Lucas 20-34-1-229, Tupa 0-1-0-0. Dallas, Aikman 12-28-2-158.
RECEIVING—New York, Chrebet 8-108, K. Johnson 6-96, Parmalee 2-6, Ward 1-10, Martin 1-6, Spence 1-2, Anderson 1-1. Dallas, E. Smith 3-36, Brazzell 2-62, LaFleur 2-18, Warren 2-6, Ismail 1-23, Ogden 1-9, Bjornson 1-4.
MISSED FIELD GOAL ATTEMPTS—New York, Hall 49.
INTERCEPTIONS—New York, Stoutmire 1-30, V. Green 1-0. Dallas, Godfrey 1-10.
KICKOFF RETURNS—New York, Stone 3-67, Glenn 1-33. Dallas, Tucker 4-89, Sanders 1-21.
PUNT RETURNS—New York, Ward 3-18. Dallas, Sanders 2-26.
SACKS—New York, Gordon 1.

BEARS 28, LIONS 10
Sunday, December 19

Detroit	3	0	0	7	10
Chicago	0	14	7	7	28

First Quarter
Det.—FG, Hanson 24, 10:25.
Second Quarter
Chi.—Engram 3 pass from McNown (Boniol kick), 12:12.
Chi.—M. Robinson 1 pass from McNown (Boniol kick), 14:53.
Third Quarter
Chi.—M. Robinson 36 pass from McNown (Boniol kick), 8:04.
Fourth Quarter
Chi.—M. Robinson 42 pass from McNown (Boniol kick), 6:38.
Det.—Batch 12 run (Hanson kick), 11:25.
Attendance—66,944.

	Detroit	Chicago
First downs	19	27
Rushes-yards	19-103	32-104
Passing	236	292
Punt returns	0-0	1-19
Kickoff returns	5-76	2-33
Interception returns	2-37	3-34
Comp.-att.-int.	23-40-3	27-36-2
Sacked-yards lost	3-17	2-9
Punts	2-46	3-28
Fumbles-lost	1-1	2-0
Penalties-yards	6-43	8-62
Time of possession	27:39	32:21

INDIVIDUAL STATISTICS
RUSHING—Detroit, Hill 13-77, Schlesinger 3-7, Batch 1-12, Frerotte 1-4, Irvin 1-3. Chicago, Enis 22-69, McNown 9-34, Milburn 1-(minus 1).
PASSING—Detroit, Frerotte 17-30-3-158, Batch 6-10-0-95. Chicago, McNown 27-36-2-301.
RECEIVING—Detroit, Morton 8-100, Sloan 5-49, Irvin 4-34, Crowell 3-41, Moore 2-24, Hill 1-5. Chicago, M. Robinson 11-170, Engram 10-94, Booker 2-8, Allred 1-12, Wetnight 1-7, Enis 1-6, Conway 1-4.
MISSED FIELD GOAL ATTEMPTS—Detroit, Hanson 50. Chicago, Boniol 30.
INTERCEPTIONS—Detroit, Rice 2-37. Chicago, Hudson 1-28, Flanigan 1-6, Cousin 1-0.
KICKOFF RETURNS—Detroit, Howard 4-64, Olivo 1-12. Chicago, Milburn 2-33.
PUNT RETURNS—Chicago, Milburn 1-19.
SACKS—Detroit, Jones 1, Porcher 1. Chicago, Colvin 1, B. Robinson 1, Simmons 1.

COLTS 24, REDSKINS 21
Sunday, December 19

Washington	3	10	0	8	21
Indianapolis	7	3	0	14	24

First Quarter
Ind.—James 37 pass from Manning (Vanderjagt kick), 8:12.
Was.—FG, Conway 23, 12:49.
Second Quarter
Was.—Connell 48 pass from B. Johnson (Conway kick), 3:40.
Ind.—FG, Vanderjagt 43, 7:40.
Was.—FG, Conway 32, 13:06.

Fourth Quarter
Ind.—Dilger 1 pass from Manning (Vanderjagt kick), 0:04.
Ind.—James 2 run (Vanderjagt kick), 9:03.
Was.—Mitchell 6 run (Westbrook pass from B. Johnson), 13:36.
Attendance—57,013.

	Washington	Indianapolis
First downs	21	24
Rushes-yards	32-151	23-88
Passing	208	291
Punt returns	3-33	2-4
Kickoff returns	3-72	4-100
Interception returns	1-0	0-0
Comp.-att.-int.	16-30-0	23-37-1
Sacked-yards lost	4-29	1-7
Punts	4-45	3-51
Fumbles-lost	2-0	3-2
Penalties-yards	6-60	5-62
Time of possession	31:16	28:44

INDIVIDUAL STATISTICS
RUSHING—Washington, Davis 14-70, Hicks 11-39, Mitchell 5-42, B. Johnson 2-0. Indianapolis, James 22-89, Manning 1-(minus 1).
PASSING—Washington, B. Johnson 16-30-0-237. Indianapolis, Manning 23-37-1-298.
RECEIVING—Washington, Mitchell 6-61, Connell 4-97, Fryar 2-23, Centers 2-16, Alexander 1-25, Westbrook 1-15. Indianapolis, Harrison 9-117, James 4-59, Pollard 3-50, Dilger 3-35, Green 2-19, Wilkins 2-18.
MISSED FIELD GOAL ATTEMPTS—Washington, Conway 49.
INTERCEPTIONS—Washington, Barber 1-0.
KICKOFF RETURNS—Washington, Mitchell 2-53, Thrash 1-19. Indianapolis, Wilkins 4-100.
PUNT RETURNS—Washington, Mitchell 3-33. Indianapolis, Wilkins 2-4.
SACKS—Washington, McMillian 1. Indianapolis, Bratzke 3, Bennett 1.

EAGLES 24, PATRIOTS 9
Sunday, December 19

New England	0	6	3	0	9
Philadelphia	10	7	7	0	24

First Quarter
Phi.—FG, N. Johnson 43, 0:50.
Phi.—Small 50 pass from Detmer (N. Johnson kick), 11:26.
Second Quarter
N.E.—FG, Vinatieri 23, 0:03.
N.E.—FG, Vinatieri 43, 11:19.
Phi.—Small 11 pass from Detmer (N. Johnson kick), 11:58.
Third Quarter
N.E.—FG, Vinatieri 46, 4:43.
Phi.—Jells 44 pass from Detmer (N. Johnson kick), 13:52.
Attendance—65,475.

	New England	Philadelphia
First downs	20	11
Rushes-yards	27-62	38-122
Passing	288	181
Punt returns	4-45	4-44
Kickoff returns	5-108	3-61
Interception returns	2-1	4-114
Comp.-att.-int.	23-49-4	10-29-2
Sacked-yards lost	6-43	0-0
Punts	6-50	11-33
Fumbles-lost	5-3	3-1
Penalties-yards	3-15	7-85
Time of possession	32:52	27:08

INDIVIDUAL STATISTICS
RUSHING—New England, Allen 14-31, Warren 9-22, Bledsoe 2-7, Ellison 1-2, Floyd 1-0. Philadelphia, Staley 29-93, Bieniemy 3-12, Watson 3-11, Detmer 2-(minus 2), Caldwell 1-8.
PASSING—New England, Bledsoe 23-49-4-331. Philadelphia, Detmer 10-29-2-181.
RECEIVING—New England, Brown 5-105, Ellison 4-50, Glenn 4-27, Warren 3-31, Coates 2-42, Allen 2-14, Jefferson 1-41, Rutledge 1-12, Brisby 1-9. Philadelphia, Small 3-62, Brown 3-60, Jells 1-44, Smith 1-14, Lewis 1-4, C. Parker 1-(minus 3).
MISSED FIELD GOAL ATTEMPTS—New England, Vinatieri 56. Philadelphia, Akers 51.
INTERCEPTIONS—New England, Bruschi 1-1, Serwanga 1-0. Philadelphia, Vincent 2-0, Harris 1-84, Trotter 1-30.

— 205 —

KICKOFF RETURNS—New England, Simmons 4-95, Ellison 1-13. Philadelphia, Rossum 3-61.
PUNT RETURNS—New England, Brown 4-45. Philadelphia, Rossum 4-44.
SACKS—Philadelphia, Mamula 3, W. Thomas 1, Dawkins 1, T. Williams 1.

RAIDERS 45, BUCCANEERS 0
Sunday, December 19

Tampa Bay	0	0	0	0—	0
Oakland	10	7	21	7—	45

First Quarter
Oak.—Brown 20 pass from Gannon (Nedney kick), 3:58.
Oak.—FG, Nedney 26, 13:02.
Second Quarter
Oak.—Wheatley 30 run (Nedney kick), 11:09.
Third Quarter
Oak.—Johnstone 13 fumble return (Nedney kick), 1:42.
Oak.—Kaufman 17 run (Nedney kick), 5:49.
Oak.—Wheatley 3 run (Nedney kick), 11:43.
Fourth Quarter
Oak.—Kaufman 75 run (Nedney kick), 4:13.
Attendance—46,395.

	Tampa Bay	Oakland
First downs	9	21
Rushes-yards	19-34	37-262
Passing	103	138
Punt returns	5-49	5-29
Kickoff returns	6-102	1-11
Interception returns	0-0	1-2
Comp.-att.-int.	17-29-1	15-28-0
Sacked-yards lost	4-39	1-3
Punts	9-45	6-41
Fumbles-lost	2-2	0-0
Penalties-yards	9-60	3-35
Time of possession	27:49	32:11

INDIVIDUAL STATISTICS
RUSHING—Tampa Bay, Dunn 7-11, Alstott 7-6, Abdullah 4-12, King 1-5. Oakland, Wheatley 19-111, Kaufman 8-122, Crockett 8-32, Hoying 2-(minus 3).
PASSING—Tampa Bay, King 17-29-1-142. Oakland, Gannon 15-26-0-141, Hoying 0-2-0-0.
RECEIVING—Tampa Bay, Dunn 5-36, Williams 4-44, Moore 3-26, Green 2-20, Emanuel 1-10, Alstott 1-4, McLeod 1-2. Oakland, Brown 4-47, Jett 4-42, Dudley 2-30, Mickens 1-9, Crockett 1-7, Ritchie 1-4, Kaufman 1-1, Wheatley 1-1.
MISSED FIELD GOAL ATTEMPTS—None.
INTERCEPTIONS—Oakland, Mincy 1-2.
KICKOFF RETURNS—Tampa Bay, Anthony 5-87, Dunn 1-15. Oakland, Kaufman 1-11.
PUNT RETURNS—Tampa Bay, Williams 3-29, Green 2-20. Oakland, Gordon 5-29.
SACKS—Tampa Bay, Sapp 1. Oakland, Barton 1, Jackson 1, Gordon 1, Team 1.

BILLS 31, CARDINALS 21
Sunday, December 19

Buffalo	14	0	3	14—	31
Arizona	0	14	0	7—	21

First Quarter
Buf.—Moulds 15 pass from Flutie (Christie kick), 3:24.
Buf.—Linton 6 run (Christie kick), 13:57.
Second Quarter
Ariz.—Bates 1 run (Jacke kick), 5:29.
Ariz.—Bates 2 run (Jacke kick), 13:45.
Third Quarter
Buf.—FG, Christie 33, 10:53.
Fourth Quarter
Buf.—Riemersma 4 pass from Flutie (Christie kick), 11:59.
Ariz.—Moore 26 pass from Plummer (Jacke kick), 13:11.
Buf.—Jones 37 kickoff return (Christie kick), 13:16.
Attendance—64,337.

	Buffalo	Arizona
First downs	25	14
Rushes-yards	41-159	21-70
Passing	217	108
Punt returns	2-18	2-45
Kickoff returns	4-89	6-129
Interception returns	1-0	2-29
Comp.-att.-int.	21-32-2	11-29-1
Sacked-yards lost	2-22	2-11
Punts	3-37	6-42
Fumbles-lost	0-0	0-0
Penalties-yards	4-58	5-20
Time of possession	39:30	20:30

INDIVIDUAL STATISTICS
RUSHING—Buffalo, Linton 21-81, Thomas 13-53, Flutie 7-25. Arizona, Murrell 12-47, Bates 8-24, Plummer 1-(minus 1).
PASSING—Buffalo, Flutie 21-32-2-239. Arizona, Plummer 11-29-1-119.
RECEIVING—Buffalo, Moulds 6-73, Riemersma 5-62, Reed 3-42, P. Price 3-34, K. Williams 2-19, Gash 1-7, Thomas 1-2. Arizona, Sanders 5-57, Moore 2-38, Hardy 2-6, Boston 1-13, Murrell 1-5.
MISSED FIELD GOAL ATTEMPTS—None.
INTERCEPTIONS—Buffalo, Greer 1-0. Arizona, Knight 1-16, Bennett 1-13.
KICKOFF RETURNS—Buffalo, K. Williams 3-52, Jones 1-37. Arizona, Bates 6-129.
PUNT RETURNS—Buffalo, K. Williams 2-18. Arizona, Cody 2-45.
SACKS—Buffalo, Hansen 1, Wiley 1. Arizona, Rice 1, Sapp 1.

VIKINGS 24, PACKERS 20
Monday, December 20

Green Bay	0	13	0	7—	20
Minnesota	0	10	7	7—	24

Second Quarter
Min.—FG, Anderson 42, 1:04.
G.B.—Levens 1 run (Longwell kick), 6:46.
G.B.—FG, Longwell 26, 9:39.
Min.—Moss 57 pass from George (Anderson kick), 10:43.
G.B.—FG, Longwell 22, 14:57.
Third Quarter
Min.—Moss 1 pass from George (Anderson kick), 13:15.
Fourth Quarter
G.B.—Thomason 9 pass from Hasselbeck (Longwell kick), 2:29.
Min.—Hoard 1 run (Anderson kick), 6:02.
Attendance—64,203.

	Green Bay	Minnesota
First downs	20	15
Rushes-yards	28-107	26-76
Passing	212	229
Punt returns	2-15	4-35
Kickoff returns	3-62	4-119
Interception returns	0-0	2-11
Comp.-att.-int.	23-40-2	16-29-0
Sacked-yards lost	4-26	1-29
Punts	7-43	6-47
Fumbles-lost	3-1	3-2
Penalties-yards	6-57	11-85
Time of possession	33:26	26:34

INDIVIDUAL STATISTICS
RUSHING—Green Bay, Levens 26-99, Favre 2-8. Minnesota, Smith 19-54, Hoard 6-5, George 1-17.
PASSING—Green Bay, Favre 22-39-2-229, Hasselbeck 1-1-0-9. Minnesota, George 16-29-0-258.
RECEIVING—Green Bay, Schroeder 6-71, Freeman 5-54, Levens 4-21, Bradford 3-43, Thomason 2-31, Henderson 2-7, Hall 1-11. Minnesota, Moss 5-131, Reed 5-73, Hatchette 4-40, Hoard 2-14.
MISSED FIELD GOAL ATTEMPTS—None.
INTERCEPTIONS—Minnesota, Wright 1-11, Griffith 1-0.
KICKOFF RETURNS—Green Bay, Mitchell 3-62. Minnesota, Tate 4-119.
PUNT RETURNS—Green Bay, Jordan 1-8, Edwards 1-7. Minnesota, Moss 4-35.
SACKS—Green Bay, K. McKenzie 1. Minnesota, Rudd 1, Hitchcock 1, Doleman 1, T. Williams 1.

WEEK 16

RESULTS

NEW ORLEANS 31, Dallas 24
Denver 17, DETROIT 7
ATLANTA 37, Arizona 14
BALTIMORE 22, Cincinnati 0
Buffalo 13, NEW ENGLAND 10 (OT)
Indianapolis 29, CLEVELAND 28
Minnesota 34, N.Y. GIANTS 17
PITTSBURGH 30, Carolina 20
ST. LOUIS 34, Chicago 12
SAN DIEGO 23, Oakland 20
SEATTLE 23, Kansas City 14
TAMPA BAY 29, Green Bay 10
TENNESSEE 41, Jacksonville 14
Washington 26, SAN FRANCISCO 20 (OT)
N.Y. Jets 38, MIAMI 31
Open date: Philadelphia

STANDINGS

AFC EAST
	W	L	T	Pct.
Indianapolis	13	2	0	.867
Buffalo	10	5	0	.667
Miami	9	6	0	.600
New England	7	8	0	.467
N.Y. Jets	7	8	0	.467

AFC CENTRAL
	W	L	T	Pct.
Jacksonville	13	2	0	.867
Tennessee	12	3	0	.800
Baltimore	8	7	0	.533
Pittsburgh	6	9	0	.400
Cincinnati	4	11	0	.267
Cleveland	2	14	0	.125

AFC WEST
	W	L	T	Pct.
Kansas City	9	6	0	.600
Seattle	9	6	0	.600
Oakland	7	8	0	.467
San Diego	7	8	0	.467
Denver	6	9	0	.400

NFC EAST
	W	L	T	Pct.
Washington	9	6	0	.600
Dallas	7	8	0	.467
N.Y. Giants	7	8	0	.467
Arizona	6	9	0	.400
Philadelphia	4	11	0	.267

NFC CENTRAL
	W	L	T	Pct.
Tampa Bay	10	5	0	.667
Minnesota	9	6	0	.600
Detroit	8	7	0	.533
Green Bay	7	8	0	.467
Chicago	6	9	0	.400

NFC WEST
	W	L	T	Pct.
St. Louis	13	2	0	.867
Carolina	7	8	0	.467
Atlanta	4	11	0	.267
San Francisco	4	11	0	.267
New Orleans	3	12	0	.200

HIGHLIGHTS

Hero of the week: Tennessee quarterback Steve McNair, who threw a career-high five touchdown passes in leading the Titans to a surprisingly easy 41-14 win over once-beaten Jacksonville. In addition to completing 23 of 33 passes overall, McNair completed 9 of 10 passes on third down against the league's No. 2-ranked defense. He accounted for the Titans' two longest offensive plays of the season with touchdown passes of 65 and 62 yards.

Goat of the week: New England kicker Adam Vinatieri, who missed a potential game-winning 33-yard field goal with six seconds left in what became a 13-10 overtime loss to Buffalo. Given a chance to make amends, Vinatieri missed a 44-yard attempt on the Patriots' first possession of overtime. That left the door open for Steve Christie, who later hit a 23-yard field goal to win the game for Buffalo.

Sub of the week: New Orleans quarterback Jake Delhomme, playing in his first regular-season NFL game, threw two touchdown passes and ran for another score in leading the Saints to a 31-24 upset win over Dallas. Delhomme, who played two years in NFL Europe but had never suited up for an NFL game, had been signed by the Saints four weeks earlier.

Comeback of the week: Trailing by nine points at the start of the fourth quarter against a team that had won just two games all season, the Indianapolis Colts rallied to beat Cleveland, 29-28, on Mike Vanderjagt's 21-yard field goal with four seconds left. Peyton Manning was superb in the final quarter, completing 10 of 11 passes on two scoring drives and picking up a pair of key first downs on scrambles.

Blowout of the week: Although the final score might indicate otherwise, the Rams had no trouble dispatching the Bears, 34-12, at the Trans World Dome. Kurt Warner completed 24 of 35 passes for 334 yards and three touchdowns in only 2½ quarters to help the Rams build a 31-0 lead. Marshall Faulk did not play after St. Louis' first offensive possession of the second half, but still finished with a career-high 258 total yards.

Nail-biter of the week: Needing a win to clinch their first division title since 1991, the Washington Redskins erased a 20-10 fourth-quarter deficit and beat San Francisco, 26-20, in overtime. The game was tied 20-20 when 49ers rookie Terry Jackson fumbled at the Washington 22-yard line with 1:38 left in regulation time. In the extra period the Redskins drove 78 yards in four plays to score the game-winning touchdown on a 33-yard pass from Brad Johnson to Larry Centers.

Hit of the week: On the first play of the third quarter in a scoreless game, Denver quarterback Brian Griese completed a 17-yard pass to Ed McCaffrey at the Broncos 40-yard line. Lions defensive back Ron Rice hit McCaffrey in the head while he was down, and the 15-yard penalty put the ball on the Lions' 45. On the next play rookie Olandis Gary broke off left tackle, made a nice move to avoid a tackler at the 10 and scored the game's first touchdown.

Oddity of the week: The Raiders scored on their first two possessions of each half in a 23-20 loss to the Chargers—and at no other time.

Top rusher: Gary carried 29 times for 185 yards in Denver's 17-7 win at Detroit.

Top passer: Johnson completed 32 of 47 passes for 471 yards and two touchdowns in Washington's 26-20 OT win at San Francisco.

Top receiver: Faulk caught 12 passes for 204 yards and one TD in the Rams' victory over Chicago.

Notes: In addition to snapping an 11-game winning streak by Jacksonville, Tennessee improved its own record to 7-0 in games in which it scored on its opening possession. ... Eddie George joined Earl Campbell, Eric Dickerson and Barry Sanders as the only players to rush for 1,200 or more yards in each of their first four NFL seasons. ... The Colts (13-2) became the first team to win 10 more games than the season before (3-13). ... Indy's Edgerrin James became the first rookie to have 10 100-yard rushing games. ... Michael McCrary's three sacks for Baltimore against Cincinnati gave him 47 sacks in his last 53 games, the most of any player during that span. ... The Cowboys were penalized 11 times in their loss to the Saints, including a holding penalty that wiped out a 97-yard kickoff return. ... Marvin

Harrison set a Colts record with 14 receptions in one game. ... Faulk joined Roger Craig as the only players to rush for 1,000 yards and catch passes for 1,000 yards in the same season. ... Washington's Brian Mitchell moved past Mel Gray to become the NFL's all-time leader in combined kick-return yards. ... The Vikings gained 146 yards on 18 plays in the second half of their 34-17 win over the Giants. ... A week after giving up 262 rushing yards in a 45-0 loss to the Raiders, the Bucs held Green Bay to 12 rushing yards in a 29-10 win. ... There were 20,172 no-shows at the Carolina-Pittsburgh game, where the wind-chill factor at game time was near zero. The crowd of 39,428 was the smallest for a Steelers home game since Bill Cowher became coach in 1992. ... The Seahawks' 23-14 win over Kansas City marked their last regular-season game at the Kingdome. It also was the Seahawks' 100th regular-season victory there. ... Tennessee and St. Louis wound up the season with the NFL's only unbeaten home records. ... Dan Marino's three TD passes against the Jets gave him 72 in his career against New York, the most touchdown passes by any quarterback against any team in NFL history.

Quote of the week: Dallas safety Darren Woodson, on losing to Delhomme and the 2-12 Saints: "They haven't played well all season. We didn't know the quarterback. We figured he wouldn't be that good. But he was."

GAME SUMMARIES

SAINTS 31, COWBOYS 24
Friday, December 24

Dallas	0	7	17	0	—24
New Orleans	10	0	7	14	—31

First Quarter
N.O.—FG, Brien 32, 10:35.
N.O.—Poole 8 pass from Delhomme (Brien kick), 13:22.
Second Quarter
Dal.—E. Smith 1 run (Murray kick), 4:24.
Third Quarter
Dal.—Tucker 20 pass from Aikman (Murray kick), 4:26.
Dal.—FG, Murray 33, 9:04.
N.O.—Kennison 51 pass from Delhomme (Brien kick), 9:50.
Dal.—LaFleur 3 pass from Aikman (Murray kick), 14:44.
Fourth Quarter
N.O.—Delhomme 4 run (Brien kick), 3:44.
N.O.—Weary 58 fumble return (Brien kick), 5:01.
Attendance—47,835.

	Dallas	New Orleans
First downs	24	18
Rushes-yards	26-122	29-61
Passing	246	249
Punt returns	1-0	2-7
Kickoff returns	6-203	5-111
Interception returns	1-5	2-22
Comp.-att.-int.	23-39-2	16-28-1
Sacked-yards lost	0-0	3-29
Punts	5-43	5-42
Fumbles-lost	1-1	2-1
Penalties-yards	11-86	6-32
Time of possession	30:27	29:33

INDIVIDUAL STATISTICS
RUSHING—Dallas, E. Smith 23-110, Thomas 3-12. New Orleans, R. Williams 23-61, Craver 3-6, Delhomme 3-(minus 6).
PASSING—Dallas, Aikman 23-39-2-246. New Orleans, Delhomme 16-27-1-278, R. Williams 0-1-0-0.
RECEIVING—Dallas, Tucker 7-128, LaFleur 4-30, Ismail 3-28, E. Smith 3-3, Bjornson 2-22, Sanders 2-10, Brazzell 1-21, Thomas 1-4. New Orleans, Poole 4-90, Kennison 3-95, R. Williams 3-31, Wilcox 3-28, Hastings 1-24, Cleeland 1-5, Franklin 1-5.
MISSED FIELD GOAL ATTEMPTS—None.
INTERCEPTIONS—Dallas, Woodson 1-5. New Orleans, Weary 1-22, Fields 1-0.
KICKOFF RETURNS—Dallas, Tucker 6-203. New Orleans, Philyaw 5-111.
PUNT RETURNS—Dallas, Sanders 1-0. New Orleans, Kennison 2-7.
SACKS—Dallas, Ekuban 1, Godfrey 1, Hambrick 1.

BRONCOS 17, LIONS 7
Saturday, December 25

Denver	0	0	10	7	—17
Detroit	0	0	0	7	— 7

Third Quarter
Den.—Gary 45 run (Elam kick), 0:42.
Den.—FG, Elam 32, 6:35.
Fourth Quarter
Den.—Carswell 1 pass from Griese (Elam kick), 1:23.
Det.—Moore 13 pass from Batch (Hanson kick), 13:04.
Attendance—73,158.

	Denver	Detroit
First downs	22	16
Rushes-yards	36-204	12-32
Passing	165	234
Punt returns	3-43	1-9
Kickoff returns	2-17	4-97
Interception returns	0-0	1-16
Comp.-att.-int.	22-30-1	21-40-0
Sacked-yards lost	1-6	5-33
Punts	5-44	8-48
Fumbles-lost	0-0	2-0
Penalties-yards	5-40	10-78
Time of possession	36:41	23:19

INDIVIDUAL STATISTICS
RUSHING—Denver, Gary 29-185, Loville 4-17, Griese 3-2. Detroit, Irvin 5-8, Hill 4-7, Batch 2-9, Crowell 1-8.
PASSING—Denver, Griese 22-30-1-171. Detroit, Batch 21-40-0-267.
RECEIVING—Denver, McCaffrey 7-65, Carswell 6-35, Chamberlain 4-52, R. Smith 4-24, Loville 1-(minus 5). Detroit, Crowell 5-95, Sloan 5-50, Moore 4-62, Morton 4-47, Schlesinger 2-11, Irvin 1-2.
MISSED FIELD GOAL ATTEMPTS—None.
INTERCEPTIONS—Detroit, Carrier 1-16.
KICKOFF RETURNS—Denver, Watson 1-17, R. Smith 1-0. Detroit, Howard 4-97.
PUNT RETURNS—Denver, Watson 3-43. Detroit, Howard 1-9.
SACKS—Denver, N. Smith 2, Tanuvasa 1, Cadrez 1, Traylor 1. Detroit, Porcher 1.

FALCONS 37, CARDINALS 14
Sunday, December 26

Arizona	0	14	0	0	—14
Atlanta	7	13	7	10	—37

First Quarter
Atl.—Mathis 23 pass from Chandler (Andersen kick), 8:01.
Second Quarter
Ariz.—Bates 1 run (Jacke kick), 0:40.
Ariz.—Bates 1 run (Jacke kick), 6:30.
Atl.—Christian 1 run (Andersen kick), 10:21.
Atl.—FG, Andersen 28, 14:18.
Atl.—FG, Andersen 24, 15:00.
Third Quarter
Atl.—Hanspard 1 run (Andersen kick), 10:21.
Fourth Quarter
Atl.—Christian 33 run (Andersen kick), 4:54.
Atl.—FG, Andersen 41, 11:57.
Attendance—47,074.

	Arizona	Atlanta
First downs	16	22
Rushes-yards	24-77	39-163
Passing	212	230
Punt returns	2-17	3-21
Kickoff returns	6-104	3-66
Interception returns	0-0	2-23

	Arizona	Atlanta
Comp.-att.-int.	15-26-2	14-23-0
Sacked-yards lost	1-5	0-0
Punts	3-44	2-44
Fumbles-lost	1-0	1-0
Penalties-yards	8-57	4-24
Time of possession	24:40	35:20

INDIVIDUAL STATISTICS

RUSHING—Arizona, Bates 14-39, Plummer 6-21, Murrell 3-10, Makovicka 1-7. Atlanta, Hanspard 26-102, Christian 9-54, Graziani 2-(minus 1), Oliver 1-8, Chandler 1-0.

PASSING—Arizona, Plummer 15-26-2-217. Atlanta, Chandler 14-23-0-230.

RECEIVING—Arizona, Hardy 4-38, Sanders 3-106, Boston 3-32, Moore 3-32, McWilliams 1-11, Bates 1-(minus 2). Atlanta, Mathis 4-41, Dwight 3-52, Christian 3-46, Baker 2-52, R. Kelly 1-29, Oliver 1-10.

MISSED FIELD GOAL ATTEMPTS—None.

INTERCEPTIONS—Atlanta, McBurrows 1-23, Booker 1-0.

KICKOFF RETURNS—Arizona, Bates 6-104. Atlanta, Oliver 3-66.

PUNT RETURNS—Arizona, Cody 2-17. Atlanta, Dwight 3-21.

SACKS—Atlanta, Smith 1.

VIKINGS 34, GIANTS 17

Sunday, December 26

Minnesota	0	14	7	13—34
N.Y. Giants	3	3	3	8—17

First Quarter
NYG—FG, Blanchard 24, 9:46.
Second Quarter
Min.—Hoard 3 run (Anderson kick), 3:01.
NYG—FG, Blanchard 43, 7:10.
Min.—Hoard 1 run (Anderson kick), 14:33.
Third Quarter
Min.—Carter 27 pass from Moss (Anderson kick), 10:31.
NYG—FG, Blanchard 42, 15:00.
Fourth Quarter
Min.—M. Williams 85 kickoff return (Anderson kick), 0:16.
NYG—Mitchell 1 pass from Collins (Collins run), 7:15.
Min.—Smith 70 run, 7:37 (two-point conversion failed).
Attendance—78,095.

	Minnesota	N.Y. Giants
First downs	18	25
Rushes-yards	25-174	27-76
Passing	204	268
Punt returns	1-(-4)	3-14
Kickoff returns	5-144	6-110
Interception returns	1-4	2-0
Comp.-att.-int.	11-22-2	31-51-1
Sacked-yards lost	1-8	5-29
Punts	4-42	2-47
Fumbles-lost	0-0	2-0
Penalties-yards	10-80	5-40
Time of possession	22:25	37:35

INDIVIDUAL STATISTICS

RUSHING—Minnesota, Smith 16-146, Hoard 6-21, M. Williams 2-3, George 1-4. New York, Montgomery 19-55, Barber 5-11, Collins 3-10.

PASSING—Minnesota, George 10-21-2-185, Moss 1-1-0-27. New York, Collins 31-51-1-297.

RECEIVING—Minnesota, Carter 5-131, Moss 3-44, Glover 2-28, Smith 1-9. New York, Toomer 9-99, Barber 8-56, Hilliard 5-62, Jurevicius 3-39, Mitchell 3-21, Cross 2-4, Patten 1-26.

MISSED FIELD GOAL ATTEMPTS—New York, Blanchard 39.

INTERCEPTIONS—Minnesota, Bass 1-4. New York, Ellsworth 1-0, Lincoln 1-0.

KICKOFF RETURNS—Minnesota, Tate 2-30, M. Williams 1-85, Morrow 1-20, Burrough 1-9. New York, Levingston 4-78, Patten 1-18, Barber 1-14.

PUNT RETURNS—Minnesota, Moss 1-(minus 4). New York, Barber 3-14.

SACKS—Minnesota, Randle 2, Griffith 1, Clemons 1, Burrough 1. New York, K. Hamilton 1.

TITANS 41, JAGUARS 14

Sunday, December 26

Jacksonville	0	7	7	0—14
Tennessee	7	17	14	3—41

First Quarter
Ten.—Roan 4 pass from McNair (Del Greco kick), 7:36.
Second Quarter
Ten.—Harris 62 pass from McNair (Del Greco kick), 0:14.
Ten.—FG, Del Greco 30, 6:04.
Jac.—Taylor 1 run (Hollis kick), 12:06.
Ten.—Thigpen 2 pass from McNair (Del Greco kick), 14:35.
Third Quarter
Ten.—Byrd 65 pass from McNair (Del Greco kick), 7:53.
Ten.—Dyson 13 pass from McNair (Del Greco kick), 11:36.
Jac.—Whitted 98 kickoff return (Hollis kick), 11:54.
Fourth Quarter
Ten.—FG, Del Greco 20, 3:40.
Attendance—66,641.

	Jacksonville	Tennessee
First downs	16	26
Rushes-yards	18-65	37-148
Passing	172	328
Punt returns	2-7	3-16
Kickoff returns	7-198	3-32
Interception returns	0-0	3-66
Comp.-att.-int.	12-33-3	26-39-0
Sacked-yards lost	4-24	0-0
Punts	6-39	4-40
Fumbles-lost	1-0	0-0
Penalties-yards	4-29	4-33
Time of possession	21:30	38:30

INDIVIDUAL STATISTICS

RUSHING—Jacksonville, Taylor 16-44, Brunell 1-14, Fiedler 1-7. Tennessee, E. George 26-102, McNair 4-34, Thomas 4-13, O'Donnell 2-(minus 2), Hentrich 1-1.

PASSING—Jacksonville, Fiedler 8-22-2-101, Brunell 4-11-1-95. Tennessee, McNair 23-33-0-291, O'Donnell 3-6-0-37.

RECEIVING—Jacksonville, J. Smith 4-104, Brady 3-32, McCardell 2-22, Jones 2-20, Taylor 1-18. Tennessee, Wycheck 9-64, Dyson 5-58, Harris 4-72, E. George 3-37, Byrd 2-71, Thigpen 2-17, Sanders 1-5, Roan 1-4.

MISSED FIELD GOAL ATTEMPTS—None.

INTERCEPTIONS—Tennessee, Rolle 3-66.

KICKOFF RETURNS—Jacksonville, Whitted 4-147, Jackson 2-45, Chamblin 1-6. Tennessee, Byrd 2-16, Mason 1-16.

PUNT RETURNS—Jacksonville, McCardell 2-7. Tennessee, Mason 3-16.

SACKS—Tennessee, Evans 1, Fisk 1, Holmes 1, Kearse 1.

RAVENS 22, BENGALS 0

Sunday, December 26

Cincinnati	0	0	0	0— 0
Baltimore	7	9	0	6—22

First Quarter
Bal.—Rhett 2 pass from Banks (Stover kick), 11:46.
Second Quarter
Bal.—FG, Stover 24, 0:57.
Bal.—FG, Stover 48, 5:07.
Bal.—FG, Stover 19, 15:00.
Fourth Quarter
Bal.—FG, Stover 30, 7:54.
Bal.—FG, Stover 19, 13:03.
Attendance—68,036.

	Cincinnati	Baltimore
First downs	15	18
Rushes-yards	25-93	32-130
Passing	148	181
Punt returns	1-6	3-47
Kickoff returns	6-138	1-7
Interception returns	1-0	2-53
Comp.-att.-int.	20-37-2	15-33-1
Sacked-yards lost	7-39	1-6
Punts	6-29	5-38
Fumbles-lost	4-1	0-0
Penalties-yards	11-87	7-53
Time of possession	31:01	28:59

INDIVIDUAL STATISTICS

RUSHING—Cincinnati, Basnight 10-41, Dillon 10-27, Blake 4-22, Groce 1-3. Baltimore, Holmes 13-59, Rhett 12-50, Evans 3-4, Banks 2-1, Johnson 1-12, J. Lewis 1-4.

1999 REVIEW Week 16

PASSING—Cincinnati, Blake 20-37-2-187. Baltimore, Banks 15-33-1-187.
RECEIVING—Cincinnati, Scott 5-83, Dillon 5-30, Pickens 4-38, Groce 2-9, Basnight 2-4, McGee 1-18, Jackson 1-5. Baltimore, Ismail 5-52, Johnson 3-82, Collins 3-41, Evans 2-9, Rhett 1-2, Holmes 1-1.
MISSED FIELD GOAL ATTEMPTS—Cincinnati, Pelfrey 20.
INTERCEPTIONS—Cincinnati, Carter 1-0. Baltimore, Woodson 1-44, Starks 1-9.
KICKOFF RETURNS—Cincinnati, Mack 5-124, Williams 1-14. Baltimore, Ismail 1-7.
PUNT RETURNS—Cincinnati, Yeast 1-6. Baltimore, J. Lewis 3-47.
SACKS—Cincinnati, Gibson 1. Baltimore, McCrary 3, Brown 1, Webster 1, Washington 1, Dalton 1.

CHARGERS 23, RAIDERS 20

Sunday, December 26

Oakland 10   0   10   0—20
San Diego 0   13   0   10—23

First Quarter
Oak.—FG, Nedney 52, 6:31.
Oak.—Crockett 1 run (Nedney kick), 8:44.
Second Quarter
S.D.—FG, Carney 48, 7:02.
S.D.—McCrary 18 pass from Harbaugh (Carney kick), 13:07.
S.D.—FG, Carney 19, 15:00.
Third Quarter
Oak.—Dudley 7 pass from Gannon (Nedney kick), 3:38.
Oak.—FG, Nedney 25, 14:34.
Fourth Quarter
S.D.—J. Graham 10 pass from Harbaugh (Carney kick), 1:42.
S.D.—FG, Carney 37, 6:51.
Attendance—63,846.

	Oakland	San Diego
First downs	18	17
Rushes-yards	24-46	21-49
Passing	248	293
Punt returns	3-28	2-43
Kickoff returns	5-80	5-102
Interception returns	1-0	1-16
Comp.-att.-int.	16-33-1	23-36-1
Sacked-yards lost	3-18	4-32
Punts	4-41	4-53
Fumbles-lost	1-0	5-0
Penalties-yards	13-100	8-91
Time of possession	31:30	28:30

INDIVIDUAL STATISTICS
RUSHING—Oakland, Wheatley 12-13, Kaufman 7-13, Gannon 3-17, Crockett 2-3. San Diego, Fazande 14-44, Harbaugh 6-5, Carney 1-0.
PASSING—Oakland, Gannon 16-33-1-266. San Diego, Harbaugh 23-36-1-325.
RECEIVING—Oakland, Jett 4-45, Dudley 4-43, Brown 3-109, Mickens 2-26, Ritchie 2-17, Wheatley 1-26. San Diego, Fletcher 7-45, F. Jones 5-81, Ricks 4-51, J. Graham 3-113, McCrary 2-21, C. Jones 1-9, Davis 1-5.
MISSED FIELD GOAL ATTEMPTS—Oakland, Nedney 52, 44.
INTERCEPTIONS—Oakland, Newman 1-0. San Diego, Seau 1-16.
KICKOFF RETURNS—Oakland, Kaufman 4-61, Branch 1-19. San Diego, Bynum 5-102.
PUNT RETURNS—Oakland, Gordon 3-28. San Diego, C. Jones 2-43.
SACKS—Oakland, Johnstone 3, Barton 1. San Diego, Hand 1, Johnson 1, Seau 0.5, Parrella 0.5.

BUCCANEERS 29, PACKERS 10

Sunday, December 26

Green Bay 0   10   0   0—10
Tampa Bay 3   6   7   13—29

First Quarter
T.B.—FG, Gramatica 49, 4:08.
Second Quarter
T.B.—FG, Gramatica 28, 0:16.
T.B.—FG, Gramatica 33, 7:54.
G.B.—FG, Longwell 46, 12:55.
G.B.—Levens 20 pass from Favre (Longwell kick), 14:39.
Third Quarter
T.B.—Dunn 8 pass from King (Gramatica kick), 6:25.

Fourth Quarter
T.B.—Alstott 5 run (pass failed), 3:30.
T.B.—Alstott 17 run (Gramatica kick), 10:19.
Attendance—65,723.

	Green Bay	Tampa Bay
First downs	14	17
Rushes-yards	12-12	37-124
Passing	231	150
Punt returns	3-12	3-16
Kickoff returns	7-118	3-70
Interception returns	1-12	2-36
Comp.-att.-int.	25-48-2	18-31-1
Sacked-yards lost	1-3	0-0
Punts	6-36	5-41
Fumbles-lost	3-2	0-0
Penalties-yards	2-20	2-25
Time of possession	23:53	36:07

INDIVIDUAL STATISTICS
RUSHING—Green Bay, Levens 10-4, Favre 2-8. Tampa Bay, Alstott 19-79, Dunn 13-25, King 5-20.
PASSING—Green Bay, Favre 25-48-2-234. Tampa Bay, King 17-30-1-133, Royals 1-1-0-17.
RECEIVING—Green Bay, Levens 9-47, Schroeder 6-54, Freeman 5-72, Thomason 3-33, Bradford 2-28. Tampa Bay, Dunn 6-48, Emanuel 4-24, Williams 2-17, Moore 1-20, Robinson 1-17, Green 1-13, Anthony 1-8, Alstott 1-3, Hape 1-0.
MISSED FIELD GOAL ATTEMPTS—None.
INTERCEPTIONS—Green Bay, T. Williams 1-12. Tampa Bay, Robinson 2-36.
KICKOFF RETURNS—Green Bay, Jordan 5-79, Mitchell 1-23, Parker 1-16. Tampa Bay, Dunn 3-70.
PUNT RETURNS—Green Bay, Jordan 3-12. Tampa Bay, Williams 3-16.
SACKS—Tampa Bay, Jones 1.

SEAHAWKS 23, CHIEFS 14

Sunday, December 26

Kansas City 0   7   7   0—14
Seattle 10   7   6   0—23

First Quarter
Sea.—FG, Peterson 31, 5:42.
Sea.—Dawkins 20 pass from Kitna (Peterson kick), 12:21.
Second Quarter
Sea.—Mayes 9 pass from Kitna (Peterson kick), 8:37.
K.C.—Johnson 4 pass from Grbac (Stoyanovich kick), 13:46.
Third Quarter
Sea.—FG, Peterson 22, 5:25.
K.C.—Horn 76 pass from Grbac (Stoyanovich kick), 6:52.
Sea.—FG, Peterson 48, 10:21.
Attendance—66,332.

	Kansas City	Seattle
First downs	17	17
Rushes-yards	22-72	28-60
Passing	230	207
Punt returns	5-30	2-40
Kickoff returns	6-113	3-45
Interception returns	0-0	3-50
Comp.-att.-int.	22-42-3	18-30-0
Sacked-yards lost	4-24	3-9
Punts	7-38	9-39
Fumbles-lost	2-0	0-0
Penalties-yards	11-64	5-55
Time of possession	28:19	31:41

INDIVIDUAL STATISTICS
RUSHING—Kansas City, Richardson 8-20, Morris 6-33, Bennett 5-14, Cloud 2-6, Grbac 1-(minus 1). Seattle, Watters 18-63, Green 7-(minus 4), Kitna 3-1.
PASSING—Kansas City, Grbac 22-42-3-254. Seattle, Kitna 18-30-0-216.
RECEIVING—Kansas City, Gonzalez 9-86, Alexander 4-42, Horn 3-92, Johnson 3-18, Richardson 2-9, Rison 1-7. Seattle, Fauria 6-84, Dawkins 4-70, Watters 2-21, Mayes 2-18, R. Brown 2-16, Galloway 2-7.
MISSED FIELD GOAL ATTEMPTS—None.
INTERCEPTIONS—Seattle, Springs 1-27, Canty 1-19, D. Williams 1-4.
KICKOFF RETURNS—Kansas City, Vanover 6-113. Seattle, Green 3-45.
PUNT RETURNS—Kansas City, Vanover 5-30. Seattle, Galloway 2-40.
SACKS—Kansas City, Patton 1, O'Neal 1, D. Williams 1. Seattle, Sinclair 2, C. Brown 1, Daniels 1.

BILLS 13, PATRIOTS 10

Sunday, December 26

Buffalo	3	0	0	7	3—13
New England	0	3	0	7	0—10

First Quarter
Buf.—FG, Christie 39, 11:00.
Second Quarter
N.E.—FG, Vinatieri 38, 15:00.
Fourth Quarter
N.E.—Allen 14 run (Vinatieri kick), 2:45.
Buf.—Linton 1 run (Christie kick), 10:37.
Overtime
Buf.—FG, Christie 23, 13:12.
Attendance—55,014.

	Buffalo	New England
First downs	23	14
Rushes-yards	41-168	34-158
Passing	206	67
Punt returns	1-(-2)	2-31
Kickoff returns	2-28	4-124
Interception returns	0-0	0-0
Comp.-att.-int.	22-35-0	10-21-0
Sacked-yards lost	3-6	6-34
Punts	5-34	8-36
Fumbles-lost	3-3	1-1
Penalties-yards	4-30	5-25
Time of possession	42:32	30:40

INDIVIDUAL STATISTICS
RUSHING—Buffalo, Linton 20-40, Thomas 15-84, Flutie 6-44. New England, Allen 27-126, Shaw 4-6, Bledsoe 3-26.
PASSING—Buffalo, Flutie 22-35-0-212. New England, Bledsoe 10-21-0-101.
RECEIVING—Buffalo, Riemersma 6-39, P. Price 5-62, Moulds 4-53, Gash 3-19, K. Williams 2-24, Collins 1-11, Linton 1-4. New England, Brisby 4-45, Shaw 2-31, Warren 2-8, Coates 1-20, Brown 1-(minus 3).
MISSED FIELD GOAL ATTEMPTS—New England, Vinatieri 44, 33, 44.
INTERCEPTIONS—None.
KICKOFF RETURNS—Buffalo, K. Williams 1-17, Gordon 1-11. New England, Brown 4-124.
PUNT RETURNS—Buffalo, K. Williams 1-(minus 2). New England, Brown 2-31.
SACKS—Buffalo, Rogers 2, B. Smith 2, P. Williams 1, S. Price 1. New England, Serwanga 1, Slade 1, Katzenmoyer 1.

STEELERS 30, PANTHERS 20

Sunday, December 26

Carolina	7	13	0	0—20
Pittsburgh	10	13	0	7—30

First Quarter
Pit.—FG, K. Brown 46, 4:21.
Pit.—Davis 102 fumble return (K. Brown kick), 11:25.
Car.—Lane 41 run (Cunningham kick), 13:05.
Second Quarter
Pit.—Huntley 25 run (two-point conversion failed), 3:57.
Car.—Jeffers 88 pass from Beuerlein (kick failed), 8:01.
Pit.—Ward 9 pass from Tomczak (K. Brown kick), 13:24.
Car.—Jeffers 43 pass from Beuerlein (Cunningham kick), 14:57.
Fourth Quarter
Pit.—Bettis 8 run (K. Brown kick), 12:34.
Attendance—39,428.

	Carolina	Pittsburgh
First downs	17	21
Rushes-yards	20-119	44-210
Passing	256	82
Punt returns	2-19	1-2
Kickoff returns	6-97	3-30
Interception returns	1-25	1-23
Comp.-att.-int.	18-35-1	13-23-1
Sacked-yards lost	1-7	1-12
Punts	4-33	4-43
Fumbles-lost	2-2	0-0
Penalties-yards	3-15	7-60
Time of possession	24:39	35:21

INDIVIDUAL STATISTICS
RUSHING—Carolina, Lane 15-90, Johnson 3-11, Beuerlein 1-14, Floyd 1-4. Pittsburgh, Bettis 33-137, Huntley 7-72, Tomczak 4-1.
PASSING—Carolina, Beuerlein 18-35-1-263. Pittsburgh, Tomczak 13-23-1-94.
RECEIVING—Carolina, Jeffers 5-160, Muhammad 4-45, Floyd 4-32, Walls 3-26, Lane 2-0. Pittsburgh, Ward 5-40, Edwards 3-36, Huntley 2-10, Witman 1-6, Shaw 1-5, Bettis 1-(minus 3).
MISSED FIELD GOAL ATTEMPTS—None.
INTERCEPTIONS—Carolina, Minter 1-25. Pittsburgh, Shields 1-23.
KICKOFF RETURNS—Carolina, Bates 6-97. Pittsburgh, Huntley 2-22, Cline 1-8.
PUNT RETURNS—Carolina, Metcalf 2-19. Pittsburgh, Ward 1-2.
SACKS—Carolina, Peter 1. Pittsburgh, Kirkland 1.

COLTS 29, BROWNS 28

Sunday, December 26

Indianapolis	0	13	6	10—29
Cleveland	7	7	14	0—28

First Quarter
Cle.—Kirby 1 run (Dawson kick), 10:50.
Second Quarter
Ind.—James 1 run (Vanderjagt kick), 0:54.
Cle.—Chiaverini 28 pass from Detmer (Dawson kick), 1:04.
Ind.—FG, Vanderjagt 41, 13:04.
Ind.—FG, Vanderjagt 19, 15:00.
Third Quarter
Cle.—Detmer 8 run (Dawson kick), 4:13.
Ind.—James 1 run (run failed), 7:56.
Cle.—Kirby 1 run (Dawson kick), 14:49.
Fourth Quarter
Ind.—James 2 run (Vanderjagt kick), 5:06.
Ind.—FG, Vanderjagt 21, 14:56.
Attendance—72,618.

	Indianapolis	Cleveland
First downs	27	17
Rushes-yards	30-120	26-141
Passing	283	173
Punt returns	4-56	1-6
Kickoff returns	5-65	5-72
Interception returns	0-0	0-0
Comp.-att.-int.	28-44-0	15-26-0
Sacked-yards lost	0-0	0-0
Punts	5-37	6-43
Fumbles-lost	1-0	0-0
Penalties-yards	0-0	6-32
Time of possession	37:20	22:40

INDIVIDUAL STATISTICS
RUSHING—Indianapolis, James 28-103, Manning 2-17. Cleveland, Abdul-Jabbar 19-84, Kirby 5-21, Edwards 1-28, Detmer 1-8.
PASSING—Indianapolis, Manning 28-44-0-283. Cleveland, Detmer 15-26-0-173.
RECEIVING—Indianapolis, Harrison 14-138, Dilger 4-56, James 4-25, Wilkins 3-28, Pollard 2-24, Green 1-12. Cleveland, I. Smith 4-48, Chiaverini 3-40, Johnson 2-29, Abdul-Jabbar 2-7, Edwards 1-25, Davis 1-13, Kirby 1-8, Bobo 1-3.
MISSED FIELD GOAL ATTEMPTS—None.
INTERCEPTIONS—None.
KICKOFF RETURNS—Indianapolis, Wilkins 5-65. Cleveland, Kirby 4-72, Saleh 1-0.
PUNT RETURNS—Indianapolis, Wilkins 4-56. Cleveland, Johnson 1-6.
SACKS—None.

RAMS 34, BEARS 12

Sunday, December 26

Chicago	0	6	0	6—12
St. Louis	0	17	14	3—34

Second Quarter
St.L.—Faulk 48 pass from Warner (Wilkins kick), 6:24.
St.L.—R. Williams 2 pass from Warner (Wilkins kick), 12:49.
St.L.—FG, Wilkins 38, 14:16.
Third Quarter
St.L.—Bruce 4 pass from Warner (Wilkins kick), 5:01.
St.L.—Wistrom 40 interception return (Wilkins kick), 6:52.
Chi.—Engram 8 pass from Matthews (kick failed), 12:00.

1999 REVIEW Week 16

— 211 —

Fourth Quarter
Chi.—Engram 4 pass from Matthews (pass failed), 3:42.
St.L.—FG, Wilkins 28, 9:55.
  Attendance—65,941.

	Chicago	St. Louis
First downs	24	23
Rushes-yards	17-69	27-115
Passing	365	361
Punt returns	0-0	4-21
Kickoff returns	5-122	1-1
Interception returns	1-0	2-42
Comp.-att.-int.	32-55-2	27-42-1
Sacked-yards lost	4-26	0-0
Punts	5-52	3-40
Fumbles-lost	2-1	2-1
Penalties-yards	10-60	8-76
Time of possession	26:15	33:45

INDIVIDUAL STATISTICS
RUSHING—Chicago, Enis 7-21, Allen 6-30, McNown 3-18, Matthews 1-0. St. Louis, Watson 11-23, Faulk 10-54, Holcombe 3-24, Bruce 2-11, Justin 1-3.
PASSING—Chicago, Matthews 23-39-1-266, McNown 9-16-1-125. St. Louis, Warner 24-35-1-334, Justin 3-7-0-27.
RECEIVING—Chicago, Engram 13-143, M. Robinson 6-93, Allen 5-63, Wetnight 4-26, Allred 2-34, Mayes 1-24, Booker 1-8. St. Louis, Faulk 12-204, Bruce 4-45, Holt 3-33, Hakim 2-40, Proehl 2-19, R. Williams 2-4, Holcombe 1-10, Robinson 1-6.
MISSED FIELD GOAL ATTEMPTS—St. Louis, Wilkins 48.
INTERCEPTIONS—Chicago, S. Harris 1-0. St. Louis, Wistrom 1-40, Jenkins 1-2.
KICKOFF RETURNS—Chicago, Milburn 5-122. St. Louis, Bly 1-1.
PUNT RETURNS—St. Louis, Horne 3-13, Hakim 1-8.
SACKS—St. Louis, Farr 1, Carter 1, Clemons 1, J. Williams 1.

REDSKINS 26, 49ERS 20
Sunday, December 26

Washington 0   7   3 10   6—26
San Francisco 7   6   7   0   0—20

First Quarter
S.F.—Garner 4 run (Richey kick), 8:55.
Second Quarter
Was.—Westbrook 65 pass from B. Johnson (Conway kick), 3:30.
S.F.—FG, Richey 29, 8:25.
S.F.—FG, Richey 25, 13:22.
Third Quarter
Was.—FG, Conway 47, 6:06.
S.F.—Stokes 5 pass from Garcia (Richey kick), 10:49.
Fourth Quarter
Was.—FG, Conway 34, 2:54.
Was.—B. Johnson 1 run (Conway kick), 11:32.
Overtime
Was.—Centers 33 pass from B. Johnson, 2:00.
  Attendance—68,329.

	Washington	San Francisco
First downs	23	24
Rushes-yards	17-57	37-250
Passing	454	168
Punt returns	1-3	1-6
Kickoff returns	5-89	5-64
Interception returns	1-10	1-4
Comp.-att.-int.	32-47-1	17-30-1
Sacked-yards lost	3-17	0-0
Punts	5-42	5-34
Fumbles-lost	2-0	1-1
Penalties-yards	6-38	1-10
Time of possession	29:30	32:30

INDIVIDUAL STATISTICS
RUSHING—Washington, Hicks 13-48, B. Johnson 2-0, Centers 1-12, Mitchell 1-(minus 3). San Francisco, Garner 16-129, Beasley 12-65, Jackson 5-16, Garcia 4-40.
PASSING—Washington, B. Johnson 32-47-1-471. San Francisco, Garcia 17-29-1-168, Rice 0-1-0-0.
RECEIVING—Washington, Westbrook 7-125, Centers 7-66, Connell 5-106, Fryar 4-60, Hicks 4-52, Mitchell 3-55, Alexander 2-7. San Francisco, Rice 5-44, Clark 4-46, Garner 3-39, Stokes 2-31, Beasley 2-6, Owens 1-2.
MISSED FIELD GOAL ATTEMPTS—None.
INTERCEPTIONS—Washington, Stevens 1-10. San Francisco, R. McDonald 1-4.
KICKOFF RETURNS—Washington, Thrash 3-36, Mitchell 2-53. San Francisco, Preston 5-64.
PUNT RETURNS—Washington, Mitchell 1-3. San Francisco, Preston 1-6.
SACKS—San Francisco, B. Young 2, Woodall 1.

JETS 38, DOLPHINS 31
Monday, December 27

N.Y. Jets 10   7   7 14—38
Miami 7   7   7 10—31

First Quarter
NYJ—K. Johnson 4 pass from Lucas (Hall kick), 6:44.
Mia.—Perry 1 pass from Marino (Mare kick), 9:23.
NYJ—FG, Hall 48, 14:53.
Second Quarter
NYJ—Coleman 98 interception return (Hall kick), 6:19.
Mia.—Pritchett 3 pass from Marino (Mare kick), 12:14.
Third Quarter
Mia.—Martin 32 pass from Marino (Mare kick), 3:59.
NYJ—Martin 1 run (Hall kick), 7:59.
Fourth Quarter
Mia.—Johnson 1 run (Mare kick), 1:28.
NYJ—Chrebet 50 pass from Lucas (Hall kick), 4:19.
NYJ—Ward 56 pass from Lucas (Hall kick), 6:04.
Mia.—FG, Mare 37, 12:40.
  Attendance—74,230.

	N.Y. Jets	Miami
First downs	16	25
Rushes-yards	25-101	24-100
Passing	189	322
Punt returns	2-11	2-12
Kickoff returns	5-103	7-166
Interception returns	3-102	0-0
Comp.-att.-int.	11-23-0	29-52-3
Sacked-yards lost	1-1	0-0
Punts	4-40	3-36
Fumbles-lost	1-1	1-0
Penalties-yards	5-44	4-28
Time of possession	24:32	35:28

INDIVIDUAL STATISTICS
RUSHING—New York, Martin 20-72, Anderson 2-15, Lucas 2-2, Parmalee 1-12. Miami, Johnson 18-83, Pritchett 5-17, Marino 1-0.
PASSING—New York, Lucas 11-23-0-190. Miami, Marino 29-52-3-322.
RECEIVING—New York, Chrebet 3-62, K. Johnson 3-29, Martin 2-25, Ward 1-56, Baxter 1-14, Anderson 1-4. Miami, McDuffie 7-79, Martin 6-102, Pritchett 4-36, Goodwin 3-14, Perry 3-8, Gadsden 2-53, Green 2-17, Johnson 1-9, Konrad 1-4.
MISSED FIELD GOAL ATTEMPTS—Miami, Mare 54.
INTERCEPTIONS—New York, Coleman 1-98, Phifer 1-4, Mickens 1-0.
KICKOFF RETURNS—New York, Stone 3-56, Glenn 2-47. Miami, Marion 6-151, Thomas 1-15.
PUNT RETURNS—New York, Ward 2-11. Miami, McDuffie 1-12, Jacquet 1-0.
SACKS—Miami, Gardener 1.

WEEK 17

RESULTS

BUFFALO 31, Indianapolis 6
CAROLINA 45, New Orleans 13
DALLAS 26, N.Y. Giants 18
GREEN BAY 49, Arizona 24
JACKSONVILLE 24, Cincinnati 7
MINNESOTA 24, Detroit 17
NEW ENGLAND 20, Baltimore 3
N.Y. JETS 19, Seattle 9
Oakland 41, KANSAS CITY 38 (OT)
PHILADELPHIA 38, St. Louis 31
San Diego 12, DENVER 6
Tampa Bay 20, CHICAGO 6
Tennessee 47, PITTSBURGH 36
WASHINGTON 21, Miami 10
ATLANTA 34, San Francisco 29
Open date: Cleveland

STANDINGS

AFC EAST
	W	L	T	Pct.
Indianapolis	13	3	0	.813
Buffalo	11	5	0	.688
Miami	9	7	0	.563
N.Y. Jets	8	8	0	.500
New England	8	8	0	.500

AFC CENTRAL
	W	L	T	Pct.
Jacksonville	14	2	0	.875
Tennessee	13	3	0	.813
Baltimore	8	8	0	.500
Pittsburgh	6	10	0	.375
Cincinnati	4	12	0	.250
Cleveland	2	14	0	.125

AFC WEST
	W	L	T	Pct.
Seattle	9	7	0	.563
Kansas City	9	7	0	.563
San Diego	8	8	0	.500
Oakland	8	8	0	.500
Denver	6	10	0	.375

NFC EAST
	W	L	T	Pct.
Washington	10	6	0	.625
Dallas	8	8	0	.500
N.Y. Giants	7	9	0	.438
Arizona	6	10	0	.375
Philadelphia	5	11	0	.313

NFC CENTRAL
	W	L	T	Pct.
Tampa Bay	11	5	0	.688
Minnesota	10	6	0	.625
Detroit	8	8	0	.500
Green Bay	8	8	0	.500
Chicago	6	10	0	.375

NFC WEST
	W	L	T	Pct.
St. Louis	13	3	0	.813
Carolina	8	8	0	.500
Atlanta	5	11	0	.313
San Francisco	4	12	0	.250
New Orleans	3	13	0	.188

HIGHLIGHTS

Hero of the week: Oakland quarterback Rich Gannon, a former Chief, stunned his former mates in his first return to Arrowhead Stadium by completing 25 of 47 passes for 324 yards and three touchdowns in leading the Raiders to a 41-38 come-from-behind win. It was an all-or-nothing game for the Chiefs, who would have captured the AFC West title with a victory but missed the playoffs completely with the loss.

Goat of the week: Jon Baker, a kickoff specialist signed by Kansas City just 12 days earlier, aided the Raiders' comeback by kicking the ball out of bounds at the start of overtime, enabling Oakland to take possession at its own 40. Gannon then completed passes of 21 and 23 yards to Rickey Dudley and Tim Brown, respectively, en route to the game-winning score: a 33-yard field goal by Joe Nedney at 3:13 of OT.

Sub of the week: Buffalo quarterback Rob Johnson, starting in place of Doug Flutie, completed 24 of 32 passes for 287 yards to lead the Bills to a stunningly easy 31-6 victory over AFC East champion Indianapolis. Johnson completed his first seven passes and engineered touchdown drives of 83, 80 and 82 yards the first three times Buffalo had the ball.. The Bills, who rolled up a season-high 419 yards, had just five TD drives of 80 or more yards in their first 15 games under Flutie.

Comeback of the week: None. Only a handful of games on the final week had any bearing on the playoff picture, and most of those that did were not close.

Blowout of the week: The Carolina Panthers, needing to win by 43 points to have any chance of making the playoffs according to the NFL's tie-breaking formula, did their best, pounding New Orleans 45-13 behind Steve Beuerlein's club-record five touchdown passes. The offensively-inept Saints did not get inside the Panthers' 40-yard line until the fourth quarter, at which point they trailed 31-0. Former Heisman Trophy winner Ricky Williams concluded a disappointing rookie season with seven rushing yards on 14 attempts.

Nail-biter of the week: The Raiders' victory over the Chiefs was a real stunner. It was their first win at Arrowhead Stadium since 1988, only their third in the last 21 games between the teams and came after Oakland erased an early 17-0 deficit. Nedney tied the game at 38-38 with a 38-yard field goal with 45 seconds left before winning it with a 33-yarder in OT. Nedney's heroics were made possible when his counterpart, Pete Stoyanovich, missed a 44-yard field goal attempt in the final minute of regulation time.

Hit of the week: Tampa Bay led Chicago, 3-0, late in the first half when Bucs defensive end Marcus Jones hit Bears rookie Cade McNown as he was attempting to pass. The ball popped free, and Steve White recovered the ball for Tampa Bay at the Chicago 14. Four plays later Mike Alstott ran around right end for a touchdown to increase the Bucs' lead to 10 points.

Oddity of the week: Chargers rookie Jermaine Fazande, who entered the game with 182 rushing yards all season, exploded for 183 yards against the Broncos to lead San Diego to a 12-6 win at Denver.

Top rusher: Fazande's 183 yards was the second-best rushing effort by a Denver opponent at Mile High Stadium. Detroit's Billy Sims had a 185-yard performance there in 1981.

Top passer: Jake Plummer completed 35 of 57 passes for 396 yards in Arizona's 49-24 loss at Green Bay.

Top receiver: Patrick Jeffers caught seven passes for 165 yards and two touchdowns in the Panthers' rout of the Saints. Jimmy Smith caught 14 passes for 165 yards in Jacksonville's 24-7 win over Cincinnati.

Notes: Only five playoff teams from 1998 repeated in '99: the Jaguars, Bills, Dolphins, Cowboys and Vikings. ... In the Rams' season-ending loss at Philadelphia, Marshall Faulk (2,429) broke Barry Sanders' NFL record for total yards in one season, and Kurt Warner (41) joined Dan Marino as the only quarterbacks to throw 40 or more TD passes in a season. ... Curtis Martin broke Freeman McNeil's Jets record for rushing yards in a season (1,464 to 1,331). ... Olandis Gary broke the Denver record for yards rushing by a rookie set by Bobby Humphrey in 1989. ... The Ravens did not allow a 100-yard rusher all season and gave up just three rushing touch-

1999 REVIEW Week 17

downs in their final 47 quarters. ... Washington's 21-10 victory over Miami was its first all season against a team with a winning record. Stephen Davis became the first Redskin since Larry Brown in 1972 to lead the NFC in rushing. ... Hours after the Packers' final game, with the team missing the playoffs for the first time since 1992, first-year coach Ray Rhodes and his entire staff were fired. ... The Broncos (6-10) became the first Super Bowl champion to finish last in its division the following year in a full season. The Giants finished last in the NFC East in 1987, but that season was interrupted by a players strike and shortened to 15 games. ... The Cardinals did not score a touchdown in the first quarter all season. ... Despite handing division champ Jacksonville (14-2) its only two losses, Tennessee became the first 13-3 team since divisional play began in 1970 to not win its division. ... The Steelers (6-10) finished with their worst record in 11 years and their worst home record (2-6) since moving into Three Rivers Stadium in 1970.

Quote of the week: Seahawks tight end Christian Fauria, on Seattle winning the AFC West despite finishing losing five of their last six games: "People are talking about getting in the back door. So what? We still got in the house."

GAME SUMMARIES

JETS 19, SEAHAWKS 9

Sunday, January 2

Seattle	6	0	3	0— 9
N.Y. Jets	3	10	3	3—19

First Quarter
Sea.—FG, Peterson 25, 4:30.
NYJ—FG, Hall 23, 10:57.
Sea.—FG, Peterson 41, 13:57.

Second Quarter
NYJ—Martin 1 run (Hall kick), 1:39.
NYJ—FG, Hall 30, 11:20.

Third Quarter
Sea.—FG, Peterson 45, 5:06.
NYJ—FG, Hall 31, 8:19.

Fourth Quarter
NYJ—FG, Hall 35, 10:39.
Attendance—78,154.

	Seattle	N.Y. Jets
First downs	14	20
Rushes-yards	12-33	41-177
Passing	233	202
Punt returns	2-16	4-34
Kickoff returns	7-190	3-74
Interception returns	2-0	2-50
Comp.-att.-int.	21-45-2	15-26-2
Sacked-yards lost	1-4	1-9
Punts	6-44	3-48
Fumbles-lost	0-0	0-0
Penalties-yards	5-44	3-25
Time of possession	22:27	37:33

INDIVIDUAL STATISTICS
RUSHING—Seattle, Watters 9-30, Green 1-4, R. Brown 1-0, Kitna 1-(minus 1). New York, Martin 34-158, Lucas 4-12, Parmalee 2-5, Anderson 1-2.
PASSING—Seattle, Kitna 21-45-2-237. New York, Lucas 15-26-2-211.
RECEIVING—Seattle, Mayes 5-64, R. Brown 5-30, Dawkins 4-66, Fauria 3-24, Watters 2-24, Galloway 1-17, Pritchard 1-12. New York, Chrebet 5-88, Martin 3-45, Anderson 3-43, K. Johnson 3-20, Ward 1-15.
MISSED FIELD GOAL ATTEMPTS—None.
INTERCEPTIONS—Seattle, Bellamy 2-0. New York, Coleman 1-34, Phifer 1-16.

KICKOFF RETURNS—Seattle, Rogers 7-190. New York, Glenn 3-74.
PUNT RETURNS—Seattle, Rogers 2-16. New York, Ward 4-34.
SACKS—Seattle, C. Brown 1. New York, Ferguson 1.

VIKINGS 24, LIONS 17

Sunday, January 2

Detroit	7	3	0	7—17
Minnesota	7	10	0	7—24

First Quarter
Min.—Smith 4 run (Anderson kick), 5:48.
Det.—Morton 6 pass from Batch (Hanson kick), 14:05.

Second Quarter
Min.—FG, Anderson 44, 2:07.
Det.—FG, Hanson 39, 7:48.
Min.—Moss 67 pass from George (Anderson kick), 9:16.

Fourth Quarter
Min.—Hoard 3 run (Anderson kick), 10:04.
Det.—Morton 36 pass from Frerotte (Hanson kick), 12:44.
Attendance—64,103.

	Detroit	Minnesota
First downs	20	20
Rushes-yards	14-16	30-137
Passing	286	242
Punt returns	1-9	2-(-6)
Kickoff returns	5-115	4-104
Interception returns	2-22	1-18
Comp.-att.-int.	31-46-1	14-24-2
Sacked-yards lost	7-55	5-33
Punts	4-44	1-41
Fumbles-lost	1-1	2-1
Penalties-yards	4-47	7-45
Time of possession	30:42	29:18

INDIVIDUAL STATISTICS
RUSHING—Detroit, Rivers 11-6, Schlesinger 3-10. Minnesota, Smith 22-97, Hoard 7-41, George 1-(minus 1).
PASSING—Detroit, Batch 17-24-0-161, Frerotte 14-22-1-180. Minnesota, George 14-24-2-275.
RECEIVING—Detroit, Morton 10-128, Crowell 8-120, Rivers 4-8, Sloan 3-40, Moore 2-16, Schlesinger 2-10, Stablein 1-12, Irvin 1-7. Minnesota, Moss 5-155, Carter 3-52, Jordan 2-13, Glover 1-23, Smith 1-13, Reed 1-13, Hoard 1-6.
MISSED FIELD GOAL ATTEMPTS—Detroit, Hanson 58. Minnesota, Anderson 52.
INTERCEPTIONS—Detroit, Rice 1-20, Kriewaldt 1-2. Minnesota, Tate 1-18.
KICKOFF RETURNS—Detroit, Talton 4-98, Howard 1-17. Minnesota, Tate 3-88, M. Williams 1-16.
PUNT RETURNS—Detroit, Stablein 1-9. Minnesota, Moss 2-(minus 6).
SACKS—Detroit, Scroggins 2, Porcher 1, Kirschke 1, Pritchett 1. Minnesota, Clemons 2.5, Randle 2, Doleman 1.5, Griffith 1.

BILLS 31, COLTS 6

Sunday, January 2

Indianapolis	3	3	0	0— 6
Buffalo	7	14	0	10—31

First Quarter
Ind.—FG, Vanderjagt 27, 5:20.
Buf.—A. Smith 21 run (Christie kick), 9:38.

Second Quarter
Buf.—P. Price 23 pass from Johnson (Christie kick), 0:53.
Ind.—FG, Vanderjagt 24, 8:22.
Buf.—Linton 3 run (Christie kick), 14:33.

Fourth Quarter
Buf.—Collins 1 pass from Johnson (Christie kick), 0:49.
Buf.—FG, Christie 19, 11:23.
Attendance—61,959.

	Indianapolis	Buffalo
First downs	13	23
Rushes-yards	19-44	31-132
Passing	182	287
Punt returns	1-5	1-6
Kickoff returns	6-100	3-42
Interception returns	0-0	1-29
Comp.-att.-int.	21-37-1	24-32-0
Sacked-yards lost	0-0	0-0
Punts	4-40	3-39

1999 REVIEW Week 17

– 214 –

	Indianapolis	Buffalo
Fumbles-lost	0-0	0-0
Penalties-yards	2-23	3-25
Time of possession	27:23	32:37

INDIVIDUAL STATISTICS

RUSHING—Indianapolis, James 18-50, Elias 1-(minus 6). Buffalo, Linton 18-60, Johnson 7-36, A. Smith 3-31, Gordon 3-5.

PASSING—Indianapolis, Manning 18-29-0-163, Walsh 3-8-1-19. Buffalo, Johnson 24-32-0-287.

RECEIVING—Indianapolis, Dilger 5-52, Harrison 4-51, James 4-33, Wilkins 3-25, Pollard 2-9, Elias 2-8, Green 1-4. Buffalo, Moulds 8-110, Reed 5-23, K. Williams 2-53, P. Price 2-31, Riemersma 2-28, Jackson 2-22, Collins 2-8, Linton 1-12.

MISSED FIELD GOAL ATTEMPTS—None.

INTERCEPTIONS—Buffalo, T. Smith 1-29.

KICKOFF RETURNS—Indianapolis, Wilkins 5-100, Austin 1-0. Buffalo, K. Williams 3-42.

PUNT RETURNS—Indianapolis, Wilkins 1-5. Buffalo, K. Williams 1-6.

SACKS—None.

PACKERS 49, CARDINALS 24

Sunday, January 2

Arizona	0	3	7	14—24
Green Bay	7	7	14	21—49

First Quarter

G.B.—Schroeder 10 pass from Favre (Longwell kick), 7:22.

Second Quarter

Ariz.—FG, Jacke 23, 1:12.
G.B.—Levens 8 run (Longwell kick), 9:01.

Third Quarter

G.B.—Levens 1 run (Longwell kick), 9:03.
Ariz.—Sanders 6 pass from Plummer (Jacke kick), 13:11.
G.B.—Mitchell 88 kickoff return (Longwell kick), 13:28.

Fourth Quarter

G.B.—Levens 5 run (Longwell kick), 2:51.
Ariz.—Bates 1 run (Jacke kick), 5:31.
G.B.—Schroeder 32 pass from Favre (Longwell kick), 12:22.
Ariz.—Cody 9 pass from Plummer (Jacke kick), 13:29.
G.B.—Levens 1 run (Longwell kick), 14:02.
Attendance—59,818.

	Arizona	Green Bay
First downs	30	26
Rushes-yards	24-80	28-176
Passing	384	299
Punt returns	0-0	1-9
Kickoff returns	8-152	4-132
Interception returns	1-6	3-4
Comp.-att.-int.	35-57-3	21-34-1
Sacked-yards lost	3-12	2-12
Punts	3-43	3-30
Fumbles-lost	2-1	2-0
Penalties-yards	3-20	3-20
Time of possession	32:00	28:00

INDIVIDUAL STATISTICS

RUSHING—Arizona, Bates 17-64, Murrell 5-13, Plummer 2-3. Green Bay, Levens 24-146, Mitchell 2-10, Favre 1-20, Hasselbeck 1-0.

PASSING—Arizona, Plummer 35-57-3-396. Green Bay, Favre 21-34-1-311.

RECEIVING—Arizona, Sanders 13-118, Moore 6-120, Murrell 5-37, Boston 4-52, Bates 3-35, Hardy 2-18, Cody 1-9, McWilliams 1-7. Green Bay, Schroeder 6-93, Thomason 4-44, Bradford 3-41, Levens 3-23, Jordan 2-54, Freeman 1-46, Mitchell 1-9, Henderson 1-1.

MISSED FIELD GOAL ATTEMPTS—Arizona, Jacke 47.

INTERCEPTIONS—Arizona, Tillman 1-6. Green Bay, M. McKenzie 2-4, Lyon 1-0.

KICKOFF RETURNS—Arizona, Bates 4-81, Cody 3-61, Makovicka 1-10. Green Bay, Mitchell 2-109, Jordan 1-19, Sharper 1-4.

PUNT RETURNS—Green Bay, Jordan 1-9.

SACKS—Arizona, Rice 2. Green Bay, Holliday 1, Vinson 1, Hunt 0.5, S. Dotson 0.5.

PATRIOTS 20, RAVENS 3

Sunday, January 2

Baltimore	0	3	0	0— 3
New England	0	13	7	0—20

Second Quarter

Bal.—FG, Stover 19, 1:27.
N.E.—FG, Vinatieri 25, 4:59.
N.E.—Bartrum 1 pass from Bledsoe (Vinatieri kick), 9:56.
N.E.—FG, Vinatieri 51, 15:00.

Third Quarter

N.E.—Eaton 23 fumble return (Vinatieri kick), 7:01.
Attendance—50,263.

	Baltimore	New England
First downs	23	12
Rushes-yards	23-119	22-49
Passing	194	102
Punt returns	3-14	4-70
Kickoff returns	3-56	2-103
Interception returns	1-0	2-0
Comp.-att.-int.	26-40-2	15-26-1
Sacked-yards lost	7-57	2-6
Punts	5-46	5-37
Fumbles-lost	2-2	0-0
Penalties-yards	9-60	3-59
Time of possession	33:14	26:46

INDIVIDUAL STATISTICS

RUSHING—Baltimore, Holmes 16-95, Evans 2-12, Banks 2-7, Rhett 2-0, Case 1-5. New England, Allen 13-26, Shaw 5-17, Bledsoe 3-0, Warren 1-6.

PASSING—Baltimore, Banks 18-26-1-163, Case 8-14-1-88. New England, Bledsoe 15-25-1-108, Brown 0-1-0-0.

RECEIVING—Baltimore, Johnson 9-114, Holmes 6-43, Ismail 5-50, Evans 4-22, Armour 2-22. New England, Brown 5-19, Coates 3-35, Warren 3-29, Brisby 1-10, Jefferson 1-10, T. Carter 1-4, Bartrum 1-1.

MISSED FIELD GOAL ATTEMPTS—None.

INTERCEPTIONS—Baltimore, McAlister 1-0. New England, Milloy 1-0, Serwanga 1-0.

KICKOFF RETURNS—Baltimore, Harris 3-56. New England, Brown 2-103.

PUNT RETURNS—Baltimore, J. Lewis 3-14. New England, Brown 4-70.

SACKS—Baltimore, Sharper 1, Siragusa 1. New England, T. Johnson 2, Thomas 2, Milloy 1, McGinest 1, Collons 1.

RAIDERS 41, CHIEFS 38

Sunday, January 2

Oakland	7	21	7	3	3—41
Kansas City	17	7	7	7	0—38

First Quarter

K.C.—Vanover 84 punt return (Stoyanovich kick), 1:57.
K.C.—Hasty 34 interception return (Stoyanovich kick), 2:14.
K.C.—FG, Stoyanovich 33, 7:29.
Oak.—Shedd 20 blocked punt return (Nedney kick), 12:11.

Second Quarter

Oak.—Crockett 12 pass from Gannon (Nedney kick), 6:26.
Oak.—Kaufman 22 pass from Gannon (Nedney kick), 11:51.
K.C.—Gonzalez 7 pass from Grbac (Stoyanovich kick), 14:06.
Oak.—Wheatley 23 pass from Gannon (Nedney kick), 14:47.

Third Quarter

K.C.—Horn 15 pass from Grbac (Stoyanovich kick), 11:56.
Oak.—Wheatley 26 run (Nedney kick), 12:57.

Fourth Quarter

K.C.—Lockett 39 pass from Grbac (Stoyanovich kick), 7:38.
Oak.—FG, Nedney 38, 14:15.

Overtime

Oak.—FG, Nedney 33, 3:13.
Attendance—79,026.

	Oakland	Kansas City
First downs	21	25
Rushes-yards	30-106	38-189
Passing	302	240
Punt returns	3-25	6-126
Kickoff returns	4-80	7-102
Interception returns	0-0	2-36
Comp.-att.-int.	25-47-2	20-39-0
Sacked-yards lost	4-22	1-3
Punts	9-43	9-35
Fumbles-lost	0-0	1-1
Penalties-yards	5-35	5-33
Time of possession	33:26	29:47

INDIVIDUAL STATISTICS

RUSHING—Oakland, Wheatley 17-86, Kaufman 9-15, Crockett 4-5. Kansas City, Bennett 20-84, Morris 9-34, Richardson 8-70, Cloud 1-1.
PASSING—Oakland, Gannon 25-47-2-324. Kansas City, Grbac 20-39-0-243.
RECEIVING—Oakland, Ritchie 8-50, Brown 6-122, Wheatley 3-34, Dudley 2-51, Mickens 2-26, Crockett 2-21, Kaufman 2-20. Kansas City, Gonzalez 6-56, Horn 4-62, Lockett 3-69, Rison 2-20, Richardson 2-9, Alexander 1-18, Morris 1-9, Bennett 1-0.
MISSED FIELD GOAL ATTEMPTS—Kansas City, Stoyanovich 44.
INTERCEPTIONS—Kansas City, Hasty 1-34, Dishman 1-2.
KICKOFF RETURNS—Oakland, Kaufman 4-80. Kansas City, Vanover 3-62, Horn 3-34, Manusky 1-6.
PUNT RETURNS—Oakland, Gordon 3-25. Kansas City, Vanover 5-116, Lockett 1-10.
SACKS—Oakland, Biekert 1. Kansas City, Hicks 1.5, Patton 1, Barndt 1, O'Neal 0.5.

BUCCANEERS 20, BEARS 6

Sunday, January 2

Tampa Bay	0	10	3	7—	20
Chicago	0	0	3	3—	6

Second Quarter
T.B.—FG, Gramatica 25, 12:44.
T.B.—Alstott 1 run (Gramatica kick), 14:44.

Third Quarter
Chi.—FG, Holmes 39, 8:14.
T.B.—FG, Gramatica 33, 12:45.

Fourth Quarter
Chi.—FG, Holmes 31, 1:36.
T.B.—Moore 6 pass from King (Gramatica kick), 7:27.
Attendance—66,944.

	Tampa Bay	Chicago
First downs	16	13
Rushes-yards	40-143	18-71
Passing	175	186
Punt returns	3-26	4-39
Kickoff returns	3-46	4-64
Interception returns	1-13	0-0
Comp.-att.-int.	18-24-0	20-42-1
Sacked-yards lost	1-3	2-10
Punts	6-43	5-48
Fumbles-lost	1-0	2-1
Penalties-yards	3-30	2-10
Time of possession	36:44	23:16

INDIVIDUAL STATISTICS

RUSHING—Tampa Bay, Alstott 22-64, Dunn 16-80, King 2-(minus 1). Chicago, Allen 12-43, McNown 5-29, Milburn 1-(minus 1).
PASSING—Tampa Bay, King 18-24-0-178. Chicago, McNown 20-42-1-196.
RECEIVING—Tampa Bay, Green 10-113, Alstott 4-19, Emanuel 1-22, McDonald 1-15, Moore 1-6, Dunn 1-3. Chicago, M. Robinson 7-84, Booker 4-29, Engram 3-32, Allen 3-26, Wetnight 3-25.
MISSED FIELD GOAL ATTEMPTS—Tampa Bay, Gramatica 48.
INTERCEPTIONS—Tampa Bay, Abraham 1-13.
KICKOFF RETURNS—Tampa Bay, Dunn 3-46. Chicago, Bennett 2-38, Milburn 2-26.
PUNT RETURNS—Tampa Bay, Williams 3-26. Chicago, Milburn 4-39.
SACKS—Tampa Bay, White 1, Jones 1. Chicago, B. Robinson 1.

EAGLES 38, RAMS 31

Sunday, January 2

St. Louis	7	10	7	7—	31
Philadelphia	3	14	7	14—	38

First Quarter
St.L.—Faulk 8 pass from Warner (Wilkins kick), 5:18.
Phi.—FG, Akers 46, 7:33.

Second Quarter
St.L.—Faulk 1 run (Wilkins kick), 3:03.
Phi.—Small 63 pass from McNabb (N. Johnson kick), 4:46.
St.L.—FG, Wilkins 47, 8:40.
Phi.—Staley 3 pass from McNabb (N. Johnson kick), 14:28.

Third Quarter
Phi.—Mamula 41 interception return (N. Johnson kick), 2:45.
St.L.—Holt 15 pass from Warner (Wilkins kick), 5:38.

Fourth Quarter
Phi.—Lewis 5 pass from McNabb (N. Johnson kick), 4:05.
Phi.—Harris 17 interception return (N. Johnson kick), 13:44.
St.L.—Holt 63 pass from Germaine (Wilkins kick), 14:01.
Attendance—60,700.

	St. Louis	Philadelphia
First downs	20	13
Rushes-yards	26-201	23-51
Passing	239	156
Punt returns	5-30	3-25
Kickoff returns	6-148	5-153
Interception returns	2-19	4-89
Comp.-att.-int.	21-40-4	15-32-2
Sacked-yards lost	5-38	3-23
Punts	4-46	7-47
Fumbles-lost	3-3	1-0
Penalties-yards	5-54	8-65
Time of possession	33:01	26:59

INDIVIDUAL STATISTICS

RUSHING—St. Louis, Holcombe 15-86, Faulk 6-79, Watson 3-3, Hakim 1-31, Germaine 1-2. Philadelphia, Staley 18-44, McNabb 5-7.
PASSING—St. Louis, Warner 12-24-2-141, Germaine 9-16-2-136. Philadelphia, McNabb 15-32-2-179.
RECEIVING—St. Louis, Holt 5-122, Proehl 5-61, Faulk 3-27, Holcombe 2-20, Hakim 2-16, Hodgins 2-11, Conwell 1-11, R. Williams 1-9. Philadelphia, Small 6-98, Brown 3-26, Lewis 2-26, Staley 2-14, C. Martin 1-9, Broughton 1-6.
MISSED FIELD GOAL ATTEMPTS—Philadelphia, N. Johnson 39.
INTERCEPTIONS—St. Louis, M. Jones 1-19, McCleon 1-0. Philadelphia, Mamula 1-41, Cook 1-29, Harris 1-17, Hauck 1-2.
KICKOFF RETURNS—St. Louis, Horne 6-148. Philadelphia, Rossum 5-153.
PUNT RETURNS—St. Louis, Hakim 3-21, Horne 2-9. Philadelphia, Rossum 3-25.
SACKS—St. Louis, M. Jones 1, Carter 1, Farr 0.5, Clemons 0.5. Philadelphia, T. Williams 2, Mamula 1, Cook 1, Team 1.

JAGUARS 24, BENGALS 7

Sunday, January 2

Cincinnati	7	0	0	0—	7
Jacksonville	7	10	0	7—	24

First Quarter
Cin.—Shaw 8 run (Pelfrey kick), 5:45.
Jac.—Taylor 13 run (Hollis kick), 9:26.

Second Quarter
Jac.—McCardell 25 pass from Fiedler (Hollis kick), 1:45.
Jac.—FG, Hollis 27, 14:39.

Fourth Quarter
Jac.—Taylor 1 run (Hollis kick), 5:41.
Attendance—70,532.

	Cincinnati	Jacksonville
First downs	13	30
Rushes-yards	18-110	36-135
Passing	126	305
Punt returns	2-9	3-30
Kickoff returns	5-123	1-16
Interception returns	0-0	2-69
Comp.-att.-int.	13-23-2	28-39-0
Sacked-yards lost	3-15	2-12
Punts	5-36	2-48
Fumbles-lost	0-0	1-1
Penalties-yards	6-64	8-49
Time of possession	22:23	37:37

INDIVIDUAL STATISTICS

RUSHING—Cincinnati, Basnight 10-86, Shaw 4-20, Blake 3-3, Groce 1-1. Jacksonville, Taylor 22-85, J. Stewart 9-42, Howard 3-10, Fiedler 2-(minus 2).
PASSING—Cincinnati, Blake 13-23-2-141. Jacksonville, Fiedler 28-39-0-317.
RECEIVING—Cincinnati, Basnight 3-58, Pickens 3-31, Scott 2-21, Groce 1-14, Battaglia 1-9, Jackson 1-7, Hundon 1-5, Shaw 1-(minus 4). Jacksonville, J. Smith 14-165, McCardell 9-108, Brady 3-32, Jones 1-13, Taylor 1-(minus 1).
MISSED FIELD GOAL ATTEMPTS—Jacksonville, Hollis 34, 28.
INTERCEPTIONS—Jacksonville, Thomas 1-36, Beasley 1-33.
KICKOFF RETURNS—Cincinnati, Mack 4-99, Williams 1-24. Jacksonville, Whitted 1-16.

PUNT RETURNS—Cincinnati, Griffin 2-9. Jacksonville, Barlow 3-30.
SACKS—Cincinnati, Gibson 1, von Oelhoffen 1. Jacksonville, Hardy 1, Walker 1, Payne 1.

CHARGERS 12, BRONCOS 6

Sunday, January 2

San Diego	0	12	0	0	—12
Denver	0	0	3	3	— 6

Second Quarter
S.D.—Fazande 1 run (kick blocked), 3:34.
S.D.—FG, Carney 25, 8:05.
S.D.—FG, Carney 28, 15:00.

Third Quarter
Den.—FG, Elam 37, 6:00.

Fourth Quarter
Den.—FG, Elam 50, 1:03.
Attendance—69,278.

	San Diego	Denver
First downs	17	15
Rushes-yards	34-194	22-44
Passing	183	191
Punt returns	3-27	4-5
Kickoff returns	3-52	3-65
Interception returns	0-0	2-12
Comp.-att.-int.	17-26-2	23-46-0
Sacked-yards lost	3-10	4-20
Punts	5-48	8-50
Fumbles-lost	4-2	3-1
Penalties-yards	6-50	6-45
Time of possession	29:15	30:45

INDIVIDUAL STATISTICS
RUSHING—San Diego, Fazande 30-183, Bynum 2-6, Harbaugh 1-5, Fletcher 1-0. Denver, Gary 18-38, Griese 2-4, Griffith 1-2, Loville 1-0.
PASSING—San Diego, Harbaugh 12-19-2-115, Moreno 5-7-0-78. Denver, Griese 23-46-0-211.
RECEIVING—San Diego, J. Graham 6-102, McCrary 3-39, Ricks 2-20, C. Jones 2-6, F. Jones 1-11, Fletcher 1-7, Bynum 1-5, Stephens 1-3. Denver, R. Smith 9-106, McCaffrey 6-54, Gary 3-11, Chamberlain 1-14, McGriff 1-13, Carswell 1-8, Loville 1-4, Griffith 1-1.
MISSED FIELD GOAL ATTEMPTS—San Diego, Carney 46.
INTERCEPTIONS—Denver, James 2-12.
KICKOFF RETURNS—San Diego, Bynum 2-38, Fletcher 1-14. Denver, Watson 2-53, Loville 1-12.
PUNT RETURNS—San Diego, C. Jones 3-27. Denver, Watson 4-5.
SACKS—San Diego, Johnson 2, Williams 1, Fontenot 1. Denver, Hasselbach 1, Tanuvasa 1, Pryce 1.

TITANS 47, STEELERS 36

Sunday, January 2

Tennessee	7	24	9	7	—47
Pittsburgh	7	0	22	7	—36

First Quarter
Ten.—Wycheck 9 pass from McNair (Del Greco kick), 5:24.
Pit.—Huntley 8 run (K. Brown kick), 12:01.

Second Quarter
Ten.—Thomas 11 run (Del Greco kick), 6:58.
Ten.—Wycheck 26 pass from O'Donnell (Del Greco kick), 13:49.
Ten.—Kearse 14 fumble return (Del Greco kick), 13:59.
Ten.—FG, Del Greco 42, 14:51.

Third Quarter
Pit.—Ward 15 pass from Tomczak (Ward pass from Tomczak), 5:42.
Ten.—Safety, M. Tomczak sacked by J. Thornton in end zone, 7:36.
Ten.—Roan 24 pass from O'Donnell (Del Greco kick), 12:04.
Pit.—Bettis 1 run (K. Brown kick), 13:21.
Pit.—Porter 46 fumble return (K. Brown kick), 13:34.

Fourth Quarter
Ten.—Walker 83 fumble return (Del Greco kick), 11:01.
Pit.—Shaw 35 pass from Tomczak (K. Brown kick), 13:18.
Attendance—48,025.

	Tennessee	Pittsburgh
First downs	21	22
Rushes-yards	32-140	29-138
Passing	197	295
Punt returns	2-8	2-22
Kickoff returns	4-60	7-167
Interception returns	1-29	1-23
Comp.-att.-int.	15-23-1	21-39-1
Sacked-yards lost	3-19	2-14
Punts	6-44	3-50
Fumbles-lost	3-2	4-3
Penalties-yards	6-56	8-96
Time of possession	33:19	26:41

INDIVIDUAL STATISTICS
RUSHING—Tennessee, Thomas 21-95, E. George 8-32, McNair 2-14, O'Donnell 1-(minus 1). Pittsburgh, Bettis 15-61, Huntley 11-78, Tomczak 2-(minus 1), Miller 1-0.
PASSING—Tennessee, O'Donnell 6-12-1-109, McNair 9-11-0-107. Pittsburgh, Tomczak 21-39-1-309.
RECEIVING—Tennessee, Wycheck 5-80, Thigpen 4-50, Dyson 2-34, Byrd 2-25, Roan 1-24, Sanders 1-3. Pittsburgh, Shaw 7-131, Ward 6-68, Edwards 3-27, Cushing 2-29, Witman 1-38, Huntley 1-11, Johnson 1-5.
MISSED FIELD GOAL ATTEMPTS—None.
INTERCEPTIONS—Tennessee, Bowden 1-29. Pittsburgh, Kirkland 1-23.
KICKOFF RETURNS—Tennessee, Mason 4-60. Pittsburgh, Zereoue 4-114, Huntley 1-29, Ward 1-24, Cline 1-0.
PUNT RETURNS—Tennessee, Byrd 2-8. Pittsburgh, Shaw 1-17, Edwards 1-5.
SACKS—Tennessee, Thornton 1, Kearse 1. Pittsburgh, Flowers 1, Porter 1, Roye 1.

COWBOYS 26, GIANTS 18

Sunday, January 2

N.Y. Giants	0	0	3	15	—18
Dallas	6	10	7	3	—26

First Quarter
Dal.—FG, Murray 20, 2:18.
Dal.—FG, Murray 21, 13:57.

Second Quarter
Dal.—Ismail 4 pass from Aikman (Murray kick), 8:25.
Dal.—FG, Murray 27, 14:35.

Third Quarter
NYG—FG, Blanchard 29, 9:36.
Dal.—Tucker 90 pass from Aikman (Murray kick), 10:46.

Fourth Quarter
NYG—Montgomery 1 run (Blanchard kick), 4:41.
Dal.—FG, Murray 40, 10:51.
NYG—Alford 7 pass from Collins (Montgomery run), 14:03.
Attendance—63,767.

	N.Y. Giants	Dallas
First downs	19	20
Rushes-yards	17-74	29-149
Passing	306	288
Punt returns	1-(-9)	1-7
Kickoff returns	5-109	3-96
Interception returns	0-0	1-0
Comp.-att.-int.	31-48-1	23-33-0
Sacked-yards lost	1-8	0-0
Punts	5-36	2-42
Fumbles-lost	1-0	1-0
Penalties-yards	5-39	7-56
Time of possession	30:02	29:58

INDIVIDUAL STATISTICS
RUSHING—New York, Montgomery 12-36, Bennett 3-35, Barber 1-3, Collins 1-0. Dallas, E. Smith 22-122, Warren 3-28, Aikman 3-(minus 2), Thomas 1-1.
PASSING—New York, Collins 31-48-1-314. Dallas, Aikman 23-32-0-288, Sanders 0-1-0-0.
RECEIVING—New York, Barber 13-100, Comella 5-37, Hilliard 5-37, Jurevicius 3-86, Toomer 2-35, Patten 1-14, Alford 1-7, Bennett 1-(minus 2). Dallas, Ismail 7-62, Tucker 4-122, Warren 3-18, LaFleur 3-17, Ogden 2-28, E. Smith 2-19, Brazzell 1-19, Lucky 1-3.
MISSED FIELD GOAL ATTEMPTS—None.
INTERCEPTIONS—Dallas, Teague 1-0.
KICKOFF RETURNS—New York, Levingston 2-43, Patten 1-26, Barber 1-23, Comella 1-17. Dallas, Tucker 2-93, Coakley 1-3.
PUNT RETURNS—New York, Barber 1-(minus 9). Dallas, Sanders 1-7.
SACKS—Dallas, Lett 1.

— 217 —

PANTHERS 45, SAINTS 13

Sunday, January 2

New Orleans	0	0	0	13	13
Carolina	10	7	14	14	45

First Quarter
Car.—FG, Cunningham 27, 2:58.
Car.—Muhammad 7 pass from Beuerlein (Cunningham kick), 12:58.

Second Quarter
Car.—Walls 37 pass from Beuerlein (Cunningham kick), 3:03.

Third Quarter
Car.—Walls 15 pass from Beuerlein (Cunningham kick), 2:54.
Car.—Jeffers 40 pass from Beuerlein (Cunningham kick), 14:06.

Fourth Quarter
N.O.—Kennison 3 pass from Delhomme (Brien kick), 2:00.
Car.—Bates 95 kickoff return (Cunningham kick), 2:21.
Car.—Jeffers 32 pass from Beuerlein (Cunningham kick), 7:36.
N.O.—Delhomme 9 run (pass failed), 14:42.
Attendance—56,929.

	New Orleans	Carolina
First downs	22	18
Rushes-yards	25-105	14-67
Passing	230	288
Punt returns	2-19	4-40
Kickoff returns	7-107	3-132
Interception returns	0-0	4-64
Comp.-att.-int.	26-49-4	22-41-0
Sacked-yards lost	3-13	6-34
Punts	7-43	6-43
Fumbles-lost	0-0	1-1
Penalties-yards	6-54	9-75
Time of possession	34:15	25:45

INDIVIDUAL STATISTICS
RUSHING—New Orleans, R. Williams 14-7, Delhomme 8-78, Poole 1-14, Craver 1-3, Perry 1-3. Carolina, Biakabutuka 8-24, Lane 4-16, Jeffers 1-23, Beuerlein 1-4.
PASSING—New Orleans, Delhomme 26-49-4-243. Carolina, Beuerlein 22-41-0-322.
RECEIVING—New Orleans, Poole 6-104, Kennison 6-44, Dawsey 5-32, R. Williams 5-5, Hastings 3-50, Franklin 1-8. Carolina, Jeffers 7-165, Muhammad 6-45, Walls 4-88, Biakabutuka 4-21, Floyd 1-3.
MISSED FIELD GOAL ATTEMPTS—None.
INTERCEPTIONS—Carolina, Minter 1-44, Alexander 1-18, Wells 1-1, Evans 1-1.
KICKOFF RETURNS—New Orleans, Philyaw 6-89, Davis 1-18. Carolina, Bates 2-123, Johnson 1-9.
PUNT RETURNS—New Orleans, Kennison 2-19. Carolina, Metcalf 4-40.
SACKS—New Orleans, Kei. Mitchell 2, B. Smith 1, Whitehead 1, Glover 1, Fields 1. Carolina, Greene 2, Peter 1.

REDSKINS 21, DOLPHINS 10

Sunday, January 2

Miami	0	3	0	7	10
Washington	0	7	7	7	21

Second Quarter
Was.—Hicks 8 run (Conway kick), 10:09.
Mia.—FG, Mare 39, 12:31.

Third Quarter
Was.—Fryar 30 pass from Peete (Conway kick), 0:54.

Fourth Quarter
Was.—Centers 4 pass from Peete (Conway kick), 8:35.
Mia.—Gadsden 4 pass from Huard (Mare kick), 11:51.
Attendance—78,106.

	Miami	Washington
First downs	25	18
Rushes-yards	26-119	30-105
Passing	270	165
Punt returns	3-5	1-11
Kickoff returns	3-73	2-46
Interception returns	0-0	2-49
Comp.-att.-int.	29-53-2	13-20-0
Sacked-yards lost	3-10	2-9
Punts	4-46	6-44
Fumbles-lost	2-2	2-0
Penalties-yards	6-88	3-25
Time of possession	34:28	25:32

INDIVIDUAL STATISTICS
RUSHING—Miami, Denson 21-80, Huard 2-22, Pritchett 2-15, Konrad 1-2. Washington, Hicks 22-53, Mitchell 4-16, Weldon 2-(minus 2), Thrash 1-37, Centers 1-1.
PASSING—Miami, Huard 18-29-1-162, Marino 11-24-1-118. Washington, B. Johnson 7-11-0-75, Peete 6-9-0-99.
RECEIVING—Miami, Konrad 10-68, Gadsden 9-114, Pritchett 3-32, Denson 3-26, McKenzie 2-18, Green 1-13, Goodwin 1-9. Washington, Centers 4-36, Westbrook 3-25, Alexander 2-38, Fryar 1-30, Mitchell 1-29, Thrash 1-17, Hicks 1-(minus 1).
MISSED FIELD GOAL ATTEMPTS—Washington, Conway 51.
INTERCEPTIONS—Washington, McMillian 2-49.
KICKOFF RETURNS—Miami, Marion 3-73. Washington, Thrash 1-27, Mitchell 1-19.
PUNT RETURNS—Miami, Jacquet 3-5. Washington, Mitchell 1-11.
SACKS—Miami, Surtain 2. Washington, Kalu 1, Boutte 1, Lang 1.

FALCONS 34, 49ERS 29

Monday, January 3

San Francisco	0	7	8	14	29
Atlanta	7	10	14	3	34

First Quarter
Atl.—Dwight 5 pass from Chandler (Andersen kick), 9:28.

Second Quarter
S.F.—Owens 4 pass from Garcia (Richey kick), 1:10.
Atl.—FG, Andersen 49, 13:52.
Atl.—Dwight 70 punt return (Andersen kick), 14:48.

Third Quarter
Atl.—Mathis 19 pass from Chandler (Andersen kick), 5:32.
Atl.—Dwight 60 pass from Chandler (Andersen kick), 11:11.
S.F.—Jervey 1 run (Stokes pass from Garcia), 14:39.

Fourth Quarter
Atl.—FG, Andersen 38, 2:09.
S.F.—Garcia 5 run (Richey kick), 5:33.
S.F.—Stokes 43 pass from Garcia (Richey kick), 12:14.
Attendance—57,980.

	San Fran.	Atlanta
First downs	23	24
Rushes-yards	25-133	21-37
Passing	373	306
Punt returns	0-0	2-79
Kickoff returns	6-111	2-45
Interception returns	0-0	0-0
Comp.-att.-int.	26-34-0	19-37-0
Sacked-yards lost	0-0	0-0
Punts	4-40	3-33
Fumbles-lost	1-1	1-0
Penalties-yards	17-148	6-40
Time of possession	30:28	29:32

INDIVIDUAL STATISTICS
RUSHING—San Francisco, Garner 9-29, Garcia 7-26, Jackson 5-35, Jervey 4-43. Atlanta, Hanspard 16-27, Christian 3-8, Chandler 2-2.
PASSING—San Francisco, Garcia 26-34-0-373. Atlanta, Chandler 19-37-0-306.
RECEIVING—San Francisco, Rice 6-143, Stokes 5-130, Owens 5-31, Streets 2-25, Beasley 2-12, Vardell 2-9, Jackson 2-3, Clark 1-18, Jervey 1-2. Atlanta, Dwight 7-162, Mathis 5-69, Santiago 3-37, German 1-17, Oliver 1-10, Christian 1-7, Hanspard 1-4.
MISSED FIELD GOAL ATTEMPTS—Atlanta, Andersen 50.
INTERCEPTIONS—None.
KICKOFF RETURNS—San Francisco, Preston 3-54, Jervey 2-53, Lynch 1-4. Atlanta, Oliver 2-45.
PUNT RETURNS—Atlanta, Dwight 2-79.
SACKS—None.

WILD-CARD GAMES

AFC

TENNESSEE 22, BUFFALO 16

Why the Titans won: They pulled off one of the most memorable plays in NFL history (see below).
Why the Bills lost: They were victimized by one of the most memorable plays in NFL history (see below).
The turning points:
1. After Al Del Greco kicked a 36-yard field goal with 1:48 left to give Tennessee a 15-13 lead, the Bills responded with a six-play, 38-yard drive to go up 16-15 on a 41-yard field goal by Steve Christie with 16 seconds left. The Bills could have run more time off the clock had quarterback Rob Johnson not lost his shoe while completing a pass to rookie wide receiver Peerless Price on the play before Christie's kick, but they were out of timeouts and coach Wade Phillips decided to kick the field goal right away, rather than run another play and possibly turn the ball over.
2. Instead of squib-kicking the ensuing kickoff, the Bills popped it up, enabling Lorenzo Neal of the Titans to field the ball cleanly at his own 24. Neal then handed it back one yard to Frank Wycheck, who threw a perfect lateral to Kevin Dyson along the left sideline. Dyson did the rest, avoiding Buffalo's coverage team by running down the sideline practically untouched. The play was reviewed to determine if Wycheck's pass had crossed the line of scrimmage (making it an illegal forward pass), but it was upheld by the officials.
Notable: The game-winning play was called Home Run Throwback and Dyson was in for it only because Derrick Mason was injured and Anthony Dorsett was suffering from cramps. Teammates had to fill Dyson in about what to do on the play as he ran on the field. It was the first kickoff return of Dyson's NFL career. ... The Titans practiced Home Run Throwback every Saturday during the regular season but had never used it in a game. It was the brainchild of special teams coach Alan Lowry, who saw replays of a similar play in a 1982 game in which SMU beat Texas Tech. ... Tennessee finished the game with five kickoff returns for 193 yards. ... Titans rookie defensive end Jevon Kearse made three tackles, including a forced fumble and a safety on two sacks. He sacked Johnson for a safety in the second quarter for the game's first points. ... Tennessee quarterback Steve McNair attempted only one pass of 20 or more yards. ... Six Titans were members the 1992 Houston Oilers team that blew a 32-point lead and lost to Buffalo, 41-38, in overtime in the biggest comeback in NFL playoff history.
Quotable: Bills safety Henry Jones: "This hurt more than the three Super Bowls I was involved in." ... Lowry: "As soon as Buffalo kicked the field goal, coach (Jeff) Fisher and I looked at each other and we said, 'This is it.' " ... Dyson: "I was amazed. I said, 'What are they calling my name for?' Isaac (Byrd, a Titans receiver) was trying to explain the play. I had seen them work it a couple of times in practice. ... Out of the 17 weeks of the season, there were probably three times where I paid attention to it." Wycheck: "It wasn't a hard pass. You just throw it like you're in your back yard." ... Johnson: "I just hope for the referee's sake that they made the right call." ... Referee Phil Luckett, who reviewed the play: "We have nothing to prove that it was a forward pass." ... Titans owner Bud Adams: "I've been watching this game for 40 years, and I've seen a lot of plays, both for us and against us, but this is the most weird way to end a game I've seen."

TITANS 22, BILLS 16
Saturday, January 8

Buffalo	0	0	7	9—16
Tennessee	0	12	0	10—22

Second Quarter
Ten.—Safety, R. Johnson fumble forced by J. Kearse out of end zone, 3:41.
Ten.—McNair 1 run (Del Greco kick), 7:05.
Ten.—FG, Del Greco 40, 15:00.
Third Quarter
Buf.—A. Smith 4 run (Christie kick), 2:32.
Fourth Quarter
Buf.—A. Smith 1 run (pass failed), 3:52.
Ten.—FG, Del Greco 36, 13:12.
Buf.—FG, Christie 41, 14:44.
Ten.—Dyson 75 kickoff return (Del Greco kick), 14:57.
Attendance—66,782.

	Buffalo	Tennessee
First downs	13	16
Rushes-yards	27-123	39-139
Passing	96	55
Punt returns	3-10	6-32
Kickoff returns	4-73	5-193
Interception returns	1-8	0-0
Comp.-att.-int.	10-22-0	13-24-1
Sacked-yards lost	6-35	3-21
Punts	8-39	7-41
Fumbles-lost	2-2	2-1
Penalties-yards	10-59	2-12
Time of possession	24:54	35:06

INDIVIDUAL STATISTICS
RUSHING—Buffalo, A. Smith 14-79, Linton 5-25, Thomas 5-10, Johnson 3-9. Tennessee, E. George 29-106, McNair 6-19, Thomas 4-14.
PASSING—Buffalo, Johnson 10-22-0-131. Tennessee, McNair 13-24-1-76.
RECEIVING—Buffalo, P. Price 5-62, Moulds 3-62, Gash 1-6, Collins 1-1. Tennessee, Wycheck 4-29, Harris 4-20, E. George 2-4, Sanders 1-11, Thigpen 1-8, Dyson 1-4.
MISSED FIELD GOAL ATTEMPTS—Tennessee, Del Greco 43.
INTERCEPTIONS—Buffalo, Winfield 1-8.
KICKOFF RETURNS—Buffalo, K. Williams 3-73, Gash 1-0. Tennessee, Mason 3-94, Byrd 1-23, Neal 1-1.
PUNT RETURNS—Buffalo, K. Williams 3-10. Tennessee, Mason 5-16, Byrd 1-16.
SACKS—Buffalo, B. Smith 2.5, Hansen 0.5. Tennessee, Kearse 2, Fisk 1, Rolle 1, Evans 1, Holmes 1.

MIAMI 20, SEATTLE 17

Why the Dolphins won: When his team needed it most, 38-year-old quarterback Dan Marino played like the Marino of old instead of an old Marino, completing four of seven passes for 84 yards while directing a game-winning, 11-play, 85-yard touchdown drive. Rookie running back J.J. Johnson scored the go-ahead touchdown on a two-yard run with 4:48 left, but the hero was Marino, who orchestrated the 37th fourth-quarter comeback of his 17-year career.

Why the Seahawks lost: In their first playoff game since 1988—the league's longest postseason drought—the Seahawks simply never got their offense untracked, thanks in part to a superb effort by the Miami defense. The Dolphins sacked quarterback Jon Kitna six times (three by end Trace Armstrong) and held the Seahawks to 171 total yards, just 32 yards (3 rushing) in the second half.

The turning points:
1. Down 10-3 at the half, the Dolphins marched 60 yards in 10 plays on their first possession after the intermission, with Marino capping the drive with a 1-yard TD pass to Oronde Gadsden. Marino, who was 5-of-8 for 28 yards in the first half, was 6-for-6 for 55 yards on the scoring drive.
2. Although rookie Charlie Rogers returned the ensuing kickoff 85 yards for a Seattle touchdown, the Dolphins bounced right back, forcing the Seahawks to punt on their next possession and then scoring the final points of the third quarter on a 50-yard Olindo Mare field goal. The field goal cut the Seahawks' lead to 17-13.
3. On what proved to be the game-winning drive, Marino completed a 23-yard pass to Tony Martin on third-and-17, a 29-yarder to Martin on second-and-7 and a 24-yarder to Gadsden on third-and-10 to set up Johnson's game-winning run.

Notable: Both teams entered the game with losses in five of their last six regular season games. ... It was Miami's first playoff road win since a 21-17 victory at Pittsburgh in the 1972 AFC championship game. ... The Dolphins did not commit a turnover for the first time in 10 games. In their previous six games they had 19 turnovers. ... Marino did not complete a pass longer than 27 yards. ... The Seahawks ran just three offensive plays in the third quarter.

Quotable: Miami coach Jimmy Johnson: "I knew we were going to win this game, and I told the team that. We had preparation this week like I haven't seen in a long time. You lose games, and your confidence gets broken. But our guys got a reprieve getting into the playoffs." ... Martin, on his 23-yard catch on third-and-17: "Those are long odds, but that's what this game is all about. Long odds. Look at what Tennessee did to Buffalo with long odds." ... Kitna: "Now that it's over for us, maybe Dan will get the Super Bowl ring he deserves to cap off a great career. He did what he had to do, particularly in the fourth quarter. He made some great throws." ... Armstrong, on his three-sack game: "I've had a bunch of twos, but not many like this." ...

Armstrong, on Marino: "Dan is a legend in this game. No one is more respected or loved on this team than Dan. It was great for him to have a great day." ... Mike Holmgren, who concluded his first season as Seahawks coach: "I am not going to remember the losses. I am going to remember that we were the AFC West champions."

DOLPHINS 20, SEAHAWKS 17
Sunday, January 9

Miami	3	0	10	7—20
Seattle	7	3	7	0—17

First Quarter
Sea.—Dawkins 9 pass from Kitna (Peterson kick), 8:42.
Mia.—FG, Mare 32, 12:55.

Second Quarter
Sea.—FG, Peterson 50, 14:15.

Third Quarter
Mia.—Gadsden 1 pass from Marino (Mare kick), 6:05.
Sea.—Rogers 85 kickoff return (Peterson kick), 6:23.
Mia.—FG, Mare 50, 12:38.

Fourth Quarter
Mia.—Johnson 2 run (Mare kick), 10:12.
Attendance—66,170.

	Miami	Seattle
First downs	18	12
Rushes-yards	37-108	20-41
Passing	191	130
Punt returns	6-63	3-24
Kickoff returns	3-88	4-159
Interception returns	2-37	0-0
Comp.-att.-int.	17-30-0	14-30-2
Sacked-yards lost	1-5	6-32
Punts	8-41	7-48
Fumbles-lost	0-0	0-0
Penalties-yards	6-67	2-10
Time of possession	34:48	25:12

INDIVIDUAL STATISTICS

RUSHING—Miami, Johnson 27-86, Denson 7-19, Pritchett 2-4, Marino 1-(minus 1). Seattle, Watters 19-40, Kitna 1-1.
PASSING—Miami, Marino 17-30-0-196. Seattle, Kitna 14-30-2-162.
RECEIVING—Miami, McDuffie 5-82, Martin 5-70, Gadsden 2-25, Johnson 2-3, Konrad 1-7, Goodwin 1-6, Perry 1-3. Seattle, Dawkins 3-35, Pritchard 3-34, Fauria 3-31, Watters 2-22, R. Brown 2-18, Galloway 1-22.
MISSED FIELD GOAL ATTEMPTS—None.
INTERCEPTIONS—Miami, Marion 1-31, Buckley 1-6.
KICKOFF RETURNS—Miami, Marion 3-88. Seattle, Rogers 4-159.
PUNT RETURNS—Miami, Jacquet 5-38, McDuffie 1-25. Seattle, Rogers 3-24.
SACKS—Miami, Armstrong 3, Thomas 1, Owens 1, Wilson 1. Seattle, Adams 1.

NFC

WASHINGTON 27, DETROIT 13

Why the Redskins won: They jumped on the Lions early and never let up. Washington converted four of its first five third-down opportunities, gained 275 yards in offense and scored 27 points before halftime. Its defense held Detroit to 23 rushing yards in the first half and intercepted two passes.

Why the Lions lost: They did little to challenge the perception that they were the weakest of the league's 12 playoff teams (the 8-8 Lions had lost their previous four games). Detroit was forced to throw on nearly every play after falling behind, and former Redskins quarterback Gus Frerotte wasn't up to the task. Frerotte, starting in place of the injured Charlie Batch, completed 21 of 46 passes for 251 yards but was intercepted two times and sacked five times. The Lions used three different players at tailback—including fullback Cory Schlesinger—but none had much success. One of Detroit's touchdowns came on a 94-yard return of a blocked field goal, the other a meaningless score on the final play of the game.

The turning points:
1. After forcing the Redskins to punt on fourth-and-5 early in the game, the Lions botched the situation by running into the punter and giving Washington a first down. Moments later, Bryant Westbrook was penalized 41 yards for pass interference. The penalty put the ball on the 1-yard line, and Stephen Davis scored the game's first touchdown on the next play.
2. After stopping the Lions on their next possession, the Redskins put together an eight-play, 87-yard drive for their second touchdown, with Davis scoring from four yards out after setting up the touchdown with a 58-yard run to the Lions 29.

Notable: The Lions had beaten the Redskins 33-17 five weeks earlier in Detroit. ... The Redskins won despite losing Davis to a knee injury after 1.5 quarters. Davis, who had missed the final 2.5 games of the regular season with injuries, still finished with 119 yards on 15 carries and scored two touchdowns. ... The one-sided game was spiced up a bit when Redskins quarterback Brad Johnson and Lions defensive end Robert Porcher got involved in a scuffle in the third quarter. In the shoving match that followed, Washington tackle Tre Johnson accidentally knocked the cap off the head of back judge Bill Leavy. Johnson was ejected from the game and later fined. ... It was Washington's first playoff game in seven years and first under coach Norv Turner. ... The Lions were penalized eight times for 93 yards in the first 17 minutes and 12 times for 126 yards overall. ... The win was Washington's 20th straight at home against the Lions since 1935.

Quotable: Detroit coach Bobby Ross: "We took a good old-fashioned beating today. I really did think we were ready to play going into the game. Early in the game, a couple of things happened that really turned it around fast for us." ... Johnson, on Davis: "We managed to win the last two games of the regular season without him, but when he's in the game it makes an unbelievable impact." ... Turner: "The first half was as good as our team can play."

REDSKINS 27, LIONS 13

Saturday, January 8

Detroit	0	0	0	13—13
Washington	14	13	0	0—27

First Quarter
Was.—Davis 1 run (Conway kick), 5:51.
Was.—Davis 4 run (Conway kick), 12:32.

Second Quarter
Was.—FG, Conway 33, 1:10.
Was.—FG, Conway 23, 5:10.
Was.—Connell 30 pass from B. Johnson (Conway kick), 13:41.

Fourth Quarter
Det.—Rice 94 blocked FG return (pass failed), 5:37.
Det.—Rivers 5 pass from Frerotte (Hanson kick), 15:00.
Attendance—79,411.

	Detroit	Washington
First downs	14	23
Rushes-yards	10-45	46-223
Passing	213	166
Punt returns	2-13	2-18
Kickoff returns	6-126	2-43
Interception returns	2-5	2-5
Comp.-att.-int.	21-46-2	15-31-2
Sacked-yards lost	5-38	1-8
Punts	7-42	4-41
Fumbles-lost	3-0	1-0
Penalties-yards	12-126	6-75
Time of possession	21:32	38:28

INDIVIDUAL STATISTICS

RUSHING—Detroit, Schlesinger 7-23, Frerotte 2-16, Rivers 1-6. Washington, Hicks 23-46, Davis 15-119, Mitchell 7-55, Centers 1-3.

PASSING—Detroit, Frerotte 21-46-2-251. Washington, B. Johnson 15-31-2-174.

RECEIVING—Detroit, Crowell 5-41, Rivers 4-24, Moore 3-69, Stablein 3-32, Morton 2-29, Irvin 2-27, Sloan 1-24, Uwaezuoke 1-5. Washington, Centers 7-61, Connell 2-35, Hicks 2-27, Westbrook 2-22, Fryar 1-17, Alexander 1-12.

MISSED FIELD GOAL ATTEMPTS—Washington, Conway 31.

INTERCEPTIONS—Detroit, Boyd 1-5, C. Brown 1-0. Washington, Bailey 1-5, Stevens 1-0.

KICKOFF RETURNS—Detroit, Talton 5-114, Irvin 1-12. Washington, Mitchell 2-43.

PUNT RETURNS—Detroit, Uwaezuoke 2-13. Washington, Mitchell 2-18.

SACKS—Detroit, Porcher 1. Washington, Shade 2, Wilkinson 1, Jones 1, Kalu 1.

MINNESOTA 27, DALLAS 10

Why the Vikings won: They had a great offensive mix and did not commit a turnover. With the Vikings unable to throw the ball effectively in the early going, running back Robert Smith repeatedly burned the Cowboys for big gains on the ground. Smith's running loosened up the defense enough to help quarterback Jeff George and receivers Randy Moss and Cris Carter step to the fore later.

Why the Cowboys lost: Besides being unable to stop Minnesota's offense, the Cowboys never seemed to recover from a number of missed opportunities early on that could have changed the complexion of the game. Given a chance to take control, the Cowboys didn't. They also committed three turnovers.

The turning points:
1. On the Cowboys' third offensive play Emmitt Smith broke free for a 65-yard run to the Vikings' 3-yard line before being hauled down by cornerback Kenny Wright. Minnesota's defense then stiffened, forcing Dallas to settle for an 18-yard field goal by stuffing Smith twice and forcing Troy Aikman to overthrow tight end David LaFleur. What should have been a 7-0 lead was just three points.
2. The Vikings were forced to punt on their next possession, but Deion Sanders muffed the kick, with Dwayne Rudd recovering for Minnesota at the Dallas 30. That set up Gary Anderson for a 47-yard field goal to tie the game 3-3.
3. The Cowboys were leading, 10-3, early in the second quarter when fullback Robert Thomas fumbled at his own 23-yard line while trying to catch a pass. Anthony Bass recovered for Minnesota and four plays later Robert Smith caught a 26-yard TD pass from George to tie the game at 10-10. The Vikings never trailed again.

Notable: The Vikings ran 24 plays from scrimmage before Moss or Carter caught a pass. Minnesota had zero passing yards in the first quarter. ... It was George's first NFL playoff victory. ... In defeat Emmitt Smith surpassed Franco Harris to become the NFL's career postseason rushing leader (1,586 yards). He also tied Thurman Thomas' record for postseason touchdowns (21). ... Robert Smith broke his own team playoff record with 140 yards rushing. ... Although the Cowboys held Carter to just one catch for five yards and a TD, Moss caught five passes for 127 yards, including a 58-yarder for the go-ahead touchdown. ... Dallas ended its season with eight straight road losses.

Quotable: Minnesota coach Dennis Green, on his team's early offensive struggles: "Our timing might have been off a little bit. They played a lot of combination coverages. We had success running and not passing so we went more to the run, and later we went to the pass. We ran the ball well and in the playoffs you have to do that." ... Sanders, on the Cowboys' defensive game plan: "They were very successful today, but I don't think anyone is going to go into a game with the Minnesota Vikings thinking they are going to beat you with the run." ... Moss:

"All week we heard about the defensive scheme in Dallas, how they were going to play us. I didn't expect a big game like that from our whole offense, but we came out and put things together."

VIKINGS 27, COWBOYS 10
Sunday, January 9

Dallas	10	0	0	0	—10
Minnesota	3	14	3	7	—27

First Quarter
Dal.—FG, Murray 18, 3:51.
Min.—FG, Anderson 47, 7:01.
Dal.—E. Smith 5 run (Murray kick), 10:00.

Second Quarter
Min.—Smith 26 pass from George (Anderson kick), 5:39.
Min.—Moss 58 pass from George (Anderson kick), 14:32.

Third Quarter
Min.—FG, Anderson 38, 11:50.

Fourth Quarter
Min.—Carter 5 pass from George (Anderson kick), 2:20.
Attendance—64,056.

	Dallas	Minnesota
First downs	18	20
Rushes-yards	16-111	38-175
Passing	278	199
Punt returns	2-6	1-9
Kickoff returns	4-69	2-27
Interception returns	0-0	1-0
Comp.-att.-int.	22-38-1	12-25-0
Sacked-yards lost	1-8	3-13
Punts	4-46	5-41
Fumbles-lost	3-2	0-0
Penalties-yards	7-60	7-50
Time of possession	24:03	35:57

INDIVIDUAL STATISTICS

RUSHING—Dallas, E. Smith 15-99, Warren 1-12. Minnesota, Smith 28-140, Hoard 6-31, Cunningham 3-(minus 4), George 1-8.

PASSING—Dallas, Aikman 22-38-1-286. Minnesota, George 12-25-0-212.

RECEIVING—Dallas, Ismail 8-163, Tucker 4-67, LaFleur 3-22, Brazzell 2-12, Thomas 2-0, E. Smith 1-14, Warren 1-4, Ogden 1-4. Minnesota, Moss 5-127, Smith 3-58, Hoard 2-15, Kleinsasser 1-7, Carter 1-5.

MISSED FIELD GOAL ATTEMPTS—Dallas, Gowin 57.

INTERCEPTIONS—Minnesota, Griffith 1-0.

KICKOFF RETURNS—Dallas, Tucker 3-60, Neufeld 1-9. Minnesota, Tate 2-27.

PUNT RETURNS—Dallas, Sanders 2-6. Minnesota, Moss 1-9.

SACKS—Dallas, Hennings 1, Myers 1, Lett 1. Minnesota, Clemons 1.

DIVISIONAL PLAYOFFS

AFC

JACKSONVILLE 62, MIAMI 7

Why the Jaguars won: They scored early and often, making a mockery out of what should have been a close game. Jacksonville's 62 points were the most scored by an AFC team in a postseason game and the most ever scored against Miami, postseason or otherwise. And it wasn't like the Jaguars were trying to run up the score. They ran the ball on 24 of 27 plays in the second half and still outscored Miami 21-0.

Why the Dolphins lost: One week after an inspiring playoff performance against Seattle, quarterback Dan Marino regressed horribly, completing two passes to Jaguars cornerback Aaron Beasley before completing one to a Dolphins receiver. He completed just 11 of 25 passes for 95 yards before getting yanked by coach Jimmy Johnson after Miami's first possession of the second half. But all the blame should not be laid at the feet of Marino, who was playing his final NFL game. When things started to snowball on his teammates, they quit.

The turning points:
1. None. The second most lopsided playoff game in NFL history doesn't have any. The Dolphins committed seven turnovers, were outgained 520-131 in total yards and were never in the game. The back-breaking touchdown, if there was one, probably was a 90-yard run by Fred Taylor with 3:46 left in the first period that increased Jacksonville's lead to 17-0. It was the longest touchdown run in NFL playoff history, with Taylor first breaking an attempted tackle by safety Calvin Jackson and then swiftly eluding cornerback Patrick Surtain on his way to the end zone. Twenty-five seconds after Taylor's score, defensive end Tony Brackens returned a Marino fumble 16 yards for another Jaguars touchdown.

Notable: The 55-point margin of victory was surpassed only by Chicago's 73-0 rout of Washington in the 1940 NFL championship game. ... Starting quarterback Mark Brunell, playing with braces on both knees, was taken out of the game by coach Tom Coughlin after the Jaguars had built a 38-0 lead. At the time, Marino had yet to complete a pass. ... Jacksonville outgained Miami, 197 yards to minus-1, in the first quarter. ... The game was Johnson's last as an NFL coach. He resigned the following day after nine seasons in the league.

Quotable: Dolphins free safety Brock Marion: "It seemed like we played the whole game in slow motion." ... Jackson: "Just last week we were on cloud nine, and now we're a pile on the ground." ... Marino: "We didn't compete. We played horrible. I've never experienced a game like this in my life, going back to the time when I was a little kid." ... Dolphins safety Shawn Wooden: "It might look like we just sat down and let them win, but we were playing our hearts out." ... Jaguars offensive tackle Leon Searcy: "They were complaining because we were still throwing in the third quarter. They thought we were running up the score. But we couldn't take a knee in the third quarter." ... Johnson: "I take the blame for this one. I tried to prepare them too much. I should have pulled back after the long trip to Seattle. It was obvious from the start that we were very dead-legged."

JAGUARS 62, DOLPHINS 7
Saturday, January 15

Miami	0	7	0	0—	7
Jacksonville	24	17	14	7—	62

First Quarter
Jac.—J. Smith 8 pass from Brunell (Hollis kick), 4:28.
Jac.—FG, Hollis 45, 8:41.
Jac.—Taylor 90 run (Hollis kick), 11:14.
Jac.—Brackens 16 fumble return (Hollis kick), 11:39.

Second Quarter
Jac.—Taylor 39 pass from Brunell (Hollis kick), 0:12.
Jac.—J. Stewart 25 run (Hollis kick), 2:55.
Jac.—FG, Hollis 28, 13:09.
Mia.—Gadsden 20 pass from Marino (Mare kick), 14:57.

Third Quarter
Jac.—J. Smith 70 pass from Fiedler (Hollis kick), 2:57.
Jac.—Whitted 38 pass from Fiedler (Hollis kick), 8:41.

Fourth Quarter
Jac.—Howard 5 run (Hollis kick), 4:23.
Attendance—78,173.

	Miami	Jacksonville
First downs	10	21
Rushes-yards	18-21	46-257
Passing	110	263
Punt returns	3-70	5-44
Kickoff returns	9-206	2-24
Interception returns	1-0	2-5
Comp.-att.-int.	16-41-2	12-20-1
Sacked-yards lost	5-31	2-14
Punts	9-40	5-39
Fumbles-lost	6-5	1-1
Penalties-yards	9-88	7-51
Time of possession	24:37	35:23

INDIVIDUAL STATISTICS

RUSHING—Miami, Johnson 8-9, Denson 6-10, Pritchett 2-10, Marino 1-0, Hutton 1-(minus 8). Jacksonville, Taylor 18-135, Howard 15-54, J. Stewart 11-62, Brunell 1-6, Shelton 1-0.

PASSING—Miami, Marino 11-25-2-95, Huard 5-16-0-46. Jacksonville, Fiedler 7-11-1-172, Brunell 5-9-0-105.

RECEIVING—Miami, Gadsden 6-62, Konrad 3-30, McDuffie 2-19, Pritchett 2-17, Johnson 2-11, Drayton 1-2. Jacksonville, J. Smith 5-136, McCardell 4-52, Taylor 1-39, Whitted 1-38, Shelton 1-12.

MISSED FIELD GOAL ATTEMPTS—Jacksonville, Hollis 39.

INTERCEPTIONS—Miami, Jackson 1-0. Jacksonville, Beasley 2-5.

KICKOFF RETURNS—Miami, Marion 4-90, Jacquet 3-77, Wilson 1-20, Drayton 1-19. Jacksonville, Whitted 1-24, Griffith 1-0.

PUNT RETURNS—Miami, Jacquet 2-47, McDuffie 1-23. Jacksonville, Barlow 5-44.

SACKS—Miami, Bowens 1, Mixon 1. Jacksonville, Walker 2, Marts 1, Brackens 1, Leroy 1.

TENNESSEE 19, INDIANAPOLIS 16

Why the Titans won: Running back Eddie George was fabulous, running for 162 yards on 26 carries and scoring the go-ahead touchdown in his first NFL playoff game. And the Titans defense, while not being credited with any sacks, kept consistent pressure on Colts quarterback Peyton Manning all day.

Why the Colts lost: Their offense, which ranked fourth in the league during the regular season, never got untracked against a good Tennessee defense. Rookie star Edgerrin James was held to 56 yards rushing, Manning completed fewer than half his passes and Marvin Harrison caught just five passes for 65 yards despite having 16 passes thrown his way. Indianapolis scored fewer than 20 points for only the fourth time in 17 games and had just three plays of more than 20 yards.

The turning points:

1. On the third play of the second half, with the Colts leading 9-6, George took a handoff from quarterback Steve McNair and sprinted 68 yards for a Tennessee touchdown. The Colts blitzed in hopes of getting to McNair; instead, they left a huge hole in the middle of the field for George to run through.

2. The Titans led, 16-9, early in the fourth quarter when the Colts' Terrence Wilkins caught a punt, tightroped down the sideline and was knocked out of bounds at the Tennessee 3-yard line. The Titans challenged the play, believing Wilkins had stepped out of bounds early on the return. Referee Johnny Grier reviewed the play and agreed, ruling Wilkins had stepped out at his own 33-yard line. The Colts subsequently went three-and-out, and Al Del Greco booted his fourth field goal of the game on the Titans' next possession.

Notable: The Titans were the only visiting team to win in the divisional round of the playoffs. ... George had 38 yards on nine carries in the first half, 124 on 17 carries in the second. ... There were no interceptions or sacks in the game. ... The win was the Titans' sixth straight, the league's longest winning streak. ... The loss dropped Jim Mora's all-time playoff coaching record to 0-5 (0-4 with the Saints, 0-1 with the Colts).

Quotable: Mora, on the replay reversal: "It was a good call. If he (Wilkins) was out of bounds, he was out of bounds. Those are the rules." ... Mora: "We just came up short against a very good team. We had trouble making a play, particularly making big plays. It was a struggle all day, both sides of the ball." ... George, on a pre-game chat he had with coach Jeff Fisher: "He asked me to relive draft day back in 1996. He told me to remember that he drafted me because he felt I could lead this team to where we are now. He challenged me to live up to the expectations." ... Titans guard Bruce Matthews, on advancing to the AFC championship game for the first time in his 17-year career: "I've always been at home by now, all my years before. This is virgin territory for me. I always told myself it didn't bother me. But it did. It's irritating to watch other teams play when you think you're better than them."

TITANS 19, COLTS 16

Sunday, January 16

Tennessee	0	6	7	6—19
Indianapolis	3	6	0	7—16

First Quarter
Ind.—FG, Vanderjagt 40, 7:47.

Second Quarter
Ten.—FG, Del Greco 49, 0:04.
Ind.—FG, Vanderjagt 40, 9:22.
Ten.—FG, Del Greco 37, 11:45.
Ind.—FG, Vanderjagt 34, 14:59.

Third Quarter
Ten.—E. George 68 run (Del Greco kick), 1:41.

Fourth Quarter
Ten.—FG, Del Greco 25, 2:03.
Ten.—FG, Del Greco 43, 10:41.
Ind.—Manning 15 run (Vanderjagt kick), 13:09.
Attendance—57,097.

	Tennessee	Indianapolis
First downs	13	19
Rushes-yards	33-197	22-78
Passing	112	227
Punt returns	3-49	2-24
Kickoff returns	2-47	6-87
Interception returns	0-0	0-0
Comp.-att.-int.	13-24-0	19-43-0
Sacked-yards lost	0-0	0-0
Punts	5-52	7-49
Fumbles-lost	1-1	1-0
Penalties-yards	9-78	7-60
Time of possession	31:05	28:55

INDIVIDUAL STATISTICS

RUSHING—Tennessee, E. George 26-162, McNair 7-35. Indianapolis, James 20-56, Manning 2-22.

PASSING—Tennessee, McNair 13-24-0-112. Indianapolis, Manning 19-43-0-227.

RECEIVING—Tennessee, Thigpen 3-19, Wycheck 3-16, E. George 3-14, Sanders 2-38, Dyson 2-25. Indianapolis, Harrison 5-65, Pathon 5-44, Wilkins 4-55, Dilger 2-12, Green 1-33, Pollard 1-10, James 1-8.

MISSED FIELD GOAL ATTEMPTS—None.

INTERCEPTIONS—None.

KICKOFF RETURNS—Tennessee, Mason 1-47, Byrd 1-0. Indianapolis, Wilkins 5-83, Pathon 1-4.

PUNT RETURNS—Tennessee, Mason 3-49. Indianapolis, Wilkins 2-24.

SACKS—None.

1999 REVIEW Divisional playoffs

NFC

TAMPA BAY 14, WASHINGTON 13

Why the Buccaneers won: Their defense was terrific, holding Washington to 26 total yards in 27 plays in the second half and forcing two turnovers, both of which were converted into touchdowns in a come-from-behind victory.

Why the Redskins lost: Their second-ranked offense was no match for the Bucs' third-ranked defense. A Washington offense that averaged 373 yards during the regular season mustered a season-low 157 in its biggest test of the year. Its longest play went for 23 yards. Even worse, the Redskins led only 3-0 at the half despite holding the Bucs' offense to 69 yards and three first downs.

The turning points:
1. The Redskins led, 13-0, with fewer than six minutes left in the third period when Tampa Bay safety John Lynch picked off a pass by Brad Johnson at the Buccaneers 27-yard line. Bucs quarterback Shaun King then completed passes of 16 yards to Warrick Dunn and 17 yards to Dave Moore before attempting a long pass to Dunn. Leomont Evans was called for pass interference, giving the Bucs a first down at the Washington 11. Two plays later Mike Alstott circled around left end for a touchdown to cut the Redskins' lead to 13-7.
2. After the teams traded punts, Bucs defensive lineman Steve White eluded Redskins tackle Kipp Vickers (playing for an ailing Andy Heck) and knocked the ball out of Johnson's hands. Warren Sapp recovered for Tampa Bay on the Redskins' 32 with 13:21 left. On the third play of the drive, King fumbled, but Dunn picked the ball up and ran 13 yards for a first down at the Washington 12 to keep the drive alive. On fourth-and-inches at the Redskins 8, Tampa Bay coach Tony Dungy spurned a field goal try, and Alstott gained five yards on the next play for a first down. Three plays later, King flipped a 1-yard touchdown pass to John Davis with 7:29 left for what proved to be the game-winning touchdown.
3. Washington's Brett Conway, who kicked three field goals of 50 or more yards during the regular season, lined up for a 52-yard game-winner with 1:17 left, but he never got a kick away. Center Dan Turk dribbled the ball back to holder Johnson, who tried to get up and throw but wound up getting sacked.

Notable: The victory was Tampa Bay's ninth in 10 games and eighth straight at home. ... Despite modest passing numbers (15 of 32 for 157 yards) King became the first rookie quarterback since the Rams' Pat Haden in 1976 to win a playoff game. ... The Redskins' only touchdown came when Brian Mitchell returned the second-half kickoff 100 yards. It was the longest TD return in NFL playoff history. ... The teams combined for 18 punts. ... Washington running back Stephen Davis was held to 37 yards on 17 carries. He had just two yards on five carries in the second half.

Quotable: Redskins guard Keith Sims: "I'm sick. We had a tremendous opportunity and we squandered it." ... Dungy: "It looks painful, but that's just the way we play. We like to play tight games." ... King, on Dunn's fumble recovery: "That was a great play by Warrick, to be so alert. I knew when that happened we were going to win." ... Lynch: "We'd like to blow somebody out. But at this point we all know that's probably not going to happen."

BUCCANEERS 14, REDSKINS 13

Saturday, January 15

Washington	0	3	10	0—13
Tampa Bay	0	0	7	7—14

Second Quarter
Was.—FG, Conway 28, 9:23.

Third Quarter
Was.—Mitchell 100 kickoff return (Conway kick), 0:19.
Was.—FG, Conway 48, 6:50.
T.B.—Alstott 2 run (Gramatica kick), 12:57.

Fourth Quarter
T.B.—J. Davis 1 pass from King (Gramatica kick), 7:31.
Attendance—65,835.

	Washington	Tampa Bay
First downs	10	12
Rushes-yards	22-46	27-44
Passing	111	142
Punt returns	5-44	1-7
Kickoff returns	3-125	4-68
Interception returns	1-12	1-0
Comp.-att.-int.	20-32-1	15-32-1
Sacked-yards lost	4-38	2-15
Punts	8-42	10-42
Fumbles-lost	2-1	1-0
Penalties-yards	4-61	2-25
Time of possession	28:25	31:35

INDIVIDUAL STATISTICS

RUSHING—Washington, Davis 17-37, Centers 1-7, Mitchell 1-1, Thrash 1-1, Hicks 1-0, Westbrook 1-0. Tampa Bay, Alstott 15-24, Dunn 11-18, King 1-2.

PASSING—Washington, B. Johnson 20-32-1-149. Tampa Bay, King 15-32-1-157.

RECEIVING—Washington, Connell 4-59, Fryar 4-30, Davis 3-26, Centers 3-8, Hicks 2-17, Mitchell 2-1, Westbrook 1-4, Alexander 1-4. Tampa Bay, Dunn 4-32, Alstott 3-17, Emanuel 2-47, Moore 2-32, Green 2-25, Williams 1-3, J. Davis 1-1.

MISSED FIELD GOAL ATTEMPTS—None.

INTERCEPTIONS—Washington, Green 1-12. Tampa Bay, Lynch 1-0.

KICKOFF RETURNS—Washington, Mitchell 1-100, Thrash 1-24, Sellers 1-1. Tampa Bay, Dunn 4-68.

PUNT RETURNS—Washington, Mitchell 5-44. Tampa Bay, Williams 1-7.

SACKS—Washington, Barber 1, Stubblefield 1. Tampa Bay, White 2, Sapp 1, Young 1.

ST. LOUIS 49, MINNESOTA 37

Why the Rams won: Although they scored touchdowns on their first and fifth plays from scrimmage, the Rams got off—for them—to a slow start offensively. Those two touchdowns were their only first-half points. Once their No. 1-ranked offense began to click on all cylinders, however, it couldn't be stopped. Quarterback Kurt Warner threw five touchdown passes to five different receivers and completed 27 of 33 passes overall, including 11 of 12 in the decisive third quarter.

Why the Vikings lost: They were helpless to stop the St. Louis offense once it got going. The Vikings came into the game with a suspect defense (27th in the regular season) and were able to tame the Rams for the first 30 minutes. But not for the second 30. Anything the Rams tried after the intermission worked to perfection.

The turning points:
1. The Vikings led, 17-14, when Tony Horne took the second-half kickoff 95 yards down the left sideline for a St. Louis touchdown. It gave the Rams a lead they never relinquished, but more important it turned the momentum in the Rams' favor and juiced a sellout home crowd.
2. After forcing the Vikings to go three-and-out on their next possession, the Rams drove 51 yards in nine plays for another touchdown, capping the drive with a one-yard run by Marshall Faulk for a 28-17 lead. The Rams failed to take advantage after recovering a Vikings fumble on the ensuing kickoff, but after another Vikings' three-and-out the Rams scored again, this time on a 13-yard Warner pass to Jeff Robinson.
3. One play after the Robinson touchdown, the Vikings fumbled again, with defensive tackle D'Marco Farr recovering for the Rams at the Minnesota 23. Four plays later Warner tossed a 1-yard TD pass to Ryan Tucker on a tackle-eligible play to increase the lead to 42-17.

Notable: The Rams set 25 team and individual playoff records. Among them were Warner's 391 yards passing and five TDs. Warner's passer rating of 143 was one of the highest in playoff history. ... It was the second-highest scoring game in playoff history, surpassed only by Philadelphia's 58-37 win over Detroit in 1995. ... Vikings quarterback Jeff George threw for 424 yards, third-most in playoff history. ... The teams combined for 881 total yards, 763 passing yards and 348 kickoff-return yards. ... It was the first home playoff game in St. Louis' 33-year NFL history.

Quotable: Rams guard Adam Timmerman, on the Vikings' pick-your-poison strategy of putting eight men "in the box" in an attempt to slow Faulk, who finished with 21 yards rushing on 11 carries: "They were daring us to pass the ball, so we had to pass the ball. There's no sense in running into eight guys when we've only got seven blockers. We kind of took what they gave us." ... Vikings defensive tackle Jerry Ball: "For them to beat us like they did and not even use Marshall Faulk as a runner, it's scary." ... Faulk: "We weren't playing our football in the first half. Coach (Dick Vermeil) made a remark at halftime like, 'Hey, we're stopping ourselves. We're going to go out there, and we're going to do the same things we've been doing. And we're going to play fast." ... Warner: "Our feeling at halftime was that we were hurting ourselves, that they couldn't stop us and we were stopping ourselves." ... Vermeil: "We went into the ballgame thinking we could take advantage of their secondary if we could pass protect really well. This (Minnesota) team, we knew, would score some points. You're not going to shut them out. But how we played in the third quarter is about as well as we can play."

RAMS 49, VIKINGS 37
Sunday, January 16

Minnesota	3	14	0	20—37
St. Louis	14	0	21	14—49

First Quarter
Min.—FG, Anderson 31, 5:37.
St.L.—Bruce 77 pass from Warner (Wilkins kick), 5:58.
St.L.—Faulk 41 pass from Warner (Wilkins kick), 10:41.

Second Quarter
Min.—Carter 22 pass from George (Anderson kick), 5:07.
Min.—Hoard 4 run (Anderson kick), 12:20.

Third Quarter
St.L.—Horne 95 kickoff return (Wilkins kick), 0:18.
St.L.—Faulk 1 run (Wilkins kick), 6:32.
St.L.—Robinson 13 pass from Warner (Wilkins kick), 14:38.

Fourth Quarter
St.L.—Tucker 1 pass from Warner (Wilkins kick), 1:24.
St.L.—R. Williams 2 pass from Warner (Wilkins kick), 6:47.
Min.—Reed 4 pass from George (Hoard run), 10:04.
Min.—Moss 44 pass from George (pass failed), 11:12.
Min.—Moss 2 pass from George (pass failed), 14:29.
Attendance—66,194.

	Minnesota	St. Louis
First downs	27	23
Rushes-yards	29-87	17-31
Passing	389	374
Punt returns	2-25	4-72
Kickoff returns	8-174	5-174
Interception returns	1-0	1-(-4)
Comp.-att.-int.	29-50-1	27-33-1
Sacked-yards lost	4-35	2-17
Punts	5-48	3-39
Fumbles-lost	2-2	2-2
Penalties-yards	10-57	10-70
Time of possession	34:11	25:49

INDIVIDUAL STATISTICS
RUSHING—Minnesota, Smith 20-64, Hoard 7-24, George 2-(minus 1). St. Louis, Faulk 11-21, Warner 3-3, Hakim 1-4, Holcombe 1-2, Lee 1-1.
PASSING—Minnesota, George 29-50-1-424. St. Louis, Warner 27-33-1-391.
RECEIVING—Minnesota, Moss 9-188, Carter 7-111, Smith 7-32, Reed 5-81, Glover 1-12. St. Louis, Holt 6-65, Faulk 5-80, Hakim 5-49, Bruce 4-133, R. Williams 2-20, Robinson 1-13, Holcombe 1-12, Proehl 1-10, Conwell 1-8, Tucker 1-1.
MISSED FIELD GOAL ATTEMPTS—St. Louis, Wilkins 42.
INTERCEPTIONS—Minnesota, Hitchcock 1-0. St. Louis, McCleon 1-(minus 4).
KICKOFF RETURNS—Minnesota, Tate 7-151, M. Williams 1-23. St. Louis, Horne 4-174, Bruce 1-0.
PUNT RETURNS—Minnesota, Moss 2-25. St. Louis, Hakim 4-72.
SACKS—Minnesota, Burrough 1, Randle 1. St. Louis, Jenkins 1, Fletcher 1, Clemons 1, Carter 1.

CONFERENCE CHAMPIONSHIPS

AFC

TENNESSEE 33, JACKSONVILLE 14

Why the Titans won: Their defense and special teams were superb. Blitzing often, the Titans forced six turnovers, sacked quarterback Mark Brunell three times and allowed the Jaguars just 1 of 9 third-down conversions.

Why the Jaguars lost: Too many mistakes—and too much poor tackling. Besides the turnovers, the Jaguars were penalized nine times for 100 yards and their receivers dropped at least half a dozen passes. The Jaguars defense allowed Titans quarterback Steve McNair, playing on a turf toe, to turn numerous near-sacks into big gains. Tennessee scored the game's final 26 points.

The turning points:

1. The Jaguars drove 62 yards in five plays for a touchdown the first time they had the ball, rekindling memories of their 62-7 wipeout of Miami a week earlier. However, this time, the opponent didn't let them run away. Derrick Mason returned the ensuing kickoff 44 yards to midfield, and the Titans tied the game nine plays later on McNair's 9-yard TD pass to Yancey Thigpen. This would be a game.

2. The Jaguars led, 14-10, at the half before the Titans drove 76 yards in six plays to take their first lead on McNair's one-yard touchdown run with 9:24 left in the third quarter. Forty-three of the 76 yards came on penalties against Jacksonville, including a 15-yarder against linebacker Kevin Hardy for roughing the passer.

3. On the Jaguars' next possession, Titans linebacker Eddie Robinson stripped tight end Kyle Brady of the ball after a catch, with Jason Fisk recovering for Tennessee at the Jacksonville 35. Frank Wycheck then caught an eight-yard pass from McNair near the goal line, only to have Hardy strip the ball away and Lonnie Marts recover for the Jaguars at the 1. However, on the Jaguars' first play, Barron Wortham stopped Fred Taylor for no gain. On the second, Fisk and Josh Evans sacked Brunell in the end zone for a safety to increase the Titans' lead to 19-14. On the ensuing free kick, Mason returned the ball 80 yards for another Tennessee touchdown, putting the Titans ahead 26-14 with 4:56 remaining in the third quarter. All told, the Titans scored 16 points in a span of 4.5 minutes to turn a 14-10 deficit into a 26-14 lead.

Notable: The Titans advanced to the Super Bowl for the first time in the franchise's 40-year history, including 37 seasons as the Houston Oilers. They became the last original AFL team to reach the NFL title game. ... The Jaguars became the first NFL team to finish a season with only three losses, with all the losses coming against the same team. ... McNair had almost as many yards rushing (91) as passing (112). His longest run was 51 yards; his longest completion was 15 yards. ... The Titans lost starting wide receiver Thigpen (broken left toe) and starting free safety Marcus Robertson (broken left ankle) to injuries in the second quarter. ... Jacksonville led the NFL in fewest turnovers (18) during the regular season while Tennessee led in fumbles forced (24).

Quotable: Jaguars coach Tom Coughlin: "However it happens, when we play Tennessee, we get a little out of our element and we turn the ball over." ... Titans owner Bud Adams, who waited 40 years for his first Super Bowl: "It's about time. I'm getting old. I didn't want to go to the Super Bowl in a wheelchair." ... Wycheck, on coach Jeff Fisher's decision to show his team a Super Bowl rap video produced by the Jaguars players: "That was great motivation, that video. Jeff didn't tell us what he was showing us. He just said he had something he wanted us to see and then he popped it on. It was real quiet in the room after it was over. Everyone was like, 'OK, we'll see if we can make them change some of those words.'"

TITANS 33, JAGUARS 14

Sunday, January 23

Tennessee	7	3	16	7	33
Jacksonville	7	7	0	0	14

First Quarter
Jac.—Brady 7 pass from Brunell (Hollis kick), 3:40.
Ten.—Thigpen 9 pass from McNair (Del Greco kick), 9:30.

Second Quarter
Jac.—J. Stewart 33 run (Hollis kick), 10:24.
Ten.—FG, Del Greco 34, 14:40.

Third Quarter
Ten.—McNair 1 run (Del Greco kick), 5:36.
Ten.—Safety, Brunell sacked by Evans and Fisk in end zone, 9:47.
Ten.—Mason 80 kickoff return (Del Greco kick), 10:04.

Fourth Quarter
Ten.—McNair 1 run (Del Greco kick), 8:01.
Attendance—75,206.

	Tennessee	Jacksonville
First downs	18	20
Rushes-yards	34-177	23-144
Passing	112	211
Punt returns	2-14	3-2
Kickoff returns	4-174	6-80
Interception returns	2-0	1-1
Comp.-att.-int.	14-23-1	19-38-2
Sacked-yards lost	1-0	3-15
Punts	5-40	3-45
Fumbles-lost	5-3	5-4
Penalties-yards	5-39	9-100
Time of possession	31:36	28:24

INDIVIDUAL STATISTICS

RUSHING—Tennessee, E. George 25-86, McNair 9-91. Jacksonville, Taylor 19-110, J. Stewart 3-35, Brunell 1-(minus 1).

PASSING—Tennessee, McNair 14-23-1-112. Jacksonville, Brunell 19-38-2-226.

RECEIVING—Tennessee, Harris 3-33, E. George 3-19, Byrd 2-19, Thigpen 2-16, Wycheck 2-12, Dyson 1-12, Neal 1-1. Jacksonville, McCardell 6-67, J. Smith 5-92, Brady 5-44, Taylor 2-16, Jones 1-7.

MISSED FIELD GOAL ATTEMPTS—None.

INTERCEPTIONS—Tennessee, Robertson 1-0, Mitchell 1-0. Jacksonville, Bryant 1-1.

KICKOFF RETURNS—Tennessee, Mason 4-174. Jacksonville, Barlow 3-58, Whitted 3-22.

PUNT RETURNS—Tennessee, Mason 2-14. Jacksonville, Barlow 3-2.

SACKS—Tennessee, Bishop 1, Holmes 1, Evans 0.5, Fisk 0.5. Jacksonville, Brackens 1.

NFC

ST. LOUIS 11, TAMPA BAY 6

Why the Rams won: Their offense, stymied most of the afternoon by a Bucs defense that played a lot of zone and applied heavy pressure, came up with its biggest play of the season as Kurt Warner and Ricky Proehl hooked up for a game-winning 30-yard touchdown pass with 4:44 left. It was the longest play of the game by a St. Louis offense which rarely resembled the juggernaut that terrorized NFL defenses all season.

Why the Buccaneers lost: On a day their defense was terrific, their offense was terrible. Tampa Bay's only points came on two field goals by rookie Martin Gramatica. Rookie quarterback Shaun King was inconsistent. The offensive line allowed five sacks. Still, the Bucs would have won the game had Warner and Proehl not hooked up for their late-game heroics.

The turning points:
1. On the Rams' first play from scrimmage, defensive end Steve White tipped and intercepted a screen pass from Warner, giving Tampa Bay possession at the St. Louis 20-yard line. The Bucs drove to the 5, but instead of scoring a touchdown (wide receiver Jacquez Green dropped a pass in the end zone) they had to settle for a 23-yard field goal. The Rams were able to tie the game on their next possession.
2. Tampa Bay led 6-5 with eight minutes left when cornerback Dre Bly intercepted a King pass intended for Warrick Dunn and returned it nine yards to give the Rams possession at the Tampa Bay 47. Six plays later the Rams scored the game's only touchdown and final points when Warner threw a pass over the shoulder of Bucs cornerback Brian Kelly and into the outstretched arms of a leaping Proehl in the left corner of the end zone.
3. On the Bucs' final possession King completed a 22-yard pass to Karl Williams to put his team at the Rams' 22 with 1:25 left. On the next play Grant Wistrom raced around left tackle Pete Pierson and sacked King for a loss of 13 yards. King then appeared to complete an 11-yard pass to Bert Emanuel, only to have the reception reversed on replay. King then fired incomplete on two more passes and the Bucs were done.

Notable: Prior to the NFC title game, the Rams had scored 30 or more points in 13 of 17 games and had not scored fewer than 21 points in any game all season. ... Proehl's winning catch was his sixth reception of the game but his first touchdown of the season. ... The Bucs held Pro Bowl running back Marshall Faulk to 49 total yards—44 rushing and 5 receiving. ... Although Warner completed passes to nine different receivers, his quarterback rating against the Bucs was nearly half (56.2) of what it had been during the regular season (109.2). ... Tampa Bay's Warren Sapp, the league's Defensive Player of the Year, had no tackles in the game.

Quotable: Proehl: "I've played 10 years in this league and never had better than 8-8 before this season. Never sniffed the playoffs. Man, I'm living a dream right now. Call that corny. But I'm living a dream." ... Rams coach Dick Vermeil, on his team escaping defeat to advance to the Super Bowl against Tennessee, which beat the Rams in Week 8: "We know what we are up against. We know we have to improve next week." ... Rams owner Georgia Frontiere, on her team advancing to the Super Bowl in Atlanta: "I grew up never liking the name Georgia. Now I love my name!" ... Sapp: "We wanted to turn the ballgame into a war. And we did. We did everything we wanted to do. Except win the war."... Warner: "Tampa Bay did a great job. But the character of this team is that when we need a play, someone steps up. Today, that was Ricky Proehl."

RAMS 11, BUCCANEERS 6
Sunday, January 23

Tampa Bay	3	0	3	0—	6
St. Louis	3	2	0	6—	11

First Quarter
T.B.—FG, Gramatica 25, 2:38.
St.L.—FG, Wilkins 24, 10:43.
Second Quarter
St.L.—Safety, S. King forced out of end zone by team, 0:05.
Third Quarter
T.B.—FG, Gramatica 23, 4:32.
Fourth Quarter
St.L.—Proehl 30 pass from Warner (pass failed), 10:16.
Attendance—66,496.

	Tampa Bay	St. Louis
First downs	12	17
Rushes-yards	23-77	21-51
Passing	126	258
Punt returns	4-45	3-25
Kickoff returns	3-60	2-38
Interception returns	3-21	2-28
Comp.-att.-int.	13-29-2	26-43-3
Sacked-yards lost	5-37	0-0
Punts	5-40	4-44
Fumbles-lost	3-0	2-0
Penalties-yards	3-15	7-48
Time of possession	26:59	33:01

INDIVIDUAL STATISTICS
RUSHING—Tampa Bay, Alstott 12-39, Dunn 9-35, King 2-3. St. Louis, Faulk 17-44, Warner 2-(minus 1), Hakim 1-6, Holcombe 1-2.
PASSING—Tampa Bay, King 13-29-2-163. St. Louis, Warner 26-43-3-258.
RECEIVING—Tampa Bay, Green 4-59, Dunn 4-37, Williams 2-28, Emanuel 1-22, Alstott 1-9, Moore 1-8. St. Louis, Holt 7-68, Proehl 6-100, Bruce 3-22, Faulk 3-5, Hakim 2-27, Holcombe 2-5, R. Williams 1-22, Robinson 1-11, Conwell 1-(minus 2).
MISSED FIELD GOAL ATTEMPTS—St. Louis, Wilkins 44.
INTERCEPTIONS—Tampa Bay, Kelly 1-15, Nickerson 1-6, White 1-0. St. Louis, Lyght 1-19, Bly 1-9.
KICKOFF RETURNS—Tampa Bay, Dunn 3-60. St. Louis, Horne 2-38.
PUNT RETURNS—Tampa Bay, Williams 4-45. St. Louis, Hakim 3-25.
SACKS—St. Louis, Farr 1, Wistrom 1, Carter 1, Clemons 1, Zgonina 1.

SUPER BOWL 34
AT GEORGIA DOME, ATLANTA, JANUARY 30, 2000

ST. LOUIS 23, TENNESSEE 16

Why the Rams won: In perhaps the most thrilling Super Bowl finish ever, linebacker Mike Jones tackled Titans wide receiver Kevin Dyson at the 1-yard line as time expired to give St. Louis its first NFL championship. The Rams, who led 16-0 late in the third quarter before Tennessee scored 16 consecutive points to tie the game, scored the go-ahead points on a 73-yard touchdown bomb from Kurt Warner to Isaac Bruce with 1:54 left. Jones' tackle made it hold up for the game-winning score.

Why the Titans lost: If their offense had been effective early, the game might not have come down to the final play. Wide receiver Yancey Thigpen missed the game with an injured foot and Steve McNair never was able to get the passing game going. In the first half he completed just 5 of 14 passes for 65 yards. Pro Bowl running back Eddie George touched the ball just eight times in the first half before exploding in the second. But by then, the Rams led 16-0.

The turning points:

1. After a disappointing first half in which their offense moved inside the Tennessee 20-yard line all five times it had the ball but netted just three field goals, the Rams came out in impressive fashion after the intermission, driving 68 yards in eight plays to increase their lead to 16-0 on a 9-yard TD pass from Warner to rookie Torry Holt.

2. After Titans kicker Al Del Greco tied the game at 16-16 on a 43-yard field goal with 2:12 left, it took St. Louis all of 18 seconds to regain the lead. Bruce, running a streak pattern on first down, got past Titans cornerback Denard Walker along the right sideline, came back slightly to grab an underthrown pass (it was underthrown because Warner was hit by defensive end Jevon Kearse) at the Tennessee 38 and then eluded overpursing safety Donald Mitchell before running untouched into the end zone.

3. The Titans started their final drive at their own 12-yard line with 1:48 left. McNair completed four of seven passes for 39 yards and scrambled twice for 14 yards to move the Titans down the field, a drive aided by a 15-yard facemask penalty against cornerback Dre Bly and two offsides penalties. After burning Tennessee's last timeout with six seconds left and the ball at the Rams' 10, McNair tossed a short pass to Dyson at the 5. As Dyson circled toward the end zone he was met by Jones near the 3-yard line. As he was going down Dyson's outstretched right arm, ball in hand, came up about 18 inches short of the Rams goal line.

Notable: Warner, the game's MVP, completed 24 of 45 passes for 414 yards, surpassing Joe Montana's Super Bowl record of 357 passing yards. ... At 63, Dick Vermeil became the oldest coach to win the Super Bowl. He also had the longest span (19 years) between Super Bowl appearances. ... Rams punter Mike Horan, two days short of his 41st birthday, became the oldest player to appear in a Super Bowl.

... The Rams rushed for just 29 yards, the fewest ever by a winning Super Bowl team.

Quotable: Rams center Mike Gruttadauria, on what it was like on the sideline on the final play of the game: "I looked to my left and to my right and looked at my teammates. Some were praying, some were chanting, some were holding hands. I think some had their eyes closed. It was tough to watch." ... Rams defensive end Grant Wistrom: "I was thinking, somebody please tackle him. Please, please, someone make that tackle."... Jones: "When he caught the ball, I was right on top of him. I was like, 'This guy is not going to get in.' "... Rams safety Keith Lyle: "That, right there, was the greatest tackle made in Super Bowl history. The rest of our lives, we'll see that shown a million times on TV, and we'll replay it over and over again in our minds." ... Vermeil: "I'd just as soon win 32-nothing. But in terms of the Super Bowl and the American football fan, it had to be great to watch."

RAMS 23, TITANS 16
Sunday, January 30

St. Louis	3	6	7	7—23
Tennessee	0	0	6	10—16

First Quarter
St.L.—FG, Wilkins 27, 12:00.

Second Quarter
St.L.—FG, Wilkins 29, 10:44.
St.L.—FG, Wilkins 28, 14:45.

Third Quarter
St.L.—Holt 9 pass from Warner (Wilkins kick), 7:40.
Ten.—George 1 run (pass failed), 14:46.

Fourth Quarter
Ten.—George 2 run (Del Greco kick), 7:39.
Ten.—FG, Del Greco 43, 12:48.
St.L.—Bruce 73 pass from Warner (Wilkins kick), 13:06.
Attendance—72,625.

	St. Louis	Tennessee
First downs	23	27
Rushes-yards	13-29	36-159
Passing	407	208
Punt returns	2-8	1-(-1)
Kickoff returns	4-55	5-122
Interception returns	0-0	0-0
Comp.-att.-int.	24-45-0	22-36-0
Sacked-yards lost	1-7	1-6
Punts	2-38.5	3-43.0
Fumbles-lost	2-0	1-0
Penalties-yards	8-60	7-45
Time of possession	23:34	36:26

INDIVIDUAL STATISTICS

RUSHING—St. Louis, Faulk 10-17, Holcombe 1-11, Warner 1-1, Horan 1-0. Tennessee, George 28-95, McNair 8-64.

PASSING—St. Louis, Warner 24-45-0-414. Tennessee, McNair 22-36-0-214.

RECEIVING—St. Louis, Holt 7-109, Bruce 6-162, Faulk 5-90, Hakim 1-17, Conwell 1-16, Proehl 1-11, R.Williams 1-9, Holcombe 1-1, Miller 1-(minus 1). Tennessee, Harris 7-64, Wycheck 5-35, Dyson 4-41, George 2-35, Byrd 2-21, Mason 2-18.

MISSED FIELD GOAL ATTEMPTS—Tennessee, Del Greco 47. St. Louis, Wilkins 34.

INTERCEPTIONS—None.

KICKOFF RETURNS—St. Louis, Horne 4-55, Morton 0-0. Tennessee, Mason 5-122.

PUNT RETURNS—St. Louis, Hakim 2-8. Tennessee, Mason 1-(minus 1).

SACKS—St. Louis, Carter 1. Tennessee, Fisk 1.

PRO BOWL

AT ALOHA STADIUM, HONOLULU, FEBRUARY 6, 2000

NFC 51, AFC 31

Why the NFC won: Its defense returned two interceptions for touchdowns and Vikings receiver Randy Moss could not be stopped. Moss, the game's most valuable player, caught nine passes for 212 yards (both Pro Bowl records) and one touchdown. Bucs fullback Mike Alstott complemented Moss' effort by scoring a Pro Bowl record three rushing touchdowns.

Why the AFC lost: It lost the turnover battle 6-1 as quarterbacks Peyton Manning, Mark Brunell and Rich Gannon combined to throw five interceptions, two of which were returned for scores. The mistakes proved crucial once the game turned into a high-scoring affair. The teams combined to score a Pro Bowl record 10 touchdowns.

The turning points:
1. The game was less than three minutes old when Cardinals cornerback Aeneas Williams intercepted Manning's second pass attempt, returning it 62 yards for a touchdown. The next time the NFC got the ball, starting quarterback Kurt Warner of the Rams completed a 48-yard pass to Moss to the AFC 5, setting up a 21-yard field goal for a 10-0 NFC lead.
2. After Manning cut the NFC's lead to 24-21 by completing a 21-yard pass to Jacksonville receiver Jimmy Smith with 20 seconds left in the second quarter, the Lions' Jason Hanson ended the half by kicking a 51-yard field goal to increase the NFC's lead to 27-21. The NFC then scored 10 unanswered points in the third period to take a 37-21 lead, effectively putting the game away.

Notable: This was the highest-scoring Pro Bowl ever, eclipsing the 64 points scored in 1980. ... Moss broke the Pro Bowl receiving record of 137 yards set by Oakland's Tim Brown in 1997. ... Smith, who caught eight passes for 119 yards for the AFC, set a record with three TD receptions. ... The teams combined for 385 kickoff-return yards, the most ever. ... The NFC's second defensive touchdown was scored by Tampa Bay's Derrick Brooks, who returned a Brunell pass 20 yards in the fourth quarter. ... Hanson's 51-yard field goal was the longest in Pro Bowl history. ... Eight members of the Super Bowl champion Rams played in the game, the most of any team.

Quotable: Moss, on the accuracy of Warner, who completed 8 of 11 passes: "He's not the MVP of the league and the Super Bowl for nothing."

NFC 51, AFC 31

Sunday, February 6

AFC	7	14	0	10—31
NFC	10	17	10	14—51

First Quarter
NFC—Williams 62 interception return (Hanson kick), 2:46.
NFC—FG Hanson 21, 10:36.
AFC—J. Smith 5 pass from Brunell (Mare kick), 14:30.

Second Quarter
NFC—Alstott 1 run (Hanson kick), 0:03.
AFC—Gonzalez 10 pass from Gannon (Mare kick), 4:55.
NFC—Alstott 3 run (Hanson kick), 10:15.
AFC—J. Smith 21 pass from Manning (Mare kick), 14:40.
NFC—FG Hanson 51, 15:00.

Third Quarter
NFC—Alstott 1 run (Hanson kick), 7:52.
NFC—FG Hanson 23, 12:57.

Fourth Quarter
AFC—FG Mare 33, 0:11.
NFC—Brooks 20 interception return (Hanson kick), 3:48.
AFC—J. Smith 52 pass from Manning (Mare kick), 8:30.
NFC—Moss 25 pass from Beuerlein (Hanson kick), 13:55.
Attendance—50,112.

	AFC	NFC
First downs	19	21
Rushes-yards	20-48	37-110
Passing	349	260
Punt returns	5-56	4-99
Kickoff returns	5-153	6-232
Interception returns	0-0	5-86
Comp.-att.-int.	27-48-5	18-31-0
Sacked-yards lost	0-0	2-12
Punts	5-47	6-44
Fumbles-lost	2-1	4-1
Penalties-yards	6-45	8-41
Time of possession	26:11	33:49

INDIVIDUAL STATISTICS

RUSHING—AFC, George 9-42, James 9-14, Dillon 1-(minus 3), Manning 1-(minus 5). NFC, Alstott 13-67, Faulk 13-39, E. Smith 7-10, Davis 1-1, B. Johnson 1-(minus 3), Beuerlein 2-(minus 4).

PASSING—AFC, Manning 17-23-2-270, Brunell 6-14-2-44, Gannon 4-11-1-35. NFC, Warner 8-11-0-123, B. Johnson 6-13-0-64, Beuerlein 4-7-0-85.

RECEIVING—AFC, J. Smith 8-119, K. Johnson 5-35, Harrison 4-35, Gonzalez 4-55, Glenn 3-69, Wycheck 1-16, James 1-11, Dillon 1-9. NFC, Moss 9-212, Carter 5-27, Muhammad 2-24, Faulk 1-5, E. Smith 1-4.

MISSED FIELD GOAL ATTEMPTS—None.

AFC SQUAD
OFFENSE
- WR— Marvin Harrison, Indianapolis*
  Jimmy Smith, Jacksonville*
  Tim Brown, Oakland
  Keyshawn Johnson, N.Y. Jets
- TE— Tony Gonzalez, Kansas City*
  Frank Wycheck, Tennessee
- T— Tony Boselli, Jacksonville*
  Jonathan Ogden, Baltimore*
  Leon Searcy, Jacksonville
  Walter Jones, Seattle
- G— Ruben Brown, Buffalo*
  Bruce Matthews, Tennessee*
  Will Shields, Kansas City
- C— Tom Nalen, Denver*
  Kevin Mawae, N.Y. Jets
  Tim Grunhard, Kansas City
- QB— Peyton Manning, Indianapolis*
  Mark Brunell, Jacksonville
  Rich Gannon, Oakland
- RB— Edgerrin James, Indianapolis*
  Corey Dillon, Cincinnati
  Eddie George, Tennessee
- FB— Sam Gash, Buffalo*

NOTE: T Boselli replaced due to injury by Jones; C Nalen replaced due to injury by Grunhard.

DEFENSE
- DE— Tony Brackens, Jacksonville*
  Jevon Kearse, Tennessee*
  Michael McCrary, Baltimore
- DT— Trevor Pryce, Denver*
  Darrell Russell, Oakland*
  Cortez Kennedy, Seattle
- OLB— Peter Boulware, Baltimore*
  Kevin Hardy, Jacksonville*
  Chad Brown, Seattle
  Mo Lewis, N.Y. Jets†
- ILB— Ray Lewis, Baltimore*
  Zach Thomas, Miami
  Junior Seau, San Diego
- CB— Sam Madison, Miami*
  Charles Woodson, Oakland*
  James Hasty, Kansas City
- SS— Lawyer Milloy, New England*
- FS— Carnell Lake, Jacksonville*
  Rod Woodson, Baltimore

NOTE: LB R. Lewis replaced due to off-field problems by Seau.

SPECIALISTS
- P— Tom Tupa, N.Y. Jets
- K— Olindo Mare, Miami
- KR— Tremain Mack, Cincinnati
- ST— Detron Smith, Denver

NFC SQUAD
OFFENSE
- WR— Isaac Bruce, St. Louis*
  Cris Carter, Minnesota*
  Randy Moss, Minnesota
  Muhsid Muhammad, Carolina
- TE— Wesley Walls, Carolina*
  David Sloan, Detroit
- T— Orlando Pace, St. Louis*
  William Roaf, New Orleans*
  Erik Williams, Dallas
- G— Larry Allen, Dallas*
  Randall McDaniel, Minnesota*
  Tre Johnson, Washington
- C— Jeff Christy, Minnesota*
  Tony Mayberry, Tampa Bay
- QB— Kurt Warner, St. Louis*
  Steve Beuerlein, Carolina
  Brad Johnson, Washington
- RB— Marshall Faulk, St. Louis*
  Stephen Davis, Washington
  Emmitt Smith, Dallas
- FB— Mike Alstott, Tampa Bay*

DEFENSE
- DE— Kevin Carter, St. Louis*
  Michael Strahan, N.Y. Giants*
  Robert Porcher, Detroit
  Simeon Rice, Arizona†
- DT— Luther Elliss, Detroit*
  Warren Sapp, Tampa Bay*
  Bryant Young, San Francisco
- OLB— Jessie Armstead, N.Y. Giants*
  Derrick Brooks, Tampa Bay*
  Dexter Coakley, Dallas
- ILB— Hardy Nickerson, Tampa Bay*
  Stephen Boyd, Detroit
- CB— Todd Lyght, St. Louis*
  Deion Sanders, Dallas*
  Aeneas Williams, Arizona
  Troy Vincent, Philadelphia
- SS— John Lynch, Tampa Bay*
- FS— Lance Schulters, San Francisco*
  Brian Dawkins, Philadelphia

NOTE: CB Sanders replaced due to injury by Vincent.

SPECIALISTS
- P— Mitch Berger, Minnesota
- K— Jason Hanson, Detroit
- KR— Glyn Milburn, Chicago
- ST— Michael Bates, Carolina

*Elected starter.
†Selected as need player.

1999 REVIEW Pro Bowl

PLAYER PARTICIPATION

COMPLETE LIST

Player, Team	GP	GS
Abdul-Jabbar, Karim, Mia.-Cle.	13	9
Abdullah, Rabih, Tampa Bay	15	1
Abdullah, Rahim, Cleveland	16	13
Abraham, Donnie, Tampa Bay	16	16
Abrams, Kevin, Detroit	1	0
Ackerman, Tom, New Orleans	16	8
Adams, Flozell, Dallas	16	16
Adams, Sam, Seattle	13	13
Agnew, Ray, St. Louis	16	16
Aguiar, Louie, Green Bay	15	0
Ahanotu, Chidi, Tampa Bay	15	15
Aikman, Troy, Dallas	14	14
Akers, David, Philadelphia	16	0
Akins, Chris, Dallas	9	0
Albright, Ethan, Buffalo	16	0
Aldridge, Allen, Detroit	16	14
Aleaga, Ink, New Orleans	8	2
Alexander, Brent, Carolina	16	16
Alexander, Derrick L., Cleveland.	16	16
Alexander, Derrick S., K.C.	15	13
Alexander, Stephen, Was.	15	15
Alford, Brian, N.Y. Giants	2	0
Allen, Eric, Oakland	16	16
Allen, James, Chicago	12	3
Allen, Larry, Dallas	11	11
Allen, Taje, St. Louis	16	2
Allen, Terry, New England	16	13
Allred, John, Chicago	16	5
Alstott, Mike, Tampa Bay	16	6
Ambrose, Ashley, New Orleans	16	16
Anders, Kimble, Kansas City	2	2
Andersen, Jason, New England	9	0
Andersen, Morten, Atlanta	16	0
Anderson, Gary, Minnesota	16	0
Anderson, Jamal, Atlanta	2	2
Anderson, Ken, Chicago	2	0
Anderson, Richie, N.Y. Jets	16	9
Anderson, Willie, Cincinnati	14	14
Andruzzi, Joseph, Green Bay	8	3
Anthony, Reidel, Tampa Bay	13	7
Araguz, Leo, Oakland	16	0
Archambeau, Lester, Atlanta	15	15
Armour, JoJuan, Cincinnati	2	0
Armour, Justin, Baltimore	15	7
Armstead, Jessie, N.Y. Giants	16	16
Armstrong, Bruce, New England.	16	16
Armstrong, Trace, Miami	16	2
Arnold, Jahine, Green Bay	1	0
Artmore, Rodney, Green Bay	5	0
Ashmore, Darryl, Oakland	16	2
Atkins, James, Baltimore	2	1
Atkins, Larry, Kansas City	9	0
Atwater, Steve, N.Y. Jets	12	11
Austin, Billy, Indianapolis	16	0
Austin, Raymond, Chicago	15	0
Avery, John, Mia.-Den.	7	0
Ayanbadejo, Obafemi, Min.-Bal.	14	0
Azumah, Jerry, Chicago	16	2
Badger, Brad, Washington	14	4
Bailey, Champ, Washington	16	16
Bailey, Karsten, Seattle	2	0
Bailey, Robert, Detroit	16	11
Baker, Eugene, Indianapolis	3	1
Baker, Jon, Kansas City	2	0
Ball, Jerry, Cle.-Min.	16	13
Banks, Antonio, Minnesota	6	1

Player, Team	GP	GS
Banks, Chris, Denver	16	1
Banks, Tavian, Jacksonville	8	1
Banks, Tony, Baltimore	12	10
Bankston, Michael, Cincinnati	16	9
Banta, Brad, Indianapolis	16	0
Barber, Kantroy, Miami	2	0
Barber, Mike, Indianapolis	16	16
Barber, Ronde, Tampa Bay	16	15
Barber, Shawn, Washington	16	16
Barber, Tiki, N.Y. Giants	16	1
Barker, Bryan, Jacksonville	16	0
Barker, Roy, Cle.-G.B.	13	3
Barlow, Reggie, Jacksonville	14	2
Barndt, Tom, Kansas City	16	13
Barnes, Lionel, St. Louis	3	0
Barnes, Pat, San Francisco	1	0
Barnhardt, Tommy, N.O.	16	0
Barrow, Micheal, Carolina	16	16
Bartholomew, Brent, Miami	2	0
Barton, Eric, Oakland	16	3
Bartrum, Mike, New England	16	0
Basnight, Michael, Cincinnati	13	1
Bass, Anthony, Minnesota	14	3
Batch, Charlie, Detroit	11	10
Bates, D'Wayne, Chicago	7	1
Bates, Mario, Arizona	16	2
Bates, Michael, Carolina	16	0
Battaglia, Marco, Cincinnati	16	0
Baxter, Fred, N.Y. Jets	14	8
Beasley, Aaron, Jacksonville	16	16
Beasley, Fred, San Francisco	13	11
Bech, Brett, New Orleans	8	0
Beede, Frank, Seattle	10	0
Bell, Myron, Cincinnati	16	16
Bell, Shonn, San Francisco	2	0
Bell, Tyrone, Green Bay	1	0
Bellamy, Jay, Seattle	16	16
Belser, Jason, Indianapolis	16	16
Bennett, Cornelius, Indianapolis	16	16
Bennett, Darren, San Diego	16	0
Bennett, Donnell, Kansas City	15	1
Bennett, Edgar, Chicago	16	2
Bennett, Sean, N.Y. Giants	9	2
Bennnett, Tommy, Arizona	15	15
Bentley, Scott, Kansas City	2	0
Berger, Mitch, Minnesota	16	0
Berry, Bert, Indianapolis	16	0
Bettis, Jerome, Pittsburgh	16	16
Beuerlein, Steve, Carolina	16	16
Beverly, Eric, Detroit	16	2
Biakabutuka, Tim, Carolina	11	11
Biekert, Greg, Oakland	16	16
Bieniemy, Eric, Philadelphia	16	0
Billups, Terry, New England	2	1
Binn, David, San Diego	16	0
Birk, Matt, Minnesota	15	0
Bishop, Blaine, Tennessee	15	15
Bishop, Greg, Atlanta	13	2
Bjornson, Eric, Dallas	16	6
Blackmon, Roosevelt, Cincinnati.	5	3
Blackshear, Jeff, Baltimore	16	16
Blackwell, Will, Pittsburgh	11	1
Blaise, Kerlin, Detroit	16	4
Blake, Jeff, Cincinnati	14	12
Blanchard, Cary, N.Y. Giants	10	0
Bledsoe, Drew, New England	16	16

Player, Team	GP	GS
Blevins, Tony, Indianapolis	15	0
Bloedorn, Greg, Seattle	9	0
Bly, Dre', St. Louis	16	2
Bobo, Orlando, Cleveland	9	1
Bock, John, Miami	7	0
Bolden, Juran, Kansas City	7	0
Bonham, Shane, S.F.-Ind.	6	0
Boniol, Chris, Chicago	10	0
Bono, Steve, Carolina	2	0
Booker, Marty, Chicago	9	4
Booker, Michael, Atlanta	13	1
Booker, Vaughn, Green Bay	14	14
Boose, Dorian, N.Y. Jets	12	0
Bordano, Chris, New Orleans	15	12
Boselli, Tony, Jacksonville	16	16
Bostic, James, Philadelphia	9	0
Bostic, Jason, Philadelphia	1	0
Boston, David, Arizona	16	8
Boulware, Peter, Baltimore	16	11
Boutte, Marc, Washington	6	0
Bowden, Joe, Tennessee	15	15
Bowens, David, Denver	16	0
Bowens, Tim, Miami	16	15
Bowie, Larry, Washington	2	0
Bownes, Fabien, Seattle	15	0
Boyd, Stephen, Detroit	14	14
Boyer, Brant, Jacksonville	16	0
Brackens, Tony, Jacksonville	16	15
Bradford, Corey, Green Bay	16	2
Bradford, Ronnie, Atlanta	16	6
Bradley, Melvin, Arizona	1	0
Brady, Jeff, Indianapolis	3	0
Brady, Kyle, Jacksonville	13	12
Braham, Rich, Cincinnati	16	16
Branch, Calvin, Oakland	16	1
Brandenburg, Dan, Buffalo	14	0
Bratzke, Chad, Indianapolis	16	16
Braxton, Tyrone, Denver	16	15
Brazzell, Chris, Dallas	5	0
Brice, Will, Cincinnati	11	0
Brien, Doug, New Orleans	16	0
Brigance, O.J., Miami	16	0
Brigham, Jeremy, Oakland	16	2
Brisby, Vincent, New England	12	1
Brister, Bubby, Denver	2	0
Brockermeyer, Blake, Chicago	15	15
Bromell, Lorenzo, Miami	15	1
Bronson, Zack, San Francisco	15	2
Brooking, Keith, Atlanta	13	13
Brooks, Barrett, Detroit	16	12
Brooks, Bobby, Oakland	1	0
Brooks, Derrick, Tampa Bay	16	16
Brooks, Macey, Chicago	9	2
Broughton, Luther, Philadelphia.	16	3
Brown, Anthony, Pittsburgh	16	11
Brown, Chad, Seattle	15	15
Brown, Cornell, Baltimore	16	5
Brown, Corwin, Detroit	13	1
Brown, Cyron, Denver	7	0
Brown, Dave, Arizona	8	5
Brown, Derek, Arizona	15	0
Brown, Doug, Washington	10	0
Brown, Eric, Denver	16	10
Brown, Ernie, Pittsburgh	3	0
Brown, Fakhir, San Diego	9	3
Brown, Gary, N.Y. Giants	3	2

Player, Team	GP	GS
Brown, Gilbert, Green Bay	16	15
Brown, J.B., Detroit	13	3
Brown, James, Miami	15	14
Brown, Jamie, Washington	1	0
Brown, Kris, Pittsburgh	16	0
Brown, Lance, Pittsburgh	16	0
Brown, Larry, Tennessee	9	0
Brown, Lomas, Cleveland	10	10
Brown, Na, Philadelphia	12	5
Brown, Omar, Atlanta	13	0
Brown, Orlando, Cleveland	15	15
Brown, Ray, San Francisco	16	16
Brown, Reggie, Seattle	16	8
Brown, Ruben, Buffalo	14	14
Brown, Tim, Oakland	16	16
Brown, Troy, New England	13	1
Brown, Wilbert, San Diego	5	0
Bruce, Isaac, St. Louis	16	16
Bruener, Mark, Pittsburgh	14	14
Brunell, Mark, Jacksonville	15	15
Bruschi, Tedy, New England	14	14
Bryant, Fernando, Jacksonville	16	16
Bryant, Junior, San Francisco	16	16
Bryant, Tony, Oakland	10	0
Brzezinski, Doug, Philadelphia	16	16
Buchanan, Ray, Atlanta	16	16
Buckey, Jeff, San Francisco	7	0
Buckley, Curtis, Washington	7	0
Buckley, Marcus, N.Y. Giants	12	0
Buckley, Terrell, Miami	16	11
Buckner, Brentson, S.F.	16	5
Bundren, Jim, Cleveland	16	1
Burke, Tom, Arizona	16	3
Burnett, Rob, Baltimore	16	16
Burns, Keith, Chicago	15	0
Burris, Jeff, Indianapolis	16	16
Burrough, John, Minnesota	10	2
Burton, Shane, Chicago	15	0
Bush, Devin, St. Louis	16	7
Bush, Lew, San Diego	16	14
Bush, Steve, Cincinnati	13	0
Butler, LeRoy, Green Bay	16	16
Bynum, Kenny, San Diego	16	5
Byrd, Isaac, Tennessee	12	6
Cadrez, Glenn, Denver	16	15
Caldwell, Mike, Philadelphia	14	2
Calloway, Chris, Atlanta	11	6
Campbell, Dan, N.Y. Giants	12	1
Campbell, Lamar, Detroit	15	2
Campbell, Mark, Cleveland	14	4
Campbell, Matt, Carolina	10	10
Cannida, James, Tampa Bay	2	1
Canty, Chris, Seattle	14	1
Carney, John, San Diego	16	0
Carpenter, Keion, Buffalo	10	0
Carpenter, Ron, St. Louis	11	0
Carrier, Mark, Detroit	15	15
Carruth, Rae, Carolina	5	5
Carswell, Dwayne, Denver	16	11
Carter, Chris, New England	15	15
Carter, Cris, Minnesota	16	16
Carter, Dale, Denver	14	14
Carter, Kevin, St. Louis	16	16
Carter, Ki-Jana, Cincinnati	3	0
Carter, Marty, Atlanta	11	11
Carter, Tom, Chi.-Cin.	14	8
Carter, Tony, New England	16	14
Carty, Johndale, Atlanta	14	0
Cascadden, Chad, N.Y. Jets	4	0
Case, Stoney, Baltimore	10	4
Centers, Larry, Washington	16	12
Chamberlain, Byron, Denver	16	0

Player, Team	GP	GS
Chamblin, Corey, Jacksonville	11	0
Chancey, Robert, Dallas	3	0
Chandler, Chris, Atlanta	12	12
Chanoine, Roger, Cleveland	1	0
Chase, Martin, Baltimore	3	0
Chavous, Corey, Arizona	15	4
Cherry, Je'Rod, New Orleans	16	0
Chester, Larry, Indianapolis	16	8
Chiaverini, Darrin, Cleveland	16	8
Childress, O.J., N.Y. Giants	4	0
Chmura, Mark, Green Bay	2	2
Chrebet, Wayne, N.Y. Jets	11	11
Christian, Bob, Atlanta	16	14
Christie, Steve, Buffalo	16	0
Christy, Jeff, Minnesota	16	16
Chryplewicz, Pete, Detroit	11	1
Claiborne, Chris, Detroit	15	13
Clark, Desmond, Denver	9	0
Clark, Greg, San Francisco	12	11
Clark, Jon, Arizona	2	0
Clark, Rico, Cin.-N.E.	9	1
Clarke, Phil, New Orleans	8	3
Clay, Willie, New Orleans	16	9
Cleeland, Cameron, N.O.	11	8
Clement, Anthony, Arizona	16	14
Clemons, Charlie, St. Louis	16	0
Clemons, Duane, Minnesota	16	9
Cline, Tony, S.F.-Pit.	10	0
Cloud, Mike, Kansas City	11	0
Coady, Rich, St. Louis	16	0
Coakley, Dexter, Dallas	16	16
Coates, Ben, New England	16	15
Cochran, Antonio, Seattle	4	0
Cody, Mac, Arizona	13	0
Coghill, George, Denver	13	5
Coleman, Ben, Jacksonville	16	12
Coleman, Marco, Washington	16	16
Coleman, Marcus, N.Y. Jets	16	10
Coleman, Roderick, Oakland	3	0
Colinet, Stalin, Min.-Cle.	14	10
Collins, Andre, Detroit	7	0
Collins, Bobby, Buffalo	14	4
Collins, Calvin, Atlanta	14	8
Collins, Cecil, Miami	8	6
Collins, Kerry, N.Y. Giants	10	7
Collins, Mo, Oakland	13	12
Collins, Ryan, Baltimore	4	3
Collins, Todd F., St. Louis	16	13
Collons, Ferric, New England	14	0
Colman, Doug, Tennessee	16	1
Colvin, Rosevelt, Chicago	11	0
Comella, Greg, N.Y. Giants	16	3
Compton, Mike, Detroit	15	15
Conaty, Bill, Buffalo	7	1
Connell, Albert, Washington	15	14
Conrad, Chris, Pittsburgh	11	3
Conway, Brett, Washington	16	0
Conway, Curtis, Chicago	9	8
Conwell, Ernie, St. Louis	3	0
Cook, Anthony, Washington	16	7
Cook, Rashard, Philadelphia	13	0
Cooper, Andre, Denver	10	1
Copeland, John, Cincinnati	16	16
Cortez, Jose, N.Y. Giants	1	0
Coryatt, Quentin, Dallas	4	1
Costello, Brad, Cincinnati	5	0
Cota, Chad, Indianapolis	15	15
Couch, Tim, Cleveland	15	14
Cousin, Terry, Chicago	16	9
Covington, Scott, Cincinnati	3	0
Cowart, Sam, Buffalo	16	16
Cox, Bryan, N.Y. Jets	12	11

Player, Team	GP	GS
Craft, Jason, Jacksonville	16	0
Craver, Aaron, New Orleans	13	10
Crawford, Keith, Green Bay	3	0
Crawford, Vernon, New England	9	0
Crockett, Henri, Atlanta	16	14
Crockett, Ray, Denver	16	16
Crockett, Zack, Jacksonville	13	1
Crosby, Clifton, St. Louis	1	0
Cross, Howard, N.Y. Giants	16	15
Crowell, Germane, Detroit	16	15
Crumpler, Carlester, Minnesota	11	1
Crutchfield, Buddy, N.Y. Jets	4	0
Culpepper, Brad, Tampa Bay	16	16
Culpepper, Daunte, Minnesota	1	0
Cummings, Joe, Buffalo	16	2
Cunningham, Randall, Min.	6	6
Cunningham, Richie, Dal.-Car.	15	0
Curry, Eric, Jacksonville	5	0
Curry, Scott, Green Bay	5	0
Curtis, Canute, Cincinnati	15	0
Cushing, Matt, Pittsburgh	7	1
Dailey, Casey, N.Y. Jets	6	0
Dalman, Chris, San Francisco	15	15
Dalton, Antico, Minnesota	2	0
Dalton, Lional, Baltimore	16	2
Daluiso, Brad, N.Y. Giants	6	0
Daniels, Phillip, Seattle	16	16
Darius, Donovin, Jacksonville	16	16
Darling, James, Philadelphia	15	10
Davidds-Garrido, Norbert, Car.	16	0
Davis, Anthony, Green Bay	14	1
Davis, Billy, Baltimore	16	0
Davis, Don, Tampa Bay	14	0
Davis, Eric, Carolina	16	16
Davis, John, Tampa Bay	16	0
Davis, Nathan, Dallas	4	0
Davis, Pernell, Philadelphia	2	0
Davis, Reggie, San Diego	16	3
Davis, Rob, Green Bay	16	0
Davis, Russell, Chicago	11	8
Davis, Stephen, Washington	14	14
Davis, Terrell, Denver	4	4
Davis, Travis, Pittsburgh	16	16
Davis, Troy, New Orleans	16	2
Davis, Tyrone, Green Bay	16	13
Davis, Wendell, Dallas	16	0
Davis, Zola, Cleveland	6	1
Dawkins, Brian, Philadelphia	16	16
Dawkins, Sean, Seattle	16	13
Dawsey, Lawrence, N.O.	10	0
Dawson, Dermontti, Pittsburgh	7	7
Dawson, Phil, Cleveland	15	0
Dearth, James, Cleveland	2	0
Deese, Derrick, San Francisco	16	16
Del Greco, Al, Tennessee	16	0
Delhomme, Jake, New Orleans	2	2
Dellenbach, Jeff, Philadelphia	16	3
DeLong, Greg, Baltimore	16	7
DeMarco, Brian, Cincinnati	7	7
Denson, Autry, Miami	6	1
Denson, Damon, New England	2	0
Denton, Tim, Washington	16	0
Dercher, Dan, San Francisco	9	0
Detmer, Koy, Philadelphia	1	1
Detmer, Ty, Cleveland	5	2
Devine, Kevin, Minnesota	2	0
Devlin, Mike, Arizona	16	0
DeVries, Jared, Detroit	2	0
Dexter, James, Arizona	8	5
Diaz, Jorge, Tampa Bay	13	11
Diaz-Infante, David, Phi.	15	0
Dilfer, Trent, Tampa Bay	10	10

– 233 –

Player, Team	GP	GS
Dilger, Ken, Indianapolis	15	15
Dillon, Corey, Cincinnati	15	15
Dimry, Charles, San Diego	12	7
DiNapoli, Gennaro, Oakland	11	9
Dingle, Antonio, G.B.-Car.	9	0
Dishman, Chris, Arizona	13	10
Dishman, Cris, Kansas City	16	0
Dixon, Andre, Detroit	4	0
Dixon, David, Minnesota	16	16
Dixon, Gerald, San Diego	14	1
Dixon, Mark, Miami	13	13
Doering, Chris, Denver	3	0
Dogins, Kevin, Tampa Bay	11	5
Doleman, Chris, Minnesota	14	12
Donnalley, Kevin, Miami	16	9
Dorsett, Anthony, Tennessee	16	1
Dotson, Earl, Green Bay	15	15
Dotson, Santana, Green Bay	12	12
Douglas, Dameane, Philadelphia	14	0
Douglas, Hugh, Philadelphia	4	2
Draft, Chris, San Francisco	7	0
Drake, Jerry, Arizona	16	16
Drakeford, Tyronne, N.O.	10	5
Drayton, Troy, Miami	14	13
Driver, Donald, Green Bay	6	0
Dronett, Shane, Atlanta	16	16
Dudley, Rickey, Oakland	16	16
Duff, Bill, Cleveland	5	0
Duffy, Roger, Pittsburgh	16	11
Dumas, Mike, San Diego	14	14
Duncan, Jamie, Tampa Bay	16	0
Dunn, Damon, Cleveland	1	0
Dunn, David, Cleveland	6	0
Dunn, Warrick, Tampa Bay	15	15
Dwight, Tim, Atlanta	12	8
Dyson, Kevin, Tennessee	16	16
Early, Quinn, N.Y. Jets	16	3
Eaton, Chad, New England	16	16
Edwards, Antonio, Carolina	14	7
Edwards, Antuan, Green Bay	16	1
Edwards, Donnie, Kansas City	16	16
Edwards, Marc, Cleveland	16	14
Edwards, Troy, Pittsburgh	16	6
Ekuban, Ebenezer, Dallas	16	2
Elam, Jason, Denver	16	0
Elias, Keith, Indianapolis	14	0
Elliott, Jumbo, N.Y. Jets	16	15
Ellis, Ed, New England	1	1
Ellis, Greg, Dallas	13	13
Ellison, Jerry, New England	12	0
Elliss, Luther, Detroit	15	14
Ellsworth, Percy, N.Y. Giants	14	14
Eloms, Joey, Seattle	4	0
Emanuel, Bert, Tampa Bay	11	10
Emmons, Carlos, Pittsburgh	16	16
Engel, Greg, Detroit	1	0
Engler, Derek, N.Y. Giants	10	4
Engram, Bobby, Chicago	16	14
Enis, Curtis, Chicago	15	12
Evans, Chuck, Baltimore	16	10
Evans, Doug, Carolina	16	16
Evans, Josh, Tennessee	11	10
Evans, Leomont, Washington	15	15
Everitt, Steve, Philadelphia	16	16
Fabini, Jason, N.Y. Jets	9	9
Fair, Terry, Detroit	11	11
Faneca, Alan, Pittsburgh	15	14
Fann, Chad, San Francisco	16	3
Farmer, Robert, N.Y. Jets	13	0
Farr, D'Marco, St. Louis	16	16
Farrior, James, N.Y. Jets	16	4
Faulk, Kevin, New England	11	2

Player, Team	GP	GS
Faulk, Marshall, St. Louis	16	16
Fauria, Christian, Seattle	16	16
Favors, Greg, Tennessee	15	0
Favre, Brett, Green Bay	16	16
Fazande, Jermaine, San Diego	7	3
Feagles, Jeff, Seattle	16	0
Ferguson, Jason, N.Y. Jets	9	9
Fiala, John, Pittsburgh	16	0
Fiedler, Jay, Jacksonville	7	1
Fields, Mark, New Orleans	14	14
Fields, Scott, Seattle	2	0
Fina, John, Buffalo	16	16
Finneran, Brian, Philadelphia	3	0
Fiore, Dave, San Francisco	16	16
Fisher, Charles, Cincinnati	1	1
Fisk, Jason, Tennessee	16	16
Flanagan, Mike, Green Bay	15	0
Flanigan, Jim, Chicago	16	16
Fletcher, London, St. Louis	16	16
Fletcher, Terrell, San Diego	15	2
Flowers, Lethon, Pittsburgh	15	15
Floyd, Chris, New England	13	0
Floyd, William, Carolina	16	16
Flutie, Doug, Buffalo	15	15
Flynn, Mike, Baltimore	12	0
Folau, Spencer, Baltimore	5	1
Foley, Glenn, Seattle	3	1
Foley, Steve, Cincinnati	16	16
Folston, James, Arizona	6	0
Fontenot, Albert, San Diego	15	15
Fontenot, Jerry, New Orleans	16	16
Forbes, Marlon, Cleveland	16	1
Ford, Henry, Tennessee	12	9
Foreman, Jay, Buffalo	7	0
Fortin, Roman, San Diego	16	16
Francis, James, Washington	10	1
Franklin, P.J., New Orleans	3	0
Frederick, Mike, Tennessee	13	0
Fredrickson, Rob, Arizona	16	16
Freeman, Antonio, Green Bay	16	16
Frerotte, Gus, Detroit	9	6
Fricke, Ben, Dallas	3	0
Friesz, John, New England	1	0
Frost, Scott, N.Y. Jets	14	0
Fryar, Irving, Washington	16	1
Fuamatu-Ma'afala, Chris, Pit.	10	0
Fuller, Corey, Cleveland	16	16
Fuller, Randy, Seattle	2	0
Gadsden, Oronde, Miami	16	7
Galloway, Joey, Seattle	8	4
Galyon, Scott, N.Y. Giants	16	0
Gammon, Kendall, New Orleans	16	0
Gandy, Wayne, Pittsburgh	16	16
Gannon, Rich, Oakland	16	16
Garcia, Frank, Carolina	16	16
Garcia, Jeff, San Francisco	13	10
Gardener, Daryl, Miami	16	15
Gardner, Barry, Philadelphia	16	5
Gardner, Derrick, Atlanta	7	0
Gardocki, Chris, Cleveland	16	0
Garner, Charlie, San Francisco	16	15
Garnes, Sam, N.Y. Giants	16	16
Garrett, Jason, Dallas	5	2
Gary, Olandis, Denver	12	12
Gash, Sam, Buffalo	15	11
George, Eddie, Tennessee	16	16
George, Jeff, Minnesota	12	10
George, Ron, Kansas City	16	0
George, Spencer, Tennessee	8	0
George, Tony, New England	16	1
Germaine, Joe, St. Louis	3	0
German, Jammi, Atlanta	14	0

Player, Team	GP	GS
Gibson, Damon, Cleveland	2	0
Gibson, Oliver, Cincinnati	16	16
Gilbert, Sean, Carolina	16	16
Gildon, Jason, Pittsburgh	16	16
Gisler, Mike, N.Y. Jets	16	0
Givens, Reggie, San Francisco	16	0
Glenn, Aaron, N.Y. Jets	16	16
Glenn, Tarik, Indianapolis	16	16
Glenn, Terry, New England	14	13
Glover, Andrew, Minnesota	16	13
Glover, Kevin, Seattle	6	6
Glover, La'Roi, New Orleans	16	0
Glover, Phil, Tennessee	1	0
Godfrey, Randall, Dallas	16	16
Goff, Mike, Cincinnati	12	1
Gogan, Kevin, Miami	16	10
Gonzalez, Pete, Pittsburgh	1	0
Gonzalez, Tony, Kansas City	15	15
Gooch, Jeff, Tampa Bay	15	0
Goodwin, Hunter, Miami	15	5
Gordon, Darrien, Oakland	16	2
Gordon, Dwayne, N.Y. Jets	16	4
Gordon, Lennox, Buffalo	8	0
Gouveia, Kurt, Washington	12	0
Gowin, Toby, Dallas	16	0
Gowins, Brian, Chicago	2	0
Gragg, Scott, N.Y. Giants	16	16
Graham, Aaron, Arizona	16	16
Graham, DeMingo, San Diego	16	10
Graham, Jay, Baltimore	4	0
Graham, Jeff, San Diego	16	11
Graham, Kent, N.Y. Giants	9	9
Gramatica, Martin, Tampa Bay	16	0
Granville, Billy, Cincinnati	16	0
Grasmanis, Paul, Denver	5	0
Gray, Carlton, Kansas City	16	0
Gray, Chris, Seattle	16	10
Graziani, Tony, Atlanta	11	3
Grbac, Elvis, Kansas City	16	16
Green, Ahman, Seattle	14	0
Green, Darrell, Washington	16	16
Green, E.G., Indianapolis	11	4
Green, Eric, N.Y. Jets	10	7
Green, Jacquez, Tampa Bay	16	10
Green, Lamont, Atlanta	1	0
Green, Victor, N.Y. Jets	16	16
Green, Yatil, Miami	8	1
Greene, Kevin, Carolina	16	16
Greene, Scott, Indianapolis	5	0
Greer, Donovan, Buffalo	16	0
Gregg, Kelly, Philadelphia	3	0
Greisen, Chris, Arizona	2	0
Griese, Brian, Denver	14	13
Griffin, Damon, Cincinnati	13	0
Griffith, Howard, Denver	16	16
Griffith, Rich, Jacksonville	16	0
Griffith, Robert, Minnesota	16	16
Groce, Clif, Cincinnati	16	15
Gruber, Paul, Tampa Bay	16	16
Grunhard, Tim, Kansas City	16	16
Gruttadauria, Mike, St. Louis	16	16
Gutierrez, Brock, Cincinnati	16	0
Habib, Brian, Seattle	16	16
Hakim, Az-zahir, St. Louis	15	0
Halapin, Mike, New Orleans	9	3
Hale, Ryan, N.Y. Giants	9	0
Haley, Charles, San Francisco	16	1
Hall, Cory, Cincinnati	16	12
Hall, John, N.Y. Jets	16	0
Hall, Lamont, Green Bay	14	0
Hall, Lemanski, Dallas	10	0
Hall, Travis, Atlanta	16	15

– 234 –

Player, Team	GP	GS
Hallen, Bob, Atlanta	16	14
Hallock, Ty, Chicago	15	4
Hambrick, Darren, Dallas	16	12
Hamilton, Bobby, N.Y. Jets	7	0
Hamilton, Conrad, N.Y. Giants	3	2
Hamilton, Keith, N.Y. Giants	16	16
Hamilton, Malcolm, Washington	4	0
Hamilton, Michael, San Diego	14	2
Hamilton, Ruffin, Atlanta	11	1
Hamiter, Uhuru, New Orleans	5	0
Hand, Norman, San Diego	14	14
Hanks, Merton, Seattle	12	1
Hansen, Brian, Washington	2	0
Hansen, Phil, Buffalo	14	14
Hanson, Chris, Green Bay	1	0
Hanson, Jason, Detroit	16	0
Hanspard, Byron, Atlanta	12	4
Hape, Patrick, Tampa Bay	15	1
Harbaugh, Jim, San Diego	14	12
Harden, Cedric, San Diego	5	0
Hardy, Kevin, Jacksonville	16	16
Hardy, Terry, Arizona	16	16
Harper, Alvin, Dallas	2	0
Harper, Dwayne, Detroit	3	1
Harris, Al, Philadelphia	16	6
Harris, Anthony, Miami	4	0
Harris, Bernardo, Green Bay	16	15
Harris, Corey, New Orleans	3	0
Harris, Corey L., Baltimore	16	0
Harris, Derrick, St. Louis	1	0
Harris, Jackie, Tennessee	12	1
Harris, James, Oakland	16	16
Harris, Johnnie, Oakland	4	0
Harris, Mark, San Francisco	16	2
Harris, Robert, N.Y. Giants	6	6
Harris, Ronnie, Atlanta	13	0
Harris, Sean, Chicago	14	10
Harris, Walt, Chicago	15	15
Harrison, Martin, Minnesota	4	0
Harrison, Marvin, Indianapolis	16	16
Harrison, Nolan, Pittsburgh	5	3
Harrison, Rodney, San Diego	6	6
Hartings, Jeff, Detroit	16	16
Harvey, Richard, Oakland	15	15
Hasselbach, Harald, Denver	16	2
Hasselbeck, Matt, Green Bay	16	0
Hastings, Andre, New Orleans	15	5
Hasty, James, Kansas City	15	15
Hatchette, Matt, Minnesota	13	0
Hauck, Tim, Philadelphia	16	15
Hawkins, Artrell, Cincinnati	14	13
Hawkins, Courtney, Pittsburgh	11	11
Hawthorne, Duane, Dallas	13	0
Hayes, Chris, N.Y. Jets	15	0
Hayes, Donald, Carolina	13	1
Heath, Rodney, Cincinnati	16	9
Heck, Andy, Washington	16	16
Hegamin, George, Tampa Bay	1	0
Heiden, Steve, San Diego	11	0
Heimburger, Craig, Green Bay	2	0
Hellestrae, Dale, Dallas	16	0
Hemsley, Nate, Dallas	6	0
Henderson, William, Green Bay	16	13
Hennings, Chad, Dallas	16	16
Henry, Kevin, Pittsburgh	16	13
Hentrich, Craig, Tennessee	16	0
Herring, Kim, Baltimore	16	16
Hetherington, Chris, Carolina	14	0
Hewitt, Chris, New Orleans	12	0
Hicks, Eric, Kansas City	16	16
Hicks, Robert, Buffalo	14	14
Hicks, Skip, Washington	10	2

Player, Team	GP	GS
Hill, Eric, San Diego	12	10
Hill, Greg, Detroit	14	8
Hill, Madre, Cleveland	5	0
Hill, Ray, Miami	16	0
Hilliard, Ike, N.Y. Giants	16	16
Hitchcock, Jimmy, Minnesota	16	16
Hoard, Leroy, Minnesota	15	3
Hobert, Billy Joe, New Orleans	9	7
Hobgood-Chittick, Nate, St.L.	10	0
Hodgins, James, St. Louis	15	0
Holcombe, Robert, St. Louis	15	7
Holdman, Warrick, Chicago	16	5
Holecek, John, Buffalo	14	14
Holland, Darius, Cleveland	15	11
Holliday, Vonnie, Green Bay	16	16
Hollier, Dwight, Miami	15	0
Hollis, Mike, Jacksonville	16	0
Holmberg, Rob, Minnesota	16	0
Holmes, Darick, Indianapolis	1	0
Holmes, Earl, Pittsburgh	16	16
Holmes, Jaret, Chicago	3	0
Holmes, Kenny, Tennessee	14	7
Holmes, Lester, Arizona	13	13
Holmes, Priest, Baltimore	9	4
Holsey, Bernard, N.Y. Giants	16	0
Holt, Torry, St. Louis	16	15
Hopkins, Brad, Tennessee	16	16
Hopson, Tyrone, San Francisco	1	0
Horan, Mike, St. Louis	8	0
Horn, Joe, Kansas City	16	1
Horne, Tony, St. Louis	12	0
Howard, Chris, Jacksonville	12	0
Howard, Desmond, G.B.-Det.	13	0
Howard, Ty, Cincinnati	12	3
Hoying, Bobby, Oakland	2	0
Huard, Damon, Miami	16	5
Hudson, Chris, Chicago	16	16
Hudson, John, N.Y. Jets	16	0
Hundon, James, Cincinnati	6	0
Hunt, Cletidus, Green Bay	11	1
Huntley, Richard, Pittsburgh	16	2
Husted, Michael, Oakland	13	0
Hutson, Tony, Dallas	2	2
Hutton, Tom, Miami	14	0
Hyder, Gaylon, St. Louis	4	0
Ingram, Steve, Jacksonville	6	0
Irvin, Ken, Buffalo	14	14
Irvin, Michael, Dallas	4	4
Irvin, Sedrick, Detroit	14	0
Irwin, Heath, New England	15	13
Ismail, Qadry, Baltimore	16	16
Ismail, Rocket, Dallas	16	14
Israel, Steve, New England	13	13
Izzo, Larry, Miami	16	0
Jacke, Chris, Arizona	16	0
Jackson, Brad, Baltimore	13	0
Jackson, Calvin, Miami	16	10
Jackson, Dexter, Tampa Bay	12	0
Jackson, Grady, Oakland	15	0
Jackson, Greg, San Diego	14	9
Jackson, John, San Diego	15	15
Jackson, Lenzie, Jacksonville	4	0
Jackson, Raymond, Cleveland	14	0
Jackson, Sheldon, Buffalo	13	4
Jackson, Steve, Tennessee	8	0
Jackson, Terry, San Francisco	16	0
Jackson, Tyoka, Tampa Bay	6	0
Jackson, Waverly, Indianapolis	16	16
Jackson, Willie, Cincinnati	16	2
Jacoby, Mitch, Kansas City	5	0
Jacox, Kendyl, San Diego	10	5
Jacquet, Nate, Miami	13	0

Player, Team	GP	GS
Jaeger, Jeff, Chicago	3	0
James, Edgerrin, Indianapolis	16	16
James, Tory, Denver	16	4
Jansen, Jon, Washington	16	16
Jasper, Edward, Atlanta	13	0
Jeffers, Patrick, Carolina	15	10
Jefferson, Greg, Philadelphia	16	6
Jefferson, Shawn, New England	16	16
Jeffries, Greg, Miami	16	0
Jells, Dietrich, Philadelphia	14	3
Jenkins, Billy, St. Louis	16	16
Jenkins, DeRon, Baltimore	16	15
Jenkins, James, Washington	16	4
Jenkins, Kerry, N.Y. Jets	16	16
Jenkins, MarTay, Arizona	3	0
Jervey, Travis, San Francisco	8	0
Jett, James, Oakland	16	11
Jett, John, Detroit	16	0
Johnson, Anthony, Carolina	16	0
Johnson, Bill, Philadelphia	6	0
Johnson, Brad, Washington	16	16
Johnson, Charles, Philadelphia	11	11
Johnson, Darrius, Denver	16	2
Johnson, Dustin, Seattle	1	0
Johnson, Ellis, Indianapolis	16	16
Johnson, J.J., Miami	13	4
Johnson, Jason, Indianapolis	16	0
Johnson, Kevin, Cleveland	16	16
Johnson, Keyshawn, N.Y. Jets	16	16
Johnson, Lee, New England	16	0
Johnson, Leon, N.Y. Jets	1	0
Johnson, LeShon, N.Y. Giants	16	4
Johnson, Lonnie, Kansas City	14	2
Johnson, Malcolm, Pittsburgh	6	0
Johnson, Norm, Philadelphia	15	0
Johnson, Olrick, NYJ-Min.	8	0
Johnson, Pat, Baltimore	10	6
Johnson, Raylee, San Diego	16	16
Johnson, Rob, Buffalo	2	1
Johnson, Ted, New England	5	5
Johnson, Tre', Washington	16	16
Johnston, Daryl, Dallas	1	0
Johnstone, Lance, Oakland	16	16
Jones, Cedric, N.Y. Giants	16	16
Jones, Charlie, San Diego	8	1
Jones, Clarence, Carolina	16	16
Jones, Damon, Jacksonville	15	8
Jones, Donta, Carolina	16	0
Jones, Ernest, Carolina	13	0
Jones, Freddie, San Diego	16	16
Jones, George, Cleveland	6	0
Jones, Greg, Washington	15	0
Jones, Henry, Buffalo	16	16
Jones, Isaac, Indianapolis	1	1
Jones, James, Detroit	16	16
Jones, Jermaine, NYJ-Chi.	2	0
Jones, Lenoy, Cleveland	16	1
Jones, Marcus, Tampa Bay	16	4
Jones, Marvin, N.Y. Jets	16	16
Jones, Mike A., St. Louis	16	16
Jones, Mike D., Tennessee	11	3
Jones, Robert, Miami	16	15
Jones, Rod, Cincinnati	16	15
Jones, Tebucky, New England	11	2
Jones, Tony, Denver	12	12
Jones, Walter, Seattle	16	16
Jordan, Andrew, Minnesota	11	1
Jordan, Charles, Sea.-G.B.	8	1
Jordan, Randy, Oakland	16	0
Jordan, Richard, Detroit	9	0
Joseph, Kerry, Seattle	16	4
Joyce, Matt, Arizona	15	15

1999 REVIEW *Player participation*

– 235 –

1999 REVIEW — Player participation

Player, Team	GP	GS
Junkin, Trey, Arizona	16	0
Jurevicius, Joe, N.Y. Giants	16	1
Jurkovic, John, Cleveland	10	9
Justin, Paul, St. Louis	10	0
Kalu, Ndukwe, Washington	12	0
Kanell, Danny, Atlanta	3	1
Kasay, John, Carolina	13	0
Katzenmoyer, Andy, N.E.	16	11
Kaufman, Napoleon, Oakland	16	5
Kearse, Jevon, Tennessee	16	16
Kelly, Brian, Tampa Bay	16	3
Kelly, Jeff, Atlanta	16	1
Kelly, Reggie, Atlanta	16	2
Kelly, Rob, New Orleans	16	7
Kelsay, Chad, Pittsburgh	6	0
Kendall, Pete, Seattle	16	16
Keneley, Matt, San Francisco	7	0
Kennedy, Cortez, Seattle	16	16
Kennedy, Lincoln, Oakland	15	15
Kennison, Eddie, New Orleans	16	16
Kent, Joey, Tennessee	8	0
Kerney, Patrick, Atlanta	16	2
Kight, Danny, Indianapolis	12	0
Killens, Terry, Tennessee	16	1
Kinchen, Brian, Carolina	16	0
King, Lamar, Seattle	14	0
King, Shaun, Tampa Bay	6	5
King, Shawn, Indianapolis	9	8
Kirby, Terry, Cleveland	16	10
Kirk, Randy, San Francisco	3	0
Kirkland, Levon, Pittsburgh	16	16
Kirschke, Travis, Detroit	15	7
Kitna, Jon, Seattle	15	15
Kleinsasser, Jimmy, Minnesota	13	7
Knight, Sammy, New Orleans	16	16
Knight, Tom, Arizona	16	11
Konrad, Rob, Miami	15	9
Koonce, George, Green Bay	15	15
Kopp, Jeff, New England	6	0
Kowalkowski, Scott, Detroit	16	3
Kozlowski, Brian, Atlanta	16	3
Kramer, Erik, San Diego	6	4
Kreutz, Olin, Chicago	16	16
Kriewaldt, Clint, Detroit	12	0
Kuberski, Bob, New England	5	0
Kuehl, Ryan, Cleveland	16	0
LaBounty, Matt, Seattle	16	1
Lacina, Corbin, Minnesota	14	0
LaFleur, David, Dallas	16	16
Lake, Carnell, Jacksonville	16	16
Landeta, Sean, Philadelphia	16	0
Landolt, Kevin, Jacksonville	1	0
Lane, Fred, Carolina	15	5
Lane, Max, New England	16	6
Lang, Kenard, Washington	16	9
Langford, Jevon, Cincinnati	12	7
Langham, Antonio, Cleveland	13	2
Lassiter, Kwamie, Arizona	16	16
Law, Ty, New England	13	13
Layman, Jason, Tennessee	15	1
Lee, Amp, St. Louis	7	0
Lee, Delphfrine, N.Y. Jets	4	0
Leeuwenburg, Jay, Cincinnati	14	9
Lepsis, Matt, Denver	16	16
Leroy, Emarlos, Jacksonville	13	0
Leshinski, Ron, Philadelphia	1	0
Lester, Tim, Dallas	5	1
Lett, Leon, Dallas	8	1
Levens, Dorsey, Green Bay	14	14
Levingston, Bashir, N.Y. Giants	12	0
Lewis, Chad, St.L.-Phi.	12	4
Lewis, Darryll, San Diego	13	8
Lewis, Jeff, Carolina	2	0
Lewis, Jermaine, Baltimore	15	6
Lewis, Mo, N.Y. Jets	16	16
Lewis, Ray, Baltimore	16	16
Lincoln, Jeremy, N.Y. Giants	15	7
Lindsay, Everett, Baltimore	16	16
Lindsey, Steve, Jacksonville	16	0
Linton, Jonathan, Buffalo	16	2
Little, Earl, N.O.-Cle.	10	0
Little, Leonard, St. Louis	6	0
Lockett, Kevin, Kansas City	16	1
Lodish, Mike, Denver	13	2
Lofton, Steve, Carolina	5	0
Logan, Ernie, N.Y. Jets	14	7
Logan, James, Seattle	16	2
Logan, Mike, Jacksonville	2	0
Long, Kevin, Tennessee	16	12
Longwell, Ryan, Green Bay	16	0
Loud, Kamil, Buffalo	7	0
Loville, Derek, Denver	10	0
Lucas, Justin, Arizona	2	0
Lucas, Ray, N.Y. Jets	9	9
Lucky, Mike, Dallas	14	4
Lyght, Todd, St. Louis	16	16
Lyle, Keith, St. Louis	9	9
Lyle, Rick, N.Y. Jets	16	16
Lynch, Ben, San Francisco	16	1
Lynch, John, Tampa Bay	16	16
Lynn, Anthony, Denver	16	0
Lyon, Billy, Green Bay	16	4
Lyons, Mitch, Pittsburgh	14	2
Machado, J.P., N.Y. Jets	5	0
Mack, Stacey, Jacksonville	12	0
Mack, Tremain, Cincinnati	12	0
Maddox, Mark, Arizona	16	2
Madison, Sam, Miami	16	16
Makovicka, Joel, Arizona	16	10
Malamala, Siupeli, N.Y. Jets	6	1
Mamula, Mike, Philadelphia	16	13
Mangum, Kris, Carolina	11	0
Mannelly, Patrick, Chicago	16	0
Manning, Peyton, Indianapolis	16	16
Manusky, Greg, Kansas City	16	0
Mare, Olindo, Miami	16	0
Marino, Dan, Miami	11	11
Marion, Brock, Miami	16	16
Marshall, Whit, Atlanta	15	0
Martin, Cecil, Philadelphia	12	5
Martin, Curtis, N.Y. Jets	16	16
Martin, Emanuel, Buffalo	7	0
Martin, Steve, Philadelphia	16	15
Martin, Tony, Miami	16	13
Martin, Wayne, New Orleans	16	16
Marts, Lonnie, Jacksonville	16	16
Maryland, Russell, Oakland	16	16
Maslowski, Mike, Kansas City	15	0
Mason, Derrick, Tennessee	13	0
Mason, Eddie, Washington	14	0
Mathews, Jason, Tennessee	5	0
Mathis, Kevin, Dallas	8	4
Mathis, Terance, Atlanta	16	16
Matthews, Bruce, Tennessee	16	16
Matthews, Shane, Chicago	8	7
Maumau, Viliami, Carolina	1	0
Mawae, Kevin, N.Y. Jets	16	16
May, Deems, Seattle	15	0
Mayberry, Jermane, Philadelphia	13	5
Mayberry, Tony, Tampa Bay	16	16
Mayes, Alonzo, Chicago	16	9
Mayes, Derrick, Seattle	16	15
Maynard, Brad, N.Y. Giants	16	0
Mays, Kivuusama, Min.-G.B.	14	0
McAfee, Fred, Tampa Bay	1	0
McAlister, Chris, Baltimore	16	12
McBride, Tod, Green Bay	15	0
McBurrows, Gerald, Atlanta	16	4
McCaffrey, Ed, Denver	15	15
McCardell, Keenan, Jacksonville	16	15
McCleon, Dexter, St. Louis	15	15
McCleskey, J.J., Arizona	16	1
McCollum, Andy, St. Louis	16	2
McCormack, Hurvin, Cleveland	13	4
McCoy, Tony, Indianapolis	10	0
McCrary, Fred, San Diego	16	14
McCrary, Michael, Baltimore	16	16
McCullough, Andy, Arizona	2	0
McCullough, George, Tennessee	5	0
McCutcheon, Daylon, Cleveland	16	15
McDaniel, Ed, Minnesota	16	16
McDaniel, Emmanuel, NYG	7	2
McDaniel, Jeremy, Buffalo	1	0
McDaniel, Randall, Minnesota	16	16
McDaniels, Pellom, Atlanta	16	0
McDonald, Darnell, Tampa Bay	8	0
McDonald, Ramos, Min.-S.F.	14	12
McDonald, Ricardo, Chicago	16	16
McDonald, Tim, San Francisco	16	16
McDuffie, O.J., Miami	12	10
McElmurry, Blaine, Jacksonville	16	0
McFarland, Anthony, Tampa Bay	14	0
McGarity, Wane, Dallas	5	1
McGarrahan, Scott, Green Bay	13	0
McGee, Tony, Cincinnati	16	16
McGinest, Willie, New England	16	16
McGlockton, Chester, K.C.	16	16
McGriff, Travis, Denver	14	0
McIver, Everett, Dallas	14	14
McKenzie, Keith, Green Bay	16	2
McKenzie, Kevin, Miami	1	0
McKenzie, Mike, Green Bay	16	16
McKenzie, Raleigh, Green Bay	16	7
McKinley, Dennis, Arizona	16	0
McKinney, Steve, Indianapolis	14	14
McKinnon, Ronald, Arizona	16	16
McLaughlin, John, Tampa Bay	12	0
McLeod, Kevin, Tampa Bay	7	0
McManus, Tom, Jacksonville	2	2
McMillian, Mark, S.F.-Was.	15	0
McNabb, Donovan, Philadelphia	12	6
McNair, Steve, Tennessee	11	11
McNeil, Ryan, Cleveland	16	14
McNown, Cade, Chicago	15	6
McQuarters, R.W., S.F.	11	4
McTyer, Tim, Cleveland	2	2
McWilliams, Johnny, Arizona	15	4
Meadows, Adam, Indianapolis	16	16
Means, Natrone, San Diego	7	5
Metcalf, Eric, Carolina	16	1
Mickell, Darren, New Orleans	1	0
Mickens, Ray, N.Y. Jets	15	5
Mickens, Terry, Oakland	16	3
Middleton, Frank, Tampa Bay	16	16
Milburn, Glyn, Chicago	16	1
Mili, Itula, Seattle	16	1
Miller, Arnold, Cleveland	9	0
Miller, Billy, Denver	10	0
Miller, Bubba, Philadelphia	14	0
Miller, Chris, Denver	3	3
Miller, Corey, Minnesota	5	2
Miller, Fred, St. Louis	16	16
Miller, Jamir, Cleveland	15	15
Miller, Jim, Chicago	5	3
Miller, Josh, Pittsburgh	16	0
Milloy, Lawyer, New England	16	16

Player, Team	GP	GS
Mills, Ernie, Dallas	11	7
Mills, John Henry, Minnesota	15	0
Milne, Brian, Cin.-Sea.	11	1
Milstead, Rod, Washington	6	0
Mims, Chris, San Diego	9	0
Mincy, Charles, Oakland	16	6
Minter, Barry, Chicago	16	16
Minter, Mike, Carolina	16	16
Miranda, Paul, Indianapolis	5	0
Mirer, Rick, N.Y. Jets	8	6
Mitchell, Basil, Green Bay	16	2
Mitchell, Brandon, New England	16	16
Mitchell, Brian, Washington	16	0
Mitchell, Donald, Tennessee	16	0
Mitchell, Jeff, Baltimore	16	16
Mitchell, Keith, New Orleans	16	16
Mitchell, Kevin, New Orleans	16	1
Mitchell, Pete, N.Y. Giants	15	6
Mitchell, Scott, Baltimore	2	2
Mixon, Kenny, Miami	11	2
Mobley, John, Denver	2	2
Mobley, Singor, Dallas	16	0
Mohr, Chris, Buffalo	16	0
Mohring, Mike, San Diego	16	1
Molden, Alex, New Orleans	13	0
Monroe, Rodrick, Atlanta	2	0
Montgomery, Joe, N.Y. Giants	7	5
Montgomery, Monty, Ind.-S.F.	7	2
Monty, Pete, N.Y. Giants	16	3
Moon, Warren, Kansas City	1	0
Moore, Damon, Philadelphia	16	1
Moore, Dave, Tampa Bay	16	16
Moore, Herman, Detroit	8	4
Moore, Jason, Denver	6	0
Moore, Larry, Indianapolis	16	16
Moore, Marty, New England	15	2
Moore, Rob, Arizona	14	14
Moore, Stevon, Baltimore	8	0
Morabito, Tim, Carolina	16	16
Moran, Sean, Buffalo	16	0
Moreno, Moses, San Diego	1	0
Morey, Sean, New England	2	0
Morgan, Don, Minnesota	2	0
Morris, Bam, Kansas City	12	8
Morris, Mike, Minnesota	16	0
Morrow, Harold, Minnesota	16	0
Morton, Johnnie, Detroit	16	12
Morton, Mike, St. Louis	16	0
Moss, Randy, Minnesota	16	16
Moss, Zefross, New England	13	13
Moulds, Eric, Buffalo	14	14
Muhammad, Muhsin, Carolina	15	15
Muhammad, Steve, Indianapolis	11	1
Mulitalo, Edwin, Baltimore	10	8
Mullen, Roderick, Carolina	15	0
Murphy, Yo, T.B.-Min.	8	0
Murray, Eddie, Dallas	4	0
Murrell, Adrian, Arizona	16	12
Myers, Greg, Cincinnati	12	4
Myers, Michael, Dallas	6	0
Myles, DeShone, Seattle	5	0
Myles, Toby, N.Y. Giants	8	0
Myslinski, Tom, Dallas	10	2
Naeole, Chris, New Orleans	15	15
Nails, Jamie, Buffalo	16	3
Nalen, Tom, Denver	16	16
Nash, Marcus, Den.-Bal.	3	1
Navies, Hannibal, Carolina	9	0
Neal, Lorenzo, Tennessee	16	14
Nedney, Joe, Ari.-Oak.	4	0
Neil, Dan, Denver	15	15
Nelson, Jim, Green Bay	16	0

Player, Team	GP	GS
Nelson, Reggie, San Diego	2	0
Nesbit, Jamar, Carolina	7	0
Neufeld, Ryan, Dallas	6	0
Neujahr, Quentin, Jacksonville	16	0
Newberry, Jeremy, S.F.	16	16
Newkirk, Robert, New Orleans	5	0
Newman, Anthony, Oakland	16	13
Newman, Keith, Buffalo	3	0
Newsome, Craig, San Francisco	7	2
Newton, Nate, Carolina	7	0
Nguyen, Dat, Dallas	16	0
Nickerson, Hardy, Tampa Bay	16	16
Noble, Brandon, Dallas	16	0
Northern, Gabe, Buffalo	16	0
Norton, Ken, San Francisco	16	16
Nutten, Tom, St. Louis	14	14
Nwokorie, Chuckie, Indianapolis	1	0
Oben, Roman, N.Y. Giants	16	16
Odom, Jason, Tampa Bay	3	3
O'Donnell, Neil, Tennessee	8	5
O'Dwyer, Matt, Cincinnati	16	16
Ofodile, A.J., Baltimore	7	3
Ogbogu, Eric, N.Y. Jets	14	0
Ogden, Jeff, Dallas	16	0
Ogden, Jonathan, Baltimore	16	16
Ogle, Kendall, Cleveland	2	0
Okeafor, Chike, San Francisco	12	0
Oldham, Chris, Pittsburgh	15	0
Oliver, Winslow, Atlanta	14	0
Olivo, Brock, Detroit	14	0
Olson, Benji, Tennessee	16	16
O'Neal, Leslie, Kansas City	16	10
O'Neill, Kevin, Detroit	4	0
Osborne, Chuck, Oakland	16	0
Ostroski, Jerry, Buffalo	15	15
Ostrowski, Phil, San Francisco	15	0
Ottis, Brad, Arizona	14	7
Owens, Dan, Detroit	8	0
Owens, Rich, Miami	16	14
Owens, Terrell, San Francisco	14	14
Oxendine, Ken, Atlanta	12	9
Pace, Orlando, St. Louis	16	16
Page, Solomon, Dallas	14	6
Palelei, Lonnie, Philadelphia	16	12
Palmer, David, Minnesota	8	2
Palmer, Mitch, Tampa Bay	4	0
Palmer, Randy, Cleveland	3	0
Parker, De'Mond, Green Bay	11	0
Parker, Glenn, Kansas City	12	11
Parker, Larry, Kansas City	10	0
Parker, Riddick, Seattle	16	3
Parker, Vaughn, San Diego	15	15
Parks, Nathan, Oakland	2	0
Parmalee, Bernie, N.Y. Jets	16	0
Parrella, John, San Diego	16	16
Parrish, Tony, Chicago	16	16
Parten, Ty, Kansas City	16	0
Pathon, Jerome, Indianapolis	10	2
Patten, David, N.Y. Giants	16	0
Patton, Marvcus, Kansas City	16	16
Paul, Tito, Washington	6	0
Paulk, Jeff, Atlanta	1	0
Paup, Bryce, Jacksonville	15	14
Payne, Seth, Jacksonville	16	16
Pederson, Doug, Philadelphia	16	9
Peete, Rodney, Washington	3	0
Pelfrey, Doug, Cincinnati	16	0
Pelshak, Troy, St. Louis	9	0
Penn, Chris, San Diego	16	3
Perry, Ed, Miami	16	1
Perry, Jason, San Diego	16	5
Perry, Marlo, Buffalo	16	0

Player, Team	GP	GS
Perry, Todd, Chicago	16	16
Perry, Wilmont, New Orleans	7	3
Peter, Christian, N.Y. Giants	16	10
Peter, Jason, Carolina	9	9
Peters, Tyrell, Baltimore	13	0
Peterson, Ben, Cincinnati	3	0
Peterson, Mike, Indianapolis	16	13
Peterson, Todd, Seattle	16	0
Peterson, Tony, San Francisco	12	0
Petitgout, Luke, N.Y. Giants	15	8
Phenix, Perry, Tennessee	16	1
Phifer, Roman, N.Y. Jets	16	12
Phillips, Joe, Minnesota	16	2
Phillips, Lawrence, S.F.	8	0
Phillips, Ryan, N.Y. Giants	16	16
Philyaw, Dino, New Orleans	13	0
Pickens, Carl, Cincinnati	16	14
Pierce, Aaron, Baltimore	10	8
Pierson, Pete, Tampa Bay	15	0
Pilgrim, Evan, Atlanta	3	1
Piller, Zach, Tennessee	8	0
Pittman, Kavika, Dallas	16	16
Pittman, Michael, Arizona	10	2
Player, Scott, Arizona	16	0
Pleasant, Anthony, N.Y. Jets	16	16
Plummer, Chad, Indianapolis	1	0
Plummer, Jake, Arizona	12	11
Pollard, Marcus, Indianapolis	16	12
Poole, Keith, New Orleans	15	15
Poole, Tyrone, Indianapolis	15	14
Pope, Daniel, Kansas City	16	0
Pope, Marquez, Cleveland	16	15
Porcher, Robert, Detroit	15	14
Porter, Daryl, Buffalo	16	0
Porter, Joey, Pittsburgh	16	0
Portilla, Jose, Atlanta	4	0
Posey, Jeff, San Francisco	16	6
Pounds, Darryl, Washington	16	0
Pourdanesh, Shar, Pittsburgh	4	2
Powell, Marvin, New Orleans	9	0
Powell, Ronnie, Cleveland	14	0
Preston, Roell, Ten.-Mia.-S.F.	7	0
Price, Peerless, Buffalo	16	4
Price, Shawn, Buffalo	15	1
Pringley, Mike, Detroit	9	0
Prioleau, Pierson, S.F.	14	5
Pritchard, Mike, Seattle	14	5
Pritchett, Kelvin, Detroit	16	2
Pritchett, Stanley, Miami	14	7
Proehl, Ricky, St. Louis	15	2
Pryce, Trevor, Denver	15	15
Pupunu, Alfred, San Diego	8	0
Purnell, Lovett, Baltimore	2	0
Purvis, Andre, Cincinnati	5	0
Pyne, Jim, Cleveland	16	16
Quarles, Shelton, Tampa Bay	16	14
Rafferty, Ian, N.Y. Jets	5	0
Rainer, Wali, Cleveland	16	15
Ramirez, Tony, Detroit	12	3
Randle, John, Minnesota	16	16
Randolph, Thomas, Ind.	15	0
Ransom, Derrick, Kansas City	10	0
Rasby, Walter, Detroit	16	6
Ray, Marcus, Oakland	8	0
Raymer, Cory, Washington	16	16
Reagor, Montae, Denver	9	0
Redmon, Anthony, Carolina	15	15
Reece, Travis, Detroit	4	0
Reed, Andre, Buffalo	16	16
Reed, Jake, Minnesota	16	8
Reed, Robert, San Diego	3	0
Reese, Ike, Philadelphia	16	0

1999 REVIEW *Player participation*

– 237 –

Player, Team	GP	GS
Reese, Izell, Dallas	8	4
Reeves, John, San Diego	5	0
Rehberg, Scott, Cleveland	15	13
Reid, Spencer, Indianapolis	12	0
Rhett, Errict, Baltimore	16	10
Rhinehart, Coby, Arizona	16	0
Rice, Jerry, San Francisco	16	16
Rice, Ron, Detroit	16	16
Rice, Simeon, Arizona	16	16
Richardson, Damien, Carolina	15	0
Richardson, Kyle, Baltimore	16	0
Richardson, Tony, Kansas City	16	16
Richey, Wade, San Francisco	16	0
Richie, David, San Francisco	1	0
Ricks, Mikhael, San Diego	16	15
Riemersma, Jay, Buffalo	14	11
Riley, Victor, Kansas City	16	16
Rison, Andre, Kansas City	15	14
Ritchie, Jon, Oakland	16	14
Rivera, Marco, Green Bay	16	16
Rivers, Ron, Detroit	7	6
Roaf, Willie, New Orleans	16	16
Roan, Michael, Tennessee	11	1
Robbins, Austin, New Orleans	14	3
Robbins, Barret, Oakland	16	16
Roberson, James, Jacksonville	2	0
Roberts, Ray, Detroit	14	14
Robertson, Marcus, Tennessee	15	15
Robinson, Bryan, Chicago	16	16
Robinson, Damien, Tampa Bay	16	16
Robinson, Eddie, Tennessee	16	16
Robinson, Eugene, Atlanta	16	16
Robinson, Jeff, St. Louis	16	9
Robinson, Marcus, Chicago	16	11
Rodenhauser, Mark, Seattle	8	0
Rodgers, Derrick, Miami	16	15
Rogers, Charlie, Seattle	12	0
Rogers, Chris, Minnesota	10	4
Rogers, Sam, Buffalo	16	16
Rogers, Tyrone, Cleveland	3	0
Rolle, Samari, Tennessee	16	0
Romanowski, Bill, Denver	16	16
Roque, Juan, Detroit	4	2
Rosenthal, Mike, N.Y. Giants	9	7
Ross, Adrian, Cincinnati	16	10
Rossum, Allen, Philadelphia	16	0
Rouen, Tom, Denver	16	0
Roundtree, Raleigh, San Diego	15	5
Royal, Andre, Indianapolis	3	3
Royals, Mark, Tampa Bay	16	0
Roye, Orpheus, Pittsburgh	16	16
Rubio, Angel, Arizona	2	0
Rucci, Todd, New England	16	15
Rucker, Mike, Carolina	16	0
Rudd, Dwayne, Minnesota	16	16
Ruddy, Tim, Miami	16	16
Ruff, Orlando, San Diego	14	0
Ruhman, Chris, Cleveland	5	2
Runyan, Jon, Tennessee	16	16
Rusk, Reggie, San Diego	9	0
Russ, Bernard, New England	6	0
Russ, Steve, Denver	8	0
Russell, Darrell, Oakland	16	16
Russell, Twan, Washington	9	0
Rutledge, Johnny, Arizona	6	0
Rutledge, Rod, New England	16	2
Salaam, Ephraim, Atlanta	16	16
Salaam, Rashaan, Cleveland	2	0
Salave'a, Joe, Tennessee	10	0
Saleh, Tarek, Cleveland	16	0
Samuel, Khari, Chicago	13	1
Sanders, Brandon, N.Y. Giants	9	2

Player, Team	GP	GS
Sanders, Chris, Tennessee	16	0
Sanders, Deion, Dallas	14	14
Sanders, Frank, Arizona	16	16
Sanderson, Scott, Tennessee	3	3
Santiago, O.J., Atlanta	14	14
Sapp, Patrick, Arizona	15	5
Sapp, Warren, Tampa Bay	15	15
Saturday, Jeff, Indianapolis	11	2
Sauer, Craig, Atlanta	16	3
Sauerbrun, Todd, Chicago	16	0
Sawyer, Corey, N.Y. Jets	5	0
Sawyer, Talance, Minnesota	2	0
Schau, Ryan, Philadelphia	1	0
Schlereth, Mark, Denver	16	16
Schlesinger, Cory, Detroit	16	11
Schneck, Mike, Pittsburgh	16	0
Schreiber, Adam, Atlanta	3	0
Schroeder, Bill, Green Bay	16	16
Schulters, Lance, San Francisco	13	13
Schulz, Kurt, Buffalo	16	16
Schwartz, Bryan, Jacksonville	8	0
Scioli, Brad, Indianapolis	10	0
Scott, Chad, Pittsburgh	13	12
Scott, Darnay, Cincinnati	16	16
Scott, Yusuf, Arizona	10	0
Scroggins, Tracy, Detroit	14	11
Scurlock, Mike, Carolina	16	0
Searcy, Leon, Jacksonville	16	16
Sears, Corey, Arizona	9	1
Seau, Junior, San Diego	14	14
Sehorn, Jason, N.Y. Giants	10	10
Sellers, Mike, Washington	16	2
Semple, Tony, Detroit	12	12
Serwanga, Kato, New England	16	3
Serwanga, Wasswa, S.F.	9	0
Shade, Sam, Washington	16	16
Shannon, Larry, Miami	2	0
Sharpe, Shannon, Denver	5	5
Sharper, Darren, Green Bay	16	16
Sharper, Jamie, Baltimore	16	16
Shaw, Bobby, Pittsburgh	15	1
Shaw, Harold, New England	8	0
Shaw, Sedrick, Cle.-Cin.	4	0
Shaw, Terrance, San Diego	8	8
Shedd, Kenny, Oakland	12	0
Shehee, Rashaan, Kansas City	9	5
Sheldon, Mike, Miami	9	0
Shelton, Daimon, Jacksonville	16	9
Shelton, L.J., Arizona	9	7
Shepherd, Leslie, Cleveland	9	5
Shields, Paul, Indianapolis	13	3
Shields, Scott, Pittsburgh	16	1
Shields, Will, Kansas City	16	16
Sidney, Dainon, Tennessee	16	2
Simien, Tracy, San Diego	8	4
Simmons, Anthony, Seattle	16	16
Simmons, Brian, Cincinnati	16	16
Simmons, Clyde, Chicago	16	0
Simmons, Jason, Pittsburgh	16	0
Simmons, Tony, New England	15	1
Simpson, Antoine, Miami	4	0
Sims, Barry, Oakland	16	10
Sims, Keith, Washington	12	12
Sinclair, Michael, Seattle	15	15
Singleton, Alshermond, T.B.	15	0
Siragusa, Tony, Baltimore	14	14
Slade, Chris, New England	16	16
Sloan, David, Detroit	16	15
Slutzker, Scott, New Orleans	11	2
Small, Torrance, Philadelphia	15	15
Smedley, Eric, Indianapolis	7	0
Smeenge, Joel, Jacksonville	15	7

Player, Team	GP	GS
Smith, Aaron, Pittsburgh	6	0
Smith, Akili, Cincinnati	7	4
Smith, Antowain, Buffalo	14	11
Smith, Brady, New Orleans	16	16
Smith, Brent, Miami	13	4
Smith, Bruce, Buffalo	16	16
Smith, Chuck, Atlanta	16	16
Smith, Darrin, Seattle	15	15
Smith, Derek M., Washington	16	16
Smith, Detron, Denver	16	0
Smith, Ed, Phi.-Det.	10	1
Smith, Emmitt, Dallas	15	15
Smith, Fernando, Baltimore	15	0
Smith, Frankie, Chicago	15	0
Smith, Hunter, Indianapolis	16	0
Smith, Irv, Cleveland	13	13
Smith, Jeff, Kansas City	15	2
Smith, Jermaine, Green Bay	10	0
Smith, Jimmy, Jacksonville	16	16
Smith, Kevin, Dallas	8	8
Smith, Lamar, New Orleans	13	2
Smith, Larry, Jacksonville	15	0
Smith, Mark, Arizona	2	0
Smith, Marquis, Cleveland	16	2
Smith, Neil, Denver	15	8
Smith, Otis, N.Y. Jets	1	1
Smith, Robert, Minnesota	13	12
Smith, Rod, Denver	15	15
Smith, Shevin, Tampa Bay	16	0
Smith, Thomas, Buffalo	16	16
Smith, Travian, Oakland	16	1
Smith, Troy, Philadelphia	1	0
Smith, Vinson, New Orleans	12	0
Snider, Matt, Green Bay	8	0
Sowell, Jerald, N.Y. Jets	16	0
Sparks, Phillippi, N.Y. Giants	11	11
Spears, Marcus, Kansas City	10	2
Spellman, Alonzo, Dallas	16	16
Spence, Blake, N.Y. Jets	10	0
Spencer, Jimmy, San Diego	14	7
Spicer, Paul, Detroit	2	0
Spikes, Cameron, St. Louis	5	0
Spikes, Takeo, Cincinnati	16	16
Spires, Greg, New England	11	0
Spriggs, Marcus, Cleveland	10	0
Spriggs, T. Marcus, Buffalo	11	2
Springs, Shawn, Seattle	16	16
Sprotte, Jimmy, Cincinnati	4	0
Staat, Jeremy, Pittsburgh	16	2
Stablein, Brian, Detroit	16	2
Stai, Brenden, Pittsburgh	16	16
Staley, Duce, Philadelphia	16	16
Stanley, Chad, San Francisco	16	0
Starks, Duane, Baltimore	16	5
Steed, Joel, Pittsburgh	14	14
Steele, Glen, Cincinnati	16	1
Stenstrom, Steve, S.F.	6	3
Stephens, Jamain, Cincinnati	7	2
Stephens, Reggie, N.Y. Giants	1	0
Stephens, Tremayne, San Diego	11	2
Stepnoski, Mark, Dallas	15	15
Steussie, Todd, Minnesota	16	16
Stevens, Matt, Washington	15	1
Stewart, James, Jacksonville	14	7
Stewart, Kordell, Pittsburgh	16	12
Stewart, Rayna, Jacksonville	14	0
Stewart, Ryan, Detroit	2	0
Still, Bryan, S.D.-Atl.	7	1
Stills, Gary, Kansas City	2	0
Stokes, J.J., San Francisco	16	4
Stokley, Brandon, Baltimore	2	0
Stoltenberg, Bryan, Carolina	16	7

– 238 –

Player, Team	GP	GS
Stone, Dwight, N.Y. Jets	16	0
Stone, Ron, N.Y. Giants	16	16
Storz, Erik, Jacksonville	7	0
Stoutmire, Omar, N.Y. Jets	12	5
Stover, Matt, Baltimore	16	0
Stoyanovich, Pete, Kansas City	16	0
Strahan, Michael, N.Y. Giants	16	16
Streets, Tai, San Francisco	2	0
Strickland, Fred, Washington	5	0
Stringer, Korey, Minnesota	16	16
Strong, Mack, Seattle	14	1
Stryzinski, Dan, Atlanta	16	0
Stubblefield, Dana, Washington	16	16
Styles, Lorenzo, St. Louis	16	0
Sullivan, Chris, New England	16	0
Supernaw, Kywin, Detroit	2	0
Surtain, Patrick, Miami	16	6
Suttle, Jason, Denver	5	0
Swann, Eric, Arizona	9	0
Swayda, Shawn, Atlanta	4	0
Swayne, Harry, Baltimore	6	6
Sweeney, Jim, Pittsburgh	6	0
Swift, Justin, Philadelphia	1	0
Swift, Michael, Carolina	15	0
Swinger, Rashod, Arizona	15	14
Sword, Sam, Oakland	10	5
Syvrud, J.J., N.Y. Jets	1	0
Szott, David, Kansas City	14	14
Tait, John, Kansas City	12	3
Talton, Tyree, Detroit	12	0
Tamm, Ralph, Kansas City	16	0
Tanuvasa, Maa, Denver	16	16
Tate, Robert, Minnesota	16	1
Taylor, Aaron, San Diego	14	14
Taylor, Bobby, Philadelphia	15	14
Taylor, Cordell, Seattle	2	0
Taylor, Fred, Jacksonville	10	9
Taylor, Jason, Miami	15	15
Teague, George, Dallas	14	14
Teague, Trey, Denver	16	4
Terrell, Daryl, New Orleans	12	1
Terry, Chris, Carolina	16	16
Terry, Corey, Jacksonville	8	0
Terry, Rick, Carolina	8	0
Testaverde, Vinny, N.Y. Jets	1	1
Thibodeaux, Keith, Atl.-Min.	11	0
Thierry, John, Cleveland	16	10
Thigpen, Yancey, Tennessee	10	10
Thomas, Chris, Was.-St.L.	8	0
Thomas, Dave, Jacksonville	15	0
Thomas, Derrick, Kansas City	16	16
Thomas, Fred, Seattle	1	0
Thomas, Henry, New England	16	16
Thomas, Hollis, Philadelphia	16	16
Thomas, Mark, Indianapolis	15	2
Thomas, Mark D., N.Y. Giants	2	0
Thomas, Orlando, Minnesota	13	12
Thomas, Randy, N.Y. Jets	16	16
Thomas, Ratcliff, Indianapolis	16	0
Thomas, Robert, Dallas	16	7
Thomas, Rodney, Tennessee	16	0
Thomas, Thurman, Buffalo	5	3
Thomas, Tra, Philadelphia	16	15
Thomas, Tre, N.Y. Giants	2	0
Thomas, William, Philadelphia	14	13
Thomas, Zach, Miami	16	16
Thomason, Jeff, Green Bay	14	2
Thompson, Bennie, Baltimore	16	0
Thompson, Derrius, Was.	1	0
Thompson, Mike, Cleveland	10	0
Thornton, John, Tennessee	16	3

Player, Team	GP	GS
Thrash, James, Washington	16	0
Tillman, Pat, Arizona	16	1
Timmerman, Adam, St. Louis	16	16
Tobeck, Robbie, Atlanta	15	15
Tolliver, Billy Joe, New Orleans	10	7
Tomczak, Mike, Pittsburgh	16	5
Tomich, Jared, New Orleans	8	6
Tongue, Reggie, Kansas City	16	16
Toomer, Amani, N.Y. Giants	16	16
Tovar, Steve, Carolina	16	6
Townsend, Deshea, Pittsburgh	16	4
Trapp, James, Baltimore	16	0
Traylor, Keith, Denver	15	15
Treu, Adam, Oakland	16	0
Trotter, Jeremiah, Philadelphia	16	16
Tuaolo, Esera, Carolina	12	0
Tubbs, Winfred, San Francisco	16	15
Tucker, Jason, Dallas	15	4
Tucker, Rex, Chicago	2	1
Tucker, Ryan, St. Louis	16	0
Tuggle, Jessie, Atlanta	14	14
Tuinei, Van, Chicago	16	8
Tuman, Jerame, Pittsburgh	7	0
Tupa, Tom, N.Y. Jets	16	0
Turk, Dan, Washington	16	0
Turk, Matt, Washington	14	0
Turley, Kyle, New Orleans	16	16
Turner, Eric, Oakland	10	10
Turner, Kevin, Philadelphia	8	7
Turner, Scott, San Diego	15	0
Tuten, Melvin, Denver	2	0
Tuten, Rick, St. Louis	8	0
Tylski, Rich, Jacksonville	10	8
Ulmer, Artie, Denver	7	0
Unutoa, Morris, Tampa Bay	12	0
Upshaw, Regan, T.B.-Jac.	7	0
Uwaezuoke, Iheanyi, Detroit	10	0
Van Dyke, Alex, Philadelphia	2	0
Van Pelt, Alex, Buffalo	1	0
Vance, Eric, Tampa Bay	6	0
Vanderjagt, Mike, Indianapolis	16	0
Vanover, Tamarick, Kansas City	14	0
Vardell, Tommy, San Francisco	6	4
Verba, Ross, Green Bay	11	10
Vickers, Kipp, Washington	11	0
Villarrial, Chris, Chicago	15	15
Vinatieri, Adam, New England	16	0
Vincent, Troy, Philadelphia	14	14
Vinson, Fred, Green Bay	16	1
Vinson, Tony, Baltimore	3	0
von Oelhoffen, Kimo, Cincinnati	16	5
Vrabel, Mike, Pittsburgh	10	0
Waddy, Jude, Green Bay	14	8
Wade, John, Jacksonville	16	16
Wadsworth, Andre, Arizona	11	7
Wahle, Mike, Green Bay	16	13
Wainright, Frank, Baltimore	16	0
Walker, Bracey, Kansas City	16	1
Walker, Brian, Seattle	5	0
Walker, Darnell, San Francisco	15	8
Walker, Denard, Tennessee	15	14
Walker, Derrick, Oakland	11	3
Walker, Gary, Jacksonville	16	16
Walker, Marquis, Oakland	16	0
Walls, Wesley, Carolina	16	16
Walsh, Chris, Minnesota	16	1
Walsh, Steve, Indianapolis	16	0
Walter, Ken, Carolina	16	0
Walz, Zack, Arizona	9	9
Ward, Dedric, N.Y. Jets	16	10
Ward, Hines, Pittsburgh	16	14

Player, Team	GP	GS
Warfield, Eric, Kansas City	16	1
Warner, Kurt, St. Louis	16	16
Warren, Chris, Dallas	16	1
Warren, Lamont, New England	16	2
Washington, Dewayne, Pit.	16	16
Washington, Keith, Baltimore	16	0
Washington, Marvin, S.F.	5	5
Washington, Ted, Buffalo	16	16
Washington, Todd, Tampa Bay	6	0
Watson, Chris, Denver	14	1
Watson, Edwin, Philadelphia	6	0
Watson, Justin, St. Louis	8	0
Watters, Ricky, Seattle	16	16
Way, Charles, N.Y. Giants	11	8
Wayne, Nate, Denver	15	0
Weary, Fred, New Orleans	16	11
Weathers, Andre, N.Y. Giants	9	0
Weaver, Jed, Philadelphia	16	10
Webb, Richmond, Miami	15	14
Webster, Larry, Baltimore	16	16
Weiner, Todd, Seattle	11	1
Welbourn, John, Philadelphia	1	1
Weldon, Casey, Washington	2	0
Wells, Dean, Carolina	16	10
Wells, Mike, Chicago	16	16
Wesley, Joe, San Francisco	8	0
West, Lyle, N.Y. Giants	6	0
Westbrook, Bryant, Detroit	10	8
Westbrook, Michael, Was.	16	16
Wetnight, Ryan, Chicago	16	4
Wheatley, Tyrone, Oakland	16	9
Wheaton, Kenny, Dallas	5	0
Wheeler, Mark, Philadelphia	13	0
Whigham, Larry, New England	16	0
White, Steve, Tampa Bay	13	13
Whitehead, Willie, New Orleans	16	3
Whitfield, Bob, Atlanta	16	16
Whiting, Brandon, Philadelphia	13	2
Whitted, Alvis, Jacksonville	14	1
Whittington, Bernard, Ind.	15	15
Whittle, Jason, N.Y. Giants	16	1
Widmer, Corey, N.Y. Giants	15	13
Wiegert, Zach, Jacksonville	16	12
Wiegmann, Casey, Chicago	16	0
Wilcox, Josh, New Orleans	8	4
Wiley, Chuck, Carolina	16	16
Wiley, Marcellus, Buffalo	16	1
Wilkins, Gabe, San Francisco	16	15
Wilkins, Jeff, St. Louis	16	0
Wilkins, Terrence, Indianapolis	16	11
Wilkinson, Dan, Washington	16	16
Williams, Aeneas, Arizona	16	16
Williams, Alfred, Denver	7	6
Williams, Ben, Philadelphia	3	0
Williams, Brian M., Green Bay	7	7
Williams, Brian S., N.Y. Giants	12	12
Williams, Charlie, Dallas	16	8
Williams, Dan, Kansas City	14	9
Williams, Darryl, Seattle	13	12
Williams, Elijah, Atlanta	15	2
Williams, Erik, Dallas	14	14
Williams, Gene, Atlanta	15	8
Williams, George, N.Y. Giants	16	0
Williams, Grant, Seattle	16	15
Williams, Jamal, San Diego	16	2
Williams, Jamel, Washington	3	0
Williams, James E., Cleveland	16	0
Williams, James O., Chicago	16	16
Williams, Jay, St. Louis	16	0
Williams, Jermaine, Oakland	15	0
Williams, K.D., Oakland	9	8

1999 REVIEW Player participation

– 239 –

Player, Team	GP	GS
Williams, Karl, Tampa Bay	13	4
Williams, Kevin L., N.Y. Jets	4	0
Williams, Kevin R., Buffalo	16	0
Williams, Moe, Minnesota	14	0
Williams, Nick, Cincinnati	11	0
Williams, Pat, Buffalo	16	0
Williams, Ricky, New Orleans	12	12
Williams, Robert, K.C.-Sea.	2	0
Williams, Rodney, Oakland	5	0
Williams, Roland, St. Louis	16	15
Williams, Sammy, Kansas City	1	0
Williams, Shaun, N.Y. Giants	11	0
Williams, Sherman, Dallas	1	0
Williams, Tony, Minnesota	16	12
Williams, Tyrone M., Phi.	4	0
Williams, U. Tyrone, Green Bay	16	16
Williams, Wally, New Orleans	6	6
Williams, Willie, Seattle	15	14
Willis, James, Seattle	16	0
Wilson, Al, Denver	16	12
Wilson, Jamie, Indianapolis	5	0
Wilson, Jerry, Miami	16	1
Wilson, Reinard, Cincinnati	15	0
Wilson, Robert, Seattle	2	0
Wilson, Troy, New Orleans	16	4
Wiltz, Jason, N.Y. Jets	12	1
Winfield, Antoine, Buffalo	16	2
Winters, Frank, Green Bay	16	16
Wisne, Jerry, Chicago	7	1
Wisniewski, Steve, Oakland	16	16
Wistrom, Grant, St. Louis	16	16
Witman, Jon, Pittsburgh	16	11
Wohlabaugh, Dave, Cleveland	15	15
Wong, Kailee, Minnesota	13	8
Woodall, Lee, San Francisco	16	16
Wooden, Shawn, Miami	15	6
Woods, Jerome, Kansas City	15	15
Woodson, Charles, Oakland	16	16
Woodson, Darren, Dallas	15	15
Woodson, Rod, Baltimore	16	16
Woody, Damien, New England	16	16
Wooten, Tito, Indianapolis	8	1
Word, Mark, Kansas City	5	0
Wortham, Barron, Tennessee	16	15
Wright, Kenny, Minnesota	16	12
Wright, Lawrence, Cincinnati	14	0
Wright, Toby, Washington	1	0
Wuerffel, Danny, New Orleans	4	0
Wunsch, Jerry, Tampa Bay	16	13
Wycheck, Frank, Tennessee	16	16
Wynn, Renaldo, Jacksonville	12	10
Yeast, Craig, Cincinnati	9	0
Young, Bryant, San Francisco	16	16
Young, Floyd, Tampa Bay	6	0
Young, Ryan, N.Y. Jets	15	7
Young, Steve, San Francisco	3	3
Zahursky, Steve, Cleveland	9	7
Zeier, Eric, Tampa Bay	2	1
Zeigler, Dusty, Buffalo	15	15
Zelenka, Joe, San Francisco	13	0
Zellner, Peppi, Dallas	13	0
Zereoue, Amos, Pittsburgh	8	0
Zgonina, Jeff, St. Louis	16	0
Zolak, Scott, Miami	1	0

PLAYERS WITH TWO OR MORE CLUBS

Player, Team	GP	GS
Abdul-Jabbar, Karim, Miami	3	3
Abdul-Jabbar, Karim, Cleveland	10	6
Avery, John, Miami	1	0
Avery, John, Denver	6	0
Ayanbedejo, Obafemi, Min.	2	0
Ayanbadejo, Obafemi, Baltimore	12	0
Ball, Jerry, Cleveland	3	3
Ball, Jerry, Minnesota	13	10
Barker, Roy, Cleveland	12	3
Barker, Roy, Green Bay	1	0
Bonham, Shane, San Francisco	3	0
Bonham, Shane, Indianapolis	3	0
Carter, Tom, Chicago	12	6
Carter, Tom, Cincinnati	2	2
Clark, Rico, Cincinnati	8	1
Clark, Rico, New England	1	0
Cline, Tony, San Francisco	8	0
Cline, Tony, Pittsburgh	2	0
Colinet, Stalin, Minnesota	3	1
Colinet, Stalin, Cleveland	11	9
Cunningham, Richie, Dallas	12	0
Cunningham, Richie, Carolina	3	0
Dingle, Antonio, Green Bay	6	0
Dingle, Antonio, Carolina	3	0
Howard, Desmond, Green Bay	8	0
Howard, Desmond, Detroit	5	0
Johnson, Olrick, N.Y. Jets	3	0
Johnson, Olrick, Minnesota	5	0
Jones, Jermaine, N.Y. Jets	1	0
Jones, Jermaine, Chicago	1	0
Jordan, Charles, Seattle	4	1
Jordan, Charles, Green Bay	4	0
Lewis, Chad, St. Louis	6	0
Lewis, Chad, Philadelphia	6	4
Little, Earl, New Orleans	1	0
Little, Earl, Cleveland	9	0
Mays, Kivuusama, Minnesota	11	0
Mays, Kivuusama, Green Bay	3	0
McDonald, Ramos, Minnesota	5	5
McDonald, Ramos, S.F.	2	0
McMillian, Mark, San Francisco	6	6
McMillian, Mark, Washington	9	0
Milne, Brian, Cincinnati	1	1
Milne, Brian, Seattle	10	0
Montgomery, Monty, Ind.	3	0
Montgomery, Monty, S.F.	4	2
Murphy, Yo, Tampa Bay	7	0
Murphy, Yo, Minnesota	1	0
Nash, Marcus, Denver	2	1
Nash, Marcus, Baltimore	1	0
Nedney, Joe, Arizona	1	0
Nedney, Joe, Oakland	3	0
Preston, Roell, Tennessee	2	0
Preston, Roell, Miami	1	0
Preston, Roell, San Francisco	4	0
Shaw, Sedrick, Cleveland	3	0
Shaw, Sedrick, Cincinnati	1	0
Smith, Ed, Philadelphia	7	1
Smith, Ed, Detroit	3	0
Still, Bryan, San Diego	4	0
Still, Bryan, Atlanta	3	1
Thibodeaux, Keith, Atlanta	8	0
Thibodeaux, Keith, Minnesota	3	0
Thomas, Chris, Washington	2	0
Thomas, Chris, St. Louis	6	0
Upshaw, Regan, Tampa Bay	1	0
Upshaw, Regan, Jacksonville	6	0
Williams, Robert, Kansas City	1	0
Williams, Robert, Seattle	1	0

ATTENDANCE

REGULAR SEASON

Team	Home Attendance	Average	NFL Rank	Road Attendance	Average	NFL Rank
Arizona	465,340	58,168	24	540,309	67,539	10
Atlanta	460,922	57,615	26	496,672	62,084	24
Baltimore	547,127	68,391	10	458,844	57,356	31
Buffalo	561,269	70,159	9	542,642	67,830	7
Carolina	489,515	61,189	21	493,822	61,728	26
Chicago	526,989	65,874	15	517,237	64,655	18
Cincinnati	404,679	50,585	30	511,363	63,920	21
Cleveland	580,934	72,617	6	482,769	60,346	28
Dallas	513,295	64,162	19	523,375	65,422	15
Denver	577,309	72,164	8	531,728	66,466	13
Detroit	579,314	72,414	7	514,996	64,375	19
Green Bay	478,900	59,863	22	547,636	68,455	4
Indianapolis	453,270	56,659	27	546,969	68,371	6
Jacksonville	540,085	67,511	12	524,496	65,562	14
Kansas City	629,545	78,693	1	495,686	61,961	25
Miami	592,161	74,020	5	547,485	68,436	5
Minnesota	513,051	64,131	20	570,672	71,334	1
N.Y. Giants	614,815	76,852	4	520,691	65,086	17
N.Y. Jets	626,258	78,282	2	522,813	65,352	16
New England	461,624	57,703	25	553,917	69,240	3
New Orleans	410,147	51,268	29	535,341	66,918	11
Oakland	398,146	49,768	31	540,706	67,588	9
Philadelphia	519,835	64,979	18	533,011	66,626	12
Pittsburgh	416,618	52,077	28	555,589	69,449	2
San Diego	477,567	59,696	23	504,560	63,070	22
San Francisco	544,231	68,029	11	496,773	62,097	23
Seattle	530,520	66,315	13	512,265	64,033	20
St. Louis	520,926	65,116	17	475,109	59,389	30
Tampa Bay	522,691	65,336	16	478,176	59,772	29
Tennessee	528,890	66,111	14	488,837	61,105	27
Washington	619,749	77,469	3	541,227	67,653	8
NFL total	16,105,716	64,942		16,105,716	64,942	

Note: Attendance figures are unofficial and are based on box scores of games.

HISTORICAL
TOP REGULAR-SEASON HOME CROWDS

Team	Attendance	Date	Site	Opponent
Arizona	73,400	October 30, 1994	Sun Devil Stadium	Pittsburgh
Atlanta	71,253	November 21, 1993	Georgia Dome	Dallas
Baltimore	69,074	December 13, 1998	Ravens Stadium	Minnesota
Buffalo	80,368	October 4, 1992	Rich Stadium	Miami
Carolina	76,136	December 10, 1995	Clemson Memorial Stadium	San Francisco
Chicago	66,944	Occurred seven times in 1999 season. Last time: January 2, 2000	Soldier Field	Tampa Bay
Cincinnati	60,284	October 17, 1971	Riverfront Stadium	Cleveland
Cleveland	85,703	September 21, 1970	Cleveland Stadium	N.Y. Jets
Dallas	80,259	November 24, 1966	Cotton Bowl	Cleveland
Denver	76,089	October 26,1986	Mile High Stadium	Seattle
Detroit	80,444	December 20, 1981	Pontiac Silverdome	Tampa Bay
Green Bay	60,766	September 1, 1997	Lambeau Field	Chicago
Indianapolis	61,282	December 14, 1997	RCA Dome	Miami
Jacksonville	74,143	December 28, 1998	ALLTEL Stadium	Pittsburgh
Kansas City	82,094	November 5, 1972	Arrowhead Stadium	Oakland
Miami	78,914	November 19, 1972	Orange Bowl	N.Y. Jets
Minnesota	64,471	November 22, 1998	Metrodome	Green Bay
New England	61,457	December 5, 1971	Schaefer Stadium*	Miami
New Orleans	83,437	November 12, 1967	Tulane Stadium	Dallas
		November 26, 1967	Tulane Stadium	Atlanta
New York Giants	78,204	October 18, 1998	Giants Stadium	Dallas
New York Jets	79,469	September 20, 1998	Giants Stadium	Indianapolis
Oakland	74,121	September 23, 1973	Memorial Stadium; Berkeley, Cal.	Miami

Team	Attendance	Date	Site	Opponent
Philadelphia	72,111	November 1, 1981	Veterans Stadium	Dallas
Pittsburgh	60,808	December 18, 1994	Three Rivers Stadium	Cleveland
St. Louis	66,065	December 19, 1999	Trans World Dome	N.Y. Giants
San Diego	68,274	October 24, 1999	Qualcomm Stadium	Green Bay
San Francisco	69,014	November 13, 1994	Candlestick Park	Dallas
Seattle	66,400	October 3, 1999	Kingdome	Oakland
Tampa Bay	73,523	December 12, 1997	Houlihan's Stadium	Green Bay
Tennessee	66,641	December 26, 1999	Adelphia Coliseum	Jacksonville
Washington	79,237	September 12, 1999	Jack Kent Cooke Stadium	Dallas

*Now known as Foxboro Stadium.

YEAR BY YEAR

NATIONAL FOOTBALL LEAGUE

Year	Regular season*	Average	Postseason†
1934	492,684 (60)	8,211	35,059 (1)
1935	638,178 (53)	12,041	15,000 (1)
1936	816,007 (54)	15,111	29,545 (1)
1937	963,039 (55)	17,510	15,878 (1)
1938	937,197 (55)	17,040	48,120 (1)
1939	1,071,200 (55)	19,476	32,279 (1)
1940	1,063,025 (55)	19,328	36,034 (1)
1941	1,108,615 (55)	20,157	55,870 (2)
1942	887,920 (55)	16,144	36,006 (1)
1943	969,128 (50)	19,383	71,315 (2)
1944	1,019,649 (50)	20,393	46,016 (1)
1945	1,270,401 (50)	25,408	32,178 (1)
1946	1,732,135 (55)	31,493	58,346 (1)
1947	1,837,437 (60)	30,624	66,268 (2)
1948	1,525,243 (60)	25,421	36,309 (1)
1949	1,391,735 (60)	23,196	27,980 (1)
1950	1,977,753 (78)	25,356	136,647 (3)
1951	1,913,019 (72)	26,570	57,522 (1)
1952	2,052,126 (72)	28,502	97,507 (2)
1953	2,164,585 (72)	30,064	54,577 (1)
1954	2,190,571 (72)	30,425	43,827 (1)
1955	2,521,836 (72)	35,026	85,693 (1)
1956	2,551,263 (72)	35,434	56,836 (1)
1957	2,836,318 (72)	39,393	119,579 (2)
1958	3,006,124 (72)	41,752	123,659 (2)
1959	3,140,000 (72)	43,617	57,545 (1)
1960	3,128,296 (78)	40,106	67,325 (1)
1961	3,986,159 (98)	40,675	39,029 (1)
1962	4,003,421 (98)	40,851	64,892 (1)
1963	4,163,643 (98)	42,486	45,801 (1)
1964	4,563,049 (98)	46,562	79,544 (1)
1965	4,634,021 (98)	47,296	100,304 (2)
1966	5,337,044 (105)	50,829	135,098 (2)
1967	5,938,924 (112)	53,026	241,754 (4)
1968	5,882,313 (112)	52,521	291,279 (4)
1969	6,096,127 (112)	54,430	242,841 (4)
1970	9,533,333 (182)	52,381	410,371 (7)
1971	10,076,035 (182)	55,363	430,244 (7)
1972	10,445,827 (182)	57,395	435,466 (7)
1973	10,730,933 (182)	58,961	458,515 (7)
1974	10,236,322 (182)	56,224	412,180 (7)
1975	10,213,193 (182)	56,116	443,811 (7)
1976	11,070,543 (196)	56,482	428,733 (7)
1977	11,018,632 (196)	56,218	483,588 (7)
1978	12,771,800 (224)	57,017	578,107 (9)
1979	13,182,039 (224)	58,848	582,266 (9)
1980	13,392,230 (224)	59,787	577,186 (9)
1981	13,606,990 (224)	60,745	587,361 (9)
1982§	7,367,438 (126)	58,472	985,952 (15)
1983	13,277,222 (224)	59,273	625,068 (9)
1984	13,398,112 (224)	59,813	614,809 (9)
1985	13,345,047 (224)	59,567	660,667 (9)
1986	13,588,551 (224)	60,663	683,901 (9)
1987‡	10,032,493 (168)	59,717	606,864 (9)
1988	13,539,848 (224)	60,446	608,204 (9)
1989	13,625,662 (224)	60,829	635,326 (9)
1990	14,266,240 (224)	63,689	797,198 (11)
1991	13,187,478 (224)	58,873	758,186 (11)
1992	13,159,387 (224)	58,747	756,005 (11)
1993	13,328,760 (224)	59,503	755,625 (11)
1994	13,479,680 (224)	60,177	719,143 (11)
1995	14,196,205 (240)	59,151	733,729 (11)
1996	13,695,748 (240)	57,066	711,601 (11)
1997	14,691,416 (240)	61,214	751,884 (11)
1998	14,977,358 (240)	62,406	776,225 (11)
1999	16,105,716 (248)	64,942	758,045 (11)

*Number of tickets sold, including no-shows; number of regular-season games in parentheses.

†Includes conference, league championship and Super Bowl games, but not Pro Bowl; number of postseason games in parentheses.

‡A 57-day players strike reduced 224-game schedule to 126 games.

§A 24-day players strike reduced 224-game schedule to 168 non-strike games.

AMERICAN FOOTBALL LEAGUE

Champ. Year	Regular season*	Average	AFL Game
1960	926,156 (56)	16,538	32,183
1961	1,002,657 (56)	17,904	29,556
1962	1,147,302 (56)	20,487	37,981
1963	1,241,741 (56)	22,174	30,127
1964	1,447,875 (56)	25,855	40,242
1965	1,782,384 (56)	31,828	30,361
1966	2,160,369 (63)	34,291	42,080
1967	2,295,697 (63)	36,439	53,330
1968	2,635,004 (70)	37,643	62,627
1969	2,843,373 (70)	40,620	53,564

*Number of regular-season games in parentheses.

TRADES

1999-2000 TRADES

(Covering June 1999 through May 2000)

JUNE 24
Seattle traded WR James McKnight to Dallas for a 2000 third-round draft choice. Seattle selected WR Darrell Jackson (Florida).

JULY 23
Green Bay traded LB Mike Morton to St. Louis for an undisclosed draft choice.

AUGUST 5
Carolina traded OL Jamie Wilson to Green Bay for an undisclosed draft choice.

AUGUST 9
San Diego traded TE John Burke to N.Y. Jets for a 2001 seventh-round draft choice.

AUGUST 13
Washington traded OT Shar Pourdanesh to Pittsburgh for a conditional 2000 draft choice.

AUGUST 20
Green Bay traded QB Rick Mirer to N.Y. Jets for an undisclosed draft choice.

AUGUST 24
Philadelphia traded QB Bobby Hoying to Oakland for a conditional 2000 sixth-round draft choice. Philadelphia selected DE John Frank (Utah).

Denver traded CB Tito Paul to Washington for an undisclosed draft choice.

AUGUST 29
Oakland traded QB Paul Justin to Rams for a 2000 seventh-round draft choice. Oakland later traded the seventh-round pick to Indianapolis.

AUGUST 30
St. Louis traded TE Mitch Jacoby to Kansas City for an undisclosed draft choice.

Green Bay traded WR Derrick Mayes to Seattle for an undisclosed draft choice.

AUGUST 31
St. Louis traded RB Greg Hill to Detroit for 2000 fifth- and seventh-round draft choices. St. Louis selected G Andrew Kline (San Diego State). St. Louis later traded the fifth-round pick to Chicago.

SEPTEMBER 1
Green Bay traded OT John Michels to Philadelphia for DE Jon Harris.

SEPTEMBER 5
Carolina traded TE Luther Broughton to Philadelphia for an undisclosed draft choice.

San Francisco traded QB Jim Druckenmiller to Miami for a conditional draft choice.

Miami traded DT Barron Tanner to Washington for a 2001 sixth-round draft choice.

Jacksonville traded CB Cordell Taylor to Seattle for a 2000 undisclosed draft choice.

SEPTEMBER 7
Green Bay traded CB Craig Newsome to San Francisco for an undisclosed draft choice.

SEPTEMBER 21
Kansas City traded CB Robert Williams to San Francisco for a 2000 conditional seventh-round choice.

Miami traded RB John Avery to Denver for WR Marcus Nash.

SEPTEMBER 28
Cleveland traded DT Jerry Ball to Minnesota for DT Stalin Colinet and a future draft choice.

OCTOBER 19
Miami traded RB Karim Abdul-Jabbar to Cleveland for a 2000 sixth-round draft choice and a 2001 conditional fifth-round choice. Miami selected DT Earnest Grant (Arkansas-Pine Bluff).

Tampa Bay traded DE Regan Upshaw to Jacksonville for an undisclosed draft choice.

JANUARY 26
Denver traded CB Tito Paul to Washington for a 2000 seventh-round draft choice and a 2001 seventh-round choice.

FEBRUARY 13
Seattle traded WR Joey Galloway to Dallas for a 2000 first-round draft choice and a 2001 first-round draft choice. Seattle selected RB Shaun Alexander (Alabama).

FEBRUARY 21
New Orleans traded WR Eddie Kennison to Chicago for a 2000 fifth-round draft choice. Chicago later traded the fifth-round pick to Indianapolis.

FEBRUARY 24
Denver traded DE David Bowens to Green Bay for an undisclosed draft choice.

MARCH 3
St. Louis traded S Billy Jenkins to Denver for a 2000 fifth-round draft choice and a 2001 conditional choice. St. Louis selected DL Brian Young (Texas-El Paso).

MARCH 9
Washington traded P Matt Turk to Miami for a 2001 conditional draft choice.

MARCH 16
Green Bay traded TE Jeff Thomason to Philadelphia for TE Kaseem Sinceno.

APRIL 4
Denver traded RB Derek Loville to St. Louis for an undisclosed draft choice.

APRIL 12
Baltimore traded 2000 first- and second-round draft choices to Denver for a 2000 first-round draft choice. Baltimore selected WR Travis Taylor (Florida). Denver selected DB Delta O' Neal (California) and S Kenoy Kennedy (Arkansas).

N.Y. Jets traded WR Keyshawn Johnson to Tampa Bay for two 2000 first-round draft choices. The Jets selected LB John

– 243 –

Abraham (South Carolina) and TE Anthony Becht (West Virginia).

APRIL 13

N.Y. Jets traded 2000 first- and second-round draft choices to San Francisco for a 2000 first-round draft choice. The Jets selected DE Shaun Ellis (Tennessee). San Francisco selected LB Julian Peterson (Michigan State) and DB Jason Webster (Texas A&M).

APRIL 14

Seattle traded RB Ahman Green and a 2000 fifth-round draft choice to Green Bay for CB Fred Vinson and a 2000 sixth-round draft choice. Seattle selected DT Tim Watson (Rowan College) and Green Bay selected KR Joey Jamison (Texas Southern).

APRIL 15-16

Carolina traded a 2000 second-round draft choice to Tampa Bay for 2000 second- and fourth-round draft choices. Tampa Bay selected Cosey Coleman G (Tennessee). Carolina selected S Deon Grant (Tennessee) and DT Alvin McKinley (Mississippi State).

Tennessee traded a 2000 second-round draft choice to Philadelphia for 2000 third- and fifth-round draft choices. Philadelphia selected G Bobby Williams (Arkansas). Tennessee selected TE Erron Kinney (Florida) and DB Aric Morris (Michigan State).

Seattle traded a 2000 third-round draft choice to San Francisco for 2000 fourth- and fifth-round draft choices. San Francisco selected LB Jeff Ulbrich (Hawaii). Seattle selected LB Isaiah Kacyvenski (Harvard). Seattle later traded the fifth-round pick to Denver.

San Francisco traded a 2000 fourth-round draft choice to Green Bay for 2000 fourth- and fifth-round draft choices. Green Bay selected LB Na'il Diggs (Ohio State). San Francisco selected S John Keith (Furman) and RB Paul Smith (Texas-El Paso).

Philadelphia traded a 2000 fourth-round draft choice to San Diego for a 2001 third-round draft choice. San Diego selected WR Trevor Gaylor (Miami of Ohio).

Chicago traded a 2000 fourth-round draft choice to St. Louis for 2000 fourth-, fifth- and seventh-round draft choices. St. Louis selected G Kaulana Noa (Hawaii). Chicago selected DB Reggie Austin (Wake Forest). Chicago later traded the fifth-round pick to San Francisco and the seventh-round pick to Cleveland.

New Orleans traded a 2000 fifth-round draft choice to Indianapolis for 2000 fifth- and sixth-round draft choices. Indianapolis selected C Matt Johnson (Brigham Young). New Orleans selected TE Austin Wheatley (Iowa) and DB Mike Hawthorne (Purdue).

Chicago traded a 2000 fifth-round draft choice to San Francisco for 2000 sixth- and seventh-round draft choices. San Francisco selected DE John Milem (Lenoir-Rhyne). Chicago selected RB Frank Murphy (Kansas State). Chicago later traded the seventh-round pick to Cleveland.

Seattle traded a 2000 fifth-round draft choice to Denver for 2000 sixth- and seventh-round choices. Denver selected WR Muneer Moore (Richmond). Seattle selected WR James Williams (Marshall). Seattle later traded the seventh-round pick to Oakland.

Chicago traded two 2000 seventh-round draft choices to Cleveland for three 2000 seventh-round draft choices. Cleveland selected DE Eric Chandler (Jackson State) and DB Rashidi Barnes (Colorado). Chicago selected DE James Cotton (Ohio State) and DB Mike Green (Louisiana-Lafayette). Chicago later traded the other seventh-round pick to Miami.

New England traded a 2000 seventh-round draft choice to San Francisco for a 2001 sixth-round draft choice. San Francisco selected QB Tim Rattay (Louisiana Tech).

Seattle traded a seventh-round draft choice to Oakland for a 2001 sixth-round draft choice. Oakland selected DB Cliffton Black (Southwest Texas State).

Chicago traded its 2000 and 2001 seventh-round draft choices to Miami for P Brent Bartholomew. Miami selected DB Jeff Harris (Georgia).

Oakland traded its 2000 seventh-round draft choice to Indianapolis for a 2001 sixth-round draft choice. Indianapolis selected DB Rodregis Brooks (Alabama-Birmingham).

APRIL 20

Carolina traded RB Fred Lane to Indianapolis for LB Spencer Reid.

APRIL 27

New Orleans traded LB Chris Bordano to Dallas for CB Kevin Mathis.

1999 STATISTICS

Rushing
Passing
Receiving
Scoring
Interceptions
Sacks
Fumbles
Field goals
Punting
Punt returns
Kickoff returns
Miscellaneous

RUSHING

TEAM

AFC

Team	Att.	Yds.	Avg.	Long	TD
Jacksonville	514	2091	4.1	52	20
Oakland	488	2084	4.3	t75	18
Kansas City	521	2082	4.0	t82	14
Cincinnati	442	2051	4.6	50	11
Buffalo	519	2040	3.9	t52	12
Pittsburgh	495	1991	4.0	52	14
N.Y. Jets	486	1961	4.0	50	7
Denver	465	1864	4.0	71	13
Tennessee	459	1811	3.9	40	19
Baltimore	431	1754	4.1	72	9
Indianapolis	419	1660	4.0	72	15
Miami	445	1453	3.3	34	8
New England	425	1426	3.4	43	9
Seattle	408	1408	3.5	45	5
San Diego	410	1246	3.0	54	10
Cleveland	313	1150	3.7	40	9
AFC total	7240	28072	3.9	t82	193
AFC average	452.5	1754.5	3.9	...	12.1

t—touchdown.

NFC

Team	Att.	Yds.	Avg.	Long	TD
San Francisco	418	2095	5.0	t68	14
St. Louis	431	2059	4.8	58	13
Dallas	493	2051	4.2	t63	16
Washington	463	2039	4.4	t76	23
Minnesota	422	1804	4.3	t70	13
Tampa Bay	502	1776	3.5	33	7
Philadelphia	424	1746	4.1	29	5
New Orleans	461	1690	3.7	33	9
Carolina	356	1525	4.3	t67	12
Green Bay	386	1519	3.9	36	13
N.Y. Giants	431	1408	3.3	40	11
Chicago	396	1387	3.5	t49	4
Detroit	356	1245	3.5	51	4
Arizona	396	1207	3.0	t58	13
Atlanta	373	1196	3.2	t33	9
NFC total	6308	24747	3.9	t76	170
NFC average	420.5	1649.8	3.9	...	11.3
NFL total	13548	52819	...	t82	363
NFL average	437.0	1703.8	3.9	...	11.7

INDIVIDUAL

BESTS OF THE SEASON

Yards, season
AFC: 1553—Edgerrin James, Indianapolis.
NFC: 1405—Stephen Davis, Washington.

Yards, game
AFC: 199—Eddie George, Tennessee vs. Oakland, Dec. 9 (28 attempts, 2 TDs).
NFC: 189—Stephen Davis, Washington vs. Arizona, Dec. 12 (37 attempts, 1 TD).

Longest gain
AFC: 82—Derrick S. Alexander, Kansas City vs. Pittsburgh, Dec. 18 (TD).
NFC: 76—Stephen Davis, Washington vs. Arizona, Dec. 12 (TD).

Attempts, season
AFC: 369—Edgerrin James, Indianapolis.
NFC: 329—Emmitt Smith, Dallas.

Attempts, game
NFC: 40—Ricky Williams, New Orleans vs. Cleveland, Oct. 31 (179 yards).
AFC: 38—Curtis Martin, N.Y. Jets vs. Arizona, Nov. 7 (131 yards).

Yards per attempt, season
NFC: 5.5—Marshall Faulk, St. Louis.
AFC: 5.2—Napoleon Kaufman, Oakland.

Touchdowns, season
NFC: 17—Stephen Davis, Washington.
AFC: 13—Edgerrin James, Indianapolis.
          James Stewart, Jacksonville.

Team leaders, yards

AFC:
Baltimore	852	Errict Rhett
Buffalo	695	Jonathan Linton
Cincinnati	1200	Corey Dillon
Cleveland	452	Terry Kirby
Denver	1159	Olandis Gary
Indianapolis	1553	Edgerrin James
Jacksonville	931	James Stewart
Kansas City	627	Donnell Bennett

AFC:
Miami	558	J.J. Johnson
New England	896	Terry Allen
N.Y. Jets	1464	Curtis Martin
Oakland	936	Tyrone Wheatley
Pittsburgh	1091	Jerome Bettis
San Diego	365	Jermaine Fazande
Seattle	1210	Ricky Watters
Tennessee	1304	Eddie George

NFC:
Arizona	553	Adrian Murrell
Atlanta	452	Ken Oxendine
Carolina	718	Tim Biakabutuka
Chicago	916	Curtis Enis
Dallas	1397	Emmitt Smith
Detroit	542	Greg Hill
Green Bay	1034	Dorsey Levens
Minnesota	1015	Robert Smith
New Orleans	884	Ricky Williams
N.Y. Giants	348	Joe Montgomery
Philadelphia	1273	Duce Staley
St. Louis	1381	Marshall Faulk
San Francisco	1229	Charlie Garner
Tampa Bay	949	Mike Alstott
Washington	1405	Stephen Davis

NFL LEADERS

Player, Team	Att.	Yds.	Avg.	Long	TD
James, Edgerrin, Indianapolis*	369	1553	4.2	72	13
Martin, Curtis, N.Y. Jets*	367	1464	4.0	50	5
Davis, Stephen, Washington	290	1405	4.8	t76	17
Smith, Emmitt, Dallas	329	1397	4.2	t63	11
Faulk, Marshall, St. Louis	253	1381	5.5	58	7
George, Eddie, Tennessee*	320	1304	4.1	40	9
Staley, Duce, Philadelphia	325	1273	3.9	29	4
Garner, Charlie, San Francisco	241	1229	5.1	53	4
Watters, Ricky, Seattle*	325	1210	3.7	45	5
Dillon, Corey, Cincinnati*	263	1200	4.6	50	5
Gary, Olandis, Denver*	276	1159	4.2	71	7
Bettis, Jerome, Pittsburgh*	299	1091	3.6	35	7
Levens, Dorsey, Green Bay	279	1034	3.7	36	9

Player, Team	Att.	Yds.	Avg.	Long	TD
Smith, Robert, Minnesota	221	1015	4.6	t70	2
Alstott, Mike, Tampa Bay	242	949	3.9	30	7
Wheatley, Tyrone, Oakland*	242	936	3.9	t30	8
Stewart, James, Jacksonville*	249	931	3.7	t44	13
Enis, Curtis, Chicago	287	916	3.2	19	3
Allen, Terry, New England*	254	896	3.5	39	8
Williams, Ricky, New Orleans	253	884	3.5	25	2
Rhett, Errict, Baltimore*	236	852	3.6	t52	5
Taylor, Fred, Jacksonville*	159	732	4.6	52	6
Biakabutuka, Tim, Carolina	138	718	5.2	t67	6
Kaufman, Napoleon, Oakland*	138	714	5.2	t75	2
Linton, Jonathan, Buffalo*	205	695	3.4	18	5
Bennett, Donnell, Kansas City*	161	627	3.9	44	8
Dunn, Warrick, Tampa Bay	195	616	3.2	33	0
Smith, Antowain, Buffalo*	165	614	3.7	t52	6
Huntley, Richard, Pittsburgh*	93	567	6.1	52	5
Johnson, J.J., Miami*	164	558	3.4	34	4

*AFC.
t—touchdown.
Leader based on yards gained.

AFC

Player, Team	Att.	Yds.	Avg.	Long	TD
Abdul-Jabbar, Karim, Mia.-Cle.	143	445	3.1	21	1
Alexander, Derrick, Kansas City	2	82	41.0	t82	1
Allen, Terry, New England	254	896	3.5	39	8
Anders, Kimble, Kansas City	32	181	5.7	46	0
Anderson, Richie, N.Y. Jets	16	84	5.3	16	0
Avery, John, Denver	5	21	4.2	11	0
Banks, Tavian, Jacksonville	23	82	3.6	21	0
Banks, Tony, Baltimore	24	93	3.9	12	0
Barker, Bryan, Jacksonville	1	6	6.0	6	0
Basnight, Michael, Cincinnati	62	308	5.0	46	0
Bennett, Darren, San Diego	1	0	0.0	0	0
Bennett, Donnell, Kansas City	161	627	3.9	44	8
Bettis, Jerome, Pittsburgh	299	1091	3.6	35	7
Blake, Jeff, Cincinnati	63	332	5.3	16	2
Bledsoe, Drew, New England	42	101	2.4	25	0
Bownes, Fabien, Seattle	1	-14	-14.0	-14	0
Brister, Bubby, Denver	2	17	8.5	17	0
Brown, Reggie, Seattle	14	38	2.7	9	0
Brown, Tim, Oakland	1	4	4.0	4	0
Brunell, Mark, Jacksonville	47	208	4.4	15	1
Bynum, Kenny, San Diego	92	287	3.1	25	1
Carter, Ki-Jana, Cincinnati	6	15	2.5	8	1
Carter, Tony, New England	6	26	4.3	9	0
Case, Stoney, Baltimore	36	141	3.9	28	3
Cloud, Mike, Kansas City	35	128	3.7	14	0
Collins, Cecil, Miami	131	414	3.2	t25	2
Couch, Tim, Cleveland	40	267	6.7	40	1
Covington, Scott, Cincinnati	2	-4	-2.0	-2	0
Crockett, Zack, Oakland	45	91	2.0	7	4
Davis, Terrell, Denver	67	211	3.1	26	2
Dawson, Phil, Cleveland	1	4	4.0	t4	1
Denson, Autry, Miami	28	98	3.5	20	0
Detmer, Ty, Cleveland	6	38	6.3	11	1
Dillon, Corey, Cincinnati	263	1200	4.6	50	5
Dyson, Kevin, Tennessee	1	3	3.0	3	0
Edwards, Marc, Cleveland	6	35	5.8	28	0
Elias, Keith, Indianapolis	13	28	2.2	8	0
Ellison, Jerry, New England	2	10	5.0	8	0
Evans, Chuck, Baltimore	38	134	3.5	12	0
Faulk, Kevin, New England	67	227	3.4	43	1
Fazande, Jermaine, San Diego	91	365	4.0	54	2
Feagles, Jeff, Seattle	2	0	0.0	0	0
Fiedler, Jay, Jacksonville	13	26	2.0	15	0
Fletcher, Terrell, San Diego	48	126	2.6	16	0
Floyd, Chris, New England	6	12	2.0	6	0
Flutie, Doug, Buffalo	88	476	5.4	t24	1
Foley, Glenn, Seattle	3	-1	-.3	0	0
Friesz, John, New England	2	-2	-1.0	-1	0

Player, Team	Att.	Yds.	Avg.	Long	TD
Fuamatu-Ma'afala, Chris, Pit.	1	4	4.0	4	0
Galloway, Joey, Seattle	1	-1	-1.0	-1	0
Gannon, Rich, Oakland	46	298	6.5	39	2
Gary, Olandis, Denver	276	1159	4.2	71	7
George, Eddie, Tennessee	320	1304	4.1	40	9
Gonzalez, Pete, Pittsburgh	2	-3	-1.5	-1	0
Gordon, Lennox, Buffalo	11	38	3.5	13	0
Grbac, Elvis, Kansas City	19	10	0.5	8	0
Green, Ahman, Seattle	26	120	4.6	21	0
Griese, Brian, Denver	46	138	3.0	23	2
Griffith, Howard, Denver	17	66	3.9	13	1
Groce, Clif, Cincinnati	8	22	2.8	8	1
Harbaugh, Jim, San Diego	34	126	3.7	16	0
Harrison, Marvin, Indianapolis	1	4	4.0	4	0
Hentrich, Craig, Tennessee	2	1	0.5	1	0
Hicks, Robert, Buffalo	1	-2	-2.0	-2	0
Holmes, Priest, Baltimore	89	506	5.7	72	1
Horn, Joe, Kansas City	2	15	7.5	9	0
Howard, Chris, Jacksonville	13	55	4.2	22	0
Hoying, Bobby, Oakland	2	-3	-1.5	-1	0
Huard, Damon, Miami	28	124	4.4	25	0
Huntley, Richard, Pittsburgh	93	567	6.1	52	5
Ismail, Qadry, Baltimore	1	4	4.0	4	0
Jacquet, Nate, Miami	1	4	4.0	4	0
James, Edgerrin, Indianapolis	369	1553	4.2	72	13
Johnson, J.J., Miami	164	558	3.4	34	4
Johnson, Kevin, Cleveland	1	-6	-6.0	-6	0
Johnson, Keyshawn, N.Y. Jets	5	6	1.2	12	0
Johnson, Lee, New England	2	13	6.5	13	0
Johnson, Leon, N.Y. Jets	1	2	2.0	2	0
Johnson, Pat, Baltimore	1	12	12.0	12	0
Johnson, Rob, Buffalo	8	61	7.6	25	0
Jones, Charlie, San Diego	1	-8	-8.0	-8	0
Jones, George, Cleveland	8	15	1.9	9	0
Jordan, Randy, Oakland	9	32	3.6	12	2
Kaufman, Napoleon, Oakland	138	714	5.2	t75	2
Kirby, Terry, Cleveland	130	452	3.5	28	6
Kitna, Jon, Seattle	35	56	1.6	10	0
Konrad, Rob, Miami	9	16	1.8	5	0
Kramer, Erik, San Diego	5	1	0.2	3	0
Lewis, Jermaine, Baltimore	5	11	2.2	4	0
Linton, Jonathan, Buffalo	205	695	3.4	18	5
Loville, Derek, Denver	40	203	5.1	t36	1
Lucas, Ray, N.Y. Jets	41	144	3.5	21	1
Lynn, Anthony, Denver	2	2	1.0	1	0
Mack, Stacey, Jacksonville	7	40	5.7	19	0
Manning, Peyton, Indianapolis	35	73	2.1	13	2
Marino, Dan, Miami	6	-6	-1.0	0	0
Martin, Curtis, N.Y. Jets	367	1464	4.0	50	5
Martin, Tony, Miami	1	-6	-6.0	-6	0
McNair, Steve, Tennessee	72	337	4.7	38	8
Means, Natrone, San Diego	112	277	2.5	15	4
Miller, Chris, Denver	8	40	5.0	13	0
Miller, Josh, Pittsburgh	2	-9	-4.5	0	0
Milne, Brian, Cincinnati	3	30	10.0	26	0
Mirer, Rick, N.Y. Jets	21	89	4.2	12	1
Mitchell, Scott, Baltimore	1	1	1.0	1	0
Mohr, Chris, Buffalo	1	0	0.0	0	0
Morris, Bam, Kansas City	120	414	3.5	24	3
Moulds, Eric, Buffalo	1	1	1.0	1	0
Neal, Lorenzo, Tennessee	2	1	0.5	t1	1
O'Donnell, Neil, Tennessee	19	1	0.1	4	0
Parmalee, Bernie, N.Y. Jets	27	133	4.9	18	0
Pope, Daniel, Kansas City	1	0	0.0	0	0
Powell, Scott, Cleveland	1	-14	-14.0	-14	0
Price, Peerless, Buffalo	1	-7	-7.0	-7	0
Pritchett, Stanley, Miami	47	158	3.4	25	1
Rhett, Errict, Baltimore	236	852	3.6	t52	5
Richardson, Tony, Kansas City	84	387	4.6	26	1
Ricks, Mikhael, San Diego	2	11	5.5	7	0
Ritchie, Jon, Oakland	5	12	2.4	5	0
Rouen, Tom, Denver	1	0	0.0	0	0

Player, Team	Att.	Yds.	Avg.	Long	TD
Salaam, Rashaan, Cleveland	1	2	2.0	2	0
Shaw, Harold, New England	9	23	2.6	12	0
Shaw, Sedrick, Cle.-Cin.	7	22	3.1	10	1
Shehee, Rashaan, Kansas City	65	238	3.7	18	1
Shelton, Daimon, Jacksonville	1	2	2.0	2	0
Shepherd, Leslie, Cleveland	1	5	5.0	5	0
Smith, Akili, Cincinnati	19	114	6.0	24	1
Smith, Antowain, Buffalo	165	614	3.7	t52	6
Smith, Detron, Denver	1	7	7.0	7	0
Sowell, Jerald, N.Y. Jets	3	5	1.7	3	0
Stephens, Tremayne, San Diego	24	61	2.5	9	3
Stewart, James, Jacksonville	249	931	3.7	t44	13
Stewart, Kordell, Pittsburgh	56	258	4.6	21	2
Stone, Dwight, N.Y. Jets	2	27	13.5	36	0
Strong, Mack, Seattle	1	0	0.0	0	0
Taylor, Fred, Jacksonville	159	732	4.6	52	6
Thomas, Rodney, Tennessee	43	164	3.8	22	1
Thomas, Thurman, Buffalo	36	152	4.2	31	0
Tomczak, Mike, Pittsburgh	16	19	1.2	17	0
Tupa, Tom, N.Y. Jets	2	8	4.0	4	0
Van Pelt, Alex, Buffalo	1	-1	-1.0	-1	0
Ward, Dedric, N.Y. Jets	1	-1	-1.0	-1	0
Ward, Hines, Pittsburgh	2	-2	-1.0	3	0
Warren, Lamont, New England	35	120	3.4	18	0
Watters, Ricky, Seattle	325	1210	3.7	45	5
Wheatley, Tyrone, Oakland	242	936	3.9	t30	8
Whitted, Alvis, Jacksonville	1	9	9.0	9	0
Wilkins, Terrence, Indianapolis	1	2	2.0	2	0
Williams, Kevin, Buffalo	1	13	13.0	13	0
Williams, Nick, Cincinnati	10	30	3.0	8	0
Witman, Jon, Pittsburgh	6	18	3.0	7	0
Yeast, Craig, Cincinnati	2	-16	-8.0	-3	0
Zereoue, Amos, Pittsburgh	18	48	2.7	8	0
Zolak, Scott, Miami	2	-2	-1.0	-1	0

*Includes both NFC and AFC statistics.
t—touchdown.

NFC

Player, Team	Att.	Yds.	Avg.	Long	TD
Abdullah, Rabih, Tampa Bay	5	12	2.4	10	0
Aikman, Troy, Dallas	21	10	0.5	7	1
Allen, James, Chicago	32	119	3.7	13	0
Alstott, Mike, Tampa Bay	242	949	3.9	30	7
Anderson, Jamal, Atlanta	19	59	3.1	20	0
Anthony, Reidel, Tampa Bay	1	2	2.0	2	0
Barber, Tiki, N.Y. Giants	62	258	4.2	30	0
Barnhardt, Tommy, New Orleans	1	4	4.0	4	0
Batch, Charlie, Detroit	28	87	3.1	t12	2
Bates, Mario, Arizona	72	202	2.8	16	9
Bates, Michael, Carolina	3	12	4.0	12	0
Beasley, Fred, San Francisco	58	276	4.8	t44	4
Bennett, Edgar, Chicago	6	28	4.7	15	0
Bennett, Sean, N.Y. Giants	29	126	4.3	40	1
Beuerlein, Steve, Carolina	27	124	4.6	16	2
Biakabutuka, Tim, Carolina	138	718	5.2	t67	6
Bieniemy, Eric, Philadelphia	12	75	6.3	28	1
Bjornson, Eric, Dallas	1	20	20.0	t20	1
Bono, Steve, Carolina	2	-2	-1.0	-1	0
Booker, Marty, Chicago	1	8	8.0	8	0
Bostic, James, Philadelphia	5	19	3.8	5	0
Boston, David, Arizona	5	0	0.0	7	0
Brooks, Macey, Chicago	1	7	7.0	7	0
Brown, Dave, Arizona	13	49	3.8	10	0
Brown, Gary, N.Y. Giants	55	177	3.2	28	0
Bruce, Isaac, St. Louis	5	32	6.4	11	0
Carruth, Rae, Carolina	1	4	4.0	4	0
Centers, Larry, Washington	13	51	3.9	12	0
Chancey, Robert, Dallas	14	57	4.1	11	0
Chandler, Chris, Atlanta	16	57	3.6	14	1
Christian, Bob, Atlanta	38	174	4.6	t33	5
Collins, Kerry, N.Y. Giants	19	36	1.9	11	2

Player, Team	Att.	Yds.	Avg.	Long	TD
Comella, Greg, N.Y. Giants	1	0	0.0	0	0
Connell, Albert, Washington	1	8	8.0	8	0
Conway, Curtis, Chicago	1	-2	-2.0	-2	0
Craver, Aaron, New Orleans	17	40	2.4	8	0
Crowell, Germane, Detroit	5	38	7.6	20	0
Culpepper, Daunte, Minnesota	3	6	2.0	9	0
Cunningham, Randall, Minnesota	10	58	5.8	14	0
Davis, Stephen, Washington	290	1405	4.8	t76	17
Davis, Troy, New Orleans	20	32	1.6	7	0
Delhomme, Jake, New Orleans	11	72	6.5	27	2
Detmer, Koy, Philadelphia	2	-2	-1.0	-1	0
Dilfer, Trent, Tampa Bay	35	144	4.1	28	0
Dunn, Warrick, Tampa Bay	195	616	3.2	33	0
Dwight, Tim, Atlanta	5	28	5.6	9	1
Engram, Bobby, Chicago	2	11	5.5	9	0
Enis, Curtis, Chicago	287	916	3.2	19	3
Faulk, Marshall, St. Louis	253	1381	5.5	58	7
Favre, Brett, Green Bay	28	142	5.1	20	0
Floyd, William, Carolina	35	78	2.2	16	3
Franklin, P.J., New Orleans	1	0	0.0	0	0
Freeman, Antonio, Green Bay	1	-2	-2.0	-2	0
Frerotte, Gus, Detroit	15	33	2.2	8	0
Garcia, Jeff, San Francisco	45	231	5.1	25	2
Garner, Charlie, San Francisco	241	1229	5.1	53	4
Garrett, Jason, Dallas	6	12	2.0	9	0
George, Jeff, Minnesota	16	41	2.6	17	0
Germaine, Joe, St. Louis	3	0	0.0	2	0
Graham, Kent, N.Y. Giants	35	132	3.8	17	1
Graziani, Tony, Atlanta	9	11	1.2	10	0
Green, Jacquez, Tampa Bay	3	8	2.7	15	0
Hakim, Az-Zahir, St. Louis	4	44	11.0	31	0
Hanspard, Byron, Atlanta	136	383	2.8	15	1
Hasselbeck, Matt, Green Bay	6	15	2.5	13	0
Hastings, Andre, New Orleans	1	4	4.0	4	0
Henderson, William, Green Bay	7	29	4.1	10	2
Hetherington, Chris, Carolina	2	7	3.5	5	0
Hicks, Skip, Washington	78	257	3.3	24	3
Hill, Greg, Detroit	144	542	3.8	45	2
Hilliard, Ike, N.Y. Giants	3	16	5.3	24	0
Hoard, Leroy, Minnesota	138	555	4.0	53	10
Hobert, Billy Joe, New Orleans	12	47	3.9	10	1
Hodgins, James, St. Louis	7	10	1.4	3	1
Holcombe, Robert, St. Louis	78	294	3.8	34	4
Holt, Torry, St. Louis	3	25	8.3	14	0
Irvin, Sedrick, Detroit	36	133	3.7	51	4
Ismail, Rocket, Dallas	13	110	8.5	t27	1
Jackson, Terry, San Francisco	15	75	5.0	11	0
Jeffers, Patrick, Carolina	2	16	8.0	23	0
Jervey, Travis, San Francisco	6	49	8.2	33	1
Jett, John, Detroit	2	-8	-4.0	0	0
Johnson, Anthony, Carolina	25	72	2.9	23	0
Johnson, Brad, Washington	26	31	1.2	12	2
Johnson, LeShon, N.Y. Giants	61	143	2.3	17	2
Justin, Paul, St. Louis	5	-1	-.2	3	0
Kennison, Eddie, New Orleans	3	20	6.7	15	0
King, Shaun, Tampa Bay	18	38	2.1	8	0
Lane, Fred, Carolina	115	475	4.1	t41	1
Lee, Amp, St. Louis	3	3	1.0	4	0
Levens, Dorsey, Green Bay	279	1034	3.7	36	9
Lewis, Jeff, Carolina	4	1	0.3	4	0
Makovicka, Joel, Arizona	8	7	0.9	7	0
Martin, Cecil, Philadelphia	3	3	1.0	2	0
Mathis, Terance, Atlanta	1	0	0.0	0	0
Matthews, Shane, Chicago	14	31	2.2	14	0
McNabb, Donovan, Philadelphia	47	313	6.7	27	0
McNown, Cade, Chicago	32	160	5.0	18	0
Metcalf, Eric, Carolina	2	20	10.0	17	0
Milburn, Glyn, Chicago	16	102	6.4	t49	1
Miller, Jim, Chicago	3	9	3.0	9	0
Mills, Ernie, Dallas	1	-1	-1.0	-1	0
Mitchell, Basil, Green Bay	29	117	4.0	15	0
Mitchell, Brian, Washington	40	220	5.5	16	1

Player, Team	Att.	Yds.	Avg.	Long	TD
Montgomery, Joe, N.Y. Giants	115	348	3.0	14	3
Morrow, Harold, Minnesota	2	1	0.5	5	0
Moss, Randy, Minnesota	4	43	10.8	15	0
Murrell, Adrian, Arizona	193	553	2.9	22	0
Oliver, Winslow, Atlanta	8	32	4.0	10	0
Olivo, Brock, Detroit	1	1	1.0	1	0
Oxendine, Ken, Atlanta	141	452	3.2	20	1
Palmer, David, Minnesota	3	12	4.0	7	0
Parker, De'Mond, Green Bay	36	184	5.1	26	2
Patten, David, N.Y. Giants	1	27	27.0	27	0
Pederson, Doug, Philadelphia	20	33	1.7	19	0
Peete, Rodney, Washington	2	-1	-.5	0	0
Perry, Wilmont, New Orleans	48	180	3.8	22	0
Phillips, Lawrence, San Francisco	30	144	4.8	t68	2
Philyaw, Dino, New Orleans	4	16	4.0	18	0
Pittman, Michael, Arizona	64	289	4.5	t58	2
Player, Scott, Arizona	1	-18	-18.0	-18	0
Plummer, Jake, Arizona	39	121	3.1	17	2
Poole, Keith, New Orleans	1	14	14.0	14	0
Powell, Marvin, New Orleans	1	1	1.0	1	0
Rice, Jerry, San Francisco	2	13	6.5	11	0
Rivers, Ron, Detroit	82	295	3.6	37	0
Sauerbrun, Todd, Chicago	1	-2	-2.0	-2	0
Schlesinger, Cory, Detroit	43	124	2.9	16	0
Smith, Emmitt, Dallas	329	1397	4.2	t63	11
Smith, Lamar, New Orleans	60	205	3.4	24	0
Smith, Robert, Minnesota	221	1015	4.6	t70	2
Staley, Duce, Philadelphia	325	1273	3.9	29	4
Stanley, Chad, San Francisco	1	0	0.0	0	0
Stenstrom, Steve, San Francisco	3	15	5.0	8	0
Tate, Robert, Minnesota	1	4	4.0	4	0
Thomas, Robert, Dallas	8	35	4.4	10	0
Thrash, James, Washington	1	37	37.0	37	0
Tillman, Pat, Arizona	1	4	4.0	4	0
Tolliver, Billy Joe, New Orleans	26	142	5.5	33	3
Toomer, Amani, N.Y. Giants	1	4	4.0	4	0
Tucker, Jason, Dallas	1	8	8.0	8	0
Turner, Kevin, Philadelphia	6	15	2.5	5	0
Vardell, Tommy, San Francisco	6	6	1.0	5	1
Warner, Kurt, St. Louis	23	92	4.0	22	1
Warren, Chris, Dallas	99	403	4.1	25	2
Watson, Edwin, Philadelphia	4	17	4.3	6	0
Watson, Justin, St. Louis	47	179	3.8	21	0
Way, Charles, N.Y. Giants	49	141	2.9	17	2
Weldon, Casey, Washington	5	-4	-.8	0	0
Westbrook, Michael, Washington	7	35	5.0	12	0
Williams, Moe, Minnesota	24	69	2.9	10	1
Williams, Ricky, New Orleans	253	884	3.5	25	2
Wuerffel, Danny, New Orleans	2	29	14.5	t29	1
Young, Steve, San Francisco	11	57	5.2	14	0
Zeier, Eric, Tampa Bay	3	7	2.3	8	0

*Includes both NFC and AFC statistics.
t—touchdown.

PLAYERS WITH TWO CLUBS

Player, Team	Att.	Yds.	Avg.	Long	TD
Abdul-Jabbar, Karim, Miami	28	95	3.4	12	1
Abdul-Jabbar, Karim, Cleveland	115	350	3.0	21	0
Shaw, Sedrick, Cleveland	3	2	0.7	3	0
Shaw, Sedrick, Cincinnati	4	20	5.0	10	1

1999 STATISTICS *Rushing*

PASSING

TEAM

AFC

Team	Att.	Comp.	Pct. Comp.	Gross Yds.	Sack	Yds. Lost	Net Yds.	Yds./ Att.	Yds./ Comp.	TD	Pct. TD	Long	Had Int.	Pct. Int.
Indianapolis	546	338	61.9	4182	14	116	4066	7.66	12.37	26	4.76	t80	17	3.1
New England	540	305	56.5	3985	56	349	3636	7.38	13.07	19	3.52	t68	21	3.9
Oakland	520	306	58.8	3850	49	241	3609	7.40	12.58	24	4.62	50	14	2.7
Miami	589	329	55.9	3736	37	251	3485	6.34	11.36	20	3.40	t69	21	3.6
Jacksonville	535	320	59.8	3716	36	221	3495	6.95	11.61	16	2.99	62	11	2.1
Denver	554	319	57.6	3646	34	227	3419	6.58	11.43	16	2.89	88	18	3.2
Seattle	525	288	54.9	3629	38	232	3397	6.91	12.60	25	4.76	51	16	3.0
San Diego	583	332	56.9	3627	46	284	3343	6.22	10.92	12	2.06	t80	24	4.1
Tennessee	527	304	57.7	3622	25	137	3485	6.87	11.91	23	4.36	t65	13	2.5
Cincinnati	548	300	54.7	3504	49	278	3226	6.39	11.68	18	3.28	t76	18	3.3
Buffalo	513	290	56.5	3478	27	185	3293	6.78	11.99	21	4.09	t54	16	3.1
Kansas City	502	295	58.8	3409	26	170	3239	6.79	11.56	22	4.38	t86	15	3.0
Baltimore	546	270	49.5	3360	56	336	3024	6.15	12.44	21	3.85	t76	20	3.7
Pittsburgh	535	301	56.3	3118	37	235	2883	5.83	10.36	19	3.55	49	18	3.4
N.Y. Jets	476	272	57.1	3001	37	210	2791	6.30	11.03	22	4.62	65	16	3.4
Cleveland	492	271	55.1	2997	60	385	2612	6.09	11.06	19	3.86	t78	15	3.0
AFC total	8531	4840	...	56860	627	3857	53003	...	...	323	...	88	273	...
AFC average	533.2	302.5	56.7	3553.8	39.2	241.1	3312.7	6.67	11.75	20.2	3.8	...	17.1	3.2

t—touchdown.

NFC

Team	Att.	Comp.	Pct. Comp.	Gross Yds.	Sack	Yds. Lost	Net Yds.	Yds./ Att.	Yds./ Comp.	TD	Pct. TD	Long	Had Int.	Pct. Int.
St. Louis	530	343	64.7	4580	33	227	4353	8.64	13.35	42	7.92	t75	15	2.8
Carolina	575	345	60.0	4447	51	286	4161	7.73	12.89	36	6.26	t88	15	2.6
Chicago	684	404	59.1	4352	38	216	4136	6.36	10.77	25	3.65	t80	22	3.2
Minnesota	530	316	59.6	4318	43	329	3989	8.15	13.66	32	6.04	t80	21	4.0
Green Bay	605	344	56.9	4132	36	232	3900	6.83	12.01	23	3.80	t74	23	3.8
Washington	537	324	60.3	4112	31	186	3926	7.66	12.69	26	4.84	t65	14	2.6
Detroit	558	326	58.4	4074	64	388	3686	7.30	12.50	22	3.94	t77	14	2.5
N.Y. Giants	602	350	58.1	4015	42	296	3719	6.67	11.47	17	2.82	t80	20	3.3
Atlanta	509	278	54.6	3691	49	345	3346	7.25	13.28	22	4.32	62	19	3.7
New Orleans	553	288	52.1	3598	41	305	3293	6.51	12.49	16	2.89	t90	30	5.4
San Francisco	560	324	57.9	3526	34	241	3285	6.30	10.88	14	2.50	62	19	3.4
Dallas	507	295	58.2	3278	24	151	3127	6.47	11.11	20	3.94	t90	13	2.6
Arizona	558	287	51.4	3085	45	282	2803	5.53	10.75	11	1.97	71	30	5.4
Tampa Bay	447	268	60.0	2781	42	303	2478	6.22	10.38	18	4.03	68	16	3.6
Philadelphia	474	235	49.6	2405	49	321	2084	5.07	10.23	18	3.80	t84	18	3.8
NFC total	8229	4727	...	56394	622	4108	52286	...	...	342	...	t90	289	...
NFC average	548.6	315.1	57.4	3759.6	41.5	273.9	3485.7	6.85	11.93	22.8	4.2	...	19.3	3.5
NFL total	16760	9567	...	113254	1249	7965	105289	...	...	665	...	t90	562	...
NFL average	540.6	308.6	57.1	3653.4	40.3	256.9	3396.4	6.76	11.84	21.5	4.0	...	18.1	3.4

INDIVIDUAL

BESTS OF THE SEASON

Highest rating, season
NFC: 109.2—Kurt Warner, St. Louis.
AFC: 90.7—Peyton Manning, Indianapolis.

Completion percentage, season
NFC: 65.1—Kurt Warner, St. Louis.
AFC: 62.1—Peyton Manning, Indianapolis.

Attempts, season
NFC: 595—Brett Favre, Green Bay.
AFC: 539—Drew Bledsoe, New England.

Completions, season
NFC: 343—Steve Beuerlein, Carolina.
AFC: 331—Peyton Manning, Indianapolis.

Yards, season
NFC: 4436—Steve Beuerlein, Carolina.
AFC: 4135—Peyton Manning, Indianapolis.

Yards, game
NFC: 471—Brad Johnson, Washington at San Francisco, Dec. 26 (32-47, 2 TDs) (OT).
437—Jeff Garcia, San Francisco at Cincinnati, Dec. 5 (33-49, 3 TDs).
AFC: 404—Peyton Manning, Indianapolis at San Diego, September 26 (29-54, 2 TDs).
Jim Harbaugh, San Diego at Minnesota, November 28 (25-39, 1 TD).

Longest gain
NFC: 90—Billy Joe Hobert (to Eddie Kennison), New Orleans vs. Atlanta, Oct. 10 (TD).
Troy Aikman (to Jason Tucker), Dallas vs. N.Y. Giants, Jan. 2 (TD).

– 250 –

AFC: 88—Brian Griese (to Byron Chamberlain), Denver vs. Green Bay, Oct. 17.

Yards per attempt, season
NFC: 8.72—Kurt Warner, St. Louis.
AFC: 7.76—Peyton Manning, Indianapolis.

Touchdown passes, season
NFC: 41—Kurt Warner, St. Louis.
AFC: 26—Peyton Manning, Indianapolis.

Touchdown passes, game
AFC: 5—Steve McNair, Tennessee vs. Jacksonville, Dec. 26 (23-33, 291 yards).
NFC: 5—Troy Aikman, Dallas at Washington, September 12 (28-49, 362 yards) (OT); Kurt Warner, St. Louis vs. San Francisco, Oct. 10 (20-23, 323 yards); Steve Beuerlein, Carolina vs. New Orleans, Jan. 2 (22-41, 322 yards).

Lowest interception percentage, season
AFC: 2.0—Mark Brunell, Jacksonville.
NFC: 2.2—Shane Matthews, Chicago.

NFL LEADERS

Player, Team	Att.	Comp.	Pct. Comp.	Yds.	Avg. Gain	TD	Pct. TD	Long	Int.	Pct. Int.	Sack	Yds. Lost	Rat. Pts.
Warner, Kurt, St. Louis	499	325	65.1	4353	8.72	41	8.2	t75	13	2.6	29	201	109.2
Beuerlein, Steve, Carolina	571	343	60.1	4436	7.77	36	6.3	t88	15	2.6	50	280	94.6
George, Jeff, Minnesota	329	191	58.1	2816	8.56	23	7.0	t80	12	3.6	28	228	94.2
Manning, Peyton, Indianapolis*	533	331	62.1	4135	7.76	26	4.9	t80	15	2.8	14	116	90.7
Johnson, Brad, Washington	519	316	60.9	4005	7.72	24	4.6	t65	13	2.5	29	177	90.0
Gannon, Rich, Oakland*	515	304	59.0	3840	7.46	24	4.7	50	14	2.7	49	241	86.5
Lucas, Ray, N.Y. Jets*	272	161	59.2	1678	6.17	14	5.1	t56	6	2.2	11	69	85.1
Batch, Charlie, Detroit	270	151	55.9	1957	7.25	13	4.8	t74	7	2.6	36	186	84.1
Frerotte, Gus, Detroit	288	175	60.8	2117	7.35	9	3.1	t77	7	2.4	28	202	83.6
Chandler, Chris, Atlanta	307	174	56.7	2339	7.62	16	5.2	t60	11	3.6	32	230	83.5
Brunell, Mark, Jacksonville*	441	259	58.7	3060	6.94	14	3.2	62	9	2.0	29	174	82.0
Grbac, Elvis, Kansas City*	499	294	58.9	3389	6.79	22	4.4	t86	15	3.0	26	170	81.7
Banks, Tony, Baltimore*	320	169	52.8	2136	6.68	17	5.3	t76	8	2.5	33	190	81.2
Aikman, Troy, Dallas	442	263	59.5	2964	6.71	17	3.8	t90	12	2.7	19	130	81.1
Matthews, Shane, Chicago	275	167	60.7	1645	5.98	10	3.6	56	6	2.2	13	79	80.6
McNair, Steve, Tennessee*	331	187	56.5	2179	6.58	12	3.6	t65	8	2.4	16	74	78.6
Garcia, Jeff, San Francisco	375	225	60.0	2544	6.78	11	2.9	62	11	2.9	15	104	77.9
Kitna, Jon, Seattle*	495	270	54.5	3346	6.76	23	4.6	51	16	3.2	32	198	77.7
Blake, Jeff, Cincinnati*	389	215	55.3	2670	6.86	16	4.1	t76	12	3.1	30	168	77.6
Dilfer, Trent, Tampa Bay	244	146	59.8	1619	6.64	11	4.5	t62	11	4.5	26	189	75.8
Tomczak, Mike, Pittsburgh*	258	139	53.9	1625	6.30	12	4.7	49	8	3.1	15	104	75.8
Griese, Brian, Denver*	452	261	57.7	3032	6.71	14	3.1	88	14	3.1	27	176	75.6
Bledsoe, Drew, New England*	539	305	56.6	3985	7.39	19	3.5	t68	21	3.9	55	342	75.6
Flutie, Doug, Buffalo*	478	264	55.2	3171	6.63	19	4.0	t54	16	3.3	26	176	75.1
Favre, Brett, Green Bay	595	341	57.3	4091	6.88	22	3.7	t74	23	3.9	35	223	74.7
Graham, Kent, N.Y. Giants	271	160	59.0	1697	6.26	9	3.3	56	9	3.3	26	184	74.6
Collins, Kerry, N.Y. Giants	331	190	57.4	2318	7.00	8	2.4	t80	11	3.3	16	112	73.3
Couch, Tim, Cleveland*	399	223	55.9	2447	6.13	15	3.8	t78	13	3.3	56	359	73.2
Harbaugh, Jim, San Diego*	434	249	57.4	2761	6.36	10	2.3	t80	14	3.2	37	208	70.6
Marino, Dan, Miami*	369	204	55.3	2448	6.63	12	3.3	62	17	4.6	9	66	67.4

*AFC.
t—touchdown.
Leader based on rating points, minimum 224 attempts.

AFC

Player, Team	Att.	Comp.	Pct. Comp.	Yds.	Avg. Gain	TD	Pct. TD	Long	Int.	Pct. Int.	Sack	Yds. Lost	Rat. Pts.
Banks, Tony, Baltimore	320	169	52.8	2136	6.68	17	5.3	t76	8	2.5	33	190	81.2
Bettis, Jerome, Pittsburgh	1	1	100.0	21	21.00	1	100.0	t21	0	0.0	0	0	158.3
Blake, Jeff, Cincinnati	389	215	55.3	2670	6.86	16	4.1	t76	12	3.1	30	168	77.6
Bledsoe, Drew, New England	539	305	56.6	3985	7.39	19	3.5	t68	21	3.9	55	342	75.6
Brister, Bubby, Denver	20	12	60.0	87	4.35	0	0.0	11	3	15.0	0	0	30.6
Brown, Troy, New England	1	0	0.0	0	0.00	0	0.0	0	0	0.0	0	0	39.6
Brunell, Mark, Jacksonville	441	259	58.7	3060	6.94	14	3.2	62	9	2.0	29	174	82.0
Case, Stoney, Baltimore	170	77	45.3	988	5.81	3	1.8	t54	8	4.7	17	116	50.3
Couch, Tim, Cleveland	399	223	55.9	2447	6.13	15	3.8	t78	13	3.3	56	359	73.2
Covington, Scott, Cincinnati	5	4	80.0	23	4.60	0	0.0	8	0	0.0	0	0	85.8
Detmer, Ty, Cleveland	91	47	51.6	548	6.02	4	4.4	35	2	2.2	4	26	75.7
Fiedler, Jay, Jacksonville	94	61	64.9	656	6.98	2	2.1	t25	2	2.1	7	47	83.5
Flutie, Doug, Buffalo	478	264	55.2	3171	6.63	19	4.0	t54	16	3.3	26	176	75.1
Foley, Glenn, Seattle	30	18	60.0	283	9.43	2	6.7	t49	0	0.0	6	34	113.6
Gannon, Rich, Oakland	515	304	59.0	3840	7.46	24	4.7	50	14	2.7	49	241	86.5
Gonzalez, Pete, Pittsburgh	1	1	100.0	8	8.00	0	0.0	8	0	0.0	0	0	100.0
Grbac, Elvis, Kansas City	499	294	58.9	3389	6.79	22	4.4	t86	15	3.0	26	170	81.7
Griese, Brian, Denver	452	261	57.7	3032	6.71	14	3.1	88	14	3.1	27	176	75.6
Harbaugh, Jim, San Diego	434	249	57.4	2761	6.36	10	2.3	t80	14	3.2	37	208	70.6
Hoying, Bobby, Oakland	5	2	40.0	10	2.00	0	0.0	7	0	0.0	0	0	47.9

Player, Team	Att.	Comp.	Pct. Comp.	Yds.	Avg. Gain	TD	Pct. TD	Long	Int.	Pct. Int.	Sack	Yds. Lost	Rat. Pts.
Huard, Damon, Miami	216	125	57.9	1288	5.96	8	3.7	t69	4	1.9	28	185	79.8
Johnson, Kevin, Cleveland	1	0	0.0	0	0.00	0	0.0	0	0	0.0	0	0	39.6
Johnson, Keyshawn, N.Y. Jets	1	0	0.0	0	0.00	0	0.0	0	0	0.0	1	9	39.6
Johnson, Rob, Buffalo	34	25	73.5	298	8.76	2	5.9	42	0	0.0	1	9	119.5
Kirby, Terry, Cleveland	1	1	100.0	2	2.00	0	0.0	2	0	0.0	0	0	79.2
Kitna, Jon, Seattle	495	270	54.5	3346	6.76	23	4.6	51	16	3.2	32	198	77.7
Kramer, Erik, San Diego	141	78	55.3	788	5.59	2	1.4	41	10	7.1	7	62	46.6
Lucas, Ray, N.Y. Jets	272	161	59.2	1678	6.17	14	5.1	t56	6	2.2	11	69	85.1
Manning, Peyton, Indianapolis	533	331	62.1	4135	7.76	26	4.9	t80	15	2.8	14	116	90.7
Marino, Dan, Miami	369	204	55.3	2448	6.63	12	3.3	62	17	4.6	9	66	67.4
McNair, Steve, Tennessee	331	187	56.5	2179	6.58	12	3.6	t65	8	2.4	16	74	78.6
Miller, Chris, Denver	81	46	56.8	527	6.51	2	2.5	42	1	1.2	7	51	79.6
Mirer, Rick, N.Y. Jets	176	95	54.0	1062	6.03	5	2.8	50	9	5.1	22	102	60.4
Mitchell, Scott, Baltimore	56	24	42.9	236	4.21	1	1.8	t28	4	7.1	6	30	31.5
Moon, Warren, Kansas City	3	1	33.3	20	6.67	0	0.0	20	0	0.0	0	0	57.6
Moreno, Moses, San Diego	7	5	71.4	78	11.14	0	0.0	45	0	0.0	1	3	108.0
O'Donnell, Neil, Tennessee	195	116	59.5	1382	7.09	10	5.1	t54	5	2.6	9	63	87.6
Pickens, Carl, Cincinnati	1	1	100.0	6	6.00	0	0.0	6	0	0.0	0	0	91.7
Reed, Robert, San Diego	0	0	...	0	...	0	...	0	0	...	1	11	...
Ricks, Mikhael, San Diego	1	0	0.0	0	0.00	0	0.0	0	0	0.0	0	0	39.6
Smith, Akili, Cincinnati	153	80	52.3	805	5.26	2	1.3	39	6	3.9	19	110	55.6
Smith, Rod, Denver	1	0	0.0	0	0.00	0	0.0	0	0	0.0	0	0	39.6
Sowell, Jerald, N.Y. Jets	1	0	0.0	0	0.00	0	0.0	0	0	0.0	0	0	39.6
Stewart, Kordell, Pittsburgh	275	160	58.2	1464	5.32	6	2.2	42	10	3.6	22	131	64.9
Testaverde, Vinny, N.Y. Jets	15	10	66.7	96	6.40	1	6.7	t27	1	6.7	0	0	78.8
Tomczak, Mike, Pittsburgh	258	139	53.9	1625	6.30	12	4.7	49	8	3.1	15	104	75.8
Tupa, Tom, N.Y. Jets	11	6	54.5	165	15.00	2	18.2	65	0	0.0	3	30	139.2
Van Pelt, Alex, Buffalo	1	1	100.0	9	9.00	0	0.0	9	0	0.0	0	0	104.2
Walsh, Steve, Indianapolis	13	7	53.8	47	3.62	0	0.0	11	2	15.4	0	0	22.4
Warren, Lamont, New England	0	0	...	0	...	0	...	...	0	...	1	7	...
Wycheck, Frank, Tennessee	1	1	100.0	61	61.00	1	100.0	t61	0	0.0	0	0	158.3
Zolak, Scott, Miami	4	0	0.0	0	0.00	0	0.0	0	0	0.0	0	0	39.6

t—touchdown.

NFC

Player, Team	Att.	Comp.	Pct. Comp.	Yds.	Avg. Gain	TD	Pct. TD	Long	Int.	Pct. Int.	Sack	Yds. Lost	Rat. Pts.
Aikman, Troy, Dallas	442	263	59.5	2964	6.71	17	3.8	t90	12	2.7	19	130	81.1
Batch, Charlie, Detroit	270	151	55.9	1957	7.25	13	4.8	t74	7	2.6	36	186	84.1
Beuerlein, Steve, Carolina	571	343	60.1	4436	7.77	36	6.3	t88	15	2.6	50	280	94.6
Bono, Steve, Carolina	1	0	0.0	0	0.00	0	0.0	0	0	0.0	0	0	39.6
Brown, Dave, Arizona	169	84	49.7	944	5.59	2	1.2	71	6	3.6	18	130	55.9
Chandler, Chris, Atlanta	307	174	56.7	2339	7.62	16	5.2	t60	11	3.6	32	230	83.5
Collins, Kerry, N.Y. Giants	331	190	57.4	2318	7.00	8	2.4	t80	11	3.3	16	112	73.3
Conway, Brett, Washington	1	0	0.0	0	0.00	0	0.0	0	0	0.0	0	0	39.6
Cunningham, Randall, Minnesota	200	124	62.0	1475	7.38	8	4.0	t61	9	4.5	15	101	79.1
Delhomme, Jake, New Orleans	76	42	55.3	521	6.86	3	3.9	t51	5	6.6	6	42	62.4
Detmer, Koy, Philadelphia	29	10	34.5	181	6.24	3	10.3	t50	2	6.9	0	0	62.6
Dilfer, Trent, Tampa Bay	244	146	59.8	1619	6.64	11	4.5	t62	11	4.5	26	189	75.8
Faulk, Marshall, St. Louis	1	0	0.0	0	0.00	0	0.0	0	0	0.0	0	0	39.6
Favre, Brett, Green Bay	595	341	57.3	4091	6.88	22	3.7	t74	23	3.9	35	223	74.7
Frerotte, Gus, Detroit	288	175	60.8	2117	7.35	9	3.1	t77	7	2.4	28	202	83.6
Garcia, Jeff, San Francisco	375	225	60.0	2544	6.78	11	2.9	62	11	2.9	15	104	77.9
Garner, Charlie, San Francisco	0	0	...	0	...	0	...	...	0	...	1	8	...
Garrett, Jason, Dallas	64	32	50.0	314	4.91	3	4.7	t37	1	1.6	5	21	73.3
George, Jeff, Minnesota	329	191	58.1	2816	8.56	23	7.0	t80	12	3.6	28	228	94.2
Germaine, Joe, St. Louis	16	9	56.3	136	8.50	1	6.3	t63	2	12.5	3	23	65.6
Graham, Kent, N.Y. Giants	271	160	59.0	1697	6.26	9	3.3	56	9	3.3	26	184	74.6
Graziani, Tony, Atlanta	118	62	52.5	759	6.43	2	1.7	62	4	3.4	12	78	64.2
Greisen, Chris, Arizona	6	1	16.7	4	0.67	0	0.0	4	0	0.0	0	0	39.6
Hasselbeck, Matt, Green Bay	10	3	30.0	41	4.10	1	10.0	19	0	0.0	1	9	77.5
Hobert, Billy Joe, New Orleans	159	85	53.5	970	6.10	6	3.8	t90	6	3.8	11	79	68.9
Johnson, Brad, Washington	519	316	60.9	4005	7.72	24	4.6	t65	13	2.5	29	177	90.0
Justin, Paul, St. Louis	14	9	64.3	91	6.50	0	0.0	27	0	0.0	1	3	82.7
Kanell, Danny, Atlanta	84	42	50.0	593	7.06	4	4.8	52	4	4.8	5	37	69.2
King, Shaun, Tampa Bay	146	89	61.0	875	5.99	7	4.8	68	4	2.7	11	78	82.4
Lewis, Jeff, Carolina	3	2	66.7	11	3.67	0	0.0	12	0	0.0	1	6	72.9
Matthews, Shane, Chicago	275	167	60.7	1645	5.98	10	3.6	56	6	2.2	13	79	80.6
McNabb, Donovan, Philadelphia	216	106	49.1	948	4.39	8	3.7	t63	7	3.2	28	204	60.1
McNown, Cade, Chicago	235	127	54.0	1465	6.23	8	3.4	t80	10	4.3	18	94	66.7

1999 STATISTICS Passing

Player, Team	Att.	Comp.	Pct. Comp.	Yds.	Avg. Gain	TD	Pct. TD	Long	Int.	Pct. Int.	Sack	Yds. Lost	Rat. Pts.
Miller, Jim, Chicago	174	110	63.2	1242	7.14	7	4.0	t77	6	3.4	7	43	83.5
Moss, Randy, Minnesota	1	1	100.0	27	27.00	1	100.0	t27	0	0.0	0	0	158.3
Pederson, Doug, Philadelphia	227	119	52.4	1276	5.62	7	3.1	t84	9	4.0	20	109	62.9
Peete, Rodney, Washington	17	8	47.1	107	6.29	2	11.8	t30	1	5.9	2	9	82.2
Pittman, Michael, Arizona	1	1	100.0	26	26.00	0	0.0	26	0	0.0	0	0	118.8
Plummer, Jake, Arizona	381	201	52.8	2111	5.54	9	2.4	63	24	6.3	27	152	50.8
Rice, Jerry, San Francisco	1	0	0.0	0	0.00	0	0.0	0	0	0.0	0	0	39.6
Royals, Mark, Tampa Bay	2	1	50.0	17	8.50	0	0.0	17	0	0.0	0	0	79.2
Sanders, Deion, Dallas	1	0	0.0	0	0.00	0	0.0	0	0	0.0	0	0	39.6
Sanders, Frank, Arizona	1	0	0.0	0	0.00	0	0.0	0	0	0.0	0	0	39.6
Small, Torrance, Philadelphia	2	0	0.0	0	0.00	0	0.0	0	0	0.0	0	0	39.6
Smith, Lamar, New Orleans	1	0	0.0	0	0.00	0	0.0	0	0	0.0	0	0	39.6
Staley, Duce, Philadelphia	0	0	...	0	...	0	...	...	0	...	1	8	...
Stenstrom, Steve, San Francisco	100	54	54.0	536	5.36	0	0.0	32	4	4.0	10	66	52.8
Tolliver, Billy Joe, New Orleans	268	139	51.9	1916	7.15	7	2.6	57	16	6.0	19	152	58.9
Warner, Kurt, St. Louis	499	325	65.1	4353	8.72	41	8.2	t75	13	2.6	29	201	109.2
Williams, Ricky, New Orleans	1	0	0.0	0	0.00	0	0.0	0	0	0.0	0	0	39.6
Wuerffel, Danny, New Orleans	48	22	45.8	191	3.98	0	0.0	22	3	6.3	5	32	30.8
Young, Steve, San Francisco	84	45	53.6	446	5.31	3	3.6	53	4	4.8	8	63	60.9
Zeier, Eric, Tampa Bay	55	32	58.2	270	4.91	0	0.0	38	1	1.8	5	36	63.4

t—touchdown.

RECEIVING

INDIVIDUAL

BESTS OF THE SEASON

Receptions, season
AFC: 116—Jimmy Smith, Jacksonville.
NFC: 96—Muhsin Muhammad, Carolina.

Receptions, game
AFC: 14—Marvin Harrison, Indianapolis at Cleveland, Dec. 26 (138 yards) (0 TDs); Jimmy Smith, Jacksonville vs. Cincinnati, Jan. 2 (165 yards) (0 TDs).
NFC: 13—Bobby Engram, Chicago at St. Louis, Dec. 26 (143 yards) (2 TDs); Frank Sanders, Arizona at Green Bay, Jan. 2 (118 yards) (1 TD); Tiki Barber, N.Y. Giants at Dallas, Jan. 2 (100 yards) (0 TDs).

Yards, season
AFC: 1663—Marvin Harrison, Indianapolis.
NFC: 1413—Randy Moss, Minnesota.

Yards, game
AFC: 258—Qadry Ismail, Baltimore at Pittsburgh, Dec. 12 (6 receptions, 3 TDs).
NFC: 204—Randy Moss, Minnesota at Chicago, Nov. 14 (12 receptions, 0 TDs); Marshall Faulk, St. Louis vs. Chicago, Dec. 26 (12 receptions, 1 TD).

Longest gain
NFC: 90—Eddie Kennison (from Billy Joe Hobert), New Orleans vs. Atlanta, Oct. 10 (TD); Jason Tucker (from Troy Aikman), Dallas vs. N.Y. Giants, Jan. 2 (TD).
AFC: 88—Byron Chamberlain (from Brian Griese), Denver vs. Green Bay, Oct. 17.

Yards per reception, season
NFC: 20.9—Tim Dwight, Atlanta.
AFC: 17.5—Shawn Jefferson, New England.

Touchdowns, season
NFC: 13—Cris Carter, Minnesota.
AFC: 12—Marvin Harrison, Indianapolis.

Team leaders, receptions

AFC:
Baltimore	68	Qadry Ismail
Buffalo	65	Eric Moulds
Cincinnati	68	Darnay Scott
Cleveland	66	Kevin Johnson
Denver	79	Rod Smith
Indianapolis	115	Marvin Harrison
Jacksonville	116	Jimmy Smith
Kansas City	76	Tony Gonzalez
Miami	67	Tony Martin
New England	69	Terry Glenn
N.Y. Jets	89	Keyshawn Johnson
Oakland	90	Tim Brown
Pittsburgh	61	Troy Edwards / Hines Ward
San Diego	57	Jeff Graham
Seattle	62	Derrick Mayes
Tennessee	69	Frank Wycheck

NFC:
Arizona	79	Frank Sanders
Atlanta	81	Terance Mathis
Carolina	96	Muhsin Muhammad
Chicago	88	Bobby Engram
Dallas	80	Raghib Ismail
Detroit	81	Germane Crowell
Green Bay	74	Antonio Freeman / Bill Schroeder
Minnesota	90	Cris Carter
New Orleans	61	Eddie Kennison

NFC:
N.Y. Giants	79	Amani Toomer
Philadelphia	49	Torrance Small
St. Louis	87	Marshall Faulk
San Francisco	67	Jerry Rice
Tampa Bay	64	Warrick Dunn
Washington	69	Larry Centers

NFL LEADERS

Player, Team	No.	Yds.	Avg.	Long	TD
Smith, Jimmy, Jacksonville*	116	1636	14.1	62	6
Harrison, Marvin, Indianapolis*	115	1663	14.5	t57	12
Muhammad, Muhsin, Carolina	96	1253	13.1	t60	8
Brown, Tim, Oakland*	90	1344	14.9	47	6
Carter, Cris, Minnesota	90	1241	13.8	68	13
Johnson, Keyshawn, N.Y. Jets*	89	1170	13.1	65	8
Engram, Bobby, Chicago	88	947	10.8	56	4
Faulk, Marshall, St. Louis	87	1048	12.0	t57	5
Robinson, Marcus, Chicago	84	1400	16.7	t80	9
Crowell, Germane, Detroit	81	1338	16.5	t77	7
Mathis, Terance, Atlanta	81	1016	12.5	52	6
Moss, Randy, Minnesota	80	1413	17.7	t67	11
Morton, Johnnie, Detroit	80	1129	14.1	48	5
Ismail, Rocket, Dallas	80	1097	13.7	t76	6
Toomer, Amani, N.Y. Giants	79	1183	15.0	t80	6
Smith, Rod, Denver*	79	1020	12.9	71	4
Sanders, Frank, Arizona	79	954	12.1	63	1
McCardell, Keenan, Jacksonville*	78	891	11.4	49	5
Bruce, Isaac, St. Louis	77	1165	15.1	60	12
Gonzalez, Tony, Kansas City*	76	849	11.2	t73	11
Freeman, Antonio, Green Bay	74	1074	14.5	51	6
Schroeder, Bill, Green Bay	74	1051	14.2	51	5
Hilliard, Ike, N.Y. Giants	72	996	13.8	46	3
McCaffrey, Ed, Denver*	71	1018	14.3	t78	7
Levens, Dorsey, Green Bay	71	573	8.1	53	1
Glenn, Terry, New England*	69	1147	16.6	67	4
Wycheck, Frank, Tennessee*	69	641	9.3	35	2
Centers, Larry, Washington	69	544	7.9	t33	3
Ismail, Qadry, Baltimore*	68	1105	16.3	t76	6
Scott, Darnay, Cincinnati*	68	1022	15.0	t76	7

*AFC.
t—touchdown.
Leader based on most passes caught.

AFC

Player, Team	No.	Yds.	Avg.	Long	TD
Abdul-Jabbar, Karim, Mia.-Cle.	17	84	4.9	21	1
Alexander, Derrick, Kansas City	54	832	15.4	t86	2
Allen, Terry, New England	14	125	8.9	38	1
Anders, Kimble, Kansas City	2	14	7.0	9	0
Anderson, Richie, N.Y. Jets	29	302	10.4	29	3
Armour, Justin, Baltimore	37	538	14.5	t54	4
Avery, John, Denver	4	24	6.0	11	0
Ayanbadejo, Obafemi, Baltimore	1	2	2.0	2	0
Banks, Tavian, Jacksonville	14	137	9.8	38	0
Barlow, Reggie, Jacksonville	16	202	12.6	31	0
Bartrum, Mike, New England	1	1	1.0	t1	1
Basnight, Michael, Cincinnati	16	172	10.8	47	0
Battaglia, Marco, Cincinnati	14	153	10.9	30	0
Baxter, Fred, N.Y. Jets	8	66	8.3	24	2
Bennett, Donnell, Kansas City	10	41	4.1	12	0
Bettis, Jerome, Pittsburgh	21	110	5.2	17	0
Blackwell, Will, Pittsburgh	20	186	9.3	26	0
Bobo, Orlando, Cleveland	1	3	3.0	3	0
Bownes, Fabien, Seattle	4	68	17.0	t49	1
Brady, Kyle, Jacksonville	32	346	10.8	30	1

— 254 —

Player, Team	No.	Yds.	Avg.	Long	TD	Player, Team	No.	Yds.	Avg.	Long	TD
Brigham, Jeremy, Oakland	8	108	13.5	29	0	Howard, Chris, Jacksonville	1	8	8.0	8	0
Brisby, Vincent, New England	18	266	14.8	40	0	Huard, Damon, Miami	1	0	0.0	0	0
Brown, Reggie, Seattle	34	228	6.7	26	1	Hundon, James, Cincinnati	1	5	5.0	5	0
Brown, Tim, Oakland	90	1344	14.9	47	6	Huntley, Richard, Pittsburgh	27	253	9.4	25	3
Brown, Troy, New England	36	471	13.1	37	1	Ismail, Qadry, Baltimore	68	1105	16.3	t76	6
Bruener, Mark, Pittsburgh	18	176	9.8	29	0	Jackson, Sheldon, Buffalo	4	34	8.5	16	0
Bush, Steve, Cincinnati	1	4	4.0	4	0	Jackson, Willie, Cincinnati	31	369	11.9	29	2
Bynum, Kenny, San Diego	16	209	13.1	t80	2	Jacoby, Mitch, Kansas City	1	6	6.0	6	0
Byrd, Isaac, Tennessee	14	261	18.6	t65	2	Jacquet, Nate, Miami	1	18	18.0	18	0
Campbell, Mark, Cleveland	9	131	14.6	21	0	James, Edgerrin, Indianapolis	62	586	9.5	54	4
Carswell, Dwayne, Denver	24	201	8.4	20	2	Jefferson, Shawn, New England	40	698	17.5	t68	6
Carter, Ki-Jana, Cincinnati	3	24	8.0	11	0	Jett, James, Oakland	39	552	14.2	43	2
Carter, Tony, New England	20	108	5.4	20	0	Johnson, J.J., Miami	15	100	6.7	17	0
Chamberlain, Byron, Denver	32	488	15.3	88	2	Johnson, Kevin, Cleveland	66	986	14.9	t64	8
Chiaverini, Darrin, Cleveland	44	487	11.1	t28	4	Johnson, Keyshawn, N.Y. Jets	89	1170	13.1	65	8
Chrebet, Wayne, N.Y. Jets	48	631	13.1	t50	3	Johnson, Lonnie, Kansas City	10	98	9.8	19	1
Clark, Desmond, Denver	1	5	5.0	5	0	Johnson, Malcolm, Pittsburgh	2	23	11.5	18	0
Cloud, Mike, Kansas City	3	25	8.3	12	0	Johnson, Pat, Baltimore	29	526	18.1	t76	3
Coates, Ben, New England	32	370	11.6	27	2	Jones, Charlie, San Diego	10	90	9.0	t44	1
Collins, Bobby, Buffalo	9	124	13.8	45	2	Jones, Damon, Jacksonville	19	221	11.6	31	4
Collins, Cecil, Miami	6	32	5.3	12	0	Jones, Freddie, San Diego	56	670	12.0	36	2
Collins, Ryan, Baltimore	4	62	15.5	28	0	Jones, Isaac, Indianapolis	1	8	8.0	8	0
Cooper, Andre, Denver	9	98	10.9	21	0	Jordan, Randy, Oakland	8	82	10.3	30	0
Crockett, Zack, Oakland	8	56	7.0	t12	1	Kaufman, Napoleon, Oakland	18	181	10.1	50	1
Cushing, Matt, Pittsburgh	2	29	14.5	22	0	Kent, Joey, Tennessee	3	42	14.0	25	0
Davis, Billy, Baltimore	6	121	20.2	73	0	Kirby, Terry, Cleveland	58	528	9.1	t78	3
Davis, Reggie, San Diego	12	137	11.4	46	1	Konrad, Rob, Miami	34	251	7.4	25	1
Davis, Terrell, Denver	3	26	8.7	10	0	Lewis, Jermaine, Baltimore	25	281	11.2	46	2
Davis, Zola, Cleveland	2	38	19.0	25	0	Linton, Jonathan, Buffalo	29	228	7.9	28	1
Dawkins, Sean, Seattle	58	992	17.1	t45	7	Lockett, Kevin, Kansas City	34	426	12.5	t39	2
DeLong, Greg, Baltimore	13	52	4.0	9	1	Loud, Kamil, Buffalo	6	66	11.0	20	0
Denson, Autry, Miami	4	28	7.0	10	0	Loville, Derek, Denver	11	50	4.5	15	0
Dilger, Ken, Indianapolis	40	479	12.0	30	2	Lyons, Mitch, Pittsburgh	8	81	10.1	25	0
Dillon, Corey, Cincinnati	31	290	9.4	23	1	Martin, Curtis, N.Y. Jets	45	259	5.8	34	0
Doering, Chris, Denver	3	22	7.3	9	0	Martin, Tony, Miami	67	1037	15.5	t69	5
Drayton, Troy, Miami	32	299	9.3	26	1	Mason, Derrick, Tennessee	8	89	11.1	31	0
Dudley, Rickey, Oakland	39	555	14.2	35	9	Mayes, Derrick, Seattle	62	829	13.4	t43	10
Dunn, David, Cleveland	1	4	4.0	4	0	McCaffrey, Ed, Denver	71	1018	14.3	t78	7
Dyson, Andre, Tennessee	54	658	12.2	t47	4	McCardell, Keenan, Jacksonville	78	891	11.4	49	5
Early, Quinn, N.Y. Jets	6	83	13.8	24	0	McCrary, Fred, San Diego	37	201	5.4	38	1
Edwards, Marc, Cleveland	27	212	7.9	t27	2	McDuffie, O.J., Miami	43	516	12.0	34	2
Edwards, Troy, Pittsburgh	61	714	11.7	41	5	McGee, Tony, Cincinnati	26	344	13.2	35	2
Elias, Keith, Indianapolis	4	16	4.0	7	0	McGriff, Travis, Denver	3	37	12.3	15	0
Ellison, Jerry, New England	4	50	12.5	23	0	McKenzie, Kevin, Miami	2	18	9.0	13	0
Evans, Chuck, Baltimore	32	235	7.3	27	1	Means, Natrone, San Diego	9	51	5.7	t12	1
Faulk, Kevin, New England	12	98	8.2	19	1	Mickens, Terry, Oakland	20	261	13.1	30	0
Fauria, Christian, Seattle	35	376	10.7	25	0	Mili, Itula, Seattle	5	28	5.6	8	1
Fletcher, Terrell, San Diego	45	360	8.0	25	0	Miller, Billy, Denver	5	59	11.8	26	0
Floyd, Chris, New England	2	16	8.0	11	0	Morris, Bam, Kansas City	7	37	5.3	9	0
Gadsden, Oronde, Miami	48	803	16.7	62	6	Moulds, Eric, Buffalo	65	994	15.3	t54	7
Galloway, Joey, Seattle	22	335	15.2	48	1	Neal, Lorenzo, Tennessee	7	27	3.9	8	2
Gannon, Rich, Oakland	1	-3	-3.0	-3	0	Ofodile, A.J., Baltimore	4	25	6.3	9	0
Gary, Olandis, Denver	21	159	7.6	21	0	Parmalee, Bernie, N.Y. Jets	15	113	7.5	23	0
Gash, Sam, Buffalo	20	163	8.2	t31	2	Pathon, Jerome, Indianapolis	14	163	11.6	38	0
George, Eddie, Tennessee	47	458	9.7	t54	4	Penn, Chris, San Diego	17	257	15.1	43	1
Glenn, Terry, New England	69	1147	16.6	67	4	Perry, Ed, Miami	3	8	2.7	5	1
Gonzalez, Tony, Kansas City	76	849	11.2	t73	11	Pickens, Carl, Cincinnati	57	737	12.9	t75	6
Goodwin, Hunter, Miami	8	55	6.9	14	0	Pierce, Aaron, Baltimore	11	102	9.3	26	0
Graham, Jeff, San Diego	57	968	17.0	54	2	Pollard, Marcus, Indianapolis	34	374	11.0	33	4
Green, E.G., Indianapolis	21	287	13.7	50	0	Powell, Ronnie, Cleveland	1	45	45.0	45	0
Green, Eric, N.Y. Jets	7	37	5.3	t10	2	Price, Peerless, Buffalo	31	393	12.7	45	3
Green, Yatil, Miami	18	234	13.0	27	0	Pritchard, Mike, Seattle	26	375	14.4	51	2
Greene, Scott, Indianapolis	1	4	4.0	4	0	Pritchett, Stanley, Miami	43	312	7.3	30	4
Griffin, Damon, Cincinnati	12	112	9.3	20	0	Pupunu, Alfred, San Diego	4	17	4.3	11	0
Griffith, Howard, Denver	26	192	7.4	20	1	Purnell, Lovett, Baltimore	2	10	5.0	5	0
Groce, Clif, Cincinnati	25	154	6.2	14	0	Reed, Andre, Buffalo	52	536	10.3	30	1
Harris, Jackie, Tennessee	26	297	11.4	t62	1	Reed, Robert, San Diego	1	1	1.0	1	0
Harrison, Marvin, Indianapolis	115	1663	14.5	t57	12	Rhett, Errict, Baltimore	24	169	7.0	t20	2
Hawkins, Courtney, Pittsburgh	30	285	9.5	23	0	Richardson, Tony, Kansas City	24	141	5.9	29	0
Hicks, Robert, Buffalo	1	-6	-6.0	-6	0	Ricks, Mikhael, San Diego	40	429	10.7	50	0
Holmes, Priest, Baltimore	13	104	8.0	t34	1	Riemersma, Jay, Buffalo	37	496	13.4	38	4
Horn, Joe, Kansas City	35	586	16.7	t76	6	Rison, Andre, Kansas City	21	218	10.4	20	0

1999 STATISTICS Receiving

Player, Team	No.	Yds.	Avg.	Long	TD
Ritchie, Jon, Oakland	45	408	9.1	t20	1
Roan, Michael, Tennessee	9	93	10.3	t24	3
Rutledge, Rod, New England	7	66	9.4	13	0
Sanders, Chris, Tennessee	20	336	16.8	t48	1
Scott, Darnay, Cincinnati	68	1022	15.0	t76	7
Seau, Junior, San Diego	2	8	4.0	6	0
Sharpe, Shannon, Denver	23	224	9.7	24	0
Shaw, Bobby, Pittsburgh	28	387	13.8	49	3
Shaw, Harold, New England	2	31	15.5	29	0
Shaw, Sedrick, Cle.-Cin.	3	4	1.3	7	0
Shehee, Rashaan, Kansas City	18	136	7.6	17	0
Shelton, Daimon, Jacksonville	12	87	7.3	13	0
Shepherd, Leslie, Cleveland	23	274	11.9	36	0
Shields, Paul, Indianapolis	4	37	9.3	21	0
Simmons, Tony, New England	19	276	14.5	t58	2
Smith, Akili, Cincinnati	1	6	6.0	6	0
Smith, Antowain, Buffalo	2	32	16.0	23	0
Smith, Detron, Denver	4	23	5.8	11	0
Smith, Irv, Cleveland	24	222	9.3	22	1
Smith, Jimmy, Jacksonville	116	1636	14.1	62	6
Smith, Rod, Denver	79	1020	12.9	71	4
Spence, Blake, N.Y. Jets	3	15	5.0	9	1
Stephens, Tremayne, San Diego	18	133	7.4	22	1
Stewart, James, Jacksonville	21	108	5.1	19	0
Stewart, Kordell, Pittsburgh	9	113	12.6	28	1
Stokley, Brandon, Baltimore	1	28	28.0	t28	1
Strong, Mack, Seattle	1	5	5.0	5	0
Taylor, Fred, Jacksonville	10	83	8.3	41	0
Thigpen, Yancey, Tennessee	38	648	17.1	35	4
Thomas, Rodney, Tennessee	9	72	8.0	26	0
Thomas, Thurman, Buffalo	3	37	12.3	t23	1
Walker, Derrick, Oakland	7	71	10.1	t21	1
Ward, Dedric, N.Y. Jets	22	325	14.8	t56	3
Ward, Hines, Pittsburgh	61	638	10.5	42	7
Warren, Lamont, New England	29	262	9.0	21	1
Watters, Ricky, Seattle	40	387	9.7	25	2
Wheatley, Tyrone, Oakland	21	196	9.3	28	3
Wiegert, Zach, Jacksonville	1	-3	-3.0	-3	0
Wilkins, Terrence, Indianapolis	42	565	13.5	t80	4
Williams, Jermaine, Oakland	1	20	20.0	20	0
Williams, Kevin, Buffalo	31	381	12.3	35	0
Williams, Nick, Cincinnati	10	96	9.6	19	0
Witman, Jon, Pittsburgh	12	106	8.8	38	0
Woodson, Charles, Oakland	1	19	19.0	19	0
Wycheck, Frank, Tennessee	69	641	9.3	35	2
Yeast, Craig, Cincinnati	3	20	6.7	8	0
Zereoue, Amos, Pittsburgh	2	17	8.5	14	0

*Includes both NFC and AFC statistics.
t—touchdown.

NFC

Player, Team	No.	Yds.	Avg.	Long	TD
Abdullah, Rabih, Tampa Bay	2	11	5.5	8	0
Alexander, Stephen, Washington	29	324	11.2	t27	3
Alford, Brian, N.Y. Giants	1	7	7.0	t7	1
Allen, James, Chicago	9	91	10.1	17	0
Allred, John, Chicago	13	102	7.8	26	1
Alstott, Mike, Tampa Bay	27	239	8.9	24	2
Anderson, Jamal, Atlanta	2	34	17.0	32	0
Anthony, Reidel, Tampa Bay	30	296	9.9	30	1
Baker, Eugene, Atlanta	7	118	16.9	36	0
Barber, Tiki, N.Y. Giants	66	609	9.2	56	2
Bates, D'Wayne, Chicago	2	19	9.5	11	0
Bates, Mario, Arizona	5	34	6.8	18	0
Bates, Michael, Carolina	1	2	2.0	2	0
Beasley, Fred, San Francisco	32	282	8.8	24	0
Bech, Brett, New Orleans	4	65	16.3	t23	1
Bennett, Edgar, Chicago	14	116	8.3	34	0
Bennett, Sean, N.Y. Giants	4	27	6.8	16	0
Biakabutuka, Tim, Carolina	23	189	8.2	32	0
Bieniemy, Eric, Philadelphia	2	28	14.0	27	0
Bjornson, Eric, Dallas	10	131	13.1	32	0
Booker, Marty, Chicago	19	219	11.5	t57	3
Bostic, James, Philadelphia	5	8	1.6	7	0
Boston, David, Arizona	40	473	11.8	43	2
Bradford, Corey, Green Bay	37	637	17.2	t74	5
Brazzell, Chris, Dallas	5	114	22.8	53	0
Brooks, Macey, Chicago	14	160	11.4	30	0
Broughton, Luther, Philadelphia	26	295	11.3	33	4
Brown, Gary, N.Y. Giants	2	2	1.0	1	0
Brown, Na, Philadelphia	18	188	10.4	27	1
Bruce, Isaac, St. Louis	77	1165	15.1	60	12
Calloway, Chris, Atlanta	22	314	14.3	33	1
Carruth, Rae, Carolina	14	200	14.3	43	0
Carter, Cris, Minnesota	90	1241	13.8	68	13
Centers, Larry, Washington	69	544	7.9	t33	3
Chmura, Mark, Green Bay	5	55	11.0	16	0
Christian, Bob, Atlanta	40	354	8.9	36	0
Chryplewicz, Pete, Detroit	2	18	9.0	13	0
Clark, Greg J., San Francisco	34	347	10.2	24	0
Cleeland, Cameron, New Orleans	26	325	12.5	31	1
Cline, Tony, San Francisco	4	45	11.3	30	0
Cody, Mac, Arizona	6	60	10.0	16	1
Comella, Greg, N.Y. Giants	8	39	4.9	26	0
Connell, Albert, Washington	62	1132	18.3	t62	7
Conway, Curtis, Chicago	44	426	9.7	t30	4
Conwell, Ernie, St. Louis	1	11	11.0	11	0
Craver, Aaron, New Orleans	19	154	8.1	29	0
Crawford, Keith, Green Bay	1	14	14.0	14	0
Cross, Howard, N.Y. Giants	9	55	6.1	12	0
Crowell, Germane, Detroit	81	1338	16.5	t77	7
Crumpler, Carlester, Minnesota	2	35	17.5	t31	1
Davis, John, Tampa Bay	2	7	3.5	6	1
Davis, Stephen, Washington	23	111	4.8	21	0
Davis, Troy, New Orleans	7	53	7.6	20	0
Davis, Tyrone, Green Bay	20	204	10.2	33	2
Dawsey, Lawrence, New Orleans	16	196	12.3	57	0
Douglas, Dameane, Philadelphia	8	79	9.9	t29	1
Driver, Donald, Green Bay	3	31	10.3	12	1
Dunn, Warrick, Tampa Bay	64	589	9.2	68	2
Dwight, Tim, Atlanta	32	669	20.9	t60	7
Emanuel, Bert, Tampa Bay	22	238	10.8	39	1
Engram, Bobby, Chicago	88	947	10.8	56	4
Enis, Curtis, Chicago	45	340	7.6	28	2
Fann, Chad, San Francisco	2	8	4.0	6	0
Faulk, Marshall, St. Louis	87	1048	12.0	t57	5
Finneran, Brian, Philadelphia	2	21	10.5	11	0
Floyd, William, Carolina	21	179	8.5	25	0
Franklin, P.J., New Orleans	2	13	6.5	8	0
Freeman, Antonio, Green Bay	74	1074	14.5	51	6
Fryar, Irving, Washington	26	254	9.8	t30	2
Garner, Charlie, San Francisco	56	535	9.6	53	2
German, Jammi, Atlanta	12	219	18.3	62	3
Glover, Andrew, Minnesota	28	327	11.7	31	1
Graham, Kent, N.Y. Giants	1	-1	-1.0	-1	0
Green, Jacquez, Tampa Bay	56	791	14.1	t62	3
Hakim, Az-Zahir, St. Louis	36	677	18.8	t75	8
Hall, Lamont, Green Bay	3	33	11.0	13	0
Hallock, Ty, Chicago	6	22	3.7	7	0
Hanspard, Byron, Atlanta	10	93	9.3	34	0
Hape, Patrick, Tampa Bay	5	12	2.4	4	1
Hardy, Terry, Arizona	30	222	7.4	23	0
Harris, Mark, San Francisco	6	66	11.0	33	0
Harris, Ronnie, Atlanta	10	164	16.4	24	0
Hastings, Andre, New Orleans	40	564	14.1	42	1
Hatchette, Matthew, Minnesota	9	180	20.0	t80	2
Hayes, Donald, Carolina	11	270	24.5	t56	2
Henderson, William, Green Bay	30	203	6.8	22	1
Hicks, Skip, Washington	8	72	9.0	25	0
Hill, Greg, Detroit	13	77	5.9	15	0
Hilliard, Ike, N.Y. Giants	72	996	13.8	46	3
Hoard, Leroy, Minnesota	17	166	9.8	29	0
Hodgins, James, St. Louis	6	35	5.8	10	0

– 256 –

Player, Team	No.	Yds.	Avg.	Long	TD
Holcombe, Robert, St. Louis	14	163	11.6	30	1
Holt, Torry, St. Louis	52	788	15.2	t63	6
Irvin, Michael, Dallas	10	167	16.7	t37	3
Irvin, Sedrick, Detroit	25	233	9.3	31	0
Ismail, Rocket, Dallas	80	1097	13.7	t76	6
Jackson, Terry, San Francisco	3	6	2.0	4	0
Jeffers, Patrick, Carolina	63	1082	17.2	t88	12
Jells, Dietrich, Philadelphia	10	180	18.0	t57	2
Jenkins, James, Washington	1	30	30.0	30	0
Jervey, Travis, San Francisco	1	2	2.0	2	0
Johnson, Anthony, Carolina	13	103	7.9	22	0
Johnson, Charles, Philadelphia	34	414	12.2	36	1
Johnson, LeShon, N.Y. Giants	12	86	7.2	28	1
Johnston, Daryl, Dallas	1	4	4.0	4	0
Jordan, Andrew, Minnesota	5	40	8.0	11	1
Jordan, Charles, Sea.-G.B.*	3	60	20.0	43	0
Jurevicius, Joe, N.Y. Giants	18	318	17.7	71	1
Kelly, Reggie, Atlanta	8	146	18.3	50	0
Kennison, Eddie, New Orleans	61	835	13.7	t90	4
Kinchen, Brian, Carolina	5	45	9.0	t26	2
Kleinsasser, Jim, Minnesota	6	13	2.2	11	0
Kozlowski, Brian, Atlanta	11	122	11.1	26	2
LaFleur, David, Dallas	35	322	9.2	25	7
Lane, Fred, Carolina	23	163	7.1	23	0
Lee, Amp, St. Louis	3	22	7.3	t15	1
Lester, Tim, Dallas	2	9	4.5	6	0
Levens, Dorsey, Green Bay	71	573	8.1	53	1
Lewis, Chad, St.L.-Phi.	8	88	11.0	21	3
Lucky, Mike, Dallas	5	25	5.0	8	0
Makovicka, Joel, Arizona	10	70	7.0	15	1
Mangum, Kris, Carolina	1	6	6.0	6	0
Martin, Cecil, Philadelphia	11	22	2.0	9	0
Mathis, Terance, Atlanta	81	1016	12.5	52	6
Mayes, Alonzo, Chicago	8	82	10.3	24	1
McCullough, Andy, Arizona	3	45	15.0	31	0
McDonald, Darnell, Tampa Bay	9	96	10.7	23	1
McGarity, Wane, Dallas	7	70	10.0	18	0
McKinley, Dennis, Arizona	1	4	4.0	4	0
McLeod, Kevin, Tampa Bay	2	5	2.5	t3	1
McNabb, Donovan, Philadelphia	1	-6	-6.0	-6	0
McWilliams, Johnny, Arizona	11	71	6.5	11	1
Metcalf, Eric, Carolina	11	133	12.1	33	0
Milburn, Glyn, Chicago	20	151	7.6	22	0
Mills, Ernie, Dallas	30	325	10.8	36	0
Mills, John Henry, Minnesota	3	30	10.0	14	0
Mitchell, Basil, Green Bay	6	48	8.0	20	0
Mitchell, Brian, Washington	31	305	9.8	36	0
Mitchell, Pete, N.Y. Giants	58	520	9.0	25	3
Monroe, Rodrick, Atlanta	1	8	8.0	8	0
Moore, Dave, Tampa Bay	23	276	12.0	t35	5
Moore, Herman, Detroit	16	197	12.3	26	2
Moore, Rob, Arizona	37	621	16.8	71	5
Morton, Johnnie, Detroit	80	1129	14.1	48	5
Moss, Randy, Minnesota	80	1413	17.7	t67	11
Muhammad, Muhsin, Carolina	96	1253	13.1	t60	8
Murphy, Yo, Tampa Bay	4	28	7.0	9	0
Murrell, Adrian, Arizona	49	335	6.8	23	0
Ogden, Jeff, Dallas	12	144	12.0	25	0
Oliver, Winslow, Atlanta	8	74	9.3	14	0
Olivo, Brock, Detroit	4	24	6.0	12	0
Owens, Terrell, San Francisco	60	754	12.6	36	4
Oxendine, Ken, Atlanta	17	172	10.1	32	1
Palmer, David, Minnesota	4	25	6.3	13	0
Parker, De'Mond, Green Bay	4	15	3.8	7	0
Patten, David, N.Y. Giants	9	115	12.8	19	0
Perry, Wilmont, New Orleans	4	26	6.5	11	0
Phillips, Lawrence, San Francisco	15	152	10.1	47	0
Philyaw, Dino, New Orleans	2	23	11.5	14	0

Player, Team	No.	Yds.	Avg.	Long	TD
Pittman, Michael, Arizona	16	196	12.3	46	0
Poole, Keith, New Orleans	42	796	19.0	t67	6
Proehl, Ricky, St. Louis	33	349	10.6	30	0
Rasby, Walter, Detroit	3	19	6.3	13	1
Reed, Jake, Minnesota	44	643	14.6	50	2
Rice, Jerry, San Francisco	67	830	12.4	62	5
Rivers, Ron, Detroit	22	173	7.9	t31	1
Robinson, Damien, Tampa Bay	1	17	17.0	17	0
Robinson, Jeff, St. Louis	6	76	12.7	30	2
Robinson, Marcus, Chicago	84	1400	16.7	t80	9
Sanders, Deion, Dallas	4	24	6.0	9	0
Sanders, Frank, Arizona	79	954	12.1	63	1
Santiago, O.J., Atlanta	15	174	11.6	46	0
Schlesinger, Cory, Detroit	21	151	7.2	25	1
Schroeder, Bill, Green Bay	74	1051	14.2	51	5
Sellers, Mike, Washington	7	105	15.0	t33	2
Sloan, David, Detroit	47	591	12.6	t74	4
Slutzker, Scott, New Orleans	11	164	14.9	42	1
Small, Torrance, Philadelphia	49	655	13.4	t84	4
Smith, Emmitt, Dallas	27	119	4.4	t14	2
Smith, Lamar, New Orleans	20	151	7.6	26	1
Smith, Robert, Minnesota	24	166	6.9	34	0
Smith, Troy, Philadelphia	1	14	14.0	14	0
Stablein, Brian, Detroit	11	119	10.8	42	1
Staley, Duce, Philadelphia	41	294	7.2	19	2
Stenstrom, Steve, San Francisco	1	9	9.0	9	0
Still, Bryan, S.D.-Atl.*	10	110	11.0	28	0
Stokes, J.J., San Francisco	34	429	12.6	47	3
Streets, Tai, San Francisco	2	25	12.5	14	0
Tate, Robert, Minnesota	1	3	3.0	3	0
Thomas, Chris, St. Louis	1	6	6.0	6	0
Thomas, Robert, Dallas	10	64	6.4	13	0
Thomason, Jeff, Green Bay	14	140	10.0	22	2
Thrash, James, Washington	3	44	14.7	25	0
Toomer, Amani, N.Y. Giants	79	1183	15.0	t80	6
Tucker, Jason, Dallas	23	439	19.1	t90	2
Tucker, Ryan, St. Louis	1	2	2.0	t2	1
Turner, Kevin, Philadelphia	9	46	5.1	14	0
Uwaezuoke, Iheanyi, Detroit	1	5	5.0	5	0
Vardell, Tommy, San Francisco	7	36	5.1	11	0
Walls, Wesley, Carolina	63	822	13.0	t37	12
Walsh, Chris, Minnesota	2	24	12.0	t18	1
Warren, Chris, Dallas	34	224	6.6	24	0
Way, Charles, N.Y. Giants	11	59	5.4	16	0
Weaver, Jed, Philadelphia	11	91	8.3	14	0
Westbrook, Michael, Washington	65	1191	18.3	t65	9
Wetnight, Ryan, Chicago	38	277	7.3	22	1
Wilcox, Josh, New Orleans	6	61	10.2	19	0
Williams, Karl, Tampa Bay	21	176	8.4	14	0
Williams, Moe, Minnesota	1	12	12.0	12	0
Williams, Ricky, New Orleans	28	172	6.1	29	0
Williams, Roland, St. Louis	25	226	9.0	24	6

*Includes both NFC and AFC statistics.
t—touchdown.

PLAYERS WITH TWO CLUBS

Player, Team	No.	Yds.	Avg.	Long	TD
Abdul-Jabbar, Karim, Miami	4	25	6.3	14	0
Abdul-Jabbar, Karim, Cleveland	13	59	4.5	21	1
Jordan, Charles, Seattle	1	6	6.0	6	0
Jordan, Charles, Green Bay	2	54	27.0	43	0
Lewis, Chad, St. Louis	1	12	12.0	12	0
Lewis, Chad, Philadelphia	7	76	10.9	21	3
Shaw, Sedrick, Cleveland	2	8	4.0	7	0
Shaw, Sedrick, Cincinnati	1	-4	-4.0	-4	0
Still, Bryan, San Diego	8	96	12.0	28	0
Still, Bryan, Atlanta	2	14	7.0	10	0

SCORING

TEAM

AFC

Team	Total TD	TD Rush	TD Pass	TD Misc.	XP	2Pt.	XPA	FG	FGA	Safeties	Total Pts.
Indianapolis	46	15	26	5	43	1	43	34	38	0	423
Jacksonville	42	20	16	6	37	4	37	31	38	3	396
Tennessee	46	19	23	4	43	1	43	21	25	4	392
Kansas City	47	14	22	11	45	0	45	21	28	0	390
Oakland	45	18	24	3	43	1	43	25	38	0	390
Seattle	34	5	25	4	32	0	32	34	40	0	338
Miami	30	8	20	2	27	0	27	39	46	1	326
Baltimore	34	9	21	4	32	1	32	28	33	1	324
Buffalo	35	12	21	2	33	1	33	25	34	0	320
Pittsburgh	35	14	19	2	30	1	31	25	29	0	317
Denver	32	13	16	3	29	1	29	29	36	2	314
N.Y. Jets	33	7	22	4	27	0	29	27	33	1	308
New England	32	9	19	4	29	0	30	26	33	0	299
Cincinnati	33	11	18	4	27	2	27	18	27	0	283
San Diego	25	10	12	3	22	1	23	31	36	1	269
Cleveland	28	9	19	0	23	1	24	8	12	0	217
AFC total	577	193	323	61	522	15	528	422	526	13	5306
AFC average	36.1	12.1	20.2	3.8	32.6	0.9	33.0	26.4	32.9	0.8	331.6

NFC

Team	Total TD	TD Rush	TD Pass	TD Misc.	XP	2Pt.	XPA	FG	FGA	Safeties	Total Pts.
St. Louis	66	13	42	11	64	2	64	20	28	1	526
Washington	54	23	26	5	49	2	50	22	32	0	443
Carolina	50	12	36	2	46	0	47	25	28	0	421
Minnesota	49	13	32	4	46	0	46	19	30	1	399
Green Bay	40	13	23	4	38	1	38	25	30	1	357
Dallas	42	16	20	6	41	0	41	19	31	1	352
Detroit	35	8	22	5	28	2	29	26	32	1	322
N.Y. Giants	32	11	17	4	28	2	28	25	30	0	299
San Francisco	33	14	14	5	30	1	31	21	23	1	295
Atlanta	34	9	22	3	34	0	34	15	21	1	285
Chicago	31	4	25	2	27	1	28	19	34	0	272
Philadelphia	29	5	18	6	27	2	27	21	31	2	272
Tampa Bay	27	7	18	2	25	0	25	27	32	1	270
New Orleans	27	9	16	2	20	3	21	24	29	0	260
Arizona	27	13	11	3	26	0	26	19	27	0	245
NFC total	576	170	342	64	529	16	535	327	438	10	5018
NFC average	38.4	11.3	22.8	4.3	35.3	1.1	35.7	21.8	29.2	0.7	334.5
NFL total	1153	363	665	125	1051	31	1063	749	964	23	10324
NFL average	37.2	11.7	21.5	4.0	33.9	1.0	34.3	24.2	31.1	0.7	333.0

INDIVIDUAL

BESTS OF THE SEASON

Points, season
AFC: 145—Mike Vanderjagt, Indianapolis.
NFC: 124—Jeff Wilkins, St. Louis.

Touchdowns, season
AFC: 17—Edgerrin James, Indianapolis.
NFC: 17—Stephen Davis, Washington.

Extra points, season
NFC: 64—Jeff Wilkins, St. Louis.
AFC: 45—Pete Stoyanovich, Kansas City.

Field goals, season
AFC: 39—Olindo Mare, Miami.
NFC: 27—Martin Gramatica, Tampa Bay.

Field goal attempts, season
AFC: 46—Olindo Mare, Miami.
NFC: 32—Brett Conway, Washington; Martin Gramatica, Tampa Bay; Jason Hanson, Detroit.

Longest field goal
AFC: 55—Jason Elam, Denver at San Diego, Nov. 7.
NFC: 53—David Akers, Philadelphia at Miami, Oct. 24; Martin Gramatica, Tampa Bay vs. Atlanta, Nov. 21.

Most points, game
NFC: 24—Az-Zahir Hakim, St. Louis at Cincinnati, Oct. 3 (4 TDs); Isaac Bruce, St. Louis vs. San Francisco, Oct. 10 (4 TDs); Dorsey Levens, Green Bay vs. Arizona, Jan. 2 (4 TDs).
AFC: 19—Olindo Mare, Miami at New England, Oct. 17 (6 FGs, 1 XP).

Team leaders, points
AFC:

Baltimore	116	Matt Stover
Buffalo	108	Steve Christie
Cincinnati	81	Doug Pelfrey
Cleveland	54	Terry Kirby
Denver	116	Jason Elam
Indianapolis	145	Mike Vanderjagt

AFC:

Team	Pts
Jacksonville	130
Kansas City	108
Miami	144
New England	107
N.Y. Jets	108
Oakland	90
Pittsburgh	105
San Diego	115
Seattle	134
Tennessee	106

NFC:

Team	Pts
Arizona	83
Atlanta	79
Carolina	99
Chicago	54
Dallas	78
Detroit	106
Green Bay	113
Minnesota	103
New Orleans	92
N.Y. Giants	73
Philadelphia	79
St. Louis	124
San Francisco	93
Tampa Bay	106
Washington	115

Mike Hollis
Pete Stoyanovich
Olindo Mare
Adam Vinatieri
John Hall
Michael Husted
Kris Brown
John Carney
Todd Peterson
Al Del Greco
Chris Jacke
Morten Andersen
John Kasay
Marcus Robinson
Emmitt Smith
Jason Hanson
Ryan Longwell
Gary Anderson
Doug Brien
Cary Blanchard
Norm Johnson
Jeff Wilkins
Wade Richey
Martin Gramatica
Brett Conway

NFL LEADERS

KICKERS

Player, Team	XPM	XPA	FGM	FGA	Tot. Pts.
Vanderjagt, Mike, Indianapolis*	43	43	34	38	145
Mare, Olindo, Miami*	27	27	39	46	144
Peterson, Todd, Seattle*	32	32	34	40	134
Hollis, Mike, Jacksonville*	37	37	31	38	130
Wilkins, Jeff, St. Louis	64	64	20	28	124
Stover, Matt, Baltimore*	32	32	28	33	116
Elam, Jason, Denver*	29	29	29	36	116
Carney, John, San Diego*	22	23	31	36	115
Conway, Brett, Washington	49	50	22	32	115
Longwell, Ryan, Green Bay	38	38	25	30	113
Stoyanovich, Pete, Kansas City*	45	45	21	28	108
Christie, Steve, Buffalo*	33	33	25	34	108
Hall, John, N.Y. Jets*	27	29	27	33	108
Vinatieri, Adam, New England*	29	30	26	33	107
Del Greco, Al, Tennessee*	43	43	21	25	106
Hanson, Jason, Detroit	28	29	26	32	106
Gramatica, Martin, Tampa Bay	25	25	27	32	106
Brown, Kris, Pittsburgh*	30	31	25	29	105
Anderson, Gary, Minnesota	46	46	19	30	103
Kasay, John, Carolina	33	33	22	25	99

*AFC.

NON-KICKERS

Player, Team	TD	RTD	PTD	MTD	2Pt.	Tot. Pts.
Davis, Stephen, Washington	17	17	0	0	1	104
James, Edgerrin, Ind.*	17	13	4	0	0	102
Carter, Cris, Minnesota	13	0	13	0	0	78
Smith, Emmitt, Dallas	13	11	2	0	0	78
Stewart, James, Jac.*	13	13	0	0	0	78
George, Eddie, Tennessee*	13	9	4	0	0	78
Faulk, Marshall, St. Louis	12	7	5	0	1	74
Bruce, Isaac, St. Louis	12	0	12	0	1	74
Harrison, Marvin, Ind.*	12	0	12	0	1	74
Walls, Wesley, Carolina	12	0	12	0	0	72
Jeffers, Patrick, Carolina	12	0	12	0	0	72
Moss, Randy, Minnesota	12	0	11	1	0	72
Wheatley, Tyrone, Oakland*	11	8	3	0	0	66
Gonzalez, Tony, Kansas City*	11	0	11	0	0	66

Player, Team	TD	RTD	PTD	MTD	2Pt.	Tot. Pts.
Hoard, Leroy, Minnesota	10	10	0	0	0	60
Levens, Dorsey, Green Bay	10	9	1	0	0	60
Mayes, Derrick, Seattle*	10	0	10	0	0	60
Westbrook, Michael, Was.	9	0	9	0	1	56
Allen, Terry, New England*	9	8	1	0	0	54
Kirby, Terry, Cleveland*	9	6	3	0	0	54
Bates, Mario, Arizona	9	9	0	0	0	54
Alstott, Mike, Tampa Bay	9	7	2	0	0	54
Dudley, Rickey, Oakland*	9	0	9	0	0	54
Robinson, Marcus, Chicago	9	0	9	0	0	54
Hakim, Az-zahir, St. Louis	9	0	8	1	0	54
Dwight, Tim, Atlanta	9	1	7	1	0	54
Bennett, Donnell, K.C.*	8	8	0	0	0	48
McNair, Steve, Tennessee*	8	8	0	0	0	48
Johnson, Keyshawn, NYJ*	8	0	8	0	0	48
Muhammad, Muhsin, Car.	8	0	8	0	0	48

*AFC.

AFC

KICKERS

Player, Team	XPM	XPA	FGM	FGA	Tot. Pts.
Brown, Kris, Pittsburgh	30	31	25	29	105
Carney, John, San Diego	22	23	31	36	115
Christie, Steve, Buffalo	33	33	25	34	108
Dawson, Phil, Cleveland	23	24	8	12	‡47
Del Greco, Al, Tennessee	43	43	21	25	106
Elam, Jason, Denver	29	29	29	36	116
Hall, John, N.Y. Jets	27	29	27	33	108
Hollis, Mike, Jacksonville	37	37	31	38	130
Husted, Michael, Oakland	30	30	20	31	90
Mare, Olindo, Miami	27	27	39	46	144
Nedney, Joe, Oakland	13	13	5	7	28
Pelfrey, Doug, Cincinnati	27	27	18	27	81
Peterson, Todd, Seattle	32	32	34	40	134
Stover, Matt, Baltimore	32	32	28	33	116
Stoyanovich, Pete, Kansas City	45	45	21	28	108
Vanderjagt, Mike, Indianapolis	43	43	34	38	145
Vinatieri, Adam, New England	29	30	26	33	107

‡Also scored a rushing TD, giving him 53 total points.

NON-KICKERS

Player, Team	TD	RTD	PTD	MTD	2Pt.	Tot. Pts.
Abdul-Jabbar, K., Mia.-Cle.	2	1	1	0	0	12
Alexander, Derrick, K.C.	3	1	2	0	0	18
Allen, Terry, New England	9	8	1	0	0	54
Anderson, Richie, N.Y. Jets	3	0	3	0	0	18
Armour, Justin, Baltimore	4	0	4	0	0	24
Barlow, Reggie, Jacksonville	1	0	0	1	0	6
Bartrum, Mike, New England	1	0	1	0	0	6
Baxter, Fred, N.Y. Jets	2	0	2	0	0	12
Beasley, Aaron, Jacksonville	2	0	0	2	0	12
Bennett, Donnell, Kansas City	8	8	0	0	0	48
Bettis, Jerome, Pittsburgh	7	7	0	0	0	42
Blake, Jeff, Cincinnati	2	2	0	0	0	12
Blevins, Tony, Indianapolis	1	0	0	1	0	6
Bownes, Fabien, Seattle	1	0	1	0	0	6
Brackens, Tony, Jacksonville	1	0	0	1	0	6
Brady, Kyle, Jacksonville	1	0	1	0	1	8
Brown, Reggie, Seattle	1	0	1	0	0	6
Brown, Tim, Oakland	6	0	6	0	0	36
Brown, Troy, New England	1	0	1	0	0	6
Brunell, Mark, Jacksonville	1	1	0	0	1	8
Bynum, Kenny, San Diego	3	1	2	0	0	18
Byrd, Isaac, Tennessee	2	0	2	0	0	12
Cadrez, Glenn, Denver	1	0	0	1	0	6
Carswell, Dwayne, Denver	2	0	2	0	0	12
Carter, Ki-Jana, Cincinnati	1	1	0	0	0	6

Player, Team	Tot. TD	RTD	PTD	MTD	2Pt.	Tot. Pts.
Case, Stoney, Baltimore	3	3	0	0	0	18
Chamberlain, Byron, Denver	2	0	2	0	0	12
Chiaverini, Darrin, Cleveland	4	0	4	0	0	24
Chrebet, Wayne, N.Y. Jets	3	0	3	0	0	18
Coates, Ben, New England	2	0	2	0	0	12
Coleman, Marcus, N.Y. Jets	1	0	0	1	0	6
Collins, Bobby, Buffalo	2	0	2	0	0	12
Collins, Cecil, Miami	2	2	0	0	0	12
Cota, Chad, Indianapolis	1	0	0	1	0	6
Couch, Tim, Cleveland	1	1	0	0	1	8
Cox, Bryan, N.Y. Jets	1	0	0	1	0	6
Craft, Jason, Jacksonville	1	0	0	1	0	6
Crockett, Zack, Oakland	5	4	1	0	0	30
Davis, Reggie, San Diego	1	0	1	0	0	6
Davis, Terrell, Denver	2	2	0	0	0	12
Davis, Travis, Pittsburgh	1	0	0	1	0	6
Dawkins, Sean, Seattle	7	0	7	0	0	42
Dawson, Phil, Cleveland	1	1	0	0	0	6
DeLong, Greg, Baltimore	1	0	1	0	0	6
Detmer, Ty, Cleveland	1	1	0	0	0	6
Dilger, Ken, Indianapolis	2	0	2	0	0	12
Dillon, Corey, Cincinnati	6	5	1	0	0	36
Dishman, Cris, Kansas City	2	0	0	2	0	12
Dixon, Gerald, San Diego	1	0	0	1	0	6
Drayton, Troy, Miami	1	0	1	0	0	6
Dudley, Rickey, Oakland	9	0	9	0	0	54
Dyson, Kevin, Tennessee	4	0	4	0	0	24
Eaton, Chad, New England	1	0	0	1	0	6
Edwards, Donnie, K.C.	2	0	0	2	0	12
Edwards, Marc, Cleveland	2	0	2	0	0	12
Edwards, Troy, Pittsburgh	5	0	5	0	0	30
Evans, Chuck, Baltimore	1	0	1	0	1	8
Faulk, Kevin, New England	2	1	1	0	0	12
Fazande, Jermaine, S.D.	2	2	0	0	0	12
Flutie, Doug, Buffalo	1	1	0	0	0	6
Gadsden, Oronde, Miami	6	0	6	0	0	36
Galloway, Joey, Seattle	1	0	1	0	0	6
Gannon, Rich, Oakland	2	2	0	0	0	12
Gary, Olandis, Denver	7	7	0	0	1	44
Gash, Sam, Buffalo	2	0	2	0	0	12
George, Eddie, Tennessee	13	9	4	0	0	78
Glenn, Terry, New England	4	0	4	0	0	24
Gonzalez, Tony, Kansas City	11	0	11	0	0	66
Graham, Jeff, San Diego	2	0	2	0	0	12
Green, Eric, N.Y. Jets	2	0	2	0	0	12
Griese, Brian, Denver	2	2	0	0	0	12
Griffith, Howard, Denver	2	1	1	0	0	12
Groce, Clif, Cincinnati	1	1	0	0	0	6
Hanks, Merton, Seattle	1	0	0	1	0	6
Harris, Corey, Baltimore	1	0	0	1	0	6
Harris, Jackie, Tennessee	1	0	1	0	1	8
Harrison, Marvin, Ind.	12	0	12	0	1	74
Hasty, James, Kansas City	2	0	0	2	0	12
Heath, Rodney, Cincinnati	1	0	0	1	0	6
Hicks, Eric, Kansas City	1	0	0	1	0	6
Holmes, Priest, Baltimore	2	1	1	0	0	12
Horn, Joe, Kansas City	6	0	6	0	0	36
Huntley, Richard, Pittsburgh	8	5	3	0	0	48
Ismail, Qadry, Baltimore	6	0	6	0	0	36
Jackson, Willie, Cincinnati	2	0	2	0	1	14
James, Edgerrin, Indianapolis	17	13	4	0	0	102
Jefferson, Shawn, N.E.	6	0	6	0	0	36
Jett, James, Oakland	2	0	2	0	1	14
Johnson, J.J., Miami	4	4	0	0	0	24
Johnson, Kevin, Cleveland	8	0	8	0	0	48
Johnson, Keyshawn, NYJ	8	0	8	0	0	48
Johnson, Lonnie, Kansas City	1	0	1	0	0	6
Johnson, Pat, Baltimore	3	0	3	0	0	18
Johnstone, Lance, Oakland	1	0	0	1	0	6
Jones, Charlie, San Diego	1	0	1	0	0	6
Jones, Damon, Jacksonville	4	0	4	0	0	24

Player, Team	Tot. TD	RTD	PTD	MTD	2Pt.	Tot. Pts.
Jones, Freddie, San Diego	2	0	2	0	0	12
Jones, Henry, Buffalo	1	0	0	1	0	6
Jordan, Randy, Oakland	2	2	0	0	0	12
Katzenmoyer, Andy, N.E.	1	0	0	1	0	6
Kaufman, Napoleon, Oakland	3	2	1	0	0	18
Kearse, Jevon, Tennessee	1	0	0	1	0	6
Kirby, Terry, Cleveland	9	6	3	0	0	54
Konrad, Rob, Miami	1	0	1	0	0	6
Law, Ty, New England	1	0	0	1	0	6
Lewis, Darryll, San Diego	2	0	0	2	0	12
Lewis, Jermaine, Baltimore	2	0	2	0	0	12
Lewis, Ray, Baltimore	0	0	0	0	0	†2
Linton, Jonathan, Buffalo	6	5	1	0	1	38
Lockett, Kevin, Kansas City	2	0	2	0	0	12
Loville, Derek, Denver	1	1	0	0	0	6
Lucas, Ray, N.Y. Jets	1	1	0	0	0	6
Mack, Tremain, Cincinnati	1	0	0	1	0	6
Madison, Sam, Miami	1	0	0	1	0	†8
Manning, Peyton, Ind.	2	2	0	0	0	12
Martin, Curtis, N.Y. Jets	5	5	0	0	0	30
Martin, Tony, Miami	5	0	5	0	0	30
Mason, Derrick, Tennessee	1	0	0	1	0	6
Mayes, Derrick, Seattle	10	0	10	0	0	60
McCaffrey, Ed, Denver	7	0	7	0	0	42
McCardell, Keenan, Jac.	5	0	5	0	1	32
McCrary, Fred, San Diego	1	0	1	0	0	6
McDuffie, O.J., Miami	2	0	2	0	0	12
McGee, Tony, Cincinnati	2	0	2	0	0	12
McGinest, Willie, N.E.	1	0	0	1	0	6
McNair, Steve, Tennessee	8	8	0	0	0	48
Means, Natrone, San Diego	5	4	1	0	0	30
Mili, Itula, Seattle	1	0	1	0	0	6
Milne, Brian, Cincinnati	0	0	0	0	1	2
Mirer, Rick, N.Y. Jets	1	1	0	0	0	6
Mitchell, Donald, Tennessee	1	0	0	1	0	6
Morris, Bam, Kansas City	3	3	0	0	0	18
Moulds, Eric, Buffalo	7	0	7	0	0	42
Neal, Lorenzo, Tennessee	3	1	2	0	0	18
Northern, Gabe, Buffalo	1	0	0	1	0	6
Ogbogu, Eric, N.Y. Jets	1	0	0	1	0	6
Penn, Chris, San Diego	1	0	1	0	0	6
Perry, Ed, Miami	1	0	1	0	0	6
Pickens, Carl, Cincinnati	6	0	6	0	0	36
Pollard, Marcus, Indianapolis	4	0	4	0	0	24
Porter, Joey, Pittsburgh	1	0	0	1	0	6
Price, Peerless, Buffalo	3	0	3	0	0	18
Pritchard, Mike, Seattle	2	0	2	0	0	12
Pritchett, Stanley, Miami	5	1	4	0	0	30
Pryce, Trevor, Denver	0	0	0	0	0	†2
Reed, Andre, Buffalo	1	0	1	0	0	6
Rhett, Errict, Baltimore	7	5	2	0	0	42
Richardson, Tony, K.C.	1	1	0	0	0	6
Ricks, Mikhael, San Diego	0	0	0	0	1	2
Riemersma, Jay, Buffalo	4	0	4	0	0	24
Ritchie, Jon, Oakland	1	0	1	0	0	6
Roan, Michael, Tennessee	3	0	3	0	0	18
Rogers, Charlie, Seattle	1	0	0	1	0	6
Romanowski, Bill, Denver	1	0	0	1	0	6
Sanders, Chris, Tennessee	1	0	1	0	0	6
Scott, Darnay, Cincinnati	7	0	7	0	0	42
Shaw, Bobby, Pittsburgh	3	0	3	0	0	18
Shaw, Sedrick, Cincinnati	1	1	0	0	0	6
Shedd, Kenny, Oakland	1	0	0	1	0	6
Shehee, Rashaan, K.C.	1	1	0	0	0	6
Simmons, Tony, N.E.	2	0	2	0	0	12
Smeenge, Joel, Jacksonville	0	0	0	0	0	†2
Smith, Akili, Cincinnati	1	1	0	0	0	6
Smith, Antowain, Buffalo	6	6	0	0	0	36
Smith, Irv, Cleveland	1	0	1	0	0	6
Smith, Jimmy, Jacksonville	6	0	6	0	1	38
Smith, Rod, Denver	4	0	4	0	0	24

Player, Team	Tot. TD	RTD	PTD	MTD	2Pt.	Tot. Pts.
Spence, Blake, N.Y. Jets	1	0	1	0	0	6
Springs, Shawn, Seattle	1	0	0	1	0	6
Starks, Duane, Baltimore	1	0	0	1	0	6
Stephens, Tremayne, S.D.	4	3	1	0	0	24
Stewart, James, Jacksonville	13	13	0	0	0	78
Stewart, Kordell, Pittsburgh	3	2	1	0	0	18
Stokley, Brandon, Baltimore	1	0	1	0	0	6
Stoutmire, Omar, N.Y. Jets	1	0	0	1	0	6
Taylor, Fred, Jacksonville	6	6	0	0	0	36
Taylor, Jason, Miami	1	0	0	1	0	6
Thigpen, Yancey, Tennessee	4	0	4	0	0	24
Thomas, Rodney, Tennessee	1	1	0	0	0	6
Thomas, Thurman, Buffalo	1	0	1	0	0	6
Thornton, John, Tennessee	0	0	0	0	0	†2
Tongue, Reggie, Kansas City	2	0	0	2	0	12
Vanover, Tamarick, K.C.	2	0	0	2	0	12
Walker, Denard, Tennessee	1	0	0	1	0	6
Walker, Derrick, Oakland	1	0	1	0	0	6
Ward, Dedric, N.Y. Jets	3	0	3	0	0	18
Ward, Hines, Pittsburgh	7	0	7	0	1	44
Warren, Lamont, N.E.	1	0	1	0	0	6
Watson, Chris, Denver	1	0	0	1	0	6
Watters, Ricky, Seattle	7	5	2	0	0	42
Wheatley, Tyrone, Oakland	11	8	3	0	0	66
Whitted, Alvis, Jacksonville	1	0	0	1	0	6
Wilkins, Terrence, Ind.	7	0	4	3	0	42
Williams, Willie, Seattle	1	0	0	1	0	6
Woodson, Charles, Oakland	1	0	0	1	0	6
Woodson, Rod, Baltimore	2	0	0	2	0	12
Wycheck, Frank, Tennessee	2	0	2	0	0	12
Yeast, Craig, Cincinnati	2	0	0	2	0	12

*Includes safety.
NOTE: Three team safeties credited to Tennessee, two to Jacksonville and one apiece to Denver, N.Y. Jets and San Diego.

NFC

KICKERS

Player, Team	XPM	XPA	FGM	FGA	Tot. Pts.
Akers, David, Philadelphia	2	2	3	6	11
Andersen, Morten, Atlanta	34	34	15	21	79
Anderson, Gary, Minnesota	46	46	19	30	103
Blanchard, Cary, N.Y. Giants	19	19	18	21	73
Boniol, Chris, Chicago	17	18	11	18	50
Brien, Doug, New Orleans	20	21	24	29	92
Conway, Brett, Washington	49	50	22	32	115
Cunningham, Richie, Dal.-Car.	44	45	15	25	89
Daluiso, Brad, N.Y. Giants	9	9	7	9	30
Gowins, Brian, Chicago	3	3	4	6	15
Gramatica, Martin, Tampa Bay	25	25	27	32	106
Hanson, Jason, Detroit	28	29	26	32	106
Holmes, Jaret, Chicago	0	0	2	2	6
Jacke, Chris, Arizona	26	26	19	27	83
Jaeger, Jeff, Chicago	7	7	2	8	13
Johnson, Norm, Philadelphia	25	25	18	25	79
Kasay, John, Carolina	33	33	22	25	99
Longwell, Ryan, Green Bay	38	38	25	30	113
Murray, Eddie, Dallas	10	10	7	9	31
Richey, Wade, San Francisco	30	31	21	23	93
Wilkins, Jeff, St. Louis	64	64	20	28	124

NON-KICKERS

Player, Team	Tot. TD	RTD	PTD	MTD	2Pt.	Tot. Pts.
Abraham, Donnie, Tampa Bay	2	0	0	2	0	12
Aikman, Troy, Dallas	1	1	0	0	0	6
Aldridge, Allen, Detroit	1	0	0	1	0	6
Alexander, Stephen, Was.	3	0	3	0	0	18
Alford, Brian, N.Y. Giants	1	0	1	0	0	6
Allred, John, Chicago	1	0	1	0	0	6
Alstott, Mike, Tampa Bay	9	7	0	2	0	54
Anthony, Reidel, Tampa Bay	1	0	1	0	0	6
Bailey, Champ, Washington	1	0	0	1	0	6
Barber, Shawn, Washington	1	0	0	1	0	6
Barber, Tiki, N.Y. Giants	3	0	2	1	0	18
Batch, Charlie, Detroit	2	2	0	0	0	12
Bates, Mario, Arizona	9	9	0	0	0	54
Bates, Michael, Carolina	2	0	0	2	0	12
Beasley, Fred, San Francisco	4	4	0	0	0	24
Bech, Brett, New Orleans	1	0	1	0	1	8
Bennett, Sean, N.Y. Giants	1	1	0	0	0	6
Beuerlein, Steve, Carolina	2	2	0	0	0	12
Blakabutuka, Tim, Carolina	6	6	0	0	0	36
Bieniemy, Eric, Philadelphia	1	1	0	0	0	6
Bjornson, Eric, Dallas	1	0	1	0	0	6
Bly, Dre', St. Louis	1	0	0	1	0	6
Booker, Marty, Chicago	3	0	3	0	0	18
Boston, David, Arizona	2	0	2	0	0	12
Bradford, Corey, Green Bay	5	0	5	0	1	32
Broughton, Luther, Phi.	4	0	4	0	0	24
Brown, Na, Philadelphia	1	0	1	0	0	6
Bruce, Isaac, St. Louis	12	0	12	0	1	74
Bryant, Junior, San Francisco	1	0	0	1	0	6
Buchanan, Ray, Atlanta	1	0	0	1	0	6
Bush, Devin, St. Louis	1	0	0	1	0	6
Calloway, Chris, Atlanta	1	0	1	0	0	6
Carter, Cris, Minnesota	13	0	13	0	0	78
Centers, Larry, Washington	3	0	3	0	0	18
Chandler, Chris, Atlanta	1	1	0	0	0	6
Christian, Bob, Atlanta	7	5	2	0	0	42
Cleeland, Cameron, N.O.	1	0	1	0	1	8
Coakley, Dexter, Dallas	1	0	0	1	0	6
Cody, Mac, Arizona	1	0	1	0	0	6
Coleman, Marco, Washington	1	0	0	1	0	6
Collins, Kerry, N.Y. Giants	2	2	0	0	1	14
Connell, Albert, Washington	7	0	7	0	0	42
Conway, Curtis, Chicago	4	0	4	0	0	24
Crowell, Germane, Detroit	7	0	7	0	1	44
Crumpler, Carlester, Min.	1	0	1	0	0	6
Culpepper, Brad, Tampa Bay	0	0	0	0	0	†2
Davis, John, Tampa Bay	1	0	1	0	0	6
Davis, Stephen, Washington	17	17	0	0	1	104
Davis, Tyrone, Green Bay	2	0	2	0	0	12
Dawkins, Brian, Philadelphia	1	0	0	1	0	6
Dawsey, Lawrence, N.O.	1	0	1	0	0	6
Delhomme, Jake, N.O.	2	2	0	0	0	12
Douglas, Dameane, Phi.	1	0	1	0	0	6
Drakeford, Tyronne, N.O.	1	0	0	1	0	6
Driver, Donald, Green Bay	1	0	1	0	0	6
Dunn, Warrick, Tampa Bay	2	0	2	0	0	12
Dwight, Tim, Atlanta	9	1	7	1	0	54
Edwards, Antuan, Green Bay	1	0	0	1	0	6
Ellis, Greg, Dallas	2	0	0	2	0	12
Elliss, Luther, Detroit	1	0	0	1	0	6
Emanuel, Bert, Tampa Bay	1	0	1	0	0	6
Engram, Bobby, Chicago	4	0	4	0	0	24
Enis, Curtis, Chicago	5	3	2	0	0	30
Fair, Terry, Detroit	2	0	0	2	0	12
Faulk, Marshall, St. Louis	12	7	5	0	1	74
Fletcher, London, St. Louis	0	0	0	0	0	†2
Floyd, William, Carolina	3	3	0	0	0	18
Fredrickson, Rob, Arizona	1	0	0	1	0	6
Freeman, Antonio, Green Bay	6	0	6	0	0	36
Fryar, Irving, Washington	2	0	2	0	0	12
Garcia, Jeff, San Francisco	2	2	0	0	0	12
Garner, Charlie, S.F.	6	4	2	0	0	36
German, Jammi, Atlanta	3	0	3	0	0	18
Glover, Andrew, Minnesota	1	0	1	0	0	6
Graham, Kent, N.Y. Giants	1	1	0	0	0	6
Green, Jacquez, Tampa Bay	3	0	3	0	0	18

1999 STATISTICS Scoring

Scoring

Player, Team	Tot. TD	RTD	PTD	MTD	2Pt.	Tot. Pts.
Hakim, Az-zahir, St. Louis	9	0	8	1	0	54
Hambrick, Darren, Dallas	0	0	0	0	0	†2
Hanspard, Byron, Atlanta	1	1	0	0	0	6
Hape, Patrick, Tampa Bay	1	0	1	0	0	6
Harris, Al, Philadelphia	1	0	0	1	0	6
Harris, Sean, Chicago	1	0	0	1	0	6
Hastings, Andre, New Orleans	1	0	1	0	0	6
Hatchette, Matthew, Min.	2	0	2	0	0	12
Hayes, Donald, Carolina	2	0	2	0	0	12
Henderson, William, G.B.	3	2	1	0	0	18
Hicks, Skip, Washington	3	3	0	0	0	18
Hill, Greg, Detroit	2	2	0	0	0	12
Hilliard, Ike, N.Y. Giants	3	0	3	0	0	18
Hoard, Leroy, Minnesota	10	10	0	0	0	60
Hobert, Billy Joe, N.O.	1	1	0	0	0	6
Hodgins, James, St. Louis	1	1	0	0	0	6
Holcombe, Robert, St. Louis	5	4	1	0	0	30
Holt, Torry, St. Louis	6	0	6	0	0	36
Horne, Tony, St. Louis	2	0	0	2	0	12
Howard, Desmond, Detroit	1	0	0	1	0	6
Irvin, Michael, Dallas	3	0	3	0	0	18
Irvin, Sedrick, Detroit	4	4	0	0	0	24
Ismail, Rocket, Dallas	7	1	6	0	0	42
Jeffers, Patrick, Carolina	12	0	12	0	0	72
Jells, Dietrich, Philadelphia	2	0	2	0	0	12
Jervey, Travis, San Francisco	1	1	0	0	0	6
Johnson, Brad, Washington	2	2	0	0	0	12
Johnson, Charles, Phi.	1	0	1	0	0	†8
Johnson, LeShon, N.Y. Giants	3	2	1	0	0	18
Jones, Mike, St. Louis	3	0	0	3	0	18
Jordan, Andrew, Minnesota	1	0	1	0	0	6
Jurevicius, Joe, N.Y. Giants	1	0	1	0	0	6
Kennison, Eddie, N.O.	4	0	4	0	1	26
Kinchen, Brian, Carolina	2	0	2	0	0	12
Kozlowski, Brian, Atlanta	2	0	2	0	0	12
LaFleur, David, Dallas	7	0	7	0	0	42
Lane, Fred, Carolina	1	1	0	0	0	6
Lassiter, Kwamie, Arizona	1	0	0	1	0	6
Lee, Amp, St. Louis	1	0	1	0	0	6
Levens, Dorsey, Green Bay	10	9	1	0	0	60
Lewis, Chad, Philadelphia	3	0	3	0	0	18
Lyght, Todd, St. Louis	1	0	0	1	0	6
Makovicka, Joel, Arizona	1	0	1	0	0	6
Mamula, Mike, Philadelphia	1	0	0	1	0	6
Mathis, Terance, Atlanta	6	0	6	0	0	36
Mayes, Alonzo, Chicago	1	0	1	0	0	6
McDonald, Darnell, Tampa Bay	1	0	1	0	0	6
McKenzie, Keith, Green Bay	2	0	0	2	0	12
McLeod, Kevin, Tampa Bay	1	0	1	0	0	6
McMillian, Mark, S.F.	1	0	0	1	0	6
McNabb, Donovan, Phi.	0	0	0	0	1	2
McNown, Cade, Chicago	0	0	0	0	1	2
McWilliams, Johnny, Arizona	1	0	1	0	0	6
Milburn, Glyn, Chicago	1	1	0	0	0	6
Minter, Barry, Chicago	1	0	0	1	0	6
Mitchell, Basil, Green Bay	1	0	0	1	0	6
Mitchell, Brian, Washington	1	1	0	0	0	6
Mitchell, Pete, N.Y. Giants	3	0	3	0	0	18
Montgomery, Joe, N.Y. Giants	3	3	0	0	1	20
Moore, Dave, Tampa Bay	5	0	5	0	0	30
Moore, Herman, Detroit	2	0	2	0	0	12
Moore, Rob, Arizona	5	0	5	0	0	30
Morton, Johnnie, Detroit	5	0	5	0	0	30
Moss, Randy, Minnesota	12	0	11	1	0	72
Muhammad, Muhsin, Car.	8	0	8	0	0	48
Oliver, Winslow, Atlanta	1	0	0	1	0	6

Player, Team	Tot. TD	RTD	PTD	MTD	2Pt.	Tot. Pts.
Owens, Terrell, San Francisco	4	0	4	0	0	24
Oxendine, Ken, Atlanta	2	1	1	0	0	12
Parker, De'Mond, Green Bay	2	2	0	0	0	12
Peter, Christian, N.Y. Giants	1	0	0	1	0	6
Phillips, Lawrence, S.F.	2	2	0	0	0	12
Pittman, Michael, Arizona	2	2	0	0	0	12
Plummer, Jake, Arizona	2	2	0	0	0	12
Poole, Keith, New Orleans	6	0	6	0	0	36
Rasby, Walter, Detroit	1	0	1	0	0	6
Reed, Jake, Minnesota	2	0	2	0	0	12
Rice, Jerry, San Francisco	5	0	5	0	0	30
Rivers, Ron, Detroit	1	0	1	0	0	6
Robinson, Jeff, St. Louis	2	0	2	0	0	12
Robinson, Marcus, Chicago	9	0	9	0	0	54
Rossum, Allen, Philadelphia	1	0	0	1	0	6
Sanders, Deion, Dallas	1	0	0	1	0	6
Sanders, Frank, Arizona	1	0	1	0	0	6
Schlesinger, Cory, Detroit	1	0	1	0	0	6
Schroeder, Bill, Green Bay	5	0	5	0	0	30
Schulters, Lance, S.F.	1	0	0	1	0	6
Sellers, Mike, Washington	2	0	2	0	0	12
Sloan, David, Detroit	4	0	4	0	0	24
Slutzker, Scott, New Orleans	1	0	1	0	0	6
Small, Torrance, Philadelphia	4	0	4	0	0	24
Smith, Emmitt, Dallas	13	11	2	0	0	78
Smith, Lamar, New Orleans	1	0	1	0	0	6
Smith, Robert, Minnesota	2	2	0	0	0	12
Stablein, Brian, Detroit	1	0	1	0	1	8
Staley, Duce, Philadelphia	6	4	2	0	0	36
Stokes, J.J., San Francisco	3	0	3	0	1	20
Strahan, Michael, N.Y. Giants	1	0	0	1	0	6
Swann, Eric, Arizona	1	0	0	1	0	6
Tate, Robert, Minnesota	1	0	0	1	0	6
Taylor, Bobby, Philadelphia	1	0	0	1	0	6
Teague, George, Dallas	2	0	0	2	0	12
Thomas, Orlando, Minnesota	1	0	0	1	0	6
Thomason, Jeff, Green Bay	2	0	2	0	0	12
Thrash, James, Washington	1	0	0	1	0	6
Tolliver, Billy Joe, N.O.	3	3	0	0	0	18
Toomer, Amani, N.Y. Giants	6	0	6	0	0	36
Tucker, Jason, Dallas	2	0	2	0	0	12
Tucker, Ryan, St. Louis	1	0	1	0	0	6
Vardell, Tommy, S.F.	1	1	0	0	0	6
Walker, Darnell, S.F.	2	0	0	2	0	12
Walls, Wesley, Carolina	12	0	12	0	0	72
Walsh, Chris, Minnesota	1	0	1	0	0	6
Warner, Kurt, St. Louis	1	1	0	0	0	6
Warren, Chris, Dallas	2	2	0	0	0	12
Way, Charles, N.Y. Giants	2	2	0	0	0	12
Weary, Fred, New Orleans	1	0	0	1	0	6
Weathers, Andre, N.Y. Giants	1	0	0	1	0	6
Weaver, Jed, Philadelphia	0	0	0	0	1	2
Westbrook, Michael, Was.	9	0	9	0	1	56
Wetnight, Ryan, Chicago	1	0	1	0	0	6
Whiting, Brandon, Phi.	1	0	0	1	0	6
Wilkinson, Dan, Washington	1	0	0	1	0	6
Williams, Moe, Minnesota	2	1	0	1	0	12
Williams, Ricky, New Orleans	2	2	0	0	0	12
Williams, Roland, St. Louis	6	0	6	0	0	36
Wistrom, Grant, St. Louis	2	0	0	2	0	12
Wuerffel, Danny, New Orleans	1	1	0	0	0	6
Young, Bryant, San Francisco	0	0	0	0	0	†2

*Includes safety.

NOTE: One team safety apiece credited to Atlanta, Detroit, Green Bay, Minnesota, and Philadelphia.

INTERCEPTIONS

TEAM

AFC

Team	No.	Yds.	Avg.	Long	TD
Seattle	30	336	11.2	42	2
Kansas City	25	378	15.1	t56	5
N.Y. Jets	24	443	18.5	t98	3
Baltimore	21	403	19.2	t66	4
Oakland	20	247	12.4	36	1
Jacksonville	19	330	17.4	t93	3
Miami	18	243	13.5	42	1
Tennessee	16	257	16.1	43	1
New England	16	110	6.9	t57	2
Denver	15	169	11.3	45	1
San Diego	15	123	8.2	68	0
Pittsburgh	14	149	10.6	25	0
Buffalo	12	180	15.0	52	0
Cincinnati	12	100	8.3	t58	1
Indianapolis	10	287	28.7	t74	1
Cleveland	8	52	6.5	14	0
AFC total	275	3807	13.8	t98	25
AFC average	17.2	237.9	13.8	...	1.6

t—touchdown.

NFC

Team	No.	Yds.	Avg.	Long	TD
St. Louis	29	567	19.6	t91	7
Philadelphia	28	625	22.3	84	5
Green Bay	26	137	5.3	60	1
Dallas	24	442	18.4	t95	4
Washington	24	375	15.6	t88	3
Tampa Bay	21	355	16.9	t55	2
New Orleans	19	138	7.3	27	0
Arizona	17	276	16.2	t78	3
N.Y. Giants	17	232	13.6	t44	2
Detroit	16	235	14.7	t41	1
Carolina	15	169	11.3	44	0
Chicago	14	229	16.4	41	1
San Francisco	13	209	16.1	t64	2
Atlanta	12	166	13.8	t52	1
Minnesota	12	66	5.5	t27	1
NFC total	287	4221	14.7	t95	33
NFC average	19.1	281.4	14.7	...	2.2
NFL total	562	8028	...	t98	58
NFL average	18.1	259.0	14.3	...	1.9

INDIVIDUAL

BESTS OF THE SEASON

Interceptions, season
AFC: 7—James Hasty, Kansas City; Sam Madison, Miami; Rod Woodson, Baltimore.
NFC: 7—Donnie Abraham, Tampa Bay; Troy Vincent, Philadelphia.

Interceptions, game
NFC: 3—Champ Bailey, Washington at Arizona, Oct. 17.
AFC: 3—Sam Madison, Miami vs. Tennessee, Nov. 7; Samari Rolle, Tennessee vs. Jacksonville, Dec. 26.

Yards, season
AFC: 200—Aaron Beasley, Jacksonville.
NFC: 151—Al Harris, Philadelphia.

Longest
AFC: 98—Marcus Coleman, N.Y. Jets at Miami, Dec. 27 (TD).
NFC: 95—George Teague, Dallas vs. Green Bay, Nov. 14 (TD).

Touchdowns, season
AFC: 2—Aaron Beasley, Jacksonville; James Hasty, Kansas City; Rod Woodson, Baltimore.
NFC: 2—Donnie Woodson, Tampa Bay; Mike A. Jones, St. Louis; George Teague, Dallas; Grant Wistrom, St. Louis.

Team leaders, interceptions
AFC:
Baltimore	7	Rod Woodson
Buffalo	3	Kurt Schulz
Cincinnati	3	Rodney Heath
Cleveland	2	Marquez Pope
Denver	5	Tory James
Indianapolis	3	Tyrone Poole
Jacksonville	6	Aaron Beasley
Kansas City	7	James Hasty
Miami	7	Sam Madison
New England	4	Lawyer Milloy
N.Y. Jets	6	Marcus Coleman
Oakland	3	Eric Allen
		Darrien Gordon
		Eric Turner
Pittsburgh	4	Scott Shields
		Dewayne Washington
San Diego	4	Darryll Lewis
		Jimmy Spencer
Seattle	5	Shawn Springs
		Willie Williams
Tennessee	4	Samari Rolle

NFC:
Arizona	2	Rob Fredrickson
		Tom Knight
		Kwamie Lassiter
		Pat Tillman
		Aeneas Williams
Atlanta	4	Ray Buchanan
Carolina	5	Eric Davis
Chicago	3	Chris Hudson
Dallas	4	Dexter Coakley
Detroit	5	Ron Rice
Green Bay	6	Mike McKenzie
Minnesota	3	Robert Griffith
New Orleans	6	Ashley Ambrose
N.Y. Giants	6	Percy Ellsworth
Philadelphia	7	Troy Vincent
St. Louis	6	Todd Lyght
San Francisco	6	Lance Schulters
Tampa Bay	7	Donnie Abraham
Washington	6	Matt Stevens

NFL LEADERS

Player, Team	No.	Yds.	Avg.	Long	TD
Woodson, Rod, Baltimore*	7	195	27.9	t66	2
Madison, Sam, Miami*	7	164	23.4	42	1
Abraham, Donnie, Tampa Bay	7	115	16.4	t55	2
Hasty, James, Kansas City*	7	98	14.0	t56	2
Vincent, Troy, Philadelphia	7	91	13.0	35	0
Beasley, Aaron, Jacksonville*	6	206	34.3	t93	2
Coleman, Marcus, N.Y. Jets*	6	165	27.5	t98	1
Schulters, Lance, San Francisco	6	127	21.2	t64	1
Lyght, Todd, St. Louis	6	112	18.7	t57	1

– 263 –

Player, Team	No.	Yds.	Avg.	Long	TD
Ellsworth, Percy, N.Y. Giants	6	80	13.3	26	0
Stevens, Matt, Washington	6	61	10.2	25	0
Ambrose, Ashley, New Orleans	6	27	4.5	16	0
McKenzie, Mike, Green Bay	6	4	0.7	4	0

*AFC.
t—touchdown.
Leader based on most interceptions.

AFC

Player, Team	No.	Yds.	Avg.	Long	TD
Abdullah, Rahim, Cleveland	1	0	0.0	0	0
Allen, Eric, Oakland	3	33	11.0	31	0
Barker, Roy, Cleveland	1	14	14.0	14	0
Beasley, Aaron, Jacksonville	6	200	33.3	t93	2
Bell, Myron, Cincinnati	1	5	5.0	5	0
Bellamy, Jay, Seattle	4	4	1.0	7	0
Biekert, Greg, Oakland	2	57	28.5	36	0
Blackmon, Roosevelt, Cincinnati	1	0	0.0	0	0
Blevins, Tony, Indianapolis	2	115	57.5	t74	1
Bowden, Joe, Tennessee	1	29	29.0	29	0
Boyer, Brant, Jacksonville	1	5	5.0	5	0
Brackens, Tony, Jacksonville	2	16	8.0	t16	1
Brown, Eric, Denver	1	13	13.0	13	0
Bruschi, Tedy, New England	1	1	1.0	1	0
Bryant, Fernando, Jacksonville	2	0	0.0	0	0
Buckley, Terrell, Miami	3	3	1.0	18	0
Burris, Jeff, Indianapolis	2	83	41.5	55	0
Canty, Chris, Seattle	3	26	8.7	19	0
Carter, Chris, New England	3	13	4.3	8	0
Carter, Dale, Denver	2	48	24.0	34	0
Carter, Tom, Chi.-Cin.*	2	36	18.0	36	0
Coghill, George, Denver	1	0	0.0	0	0
Coleman, Marcus, N.Y. Jets	6	165	27.5	t98	1
Copeland, John, Cincinnati	2	16	8.0	12	0
Cox, Bryan, N.Y. Jets	1	27	27.0	t27	1
Crockett, Ray, Denver	2	14	7.0	10	0
Darius, Donovin, Jacksonville	4	37	9.3	29	0
Davis, Travis, Pittsburgh	1	1	1.0	1	0
Dimry, Charles, San Diego	2	1	0.5	1	0
Dishman, Cris, Kansas City	5	95	19.0	t47	1
Dorsett, Anthony, Tennessee	1	43	43.0	43	0
Dumas, Mike, San Diego	2	92	46.0	68	0
Edwards, Donnie, Kansas City	5	50	10.0	t28	1
Emmons, Carlos, Pittsburgh	1	22	22.0	22	0
Fisk, Jason, Tennessee	1	17	17.0	17	0
Glenn, Aaron, N.Y. Jets	3	20	6.7	12	0
Gordon, Darrien, Oakland	3	44	14.7	28	0
Green, Victor, N.Y. Jets	5	92	18.4	32	0
Greer, Donovan, Buffalo	1	0	0.0	0	0
Hall, Cory, Cincinnati	1	0	0.0	0	0
Hanks, Merton, Seattle	2	30	15.0	t23	1
Harris, Corey, Baltimore	1	24	24.0	t24	1
Harrison, Rodney, San Diego	1	0	0.0	0	0
Hasty, James, Kansas City	7	98	14.0	t56	2
Heath, Rodney, Cincinnati	3	72	24.0	t58	1
Holecek, John, Buffalo	1	35	35.0	35	0
Holmes, Kenny, Tennessee	2	17	8.5	19	0
Irvin, Ken, Buffalo	1	1	1.0	1	0
Israel, Steve, New England	1	0	0.0	0	0
Jackson, Steve, Tennessee	1	2	2.0	2	0
James, Tory, Denver	5	59	11.8	45	0
Johnstone, Lance, Oakland	1	0	0.0	0	0
Jones, Lenoy, Cleveland	1	3	3.0	3	0
Jones, Marvin, N.Y. Jets	1	15	15.0	15	0
Joseph, Kerry, Seattle	3	82	27.3	40	0
Katzenmoyer, Andy, New England	1	57	57.0	t57	1
Kennedy, Cortez, Seattle	2	12	6.0	7	0
Kirkland, Levon, Pittsburgh	1	23	23.0	23	0
Law, Ty, New England	2	20	10.0	t27	1
Lewis, Darryll, San Diego	4	9	2.3	5	0
Lewis, Ray, Baltimore	3	97	32.3	60	0

Player, Team	No.	Yds.	Avg.	Long	TD
Little, Earl, Cleveland	1	0	0.0	0	0
Madison, Sam, Miami	7	164	23.4	42	1
Marion, Brock, Miami	2	30	15.0	28	0
Martin, Emanuel, Buffalo	1	0	0.0	0	0
Marts, Lonnie, Jacksonville	1	10	10.0	10	0
Maryland, Russell, Oakland	1	2	2.0	2	0
McAlister, Chris, Baltimore	5	28	5.6	21	0
McCutcheon, Daylon, Cleveland	1	12	12.0	12	0
McElmurry, Blaine, Jacksonville	1	26	26.0	26	0
McGlockton, Chester, Kansas City	1	30	30.0	30	0
Mickens, Ray, N.Y. Jets	2	2	1.0	2	0
Milloy, Lawyer, New England	4	17	4.3	17	0
Mincy, Charles, Oakland	2	23	11.5	21	0
Mitchell, Donald, Tennessee	1	42	42.0	t42	1
Myers, Greg, Cincinnati	1	0	0.0	0	0
Newman, Anthony, Oakland	2	16	8.0	16	0
Oldham, Chris, Pittsburgh	1	9	9.0	9	0
Patton, Marvcus, Kansas City	1	0	0.0	0	0
Phifer, Roman, N.Y. Jets	2	20	10.0	16	0
Poole, Tyrone, Indianapolis	3	85	28.3	38	0
Pope, Marquez, Cleveland	2	15	7.5	13	0
Pryce, Trevor, Denver	1	0	0.0	0	0
Randolph, Thomas, Indianapolis	1	0	0.0	0	0
Robertson, Marcus, Tennessee	1	3	3.0	3	0
Rodgers, Derrick, Miami	1	5	5.0	5	0
Rogers, Sam, Buffalo	1	24	24.0	24	0
Rolle, Samari, Tennessee	4	65	16.3	30	0
Romanowski, Bill, Denver	3	35	11.7	t18	1
Roye, Orpheus, Pittsburgh	1	2	2.0	2	0
Schulz, Kurt, Buffalo	3	26	8.7	26	0
Scott, Chad, Pittsburgh	1	16	16.0	16	0
Seau, Junior, San Diego	1	16	16.0	16	0
Serwanga, Kato, New England	3	2	0.7	2	0
Shields, Scott, Pittsburgh	4	75	18.8	25	0
Sidney, Dainon, Tennessee	3	12	4.0	7	0
Simien, Tracy, San Diego	1	4	4.0	4	0
Slade, Chris, New England	1	0	0.0	0	0
Smith, Darrin, Seattle	1	0	0.0	0	0
Smith, Thomas, Buffalo	1	29	29.0	29	0
Spencer, Jimmy, San Diego	4	1	0.3	1	0
Spikes, Takeo, Cincinnati	2	7	3.5	7	0
Springs, Shawn, Seattle	5	77	15.4	42	0
Starks, Duane, Baltimore	5	59	11.8	t43	1
Stoutmire, Omar, N.Y. Jets	2	97	48.5	t67	1
Surtain, Patrick, Miami	2	28	14.0	28	0
Taylor, Jason, Miami	1	0	0.0	0	0
Thierry, John, Cleveland	1	8	8.0	8	0
Thomas, Dave, Jacksonville	2	36	18.0	36	0
Thomas, Derrick, Kansas City	1	20	20.0	20	0
Thomas, Ratcliff, Indianapolis	1	0	0.0	0	0
Thomas, Zach, Miami	1	0	0.0	0	0
Tongue, Reggie, Kansas City	1	80	80.0	t46	1
Turner, Eric, Oakland	3	43	14.3	24	0
Walker, Brian, Seattle	1	21	21.0	21	0
Walker, Denard, Tennessee	1	27	27.0	27	0
Walker, Marquise, Oakland	1	0	0.0	0	0
Warfield, Eric, Kansas City	3	0	0.0	0	0
Washington, Dewayne, Pittsburgh	4	1	0.3	1	0
Wiley, Marcellus, Buffalo	1	52	52.0	52	0
Williams, Darryl, Seattle	4	41	10.3	21	0
Williams, K.D., Oakland	1	14	14.0	14	0
Williams, Willie, Seattle	5	43	8.6	t40	1
Wilson, Jerry, Miami	1	13	13.0	13	0
Wiltz, Jason, N.Y. Jets	2	5	2.5	5	0
Winfield, Antoine, Buffalo	2	13	6.5	10	0
Woods, Jerome, Kansas City	1	5	5.0	5	0
Woodson, Charles, Oakland	1	15	15.0	t15	1
Woodson, Rod, Baltimore	7	195	27.9	t66	2
Wooten, Tito, Indianapolis	1	4	4.0	4	0

*Includes both NFC and AFC statistics.
t—touchdown.

NFC

Player, Team	No.	Yds.	Avg.	Long	TD
Abraham, Donnie, Tampa Bay	7	115	16.4	t55	2
Alexander, Brent, Carolina	2	18	9.0	18	0
Allen, Taje, St. Louis	2	76	38.0	40	0
Ambrose, Ashley, New Orleans	6	27	4.5	16	0
Armstead, Jessie, N.Y. Giants	2	35	17.5	31	0
Bailey, Champ, Washington	5	55	11.0	t59	1
Bailey, Robert, Detroit	2	39	19.5	31	0
Barber, Ronde, Tampa Bay	2	60	30.0	43	0
Barber, Shawn, Washington	2	70	35.0	t70	1
Bass, Anthony, Minnesota	1	4	4.0	4	0
Bennett, Tommy, Arizona	1	13	13.0	13	0
Bly, Dre', St. Louis	3	53	17.7	t53	1
Booker, Michael, Atlanta	2	10	5.0	10	0
Boyd, Stephen, Detroit	1	18	18.0	18	0
Brooks, Derrick, Tampa Bay	4	61	15.3	38	0
Buchanan, Ray, Atlanta	4	81	20.3	t52	1
Burns, Keith, Chicago	1	15	15.0	15	0
Burton, Shane, Chicago	1	37	37.0	37	0
Bush, Devin, St. Louis	2	45	22.5	t45	1
Butler, LeRoy, Green Bay	2	0	0.0	0	0
Caldwell, Mike, Philadelphia	1	12	12.0	12	0
Carrier, Mark, Detroit	3	16	5.3	16	0
Carter, Marty, Atlanta	1	4	4.0	4	0
Chavous, Corey, Arizona	1	1	1.0	1	0
Clay, Willie, New Orleans	3	32	10.7	24	0
Clemons, Charlie, St. Louis	1	0	0.0	0	0
Coady, Rich, St. Louis	1	11	11.0	11	0
Coakley, Dexter, Dallas	4	119	29.8	t46	1
Cook, Rashard, Philadelphia	1	29	29.0	29	0
Cousin, Terry, Chicago	2	1	0.5	1	0
Darling, James, Philadelphia	1	33	33.0	33	0
Davis, Eric, Carolina	5	49	9.8	16	0
Dawkins, Brian, Philadelphia	4	127	31.8	t67	1
Drake, Jerry, Arizona	1	0	0.0	0	0
Edwards, Antuan, Green Bay	4	26	6.5	t26	1
Ellis, Greg, Dallas	1	87	87.0	t87	1
Ellsworth, Percy, N.Y. Giants	6	80	13.3	26	0
Evans, Doug, Carolina	2	1	0.5	1	0
Fair, Terry, Detroit	3	49	16.3	t41	1
Fields, Mark, New Orleans	2	0	0.0	0	0
Flanigan, Jim, Chicago	1	6	6.0	6	0
Fredrickson, Rob, Arizona	2	57	28.5	t34	1
Garnes, Sam, N.Y. Giants	2	7	3.5	4	0
Gilbert, Sean, Carolina	1	4	4.0	4	0
Godfrey, Randall, Dallas	1	10	10.0	10	0
Green, Darrell, Washington	3	33	11.0	25	0
Griffith, Robert, Minnesota	3	0	0.0	0	0
Hambrick, Darren, Dallas	2	44	22.0	25	0
Harris, Al, Philadelphia	4	151	37.8	84	1
Harris, Sean, Chicago	1	0	0.0	0	0
Harris, Walt, Chicago	1	-1	-1.0	-1	0
Hauck, Tim, Philadelphia	1	2	2.0	2	0
Hawthorne, Duane, Dallas	3	-2	-.7	0	0
Hitchcock, Jimmy, Minnesota	2	0	0.0	0	0
Hudson, Chris, Chicago	3	28	9.3	28	0
Jenkins, Billy, St. Louis	2	16	8.0	14	0
Jones, Mike, St. Louis	4	96	24.0	t44	2
Kelly, Brian, Tampa Bay	1	26	26.0	26	0
Kelly, Rob, New Orleans	1	6	6.0	6	0
Knight, Sammy, New Orleans	1	0	0.0	0	0
Knight, Tom, Arizona	2	16	8.0	16	0
Kowalkowski, Scott, Detroit	1	29	29.0	29	0
Kriewaldt, Clint, Detroit	1	2	2.0	2	0
Lassiter, Kwamie, Arizona	2	110	55.0	t78	1
Levingston, Bashir, N.Y. Giants	1	34	34.0	34	0
Lincoln, Jeremy, N.Y. Giants	1	0	0.0	0	0
Lyght, Todd, St. Louis	6	112	18.7	t57	1
Lyle, Keith, St. Louis	2	10	5.0	10	0
Lynch, John, Tampa Bay	2	32	16.0	28	0

Player, Team	No.	Yds.	Avg.	Long	TD
Lyon, Billy, Green Bay	1	0	0.0	0	0
Mamula, Mike, Philadelphia	1	41	41.0	t41	1
McBurrows, Gerald, Atlanta	2	64	32.0	41	0
McCleon, Dexter, St. Louis	4	17	4.3	14	0
McCleskey, J.J., Arizona	1	2	2.0	2	0
McDonald, Ramos, San Francisco	1	4	4.0	4	0
McDonald, Tim, San Francisco	2	18	9.0	18	0
McKenzie, Mike, Green Bay	6	4	0.7	4	0
McKinnon, Ronald, Arizona	1	0	0.0	0	0
McMillian, Mark, S.F.-Was.	2	24	12.0	24	0
McQuarters, R.W., San Francisco	1	25	25.0	25	0
Miller, Corey, Minnesota	1	0	0.0	0	0
Minter, Barry, Chicago	2	66	33.0	t34	1
Minter, Mike, Carolina	3	69	23.0	44	0
Mitchell, Keith, New Orleans	3	22	7.3	18	0
Molden, Alex, New Orleans	1	2	2.0	2	0
Moore, Damon, Philadelphia	1	28	28.0	28	0
Nelson, Jim, Green Bay	1	0	0.0	0	0
Nguyen, Dat, Dallas	1	6	6.0	6	0
Nickerson, Hardy, Tampa Bay	2	18	9.0	18	0
Parrish, Tony, Chicago	1	41	41.0	41	0
Phillips, Ryan, N.Y. Giants	1	0	0.0	0	0
Pounds, Darryl, Washington	3	37	12.3	25	0
Randle, John, Minnesota	1	1	1.0	1	0
Reese, Izell, Dallas	3	28	9.3	24	0
Rice, Ron, Detroit	5	82	16.4	33	0
Richardson, Damien, Carolina	1	27	27.0	27	0
Robinson, Damien, Tampa Bay	2	36	18.0	36	0
Robinson, Eugene, Atlanta	3	7	2.3	7	0
Sanders, Deion, Dallas	3	2	0.7	2	0
Schulters, Lance, San Francisco	6	127	21.2	t64	1
Sehorn, Jason, N.Y. Giants	1	-4	-4.0	-4	0
Shade, Sam, Washington	2	7	3.5	7	0
Sharper, Darren, Green Bay	3	12	4.0	9	0
Singleton, Alshermond, T.B.	1	7	7.0	7	0
Smith, Derek, Washington	1	0	0.0	0	0
Smith, Jermaine, Green Bay	1	2	2.0	2	0
Smith, Kevin, Dallas	1	16	16.0	16	0
Sparks, Phillippi, N.Y. Giants	1	28	28.0	28	0
Stevens, Matt, Washington	6	61	10.2	25	0
Strahan, Michael, N.Y. Giants	1	44	44.0	t44	1
Swann, Eric, Arizona	1	42	42.0	t42	1
Tate, Robert, Minnesota	1	18	18.0	18	0
Taylor, Bobby, Philadelphia	4	59	14.8	28	1
Teague, George, Dallas	3	127	42.3	t95	2
Thomas, Orlando, Minnesota	2	32	16.0	t27	1
Tillman, Pat, Arizona	2	7	3.5	6	0
Trotter, Jeremiah, Philadelphia	2	30	15.0	30	0
Tubbs, Winfred, San Francisco	1	8	8.0	8	0
Vincent, Troy, Philadelphia	7	91	13.0	35	0
Vinson, Fred, Green Bay	2	21	10.5	21	0
Wadsworth, Andre, Arizona	1	23	23.0	23	0
Walker, Darnell, San Francisco	1	27	27.0	t27	1
Weary, Fred, New Orleans	2	49	24.5	27	0
Weathers, Andre, N.Y. Giants	1	8	8.0	t8	1
Wells, Dean, Carolina	1	1	1.0	1	0
Whiting, Brandon, Philadelphia	1	22	22.0	t22	1
Wilkinson, Dan, Washington	1	88	88.0	t88	1
Williams, Aeneas, Arizona	2	5	2.5	8	0
Williams, Brian, Green Bay	2	60	30.0	60	0
Williams, Tyrone, Green Bay	4	12	3.0	12	0
Wistrom, Grant, St. Louis	2	131	65.5	t91	2
Woodson, Darren, Dallas	2	5	2.5	5	0
Wright, Kenny, Minnesota	1	11	11.0	11	0

t—touchdown.

PLAYERS WITH TWO CLUBS

Player, Team	No.	Yds.	Avg.	Long	TD
Carter, Tom, Chicago	1	36	36.0	36	0
Carter, Tom, Cincinnati	0	0	0.0	0	0
McMillian, Mark, San Francisco	1	0	0.0	0	0
McMillian, Mark, Washington	1	24	24.0	24	0

SACKS

TEAM

AFC

Team	Sacks	Yards
Jacksonville	57	373
Tennessee	54	305
Denver	50	283
Baltimore	49	291
Oakland	44	309
New England	42	268
Indianapolis	41	269
San Diego	41	263
Kansas City	40	286
Pittsburgh	39	241
Miami	39	240
Seattle	38	252
Buffalo	37	214
Cincinnati	35	229
N.Y. Jets	26	184
Cleveland	25	147
AFC total	**657**	**4154**
AFC average	**41.1**	**259.6**

NFC

Team	Sacks	Yards
St. Louis	57	358
Detroit	50	340
Minnesota	46	272
New Orleans	45	277
Tampa Bay	43	291
Atlanta	40	258
Washington	40	221
Philadelphia	37	272
Chicago	37	257
Carolina	35	235
Dallas	35	217
Arizona	33	229
San Francisco	32	227
N.Y. Giants	32	172
Green Bay	30	185
NFC total	**592**	**3811**
NFC average	**39.5**	**254.1**
NFL total	**1249**	**7965**
NFL average	**40.3**	**256.9**

INDIVIDUAL

BESTS OF THE SEASON

Sacks, season
NFC: 17.0—Kevin Carter, St. Louis.
AFC: 14.5—Jevon Kearse, Tennessee.

Sacks, game
AFC: 3.5—Michael McCrary, Baltimore vs. Tennessee, Dec. 5.
NFC: 3.0—Held by many players.

NFL LEADERS

Player, Team	No.
Carter, Kevin, St. Louis	17.0
Rice, Simeon, Arizona	16.5
Porcher, Robert, Detroit	15.0
Kearse, Jevon, Tennessee*	14.5
Pryce, Trevor, Denver*	13.0
Sapp, Warren, Tampa Bay	12.5
Brackens, Tony, Jacksonville*	12.0
Greene, Kevin, Carolina	12.0
Bratzke, Chad, Indianapolis*	12.0
McCrary, Michael, Baltimore*	11.5
Young, Bryant, San Francisco	11.0
Johnson, Raylee, San Diego*	10.5
Hardy, Kevin, Jacksonville*	10.5
Johnstone, Lance, Oakland*	10.0
Boulware, Peter, Baltimore*	10.0
Smith, Chuck, Atlanta	10.0
Randle, John, Minnesota	10.0
Walker, Gary, Jacksonville*	10.0
Russell, Darrell, Oakland*	9.5
*AFC.	

AFC

Player, Team	No.
Adams, Sam, Seattle	1.0
Alexander, Derrick, Cleveland	2.5
Armstrong, Trace, Miami	7.5
Bankston, Michael, Cincinnati	6.0
Barker, Roy, Cleveland	2.0

Player, Team	No.
Barndt, Tom, Kansas City	2.5
Barton, Eric, Oakland	3.0
Beasley, Aaron, Jacksonville	1.5
Bell, Myron, Cincinnati	2.0
Belser, Jason, Indianapolis	1.0
Bennett, Cornelius, Indianapolis	5.0
Berry, Bert, Indianapolis	1.0
Biekert, Greg, Oakland	2.0
Bishop, Blaine, Tennessee	2.5
Blevins, Tony, Indianapolis	1.0
Boulware, Peter, Baltimore	10.0
Bowden, Joe, Tennessee	3.5
Bowens, David, Denver	1.0
Bowens, Tim, Miami	1.5
Boyer, Brant, Jacksonville	4.0
Brackens, Tony, Jacksonville	12.0
Bratzke, Chad, Indianapolis	12.0
Braxton, Tyrone, Denver	1.0
Bromell, Lorenzo, Miami	5.0
Brown, Chad, Seattle	5.5
Brown, Cornell, Baltimore	1.0
Brown, Eric, Denver	1.5
Brown, Lance, Pittsburgh	1.0
Bruschi, Tedy, New England	2.0
Bryant, Tony, Oakland	4.5
Buckley, Terrell, Miami	1.0
Burnett, Rob, Baltimore	6.5
Burris, Jeff, Indianapolis	2.0
Bush, Lewis, San Diego	1.0
Cadrez, Glenn, Denver	7.0
Carter, Chris, New England	1.0
Chester, Larry, Indianapolis	1.0
Collons, Ferric, New England	2.0
Copeland, John, Cincinnati	4.0
Cowart, Sam, Buffalo	1.0
Crockett, Ray, Denver	2.0
Cummings, Joe, Buffalo	1.0
Curry, Eric, Jacksonville	0.5
Curtis, Canute, Cincinnati	1.0
Dalton, Lionel, Baltimore	1.0

1999 STATISTICS Sacks

Player, Team	No.
Daniels, Phillip, Seattle	9.0
Dixon, Gerald, San Diego	4.0
Dumas, Mike, San Diego	2.0
Eaton, Chad, New England	3.0
Edwards, Donnie, Kansas City	3.0
Emmons, Carlos, Pittsburgh	6.0
Evans, Josh, Tennessee	3.5
Farrior, James, N.Y. Jets	2.0
Ferguson, Jason, N.Y. Jets	1.0
Fisk, Jason, Tennessee	4.0
Flowers, Lethon, Pittsburgh	5.0
Foley, Steve, Cincinnati	3.5
Fontenot, Al, San Diego	5.0
Ford, Henry, Tennessee	5.5
Frederick, Mike, Tennessee	0.5
Gardener, Daryl, Miami	5.0
Gibson, Oliver, Cincinnati	4.5
Gildon, Jason, Pittsburgh	8.5
Gordon, Darrien, Oakland	1.0
Gordon, Dwayne, N.Y. Jets	1.0
Hand, Norman, San Diego	4.0
Hanks, Merton, Seattle	2.0
Hansen, Phil, Buffalo	6.0
Harden, Cedric, San Diego	0.5
Hardy, Kevin, Jacksonville	10.5
Harris, Corey, Baltimore	1.0
Harris, James, Oakland	2.5
Harrison, Rodney, San Diego	1.0
Harvey, Richard, Oakland	2.0
Hasselbach, Harald, Denver	2.5
Hasty, James, Kansas City	1.0
Henry, Kevin, Pittsburgh	1.0
Hicks, Eric, Kansas City	4.0
Holecek, John, Buffalo	1.0
Holland, Darius, Cleveland	2.0
Holmes, Kenny, Tennessee	4.0
Israel, Steve, New England	1.0
Jackson, Calvin, Miami	1.0
Jackson, Grady, Oakland	4.0
Jackson, Steve, Tennessee	0.5
Jenkins, DeRon, Baltimore	1.0
Johnson, Ellis, Indianapolis	7.5
Johnson, Raylee, San Diego	10.5
Johnson, Ted, New England	2.0
Johnstone, Lance, Oakland	10.0
Jones, Marvin, N.Y. Jets	1.0
Jones, Mike D., Tennessee	1.0
Katzenmoyer, Andy, New England	3.5
Kearse, Jevon, Tennessee	14.5
Kennedy, Cortez, Seattle	6.5
King, Lamar, Seattle	2.0
King, Shawn, Indianapolis	1.5
Kirkland, Levon, Pittsburgh	2.0
LaBounty, Matt, Seattle	2.0
Lake, Carnell, Jacksonville	3.5
Law, Ty, New England	0.5
Lewis, Mo, N.Y. Jets	5.5
Lewis, Ray, Baltimore	3.5
Logan, Ernie, N.Y. Jets	3.0
Lyle, Rick, N.Y. Jets	1.0
Marion, Brock, Miami	1.0
Marts, Lonnie, Jacksonville	2.0
Maryland, Russell, Oakland	1.5
McCormack, Hurvin, Cleveland	2.0
McCrary, Michael, Baltimore	11.5
McCutcheon, Daylon, Cleveland	1.0
McGinest, Willie, New England	9.0
McGlockton, Chester, Kansas City	1.5
McNeil, Ryan, Cleveland	1.0
Mickens, Ray, N.Y. Jets	2.0
Miller, Arnold, Cleveland	1.0
Miller, Jamir, Cleveland	4.5
Milloy, Lawyer, New England	2.0
Mitchell, Brandon, New England	3.0
Mohring, Mike, San Diego	2.0
Moran, Sean, Buffalo	0.5
Northern, Gabe, Buffalo	3.5
Ogbogu, Eric, N.Y. Jets	1.0
Oldham, Chris, Pittsburgh	3.0
O'Neal, Leslie, Kansas City	5.5
Osborne, Chuck, Oakland	1.0
Owens, Rich, Miami	8.5
Parker, Riddick, Seattle	2.0
Parrella, John, San Diego	5.5
Patton, Marvcus, Kansas City	6.5
Paup, Bryce, Jacksonville	1.0
Payne, Seth, Jacksonville	1.5
Perry, Marlo, Buffalo	1.5
Peterson, Mike, Indianapolis	3.0
Phifer, Roman, N.Y. Jets	4.5
Pleasant, Anthony, N.Y. Jets	2.0
Poole, Tyrone, Indianapolis	1.0
Porter, Joey, Pittsburgh	2.0
Price, Shawn, Buffalo	2.5
Pryce, Trevor, Denver	13.0
Rainer, Wali, Cleveland	1.0
Ransom, Derrick, Kansas City	1.0
Roberson, James, Jacksonville	1.0
Robertson, Marcus, Tennessee	0.5
Robinson, Eddie, Tennessee	6.0
Rogers, Sam, Buffalo	3.0
Rolle, Samari, Tennessee	3.0
Ross, Adrian, Cincinnati	1.0
Royal, Andre, Indianapolis	1.0
Roye, Orpheus, Pittsburgh	4.5
Russell, Darrell, Oakland	9.5
Seau, Junior, San Diego	3.5
Serwanga, Kato, New England	1.0
Sharper, Jamie, Baltimore	4.0
Shields, Scott, Pittsburgh	1.0
Simien, Tracy, San Diego	1.0
Simmons, Brian, Cincinnati	3.0
Sinclair, Michael, Seattle	6.0
Siragusa, Tony, Baltimore	3.5
Slade, Chris, New England	4.5
Smeenge, Joel, Jacksonville	5.0
Smith, Bruce, Buffalo	7.0
Smith, Darrin, Seattle	1.0
Smith, Fernando, Baltimore	2.0
Smith, Larry, Jacksonville	3.0
Smith, Neil, Denver	6.5
Spikes, Takeo, Cincinnati	3.0
Spires, Greg, New England	0.5
Steed, Joel, Pittsburgh	3.0
Stoutmire, Omar, N.Y. Jets	1.0
Sullivan, Chris, New England	1.0
Surtain, Patrick, Miami	2.0
Sword, Sam, Oakland	1.0
Tanuvasa, Maa, Denver	7.0
Taylor, Jason, Miami	2.5
Thierry, John, Cleveland	7.0
Thomas, Derrick, Kansas City	7.0
Thomas, Henry, New England	3.0
Thomas, Mark, Indianapolis	3.0
Thomas, Zach, Miami	1.0
Thornton, John, Tennessee	4.5
Tongue, Reggie, Kansas City	2.0
Trapp, James, Baltimore	1.0
Traylor, Keith, Denver	1.5
von Oelhoffen, Kimo, Cincinnati	4.0
Vrabel, Mike, Pittsburgh	2.0
Walker, Gary, Jacksonville	10.0

Player, Team	No.
Walker, Marquise, Oakland	1.0
Washington, Keith, Baltimore	1.0
Washington, Ted, Buffalo	2.5
Wayne, Nate, Denver	2.0
Webster, Larry, Baltimore	2.0
Whigham, Larry, New England	3.0
Whittington, Bernard, Indianapolis	1.0
Wiley, Marcellus, Buffalo	5.0
Williams, Alfred, Denver	4.0
Williams, Dan, Kansas City	5.0
Williams, Jamal, San Diego	1.0
Williams, K.D., Oakland	1.0
Williams, Pat, Buffalo	2.5
Wilson, Al, Denver	1.0
Wilson, Jerry, Miami	3.0
Wilson, Reinard, Cincinnati	3.0
Wiltz, Jason, N.Y. Jets	1.0
Wortham, Barron, Tennessee	0.5
Wynn, Renaldo, Jacksonville	1.5

NFC

Player, Team	No.
Abraham, Donnie, Tampa Bay	2.0
Agnew, Ray, St. Louis	2.5
Ahanotu, Chidi, Tampa Bay	6.5
Aldridge, Allen, Detroit	3.0
Allen, Taje, St. Louis	0.5
Archambeau, Lester, Atlanta	5.5
Armstead, Jessie, N.Y. Giants	9.0
Bailey, Champ, Washington	1.0
Bailey, Robert, Detroit	2.0
Ball, Jerry, Cle.-Min.*	2.0
Barber, Ronde, Tampa Bay	1.0
Barber, Shawn, Washington	1.0
Barrow, Micheal, Carolina	4.0
Booker, Vaughn, Green Bay	3.5
Boutte, Marc, Washington	1.0
Brooking, Keith, Atlanta	2.0
Brooks, Derrick, Tampa Bay	2.0
Bryant, Junior, San Francisco	4.5
Buchanan, Ray, Atlanta	1.0
Buckner, Brentson, San Francisco	1.0
Burke, Tom, Arizona	2.5
Burrough, John, Minnesota	1.0
Burton, Shane, Chicago	3.0
Butler, LeRoy, Green Bay	1.0
Caldwell, Mike, Philadelphia	1.0
Carter, Kevin, St. Louis	17.0
Claiborne, Chris, Detroit	1.5
Clemons, Charlie, St. Louis	3.0
Clemons, Duane, Minnesota	9.0
Coakley, Dexter, Dallas	1.0
Coleman, Marco, Washington	6.5
Colvin, Rosevelt, Chicago	2.0
Cook, Anthony, Washington	3.0
Cook, Rashard, Philadelphia	1.0
Crockett, Henri, Atlanta	1.5
Culpepper, Brad, Tampa Bay	6.0
Davis, Russell, Chicago	2.0
Dawkins, Brian, Philadelphia	1.5
Doleman, Chris, Minnesota	8.0
Dotson, Santana, Green Bay	2.5
Douglas, Hugh, Philadelphia	2.0
Drake, Jerry, Arizona	1.0
Dronett, Shane, Atlanta	6.5
Edwards, Antonio, Carolina	2.0
Ekuban, Ebenezer, Dallas	2.5
Ellis, Greg, Dallas	7.5
Elliss, Luther, Detroit	3.5
Farr, D'Marco, St. Louis	8.5

Player, Team	No.
Fields, Mark, New Orleans	4.0
Flanigan, Jim, Chicago	6.0
Fletcher, London, St. Louis	3.0
Francis, James, Washington	0.5
Fredrickson, Rob, Arizona	2.0
Galyon, Scott, N.Y. Giants	1.0
Garnes, Sam, N.Y. Giants	1.0
Gilbert, Sean, Carolina	2.5
Glover, La'Roi, New Orleans	8.5
Godfrey, Randall, Dallas	1.0
Greene, Kevin, Carolina	12.0
Griffith, Robert, Minnesota	4.0
Haley, Charles, San Francisco	3.0
Hall, Travis, Atlanta	4.5
Hambrick, Darren, Dallas	2.5
Hamilton, Keith, N.Y. Giants	4.0
Harris, Robert, N.Y. Giants	1.0
Harris, Walt, Chicago	1.0
Hennings, Chad, Dallas	5.0
Hewitt, Chris, New Orleans	1.0
Hitchcock, Jimmy, Minnesota	2.0
Hobgood-Chittick, Nate, St. Louis	0.5
Holdman, Warrick, Chicago	2.0
Holliday, Vonnie, Green Bay	6.0
Hudson, Chris, Chicago	1.0
Hunt, Cletidus, Green Bay	0.5
Jackson, Tyoka, Tampa Bay	1.0
Jefferson, Greg, Philadelphia	4.0
Jenkins, Billy, St. Louis	1.0
Johnson, Bill, Philadelphia	1.0
Jones, Cedric, N.Y. Giants	7.5
Jones, Ernest, Carolina	2.5
Jones, Greg, Washington	0.5
Jones, James, Detroit	7.0
Jones, Marcus, Tampa Bay	7.0
Jones, Mike, St. Louis	1.0
Kalu, Ndukwe, Washington	3.5
Kerney, Patrick, Atlanta	2.5
Kirschke, Travis, Detroit	2.0
Kowalkowski, Scott, Detroit	1.0
Lang, Kenard, Washington	6.0
Lett, Leon, Dallas	1.5
Lyght, Todd, St. Louis	2.5
Lyle, Keith, St. Louis	1.0
Lynch, John, Tampa Bay	0.5
Lyon, Billy, Green Bay	2.0
Mamula, Mike, Philadelphia	8.5
Martin, Steve, Philadelphia	2.0
Martin, Wayne, New Orleans	4.5
McBurrows, Gerald, Atlanta	1.0
McCleon, Dexter, St. Louis	1.5
McDaniel, Ed, Minnesota	2.0
McDonald, Ricardo, Chicago	0.5
McDonald, Tim, San Francisco	2.0
McFarland, Anthony, Tampa Bay	1.0
McKenzie, Keith, Green Bay	8.0
McKinnon, Ronald, Arizona	1.0
McMillian, Mark, Washington	1.5
Minter, Barry, Chicago	3.0
Minter, Mike, Carolina	1.0
Mitchell, Keith, New Orleans	3.5
Nguyen, Dat, Dallas	1.0
Nickerson, Hardy, Tampa Bay	0.5
Noble, Brandon, Dallas	3.0
Norton, Ken, San Francisco	1.0
Okeafor, Chike, San Francisco	1.0
Ottis, Brad, Arizona	1.0
Owens, Dan, Detroit	1.0
Peter, Jason, Carolina	4.5
Phillips, Joe, Minnesota	1.0
Pittman, Kavika, Dallas	3.0

Player, Team	No.
Porcher, Robert, Detroit	15.0
Posey, Jeff, San Francisco	2.0
Pounds, Darryl, Washington	1.0
Pringley, Mike, Detroit	1.5
Pritchett, Kelvin, Detroit	1.0
Randle, John, Minnesota	10.0
Reese, Ike, Philadelphia	3.0
Rice, Ron, Detroit	1.0
Rice, Simeon, Arizona	16.5
Richardson, Damien, Carolina	1.0
Robbins, Austin, New Orleans	2.0
Robinson, Bryan, Chicago	5.0
Robinson, Damien, Tampa Bay	0.5
Rucker, Mike, Carolina	3.0
Rudd, Dwayne, Minnesota	3.0
Sapp, Patrick, Arizona	1.0
Sapp, Warren, Tampa Bay	12.5
Sauer, Craig, Atlanta	1.0
Scroggins, Tracy, Detroit	8.5
Shade, Sam, Washington	1.5
Sharper, Darren, Green Bay	1.0
Simmons, Clyde, Chicago	7.0
Singleton, Alshermond, Tampa Bay	0.5
Smith, Brady, New Orleans	6.0
Smith, Chuck, Atlanta	10.0
Smith, Derek, Washington	1.0
Smith, Frankie, Chicago	1.0
Smith, Jermaine, Green Bay	0.5
Spellman, Alonzo, Dallas	5.0
Stevens, Matt, Washington	1.0
Stewart, Ryan, Detroit	1.0
Strahan, Michael, N.Y. Giants	5.5
Stubblefield, Dana, Washington	3.0
Swann, Eric, Arizona	4.0
Swinger, Rashod, Arizona	1.0
Thomas, Hollis, Philadelphia	1.0
Thomas, William, Philadelphia	2.5
Tomich, Jared, New Orleans	3.0

Player, Team	No.
Trotter, Jeremiah, Philadelphia	2.5
Tuaolo, Esera, Carolina	1.0
Tubbs, Winfred, San Francisco	2.0
Tuggle, Jessie, Atlanta	3.5
Tuinei, Van, Chicago	2.5
Vincent, Troy, Philadelphia	1.0
Vinson, Fred, Green Bay	1.0
Waddy, Jude, Green Bay	1.0
Wadsworth, Andre, Arizona	2.0
Walker, Darnell, San Francisco	1.0
Walz, Zack, Arizona	1.0
Wells, Dean, Carolina	0.5
Wells, Mike, Chicago	1.0
White, Steve, Tampa Bay	2.0
Whitehead, William, New Orleans	7.0
Whiting, Brandon, Philadelphia	1.0
Widmer, Corey, N.Y. Giants	3.0
Wilkins, Gabe, San Francisco	1.0
Wilkinson, Dan, Washington	8.0
Williams, Brian, Green Bay	2.0
Williams, Jay, St. Louis	4.0
Williams, Tony, Minnesota	5.0
Williams, Tyrone, Philadelphia	3.0
Wilson, Troy, New Orleans	5.5
Wistrom, Grant, St. Louis	6.5
Woodall, Lee, San Francisco	2.5
Woodson, Darren, Dallas	1.0
Young, Bryant, San Francisco	11.0
Zellner, Peppi, Dallas	1.0
Zgonina, Jeff, St. Louis	4.5

*Includes both NFC and AFC statistics.

PLAYERS WITH TWO CLUBS

Player, Team	No.
Ball, Jerry, Cleveland	1.0
Ball, Jerry, Minnesota	1.0

FUMBLES

TEAM

AFC

Team	Fum.	Own Fum. Rec.	Own Fum. *O.B.	Own Fum. Lost	TD	Opp Fum. Rec.	TD	†Yards	Total Rec.
Buffalo	17	5	1	11	0	9	1	75	14
Tennessee	17	8	0	9	0	24	2	96	32
Jacksonville	18	11	0	7	0	11	1	43	22
Pittsburgh	19	10	2	7	0	14	2	146	24
Kansas City	22	11	2	9	0	20	4	178	31
N.Y. Jets	22	14	2	6	0	11	1	-20	25
Oakland	22	6	1	15	0	13	1	107	19
Miami	23	7	3	13	0	10	1	33	17
Baltimore	24	12	1	11	0	10	0	-25	22
Indianapolis	25	9	5	11	1	13	1	0	22
New England	27	14	1	12	0	15	2	16	29
Cleveland	29	13	0	16	0	12	0	3	25
San Diego	29	18	0	11	0	12	2	6	30
Seattle	31	11	3	17	0	6	0	-14	17
Denver	33	21	2	10	0	11	1	1	32
Cincinnati	34	19	1	14	0	15	0	-14	34
AFC total	392	189	24	179	1	206	19	631	395
AFC average	24.5	11.8	1.5	11.2	0.1	12.9	1.2	39.4	24.7

*Fumbled out of bounds.
†Includes all fumble yardage (aborted plays and recoveries of own and opponents' fumbles).

NFC

Team	Fum.	Own Fum. Rec.	Own Fum. *O.B.	Own Fum. Lost	TD	Opp Fum. Rec.	TD	†Yards	Total Rec.
Detroit	21	10	3	8	0	16	3	100	26
Dallas	22	10	2	10	0	9	1	60	19
Atlanta	24	7	1	16	0	6	0	11	13
Carolina	24	5	0	19	0	14	0	37	19
Minnesota	24	4	1	19	0	18	0	8	22
Tampa Bay	25	4	2	19	0	9	0	-15	13
New Orleans	26	16	1	9	0	15	2	79	31
Green Bay	28	13	3	12	0	15	2	68	28
N.Y. Giants	29	14	3	12	0	7	1	26	21
San Francisco	29	15	1	13	0	7	3	95	22
St. Louis	30	11	3	16	0	7	1	100	18
Arizona	31	18	3	10	0	10	0	-4	28
Washington	31	15	5	11	0	13	1	43	28
Chicago	32	17	0	15	0	19	1	2	36
Philadelphia	33	11	1	21	0	18	0	32	29
NFC total	409	170	29	210	0	183	15	642	353
NFC average	27.3	11.3	1.9	14.0	0.0	12.2	1.0	42.8	23.5
NFL total	801	359	53	389	1	389	34	1273	748
NFL average	25.8	11.6	1.7	12.5	0.0	12.5	1.1	41.1	24.1

INDIVIDUAL

BESTS OF THE SEASON

Fumbles, season
AFC: 16—Brian Griese, Denver.
NFC: 12—Steve Beuerlein, Carolina; Brad Johnson, Washington.

Fumbles, game
AFC: 4—Jim Harbaugh, San Diego vs. Oakland, Dec. 26.
NFC: 4—Kurt Warner, St. Louis at Tennessee, Oct. 31.

Own fumbles recovered, season
AFC: 9—Brian Griese, Denver.
NFC: 5—Tiki Barber, N.Y. Giants; Jake Plummer, Arizona.

Own fumbles recovered, game
AFC: 3—Mark Brunell, Jacksonville vs. Denver, Dec. 13.
NFC: 2—Held by many players.

Opponents' fumbles recovered, season
AFC: 4—Ryan McNeil, Cleveland; Takeo Spikes, Cincinnati.
NFC: 4—Duane Clemons, Minnesota; Keith McKenzie, Green Bay.

Opponents' fumbles recovered, game
AFC: 2—Phil Hansen, Buffalo vs. Philadelphia, Sept. 26; Fernando Smith, Baltimore at Atlanta, Oct. 3; Ryan McNeil, Cleveland vs. New England, Oct. 3; Barron Wortham, Tennessee vs. St. Louis, Oct. 31; Reggie Tongue, Kansas City at Tampa Bay, Nov. 14.
NFC: 1—Held by many players.

Yards returning fumbles, season
AFC: 120—Travis Davis, Pittsburgh.
NFC: 98—Greg Ellis, Dallas.

Longest fumble return
AFC: 102—Travis Davis, Pittsburgh vs. Carolina, Dec. 26 (TD).
NFC: 98—Greg Ellis, Dallas vs. Arizona, Oct. 3 (TD).

AFC

Player, Team	Fum.	Own Rec.	Opp. Rec.	Yds.	Tot. Rec.	TD
Abdul-Jabbar, Karim, Cle.	0	1	0	0	1	0
Adams, Sam, Seattle	0	0	1	0	1	0
Albright, Ethan, Buffalo	1	0	0	-8	0	0
Allen, Eric, Oakland	0	0	1	0	1	0
Allen, Terry, New England	8	1	0	0	1	0
Anders, Kimble, Kansas City	1	0	0	0	0	0
Anderson, Willie, Cincinnati	0	1	0	0	1	0
Armstrong, Bruce, N.E.	0	1	0	0	1	0
Austin, Billy, Indianapolis	0	1	0	0	1	0
Banks, Tony, Baltimore	11	2	0	0	2	0
Barber, Mike, Indianapolis	0	1	0	0	1	0
Barlow, Reggie, Jacksonville	4	1	0	0	1	0
Barndt, Tom, Kansas City	0	0	1	0	1	0
Bartrum, Mike, New England	1	0	0	-7	0	0
Basnight, Michael, Cincinnati	1	1	0	0	1	0
Baxter, Fred, N.Y. Jets	0	1	0	0	1	0
Bellamy, Jay, Seattle	0	1	0	0	1	0
Bennett, Cornelius, Ind.	0	0	2	0	2	0
Bennett, Donnell, Kansas City	1	0	0	0	0	0
Bettis, Jerome, Pittsburgh	2	3	0	1	3	0
Binn, David, San Diego	1	0	0	-36	0	0
Bishop, Blaine, Tennessee	0	0	2	0	2	0
Blackwell, Will, Pittsburgh	1	0	0	0	0	0
Blake, Jeff, Cincinnati	12	7	0	-28	7	0
Bledsoe, Drew, New England	8	6	0	-13	6	0
Blevins, Tony, Indianapolis	0	0	2	2	2	0
Bloedorn, Greg, Seattle	1	0	0	-6	0	0
Boose, Dorian, N.Y. Jets	0	0	1	0	1	0
Boselli, Tony, Jacksonville	0	3	0	0	3	0
Bowden, Joe, Tennessee	0	0	3	11	3	0
Bowens, David, Denver	0	1	0	0	1	0
Brackens, Tony, Jacksonville	0	0	2	6	2	0
Braham, Rich, Cincinnati	0	1	0	0	1	0
Bratzke, Chad, Indianapolis	1	0	1	3	1	0
Brice, Will, Cincinnati	0	1	0	0	1	0
Brown, Chad, Seattle	0	0	1	0	1	0
Brown, Eric, Denver	2	1	0	0	1	0
Brown, Reggie, Seattle	1	0	0	0	0	0
Brown, Troy, New England	1	1	1	0	2	0
Bruener, Mark, Pittsburgh	0	2	0	4	2	0
Brunell, Mark, Jacksonville	6	3	0	-2	3	0
Bruschi, Tedy, New England	0	0	1	0	1	0
Bryant, Fernando, Jac.	0	0	3	27	3	0
Buckley, Terrell, Miami	1	0	0	0	0	0
Bush, Lewis, San Diego	0	0	1	0	1	0
Bynum, Kenny, San Diego	3	3	0	0	3	0
Byrd, Isaac, Tennessee	1	0	0	0	0	0
Cadrez, Glenn, Denver	0	1	3	74	4	1
Campbell, Mark, Cleveland	0	2	0	0	2	0
Carney, John, San Diego	0	1	0	0	1	0
Carter, Chris, New England	0	1	1	0	2	0
Carter, Tony, New England	0	1	0	0	1	0
Case, Stoney, Baltimore	2	2	0	-3	2	0
Chester, Larry, Indianapolis	0	0	1	0	1	0
Chiaverini, Darrin, Cleveland	0	1	0	0	1	0
Christie, Steve, Buffalo	0	1	0	0	1	0
Coleman, Marcus, N.Y. Jets	0	0	1	0	1	0
Collins, Cecil, Miami	2	1	0	0	1	0
Cota, Chad, Indianapolis	0	0	1	25	1	1
Couch, Tim, Cleveland	14	4	0	-11	4	0
Cowart, Sam, Buffalo	0	0	1	0	1	0
Cox, Bryan, N.Y. Jets	0	0	1	0	1	0
Craft, Jason, Jacksonville	0	0	1	23	1	1
Crockett, Ray, Denver	0	0	1	0	1	0

Player, Team	Fum.	Own Rec.	Opp. Rec.	Yds.	Tot. Rec.	TD
Davis, Billy, Baltimore	0	0	1	0	1	0
Davis, Reggie, San Diego	0	0	1	0	1	0
Davis, Terrell, Denver	1	1	0	0	1	0
Davis, Travis, Pittsburgh	0	0	1	102	1	1
Dawkins, Sean, Seattle	1	0	0	0	0	0
Dilger, Ken, Indianapolis	1	1	0	0	1	0
Dillon, Corey, Cincinnati	3	1	0	0	1	0
Dishman, Cris, Kansas City	0	1	2	40	3	1
Dixon, Gerald, San Diego	0	0	1	27	1	1
Dunn, David, Cleveland	3	1	0	0	1	0
Eaton, Chad, New England	0	0	3	53	3	1
Edwards, Donnie, K.C.	0	0	2	79	2	1
Edwards, Marc, Cleveland	1	0	0	0	0	0
Edwards, Troy, Pittsburgh	4	2	1	0	3	0
Emmons, Carlos, Pittsburgh	0	0	3	2	3	0
Evans, Chuck, Baltimore	0	1	0	0	1	0
Evans, Josh, Tennessee	0	0	2	0	2	0
Farmer, Robert, N.Y. Jets	1	1	0	0	1	0
Faulk, Kevin, New England	3	0	0	-9	0	0
Fauria, Christian, Seattle	1	0	0	0	0	0
Favors, Gregory, Tennessee	0	0	1	0	1	0
Fazande, Jermaine, S.D.	2	0	0	0	0	0
Fiedler, Jay, Jacksonville	1	0	0	0	0	0
Fletcher, Terrell, San Diego	1	1	0	0	1	0
Flutie, Doug, Buffalo	6	1	0	-5	1	0
Foley, Glenn, Seattle	1	0	0	0	0	0
Foley, Steve, Cincinnati	0	0	2	0	2	0
Fontenot, Al, San Diego	0	0	1	0	1	0
Ford, Henry, Tennessee	0	0	2	0	2	0
Fortin, Roman, San Diego	0	2	0	0	2	0
Fuller, Corey, Cleveland	0	0	2	0	2	0
Gannon, Rich, Oakland	8	1	0	-5	1	0
Gardener, Daryl, Miami	0	0	1	33	1	0
Gary, Olandis, Denver	2	1	0	0	1	0
Gash, Sam, Buffalo	0	1	0	0	1	0
George, Eddie, Tennessee	5	1	0	0	1	0
Gibson, Oliver, Cincinnati	0	0	1	0	1	0
Glenn, Aaron, N.Y. Jets	0	0	1	0	1	0
Glenn, Terry, New England	2	1	0	0	1	0
Goff, Mike, Cincinnati	0	1	0	0	1	0
Gogan, Kevin, Miami	0	1	0	0	1	0
Gonzalez, Tony, Kansas City	2	1	0	0	1	0
Goodwin, Hunter, Miami	1	0	0	0	0	0
Gordon, Darrien, Oakland	3	1	1	40	2	0
Gray, Chris, Seattle	0	1	0	0	1	0
Grbac, Elvis, Kansas City	7	1	0	0	1	0
Green, Ahman, Seattle	2	1	0	0	1	0
Green, Victor, N.Y. Jets	0	0	2	9	2	0
Griese, Brian, Denver	16	9	0	-46	9	0
Griffin, Damon, Cincinnati	5	2	0	0	2	0
Griffith, Howard, Denver	0	1	0	0	1	0
Grunhard, Tim, Kansas City	0	1	0	0	1	0
Hall, Cory, Cincinnati	0	0	1	0	1	0
Hansen, Phil, Buffalo	0	0	2	24	2	0
Harbaugh, Jim, San Diego	12	4	0	-20	4	0
Hardy, Kevin, Jacksonville	0	0	1	0	1	0
Harrison, Marvin, Indianapolis	2	1	0	0	1	0
Harrison, Nolan, Pittsburgh	0	0	1	0	1	0
Hawkins, Artrell, Cincinnati	0	0	1	0	1	0
Heath, Rodney, Cincinnati	0	0	2	-4	2	0
Hentrich, Craig, Tennessee	0	1	1	0	2	0
Herring, Kim, Baltimore	0	0	2	0	2	0
Hicks, Eric, Kansas City	0	0	2	44	2	1
Hill, Raymond, Miami	0	1	0	1	1	0
Holland, Darius, Cleveland	0	0	1	14	1	0
Hollier, Dwight, Miami	0	1	0	0	1	0
Holmes, Earl, Pittsburgh	0	0	1	0	1	0
Holmes, Priest, Baltimore	0	1	0	0	1	0
Horn, Joe, Kansas City	0	1	0	0	1	0
Huard, Damon, Miami	3	1	0	-5	1	0

1999 STATISTICS — Fumbles

Player, Team	Fum.	Own Rec.	Opp. Rec.	Yds.	Tot. Rec.	TD
Huntley, Richard, Pittsburgh...	3	0	0	0	0	0
Ismail, Qadry, Baltimore	2	0	0	0	0	0
Israel, Steve, New England	0	0	2	0	2	0
Izzo, Larry, Miami	0	0	1	0	1	0
Jackson, Brad, Baltimore........	0	0	1	0	1	0
Jackson, Grady, Oakland.........	0	0	1	0	1	0
Jackson, Greg, San Diego.......	0	0	1	0	1	0
Jackson, Steve, Tennessee	0	1	1	0	2	0
Jackson, Willie, Cincinnati.......	1	1	0	0	1	0
Jacquet, Nate, Miami	1	0	0	0	0	0
James, Edgerrin, Indianapolis.	8	2	0	0	2	0
Jefferson, Shawn, N.E.	0	1	0	0	1	0
Jenkins, Kerry, N.Y. Jets	0	1	0	0	1	0
Johnson, Darrius, Denver........	0	1	1	0	2	0
Johnson, Ellis, Indianapolis	0	0	1	0	1	0
Johnson, J.J., Miami	2	1	0	0	1	0
Johnson, Kevin, Cleveland......	1	1	0	0	1	0
Johnson, Leon, N.Y. Jets	1	0	0	0	0	0
Johnson, Pat, Baltimore..........	1	1	0	12	1	0
Johnson, Raylee, San Diego ...	0	0	1	0	1	0
Johnstone, Lance, Oakland.....	0	0	1	13	1	1
Jones, Charlie, San Diego	1	1	0	0	1	0
Jones, Lenoy, Cleveland	1	0	0	0	0	0
Jones, Marvin, N.Y. Jets	0	0	1	0	1	0
Jones, Mike D., Tennessee	0	0	1	0	1	0
Jones, Walter, Seattle	0	1	0	0	1	0
Jordan, Randy, Oakland..........	2	0	0	0	0	0
Joseph, Kerry, Seattle	0	0	1	0	1	0
Kaufman, Napoleon, Oakland..	3	2	0	0	2	0
Kearse, Jevon, Tennessee.......	0	0	1	14	1	1
Killens, Terry, Tennessee.........	0	0	1	0	1	0
Kirby, Terry, Cleveland	4	2	0	0	2	0
Kirkland, Levon, Pittsburgh	0	0	2	0	2	0
Kitna, Jon, Seattle...................	14	6	0	-9	6	0
Konrad, Rob, Miami	3	1	0	0	1	0
Kramer, Erik, San Diego..........	3	1	0	-7	1	0
Law, Ty, New England	1	0	1	0	1	0
Leeuwenburg, Jay, Cincinnati .	1	0	0	0	0	0
Lewis, Darryll, San Diego	0	0	2	42	2	1
Lewis, Jermaine, Baltimore.....	1	0	1	0	1	0
Lewis, Mo, N.Y. Jets	0	0	1	0	1	0
Lewis, Ray, Baltimore	1	0	0	0	0	0
Linton, Jonathan, Buffalo........	4	1	0	0	1	0
Little, Earl, Cleveland	1	0	0	0	0	0
Long, Kevin, Tennessee	1	0	0	-10	0	0
Loville, Derek, Denver.............	1	0	0	-12	0	0
Lucas, Ray, N.Y. Jets	8	4	0	-28	4	0
Lynn, Anthony, Denver............	0	0	1	0	1	0
Machado, J.P., N.Y. Jets	0	1	0	0	1	0
Mack, Tremain, Cincinnati......	3	1	0	0	1	0
Manning, Peyton, Ind.	6	2	0	-5	2	0
Manusky, Greg, Kansas City ...	0	0	1	0	1	0
Marino, Dan, Miami	5	0	0	0	0	0
Marion, Brock, Miami	2	0	1	0	1	0
Marts, Lonnie, Jacksonville	0	0	2	3	2	0
Martin, Curtis, N.Y. Jets	2	2	0	0	2	0
Maryland, Russell, Oakland....	0	0	1	0	1	0
May, Deems, Seattle	1	0	0	-12	0	0
Mayes, Derrick, Seattle...........	1	0	0	0	0	0
McCardell, Keenan, Jac.	1	1	0	0	1	0
McCrary, Michael, Baltimore...	0	0	1	0	1	0
McDuffie, O.J., Miami	2	0	0	0	0	0
McGinest, Willie, N.E.	0	0	2	2	2	1
McGlockton, Chester, K.C.	1	0	1	-2	1	0
McGriff, Travis, Denver	1	1	0	0	1	0
McKenzie, Kevin, Miami..........	1	0	0	0	0	0
McNair, Steve, Tennessee	3	1	0	0	1	0
McNeil, Ryan, Cleveland	0	0	4	0	4	0
Mickens, Terry, Oakland.........	1	0	0	0	0	0
Mili, Itula, Seattle	1	0	0	0	0	0

Player, Team	Fum.	Own Rec.	Opp. Rec.	Yds.	Tot. Rec.	TD
Miller, Chris, Denver	2	0	0	-6	0	0
Miller, Josh, Pittsburgh...........	1	0	0	-11	0	0
Milloy, Lawyer, New England ..	0	0	2	0	2	0
Mincy, Charles, Oakland	0	0	1	0	1	0
Mirer, Rick, N.Y. Jets	3	2	0	-1	2	0
Mitchell, Brandon, N.E.	0	0	1	0	1	0
Mitchell, Donald, Tennessee ...	0	0	1	0	1	0
Mitchell, Jeff, Baltimore..........	2	0	0	-36	0	0
Mitchell, Scott, Baltimore	1	0	0	0	0	0
Moore, Larry, Indianapolis......	2	0	0	-25	0	0
Morris, Bam, Kansas City	3	1	0	0	1	0
Moulds, Eric, Buffalo	1	0	0	0	0	0
Myers, Greg, Cincinnati	0	0	1	21	1	0
Newman, Anthony, Oakland...	0	0	1	0	1	0
Northern, Gabe, Buffalo	0	0	1	59	1	1
O'Donnell, Neil, Tennessee	5	3	0	-14	3	0
Ogbogu, Eric, N.Y. Jets	0	0	2	0	2	1
Ogden, Jonathan, Baltimore ...	0	2	0	2	2	0
Oldham, Chris, Pittsburgh	0	0	1	0	1	0
Olson, Benji, Tennessee	0	1	0	0	1	0
Ostroski, Jerry, Buffalo	1	0	0	-2	0	0
Owens, Rich, Miami................	0	0	1	0	1	0
Parker, Larry, Kansas City	1	0	0	0	0	0
Parker, Vaughn, San Diego	0	1	0	0	1	0
Patton, Marvcus, Kansas City .	0	0	3	0	3	0
Penn, Chris, San Diego...........	3	1	0	0	1	0
Perry, Jason, San Diego	0	0	1	0	1	0
Peterson, Mike, Indianapolis...	0	0	1	0	1	0
Pickens, Carl, Cincinnati	1	0	0	0	0	0
Pierce, Aaron, Baltimore	1	0	0	0	0	0
Pollard, Marcus, Indianapolis .	2	0	0	0	0	0
Pope, Daniel, Kansas City	1	1	0	-11	1	0
Porter, Joey, Pittsburgh	0	0	2	50	2	1
Powell, Ronnie, Cleveland	3	0	0	0	0	0
Pryce, Trevor, Denver	0	0	1	0	1	0
Randolph, Thomas, Ind.	0	0	1	0	1	0
Reed, Andre, Buffalo	0	1	0	0	1	0
Reed, Robert, San Diego	1	0	0	0	0	0
Rehberg, Scott, Cleveland	0	1	0	0	1	0
Richardson, Tony, K.C.	1	0	0	0	0	0
Robbins, Barret, Oakland........	0	1	0	0	1	0
Robinson, Eddie, Tennessee ...	0	0	3	1	3	0
Rodgers, Derrick, Miami.........	0	0	2	0	2	0
Rogers, Charlie, Seattle	3	0	0	0	0	0
Rogers, Sam, Buffalo	0	0	2	7	2	0
Rolle, Samari, Tennessee........	1	0	1	3	1	0
Romanowski, Bill, Denver.......	1	1	0	0	1	0
Rouen, Tom, Denver...............	1	0	0	0	0	0
Roye, Orpheus, Pittsburgh	0	0	1	0	1	0
Russell, Darrell, Oakland.........	0	0	1	0	1	0
Rutledge, Rod, New England ..	1	0	0	0	0	0
Saleh, Tarek, Cleveland	0	0	1	0	1	0
Schulz, Kurt, Buffalo...............	0	0	1	0	1	0
Seau, Junior, San Diego	0	0	1	0	1	0
Serwanga, Kato, New England.	0	0	1	0	1	0
Shaw, Sedrick, Cleveland........	1	0	0	0	0	0
Shehee, Rashaan, Kansas City.	1	0	0	0	0	0
Shelton, Daimon, Jacksonville.	0	0	1	0	1	0
Shields, Will, Kansas City	0	1	0	0	1	0
Simien, Tracy, San Diego	0	0	1	0	1	0
Simmons, Brian, Cincinnati	0	0	1	0	1	0
Simmons, Jason, Pittsburgh ...	0	1	0	0	1	0
Simmons, Tony, New England .	1	0	0	0	0	0
Sinclair, Michael, Seattle.........	0	0	1	13	1	0
Siragusa, Tony, Baltimore.......	0	1	0	0	1	0
Smith, Akili, Cincinnati............	4	1	0	-3	1	0
Smith, Antowain, Buffalo	4	0	0	0	0	0
Smith, Bruce, Buffalo..............	0	0	1	0	1	0
Smith, Detron, Denver............	0	0	1	0	1	0
Smith, Fernando, Baltimore	0	0	3	0	3	0

Player, Team	Fum.	Own Rec.	Opp. Rec.	Yds.	Tot. Rec.	TD
Smith, Jimmy, Jacksonville	1	0	0	0	0	0
Smith, Rod, Denver	1	0	0	0	0	0
Smith, Thomas, Buffalo	0	0	1	0	1	0
Smith, Travian, Oakland	0	0	1	1	1	0
Spears, Marcus, Kansas City ..	0	1	0	0	1	0
Spikes, Takeo, Cincinnati	0	0	4	0	4	0
Springs, Shawn, Seattle	0	0	1	0	1	0
Steed, Joel, Pittsburgh	0	0	1	4	1	0
Stephens, Tremayne, S.D.	2	3	0	0	3	0
Stewart, James, Jacksonville ..	4	1	0	0	1	0
Stewart, Kordell, Pittsburgh....	4	1	0	0	1	0
Stewart, Rayna, Jacksonville ..	0	1	0	0	1	0
Stone, Dwight, N.Y. Jets	3	2	0	0	2	0
Stoutmire, Omar, N.Y. Jets	0	0	1	0	1	0
Szott, Dave, Kansas City	0	1	0	0	1	0
Taylor, Jason, Miami	0	0	2	4	2	1
Teague, Trey, Denver	1	0	0	-9	0	0
Thigpen, Yancey, Tennessee ...	1	0	0	0	0	0
Thomas, Derrick, Kansas City.	0	0	1	0	1	0
Thomas, Mark, Indianapolis ...	0	0	1	0	1	0
Thompson, Mike, Cleveland....	0	0	2	0	2	0
Tomczak, Mike, Pittsburgh	3	0	0	-6	0	0
Tongue, Reggie, Kansas City ..	0	0	3	9	3	1
Treu, Adam, Oakland	1	0	0	0	0	0
Tupa, Tom, N.Y. Jets	1	0	0	0	0	0
Turner, Eric, Oakland	0	0	2	34	2	0
Turner, Scott, San Diego	0	0	1	0	1	0
Vanover, Tamarick, K.C.	3	1	0	0	1	0
von Oelhoffen, Kimo, Cin.	0	0	1	0	1	0
Vrabel, Mike, Pittsburgh	0	1	0	0	1	0
Wade, John, Jacksonville	1	0	0	-14	0	0
Walker, Brian, Seattle	0	1	0	0	1	0
Walker, Denard, Tennessee	0	0	1	83	1	1
Walker, Derrick, Oakland	1	0	0	0	0	0
Ward, Dedric, N.Y. Jets	2	0	0	0	0	0
Ward, Hines, Pittsburgh	1	0	0	0	0	0
Washington, Keith, Baltimore .	1	1	0	0	1	0
Watson, Chris, Denver	5	2	1	0	3	0
Watters, Ricky, Seattle	4	0	0	0	0	0
Wheatley, Tyrone, Oakland......	3	1	0	0	1	0
Wiegert, Zach, Jacksonville ...	0	1	0	0	1	0
Wilkins, Terrence, Ind.	3	1	0	0	1	1
Williams, Dan, Kansas City	0	0	2	0	2	0
Williams, Darryl, Seattle	0	0	1	0	1	0
Williams, James, Cleveland ...	0	0	2	0	2	0
Williams, K.D., Oakland	0	0	1	0	1	0
Williams, Kevin, N.Y. Jets	1	0	0	0	0	0
Williams, Nick, Cincinnati	1	0	0	0	0	0
Williams, Robert, Kansas City.	0	0	1	0	1	0
Wilson, Al, Denver	0	0	2	0	2	0
Wooden, Shawn, Miami	0	0	2	0	2	0
Woods, Jerome, Kansas City..	0	0	1	19	1	0
Woodson, Charles, Oakland...	0	0	1	24	1	0
Woodson, Rod, Baltimore	1	2	0	0	2	0
Woody, Damien, New England.	1	1	0	-10	1	0
Wooten, Tito, Indianapolis	0	0	2	0	2	0
Wortham, Barron, Tennessee..	0	0	3	8	3	0
Wright, Lawrence, Cincinnati..	0	0	1	0	1	0
Wynn, Renaldo, Jacksonville ..	0	0	1	0	1	0
Yeast, Craig, Cincinnati	2	1	0	0	1	0

NFC

Player, Team	Fum.	Own Rec.	Opp. Rec.	Yds.	Tot. Rec.	TD
Adams, Flozell, Dallas	0	1	0	0	1	0
Aikman, Troy, Dallas	8	2	0	-12	2	0
Aldridge, Allen, Detroit	1	0	1	8	1	0
Alstott, Mike, Tampa Bay	6	0	0	0	0	0
Ambrose, Ashley, N.O.	0	0	2	29	2	0
Anthony, Reidel, Tampa Bay ...	1	0	0	0	0	0
Banks, Antonio, Minnesota.....	0	0	1	0	1	0
Barber, Tiki, N.Y. Giants	5	5	0	0	5	0
Barnhardt, Tommy, N.O.	1	1	0	0	1	0
Barrow, Micheal, Carolina	0	0	1	0	1	0
Batch, Charlie, Detroit	4	0	0	0	0	0
Bates, Mario, Arizona	2	0	1	0	1	0
Bates, Michael, Carolina	1	0	0	0	0	0
Beasley, Fred, San Francisco ..	2	2	0	0	2	0
Bennett, Edgar, Chicago	1	0	0	0	0	0
Bennett, Tommy, Arizona	0	0	1	0	1	0
Berger, Mitch, Minnesota	0	0	1	0	1	0
Beuerlein, Steve, Carolina	12	0	0	-4	0	0
Biakabutuka, Tim, Carolina	3	0	0	0	0	0
Bostic, James, Philadelphia	2	0	0	0	0	0
Boston, David, Arizona	2	1	0	0	1	0
Bowie, Larry, Washington	1	0	0	0	0	0
Bradford, Corey, Green Bay	1	0	0	0	0	0
Brooks, Derrick, Tampa Bay	0	0	2	4	2	0
Brooks, Macey, Chicago	0	0	1	0	1	0
Broughton, Luther, Phi.	0	1	0	0	1	0
Brown, Dave, Arizona	4	1	0	0	1	0
Brown, Doug, Washington	0	0	1	0	1	0
Brown, Gary, N.Y. Giants	1	0	0	0	0	0
Brown, Ray, San Francisco	0	2	0	0	2	0
Bryant, Junior, San Francisco.	0	0	1	0	1	1
Burns, Keith, Chicago	0	0	1	0	1	0
Bush, Devin, St. Louis	0	1	1	31	2	0
Butler, LeRoy, Green Bay	0	0	1	0	1	0
Caldwell, Mike, Philadelphia ...	0	0	1	0	1	0
Carrier, Mark, Detroit	0	0	1	6	1	0
Carter, Kevin, St. Louis	0	0	2	0	2	0
Carter, Marty, Atlanta	0	0	1	0	1	0
Carter, Tom, Chicago	0	0	1	21	1	0
Centers, Larry, Washington	2	1	0	0	1	0
Chandler, Chris, Atlanta	7	4	0	-14	4	0
Christian, Bob, Atlanta	1	0	0	0	0	0
Claiborne, Chris, Detroit	0	0	3	27	3	0
Clark, Greg J., San Francisco..	1	0	0	0	0	0
Cleeland, Cameron, N.O.	1	0	0	0	0	0
Clemons, Charlie, St. Louis	0	0	1	0	1	0
Clemons, Duane, Minnesota ...	0	0	4	0	4	0
Cody, Mac, Arizona	2	1	0	0	1	0
Coleman, Marco, Washington.	0	0	1	42	1	1
Collins, Andre, Detroit	0	0	1	0	1	0
Collins, Kerry, N.Y. Giants	11	2	0	-27	2	0
Colvin, Rosevelt, Chicago	0	0	1	0	1	0
Compton, Mike, Detroit	0	2	0	8	2	0
Connell, Albert, Washington ...	1	1	0	0	1	0
Conway, Brett, Washington	0	1	0	0	1	0
Conway, Curtis, Chicago	2	0	0	0	0	0
Cook, Anthony, Washington ...	0	0	1	0	1	0
Cousin, Terry, Chicago	0	0	1	0	1	0
Craver, Aaron, New Orleans....	1	1	0	0	1	0
Crowell, Germane, Detroit	1	1	0	0	1	0
Culpepper, Daunte, Minnesota.	1	1	0	-2	1	0
Cunningham, Randall, Min. ...	2	0	0	-1	0	0
Davis, Eric, Carolina	1	0	1	0	1	0
Davis, Stephen, Washington...	4	2	0	0	2	0
Davis, Troy, New Orleans	1	0	0	0	0	0
Dawkins, Brian, Philadelphia...	0	1	1	0	2	0
Deese, Derrick, San Francisco.	0	4	0	0	4	0
Delhomme, Jake, New Orleans	1	0	0	0	0	0
Diaz, Jorge, Tampa Bay	0	1	0	0	1	0
Dilfer, Trent, Tampa Bay	6	0	0	-4	0	0
Doleman, Chris, Minnesota	0	0	2	7	2	0
Drake, Jerry, Arizona	0	0	1	0	1	0
Drakeford, Tyronne, N.O.	0	0	1	20	1	1
Dronett, Shane, Atlanta	0	0	1	15	1	0
Dunn, Warrick, Tampa Bay	3	1	0	0	1	0
Dwight, Tim, Atlanta	2	0	0	0	0	0
Edwards, Antuan, Green Bay ..	1	0	0	0	0	0

– 273 –

Player, Team	Fum.	Own Rec.	Opp. Rec.	Yds.	Tot. Rec.	TD
Ellis, Greg, Dallas	0	0	1	98	1	1
Elliss, Luther, Detroit	0	0	2	11	2	1
Ellsworth, Percy, N.Y. Giants	0	0	1	15	1	0
Engram, Bobby, Chicago	2	1	1	0	2	0
Enis, Curtis, Chicago	4	2	0	0	2	0
Evans, Leomont, Washington	0	0	1	0	1	0
Everitt, Steve, Philadelphia	0	1	0	0	1	0
Fair, Terry, Detroit	2	0	1	35	1	1
Fann, Chad, San Francisco	1	1	0	0	1	0
Faulk, Marshall, St. Louis	2	0	0	0	0	0
Favre, Brett, Green Bay	9	1	0	-2	1	0
Fields, Mark, New Orleans	0	0	1	0	1	0
Flanigan, Jim, Chicago	0	0	1	98	1	0
Floyd, William, Carolina	1	1	0	0	1	0
Fontenot, Jerry, New Orleans	0	1	0	0	1	0
Fredrickson, Rob, Arizona	0	0	1	0	1	0
Freeman, Antonio, Green Bay	1	1	0	0	1	0
Frerotte, Gus, Detroit	3	1	0	0	1	0
Garcia, Frank, Carolina	0	2	0	0	2	0
Garcia, Jeff, San Francisco	5	1	0	-1	1	0
Gardner, Barry, Philadelphia	0	0	1	20	1	0
Garner, Charlie, San Francisco	4	0	0	0	0	0
George, Jeff, Minnesota	8	2	0	0	2	0
Germaine, Joe, St. Louis	1	0	0	0	0	0
Givens, Reggie, San Francisco	1	0	0	0	0	0
Glover, La'Roi, New Orleans	0	0	1	2	1	0
Gragg, Scott, N.Y. Giants	0	1	0	0	1	0
Graham, Aaron, Arizona	1	1	0	0	1	0
Graham, Kent, N.Y. Giants	4	2	0	0	2	0
Gramatica, Martin, Tampa Bay	0	0	1	0	1	0
Graziani, Tony, Atlanta	4	2	0	-8	2	0
Green, Darrell, Washington	0	0	1	4	1	0
Green, Jacquez, Tampa Bay	1	0	0	0	0	0
Greene, Kevin, Carolina	0	0	3	8	3	1
Hakim, Az-Zahir, St. Louis	6	3	0	0	3	0
Hall, Travis, Atlanta	0	0	1	0	1	0
Hallock, Ty, Chicago	0	0	1	0	1	0
Hamilton, Keith, N.Y. Giants	0	0	2	0	2	0
Hanspard, Byron, Atlanta	1	0	0	0	0	0
Hardy, Terry, Arizona	1	0	0	0	0	0
Harris, Al, Philadelphia	1	0	0	0	0	0
Harris, Bernardo, Green Bay	0	1	0	0	1	0
Harris, Mark, San Francisco	1	0	0	0	0	0
Harris, Ronnie, Atlanta	1	0	0	0	0	0
Harris, Sean, Chicago	0	0	2	0	2	1
Harris, Walt, Chicago	0	0	1	0	1	0
Hartings, Jeff, Detroit	0	2	0	1	2	0
Hasselbeck, Matt, Green Bay	1	1	0	-16	1	0
Hauck, Tim, Philadelphia	0	0	1	0	1	0
Henderson, William, G.B.	1	0	0	0	0	0
Hetherington, Chris, Carolina	0	0	1	0	1	0
Hicks, Skip, Washington	1	0	0	0	0	0
Hill, Greg, Detroit	1	0	0	0	0	0
Hoard, Leroy, Minnesota	4	0	0	0	0	0
Hobert, Billy Joe, N.O.	2	1	0	-8	1	0
Holcombe, Robert, St. Louis	4	0	0	0	0	0
Holdman, Warrick, Chicago	0	0	1	33	1	0
Holliday, Vonnie, Green Bay	0	0	1	0	1	0
Holmes, Lester, Arizona	0	1	0	0	1	0
Holsey, Bernard, N.Y. Giants	0	1	0	1	1	0
Holt, Torry, St. Louis	4	1	0	0	1	0
Hunt, Cletidus, Green Bay	0	0	1	0	1	0
Irvin, Sedrick, Detroit	2	0	0	0	0	0
Ismail, Rocket, Dallas	1	0	0	0	0	0
Jackson, Terry, San Francisco	1	0	0	0	0	0
Jeffers, Patrick, Carolina	0	1	0	3	1	0
Jefferson, Greg, Philadelphia	0	0	2	4	2	0
Jett, John, Detroit	1	0	0	0	0	0
Johnson, Anthony, Carolina	1	0	0	0	0	0
Johnson, Brad, Washington	12	2	0	-8	2	0

Player, Team	Fum.	Own Rec.	Opp. Rec.	Yds.	Tot. Rec.	TD
Johnson, Charles, Phi.	2	1	0	0	1	0
Johnson, LeShon, N.Y. Giants	2	0	0	0	0	0
Johnson, Tre', Washington	0	3	0	0	3	0
Johnston, Daryl, Dallas	0	1	0	0	1	0
Jones, Donta, Carolina	0	0	1	0	1	0
Jones, James, Detroit	0	0	1	0	1	0
Jones, Mike, St. Louis	1	0	2	42	2	1
Jordan, Charles, Green Bay	1	1	0	0	1	0
Joyce, Matt, Arizona	0	1	0	0	1	0
Jurevicius, Joe, N.Y. Giants	1	0	0	0	0	0
Kelly, Jeff, Atlanta	0	0	1	0	1	0
Kelly, Rob, New Orleans	0	0	1	0	1	0
Kennison, Eddie, New Orleans	6	4	0	0	4	0
Kinchen, Brian, Carolina	0	0	1	0	1	0
King, Shaun, Tampa Bay	4	1	0	0	1	0
Kirschke, Travis, Detroit	0	0	1	0	1	0
Kleinsasser, Jim, Minnesota	2	0	0	0	0	0
Knight, Sammy, New Orleans	0	0	1	0	1	0
Kozlowski, Brian, Atlanta	1	0	0	0	0	0
Kreutz, Olin, Chicago	1	2	0	-17	2	0
LaFleur, David, Dallas	0	1	0	0	1	0
Landeta, Sean, Philadelphia	1	1	0	0	1	0
Lane, Fred, Carolina	1	0	0	0	0	0
Lang, Kenard, Washington	0	0	1	0	1	0
Lassiter, Kwamie, Arizona	0	0	2	0	2	0
Lee, Amp, St. Louis	1	0	0	0	0	0
Lett, Leon, Dallas	0	0	2	0	2	0
Levens, Dorsey, Green Bay	5	0	0	0	0	0
Levingston, Bashir, NYG	1	0	0	0	0	0
Makovicka, Joel, Arizona	1	1	0	0	1	0
Mamula, Mike, Philadelphia	0	0	2	0	2	0
Martin, Steve, Philadelphia	0	0	1	0	1	0
Martin, Wayne, New Orleans	0	0	2	0	2	0
Mathis, Kevin, Dallas	1	1	0	0	1	0
Matthews, Shane, Chicago	7	2	0	-14	2	0
Mayberry, Tony, Tampa Bay	1	0	0	-15	0	0
McBride, Tod, Green Bay	0	0	2	0	2	0
McBurrows, Gerald, Atlanta	0	0	1	0	1	0
McDaniel, Ed, Minnesota	0	0	2	0	2	0
McDonald, Tim, S.F.	0	0	1	0	1	0
McGarrahan, Scott, G.B.	0	1	0	0	1	0
McIver, Everett, Dallas	0	1	0	0	1	0
McKenzie, Keith, Green Bay	0	0	4	63	4	2
McKinley, Dennis, Arizona	0	1	1	0	2	0
McKinnon, Ronald, Arizona	0	0	1	0	1	0
McMillian, Mark, S.F.-Was.	1	0	1	41	1	1
McNabb, Donovan, Phi.	8	0	0	-3	0	0
McNown, Cade, Chicago	6	2	0	-2	2	0
McQuarters, R.W., S.F.	1	0	0	0	0	0
McWilliams, Johnny, Arizona	1	1	0	0	1	0
Metcalf, Eric, Carolina	2	0	0	0	0	0
Milburn, Glyn, Chicago	4	2	0	0	2	0
Miller, Jim, Chicago	4	3	0	-19	3	0
Minter, Barry, Chicago	0	0	1	0	1	0
Minter, Mike, Carolina	0	0	2	30	2	0
Mitchell, Basil, Green Bay	2	1	1	0	2	0
Mitchell, Brian, Washington	2	1	1	5	2	0
Mitchell, Keith, New Orleans	0	0	1	0	1	0
Mitchell, Pete, N.Y. Giants	1	0	0	0	0	0
Montgomery, Joe, N.Y. Giants	2	0	0	0	0	0
Moore, Damon, Philadelphia	0	0	1	0	1	0
Morrow, Harold, Minnesota	0	0	1	0	1	0
Moss, Randy, Minnesota	3	0	0	0	0	0
Muhammad, Muhsin, Carolina	1	0	0	0	0	0
Murphy, Yo, Minnesota	1	0	0	0	0	0
Murrell, Adrian, Arizona	4	0	0	0	0	0
Nelson, Jim, Green Bay	0	0	1	0	1	0
Noble, Brandon, Dallas	0	0	1	0	1	0
Nutten, Tom, St. Louis	0	1	0	0	1	0
Oben, Roman, N.Y. Giants	0	2	0	0	2	0

		Own	Opp.		Tot.	
Player, Team	Fum.	Rec.	Rec.	Yds.	Rec.	TD
Oliver, Winslow, Atlanta	2	0	0	0	0	0
Olivo, Brock, Detroit	0	0	1	0	1	0
Owens, Terrell, San Francisco	1	0	0	0	0	0
Oxendine, Ken, Atlanta	5	0	0	0	0	0
Palmer, David, Minnesota	1	0	0	0	0	0
Parker, De'Mond, Green Bay	1	1	1	0	2	0
Pederson, Doug, Philadelphia	7	0	0	0	0	0
Perry, Todd, Chicago	0	1	0	0	1	0
Perry, Wilmont, New Orleans	0	1	0	0	1	0
Peter, Christian, N.Y. Giants	0	0	1	38	1	1
Peterson, Tony, S.F.	1	0	0	0	0	0
Phillips, Lawrence, S.F.	2	2	0	0	2	0
Philyaw, Dino, New Orleans	1	1	0	0	1	0
Pittman, Kavika, Dallas	0	0	2	0	2	0
Pittman, Michael, Arizona	3	1	0	0	1	0
Plummer, Jake, Arizona	7	5	0	-4	5	0
Pounds, Darryl, Washington	1	0	1	2	1	0
Preston, Roell, San Francisco	1	1	0	0	1	0
Quarles, Shelton, Tampa Bay	0	0	1	0	1	0
Ramirez, Tony, Detroit	0	1	0	0	1	0
Randle, John, Minnesota	0	0	3	0	3	0
Raymer, Cory, Washington	0	1	0	0	1	0
Rice, Ron, Detroit	0	0	1	0	1	0
Rice, Simeon, Arizona	0	0	1	0	1	0
Rivera, Marco, Green Bay	0	1	0	0	1	0
Roaf, William, New Orleans	0	1	0	0	1	0
Robbins, Austin, New Orleans	0	0	1	0	1	0
Roberts, Ray, Detroit	0	1	0	0	1	0
Robinson, Damien, T.B.	0	0	2	0	2	0
Rossum, Allen, Philadelphia	6	2	0	0	2	0
Rudd, Dwayne, Minnesota	0	0	1	0	1	0
Samuel, Khari, Chicago	0	0	1	0	1	0
Sanders, Deion, Dallas	1	0	0	0	0	0
Sanders, Frank, Arizona	2	1	0	0	1	0
Sapp, Warren, Tampa Bay	0	0	2	0	2	0
Sauerbrun, Todd, Detroit	1	0	0	0	0	0
Schlesinger, Cory, Detroit	4	1	0	0	1	0
Schroeder, Bill, Green Bay	3	0	0	0	0	0
Scroggins, Tracy, Detroit	0	0	2	4	2	0
Scurlock, Mike, Carolina	0	0	1	0	1	0
Sehorn, Jason, N.Y. Giants	1	0	0	-1	0	0
Sellers, Mike, Washington	1	0	0	0	0	0
Shade, Sam, Washington	0	0	1	0	1	0
Sharper, Darren, Green Bay	0	0	1	9	1	0
Simmons, Clyde, Chicago	0	0	1	0	1	0
Slutzker, Scott, New Orleans	1	0	0	0	0	0
Smith, Brady, New Orleans	0	0	2	0	2	0
Smith, Chuck, Atlanta	0	0	1	18	1	0
Smith, Derek, Washington	0	0	1	0	1	0
Smith, Emmitt, Dallas	5	1	0	0	1	0
Smith, Frankie, Chicago	0	0	1	0	1	0
Smith, Jermaine, Green Bay	1	0	0	0	0	0
Smith, Lamar, New Orleans	1	0	0	0	0	0
Smith, Robert, Minnesota	1	0	0	0	0	0
Sparks, Phillippi, N.Y. Giants	0	1	0	0	1	0
Spellman, Alonzo, Dallas	0	0	1	0	1	0
Stablein, Brian, Detroit	1	1	0	0	1	0
Staley, Duce, Philadelphia	5	2	0	0	2	0
Stanley, Chad, San Francisco	0	1	0	0	1	0
Stenstrom, Steve, S.F.	3	0	0	-1	0	0
Stepnoski, Mark, Dallas	1	1	0	-26	1	0
Steussie, Todd, Minnesota	0	1	0	0	1	0
Stevens, Matt, Washington	0	0	1	0	1	0
Stokes, J.J., San Francisco	1	1	0	0	1	0

		Own	Opp.		Tot.	
Player, Team	Fum.	Rec.	Rec.	Yds.	Rec.	TD
Strahan, Michael, N.Y. Giants	0	0	2	0	2	0
Stubblefield, Dana, Was.	0	0	1	0	1	0
Styles, Lorenzo, St. Louis	0	1	0	0	1	0
Swift, Michael, Carolina	0	0	1	0	1	0
Tate, Robert, Minnesota	1	0	0	0	0	0
Taylor, Bobby, Philadelphia	0	0	3	0	3	0
Teague, George, Dallas	0	0	1	0	1	0
Terry, Chris, Carolina	0	1	1	0	2	0
Thomas, Hollis, Philadelphia	0	0	1	2	1	0
Thomas, Orlando, Minnesota	0	0	1	0	1	0
Thomas, Tra, Philadelphia	0	1	0	0	1	0
Thomas, William, Philadelphia	0	0	1	9	1	0
Tillman, Pat, Arizona	1	1	0	0	1	0
Timmerman, Adam, St. Louis	0	1	0	0	1	0
Tobeck, Robbie, Atlanta	0	1	0	0	1	0
Tolliver, Billy Joe, N.O.	4	2	0	-24	2	0
Trotter, Jeremiah, Philadelphia	0	0	1	0	1	0
Tuaolo, Esera, Carolina	0	0	1	0	1	0
Tubbs, Winfred, S.F.	0	0	1	0	1	0
Tucker, Jason, Dallas	1	1	0	0	1	0
Tuinei, Van, Chicago	0	0	2	0	2	0
Turk, Matt, Washington	1	0	0	0	0	0
Turner, Kevin, Philadelphia	1	1	0	0	1	0
Uwaezuoke, Iheanyi, Detroit	1	0	0	0	0	0
Verba, Ross, Green Bay	0	1	0	2	1	0
Villarrial, Chris, Chicago	0	2	0	0	2	0
Wahle, Mike, Green Bay	0	1	0	0	1	0
Walker, Darnell, S.F.	0	0	2	71	2	1
Walls, Wesley, Carolina	1	0	0	0	0	0
Warner, Kurt, St. Louis	9	0	0	-4	0	0
Warren, Chris, Dallas	4	0	0	0	0	0
Watson, Justin, St. Louis	2	0	0	0	0	0
Weary, Fred, New Orleans	0	2	2	60	4	1
Weathers, Andre, N.Y. Giants	0	0	1	0	1	0
Weldon, Casey, Washington	1	1	0	-2	1	0
Wells, Mike, Chicago	0	0	1	0	1	0
Westbrook, Bryant, Detroit	0	0	1	0	1	0
Westbrook, Michael, Was.	3	1	0	0	1	0
Wheeler, Mark, Philadelphia	0	0	1	0	1	0
White, Steve, Tampa Bay	0	0	1	0	1	0
Wilkinson, Dan, Washington	0	0	1	0	1	0
Williams, Aeneas, Arizona	0	1	1	0	2	0
Williams, Brian, Green Bay	0	1	0	0	1	0
Williams, Charlie, Dallas	0	0	1	0	1	0
Williams, Karl, Tampa Bay	2	1	0	0	1	0
Williams, Ricky, New Orleans	6	1	0	0	1	0
Williams, Roland, St. Louis	0	2	0	0	2	0
Williams, Tony, Minnesota	0	0	1	0	1	0
Williams, U. Tyrone, G.B.	1	0	2	12	2	0
Williams, Tyrone, Philadelphia	0	0	1	0	1	0
Winters, Frank, Green Bay	0	1	0	0	1	0
Wistrom, Grant, St. Louis	1	0	1	31	1	0
Wong, Kailee, Minnesota	0	0	1	4	1	0
Young, Steve, San Francisco	2	0	0	0	0	0
Zeier, Eric, Tampa Bay	1	0	0	0	0	0
Zelenka, Joe, San Francisco	1	0	1	-15	1	0

PLAYERS WITH TWO CLUBS

		Own	Opp.		Tot.	
Player, Team	Fum.	Rec.	Rec.	Yds.	Rec.	TD
McMillian, Mark, S.F.	0	0	1	41	1	1
McMillian, Mark, Washington	1	0	0	0	0	0

FIELD GOALS

TEAM

AFC

Team	Made	Att.	Pct.	Long
Indianapolis	34	38	.895	53
Pittsburgh	25	29	.862	51
San Diego	31	36	.861	50
Seattle	34	40	.850	51
Baltimore	28	33	.848	50
Miami	39	46	.848	54
Tennessee	21	25	.840	50
N.Y. Jets	27	33	.818	48
Jacksonville	31	38	.816	49
Denver	29	36	.806	55
New England	26	33	.788	51
Kansas City	21	28	.750	51
Buffalo	25	34	.735	52
Cincinnati	18	27	.667	50
Cleveland	8	12	.667	49
Oakland	25	38	.658	52
AFC total	422	526	...	55
AFC average	26.4	32.9	.802	...

NFC

Team	Made	Att.	Pct.	Long
San Francisco	21	23	.913	52
Carolina	25	28	.893	52
Tampa Bay	27	32	.844	53
Green Bay	25	30	.833	50
N.Y. Giants	25	30	.833	48
New Orleans	24	29	.828	52
Detroit	26	32	.813	52
St. Louis	20	28	.714	51
Atlanta	15	21	.714	49
Arizona	19	27	.704	49
Washington	22	32	.688	51
Philadelphia	21	31	.677	53
Minnesota	19	30	.633	44
Dallas	19	31	.613	47
Chicago	19	34	.559	52
NFC total	327	438	...	53
NFC average	21.8	29.2	.747	...
NFL total	749	964	...	55
NFL average	24.2	31.1	.777	...

INDIVIDUAL

BESTS OF THE SEASON

Field goal percentage, season
NFC: .913—Wade Richey, San Francisco.
AFC: .895—Mike Vanderjagt, Indianapolis.

Field goals, season
AFC: 39—Olindo Mare, Miami.
NFC: 27—Martin Gramatica, Tampa Bay.

Field goal attempts, season
AFC: 46—Olindo Mare, Miami.
NFC: 32—Brett Conway, Washington; Martin Gramatica, Tampa Bay; Jason Hanson, Detroit.

Longest field goal
AFC: 55—Jason Elam, Denver at San Diego, Nov. 7.
NFC: 53—David Akers, Philadelphia at Miami, Oct. 24; Martin Gramatica, Tampa Bay vs. Atlanta, Nov. 21.

Average yards made, season
NFC: 39.2—Jason Hanson, Detroit.
AFC: 36.8—Jason Elam, Denver.

NFL LEADERS

Team	Made	Att.	Pct.	Long
Richey, Wade, San Francisco	21	23	.913	52
Vanderjagt, Mike, Indianapolis*	34	38	.895	53
Kasay, John, Carolina	22	25	.880	52
Brown, Kris, Pittsburgh*	25	29	.862	51
Carney, John, San Diego*	31	36	.861	50
Blanchard, Cary, N.Y. Giants	18	21	.857	48
Peterson, Todd, Seattle*	34	40	.850	51
Stover, Matt, Baltimore*	28	33	.848	50
Mare, Olindo, Miami*	39	46	.848	54
Gramatica, Martin, Tampa Bay	27	32	.844	53

*AFC.
Leader based on percentage, minimum 16 attempts.

AFC

Player, Team	1-19	20-29	30-39	40-49	Over	Totals	Avg. Yds. Att.	Avg. Yds. Made	Avg. Yds. Miss	Long
Brown, Kris	2-2	5-5	9-10	8-11	1-1	25-29	36.3	35.4	42.5	51
Pittsburgh	1.000	1.000	.900	.727	1.000	.862				
Carney, John	2-2	13-13	6-8	9-12	1-1	31-36	33.8	32.5	41.8	50
San Diego	1.000	1.000	.750	.750	1.000	.861				
Christie, Steve	2-2	10-10	7-10	3-9	3-3	25-34	35.4	32.9	42.3	52
Buffalo	1.000	1.000	.700	.333	1.000	.735				
Dawson, Phil	0-0	2-2	3-5	3-5	0-0	8-12	38.1	36.3	41.8	49
Cleveland	...	1.000	.600	.600	...	.667				
Del Greco, Al	1-1	8-8	7-9	4-6	1-1	21-25	33.6	32.5	39.0	50
Tennessee	1.000	1.000	.778	.667	1.000	.840				
Elam, Jason	1-1	8-8	7-8	8-11	5-8	29-36	39.2	36.8	49.0	55
Denver	1.000	1.000	.875	.727	.625	.806				
Hall, John	0-0	3-4	17-17	7-12	0-0	27-33	37.0	35.7	42.7	48
N.Y. Jets	...	.750	1.000	.583	...	.818				
Hollis, Mike	0-0	12-13	8-9	10-15	1-1	31-38	35.1	33.5	42.4	50
Jacksonville	...	.923	.889	.667	1.000	.816				
Husted, Michael	2-2	3-3	7-11	8-12	0-3	20-31	38.2	35.2	43.8	49
Oakland	1.000	1.000	.636	.667	.000	.645				

Player, Team	1-19	20-29	30-39	40-49	Over	Totals	Avg. Yds. Att.	Avg. Yds. Made	Avg. Yds. Miss	Long
Mare, Olindo	1-1	9-9	17-17	9-14	3-5	39-46	36.9	35.0	47.3	54
Miami	1.000	1.000	1.000	.643	.600	.848				
Nedney, Joe	0-0	2-2	2-2	0-1	1-2	5-7	38.6	34.8	48.0	52
Oakland	...	1.000	1.000	.000	.500	.714				
Pelfrey, Doug	1-1	9-11	7-12	0-2	1-1	18-27	32.2	31.4	33.8	50
Cincinnati	1.000	.818	.583	.000	1.000	.667				
Peterson, Todd	1-1	10-10	8-11	14-16	1-2	34-40	36.4	35.5	41.3	51
Seattle	1.000	1.000	.727	.875	.500	.850				
Stover, Matt	4-4	9-9	6-8	7-7	2-5	28-33	35.1	33.0	46.8	50
Baltimore	1.000	1.000	.750	1.000	.400	.848				
Stoyanovich, Pete	1-1	7-7	5-6	7-13	1-1	21-28	37.2	35.0	43.6	51
Kansas City	1.000	1.000	.833	.538	1.000	.750				
Vanderjagt, Mike	2-2	10-10	11-13	10-11	1-2	34-38	34.9	33.9	43.3	53
Indianapolis	1.000	1.000	.846	.909	.500	.895				
Vinatieri, Adam	1-1	14-14	5-7	5-9	1-2	26-33	33.5	31.0	42.7	51
New England	1.000	1.000	.714	.556	.500	.788				

NFC

Player, Team	1-19	20-29	30-39	40-49	Over	Totals	Avg. Yds. Att.	Avg. Yds. Made	Avg. Yds. Miss	Long
Akers, David	0-0	0-0	0-0	2-3	1-3	3-6	50.7	49.0	52.3	53
Philadelphia	...	...	...	.667	.333	.500				
Andersen, Morten	1-1	5-5	5-8	4-6	0-1	15-21	36.0	33.5	42.2	49
Atlanta	1.000	1.000	.625	.667	.000	.714				
Anderson, Gary	0-0	6-8	9-11	4-9	0-2	19-30	35.7	32.9	40.4	44
Minnesota	...	.750	.818	.444	.000	.633				
Blanchard, Cary	0-0	7-7	2-4	9-10	0-0	18-21	35.0	34.5	38.3	48
N.Y. Giants	...	1.000	.500	.900	...	.857				
Boniol, Chris	0-0	6-6	2-6	3-5	0-1	11-18	34.4	32.2	37.9	46
Chicago	...	1.000	.333	.600	.000	.611				
Brien, Doug	0-0	9-11	6-7	7-9	2-2	24-29	35.8	35.4	37.4	52
New Orleans	...	.818	.857	.778	1.000	.828				
Conway, Brett	0-0	7-9	6-7	6-7	3-9	22-32	38.8	35.9	45.3	51
Washington	...	.778	.857	.857	.333	.688				
Cunningham, Richie	0-0	6-8	5-6	4-10	0-1	15-25	35.8	32.9	40.2	47
Dal.-Car.	...	.750	.833	.400	.000	.600				
Daluiso, Brad	0-0	4-4	3-3	0-2	0-0	7-9	31.2	28.3	41.5	36
N.Y. Giants	...	1.000	1.000	.000	...	.778				
Gowins, Brian	0-0	3-3	0-0	1-2	0-1	4-6	35.8	29.3	49.0	43
Chicago	...	1.000	...	.500	.000	.667				
Gramatica, Martin	0-0	8-8	10-12	6-8	3-4	27-32	37.2	36.0	43.4	53
Tampa Bay	...	1.000	.833	.750	.750	.844				
Hanson, Jason	0-0	8-8	4-4	10-12	4-8	26-32	41.6	39.2	52.2	52
Detroit	...	1.000	1.000	.833	.500	.813				
Holmes, Jaret	0-0	0-0	2-2	0-0	0-0	2-2	35.0	35.0	...	39
Chicago	...	...	1.000	...	...	1.000				
Jacke, Chris	0-0	5-5	10-12	4-7	0-3	19-27	37.1	33.8	44.9	49
Arizona	...	1.000	.833	.571	.000	.704				
Jaeger, Jeff	0-0	0-0	0-2	1-5	1-1	2-8	44.1	46.5	43.3	52
Chicago	...	...	.000	.200	1.000	.250				
Johnson, Norm	0-0	8-9	5-8	5-6	0-2	18-25	35.1	33.7	38.9	49
Philadelphia	...	.889	.625	.833	.000	.720				
Kasay, John	1-1	8-8	6-6	5-6	2-4	22-25	35.0	32.9	50.7	52
Carolina	1.000	1.000	1.000	.833	.500	.880				
Longwell, Ryan	0-0	8-9	8-9	8-10	1-2	25-30	35.8	35.1	39.4	50
Green Bay	...	.889	.889	.800	.500	.833				
Murray, Eddie	0-0	3-3	3-4	1-2	0-0	7-9	31.9	29.3	41.0	40
Dallas	...	1.000	.750	.500	...	.778				
Richey, Wade	1-1	7-7	7-8	5-6	1-1	21-23	34.2	33.3	44.0	52
San Francisco	1.000	1.000	.875	.833	1.000	.913				
Wilkins, Jeff	1-1	5-5	6-7	7-11	1-4	20-28	38.9	36.3	45.6	51
St. Louis	1.000	1.000	.857	.636	.250	.714				

PLAYERS WITH TWO CLUBS

Player, Team	1-19	20-29	30-39	40-49	Over	Totals	Avg. Yds. Att.	Avg. Yds. Made	Avg. Yds. Miss	Long
Cunningham, Richie	0-0	4-6	5-6	3-9	0-1	12-22	36.5	33.5	40.2	47
Dallas	...	.667	.833	.333	.000	.545				
Cunningham, Richie	0-0	2-2	0-0	1-1	0-0	3-3	30.3	30.3	-	43
Carolina	...	1.000	...	1.000	...	1.000				

PUNTING

TEAM

AFC

Team	Total Punts	Yards	Long	Avg.	TB	Blocked	Opp. Ret.	Ret. Yards	Inside 20	Net Avg.
Denver	84	3908	65	46.5	16	0	43	600	19	35.6
Pittsburgh	84	3795	75	45.2	10	0	39	392	27	38.1
N.Y. Jets	82	3693	69	45.0	7	0	47	427	26	38.1
San Diego	89	3910	60	43.9	6	0	41	343	32	38.7
Cleveland	106	4645	61	43.8	11	0	68	762	20	34.6
Tennessee	90	3824	78	42.5	3	0	45	335	35	38.1
Baltimore	104	4355	63	41.9	10	1	43	468	39	35.5
Jacksonville	78	3260	83	41.8	6	0	37	259	32	36.9
New England	90	3735	58	41.5	14	0	36	345	23	34.6
Indianapolis	60	2467	61	41.1	8	2	29	469	16	30.6
Miami	81	3322	63	41.0	4	0	42	424	23	34.8
Kansas City	104	4253	64	40.9	10	2	46	406	21	35.1
Seattle	84	3425	59	40.8	5	0	36	370	34	35.2
Oakland	77	3045	56	39.5	4	1	38	479	25	32.3
Buffalo	73	2840	60	38.9	7	0	23	226	20	33.9
Cincinnati	84	3219	72	38.3	5	2	45	498	13	31.2
AFC total	1370	57696	83	...	126	8	658	6803	405	...
AFC average	85.6	3606.0	...	42.1	7.9	0.5	41.1	425.2	25.3	35.3

Leader based on average.

NFC

Team	Total Punts	Yards	Long	Avg.	TB	Blocked	Opp. Ret.	Ret. Yards	Inside 20	Net Avg.
Minnesota	61	2769	75	45.4	9	0	28	246	18	38.4
Dallas	81	3500	64	43.2	10	0	43	459	24	35.1
Tampa Bay	90	3882	66	43.1	8	0	49	360	23	37.4
Detroit	86	3637	62	42.3	12	0	42	402	27	34.8
Arizona	94	3948	60	42.0	8	0	53	340	18	36.7
Philadelphia	108	4524	60	41.9	12	1	59	490	21	35.1
Washington	71	2926	57	41.2	11	0	27	279	17	34.2
St. Louis	60	2464	70	41.1	11	0	23	155	17	34.8
N.Y. Giants	89	3651	63	41.0	6	0	38	405	31	35.1
Chicago	85	3478	65	40.9	10	0	36	266	20	34.6
New Orleans	83	3282	52	39.5	5	0	43	283	15	34.9
Atlanta	80	3163	55	39.5	4	0	26	119	27	37.1
Carolina	65	2562	56	39.4	1	0	32	158	18	36.7
Green Bay	80	3130	64	39.1	4	0	39	333	21	34.0
San Francisco	75	2883	70	38.4	9	2	33	399	21	30.7
NFC total	1208	49799	75	...	120	3	571	4694	318	...
NFC average	80.5	3319.9	...	41.2	8.0	0.2	38.1	312.9	21.2	35.4
NFL total	2578	107495	83	...	246	11	1229	11497	723	...
NFL average	83.2	3467.6	...	41.7	7.9	0.4	39.6	370.9	23.3	35.3

INDIVIDUAL

BESTS OF THE SEASON

Average yards per punt, season
AFC: 46.5—Tom Rouen, Denver.
NFC: 45.4—Mitch Berger, Minnesota.

Net average yards per punt, season
AFC: 38.7—Darren Bennett, San Diego.
NFC: 38.4—Mitch Berger, Minnesota.

Longest
AFC: 83—Bryan Barker, Jacksonville at N.Y. Jets, Oct. 11.
NFC: 75—Mitch Berger, Minnesota vs. San Francisco, Oct. 24.

Punts, season
NFC: 107—Sean Landeta, Philadelphia.
AFC: 106—Chris Gardocki, Cleveland.

Punts, game
NFC: 12—Brad Maynard, N.Y. Giants at Tampa Bay, Sept. 12 (526 yards).
AFC: 10—Chris Gardocki, Cleveland at Baltimore, Sept. 26 (447 yards); Lee Johnson, New England at Arizona, Oct. 31 (376 yards).

NFL LEADERS

Player, Team	Net Punts	Yards	Long	Avg.	Total Punts	TB	Blk.	Opp. Ret.	Ret. Yds.	In 20	Net Avg.
Rouen, Tom, Denver*	84	3908	65	46.5	84	16	0	43	600	19	35.6
Berger, Mitch, Minnesota	61	2769	75	45.4	61	9	0	28	246	18	38.4

Player, Team	Net Punts	Yards	Long	Avg.	Total Punts	TB	Blk.	Opp. Ret.	Ret. Yds.	In 20	Net Avg.
Miller, Josh, Pittsburgh*	84	3795	75	45.2	84	10	0	39	392	27	38.1
Tupa, Tom, N.Y. Jets*	81	3659	69	45.2	81	7	0	47	427	25	38.2
Bennett, Darren, San Diego*	89	3910	60	43.9	89	6	0	41	343	32	38.7
Gardocki, Chris, Cleveland*	106	4645	61	43.8	106	11	0	68	762	20	34.6
Gowin, Toby, Dallas	81	3500	64	43.2	81	10	0	43	459	24	35.1
Royals, Mark, Tampa Bay	90	3882	66	43.1	90	8	0	49	360	23	37.4
Hentrich, Craig, Tennessee*	90	3824	78	42.5	90	3	0	45	335	35	38.1
Smith, Hunter, Indianapolis*	58	2467	61	42.5	60	8	2	29	469	16	30.6
Richardson, Kyle, Baltimore*	103	4355	63	42.3	104	10	1	43	468	39	35.5
Jett, John, Detroit	86	3637	62	42.3	86	12	0	42	402	27	34.8
Landeta, Sean, Philadelphia	107	4524	60	42.3	108	12	1	59	490	21	35.1
Player, Scott, Arizona	94	3948	60	42.0	94	8	0	53	340	18	36.7
Barker, Bryan, Jacksonville*	78	3260	83	41.8	78	6	0	37	259	32	36.9
Pope, Daniel, Kansas City*	101	4218	64	41.8	103	10	2	46	406	20	35.1

*AFC.
Leader based on average, minimum 40 punts.

AFC

Player, Team	Net Punts	Yards	Long	Avg.	Total Punts	TB	Blk.	Opp. Ret.	Ret. Yds.	In 20	Net Avg.
Araguz, Leo, Oakland	76	3045	56	40.1	77	4	1	38	479	25	32.3
Barker, Bryan, Jacksonville	78	3260	83	41.8	78	6	0	37	259	32	36.9
Bartholomew, Brent, Miami	7	308	51	44.0	7	1	0	4	60	1	32.6
Bennett, Darren, San Diego	89	3910	60	43.9	89	6	0	41	343	32	38.7
Brice, Will, Cincinnati	60	2475	72	41.3	62	4	2	36	406	12	32.1
Costello, Brad, Cincinnati	22	744	44	33.8	22	1	0	9	92	1	28.7
Feagles, Jeff, Seattle	84	3425	59	40.8	84	5	0	36	370	34	35.2
Gardocki, Chris, Cleveland	106	4645	61	43.8	106	11	0	68	762	20	34.6
Hall, John, N.Y. Jets	1	34	34	34.0	1	0	0	0	0	1	34.0
Hentrich, Craig, Tennessee	90	3824	78	42.5	90	3	0	45	335	35	38.1
Hutton, Tom, Miami	73	2978	63	40.8	73	3	0	37	358	22	35.1
Johnson, Lee, New England	90	3735	58	41.5	90	14	0	36	345	23	34.6
Mare, Olindo, Miami	1	36	36	36.0	1	0	0	1	6	0	30.0
Miller, Josh, Pittsburgh	84	3795	75	45.2	84	10	0	39	392	27	38.1
Mohr, Chris, Buffalo	73	2840	60	38.9	73	7	0	23	226	20	33.9
Pope, Daniel, Kansas City	101	4218	64	41.8	103	10	2	46	406	20	35.1
Richardson, Kyle, Baltimore	103	4355	63	42.3	104	10	1	43	468	39	35.5
Rouen, Tom, Denver	84	3908	65	46.5	84	16	0	43	600	19	35.6
Smith, Hunter, Indianapolis	58	2467	61	42.5	60	8	2	29	469	16	30.6
Stoyanovich, Pete, Kansas City	1	35	35	35.0	1	0	0	0	0	1	35.0
Tupa, Tom, N.Y. Jets	81	3659	69	45.2	81	7	0	47	427	25	38.2

NFC

Player, Team	Net Punts	Yards	Long	Avg.	Total Punts	TB	Blk.	Opp. Ret.	Ret. Yds.	In 20	Net Avg.
Aguiar, Louie, Green Bay	75	2954	64	39.4	75	4	0	37	330	20	33.9
Barnhardt, Tommy, New Orleans	82	3262	52	39.8	82	5	0	43	283	14	35.1
Berger, Mitch, Minnesota	61	2769	75	45.4	61	9	0	28	246	18	38.4
Brien, Doug, New Orleans	1	20	20	20.0	1	0	0	0	0	1	20.0
Gowin, Toby, Dallas	81	3500	64	43.2	81	10	0	43	459	24	35.1
Hansen, Brian, Washington	9	362	49	40.2	9	1	0	5	120	1	24.7
Hanson, Chris, Green Bay	4	157	44	39.3	4	0	0	2	3	0	38.5
Horan, Mike, St. Louis	26	1048	57	40.3	26	4	0	11	51	7	35.3
Jett, John, Detroit	86	3637	62	42.3	86	12	0	42	402	27	34.8
Landeta, Sean, Philadelphia	107	4524	60	42.3	108	12	1	59	490	21	35.1
Longwell, Ryan, Green Bay	1	19	19	19.0	1	0	0	0	0	1	19.0
Maynard, Brad, N.Y. Giants	89	3651	63	41.0	89	6	0	38	405	31	35.1
Player, Scott, Arizona	94	3948	60	42.0	94	8	0	53	340	18	36.7
Richey, Wade, San Francisco	4	146	45	36.5	4	0	0	2	25	1	30.3
Royals, Mark, Tampa Bay	90	3882	66	43.1	90	8	0	49	360	23	37.4
Sauerbrun, Todd, Chicago	85	3478	65	40.9	85	10	0	36	266	20	35.4
Stanley, Chad, San Francisco	69	2737	70	39.7	71	9	2	31	374	20	30.7
Stryzinski, Dan, Atlanta	80	3163	55	39.5	80	4	0	26	119	27	37.1
Turk, Matt, Washington	62	2564	57	41.4	62	10	0	22	159	16	35.6
Tuten, Rick, St. Louis	32	1359	70	42.5	32	7	0	11	101	9	34.9
Walter, Ken, Carolina	65	2562	56	39.4	65	1	0	32	158	18	36.7
Wilkins, Jeff, St. Louis	2	57	34	28.5	2	0	0	1	3	1	27.0

PUNT RETURNS

TEAM

AFC

Team	No.	FC	Yds.	Avg.	Long	TD
Seattle	30	24	419	14.0	t94	1
Kansas City	58	19	706	12.2	t84	2
Cincinnati	35	10	410	11.7	t86	2
New England	48	17	495	10.3	52	0
Jacksonville	45	21	462	10.3	t74	1
Buffalo	34	17	347	10.2	27	0
Miami	44	13	432	9.8	45	0
Indianapolis	41	18	388	9.5	t39	1
Oakland	42	14	397	9.5	78	0
Pittsburgh	42	14	377	9.0	48	0
Tennessee	40	17	358	9.0	t65	1
San Diego	34	25	290	8.5	33	0
Baltimore	59	20	452	7.7	33	0
Denver	54	10	409	7.6	t81	1
N.Y. Jets	43	14	319	7.4	23	0
Cleveland	25	13	162	6.5	15	0
AFC total	674	266	6423	9.5	t94	9
AFC average	42.1	16.6	401.4	9.5	...	0.6

t—touchdown.

NFC

Team	No.	FC	Yds.	Avg.	Long	TD
Atlanta	32	17	372	11.6	t70	2
N.Y. Giants	45	13	520	11.6	t85	1
Chicago	30	19	346	11.5	54	0
Dallas	41	9	440	10.7	76	1
Arizona	47	13	489	10.4	43	0
Detroit	38	16	386	10.2	t68	1
St. Louis	52	25	498	9.6	t84	1
Philadelphia	29	18	250	8.6	39	0
Minnesota	32	13	269	8.4	t64	1
Tampa Bay	43	26	357	8.3	31	0
Washington	41	14	332	8.1	33	0
New Orleans	35	23	258	7.4	18	0
Green Bay	29	13	212	7.3	45	0
Carolina	35	18	241	6.9	30	0
San Francisco	26	13	104	4.0	32	0
NFC total	555	250	5074	9.1	t85	7
NFC average	37.0	16.7	338.3	9.1	...	0.5
NFL total	1229	516	11497	...	t94	16
NFL average	39.6	16.6	370.9	9.4	...	0.5

INDIVIDUAL

BESTS OF THE SEASON

Yards per attempt, season
AFC: 14.5—Charlie Rogers, Seattle.
NFC: 11.7—Mac Cody, Arizona.

Yards, season
AFC: 627—Tamarick Vanover, Kansas City.
NFC: 506—Tiki Barber, N.Y. Giants.

Yards, game
NFC: 147—Az-Zahir Hakim, St. Louis at Cincinnati, Oct. 3 (5 returns, 1 TD).
AFC: 139—Tamarick Vanover, Kansas City at Denver, Dec. 5 (7 returns, 1 TD).

Longest
AFC: 94—Charlie Rogers, Seattle at Pittsburgh, Sept. 26 (TD).
NFC: 85—Tiki Barber, N.Y. Giants vs. Dallas, Oct. 18 (TD).

Returns, season
AFC: 57—Jermaine Lewis, Baltimore.

Returns, game
AFC: 44—Tiki Barber, N.Y. Giants; Az-Zahir Hakim, St. Louis.

Returns, game
AFC: 7—Tamarick Vanover, Kansas City vs. Detroit, Sept. 26 (104 yards); Jermaine Lewis, Baltimore at Cleveland, Nov. 7 (49 yards); Tamarick Vanover, Kansas City at Denver, Dec. 5 (139 yards, 1 TD); Jermaine Lewis, Baltimore vs. New Orleans, Dec. 19 (34 yards).
NFC: 7—Az-Zahir Hakim, St. Louis at Tennessee, Oct. 31 (68 yards).

Fair catches, season
NFC: 23—Eddie Kennison, New Orleans.
AFC: 19—Chris Penn, San Diego.

Touchdowns, season
AFC: 2—Tamarick Vanover, Kansas City; Craig Yeast, Cincinnati.
NFC: 1—Held by many players.

NFL LEADERS

Player, Team	No.	FC	Yds.	Avg.	Long	TD
Rogers, Charlie, Seattle*	22	18	318	14.5	t94	1
Jacquet, Nate, Miami*	28	0	351	12.5	45	0

Player, Team	No.	FC	Yds.	Avg.	Long	TD
Vanover, Tamarick, K.C.*	51	18	627	12.3	t84	2
Cody, Mac, Arizona	32	12	373	11.7	31	0
Milburn, Glyn, Chicago	30	19	346	11.5	54	0
Barber, Tiki, N.Y. Giants	44	13	506	11.5	t85	1
Sanders, Deion, Dallas	30	1	344	11.5	76	1
Dwight, Tim, Atlanta	20	12	220	11.0	t70	1
Barlow, Reggie, Jacksonville*	38	17	414	10.9	t74	1
Brown, Troy, New England*	38	13	405	10.7	52	0
Hakim, Az-Zahir, St. Louis	44	22	461	10.5	t84	1
Williams, Kevin, Buffalo*	33	17	331	10.0	27	0
Wilkins, Terrence, Ind.*	41	17	388	9.5	t39	1
Gordon, Darrien, Oakland*	42	14	397	9.5	78	0
Edwards, Troy, Pittsburgh*	25	4	234	9.4	48	0
Rossum, Allen, Philadelphia	28	17	250	8.9	39	0
Green, Jacquez, Tampa Bay	23	14	204	8.9	31	0

*AFC.
t—touchdown.
Leader based on average return, minimum 20.

AFC

Player, Team	No.	FC	Yds.	Avg.	Long	TD
Barlow, Reggie, Jacksonville	38	17	414	10.9	t74	1
Blackwell, Will, Pittsburgh	1	1	39	39.0	39	0
Brown, Troy, New England	38	13	405	10.7	52	0
Buckley, Terrell, Miami	8	5	13	1.6	8	0
Byrd, Isaac, Tennessee	2	0	8	4.0	8	0
Coghill, George, Denver	3	1	25	8.3	10	0
Dunn, David, Cleveland	4	1	25	6.3	13	0
Edwards, Troy, Pittsburgh	25	4	234	9.4	48	0
Faulk, Kevin, New England	10	4	90	9.0	20	0
Galloway, Joey, Seattle	3	1	54	18.0	21	0
George, Spencer, Tennessee	1	0	18	18.0	18	0
Gibson, Damon, Cleveland	2	2	9	4.5	8	0
Gordon, Darrien, Oakland	42	14	397	9.5	78	0
Griffin, Damon, Cincinnati	23	3	195	8.5	34	0
Hawkins, Courtney, Pittsburgh	11	6	49	4.5	14	0
Horn, Joe, Kansas City	1	0	18	18.0	18	0
Jackson, Willie, Cincinnati	2	1	6	3.0	8	0
Jacquet, Nate, Miami	28	0	351	12.5	45	0
Johnson, Kevin, Cleveland	19	10	128	6.7	15	0

– 280 –

Player, Team	No.	FC	Yds.	Avg.	Long	TD
Johnson, Leon, N.Y. Jets	1	1	6	6.0	6	0
Jones, Charlie, San Diego	9	6	93	10.3	33	0
Joseph, Kerry, Seattle	0	2	0	...	...	0
Lewis, Jermaine, Baltimore	57	18	452	7.9	33	0
Lockett, Kevin, Kansas City	1	0	10	10.0	10	0
Logan, Mike, Jacksonville	1	0	7	7.0	7	0
Mason, Derrick, Tennessee	26	15	225	8.7	t65	1
McCardell, Keenan, Jac.	6	4	41	6.8	19	0
McDuffie, O.J., Miami	7	8	62	8.9	21	0
McGriff, Travis, Denver	7	1	50	7.1	20	0
Parker, Larry, Kansas City	5	1	51	10.2	35	0
Pathon, Jerome, Indianapolis	0	1	0	...	...	0
Penn, Chris, San Diego	21	19	148	7.0	18	0
Price, Peerless, Buffalo	1	0	16	16.0	16	0
Reed, Robert, San Diego	3	0	49	16.3	21	0
Rogers, Charlie, Seattle	22	18	318	14.5	t94	1
Rolle, Samari, Tennessee	1	0	23	23.0	23	0
Sawyer, Corey, N.Y. Jets	4	1	25	6.3	11	0
Shaw, Bobby, Pittsburgh	4	3	53	13.3	17	0
Sidney, Dainon, Tennessee	1	0	4	4.0	4	0
Thigpen, Yancey, Tennessee	1	0	21	21.0	21	0
Turner, Scott, San Diego	1	0	0	0.0	0	0
Vanover, Tamarick, K.C.	51	18	627	12.3	t84	2
Ward, Dedric, N.Y. Jets	38	12	288	7.6	23	0
Ward, Hines, Pittsburgh	1	0	2	2.0	2	0
Watson, Chris, Denver	44	8	334	7.6	t81	1
Wilkins, Terrence, Ind.	41	17	388	9.5	t39	1
Williams, Kevin, Buffalo	33	17	331	10.0	27	0
Woodson, Rod, Baltimore	2	2	0	0.0	7	0
Yeast, Craig, Cincinnati	10	6	209	20.9	t86	2

t—touchdown.

NFC

Player, Team	No.	FC	Yds.	Avg.	Long	TD
Barber, Tiki, N.Y. Giants	44	13	506	11.5	t85	1
Boston, David, Arizona	7	0	62	8.9	43	0
Brown, Na, Philadelphia	0	1	0	...	...	0
Cody, Mac, Arizona	32	12	373	11.7	31	0
Dwight, Tim, Atlanta	20	12	220	11.0	t70	1
Edwards, Antuan, Green Bay	10	4	90	9.0	45	0
Fair, Terry, Detroit	11	4	97	8.8	36	0
Givens, Reggie, San Francisco	1	0	0	0.0	0	0
Green, Jacquez, Tampa Bay	23	14	204	8.9	31	0
Hakim, Az-Zahir, St. Louis	44	22	461	10.5	t84	1
Harris, Mark, San Francisco	4	2	8	2.0	5	0
Holt, Torry, St. Louis	3	2	15	5.0	11	0
Horne, Tony, St. Louis	5	0	22	4.4	9	0
Howard, Desmond, G.B.-Det.	18	10	208	11.6	t68	1
Irvin, Sedrick, Detroit	2	0	15	7.5	15	0
Johnson, Anthony, Carolina	1	0	3	3.0	3	0
Johnson, Charles, Phi.	1	0	0	0.0	0	0
Jordan, Charles, Sea.-G.B.*	10	5	76	7.6	15	0
Kennison, Eddie, New Orleans	35	23	258	7.4	18	0
Knight, Tom, Arizona	3	1	38	12.7	27	0
McCleskey, J.J., Arizona	1	0	0	0.0	0	0
McGarity, Wane, Dallas	3	4	16	5.3	9	0
McQuarters, R.W., S.F.	18	3	90	5.0	32	0
Metcalf, Eric, Carolina	34	18	238	7.0	30	0
Milburn, Glyn, Chicago	30	19	346	11.5	54	0
Mitchell, Basil, Green Bay	2	0	0	0.0	0	0
Mitchell, Brian, Washington	40	14	332	8.3	33	0
Moss, Randy, Minnesota	17	4	162	9.5	t64	1
Murphy, Yo, Minnesota	3	0	14	4.7	7	0
Ogden, Jeff, Dallas	4	2	28	7.0	10	0
Oliver, Winslow, Atlanta	12	5	152	12.7	t58	1
Palmer, David, Minnesota	12	5	93	7.8	18	0
Pittman, Michael, Arizona	4	0	16	4.0	7	0
Pounds, Darryl, Washington	1	0	0	0.0	0	0
Preston, Roell, Ten.-Mia.-S.F.*	12	10	71	5.9	12	0
Proehl, Ricky, St. Louis	0	1	0	...	...	0
Rossum, Allen, Philadelphia	28	17	250	8.9	39	0
Sanders, Deion, Dallas	30	1	344	11.5	76	1
Stablein, Brian, Detroit	1	0	9	9.0	9	0
Tate, Robert, Minnesota	0	4	0	...	...	0
Toomer, Amani, N.Y. Giants	1	0	14	14.0	14	0
Tucker, Jason, Dallas	4	2	52	13.0	41	0
Uwaezuoke, Iheanyi, Detroit	18	9	150	8.3	20	0
Williams, Karl, Tampa Bay	20	12	153	7.7	30	0

t—touchdown.
*Includes both AFC and NFC statistics.

PLAYERS WITH TWO CLUBS

Player, Team	No.	FC	Yds.	Avg.	Long	TD
Howard, Desmond, Green Bay	12	7	93	7.8	20	0
Howard, Desmond, Detroit	6	3	115	19.2	t68	1
Jordan, Charles, Seattle	5	3	47	9.4	15	0
Jordan, Charles, Green Bay	5	2	29	5.8	13	0
Preston, Roell, Tennessee	8	2	59	7.4	12	0
Preston, Roell, Miami	1	0	6	6.0	6	0
Preston, Roell, San Francisco	3	8	6	2.0	6	0

KICKOFF RETURNS

TEAM

AFC

Team	No.	Yds.	Avg.	Long	TD
New England	62	1498	24.2	95	0
Cincinnati	84	2020	24.0	t99	1
Miami	72	1713	23.8	93	0
N.Y. Jets	67	1571	23.4	81	0
Seattle	68	1547	22.8	61	0
Denver	63	1398	22.2	71	0
Indianapolis	67	1397	20.9	t97	1
Baltimore	54	1098	20.3	66	0
Buffalo	51	1001	19.6	62	1
Pittsburgh	57	1110	19.5	44	0
Cleveland	89	1725	19.4	43	0
Jacksonville	46	881	19.2	t98	1
San Diego	69	1312	19.0	37	0
Kansas City	63	1182	18.8	29	0
Oakland	61	1140	18.7	48	0
Tennessee	56	1042	18.6	41	0
AFC total	1029	21635	21.0	t99	4
AFC average	64.3	1352.2	21.0	...	0.3

t—touchdown.

NFC

Team	No.	Yds.	Avg.	Long	TD
St. Louis	54	1354	25.1	t101	2
Dallas	58	1372	23.7	79	0
Philadelphia	69	1612	23.4	t89	1
Minnesota	70	1597	22.8	t85	2
Carolina	66	1475	22.3	t100	2
Chicago	68	1491	21.9	93	0
Arizona	64	1403	21.9	68	0
N.Y. Giants	69	1502	21.8	45	0
New Orleans	79	1639	20.7	55	0
San Francisco	77	1579	20.5	75	0
Washington	63	1290	20.5	t95	1
Tampa Bay	55	1116	20.3	55	0
Detroit	72	1445	20.1	91	0
Atlanta	76	1445	19.0	40	0
Green Bay	66	1241	18.8	t88	1
NFC total	1006	21561	21.4	t101	9
NFC average	67.1	1437.4	21.4	...	0.6
NFL total	2035	43196	...	t101	13
NFL average	65.6	1393.4	21.2	...	0.4

INDIVIDUAL

BESTS OF THE SEASON

Yards per attempt, season
NFC: 29.7—Tony Horne, St. Louis.
AFC: 27.1—Tremain Mack, Cincinnati.

Yards, season
AFC: 1524—Brock Marion, Miami.
NFC: 1426—Glyn Milburn, Chicago.

Yards, game
NFC: 222—Allen Rossum, Philadelphia vs. Washington, Nov. 14 (5 returns, 1 TD).
AFC: 190—Charlie Rogers, Seattle at N.Y. Jets, Jan. 2 (7 returns, 0 TDs).

Longest
NFC: 101—Tony Horne, St. Louis at Atlanta, Oct. 17 (TD).
AFC: 99—Tremain Mack, Cleveland vs. Cincinnati, Nov. 14 (TD).

Returns, season
AFC: 63—Brock Marion, Miami.
NFC: 61—Glyn Milburn, Chicago.

Returns, game
NFC: 8—Allen Rossum, Philadelphia vs. Indianapolis, Nov. 21 (192 yards, 0 TDs).
AFC: 7—Tremain Mack, Cincinnati at Seattle, Nov. 7 (132 yards, 0 TDs); Napoleon Kaufman, Oakland vs. Kansas City, Nov. 28 (141 yards, 0 TDs); Brock Marion, Miami at N.Y. Jets, Dec. 12 (143 yards, 0 TDs); Charlie Rogers, Seattle at N.Y. Jets, Jan. 2 (190 yards, 0 TDs).

Touchdowns, season
NFC: 2—Michael Bates, Carolina; Tony Horne, St. Louis.
AFC: 1—Henry Jones, Buffalo; Tremain Mack, Cincinnati; Alvis Whitted, Jacksonville; Terrence Wilkins, Indianapolis.

NFL LEADERS

Player, Team	No.	Yds.	Avg.	Long	TD
Horne, Tony, St. Louis	30	892	29.7	t101	2
Tucker, Jason, Dallas	22	613	27.9	79	0
Mack, Tremain, Cincinnati*	51	1382	27.1	t99	1
Tate, Robert, Minnesota	25	627	25.1	t76	1

Player, Team	No.	Yds.	Avg.	Long	TD
Rossum, Allen, Philadelphia	54	1347	24.9	t89	1
Bates, Michael, Carolina	52	1287	24.8	t100	2
Stone, Dwight, N.Y. Jets*	28	689	24.6	50	0
Marion, Brock, Miami*	62	1524	24.6	93	0
Levingston, Bashir, N.Y. Giants	22	532	24.2	35	0
Faulk, Kevin, New England*	39	943	24.2	95	0
Watson, Chris, Denver*	48	1138	23.7	71	0
Bates, Mario, Arizona	52	1231	23.7	68	0
Milburn, Glyn, Chicago	61	1426	23.4	93	0
Palmer, David, Minnesota	27	621	23.0	51	0
Green, Ahman, Seattle*	36	818	22.7	54	0

*AFC.
t—touchdown.
Leader based on average return, minimum 20.

AFC

Player, Team	No.	Yds.	Avg.	Long	TD
Ashmore, Darryl, Oakland	1	0	0.0	0	0
Austin, Billy, Indianapolis	1	0	0.0	0	0
Avery, John, Mia.-Den.	9	192	21.3	33	0
Banks, Tavian, Jacksonville	5	78	15.6	20	0
Barlow, Reggie, Jacksonville	19	396	20.8	56	0
Bennett, Donnell, Kansas City	3	51	17.0	24	0
Blackwell, Will, Pittsburgh	14	282	20.1	37	0
Bownes, Fabien, Seattle	2	40	20.0	33	0
Branch, Calvin, Oakland	6	96	16.0	20	0
Brown, Troy, New England	8	271	33.9	54	0
Bynum, Kenny, San Diego	37	781	21.1	37	0
Byrd, Isaac, Tennessee	2	16	8.0	9	0
Campbell, Mark, Cleveland	3	28	9.3	10	0
Chamblin, Corey, Jacksonville	1	6	6.0	6	0
Chiaverini, Darrin, Cleveland	2	35	17.5	22	0
Cline, Tony, Pittsburgh	2	8	4.0	8	0
Cloud, Mike, Kansas City	2	28	14.0	18	0
Collins, Bobby, Buffalo	1	6	6.0	6	0
DeLong, Greg, Baltimore	f1	11	11.0	11	0
Dillon, Corey, Cincinnati	1	4	4.0	4	0
Dunn, David, Cleveland	9	180	20.0	27	0
Edwards, Troy, Pittsburgh	13	234	18.0	44	0
Elias, Keith, Indianapolis	5	82	16.4	21	0

Player, Team	No.	Yds.	Avg.	Long	TD
Ellison, Jerry, New England	1	13	13.0	13	0
Farmer, Robert, N.Y. Jets	4	84	21.0	30	0
Faulk, Kevin, New England	39	943	24.2	95	0
Fauria, Christian, Seattle	2	15	7.5	8	0
Fletcher, Terrell, San Diego	7	112	16.0	22	0
Fuamatu-Ma'afala, Chris, Pit.	1	9	9.0	9	0
Gash, Sam, Buffalo	1	13	13.0	13	0
George, Spencer, Tennessee	4	63	15.8	22	0
Glenn, Aaron, N.Y. Jets	27	601	22.3	46	0
Gordon, Lennox, Buffalo	1	11	11.0	11	0
Green, Ahman, Seattle	36	818	22.7	54	0
Greene, Scott, Indianapolis	1	14	14.0	14	0
Griffin, Damon, Cincinnati	15	296	19.7	42	0
Harris, Corey, Baltimore	38	843	22.2	66	0
Hill, Madre, Cleveland	8	137	17.1	27	0
Horn, Joe, Kansas City	9	165	18.3	28	0
Huntley, Richard, Pittsburgh	15	336	22.4	41	0
Ismail, Qadry, Baltimore	4	55	13.8	19	0
Jackson, Lenzie, Jacksonville	3	58	19.3	23	0
Jackson, Willie, Cincinnati	6	179	29.8	46	0
Jacquet, Nate, Miami	1	26	26.0	26	0
Johnson, J.J., Miami	2	26	13.0	19	0
Johnson, Kevin, Cleveland	1	25	25.0	25	0
Johnson, Leon, N.Y. Jets	2	31	15.5	17	0
Johnson, Lonnie, Kansas City	1	11	11.0	11	0
Jones, Damon, Jacksonville	f0	0	...	...	0
Jones, George, Cleveland	1	12	12.0	12	0
Jones, Henry, Buffalo	1	37	37.0	t37	1
Jones, Tebucky, New England	5	113	22.6	28	0
Jordan, Randy, Oakland	10	207	20.7	28	0
Joseph, Kerry, Seattle	6	132	22.0	61	0
Kaufman, Napoleon, Oakland	42	831	19.8	48	0
Kent, Joey, Tennessee	2	24	12.0	13	0
Kirby, Terry, Cleveland	11	230	20.9	28	0
Lewis, Jermaine, Baltimore	8	158	19.8	25	0
Little, Earl, Cleveland	2	34	17.0	20	0
Logan, Mike, Jacksonville	1	25	25.0	25	0
Loud, Kamil, Buffalo	2	26	13.0	15	0
Loville, Derek, Denver	2	22	11.0	12	0
Lyons, Mitch, Pittsburgh	3	42	14.0	17	0
Mack, Stacey, Jacksonville	6	112	18.7	32	0
Mack, Tremain, Cincinnati	51	1382	27.1	t99	1
Manusky, Greg, Kansas City	2	6	3.0	6	0
Marion, Brock, Miami	62	1524	24.6	93	0
Mason, Derrick, Tennessee	41	805	19.6	41	0
McAlister, Chris, Baltimore	1	12	12.0	12	0
McCardell, Keenan, Jacksonville	f2	19	9.5	10	0
McCrary, Fred, San Diego	1	4	4.0	4	0
McDuffie, O.J., Miami	1	17	17.0	17	0
Miller, Billy, Denver	4	79	19.8	30	0
Mincy, Charles, Oakland	1	0	0.0	0	0
Muhammad, Steve, Indianapolis	2	41	20.5	22	0
Neal, Lorenzo, Tennessee	2	15	7.5	14	0
Parker, Larry, Kansas City	1	24	24.0	24	0
Parten, Ty, Kansas City	1	11	11.0	11	0
Pathon, Jerome, Indianapolis	6	123	20.5	31	0
Pierce, Aaron, Baltimore	1	7	7.0	7	0
Porter, Daryl, Buffalo	2	41	20.5	24	0
Powell, Ronnie, Cleveland	44	986	22.4	43	0
Price, Peerless, Buffalo	1	27	27.0	27	0
Reed, Robert, San Diego	5	72	14.4	21	0
Rogers, Charlie, Seattle	18	465	25.8	49	0
Saleh, Tarek, Cleveland	5	43	8.6	14	0
Shelton, Daimon, Jacksonville	1	0	0.0	0	0
Shields, Paul, Indianapolis	1	3	3.0	3	0
Simmons, Tony, New England	6	132	22.0	29	0
Smith, Detron, Denver	1	12	12.0	11	0
Smith, Irv, Cleveland	3	15	5.0	10	0
Smith, Rod, Denver	1	10	10.0	10	0
Springs, Shawn, Seattle	1	15	15.0	15	0
Stephens, Tremayne, San Diego	18	335	18.6	28	0
Still, Bryan, San Diego	1	8	8.0	8	0
Stone, Dwight, N.Y. Jets	28	689	24.6	50	0
Sullivan, Chris, New England	1	1	1.0	1	0
Thomas, Zach, Miami	1	15	15.0	15	0
Treu, Adam, Oakland	1	6	6.0	6	0
Vanover, Tamarick, Kansas City	44	886	20.1	29	0
Vrabel, Mike, Pittsburgh	1	6	6.0	6	0
Ward, Hines, Pittsburgh	1	24	24.0	24	0
Warren, Lamont, New England	2	25	12.5	16	0
Washington, Keith, Baltimore	1	12	12.0	12	0
Watson, Chris, Denver	48	1138	23.7	71	0
Whitted, Alvis, Jacksonville	8	187	23.4	t98	1
Wilkins, Terrence, Indianapolis	51	1134	22.2	t97	1
Williams, Kevin R., Buffalo	42	840	20.0	62	0
Williams, Kevin, N.Y. Jets	6	166	27.7	81	0
Williams, Nick, Cincinnati	8	109	13.6	24	0
Wilson, Jerry, Miami	3	50	16.7	23	0
Yeast, Craig, Cincinnati	3	50	16.7	22	0
Zereoue, Amos, Pittsburgh	7	169	24.1	35	0

t—touchdown.
f—includes at least one fair catch.

NFC

Player, Team	No.	Yds.	Avg.	Long	TD
Alstott, Mike, Tampa Bay	1	19	19.0	19	0
Anthony, Reidel, Tampa Bay	21	434	20.7	39	0
Barber, Tiki, N.Y. Giants	12	266	22.2	41	0
Bates, Mario, Arizona	52	1231	23.7	68	0
Bates, Michael, Carolina	52	1287	24.8	t100	2
Bech, Brett, New Orleans	1	12	12.0	12	0
Bennett, Edgar, Chicago	3	53	17.7	20	0
Bieniemy, Eric, Philadelphia	10	210	21.0	30	0
Bly, Dre', St. Louis	f1	1	1.0	1	0
Bowie, Larry, Washington	1	0	0.0	0	0
Broughton, Luther, Philadelphia	1	5	5.0	5	0
Burrough, John, Minnesota	1	9	9.0	9	0
Carpenter, Ron, St. Louis	16	406	25.4	43	0
Coakley, Dexter, Dallas	1	3	3.0	3	0
Cody, Mac, Arizona	4	76	19.0	29	0
Comella, Greg, N.Y. Giants	2	31	15.5	17	0
Craver, Aaron, New Orleans	1	3	3.0	3	0
Davis, Troy, New Orleans	20	424	21.2	35	0
Dawsey, Lawrence, New Orleans	1	20	20.0	20	0
Dishman, Chris, Arizona	1	9	9.0	9	0
Dunn, Warrick, Tampa Bay	8	156	19.5	34	0
Dwight, Tim, Atlanta	44	944	21.5	40	0
Fair, Terry, Detroit	34	752	22.1	91	0
Fletcher, London, St. Louis	2	13	6.5	13	0
Gammon, Kendall, New Orleans	1	9	9.0	9	0
German, Jammi, Atlanta	1	1	1.0	1	0
Green, Jacquez, Tampa Bay	10	185	18.5	29	0
Hakim, Az-Zahir, St. Louis	2	35	17.5	20	0
Hallock, Ty, Chicago	2	10	5.0	7	0
Harris, Mark, San Francisco	2	26	13.0	15	0
Harris, Ronnie, Atlanta	1	5	5.0	5	0
Henderson, William, Green Bay	2	23	11.5	16	0
Hetherington, Chris, Carolina	1	16	16.0	16	0
Hodgins, James, St. Louis	2	4	2.0	4	0
Horne, Tony, St. Louis	f30	892	29.7	t101	2
Howard, Desmond, G.B.-Det.	34	662	19.5	35	0
Irvin, Sedrick, Detroit	3	21	7.0	21	0
Jenkins, James, Washington	1	10	10.0	10	0
Jervey, Travis, San Francisco	8	191	23.9	48	0
Johnson, Anthony, Carolina	1	9	9.0	9	0
Jordan, Andrew, Minnesota	1	0	0.0	0	0
Jordan, Charles, Sea.-G.B.*	9	157	17.4	24	0
Kinchen, Brian, Carolina	3	29	9.7	15	0
Kleinsasser, Jim, Minnesota	1	0	0.0	0	0
Kozlowski, Brian, Atlanta	2	19	9.5	10	0
Lane, Fred, Carolina	3	58	19.3	22	0
Lassiter, Kwamie, Arizona	1	13	13.0	13	0

1999 STATISTICS Kickoff returns

Player, Team	No.	Yds.	Avg.	Long	TD
Levingston, Bashir, N.Y. Giants	22	532	24.2	35	0
Lynch, Ben, San Francisco	1	4	4.0	4	0
Makovicka, Joel, Arizona	1	10	10.0	10	0
Mangum, Kris, Carolina	2	20	10.0	13	0
Marshall, Whit, Atlanta	1	-2	-2.0	-2	0
Mathis, Kevin, Dallas	18	408	22.7	37	0
McCollum, Andy, St. Louis	1	3	3.0	3	0
McKenzie, Raleigh, Green Bay	1	13	13.0	13	0
McQuarters, R.W., San Francisco	26	568	21.8	37	0
Metcalf, Eric, Carolina	4	56	14.0	31	0
Milburn, Glyn, Chicago	61	1426	23.4	93	0
Milstead, Rod, Washington	1	0	0.0	0	0
Mitchell, Basil, Green Bay	21	464	22.1	t88	1
Mitchell, Brian, Washington	43	893	20.8	45	0
Morrow, Harold, Minnesota	1	20	20.0	20	0
Morton, Johnnie, Detroit	1	22	22.0	22	0
Murphy, Yo, T.B.-Min.	18	387	21.5	55	0
Noble, Brandon, Dallas	1	9	9.0	9	0
Ogden, Jeff, Dallas	12	252	21.0	29	0
Oliver, Winslow, Atlanta	24	441	18.4	28	0
Olivo, Brock, Detroit	11	198	18.0	25	0
Palmer, David, Minnesota	27	621	23.0	51	0
Parker, De'Mond, Green Bay	15	268	17.9	40	0
Patten, David, N.Y. Giants	33	673	20.4	45	0
Perry, Wilmont, New Orleans	2	6	3.0	16	0
Peterson, Tony, San Francisco	2	10	5.0	10	0
Phillips, Lawrence, San Francisco	19	415	21.8	75	0
Philyaw, Dino, New Orleans	53	1165	22.0	55	0
Pittman, Michael, Arizona	2	31	15.5	22	0
Preston, Roell, Ten.-S.F.*	21	411	19.6	58	0
Prioleau, Pierson, San Francisco	3	73	24.3	32	0
Rossum, Allen, Philadelphia	54	1347	24.9	t89	1
Sanders, Deion, Dallas	4	87	21.8	31	0

Player, Team	No.	Yds.	Avg.	Long	TD
Schlesinger, Cory, Detroit	2	33	16.5	20	0
Schroeder, Bill, Green Bay	1	10	10.0	10	0
Sellers, Mike, Washington	3	32	10.7	16	0
Sharper, Darren, Green Bay	1	4	4.0	4	0
Smith, Ed, Philadelphia	1	1	1.0	1	0
Talton, Tyree, Detroit	6	121	20.2	38	0
Tate, Robert, Minnesota	25	627	25.1	t76	1
Thrash, James, Washington	14	355	25.4	t95	1
Tillman, Pat, Arizona	3	33	11.0	18	0
Tucker, Jason, Dallas	22	613	27.9	79	0
Tuinei, Van, Chicago	1	0	0.0	0	0
Whiting, Brandon, Philadelphia	3	49	16.3	21	0
Wiegmann, Casey, Chicago	1	2	2.0	2	0
Williams, Elijah, Atlanta	3	37	12.3	18	0
Williams, Karl, Tampa Bay	1	15	15.0	15	0
Williams, Moe, Minnesota	10	240	24.0	t85	1

t—touchdown.
f—includes at least one fair catch.

PLAYERS WITH TWO CLUBS

Player, Team	No.	Yds.	Avg.	Long	TD
Avery, John, Miami	2	55	27.5	33	0
Avery, John, Denver	7	137	19.6	25	0
Howard, Desmond, Green Bay	19	364	19.2	31	0
Howard, Desmond, Detroit	15	298	19.9	35	0
Jordan, Charles, Seattle	3	62	20.7	24	0
Jordan, Charles, Green Bay	6	95	15.8	22	0
Murphy, Yo, Tampa Bay	14	307	21.9	55	0
Murphy, Yo, Minnesota	4	80	20.0	24	0
Preston, Roell, Tennessee	5	119	23.8	29	0
Preston, Roell, San Francisco	16	292	18.3	58	0

MISCELLANEOUS

CLUB RANKINGS BY YARDS

Team	OFFENSE Total	Rush	Pass	DEFENSE Total	Rush	Pass
Arizona	29	29	27	22	30	10
Atlanta	27	30	17	16	29	9
Baltimore	24	16	25	2	2	6
Buffalo	11	8	T19	*1	4	*1
Carolina	6	20	2	26	24	23
Chicago	8	26	3	29	23	29
Cincinnati	15	T6	23	25	16	28
Cleveland	31	31	29	31	31	11
Dallas	16	T6	24	9	6	13
Denver	14	12	15	7	19	8
Detroit	21	28	9	18	9	27
Green Bay	9	21	7	19	22	18
Indianapolis	4	19	4	15	18	19
Jacksonville	7	2	12	4	7	3
Kansas City	12	4	22	14	11	16
Miami	20	22	T13	5	8	5
Minnesota	3	14	5	27	14	30
New England	18	23	10	8	21	7
New Orleans	19	18	T19	20	20	21
N.Y. Giants	17	T24	8	13	13	14
N.Y. Jets	25	11	28	21	17	24
Oakland	5	3	11	10	12	12
Philadelphia	30	17	31	24	28	15
Pittsburgh	22	10	26	11	26	4
St. Louis	*1	5	*1	6	*1	20
San Diego	26	27	18	12	3	22
San Francisco	10	*1	21	28	15	31
Seattle	23	T24	16	23	25	17
Tampa Bay	28	15	30	3	5	2
Tennessee	13	13	T13	17	10	25
Washington	2	9	6	30	27	26

*NFL leader.

TAKEAWAYS/GIVEAWAYS

AFC

	TAKEAWAYS Int.	Fum.	Tot.	GIVEAWAYS Int.	Fum.	Tot.	Net Diff.
Kansas City	25	20	45	15	9	24	21
Tennessee	16	24	40	13	9	22	18
N.Y. Jets	24	11	35	16	6	22	13
Jacksonville	19	11	30	11	7	18	12
Oakland	20	13	33	14	15	29	4
Pittsburgh	14	14	28	18	7	25	3
Seattle	30	6	36	16	17	33	3
Baltimore	21	10	31	20	11	31	0
Denver	15	11	26	18	10	28	-2
New England	16	15	31	21	12	33	-2
Cincinnati	12	15	27	18	14	32	-5
Indianapolis	10	13	23	17	11	28	-5
Buffalo	12	9	21	16	11	27	-6
Miami	18	10	28	21	13	34	-6
San Diego	15	12	27	24	11	35	-8
Cleveland	8	12	20	15	16	31	-11

NFC

	TAKEAWAYS Int.	Fum.	Tot.	GIVEAWAYS Int.	Fum.	Tot.	Net Diff.
Washington	24	13	37	14	11	25	12
Dallas	24	9	33	13	10	23	10
Detroit	16	16	32	14	8	22	10
Philadelphia	28	18	46	18	21	39	7
Green Bay	26	15	41	23	13	36	5
St. Louis	29	7	36	15	16	31	5
Chicago	14	19	33	22	15	37	-4
Tampa Bay	21	10	31	16	19	35	-4
Carolina	15	14	29	15	19	34	-5
New Orleans	19	15	34	30	9	39	-5
N.Y. Giants	17	7	24	20	12	32	-8
Minnesota	12	18	30	21	19	40	-10
San Francisco	13	7	20	19	13	32	-12
Arizona	17	10	27	30	10	40	-13
Atlanta	12	6	18	19	16	35	-17

CLUB LEADERS

	Offense	Defense
First downs	Was. 338	T.B. 228
Rushing	Dal. 129	St.L. 53
Passing	Car. 208	Pit. 142
Penalty	Ind. 38	T.B. 9
Rushes	K.C. 521	St.L. 338
Net yards gained	S.F. 2095	St.L. 1189
Average gain	S.F. 5.0	S.D. 3.1
Passes attempted	Chi. 684	Pit. 463
Completed	Chi. 404	Pit. 245
Percent completed	St.L. 64.7	T.B. 52.7
Total yards gained	St.L. 4580	Buf. 2889
Times sacked	Ind. 14	Jac., St.L. 57
Yards lost	Ind. 116	Jac. 373
Net yards gained	St.L. 4353	Buf. 2675
Net yards per pass play	St.L. 7.7	Bal. 4.6
Yards gained per completion	Min. 13.7	Bal. 10.0
Combined net yards gained	St.L. 6412	Buf. 4045
Percent total yards rushing	Phi. 45.6	St.L. 25.3
Percent total yards passing	Chi. 74.9	Cle. 54.7
Ball-control plays	Chi. 1118	Mia. 936
Average yards per play	St.L. 6.5	Bal. 4.1
Avg. time of possession	Buf. 32:12	—
Third-down efficiency	St.L. 46.9	Mia. 28.8
Interceptions	—	Sea. 30
Yards returned	—	Phi. 625
Returned for TD	—	St.L. 7
Punts	Phi. 108	—
Yards punted	Cle. 4645	—
Average yards per punt	Den. 46.5	—
Punt returns	Bal. 59	Buf., St.L. 23
Yards returned	K.C. 706	Atl. 119
Average yds. per return	Sea. 14.0	Atl. 4.6
Returned for TD	3 tied with 2	—
Kickoff returns	Cle. 89	Cle. 42
Yards returned	Cin. 2020	CLe. 764
Average yards per return	St.L. 25.1	Chi. 16.6
Returned for TD	3 tied with 2	—
Total points scored	St.L. 526	Jac. 217
Total TDs	St.L. 66	Buf., T.B. 23
TDs rushing	Was. 23	St.L. 4
TDs passing	St.L. 42	T.B. 11
TDs on ret. and recov.	K.C., St.L. 11	Jac. 0
Extra point kicks	St.L. 64	3 tied with 2
2-Pt. conversions	Jac. 4	—
Safeties	Ten. 4	—
Field goals made	Mia. 39	Ten. 15
Field goals attempted	Mia. 46	Jac. 18
Percent successful	S.F. 91.3	NYG 64.9

– 285 –

TEAM-BY-TEAM SUMMARIES

AFC

OFFENSE

	Bal.	Buf.	Cin.	Cle.	Den.	Ind.	Jac.	K.C.	Mia.	N.E.	NYJ	Oak.	Pit.	S.D.	Sea.	Ten.
First downs	259	313	293	220	308	327	331	282	287	280	268	326	295	262	276	294
Rushing	87	117	111	64	107	89	116	108	81	72	111	110	111	69	65	109
Passing	148	173	161	134	168	200	194	164	188	184	139	196	159	171	179	167
Penalty	24	23	21	22	33	38	21	10	18	24	18	20	25	22	32	18
Rushes	431	519	442	313	465	419	514	521	445	425	486	488	495	410	408	459
Net yards gained	1754	2040	2051	1150	1864	1660	2091	2082	1453	1426	1961	2084	1991	1246	1408	1811
Average gain	4.1	3.9	4.6	3.7	4.0	4.0	4.1	4.0	3.3	3.4	4.0	4.3	4.0	3.0	3.5	3.9
Average yards per game	109.6	127.5	128.2	71.9	116.5	103.8	130.7	130.1	90.8	89.1	122.6	130.3	124.4	77.9	88.0	113.2
Passes attempted	546	513	548	492	554	546	535	502	589	540	476	520	535	583	525	527
Completed	270	290	300	271	319	338	320	295	329	305	272	306	301	332	288	304
Percent completed	49.5	56.5	54.7	55.1	57.6	61.9	59.8	58.8	55.9	56.5	57.1	58.8	56.3	56.9	54.9	57.7
Total yards gained	3360	3478	3504	2997	3646	4182	3716	3409	3736	3985	3001	3850	3118	3627	3629	3622
Times sacked	56	27	49	60	34	14	36	26	37	56	37	49	37	46	38	25
Yards lost	336	185	278	385	227	116	221	170	251	349	210	241	235	284	232	137
Net yards gained	3024	3293	3226	2612	3419	4066	3495	3239	3485	3636	2791	3609	2883	3343	3397	3485
Average yards per game	189.0	205.8	201.6	163.3	213.7	254.1	218.4	202.4	217.8	227.3	174.4	225.6	180.2	208.9	212.3	217.8
Net yards per pass play	5.02	6.10	5.40	4.73	5.81	7.26	6.12	6.13	5.57	6.10	5.44	6.34	5.04	5.31	6.03	6.31
Yards gained per completion	12.44	11.99	11.68	11.06	11.43	12.37	11.61	11.56	11.36	13.07	11.03	12.58	10.36	10.92	12.60	11.91
Combined net yards gained	4778	5333	5277	3762	5283	5726	5586	5321	4938	5062	4752	5693	4874	4589	4805	5296
Percent total yards rushing	36.7	38.3	38.9	30.6	35.3	29.0	37.4	39.1	29.4	28.2	41.3	36.6	40.8	27.2	29.3	34.2
Percent total yards passing	63.3	61.7	61.1	69.4	64.7	71.0	62.6	60.9	70.6	71.8	58.7	63.4	59.2	72.8	70.7	65.8
Average yards per game	298.6	333.3	329.8	235.1	330.2	357.9	349.1	332.6	308.6	316.4	297.0	355.8	304.6	286.8	300.3	331.0
Ball-control plays	1033	1059	1039	865	1053	979	1085	1049	1071	1021	999	1057	1067	1039	971	1011
Average yards per play	4.6	5.0	5.1	4.3	5.0	5.8	5.1	5.1	4.6	5.0	4.8	5.4	4.6	4.4	4.9	5.2
Average time of possession	29:24	32:12	29:59	23:38	31:06	30:45	31:57	30:20	31:34	28:49	30:45	32:06	31:28	30:00	27:48	31:30
Third-down efficiency	28.4	40.8	39.6	29.1	36.7	39.2	40.0	39.5	33.9	35.4	34.5	39.4	38.5	36.8	32.4	38.2
Had intercepted	20	16	18	15	18	17	11	15	21	21	16	14	18	24	16	13
Yards opponents returned	220	288	305	153	231	189	149	166	567	299	148	239	304	196	210	227
Returned by oppponents for TD	3	1	1	1	1	2	0	1	7	1	0	2	3	1	0	2
Punts	104	73	84	106	84	60	78	104	81	90	82	77	84	89	84	90
Yards punted	4355	2840	3219	4645	3908	2467	3260	4253	3322	3735	3693	3045	3795	3910	3425	3824
Average yards per punt	41.9	38.9	38.3	43.8	46.5	41.1	41.8	40.9	41.0	41.5	45.0	39.5	45.2	43.9	40.8	42.5
Punt returns	59	34	35	25	54	41	45	58	44	48	43	42	42	34	30	40
Yards returned	452	347	410	162	409	388	462	706	432	495	319	397	377	290	419	358
Average yards per return	7.7	10.2	11.7	6.5	7.6	9.5	10.3	12.2	9.8	10.3	7.4	9.5	9.0	8.5	14.0	9.0
Returned for TD	0	0	2	0	1	1	1	2	0	0	0	0	0	0	1	1
Kickoff returns	54	51	84	89	63	67	46	63	72	62	67	61	57	69	68	56
Yards returned	1098	1001	2020	1725	1398	1397	881	1182	1713	1498	1571	1140	1110	1312	1547	1042
Average yards per return	20.3	19.6	24.0	19.4	22.2	20.9	19.2	18.8	23.8	24.2	23.4	18.7	19.5	19.0	22.8	18.6
Returned for TD	0	1	1	0	0	1	1	0	0	0	0	0	0	0	0	0
Fumbles	24	17	34	29	33	25	18	22	23	27	22	22	19	29	31	17
Lost	11	11	14	16	10	11	7	9	13	12	6	15	7	11	17	9
Out of bounds	1	1	1	0	2	5	0	2	3	1	2	1	2	0	3	0
Recovered for TD	0	0	0	0	0	1	0	0	0	0	0	0	0	0	0	0
Penalties	125	97	126	92	114	81	90	126	111	95	87	98	119	104	98	114
Yards penalized	1010	789	1027	714	872	683	755	982	936	812	771	825	945	823	883	1069
Total points scored	324	320	283	217	314	423	396	390	326	299	308	390	317	269	338	392
Total TDs	34	35	33	28	32	46	42	47	30	32	33	45	35	25	34	46
TDs rushing	9	12	11	9	13	15	20	14	8	9	7	18	14	10	5	19
TDs passing	21	21	18	19	16	26	16	22	20	19	22	24	19	12	25	23
TDs on returns and recoveries	4	2	4	0	3	5	6	11	2	4	4	3	2	3	4	4
Extra point kicks	32	33	27	23	29	43	37	45	27	27	29	43	30	22	32	43
Extra point kick attempts	32	33	27	24	29	43	37	45	27	30	29	43	31	23	32	43
2-Pt. conversions	1	1	2	1	1	1	4	0	0	0	1	1	1	0	1	1
2-Pt. conversions attempts	1	1	6	4	1	3	5	2	3	2	4	2	4	2	2	3
Safeties	1	0	1	0	2	0	3	0	1	0	1	0	0	1	0	4
Field goals made	28	25	18	8	29	34	31	21	39	26	27	25	25	31	34	21
Field goals attempted	33	34	27	12	36	38	38	28	46	33	33	38	29	36	40	25
Percent successful	84.8	73.5	66.7	66.7	80.6	89.5	81.6	75.0	84.8	78.8	81.8	65.8	86.2	86.1	85.0	84.0
Extra points	33	34	29	24	30	44	41	45	27	29	27	44	31	23	32	44
Field goals blocked	1	0	2	0	1	2	1	0	1	0	0	1	1	0	0	0

– 286 –

DEFENSE

	K.C.	Mia.	N.E.	NYJ	Bal. Oak.	Buf. Pit.	Cin. S.D.	Cle. Sea.	Den. Ten.	Ind.	Jac.
First downs	260	244	316	368	267	304	248	252	281	299	266	260	279	313	300
Rushing	70	73	99	161	88	92	72	80	79	106	97	85	92	77	107	81
Passing	158	144	189	187	154	192	159	173	145	154	180	161	142	181	183	193
Penalty	32	27	28	20	25	20	17	28	28	21	22	20	26	21	23	26
Rushes	392	407	454	610	440	406	373	415	413	486	430	398	451	432	484	383
Net yards gained	1231	1370	1699	2736	1737	1715	1444	1557	1476	1795	1703	1559	1958	1321	1934	1550
Average gain	3.1	3.4	3.7	4.5	3.9	4.2	3.9	3.8	3.6	3.7	4.0	3.9	4.3	3.1	4.0	4.0
Average yards per game	76.9	85.6	106.2	171.0	108.6	107.2	90.3	97.3	92.3	112.2	106.4	97.4	122.4	82.6	120.9	96.9
Passes attempted	599	506	522	523	471	561	521	578	484	520	574	539	463	549	582	557
Completed	328	269	312	331	273	328	291	317	256	293	319	302	245	315	320	312
Percent completed	54.8	53.2	59.8	63.3	58.0	58.5	55.9	54.8	52.9	56.3	55.6	56.0	52.9	57.4	55.0	56.0
Total yards gained	3282	2889	4027	3457	3299	3775	3263	3168	3168	3281	3860	3630	3167	3847	3744	4000
Times sacked	49	37	35	25	50	41	57	40	39	42	26	44	39	41	38	54
Yards lost	291	214	229	147	283	269	373	286	240	268	184	309	241	263	252	305
Net yards gained	2991	2675	3798	3310	3016	3506	2890	3482	2928	3013	3676	3321	2926	3584	3492	3695
Average yards per game	186.9	167.2	237.4	206.9	188.5	219.1	180.6	217.6	183.0	188.3	229.8	207.6	182.9	224.0	218.3	230.9
Net yards per pass play	4.62	4.93	6.82	6.04	5.79	5.82	5.00	5.63	5.60	5.36	6.13	5.70	5.83	6.07	5.63	6.05
Yards gained per completion	10.01	10.74	12.91	10.44	12.08	11.51	11.21	11.89	12.38	11.20	12.10	12.02	12.93	12.21	11.70	12.82
Combined net yards gained	4222	4045	5497	6046	4753	5221	4334	5039	4404	4808	5379	4880	4884	4905	5426	5245
Percent total yards rushing	29.2	33.9	30.9	45.3	36.5	32.8	33.3	30.9	33.5	37.3	31.7	31.9	40.1	26.9	35.6	29.6
Percent total yards passing	70.8	66.1	69.1	54.7	63.5	67.2	66.7	69.1	66.5	62.7	68.3	68.1	59.9	73.1	64.4	70.4
Average yards per game	263.9	252.8	343.6	377.9	297.1	326.3	270.9	314.9	275.3	300.5	336.2	305.0	305.3	306.6	339.1	327.8
Ball-control plays	1040	950	1011	1158	961	1008	951	1033	936	1048	1030	981	953	1022	1104	994
Average yards per play	4.1	4.3	5.4	5.2	4.9	5.2	4.6	4.9	4.7	4.6	5.2	5.0	5.1	4.8	4.9	5.3
Average time of possession	30:36	27:48	30:01	36:22	28:54	29:15	28:03	29:40	28:26	31:11	29:15	27:54	28:32	30:00	32:12	28:30
Third-down efficiency	34.1	31.4	40.7	46.8	31.5	35.1	33.5	30.2	28.8	35.1	40.7	33.0	31.5	36.7	37.2	35.0
Intercepted by	21	12	12	8	15	10	19	25	18	16	24	20	14	15	30	16
Yards returned by	403	180	100	52	169	287	330	378	243	110	443	247	149	123	336	257
Returned for TD	4	0	1	0	1	1	3	5	1	2	3	1	0	0	2	1
Punts	115	93	71	66	92	83	96	98	85	95	78	82	92	85	81	80
Yards punted	4854	3875	3136	2702	4011	3437	3976	4260	3495	3914	3190	3542	3737	3439	3398	3435
Average yards per punt	42.2	41.7	44.2	40.9	43.6	41.4	41.4	43.5	41.1	41.2	40.9	43.2	40.6	40.5	42.0	42.9
Punt returns	43	23	45	68	43	29	37	46	42	36	47	38	39	41	36	45
Yards returned	468	226	498	762	600	469	259	406	424	345	427	479	392	343	370	335
Average yards per return	10.9	9.8	11.1	11.2	14.0	16.2	7.0	8.8	10.1	9.6	9.1	12.6	10.1	8.4	10.3	7.4
Returned for TD	1	0	1	2	1	0	0	0	0	0	0	1	1	0	1	0
Kickoff returns	70	68	57	42	70	83	64	78	58	64	63	77	67	67	81	76
Yards returned	1479	1504	1068	764	1457	1822	1474	1544	1282	1441	1589	1626	1209	1550	1500	1596
Average yards per return	21.1	22.1	18.7	18.2	20.8	22.0	23.0	19.8	22.1	22.5	25.2	21.1	18.0	23.1	18.5	21.0
Returned for TD	0	0	0	0	0	0	1	0	1	0	0	0	0	0	0	2
Fumbles	25	14	27	25	29	22	31	31	19	29	24	26	29	30	17	39
Recovered by	10	9	15	12	11	13	11	20	10	15	11	13	14	12	6	24
Out of bounds	2	1	1	3	0	0	4	0	1	0	4	1	1	4	1	1
Recovered for TD	0	0	0	0	0	0	0	0	0	0	0	0	0	0	0	0
Penalties	122	97	105	88	114	130	93	107	80	102	76	114	101	117	128	128
Yards penalized	1118	790	835	776	1016	1093	728	787	708	775	685	861	813	909	985	1010
Total points scored	277	229	460	437	318	333	217	322	336	284	309	329	320	316	298	324
Total TDs	31	23	53	49	35	36	24	38	35	30	33	36	36	34	30	39
TDs rushing	6	9	22	29	15	12	6	10	6	6	16	10	10	8	9	8
TDs passing	20	12	28	17	17	21	18	24	19	23	16	22	20	24	19	26
TDs on returns and recoveries	5	2	3	3	3	3	0	4	10	1	1	4	6	2	2	5
Extra point kicks	26	22	49	40	31	31	22	33	33	27	33	33	34	34	26	33
Extra point kick attempts	27	22	50	41	32	31	22	33	35	27	33	33	35	34	27	33
2-Pt. conversions	4	0	2	1	1	2	0	2	0	0	0	0	0	0	0	4
2-Pt. conversions attempted	4	1	3	8	3	5	2	5	0	3	0	2	1	0	2	6
Safeties	0	0	1	1	0	2	0	0	0	1	0	1	5	0	1	2
Field goals made	19	23	29	33	25	26	17	19	31	25	26	26	20	26	30	15
Field goals attempted	25	31	32	39	29	29	18	25	40	30	31	32	26	38	38	22
Percent successful	76.0	74.2	90.6	84.6	86.2	89.7	94.4	76.0	77.5	83.3	83.9	81.3	76.9	68.4	78.9	68.2
Extra points	30	22	51	41	32	33	22	35	33	27	33	33	34	34	26	37
Field goals blocked	2	2	1	0	0	1	0	1	1	0	0	1	0	0	1	0

1999 STATISTICS Miscellaneous

NFC
OFFENSE

	Ari.	Atl.	Car.	Chi.	Dal.	Det.	G.B.	Min.	N.O.	NYG	Phi.	S.F.	St.L.	T.B.	Was.
First downs	254	273	307	302	295	269	314	324	288	308	218	300	335	245	338
Rushing	77	68	78	82	129	67	87	96	97	87	76	102	102	97	121
Passing	150	179	208	203	139	179	196	192	159	197	123	172	207	132	183
Penalty	27	26	21	17	27	23	31	36	32	24	19	26	26	16	34
Rushes	396	373	356	396	493	356	386	422	461	431	424	418	431	502	463
Net yards gained	1207	1196	1525	1387	2051	1245	1519	1804	1690	1408	1746	2095	2059	1776	2039
Average gain	3.0	3.2	4.3	3.5	4.2	3.5	3.9	4.3	3.7	3.3	4.1	5.0	4.8	3.5	4.4
Average yards per game	75.4	74.8	95.3	86.7	128.2	77.8	94.9	112.8	105.6	88.0	109.1	130.9	128.7	111.0	127.4
Passes attempted	558	509	575	684	507	558	605	530	553	602	474	560	530	447	537
Completed	287	278	345	404	295	326	344	316	288	350	235	324	343	268	324
Percent completed	51.4	54.6	60.0	59.1	58.2	58.4	56.9	59.6	52.1	58.1	49.6	57.9	64.7	60.0	60.3
Total yards gained	3085	3691	4447	4352	3278	4074	4132	4318	3598	4015	2405	3526	4580	2781	4112
Times sacked	45	49	51	38	24	64	36	43	41	42	49	34	33	42	31
Yards lost	282	345	286	216	151	388	232	329	305	296	321	241	227	303	186
Net yards gained	2803	3346	4161	4136	3127	3686	3900	3989	3293	3719	2084	3285	4353	2478	3926
Average yards per game	175.2	209.1	260.1	258.5	195.4	230.4	243.8	249.3	205.8	232.4	130.3	205.3	272.1	154.9	245.4
Net yards per pass play	4.65	6.00	6.65	5.73	5.89	5.93	6.08	6.96	5.54	5.77	3.98	5.53	7.73	5.07	6.91
Yards gained per completion	10.75	13.28	12.89	10.77	11.11	12.50	12.01	13.66	12.49	11.47	10.23	10.88	13.35	10.38	12.69
Combined net yards gained	4010	4542	5686	5523	5178	4931	5419	5793	4983	5127	3830	5380	6412	4254	5965
Percent total yards rushing	30.1	26.3	26.8	25.1	39.6	25.2	28.0	31.1	33.9	27.5	45.6	38.9	32.1	41.7	34.2
Percent total yards passing	69.9	73.7	73.2	74.9	60.4	74.8	72.0	68.9	66.1	72.5	54.4	61.1	67.9	58.3	65.8
Average yards per game	250.6	283.9	355.4	345.2	323.6	308.2	338.7	362.1	311.4	320.4	239.4	336.3	400.8	265.9	372.8
Ball-control plays	999	931	982	1118	1024	978	1027	995	1055	1075	947	1012	994	991	1031
Average yards per play	4.0	4.9	5.8	4.9	5.1	5.0	5.3	5.8	4.7	4.8	4.0	5.3	6.5	4.3	5.8
Average time of possession	27:10	28:44	29:23	29:24	31:51	29:15	29:13	29:21	30:54	30:31	27:03	30:17	31:50	32:11	29:33
Third-down efficiency	32.6	34.7	38.3	36.8	35.2	36.5	36.8	43.6	33.6	36.2	31.1	34.0	46.9	35.2	37.9
Had intercepted	30	19	15	22	13	14	23	21	30	20	18	19	15	16	14
Yards opponents returned	336	365	267	359	100	174	338	302	483	322	266	286	266	144	129
Returned by opponents for TD	2	3	3	2	0	1	2	3	4	5	2	2	2	1	0
Punts	94	80	65	85	81	86	80	61	83	89	108	75	60	90	71
Yards punted	3948	3163	2562	3478	3500	3637	3130	2769	3282	3651	4524	2883	2464	3882	2926
Average yards per punt	42.0	39.5	39.4	40.9	43.2	42.3	39.1	45.4	39.5	41.0	41.9	38.4	41.1	43.1	41.2
Punt returns	47	32	35	30	41	38	29	32	35	45	29	26	52	43	41
Yards returned	489	372	241	346	440	386	212	269	258	520	250	104	498	357	332
Average yards per return	10.4	11.6	6.9	11.5	10.7	10.2	7.3	8.4	7.4	11.6	8.6	4.0	9.6	8.3	8.1
Returned for TD	0	2	0	0	1	1	0	1	0	1	0	0	1	0	0
Kickoff returns	64	76	66	68	58	72	66	70	79	69	69	77	54	55	63
Yards returned	1403	1445	1475	1491	1372	1445	1241	1597	1639	1502	1612	1579	1354	1116	1290
Average yards per return	21.9	19.0	22.3	21.9	23.7	20.1	18.8	22.8	20.7	21.8	23.4	20.5	25.1	20.3	20.5
Returned for TD	0	0	2	0	0	0	1	2	0	0	1	0	2	0	1
Fumbles	31	24	24	32	22	21	28	24	26	29	33	29	30	25	31
Lost	10	16	19	15	10	8	13	19	9	12	21	13	16	19	11
Out of bounds	3	1	0	0	2	3	0	1	0	3	1	1	3	2	5
Recovered for TD	0	0	0	0	0	0	0	0	0	0	0	0	0	0	0
Penalties	70	110	106	117	136	110	100	114	110	98	102	120	113	75	104
Yards penalized	481	968	857	915	1196	995	808	955	877	906	905	1045	889	583	808
Total points scored	245	285	421	272	352	322	357	399	260	299	272	295	526	270	443
Total TDs	27	34	50	31	42	35	40	49	27	32	29	33	66	27	54
TDs rushing	13	9	12	4	16	8	13	13	9	11	5	14	13	7	23
TDs passing	11	22	36	25	20	22	23	32	16	17	18	14	42	18	26
TDs on returns and recoveries	3	3	2	2	6	5	4	4	2	4	6	5	11	2	5
Extra point kicks	26	34	46	27	41	28	38	46	20	28	27	30	64	25	49
Extra point kick attempts	26	34	47	28	41	29	38	46	21	28	27	31	64	25	50
2-Pt. conversions	0	0	0	1	0	2	1	0	3	2	2	1	2	0	2
2-Pt. conversions attempts	1	0	3	3	0	6	2	3	6	3	2	2	2	2	3
Safeties	0	1	0	0	1	1	1	1	0	0	2	1	1	1	0
Field goals made	19	15	25	19	19	26	25	19	24	25	21	21	20	27	22
Field goals attempted	27	21	28	34	31	32	30	30	29	30	31	23	28	32	32
Percent successful	70.4	71.4	89.3	55.9	61.3	81.3	83.3	63.3	82.8	83.3	67.7	91.3	71.4	84.4	68.8
2-Pt. conversions	0	0	0	1	0	2	1	0	3	2	2	1	2	0	2
Extra points	26	34	46	28	41	30	39	46	23	30	29	31	66	25	51
Field goals blocked	1	1	0	0	0	0	3	3	0	0	1	1	0	2	2

DEFENSE

	Ari.	Atl.	Car.	Chi.	Dal.	Det.	G.B.	Min.	N.O.	NYG	Phi.	S.F.	St.L.	T.B.	Was.
First downs	301	293	331	310	266	305	304	320	297	270	328	315	263	228	322
Rushing	128	111	115	89	81	87	103	83	105	81	125	91	53	75	107
Passing	157	149	189	196	154	185	177	213	170	170	171	192	189	144	193
Penalty	16	33	27	25	31	33	24	24	22	19	32	32	21	9	22
Rushes	542	487	450	438	417	393	472	413	432	447	519	426	338	361	439
Net yards gained	2265	2072	1898	1882	1442	1531	1804	1617	1774	1560	2001	1619	1189	1407	1973
Average gain	4.2	4.3	4.2	4.3	3.5	3.9	3.8	3.9	4.1	3.5	3.9	3.8	3.5	3.9	4.5
Average yards per game	141.6	129.5	118.6	117.6	90.1	95.7	112.8	101.1	110.9	97.5	125.1	101.2	74.3	87.9	123.3
Passes attempted	493	468	557	583	545	574	538	606	489	511	568	521	596	573	589
Completed	294	274	327	354	297	359	304	373	291	295	322	317	319	302	328
Percent completed	59.6	58.5	58.7	60.7	54.5	62.5	56.5	61.6	59.5	57.7	56.7	60.8	53.5	52.7	55.7
Total yards gained	3386	3409	3840	4079	3615	4100	3690	4252	3821	3593	3733	4295	3867	3164	3953
Times sacked	33	40	35	37	35	50	30	46	45	32	37	32	57	43	40
Yards lost	229	258	235	257	217	340	185	272	277	172	272	227	358	291	221
Net yards gained	3157	3151	3605	3822	3398	3760	3505	3980	3544	3421	3461	4068	3509	2873	3732
Average yards per game	197.3	196.9	225.3	238.9	212.4	235.0	219.1	248.8	221.5	213.8	216.3	254.3	219.3	179.6	233.3
Net yards per pass play	6.00	6.20	6.09	6.16	5.86	6.03	6.17	6.10	6.64	6.30	5.72	7.36	5.37	4.66	5.93
Yards gained per completion	11.52	12.44	11.74	11.52	12.17	11.42	12.14	11.40	13.13	12.18	11.59	13.55	12.12	10.48	12.05
Combined net yards gained	5422	5223	5503	5704	4840	5291	5309	5597	5318	4981	5462	5687	4698	4280	5705
Percent total yards rushing	41.8	39.7	34.5	33.0	29.8	28.9	34.0	28.9	33.4	31.3	36.6	28.5	25.3	32.9	34.6
Percent total yards passing	58.2	60.3	65.5	67.0	70.2	71.1	66.0	71.1	66.6	68.7	63.4	71.5	74.7	67.1	65.4
Average yards per game	338.9	326.4	343.9	356.5	302.5	330.7	331.8	349.8	332.4	311.3	341.4	355.4	293.6	267.5	356.6
Ball-control plays	1068	995	1042	1058	997	1017	1040	1065	966	990	1124	979	991	977	1068
Average yards per play	5.1	5.2	5.3	5.4	4.9	5.2	5.1	5.3	5.5	5.0	4.9	5.8	4.7	4.4	5.3
Average time of possession	32:51	31:16	30:37	30:36	28:09	30:45	30:47	30:39	29:06	29:29	32:57	29:43	28:10	27:49	30:27
Third-down efficiency	40.5	39.1	41.6	40.6	32.1	39.4	39.0	39.2	38.7	33.8	37.8	40.1	33.8	32.3	39.2
Intercepted by	17	12	15	14	24	16	26	12	19	17	28	13	29	21	24
Yards returned by	276	166	169	229	442	235	137	66	138	232	625	209	567	355	375
Returned for TD	3	1	0	1	4	1	1	1	0	0	2	5	2	7	2	3
Punts	89	72	74	80	93	82	69	69	77	78	73	69	86	101	74
Yards punted	3775	2875	2924	3115	3836	3442	2954	2855	3183	3428	3011	2714	3674	4150	3158
Average yards per punt	42.4	39.9	39.5	38.9	41.2	42.0	42.8	41.4	41.3	43.9	41.2	39.3	42.7	41.1	42.7
Punt returns	53	26	32	36	43	42	39	28	43	38	59	33	23	49	27
Yards returned	340	119	158	266	459	402	333	246	283	405	490	399	155	360	279
Average yards per return	6.4	4.6	4.9	7.4	10.7	9.6	8.5	8.8	6.6	10.7	8.3	12.1	6.7	7.3	10.3
Returned for TD	0	0	0	0	1	0	0	0	1	1	0	2	0	0	2
Kickoff returns	59	55	76	57	62	60	72	69	60	53	57	47	85	61	77
Yards returned	1224	1221	1425	948	1259	1242	1565	1423	1473	1152	1305	1093	2115	1074	1772
Average yards per return	20.7	22.2	18.8	16.6	20.3	20.7	21.7	20.6	24.6	21.7	22.9	23.3	24.9	17.6	23.0
Returned for TD	2	2	0	0	0	1	0	0	1	1	0	1	0	0	1
Fumbles	28	16	22	29	23	32	36	31	22	23	38	18	21	23	22
Recovered	10	6	14	19	9	16	15	18	15	7	18	7	7	10	13
Out of bounds	4	2	1	1	3	2	3	2	0	2	4	2	0	1	2
Recovered for TD	0	0	0	0	1	0	0	0	0	0	0	0	0	0	0
Penalties	112	126	109	89	107	105	99	108	124	92	89	96	114	88	102
Yards penalized	938	980	877	720	862	839	993	880	1006	750	719	760	1007	727	1137
Total points scored	382	380	381	341	276	323	341	335	434	358	357	453	242	235	377
Total TDs	48	43	47	38	28	36	39	35	55	41	36	53	26	23	43
TDs rushing	17	18	13	11	6	12	16	9	15	13	12	11	4	8	16
TDs passing	25	20	26	23	19	21	20	20	34	20	22	36	19	11	23
TDs on returns and recoveries	6	5	8	4	3	3	3	6	6	8	2	6	3	4	4
Extra point kicks	44	40	42	38	24	31	35	32	54	38	33	50	22	23	38
Extra point kick attempts	45	40	43	38	24	31	35	32	54	39	33	50	23	23	38
2-Pt. conversions	0	1	0	0	3	2	0	2	1	0	0	1	2	0	3
2-Pt. conversions attempted	3	2	4	4	4	5	4	3	1	2	2	2	3	0	4
Safeties	1	1	0	0	0	3	0	1	0	1	0	1	0	1	0
Field goals made	16	26	19	25	26	22	24	29	16	24	36	27	20	24	25
Field goals attempted	24	35	25	36	33	29	31	42	23	37	45	32	26	31	30
Percent successful	66.7	74.3	76.0	69.4	78.8	75.9	77.4	69.0	69.6	64.9	80.0	84.4	76.9	77.4	83.3
Extra points	44	41	42	38	27	33	35	34	55	38	33	51	24	23	41
Field goals blocked	0	3	0	4	2	1	0	0	0	2	0	1	0	1	0

1999 STATISTICS Miscellaneous

AFC, NFC, AND NFL SUMMARIES

	AFC Offense Total	AFC Offense Average	AFC Defense Total	AFC Defense Average	NFC Offense Total	NFC Offense Average	NFC Defense Total	NFC Defense Average	NFL Total	NFL Average
First downs	4621	288.8	4538	283.6	4370	291.3	4453	296.9	8991	290.0
Rushing	1527	95.4	1459	91.2	1366	91.1	1434	95.6	2893	93.3
Passing	2725	170.3	2695	168.4	2619	174.6	2649	176.6	5344	172.4
Penalty	369	23.1	384	24.0	385	25.7	370	24.7	754	24.3
Rushes	7240	452.5	6974	435.9	6308	420.5	6574	438.3	13548	437.0
Net yards gained	28072	1754.5	26785	1674.1	24747	1549.8	26034	1735.6	52819	1703.8
Average gain	....	3.9	....	3.8	....	3.9	....	4.0	....	3.9
Average yards per game	....	109.7	....	104.6	....	103.1	....	108.5	....	106.5
Passes attempted	8531	533.2	8549	534.3	8229	548.6	8211	547.4	16760	540.6
Completed	4840	302.5	4811	300.7	4727	315.1	4756	317.1	9567	308.6
Percent completed	....	56.7	....	56.3	....	57.4	....	57.9	....	57.1
Total yards gained	56860	3553.8	56457	3528.6	56394	3759.6	56797	3786.5	113254	3653.4
Times sacked	627	39.2	657	41.1	622	41.5	592	39.5	1249	40.3
Yards lost	3857	241.1	4154	259.6	4108	273.9	3811	254.1	7965	256.9
Net yards gained	53003	3312.7	52303	3268.9	52286	3485.7	52986	3532.4	105289	3396.4
Average yards per game	....	207.0	....	204.3	....	217.9	....	220.8	....	212.3
Net yards per pass play	....	5.79	....	5.68	....	5.91	....	6.02	....	5.85
Yards gained per completion	....	11.75	....	11.73	....	11.93	....	11.94	....	11.84
Combined net yards gained	81075	5067.2	79088	4943.0	77033	5135.5	79020	5268.0	158108	5100.3
Percent total yards rushing	....	34.6	....	33.9	....	32.1	....	32.9	....	33.4
Percent total yards passing	....	65.4	....	66.1	....	67.9	....	67.1	....	66.6
Average yards per game	....	316.7	....	308.9	....	321.0	....	329.3	....	318.8
Ball-control plays	16398	1024.9	16180	1011.3	15159	1010.6	15377	1025.1	31557	1018.0
Average yards per play	....	4.9	....	4.9	....	5.1	....	5.1	....	5.0
Third-down efficiency	....	36.4	....	35.2	....	36.5	....	37.8	....	36.5
Interceptions	273	17.1	275	17.2	289	19.3	287	19.1	562	18.1
Yards returned	3891	243.2	3807	237.9	4137	275.8	4221	281.4	8034	259.2
Returned for TD	26	1.6	25	1.6	32	2.1	33	2.1	58	1.9
Punts	1370	85.6	1392	87.0	1208	80.5	1186	79.1	2578	83.2
Yards punted	57696	3606.0	58401	3650.1	49799	3319.9	49094	3272.9	107495	3467.6
Average yards per punt	....	42.1	....	42.0	....	41.2	....	41.4	....	41.7
Punt returns	674	42.1	658	41.1	555	37.0	571	38.1	1229	39.6
Yards returned	6423	401.4	6803	425.2	5074	338.3	4694	312.9	11497	370.9
Average yards per return	....	9.5	....	10.3	....	9.1	....	8.2	....	9.4
Returned for TD	9	0.6	9	0.6	7	0.5	7	0.5	16	0.5
Kickoff returns	1029	64.3	1085	67.8	1006	67.1	950	63.3	2035	65.6
Yards returned	21635	1352.2	22905	1431.6	21561	1437.4	20291	1352.7	43196	1393.4
Average yards per return	....	21.0	....	21.1	....	21.4	....	21.4	....	21.2
Returned for TD	4	0.3	4	0.3	9	0.6	9	0.6	13	0.4
Fumbles	392	24.5	417	26.1	409	27.3	384	25.6	801	25.8
Lost	179	11.2	206	12.9	211	14.1	184	12.3	390	12.6
Out of bounds	24	1.5	24	1.5	29	1.9	29	1.9	53	1.7
Own recovered for TD	1	0.1	0	0.0	0	0.0	1	0.1	1	0.0
Opponents recovered by	206	12.9	179	11.2	183	12.2	210	14.0	389	12.5
Opponents recovered for TD	19	1.2	13	0.8	15	1.0	21	1.4	34	1.1
Penalties	1677	104.8	1702	106.4	1585	105.7	1560	104.0	3262	105.2
Yards penalized	13896	868.5	13889	868.1	13188	879.2	13195	879.7	27084	873.7
Total points scored	5306	331.6	5109	319.3	5018	334.5	5215	347.7	10324	333.0
Total TDs	577	36.1	562	35.1	576	38.4	591	39.4	1153	37.2
TDs rushing	193	12.1	182	11.4	170	11.3	181	12.1	363	11.7
TDs passing	323	20.2	326	20.4	342	22.8	339	22.6	665	21.5
TDs on returns and recoveries	61	3.8	54	3.4	64	4.3	71	4.7	125	4.0
Extra point kicks	522	32.6	507	31.7	529	35.3	544	36.3	1051	33.9
Extra point kick attempts	528	33.0	515	32.2	535	35.7	548	36.5	1063	34.3
2-Pt. conversions	15	0.9	16	1.0	16	1.1	15	1.0	31	1.0
2-Pt. conversion attempts	46	2.9	45	2.8	38	2.5	39	2.6	84	2.7
Safeties	13	0.8	14	0.9	10	0.7	9	0.6	23	0.7
Field goals made	422	26.4	390	24.4	327	21.8	359	23.9	749	24.2
Field goals attempted	526	32.9	485	30.3	438	29.2	479	31.9	964	31.1
Percent successful	....	80.2	....	80.4	....	74.7	....	74.9	....	77.7

TOP REGULAR-SEASON PERFORMANCES

RUSHING

Player, Team	Opponent	Date	Att.	Yds.	TD
Eddie George, Tennessee	vs. Oakland	December 9	28	199	2
Corey Dillon, Cincinnati	vs. Cleveland	December 12	28	192	3
Stephen Davis, Washington	vs. Arizona	December 12	37	189	1
Olandis Gary, Denver	at Detroit	December 25	29	185	1
Stephen Davis, Washington	vs. N.Y. Giants	November 21	33	183	1
Olandis Gary, Denver	vs. Seattle	December 19*	22	183	0
Jermaine Fazande, San Diego	at Denver	January 2	30	183	1
Marshall Faulk, St. Louis	at Atlanta	October 17	18	181	1
Ricky Williams, New Orleans	vs. Cleveland	October 31	40	179	0
Corey Dillon, Cincinnati	at Cleveland	October 10	28	168	0
Charlie Garner, San Francisco	vs. Pittsburgh	November 7	20	166	1
Curtis Martin, N.Y. Jets	vs. Seattle	January 2	34	158	1
Eddie George, Tennessee	at New Orleans	October 17	28	155	0
Marshall Faulk, St. Louis	at New Orleans	December 12	29	154	1
Dorsey Levens, Green Bay	at Detroit	September 19	29	153	1
Edgerrin James, Indianapolis	at Philadelphia	November 21	22	152	2
Curtis Martin, N.Y. Jets	at New England	November 15	31	149	1
Robert Smith, Minnesota	at N.Y. Giants	December 26	16	146	1
Dorsey Levens, Green Bay	vs. Arizona	January 2	24	146	4
James Stewart, Jacksonville	vs. Pittsburgh	December 2	30	145	1
Stephen Davis, Washington	vs. Chicago	October 31	12	143	2
Kimble Anders, Kansas City	vs. Denver	September 19	22	142	0
Tshimanga Biakabutuka, Carolina	at Washington	October 3	12	142	3
Duce Staley, Philadelphia	at Carolina	November 7	17	140	1
Emmitt Smith, Dallas	at Minnesota	November 8	13	140	2
Jerome Bettis, Pittsburgh	vs. Carolina	December 26	33	137	1
Fred Taylor, Jacksonville	at Cleveland	December 19	26	136	1
Errict Rhett, Baltimore	at Atlanta	October 3*	27	136	0
Michael Pittman, Arizona	vs. Detroit	November 14	23	133	1
Marshall Faulk, St. Louis	vs. Cleveland	October 24	16	133	1
Ricky Watters, Seattle	vs. Cincinnati	November 7	27	133	0
Corey Dillon, Cincinnati	vs. San Francisco	December 5	25	133	1
Tshimanga Biakabutuka, Carolina	vs. Cincinnati	September 26	8	132	2
Curtis Martin, N.Y. Jets	vs. Arizona	November 7	38	131	0
Mike Alstott, Tampa Bay	vs. Denver	September 26	25	131	1
Priest Holmes, Baltimore	at Pittsburgh	December 12	18	130	1
Edgerrin James, Indianapolis	at Miami	December 5	23	130	2
Charlie Garner, San Francisco	vs. Washington	December 26*	16	129	1
Curtis Martin, N.Y. Jets	vs. Indianapolis	October 17	23	128	0
Fred Taylor, Jacksonville	at Cincinnati	October 31	15	128	1
Emmitt Smith, Dallas	at Arizona	November 21	29	127	0
Stephen Davis, Washington	at N.Y. Giants	September 19	23	126	3
Antowain Smith, Buffalo	vs. Miami	November 14	29	126	0
Terry Allen, New England	vs. Buffalo	December 26*	27	126	1
Marshall Faulk, St. Louis	at San Francisco	November 21	21	126	0
Ricky Watters, Seattle	at Green Bay	November 1	31	125	0
Olandis Gary, Denver	vs. Green Bay	October 17	37	124	1
James Stewart, Jacksonville	at Carolina	September 19	27	124	2
Fred Taylor, Jacksonville	at Atlanta	November 7	27	124	0
Curtis Martin, N.Y. Jets	at Oakland	October 24	26	123	0
Eddie George, Tennessee	at Cincinnati	November 14	29	123	2
Greg Hill, Detroit	vs. Tampa Bay	October 31	16	123	0
Napoleon Kaufman, Oakland	vs. Tampa Bay	December 19	8	122	2
Emmitt Smith, Dallas	vs. N.Y. Giants	January 2	22	122	0
Duce Staley, Philadelphia	vs. Washington	November 14	28	122	1
Stephen Davis, Washington	at Philadelphia	November 14	25	122	2
Corey Dillon, Cincinnati	at Pittsburgh	November 28	23	120	0
Robert Smith, Minnesota	at Kansas City	December 12	21	118	0
Edgerrin James, Indianapolis	at New England	September 19	32	118	1
Marshall Faulk, St. Louis	at Carolina	December 5	22	118	0
Edgerrin James, Indianapolis	vs. Dallas	October 31	27	117	0
Mike Alstott, Tampa Bay	at New Orleans	November 7	25	117	0
Errict Rhett, Baltimore	at Cleveland	November 7	17	117	2
Ricky Watters, Seattle	at Denver	December 19*	16	115	1
Emmitt Smith, Dallas	at Philadelphia	October 10	30	114	0
Errict Rhett, Baltimore	vs. Cleveland	September 26	22	113	0
Curtis Martin, N.Y. Jets	at Dallas	December 19	26	113	0
Corey Dillon, Cincinnati	at Carolina	September 26	20	113	0
Eddie George, Tennessee	at Cleveland	November 28	26	113	2
Antowain Smith, Buffalo	vs. N.Y. Jets	September 19	30	113	1
De'Mond Parker, Green Bay	at Chicago	December 5	19	113	2
Edgerrin James, Indianapolis	vs. Buffalo	September 12	26	112	1

– 291 –

Player, Team	Opponent	Date	Att.	Yds.	TD
Joe Montgomery, N.Y. Giants	vs. N.Y. Jets	December 5	38	111	1
Tyrone Wheatley, Oakland	vs. Tampa Bay	December 19	19	111	2
Edgerrin James, Indianapolis	at N.Y. Jets	October 17	26	111	0
Jerome Bettis, Pittsburgh	at Cincinnati	October 17	26	111	2
Duce Staley, Philadelphia	vs. Arizona	September 12	21	111	1
Ricky Williams, New Orleans	at N.Y. Giants	October 24	24	111	0
Emmitt Smith, Dallas	vs. N.Y. Jets	December 19	19	110	0
Emmitt Smith, Dallas	at New Orleans	December 24	23	110	1
Duce Staley, Philadelphia	vs. Dallas	October 10	22	110	0
Emmitt Smith, Dallas	at Washington	September 12*	23	109	1
Stephen Davis, Washington	vs. Dallas	September 12*	24	109	2
Edgerrin James, Indianapolis	vs. Kansas City	November 7	20	109	0
Emmitt Smith, Dallas	vs. Atlanta	September 20	29	109	2
Edgerrin James, Indianapolis	at N.Y. Giants	November 14	16	108	0
Olandis Gary, Denver	at San Diego	November 7	30	108	2
Ricky Watters, Seattle	at Kansas City	November 21	24	107	2
Charlie Garner, San Francisco	vs. Atlanta	December 12	26	107	1
Robert Smith, Minnesota	vs. Chicago	October 10	12	107	0
J.J. Johnson, Miami	vs. New England	November 21	31	106	1
Terry Allen, New England	vs. Denver	October 24	17	106	2
Leroy Hoard, Minnesota	vs. San Francisco	October 24	17	105	1
Marshall Faulk, St. Louis	vs. Atlanta	September 26	17	105	0
Dorsey Levens, Green Bay	vs. Seattle	November 1	24	104	0
Robert Smith, Minnesota	vs. San Diego	November 28	20	104	0
Edgerrin James, Indianapolis	at Cleveland	December 26	28	103	3
Emmitt Smith, Dallas	vs. Miami	November 25	31	103	0
Lawrence Phillips, San Francisco	at Arizona	September 27	9	102	1
Eddie George, Tennessee	vs. Jacksonville	December 26	26	102	0
Marshall Faulk, St. Louis	vs. New Orleans	November 28	18	102	2
Byron Hanspard, Atlanta	vs. Arizona	December 26	26	102	1
Errict Rhett, Baltimore	vs. Pittsburgh	September 19	22	101	1
Duce Staley, Philadelphia	at Chicago	October 17	23	101	0
Edgerrin James, Indianapolis	vs. New England	December 12	20	101	0
Priest Holmes, Baltimore	vs. Tennessee	December 5	9	100	0
Tyrone Wheatley, Oakland	at Seattle	October 3	20	100	1

*Overtime game.

PASSING

Player, Team	Opponent	Date	Att.	Comp.	Yds.	TD	Int.
Brad Johnson, Washington	at San Francisco	December 26*	47	32	471	2	1
Jeff Garcia, San Francisco	at Cincinnati	December 5	49	33	437	3	1
Jim Miller, Chicago	vs. Minnesota	November 14*	48	34	422	3	1
Peyton Manning, Indianapolis	at San Diego	September 26	54	29	404	2	1
Jim Harbaugh, San Diego	at Minnesota	November 28	39	25	404	1	1
Jake Plummer, Arizona	at Green Bay	January 2	57	35	396	2	3
Dan Marino, Miami	at Indianapolis	October 10	38	25	393	2	0
Drew Bledsoe, New England	at Cleveland	October 3	43	29	393	1	0
Brett Favre, Green Bay	vs. Tampa Bay	October 10	40	22	390	2	0
Brad Johnson, Washington	vs. Dallas	September 12*	33	20	382	2	0
Drew Bledsoe, New England	at Indianapolis	December 12	44	31	379	1	1
Gus Frerotte, Detroit	at Arizona	November 14	39	24	375	2	0
Jeff George, Minnesota	at Chicago	November 14*	44	25	374	3	1
Jeff Garcia, San Francisco	at Atlanta	January 3	34	26	373	2	0
Steve Beuerlein, Carolina	at Green Bay	December 12	42	29	373	3	1
Steve Beuerlein, Carolina	vs. San Francisco	December 18	38	27	368	4	0
Randall Cunningham, Minnesota	vs. Oakland	September 19	39	23	364	2	2
Jeff George, Minnesota	vs. San Diego	November 28	43	28	363	4	2
Brian Griese, Denver	vs. Green Bay	October 17	31	19	363	2	1
Troy Aikman, Dallas	at Washington	September 12*	49	28	362	5	3
Jim Miller, Chicago	at San Diego	November 21*	38	25	357	1	0
Neil O'Donnell, Tennessee	at San Francisco	October 3	40	20	355	2	1
Billy Joe Tolliver, New Orleans	vs. Tennessee	October 17	45	28	354	2	2
Rich Gannon, Oakland	vs. N.Y. Jets	October 24	51	26	352	2	1
Mark Brunell, Jacksonville	vs. New Orleans	November 21	30	19	351	2	1
Kurt Warner, St. Louis	at Carolina	December 5	31	22	351	3	2
Kurt Warner, St. Louis	at New Orleans	December 12	31	21	346	2	1
Steve McNair, Tennessee	vs. Cincinnati	September 12	32	21	341	3	1
Kerry Collins, N.Y. Giants	vs. N.Y. Jets	December 5	29	17	341	3	0
Drew Bledsoe, New England	at N.Y. Jets	September 12	30	21	340	1	1
Mark Brunell, Jacksonville	at Baltimore	November 28	47	27	338	2	2
Brad Johnson, Washington	vs. Carolina	October 3	33	20	337	4	0
Kurt Warner, St. Louis	vs. Chicago	December 26	35	24	334	3	0
Drew Bledsoe, New England	at Kansas City	October 10	45	23	334	2	2
Steve Beuerlein, Carolina	at Washington	October 3	47	23	334	1	1
Jeff Blake, Cincinnati	vs. San Francisco	December 5	30	21	334	4	0
Brett Favre, Green Bay	vs. Oakland	September 12	47	28	333	4	3

Player, Team	Opponent	Date	Att.	Comp.	Yds.	TD	Int.
Tony Banks, Baltimore	vs. Tennessee	December 5	31	18	332	4	0
Drew Bledsoe, New England	at Philadelphia	December 19	49	23	331	0	4
Kurt Warner, St. Louis	at Tennessee	October 31	46	29	328	3	0
Jim Harbaugh, San Diego	vs. Oakland	December 26	36	23	325	2	1
Rich Gannon, Oakland	at Kansas City	January 2*	47	25	324	3	2
Kurt Warner, St. Louis	vs. San Francisco	October 10	23	20	323	5	1
Dan Marino, Miami	vs. N.Y. Jets	December 27	52	29	322	3	3
Steve Beuerlein, Carolina	vs. New Orleans	January 2	41	22	322	5	0
Elvis Grbac, Kansas City	vs. Seattle	November 21	49	30	320	0	1
Kurt Warner, St. Louis	vs. N.Y. Giants	December 19	32	18	319	2	0
Jay Fiedler, Jacksonville	vs. Cincinnati	January 2	39	28	317	1	0
Brian Griese, Denver	at New England	October 24	38	25	316	1	0
Chris Chandler, Atlanta	at Carolina	November 28	42	24	315	4	0
Kerry Collins, N.Y. Giants	at Dallas	January 2	48	31	314	1	1
Peyton Manning, Indianapolis	vs. Dallas	October 31	34	22	313	1	0
Brad Johnson, Washington	at Philadelphia	November 14	33	18	313	2	3
Dan Marino, Miami	vs. Indianapolis	December 5	38	24	313	3	1
Brett Favre, Green Bay	vs. Arizona	January 2	34	21	311	2	1
Neil O'Donnell, Tennessee	vs. Cleveland	September 19	40	31	310	1	0
Kurt Warner, St. Louis	at Cincinnati	October 3	21	17	310	3	0
Kurt Warner, St. Louis	vs. Baltimore	September 12	44	28	309	3	2
Gus Frerotte, Detroit	vs. Chicago	November 25	42	29	309	2	0
Randall Cunningham, Minnesota	vs. Chicago	October 10	47	25	309	1	3
Mike Tomczak, Pittsburgh	vs. Tennessee	January 2	39	21	309	2	1
Brett Favre, Green Bay	vs. Detroit	November 21	40	26	309	1	0
Mark Brunell, Jacksonville	vs. Pittsburgh	December 2	37	25	308	1	0
Chris Chandler, Atlanta	vs. San Francisco	January 3	37	19	306	3	0
Kurt Warner, St. Louis	at Detroit	November 7	42	25	305	3	2
Brett Favre, Green Bay	vs. Minnesota	September 26	39	24	304	1	0
Jeff Garcia, San Francisco	at Carolina	December 18	46	29	303	2	1
Brett Favre, Green Bay	vs. Carolina	December 12	38	26	302	2	1
Cade McNown, Chicago	vs. Detroit	December 19	36	27	301	4	2
Trent Dilfer, Tampa Bay	at Minnesota	October 3	39	25	301	2	1
Doug Flutie, Buffalo	at Indianapolis	September 12	42	22	300	1	2
Steve Beuerlein, Carolina	at San Francisco	October 17	36	23	300	4	3

*Overtime game.

RECEIVING

Player, Team	Opponent	Date	Rec.	Yds.	TD
Qadry Ismail, Baltimore	at Pittsburgh	December 12	6	258	3
Jimmy Smith, Jacksonville	vs. New Orleans	November 21	9	220	1
Terry Glenn, New England	at Cleveland	October 3	13	214	1
Randy Moss, Minnesota	at Chicago	November 14*	12	204	0
Marshall Faulk, St. Louis	vs. Chicago	December 26	12	204	1
Marvin Harrison, Indianapolis	at San Diego	September 26	13	196	1
Keyshawn Johnson, N.Y. Jets	vs. New England	September 12	8	194	1
Tim Brown, Oakland	vs. N.Y. Jets	October 24	11	190	1
Amani Toomer, N.Y. Giants	vs. N.Y. Jets	December 5	6	181	3
Marcus Robinson, Chicago	vs. Detroit	December 19	11	170	3
Tony Martin, Miami	at Indianapolis	October 10	10	166	1
Terance Mathis, Atlanta	at Pittsburgh	October 25	12	166	1
Patrick Jeffers, Carolina	vs. New Orleans	January 2	7	165	2
Jimmy Smith, Jacksonville	vs. Cincinnati	January 2	14	165	0
Jacquez Green, Tampa Bay	vs. Kansas City	November 14	7	164	1
Germane Crowell, Detroit	vs. St. Louis	November 7	8	163	0
Marcus Robinson, Chicago	at San Diego	November 21*	6	163	1
Tim Dwight, Atlanta	vs. San Francisco	January 3	7	162	2
Amani Toomer, N.Y. Giants	at St. Louis	December 19	9	162	0
Kevin Dyson, Tennessee	vs. Cincinnati	September 12	9	162	1
Marcus Robinson, Chicago	at Washington	October 31	9	161	2
Patrick Jeffers, Carolina	at Pittsburgh	December 26	5	160	2
Michael Westbrook, Washington	vs. Dallas	September 12*	5	159	1
Bill Schroeder, Green Bay	vs. Tampa Bay	October 10	7	158	0
Jerry Rice, San Francisco	at Cincinnati	December 5	9	157	2
Marvin Harrison, Indianapolis	vs. Cincinnati	October 24	8	156	1
Randy Moss, Minnesota	vs. Detroit	January 2	5	155	0
Derrick Alexander, Kansas City	at Chicago	September 12	6	154	1
Antonio Freeman, Green Bay	vs. Tampa Bay	October 10	7	152	2
Michael Westbrook, Washington	at Philadelphia	November 14	4	152	1
Isaac Bruce, St. Louis	at Cincinnati	October 3	6	152	0
Muhsin Muhammad, Carolina	at Washington	October 3	8	151	0
Rocket Ismail, Dallas	at Washington	September 12*	8	149	1
Marcus Robinson, Chicago	vs. Minnesota	November 14*	7	148	0
Terry Glenn, New England	at Indianapolis	December 12	9	148	0
Eric Moulds, Buffalo	at Indianapolis	September 12	10	147	0
Patrick Jeffers, Carolina	at Green Bay	December 12	8	147	2

Player, Team	Opponent	Date	Rec.	Yds.	TD
Terrell Owens, San Francisco	at Cincinnati	December 5	9	145	0
Keyshawn Johnson, N.Y. Jets	vs. Miami	December 12	11	144	2
Cris Carter, Minnesota	at Denver	October 31	8	144	2
Bobby Engram, Chicago	at St. Louis	December 26	13	143	2
Yancey Thigpen, Tennessee	at San Francisco	October 3	6	143	1
Jerry Rice, San Francisco	at Atlanta	January 3	6	143	0
Germane Crowell, Detroit	at Arizona	November 14	5	142	1
Germane Crowell, Detroit	at Seattle	September 12	7	141	2
Jeff Graham, San Diego	at Minnesota	November 28	6	141	0
Cris Carter, Minnesota	at Chicago	November 14*	9	141	3
Michael Westbrook, Washington	vs. Carolina	October 3	8	140	2
Jimmy Smith, Jacksonville	vs. San Francisco	September 12	6	139	0
Marvin Harrison, Indianapolis	at Cleveland	December 26	14	138	1
Patrick Jeffers, Carolina	vs. San Francisco	December 18	8	138	1
Eddie Kennison, New Orleans	vs. Atlanta	October 10	4	138	1
Derrick Mayes, Seattle	at Chicago	September 19	7	137	1
Albert Connell, Washington	vs. Dallas	September 12*	4	137	1
Marcus Robinson, Chicago	vs. Philadelphia	October 17	4	136	1
Cris Carter, Minnesota	vs. San Diego	November 28	11	136	2
Kevin Johnson, Cleveland	at Cincinnati	December 12	7	135	0
Jimmy Smith, Jacksonville	at Cleveland	December 19	8	134	0
Isaac Bruce, St. Louis	vs. San Francisco	October 10	5	134	4
Marty Booker, Chicago	vs. Minnesota	November 14*	7	134	2
Albert Connell, Washington	vs. Carolina	October 3	5	134	2
Donald Hayes, Carolina	vs. Atlanta	November 28	5	133	1
Jimmy Smith, Jacksonville	at Baltimore	November 28	10	132	1
Cris Carter, Minnesota	at N.Y. Giants	December 26	5	131	1
Randy Moss, Minnesota	vs. Green Bay	December 20	5	131	2
Bobby Shaw, Pittsburgh	vs. Tennessee	January 2	7	131	1
Kevin Johnson, Cleveland	vs. New England	October 3	6	131	1
J.J. Stokes, San Francisco	at Atlanta	January 3	5	130	1
Jimmy Smith, Jacksonville	vs. Tennessee	September 26	10	129	1
Johnnie Morton, Detroit	at Minnesota	January 2	10	128	2
Jason Tucker, Dallas	at New Orleans	December 24	7	128	1
Randy Moss, Minnesota	vs. San Diego	November 28	7	127	1
Muhsin Muhammad, Carolina	vs. San Francisco	December 18	11	126	3
Michael Westbrook, Washington	at San Francisco	December 26*	7	125	1
Ed McCaffrey, Denver	at Seattle	November 14	6	125	1
Marvin Harrison, Indianapolis	at Miami	December 5	8	125	1
Rocket Ismail, Dallas	vs. Miami	November 25	5	125	1
Randy Moss, Minnesota	at Detroit	October 17	10	125	1
Muhsin Muhammad, Carolina	at St. Louis	November 14	9	125	0
E.G. Green, Indianapolis	vs. Buffalo	September 12	5	124	0
Jimmy Smith, Jacksonville	vs. Pittsburgh	December 2	10	124	1
Byron Chamberlain, Denver	vs. Green Bay	October 17	3	123	0
Amani Toomer, N.Y. Giants	vs. Philadelphia	October 3	8	123	0
Oronde Gadsden, Miami	at Indianapolis	October 10	4	123	1
Darnay Scott, Cincinnati	at Pittsburgh	November 28	4	123	1
Torry Holt, St. Louis	at Philadelphia	January 2	5	122	2
Tim Brown, Oakland	at Kansas City	January 2*	6	122	0
Michael Irvin, Dallas	at Washington	September 12*	5	122	2
Eric Moulds, Buffalo	vs. Pittsburgh	October 10	6	122	1
Terry Glenn, New England	vs. Indianapolis	September 19	7	122	0
Randy Moss, Minnesota	vs. Chicago	October 10	8	122	0
Jason Tucker, Dallas	vs. N.Y. Giants	January 2	4	122	1
Az-zahir Hakim, St. Louis	at Carolina	December 5	4	122	0
Germane Crowell, Detroit	vs. Washington	December 5	5	122	0
Marvin Harrison, Indianapolis	vs. Buffalo	September 12	8	121	2
Bobby Engram, Chicago	at San Diego	November 21*	8	121	0
Ike Hilliard, N.Y. Giants	vs. N.Y. Jets	December 5	6	121	0
Tim Brown, Oakland	vs. Chicago	September 26	9	121	1
Randy Moss, Minnesota	vs. Tampa Bay	October 3	4	120	2
Germane Crowell, Detroit	at Minnesota	January 2	8	120	0
Rob Moore, Arizona	at Green Bay	January 2	6	120	0
Terrell Owens, San Francisco	vs. St. Louis	November 21	6	120	0
Torrance Small, Philadelphia	vs. N.Y. Giants	October 31*	4	119	1
Johnnie Morton, Detroit	vs. Green Bay	September 19	4	118	0
Tony Martin, Miami	at New England	October 17	7	118	1
Marvin Harrison, Indianapolis	vs. New England	December 12	6	118	0
Frank Sanders, Arizona	at Green Bay	January 2	13	118	1
Muhsin Muhammad, Carolina	vs. Cincinnati	September 26	8	117	0
Tim Brown, Oakland	vs. San Diego	November 14	7	117	0
Derrick Alexander, Kansas City	vs. Denver	September 19	6	117	0
Marvin Harrison, Indianapolis	vs. Washington	December 19	9	117	0
Rod Smith, Denver	vs. Minnesota	October 31	7	117	0
Cris Carter, Minnesota	vs. Dallas	November 8	9	116	1
Ed McCaffrey, Denver	vs. Green Bay	October 17	5	116	2

Player, Team	Opponent	Date	Rec.	Yds.	TD
Warrick Dunn, Tampa Bay	vs. Detroit	December 12	6	115	0
Qadry Ismail, Baltimore	vs. New Orleans	December 19	7	115	1
Jimmy Smith, Jacksonville	at Carolina	September 19	10	115	0
Jeff Graham, San Diego	at Seattle	December 12	9	114	0
Ike Hilliard, N.Y. Giants	vs. Washington	September 19	8	114	1
Sean Dawkins, Seattle	at Kansas City	November 21	5	114	1
Oronde Gadsden, Miami	at Washington	January 2	9	114	1
Patrick Johnson, Baltimore	at New England	January 2	9	114	0
Jeff Graham, San Diego	vs. Oakland	December 26	3	113	1
Andre Hastings, New Orleans	at St. Louis	November 28	9	113	0
Shawn Jefferson, New England	at Arizona	October 31	3	113	2
Keenan McCardell, Jacksonville	vs. Pittsburgh	December 2	5	113	0
Jacquez Green, Tampa Bay	at Chicago	January 2	10	113	0
Terry Glenn, New England	at N.Y. Jets	September 12	7	113	0
Qadry Ismail, Baltimore	vs. Tennessee	December 5	5	113	0
Derrick Alexander, Kansas City	vs. San Diego	October 31	2	113	1
Tim Brown, Oakland	vs. Miami	October 31	7	113	0
Torry Holt, St. Louis	at New Orleans	December 12	6	113	0
Germane Crowell, Detroit	at Green Bay	November 21	8	112	1
Isaac Bruce, St. Louis	at Carolina	December 5	6	111	0
Terrence Wilkins, Indianapolis	at Philadelphia	November 21	4	111	1
Antonio Freeman, Green Bay	vs. Oakland	September 12	7	111	1
Ed McCaffrey, Denver	at New England	October 24	5	111	0
Eric Moulds, Buffalo	vs. Indianapolis	January 2	8	110	0
Albert Connell, Washington	at Arizona	October 17	8	110	0
Antonio Freeman, Green Bay	at Dallas	November 14	6	110	1
Johnnie Morton, Detroit	at Arizona	November 14	4	110	0
Darnay Scott, Cincinnati	at Cleveland	October 10	8	110	0
Tim Brown, Oakland	at San Diego	December 26	3	109	0
Marvin Harrison, Indianapolis	at N.Y. Giants	November 14	6	109	2
Tony Martin, Miami	vs. Indianapolis	December 5	6	109	1
Michael Westbrook, Washington	at Detroit	December 5	5	108	1
Darrin Chiaverini, Cleveland	vs. Jacksonville	December 19	10	108	1
Jake Reed, Minnesota	at Green Bay	September 26	6	108	0
Keenan McCardell, Jacksonville	vs. Cincinnati	January 2	9	108	1
Wayne Chrebet, N.Y. Jets	at Dallas	December 19	8	108	0
Carl Pickens, Cincinnati	vs. San Francisco	December 5	7	107	2
Tony Simmons, New England	at Kansas City	October 10	7	107	0
Patrick Jeffers, Carolina	vs. St. Louis	December 5	7	107	1
Johnnie Morton, Detroit	at Tampa Bay	December 12	7	107	0
Rod Smith, Denver	vs. San Diego	January 2	9	106	0
Corey Bradford, Green Bay	vs. Seattle	November 1	3	106	1
Peerless Price, Buffalo	at Seattle	October 24	5	106	1
Rod Smith, Denver	vs. Kansas City	December 5	8	106	0
Frank Sanders, Arizona	at Atlanta	December 26	3	106	0
Albert Connell, Washington	at San Francisco	December 26*	5	106	0
Amani Toomer, N.Y. Giants	vs. Washington	September 19	5	105	0
Ed McCaffrey, Denver	vs. Miami	September 13	6	105	3
Sean Dawkins, Seattle	at Pittsburgh	September 26	5	105	0
Marvin Harrison, Indianapolis	at New England	September 19	7	105	3
Derrick Mayes, Seattle	vs. Buffalo	October 24	6	105	2
Troy Brown, New England	at Philadelphia	December 19	5	105	0
Keith Poole, New Orleans	at Carolina	January 2	6	104	0
Jimmy Smith, Jacksonville	at Tennessee	December 26	4	104	0
Carl Pickens, Cincinnati	at Seattle	November 7	4	104	1
Oronde Gadsden, Miami	vs. Indianapolis	December 5	6	103	1
Curtis Conway, Chicago	vs. New Orleans	October 3	8	103	2
Muhsin Muhammad, Carolina	vs. Jacksonville	September 19	4	103	1
Tim Dwight, Atlanta	at Carolina	November 28	5	102	0
Jeff Graham, San Diego	at Denver	January 2	6	102	0
Rob Moore, Arizona	at N.Y. Giants	November 28	7	102	1
Tony Martin, Miami	vs. N.Y. Jets	December 27	6	102	1
Keenan McCardell, Jacksonville	at Baltimore	November 28	8	102	0
Isaac Bruce, St. Louis	at New Orleans	December 12	4	102	0
Derrick Alexander, Kansas City	vs. Seattle	November 21	8	101	0
David Boston, Arizona	vs. N.Y. Giants	October 10	8	101	1
Rocket Ismail, Dallas	vs. Arizona	October 3	4	101	1
Tony Martin, Miami	at Denver	September 13	4	101	0
Ike Hilliard, N.Y. Giants	at Washington	November 21	4	101	0
Tiki Barber, N.Y. Giants	at Dallas	January 2	13	100	0
Jake Reed, Minnesota	vs. Oakland	September 19	5	100	0
Johnnie Morton, Detroit	at Chicago	December 19	8	100	0
Chris Sanders, Tennessee	vs. Atlanta	December 19	5	100	1

*Overtime game.

RED-ZONE STATISTICS (INSIDE OPPONENTS 20-YARD LINE)

OFFENSE

TOTAL SCORES

Team	Series	TD Rush	TD Pass	Total TDs	TD Efficiency Pct.	FGM	Total Scores	Scoring Efficiency Pct.
Indianapolis	60	13	13	27	45.00	24	51	85.00
Jacksonville	63	17	12	29	46.03	20	49	77.78
St. Louis	56	12	25	37	66.07	11	48	85.71
Oakland	56	15	16	31	55.36	15	46	82.14
Miami	51	7	14	21	41.18	25	46	90.20
Green Bay	53	12	17	29	54.72	16	45	84.91
Tennessee	50	18	13	31	62.00	14	45	90.00
Washington	52	21	10	31	59.62	13	44	84.62
Buffalo	52	9	15	24	46.15	19	43	82.69
Minnesota	59	12	18	30	50.85	13	43	72.88
Pittsburgh	50	12	15	27	54.00	16	43	86.00
Carolina	49	7	20	27	55.10	16	43	87.76
N.Y. Jets	51	6	14	20	39.22	20	40	78.43
San Diego	48	10	9	19	39.58	21	40	83.33
Dallas	48	12	13	25	52.08	14	39	81.25
Cincinnati	54	11	12	23	42.59	15	38	70.37
N.Y. Giants	45	11	11	22	48.89	16	38	84.44
Denver	46	9	10	19	41.30	18	37	80.43
Kansas City	41	12	13	25	60.98	12	37	90.24
New England	46	8	9	17	36.96	20	37	80.43
San Francisco	45	12	9	21	46.67	16	37	82.22
Seattle	42	5	13	18	42.86	18	36	85.71
Arizona	42	12	9	21	50.00	14	35	83.33
Tampa Bay	45	4	11	15	33.33	19	34	75.56
New Orleans	45	8	10	18	40.00	15	33	73.33
Baltimore	41	6	8	14	34.15	19	33	80.49
Atlanta	42	8	14	22	52.38	10	32	76.19
Chicago	48	3	14	17	35.42	13	30	62.50
Detroit	36	7	12	19	52.78	11	30	83.33
Cleveland	28	9	11	20	71.43	5	25	89.29
Philadelphia	31	2	9	11	35.48	14	25	80.65
Totals	1475	310	399	710	48.14	492	1202	81.49
Average	47.6	10.0	12.9	22.9	48.14	15.9	38.8	81.49

SCORING EFFICIENCY

Team	Series	TD Rush	TD Pass	Total TDs	TD Efficiency Pct.	FGM	Total Scores	Scoring Efficiency Pct.
Kansas City	41	12	13	25	60.98	12	37	90.24
Miami	51	7	14	21	41.18	25	46	90.20
Tennessee	50	18	13	31	62.00	14	45	90.00
Cleveland	28	9	11	20	71.43	5	25	89.29
Carolina	49	7	20	27	55.10	16	43	87.76
Pittsburgh	50	12	15	27	54.00	16	43	86.00
St. Louis	56	12	25	37	66.07	11	48	85.71
Seattle	42	5	13	18	42.86	18	36	85.71
Indianapolis	60	13	13	27	45.00	24	51	85.00
Green Bay	53	12	17	29	54.72	16	45	84.91
Washington	52	21	10	31	59.62	13	44	84.62
N.Y. Giants	45	11	11	22	48.89	16	38	84.44
San Diego	48	10	9	19	39.58	21	40	83.33
Arizona	42	12	9	21	50.00	14	35	83.33
Detroit	36	7	12	19	52.78	11	30	83.33
Buffalo	52	9	15	24	46.15	19	43	82.69
San Francisco	45	12	9	21	46.67	16	37	82.22
Oakland	56	15	16	31	55.36	15	46	82.14
Dallas	48	12	13	25	52.08	14	39	81.25
Philadelphia	31	2	9	11	35.48	14	25	80.65
Baltimore	41	6	8	14	34.15	19	33	80.49
Denver	46	9	10	19	41.30	18	37	80.43
New England	46	8	9	17	36.96	20	37	80.43
N.Y. Jets	51	6	14	20	39.22	20	40	78.43
Jacksonville	63	17	12	29	46.03	20	49	77.78
Atlanta	42	8	14	22	52.38	10	32	76.19
Tampa Bay	45	4	11	15	33.33	19	34	75.56
New Orleans	45	8	10	18	40.00	15	33	73.33
Minnesota	59	12	18	30	50.85	13	43	72.88
Cincinnati	54	11	12	23	42.59	15	38	70.37
Chicago	48	3	14	17	35.42	13	30	62.50
Totals	1475	310	399	710	48.14	492	1202	81.49
Average	47.6	10.0	12.9	22.9	48.14	15.9	38.8	81.49

1999 STATISTICS Miscellaneous

DEFENSE
TOTAL SCORES

Team	Series	TD Rush	TD Pass	Total TDs	TD Efficiency Pct.	FGM	Total Scores	Scoring Efficiency Pct.
Tampa Bay	32	6	5	11	34.38	14	25	78.13
Miami	38	5	7	12	31.58	17	29	76.32
Pittsburgh	40	7	10	17	42.50	12	29	72.50
Jacksonville	36	6	12	18	50.00	11	29	80.56
St. Louis	36	4	15	19	52.78	11	30	83.33
Dallas	39	6	7	14	35.90	17	31	79.49
Buffalo	39	9	8	17	43.59	16	33	84.62
Tennessee	47	8	16	24	51.06	9	33	70.21
Kansas City	48	9	14	23	47.92	11	34	70.83
Baltimore	42	6	14	20	47.62	14	34	80.95
Minnesota	46	6	10	16	34.78	19	35	76.09
Detroit	49	10	11	21	42.86	15	36	73.47
New England	42	5	14	19	45.24	18	37	88.10
Arizona	45	13	14	27	60.00	10	37	82.22
Denver	43	13	10	23	53.49	15	38	88.37
Chicago	49	8	14	22	44.90	17	39	79.59
Oakland	43	8	15	23	53.49	16	39	90.70
Carolina	48	10	17	27	56.25	12	39	81.25
San Diego	48	7	15	22	45.83	18	40	83.33
New Orleans	51	14	16	30	58.82	11	41	80.39
N.Y. Giants	52	11	13	24	46.15	17	41	78.85
N.Y. Jets	49	12	9	21	42.86	20	41	83.67
Seattle	50	9	14	23	46.00	18	41	82.00
Indianapolis	48	9	14	23	47.92	19	42	87.50
Washington	51	13	15	28	54.90	14	42	82.35
Green Bay	59	14	12	26	44.07	17	43	72.88
Atlanta	50	17	9	26	52.00	19	45	90.00
San Francisco	54	10	21	31	57.41	16	47	87.04
Philadelphia	65	11	16	27	41.54	25	52	80.00
Cincinnati	69	19	19	38	55.07	21	59	85.51
Cleveland	67	25	13	38	56.72	23	61	91.04
Totals	1475	310	399	710	48.14	492	1202	81.49
Average	47.6	10.0	12.9	22.9	48.14	15.9	38.8	81.49

SCORING EFFICIENCY

Team	Series	TD Rush	TD Pass	Total TDs	TD Efficiency Pct.	FGM	Total Scores	Scoring Efficiency Pct.
Tennessee	47	8	16	24	51.06	9	33	70.21
Kansas City	48	9	14	23	47.92	11	34	70.83
Pittsburgh	40	7	10	17	42.50	12	29	72.50
Green Bay	59	14	12	26	44.07	17	43	72.88
Detroit	49	10	11	21	42.86	15	36	73.47
Minnesota	46	6	10	16	34.78	19	35	76.09
Miami	38	5	7	12	31.58	17	29	76.32
Tampa Bay	32	6	5	11	34.38	14	25	78.13
N.Y. Giants	52	11	13	24	46.15	17	41	78.85
Dallas	39	6	7	14	35.90	17	31	79.49
Chicago	49	8	14	22	44.90	17	39	79.59
Philadelphia	65	11	16	27	41.54	25	52	80.00
New Orleans	51	14	16	30	58.82	11	41	80.39
Jacksonville	36	6	12	18	50.00	11	29	80.56
Baltimore	42	6	14	20	47.62	14	34	80.95
Carolina	48	10	17	27	56.25	12	39	81.25
Seattle	50	9	14	23	46.00	18	41	82.00
Arizona	45	13	14	27	60.00	10	37	82.22
Washington	51	13	15	28	54.90	14	42	82.35
St. Louis	36	4	15	19	52.78	11	30	83.33
San Diego	48	7	15	22	45.83	18	40	83.33
N.Y. Jets	49	12	9	21	42.86	20	41	83.67
Buffalo	39	9	8	17	43.59	16	33	84.62
Cincinnati	69	19	19	38	55.07	21	59	85.51
San Francisco	54	10	21	31	57.41	16	47	87.04
Indianapolis	48	9	14	23	47.92	19	42	87.50
New England	42	5	14	19	45.24	18	37	88.10
Denver	43	13	10	23	53.49	15	38	88.37
Atlanta	50	17	9	26	52.00	19	45	90.00
Oakland	43	8	15	23	53.49	16	39	90.70
Cleveland	67	25	13	38	56.72	23	61	91.04
Totals	1475	310	399	710	48.14	492	1202	81.49
Average	47.6	10.0	12.9	22.9	48.14	15.9	38.8	81.49

HISTORY

Championship games
Year-by-year standings
Super Bowls
Pro Bowls
Records
Statistical leaders
Coaching records
Hall of Fame
The Sporting News awards
Team by team

CHAMPIONSHIP GAMES
NFL (1933-1969); NFC (1970-1999)
RESULTS

Sea.	Date	Winner (Share)	Loser (Share)	Score	Site	Attendance
1933	Dec. 17	Chicago Bears ($210.34)	N.Y. Giants ($140.22)	23-21	Chicago	26,000
1934	Dec. 9	N.Y. Giants ($621)	Chicago Bears ($414.02)	30-13	N.Y. Giants	35,059
1935	Dec. 15	Detroit ($313.35)	N.Y. Giants ($200.20)	26-7	Detroit	15,000
1936	Dec. 13	Green Bay ($250)	Boston Redskins ($180)	21-6	N.Y. Giants	29,545
1937	Dec. 12	Washington ($225.90)	Chicago Bears ($127.78)	28-21	Chicago	15,870
1938	Dec. 11	N.Y. Giants ($504.45)	Green Bay ($368.81)	23-17	N.Y. Giants	48,120
1939	Dec. 10	Green Bay ($703.97)	N.Y. Giants ($455.57)	27-0	Milwaukee	32,279
1940	Dec. 8	Chicago Bears ($873)	Washington ($606)	73-0	Washington	36,034
1941	Dec. 21	Chicago Bears ($430)	N.Y. Giants ($288)	37-9	Chicago	13,341
1942	Dec. 13	Washington ($965)	Chicago Bears ($637)	14-6	Washington	36,006
1943	Dec. 26	Chicago Bears ($1,146)	Washington ($765)	41-21	Chicago	34,320
1944	Dec. 17	Green Bay ($1,449)	N.Y. Giants ($814)	14-7	N.Y. Giants	46,016
1945	Dec. 16	Cleveland Rams ($1,469)	Washington ($902)	15-14	Cleveland	32,178
1946	Dec. 15	Chicago Bears ($1,975)	N.Y. Giants ($1,295)	24-14	N.Y. Giants	58,346
1947	Dec. 28	Chi. Cardinals ($1,132)	Philadelphia ($754)	28-21	Chicago	30,759
1948	Dec. 19	Philadelphia ($1,540)	Chi. Cardinals ($874)	7-0	Philadelphia	36,309
1949	Dec. 18	Philadelphia ($1,094)	L.A. Rams ($739)	14-0	L.A. Rams	27,980
1950	Dec. 24	Cleveland Browns ($1,113)	L.A. Rams ($686)	30-28	Cleveland	29,751
1951	Dec. 23	L. A. Rams ($2,108)	Cleve. Browns ($1,483)	24-17	L.A. Rams	57,522
1952	Dec. 28	Detroit ($2,274)	Cleveland Browns ($1,712)	17-7	Cleveland	50,934
1953	Dec. 27	Detroit ($2,424)	Cleveland Browns ($1,654)	17-16	Detroit	54,577
1954	Dec. 26	Cleveland Browns ($2,478)	Detroit ($1,585)	56-10	Cleveland	43,827
1955	Dec. 26	Cleveland Browns ($3,508)	L.A. Rams ($2,316)	38-14	L.A. Rams	85,693
1956	Dec. 30	N.Y. Giants ($3,779)	Chicago Bears ($2,485)	47-7	N.Y. Giants	56,836
1957	Dec. 29	Detroit ($4,295)	Cleveland Browns ($2,750)	59-14	Detroit	55,263
1958	Dec. 28	Baltimore ($4,718)	N.Y. Giants ($3,111)	23-17*	N.Y. Giants	64,185
1959	Dec. 27	Baltimore ($4,674)	N.Y. Giants ($3,083)	31-16	Baltimore	57,545
1960	Dec. 26	Philadelphia ($5,116)	Green Bay ($3,105)	17-13	Philadelphia	67,325
1961	Dec. 31	Green Bay ($5,195)	N.Y. Giants ($3,339)	37-0	Green Bay	39,029
1962	Dec. 30	Green Bay ($5,888)	N.Y. Giants ($4,166)	16-7	N.Y. Giants	64,892
1963	Dec. 29	Chicago Bears ($5,899)	N.Y. Giants ($4,218)	14-10	Chicago	45,801
1964	Dec. 27	Cleveland Browns ($8,052)	Baltimore ($5,571)	27-0	Cleveland	79,544
1965	Jan. 2	Green Bay ($7,819)	Cleveland Browns ($5,288)	23-12	Green Bay	50,777
1966	Jan. 1	Green Bay ($9,813)	Dallas ($6,527)	34-27	Dallas	74,152
1967	Dec. 31	Green Bay ($7,950)	Dallas ($5,299)	21-17	Green Bay	50,861
1968	Dec. 29	Baltimore ($9,306)	Cleveland Browns ($5,963)	34-0	Cleveland	78,410
1969	Jan. 4	Minnesota ($7,930)	Cleveland Browns ($5,118)	27-7	Minnesota	46,503
1970	Jan. 3	Dallas ($8,500)	San Francisco ($5,500)	17-10	San Francisco	59,364
1971	Jan. 2	Dallas ($8,500)	San Francisco ($5,500)	14-3	Dallas	63,409
1972	Dec. 31	Washington ($8,500)	Dallas ($5,500)	26-3	Washington	53,129
1973	Dec. 30	Minnesota ($8,500)	Dallas ($5,500)	27-10	Dallas	64,422
1974	Dec. 29	Minnesota ($8,500)	L.A. Rams ($5,500)	14-10	Minnesota	48,444
1975	Jan. 4	Dallas ($8,500)	L.A. Rams ($5,500)	37-7	L.A. Rams	88,919
1976	Dec. 26	Minnesota ($8,500)	L.A. Rams ($5,500)	24-13	Minnesota	48,379
1977	Jan. 1	Dallas ($9,000)	Minnesota ($9,000)	23-6	Dallas	64,293
1978	Jan. 7	Dallas ($9,000)	L.A. Rams ($9,000)	28-0	L.A. Rams	71,086
1979	Jan. 6	L.A. Rams ($9,000)	Tampa Bay ($9,000)	9-0	Tampa Bay	72,033
1980	Jan. 11	Philadelphia ($9,000)	Dallas ($9,000)	20-7	Philadelphia	70,696
1981	Jan. 10	San Francisco ($9,000)	Dallas ($9,000)	28-27	San Francisco	60,525
1982	Jan. 22	Washington ($18,000)	Dallas ($18,000)	31-17	Washington	55,045
1983	Jan. 8	Washington ($18,000)	San Francisco ($18,000)	24-21	Washington	55,363
1984	Jan. 6	San Francisco ($18,000)	Chicago Bears ($18,000)	23-0	San Francisco	61,040
1985	Jan. 12	Chicago Bears ($18,000)	L.A. Rams ($18,000)	24-0	Chicago	63,522
1986	Jan. 11	N. Y. Giants ($18,000)	Washington ($18,000)	17-0	N.Y. Giants	76,633
1987	Jan. 17	Washington ($18,000)	Minnesota ($18,000)	17-10	Washington	55,212
1988	Jan. 8	San Francisco ($18,000)	Chicago Bears ($18,000)	28-3	Chicago	64,830
1989	Jan. 14	San Francisco ($18,000)	L.A. Rams ($18,000)	30-3	San Francisco	64,769
1990	Jan. 20	N. Y. Giants ($18,000)	San Francisco ($18,000)	15-13	San Francisco	65,750
1991	Jan. 12	Washington ($18,000)	Detroit ($18,000)	41-10	Washington	55,585
1992	Jan. 17	Dallas ($18,000)	San Francisco ($18,000)	30-20	San Francisco	64,920
1993	Jan. 23	Dallas ($23,500)	San Francisco ($23,500)	38-21	Dallas	64,902
1994	Jan. 15	San Francisco ($26,000)	Dallas ($26,000)	38-28	San Francisco	69,125
1995	Jan. 14	Dallas ($27,000)	Green Bay ($27,000)	38-27	Dallas	65,135
1996	Jan. 12	Green Bay ($29,000)	Carolina ($29,000)	30-13	Green Bay	60,216
1997	Jan. 11	Green Bay ($30,000)	San Francisco ($30,000)	23-10	San Francisco	68,987
1998	Jan. 17	Atlanta ($32,500)	Minnesota ($32,500)	30-27*	Minnesota	64,060
1999	Jan. 23	St. Louis ($33,000)	Tampa Bay ($33,000)	11-6	St. Louis	66,496

*Overtime.

COMPOSITE STANDINGS

	W	L	Pct.	PF	PA		W	L	Pct.	PF	PA
Atlanta Falcons	1	0	1.000	30	27	Dallas Cowboys	8	8	.500	361	319
Philadelphia Eagles	4	1	.800	79	48	Phoenix Cardinals*	1	1	.500	28	28
Green Bay Packers	10	3	.769	303	177	San Francisco 49ers	5	7	.417	245	222
Baltimore Colts	3	1	.750	88	60	Cleveland Browns	4	7	.364	224	253
Detroit Lions	4	2	.667	139	141	New York Giants	5	11	.313	240	322
Washington Redskins†	7	5	.583	222	255	St. Louis Rams‡	4	9	.308	134	276
Minnesota Vikings	4	3	.571	135	110	Carolina Panthers	0	1	.000	13	30
Chicago Bears	7	6	.538	286	245	Tampa Bay Buccaneers	0	2	.000	6	20

*Both games played when franchise was in Chicago; won 28-21, lost 7-0.
†One game played when franchise was in Boston; lost 21-6.
‡One game played when franchise was in Cleveland; won 15-14. 11 games played when franchise was in Los Angeles, record of 2-9.

AFL (1960-1969); AFC (1970-1999)

RESULTS

Sea.	Date	Winner (Share)	Loser (Share)	Score	Site	Attendance
1960	Jan. 1	Houston ($1,025)	L.A. Chargers ($718)	24-16	Houston	32,183
1961	Dec. 24	Houston ($1,792)	San Diego ($1,111)	10-3	San Diego	29,556
1962	Dec. 23	Dallas Texans ($2,206)	Houston ($1,471)	20-17*	Houston	37,981
1963	Jan. 5	San Diego ($2,498)	Boston Patriots ($1,596)	51-10	San Diego	30,127
1964	Dec. 26	Buffalo ($2,668)	San Diego ($1,738)	20-7	Buffalo	40,242
1965	Dec. 26	Buffalo ($5,189)	San Diego ($3,447)	23-0	San Diego	30,361
1966	Jan. 1	Kansas City ($5,309)	Buffalo ($3,799)	31-7	Buffalo	42,080
1967	Dec. 31	Oakland ($6,321)	Houston ($4,996)	40-7	Oakland	53,330
1968	Dec. 29	N.Y. Jets ($7,007)	Oakland ($5,349)	27-23	New York	62,627
1969	Jan. 4	Kansas City ($7,755)	Oakland ($6,252)	17-7	Oakland	53,564
1970	Jan. 3	Baltimore ($8,500)	Oakland ($5,500)	27-17	Baltimore	54,799
1971	Jan. 2	Miami ($8,500)	Baltimore ($5,500)	21-0	Miami	76,622
1972	Dec. 31	Miami ($8,500)	Pittsburgh ($5,500)	21-17	Pittsburgh	50,845
1973	Dec. 30	Miami ($8,500)	Oakland ($5,500)	27-10	Miami	79,325
1974	Dec. 29	Pittsburgh ($8,500)	Oakland ($5,500)	24-13	Oakland	53,800
1975	Jan. 4	Pittsburgh ($8,500)	Oakland ($5,500)	16-10	Pittsburgh	50,609
1976	Dec. 28	Oakland ($8,500)	Pittsburgh ($5,500)	24-7	Oakland	53,821
1977	Jan. 1	Denver ($9,000)	Oakland ($9,000)	20-17	Denver	75,044
1978	Jan. 7	Pittsburgh ($9,000)	Houston ($9,000)	34-5	Pittsburgh	50,725
1979	Jan. 6	Pittsburgh ($9,000)	Houston ($9,000)	27-13	Pittsburgh	50,475
1980	Jan. 11	Oakland ($9,000)	San Diego ($9,000)	34-27	San Diego	52,428
1981	Jan. 10	Cincinnati ($9,000)	San Diego ($9,000)	27-7	Cincinnati	46,302
1982	Jan. 23	Miami ($18,000)	N.Y. Jets ($18,000)	14-0	Miami	67,396
1983	Jan. 8	L.A. Raiders ($18,000)	Seattle ($18,000)	30-14	Los Angeles	88,734
1984	Jan. 6	Miami ($18,000)	Pittsburgh ($18,000)	45-28	Miami	76,029
1985	Jan. 12	New England ($18,000)	Miami ($18,000)	31-14	Miami	74,978
1986	Jan. 11	Denver ($18,000)	Cleveland ($18,000)	23-20*	Cleveland	79,915
1987	Jan. 17	Denver ($18,000)	Cleveland ($18,000)	38-33	Denver	75,993
1988	Jan. 8	Cincinnati ($18,000)	Buffalo ($18,000)	21-10	Cincinnati	59,747
1989	Jan. 14	Denver ($18,000)	Cleveland ($18,000)	37-21	Denver	76,046
1990	Jan. 20	Buffalo ($18,000)	L.A. Raiders ($18,000)	51-3	Buffalo	80,234
1991	Jan. 12	Buffalo ($18,000)	Denver ($18,000)	10-7	Buffalo	80,272
1992	Jan. 17	Buffalo ($18,000)	Miami ($18,000)	29-10	Miami	72,703
1993	Jan. 23	Buffalo ($23,500)	Kansas City ($23,500)	30-13	Buffalo	76,642
1994	Jan. 15	San Diego ($26,000)	Pittsburgh ($26,000)	17-13	Pittsburgh	61,545
1995	Jan. 14	Pittsburgh ($27,000)	Indianapolis ($27,000)	20-16	Pittsburgh	61,062
1996	Jan. 12	New England ($29,000)	Jacksonville ($29,000)	20-6	New England	60,190
1997	Jan. 11	Denver ($30,000)	Pittsburgh ($30,000)	24-21	Pittsburgh	61,382
1998	Jan. 17	Denver ($32,500)	N.Y. Jets ($32,500)	23-10	Denver	75,482
1999	Jan. 23	Tennessee ($33,000)	Jacksonville ($33,000)	33-14	Jacksonville	75,206

*Overtime.

COMPOSITE STANDINGS

	W	L	Pct.	PF	PA		W	L	Pct.	PF	PA
Cincinnati Bengals	2	0	1.000	48	17	New York Jets	1	2	.333	37	60
Denver Broncos	6	1	.857	172	132	Indianapolis Colts∞	1	2	.333	43	58
Buffalo Bills	6	2	.750	180	92	Oakland Raiders§	4	8	.333	228	264
Kansas City Chiefs†	3	1	.750	81	61	San Diego Chargers*	2	6	.250	128	161
Miami Dolphins	5	2	.714	152	115	Seattle Seahawks	0	1	.000	14	30
New England Patriots‡	2	1	.667	61	71	Jacksonville Jaguars	0	2	.000	20	53
Pittsburgh Steelers	5	5	.500	207	188	Cleveland Browns	0	3	.000	74	98
Tennessee Titans▲	3	4	.429	109	154						

– 301 –

*One game played when franchise was in Los Angeles; lost 24-16.
†One game played when franchise was in Dallas (Texans); won 20-17.
‡One game played when franchise was in Boston; lost 51-10.
§Two games played when franchise was in Los Angeles; record of 1-1.
∞Two games played when franchise was in Baltimore; record of 1-1.
▲Six games played when franchise was in Houston (Oilers); record of 2-4.

POSTSEASON GAME COMPOSITE STANDINGS

	W	L	Pct.	PF	PA		W	L	Pct.	PF	PA
Green Bay Packers	22	10	.688	772	558	Philadelphia Eagles	9	11	.450	356	369
San Francisco 49ers	24	15	.615	984	759	St. Louis Rams†	16	20	.444	584	756
Dallas Cowboys	32	21	.604	1271	979	New York Giants	14	19	.424	551	616
Washington Redskins‡	22	15	.595	778	652	Kansas City Chiefs*	8	11	.421	301	384
Denver Broncos	16	11	.593	613	636	Minnesota Vikings	16	22	.421	745	856
Pittsburgh Steelers	21	15	.583	801	707	Cincinnati Bengals	5	7	.417	246	257
Oakland Raiders♦	21	15	.583	855	659	Detroit Lions	7	10	.412	365	404
Miami Dolphins	19	17	.528	754	784	New England Patriots§	7	10	.412	320	357
Chicago Bears	14	14	.500	579	552	Atlanta Falcons	4	6	.400	208	260
Jacksonville Jaguars	4	4	.500	208	200	San Diego Chargers▲	7	11	.389	332	428
Carolina Panthers	1	1	.500	39	47	Seattle Seahawks	3	5	.375	145	159
Buffalo Bills	14	15	.483	681	658	Tampa Bay Buccaneers	3	5	.375	88	149
Indianapolis Colts■	10	11	.476	376	408	Cleveland Browns	11	19	.367	596	702
New York Jets	6	7	.462	260	247	Arizona Cardinals∞	2	5	.286	122	182
Tennessee Titans▼	12	14	.462	461	602	New Orleans Saints	0	4	.000	56	123

*One game played when franchise was in Dallas (Texans); won 20-17.
†One game played when franchise was in Cleveland; won 15-14. 32 games played when franchise was in Los Angeles; record of 12-20.
‡One game played when franchise was in Boston; lost 21-6.
§Two games played when franchise was in Boston; won 26-8, lost 51-10.
∞Two games played when franchise was in Chicago; won 28-21, lost 7-0. Three games played when franchise was in St. Louis; lost 35-23, lost 30-14, lost 41-16.
▲One game played when franchise was in Los Angeles; lost 24-16.
♦12 games played when franchise was in Los Angeles; record of 6-6.
■15 games played when franchise was in Baltimore; record of 8-7.
▼22 games played when franchise was in Houston; record of 9-13.

CHAMPIONS OF DEFUNCT PRO FOOTBALL LEAGUES

ALL-AMERICAN FOOTBALL CONFERENCE

Year	Winner	Coach	Loser	Coach	Score, Site
1946	Cleveland Browns	Paul Brown	N.Y. Yankees	Ray Flaherty	14-9, Cleveland
1947	Cleveland Browns	Paul Brown	N.Y. Yankees	Ray Flaherty	14-3, New York
1948	Cleveland Browns	Paul Brown	Buffalo Bills	Red Dawson	49-7, Cleveland
1949	Cleveland Browns	Paul Brown	S.F. 49ers	Buck Shaw	21-7, Cleveland

NOTE: Cleveland Browns and San Francisco 49ers joined the NFL after the AAFC folded in 1949.

WORLD FOOTBALL LEAGUE

Year	Winner	Coach	Loser	Coach	Score, Site
1974	Birmingham Americans	Jack Gotta	Florida Blazers	Jack Pardee	22-21, Birmingham
1975	League folded October 22				

UNITED STATES FOOTBALL LEAGUE

Year	Winner	Coach	Loser	Coach	Score, Site
1983	Michigan Panthers	Jim Stanley	Philadelphia Stars	Jim Mora	24-22, Denver
1984	Philadelphia Stars	Jim Mora	Arizona Wranglers	George Allen	23-3, Tampa
1985	Baltimore Stars	Jim Mora	Oakland Invaders	Charlie Sumner	28-24, E. Rutherford, N.J.

YEAR-BY-YEAR STANDINGS

1920

Team	W	L	T	Pct.
Akron Pros*	8	0	3	1.000
Decatur Staleys	10	1	2	.909
Buffalo All-Americans	9	1	1	.900
Chicago Cardinals	6	2	2	.750
Rock Island Independents	6	2	2	.750
Dayton Triangles	5	2	2	.714
Rochester Jeffersons	6	3	2	.667
Canton Bulldogs	7	4	2	.636
Detroit Heralds	2	3	3	.400
Cleveland Tigers	2	4	2	.333
Chicago Tigers	2	5	1	.286
Hammond Pros	2	5	0	.286
Columbus Panhandles	2	6	2	.250
Muncie Flyers	0	1	0	.000

*No official standings were maintained for the 1920 season, and the championship was awarded to the Akron Pros in a League meeting on April 30, 1921. Clubs played schedules which included games against non-league opponents. Records of clubs against all opponents are listed above.

1921

Team	W	L	T	Pct.
Chicago Staleys	9	1	1	.900
Buffalo All-Americans	9	1	2	.900
Akron Pros	8	3	1	.727
Canton Bulldogs	5	2	3	.714
Rock Island Independents	4	2	1	.667
Evansville Crimson Giants	3	2	0	.600
Green Bay Packers	3	2	1	.600
Dayton Triangles	4	4	1	.500
Chicago Cardinals	3	3	2	.500
Rochester Jeffersons	2	3	0	.400
Cleveland Indians	3	5	0	.375
Washington Senators	1	2	0	.333
Cincinnati Celts	1	3	0	.250
Hammond Pros	1	3	1	.250
Minneapolis Marines	1	3	1	.250
Detroit Heralds	1	5	1	.167
Columbus Panhandles	1	8	0	.111
Tonawanda Kardex	0	1	0	.000
Muncie Flyers	0	2	0	.000
Louisville Brecks	0	2	0	.000
New York Giants	0	2	0	.000

1922

Team	W	L	T	Pct.
Canton Bulldogs	10	0	2	1.000
Chicago Bears	9	3	0	.750
Chicago Cardinals	8	3	0	.727
Toledo Maroons	5	2	2	.714
Rock Island Independents	4	2	1	.667
Racine Legion	6	4	1	.600
Dayton Triangles	4	3	1	.571
Green Bay Packers	4	3	3	.571
Buffalo All-Americans	5	4	1	.556
Akron Pros	3	5	2	.375
Milwaukee Badgers	2	4	3	.333
Oorang Indians	2	6	0	.250
Minneapolis Marines	1	3	0	.250
Louisville Brecks	1	3	0	.250
Evansville Crimson Giants	0	3	0	.000
Rochester Jeffersons	0	4	1	.000
Hammond Pros	0	5	1	.000
Columbus Panhandles	0	7	0	.000

1923

Team	W	L	T	Pct.
Canton Bulldogs	11	0	1	1.000
Chicago Bears	9	2	1	.818
Green Bay Packers	7	2	1	.778
Milwaukee Badgers	7	2	3	.778
Cleveland Indians	3	1	3	.750
Chicago Cardinals	8	4	0	.667
Duluth Kelleys	4	3	0	.571
Columbus Tigers	5	4	1	.556
Buffalo All-Americans	4	4	3	.500
Racine Legion	4	4	2	.500
Toledo Maroons	2	3	2	.400
Rock Island Independents	2	3	3	.400
Minneapolis Marines	2	5	2	.286
St. Louis All-Stars	1	4	2	.200
Hammond Pros	1	5	1	.167
Dayton Triangles	1	6	1	.143
Akron Indians	1	6	0	.143
Oorang Indians	1	10	0	.091
Rochester Jeffersons	0	2	0	.000
Louisville Brecks	0	3	0	.000

1924

Team	W	L	T	Pct.
Cleveland Bulldogs	7	1	1	.875
Chicago Bears	6	1	4	.857
Frankford Yellow Jackets	11	2	1	.846
Duluth Kelleys	5	1	0	.833
Rock Island Independents	6	2	2	.750
Green Bay Packers	7	4	0	.636
Racine Legion	4	3	3	.571
Chicago Cardinals	5	4	1	.556
Buffalo Bisons	6	5	0	.545
Columbus Tigers	4	4	0	.500
Hammond Pros	2	2	1	.500
Milwaukee Badgers	5	8	0	.385
Akron Indians	2	6	0	.250
Dayton Triangles	2	6	0	.250
Kansas City Blues	2	7	0	.222
Kenosha Maroons	0	5	1	.000
Minneapolis Marines	0	6	0	.000
Rochester Jeffersons	0	7	0	.000

1925

Team	W	L	T	Pct.
Chicago Cardinals	11	2	1	.846
Pottsville Maroons	10	2	0	.833
Detroit Panthers	8	2	2	.800
New York Giants	8	4	0	.667
Akron Indians	4	2	2	.667
Frankford Yellow Jackets	13	7	0	.650
Chicago Bears	9	5	3	.643
Rock Island Independents	5	3	3	.625
Green Bay Packers	8	5	0	.615
Providence Steam Roller	6	5	1	.545
Canton Bulldogs	4	4	0	.500
Cleveland Bulldogs	5	8	1	.385
Kansas City Cowboys	2	5	1	.286
Hammond Pros	1	4	0	.200
Buffalo Bisons	1	6	2	.143
Duluth Kelleys	0	3	0	.000
Rochester Jeffersons	0	6	1	.000
Milwaukee Badgers	0	6	0	.000
Dayton Triangles	0	7	1	.000
Columbus Tigers	0	9	0	.000

HISTORY Year-by-year standings

– 303 –

HISTORY Year-by-year standings

1926

Team	W	L	T	Pct.
Frankford Yellow Jackets	14	1	1	.933
Chicago Bears	12	1	3	.923
Pottsville Maroons	10	2	1	.833
Kansas City Cowboys	8	3	0	.727
Green Bay Packers	7	3	3	.700
Los Angeles Buccaneers	6	3	1	.667
New York Giants	8	4	1	.667
Duluth Eskimos	6	5	3	.545
Buffalo Rangers	4	4	2	.500
Chicago Bulldogs	5	6	1	.455
Providence Steam Roller	5	7	1	.417
Detroit Panthers	4	6	2	.400
Hartford Blues	3	7	0	.300
Brooklyn Lions	3	8	0	.273
Milwaukee Badgers	2	7	0	.222
Akron Pros	1	4	3	.200
Dayton Triangles	1	4	1	.200
Racine Tornadoes	1	4	0	.200
Columbus Tigers	1	6	0	.143
Canton Bulldogs	1	9	3	.100
Hammond Pros	0	4	0	.000
Louisville Colonels	0	4	0	.000

1927

Team	W	L	T	Pct.
New York Giants	11	1	1	.917
Green Bay Packers	7	2	1	.778
Chicago Bears	9	3	2	.750
Cleveland Bulldogs	8	4	1	.667
Providence Steam Roller	8	5	1	.615
New York Yankees	7	8	1	.467
Frankford Yellow Jackets	6	9	3	.400
Pottsville Maroons	5	8	0	.385
Chicago Cardinals	3	7	1	.300
Dayton Triangles	1	6	1	.143
Duluth Eskimos	1	8	0	.111
Buffalo Bisons	0	5	0	.000

1928

Team	W	L	T	Pct.
Providence Steam Roller	8	1	2	.889
Frankford Yellow Jackets	11	3	2	.786
Detroit Wolverines	7	2	1	.778
Green Bay Packers	6	4	3	.600
Chicago Bears	7	5	1	.583
New York Giants	4	7	2	.364
New York Yankees	4	8	1	.333
Pottsville Maroons	2	8	0	.200
Chicago Cardinals	1	5	0	.167
Dayton Triangles	0	7	0	.000

1929

Team	W	L	T	Pct.
Green Bay Packers	12	0	1	1.000
New York Giants	13	1	1	.929
Frankford Yellow Jackets	9	4	5	.692
Chicago Cardinals	6	6	1	.500
Boston Bulldogs	4	4	0	.500
Orange Tornadoes	3	4	4	.429
Staten Island Stapletons	3	4	3	.429
Providence Steam Roller	4	6	2	.400
Chicago Bears	4	9	2	.308
Buffalo Bisons	1	7	1	.125
Minneapolis Red Jackets	1	9	0	.100
Dayton Triangles	0	6	0	.000

1930

Team	W	L	T	Pct.
Green Bay Packers	10	3	1	.769
New York Giants	13	4	0	.765
Chicago Bears	9	4	1	.692
Brooklyn Dodgers	7	4	1	.636
Providence Steam Roller	6	4	1	.600
Staten Island Stapletons	5	5	2	.500
Chicago Cardinals	5	6	2	.455
Portsmouth Spartans	5	6	3	.455
Frankford Yellow Jackets	4	13	1	.222
Minneapolis Red Jackets	1	7	1	.125
Newark Tornadoes	1	10	1	.091

1931

Team	W	L	T	Pct.
Green Bay Packers	12	2	0	.857
Portsmouth Spartans	11	3	0	.786
Chicago Bears	8	5	0	.615
Chicago Cardinals	5	4	0	.556
New York Giants	7	6	1	.538
Providence Steam Roller	4	4	3	.500
Staten Island Stapletons	4	6	1	.400
Cleveland Indians	2	8	0	.200
Brooklyn Dodgers	2	12	0	.143
Frankford Yellow Jackets	1	6	1	.143

1932

Team	W	L	T	Pct.
Chicago Bears	7	1	6	.875
Green Bay Packers	10	3	1	.769
Portsmouth Spartans	6	2	4	.750
Boston Braves	4	4	2	.500
New York Giants	4	6	2	.400
Brooklyn Dodgers	3	9	0	.250
Chicago Cardinals	2	6	2	.250
Staten Island Stapletons	2	7	3	.222

NOTE: Chicago Bears and Portsmouth finished regularly scheduled games tied for first place. Bears won playoff game, which counted in standings, 9-0.

1933

EASTERN DIVISION

Team	W	L	T	Pct.	PF	PA
N.Y. Giants	11	3	0	.786	244	101
Brooklyn	5	4	1	.556	93	54
Boston	5	5	2	.500	103	97
Philadelphia	3	5	1	.375	77	158
Pittsburgh	3	6	2	.333	67	208

WESTERN DIVISION

Team	W	L	T	Pct.	PF	PA
Chicago Bears	10	2	1	.833	133	82
Portsmouth	6	5	0	.545	128	87
Green Bay	5	7	1	.417	170	107
Cincinnati	3	6	1	.333	38	110
Chi. Cardinals	1	9	1	.100	52	101

PLAYOFFS

NFL championship
Chicago Bears 23 vs. N.Y. Giants 21

– 304 –

1934

EASTERN DIVISION
Team	W	L	T	Pct.	PF	PA
N.Y. Giants	8	5	0	.615	147	107
Boston	6	6	0	.500	107	94
Brooklyn	4	7	0	.364	61	153
Philadelphia	4	7	0	.364	127	85
Pittsburgh	2	10	0	.167	51	206

WESTERN DIVISION
Team	W	L	T	Pct.	PF	PA
Chicago Bears	13	0	0	1.000	286	86
Detroit	10	3	0	.769	238	59
Green Bay	7	6	0	.538	156	112
Chi. Cardinals	5	6	0	.455	80	84
St. Louis	1	2	0	.333	27	61
Cincinnati	0	8	0	.000	10	243

PLAYOFFS
NFL championship
N.Y. Giants 30 vs. Chicago Bears 13

1935

EASTERN DIVISION
Team	W	L	T	Pct.	PF	PA
N.Y. Giants	9	3	0	.750	180	96
Brooklyn	5	6	1	.455	90	141
Pittsburgh	4	8	0	.333	100	209
Boston	2	8	1	.200	65	123
Philadelphia	2	9	0	.182	60	179

NOTE: One game between Boston and Philadelphia was cancelled.

WESTERN DIVISION
Team	W	L	T	Pct.	PF	PA
Detroit	7	3	2	.700	191	111
Green Bay	8	4	0	.667	181	96
Chicago Bears	6	4	2	.600	192	106
Chi. Cardinals	6	4	2	.600	99	97

PLAYOFFS
NFL championship
Detroit 26 vs. N.Y. Giants 7

1936

EASTERN DIVISION
Team	W	L	T	Pct.	PF	PA
Boston	7	5	0	.583	149	110
Pittsburgh	6	6	0	.500	98	187
N.Y. Giants	5	6	1	.455	115	163
Brooklyn	3	8	1	.273	92	161
Philadelphia	1	11	0	.083	51	206

WESTERN DIVISION
Team	W	L	T	Pct.	PF	PA
Green Bay	10	1	1	.909	248	118
Chicago Bears	9	3	0	.750	222	94
Detroit	8	4	0	.667	235	102
Chi. Cardinals	3	8	1	.273	74	143

PLAYOFFS
NFL championship
Green Bay 21, Boston 6, at New York.

1937

EASTERN DIVISION
Team	W	L	T	Pct.	PF	PA
Washington	8	3	0	.727	195	120
N.Y. Giants	6	3	2	.667	128	109
Pittsburgh	4	7	0	.364	122	145
Brooklyn	3	7	1	.300	82	174
Philadelphia	2	8	1	.200	86	177

WESTERN DIVISION
Team	W	L	T	Pct.	PF	PA
Chicago Bears	9	1	1	.900	201	100
Green Bay	7	4	0	.636	220	122
Detroit	7	4	0	.636	180	105
Chi. Cardinals	5	5	1	.500	135	165
Cleveland	1	10	0	.091	75	207

PLAYOFFS
NFL championship
Washington 28 at Chicago Bears 21

1938

EASTERN DIVISION
Team	W	L	T	Pct.	PF	PA
N.Y. Giants	8	2	1	.800	194	79
Washington	6	3	2	.667	148	154
Brooklyn	4	4	3	.500	131	161
Philadelphia	5	6	0	.455	154	164
Pittsburgh	2	9	0	.182	79	169

WESTERN DIVISION
Team	W	L	T	Pct.	PF	PA
Green Bay	8	3	0	.727	223	118
Detroit	7	4	0	.636	119	108
Chicago Bears	6	5	0	.545	194	148
Cleveland	4	7	0	.364	131	215
Chi. Cardinals	2	9	0	.182	111	168

PLAYOFFS
NFL championship
N.Y. Giants 23 vs. Green Bay 17

1939

EASTERN DIVISION
Team	W	L	T	Pct.	PF	PA
N.Y. Giants	9	1	1	.900	168	85
Washington	8	2	1	.800	242	94
Brooklyn	4	6	1	.400	108	219
Philadelphia	1	9	1	.100	105	200
Pittsburgh	1	9	1	.100	114	216

WESTERN DIVISION
Team	W	L	T	Pct.	PF	PA
Green Bay	9	2	0	.818	233	153
Chicago Bears	8	3	0	.727	298	157
Detroit	6	5	0	.545	145	150
Cleveland	5	5	1	.500	195	164
Chi. Cardinals	1	10	0	.091	84	254

PLAYOFFS
NFL championship
Green Bay 27 vs. N.Y. Giants 0

1940

EASTERN DIVISION
Team	W	L	T	Pct.	PF	PA
Washington	9	2	0	.818	245	142
Brooklyn	8	3	0	.727	186	120
N.Y. Giants	6	4	1	.600	131	133
Pittsburgh	2	7	2	.222	60	178
Philadelphia	1	10	0	.091	111	211

WESTERN DIVISION
Team	W	L	T	Pct.	PF	PA
Chicago Bears	8	3	0	.727	238	152
Green Bay	6	4	1	.600	238	155
Detroit	5	5	1	.500	138	153
Cleveland	4	6	1	.400	171	191
Chi. Cardinals	2	7	2	.222	139	222

PLAYOFFS
NFL championship
Chicago Bears 73 at Washington 0

HISTORY Year-by-year standings

– 305 –

HISTORY *Year-by-year standings*

1941

EASTERN DIVISION
Team	W	L	T	Pct.	PF	PA
N.Y. Giants	8	3	0	.727	238	114
Brooklyn	7	4	0	.636	158	127
Washington	6	5	0	.545	176	174
Philadelphia	2	8	1	.200	119	218
Pittsburgh	1	9	1	.100	103	276

WESTERN DIVISION
Team	W	L	T	Pct.	PF	PA
Chicago Bears	10	1	0	.909	396	147
Green Bay	10	1	0	.909	258	120
Detroit	4	6	1	.400	121	195
Chi. Cardinals	3	7	1	.300	127	197
Cleveland	2	9	0	.182	116	244

PLAYOFFS
Western Division playoff
Chicago Bears 33 vs. Green Bay 14
NFL championship
Chicago Bears 37 vs. N.Y. Giants 9

1942

EASTERN DIVISION
Team	W	L	T	Pct.	PF	PA
Washington	10	1	0	.909	227	102
Pittsburgh	7	4	0	.636	167	119
N.Y. Giants	5	5	1	.500	155	139
Brooklyn	3	8	0	.273	100	168
Philadelphia	2	9	0	.182	134	239

WESTERN DIVISION
Team	W	L	T	Pct.	PF	PA
Chicago Bears	11	0	0	1.000	376	84
Green Bay	8	2	1	.800	300	215
Cleveland	5	6	0	.455	150	207
Chi. Cardinals	3	8	0	.273	98	209
Detroit	0	11	0	.000	38	263

PLAYOFFS
NFL championship
Washington 14 vs. Chicago Bears 6

1943

EASTERN DIVISION
Team	W	L	T	Pct.	PF	PA
Washington	6	3	1	.667	229	137
N.Y. Giants	6	3	1	.667	197	170
Phil.-Pitt.	5	4	1	.556	225	230
Brooklyn	2	8	0	.200	65	234

NOTE: Cleveland Rams did not play in 1943.

WESTERN DIVISION
Team	W	L	T	Pct.	PF	PA
Chicago Bears	8	1	1	.889	303	157
Green Bay	7	2	1	.778	264	172
Detroit	3	6	1	.333	178	218
Chi. Cardinals	0	10	0	.000	95	238

PLAYOFFS
Eastern Division playoff
Washington 28 at N.Y. Giants 0
NFL championship
Chicago Bears 41 vs. Washington 21

1944

EASTERN DIVISION
Team	W	L	T	Pct.	PF	PA
N.Y. Giants	8	1	1	.889	206	75
Philadelphia	7	1	2	.875	267	131
Washington	6	3	1	.667	169	180
Boston	2	8	0	.200	82	233
Brooklyn	0	10	0	.000	69	166

WESTERN DIVISION
Team	W	L	T	Pct.	PF	PA
Green Bay	8	2	0	.800	238	141
Chicago Bears	6	3	1	.667	258	172
Detroit	6	3	1	.667	216	151
Cleveland	4	6	0	.400	188	224
Card-Pitt	0	10	0	.000	108	328

PLAYOFFS
NFL championship
Green Bay 14 at N.Y. Giants 7

1945

EASTERN DIVISION
Team	W	L	T	Pct.	PF	PA
Washington	8	2	0	.800	209	121
Philadelphia	7	3	0	.700	272	133
N.Y. Giants	3	6	1	.333	179	198
Boston	3	6	1	.333	123	211
Pittsburgh	2	8	0	.200	79	220

WESTERN DIVISION
Team	W	L	T	Pct.	PF	PA
Cleveland	9	1	0	.900	244	136
Detroit	7	3	0	.700	195	194
Green Bay	6	4	0	.600	258	173
Chicago Bears	3	7	0	.300	192	235
Chi. Cardinals	1	9	0	.100	98	228

PLAYOFFS
NFL championship
Cleveland 15 vs. Washington 14

1946

AAFC

EASTERN DIVISION
Team	W	L	T	Pct.	PF	PA
New York	10	3	1	.769	270	192
Brooklyn	3	10	1	.231	226	339
Buffalo	3	10	1	.231	249	370
Miami	3	11	0	.154	167	378

WESTERN DIVISION
Team	W	L	T	Pct.	PF	PA
Cleveland	12	2	0	.857	423	137
San Francisco	9	5	0	.643	307	189
Los Angeles	7	5	2	.583	305	290
Chicago	5	6	3	.455	263	315

PLAYOFFS
AAFC championship
Cleveland 14 vs. New York 9

NFL

EASTERN DIVISION
Team	W	L	T	Pct.	PF	PA
N.Y. Giants	7	3	1	.700	236	162
Philadelphia	6	5	0	.545	231	220
Washington	5	5	1	.500	171	191
Pittsburgh	5	5	1	.500	136	117
Boston	2	8	1	.200	189	273

WESTERN DIVISION
Team	W	L	T	Pct.	PF	PA
Chicago Bears	8	2	1	.800	289	193
Los Angeles	6	4	1	.600	277	257
Green Bay	6	5	0	.545	148	158
Chi. Cardinals	6	5	0	.545	260	198
Detroit	1	10	0	.091	142	310

PLAYOFFS
NFL championship
Chicago Bears 24 at N.Y. Giants 14

1947

AAFC

EASTERN DIVISION
Team	W	L	T	Pct.	PF	PA
New York	11	2	1	.846	378	239
Buffalo	8	4	2	.667	320	288
Brooklyn	3	10	1	.231	181	340
Baltimore	2	11	1	.154	167	377

WESTERN DIVISION
Team	W	L	T	Pct.	PF	PA
Cleveland	12	1	1	.923	410	185
San Francisco	8	4	2	.667	327	264
Los Angeles	7	7	0	.500	328	256
Chicago	1	13	0	.071	263	425

PLAYOFFS
AAFC championship
Cleveland 14 at New York 3

NFL

EASTERN DIVISION
Team	W	L	T	Pct.	PF	PA
Philadelphia	8	4	0	.667	308	242
Pittsburgh	8	4	0	.667	240	259
Boston	4	7	1	.364	168	256
Washington	4	8	0	.333	295	367
N.Y. Giants	2	8	2	.200	190	309

WESTERN DIVISION
Team	W	L	T	Pct.	PF	PA
Chi. Cardinals	9	3	0	.750	306	231
Chicago Bears	8	4	0	.667	363	241
Green Bay	6	5	1	.545	274	210
Los Angeles	6	6	0	.500	259	214
Detroit	3	9	0	.250	231	305

PLAYOFFS
Eastern Division playoff
Philadelphia 21 at Pittsburgh 0
NFL championship
Chicago Cardinals 28 vs. Philadelphia 21

1948

AAFC

EASTERN DIVISION
Team	W	L	T	Pct.	PF	PA
Buffalo	7	7	0	.500	360	358
Baltimore	7	7	0	.500	333	327
New York	6	8	0	.429	265	301
Brooklyn	2	12	0	.143	253	387

WESTERN DIVISION
Team	W	L	T	Pct.	PF	PA
Cleveland	14	0	0	1.000	389	190
San Francisco	12	2	0	.857	495	248
Los Angeles	7	7	0	.500	258	305
Chicago	1	13	0	.071	202	439

PLAYOFFS
Eastern Division playoff
Buffalo 28 vs. Baltimore 17
AAFC championship
Cleveland 49 vs. Buffalo 7

NFL

EASTERN DIVISION
Team	W	L	T	Pct.	PF	PA
Philadelphia	9	2	1	.818	376	156
Washington	7	5	0	.583	291	287
N.Y. Giants	4	8	0	.333	297	388
Pittsburgh	4	8	0	.333	200	243
Boston	3	9	0	.250	174	372

WESTERN DIVISION
Team	W	L	T	Pct.	PF	PA
Chi. Cardinals	11	1	0	.917	395	226
Chicago Bears	10	2	0	.833	375	151
Los Angeles	6	5	1	.545	327	269
Green Bay	3	9	0	.250	154	290
Detroit	2	10	0	.167	200	407

PLAYOFFS
NFL championship
Philadelphia 7 vs. Chicago Cardinals 0

1949

AAFC

Team	W	L	T	Pct.	PF	PA
Cleveland	9	1	2	.900	339	171
San Francisco	9	3	0	.750	416	227
Brooklyn-N.Y.	8	4	0	.667	196	206
Buffalo	5	5	2	.500	236	256
Chicago	4	8	0	.333	179	268
Los Angeles	4	8	0	.333	253	322
Baltimore	1	11	0	.083	172	341

PLAYOFFS
AAFC Semifinals
Cleveland 31 vs. Buffalo 21
San Francisco 17 vs. Brooklyn-N.Y. 7
AAFC championship
Cleveland 21 vs. San Francisco 7

NFL

EASTERN DIVISION
Team	W	L	T	Pct.	PF	PA
Philadelphia	11	1	0	.917	364	134
Pittsburgh	6	5	1	.545	224	214
N.Y. Giants	6	6	0	.500	287	298
Washington	4	7	1	.364	268	339
N.Y. Bulldogs	1	10	1	.091	153	365

WESTERN DIVISION
Team	W	L	T	Pct.	PF	PA
Los Angeles	8	2	2	.800	360	239
Chicago Bears	9	3	0	.750	332	218
Chi. Cardinals	6	5	1	.545	360	301
Detroit	4	8	0	.333	237	259
Green Bay	2	10	0	.167	114	329

PLAYOFFS
NFL championship
Philadelphia 14 at Los Angeles 0

1950

AMERICAN CONFERENCE
Team	W	L	T	Pct.	PF	PA
Cleveland	10	2	0	.833	310	144
N.Y. Giants	10	2	0	.833	268	150
Philadelphia	6	6	0	.500	254	141
Pittsburgh	6	6	0	.500	180	195
Chi. Cardinals	5	7	0	.417	233	287
Washington	3	9	0	.250	232	326

NATIONAL CONFERENCE
Team	W	L	T	Pct.	PF	PA
Los Angeles	9	3	0	.750	466	309
Chicago Bears	9	3	0	.750	279	207
N.Y. Yanks	7	5	0	.583	366	367
Detroit	6	6	0	.500	321	285
Green Bay	3	9	0	.250	244	406
San Francisco	3	9	0	.250	213	300
Baltimore	1	11	0	.083	213	462

PLAYOFFS
American Conference playoff
Cleveland 8 vs. N.Y. Giants 3
National Conference playoff
Los Angeles 24 vs. Chicago Bears 14
NFL championship
Cleveland 30 vs. Los Angeles 28

HISTORY Year-by-year standings

– 307 –

1951

AMERICAN CONFERENCE

Team	W	L	T	Pct.	PF	PA
Cleveland	11	1	0	.917	331	152
N.Y. Giants	9	2	1	.818	254	161
Washington	5	7	0	.417	183	296
Pittsburgh	4	7	1	.364	183	235
Philadelphia	4	8	0	.333	234	264
Chi. Cardinals	3	9	0	.250	210	287

NATIONAL CONFERENCE

Team	W	L	T	Pct.	PF	PA
Los Angeles	8	4	0	.667	392	261
Detroit	7	4	1	.636	336	259
San Francisco	7	4	1	.636	255	205
Chicago Bears	7	5	0	.583	286	282
Green Bay	3	9	0	.250	254	375
N.Y. Yanks	1	9	2	.100	241	382

PLAYOFFS
NFL championship
Los Angeles 24 vs. Cleveland 17

1952

AMERICAN CONFERENCE

Team	W	L	T	Pct.	PF	PA
Cleveland	8	4	0	.667	310	213
N.Y. Giants	7	5	0	.583	234	231
Philadelphia	7	5	0	.583	252	271
Pittsburgh	5	7	0	.417	300	273
Chi. Cardinals	4	8	0	.333	172	221
Washington	4	8	0	.333	240	287

NATIONAL CONFERENCE

Team	W	L	T	Pct.	PF	PA
Detroit	9	3	0	.750	344	192
Los Angeles	9	3	0	.750	349	234
San Francisco	7	5	0	.583	285	221
Green Bay	6	6	0	.500	295	312
Chicago Bears	5	7	0	.417	245	326
Dallas Texans	1	11	0	.083	182	427

PLAYOFFS
National Conference playoff
Detroit 31 vs. Los Angeles 21
NFL championship
Detroit 17 at Cleveland 7

1953

EASTERN CONFERENCE

Team	W	L	T	Pct.	PF	PA
Cleveland	11	1	0	.917	348	162
Philadelphia	7	4	1	.636	352	215
Washington	6	5	1	.545	208	215
Pittsburgh	6	6	0	.500	211	263
N.Y. Giants	3	9	0	.250	179	277
Chi. Cardinals	1	10	1	.091	190	337

WESTERN CONFERENCE

Team	W	L	T	Pct.	PF	PA
Detroit	10	2	0	.833	271	205
San Francisco	9	3	0	.750	372	237
Los Angeles	8	3	1	.727	366	236
Chicago Bears	3	8	1	.273	218	262
Baltimore	3	9	0	.250	182	350
Green Bay	2	9	1	.182	200	338

PLAYOFFS
NFL championship
Detroit 17 vs. Cleveland 16

1954

EASTERN CONFERENCE

Team	W	L	T	Pct.	PF	PA
Cleveland	9	3	0	.750	336	162
Philadelphia	7	4	1	.636	284	230
N.Y. Giants	7	5	0	.583	293	184
Pittsburgh	5	7	0	.417	219	263
Washington	3	9	0	.250	207	432
Chi. Cardinals	2	10	0	.167	183	347

WESTERN CONFERENCE

Team	W	L	T	Pct.	PF	PA
Detroit	9	2	1	.818	337	189
Chicago Bears	8	4	0	.667	301	279
San Francisco	7	4	1	.636	313	251
Los Angeles	6	5	1	.545	314	285
Green Bay	4	8	0	.333	234	251
Baltimore	3	9	0	.250	131	279

PLAYOFFS
NFL championship
Cleveland 56 vs. Detroit 10

1955

EASTERN CONFERENCE

Team	W	L	T	Pct.	PF	PA
Cleveland	9	2	1	.818	349	218
Washington	8	4	0	.667	246	222
N.Y. Giants	6	5	1	.545	267	223
Chi. Cardinals	4	7	1	.364	224	252
Philadelphia	4	7	1	.364	248	231
Pittsburgh	4	8	0	.333	195	285

WESTERN CONFERENCE

Team	W	L	T	Pct.	PF	PA
Los Angeles	8	3	1	.727	260	231
Chicago Bears	8	4	0	.667	294	251
Green Bay	6	6	0	.500	258	276
Baltimore	5	6	1	.455	214	239
San Francisco	4	8	0	.333	216	298
Detroit	3	9	0	.250	230	275

PLAYOFFS
NFL championship
Cleveland 38 at Los Angeles 14

1956

EASTERN CONFERENCE

Team	W	L	T	Pct.	PF	PA
N.Y. Giants	8	3	1	.727	264	197
Chi. Cardinals	7	5	0	.583	240	182
Washington	6	6	0	.500	183	225
Cleveland	5	7	0	.417	167	177
Pittsburgh	5	7	0	.417	217	250
Philadelphia	3	8	1	.273	143	215

WESTERN CONFERENCE

Team	W	L	T	Pct.	PF	PA
Chicago Bears	9	2	1	.818	363	246
Detroit	9	3	0	.750	300	188
San Francisco	5	6	1	.455	233	284
Baltimore	5	7	0	.417	270	322
Green Bay	4	8	0	.333	264	342
Los Angeles	4	8	0	.333	291	307

PLAYOFFS
NFL championship
N.Y. Giants 47 vs. Chicago Bears 7

HISTORY *Year-by-year standings*

– 308 –

1957

EASTERN CONFERENCE
Team	W	L	T	Pct.	PF	PA
Cleveland	9	2	1	.818	269	172
N.Y. Giants	7	5	0	.583	254	211
Pittsburgh	6	6	0	.500	161	178
Washington	5	6	1	.455	251	230
Philadelphia	4	8	0	.333	173	230
Chi. Cardinals	3	9	0	.250	200	299

WESTERN CONFERENCE
Team	W	L	T	Pct.	PF	PA
Detroit	8	4	0	.667	251	231
San Francisco	8	4	0	.667	260	264
Baltimore	7	5	0	.583	303	235
Los Angeles	6	6	0	.500	307	278
Chicago Bears	5	7	0	.417	203	211
Green Bay	3	9	0	.250	218	311

PLAYOFFS
Western Conference playoff
Detroit 31 at San Francisco 27
NFL championship
Detroit 59 vs. Cleveland 14

1958

EASTERN CONFERENCE
Team	W	L	T	Pct.	PF	PA
N.Y. Giants	9	3	0	.750	246	183
Cleveland	9	3	0	.750	302	217
Pittsburgh	7	4	1	.636	261	230
Washington	4	7	1	.364	214	268
Chi. Cardinals	2	9	1	.182	261	356
Philadelphia	2	9	1	.182	235	306

WESTERN CONFERENCE
Team	W	L	T	Pct.	PF	PA
Baltimore	9	3	0	.750	381	203
Chicago Bears	8	4	0	.667	298	230
Los Angeles	8	4	0	.667	344	278
San Francisco	6	6	0	.500	257	324
Detroit	4	7	1	.364	261	276
Green Bay	1	10	1	.091	193	382

PLAYOFFS
Eastern Conference playoff
N.Y. Giants 10 vs. Cleveland 0
NFL championship
Baltimore 23 at N.Y. Giants 17 (OT)

1959

EASTERN CONFERENCE
Team	W	L	T	Pct.	PF	PA
N.Y. Giants	10	2	0	.833	284	170
Cleveland	7	5	0	.583	270	214
Philadelphia	7	5	0	.583	268	278
Pittsburgh	6	5	1	.545	257	216
Washington	3	9	0	.250	185	350
Chi. Cardinals	2	10	0	.167	234	324

WESTERN CONFERENCE
Team	W	L	T	Pct.	PF	PA
Baltimore	9	3	0	.750	374	251
Chicago Bears	8	4	0	.667	252	196
Green Bay	7	5	0	.583	248	246
San Francisco	7	5	0	.583	255	237
Detroit	3	8	1	.273	203	275
Los Angeles	2	10	0	.167	242	315

PLAYOFFS
NFL championship
Baltimore 31 vs. N.Y. Giants 16

1960

AFL

EASTERN DIVISION
Team	W	L	T	Pct.	PF	PA
Houston	10	4	0	.714	379	285
N.Y. Titans	7	7	0	.500	382	399
Buffalo	5	8	1	.385	296	303
Boston Patriots	5	9	0	.357	286	349

WESTERN DIVISION
Team	W	L	T	Pct.	PF	PA
L.A. Chargers	10	4	0	.714	373	336
Dallas Texans	8	6	0	.571	362	253
Oakland	6	8	0	.429	319	388
Denver	4	9	1	.308	309	393

PLAYOFFS
AFL championship
Houston 24 vs. L.A. Chargers 16

NFL

EASTERN CONFERENCE
Team	W	L	T	Pct.	PF	PA
Philadelphia	10	2	0	.833	321	246
Cleveland	8	3	1	.727	362	217
N.Y. Giants	6	4	2	.600	271	261
St. Louis	6	5	1	.545	288	230
Pittsburgh	5	6	1	.455	240	275
Washington	1	9	2	.100	178	309

WESTERN CONFERENCE
Team	W	L	T	Pct.	PF	PA
Green Bay	8	4	0	.667	332	209
Detroit	7	5	0	.583	239	212
San Francisco	7	5	0	.583	208	205
Baltimore	6	6	0	.500	288	234
Chicago	5	6	1	.455	194	299
L.A. Rams	4	7	1	.364	265	297
Dallas Cowboys	0	11	1	.000	177	369

PLAYOFFS
NFL championship
Philadelphia 17 vs. Green Bay 13

1961

AFL

EASTERN DIVISION
Team	W	L	T	Pct.	PF	PA
Houston	10	3	1	.769	513	242
Boston Patriots	9	4	1	.692	413	313
N.Y. Titans	7	7	0	.500	301	390
Buffalo	6	8	0	.429	294	342

WESTERN DIVISION
Team	W	L	T	Pct.	PF	PA
San Diego	12	2	0	.857	396	219
Dallas Texans	6	8	0	.429	334	343
Denver	3	11	0	.214	251	432
Oakland	2	12	0	.143	237	458

PLAYOFFS
AFL championship
Houston 10 at San Diego 3

HISTORY Year-by-year standings

– 309 –

HISTORY — Year-by-year standings

NFL

EASTERN CONFERENCE

Team	W	L	T	Pct.	PF	PA
N.Y. Giants	10	3	1	.769	368	220
Philadelphia	10	4	0	.714	361	297
Cleveland	8	5	1	.615	319	270
St. Louis	7	7	0	.500	279	267
Pittsburgh	6	8	0	.429	295	287
Dallas Cowboys	4	9	1	.308	236	380
Washington	1	12	1	.077	174	392

WESTERN CONFERENCE

Team	W	L	T	Pct.	PF	PA
Green Bay	11	3	0	.786	391	223
Detroit	8	5	1	.615	270	258
Baltimore	8	6	0	.571	302	307
Chicago	8	6	0	.571	326	302
San Francisco	7	6	1	.538	346	272
Los Angeles	4	10	0	.286	263	333
Minnesota	3	11	0	.214	285	407

PLAYOFFS

NFL championship
Green Bay 37 vs. N.Y. Giants 0

1962
AFL

EASTERN DIVISION

Team	W	L	T	Pct.	PF	PA
Houston	11	3	0	.786	387	270
Boston Patriots	9	4	1	.692	346	295
Buffalo	7	6	1	.538	309	272
N.Y. Titans	5	9	0	.357	278	423

WESTERN DIVISION

Team	W	L	T	Pct.	PF	PA
Dallas Texans	11	3	0	.786	389	233
Denver	7	7	0	.500	353	334
San Diego	4	10	0	.286	314	392
Oakland	1	13	0	.071	213	370

PLAYOFFS

AFL championship
Dallas Texans 20 at Houston 17 (OT)

NFL

EASTERN CONFERENCE

Team	W	L	T	Pct.	PF	PA
N.Y. Giants	12	2	0	.857	398	283
Pittsburgh	9	5	0	.643	312	363
Cleveland	7	6	1	.538	291	257
Washington	5	7	2	.417	305	376
Dallas Cowboys	5	8	1	.385	398	402
St. Louis	4	9	1	.308	287	361
Philadelphia	3	10	1	.231	282	356

WESTERN CONFERENCE

Team	W	L	T	Pct.	PF	PA
Green Bay	13	1	0	.929	415	148
Detroit	11	3	0	.786	315	177
Chicago	9	5	0	.643	321	287
Baltimore	7	7	0	.500	293	288
San Francisco	6	8	0	.429	282	331
Minnesota	2	11	1	.154	254	410
Los Angeles	1	12	1	.077	220	334

PLAYOFFS

NFL championship
Green Bay 16 at N.Y. Giants 7

1963
AFL

EASTERN DIVISION

Team	W	L	T	Pct.	PF	PA
Boston Patriots	7	6	1	.538	327	257
Buffalo	7	6	1	.538	304	291
Houston	6	8	0	.429	302	372
N.Y. Jets	5	8	1	.385	249	399

WESTERN DIVISION

Team	W	L	T	Pct.	PF	PA
San Diego	11	3	0	.786	399	256
Oakland	10	4	0	.714	363	288
Kansas City	5	7	2	.417	347	263
Denver	2	11	1	.154	301	473

PLAYOFFS

Eastern Division playoff
Boston 26 at Buffalo 8
AFL championship
San Diego 51 vs. Boston 10

NFL

EASTERN CONFERENCE

Team	W	L	T	Pct.	PF	PA
N.Y. Giants	11	3	0	.786	448	280
Cleveland	10	4	0	.714	343	262
St. Louis	9	5	0	.643	341	283
Pittsburgh	7	4	3	.636	321	295
Dallas	4	10	0	.286	305	378
Washington	3	11	0	.214	279	398
Philadelphia	2	10	2	.167	242	381

WESTERN CONFERENCE

Team	W	L	T	Pct.	PF	PA
Chicago	11	1	2	.917	301	144
Green Bay	11	2	1	.846	369	206
Baltimore	8	6	0	.571	316	285
Detroit	5	8	1	.385	326	265
Minnesota	5	8	1	.385	309	390
Los Angeles	5	9	0	.357	210	350
San Francisco	2	12	0	.143	198	391

PLAYOFFS

NFL championship
Chicago 14 vs. N.Y. Giants 10

1964
AFL

EASTERN DIVISION

Team	W	L	T	Pct.	PF	PA
Buffalo	12	2	0	.857	400	242
Boston Patriots	10	3	1	.769	365	297
N.Y. Jets	5	8	1	.385	278	315
Houston	4	10	0	.286	310	355

WESTERN DIVISION

Team	W	L	T	Pct.	PF	PA
San Diego	8	5	1	.615	341	300
Kansas City	7	7	0	.500	366	306
Oakland	5	7	2	.417	303	350
Denver	2	11	1	.154	240	438

PLAYOFFS

AFL championship
Buffalo 20 vs. San Diego 7

– 310 –

NFL

EASTERN CONFERENCE
Team	W	L	T	Pct.	PF	PA
Cleveland	10	3	1	.769	415	293
St. Louis	9	3	2	.750	357	331
Philadelphia	6	8	0	.429	312	313
Washington	6	8	0	.429	307	305
Dallas	5	8	1	.385	250	289
Pittsburgh	5	9	0	.357	253	315
N.Y. Giants	2	10	2	.167	241	399

WESTERN CONFERENCE
Team	W	L	T	Pct.	PF	PA
Baltimore	12	2	0	.857	428	225
Green Bay	8	5	1	.615	342	245
Minnesota	8	5	1	.615	355	296
Detroit	7	5	2	.583	280	260
Los Angeles	5	7	2	.417	283	339
Chicago	5	9	0	.357	260	379
San Francisco	4	10	0	.286	236	330

PLAYOFFS
NFL championship
Cleveland 27 vs. Baltimore 0

1965

AFL

EASTERN DIVISION
Team	W	L	T	Pct.	PF	PA
Buffalo	10	3	1	.769	313	226
N.Y. Jets	5	8	1	.385	285	303
Boston Patriots	4	8	2	.333	244	302
Houston	4	10	0	.286	298	429

WESTERN DIVISION
Team	W	L	T	Pct.	PF	PA
San Diego	9	2	3	.818	340	227
Oakland	8	5	1	.615	298	239
Kansas City	7	5	2	.583	322	285
Denver	4	10	0	.286	303	392

PLAYOFFS
AFL championship
Buffalo 23 at San Diego 0

NFL

EASTERN CONFERENCE
Team	W	L	T	Pct.	PF	PA
Cleveland	11	3	0	.786	363	325
Dallas	7	7	0	.500	325	280
N.Y. Giants	7	7	0	.500	270	338
Washington	6	8	0	.429	257	301
Philadelphia	5	9	0	.357	363	359
St. Louis	5	9	0	.357	296	309
Pittsburgh	2	12	0	.143	202	397

WESTERN CONFERENCE
Team	W	L	T	Pct.	PF	PA
Green Bay	10	3	1	.769	316	224
Baltimore	10	3	1	.769	389	284
Chicago	9	5	0	.643	409	275
San Francisco	7	6	1	.538	421	402
Minnesota	7	7	0	.500	383	403
Detroit	6	7	1	.462	257	295
Los Angeles	4	10	0	.286	269	328

PLAYOFFS
Western Conference playoff
Green Bay 13 vs. Baltimore 10 (OT)
NFL championship
Green Bay 23 vs. Cleveland 12

1966

AFL

EASTERN DIVISION
Team	W	L	T	Pct.	PF	PA
Buffalo	9	4	1	.692	358	255
Boston Patriots	8	4	2	.667	315	283
N.Y. Jets	6	6	2	.500	322	312
Houston	3	11	0	.214	335	396
Miami	3	11	0	.214	213	362

WESTERN DIVISION
Team	W	L	T	Pct.	PF	PA
Kansas City	11	2	1	.846	448	276
Oakland	8	5	1	.615	315	288
San Diego	7	6	1	.538	335	284
Denver	4	10	0	.286	196	381

PLAYOFFS
AFL championship
Kansas City 31 at Buffalo 7

NFL

EASTERN CONFERENCE
Team	W	L	T	Pct.	PF	PA
Dallas	10	3	1	.769	445	239
Cleveland	9	5	0	.643	403	259
Philadelphia	9	5	0	.643	326	340
St. Louis	8	5	1	.615	264	265
Washington	7	7	0	.500	351	355
Pittsburgh	5	8	1	.385	316	347
Atlanta	3	11	0	.214	204	437
N.Y. Giants	1	12	1	.077	263	501

WESTERN CONFERENCE
Team	W	L	T	Pct.	PF	PA
Green Bay	12	2	0	.857	335	163
Baltimore	9	5	0	.643	314	226
Los Angeles	8	6	0	.571	289	212
San Francisco	6	6	2	.500	320	325
Chicago	5	7	2	.417	234	272
Detroit	4	9	1	.308	206	317
Minnesota	4	9	1	.308	292	304

PLAYOFFS
NFL championship
Green Bay 34 at Dallas 27
Super Bowl 1
Green Bay 35, Kansas City 10, at Los Angeles.

1967

AFL

EASTERN DIVISION
Team	W	L	T	Pct.	PF	PA
Houston	9	4	1	.692	258	199
N.Y. Jets	8	5	1	.615	371	329
Buffalo	4	10	0	.286	237	285
Miami	4	10	0	.286	219	407
Boston Patriots	3	10	1	.231	280	389

WESTERN DIVISION
Team	W	L	T	Pct.	PF	PA
Oakland	13	1	0	.929	468	233
Kansas City	9	5	0	.643	408	254
San Diego	8	5	1	.615	360	352
Denver	3	11	0	.214	256	409

PLAYOFFS
AFL championship
Oakland 40 vs. Houston 7

HISTORY *Year-by-year standings*

NFL

EASTERN CONFERENCE

CAPITOL DIVISION

Team	W	L	T	Pct.	PF	PA
Dallas	9	5	0	.643	342	268
Philadelphia	6	7	1	.462	351	409
Washington	5	6	3	.455	347	353
New Orleans	3	11	0	.214	233	379

CENTURY DIVISION

Team	W	L	T	Pct.	PF	PA
Cleveland	9	5	0	.643	334	297
N.Y. Giants	7	7	0	.500	369	379
St. Louis	6	7	1	.462	333	356
Pittsburgh	4	9	1	.308	281	320

WESTERN CONFERENCE

COASTAL DIVISION

Team	W	L	T	Pct.	PF	PA
Los Angeles	11	1	2	.917	398	196
Baltimore	11	1	2	.917	394	198
San Francisco	7	7	0	.500	273	337
Atlanta	1	12	1	.077	175	422

CENTRAL DIVISION

Team	W	L	T	Pct.	PF	PA
Green Bay	9	4	1	.692	332	209
Chicago	7	6	1	.538	239	218
Detroit	5	7	2	.417	260	259
Minnesota	3	8	3	.273	233	294

PLAYOFFS

Conference championships
Dallas 52 vs. Cleveland 14
Green Bay 28 vs. Los Angeles 7

NFL championship
Green Bay 21 vs. Dallas 17

Super Bowl 2
Green Bay 33, Oakland 14, at Miami.

1968

AFL

EASTERN DIVISION

Team	W	L	T	Pct.	PF	PA
N.Y. Jets	11	3	0	.786	419	280
Houston	7	7	0	.500	303	248
Miami	5	8	1	.385	276	355
Boston Patriots	4	10	0	.286	229	406
Buffalo	1	12	1	.077	199	367

WESTERN DIVISION

Team	W	L	T	Pct.	PF	PA
Oakland	12	2	0	.857	453	233
Kansas City	12	2	0	.857	371	170
San Diego	9	5	0	.643	382	310
Denver	5	9	0	.357	255	404
Cincinnati	3	11	0	.214	215	329

PLAYOFFS

Western Division playoff
Oakland 41 vs. Kansas City 6

AFL championship
N.Y. Jets 27 vs. Oakland 23

NFL

EASTERN CONFERENCE

CAPITOL DIVISION

Team	W	L	T	Pct.	PF	PA
Dallas	12	2	0	.857	431	186
N.Y. Giants	7	7	0	.500	294	325
Washington	5	9	0	.357	249	358
Philadelphia	2	12	0	.143	202	351

CENTURY DIVISION

Team	W	L	T	Pct.	PF	PA
Cleveland	10	4	0	.714	394	273
St. Louis	9	4	1	.692	325	289
New Orleans	4	9	1	.308	246	327
Pittsburgh	2	11	1	.154	244	397

WESTERN CONFERENCE

COASTAL DIVISION

Team	W	L	T	Pct.	PF	PA
Baltimore	13	1	0	.929	402	144
Los Angeles	10	3	1	.769	312	200
San Francisco	7	6	1	.538	303	310
Atlanta	2	12	0	.143	170	389

CENTRAL DIVISION

Team	W	L	T	Pct.	PF	PA
Minnesota	8	6	0	.571	282	242
Chicago	7	7	0	.500	250	333
Green Bay	6	7	1	.462	281	227
Detroit	4	8	2	.333	207	241

PLAYOFFS

Conference championships
Cleveland 31 vs. Dallas 20
Baltimore 24 vs. Minnesota 14

NFL championship
Baltimore 34 at Cleveland 0

Super Bowl 3
N.Y. Jets 16, Baltimore 7, at Miami.

1969

AFL

EASTERN DIVISION

Team	W	L	T	Pct.	PF	PA
N.Y. Jets	10	4	0	.714	353	269
Houston	6	6	2	.500	278	279
Boston Patriots	4	10	0	.286	266	316
Buffalo	4	10	0	.286	230	359
Miami	3	10	1	.231	233	332

WESTERN DIVISION

Team	W	L	T	Pct.	PF	PA
Oakland	12	1	1	.923	377	242
Kansas City	11	3	0	.786	359	177
San Diego	8	6	0	.571	288	276
Denver	5	8	1	.385	297	344
Cincinnati	4	9	1	.308	280	367

PLAYOFFS

Divisional games
Kansas City 13 at N.Y. Jets 6
Oakland 56 vs. Houston 7

AFL championship
Kansas City 17 at Oakland 7

NFL

EASTERN CONFERENCE

CAPITOL DIVISION

Team	W	L	T	Pct.	PF	PA
Dallas	11	2	1	.846	369	223
Washington	7	5	2	.583	307	319
New Orleans	5	9	0	.357	311	393
Philadelphia	4	9	1	.308	279	377

CENTURY DIVISION

Team	W	L	T	Pct.	PF	PA
Cleveland	10	3	1	.769	351	300
N.Y. Giants	6	8	0	.429	264	298
St. Louis	4	9	1	.308	314	389
Pittsburgh	1	13	0	.071	218	404

WESTERN CONFERENCE

COASTAL DIVISION

Team	W	L	T	Pct.	PF	PA
Los Angeles	11	3	0	.786	320	243
Baltimore	8	5	1	.615	279	268
Atlanta	6	8	0	.429	276	268
San Francisco	4	8	2	.333	277	319

CENTRAL DIVISION

Team	W	L	T	Pct.	PF	PA
Minnesota	12	2	0	.857	379	133
Detroit	9	4	1	.692	259	188
Green Bay	8	6	0	.571	269	221
Chicago	1	13	0	.071	210	339

PLAYOFFS

Conference championships
Cleveland 38 at Dallas 14
Minnesota 23 vs. Los Angeles 20

NFL championship
Minnesota 27 vs. Cleveland 7

Super Bowl 4
Kansas City 23, Minnesota 7, at New Orleans.

1970

AMERICAN CONFERENCE

EASTERN DIVISION

Team	W	L	T	Pct.	PF	PA
Baltimore*	11	2	1	.846	321	234
Miami†	10	4	0	.714	297	228
N.Y. Jets	4	10	0	.286	255	286
Buffalo	3	10	1	.231	204	337
Boston Patriots	2	12	0	.143	149	361

CENTRAL DIVISION

Team	W	L	T	Pct.	PF	PA
Cincinnati*	8	6	0	.571	312	255
Cleveland	7	7	0	.500	286	265
Pittsburgh	5	9	0	.357	210	272
Houston	3	10	1	.231	217	352

WESTERN DIVISION

Team	W	L	T	Pct.	PF	PA
Oakland*	8	4	2	.667	300	293
Kansas City	7	5	2	.583	272	244
San Diego	5	6	3	.455	282	278
Denver	5	8	1	.385	253	264

*Division champion.
†Wild-card team.

NATIONAL CONFERENCE

EASTERN DIVISION

Team	W	L	T	Pct.	PF	PA
Dallas*	10	4	0	.714	299	221
N.Y. Giants	9	5	0	.643	301	270
St. Louis	8	5	1	.615	325	228
Washington	6	8	0	.429	297	314
Philadelphia	3	10	1	.231	241	332

CENTRAL DIVISION

Team	W	L	T	Pct.	PF	PA
Minnesota*	12	2	0	.857	335	143
Detroit†	10	4	0	.714	347	202
Chicago	6	8	0	.429	256	261
Green Bay	6	8	0	.429	196	293

WESTERN DIVISION

Team	W	L	T	Pct.	PF	PA
San Francisco*	10	3	1	.769	352	267
Los Angeles	9	4	1	.692	325	202
Atlanta	4	8	2	.333	206	261
New Orleans	2	11	1	.154	172	347

PLAYOFFS

AFC divisional games
Baltimore 17 vs. Cincinnati 0
Oakland 21 vs. Miami 14

AFC championship
Baltimore 27 vs. Oakland 17

NFC divisional games
Dallas 5 vs. Detroit 0
San Francisco 17 at Minnesota 14

NFC championship
Dallas 17 at San Francisco 10

Super Bowl 5
Baltimore 16, Dallas 13, at Miami.

1971

AMERICAN CONFERENCE

EASTERN DIVISION

Team	W	L	T	Pct.	PF	PA
Miami*	10	3	1	.769	315	174
Baltimore†	10	4	0	.714	313	140
New England	6	8	0	.429	238	325
N.Y. Jets	6	8	0	.429	212	299
Buffalo	1	13	0	.071	184	394

CENTRAL DIVISION

Team	W	L	T	Pct.	PF	PA
Cleveland*	9	5	0	.643	285	273
Pittsburgh	6	8	0	.429	246	292
Houston	4	9	1	.308	251	330
Cincinnati	4	10	0	.286	284	265

WESTERN DIVISION

Team	W	L	T	Pct.	PF	PA
Kansas City*	10	3	1	.769	302	208
Oakland	8	4	2	.667	344	278
San Diego	6	8	0	.429	311	341
Denver	4	9	1	.308	203	275

*Division champion.
†Wild-card team.

NATIONAL CONFERENCE

EASTERN DIVISION

Team	W	L	T	Pct.	PF	PA
Dallas*	11	3	0	.786	406	222
Washington†	9	4	1	.692	276	190
Philadelphia	6	7	1	.462	221	302
St. Louis	4	9	1	.308	231	279
N.Y. Giants	4	10	0	.286	228	362

CENTRAL DIVISION

Team	W	L	T	Pct.	PF	PA
Minnesota*	11	3	0	.786	245	139
Detroit	7	6	1	.538	341	286
Chicago	6	8	0	.429	185	276
Green Bay	4	8	2	.333	274	298

WESTERN DIVISION

Team	W	L	T	Pct.	PF	PA
San Francisco*	9	5	0	.643	300	216
Los Angeles	8	5	1	.615	313	260
Atlanta	7	6	1	.538	274	277
New Orleans	4	8	2	.333	266	347

PLAYOFFS

AFC divisional games
Miami 27 at Kansas City 24 (OT)
Baltimore 20 at Cleveland 3

AFC championship
Miami 21 vs. Baltimore 0

NFC divisional games
Dallas 20 at Minnesota 12
San Francisco 24 vs. Washington 20

NFC championship
Dallas 14 vs. San Francisco 3

Super Bowl 6
Dallas 24, Miami 3, at New Orleans.

FOOTBALL COMES TO MONDAY NIGHT

Although few people at the time could have guessed at the kind of popularity the show would come to enjoy, ABC's Monday Night Football debuted on September 21, 1970 with the telecast of a Jets-Browns game from Cleveland Stadium. With 85,703 fans looking on, coach Blanton Collier's Browns beat Weeb Ewbank's Jets, 31-21. Though the game had little of the excitement of future Monday night encounters, it did have a few noteworthy accomplishments. Jets quarterback Joe Namath completed 19 of 32 passes for 299 yards and one touchdown, but he also was intercepted three times, turnovers that proved crucial to the Browns' victory. Homer Jones returned a kickoff 94 yards for a Cleveland touchdown.

1972

AMERICAN CONFERENCE

EASTERN DIVISION

Team	W	L	T	Pct.	PF	PA
Miami*	14	0	0	1.000	385	171
N.Y. Jets	7	7	0	.500	367	324
Baltimore	5	9	0	.357	235	252
Buffalo	4	9	1	.321	257	377
New England	3	11	0	.214	192	446

CENTRAL DIVISION

Team	W	L	T	Pct.	PF	PA
Pittsburgh*	11	3	0	.786	343	175
Cleveland†	10	4	0	.714	268	249
Cincinnati	8	6	0	.571	299	229
Houston	1	13	0	.071	164	380

WESTERN DIVISION

Team	W	L	T	Pct.	PF	PA
Oakland*	10	3	1	.750	365	248
Kansas City	8	6	0	.571	287	254
Denver	5	9	0	.357	325	350
San Diego	4	9	1	.321	264	344

NATIONAL CONFERENCE

EASTERN DIVISION

Team	W	L	T	Pct.	PF	PA
Washington*	11	3	0	.786	336	218
Dallas†	10	4	0	.714	319	240
N.Y. Giants	8	6	0	.571	331	247
St. Louis	4	9	1	.321	193	303
Philadelphia	2	11	1	.179	145	352

CENTRAL DIVISION

Team	W	L	T	Pct.	PF	PA
Green Bay*	10	4	0	.714	304	226
Detroit	8	5	1	.607	339	290
Minnesota	7	7	0	.500	301	252
Chicago	4	9	1	.321	225	275

WESTERN DIVISION

Team	W	L	T	Pct.	PF	PA
San Francisco*	8	5	1	.607	353	249
Atlanta	7	7	0	.500	269	274
Los Angeles	6	7	1	.464	291	286
New Orleans	2	11	1	.179	215	361

PLAYOFFS

AFC divisional games
Pittsburgh 13 vs. Oakland 7
Miami 20 vs. Cleveland 14

AFC championship
Miami 21 at Pittsburgh 17

NFC divisional games
Dallas 30 at San Francisco 28
Washington 16 vs. Green Bay 3

NFC championship
Washington 26 vs. Dallas 3

Super Bowl 7
Miami 14, Washington 7, at Los Angeles.

*Division champion.
†Wild-card team.

1973

AMERICAN CONFERENCE

EASTERN DIVISION

Team	W	L	T	Pct.	PF	PA
Miami*	12	2	0	.857	343	150
Buffalo	9	5	0	.643	259	230
New England	5	9	0	.357	258	300
Baltimore	4	10	0	.286	226	341
N.Y. Jets	4	10	0	.286	240	306

CENTRAL DIVISION

Team	W	L	T	Pct.	PF	PA
Cincinnati*	10	4	0	.714	286	231
Pittsburgh†	10	4	0	.714	347	210
Cleveland	7	5	2	.571	234	255
Houston	1	13	0	.071	199	447

WESTERN DIVISION

Team	W	L	T	Pct.	PF	PA
Oakland*	9	4	1	.679	292	175
Denver	7	5	2	.571	354	296
Kansas City	7	5	2	.571	231	192
San Diego	2	11	1	.179	188	386

NATIONAL CONFERENCE

EASTERN DIVISION

Team	W	L	T	Pct.	PF	PA
Dallas*	10	4	0	.714	382	203
Washington†	10	4	0	.714	325	198
Philadelphia	5	8	1	.393	310	393
St. Louis	4	9	1	.321	286	365
N.Y. Giants	2	11	1	.179	226	362

CENTRAL DIVISION

Team	W	L	T	Pct.	PF	PA
Minnesota*	12	2	0	.857	296	168
Detroit	6	7	1	.464	271	247
Green Bay	5	7	2	.429	202	259
Chicago	3	11	0	.214	195	334

WESTERN DIVISION

Team	W	L	T	Pct.	PF	PA
Los Angeles*	12	2	0	.857	388	178
Atlanta	9	5	0	.643	318	224
New Orleans	5	9	0	.357	163	312
San Francisco	5	9	0	.357	262	319

PLAYOFFS

AFC divisional games
Oakland 33 vs. Pittsburgh 14
Miami 34 vs. Cincinnati 16

AFC championship
Miami 27 vs. Oakland 10

NFC divisional games
Minnesota 27 vs. Washington 20
Dallas 27 vs. Los Angeles 16

NFC championship
Minnesota 27 at Dallas 10

Super Bowl 8
Miami 24, Minnesota 7, at Houston.

*Division champion.
†Wild-card team.

1974

AMERICAN CONFERENCE

EASTERN DIVISION

Team	W	L	T	Pct.	PF	PA
Miami*	11	3	0	.786	327	216
Buffalo†	9	5	0	.643	264	244
New England	7	7	0	.500	348	289
N.Y. Jets	7	7	0	.500	279	300
Baltimore	2	12	0	.143	190	329

CENTRAL DIVISION

Team	W	L	T	Pct.	PF	PA
Pittsburgh*	10	3	1	.750	305	189
Cincinnati	7	7	0	.500	283	259
Houston	7	7	0	.500	236	282
Cleveland	4	10	0	.286	251	344

WESTERN DIVISION

Team	W	L	T	Pct.	PF	PA
Oakland*	12	2	0	.857	355	228
Denver	7	6	1	.536	302	294
Kansas City	5	9	0	.357	233	293
San Diego	5	9	0	.357	212	285

NATIONAL CONFERENCE

EASTERN DIVISION

Team	W	L	T	Pct.	PF	PA
St. Louis*	10	4	0	.714	285	218
Washington†	10	4	0	.714	320	196
Dallas	8	6	0	.571	297	235
Philadelphia	7	7	0	.500	242	217
N.Y. Giants	2	12	0	.143	195	299

CENTRAL DIVISION

Team	W	L	T	Pct.	PF	PA
Minnesota*	10	4	0	.714	310	195
Detroit	7	7	0	.500	256	270
Green Bay	6	8	0	.429	210	206
Chicago	4	10	0	.286	152	279

WESTERN DIVISION

Team	W	L	T	Pct.	PF	PA
Los Angeles*	10	4	0	.714	263	181
San Francisco	6	8	0	.429	226	236
New Orleans	5	9	0	.357	166	263
Atlanta	3	11	0	.214	111	271

PLAYOFFS

AFC divisional games
Oakland 28 vs. Miami 26
Pittsburgh 32 vs. Buffalo 14

AFC championship
Pittsburgh 24 at Oakland 13

NFC divisional games
Minnesota 30 vs. St. Louis 14
Los Angeles 19 vs. Washington 10

NFC championship
Minnesota 14 vs. Los Angeles 10

Super Bowl 9
Pittsburgh 16, Minnesota 6, at New Orleans.

*Division champion.
†Wild-card team.

1975

AMERICAN CONFERENCE

EASTERN DIVISION

Team	W	L	T	Pct.	PF	PA
Baltimore*	10	4	0	.714	395	269
Miami	10	4	0	.714	357	222
Buffalo	8	6	0	.571	420	355
New England	3	11	0	.214	258	358
N.Y. Jets	3	11	0	.214	258	433

CENTRAL DIVISION

Team	W	L	T	Pct.	PF	PA
Pittsburgh*	12	2	0	.857	373	162
Cincinnati†	11	3	0	.786	340	246
Houston	10	4	0	.714	293	226
Cleveland	3	11	0	.214	218	372

WESTERN DIVISION

Team	W	L	T	Pct.	PF	PA
Oakland*	11	3	0	.786	375	255
Denver	6	8	0	.429	254	307
Kansas City	5	9	0	.357	282	341
San Diego	2	12	0	.143	189	345

*Division champion.
†Wild-card team.

NATIONAL CONFERENCE

EASTERN DIVISION

Team	W	L	T	Pct.	PF	PA
St. Louis*	11	3	0	.786	356	276
Dallas†	10	4	0	.714	350	268
Washington	8	6	0	.571	325	276
N.Y. Giants	5	9	0	.357	216	306
Philadelphia	4	10	0	.286	225	302

CENTRAL DIVISION

Team	W	L	T	Pct.	PF	PA
Minnesota*	12	2	0	.857	377	180
Detroit	7	7	0	.500	245	262
Chicago	4	10	0	.286	191	379
Green Bay	4	10	0	.286	226	285

WESTERN DIVISION

Team	W	L	T	Pct.	PF	PA
Los Angeles*	12	2	0	.857	312	135
San Francisco	5	9	0	.357	255	286
Atlanta	4	10	0	.286	240	289
New Orleans	2	12	0	.143	165	360

PLAYOFFS

AFC divisional games
Pittsburgh 28 vs. Baltimore 10
Oakland 31 vs. Cincinnati 28
AFC championship
Pittsburgh 16 vs. Oakland 10
NFC divisional games
Los Angeles 35 vs. St. Louis 23
Dallas 17 at Minnesota 14
NFC championship
Dallas 37 at Los Angeles 7
Super Bowl 10
Pittsburgh 21, Dallas 17, at Miami.

1976

AMERICAN CONFERENCE

EASTERN DIVISION

Team	W	L	T	Pct.	PF	PA
Baltimore*	11	3	0	.786	417	246
New England†	11	3	0	.786	376	236
Miami	6	8	0	.429	263	264
N.Y. Jets	3	11	0	.214	169	383
Buffalo	2	12	0	.143	245	363

CENTRAL DIVISION

Team	W	L	T	Pct.	PF	PA
Pittsburgh*	10	4	0	.714	342	138
Cincinnati	10	4	0	.714	335	210
Cleveland	9	5	0	.643	267	287
Houston	5	9	0	.357	222	273

WESTERN DIVISION

Team	W	L	T	Pct.	PF	PA
Oakland*	13	1	0	.929	350	237
Denver	9	5	0	.643	315	206
San Diego	6	8	0	.429	248	285
Kansas City	5	9	0	.357	290	376
Tampa Bay	0	14	0	.000	125	412

*Division champion.
†Wild-card team.

NATIONAL CONFERENCE

EASTERN DIVISION

Team	W	L	T	Pct.	PF	PA
Dallas*	11	3	0	.786	296	194
Washington†	10	4	0	.714	291	217
St. Louis	10	4	0	.714	309	267
Philadelphia	4	10	0	.286	165	286
N.Y. Giants	3	11	0	.214	170	250

CENTRAL DIVISION

Team	W	L	T	Pct.	PF	PA
Minnesota*	11	2	1	.821	305	176
Chicago	7	7	0	.500	253	216
Detroit	6	8	0	.429	262	220
Green Bay	5	9	0	.357	218	299

WESTERN DIVISION

Team	W	L	T	Pct.	PF	PA
Los Angeles*	10	3	1	.750	351	190
San Francisco	8	6	0	.571	270	190
Atlanta	4	10	0	.286	172	312
New Orleans	4	10	0	.286	253	346
Seattle	2	12	0	.143	229	429

PLAYOFFS

AFC divisional games
Oakland 24 vs. New England 21
Pittsburgh 40 at Baltimore 14
AFC championship
Oakland 24 vs. Pittsburgh 7
NFC divisional games
Minnesota 35 vs. Washington 20
Los Angeles 14 at Dallas 12
NFC championship
Minnesota 24 vs. Los Angeles 13
Super Bowl 11
Oakland 32, Minnesota 14, at Pasadena, Calif.

HISTORY Year-by-year standings

THE '76 BUCS: THE WRONG KIND OF FAME

Four seasons after the Miami Dolphins went through an entire season without losing a game, another Florida team also made NFL history, but not the kind it would have preferred. In their inaugural season the Tampa Bay Buccaneers failed to win a game, going 0-16 as a member of the AFC's Western Division. Coach John McKay's Bucs scored a league-low 125 points and allowed 412, a total surpassed only by the league's other 1976 expansion team, the Seattle Seahawks. Tampa Bay failed to score more than 20 points in any game and did not come within three points of winning a game. One of those three-point defeats came in Week 6, when the Seahawks beat the Bucs, 13-10, a victory preserved when veteran linebacker Mike Curtis blocked a 35-yard field goal attempt by Bucs kicker Dave Green with 42 seconds left.

1977

AMERICAN CONFERENCE

EASTERN DIVISION

Team	W	L	T	Pct.	PF	PA
Baltimore*	10	4	0	.714	295	221
Miami	10	4	0	.714	313	197
New England	9	5	0	.643	278	217
N.Y. Jets	3	11	0	.214	191	300
Buffalo	3	11	0	.214	160	313

CENTRAL DIVISION

Team	W	L	T	Pct.	PF	PA
Pittsburgh*	9	5	0	.643	283	243
Houston	8	6	0	.571	299	230
Cincinnati	8	6	0	.571	238	235
Cleveland	6	8	0	.429	269	267

WESTERN DIVISION

Team	W	L	T	Pct.	PF	PA
Denver*	12	2	0	.857	274	148
Oakland†	11	3	0	.786	351	230
San Diego	7	7	0	.500	222	205
Seattle	5	9	0	.357	282	373
Kansas City	2	12	0	.143	225	349

*Division champion.
†Wild-card team.

NATIONAL CONFERENCE

EASTERN DIVISION

Team	W	L	T	Pct.	PF	PA
Dallas*	12	2	0	.857	345	212
Washington	9	5	0	.643	196	189
St. Louis	7	7	0	.500	272	287
Philadelphia	5	9	0	.357	220	207
N.Y. Giants	5	9	0	.357	181	265

CENTRAL DIVISION

Team	W	L	T	Pct.	PF	PA
Minnesota*	9	5	0	.643	231	227
Chicago†	9	5	0	.643	255	253
Detroit	6	8	0	.429	183	252
Green Bay	4	10	0	.286	134	219
Tampa Bay	2	12	0	.143	103	223

WESTERN DIVISION

Team	W	L	T	Pct.	PF	PA
Los Angeles*	10	4	0	.714	302	146
Atlanta	7	7	0	.500	179	129
San Francisco	5	9	0	.357	220	260
New Orleans	3	11	0	.214	232	336

PLAYOFFS

AFC divisional games
Denver 34 vs. Pittsburgh 21
Oakland 37 at Baltimore 31 (OT)

AFC championship
Denver 20 vs. Oakland 17

NFC divisional games
Dallas 37 vs. Chicago 7
Minnesota 14 at Los Angeles 7

NFC championship
Dallas 23 vs. Minnesota 6

Super Bowl 12
Dallas 27, Denver 10, at New Orleans.

1978

AMERICAN CONFERENCE

EASTERN DIVISION

Team	W	L	T	Pct.	PF	PA
New England*	11	5	0	.688	358	286
Miami†	11	5	0	.688	372	254
N.Y. Jets	8	8	0	.500	359	364
Buffalo	5	11	0	.313	302	354
Baltimore	5	11	0	.313	239	421

CENTRAL DIVISION

Team	W	L	T	Pct.	PF	PA
Pittsburgh*	14	2	0	.875	356	195
Houston†	10	6	0	.625	283	298
Cleveland	8	8	0	.500	334	356
Cincinnati	4	12	0	.250	252	284

WESTERN DIVISION

Team	W	L	T	Pct.	PF	PA
Denver*	10	6	0	.625	282	198
Oakland	9	7	0	.563	311	283
Seattle	9	7	0	.563	345	358
San Diego	9	7	0	.563	355	309
Kansas City	4	12	0	.250	243	327

*Division champion.
†Wild-card team.

NATIONAL CONFERENCE

EASTERN DIVISION

Team	W	L	T	Pct.	PF	PA
Dallas*	12	4	0	.750	384	208
Philadelphia†	9	7	0	.563	270	250
Washington	8	8	0	.500	273	283
St. Louis	6	10	0	.375	248	296
N.Y. Giants	6	10	0	.375	264	298

CENTRAL DIVISION

Team	W	L	T	Pct.	PF	PA
Minnesota*	8	7	1	.531	294	306
Green Bay	8	7	1	.531	249	269
Detroit	7	9	0	.438	290	300
Chicago	7	9	0	.438	253	274
Tampa Bay	5	11	0	.313	241	259

WESTERN DIVISION

Team	W	L	T	Pct.	PF	PA
Los Angeles*	12	4	0	.750	316	245
Atlanta†	9	7	0	.563	240	290
New Orleans	7	9	0	.438	281	298
San Francisco	2	14	0	.125	219	350

PLAYOFFS

AFC wild-card game
Houston 17 at Miami 9

AFC divisional games
Houston 31 at New England 14
Pittsburgh 33 vs. Denver 10

AFC championship
Pittsburgh 34 vs. Houston 5

NFC wild-card game
Atlanta 14 vs. Philadelphia 13

NFC divisional games
Dallas 27 vs. Atlanta 20
Los Angeles 34 vs. Minnesota 10

NFC championship
Dallas 28 at Los Angeles 0

Super Bowl 13
Pittsburgh 35, Dallas 31, at Miami.

SMASHING DEBUT FOR BIG EARL

Houston running back Earl Campbell, winner of the Heisman Trophy at Texas the year before and the league's top draft pick, gave NFL fans a preview of things to come by rushing for a league-high 1,450 yards and scoring 13 touchdowns in one of the most electrifying rookie seasons in NFL history. Campbell dethroned defending league rushing champ Walter Payton by 55 yards despite carrying the ball 31 fewer times. More important, he took a team that had not been to the playoffs in eight years to the AFC championship game. Campbell's best game of 1978 came under the brightest of lights: a 199-yard, four-touchdown performance in a 35-30 victory over Miami on Monday, November 20. He capped his big evening by scoring the Oilers' final touchdown on an 81-yard run in the fourth quarter.

1979

AMERICAN CONFERENCE

EASTERN DIVISION

Team	W	L	T	Pct.	PF	PA
Miami*	10	6	0	.625	341	257
New England	9	7	0	.563	411	326
N.Y. Jets	8	8	0	.500	337	383
Buffalo	7	9	0	.438	268	279
Baltimore	5	11	0	.313	271	351

CENTRAL DIVISION

Team	W	L	T	Pct.	PF	PA
Pittsburgh*	12	4	0	.750	416	262
Houston†	11	5	0	.688	362	331
Cleveland	9	7	0	.563	359	352
Cincinnati	4	12	0	.250	337	421

WESTERN DIVISION

Team	W	L	T	Pct.	PF	PA
San Diego*	12	4	0	.750	411	246
Denver†	10	6	0	.625	289	262
Seattle	9	7	0	.563	378	372
Oakland	9	7	0	.563	365	337
Kansas City	7	9	0	.438	238	262

*Division champion.
†Wild-card team.

NATIONAL CONFERENCE

EASTERN DIVISION

Team	W	L	T	Pct.	PF	PA
Dallas*	11	5	0	.688	371	313
Philadelphia†	11	5	0	.688	339	282
Washington	10	6	0	.625	348	295
N.Y. Giants	6	10	0	.375	237	323
St. Louis	5	11	0	.313	307	358

CENTRAL DIVISION

Team	W	L	T	Pct.	PF	PA
Tampa Bay*	10	6	0	.625	273	237
Chicago†	10	6	0	.625	306	249
Minnesota	7	9	0	.438	259	337
Green Bay	5	11	0	.313	246	316
Detroit	2	14	0	.125	219	365

WESTERN DIVISION

Team	W	L	T	Pct.	PF	PA
Los Angeles*	9	7	0	.563	323	309
New Orleans	8	8	0	.500	370	360
Atlanta	6	10	0	.375	300	388
San Francisco	2	14	0	.125	308	416

PLAYOFFS

AFC wild-card game
Houston 13 vs. Denver 7
AFC divisional games
Houston 17 at San Diego 14
Pittsburgh 34 vs. Miami 14
AFC championship
Pittsburgh 27 vs. Houston 13
NFC wild-card game
Philadelphia 27 vs. Chicago 17
NFC divisional games
Tampa Bay 24 vs. Philadelphia 17
Los Angeles 21 at Dallas 19
NFC championship
Los Angeles 9 at Tampa Bay 0
Super Bowl 14
Pittsburgh 31, Los Angeles 19, at Pasadena, Calif.

1980

AMERICAN CONFERENCE

EASTERN DIVISION

Team	W	L	T	Pct.	PF	PA
Buffalo*	11	5	0	.688	320	260
New England	10	6	0	.625	441	325
Miami	8	8	0	.500	266	305
Baltimore	7	9	0	.438	355	387
N.Y. Jets	4	12	0	.250	302	395

CENTRAL DIVISION

Team	W	L	T	Pct.	PF	PA
Cleveland*	11	5	0	.688	357	310
Houston†	11	5	0	.688	295	251
Pittsburgh	9	7	0	.563	352	313
Cincinnati	6	10	0	.375	244	312

WESTERN DIVISION

Team	W	L	T	Pct.	PF	PA
San Diego*	11	5	0	.688	418	327
Oakland†	11	5	0	.688	364	306
Kansas City	8	8	0	.500	319	336
Denver	8	8	0	.500	310	323
Seattle	4	12	0	.250	291	408

*Division champion.
†Wild-card team.

NATIONAL CONFERENCE

EASTERN DIVISION

Team	W	L	T	Pct.	PF	PA
Philadelphia*	12	4	0	.750	384	222
Dallas†	12	4	0	.750	454	311
Washington	6	10	0	.375	261	293
St. Louis	5	11	0	.313	299	350
N.Y. Giants	4	12	0	.250	249	425

CENTRAL DIVISION

Team	W	L	T	Pct.	PF	PA
Minnesota*	9	7	0	.563	317	308
Detroit	9	7	0	.563	334	272
Chicago	7	9	0	.438	304	264
Tampa Bay	5	10	1	.344	271	341
Green Bay	5	10	1	.344	231	371

WESTERN DIVISION

Team	W	L	T	Pct.	PF	PA
Atlanta*	12	4	0	.750	405	272
Los Angeles†	11	5	0	.688	424	289
San Francisco	6	10	0	.375	320	415
New Orleans	1	15	0	.063	291	487

PLAYOFFS

AFC wild-card game
Oakland 27 vs. Houston 7
AFC divisional games
San Diego 20 vs. Buffalo 14
Oakland 14 at Cleveland 12
AFC championship
Oakland 34 at San Diego 27
NFC wild-card game
Dallas 34 vs. Los Angeles 13
NFC divisional games
Philadelphia 31 vs. Minnesota 16
Dallas 30 at Atlanta 27
NFC championship
Philadelphia 20 vs. Dallas 7
Super Bowl 15
Oakland 27, Philadelphia 10, at New Orleans.

AIR CORYELL TAKES TO THE SKIES

Although their season would end in disappointment—a loss to Oakland in the AFC championship game—few teams were more exciting to watch in 1980 than coach Don Coryell's San Diego Chargers. Only eight receivers caught passes for 1,000 or more yards that year, but San Diego had three of them: John Jefferson (who led the league with 1,340 yards), Kellen Winslow (1,290) and Charlie Joiner (1,132). It marked the first time in history that three receivers on the same team each topped 1,000 yards in the same season. In addition, Winslow caught 89 passes to set a record for receptions by a tight end and Jefferson became the first player to begin his NFL career with three consecutive 1,000-yard seasons. Not surprisingly, the Chargers won the AFC West title for the second year in a row, the only team to repeat from the 1979 season.

1981

AMERICAN CONFERENCE

EASTERN DIVISION
Team	W	L	T	Pct.	PF	PA
Miami*	11	4	1	.719	345	275
N.Y. Jets†	10	5	1	.656	355	287
Buffalo†	10	6	0	.625	311	276
Baltimore	2	14	0	.125	259	533
New England	2	14	0	.125	322	370

CENTRAL DIVISION
Team	W	L	T	Pct.	PF	PA
Cincinnati*	12	4	0	.750	421	304
Pittsburgh	8	8	0	.500	356	297
Houston	7	9	0	.438	281	355
Cleveland	5	11	0	.313	276	375

WESTERN DIVISION
Team	W	L	T	Pct.	PF	PA
San Diego*	10	6	0	.625	478	390
Denver	10	6	0	.625	321	289
Kansas City	9	7	0	.563	343	290
Oakland	7	9	0	.438	273	343
Seattle	6	10	0	.375	322	388

*Division champion.
†Wild-card team.

NATIONAL CONFERENCE

EASTERN DIVISION
Team	W	L	T	Pct.	PF	PA
Dallas*	12	4	0	.750	367	277
Philadelphia†	10	6	0	.625	368	221
N.Y. Giants†	9	7	0	.563	295	257
Washington	8	8	0	.500	347	349
St. Louis	7	9	0	.438	315	408

CENTRAL DIVISION
Team	W	L	T	Pct.	PF	PA
Tampa Bay*	9	7	0	.563	315	268
Detroit	8	8	0	.500	397	322
Green Bay	8	8	0	.500	324	361
Minnesota	7	9	0	.438	325	369
Chicago	6	10	0	.375	253	324

WESTERN DIVISION
Team	W	L	T	Pct.	PF	PA
San Francisco*	13	3	0	.813	357	250
Atlanta	7	9	0	.438	426	355
Los Angeles	6	10	0	.375	303	351
New Orleans	4	12	0	.250	207	378

PLAYOFFS

AFC wild-card game
Buffalo 31 at New York Jets 27
AFC divisional games
San Diego 41 at Miami 38 (OT)
Cincinnati 28 vs. Buffalo 21
AFC championship
Cincinnati 27 vs. San Diego 7
NFC wild-card game
N.Y. Giants 27 at Philadelphia 21
NFC divisional games
Dallas 38 vs. Tampa Bay 0
San Francisco 38 vs. N.Y. Giants 24
NFC championship
San Francisco 28 vs. Dallas 27
Super Bowl 16
San Francisco 26, Cincinnati 21, at Pontiac, Mich.

1982

AMERICAN CONFERENCE
Team	W	L	T	Pct.	PF	PA
L.A. Raiders	8	1	0	.889	260	200
Miami	7	2	0	.778	198	131
Cincinnati	7	2	0	.778	232	177
Pittsburgh	6	3	0	.667	204	146
San Diego	6	3	0	.667	288	221
N.Y. Jets	6	3	0	.667	245	166
New England	5	4	0	.556	143	157
Cleveland	4	5	0	.444	140	182
Buffalo	4	5	0	.444	150	154
Seattle	4	5	0	.444	127	147
Kansas City	3	6	0	.333	176	184
Denver	2	7	0	.222	148	226
Houston	1	8	0	.111	136	245
Baltimore	0	8	1	.056	113	236

NATIONAL CONFERENCE
Team	W	L	T	Pct.	PF	PA
Washington	8	1	0	.889	190	128
Dallas	6	3	0	.667	226	145
Green Bay	5	3	1	.611	226	169
Minnesota	5	4	0	.556	187	198
Atlanta	5	4	0	.556	183	199
St. Louis	5	4	0	.556	135	170
Tampa Bay	5	4	0	.556	158	178
Detroit	4	5	0	.444	181	176
New Orleans	4	5	0	.444	129	160
N.Y. Giants	4	5	0	.444	164	160
San Francisco	3	6	0	.333	209	206
Chicago	3	6	0	.333	141	174
Philadelphia	3	6	0	.333	191	195
L.A. Rams	2	7	0	.222	200	250

As a result of a 57-day players' strike, the 1982 NFL regular season schedule was reduced from 16 weeks to 9. At the conclusion of the regular season, a 16-team Super Bowl Tournament was held. Eight teams from each conference were seeded 1 through 8 based on their records during regular season play.
  Miami finished ahead of Cincinnati based on a better conference record. Pittsburgh won common games tiebreaker with San Diego after New York Jets were eliminated from three-way tie based on conference record. Cleveland finished ahead of Buffalo and Seattle based on better conference record. Minnesota, Atlanta, St. Louis and Tampa Bay seeds were determined by best won-lost record in conference games. Detroit finished ahead of New Orleans and the New York Giants based on a better conference record.

PLAYOFFS

AFC first round
Miami 28 vs. New England 13
L.A. Raiders 27 vs. Cleveland 10
New York Jets 44 at Cincinnati 17
San Diego 31 at Pittsburgh 28
AFC second round
N.Y. Jets 17 at L.A. Raiders 14
Miami 34 vs. San Diego 13
AFC championship
Miami 14 vs. New York Jets 0
NFC first round
Washington 31 vs. Detroit 7
Green Bay 41 vs. St. Louis 16
Minnesota 30 vs. Atlanta 24
Dallas 30 vs. Tampa Bay 17
NFC second round
Washington 21 vs. Minnesota 7
Dallas 37 vs. Green Bay 26
NFC championship
Washington 31 vs. Dallas 17
Super Bowl 17
Washington 27, Miami 17, at Pasadena, Calif.

LT: A ROOKIE TO REMEMBER

The 1981 season was a big one for rookies (six made the Pro Bowl), but none had more impact than Giants linebacker Lawrence Taylor, who had no problem adjusting to the pro game after an All-American career at North Carolina. The second player drafted in 1981, Taylor was simply marvelous, helping to make a good New York defense with veterans like linebacker Harry Carson and cornerback Mark Haynes great. In 16 games (all starts) Taylor had 133 tackles, 10.5 sacks, recovered a fumble and intercepted a pass. He followed that up with 14 tackles and two sacks in two playoff games, the Giants' first postseason action since 1963. For his efforts Taylor was a unanimous All-NFL first-team selection, a Pro Bowl starter and the Associated Press Defensive Player of the Year.

1983

AMERICAN CONFERENCE
EASTERN DIVISION
Team	W	L	T	Pct.	PF	PA
Miami*	12	4	0	.750	389	250
New England	8	8	0	.500	274	289
Buffalo	8	8	0	.500	283	351
Baltimore	7	9	0	.438	264	354
N.Y. Jets	7	9	0	.438	313	331

CENTRAL DIVISION
Team	W	L	T	Pct.	PF	PA
Pittsburgh*	10	6	0	.625	355	303
Cleveland	9	7	0	.563	356	342
Cincinnati	7	9	0	.438	346	302
Houston	2	14	0	.125	288	460

WESTERN DIVISION
Team	W	L	T	Pct.	PF	PA
L.A. Raiders*	12	4	0	.750	442	338
Seattle†	9	7	0	.563	403	397
Denver†	9	7	0	.563	302	327
San Diego	6	10	0	.375	358	462
Kansas City	6	10	0	.375	386	367

*Division champion.
†Wild-card team.

NATIONAL CONFERENCE
EASTERN DIVISION
Team	W	L	T	Pct.	PF	PA
Washington*	14	2	0	.875	541	332
Dallas†	12	4	0	.750	479	360
St. Louis	8	7	1	.531	374	428
Philadelphia	5	11	0	.313	233	322
N.Y. Giants	3	12	1	.219	267	347

CENTRAL DIVISION
Team	W	L	T	Pct.	PF	PA
Detroit*	9	7	0	.563	347	286
Green Bay	8	8	0	.500	429	439
Chicago	8	8	0	.500	311	301
Minnesota	8	8	0	.500	316	348
Tampa Bay	2	14	0	.125	241	380

WESTERN DIVISION
Team	W	L	T	Pct.	PF	PA
San Francisco*	10	6	0	.625	432	293
L.A. Rams†	9	7	0	.563	361	344
New Orleans	8	8	0	.500	319	337
Atlanta	7	9	0	.438	370	389

PLAYOFFS
AFC wild-card game
Seattle 31 vs. Denver 7
AFC divisional games
Seattle 27 at Miami 20
L.A. Raiders 38 vs. Pittsburgh 10
AFC championship game
L.A. Raiders 30 vs. Seattle 14
NFC wild-card game
Los Angeles Rams 24 at Dallas 17
NFC divisional games
San Francisco 24 vs. Detroit 23
Washington 51 vs. L.A. Rams 7
NFC championship
Washington 24 vs. San Francisco 21
Super Bowl 18
L.A. Raiders 38, Washington 9, at Tampa, Fla.

1984

AMERICAN CONFERENCE
EASTERN DIVISION
Team	W	L	T	Pct.	PF	PA
Miami*	14	2	0	.875	513	298
New England	9	7	0	.563	362	352
N.Y. Jets	7	9	0	.438	332	364
Indianapolis	4	12	0	.250	239	414
Buffalo	2	14	0	.125	250	454

CENTRAL DIVISION
Team	W	L	T	Pct.	PF	PA
Pittsburgh*	9	7	0	.563	387	310
Cincinnati	8	8	0	.500	339	339
Cleveland	5	11	0	.313	250	297
Houston	3	13	0	.188	240	437

WESTERN DIVISION
Team	W	L	T	Pct.	PF	PA
Denver*	13	3	0	.813	353	241
Seattle†	12	4	0	.750	418	282
L.A. Raiders†	11	5	0	.688	368	278
Kansas City	8	8	0	.500	314	324
San Diego	7	9	0	.438	394	413

*Division champion.
†Wild-card team.

NATIONAL CONFERENCE
EASTERN DIVISION
Team	W	L	T	Pct.	PF	PA
Washington*	11	5	0	.688	426	310
N.Y. Giants†	9	7	0	.563	299	301
St. Louis	9	7	0	.563	423	345
Dallas	9	7	0	.563	308	308
Philadelphia	6	9	1	.406	278	320

CENTRAL DIVISION
Team	W	L	T	Pct.	PF	PA
Chicago*	10	6	0	.625	325	248
Green Bay	8	8	0	.500	390	309
Tampa Bay	6	10	0	.375	335	380
Detroit	4	11	1	.281	283	408
Minnesota	3	13	0	.188	276	484

WESTERN DIVISION
Team	W	L	T	Pct.	PF	PA
San Francisco*	15	1	0	.938	475	227
L.A. Rams†	10	6	0	.625	346	316
New Orleans	7	9	0	.438	298	361
Atlanta	4	12	0	.250	281	382

PLAYOFFS
AFC wild-card game
Seattle 13 vs. Los Angeles Raiders 7
AFC divisional games
Miami 31 vs. Seattle 10
Pittsburgh 24 at Denver 17
AFC championship
Miami 45 vs. Pittsburgh 28
NFC wild-card game
N.Y. Giants 16 at L.A. Rams 13
NFC divisional games
San Francisco 21 vs. N.Y. Giants 10
Chicago 23 at Washington 19
NFC championship
San Francisco 23 vs. Chicago 0
Super Bowl 19
San Francisco 38, Miami 16, at Palo Alto, Calif.

CAPITAL GAINS FOR THE REDSKINS
Although they failed to successfully defend their Super Bowl championship, the Washington Redskins did just about everything else right in 1983, especially on offense. Washington scored 541 points, the most in NFL history and 62 more than the next highest scoring team that year. Running back John Riggins scored a record 24 touchdowns, rushed for a club-record 1,347 yards and set a league mark by rushing for a TD in 13 consecutive games. Mark Moseley's 161 points set a new league standard for kickers. But as good as Riggins and Moseley were, the league's Most Valuable Player, in voting conducted by the Associated Press, was quarterback Joe Theismann, who threw 29 TD passes, compiled a 97.0 passer rating and had streaks of 161 and 104 consecutive passes without an interception.

– 319 –

HISTORY — *Year-by-year standings*

1985

AMERICAN CONFERENCE

EASTERN DIVISION

Team	W	L	T	Pct.	PF	PA
Miami*	12	4	0	.750	428	320
N.Y. Jets†	11	5	0	.688	393	264
New England†	11	5	0	.688	362	290
Indianapolis	5	11	0	.313	320	386
Buffalo	2	14	0	.125	200	381

CENTRAL DIVISION

Team	W	L	T	Pct.	PF	PA
Cleveland*	8	8	0	.500	287	294
Cincinnati	7	9	0	.438	441	437
Pittsburgh	7	9	0	.438	379	355
Houston	5	11	0	.313	284	412

WESTERN DIVISION

Team	W	L	T	Pct.	PF	PA
L.A. Raiders*	12	4	0	.750	354	308
Denver	11	5	0	.688	380	329
Seattle	8	8	0	.500	349	303
San Diego	8	8	0	.500	467	435
Kansas City	6	10	0	.375	317	360

*Division champion.
†Wild-card team.

NATIONAL CONFERENCE

EASTERN DIVISION

Team	W	L	T	Pct.	PF	PA
Dallas*	10	6	0	.625	357	333
N.Y. Giants†	10	6	0	.625	399	283
Washington	10	6	0	.625	297	312
Philadelphia	7	9	0	.438	286	310
St. Louis	5	11	0	.313	278	414

CENTRAL DIVISION

Team	W	L	T	Pct.	PF	PA
Chicago*	15	1	0	.938	456	198
Green Bay	8	8	0	.500	337	355
Minnesota	7	9	0	.438	346	359
Detroit	7	9	0	.438	307	366
Tampa Bay	2	14	0	.125	294	448

WESTERN DIVISION

Team	W	L	T	Pct.	PF	PA
L.A. Rams*	11	5	0	.688	340	277
San Francisco†	10	6	0	.625	411	263
New Orleans	5	11	0	.313	294	401
Atlanta	4	12	0	.250	282	452

PLAYOFFS

AFC wild-card game
New England 26 at N.Y. Jets 14
AFC divisional games
Miami 24 vs. Cleveland 21
New England 27 at L.A. Raiders 20
AFC championship
New England 31 at Miami 14
NFC wild-card game
N.Y. Giants 17 vs. San Francisco 3
NFC divisional games
Los Angeles Rams 20 vs. Dallas 0
Chicago 21 vs. New York Giants 0
NFC championship
Chicago 24 vs. Los Angeles Rams 0
Super Bowl 20
Chicago 46, New England 10, at New Orleans.

1986

AMERICAN CONFERENCE

EASTERN DIVISION

Team	W	L	T	Pct.	PF	PA
New England*	11	5	0	.688	412	307
N.Y. Jets†	10	6	0	.625	364	386
Miami	8	8	0	.500	430	405
Buffalo	4	12	0	.250	287	348
Indianapolis	3	13	0	.188	229	400

CENTRAL DIVISION

Team	W	L	T	Pct.	PF	PA
Cleveland*	12	4	0	.750	391	310
Cincinnati	10	6	0	.625	409	394
Pittsburgh	6	10	0	.375	307	336
Houston	5	11	0	.313	274	329

WESTERN DIVISION

Team	W	L	T	Pct.	PF	PA
Denver*	11	5	0	.688	378	327
Kansas City†	10	6	0	.625	358	326
Seattle	10	6	0	.625	366	293
L.A. Raiders	8	8	0	.500	323	346
San Diego	4	12	0	.250	335	396

*Division champion.
†Wild-card team.

NATIONAL CONFERENCE

EASTERN DIVISION

Team	W	L	T	Pct.	PF	PA
N.Y. Giants*	14	2	0	.875	371	236
Washington†	12	4	0	.750	368	296
Dallas	7	9	0	.438	346	337
Philadelphia	5	10	1	.344	256	312
St. Louis	4	11	1	.281	218	351

CENTRAL DIVISION

Team	W	L	T	Pct.	PF	PA
Chicago*	14	2	0	.875	352	187
Minnesota	9	7	0	.563	398	273
Detroit	5	11	0	.313	277	326
Green Bay	4	12	0	.250	254	418
Tampa Bay	2	14	0	.125	239	473

WESTERN DIVISION

Team	W	L	T	Pct.	PF	PA
San Francisco*	10	5	1	.656	374	247
L.A. Rams†	10	6	0	.625	309	267
Atlanta	7	8	1	.469	280	280
New Orleans	7	9	0	.438	288	287

PLAYOFFS

AFC wild-card game
N.Y. Jets 35 vs. Kansas City 15
AFC divisional games
Cleveland 23 vs. N.Y. Jets 20 (OT)
Denver 22 vs. New England 17
AFC championship
Denver 23 at Cleveland 20 (OT)
NFC wild-card game
Washington 19 vs. L.A. Rams 7
NFC divisional games
Washington 27 at Chicago 13
N.Y. Giants 49 vs. San Francisco 3
NFC championship
N.Y. Giants 17 vs. Washington 0
Super Bowl 21
New York Giants 39, Denver 20, at Pasadena, Calif.

DA BEARS

The 1985 Chicago Bears may not have been the best team ever, but they were certainly among the most colorful. Running back Walter Payton suggested his teammates could have stepped right from the pages of "One Flew Over the Cuckoo's Nest." Rookie defensive tackle William Perry, whose girth earned him the nickname "The Refrigerator," said "I was big when I was little" when queried about his weight. The players cut a popular music video "The Super Bowl Shuffle"—while the regular season was still in progress. But there were good reasons for the cockiness: the Bears were good. They scored 456 points and allowed 198, one of the lowest totals ever for a 16-game season. Their final record, including the playoffs, was 18-1, and they outscored their three postseason opponents by a combined 91-10. Chicago's 46-10 rout of New England in the Super Bowl was the most lopsided in the game's first 20 years.

1987

AMERICAN CONFERENCE

EASTERN DIVISION

Team	W	L	T	Pct.	PF	PA
Indianapolis*	9	6	0	.600	300	238
New England	8	7	0	.533	320	293
Miami	8	7	0	.533	362	335
Buffalo	7	8	0	.467	270	305
N.Y. Jets	6	9	0	.400	334	360

CENTRAL DIVISION

Team	W	L	T	Pct.	PF	PA
Cleveland*	10	5	0	.667	390	239
Houston†	9	6	0	.600	345	349
Pittsburgh	8	7	0	.533	285	299
Cincinnati	4	11	0	.267	285	370

WESTERN DIVISION

Team	W	L	T	Pct.	PF	PA
Denver*	10	4	1	.700	379	288
Seattle†	9	6	0	.600	371	314
San Diego	8	7	0	.533	253	317
L.A. Raiders	5	10	0	.333	301	289
Kansas City	4	11	0	.267	273	388

*Division champion.
†Wild-card team.

NOTE: The 1987 NFL regular season was reduced from 224 games to 210 (16 to 15 for each team) due to players' strike.

NATIONAL CONFERENCE

EASTERN DIVISION

Team	W	L	T	Pct.	PF	PA
Washington*	11	4	0	.733	379	285
Dallas	7	8	0	.467	340	348
St. Louis	7	8	0	.467	362	368
Philadelphia	7	8	0	.467	337	380
N.Y. Giants	6	9	0	.400	280	312

CENTRAL DIVISION

Team	W	L	T	Pct.	PF	PA
Chicago*	11	4	0	.733	356	282
Minnesota†	8	7	0	.533	336	335
Green Bay	5	9	1	.367	255	300
Tampa Bay	4	11	0	.267	286	360
Detroit	4	11	0	.267	269	384

WESTERN DIVISION

Team	W	L	T	Pct.	PF	PA
San Francisco*	13	2	0	.867	459	253
New Orleans†	12	3	0	.800	422	283
L.A. Rams	6	9	0	.400	317	361
Atlanta	3	12	0	.200	205	436

PLAYOFFS

AFC wild-card game
Houston 23 vs. Seattle 20 (OT)
AFC divisional games
Cleveland 38 vs. Indianapolis 21
Denver 34 vs. Houston 10
AFC championship
Denver 38 vs. Cleveland 33
NFC wild-card game
Minnesota 44 at New Orleans 10
NFC divisional games
Minnesota 36 at San Francisco 24
Washington 21 at Chicago 17
NFC championship
Washington 17 vs. Minnesota 10
Super Bowl 22
Washington 42, Denver 10, at San Diego.

1988

AMERICAN CONFERENCE

EASTERN DIVISION

Team	W	L	T	Pct.	PF	PA
Buffalo*	12	4	0	.750	329	237
Indianapolis	9	7	0	.563	354	315
New England	9	7	0	.563	250	284
N.Y. Jets	8	7	1	.531	372	354
Miami	6	10	0	.375	319	380

CENTRAL DIVISION

Team	W	L	T	Pct.	PF	PA
Cincinnati*	12	4	0	.750	448	329
Cleveland†	10	6	0	.625	304	288
Houston†	10	6	0	.625	424	365
Pittsburgh	5	11	0	.313	336	421

WESTERN DIVISION

Team	W	L	T	Pct.	PF	PA
Seattle*	9	7	0	.563	339	329
Denver	8	8	0	.500	327	352
L.A. Raiders	7	9	0	.438	325	369
San Diego	6	10	0	.375	231	332
Kansas City	4	11	1	.281	254	320

*Division champion.
†Wild-card team.

NATIONAL CONFERENCE

EASTERN DIVISION

Team	W	L	T	Pct.	PF	PA
Philadelphia*	10	6	0	.625	379	319
N.Y. Giants	10	6	0	.625	359	304
Washington	7	9	0	.438	345	387
Phoenix	7	9	0	.438	344	398
Dallas	3	13	0	.188	265	381

CENTRAL DIVISION

Team	W	L	T	Pct.	PF	PA
Chicago*	12	4	0	.750	312	215
Minnesota†	11	5	0	.688	406	233
Tampa Bay	5	11	0	.313	261	350
Detroit	4	12	0	.250	220	313
Green Bay	4	12	0	.250	240	315

WESTERN DIVISION

Team	W	L	T	Pct.	PF	PA
San Francisco*	10	6	0	.625	369	294
L.A. Rams†	10	6	0	.625	407	293
New Orleans	10	6	0	.625	312	283
Atlanta	5	11	0	.313	244	315

PLAYOFFS

AFC wild-card game
Houston 24 at Cleveland 23
AFC divisional games
Cincinnati 21 vs. Seattle 13
Buffalo 17 vs. Houston 10
AFC championship
Cincinnati 21 vs. Buffalo 10
NFC wild-card game
Minnesota 28 vs. L.A. Rams 17
NFC divisional games
Chicago 20 vs. Philadelphia 12
San Francisco 34 vs. Minnesota 9
NFC championship
San Francisco 28 at Chicago 3
Super Bowl 23
San Francisco 20, Cincinnati 16, at Miami.

HISTORY *Year-by-year standings*

REPLACEMENT BALL

Frustrated in their attempts to gain a fairer form of unrestricted free agency, NFL players went on strike for the second time in league history on September 22, 1987. The work stoppage forced the cancellation of all Week 3 games and brought about three subsequent weeks of what came to be called "replacement football." With their regular players on strike, team owners quickly assembled new squads consisting of former NFL and United States Football League players, castoffs and amateur dreamers willing to cross a picket line. The result? There was a wide discrepancy in the quality of the teams, depending largely on how much effort management invested in assembling new rosters. The defending Super Bowl champion Giants, for example, lost all three of their replacement games (which counted in the standings) and never recovered once their regular players returned, finishing the season 6-9 and out of the playoffs. The Redskins, meanwhile, went 3-0 in replacement ball, helping to propel them to an 11-4 regular-season finish en route to the club's second Super Bowl title in six years.

HISTORY *Year-by-year standings*

1989

AMERICAN CONFERENCE

EASTERN DIVISION

Team	W	L	T	Pct.	PF	PA
Buffalo*	9	7	0	.563	409	317
Indianapolis	8	8	0	.500	298	301
Miami	8	8	0	.500	331	379
New England	5	11	0	.313	297	391
N.Y. Jets	4	12	0	.250	253	411

CENTRAL DIVISION

Team	W	L	T	Pct.	PF	PA
Cleveland*	9	6	1	.594	334	254
Houston†	9	7	0	.563	365	412
Pittsburgh†	9	7	0	.563	265	326
Cincinnati	8	8	0	.500	404	285

WESTERN DIVISION

Team	W	L	T	Pct.	PF	PA
Denver*	11	5	0	.688	362	226
Kansas City	8	7	1	.531	318	286
L.A. Raiders	8	8	0	.500	315	297
Seattle	7	9	0	.438	241	327
San Diego	6	10	0	.375	266	290

*Division champion.
†Wild-card team.

NATIONAL CONFERENCE

EASTERN DIVISION

Team	W	L	T	Pct.	PF	PA
N.Y. Giants*	12	4	0	.750	348	252
Philadelphia†	11	5	0	.688	342	274
Washington	10	6	0	.625	386	308
Phoenix	5	11	0	.313	258	377
Dallas	1	15	0	.063	204	393

CENTRAL DIVISION

Team	W	L	T	Pct.	PF	PA
Minnesota*	10	6	0	.625	351	275
Green Bay	10	6	0	.625	362	356
Detroit	7	9	0	.438	312	364
Chicago	6	10	0	.375	358	377
Tampa Bay	5	11	0	.313	320	419

WESTERN DIVISION

Team	W	L	T	Pct.	PF	PA
San Francisco*	14	2	0	.875	442	253
L.A. Rams†	11	5	0	.688	426	344
New Orleans	9	7	0	.563	386	301
Atlanta	3	13	0	.188	279	437

PLAYOFFS

AFC wild-card game
Pittsburgh 26 at Houston 23 (OT)
AFC divisional games
Cleveland 34 vs. Buffalo 30
Denver 24 vs. Pittsburgh 23
AFC championship
Denver 37 vs. Cleveland 21
NFC wild-card game
L.A. Rams 21 at Philadelphia 7
NFC divisional games
L.A. Rams 19 at N.Y. Giants 13 (OT)
San Francisco 41 vs. Minnesota 13
NFC championship
San Francisco 30 vs. L.A. Rams 3
Super Bowl 24
San Francisco 55, Denver 10, at New Orleans.

1990

AMERICAN CONFERENCE

EASTERN DIVISION

Team	W	L	T	Pct.	PF	PA
Buffalo*	13	3	0	.813	428	263
Miami†	12	4	0	.750	336	242
Indianapolis	7	9	0	.438	281	353
N.Y. Jets	6	10	0	.375	295	345
New England	1	15	0	.063	181	446

CENTRAL DIVISION

Team	W	L	T	Pct.	PF	PA
Cincinnati*	9	7	0	.563	360	352
Houston†	9	7	0	.563	405	307
Pittsburgh	9	7	0	.563	292	240
Cleveland	3	13	0	.188	228	462

WESTERN DIVISION

Team	W	L	T	Pct.	PF	PA
L.A. Raiders*	12	4	0	.750	337	268
Kansas City†	11	5	0	.688	369	257
Seattle	9	7	0	.563	306	286
San Diego	6	10	0	.375	315	281
Denver	5	11	0	.313	331	374

*Division champion.
†Wild-card team.

NATIONAL CONFERENCE

EASTERN DIVISION

Team	W	L	T	Pct.	PF	PA
N.Y. Giants*	13	3	0	.813	335	211
Philadelphia†	10	6	0	.625	396	299
Washington†	10	6	0	.625	381	301
Dallas	7	9	0	.438	244	308
Phoenix	5	11	0	.313	268	396

CENTRAL DIVISION

Team	W	L	T	Pct.	PF	PA
Chicago*	11	5	0	.688	348	280
Tampa Bay	6	10	0	.375	264	367
Detroit	6	10	0	.375	373	413
Green Bay	6	10	0	.375	271	347
Minnesota	6	10	0	.375	351	326

WESTERN DIVISION

Team	W	L	T	Pct.	PF	PA
San Francisco*	14	2	0	.875	353	239
New Orleans†	8	8	0	.500	274	275
L.A. Rams	5	11	0	.313	345	412
Atlanta	5	11	0	.313	348	365

PLAYOFFS

AFC wild-card playoffs
Miami 17 vs. Kansas City 16
Cincinnati 41 vs. Houston 14
AFC divisional playoffs
Buffalo 44 vs. Miami 34
L.A. Raiders 20 vs. Cincinnati 10
AFC championship
Buffalo 51 vs. L.A. Raiders 3
NFC wild-card playoffs
Washington 20 at Philadelphia 6
Chicago 16 vs. New Orleans 6
NFC divisional playoffs
San Francisco 28 vs. Washington 10
N.Y. Giants 31 vs. Chicago 3
NFC championship
N.Y. Giants 15 at San Francisco 13
Super Bowl 25
N.Y. Giants 20 vs. Buffalo 19, at Tampa, Fla.

GIANTS AND BILLS GO DOWN TO THE WIRE

One year after the most lopsided Super Bowl ever, the Giants and Bills staged the closest, with New York edging Buffalo, 20-19, at Tampa Stadium in Super Bowl 25 when Bills kicker Scott Norwood missed a 47-yard field goal attempt with eight seconds left. Although Norwood wore the goat horns afterward, his teammates did little early in the contest to prevent the game from coming down to a last-minute kick. A Buffalo offense that had scored a league-high 428 points during the regular season and 95 in the first two playoff games did little in its biggest test of the season. Only running back Thurman Thomas (135 yards rushing) had what could be considered a superior game. The Giants' offense, meanwhile, put together scoring drives of 87, 75 and 74 yards. A 14-play, 75-yard drive that took 9 minutes, 29 seconds off the clock went into the books as the most time-consuming drive in Super Bowl history.

1991

AMERICAN CONFERENCE

EASTERN DIVISION

Team	W	L	T	Pct.	PF	PA
Buffalo*	13	3	0	.813	458	318
N.Y. Jets†	8	8	0	.500	314	293
Miami	8	8	0	.500	343	349
New England	6	10	0	.375	211	305
Indianapolis	1	15	0	.063	143	381

CENTRAL DIVISION

Team	W	L	T	Pct.	PF	PA
Houston*	11	5	0	.688	386	251
Pittsburgh	7	9	0	.438	292	344
Cleveland	6	10	0	.375	293	298
Cincinnati	3	13	0	.188	263	435

WESTERN DIVISION

Team	W	L	T	Pct.	PF	PA
Denver*	12	4	0	.750	304	235
Kansas City†	10	6	0	.625	322	252
L.A. Raiders†	9	7	0	.563	298	297
Seattle	7	9	0	.438	276	261
San Diego	4	12	0	.250	274	342

*Division champion.
†Wild-card team.

NATIONAL CONFERENCE

EASTERN DIVISION

Team	W	L	T	Pct.	PF	PA
Washington*	14	2	0	.875	485	224
Dallas†	11	5	0	.688	342	310
Philadelphia	10	6	0	.625	285	244
N.Y. Giants	8	8	0	.500	281	297
Phoenix	4	12	0	.250	196	344

CENTRAL DIVISION

Team	W	L	T	Pct.	PF	PA
Detroit*	12	4	0	.750	339	295
Chicago†	11	5	0	.688	299	269
Minnesota	8	8	0	.500	301	306
Green Bay	4	12	0	.250	273	313
Tampa Bay	3	13	0	.188	199	365

WESTERN DIVISION

Team	W	L	T	Pct.	PF	PA
New Orleans*	11	5	0	.688	341	211
Atlanta†	10	6	0	.625	361	338
San Francisco	10	6	0	.625	393	239
L.A. Rams	3	13	0	.188	234	390

PLAYOFFS

AFC wild-card playoffs
Kansas City 10 vs. L.A. Raiders 6
Houston 17 vs. N.Y. Jets 10

AFC divisional playoffs
Denver 26 vs. Houston 24
Buffalo 37 vs. Kansas City 14

AFC championship
Buffalo 10 vs. Denver 7

NFC wild-card playoffs
Atlanta 27 at New Orleans 20
Dallas 17 at Chicago 13

NFC divisional playoffs
Washington 24 vs. Atlanta 7
Detroit 38 vs. Dallas 6

NFC championship
Washington 41 vs. Detroit 10

Super Bowl 26
Washington 37 vs. Buffalo 24, at Minneapolis.

1992

AMERICAN CONFERENCE

EASTERN DIVISION

Team	W	L	T	Pct.	PF	PA
Miami*	11	5	0	.688	340	281
Buffalo†	11	5	0	.688	381	283
Indianapolis	9	7	0	.563	216	302
N.Y. Jets	4	12	0	.250	220	315
New England	2	14	0	.125	205	363

CENTRAL DIVISION

Team	W	L	T	Pct.	PF	PA
Pittsburgh*	11	5	0	.688	299	225
Houston†	10	6	0	.625	352	258
Cleveland	7	9	0	.438	272	275
Cincinnati	5	11	0	.313	274	364

WESTERN DIVISION

Team	W	L	T	Pct.	PF	PA
San Diego*	11	5	0	.688	335	241
Kansas City†	10	6	0	.625	348	282
Denver	8	8	0	.500	262	329
L.A. Raiders	7	9	0	.438	249	281
Seattle	2	14	0	.125	140	312

*Division champion.
†Wild-card team.

NATIONAL CONFERENCE

EASTERN DIVISION

Team	W	L	T	Pct.	PF	PA
Dallas*	13	3	0	.813	409	243
Philadelphia†	11	5	0	.688	354	245
Washington†	9	7	0	.563	300	255
N.Y. Giants	6	10	0	.375	306	367
Phoenix	4	12	0	.250	243	332

CENTRAL DIVISION

Team	W	L	T	Pct.	PF	PA
Minnesota*	11	5	0	.688	374	249
Green Bay	9	7	0	.563	276	296
Tampa Bay	5	11	0	.313	267	365
Chicago	5	11	0	.313	295	361
Detroit	5	11	0	.313	273	332

WESTERN DIVISION

Team	W	L	T	Pct.	PF	PA
San Francisco*	14	2	0	.875	431	236
New Orleans†	12	4	0	.750	330	202
Atlanta	6	10	0	.375	327	414
L.A. Rams	6	10	0	.375	313	383

PLAYOFFS

AFC wild-card playoffs
San Diego 17 vs. Kansas City 0
Buffalo 41 vs. Houston 38 (OT)

AFC divisional playoffs
Buffalo 24 at Pittsburgh 3
Miami 31 vs. San Diego 0

AFC championship
Buffalo 29 at Miami 10

NFC wild-card playoffs
Washington 24 at Minnesota 7
Philadelphia 36 at New Orleans 20

NFC divisional playoffs
San Francisco 20 vs. Washington 13
Dallas 34 vs. Philadelphia 10

NFC championship
Dallas 30 at San Francisco 20

Super Bowl 27
Dallas 52 vs. Buffalo 17, at Pasadena, Calif.

HISTORY *Year-by-year standings*

COWBOYS HIT THE HEIGHTS AGAIN

Three years after hitting the lowest point in franchise history, the Dallas Cowboys were back on top of the football world following a 52-17 romp over Buffalo in Super Bowl 27. In their fourth year under Jimmy Johnson, who replaced legendary coach Tom Landry following an ownership change in February 1989, the Cowboys won a franchise-record 13 regular season games and rolled through the playoffs, beating the Eagles, 49ers and Bills by a combined score of 116-47. Troy Aikman, the first player Johnson drafted after taking over, was superb in the playoffs, compiling an NFL-record 116.7 quarterback rating in the three games. With the win Johnson joined Paul Brown as the only men to coach championship teams in both college and the NFL.

HISTORY — *Year-by-year standings*

1993

AMERICAN CONFERENCE

EASTERN DIVISION

Team	W	L	T	Pct.	PF	PA
Buffalo*	12	4	0	.750	329	242
Miami	9	7	0	.563	349	351
N.Y. Jets	8	8	0	.500	270	247
New England	5	11	0	.313	238	286
Indianapolis	4	12	0	.250	189	378

CENTRAL DIVISION

Team	W	L	T	Pct.	PF	PA
Houston*	12	4	0	.750	368	238
Pittsburgh†	9	7	0	.563	308	281
Cleveland	7	9	0	.438	304	307
Cincinnati	3	13	0	.188	187	319

WESTERN DIVISION

Team	W	L	T	Pct.	PF	PA
Kansas City*	11	5	0	.688	328	291
L.A. Raiders†	10	6	0	.625	306	326
Denver†	9	7	0	.563	373	284
San Diego	8	8	0	.500	322	290
Seattle	6	10	0	.375	280	314

*Division champion.
†Wild-card team.

NATIONAL CONFERENCE

EASTERN DIVISION

Team	W	L	T	Pct.	PF	PA
Dallas*	12	4	0	.750	376	229
N.Y. Giants†	11	5	0	.688	288	205
Philadelphia	8	8	0	.500	293	315
Phoenix	7	9	0	.438	326	269
Washington	4	12	0	.250	230	345

CENTRAL DIVISION

Team	W	L	T	Pct.	PF	PA
Detroit*	10	6	0	.625	298	292
Minnesota†	9	7	0	.563	277	290
Green Bay†	9	7	0	.563	340	282
Chicago	7	9	0	.438	234	230
Tampa Bay	5	11	0	.313	237	376

WESTERN DIVISION

Team	W	L	T	Pct.	PF	PA
San Francisco*	10	6	0	.625	473	295
New Orleans	8	8	0	.500	317	343
Atlanta	6	10	0	.375	316	385
L.A. Rams	5	11	0	.313	221	367

PLAYOFFS

AFC wild-card playoffs
Kansas City 27 vs. Pittsburgh 24 (OT)
L.A. Raiders 42 vs. Denver 24

AFC divisional playoffs
Buffalo 29 vs. L.A. Raiders 23
Kansas City 28 at Houston 20

AFC championship
Buffalo 30 vs. Kansas City 13

NFC wild-card playoffs
Green Bay 28 at Detroit 24
N.Y. Giants 17 vs. Minnesota 10

NFC divisional playoffs
San Francisco 44 vs. N.Y. Giants 3
Dallas 27 vs. Green Bay 17

NFC championship
Dallas 38 vs. San Francisco 21

Super Bowl 28
Dallas 30 vs. Buffalo 13, at Atlanta.

1994

AMERICAN CONFERENCE

EASTERN DIVISION

Team	W	L	T	Pct.	PF	PA
Miami*	10	6	0	.625	389	327
New England†	10	6	0	.625	351	312
Indianapolis	8	8	0	.500	307	320
Buffalo	7	9	0	.438	340	356
N.Y. Jets	6	10	0	.375	264	320

CENTRAL DIVISION

Team	W	L	T	Pct.	PF	PA
Pittsburgh*	12	4	0	.750	316	234
Cleveland†	11	5	0	.688	340	204
Cincinnati	3	13	0	.188	276	406
Houston	2	14	0	.125	226	352

WESTERN DIVISION

Team	W	L	T	Pct.	PF	PA
San Diego*	11	5	0	.688	381	306
Kansas City†	9	7	0	.563	319	298
L.A. Raiders	9	7	0	.563	303	327
Denver	7	9	0	.438	347	396
Seattle	6	10	0	.375	287	323

*Division champion.
†Wild-card team.

NATIONAL CONFERENCE

EASTERN DIVISION

Team	W	L	T	Pct.	PF	PA
Dallas*	12	4	0	.750	414	248
N.Y. Giants	9	7	0	.563	279	305
Arizona	8	8	0	.500	235	267
Philadelphia	7	9	0	.438	308	308
Washington	3	13	0	.188	320	412

CENTRAL DIVISION

Team	W	L	T	Pct.	PF	PA
Minnesota*	10	6	0	.625	356	314
Detroit†	9	7	0	.563	357	342
Green Bay†	9	7	0	.563	382	287
Chicago†	9	7	0	.563	271	307
Tampa Bay	6	10	0	.375	251	351

WESTERN DIVISION

Team	W	L	T	Pct.	PF	PA
San Francisco*	13	3	0	.813	505	296
New Orleans	7	9	0	.438	348	407
Atlanta	7	9	0	.438	313	389
L.A. Rams	4	12	0	.250	286	365

PLAYOFFS

AFC wild-card playoffs
Miami 27 vs. Kansas City 17
Cleveland 20 vs. New England 13

AFC divisional playoffs
Pittsburgh 29 vs. Cleveland 9
San Diego 22 vs. Miami 21

AFC championship
San Diego 17 at Pittsburgh 13

NFC wild-card playoffs
Green Bay 16 vs. Detroit 12
Chicago 35 at Minnesota 18

NFC divisional playoffs
San Francisco 44 vs. Chicago 15
Dallas 35 vs. Green Bay 9

NFC championship
San Francisco 38 vs. Dallas 28

Super Bowl 29
San Francisco 49 vs. San Diego 26 at Miami.

MONTANA IN THE MIDWEST

Although he was unable to take the Chiefs to the same heights he did the San Francisco 49ers a decade earlier, Joe Montana closed out his illustrious career with two relatively productive, if injury plagued, seasons in Kansas City. Montana, who never completely recovered from injuries suffered in the 1990 NFC title game against the Giants (broken right hand, bruised sternum) that forced him to miss the entire 1991 season and all but one game in '92, played only 38 of 64 quarters for the Chiefs in 1993. Nevertheless, he was the AFC's No. 2-rated quarterback and guided Kansas City to within one game of the Super Bowl. Using the old Montana magic, he spearheaded come-from-behind playoff victories over the Steelers and Oilers before the Chiefs finally succumbed, 30-13, at Buffalo in the AFC championship game.

1995

AMERICAN CONFERENCE

EASTERN DIVISION
	W	L	T	Pct.	Pts.	Opp.
Buffalo*	10	6	0	.625	350	335
Indianapolis†	9	7	0	.563	331	316
Miami†	9	7	0	.563	398	332
New England	6	10	0	.375	294	377
N.Y. Jets	3	13	0	.188	233	384

CENTRAL DIVISION
	W	L	T	Pct.	Pts.	Opp.
Pittsburgh*	11	5	0	.689	407	327
Cincinnati	7	9	0	.438	349	374
Houston	7	9	0	.438	348	324
Cleveland	5	11	0	.313	289	356
Jacksonville	4	12	0	.250	275	404

WESTERN DIVISION
	W	L	T	Pct.	Pts.	Opp.
Kansas City*	13	3	0	.813	358	241
San Diego†	9	7	0	.563	321	323
Seattle	8	8	0	.500	363	366
Denver	8	8	0	.500	388	345
Oakland	8	8	0	.500	348	332

*Division champion.
†Wild-card team.

NATIONAL CONFERENCE

EASTERN DIVISION
	W	L	T	Pct.	Pts.	Opp.
Dallas*	12	4	0	.750	435	291
Philadelphia†	10	6	0	.625	318	338
Washington	6	10	0	.375	326	359
N.Y. Giants	5	11	0	.313	290	340
Arizona	4	12	0	.250	275	422

CENTRAL DIVISION
	W	L	T	Pct.	Pts.	Opp.
Green Bay*	11	5	0	.689	404	314
Detroit†	10	6	0	.625	436	336
Chicago	9	7	0	.563	392	360
Minnesota	8	8	0	.500	412	385
Tampa Bay	7	9	0	.438	238	335

WESTERN DIVISION
	W	L	T	Pct.	Pts.	Opp.
San Francisco*	11	5	0	.688	457	258
Atlanta†	9	7	0	.563	362	349
St. Louis	7	9	0	.438	309	418
Carolina	7	9	0	.438	289	325
New Orleans	7	9	0	.438	319	348

PLAYOFFS

AFC wild-card playoffs
Buffalo 37 vs. Miami 22
Indianapolis 35 at San Diego 20
AFC divisional playoffs
Pittsburgh 40 vs. Buffalo 21
Indianapolis 10 at Kansas City 7
AFC championship
Pittsburgh 20 vs. Indianapolis 16
NFC wild-card playoffs
Philadelphia 58 vs. Detroit 37
Green Bay 37 vs. Atlanta 20
NFC divisional playoffs
Green Bay 27 at San Francisco 17
Dallas 30 vs. Philadelphia 11
NFC championship
Dallas 38 vs. Green Bay 27
Super Bowl 30
Dallas 27 vs Pittsburgh 17, at Tempe, Ariz.

1996

AMERICAN CONFERENCE

EASTERN DIVISION
	W	L	T	Pct.	Pts.	Opp.
New England*	11	5	0	.687	418	313
Buffalo†	10	6	0	.625	319	266
Indianapolis†	9	7	0	.563	317	334
Miami	8	8	0	.500	339	325
N.Y. Jets	1	15	0	.063	279	454

CENTRAL DIVISION
	W	L	T	Pct.	Pts.	Opp.
Pittsburgh*	10	6	0	.625	344	257
Jacksonville†	9	7	0	.563	325	335
Cincinnati	8	8	0	.500	372	369
Houston	8	8	0	.500	345	319
Baltimore	4	12	0	.250	371	441

WESTERN DIVISION
	W	L	T	Pct.	Pts.	Opp.
Denver*	13	3	0	.813	391	275
Kansas City	9	7	0	.563	297	300
San Diego	8	8	0	.500	310	376
Oakland	7	9	0	.438	340	293
Seattle	7	9	0	.438	317	376

*Division champion.
†Wild-card team.

NATIONAL CONFERENCE

EASTERN DIVISION
	W	L	T	Pct.	Pts.	Opp.
Dallas*	10	6	0	.625	286	250
Philadelphia†	10	6	0	.625	363	341
Washington	9	7	0	.563	364	312
Arizona	7	9	0	.438	300	397
N.Y. Giants	6	10	0	.375	242	297

CENTRAL DIVISION
	W	L	T	Pct.	Pts.	Opp.
Green Bay*	13	3	0	.813	456	210
Minnesota†	9	7	0	.563	298	315
Chicago	7	9	0	.438	283	305
Tampa Bay	6	10	0	.375	221	293
Detroit	5	11	0	.313	302	368

WESTERN DIVISION
	W	L	T	Pct.	Pts.	Opp.
Carolina*	12	4	0	.750	367	218
San Francisco†	12	4	0	.750	398	257
St. Louis	6	10	0	.375	303	409
Atlanta	3	13	0	.188	309	465
New Orleans	3	13	0	.188	229	339

PLAYOFFS

AFC wild-card playoffs
Jacksonville 30, Buffalo 27
Pittsburgh 42, Indianapolis 14
AFC divisional playoffs
Jacksonville 30, Denver 27
New England 28, Pittsburgh 3
AFC championship
New England 20, Jacksonville 16
NFC wild-card playoffs
Dallas 40, Minnesota 15
San Francisco 14, Philadelphia 0
NFC divisional playoffs
Green Bay 35, San Francisco 14
Carolina 26, Dallas 17
NFC championship
Green Bay 30, Carolina 13
Super Bowl 31
Green Bay 35, New England 21, at New Orleans.

LOMBARDI WOULD BE PROUD

Six coaches and 29 years after last winning the Super Bowl, the Green Bay Packers were NFL champions again following a 35-21 victory over New England in Super Bowl 31. The title was not unexpected, despite the many years that had passed since the franchise's last title in Vince Lombardi's final season as coach. The Packers scored the most points of any team and allowed the fewest en route to finishing the 1996 regular season at 13-3. They had the league's best player in quarterback Brett Favre and arguably its best coach (Mike Holmgren) and best general manager (Ron Wolf). Just as important, the '96 Packers were a playoff-hardened team, having lost to Dallas in the NFC title game the previous year and been ousted in the second round in each of the two seasons before that.

1997

AMERICAN CONFERENCE
EASTERN DIVISION
	W	L	T	Pct.	Pts.	Opp.
New England*	10	6	0	.625	369	289
Miami†	9	7	0	.563	339	327
N.Y. Jets	9	7	0	.563	348	287
Buffalo	6	10	0	.375	255	367
Indianapolis	3	13	0	.188	313	401

CENTRAL DIVISION
	W	L	T	Pct.	Pts.	Opp.
Pittsburgh*	11	5	0	.688	372	307
Jacksonville†	11	5	0	.688	394	318
Tennessee	8	8	0	.500	333	310
Cincinnati	7	9	0	.438	355	405
Baltimore	6	9	1	.406	326	345

WESTERN DIVISION
	W	L	T	Pct.	Pts.	Opp.
Kansas City*	13	3	0	.813	375	232
Denver†	12	4	0	.750	472	287
Seattle	8	8	0	.500	365	362
Oakland	4	12	0	.250	324	419
San Diego	4	12	0	.250	266	425

*Division champion.
†Wild-card team.

NATIONAL CONFERENCE
EASTERN DIVISION
	W	L	T	Pct.	Pts.	Opp.
N.Y. Giants*	10	5	1	.656	307	265
Washington	8	7	1	.531	327	289
Philadelphia	6	9	1	.406	317	372
Dallas	6	10	0	.375	304	314
Arizona	4	12	0	.250	283	379

CENTRAL DIVISION
	W	L	T	Pct.	Pts.	Opp.
Green Bay*	13	3	0	.813	422	282
Tampa Bay†	10	6	0	.625	299	263
Detroit†	9	7	0	.563	379	306
Minnesota†	9	7	0	.563	354	359
Chicago	4	12	0	.250	263	421

WESTERN DIVISION
	W	L	T	Pct.	Pts.	Opp.
San Francisco*	13	3	0	.813	375	265
Carolina	7	9	0	.438	265	314
Atlanta	7	9	0	.438	320	361
New Orleans	6	10	0	.375	237	327
St. Louis	5	11	0	.313	299	359

PLAYOFFS
AFC wild-card playoffs
Denver 42, Jacksonville 17
New England 17, Miami 3
AFC divisional playoffs
Pittsburgh 7, New England 6
Denver 14, Kansas City 10
AFC championship
Denver 24, Pittsburgh 21
NFC wild-card playoffs
Minnesota 23, N.Y. Giants 22
Tampa Bay 20, Detroit 10
NFC divisional playoffs
San Francisco 38, Minnesota 22
Green Bay 21, Tampa Bay 7
NFC championship
Green Bay 23, San Francisco 10
Super Bowl 32
Denver 31, Green Bay 24, at San Diego.

1998

AMERICAN CONFERENCE
EASTERN DIVISION
	W	L	T	Pct.	Pts.	Opp.
N.Y. Jets*	12	4	0	.750	416	266
Buffalo†	10	6	0	.625	400	333
Miami†	10	6	0	.625	321	265
New England†	9	7	0	.563	337	329
Indianapolis	3	13	0	.188	310	444

CENTRAL DIVISION
	W	L	T	Pct.	Pts.	Opp.
Jacksonville*	11	5	0	.688	392	338
Tennessee	8	8	0	.500	330	320
Pittsburgh	7	9	0	.438	263	303
Baltimore	6	10	0	.375	269	335
Cincinnati	3	13	0	.188	268	452

WESTERN DIVISION
	W	L	T	Pct.	Pts.	Opp.
Denver*	14	2	0	.875	501	309
Oakland	8	8	0	.500	288	356
Seattle	8	8	0	.500	372	310
Kansas City	7	9	0	.438	327	363
San Diego	5	11	0	.313	241	342

*Division champion.
†Wild-card team.

NATIONAL CONFERENCE
EASTERN DIVISION
	W	L	T	Pct.	Pts.	Opp.
Dallas*	10	6	0	.625	381	275
Arizona†	9	7	0	.563	325	378
N.Y. Giants	8	8	0	.500	287	309
Washington	6	10	0	.375	319	421
Philadelphia	3	13	0	.188	161	344

CENTRAL DIVISION
	W	L	T	Pct.	Pts.	Opp.
Minnesota*	15	1	0	.938	556	296
Green Bay†	11	5	0	.688	408	319
Tampa Bay	8	8	0	.500	314	295
Detroit	5	11	0	.313	306	378
Chicago	4	12	0	.250	276	368

WESTERN DIVISION
	W	L	T	Pct.	Pts.	Opp.
Atlanta*	14	2	0	.875	442	289
San Francisco†	12	4	0	.750	479	328
New Orleans	6	10	0	.375	305	359
Carolina	4	12	0	.250	336	413
St. Louis	4	12	0	.250	285	378

PLAYOFFS
AFC wild-card playoffs
Miami 24, Buffalo 17
Jacksonville 25, New England 10
AFC divisional playoffs
Denver 38, Miami 3
New York Jets 34, Jacksonville 24
AFC championship
Denver 23, New York Jets 10
NFC wild-card playoffs
Arizona 20, Dallas 7
San Francisco 30, Green Bay 27
NFC divisional playoffs
Atlanta 20, San Francisco 18
Minnesota 41, Arizona 21
NFC championship
Atlanta 30, Minnesota 27 (OT)
Super Bowl 33
Denver 34, Atlanta 19, at Miami.

ELWAY, BRONCOS REACH THE TOP

One year after a humbling first-round playoff loss at home to Jacksonville, the Denver Broncos made sure history did not repeat, whipping the Jaguars, 42-17, in a first-round rematch at Mile High Stadium. That was impressive, but what happened next was more impressive: three straight road playoff victories and the franchise's first-ever Super Bowl title. Prior to the three-game winning streak, the Broncos had won just one other road playoff game in their 37-year history. Although running back Terrell Davis was the Broncos' star and won Super Bowl 32 MVP honors, their leader was veteran quarterback John Elway, who finally scaled the NFL mountaintop after three crushing Super Bowl defeats earlier in his career. Denver thus became the first AFC team in 14 years and only the second wild-card team to win the Super Bowl.

SUPER BOWLS

SUMMARIES

SUPER BOWL 1
JANUARY 15, 1967, AT LOS ANGELES
Kansas City (AFL) 0   10   0   0 — 10
Green Bay (NFL) 7   7   14   7 — 35
Winning coach—Vince Lombardi.
Most Valuable Player—Bart Starr.
Attendance—61,946.

SUPER BOWL 2
JANUARY 14, 1968, AT MIAMI
Green Bay (NFL) 3   13   10   7 — 33
Oakland (AFL) 0   7   0   7 — 14
Winning coach—Vince Lombardi.
Most Valuable Player—Bart Starr.
Attendance—75,546.

SUPER BOWL 3
JANUARY 12, 1969, AT MIAMI
New York (AFL) 0   7   6   3 — 16
Baltimore (NFL) 0   0   0   7 — 7
Winning coach—Weeb Ewbank.
Most Valuable Player—Joe Namath.
Attendance—75,389.

SUPER BOWL 4
JANUARY 11, 1970, AT NEW ORLEANS
Minnesota (NFL) 0   0   7   0 — 7
Kansas City (AFL) 3   13   7   0 — 23
Winning coach—Hank Stram.
Most Valuable Player—Len Dawson.
Attendance—80,562.

SUPER BOWL 5
JANUARY 17, 1971, AT MIAMI
Baltimore (AFC) 0   6   0   10 — 16
Dallas (NFC) 3   10   0   0 — 13
Winning coach—Don McCafferty.
Most Valuable Player—Chuck Howley.
Attendance—79,204.

SUPER BOWL 6
JANUARY 16, 1972, AT NEW ORLEANS
Dallas (NFC) 3   7   7   7 — 24
Miami (AFC) 0   3   0   0 — 3
Winning coach—Tom Landry.
Most Valuable Player—Roger Staubach.
Attendance—81,023.

SUPER BOWL 7
JANUARY 14, 1973, AT LOS ANGELES
Miami (AFC) 7   7   0   0 — 14
Washington (NFC) 0   0   0   7 — 7
Winning coach—Don Shula.
Most Valuable Player—Jake Scott.
Attendance—90,182.

SUPER BOWL 8
JANUARY 13, 1974, AT HOUSTON
Minnesota (NFC) 0   0   0   7 — 7
Miami (AFC) 14   3   7   0 — 24
Winning coach—Don Shula.
Most Valuable Player—Larry Csonka.
Attendance—71,882.

SUPER BOWL 9
JANUARY 12, 1975, AT NEW ORLEANS
Pittsburgh (AFC) 0   2   7   7 — 16
Minnesota (NFC) 0   0   0   6 — 6
Winning coach—Chuck Noll.
Most Valuable Player—Franco Harris.
Attendance—80,997.

SUPER BOWL 10
JANUARY 18, 1976, AT MIAMI
Dallas (NFC) 7   3   0   7 — 17
Pittsburgh (AFC) 7   0   0   14 — 21
Winning coach—Chuck Noll.
Most Valuable Player—Lynn Swann.
Attendance—80,187.

SUPER BOWL 11
JANUARY 9, 1977, AT PASADENA, CALIF.
Oakland (AFC) 0   16   3   13 — 32
Minnesota (NFC) 0   0   7   7 — 14
Winning coach—John Madden.
Most Valuable Player—Fred Biletnikoff.
Attendance—103,428.

SUPER BOWL 12
JANUARY 15, 1978, AT NEW ORLEANS
Dallas (NFC) 10   3   7   7 — 27
Denver (AFC) 0   0   10   0 — 10
Winning coach—Tom Landry.
Most Valuable Players—Harvey Martin and Randy White.
Attendance—75,804.

SUPER BOWL 13
JANUARY 21, 1979, AT MIAMI
Pittsburgh (AFC) 7   14   0   14 — 35
Dallas (NFC) 7   7   3   14 — 31
Winning coach—Chuck Noll.
Most Valuable Player—Terry Bradshaw.
Attendance—78,656.

SUPER BOWL 14
JANUARY 20, 1980, PASADENA, CALIF.
Los Angeles (NFC) 7   6   6   0 — 19
Pittsburgh (AFC) 3   7   7   14 — 31
Winning coach—Chuck Noll.
Most Valuable Player—Terry Bradshaw.
Attendance—103,985.

SUPER BOWL 15
JANUARY 25, 1981, AT NEW ORLEANS
Oakland (AFC) 14   0   10   3 — 27
Philadelphia (NFC) 0   3   0   7 — 10
Winning coach—Tom Flores.
Most Valuable Player—Jim Plunkett.
Attendance—75,500.

SUPER BOWL 16
JANUARY 24, 1982, AT PONTIAC, MICH.
San Francisco (NFC) 7   13   0   6 — 26
Cincinnati (AFC) 0   0   7   14 — 21
Winning coach—Bill Walsh.
Most Valuable Player—Joe Montana.
Attendance—81,270.

HISTORY *Super Bowls*

HISTORY Super Bowls

SUPER BOWL 17
JANUARY 30, 1983, AT PASADENA, CALIF.
Miami (AFC) 7   10   0   0 — 17
Washington (NFC) 0   10   3   14 — 27
Winning coach—Joe Gibbs.
Most Valuable Player—John Riggins.
Attendance—103,667.

SUPER BOWL 18
JANUARY 22, 1984, AT TAMPA
Washington (NFC) 0   3   6   0 — 9
Los Angeles (AFC) 7   14 14   3 — 38
Winning coach—Tom Flores.
Most Valuable Player—Marcus Allen.
Attendance—72,920.

SUPER BOWL 19
JANUARY 20, 1985, AT PALO ALTO, CALIF.
Miami (AFC) 10   6   0   0 — 16
San Francisco (NFC) 7   21 10   0 — 38
Winning coach—Bill Walsh.
Most Valuable Player—Joe Montana.
Attendance—84,059.

SUPER BOWL 20
JANUARY 26, 1986, AT NEW ORLEANS
Chicago (NFC) .... 13 10 21   2 — 46
New England (AFC) 3   0   0   7 — 10
Winning coach—Mike Ditka.
Most Valuable Player—Richard Dent.
Attendance—73,818.

SUPER BOWL 21
JANUARY 25, 1987, AT PASADENA, CALIF.
Denver (AFC) 10   0   0   10 — 20
N.Y. Giants (NFC) 7   2 17   13 — 39
Winning coach—Bill Parcells.
Most Valuable Player—Phil Simms.
Attendance—101,063.

SUPER BOWL 22
JANUARY 31, 1988, AT SAN DIEGO
Washington (NFC) 0   35   0   7 — 42
Denver (AFC) 10   0   0   0 — 10
Winning coach—Joe Gibbs.
Most Valuable Player—Doug Williams.
Attendance—73,302.

SUPER BOWL 23
JANUARY 22, 1989, AT MIAMI
Cincinnati (AFC) 0   3 10   3 — 16
San Francisco (NFC) 3   0   3   14 — 20
Winning coach—Bill Walsh.
Most Valuable Player—Jerry Rice.
Attendance—75,179.

SUPER BOWL 24
JANUARY 28, 1990, AT NEW ORLEANS
San Francisco (NFC) .... 13 14 14   14 — 55
Denver (AFC) 3   0   7   0 — 10
Winning coach—George Seifert.
Most Valuable Player—Joe Montana.
Attendance—72,919.

SUPER BOWL 25
JANUARY 27, 1991, AT TAMPA
Buffalo (AFC) 3   9   0   7 — 19
New York (NFC) 3   7   7   3 — 20
Winning coach—Bill Parcells.
Most Valuable Player—Ottis Anderson.
Attendance—73,813.

SUPER BOWL 26
JANUARY 26, 1992, AT MINNEAPOLIS
Washington (NFC) 0   17 14   6 — 37
Buffalo (AFC) 0   0 10   14 — 24
Winning coach—Joe Gibbs.
Most Valuable Player—Mark Rypien.
Attendance—63,130.

SUPER BOWL 27
JANUARY 31, 1993, AT PASADENA, CALIF.
Buffalo (AFC) 7   3   7   0 — 17
Dallas (NFC) .... 14 14   3   21 — 52
Winning coach—Jimmy Johnson.
Most Valuable Player—Troy Aikman.
Attendance—98,374.

SUPER BOWL 28
JANUARY 30, 1994, AT ATLANTA, GA.
Dallas (NFC) 6   0 14   10 — 30
Buffalo (AFC) 3   10   0   0 — 13
Winning coach—Jimmy Johnson.
Most Valuable Player—Emmitt Smith.
Attendance—72,817.

SUPER BOWL 29
JANUARY 29, 1995, AT MIAMI, FLA.
San Diego (AFC) 7   3   8   8 — 26
San Francisco (NFC) .... 14 14 14   7 — 49
Winning coach—George Seifert.
Most Valuable Player—Steve Young.
Attendance—74,107.

SUPER BOWL 30
JANUARY 28, 1996, AT TEMPE, ARIZ.
Dallas (NFC) 10   3   7   7 — 27
Pittsburgh (AFC) 0   7   0   10 — 17
Winning coach—Barry Switzer.
Most Valuable Player—Larry Brown.
Attendance—76,347.

SUPER BOWL 31
JANUARY 26, 1997, AT NEW ORLEANS
New England (AFC) 14   0   7   0 — 21
Green Bay (NFC) .... 10 17   8   0 — 35
Winning coach—Mike Holmgren.
Most Valuable Player—Desmond Howard.
Attendance—72,301.

SUPER BOWL 32
JANUARY 25, 1998, AT SAN DIEGO
Green Bay (NFC) 7   7   3   7 — 24
Denver (AFC) 7   10   7   7 — 31
Winning coach—Mike Shanahan.
Most Valuable Player—Terrell Davis.
Attendance—68,912.

SUPER BOWL 33
JANUARY 31, 1999, AT MIAMI
Denver (AFC) 7   10   0   17 — 34
Atlanta (NFC) 3   3   0   13 — 19
Winning coach—Mike Shanahan.
Most Valuable Player—John Elway.
Attendance—74,803.

SUPER BOWL 34
JANUARY 30, 2000, AT ATLANTA
St. Louis (NFC) 3   6   7   7 — 23
Tennessee (AFC) 0   0   6   10 — 16
Winning coach—Dick Vermeil.
Most Valuable Player—Kurt Warner.
Attendance—72,625.

PRO BOWLS

RESULTS

Date	Site	Winning team, score	Losing team, score	Att.
1-15-39	Wrigley Field, Los Angeles	New York Giants, 13	Pro All-Stars, 10	†20,000
1-14-40	Gilmore Stadium, Los Angeles	Green Bay Packers, 16	NFL All-Stars, 7	†18,000
12-29-40	Gilmore Stadium, Los Angeles	Chicago Bears, 28	NFL All-Stars, 14	21,624
1-4-42	Polo Grounds, New York	Chicago Bears, 35	NFL All-Stars, 24	17,725
12-27-42	Shibe Park, Philadelphia	NFL All-Stars, 17	Washington Redskins, 14	18,671
1943-50	No game was played.			
1-14-51	Los Angeles Memorial Coliseum	American Conference, 28	National Conference, 27	53,676
1-12-52	Los Angeles Memorial Coliseum	National Conference, 30	American Conference, 13	19,400
1-10-53	Los Angeles Memorial Coliseum	National Conference, 27	American Conference, 7	34,208
1-17-54	Los Angeles Memorial Coliseum	East, 20	West, 9	44,214
1-16-55	Los Angeles Memorial Coliseum	West, 26	East, 19	43,972
1-15-56	Los Angeles Memorial Coliseum	East, 31	West, 30	37,867
1-13-57	Los Angeles Memorial Coliseum	West, 19	East, 10	44,177
1-12-58	Los Angeles Memorial Coliseum	West, 26	East, 7	66,634
1-11-59	Los Angeles Memorial Coliseum	East, 28	West, 21	72,250
1-17-60	Los Angeles Memorial Coliseum	West, 38	East, 21	56,876
1-15-61	Los Angeles Memorial Coliseum	West, 35	East, 31	62,971
1-7-62*	Balboa Stadium, San Diego	West, 47	East, 27	20,973
1-14-62	Los Angeles Memorial Coliseum	West, 31	East, 30	57,409
1-13-63*	Balboa Stadium, San Diego	West, 21	East, 14	27,641
1-13-63	Los Angeles Memorial Coliseum	East, 30	West, 20	61,374
1-12-64	Los Angeles Memorial Coliseum	West, 31	East, 17	67,242
1-19-64*	Balboa Stadium, San Diego	West, 27	East, 24	20,016
1-10-65	Los Angeles Memorial Coliseum	West, 34	East, 14	60,598
1-16-65*	Jeppesen Stadium, Houston	West, 38	East, 14	15,446
1-15-66*	Rice Stadium, Houston	AFL All-Stars, 30	Buffalo Bills, 19	35,572
1-15-66	Los Angeles Memorial Coliseum	East, 36	West, 7	60,124
1-21-67*	Oakland-Alameda County Coliseum	East, 30	West, 23	18,876
1-22-67	Los Angeles Memorial Coliseum	East, 20	West, 10	15,062
1-21-68*	Gator Bowl, Jacksonville, Fla.	East, 25	West, 24	40,103
1-21-68	Los Angeles Memorial Coliseum	West, 38	East, 20	53,289
1-19-69*	Gator Bowl, Jacksonville, Fla.	West, 38	East, 25	41,058
1-19-69	Los Angeles Memorial Coliseum	West, 10	East, 7	32,050
1-17-70*	Astrodome, Houston	West, 26	East, 3	30,170
1-18-70	Los Angeles Memorial Coliseum	West, 16	East, 13	57,786
1-24-71	Los Angeles Memorial Coliseum	NFC, 27	AFC, 6	48,222
1-23-72	Los Angeles Memorial Coliseum	AFC, 26	NFC, 13	53,647
1-21-73	Texas Stadium, Irving	AFC, 33	NFC, 28	37,091
1-20-74	Arrowhead Stadium, Kansas City	AFC, 15	NFC, 13	66,918
1-20-75	Orange Bowl, Miami	NFC, 17	AFC, 10	26,484
1-26-76	Louisiana Superdome, New Orleans	NFC, 23	AFC, 20	30,546
1-17-77	Kingdome, Seattle	AFC, 24	NFC, 14	64,752
1-23-78	Tampa Stadium	NFC, 14	AFC, 13	51,337
1-29-79	Los Angeles Memorial Coliseum	NFC, 13	AFC, 7	46,281
1-27-80	Aloha Stadium, Honolulu	NFC, 37	AFC, 27	49,800
2-1-81	Aloha Stadium, Honolulu	NFC, 21	AFC, 7	50,360
1-31-82	Aloha Stadium, Honolulu	AFC, 16	NFC, 13	50,402
2-6-83	Aloha Stadium, Honolulu	NFC, 20	AFC, 19	49,883
1-29-84	Aloha Stadium, Honolulu	NFC, 45	AFC, 3	50,445
1-27-85	Aloha Stadium, Honolulu	AFC, 22	NFC, 14	50,385
2-2-86	Aloha Stadium, Honolulu	NFC, 28	AFC, 24	50,101
2-1-87	Aloha Stadium, Honolulu	AFC, 10	NFC, 6	50,101
2-7-88	Aloha Stadium, Honolulu	AFC, 15	NFC, 6	50,113
1-29-89	Aloha Stadium, Honolulu	NFC, 34	AFC, 3	50,113
2-4-90	Aloha Stadium, Honolulu	NFC, 27	AFC, 21	50,445
2-3-91	Aloha Stadium, Honolulu	AFC, 23	NFC, 21	50,345
2-2-92	Aloha Stadium, Honolulu	NFC, 21	AFC, 15	50,209
2-7-93	Aloha Stadium, Honolulu	AFC, 23 (OT)	NFC, 20	50,007
2-6-94	Aloha Stadium, Honolulu	NFC, 17	AFC, 3	50,026
2-5-95	Aloha Stadium, Honolulu	AFC, 41	NFC, 13	49,121
2-4-96	Aloha Stadium, Honolulu	NFC, 20	AFC, 13	50,034
2-2-97	Aloha Stadium, Honolulu	AFC, 26 (OT)	NFC, 23	50,031
2-1-98	Aloha Stadium, Honolulu	AFC, 29	NFC, 24	49,995
2-7-99	Aloha Stadium, Honolulu	AFC, 23	NFC, 10	50,075
2-6-00	Aloha Stadium, Honolulu	NFC, 51	AFC, 31	50,112

*AFL game.
†Estimated figure.

OUTSTANDING PLAYER AWARDS

Year—Name, team
1951— Otto Graham, Cleveland Browns
1952— Dan Towler, Los Angeles Rams
1953— Dan Doll, Detroit Lions
1954— Chuck Bednarik, Philadelphia Eagles
1955— Billy Wilson, San Francisco 49ers
1956— Ollie Matson, Chicago Cardinals
1957— Bert Rechichar, Baltimore Colts (back)
　　　Ernie Stautner, Pittsburgh Steelers (lineman)
1958— Hugh McElhenny, San Francisco 49ers (back)
　　　Gene Brito, Washington Redskins (lineman)
1959— Frank Gifford, New York Giants (back)
　　　Doug Atkins, Chicago Bears (lineman)
1960— Johnny Unitas, Baltimore Colts (back)
　　　Gene Lipscomb, Baltimore Colts (lineman)
1961— Johnny Unitas, Baltimore Colts (back)
　　　Sam Huff, New York Giants (lineman)
1962— Cotton Davidson, Dallas Texans*
　　　Jim Brown, Cleveland Browns (back)
　　　Henry Jordan, Green Bay Packers (lineman)
1963— Curtis McClinton, Dallas Texans* (offense)
　　　Earl Faison, San Diego Chargers* (defense)
　　　Jim Brown, Cleveland Browns (back)
　　　Gene Lipscomb, Pittsburgh Steelers (lineman)
1964— Keith Lincoln, San Diego Chargers* (offense)
　　　Archie Matsos, Oakland Raiders* (defense)
　　　Johnny Unitas, Baltimore Colts (back)
　　　Gino Marchetti, Baltimore Colts (lineman)
1965— Keith Lincoln, San Diego Chargers* (offense)
　　　Willie Brown, Denver Broncos* (defense)
　　　Fran Tarkenton, Minnesota Vikings (back)
　　　Terry Barr, Detroit Lions (lineman)
1966— Joe Namath, New York Jets* (offense)
　　　Frank Buncom, San Diego Chargers* (defense)
　　　Jim Brown, Cleveland Browns (back)
　　　Dale Meinert, St. Louis Cardinals (lineman)
1967— Babe Parilli, Boston Patriots* (offense)
　　　Verlon Biggs, New York Jets* (defense)
　　　Gale Sayers, Chicago Bears (back)
　　　Floyd Peters, Philadelphia Eagles (lineman)
1968— Joe Namath, New York Jets* (offense)
　　　Don Maynard, New York Jets* (offense)
　　　Speedy Duncan, San Diego Chargers (defense)
　　　Gale Sayers, Chicago Bears (back)
　　　Dave Robinson, Green Bay Packers (lineman)

Year—Name, team
1969— Len Dawson, Kansas City Chiefs* (offense)
　　　George Webster, Houston* (defense)
　　　Roman Gabriel, Los Angeles Rams (back)
　　　Merlin Olsen, Los Angeles Rams (lineman)
1970— John Hadl, San Diego Chargers*
　　　Gale Sayers, Chicago Bears (back)
　　　George Andrie, Dallas Cowboys (lineman)
1971— Mel Renfro, Dallas Cowboys (back)
　　　Fred Carr, Green Bay Packers (lineman)
1972— Jan Stenerud, Kansas City Chiefs (offense)
　　　Willie Lanier, Kansas City Chiefs (defense)
1973— O.J. Simpson, Buffalo Bills
1974— Garo Yepremian, Miami Dolphins
1975— James Harris, Los Angeles Rams
1976— Billy Johnson, Houston Oilers
1977— Mel Blount, Pittsburgh Steelers
1978— Walter Payton, Chicago Bears
1979— Ahmad Rashad, Minnesota Vikings
1980— Chuck Muncie, New Orleans Saints
1981— Eddie Murray, Detroit Lions
1982— Kellen Winslow, San Diego Chargers
　　　Lee Roy Selmon, Tampa Bay Buccaneers
1983— Dan Fouts, San Diego Chargers
　　　John Jefferson, Green Bay Packers
1984— Joe Theismann, Washington Redskins
1985— Mark Gastineau, New York Jets
1986— Phil Simms, New York Giants
1987— Reggie White, Philadelphia Eagles
1988— Bruce Smith, Buffalo Bills
1989— Randall Cunningham, Philadelphia Eagles
1990— Jerry Gray, Los Angeles Rams
1991— Jim Kelly, Buffalo Bills
1992— Michael Irvin, Dallas Cowboys
1993— Steve Tasker, Buffalo Bills
1994— Andre Rison, Atlanta Falcons
1995— Marshall Faulk, Indianapolis Colts
1996— Jerry Rice, San Francisco 49ers
1997— Mark Brunell, Jacksonville Jaguars
1998— Warren Moon, Seattle Seahawks
1999— Ty Law, New England Patriots
　　　Keyshawn Johnson, New York Jets
2000— Randy Moss, Minnesota Vikings
*AFL game.

RECORDS

INDIVIDUAL SERVICE
PLAYERS

Most years played
26—George Blanda, Chicago Bears, Baltimore, Houston, Oakland, 1949 through 1975, except 1959.

Most years with one club
20—Jackie Slater, L.A. Rams, St. Louis Rams, 1976 through 1995.

Most games played, career
340—George Blanda, Chicago Bears, Baltimore, Houston, Oakland, 1949 through 1975, except 1959.

Most consecutive games played, career
282—Jim Marshall, Cleveland, Minnesota, September 25, 1960 through December 16, 1979.

COACHES

Most years as head coach
40—George Halas, Chicago Bears, 1920 through 1929, 1933 through 1942, 1946 through 1955 and 1958 through 1967.

Most games won as head coach
328—Don Shula, Baltimore, 1963 through 1969; Miami, 1970 through 1995.

Most games lost as head coach
162—Tom Landry, Dallas, 1960 through 1988.

INDIVIDUAL OFFENSE
RUSHING
YARDS

Most yards, career
16,726—Walter Payton, Chicago, 1975 through 1987.

Most yards, season
2,105—Eric Dickerson, Los Angeles Rams, 1984.

Most years leading league in yards
8—Jim Brown, Cleveland, 1957 through 1965, except 1962.

Most consecutive years leading league in yards
5—Jim Brown, Cleveland, 1957 through 1961.

Most years with 1,000 or more yards
10—Walter Payton, Chicago, 1976 through 1986, except 1982.
Barry Sanders, Detroit, 1989 through 1998.

Most consecutive years with 1,000 or more yards
10—Barry Sanders, Detroit, 1989 through 1998.

Most yards, game
275—Walter Payton, Chicago vs. Minnesota, November 20, 1977.

Most games with 200 or more yards, career
6—O.J. Simpson, Buffalo, San Francisco, 1969 through 1979.

Most games with 200 or more yards, season
4—Earl Campbell, Houston, 1980.

Most consecutive games with 200 or more yards, season
2—O.J. Simpson, Buffalo, December 9 through 16, 1973.
O.J. Simpson, Buffalo, November 25 through December 5, 1976.
Earl Campbell, Houston, October 19 through 26, 1980.

Most games with 100 or more yards, career
77—Walter Payton, Chicago, 1975 through 1987.

Most games with 100 or more yards, season
14—Barry Sanders, Detroit, 1997.

Most consecutive games with 100 or more yards, career
14—Barry Sanders, Detroit, September 14 through December 21, 1997.

Most consecutive games with 100 or more yards, season
14—Barry Sanders, Detroit, September 14 through December 21, 1997.

Longest run from scrimmage
99 yards—Tony Dorsett, Dallas at Minnesota, January 3, 1983 (touchdown).

ATTEMPTS

Most attempts, career
3,838—Walter Payton, Chicago, 1975 through 1987.

Most attempts, season
410—Jamal Anderson, Atlanta, 1998.

Most attempts, game
45—Jamie Morris, Washington at Cincinnati, December 17, 1988, overtime.
43—Butch Woolfolk, New York Giants at Philadelphia, November 20, 1983.
James Wilder, Tampa Bay vs. Green Bay, September 30, 1984, overtime.

Most years leading league in attempts
6—Jim Brown, Cleveland, 1958 through 1965, except 1960 and 1962.

Most consecutive years leading league in attempts
4—Steve Van Buren, Philadelphia, 1947 through 1950.
Walter Payton, Chicago, 1976 through 1979.

TOUCHDOWNS

Most touchdowns, career
136—Emmitt Smith, Dallas, 1990 through 1999.

Most touchdowns, season
25—Emmitt Smith, Dallas, 1995.

Most years leading league in touchdowns
5—Jim Brown, Cleveland, 1957 through 1959, 1963, 1965.

Most consecutive years leading league in touchdowns
3—Steve Van Buren, Philadelphia, 1947 through 1949.
Jim Brown, Cleveland, 1957 through 1959.
Abner Haynes, Dallas Texans, 1960 through 1962.
Cookie Gilchrist, Buffalo, 1962 through 1964.
Leroy Kelly, Cleveland, 1966 through 1968.

Most touchdowns, game
6—Ernie Nevers, Chicago Cardinals vs. Chicago Bears, November 28, 1929.

Most consecutive games with one or more touchdowns, career
13—John Riggins, Washington, December 26, 1982 through November 27, 1983.
George Rogers, Washington, November 24, 1985 through November 2, 1986.

Most consecutive games with one or more touchdowns, season
12—John Riggins, Washington, September 5 through November 27, 1983.

PASSING
PASSER RATING

Highest rating, career (1,500 or more attempts)
96.8—Steve Young, Tampa Bay, San Francisco, 1985 through 1999.

Highest rating, season (qualifiers)
112.8—Steve Young, San Francisco, 1994.

ATTEMPTS

Most attempts, career
8,358—Dan Marino, Miami, 1983 through 1999.

Most attempts, season
691—Drew Bledsoe, New England, 1994.

Most years leading league in attempts
5—Dan Marino, Miami, 1984, 1986, 1988, 1992, 1997.

Most consecutive years leading league in attempts
3—Johnny Unitas, Baltimore, 1959 through 1961.
George Blanda, Houston, 1963 through 1965.

Most attempts, game
70—Drew Bledsoe, New England vs. Minnesota, November 13, 1994 (overtime).
68—George Blanda, Houston vs. Buffalo, November 1, 1964.

COMPLETIONS

Most completions, career
4,967—Dan Marino, Miami, 1983 through 1999.

Most completions, season
404—Warren Moon, Houston, 1991.

Most years leading league in completions
6—Dan Marino, Miami, 1984, 1985, 1986, 1988, 1992, 1997.

Most consecutive years leading league in completions
3—George Blanda, Houston, 1963 through 1965.
Dan Marino, Miami, 1984 through 1986.

Most completions, game
45—Drew Bledsoe, New England vs. Minnesota, November 13, 1994 (overtime).
42—Richard Todd, New York Jets vs. San Francisco, September 21, 1980.

YARDS

Most yards, career
61,361—Dan Marino, Miami, 1983 through 1999.

Most yards, season
5,084—Dan Marino, Miami, 1984.

Most years leading league in yards
5—Sonny Jurgensen, Philadelphia, Washington, 1961, 1962, 1966, 1967, 1969.
Dan Marino, Miami, 1984 through 1986, 1988, 1992.

Most consecutive years leading league in yards
4—Dan Fouts, San Diego, 1979 through 1982.

Most years with 3,000 or more yards
13—Dan Marino, Miami, 1984 through 1998, except 1993 and 1996.

Most yards, game
554—Norm Van Brocklin, Los Angeles at New York Yanks, September 28, 1951.

Most games with 400 or more yards, career
13—Dan Marino, Miami, 1983 through 1996.

Most games with 400 or more yards, season
4—Dan Marino, Miami, 1984.

Most consecutive games with 400 or more yards, season
2—Dan Fouts, San Diego, December 11 through 20, 1982.
Dan Marino, Miami, December 2 through 9, 1984.
Phil Simms, New York Giants, October 6 through 13, 1985.

Most games with 300 or more yards, career
63—Dan Marino, Miami, 1983 through 1999.

Most games with 300 or more yards, season
9—Dan Marino, Miami, 1984.
Warren Moon, Houston, 1990.
Kurt Warner, St. Louis, 1999.

Most consecutive games with 300 or more yards, season
6—Steve Young, San Francisco, September 6 through October 18, 1998.

Longest pass completion
99 yards—Frank Filchock, Washington vs. Pittsburgh, October 15, 1939 (touchdown).
George Izo, Washington at Cleveland, September 15, 1963 (touchdown).
Karl Sweetan, Detroit at Baltimore, October 16, 1966 (touchdown).
Sonny Jurgensen, Washington at Chicago, September 15, 1968 (touchdown).
Jim Plunkett, Los Angeles Raiders vs. Washington, October 2, 1983 (touchdown).
Ron Jaworski, Philadelphia vs. Atlanta, November 10, 1985 (touchdown).
Stan Humphries, San Diego at Seattle, September 18, 1994 (touchdown).
Brett Favre, Green Bay at Chicago, September 11, 1995 (touchdown).

YARDS PER ATTEMPT

Most yards per attempt, career (1,500 or more attempts)
8.63—Otto Graham, Cleveland, 1950 through 1955 (13,499 yards, 1,565 attempts).

Most yards per attempt, season (qualifiers)
11.17—Tommy O'Connell, Cleveland, 1957 (1,229 yards, 110 attempts).

Most years leading league in yards per attempt
7—Sid Luckman, Chicago Bears, 1939 through 1943, 1946, 1947.

Most consecutive years leading league in yards per attempt
5—Sid Luckman, Chicago Bears, 1939 through 1943.

Most yards per attempt, game (20 or more attempts)
18.58—Sammy Baugh, Washington vs. Boston, October 31, 1948 (446 yards, 24 attempts).

TOUCHDOWNS

Most touchdowns, career
420—Dan Marino, Miami, 1983 through 1999.

Most touchdowns, season
48—Dan Marino, Miami, 1984.

Most years leading league in touchdowns
4—Johnny Unitas, Baltimore, 1957 through 1960.
Len Dawson, Dallas Texans, Kansas City, 1962 through 1966, except 1964.
Steve Young, San Francisco, 1992 through 1994, 1998.

Most consecutive years leading league in touchdowns
4—Johnny Unitas, Baltimore, 1957 through 1960.

Most touchdowns, game
7—Sid Luckman, Chicago Bears at New York Giants, November 14, 1943.
Adrian Burk, Philadelphia at Washington, October 17, 1954.
George Blanda, Houston vs. New York Titans, November 19, 1961.
Y.A. Tittle, New York Giants vs. Washington, October 28, 1962.
Joe Kapp, Minnesota vs. Baltimore, September 28, 1969.

INTERCEPTIONS

Most interceptions, career
277—George Blanda, Chicago Bears, Baltimore, Houston, Oakland, 1949 through 1975, except 1959.

Most interceptions, season
42—George Blanda, Houston, 1962.

Most interceptions, game
8—Jim Hardy, Chicago Cardinals vs. Philadelphia, September 24, 1950.

Most attempts with no interceptions, game
70—Drew Bledsoe, New England vs. Minnesota, November 13, 1994 (overtime).
63—Rich Gannon, Minnesota at New England, October 20, 1991 (overtime).
60—Davey O'Brien, Philadelphia at Washington, December 1, 1940.

INTERCEPTION PERCENTAGE

Lowest interception percentage, career (1,500 or more attempts)
2.03—Neil O'Donnell, Pittsburgh, N.Y. Jets, Cincinnati, Tennessee, 1991 through 1999 (3,057 attempts, 62 interceptions).

Lowest interception percentage, season (qualifiers)
0.66—Joe Ferguson, Buffalo, 1976 (151 attempts, one interception).

Most years leading league in lowest interception percentage
5—Sammy Baugh, Washington, 1940, 1942, 1944, 1945, 1947.

SACKS (SINCE 1963)

Most times sacked, career
516—John Elway, Denver, 1983 through 1998.

Most times sacked, season
72—Randall Cunningham, Philadelphia, 1986.

Most times sacked, game
12—Bert Jones, Baltimore vs. St. Louis, October 26, 1980.
Warren Moon, Houston vs. Dallas, September 29, 1985.

RECEIVING

RECEPTIONS

Most receptions, career
1,206—Jerry Rice, San Francisco, 1985 through 1999.

Most receptions, season
123—Herman Moore, Detroit, 1995.

Most years leading league in receptions
8—Don Hutson, Green Bay, 1936 through 1945, except 1938 and 1940.

Most consecutive years leading league in receptions
5—Don Hutson, Green Bay, 1941 through 1945.

Most receptions, game
18—Tom Fears, Los Angeles vs. Green Bay, December 3, 1950.

Most consecutive games with one or more receptions
209—Jerry Rice, San Francisco, December 9, 1985 through January 3, 2000 (current).

YARDS

Most yards, career
18,442—Jerry Rice, San Francisco, 1985 through 1999.

Most yards, season
1,848—Jerry Rice, San Francisco, 1995.

Most years leading league in yards
7—Don Hutson, Green Bay, 1936 through 1944, except 1937 and 1940.

Most consecutive years leading league in yards
4—Don Hutson, Green Bay, 1941 through 1944.

Most years with 1,000 or more yards
12—Jerry Rice, San Francisco, 1986 through 1998, except 1997.

Most yards, game
336—Willie Anderson, Los Angeles Rams at New Orleans, November 26, 1989 (overtime).
309—Stephone Paige, Kansas City vs. San Diego, December 22, 1985.

Most games with 200 or more yards, career
5—Lance Alworth, San Diego, Dallas, 1962 through 1972.

Most games with 200 or more yards, season
3—Charley Hennigan, Houston, 1961.

Most games with 100 or more yards, career
66—Jerry Rice, San Francisco, 1985 through 1999.

Most games with 100 or more yards, season
11—Michael Irvin, Dallas, 1995.

Most consecutive games with 100 or more yards, season
7—Charley Hennigan, Houston, 1961.
Bill Groman, Houston, 1961.
Michael Irvin, Dallas, 1995.

Longest reception
99 yards—Andy Farkas, Washington vs. Pittsburgh, October 15, 1939 (touchdown).
Bobby Mitchell, Washington at Cleveland, September 15, 1963 (touchdown).
Pat Studstill, Detroit at Baltimore, October 16, 1966 (touchdown).
Gerry Allen, Washington at Chicago, September 15, 1968 (touchdown).
Cliff Branch, Los Angeles Raiders vs. Washington, October 2, 1983 (touchdown).
Mike Quick, Philadelphia vs. Atlanta, November 10, 1985 (touchdown).
Tony Martin, San Diego at Seattle, September 18, 1994 (touchdown).
Robert Brooks, Green Bay at Chicago, September 11, 1995 (touchdown).

TOUCHDOWNS

Most touchdowns, career
169—Jerry Rice, San Francisco, 1985 through 1999.

Most touchdowns, season
22—Jerry Rice, San Francisco, 1987.

Most years leading league in touchdowns
9—Don Hutson, Green Bay, 1935 through 1944, except 1939.

Most consecutive years leading league in touchdowns
5—Don Hutson, Green Bay, 1940 through 1944.

Most touchdowns, game
5—Bob Shaw, Chicago Cardinals vs. Baltimore, October 2, 1950.
Kellen Winslow, San Diego at Oakland, November 22, 1981.
Jerry Rice, San Francisco at Atlanta, October 14, 1990.

Most consecutive games with one or more touchdowns
13—Jerry Rice, San Francisco, December 19, 1986 through December 27, 1987.

COMBINED NET YARDS

(Rushing, receiving, interception returns, punt returns, kickoff returns and fumble returns)

ATTEMPTS

Most attempts, career
4,368—Walter Payton, Chicago, 1975 through 1987.

Most attempts, season
496—James Wilder, Tampa Bay, 1984.

Most attempts, game
48—James Wilder, Tampa Bay at Pittsburgh, October 30, 1983.

YARDS

Most yards, career
21,803—Walter Payton, Chicago, 1975 through 1987.

Most yards, season
2,535—Lionel James, San Diego, 1985.

Most years leading league in yards
5—Jim Brown, Cleveland, 1958 through 1961, 1964.

Most consecutive years leading league in yards
4—Jim Brown, Cleveland, 1958 through 1961.

Most yards, game
404—Glyn Milburn, Denver vs. Seattle, December 10, 1995.

HISTORY Records

SCORING

POINTS

Most points, career
2,002—George Blanda, Chicago Bears, Baltimore, Houston, Oakland, 1949 through 1975, except 1959.

Most points, season
176—Paul Hornung, Green Bay, 1960.

Most years leading league in points
5—Don Hutson, Green Bay, 1940 through 1944.
Gino Cappelletti, Boston, 1961 through 1966, except 1962.

Most consecutive years leading league in points
5—Don Hutson, Green Bay, 1940 through 1944.

Most years with 100 or more points
12—Morten Andersen, New Orleans, Atlanta, 1985 through 1998, except 1990 and 1996.

Most points, game
40—Ernie Nevers, Chicago Cardinals vs. Chicago Bears, November 28, 1929.

Most consecutive games with one or more points
254—Morten Andersen, New Orleans, Atlanta, December 11, 1983 through January 3, 2000 (current).

TOUCHDOWNS

Most touchdowns, career
180—Jerry Rice, San Francisco, 1985 through 1999.

Most touchdowns, season
25—Emmitt Smith, Dallas, 1995.

Most years leading league in touchdowns
8—Don Hutson, Green Bay, 1935 through 1938 and 1941 through 1944.

Most consecutive years leading league in touchdowns
4—Don Hutson, Green Bay, 1935 through 1938 and 1941 through 1944.

Most touchdowns, game
6—Ernie Nevers, Chicago Cardinals vs. Chicago Bears, November 28, 1929.
Dub Jones, Cleveland vs. Chicago Bears, November 25, 1951.
Gale Sayers, Chicago vs. San Francisco, December 12, 1965.

Most consecutive games with one or more touchdowns
18—Lenny Moore, Baltimore, October 27, 1963 through September 19, 1965.

EXTRA POINTS

Most extra points attempted, career
959—George Blanda, Chicago Bears, Baltimore, Houston, Oakland, 1949 through 1975, except 1959.

Most extra points made, career
943—George Blanda, Chicago Bears, Baltimore, Houston, Oakland, 1949 through 1975, except 1959.

Most extra points attempted, season
70—Uwe von Schamann, Miami, 1984.

Most extra points made, season
66—Uwe von Schamann, Miami, 1984.

Most extra points attempted, game
10—Charlie Gogolak, Washington vs. New York Giants, November 27, 1966.

Most extra points made, game
9—Pat Harder, Chicago Cardinals at New York Giants, October 17, 1948.
Bob Waterfield, Los Angeles vs. Baltimore, October 22, 1950.
Charlie Gogolak, Washington vs. New York Giants, November 27, 1966.

FIELD GOALS AND FIELD-GOAL PERCENTAGE

Most field goals attempted, career
637—George Blanda, Chicago Bears, Baltimore, Houston, Oakland, 1949 through 1975, except 1959.

Most field goals made, career
439—Gary Anderson, Pittsburgh, Philadelphia, San Francisco, Minnesota, 1982 through 1999.

Most field goals attempted, season
49—Bruce Gossett, Los Angeles, 1966.
Curt Knight, Washington, 1971.

Most field goals made, season
39—Olindo Mare, Miami, 1999.

Most field goals attempted, game
9—Jim Bakken, St. Louis at Pittsburgh, September 24, 1967.

Most field goals made, game
7—Jim Bakken, St. Louis at Pittsburgh, September 24, 1967.
Rich Karlis, Minnesota vs. Los Angeles Rams, November 5, 1989 (overtime).
Chris Boniol, Dallas vs. Green Bay, November 18, 1996.

Most field goals made, one quarter
4—Garo Yepremian, Detroit vs. Minnesota, November 13, 1966, second quarter.
Curt Knight, Washington at New York Giants, November 15, 1970, second quarter.
Roger Ruzek, Dallas vs. New York Giants, November 2, 1987, fourth quarter.

Most consecutive games with one or more field goals made, career
31—Fred Cox, Minnesota, November 17, 1968 through December 5, 1970.

Most consecutive field goals made, career
40—Gary Anderson, San Francisco, Minnesota, December 15, 1997 through December 26, 1998.

Most field goals of 50 or more yards, career
35—Morten Andersen, New Orleans, Atlanta, 1982 through 1999.

Most field goals of 50 or more yards, season
8—Morten Andersen, Atlanta, 1995.

Most field goals of 50 or more yards, game
3—Morten Andersen, Atlanta vs. New Orleans, December 10, 1995.

Longest field goal made
63 yards—Tom Dempsey, New Orleans vs. Detroit, November 8, 1970.
Jason Elam, Denver vs. Jacksonville, October 25, 1998.

Highest field-goal percentage, career (100 or more made)
81.67—John Carney, Tampa Bay, L.A. Rams, San Diego, 1988 through 1999 (300 attempted, 245 made).

Highest field-goal percentage, season (qualifiers)
100.00—Tony Zendejas, Los Angeles Rams, 1991 (17 made).
Gary Anderson, Minnesota, 1998 (35 made).

SAFETIES

Most safeties, career
4—Ted Hendricks, Baltimore, Green Bay, Oakland, Los Angeles Raiders, 1969 through 1983.
Doug English, Detroit, 1975 through 1985, except 1980.

Most safeties, season
2—Held by many players.

Most safeties, game
2—Fred Dryer, Los Angeles vs. Green Bay, October 21, 1973.

PUNTING

Most punts, career
1,154—Dave Jennings, New York Giants, New York Jets, 1974 through 1987.

Most punts, season
114—Bob Parsons, Chicago, 1981.

Most seasons leading league in punting
4—Sammy Baugh, Washington, 1940 through 1943.
  Jerrel Wilson, Kansas City, 1965, 1968, 1972, 1973.

Most consecutive seasons leading league in punting
4—Sammy Baugh, Washington, 1940 through 1943.

Most punts, game
16— Leo Araguz, Oakland vs. San Diego, October 11, 1998.

Longest punt
98 yards—Steve O'Neal, New York Jets at Denver, September 21, 1969.

FUMBLES

Most fumbles, career
160—Warren Moon, Houston, Minnesota, Seattle, Kansas City, 1984 through 1999.

Most fumbles, season
21—Tony Banks, St. Louis, 1996.

Most fumbles, game
7—Len Dawson, Kansas City vs. San Diego, November 15, 1964.

PUNT RETURNS

Most punt returns, career
349—Dave Meggett, N.Y. Giants, New England, N.Y. Jets, 1989 through 1998.

Most punt returns, season
70—Danny Reece, Tampa Bay, 1979.

Most years leading league in punt returns
3—Les "Speedy" Duncan, San Diego, Washington, 1965, 1966, 1971.
  Rick Upchurch, Denver, 1976, 1978, 1982.

Most punt returns, game
11—Eddie Brown, Washington at Tampa Bay, October 9, 1977.

YARDS

Most yards, career
3,708—Dave Meggett, N.Y. Giants, New England, N.Y. Jets, 1989 through 1998.

Most yards, season
875—Desmond Howard, Green Bay, 1996.

Most yards, game
207—LeRoy Irvin, Los Angeles at Atlanta, October 11, 1981.

Longest punt return
103 yards—Robert Bailey, Los Angeles Rams at New Orleans, October 23, 1994 (touchdown).

FAIR CATCHES

Most fair catches, career
151—Brian Mitchell, Washington, 1990 through 1999.

Most fair catches, season
27—Leo Lewis, Minnesota, 1989.

Most fair catches, game
7—Lem Barney, Detroit vs. Chicago, November 21, 1976.
  Bobby Morse, Philadelphia vs. Buffalo, December 27, 1987.

TOUCHDOWNS

Most touchdowns, career
9—Eric Metcalf, Cleveland, Atlanta, San Diego, Arizona, Carolina, 1989 through 1999.

Most touchdowns, season
4—Jack Christiansen, Detroit, 1951.
  Rick Upchurch, Denver, 1976.

Most touchdowns, game
2—Jack Christiansen, Detroit vs. Los Angeles, October 14, 1951.
  Jack Christiansen, Detroit vs. Green Bay, November 22, 1951.
  Dick Christy, New York Titans vs. Denver, September 24, 1961.
  Rick Upchurch, Denver vs. Cleveland, September 26, 1976.
  LeRoy Irvin, Los Angeles at Atlanta, October 11, 1981.
  Vai Sikahema, St. Louis vs. Tampa Bay, December 21, 1986.
  Todd Kinchen, Los Angeles Rams vs. Atlanta, December 27, 1992.
  Eric Metcalf, San Diego at Cincinnati, November 2, 1997.
  Darrien Gordon, Denver vs. Carolina, November 9, 1997.
  Jermaine Lewis, Baltimore vs. Seattle, December 7, 1997.

KICKOFF RETURNS

Most kickoff returns, career
421—Mel Gray, New Orleans, Detroit, Houston, Tennessee, Philadelphia, 1986 through 1997.
  Brian Mitchell, Washington, 1990 through 1999.

Most kickoff returns, season
70—Tyrone Hughes, New Orleans, 1996.

Most years leading league in kickoff returns
3—Abe Woodson, San Francisco, 1959, 1962, 1963.
  Tyrone Hughes, New Orleans, 1994 through 1996.

Most kickoff returns, game
10—Desmond Howard, Oakland at Seattle, October 26, 1997.

YARDS

Most yards, career
10,250—Mel Gray, New Orleans, Detroit, Houston, Tennessee, Philadelphia, 1986 through 1997.

Most yards, season
1,791—Tyrone Hughes, New Orleans, 1996.

Most years leading league in yards
3—Bruce Harper, New York Jets, 1977 through 1979.
  Tyrone Hughes, New Orleans, 1994 through 1996.

Most yards, game
304—Tyrone Hughes, New Orleans vs. Los Angeles Rams, October 23, 1994.

Longest kickoff return
106 yards—Al Carmichael, Green Bay vs. Chicago Bears, October 7, 1956 (touchdown).
  Noland Smith, Kansas City at Denver, December 17, 1967.
  Roy Green, St. Louis at Dallas, October 21, 1979.

TOUCHDOWNS

Most touchdowns, career
6—Ollie Matson, Chicago Cardinals, Los Angeles Rams, Detroit, Philadelphia, 1952 through 1964, except 1953.
  Gale Sayers, Chicago, 1965 through 1971.
  Travis Williams, Green Bay, Los Angeles, 1967 through 1971.
  Mel Gray, New Orleans, Detroit, Houston, Tennessee, Philadelphia, 1986 through 1997.

Most touchdowns, season
4—Travis Williams, Green Bay, 1967.
  Cecil Turner, Chicago, 1970.

Most touchdowns, game
2—Timmy Brown, Philadelphia vs. Dallas, November 6, 1966.
  Travis Williams, Green Bay vs. Cleveland, November 12, 1967.
  Ron Brown, Los Angeles Rams vs. Green Bay, November 24, 1985.
  Tyrone Hughes, New Orleans vs. Los Angeles Rams, October 23, 1994.

COMBINED KICK RETURNS
(KICKOFFS AND PUNTS)

Most kick returns, career
738—Brian Mitchell, Washington, 1990 through 1999.

Most kick returns, season
102—Glyn Milburn, Detroit, 1997.

Most kick returns, game
13—Stump Mitchell, St. Louis at Atlanta, October 18, 1981.
Ron Harris, New England at Pittsburgh, December 5, 1993.

YARDS

Most yards, career
13,062—Brian Mitchell, Washington, 1990 through 1999.

Most yards, season
1,943—Tyrone Hughes, New Orleans, 1996.

Most yards, game
347—Tyrone Hughes, New Orleans vs. Los Angeles Rams, October 23, 1994.

TOUCHDOWNS

Most touchdowns, career
11—Eric Metcalf, Cleveland, Atlanta, San Diego, Arizona, Carolina, 1989 through 1999.

Most touchdowns, season
4—Jack Christiansen, Detroit, 1951.
Emlen Tunnell, New York Giants, 1951.
Gale Sayers, Chicago, 1967.
Travis Williams, Green Bay, 1967.
Cecil Turner, Chicago, 1970.
Billy "White Shoes" Johnson, Houston, 1975.
Rick Upchurch, Denver, 1976.

Most touchdowns, game
2—Held by many players.

INDIVIDUAL DEFENSE
INTERCEPTIONS

Most interceptions, career
81—Paul Krause, Washington, Minnesota, 1964 through 1979.

Most interceptions, season
14—Dick "Night Train" Lane, Los Angeles, 1952.

Most interceptions, game
4—Held by many players.

Most consecutive games with one or more interceptions
8—Tom Morrow, Oakland, 1962 through 1963.

Most yards on interceptions, career
1,282—Emlen Tunnell, New York Giants, Green Bay, 1948 through 1961.

Most yards on interceptions, season
349—Charlie McNeil, San Diego, 1961.

Most yards on interceptions, game
177—Charlie McNeil, San Diego vs. Houston, September 24, 1961.

Longest interception return
103—Vencie Glenn, San Diego vs. Denver, November 29, 1987.
Louis Oliver, Miami vs. Buffalo, October 4, 1992.
(Note: James Willis, 14 yards, and Troy Vincent, 90 yards, combined for a 104-yard interception return for Philadelphia vs. Dallas, November 3, 1996.)

TOUCHDOWNS

Most touchdowns, career
9—Ken Houston, Houston, Washington, 1967 through 1980.
Rod Woodson, Pittsburgh, San Francisco, Baltimore, 1987 through 1999.

Most touchdowns, season
4—Ken Houston, Houston, 1971.
Jim Kearney, Kansas City, 1972.
Eric Allen, Philadelphia, 1993.

Most touchdowns, game
2—Held by many players.

FUMBLES RECOVERED

Most fumbles recovered (own and opponents'), career
55—Warren Moon, Houston, Minnesota, Seattle, 1984 through 1998.

Most fumbles recovered (own), career
55—Warren Moon, Houston, Minnesota, Seattle, 1984 through 1998.

Most opponents' fumbles recovered, career
29—Jim Marshall, Cleveland, Minnesota, 1960 through 1979.

Most fumbles recovered (own and opponents'), season
9—Don Hultz, Minnesota, 1963.
Dave Krieg, Seattle, 1989.

Most fumbles recovered (own), season
9—Dave Krieg, Seattle, 1989.

Most opponents' fumbles recovered, season
9—Don Hultz, Minnesota, 1963.

Most fumbles recovered (own and opponents'), game
4—Otto Graham, Cleveland at New York Giants, October 25, 1953.
Sam Etcheverry, St. Louis at New York Giants, September 17, 1961.
Roman Gabriel, Los Angeles at San Francisco, October 12, 1969.
Joe Ferguson, Buffalo vs. Miami, September 18, 1977.
Randall Cunningham, Philadelphia at Los Angeles Raiders, November 30, 1986 (overtime).

Most fumbles recovered (own), game
4—Otto Graham, Cleveland at New York Giants, October 25, 1953.
Sam Etcheverry, St. Louis at New York Giants, September 17, 1961.
Roman Gabriel, Los Angeles at San Francisco, October 12, 1969.
Joe Ferguson, Buffalo vs. Miami, September 18, 1977.
Randall Cunningham, Philadelphia at Los Angeles Raiders, November 30, 1986 (overtime).

Most opponents' fumbles recovered, game
3—Held by many players.

Longest fumble return
104 yards—Jack Tatum, Oakland at Green Bay, September 24, 1972 (touchdown).

TOUCHDOWNS

Most touchdowns (own and opponents' recovered), career
5—Jessie Tuggle, Atlanta, 1987 through 1998.

Most touchdowns (own recovered), career
2—Held by many players.

Most touchdowns (opponents' recovered), career
4—Jessie Tuggle, Atlanta, 1987 through 1992.

Most touchdowns, season
2—Held by many players.

Most touchdowns, game
2—Fred "Dippy" Evans, Chicago Bears vs. Washington, November 28, 1948.

SACKS (SINCE 1982)

Most sacks, career
192.5—Reggie White, Philadelphia, Green Bay, 1985 through 1998.

– 336 –

Most sacks, season
22—Mark Gastineau, New York Jets, 1984.
Most sacks, game
7—Derrick Thomas, Kansas City vs. Seattle, November 11, 1990.

TEAM MISCELLANEOUS
CHAMPIONSHIPS

Most league championships won
12—Green Bay, 1929, 1930, 1931, 1936, 1939, 1944, 1961, 1962, 1965, 1966, 1967, 1996.
Most consecutive league championships won
3—Green Bay, 1929 through 1931.
 Green Bay, 1965 through 1967.
Most first-place finishes during regular season (since 1933)
18—Cleveland Browns, 1950 through 1955, 1957, 1964, 1965, 1967, 1968, 1969, 1971, 1980, 1985, 1986, 1987, 1989.
Most consecutive first-place finishes during regular season (since 1933)
7—Los Angeles, 1973 through 1979.

GAMES WON

Most games won, season
15—San Francisco, 1984.
 Chicago, 1985.
 Minnesota, 1998.
Most consecutive games won, season
14—Miami, September 17 through December 16, 1972.
Most consecutive games won from start of season
14—Miami, September 17 through December 16, 1972 (entire season).
Most consecutive games won at end of season
14—Miami, September 17 through December 16, 1972 (entire season).
Most consecutive undefeated games, season
14—Miami, September 17 through December 16, 1972 (entire season).
Most consecutive games won
17—Chicago Bears, November 26, 1933 through December 2, 1934.
Most consecutive undefeated games
25—Canton, 1921 through 1923 (won 22, tied three).
Most consecutive home games won
27—Miami, October 17, 1971 through December 15, 1974.
Most consecutive undefeated home games
30—Green Bay, 1928 through 1933 (won 27, tied three).
Most consecutive road games won
18—San Francisco, November 27, 1988 through December 30, 1990.
Most consecutive undefeated road games
18—San Francisco, November 27, 1988 through December 30, 1990 (won 18).

GAMES LOST

Most games lost, season
15—New Orleans, 1980.
 Dallas, 1989.
 New England, 1990.
 Indianapolis, 1991.
 New York Jets, 1996.
Most consecutive games lost
26—Tampa Bay, September 12, 1976 through December 4, 1977.

Most consecutive winless games
26—Tampa Bay, September 12, 1976 through December 4, 1977 (lost 26).
Most consecutive games lost, season
14—Tampa Bay, September 12 through December 12, 1976.
 New Orleans, September 7 through December 7, 1980.
 Baltimore, September 13 through December 13, 1981.
 New England, September 23 through December 30, 1990.
Most consecutive games lost from start of season
14—Tampa Bay, September 12 through December 12, 1976 (entire season).
 New Orleans, September 7 through December 7, 1980.
Most consecutive games lost at end of season
14—Tampa Bay, September 12 through December 12, 1976 (entire season).
 New England, September 23 through December 30, 1990.
Most consecutive winless games, season
14—Tampa Bay, September 12 through December 12, 1976 (lost 14; entire season).
 New Orleans, September 7 through December 7, 1980 (lost 14).
 Baltimore, September 13 through December 13, 1981 (lost 14).
 New England, September 23 through December 30, 1990 (lost 14).
Most consecutive home games lost
14—Dallas, October 9, 1988 through December 24, 1989.
Most consecutive winless home games
14—Dallas, October 9, 1988 through December 24, 1989 (lost 14).
Most consecutive road games lost
23—Houston, September 27, 1981 through November 4, 1984.
Most consecutive winless road games
23—Houston, September 27, 1981 through November 4, 1984 (lost 23).

TIE GAMES

Most tie games, season
6—Chicago Bears, 1932.
Most consecutive tie games
3—Chicago Bears, September 25 through October 9, 1932.

TEAM OFFENSE
RUSHING

Most years leading league in rushing
16—Chicago Bears, 1932, 1934, 1935, 1939, 1940, 1941, 1942, 1951, 1955, 1956, 1968, 1977, 1983, 1984, 1985, 1986.
Most consecutive years leading league in rushing
4—Chicago Bears, 1939 through 1942.
 Chicago Bears, 1983 through 1986.

ATTEMPTS

Most attempts, season
681—Oakland, 1977.
Most attempts, game
72—Chicago Bears vs. Brooklyn, October 20, 1935.
Most attempts by both teams, game
108—Chicago Cardinals 70, Green Bay 38, December 5, 1948.
Fewest attempts, game
6—Chicago Cardinals at Boston, October 29, 1933.
Fewest attempts by both teams, game
35—New Orleans 20, Seattle 15, September 1, 1991.

YARDS

Most yards, season
3,165—New England, 1978.

Fewest yards, season
298—Philadelphia, 1940.

Most yards, game
426—Detroit vs. Pittsburgh, November 4, 1934.

Most yards by both teams, game
595—Los Angeles 371, New York Yanks 224, November 18, 1951.

Fewest yards, game
-53—Detroit at Chicago Cardinals, October 17, 1943.

Fewest yards by both teams, game
-15—Detroit -53, Chicago Cardinals 38, October 17, 1943.

TOUCHDOWNS

Most touchdowns, season
36—Green Bay, 1962.

Fewest touchdowns, season
1—Brooklyn, 1934.

Most touchdowns, game
7—Los Angeles vs. Atlanta, December 4, 1976.

Most touchdowns by both teams, game
8—Los Angeles 6, New York Yanks 2, November 18, 1951.
  Chicago Bears 5, Green Bay 3, November 6, 1955.
  Cleveland 6, Los Angeles 2, November 24, 1957.

PASSING

ATTEMPTS

Most attempts, season
709—Minnesota, 1981.

Fewest attempts, season
102—Cincinnati, 1933.

Most attempts, game
70—New England vs. Minnesota, November 13, 1994 (overtime).
68—Houston at Buffalo, November 1, 1964.

Most attempts by both teams, game
112—New England 70, Minnesota 42, November 13, 1994 (overtime).
104—Miami 55, New York Jets 49, October 18, 1987 (overtime).
102—San Francisco 57, Atlanta 45, October 6, 1985.

Fewest attempts, game
0—Green Bay vs. Portsmouth, October 8, 1933.
  Detroit at Cleveland, September 10, 1937.
  Pittsburgh vs. Brooklyn, November 16, 1941.
  Pittsburgh vs. Los Angeles, November 13, 1949.
  Cleveland vs. Philadelphia, December 3, 1950.

Fewest attempts by both teams, game
4—Detroit 3, Chicago Cardinals 1, November 3, 1935.
  Cleveland 4, Detroit 0, September 10, 1937.

COMPLETIONS

Most completions, season
432—San Francisco, 1995.

Fewest completions, season
25—Cincinnati, 1933.

Most completions, game
45—New England vs. Minnesota, November 13, 1994 (overtime).
42—New York Jets vs. San Francisco, September 21, 1980.

Most completions by both teams, game
71—New England 45, Minnesota 26, November 13, 1994 (overtime).
68—San Francisco 37, Atlanta 31, October 6, 1985.

Fewest completions, game
0—Held by many teams. Last team: Buffalo vs. New York Jets, September 29, 1974.

Fewest completions by both teams, game
1—Philadelphia 1, Chicago Cardinals 0, November 8, 1936.
  Cleveland 1, Detroit 0, September 10, 1937.
  Detroit 1, Chicago Cardinals 0, September 15, 1940.
  Pittsburgh 1, Brooklyn 0, November 29, 1942.

YARDS

Most yards, season
5,018—Miami, 1984.

Most years leading league in yards
10—San Diego, 1965, 1968, 1971, 1978 through 1983, 1985.

Most consecutive years leading league in yards
6—San Diego, 1978 through 1983.

Fewest yards, season
302—Chicago Cardinals, 1934.

Most yards, game
554—Los Angeles at New York Yanks, September 28, 1951.

Most yards by both teams, game
884—New York Jets 449, Miami 435, September 21, 1986 (overtime).
883—San Diego 486, Cincinnati 397, December 20, 1982.

Fewest yards, game
-53—Denver at Oakland, September 10, 1967.

Fewest yards by both teams, game
-11—Green Bay -10, Dallas -1, October 24, 1965.

TOUCHDOWNS

Most touchdowns, season
49—Miami, 1984.

Fewest touchdowns, season
0—Cincinnati, 1933.
  Pittsburgh, 1945.

Most touchdowns, game
7—Chicago Bears at New York Giants, November 14, 1943.
  Philadelphia at Washington, October 17, 1954.
  Houston vs. New York Titans, November 19, 1961.
  Houston vs. New York Titans, October 14, 1962.
  New York Giants vs. Washington, October 28, 1962.
  Minnesota vs. Baltimore, September 28, 1969.
  San Diego at Oakland, November 22, 1981.

Most touchdowns by both teams, game
12—New Orleans 6, St. Louis 6, November 2, 1969.

INTERCEPTIONS

Most interceptions, season
48—Houston, 1962.

Fewest interceptions, season
5—Cleveland, 1960.
  Green Bay, 1966.
  Kansas City, 1990.
  New York Giants, 1990.

Most interceptions, game
9—Detroit vs. Green Bay, October 24, 1943.
  Pittsburgh vs. Philadelphia, December 12, 1965.

Most interceptions by both teams, game
13—Denver 8, Houston 5, December 2, 1962.

SACKS

Most sacks allowed, season
104—Philadelphia, 1986.

Most years leading league in fewest sacks allowed
10—Miami, 1973 and 1982 through 1990.

Most consecutive years leading league in fewest sacks allowed
9—Miami, 1982 through 1990.

Fewest sacks allowed, season
7—Miami, 1988.

Most sacks allowed, game
12—Pittsburgh at Dallas, November 20, 1966.
Baltimore vs. St. Louis, October 26, 1980.
Detroit vs. Chicago, December 16, 1984.
Houston vs. Dallas, September 29, 1985.

Most sacks allowed by both teams, game
18—Green Bay 10, San Diego 8, September 24, 1978.

SCORING

POINTS

Most points, season
556—Minnesota, 1998.

Most points, game
72—Washington vs. New York Giants, November 27, 1966.

Most points by both teams, game
113—Washington 72, New York Giants 41, November 27, 1966.

Fewest points by both teams, game
0—Occurred many times. Last time: New York Giants 0, Detroit 0, November 7, 1943.

Most points in a shutout victory
64—Philadelphia vs. Cincinnati, November 6, 1934.

Fewest points in a shutout victory
2—Green Bay at Chicago Bears, October 16, 1932.
Chicago Bears at Green Bay, September 18, 1938.

Most points in first half of game
49—Green Bay vs. Tampa Bay, October 2, 1983.

Most points in first half of game by both teams
70—Houston 35, Oakland 35, December 22, 1963.

Most points in second half of game
49—Chicago Bears at Philadelphia, November 30, 1941.

Most points in second half of game by both teams
65—Washington 38, New York Giants 27, November 27, 1966.

Most points in one quarter
41—Green Bay vs. Detroit, October 7, 1945, second quarter.
Los Angeles vs. Detroit, October 29, 1950, third quarter.

Most points in one quarter by both teams
49—Oakland 28, Houston 21, December 22, 1963, second quarter.

Most points in first quarter
35—Green Bay vs. Cleveland, November 12, 1967.

Most points in first quarter by both teams
42—Green Bay 35, Cleveland 7, November 12, 1967.

Most points in second quarter
41—Green Bay vs. Detroit, October 7, 1945.

Most points in second quarter by both teams
49—Oakland 28, Houston 21, December 22, 1963.

Most points in third quarter
41—Los Angeles vs. Detroit, October 29, 1950.

Most points in third quarter by both teams
48—Los Angeles 41, Detroit 7, October 29, 1950.

Most points in fourth quarter
31—Oakland vs. Denver, December 17, 1960.
Oakland vs. San Diego, December 8, 1963.
Atlanta at Green Bay, September 13, 1981.

Most points in fourth quarter by both teams
42—Chicago Cardinals 28, Philadelphia 14, December 7, 1947.
Green Bay 28, Chicago Bears 14, November 6, 1955.
New York Jets 28, Boston 14, October 27, 1968.
Pittsburgh 21, Cleveland 21, October 18, 1969.

Most consecutive games without being shut out
354—San Francisco, October 16, 1977 through January 3, 2000 (current).

TIMES SHUT OUT

Most times shut out, season
8—Frankford, 1927 (lost six, tied two).
Brooklyn, 1931 (lost eight).

Most consecutive times shut out
8—Rochester, 1922 through 1924 (lost eight).

TOUCHDOWNS

Most touchdowns, season
70—Miami, 1984.

Most years leading league in touchdowns
13—Chicago Bears, 1932, 1934, 1935, 1939, 1941, 1942, 1943, 1944, 1946, 1947, 1948, 1956, 1965.

Most consecutive years leading league in touchdowns
4—Chicago Bears, 1941 through 1944.
Los Angeles, 1949 through 1952.

Most touchdowns, game
10—Philadelphia vs. Cincinnati, November 6, 1934.
Los Angeles vs. Baltimore, October 22, 1950.
Washington vs. New York Giants, November 27, 1966.

Most touchdowns by both teams, game
16—Washington 10, New York Giants 6, November 27, 1966.

Most consecutive games with one or more touchdowns
166—Cleveland, 1957 through 1969.

EXTRA POINTS

Most extra points, season
66—Miami, 1984.

Fewest extra points, season
2—Chicago Cardinals, 1933.

Most extra points, game
10—Los Angeles vs. Baltimore, October 22, 1950.

Most extra points by both teams, game
14—Chicago Cardinals 9, New York Giants 5, October 17, 1948.
Houston 7, Oakland 7, December 22, 1963.
Washington 9, New York Giants 5, November 27, 1966.

FIELD GOALS

Most field goals attempted, season
49—Los Angeles, 1966.
Washington, 1971.

Most field goals made, season
39—Miami, 1999.

Most field goals attempted, game
9—St. Louis at Pittsburgh, September 24, 1967.

Most field goals made, game
7—St. Louis at Pittsburgh, September 24, 1967.
Minnesota vs. Los Angeles Rams, November 5, 1989 (overtime).

Most field goals attempted by both teams, game
11—St. Louis 6, Pittsburgh 5, November 13, 1966.
Washington 6, Chicago 5, November 14, 1971.
Green Bay 6, Detroit 5, September 29, 1974.
Washington 6, New York Giants 5, November 14, 1976.

Most field goals made by both teams, game
8—Cleveland 4, St. Louis 4, September 20, 1964.
Chicago 5, Philadelphia 3, October 20, 1968.
Washington 5, Chicago 3, November 14, 1971.
Kansas City 5, Buffalo 3, December 19, 1971.
Detroit 4, Green Bay 4, September 29, 1974.
Cleveland 5, Denver 3, October 19, 1975.

New England 4, San Diego 4, November 9, 1975.
San Francisco 6, New Orleans 2, October 16, 1983.
Seattle 5, Los Angeles Raiders 3, December 18, 1988.

Most consecutive games with one or more field goals made
31—Minnesota, November 17, 1968 through December 5, 1970.

SAFETIES

Most safeties, season
4—Cleveland, 1927.
Detroit, 1962.
Seattle, 1993.

Most safeties, game
3—Los Angeles Rams vs. New York Giants, September 30, 1984.

Most safeties by both teams, game
3—Los Angeles Rams 3, New York Giants 0, September 30, 1984.

FIRST DOWNS

Most first downs, season
387—Miami, 1984.

Most first downs, game
39—New York Jets vs. Miami, November 27, 1988.
Washington at Detroit, November 4, 1990 (overtime).

Most first downs by both teams, game
62—San Diego 32, Seattle 30, September 15, 1985.

PUNTING

Most punts, season
114—Chicago, 1981.

Fewest punts, season
23—San Diego, 1982.

Most punts, game
17—Chicago Bears vs. Green Bay, October 22, 1933.
Cincinnati vs. Pittsburgh, October 22, 1933.

Most punts by both teams, game
31—Chicago Bears 17, Green Bay 14, October 22, 1933.
Cincinnati 17, Pittsburgh 14, October 22, 1933.

Fewest punts, game
0—Held by many teams.

Fewest punts by both teams, game
0—Buffalo 0, San Francisco 0, September 13, 1992.

FUMBLES

Most fumbles, season
56—Chicago Bears, 1938.
San Francisco, 1978.

Fewest fumbles, season
8—Cleveland, 1959.

Most fumbles, game
10—Philadelphia/Pittsburgh vs. New York, October 9, 1943.
Detroit at Minnesota, November 12, 1967.
Kansas City vs. Houston, October 12, 1969.
San Francisco at Detroit, December 17, 1978.

Most fumbles by both teams, game
14—Washington 8, Pittsburgh 6, November 14, 1937.
Chicago Bears 7, Cleveland 7, November 24, 1940.
St. Louis 8, New York Giants 6, September 17, 1961.
Kansas City 10, Houston 4, October 12, 1969.

LOST

Most fumbles lost, season
36—Chicago Cardinals, 1959.

Fewest fumbles lost, season
3—Philadelphia, 1938.
Minnesota, 1980.

Most fumbles lost, game
8—St. Louis at Washington, October 25, 1976.
Cleveland at Pittsburgh, December 23, 1990.

RECOVERED

Most fumbles recovered (own and opponents'), season
58—Minnesota, 1963.

Fewest fumbles recovered (own and opponents'), season
9—San Francisco, 1982.

Most fumbles recovered (own and opponents'), game
10—Denver vs. Buffalo, December 13, 1964.
Pittsburgh vs. Houston, December 9, 1973.
Washington vs. St. Louis, October 25, 1976.

Most fumbles recovered (own), season
37—Chicago Bears, 1938.

Fewest fumbles recovered (own), season
2—Washington, 1958.

TOUCHDOWNS

Most touchdowns on fumbles recovered (own and opponents'), season
5—Chicago Bears, 1942.
Los Angeles, 1952.
San Francisco, 1965.
Oakland, 1978.

Most touchdowns on own fumbles recovered, season
2—Held by many teams. Last team: Miami, 1996.

Most touchdowns on fumbles recovered (own and opponents'), game
2—Held by many teams.

Most touchdowns on fumbles recovered (own and opponents'), game
3—Detroit 2, Minnesota 1, December 9, 1962.
Green Bay 2, Dallas 1, November 29, 1964.
Oakland 2, Buffalo 1, December 24, 1967.

Most touchdowns on own fumbles recovered, game
1—Held by many teams.

Most touchdowns on opponents' fumbles recovered by both teams, game
3—Green Bay 2, Dallas 1, November 29, 1964.
Oakland 2, Buffalo 1, December 24, 1967.

TURNOVERS

Most turnovers, season
63—San Francisco, 1978.

Fewest turnovers, season
12—Kansas City, 1982.

Most turnovers, game
12—Detroit vs. Chicago Bears, November 22, 1942.
Chicago Cardinals vs. Philadelphia, September 24, 1950.
Pittsburgh vs. Philadelphia, December 12, 1965.

Most turnovers by both teams, game
17—Detroit 12, Chicago Bears 5, November 22, 1942.
Boston 9, Philadelphia 8, December 8, 1946.

PUNT RETURNS

Most punt returns, season
71—Pittsburgh, 1976.
Tampa Bay, 1979.
Los Angeles Raiders, 1985.

Fewest punt returns, season
12—Baltimore, 1981.
San Diego, 1982.

Most punt returns, game
12—Philadelphia at Cleveland, December 3, 1950.

Most punt returns by both teams, game
17—Philadelphia 12, Cleveland 5, December 3, 1950.

YARDS

Most yards, season
785—Los Angeles Raiders, 1985.

Fewest yards, season
27—St. Louis, 1965.

Most yards, game
231—Detroit vs. San Francisco, October 6, 1963.

Most yards by both teams, game
282—Los Angeles 219, Atlanta 63, October 11, 1981.

TOUCHDOWNS

Most touchdowns, season
5—Chicago Cardinals, 1959.

Most touchdowns, game
2—Held by many teams. Last team: Cleveland vs. Pittsburgh, October 24, 1993.

Most touchdowns by both teams, game
2—Occurred many times. Last time: Cleveland 2, Pittsburgh 0, October 24, 1993.

KICKOFF RETURNS

Most kickoff returns, season
89—Cleveland, 1999.

Fewest kickoff returns, season
17—New York Giants, 1944.

Most kickoff returns, game
12—New York Giants at Washington, November 27, 1966.

Most kickoff returns by both teams, game
19—New York Giants 12, Washington 7, November 27, 1966.

YARDS

Most yards, season
1,973—New Orleans, 1980.

Fewest yards, season
282—New York Giants, 1940.

Most yards, game
362—Detroit at Los Angeles, October 29, 1950.

Most yards by both teams, game
560—Detroit 362, Los Angeles 198, October 29, 1950.

TOUCHDOWNS

Most touchdowns, season
4—Green Bay, 1967.
  Chicago, 1970.
  Detroit, 1994.

Most touchdowns, game
2—Chicago Bears at Green Bay, September 22, 1940.
  Chicago Bears vs. Green Bay, November 9, 1952.
  Philadelphia vs. Dallas, November 6, 1966.
  Green Bay vs. Cleveland, November 12, 1967.
  Los Angeles Rams vs. Green Bay, November 24, 1985.
  New Orleans vs. Los Angeles Rams, October 23, 1994.

Most touchdowns by both teams, game (each team scoring)
2—Occurred many times. Last time: Houston 1, Pittsburgh 1, December 4, 1988.

PENALTIES

Most penalties, season
158—Kansas City, 1998.

Fewest penalties, season
19—Detroit, 1937.

Most penalties, game
22—Brooklyn at Green Bay, September 17, 1944.
  Chicago Bears at Philadelphia, November 26, 1944.
  San Francisco at Buffalo, October 4, 1998.

Most penalties by both teams, game
37—Cleveland 21, Chicago Bears 16, November 25, 1951.

Fewest penalties, game
0—Held by many teams. Last team: San Francisco vs. Philadelphia, November 29, 1992.

Fewest penalties by both teams, game
0—Brooklyn 0, Pittsburgh 0, October 28, 1934.
  Brooklyn 0, Boston 0, September 28, 1936.
  Cleveland 0, Chicago Bears 0, October 9, 1938.
  Pittsburgh 0, Philadelphia 0, November 10, 1940.

YARDS PENALIZED

Most yards penalized, season
1,304—Kansas City, 1998.

Fewest yards penalized, season
139—Detroit, 1937.

Most yards penalized, game
209—Cleveland vs. Chicago Bears, November 25, 1951.

Most yards penalized by both teams, game
374—Cleveland 209, Chicago Bears 165, November 25, 1951.

Fewest yards penalized, game
0—Held by many teams. Last team: San Francisco vs. Philadelphia, November 29, 1992.

Fewest yards penalized by both teams, game
0—Brooklyn 0, Pittsburgh 0, October 28, 1934.
  Brooklyn 0, Boston 0, September 28, 1936.
  Cleveland 0, Chicago Bears 0, October 9, 1938.
  Pittsburgh 0, Philadelphia 0, November 10, 1940.

TEAM DEFENSE
RUSHING

YARDS ALLOWED

Most yards allowed, season
3,228—Buffalo, 1978.

Fewest yards allowed, season
519—Chicago Bears, 1942.

TOUCHDOWNS ALLOWED

Most touchdowns allowed, season
36—Oakland, 1961.

Fewest touchdowns allowed, season
2—Detroit, 1934.
  Dallas, 1968.
  Minnesota, 1971.

PASSING

YARDS ALLOWED

Most yards allowed, season
4,751—Atlanta, 1995.

Fewest yards allowed, season
545—Philadelphia, 1934.

TOUCHDOWNS ALLOWED

Most touchdowns allowed, season
40—Denver, 1963.

Fewest touchdowns allowed, season
1—Portsmouth, 1932.
  Philadelphia, 1934.

YARDS ALLOWED

(RUSHING AND PASSING)

Most yards allowed rushing and passing, season
6,793—Baltimore, 1981.

Fewest yards allowed rushing and passing, season
1,539—Chicago Cardinals, 1934.

SCORING

POINTS ALLOWED

Most points allowed, season
533—Baltimore, 1981.

Fewest points allowed, season (since 1932)
44—Chicago Bears, 1932.

SHUTOUTS

Most shutouts, season
10—Pottsville, 1926 (won nine, tied one).
New York Giants, 1927 (won nine, tied one).

Most consecutive shutouts
13—Akron, 1920 through 1921 (won 10, tied three).

TOUCHDOWNS ALLOWED

Most touchdowns allowed, season
68—Baltimore, 1981.

Fewest touchdowns allowed, season (since 1932)
6—Chicago Bears, 1932.
Brooklyn, 1933.

FIRST DOWNS ALLOWED

Most first downs allowed, season
406—Baltimore, 1981.

Fewest first downs allowed, season
77—Detroit, 1935.

Most first downs allowed by rushing, season
179—Detroit, 1985.

Fewest first downs allowed by rushing, season
35—Chicago Bears, 1942.

Most first downs allowed by passing, season
230—Atlanta, 1995.

Fewest first downs allowed by passing, season
33—Chicago Bears, 1943.

Most first downs allowed by penalties, season
56—Kansas City, 1998.

Fewest first downs allowed by penalties, season
1—Boston, 1944.

INTERCEPTIONS

Most interceptions, season
49—San Diego, 1961.

Fewest interceptions, season
3—Houston, 1982.

Most interceptions, game
9—Green Bay at Detroit, October 24, 1943.
Philadelphia at Pittsburgh, December 12, 1965.

Most yards returning interceptions, season
929—San Diego, 1961.

Fewest yards returning interceptions, season
5—Los Angeles, 1959.

Most yards returning interceptions, game
325—Seattle vs. Kansas City, November 4, 1984.

Most touchdowns returning interceptions, season
9—San Diego, 1961.

Most touchdowns returning interceptions, game
4—Seattle vs. Kansas City, November 4, 1984.

Most touchdowns returning interceptions by both teams, game
4—Philadelphia 3, Pittsburgh 1, December 12, 1965.
Seattle 4, Kansas City 0, November 4, 1984.

FUMBLES

Most opponents' fumbles forced, season
50—Minnesota, 1963.
San Francisco, 1978.

Fewest opponents' fumbles forced, season
11—Cleveland, 1956.
Baltimore, 1982.
Tennessee, 1998.

RECOVERED

Most opponents' fumbles recovered, season
31—Minnesota, 1963.

Fewest opponents' fumbles recovered, season
3—Los Angeles, 1974.

Most opponents' fumbles recovered, game
8—Washington vs. St. Louis, October 25, 1976.
Pittsburgh vs. Cleveland, December 23, 1990.

TOUCHDOWNS

Most touchdowns on opponents' fumbles recovered, season
4—Held by many teams. Last team: Cincinnati, 1998.

Most touchdowns on opponents' fumbles recovered, game
2—Held by many teams. Last team: Cincinnati at Pittsburgh, December 20, 1998.

TURNOVERS

Most opponents' turnovers, season
66—San Diego, 1961.

Fewest opponents' turnovers, season
11—Baltimore, 1982.

Most opponents' turnovers, game
12—Chicago Bears at Detroit, November 22, 1942.
Philadelphia at Chicago Cardinals, September 24, 1950.
Philadelphia at Pittsburgh, December 12, 1965.

SACKS

Most sacks, season
72—Chicago, 1984.

Fewest sacks, season
11—Baltimore, 1982.

Most sacks, game
12—Dallas at Pittsburgh, November 20, 1966.
St. Louis at Baltimore, October 26, 1980.
Chicago at Detroit, December 16, 1984.
Dallas at Houston, September 29, 1985.

PUNTS RETURNED

Most punts returned by opponents, season
71—Tampa Bay, 1976.
Tampa Bay, 1977.

Fewest punts returned by opponents, season
7—Washington, 1962.
San Diego, 1982.

Most yards allowed on punts returned by opponents, season
932—Green Bay, 1949.

Fewest yards allowed on punts returned by opponents, season
22—Green Bay, 1967.

Most touchdowns allowed on punts returned by opponents, season
4—New York, 1959.
   Atlanta, 1992.

KICKOFFS RETURNED

Most kickoffs returned by opponents, season
91—Washington, 1983.

Fewest kickoffs returned by opponents, season
10—Brooklyn, 1943.

Most yards allowed on kickoffs returned by opponents, season
2,045—Kansas City, 1966.

Fewest yards allowed on kickoffs returned by opponents, season
225—Brooklyn, 1943.

Most touchdowns allowed on kickoffs returned by opponents, season
4—Minnesota, 1998.

STATISTICAL LEADERS

CAREER MILESTONES

TOP 20 RUSHERS

Player	League	Years	Att.	Yds.	Avg.	Long	TD
Walter Payton	NFL	13	3838	16726	4.4	76	110
Barry Sanders	NFL	10	3062	15269	5.0	85	99
Emmitt Smith*	NFL	10	3243	13963	4.3	75	136
Eric Dickerson	NFL	11	2996	13259	4.4	85	90
Tony Dorsett	NFL	12	2936	12739	4.3	99	77
Jim Brown	NFL	9	2359	12312	5.2	80	106
Marcus Allen	NFL	16	3022	12243	4.1	61	123
Franco Harris	NFL	13	2949	12120	4.1	75	91
Thurman Thomas*	NFL	12	2849	11938	4.2	80	65
John Riggins	NFL	14	2916	11352	3.9	66	104
O.J. Simpson	AFL-NFL	11	2404	11236	4.7	94	61
Ottis Anderson	NFL	14	2562	10273	4.0	76	81
Joe Perry	AAFC-NFL	16	1929	9723	5.0	78	71
Earl Campbell	NFL	8	2187	9407	4.3	81	74
Ricky Watters*	NFL	8	2272	9083	4.0	57	70
Jim Taylor	NFL	10	1941	8597	4.4	84	83
Jerome Bettis*	NFL	7	2106	8463	4.0	71	41
Earnest Byner	NFL	14	2095	8261	3.9	54	56
Herschel Walker	NFL	12	1954	8225	4.2	91	61
Roger Craig	NFL	11	1991	8189	4.1	71	56

*Active through 1999 season.

TOP 20 PASSERS

Player	League	Years	Att.	Comp.	Yds.	TD	Int.	Rating Pts.
Steve Young*	NFL	15	4149	2667	33124	232	107	96.8
Joe Montana	NFL	15	5391	3409	40551	273	139	92.3
Brett Favre*	NFL	9	4352	2659	30894	235	141	87.1
Otto Graham	AAFC-NFL	10	2626	1464	23584	174	135	86.6
Dan Marino*	NFL	17	8358	4967	61361	420	252	86.4
Mark Brunell*	NFL	7	2160	1297	15572	86	52	85.4
Jim Kelly	NFL	11	4779	2874	35467	237	175	84.4
Roger Staubach	NFL	11	2958	1685	22700	153	109	83.4
Neil Lomax	NFL	8	3153	1817	22771	136	90	82.7
Troy Aikman*	NFL	11	4453	2742	31310	158	127	82.64
Sonny Jurgensen	NFL	18	4262	2433	32224	255	189	82.63
Len Dawson	NFL-AFL	19	3741	2136	28711	239	183	82.56
Neil O'Donnell*	NFL	9	3057	1766	20408	114	62	82.0
Ken Anderson	NFL	16	4475	2654	32838	197	160	81.9
Bernie Kosar	NFL	12	3365	1994	23301	124	87	81.8
Danny White	NFL	13	2950	1761	21959	155	132	81.7
Dave Krieg	NFL	19	5311	3105	38147	261	199	81.5
Randall Cunningham*	NFL	14	4075	2301	28557	198	128	81.4
Chris Chandler*	NFL	11	2894	1668	20865	135	101	81.2
Steve Beuerlein*	NFL	11	2615	1469	19002	120	84	81.09
Boomer Esiason	NFL	14	5205	2969	37920	247	184	81.06

*Active through 1999 season.

TOP 20 RECEIVERS

Player	League	Years	No.	Yds.	Avg.	Long	TD
Jerry Rice*	NFL	15	1206	18442	15.3	96	169
Andre Reed*	NFL	15	941	13095	13.9	83	86
Art Monk	NFL	16	940	12721	13.5	79	68
Cris Carter*	NFL	13	924	11688	12.6	80	114
Steve Largent	NFL	14	819	13089	16.0	74	100
Henry Ellard	NFL	16	814	13777	16.9	81	65
Irving Fryar*	NFL	16	810	12237	15.1	80	79
Tim Brown*	NFL	12	770	10944	14.2	80	75
James Lofton	NFL	16	764	14004	18.3	80	75
Charlie Joiner	AFL-NFL	18	750	12146	16.2	87	65
Michael Irvin*	NFL	12	750	11904	15.9	87	65
Andre Rison*	NFL	11	702	9599	13.7	80	78
Gary Clark	NFL	11	699	10856	15.5	84	65
Ozzie Newsome	NFL	13	662	7980	12.1	74	47

Player	League	Years	No.	Yds.	Avg.	Long	TD
Charley Taylor	NFL	13	649	9110	14.0	88	79
Drew Hill	NFL	15	634	9831	15.5	81	60
Don Maynard	NFL-AFL	15	633	11834	18.7	87	88
Raymond Berry	NFL	13	631	9275	14.7	70	68
Rob Moore*	NFL	10	628	9368	14.9	71	49
Herman Moore*	NFL	9	626	8664	13.8	93	59

*Active through 1999 season.

TOP 20 SCORERS

Player	League	Years	TD	XP Made	FG Made	Total
George Blanda	NFL-AFL	26	9	943	335	2002
Gary Anderson*	NFL	18	0	631	439	1948
Morten Andersen*	NFL	18	0	592	416	1840
Norm Johnson*	NFL	18	0	638	366	1736
Nick Lowery	NFL	18	0	562	383	1711
Jan Stenerud	AFL-NFL	19	0	580	373	1699
Lou Groza	AAFC-NFL	21	1	810	264	1608
Eddie Murray*	NFL	18	0	531	344	1563
Pat Leahy	NFL	18	0	558	304	1470
Al Del Greco*	NFL	16	0	506	320	1466
Jim Turner	AFL-NFL	16	1	521	304	1439
Matt Bahr	NFL	17	0	522	300	1422
Mark Moseley	NFL	16	0	482	300	1382
Jim Bakken	NFL	17	0	534	282	1380
Fred Cox	NFL	15	0	519	282	1365
Jim Breech	NFL	14	0	517	243	1246
Chris Bahr	NFL	14	0	490	241	1213
Kevin Butler	NFL	13	0	413	265	1208
Pete Stoyanovich*	NFL	11	0	394	267	1195
Gino Cappelletti	AFL-NFL	11	42	350	†176	†1130

*Active through 1999 season.
†Includes four two-point conversions.

YEAR BY YEAR

AFC

RUSHING
(Based on most net yards)

	Net Yds.	Att.	TD
1960—Abner Haynes, Dallas	875	156	9
1961—Billy Cannon, Houston	948	200	6
1962—Cookie Gilchrist, Buffalo	1096	214	13
1963—Clem Daniels, Oakland	1099	215	3
1964—Cookie Gilchrist, Buffalo	981	230	6
1965—Paul Lowe, San Diego	1121	222	7
1966—Jim Nance, Boston	1458	299	11
1967—Jim Nance, Boston	1216	269	7
1968—Paul Robinson, Cincinnati	1023	238	8
1969—Dick Post, San Diego	873	182	6
1970—Floyd Little, Denver	901	209	3
1971—Floyd Little, Denver	1133	284	6
1972—O.J. Simpson, Buffalo	1251	292	6
1973—O.J. Simpson, Buffalo	2003	332	12
1974—Otis Armstrong, Denver	1407	263	9
1975—O.J. Simpson, Buffalo	1817	329	16
1976—O.J. Simpson, Buffalo	1503	290	8
1977—Mark van Eeghen, Oakland	1273	324	7
1978—Earl Campbell, Houston	1450	302	13
1979—Earl Campbell, Houston	1697	368	19
1980—Earl Campbell, Houston	1934	373	13
1981—Earl Campbell, Houston	1376	361	10
1982—Freeman McNeil, N.Y. Jets	786	151	6
1983—Curt Warner, Seattle	1449	335	13
1984—Earnest Jackson, San Diego	1179	296	8
1985—Marcus Allen, L.A. Raiders	1759	380	11
1986—Curt Warner, Seattle	1481	319	13
1987—Eric Dickerson, Indianapolis	1288	283	6
1988—Eric Dickerson, Indianapolis	1659	388	14
1989—Christian Okoye, Kansas City	1480	370	12
1990—Thurman Thomas, Buffalo	1297	271	11
1991—Thurman Thomas, Buffalo	1407	288	7
1992—Barry Foster, Pittsburgh	1690	390	11
1993—Thurman Thomas, Buffalo	1315	355	6
1994—Chris Warren, Seattle	1545	333	9
1995—Curtis Martin, New England	1487	368	14
1996—Terrell Davis, Denver	1538	345	13
1997—Terrell Davis, Denver	1750	369	15
1998—Terrell Davis, Denver	2008	392	21
1999—Edgerrin James, Indianapolis	1553	369	13

PASSING
(Based on highest passer rating among qualifiers*)

	Att.	Com.	Yds.	TD	Int.	Rat.
1960—Jack Kemp, Chargers	406	211	3018	20	25	67.1
1961—George Blanda, Hou.	362	187	3330	36	22	91.3
1962—Len Dawson, Dal.	310	189	2759	29	17	98.3
1963—Tobin Rote, S.D.	286	170	2510	20	17	86.7
1964—Len Dawson, K.C.	354	199	2879	30	18	89.9
1965—John Hadl, S.D.	348	174	2798	20	21	71.3
1966—Len Dawson, K.C.	284	159	2527	26	10	101.7
1967—Daryle Lamonica, Oak.	425	220	3228	30	20	80.8
1968—Len Dawson, K.C.	224	131	2109	17	9	98.6
1969—Greg Cook, Cin.	197	106	1854	15	11	88.3
1970—Daryle Lamonica, Oak.	356	179	2516	22	15	76.5
1971—Bob Griese, Mia.	263	145	2089	19	9	90.9
1972—Earl Morrall, Mia.	150	83	1360	11	7	91.0
1973—Ken Stabler, Oak.	260	163	1997	14	10	88.5
1974—Ken Anderson, Cin.	328	213	2667	18	10	95.9
1975—Ken Anderson, Cin.	377	228	3169	21	11	94.1
1976—Ken Stabler, Oak.	291	194	2737	27	17	103.7
1977—Bob Griese, Mia.	307	180	2252	22	13	88.0
1978—Terry Bradshaw, Pit.	368	207	2915	28	20	84.8

– 345 –

HISTORY Statistical leaders

	Att.	Com.	Yds.	TD	Int.	Rat.
1979— Dan Fouts, S.D.	530	332	4082	24	24	82.6
1980— Brian Sipe, Cle.	554	337	4132	30	14	91.4
1981— Ken Anderson, Cin.	479	300	3754	29	10	98.5
1982— Ken Anderson, Cin.	309	218	2495	12	9	95.5
1983— Dan Marino, Mia.	296	173	2210	20	6	96.0
1984— Dan Marino, Mia.	564	362	5084	48	17	108.9
1985— Ken O'Brien, NYJ	488	297	3888	25	8	96.2
1986— Dan Marino, Mia.	623	378	4746	44	23	92.5
1987— Bernie Kosar, Cle.	389	241	3033	22	9	95.4
1988— Boomer Esiason, Cin.	388	223	3572	28	14	97.4
1989— Boomer Esiason, Cin.	455	258	3525	28	11	92.1
1990— Jim Kelly, Buf.	346	219	2829	24	9	101.2
1991— Jim Kelly, Buf.	474	304	3844	33	17	97.6
1992— Warren Moon, Hou.	346	224	2521	18	12	89.3
1993— John Elway, Den.	551	348	4030	25	10	92.8
1994— Dan Marino, Mia.	615	385	4453	30	17	89.2
1995— Jim Harbaugh, Ind.	314	200	2575	17	5	100.7
1996— John Elway, Den.	466	287	3328	26	14	89.2
1997— Mark Brunell, Jac.	435	264	3281	18	7	†91.17
1998— Vinny Testaverde, NYJ	421	259	3256	29	7	101.6
1999— Peyton Manning, Ind.	533	331	4135	26	15	90.7

*This chart includes passer rating points for all leaders, although the same rating system was not used for determining leading quarterbacks prior to 1973. The old system was less equitable, yet similar to the new in that the rating was based on percentage of completions, touchdown passes, percentage of interceptions and average gain in yards.

†Brunell and Jeff George of Oakland (521, 290, 3917, 29, 9), tied with 91.2 rating points, but rounded to another decimal place, Brunell's rating is higher, 91.17 to 91.15.

RECEIVING
(Based on most receptions)

	No.	Yds.	TD
1960— Lionel Taylor, Denver	92	1235	12
1961— Lionel Taylor, Denver	100	1176	4
1962— Lionel Taylor, Denver	77	908	4
1963— Lionel Taylor, Denver	78	1101	10
1964— Charley Hennigan, Houston	101	1546	8
1965— Lionel Taylor, Denver	85	1131	6
1966— Lance Alworth, San Diego	73	1383	13
1967— George Sauer, N.Y. Jets	75	1189	6
1968— Lance Alworth, San Diego	68	1312	10
1969— Lance Alworth, San Diego	64	1003	4
1970— Marlin Briscoe, Buffalo	57	1036	8
1971— Fred Biletnikoff, Oakland	61	929	9
1972— Fred Biletnikoff, Oakland	58	802	7
1973— Fred Willis, Houston	57	371	1
1974— Lydell Mitchell, Baltimore	72	544	2
1975— Reggie Rucker, Cleveland	60	770	3
Lydell Mitchell, Baltimore	60	544	4
1976— MacArthur Lane, Kansas City	66	686	1
1977— Lydell Mitchell, Baltimore	71	620	4
1978— Steve Largent, Seattle	71	1168	8
1979— Joe Washington, Baltimore	82	750	3
1980— Kellen Winslow, San Diego	89	1290	9
1981— Kellen Winslow, San Diego	88	1075	10
1982— Kellen Winslow, San Diego	54	721	6
1983— Todd Christensen, L.A. Raiders	92	1247	12
1984— Ozzie Newsome, Cleveland	89	1001	5
1985— Lionel James, San Diego	86	1027	6
1986— Todd Christensen, L.A. Raiders	95	1153	8
1987— Al Toon, N.Y. Jets	68	976	5
1988— Al Toon, N.Y. Jets	93	1067	5
1989— Andre Reed, Buffalo	88	1312	9
1990— Haywood Jeffires, Houston	74	1048	8
Drew Hill, Houston	74	1019	5
1991— Haywood Jeffires, Houston	100	1181	7
1992— Haywood Jeffires, Houston	90	913	9
1993— Reggie Langhorne, Indianapolis	85	1038	3
1994— Ben Coates, New England	96	1174	7
1995— Carl Pickens, Cincinnati	99	1234	17
1996— Carl Pickens, Cincinnati	100	1180	12

	No.	Yds.	TD
1997— Tim Brown, Oakland	104	1408	5
1998— O.J. McDuffie, Miami	90	1050	7
1999— Jimmy Smith, Jacksonville	116	1636	6

SCORING
(Based on most total points)

	TD	PAT	FG	Tot.
1960— Gene Mingo, Denver	6	33	18	123
1961— Gino Cappelletti, Boston	8	48	17	147
1962— Gene Mingo, Denver	4	32	27	137
1963— Gino Cappelletti, Boston	2	35	22	113
1964— Gino Cappelletti, Boston	7	36	25	155
1965— Gino Cappelletti, Boston	9	27	17	132
1966— Gino Cappelletti, Boston	6	35	16	119
1967— George Blanda, Oakland	0	56	20	116
1968— Jim Turner, N.Y. Jets	0	43	34	145
1969— Jim Turner, N.Y. Jets	0	33	32	129
1970— Jan Stenerud, Kansas City	0	26	30	116
1971— Garo Yepremian, Miami	0	33	28	117
1972— Bobby Howfield, N.Y. Jets	0	40	27	121
1973— Roy Gerela, Pittsburgh	0	36	29	123
1974— Roy Gerela, Pittsburgh	0	33	20	93
1975— O.J. Simpson, Buffalo	23	0	0	138
1976— Toni Linhart, Baltimore	0	49	20	109
1977— Errol Mann, Oakland	0	39	20	99
1978— Pat Leahy, N.Y. Jets	0	41	22	107
1979— John Smith, New England	0	46	23	115
1980— John Smith, New England	0	51	26	129
1981— Jim Breech, Cincinnati	0	49	22	115
Nick Lowery, Kansas City	0	37	26	115
1982— Marcus Allen, L.A. Raiders	14	0	0	84
1983— Gary Anderson, Pittsburgh	0	38	27	119
1984— Gary Anderson, Pittsburgh	0	45	24	117
1985— Gary Anderson, Pittsburgh	0	40	33	139
1986— Tony Franklin, New England	0	44	32	140
1987— Jim Breech, Cincinnati	0	25	24	97
1988— Scott Norwood, Buffalo	0	33	32	129
1989— David Treadwell, Denver	0	39	27	120
1990— Nick Lowery, Kansas City	0	37	34	139
1991— Pete Stoyanovich, Miami	0	28	31	121
1992— Pete Stoyanovich, Miami	0	34	30	124
1993— Jeff Jaeger, L.A. Raiders	0	27	35	132
1994— John Carney, San Diego	0	33	34	135
1995— Norm Johnson, Pittsburgh	0	39	34	141
1996— Cary Blanchard, Indianapolis	0	27	36	135
1997— Mike Hollis, Jacksonville	0	41	31	134
1998— Steve Christie, Buffalo	0	41	33	140
1999— Mike Vanderjagt, Indianapolis	0	43	34	145

FIELD GOALS

	No.
1960— Gene Mingo, Denver	18
1961— Gino Cappelletti, Boston	17
1962— Gene Mingo, Denver	27
1963— Gino Cappelletti, Boston	22
1964— Gino Cappelletti, Boston	25
1965— Pete Gogolak, Buffalo	28
1966— Mike Mercer, Oakland-Kansas City	21
1967— Jan Stenerud, Kansas City	21
1968— Jim Turner, N.Y. Jets	34
1969— Jim Turner, N.Y. Jets	32
1970— Jan Stenerud, Kansas City	30
1971— Garo Yepremian, Miami	28
1972— Roy Gerela, Pittsburgh	28
1973— Roy Gerela, Pittsburgh	29
1974— Roy Gerela, Pittsburgh	20
1975— Jan Stenerud, Kansas City	22
1976— Jan Stenerud, Kansas City	21
1977— Errol Mann, Oakland	20
1978— Pat Leahy, N.Y. Jets	22
1979— John Smith, New England	23
1980— John Smith, New England	26
Fred Steinfort, Denver	26

		No.
1981—	Nick Lowery, Kansas City	26
1982—	Nick Lowery, Kansas City	19
1983—	Raul Allegre, Baltimore	30
1984—	Gary Anderson, Pittsburgh	24
	Matt Bahr, Cleveland	24
1985—	Gary Anderson, Pittsburgh	33
1986—	Tony Franklin, New England	32
1987—	Dean Biasucci, Indianapolis	24
	Jim Breech, Cincinnati	24
1988—	Scott Norwood, Buffalo	32
1989—	David Treadwell, Denver	27
1990—	Nick Lowery, Kansas City	34
1991—	Pete Stoyanovich, Miami	31
1992—	Pete Stoyanovich, Miami	30
1993—	Jeff Jaeger, L.A. Raiders	35
1994—	John Carney, San Diego	34
1995—	Norm Johnson, Pittsburgh	34
1996—	Cary Blanchard, Indianapolis	36
1997—	Cary Blanchard, Indianapolis	32
1998—	Al Del Greco, Tennessee	36
1999—	Olinda Mare, Miami	39

INTERCEPTIONS

		No.	Yds.
1960—	Austin Gonsoulin, Denver	11	98
1961—	Bill Atkins, Buffalo	10	158
1962—	Lee Riley, N.Y. Jets	11	122
1963—	Fred Glick, Houston	12	180
1964—	Dainard Paulson, N.Y. Jets	12	157
1965—	W.K. Hicks, Houston	9	156
1966—	Johnny Robinson, Kansas City	10	136
	Bobby Hunt, Kansas City	10	113
1967—	Miller Farr, Houston	10	264
	Tom Janik, Buffalo	10	222
	Dick Westmoreland, Miami	10	127
1968—	Dave Grayson, Oakland	10	195
1969—	Emmitt Thomas, Kansas City	9	146
1970—	Johnny Robinson, Kansas City	10	155
1971—	Ken Houston, Houston	9	220
1972—	Mike Sensibaugh, Kansas City	8	65
1973—	Dick Anderson, Miami	8	136
	Mike Wagner, Pittsburgh	8	134
1974—	Emmitt Thomas, Kansas City	12	214
1975—	Mel Blount, Pittsburgh	11	121
1976—	Ken Riley, Cincinnati	9	141
1977—	Lyle Blackwood, Baltimore	10	163
1978—	Thom Darden, Cleveland	10	200
1979—	Mike Reinfeldt, Houston	12	205
1980—	Lester Hayes, Oakland	13	273
1981—	John Harris, Seattle	10	155
1982—	Ken Riley, Cincinnati	5	88
	Bobby Jackson, N.Y. Jets	5	84
	Dwayne Woodruff, Pittsburgh	5	53
	Donnie Shell, Pittsburgh	5	27
1983—	Ken Riley, Cincinnati	8	89
	Vann McElroy, Los Angeles	8	68
1984—	Kenny Easley, Seattle	10	126
1985—	Eugene Daniel, Indianapolis	8	53
	Albert Lewis, Kansas City	8	59
1986—	Deron Cherry, Kansas City	9	150
1987—	Mike Prior, Indianapolis	6	57
	Mark Kelso, Buffalo	6	25
	Keith Bostic, Houston	6	-14
1988—	Erik McMillan, N.Y. Jets	8	168
1989—	Felix Wright, Cleveland	9	91
1990—	Richard Johnson, Houston	8	100
1991—	Ronnie Lott, L.A. Raiders	8	52
1992—	Henry Jones, Buffalo	8	263
1993—	Nate Odomes, Buffalo	9	65
	Eugene Robinson, Seattle	9	80
1994—	Eric Turner, Cleveland	9	199

		No.	Yds.
1995—	Willie Williams, Pittsburgh	7	122
1996—	Tyrone Braxton, Denver	9	128
1997—	Mark McMillian, Kansas City	8	274
	Darryl Williams, Seattle	8	172
1998—	Ty Law, New England	9	133
1999—	Rod Woodson, Baltimore	7	195
	Sam Madison, Miami	7	164
	James Hasty, Kansas City	7	98

PUNTING
(Based on highest average yardage per punt by qualifiers)

		No.	Avg.
1960—	Paul Maguire, L.A. Chargers	43	40.5
1961—	Bill Atkins, Buffalo	85	44.5
1962—	Jim Fraser, Denver	55	43.6
1963—	Jim Fraser, Denver	81	44.4
1964—	Jim Fraser, Denver	73	44.2
1965—	Jerrel Wilson, Kansas City	69	45.4
1966—	Bob Scarpitto, Denver	76	45.8
1967—	Bob Scarpitto, Denver	105	44.9
1968—	Jerrel Wilson, Kansas City	63	45.1
1969—	Dennis Partee, San Diego	71	44.6
1970—	Dave Lewis, Cincinnati	79	46.2
1971—	Dave Lewis, Cincinnati	72	44.8
1972—	Jerrel Wilson, Kansas City	66	44.8
1973—	Jerrel Wilson, Kansas City	80	45.5
1974—	Ray Guy, Oakland	74	42.2
1975—	Ray Guy, Oakland	68	43.8
1976—	Marv Bateman, Buffalo	86	42.8
1977—	Ray Guy, Oakland	59	43.4
1978—	Pat McInally, Cincinnati	91	43.1
1979—	Bob Grupp, Kansas City	89	43.6
1980—	Luke Prestridge, Denver	70	43.9
1981—	Pat McInally, Cincinnati	72	45.4
1982—	Luke Prestridge, Denver	45	45.0
1983—	Rohn Stark, Baltimore	91	45.3
1984—	Jim Arnold, Kansas City	98	44.9
1985—	Rohn Stark, Indianapolis	78	45.9
1986—	Rohn Stark, Indianapolis	76	45.2
1987—	Ralf Mojsiejenko, San Diego	67	42.9
1988—	Harry Newsome, Pittsburgh	65	45.4
1989—	Greg Montgomery, Houston	56	43.3
1990—	Mike Horan, Denver	58	44.4
1991—	Reggie Roby, Miami	54	45.7
1992—	Greg Montgomery, Houston	53	46.9
1993—	Greg Montgomery, Houston	54	45.6
1994—	Jeff Gossett, L.A. Raiders	77	43.9
1995—	Rick Tuten, Seattle	83	45.0
1996—	John Kidd, Miami	78	46.3
1997—	Tom Tupa, New England	71	45.7
1998—	Craig Hentrich, Tennessee	69	47.2
1999—	Tom Rouen, Denver	84	46.5

PUNT RETURNS
(Based on most total yards)

		No.	Yds.	Avg.
1960—	Abner Haynes, Dallas	14	215	15.4
1961—	Dick Christy, N.Y. Jets	18	383	21.3
1962—	Dick Christy, N.Y. Jets	15	250	16.7
1963—	Claude Gibson, Oakland	26	307	11.8
1964—	Bobby Jancik, Houston	12	220	18.3
1965—	Leslie Duncan, San Diego	30	464	15.5
1966—	Leslie Duncan, San Diego	18	238	13.2
1967—	Floyd Little, Denver	16	270	16.9
1968—	Noland Smith, Kansas City	18	270	15.0
1969—	Bill Thompson, Denver	25	288	11.5
1970—	Ed Podolak, Kansas City	23	311	13.5
1971—	Leroy Kelly, Cleveland	30	292	9.7
1972—	Chris Farasopolous, N.Y. Jets	17	179	10.5
1973—	Ron Smith, San Diego	27	352	15.0
1974—	Lemar Parrish, Cincinnati	18	338	18.8
1975—	Billy Johnson, Houston	40	612	18.8

HISTORY *Statistical leaders*

	No.	Yds.	Avg.
1976—Rick Upchurch, Denver	39	536	13.7
1977—Billy Johnson, Houston	30	539	15.4
1978—Rick Upchurch, Denver	36	493	13.7
1979—Tony Nathan, Miami	28	306	10.9
1980—J.T. Smith, Kansas City	40	581	14.5
1981—James Brooks, San Diego	22	290	13.2
1982—Rick Upchurch, Denver	15	242	16.1
1983—Kirk Springs, N.Y. Jets	23	287	12.5
1984—Mike Martin, Cincinnati	24	376	15.7
1985—Irving Fryar, New England	37	520	14.1
1986—Bobby Joe Edmonds, Seattle	34	419	12.3
1987—Bobby Joe Edmonds, Seattle	20	251	12.6
1988—Jojo Townsell, N.Y. Jets	35	409	11.7
1989—Clarence Verdin, Indianapolis	23	296	12.9
1990—Clarence Verdin, Indianapolis	31	396	12.8
1991—Rod Woodson, Pittsburgh	28	320	11.4
1992—Rod Woodson, Pittsburgh	32	364	11.4
1993—Tim Brown, L.A. Raiders	40	465	11.6
1994—Tim Brown, L.A. Raiders	40	487	12.2
1995—Tamarick Vanover, Kansas City	51	540	10.6
1996—David Meggett, New England	52	588	11.3
1997—Leon Johnson, N.Y. Jets	51	619	12.1
1998—Reggie Barlow, Jacksonville	43	555	12.9
1999—Charlie Rogers, Seattle	22	318	14.5

	No.	Yds.	Avg.
1977—Raymond Clayborn, New England	20	869	31.0
1978—Keith Wright, Cleveland	30	789	26.3
1979—Larry Brunson, Oakland	17	441	25.9
1980—Horace Ivory, New England	36	992	27.6
1981—Carl Roaches, Houston	28	769	27.5
1982—Mike Mosley, Buffalo	18	487	27.1
1983—Fulton Walker, Miami	36	962	26.7
1984—Bobby Humphrey, N.Y. Jets	22	675	30.7
1985—Glen Young, Cleveland	35	898	25.7
1986—Lupe Sanchez, Pittsburgh	25	591	23.6
1987—Paul Palmer, Kansas City	38	923	24.3
1988—Tim Brown, L.A. Raiders	41	1098	26.8
1989—Rod Woodson, Pittsburgh	36	982	27.3
1990—Kevin Clark, Denver	20	505	25.3
1991—Nate Lewis, San Diego	23	578	25.1
1992—Jon Vaughn, New England	20	564	28.2
1993—Clarence Verdin, Indianapolis	50	1050	21.0
1994—Andre Coleman, San Diego	49	1293	26.4
1995—Andre Coleman, San Diego	62	1411	22.8
1996—Mel Gray, Houston	50	1224	24.5
1997—Kevin Williams, Arizona	59	1459	24.7
1998—Vaughn Hebron, Denver	46	1216	26.4
1999—Tremain Mack, Cincinnati	51	1382	27.1

KICKOFF RETURNS
(Based on most total yards)

	No.	Yds.	Avg.
1960—Ken Hall, Houston	19	594	31.3
1961—Dave Grayson, Dallas	16	453	28.3
1962—Bobby Jancik, Houston	24	726	30.3
1963—Bobby Jancik, Houston	45	1317	29.3
1964—Bo Roberson, Oakland	36	975	27.1
1965—Abner Haynes, Denver	34	901	26.5
1966—Goldie Sellers, Denver	19	541	28.5
1967—Zeke Moore, Houston	14	405	28.9
1968—George Atkinson, Oakland	32	802	25.1
1969—Bill Thompson, Denver	19	594	31.3
1970—Jim Duncan, Baltimore	20	707	35.4
1971—Mercury Morris, Miami	15	423	28.2
1972—Bruce Laird, Baltimore	29	843	29.1
1973—Wallace Francis, Buffalo	23	687	29.9
1974—Greg Pruitt, Cleveland	22	606	27.5
1975—Harold Hart, Oakland	17	518	30.5
1976—Duriel Harris, Miami	17	559	32.9

SACKS

	No.
1982—Jesse Baker, Houston	7.5
1983—Mark Gastineau, N.Y. Jets	19.0
1984—Mark Gastineau, N.Y. Jets	22.0
1985—Andre Tippett, New England	16.5
1986—Sean Jones, L.A. Raiders	15.5
1987—Andre Tippett, New England	12.5
1988—Greg Townsend, L.A. Raiders	11.5
1989—Lee Williams, San Diego	14.0
1990—Derrick Thomas, Kansas City	20.0
1991—William Fuller, Houston	15.0
1992—Leslie O'Neal, San Diego	17.0
1993—Neil Smith, Kansas City	15.0
1994—Kevin Greene, Pittsburgh	14.0
1995—Bryce Paup, Buffalo	17.5
1996—Michael McCrary, Seattle	13.5
Bruce Smith, Buffalo	13.5
1997—Bruce Smith, Buffalo	15.0
1998—Michael Sinclair, Seattle	16.5
1999—Jevon Kearse, Tennessee	14.5

NFC

RUSHING
(Based on most net yards)

	Net Yds.	Att.	TD
1960—Jim Brown, Cleveland	1257	215	9
1961—Jim Brown, Cleveland	1408	305	8
1962—Jim Taylor, Green Bay	1474	272	19
1963—Jim Brown, Cleveland	1863	291	12
1964—Jim Brown, Cleveland	1446	280	7
1965—Jim Brown, Cleveland	1544	289	17
1966—Gale Sayers, Chicago	1231	229	8
1967—Leroy Kelly, Cleveland	1205	235	11
1968—Leroy Kelly, Cleveland	1239	248	16
1969—Gale Sayers, Chicago	1032	236	8
1970—Larry Brown, Washington	1125	237	5
1971—John Brockington, Green Bay	1105	216	4
1972—Larry Brown, Washington	1216	285	8
1973—John Brockington, Green Bay	1144	265	3
1974—Lawrence McCutcheon, L.A. Rams	1109	236	3
1975—Jim Otis, St. Louis	1076	269	5
1976—Walter Payton, Chicago	1390	311	13
1977—Walter Payton, Chicago	1852	339	14
1978—Walter Payton, Chicago	1395	333	11

	Net Yds.	Att.	TD
1979—Walter Payton, Chicago	1610	369	14
1980—Walter Payton, Chicago	1460	317	6
1981—George Rogers, New Orleans	1674	378	13
1982—Tony Dorsett, Dallas	745	177	5
1983—Eric Dickerson, L.A. Rams	1808	390	18
1984—Eric Dickerson, L.A. Rams	2105	379	14
1985—Gerald Riggs, Atlanta	1719	397	10
1986—Eric Dickerson, L.A. Rams	1821	404	11
1987—Charles White, L.A. Rams	1374	324	11
1988—Herschel Walker, Dallas	1514	361	5
1989—Barry Sanders, Detroit	1470	280	14
1990—Barry Sanders, Detroit	1304	255	13
1991—Emmitt Smith, Dallas	1563	365	12
1992—Emmitt Smith, Dallas	1713	373	18
1993—Emmitt Smith, Dallas	1486	283	9
1994—Barry Sanders, Detroit	1883	331	7
1995—Emmitt Smith, Dallas	1773	377	25
1996—Barry Sanders, Detroit	1553	307	11
1997—Barry Sanders, Detroit	2053	335	11
1998—Jamal Anderson, Atlanta	1846	410	14
1999—Stephen Davis, Washington	1405	290	17

PASSING
(Based on highest passer rating among qualifiers*)

		Att.	Com.	Yds.	TD	Int.	Rat.
1960—	Milt Plum, Cle.	250	151	2297	21	5	110.4
1961—	Milt Plum, Cle.	302	177	2416	18	10	90.3
1962—	Bart Starr, G.B.	285	178	2438	12	9	90.7
1963—	Y.A. Tittle, NYG	367	221	3145	36	14	104.8
1964—	Bart Starr, G.B.	272	163	2144	15	4	97.1
1965—	Rudy Bukich, Chi.	312	176	2641	20	9	93.7
1966—	Bart Starr, G.B.	251	156	2257	14	3	105.0
1967—	Sonny Jurgensen, Was.	508	288	3747	31	16	87.3
1968—	Earl Morrall, Bal.	317	182	2909	26	17	93.2
1969—	Sonny Jurgensen, Was.	442	274	3102	22	15	85.4
1970—	John Brodie, S.F.	378	223	2941	24	10	93.8
1971—	Roger Staubach, Dal.	211	126	1882	15	4	104.8
1972—	Norm Snead, NYG	325	196	2307	17	12	84.0
1973—	Roger Staubach, Dal.	286	179	2428	23	15	94.6
1974—	Sonny Jurgensen, Was.	167	107	1185	11	5	94.6
1975—	Fran Tarkenton, Min.	425	273	2994	25	13	91.7
1976—	James Harris, L.A.	158	91	1460	8	6	89.8
1977—	Roger Staubach, Dal.	361	210	2620	18	9	87.1
1978—	Roger Staubach, Dal.	413	231	3190	25	16	84.9
1979—	Roger Staubach, Dal.	461	267	3586	27	11	92.4
1980—	Ron Jaworski, Phi.	451	257	3529	27	12	90.0
1981—	Joe Montana, S.F.	488	311	3565	19	12	88.4
1982—	Joe Theismann, Was.	252	161	2033	13	9	91.3
1983—	Steve Bartkowski, Atl.	432	274	3167	22	5	97.6
1984—	Joe Montana, S.F.	432	279	3630	28	10	102.9
1985—	Joe Montana, S.F.	494	303	3653	27	13	91.3
1986—	Tommy Kramer, Min.	372	208	3000	24	10	92.6
1987—	Joe Montana, S.F.	398	266	3054	31	13	102.1
1988—	Wade Wilson, Min.	332	204	2746	15	9	91.5
1989—	Joe Montana, S.F.	386	271	3521	26	8	112.4
1990—	Phil Simms, NYG	311	184	2284	15	4	92.7
1991—	Steve Young, S.F.	279	180	2517	17	8	101.8
1992—	Steve Young, S.F.	402	268	3465	25	7	107.0
1993—	Steve Young, S.F.	462	314	4023	29	16	101.5
1994—	Steve Young, S.F.	461	324	3969	35	10	112.8
1995—	Brett Favre, G.B.	570	359	4413	38	13	99.5
1996—	Steve Young, S.F.	316	214	2410	14	6	97.2
1997—	Steve Young, S.F.	356	241	3029	19	6	104.7
1998—	Ran. Cunningham, Min.	425	259	3704	34	10	106.0
1999—	Kurt Warner, St.L.	499	325	4353	41	13	109.2

*This chart includes passer rating points for all leaders, although the same rating system was not used for determining leading quarterbacks prior to 1973. The old system was less equitable, yet similar to the new in that the rating was based on percentage of completions, touchdown passes, percentage of interceptions and average gain in yards.

RECEIVING
(Based on most receptions)

		No.	Yds.	TD
1960—	Raymond Berry, Baltimore	74	1298	10
1961—	Jim Phillips, L.A. Rams	78	1092	5
1962—	Bobby Mitchell, Washington	72	1384	11
1963—	Bobby Joe Conrad, St. Louis	73	967	10
1964—	Johnny Morris, Chicago	93	1200	10
1965—	Dave Parks, San Francisco	80	1344	12
1966—	Charley Taylor, Washington	72	1119	12
1967—	Charley Taylor, Washington	70	990	9
1968—	Clifton McNeil, San Francisco	71	994	7
1969—	Dan Abramowicz, New Orleans	73	1015	7
1970—	Dick Gordon, Chicago	71	1026	13
1971—	Bob Tucker, N.Y. Giants	59	791	4
1972—	Harold Jackson, Philadelphia	62	1048	4
1973—	Harold Carmichael, Philadelphia	67	1116	9
1974—	Charles Young, Philadelphia	63	696	3
1975—	Chuck Foreman, Minnesota	73	691	9
1976—	Drew Pearson, Dallas	58	806	6
1977—	Ahmad Rashad, Minnesota	51	681	2

		No.	Yds.	TD
1978—	Rickey Young, Minnesota	88	704	5
1979—	Ahmad Rashad, Minnesota	80	1156	9
1980—	Earl Cooper, San Francisco	83	567	4
1981—	Dwight Clark, San Francisco	85	1105	4
1982—	Dwight Clark, San Francisco	60	913	5
1983—	Roy Green, St. Louis	78	1227	14
	Charlie Brown, Washington	78	1225	8
	Earnest Gray, N.Y. Giants	78	1139	5
1984—	Art Monk, Washington	106	1372	7
1985—	Roger Craig, San Francisco	92	1016	6
1986—	Jerry Rice, San Francisco	86	1570	15
1987—	J.T. Smith, St. Louis	91	1117	8
1988—	Henry Ellard, L.A. Rams	86	1414	10
1989—	Sterling Sharpe, Green Bay	90	1423	12
1990—	Jerry Rice, San Francisco	100	1502	13
1991—	Michael Irvin, Dallas	93	1523	8
1992—	Sterling Sharpe, Green Bay	108	1461	13
1993—	Sterling Sharpe, Green Bay	112	1274	11
1994—	Cris Carter, Minnesota	122	1256	7
1995—	Herman Moore, Detroit	123	1686	14
1996—	Jerry Rice, San Francisco	108	1254	8
1997—	Herman Moore, Detroit	104	1293	8
1998—	Frank Sanders, Arizona	89	1145	3
1999—	Muhsid Muhammad, Carolina	96	1253	8

SCORING
(Based on most total points)

		TD	PAT	FG	Tot.
1960—	Paul Hornung, Green Bay	15	41	15	176
1961—	Paul Hornung, Green Bay	10	41	15	146
1962—	Jim Taylor, Green Bay	19	0	0	114
1963—	Don Chandler, N.Y. Giants	0	52	18	106
1964—	Lenny Moore, Baltimore	20	0	0	120
1965—	Gale Sayers, Chicago	22	0	0	132
1966—	Bruce Gossett, L.A. Rams	0	29	28	113
1967—	Jim Bakken, St. Louis	0	36	27	117
1968—	Leroy Kelly, Cleveland	20	0	0	120
1969—	Fred Cox, Minnesota	0	43	26	121
1970—	Fred Cox, Minnesota	0	35	30	125
1971—	Curt Knight, Washington	0	27	29	114
1972—	Chester Marcol, Green Bay	0	29	33	128
1973—	David Ray, L.A. Rams	0	40	30	130
1974—	Chester Marcol, Green Bay	0	19	25	94
1975—	Chuck Foreman, Minnesota	22	0	0	132
1976—	Mark Moseley, Washington	0	31	22	97
1977—	Walter Payton, Chicago	16	0	0	96
1978—	Frank Corral, L.A. Rams	0	31	29	118
1979—	Mark Moseley, Washington	0	39	25	114
1980—	Ed Murray, Detroit	0	35	27	116
1981—	Ed Murray, Detroit	0	46	25	121
	Rafael Septien, Dallas	0	40	27	121
1982—	Wendell Tyler, L.A. Rams	13	0	0	78
1983—	Mark Moseley, Washington	0	62	33	161
1984—	Ray Wersching, S.F.	0	56	25	131
1985—	Kevin Butler, Chicago	0	51	31	144
1986—	Kevin Butler, Chicago	0	36	28	120
1987—	Jerry Rice, San Francisco	23	0	0	138
1988—	Mike Cofer, San Francisco	0	40	27	121
1989—	Mike Cofer, San Francisco	0	49	29	136
1990—	Chip Lohmiller, Washington	0	41	30	131
1991—	Chip Lohmiller, Washington	0	56	31	149
1992—	Morten Andersen, New Orleans	0	33	29	120
	Chip Lohmiller, Washington	0	30	30	120
1993—	Jason Hanson, Detroit	0	28	34	130
1994—	Fuad Reveiz, Minnesota	0	30	34	132
1995—	Emmitt Smith, Dallas	25	0	0	150
1996—	John Kasay, Carolina	0	34	37	145
1997—	Richie Cunningham, Dallas	0	24	34	126
1998—	Gary Anderson, Minnesota	0	59	35	164
1999—	Jeff Wilkins, St. Louis	0	64	20	124

HISTORY Statistical leaders

– 349 –

FIELD GOALS

Year	Player	No.
1960—	Tommy Davis, San Francisco	19
1961—	Steve Myhra, Baltimore	21
1962—	Lou Michaels, Pittsburgh	26
1963—	Jim Martin, Baltimore	24
1964—	Jim Bakken, St. Louis	25
1965—	Fred Cox, Minnesota	23
1966—	Bruce Gossett, L.A. Rams	28
1967—	Jim Bakken, St. Louis	27
1968—	Mac Percival, Chicago	25
1969—	Fred Cox, Minnesota	26
1970—	Fred Cox, Minnesota	30
1971—	Curt Knight, Washington	29
1972—	Chester Marcol, Green Bay	33
1973—	David Ray, L.A. Rams	30
1974—	Chester Marcol, Green Bay	25
1975—	Toni Fritsch, Dallas	22
1976—	Mark Moseley, Washington	22
1977—	Mark Moseley, Washington	21
1978—	Frank Corral, L.A. Rams	29
1979—	Mark Moseley, Washington	25
1980—	Eddie Murray, Detroit	27
1981—	Rafael Septien, Dallas	27
1982—	Mark Moseley, Washington	20
1983—	Ali Haji-Sheikh, N.Y. Giants	35
1984—	Paul McFadden, Philadelphia	30
1985—	Morten Andersen, New Orleans	31
	Kevin Butler, Chicago	31
1986—	Kevin Butler, Chicago	28
1987—	Morten Andersen, New Orleans	28
1988—	Mike Cofer, San Francisco	27
1989—	Rich Karlis, Minnesota	31
1990—	Chip Lohmiller, Washington	30
1991—	Chip Lohmiller, Washington	31
1992—	Chip Lohmiller, Washington	30
1993—	Jason Hanson, Detroit	34
1994—	Fuad Reveiz, Minnesota	34
1995—	Morten Andersen, Atlanta	31
1996—	John Kasay, Carolina	37
1997—	Richie Cunningham, Dallas	34
1998—	Gary Anderson, Minnesota	35
1999—	Martin Gramatica, Tampa Bay	27

INTERCEPTIONS

Year	Player	No.	Yds.
1960—	Dave Baker, San Francisco	10	96
	Jerry Norton, St. Louis	10	96
1961—	Dick Lynch, N.Y. Giants	9	60
1962—	Willie Wood, Green Bay	9	132
1963—	Dick Lynch, N.Y. Giants	9	251
	Rosie Taylor, Chicago	9	172
1964—	Paul Krause, Washington	12	140
1965—	Bobby Boyd, Baltimore	9	78
1966—	Larry Wilson, St. Louis	10	180
1967—	Lem Barney, Detroit	10	232
	Dave Whitsell, New Orleans	10	178
1968—	Willie Williams, N.Y. Giants	10	103
1969—	Mel Renfro, Dallas	10	118
1970—	Dick Le Beau, Detroit	9	96
1971—	Bill Bradley, Philadelphia	11	248
1972—	Bill Bradley, Philadelphia	9	73
1973—	Bob Bryant, Minnesota	7	105
1974—	Ray Brown, Atlanta	8	164
1975—	Paul Krause, Minnesota	10	201
1976—	Monte Jackson, L.A. Rams	10	173
1977—	Rolland Lawrence, Atlanta	7	138
1978—	Ken Stone, St. Louis	9	139
	Willie Buchanon, Green Bay	9	93
1979—	Lemar Parrish, Washington	9	65
1980—	Nolan Cromwell, L.A. Rams	8	140
1981—	Everson Walls, Dallas	11	133
1982—	Everson Walls, Dallas	7	61
1983—	Mark Murphy, Washington	9	127
1984—	Tom Flynn, Green Bay	9	106
1985—	Everson Walls, Dallas	9	31
1986—	Ronnie Lott, San Francisco	10	134
1987—	Barry Wilburn, Washington	9	135
1988—	Scott Case, Atlanta	10	47
1989—	Eric Allen, Philadelphia	8	38
1990—	Mark Carrier, Chicago	10	39
1991—	Ray Crockett, Detroit	6	141
	Tim McKyer, Atlanta	6	24
	Deion Sanders, Atlanta	6	119
	Aeneas Williams, Phoenix	6	60
1992—	Aubray McMillian, Minnesota	8	157
1993—	Deion Sanders, Atlanta	7	91
1994—	Aeneas Williams, Arizona	9	89
1995—	Orlando Thomas, Minnesota	9	108
1996—	Keith Lyle, St. Louis	9	152
1997—	Ryan McNeil, St. Louis	9	127
1998—	Kwamie Lassiter, Arizona	8	80
1999—	Donnie Abraham, Tampa Bay	7	115
	Troy Vincent, Philadelphia	7	91

PUNTING
(Based on highest average yardage per punt by qualifiers)

Year	Player	No.	Avg.
1960—	Jerry Norton, St. Louis	39	45.6
1961—	Yale Lary, Detroit	52	48.4
1962—	Tommy Davis, San Francisco	48	45.8
1963—	Yale Lary, Detroit	35	48.9
1964—	Bobby Walden, Minnesota	72	46.4
1965—	Gary Collins, Cleveland	65	46.7
1966—	David Lee, Baltimore	49	45.6
1967—	Billy Lothridge, Atlanta	87	43.7
1968—	Billy Lothridge, Atlanta	75	44.3
1969—	David Lee, Baltimore	50	45.3
1970—	Julian Fagan, New Orleans	77	42.5
1971—	Tom McNeill, Philadelphia	73	42.0
1972—	Dave Chapple, L.A. Rams	53	44.2
1973—	Tom Wittum, San Francisco	79	43.7
1974—	Tom Blanchard, New Orleans	88	42.1
1975—	Herman Weaver, Detroit	80	42.0
1976—	John James, Atlanta	101	42.1
1977—	Tom Blanchard, New Orleans	82	42.4
1978—	Tom Skladany, Detroit	86	42.5
1979—	Dave Jennings, N.Y. Giants	104	42.7
1980—	Dave Jennings, N.Y. Giants	94	44.8
1981—	Tom Skladany, Detroit	64	43.5
1982—	Carl Birdsong, St. Louis	54	43.8
1983—	Frank Garcia, Tampa Bay	95	42.2
1984—	Brian Hansen, New Orleans	69	43.8
1985—	Rick Donnelly, Atlanta	59	43.6
1986—	Sean Landeta, N.Y. Giants	79	44.8
1987—	Rick Donnelly, Atlanta	61	44.0
1988—	Jim Arnold, Detroit	97	42.4
1989—	Rich Camarillo, Phoenix	76	43.4
1990—	Sean Landeta, N.Y. Giants	75	44.1
1991—	Harry Newsome, Minnesota	68	45.5
1992—	Harry Newsome, Minnesota	72	45.0
1993—	Jim Arnold, Detroit	72	44.5
1994—	Sean Landeta, L.A. Rams	78	44.8
1995—	Sean Landeta, St. Louis	83	44.3
1996—	Matt Turk, Washington	75	45.1
1997—	Mark Royals, New Orleans	88	45.9
1998—	Mark Royals, New Orleans	88	45.6
1999—	Mitch Berger, Minnesota	61	45.4

PUNT RETURNS
(Based on most total yards)

Year	Player	No.	Yds.	Avg.
1960—	Abe Woodson, San Francisco	13	174	13.4
1961—	Willie Wood, Green Bay	14	225	16.1

HISTORY Statistical leaders

Year	Player	No.	Yds.	Avg.
1962	Pat Studstill, Detroit	29	457	15.8
1963	Dick James, Washington	16	214	13.4
1964	Tommy Watkins, Detroit	16	238	14.9
1965	Leroy Kelly, Cleveland	17	265	15.6
1966	Johnny Roland, St. Louis	20	221	11.1
1967	Ben Davis, Cleveland	18	229	12.7
1968	Bob Hayes, Dallas	15	312	20.8
1969	Alvin Haymond, L.A. Rams	33	435	13.2
1970	Bruce Taylor, San Francisco	43	516	12.0
1971	Les Duncan, Washington	22	233	10.6
1972	Ken Ellis, Green Bay	14	215	15.4
1973	Bruce Taylor, San Francisco	15	207	13.8
1974	Dick Jauron, Detroit	17	286	16.8
1975	Terry Metcalf, St. Louis	23	285	12.4
1976	Eddie Brown, Washington	48	646	13.5
1977	Larry Marshall, Philadelphia	46	489	10.6
1978	Jackie Wallace, L.A. Rams	52	618	11.9
1979	John Sciarra, Philadelphia	16	182	11.4
1980	Kenny Johnson, Atlanta	23	281	12.2
1981	LeRoy Irvin, L.A. Rams	46	615	13.4
1982	Billy Johnson, Atlanta	24	273	11.4
1983	Henry Ellard, L.A. Rams	16	217	13.6
1984	Henry Ellard, L.A. Rams	30	403	13.4
1985	Henry Ellard, L.A. Rams	37	501	13.5
1986	Vai Sikahema, St. Louis	43	522	12.1
1987	Mel Gray, New Orleans	24	352	14.7
1988	John Taylor, San Francisco	44	556	12.6
1989	Walter Stanley, Detroit	36	496	13.8
1990	Johnny Bailey, Chicago	36	399	11.1
1991	Mel Gray, Detroit	25	385	15.4
1992	Johnny Bailey, Phoenix	20	263	13.2
1993	Tyrone Hughes, New Orleans	37	503	13.6
1994	Brian Mitchell, Washington	32	452	14.1
1995	Eric Guliford, Carolina	43	475	11.0
1996	Desmond Howard, Green Bay	58	875	15.1
1997	Karl Williams, Tampa Bay	46	597	13.0
1998	Brian Mitchell, Washington	44	506	11.5
1999	Glyn Milburn, Chicago	29	346	11.9

KICKOFF RETURNS
(Based on most total yards)

Year	Player	No.	Yds.	Avg.
1960	Tom Moore, Green Bay	12	397	33.1
1961	Dick Bass, L.A. Rams	23	698	30.3
1962	Abe Woodson, San Francisco	37	1157	31.3
1963	Abe Woodson, San Francisco	29	935	32.3
1964	Clarence Childs, N.Y. Giants	34	987	29.0
1965	Tommy Watkins, Detroit	17	584	34.4
1966	Gale Sayers, Chicago	23	718	31.2
1967	Travis Williams, Green Bay	18	739	41.1
1968	Preston Pearson, Baltimore	15	527	35.1
1969	Bobby Williams, Detroit	17	563	33.1
1970	Cecil Turner, Chicago	23	752	32.7
1971	Travis Williams, L.A. Rams	25	743	29.7
1972	Ron Smith, Chicago	30	924	30.8
1973	Carl Garrett, Chicago	16	486	30.4
1974	Terry Metcalf, St. Louis	20	623	31.2
1975	Walter Payton, Chicago	14	444	31.7
1976	Cullen Bryant, L.A. Rams	16	459	28.7
1977	Wilbert Montgomery, Phila.	23	619	26.9
1978	Steve Odom, Green Bay	25	677	27.1
1979	Jimmy Edwards, Minnesota	44	1103	25.1
1980	Rich Mauti, New Orleans	31	798	27.6
1981	Mike Nelms, Washington	37	1099	29.7
1982	Alvin Hall, Detroit	16	426	26.6
1983	Darrin Nelson, Minnesota	18	445	24.7
1984	Barry Redden, L.A. Rams	23	530	23.0
1985	Ron Brown, L.A. Rams	28	918	32.8
1986	Dennis Gentry, Chicago	20	576	28.8
1987	Sylvester Stamps, Atlanta	24	660	27.5
1988	Donnie Elder, Tampa Bay	34	772	22.7
1989	Mel Gray, Detroit	24	640	26.7
1990	Dave Meggett, N.Y. Giants	21	492	23.4
1991	Mel Gray, Detroit	36	929	25.8
1992	Deion Sanders, Atlanta	40	1067	26.7
1993	Tony Smith, Atlanta	38	948	24.9
1994	Tyrone Hughes, New Orleans	63	1556	24.7
1995	Tyrone Hughes, New Orleans	66	1617	24.5
1996	Tyrone Hughes, New Orleans	70	1791	25.6
1997	Glyn Milburn, Detroit	55	1315	23.9
1998	Glyn Milburn, Chicago	62	1550	25.0
1999	Tony Horne, St. Louis	30	892	29.7

SACKS

Year	Player	No.
1982	Doug Martin, Minnesota	11.5
1983	Fred Dean, San Francisco	17.5
1984	Richard Dent, Chicago	17.5
1985	Richard Dent, Chicago	17.0
1986	Lawrence Taylor, N.Y. Giants	20.5
1987	Reggie White, Philadelphia	21.0
1988	Reggie White, Philadelphia	18.0
1989	Chris Doleman, Minnesota	21.0
1990	Charles Haley, San Francisco	16.0
1991	Pat Swilling, New Orleans	17.0
1992	Clyde Simmons, Philadelphia	19.0
1993	Renaldo Turnbull, New Orleans	13.0
	Reggie White, Green Bay	13.0
1994	Ken Harvey, Washington	13.5
	John Randle, Minnesota	13.5
1995	William Fuller, Philadelphia	13.0
	Wayne Martin, New Orleans	13.0
1996	Kevin Greene, Carolina	14.5
1997	John Randle, Minnesota	15.5
1998	Reggie White, Green Bay	16.0
1999	Kevin Carter, St. Louis	17.0

COACHING RECORDS

COACHES WITH 100 CAREER VICTORIES

(Ranked according to career wins)

	Yrs.	REGULAR SEASON Won	Lost	Tied	Pct.	POSTSEASON Won	Lost	Pct.	CAREER Won	Lost	Tied	Pct.
Don Shula	33	328	156	6	.676	19	17	.528	347	173	6	.665
George Halas	40	318	148	31	.671	6	3	.667	324	151	31	.671
Tom Landry	29	250	162	6	.605	20	16	.556	270	178	6	.605
Curly Lambeau	33	226	132	22	.624	3	2	.600	229	134	22	.623
Chuck Noll	23	193	148	1	.566	16	8	.667	209	156	1	.572
Chuck Knox	22	186	147	1	.558	7	11	.389	193	158	1	.550
*Dan Reeves	19	167	128	1	.566	10	8	.556	177	136	1	.565
Paul Brown	21	166	100	6	.621	4	9	.308	170	109	6	.607
Bud Grant	18	158	96	5	.620	10	12	.455	168	108	5	.607
Steve Owen	23	153	100	17	.598	2	8	.200	155	108	17	.584
Marv Levy	17	143	112	0	.561	11	8	.579	154	120	0	.562
Marty Schottenheimer	15	145	85	1	.630	5	11	.313	150	96	1	.609
*Bill Parcells	15	138	100	1	.579	11	6	.647	149	106	1	.584
Joe Gibbs	12	124	60	0	.674	16	5	.762	140	65	0	.683
Hank Stram	17	131	97	10	.571	5	3	.625	136	100	10	.573
Weeb Ewbank	20	130	129	7	.502	4	1	.800	134	130	7	.507
*Mike Ditka	14	121	95	0	.560	6	6	.500	127	101	0	.557
Sid Gillman	18	122	99	7	.550	1	5	.167	123	104	7	.541
George Allen	12	116	47	5	.705	4	7	.364	120	54	5	.684
*George Seifert	9	106	38	0	.736	10	5	.667	116	43	0	.730
Don Coryell	14	111	83	1	.572	3	6	.333	114	89	1	.561
John Madden	10	103	32	7	.750	9	7	.563	112	39	7	.731
*Jim Mora	13	109	90	0	.548	0	5	.000	109	95	0	.534
Buddy Parker	15	104	75	9	.577	3	2	.600	107	77	9	.578
Vince Lombardi	10	96	34	6	.728	9	1	.900	105	35	6	.740
Bill Walsh	10	92	59	1	.609	10	4	.714	102	63	1	.617

*Active NFL coaches in 1999.

ACTIVE COACHES CAREER RECORDS

(Ranked according to career NFL percentages)

	Yrs.	REGULAR SEASON Won	Lost	Tied	Pct.	POSTSEASON Won	Lost	Pct.	CAREER Won	Lost	Tied	Pct.
George Seifert	9	106	38	0	.736	10	5	.667	116	43	0	.730
Mike Holmgren	8	84	44	0	.656	9	6	.600	93	50	0	.650
Mike Shanahan	7	61	39	0	.610	7	1	.875	68	40	0	.630
Dennis Green	8	81	47	0	.633	3	7	.300	84	54	0	.609
Tom Coughlin	5	49	31	0	.613	4	4	.500	53	35	0	.602
Steve Mariucci	3	29	19	0	.604	2	2	.500	31	21	0	.596
Bill Cowher	8	77	51	0	.602	5	6	.455	82	57	0	.590
Dan Reeves	19	167	128	1	.566	10	8	.556	177	136	1	.565
Gunther Cunningham	1	9	7	0	.563	0	0	.000	9	7	0	.563
Mike Ditka	14	121	95	0	.560	6	6	.500	127	101	0	.557
Tony Dungy	4	35	29	0	.547	2	2	.500	37	31	0	.544
Wade Phillips	5	38	30	0	.559	0	3	.000	38	33	0	.535
Jim Mora	13	109	90	0	.548	0	5	.000	109	95	0	.534
USFL Totals	3	41	12	1	.769	7	1	.875	48	13	1	.782
Jeff Fisher	6	45	41	0	.523	3	1	.750	48	42	0	.533
Bobby Ross	8	69	59	0	.539	3	5	.375	72	64	0	.529
Jim Fassel	3	25	22	1	.531	0	1	.000	25	23	1	.520
Jon Gruden	2	16	16	0	.500	0	0	.000	16	16	0	.500
Brian Billick	1	8	8	0	.500	0	0	.000	8	8	0	.500
Mike Riley	1	8	8	0	.500	0	0	.000	8	8	0	.500
Bill Belichick	5	36	44	0	.450	1	1	.500	37	45	0	.451
Norv Turner	6	42	53	1	.443	1	1	.500	43	54	1	.444
Dave Wannstedt	6	40	56	0	.417	1	1	.500	41	57	0	.418
Vince Tobin	4	26	38	0	.406	1	1	.500	27	39	0	.409
Bruce Coslet	8	47	74	0	.388	0	1	.000	47	75	0	.385
Dick Jauron	1	6	10	0	.375	0	0	.000	6	10	0	.375
Andy Reid	1	5	11	0	.313	0	0	.000	5	11	0	.313
Chris Palmer	1	2	14	0	.125	0	0	.000	2	14	0	.125
Dave Campo	0	0	0	0	.000	0	0	.000	0	0	0	.000
Jim Haslett	0	0	0	0	.000	0	0	.000	0	0	0	.000
Mike Martz	0	0	0	0	.000	0	0	.000	0	0	0	.000
Mike Sherman	0	0	0	0	.000	0	0	.000	0	0	0	.000

HALL OF FAME

ROSTER OF MEMBERS
FIVE NEW INDUCTEES IN 2000

Howie Long, Ronnie Lott, Joe Montana, Dan Rooney and Dave Wilcox were inducted into Pro Football's Hall of Fame in 2000, expanding the list of former stars honored at Canton, Ohio, to 204.

Name	Elec. year	College	Pos.	NFL teams
Adderley, Herb	1980	Michigan State	CB	Green Bay Packers, 1961-69; Dallas Cowboys, 1970-72
Alworth, Lance†	1978	Arkansas	WR	San Diego Chargers, 1962-70; Dallas Cowboys, 1971-72.
Atkins, Doug	1982	Tennessee	DE	Cleveland Browns, 1953-54; Chicago Bears, 1955-66; New Orleans Saints, 1967-69
Badgro, Morris (Red)	1981	Southern California	E	New York Yankees, 1926; New York Giants, 1930-35
Barney, Lem	1992	Jackson State	CB	Detroit Lions, 1967-77
Battles, Cliff	1968	W. Virginia Wesleyan	HB/QB	Boston Braves, Boston Redskins, Washington Redskins, 1932-37; coach, Brooklyn Dodgers, 1946-47
Baugh, Sammy	1963	Texas Christian	QB	Washington Redskins, 1937-52; coach, New York Titans, 1960-61; Houston Oilers, 1964
Bednarik, Chuck	1967	Pennsylvania	C/LB	Philadelphia Eagles, 1949-62
Bell, Bert	1963	Pennsylvania	*	NFL Commissioner, 1946-59
Bell, Bobby	1983	Minnesota	LB	Kansas City Chiefs, 1963-74
Berry, Raymond†	1973	Southern Methodist	E	Baltimore Colts, 1955-67; coach, New England Patriots, 1984-89
Bidwill, Charles W.	1967	Loyola	*	Owner, Chicago Cardinals, 1933-47
Biletnikoff, Fred	1988	Florida State	WR	Oakland Raiders, 1965-78
Blanda, George†	1981	Kentucky	QB/PK	Chicago Bears, 1949-58; Baltimore Colts, 1950; Houston Oilers, 1960-66; Oakland Raiders, 1967-73
Blount, Mel†	1989	Southern	CB	Pittsburgh Steelers, 1970-83
Bradshaw, Terry†	1989	Louisiana Tech	QB	Pittsburgh Steelers, 1970-83
Brown, Jim†	1971	Syracuse	FB	Cleveland Browns, 1957-65
Brown, Paul	1967	Miami of Ohio	*	Coach, Cleveland Browns, 1946-62; Cincinnati Bengals, 1968-75
Brown, Roosevelt	1975	Morgan State	T	New York Giants, 1953-66
Brown, Willie†	1984	Grambling	DB	Denver Broncos, 1963-66; Oakland Raiders, 1967-78
Buchanan, Buck	1990	Grambling	DT	Kansas City Chiefs, 1963-75
Butkus, Dick†	1979	Illinois	LB	Chicago Bears, 1965-73
Campbell, Earl†	1991	Texas	RB	Houston Oilers, 1978-84; New Orleans Saints, 1984-85
Canadeo, Tony	1974	Gonzaga	HB	Green Bay Packers, 1941-44, 46-52
Carr, Joe	1963			NFL President, 1921-39
Chamberlin, Guy	1965	Nebraska	E/WB*	Player/coach, Canton Bulldogs, Cleveland, Frankford Yellowjackets, Chicago Bears, Chicago Cardinals, 1919-28
Christiansen, Jack	1970	Colorado A&M	DB	Detroit Lions, 1951-58; coach, San Francisco 49ers, 1963-67
Clark, Dutch	1963	Colorado College	QB	Portsmouth Spartans, Detroit Lions, 1931-38
Connor, George	1975	Notre Dame	T/LB	Chicago Bears, 1948-55
Conzelman, Jimmy	1964	Washington (Mo.)	HB*	Coach/executive, Decatur, Rock Island, Milwaukee, Detroit, Providence, Chicago Cardinals, 1920-48
Creekmur, Lou	1996	William & Mary	T/G	Detroit Lions, 1950-59
Csonka, Larry	1987	Syracuse	RB	Miami Dolphins, 1968-74, 79; New York Giants, 1976-78
Davis, Al	1992	Syracuse	*	Coach/general manager/president, Oakland-Los Angeles Raiders, 1963-present
Davis, Willie	1981	Grambling	DE	Cleveland Browns, 1958-59; Green Bay Packers, 1960-69
Dawson, Len	1987	Purdue	QB	Pittsburgh Steelers, 1957-58; Cleveland Browns, 1960-61; Dallas Texans, 1962; Kansas City Chiefs, 1963-75
Dickerson, Eric†	1999	Southern Methodist	RB	Los Angeles Rams, 1983-87; Indianapolis Colts, 1987-91; Los Angeles Raiders, 1992; Atlanta Falcons, 1993
Dierdorf, Dan	1996	Michigan	T/C	St. Louis Cardinals, 1971-83
Ditka, Mike	1988	Pittsburgh	TE	Chicago Bears, 1961-66; Philadelphia Eagles, 1967-68; Dallas Cowboys, 1969-72; coach, Chicago Bears, 1982-92; New Orleans Saints, 1997-99
Donovan, Art	1968	Boston College	DT	Baltimore Colts, New York Yanks, Dallas Texans, 1950-61
Dorsett, Tony	1994	Pittsburgh	RB	Dallas Cowboys, 1977-87; Denver Broncos, 1988
Driscoll, Paddy	1965	Northwestern	TB/HB/QB	Player/coach, Chicago Cardinals, Chicago Bears, 1919-31, 41-68
Dudley, Bill	1966	Virginia	HB	Pittsburgh Steelers, Detroit Lions, Washington Redskins, 1942-53
Edwards, Turk	1969	Washington State	T	Boston Braves, Boston Redskins, Washington Redskins, 1932-40
Ewbank, Weeb	1978	Miami of Ohio	*	Coach, Baltimore Colts, 1954-62; New York Jets, 1963-73
Fears, Tom	1970	Santa Clara	E	Los Angeles Rams, 1948-56; coach, New Orleans Saints, 1967-70
Finks, Jim	1995	Tulsa	QB*	Pittsburgh Steelers, 1949-55; administrator, Minnesota Vikings, 1964-73; Chicago Bears, 1974-86; New Orleans Saints, 1987-93

– 353 –

HISTORY *Hall of Fame*

Name	Elec. year	College	Pos.	NFL teams
Flaherty, Ray	1976	Gonzaga	E*	Player/coach, Los Angeles Wildcats, New York Yankees, AFL; New York Giants, Boston Redskins, Washington Redskins, New York Yankees, AAFC; Chicago Hornets, 1926-49
Ford, Len	1976	Michigan	E	Los Angeles Dons, Cleveland Browns, 1948-58
Fortmann, Danny	1965	Colgate	G	Chicago Bears, 1936-43
Fouts, Dan†	1993	Oregon	QB	San Diego Chargers, 1973-87
Gatski, Frank	1985	Marshall	C	Cleveland Browns, 1946-56; Detroit Lions, 1957
George, Bill	1974	Wake Forest	LB	Chicago Bears, Los Angeles Rams, 1952-66
Gibbs, Joe	1996	San Diego State	*	Washington Redskins, 1981-92
Gifford, Frank	1977	Southern California	HB/E	New York Giants, 1952-60, 62-64
Gillman, Sid	1983	Ohio State	E*	Cleveland Rams, 1936; coach, Los Angeles Rams, 1955-59; Los Angeles Chargers, 1960; San Diego Chargers, 1961-69, 71; Houston Oilers, 1973-74
Graham, Otto	1965	Northwestern	QB	Cleveland Browns, 1946-55; coach, Washington Redskins, 1966-68
Grange, Red	1963	Illinois	HB	Chicago Bears, 1925, 29-34; New York Yankees, 1926-27
Grant, Bud	1994	Minnesota	WR*	Philadelphia Eagles, 1951-52; coach, Minnesota Vikings, 1967-83, 1985
Greene, Joe†	1987	North Texas State	DT	Pittsburgh Steelers, 1969-81
Gregg, Forrest†	1977	Southern Methodist	T	Green Bay Packers, Dallas Cowboys, 1956, 58-71; coach, Cleveland Browns, 1975-77; Cincinnati Bengals, 1980-83; Green Bay Packers, 1984-87
Griese, Bob	1990	Purdue	QB	Miami Dolphins, 1967-80
Groza, Lou	1974	Ohio State	T/PK	Cleveland Browns, 1946-59, 61-67
Guyon, Joe	1966	Carlisle, Georgia Tech	HB	Canton Bulldogs, Cleveland Indians, Oorang Indians, Rock Island Independents, Kansas City Cowboys, New York Giants, 1918-27
Halas, George	1963	Illinois	E*	Player/coach/ founder, Chicago Bears, 1920-83
Ham, Jack†	1988	Penn State	LB	Pittsburgh Steelers, 1971-82
Hannah, John†	1991	Alabama	G	New England Patriots, 1973-85
Harris, Franco†	1990	Penn State	RB	Pittsburgh Steelers, 1972-83; Seattle Seahawks, 1984
Haynes, Mike	1997	Arizona State	CB	New England Patriots, 1976-82; Los Angeles Raiders, 1983-89
Healey, Ed	1964	Dartmouth	T	Rock Island, Chicago Bears, 1920-27
Hein, Mel	1963	Washington State	C	New York Giants, 1931-45
Hendricks, Ted	1990	Miami, Fla.	LB	Baltimore Colts, 1969-73; Green Bay Packers, 1974; Oakland/Los Angeles Raiders, 1975-83
Henry, Wilbur	1963	Wash'ton & Jefferson	T	Canton Bulldogs, Akron Indians, New York Giants, Pottsville Maroons, Pittsburgh Steelers, 1920-30
Herber, Arnie	1966	Regis	HB	Green Bay Packers, New York Giants, 1930-45
Hewitt, Bill	1971	Michigan	E	Chicago Bears, 1932-36; Philadelphia Eagles, 1937-39; Philadelphia/Pittsburgh, 1943
Hinkle, Clarke	1964	Bucknell	FB	Green Bay Packers, 1932-41
Hirsch, Elroy (Crazylegs)	1968	Wisconsin	E/HB	Chicago Rockets, Los Angeles Rams, 1946-57
Hornung, Paul	1986	Notre Dame	RB	Green Bay Packers, 1957-62, 64-66
Houston, Ken†	1986	Prairie View	DB	Houston Oilers, 1967-72; Washington Redskins, 1973-80
Hubbard, Cal	1963	Centenary, Geneva	T/E	New York Giants, Green Bay Packers, Pittsburgh Steelers, 1927-36
Huff, Sam	1982	West Virginia	LB	New York Giants, 1956-63; Washington Redskins, 1964-67, 69
Hunt, Lamar	1972	Southern Methodist	*	Founder, American Football League, 1959; president, Dallas Texans, 1960-62; Kansas City Chiefs, 1963-present
Hutson, Don	1963	Alabama	E	Green Bay Packers, 1935-45
Johnson, Jimmy	1994	UCLA	DB	San Francisco 49ers, 1961-76
Johnson, John Henry	1987	Arizona State	FB	San Francisco 49ers, 1954-56; Detroit Lions, 1957-59; Pittsburgh Steelers, 1960-65; Houston Oilers, 1966
Joiner, Charlie	1996	Grambling	WR	Houston Oilers, 1969-72; Cincinnati Bengals, 1972-75; San Diego Chargers, 1976-86
Jones, Deacon†	1980	South Carolina State	DE	Los Angeles Rams, 1961-71; San Diego Chargers, 1972-73; Washington Redskins, 1974
Jones, Stan	1991	Maryland	G/DT	Chicago Bears, 1954-65; Washington Redskins, 1966
Jordan, Henry	1995	Virginia	DT	Cleveland Browns, 1957-58; Green Bay Packers, 1959-69
Jurgensen, Sonny	1983	Duke	QB	Philadelphia Eagles, 1957-63; Washington Redskins, 1964-74
Kelly, Leroy	1994	Morgan State	RB	Cleveland Browns, 1964-73
Kiesling, Walter	1966	St. Thomas	G/T*	Player/coach, Duluth Eskimos, Pottsville Maroons, Boston Braves, Chicago Cardinals, Chicago Bears, Green Bay Packers, Pittsburgh Steelers, 1926-56
Kinard, Frank (Bruiser)	1971	Mississippi	T	Brooklyn Dodgers, 1938-45; New York Yankees, 1946-47
Krause, Paul	1998	Iowa	S	Washington Redskins, 1964-67; Minnesota Vikings, 1968-79
Lambeau, Curly	1963	Notre Dame	TB/FB/E*	Founder/player/coach, Green Bay Packers, 1919-49
Lambert, Jack†	1990	Kent State	LB	Pittsburgh Steelers, 1974-84
Landry, Tom†	1990	Texas	*	Coach, Dallas Cowboys, 1960-88
Lane, Dick (Night Train)	1974	Scottsbluff J.C.	DB	Los Angeles Rams, Chicago Cardinals, Detroit Lions, 1952-65
Langer, Jim†	1987	South Dakota State	C	Miami Dolphins, 1970-79; Minnesota Vikings, 1980-81

– 354 –

Name	Elec. year	College	Pos.	NFL teams
Lanier, Willie	1986	Morgan State	LB	Kansas City Chiefs, 1967-77
Largent, Steve†	1995	Tulsa	WR	Seattle Seahawks, 1976-89
Lary, Yale	1979	Texas A&M	DB	Detroit Lions, 1952-53, 56-64
Lavelli, Dante	1975	Ohio State	E	Cleveland Browns, 1946-56
Layne, Bobby	1967	Texas	QB	Chicago Bears, New York Bulldogs, Detroit Lions, Pittsburgh Steelers, 1948-62
Leemans, Tuffy	1978	George Washington	FB	New York Giants, 1936-43
Lilly, Bob†	1980	Texas Christian	DT	Dallas Cowboys, 1961-74
Little, Larry	1993	Bethune Cookman	G	San Diego Chargers, 1967-68; Miami Dolphins, 1969-80
Lombardi, Vince	1971	Fordham	*	Coach, Green Bay Packers, 1959-67; Washington Redskins, 1969
Long, Howie	2000	Villanova	DE	Oakland/Los Angeles Raiders, 1981-93
Lott, Ronnie†	2000	Southern California	DB	San Francisco 49ers, 1981-90; Los Angeles Raiders, 1991-92; New York Jets, 1993-94
Luckman, Sid	1965	Columbia	QB	Chicago Bears, 1939-50
Lyman, Roy (Link)	1964		T	Canton Bulldogs, Cleveland, Chicago Bears, 1922-34
Mack, Tom	1999	Michigan	G	Los Angeles Rams, 1966-78
Mackey, John	1992	Syracuse	TE	Baltimore Colts, 1963-71; San Diego Chargers, 1972
Mara, Tim	1963		*	Founder, New York Giants, 1925-65
Mara, Wellington	1997	Fordham	*	President, New York Giants, 1965-present
Marchetti, Gino†	1972	San Francisco	DE	Dallas Texans, 1952; Baltimore Colts, 1953-66
Marshall, George Preston	1963		*	Founder, Washington Redskins, 1932-65
Matson, Ollie†	1972	San Francisco	HB	Chicago Cardinals, 1952, 54-58; Los Angeles Rams, 1959-62; Detroit Lions, 1963; Philadelphia Eagles, 1964-66
Maynard, Don	1987	Texas Western College	WR	New York Giants, 1958; New York Jets, 1960-72; St. Louis Cardinals, 1973
McAfee, George	1966	Duke	HB	Chicago Bears, 1940-41, 45-50
McCormack, Mike	1984	Kansas	T	New York Yanks, 1951; Cleveland Browns, 1954-62
McDonald, Tommy	1998	Oklahoma	WR	Philadelphia Eagles,1957-63; Dallas Cowboys, 1964; Los Angeles Rams, 1965-66; Atlanta Falcons, 1967; Cleveland Browns,1968
McElhenny, Hugh†	1970	Washington	HB	San Francisco 49ers, Minnesota Vikings, New York Giants, Detroit Lions, 1952-64
McNally, Johnny Blood	1963	St. John's	HB	Milwaukee Badgers, Duluth Eskimos, Pottsville Maroons, Green Bay Packers, Pittsburgh Steelers, 1925-39
Michalske, August (Mike)	1964	Penn State	G	New York Yankees, Green Bay Packers, 1927-37
Millner, Wayne	1968	Notre Dame	E	Boston Redskins, Washington Redskins, 1936-41, 45
Mitchell, Bobby	1983	Illinois	RB/FL/WR	Cleveland Browns, 1958-61; Washington Redskins, 1962-68
Mix, Ron	1979	Southern California	T	Los Angeles Chargers, 1960; San Diego Chargers, 1961-69; Oakland Raiders, 1971
Montana, Joe†	2000	Notre Dame	QB	San Francisco 49ers, 1979-92; Kansas City Chiefs, 1993-94
Moore, Lenny	1975	Penn State	HB	Baltimore Colts, 1956-67
Motley, Marion	1968	Nevada	FB/LB	Cleveland Browns, Pittsburgh Steelers, 1946-55
Munoz, Anthony†	1998	Southern California	OT	Cincinnati Bengals, 1980-92
Musso, George	1982	Milliken	G/DT	Chicago Bears, 1933-44
Nagurski, Bronko	1963	Minnesota	FB/T	Chicago Bears, 1930-37, 43
Namath, Joe	1985	Alabama	QB	New York Jets, 1965-76; Los Angeles Rams, 1977
Neale, Earle (Greasy)	1969	W. Virginia Wesleyan	*	Coach, Philadelphia Eagles, 1941-50
Nevers, Ernie	1963	Stanford	FB	Duluth Eskimos, Chicago Cardinals, 1926-37
Newsome, Ozzie	1999	Alabama	TE	Cleveland Browns, 1978-90
Nitschke, Ray†	1978	Illinois	LB	Green Bay Packers, 1958-72
Noll, Chuck†	1993	Dayton	*	Coach, Pittsburgh Steelers, 1969-91
Nomellini, Leo†	1969	Minnesota	DT	San Francisco 49ers, 1953-63
Olsen, Merlin†	1982	Utah State	DT	Los Angeles Rams, 1962-76
Otto, Jim†	1980	Miami, Fla.	C	Oaklland Raiders, 1960-74
Owen, Steve	1966	Phillips	T/G	Player/coach, Kansas City Cowboys, New York Giants, 1924-53
Page, Alan	1988	Notre Dame	DT	Minnesota Vikings, 1967-78; Chicago Bears, 1978-81
Parker, Clarence (Ace)	1972	Duke	HB	Brooklyn Dodgers, 1937-41; Boston Yanks, 1945; New York Yankees, 1946
Parker, Jim†	1973	Ohio State	G	Baltimore Colts, 1957-67
Payton, Walter†	1993	Jackson State	RB	Chicago Bears, 1975-87
Perry, Joe†	1969	Compton J.C.	FB	San Francisco 49ers, Baltimore Colts, 1948-63
Pihos, Pete	1970	Indiana	E	Philadelphia Eagles, 1947-55
Ray, Hugh (Shorty)	1966	Illinois	*	NFL technical adviser and supervisor of officials, 1938-56
Reeves, Daniel F.	1967	Georgetown	*	Founder, Los Angeles Rams, 1941-71
Renfro, Mel	1996	Oregon	DB	Dallas Cowboys, 1964-77
Riggins, John	1992	Kansas	FB	New York Jets, 1971-75; Washington Redskins, 1976-85
Ringo, Jim	1981	Syracuse	C	Green Bay Packers, 1953-63; Philadelphia Eagles, 1964-67
Robustelli, Andy	1971	Arnold	DE	Los Angeles Rams, 1951-55; New York Giants, 1956-64
Rooney, Arthur J.	1964	Georgetown	*	Founder, Pittsburgh Steelers, 1933-82
Rooney, Dan	2000	Duquesne	*	Pittsburgh Steelers, 1955-present
Rozelle, Pete	1985	San Francisco	*	NFL Commissioner, 1960-89

HISTORY Hall of Fame

HISTORY — Hall of Fame

Name	Elec. year	College	Pos.	NFL teams
St. Clair, Bob	1990	Tulsa	T	San Francisco 49ers, 1953-63
Sayers, Gale†	1977	Kansas	RB	Chicago Bears, 1965-71
Schmidt, Joe	1973	Pittsburgh	LB	Detroit Lions, 1953-65; coach, Detroit Lions, 1967-72
Schramm, Tex	1991	Texas	*	President/general manager, Dallas Cowboys, 1960-88
Selmon, Lee Roy	1995	Oklahoma	DE	Tampa Bay Buccaneers, 1976-84
Shaw, Billy	1999	Georgia Tech	G	Buffalo Bills, 1961-69
Shell, Art	1989	Md.-Eastern Shore	T	Oakland-Los Angeles Raiders, 1968-82; coach, Los Angeles Raiders, 1989-94
Shula, Don†	1997	John Carroll	DB	Cleveland Browns, 1951-52; Baltimore Colts, 1953-56; Washington Redskins, 1957; coach, Baltimore Colts, 1963-69, Miami Dolphins, 1970-95
Simpson, O.J.†	1985	Southern California	RB	Buffalo Bills, 1969-77; San Francisco 49ers, 1978
Singletary, Mike†	1998	Baylor	LB	Chicago Bears, 1981-92
Smith, Jackie	1994	N'western Louisiana	TE	St. Louis Cardinals, 1963-77; Dallas Cowboys, 1978
Starr, Bart†	1977	Alabama	QB	Green Bay Packers, 1956-71; coach, Green Bay Packers, 1975-83
Staubach, Roger†	1985	Navy	QB	Dallas Cowboys, 1969-79
Stautner, Ernie†	1969	West Virginia	DT	Pittsburgh Steelers, 1950-63
Stenerud, Jan†	1991	Montana State	PK	Kansas City Chiefs, 1967-79; Green Bay Packers, 1980-83; Minnesota Vikings, 1984-85
Stephenson, Dwight	1998	Alabama	C	Miami Dolphins, 1980-87
Strong, Ken	1967	New York U.	HB/PK	Staten Island Stapletons, New York Yankees, New York Giants, 1929-39, 44-47
Stydahar, Joe	1967	West Virginia	T	Chicago Bears, 1936-42, 45-46
Tarkenton, Fran	1986	Georgia	QB	Minnesota Vikings, 1961-66, 72-78; New York Giants, 1967-71
Taylor, Charley	1984	Arizona State	WR	Washington Redskins, 1964-75, 77
Taylor, Lawrence†	1999	North Carolina	LB	New York Giants, 1981-93
Taylor, Jim	1976	Louisiana State	FB	Green Bay Packers, 1958-66; New Orleans Saints, 1967
Thorpe, Jim	1963	Carlisle	HB	Canton Bulldogs, Oorang Indians, Cleveland Indians, Toledo Maroons, Rock Island Independents, New York Giants, 1915-26, 29
Tittle, Y.A.	1971	Louisiana State	QB	Baltimore Colts, 1948-50; San Francisco 49ers, 1951-60; New York Giants, 1961-64
Trafton, George	1964	Notre Dame	C	Chicago Bears, 1920-32
Trippi, Charlie	1968	Georgia	HB	Chicago Cardinals, 1947-55
Tunnell, Emlen	1967	Iowa	DB	New York Giants, Green Bay Packers, 1948-61
Turner, Clyde (Bulldog)	1966	Hardin-Simmons	C/LB	Chicago Bears, 1940-52; coach, New York Titans, 1962
Unitas, John†	1979	Louisville	QB	Baltimore Colts, 1956-72; San Diego Chargers, 1973
Upshaw, Gene†	1987	Texas A&I	G	Oakland Raiders, 1967-81
Van Brocklin, Norm	1971	Oregon	QB	Los Angeles Rams, 1949-57; Philadelphia Eagles, 1958-60; coach, Minnesota Vikings, 1961-66; Atlanta Falcons, 1968-74
Van Buren, Steve	1965	Louisiana State	HB	Philadelphia Eagles, 1944-51
Walker, Doak	1986	Southern Methodist	RB	Detroit Lions, 1950-55
Walsh, Bill	1993	San Jose State	*	Coach, San Francisco 49ers, 1979-88
Warfield, Paul†	1983	Ohio State	WR	Cleveland Browns, 1964-69, 76-77; Miami Dolphins, 1970-74
Waterfield, Bob	1965	UCLA	QB	Cleveland Rams, Los Angeles Rams, 1945-52; coach, Los Angeles Rams, 1960-62
Webster, Mike	1997	Wisconsin	C-G	Pittsburgh Steelers, 1974-88; Kansas City Chiefs, 1989-90
Weinmeister, Arnie	1984	Washington	T	New York Yankees, 1948-49; New York Giants, 1950-53
White, Randy	1994	Maryland	DT	Dallas Cowboys, 1975-88
Wilcox, Dave	2000	Oregon	LB	San Francisco 49ers, 1964-74
Willis, Bill	1977	Ohio State	G	Cleveland Browns, 1946-53
Wilson, Larry†	1978	Utah	DB	St. Louis Cardinals, 1960-72
Winslow, Kellen	1995	Missouri	TE	San Diego Chargers, 1979-87
Wojciechowicz, Alex	1968	Fordham	C/LB	Detroit Lions, Philadelphia Eagles, 1938-50
Wood, Willie	1989	Southern California	S	Green Bay Packers, 1960-71

*Hall of Fame member was selected for contributions other than as a player.
†Elected his first year of eligibility.
Abbreviations of positions: C—Center, CB—Cornerback, DB—Defensive back, DE—Defensive end, DT—Defensive tackle, E—End, FB—Fullback, FL—Flanker, G—Guard, HB—Halfback, LB—Linebacker, PK—Placekicker, QB—Quarterback, RB—Running back, S—Safety, T—Tackle, TB—Tailback, TE—Tight end.

THE SPORTING NEWS AWARDS

PLAYER OF THE YEAR

1954—Lou Groza, OT/K, Cleveland
1955—Otto Graham, QB, Cleveland
1956—Frank Gifford, HB, N.Y. Giants
1957—Jim Brown, RB, Cleveland
1958—Jim Brown, RB, Cleveland
1959—Johnny Unitas, QB, Baltimore
1960—Norm Van Brocklin, QB, Philadelphia
1961—Paul Hornung, HB, Green Bay
1962—Y.A. Tittle, QB, N.Y. Giants
1963—Y.A. Tittle, QB, N.Y. Giants
1964—Johnny Unitas, QB, Baltimore
1965—Jim Brown, RB, Cleveland
1966—Bart Starr, QB, Green Bay
1967—Johnny Unitas, QB, Baltimore
1968—Earl Morrall, QB, Baltimore
1969—Roman Gabriel, QB, L.A. Rams
1970—NFC: John Brodie, QB, San Francisco
      AFC: George Blanda, QB/PK, Oakland
1971—NFC: Roger Staubach, QB, Dallas
      AFC: Bob Griese, QB, Miami
1972—NFC: Larry Brown, RB, Washington
      AFC: Earl Morrall, QB, Miami
1973—NFC: John Hadl, QB, L.A. Rams
      AFC: O.J. Simpson, RB, Buffalo
1974—NFC: Chuck Foreman, RB, Minnesota
      AFC: Ken Stabler, QB, Oakland
1975—NFC: Fran Tarkenton, QB, Minnesota
      AFC: O.J. Simpson, RB, Buffalo
1976—NFC: Walter Payton, RB, Chicago
      AFC: Ken Stabler, QB, Oakland
1977—NFC: Walter Payton, RB, Chicago
      AFC: Craig Morton, QB, Denver
1978—NFC: Archie Manning, QB, New Orleans
      AFC: Earl Campbell, RB, Houston
1979—NFC: Ottis Anderson, RB, St. Louis
      AFC: Dan Fouts, QB, San Diego
1980—Brian Sipe, QB, Cleveland
1981—Ken Anderson, QB, Cincinnati
1982—Mark Moseley, PK, Washington
1983—Eric Dickerson, RB, L.A. Rams
1984—Dan Marino, QB, Miami
1985—Marcus Allen, RB, L.A. Raiders
1986—Lawrence Taylor, LB, N.Y. Giants
1987—Jerry Rice, WR, San Francisco
1988—Boomer Esiason, QB, Cincinnati
1989—Joe Montana, QB, San Francisco
1990—Jerry Rice, WR, San Francisco
1991—Thurman Thomas, RB, Buffalo
1992—Steve Young, QB, San Francisco
1993—Emmitt Smith, RB, Dallas
1994—Steve Young, QB, San Francisco
1995—Brett Favre, QB, Green Bay
1996—Brett Favre, QB, Green Bay
1997—Barry Sanders, RB, Detroit
1998—Terrell Davis, RB, Denver
1999—Kurt Warner, QB, St. Louis
      NOTE: From 1970-79, a player was selected as Player of the Year for both the NFC and AFC. In 1980 The Sporting News reinstated the selection of one player as Player of the Year for the entire NFL.

ROOKIE OF THE YEAR

1955—Alan Ameche, FB, Baltimore
1956—J.C. Caroline, HB, Chicago
1957—Jim Brown, FB, Cleveland
1958—Bobby Mitchell, HB, Cleveland
1959—Nick Pietrosante, FB, Detroit
1960—Gail Cogdill, E, Detroit
1961—Mike Ditka, E, Chicago
1962—Ronnie Bull, HB, Chicago
1963—Paul Flatley, WR, Minnesota
1964—Charley Taylor, HB, Washington
1965—Gale Sayers, RB, Chicago
1966—Tommy Nobis, LB, Atlanta
1967—Mel Farr, RB, Detroit
1968—Earl McCullouch, WR, Detroit
1969—Calvin Hill, RB, Dallas
1970—NFC: Bruce Taylor, CB, San Francisco
      AFC: Dennis Shaw, QB, Buffalo
1971—NFC: John Brockington, RB, Green Bay
      AFC: Jim Plunkett, QB, New England
1972—NFC: Chester Marcol, PK, Green Bay
      AFC: Franco Harris, RB, Pittsburgh
1973—NFC: Chuck Foreman, RB, Minnesota
      AFC: Boobie Clark, RB, Cincinnati
1974—NFC: Wilbur Jackson, RB, San Francisco
      AFC: Don Woods, RB, San Diego
1975—NFC: Steve Bartkowski, QB, Atlanta
      AFC: Robert Brazile, LB, Houston
1976—NFC: Sammy White, WR, Minnesota
      AFC: Mike Haynes, CB, New England
1977—NFC: Tony Dorsett, RB, Dallas
      AFC: A.J. Duhe, DT, Miami
1978—NFC: Al Baker, DE, Detroit
      AFC: Earl Campbell, RB, Houston
1979—NFC: Ottis Anderson, RB, St. Louis
      AFC: Jerry Butler, WR, Buffalo
1980—Billy Sims, RB, Detroit
1981—George Rogers, RB, New Orleans
1982—Marcus Allen, RB, L.A. Raiders
1983—Dan Marino, QB, Miami
1984—Louis Lipps, WR, Pittsburgh
1985—Eddie Brown, WR, Cincinnati
1986—Rueben Mayes, RB, New Orleans
1987—Robert Awalt, TE, St. Louis
1988—Keith Jackson, TE, Philadelphia
1989—Barry Sanders, RB, Detroit
1990—Richmond Webb, T, Miami
1991—Mike Croel, LB, Denver
1992—Santana Dotson, DL, Tampa Bay
1993—Jerome Bettis, RB, L.A. Rams
1994—Marshall Faulk, RB, Indianapolis
1995—Curtis Martin, RB, New England
1996—Eddie George, RB, Houston
1997—Warrick Dunn, RB, Tampa Bay
1998—Randy Moss, WR, Minnesota
1999—Edgerrin James, RB, Indianapolis
      NOTE: In 1980, The Sporting News began selecting one rookie as Rookie of the Year for the entire NFL.

NFL COACH OF THE YEAR

1947—Jimmy Conzelman, Chi. Cardinals
1948—Earle (Greasy) Neale, Philadelphia
1949—Paul Brown, Cleveland (AAFC)
1950—Steve Owen, N.Y. Giants
1951—Paul Brown, Cleveland
1952—J. Hampton Pool, L.A. Rams
1953—Paul Brown, Cleveland
1954—None

1955—Joe Kuharich, Washington
1956—Jim Lee Howell, N.Y. Giants
1957—None
1958—None
1959—None
1960—None
1961—Vince Lombardi, Green Bay
1962—None
1963—George Halas, Chicago
1964—Don Shula, Baltimore
1965—George Halas, Chicago
1966—Tom Landry, Dallas
1967—George Allen, L.A. Rams
1968—Don Shula, Baltimore
1969—Bud Grant, Minnesota
1970—Don Shula, Miami
1971—George Allen, Washington
1972—Don Shula, Miami
1973—Chuck Knox, L.A. Rams
1974—Don Coryell, St. Louis
1975—Ted Marchibroda, Baltimore
1976—Chuck Fairbanks, New England
1977—Red Miller, Denver
1978—Jack Patera, Seattle
1979—Dick Vermeil, Philadelphia
1980—Chuck Knox, Buffalo
1981—Bill Walsh, San Francisco
1982—Joe Gibbs, Washington
1983—Joe Gibbs, Washington
1984—Chuck Knox, Seattle
1985—Mike Ditka, Chicago
1986—Bill Parcells, N.Y. Giants
1987—Jim Mora, New Orleans
1988—Marv Levy, Buffalo
1989—Lindy Infante, Green Bay
1990—George Seifert, San Francisco
1991—Joe Gibbs, Washington
1992—Bill Cowher, Pittsburgh
1993—Dan Reeves, N.Y. Giants
1994—George Seifert, San Francisco
1995—Ray Rhodes, Philadelphia
1996—Dom Capers, Carolina
1997—Jim Fassel, N.Y. Giants
1998—Dan Reeves, Atlanta
1999—Dick Vermeil, St. Louis

NFL EXECUTIVE OF THE YEAR

1955—Dan Reeves, L.A. Rams
1956—George Halas, Chicago
1972—Dan Rooney, Pittsburgh
1973—Jim Finks, Minnesota
1974—Art Rooney, Pittsburgh
1975—Joe Thomas, Baltimore
1976—Al Davis, Oakland
1977—Tex Schramm, Dallas
1978—John Thompson, Seattle
1979—John Sanders, San Diego
1980—Eddie LeBaron, Atlanta
1981—Paul Brown, Cincinnati
1982—Bobby Beathard, Washington
1983—Bobby Beathard, Washington
1984—George Young, N.Y. Giants
1985—Mike McCaskey, Chicago
1986—George Young, N.Y. Giants
1987—Jim Finks, New Orleans
1988—Bill Polian, Buffalo
1989—John McVay, San Francisco
1990—George Young, N.Y. Giants
1991—Bill Polian, Buffalo
1992—Ron Wolf, Green Bay
1993—George Young, N.Y. Giants
1994—Carmen Policy, San Francisco
1995—Bill Polian, Carolina
1996—Bill Polian, Carolina
1997—George Young, N.Y. Giants
1998—Jeff Diamond, Minnesota
1999—Bill Polian, Indianapolis

NOTE: The Executive of the Year Award was not given from 1957-71.

1999 NFL ALL-PRO TEAM

OFFENSE

WR—Marvin Harrison, Indianapolis
   Isaac Bruce, St. Louis
TE—Tony Gonzalez, Kansas City
T—Tony Boselli, Jacksonville
   Orlando Pace, St. Louis
C—(tie) Tom Nalen, Denver
   Kevin Mawae, N.Y. Jets
G—Larry Allen, Dallas
   Will Shields, Kansas City
QB—Kurt Warner, St. Louis
RB—Marshall Faulk, St. Louis
   Edgerrin James, Indianapolis

DEFENSE

DE—Kevin Carter, St. Louis
   Jevon Kearse, Tennessee
DT—Warren Sapp, Tampa Bay
   Darrell Russell, Oakland
LB—Ray Lewis, Baltimore
   Derrick Brooks, Tampa Bay
   Kevin Hardy, Jacksonville
CB—Sam Madison, Miami
   Deion Sanders, Dallas
S—Lawyer Milloy, New England
   John Lynch, Tampa Bay

SPECIALISTS

PR—Glyn Milburn, Chicago
KR—Tony Horne, St. Louis
K—Olindo Mare, Miami
P—Mitch Berger, Minnesota

TEAM BY TEAM

ARIZONA CARDINALS
YEAR-BY-YEAR RECORDS

HISTORY — Team by team

		REGULAR SEASON						PLAYOFFS			
Year	W	L	T	Pct.	PF	PA	Finish	W	L	Highest round	Coach
1920*	6	2	2	.750	...	...	T4th				Paddy Driscoll
1921*	3	3	2	.500	...	...	T8th				Paddy Driscoll
1922*	8	3	0	.727	...	...	3rd				Paddy Driscoll
1923*	8	4	0	.667	...	...	6th				Arnold Horween
1924*	5	4	1	.556	...	...	8th				Arnold Horween
1925*	11	2	1	.846	...	...	1st				Norman Barry
1926*	5	6	1	.455	...	...	10th				Norman Barry
1927*	3	7	1	.300	...	...	9th				Guy Chamberlin
1928*	1	5	0	.167	...	...	9th				Fred Gillies
1929*	6	6	1	.500	...	...	T4th				Dewey Scanlon
1930*	5	6	2	.455	...	...	T7th				Ernie Nevers
1931*	5	4	0	.556	...	...	4th				LeRoy Andrews, E. Nevers
1932*	2	6	2	.250	...	...	7th				Jack Chevigny
1933*	1	9	1	.100	52	101	5th/Western Div.	—	—		Paul Schissler
1934*	5	6	0	.455	80	84	4th/Western Div.	—	—		Paul Schissler
1935*	6	4	2	.600	99	97	T3rd/Western Div.	—	—		Milan Creighton
1936*	3	8	1	.273	74	143	4th/Western Div.	—	—		Milan Creighton
1937*	5	5	1	.500	135	165	4th/Western Div.	—	—		Milan Creighton
1938*	2	9	0	.182	111	168	5th/Western Div.	—	—		Milan Creighton
1939*	1	10	0	.091	84	254	5th/Western Div.	—	—		Ernie Nevers
1940*	2	7	2	.222	139	222	5th/Western Div.	—	—		Jimmy Conzelman
1941*	3	7	1	.300	127	197	4th/Western Div.	—	—		Jimmy Conzelman
1942*	3	8	0	.273	98	209	4th/Western Div.	—	—		Jimmy Conzelman
1943*	0	10	0	.000	95	238	4th/Western Div.	—	—		Phil Handler
1944†	0	10	0	.000	108	328	5th/Western Div.	—	—		P. Handler-Walt Kiesling
1945*	1	9	0	.100	98	228	5th/Western Div.	—	—		Phil Handler
1946*	6	5	0	.545	260	198	T3rd/Western Div.	—	—		Jimmy Conzelman
1947*	9	3	0	.750	306	231	1st/Western Div.	1	0	NFL champ	Jimmy Conzelman
1948*	11	1	0	.917	395	226	1st/Western Div.	0	1	NFL championship game	Jimmy Conzelman
1949*	6	5	1	.545	360	301	3rd/Western Div.	—	—		P. Handler-Buddy Parker
1950*	5	7	0	.417	233	287	5th/American Conf.	—	—		Curly Lambeau
1951*	3	9	0	.250	210	287	6th/American Conf.	—	—		Curly Lambeau, P. Handler-Cecil Isbell
1952*	4	8	0	.333	172	221	T5th/American Conf.	—	—		Joe Kuharich
1953*	1	10	1	.091	190	337	6th/Eastern Conf.	—	—		Joe Stydahar
1954*	2	10	0	.167	183	347	6th/Eastern Conf.	—	—		Joe Stydahar
1955*	4	7	1	.364	224	252	T4th/Eastern Conf.	—	—		Ray Richards
1956*	7	5	0	.583	240	182	2nd/Eastern Conf.	—	—		Ray Richards
1957*	3	9	0	.250	200	299	6th/Eastern Conf.	—	—		Ray Richards
1958*	2	9	1	.182	261	356	T5th/Eastern Conf.	—	—		Pop Ivy
1959*	2	10	0	.167	234	324	6th/Eastern Conf.	—	—		Pop Ivy
1960‡	6	5	1	.545	288	230	4th/Eastern Conf.	—	—		Pop Ivy
1961‡	7	7	0	.500	279	267	4th/Eastern Conf.	—	—		Pop Ivy
1962‡	4	9	1	.308	287	361	6th/Eastern Conf.	—	—		Wally Lemm
1963‡	9	5	0	.643	341	283	3rd/Eastern Conf.	—	—		Wally Lemm
1964‡	9	3	2	.750	357	331	2nd/Eastern Conf.	—	—		Wally Lemm
1965‡	5	9	0	.357	296	309	T5th/Eastern Conf.	—	—		Wally Lemm
1966‡	8	5	1	.615	264	265	4th/Eastern Conf.	—	—		Charley Winner
1967‡	6	7	1	.462	333	356	3rd/Century Div.	—	—		Charley Winner
1968‡	9	4	1	.692	325	289	2nd/Century Div.	—	—		Charley Winner
1969‡	4	9	1	.308	314	389	3rd/Century Div.	—	—		Charley Winner
1970‡	8	5	1	.615	325	228	3rd/NFC Eastern Div.	—	—		Charley Winner
1971‡	4	9	1	.308	231	279	4th/NFC Eastern Div.	—	—		Bob Hollway
1972‡	4	9	1	.308	193	303	4th/NFC Eastern Div.	—	—		Bob Hollway
1973‡	4	9	1	.308	286	365	4th/NFC Eastern Div.	—	—		Don Coryell
1974‡	10	4	0	.714	285	218	1st/NFC Eastern Div.	0	1	NFC div. playoff game	Don Coryell
1975‡	11	3	0	.786	356	276	1st/NFC Eastern Div.	0	1	NFC div. playoff game	Don Coryell
1976‡	10	4	0	.714	309	267	3rd/NFC Eastern Div.	—	—		Don Coryell
1977‡	7	7	0	.500	272	287	3rd/NFC Eastern Div.	—	—		Don Coryell
1978‡	6	10	0	.375	248	296	T4th/NFC Eastern Div.	—	—		Bud Wilkinson
1979‡	5	11	0	.313	307	358	4th/NFC Eastern Div.	—	—		B. Wilkinson, Larry Wilson
1980‡	5	11	0	.313	299	350	4th/NFC Eastern Div.	—	—		Jim Hanifan
1981‡	7	9	0	.438	315	408	5th/NFC Eastern Div.	—	—		Jim Hanifan
1982‡	5	4	0	.556	135	170	T4th/NFC	0	1	NFC first-round pl. game	Jim Hanifan

HISTORY Team by team

Year	W	L	T	Pct.	PF	PA	Finish	W	L	Highest round	Coach
1983‡	8	7	1	.531	374	428	3rd/NFC Eastern Div.	—	—		Jim Hanifan
1984‡	9	7	0	.563	423	345	T3rd/NFC Eastern Div.	—	—		Jim Hanifan
1985‡	5	11	0	.313	278	414	5th/NFC Eastern Div.	—	—		Jim Hanifan
1986‡	4	11	1	.281	218	351	5th/NFC Eastern Div.	—	—		Gene Stallings
1987‡	7	8	0	.467	362	368	T2nd/NFC Eastern Div.	—	—		Gene Stallings
1988§	7	9	0	.438	344	398	T3rd/NFC Eastern Div.	—	—		Gene Stallings
1989§	5	11	0	.313	258	377	4th/NFC Eastern Div.	—	—		G. Stallings, Hank Kuhlmann
1990§	5	11	0	.313	268	396	5th/NFC Eastern Div.	—	—		Joe Bugel
1991§	4	12	0	.250	196	344	5th/NFC Eastern Div.	—	—		Joe Bugel
1992§	4	12	0	.250	243	332	5th/NFC Eastern Div.	—	—		Joe Bugel
1993§	7	9	0	.438	326	269	4th/NFC Eastern Div.	—	—		Joe Bugel
1994	8	8	0	.500	235	267	3rd/NFC Eastern Div.	—	—		Buddy Ryan
1995	4	12	0	.250	275	422	5th/NFC Eastern Div.	—	—		Buddy Ryan
1996	7	9	0	.438	300	397	4th/NFC Eastern Div.	—	—		Vince Tobin
1997	4	12	0	.250	283	379	5th/NFC Eastern Div.	—	—		Vince Tobin
1998	9	7	0	.563	325	378	2nd/NFC Eastern Div.	1	1	NFC div. playoff game	Vince Tobin
1999	6	10	0	.375	245	382	4th/NFC Eastern Div.	—	—		Vince Tobin

*Chicago Cardinals.
†Card-Pitt, a combined squad of Chicago Cardinals and Pittsburgh Steelers.
‡St. Louis Cardinals.
§Phoenix Cardinals.

FIRST-ROUND DRAFT PICKS

1936—Jim Lawrence, B, Texas Christian
1937—Ray Buivid, B, Marquette
1938—Jack Robbins, B, Arkansas
1939—Charles Aldrich, C, Texas Christian*
1940—George Cafego, B, Tennessee*
1941—John Kimbrough, B, Texas A&M
1942—Steve Lach, B, Duke
1943—Glenn Dobbs, B, Tulsa
1944—Pat Harder, B, Wisconsin*
1945—Charley Trippi, B, Georgia*
1946—Dub Jones, B, Louisiana State
1947—DeWitt (Tex) Coulter, T, Army
1948—Jim Spavital, B, Oklahoma A&M
1949—Bill Fischer, G, Notre Dame
1950—None
1951—Jerry Groom, C, Notre Dame
1952—Ollie Matson, B, San Francisco
1953—Johnny Olszewski, QB, California
1954—Lamar McHan, B, Arkansas
1955—Max Boydston, E, Oklahoma
1956—Joe Childress, B, Auburn
1957—Jerry Tubbs, C, Oklahoma
1958—King Hill, B, Rice*
1959—Billy Stacy, B, Mississippi State
1960—George Izo, QB, Notre Dame
1961—Ken Rice, T, Auburn
1962—Fate Echols, DT, Northwestern
Irv Goode, C, Kentucky
1963—Jerry Stovall, DB, Louisiana State
Don Brumm, E, Purdue
1964—Ken Kortas, DT, Louisville
1965—Joe Namath, QB, Alabama
1966—Carl McAdams, LB, Oklahoma
1967—Dave Williams, WR, Washington
1968—MacArthur Lane, RB, Utah State
1969—Roger Wehrli, DB, Missouri

1970—Larry Stegent, RB, Texas A&M
1971—Norm Thompson, DB, Utah
1972—Bobby Moore, RB, Oregon
1973—Dave Butz, DT, Purdue
1974—J.V. Cain, TE, Colorado
1975—Tim Gray, DB, Texas A&M
1976—Mike Dawson, DT, Arizona
1977—Steve Pisarkiewicz, QB, Missouri
1978—Steve Little, K, Arkansas
Ken Greene, DB, Washington St.
1979—Ottis Anderson, RB, Miami (Fla.)
1980—Curtis Greer, DE, Michigan
1981—E.J. Junior, LB, Alabama
1982—Luis Sharpe, T, UCLA
1983—Leonard Smith, DB, McNeese State
1984—Clyde Duncan, WR, Tennessee
1985—Freddie Joe Nunn, LB, Mississippi
1986—Anthony Bell, LB, Michigan St.
1987—Kelly Stouffer, QB, Colorado St.
1988—Ken Harvey, LB, California
1989—Eric Hill, LB, Louisiana State
Joe Wolf, G, Boston College
1990—None
1991—Eric Swann, DL, None
1992—None
1993—Garrison Hearst, RB, Georgia
Ernest Dye, T, South Carolina
1994—Jamir Miller, LB, UCLA
1995—None
1996—Simeon Rice, DE, Illinois
1997—Tom Knight, DB, Iowa
1998—Andre Wadsworth, DE, Florida State
1999—David Boston, WR, Ohio State
L.J. Shelton, T, Eastern Michigan
2000—Thomas Jones, RB, Virginia
*First player chosen in draft.

FRANCHISE RECORDS

Most rushing yards, career
7,999—Ottis Anderson
Most rushing yards, season
1,605—Ottis Anderson, 1979
Most rushing yards, game
214—LeShon Johnson at N.O., Sept. 22, 1996

Most rushing touchdowns, season
14—John David Crow, 1962
Most passing attempts, season
560—Neil Lomax, 1984
Most passing attempts, game
61—Neil Lomax at S.D., Sept. 20, 1987

Most passes completed, season
345—Neil Lomax, 1984
Most passes completed, game
37—Neil Lomax at Was., Dec. 16, 1984
Kent Graham vs. St.L., Sept. 29, 1996 (OT)

Most passing yards, career
34,639—Jim Hart
Most passing yards, season
4,614—Neil Lomax, 1984
Most passing yards, game
522—Boomer Esiason at Was., Nov. 10, 1996 (OT)
468—Neil Lomax at Was., Dec. 16, 1984
Most touchdown passes, season
28—Charley Johnson, 1963
Neil Lomax, 1984
Most pass receptions, career
535—Larry Centers

Most pass receptions, season
101—Larry Centers, 1995
Most pass receptions, game
16—Sonny Randle at NYG, Nov. 4, 1962
Most receiving yards, career
8,497—Roy Green
Most receiving yards, season
1,555—Roy Green, 1984
Most receiving yards, game
256—Sonny Randle vs. NYG, Nov. 4, 1962
Most receiving touchdowns, season
16—Sonny Randle, 1960

Most touchdowns, career
69—Roy Green
Most field goals, season
30—Greg Davis, 1995
Longest field goal
55 yards—Greg Davis at Sea., Dec. 19, 1993
Greg Davis at Det., Sept. 17, 1995
Most interceptions, career
52—Larry Wilson
Most interceptions, season
12—Bob Nussbaumer, 1949

SERIES RECORDS

Arizona vs.: Atlanta 13-7; Baltimore, 1-0; Buffalo 3-4; Carolina 0-1; Chicago 26-54-6; Cincinnati 2-4; Cleveland 10-32-3; Dallas 24-50-1; Denver 0-4-1; Detroit 17-28-3; Green Bay 21-42-4; Indianapolis 6-6; Jacksonville 0-0; Kansas City 1-5-1; Miami 0-8; Minnesota 8-7; New England 6-4; New Orleans 12-10; N.Y. Giants 39-74-2; N.Y. Jets 2-3; Oakland 1-3; Philadelphia 51-49-5; Pittsburgh 21-30-3; St. Louis 14-16-2; San Diego 2-6; San Francisco 9-11; Seattle 5-1; Tampa Bay 7-7; Tennessee 4-3; Washington 41-63-1.
NOTE: Includes records for entire franchise, from 1920 to present.

COACHING RECORDS

LeRoy Andrews, 0-1-0; Norman Barry, 16-8-2; Joe Bugel, 20-44-0; Guy Chamberlain, 3-7-1; Jack Chevigny, 2-6-2; Jimmy Conzelman, 34-31-3 (1-1); Don Coryell, 42-27-1 (0-2); Milan Creighton, 16-26-4; Paddy Driscoll, 17-8-4; Chuck Drulis-Ray Prochaska-Ray Willsey*, 2-0-0; Fred Gillies, 1-5-0; Phil Handler, 1-29-0; Phil Handler-Cecil Isbell*, 1-1-0; Phil Handler-Buddy Parker*, 2-4-0; Jim Hanifan, 39-49-1 (0-1); Bob Hollway, 8-18-2; Arnold Horween, 13-8-1; Frank Ivy, 17-29-2; Joe Kuharich, 4-8-0; Hank Kuhlmann, 0-5-0; Curly Lambeau, 7-15-0; Wally Lemm, 27-26-3; Ernie Nevers, 11-19-2; Buddy Parker, 4-1-1; Ray Richards, 14-21-1; Buddy Ryan, 12-20-0; Dewey Scanlon, 6-6-1; Paul Schissler, 6-15-1; Gene Stallings, 23-34-1; Joe Stydahar, 3-20-1; Vince Tobin, 26-38-0 (1-1); Bud Wilkinson, 9-20-0; Larry Wilson, 2-1-0; Charley Winner, 35-30-5.
NOTE: Playoff games in parentheses.
*Co-coaches.

RETIRED UNIFORM NUMBERS

No.	Player
8	Larry Wilson
77	Stan Mauldin
88	J.V. Cain
99	Marshall Goldberg

ATLANTA FALCONS
YEAR-BY-YEAR RECORDS

Year	W	L	T	Pct.	PF	PA	Finish	W	L	Highest round	Coach
1966	3	11	0	.214	204	437	7th/Eastern Conf.	—	—		Norb Hecker
1967	1	12	1	.077	175	422	4th/Coastal Div.	—	—		Norb Hecker
1968	2	12	0	.143	170	389	4th/Coastal Div.	—	—		N. Hecker, N. Van Brocklin
1969	6	8	0	.429	276	268	3rd/Coastal Div.	—	—		Norm Van Brocklin
1970	4	8	2	.333	206	261	3rd/NFC Western Div.	—	—		Norm Van Brocklin
1971	7	6	1	.538	274	277	3rd/NFC Western Div.	—	—		Norm Van Brocklin
1972	7	7	0	.500	269	274	2nd/NFC Western Div.	—	—		Norm Van Brocklin
1973	9	5	0	.643	318	224	2nd/NFC Western Div.	—	—		Norm Van Brocklin
1974	3	11	0	.214	111	271	4th/NFC Western Div.	—	—		N. Van Brocklin, M. Campbell
1975	4	10	0	.286	240	289	3rd/NFC Western Div.	—	—		Marion Campbell
1976	4	10	0	.286	172	312	T3rd/NFC Western Div.	—	—		M. Campbell, Pat Peppler
1977	7	7	0	.500	179	129	2nd/NFC Western Div.	—	—		Leeman Bennett
1978	9	7	0	.563	240	290	2nd/NFC Western Div.	1	1	NFC div. playoff game	Leeman Bennett
1979	6	10	0	.375	300	388	3rd/NFC Western Div.	—	—		Leeman Bennett
1980	12	4	0	.750	405	272	1st/NFC Western Div.	0	1	NFC div. playoff game	Leeman Bennett
1981	7	9	0	.438	426	355	2nd/NFC Western Div.	—	—		Leeman Bennett
1982	5	4	0	.556	183	199	T4th/NFC	0	1	NFC first-round pl. game	Leeman Bennett
1983	7	9	0	.438	370	389	4th/NFC Western Div.	—	—		Dan Henning
1984	4	12	0	.250	281	382	4th/NFC Western Div.	—	—		Dan Henning
1985	4	12	0	.250	282	452	4th/NFC Western Div.	—	—		Dan Henning
1986	7	8	1	.469	280	280	3rd/NFC Western Div.	—	—		Dan Henning
1987	3	12	0	.200	205	436	4th/NFC Western Div.	—	—		Marion Campbell
1988	5	11	0	.313	244	315	4th/NFC Western Div.	—	—		Marion Campbell
1989	3	13	0	.188	279	437	4th/NFC Western Div.	—	—		M. Campbell, Jim Hanifan
1990	5	11	0	.313	348	365	T3rd/NFC Western Div.	—	—		Jerry Glanville
1991	10	6	0	.625	361	338	2nd/NFC Western Div.	1	1	NFC div. playoff game	Jerry Glanville
1992	6	10	0	.375	327	414	T3rd/NFC Western Div.	—	—		Jerry Glanville
1993	6	10	0	.375	316	385	3rd/NFC Western Div.	—	—		Jerry Glanville

HISTORY — Team by team

REGULAR SEASON / PLAYOFFS

Year	W	L	T	Pct.	PF	PA	Finish	W	L	Highest round	Coach
1994	7	9	0	.438	313	389	T2nd/NFC Western Div.	—	—		June Jones
1995	9	7	0	.563	362	349	2nd/NFC Western Div.	0	1	NFC wild-card game	June Jones
1996	3	13	0	.188	309	465	T4th/NFC Western Div.	—	—		June Jones
1997	7	9	0	.438	320	361	T2nd/NFC Western Div.	—	—		Dan Reeves
1998	14	2	0	.875	442	289	1st/NFC Western Div.	2	1	Super Bowl	Dan Reeves
1999	5	11	0	.313	285	380	3rd/NFC Western Div.	—	—		Dan Reeves

FIRST-ROUND DRAFT PICKS

1966—Tommy Nobis, LB, Texas*
Randy Johnson, QB, Texas A&I
1967—None
1968—Claude Humphrey, DE, Tennessee State
1969—George Kunz, T, Notre Dame
1970—John Small, LB, Citadel
1971—Joe Profit, RB, Northeast Louisiana State
1972—Clarence Ellis, DB, Notre Dame
1973—None
1974—None
1975—Steve Bartkowski, QB, California*
1976—Bubba Bean, RB, Texas A&M
1977—Warren Bryant, T, Kentucky
Wilson Faumuina, DT, San Jose State
1978—Mike Kenn, T, Michigan
1979—Don Smith, DE, Miami (Fla.)
1980—Junior Miller, TE, Nebraska
1981—Bobby Butler, DB, Florida State
1982—Gerald Riggs, RB, Arizona State
1983—Mike Pitts, DE, Alabama
1984—Rick Bryan, DT, Oklahoma
1985—Bill Fralic, T, Pittsburgh
1986—Tony Casillas, DT, Oklahoma
Tim Green, LB, Syracuse
1987—Chris Miller, QB, Oregon
1988—Aundray Bruce, LB, Auburn*
1989—Deion Sanders, DB, Florida State
Shawn Collins, WR, Northern Arizona
1990—Steve Broussard, RB, Washington State
1991—Bruce Pickens, CB, Nebraska
Mike Pritchard, WR, Colorado
1992—Bob Whitfield, T, Stanford
Tony Smith, RB, Southern Mississippi
1993—Lincoln Kennedy, T, Washington
1994—None
1995—Devin Bush, DB, Florida State
1996—None
1997—Michael Booker, DB, Nebraska
1998—Keith Brooking, LB, Georgia Tech
1999—Patrick Kerney, DE, Virginia
2000—None
*First player chosen in draft.

FRANCHISE RECORDS

Most rushing yards, career
6,631—Gerald Riggs
Most rushing yards, season
1,846—Jamal Anderson, 1998
Most rushing yards, game
202—Gerald Riggs at N.O., Sept. 2, 1984
Most rushing touchdowns, season
14—Jamal Anderson, 1998
Most passing attempts, season
557—Jeff George, 1995
Most passing attempts, game
66—Chris Miller vs. Det., Dec. 24, 1989
Most passes completed, season
336—Jeff George, 1995
Most passes completed, game
37—Chris Miller vs. Det., Dec. 24, 1989
Most passing yards, career
23,468—Steve Bartkowski
Most passing yards, season
4,143—Jeff George, 1995

Most passing yards, game
416—Steve Bartkowski vs. Pit., Nov. 15, 1981
Most touchdown passes, season
31—Steve Bartkowski, 1980
Most pass receptions, career
465—Terance Mathis
Most pass receptions, season
111—Terance Mathis, 1994
Most pass receptions, game
15—William Andrews vs. Pit., Nov. 15, 1981
Most receiving yards, career
6,257—Alfred Jenkins
Most receiving yards, season
1,358—Alfred Jenkins, 1981
Most receiving yards, game
198—Terance Mathis at N.O., Dec. 13, 1998

Most receiving touchdowns, season
15—Andre Rison, 1993
Most touchdowns, career
56—Andre Rison
Most field goals, season
31—Morten Andersen, 1995
Longest field goal
59 yards—Morten Andersen vs. S.F., Dec. 24, 1995
Most interceptions, career
39—Rolland Lawrence
Most interceptions, season
10—Scott Case, 1988
Most sacks, career
62.5—Claude Humphrey
Most sacks, season
16—Joel Williams, 1980

SERIES RECORDS

Atlanta vs.: Arizona 7-13; Baltimore 0-1; Buffalo 3-4; Carolina 5-5; Chicago 10-9; Cincinnati 2-7; Cleveland 2-8; Dallas 6-12; Denver 3-6; Detroit 7-20; Green Bay 9-10; Indianapolis 1-10; Jacksonville 0-2; Kansas City 0-4; Miami 2-6; Minnesota 6-14; New England 6-3; New Orleans 37-24; N.Y. Giants 7-6; N.Y. Jets 4-4; Oakland 3-6; Philadelphia 9-9-1; Pittsburgh 1-11; St. Louis 23-41-2; San Diego 5-1; San Francisco 24-41-1; Seattle 2-4; Tampa Bay 8-8; Tennessee 5-5; Washington 4-13-1.

COACHING RECORDS

Leeman Bennett, 46-41-0 (1-3); Marion Campbell, 17-51-0; Jerry Glanville, 27-37-0 (1-1); Jim Hanifan, 0-4-0; Norb Hecker, 4-26-1; Dan Henning, 22-41-1; June Jones, 19-29-0 (0-1); Pat Peppler, 3-6-0; Dan Reeves, 26-22-0 (2-1); Norm Van Brocklin, 37-49-3.
NOTE: Playoff games in parentheses.

RETIRED UNIFORM NUMBERS

No.	Player
10	Steve Bartkowski
31	William Andrews
57	Jeff Van Note
60	Tommy Nobis

BALTIMORE RAVENS

YEAR-BY-YEAR RECORDS

		REGULAR SEASON					PLAYOFFS		
Year	W	L	T	Pct.	PF	PA	Finish	W	L	Highest round	Coach
1996	4	12	0	.250	371	441	5th/AFC Central Div.	—	—		Ted Marchibroda
1997	6	9	1	.406	326	345	5th/AFC Central Div.	—	—		Ted Marchibroda
1998	6	10	0	.375	269	335	4th/AFC Central Div.	—	—		Ted Marchibroda
1999	8	8	0	.500	324	277	3rd/AFC Central Div.	—	—		Brian Billick

FIRST-ROUND DRAFT PICKS

1996—Jonathan Ogden, T, UCLA
   Ray Lewis, LB, Miami (Fla.)
1997—Peter Boulware, DE, Florida State

1998—Duane Starks, DB, Miami (Fla.)
1999—Chris McAlister, DB, Arizona

2000—Jamal Lewis, RB, Tennessee
   Travis Taylor, WR, Florida

FRANCHISE RECORDS

Most rushing yards, career
1,514—Priest Holmes
Most rushing yards, season
1,008—Priest Holmes, 1998
Most rushing yards, game
227—Priest Holmes at Cin., Nov. 22, 1998
Most rushing touchdowns, season
7—Priest Holmes, 1998
Most passing attempts, season
549—Vinny Testaverde, 1996
Most passing attempts, game
51—Vinny Testaverde vs. St.L., Oct. 27, 1996 (OT)
50—Vinny Testaverde vs. Jac., Nov. 24, 1996 (OT)
47—Vinny Testaverde vs. Pit., Oct. 5, 1997
   Vinny Testaverde at Mia., Oct. 19, 1997
Most passes completed, season
325—Vinny Testaverde, 1996
Most passes completed, game
32—Vinny Testaverde vs. Mia., Oct. 19, 1997

Most passing yards, career
7,148—Vinny Testaverde
Most passing yards, season
4,177—Vinny Testaverde, 1996
Most passing yards, game
429—Vinny Testaverde vs. St.L., Oct. 27, 1996 (OT)
366—Vinny Testaverde vs. Jac., Nov. 24, 1996 (OT)
353—Vinny Testaverde vs. N.E., Oct. 6, 1996
Most touchdown passes, season
33—Vinny Testaverde, 1996
Most pass receptions, career
183—Michael Jackson
Most pass receptions, season
76—Michael Jackson, 1996
Most pass receptions, game
13—Priest Holmes vs. Ten., Oct. 11, 1998
Most receiving yards, career
2,596—Michael Jackson
Most receiving yards, season
1,201—Michael Jackson, 1996

Most receiving yards, game
258—Qadry Ismail at Pit., Dec. 12, 1999
Most receiving touchdowns, season
14—Michael Jackson, 1996
Most touchdowns, career
19—Jermaine Lewis
Most field goals, season
28—Matt Stover, 1999
Longest field goal
50 yards—Matt Stover vs. St.L., Oct. 27, 1996
   Matt Stover at Ten., Oct. 10, 1999
   Matt Stover at Cin., Nov. 21, 1999
Most interceptions, career
13—Rod Woodson
Most interceptions, season
7—Rod Woodson, 1999
Most sacks, career
35.0—Michael McCrary
Most sacks, season
14.5—Michael McCrary, 1998

SERIES RECORDS

Baltimore vs.: Arizona, 0-1; Atlanta, 1-0; Buffalo 0-1; Carolina 0-1; Chicago 0-1; Cincinnati 5-3; Cleveland 2-0; Denver 0-1; Detroit 1-0; Green Bay 0-1; Indianapolis 1-1; Jacksonville 0-8; Kansas City 0-1; Miami, 0-1; Minnesota 0-1; New England 0-2; New Orleans 2-0; N.Y. Giants, 1-0; N.Y. Jets, 1-1; Oakland 2-0; Philadelphia, 0-0-1; Pittsburgh 2-6; St. Louis 1-1; San Diego, 0-2; San Francisco 0-1; Seattle, 1-0; Tennessee 3-5; Washington, 1-0.

COACHING RECORDS

Brian Billick, 8-8-0; Ted Marchibroda, 16-31-1.

RETIRED UNIFORM NUMBERS

No.	Player
	None

BUFFALO BILLS

YEAR-BY-YEAR RECORDS

		REGULAR SEASON						PLAYOFFS			
Year	W	L	T	Pct.	PF	PA	Finish	W	L	Highest round	Coach
1960*	5	8	1	.385	296	303	3rd/Eastern Div.	—	—		Buster Ramsey
1961*	6	8	0	.429	294	342	4th/Eastern Div.	—	—		Buster Ramsey
1962*	7	6	1	.538	309	272	3rd/Eastern Div.	—	—		Lou Saban
1963*	7	6	1	.538	304	291	2nd/Eastern Div.	0	1	E. Div. championship game	Lou Saban
1964*	12	2	0	.857	400	242	1st/Eastern Div.	1	0	AFL champ	Lou Saban
1965*	10	3	1	.769	313	226	1st/Eastern Div.	1	0	AFL champ	Lou Saban
1966*	9	4	1	.692	358	255	1st/Eastern Div.	0	1	AFL championship game	Joe Collier

HISTORY Team by team

– 363 –

HISTORY — Team by team

REGULAR SEASON / PLAYOFFS

Year	W	L	T	Pct.	PF	PA	Finish	W	L	Highest round	Coach
1967*	4	10	0	.286	237	285	T3rd/Eastern Div.	—	—		Joe Collier
1968*	1	12	1	.077	199	367	5th/Eastern Div.	—	—		J. Collier, H. Johnson
1969*	4	10	0	.286	230	359	T3rd/Eastern Div.	—	—		John Rauch
1970	3	10	1	.231	204	337	4th/AFC Eastern Div.	—	—		John Rauch
1971	1	13	0	.071	184	394	5th/AFC Eastern Div.	—	—		Harvey Johnson
1972	4	9	1	.321	257	377	4th/AFC Eastern Div.	—	—		Lou Saban
1973	9	5	0	.643	259	230	2nd/AFC Eastern Div.	—	—		Lou Saban
1974	9	5	0	.643	264	244	2nd/AFC Eastern Div.	0	1	AFC div. playoff game	Lou Saban
1975	8	6	0	.571	420	355	3rd/AFC Eastern Div.	—	—		Lou Saban
1976	2	12	0	.143	245	363	5th/AFC Eastern Div.	—	—		Lou Saban, Jim Ringo
1977	3	11	0	.214	160	313	T4th/AFC Eastern Div.	—	—		Jim Ringo
1978	5	11	0	.313	302	354	T4th/AFC Eastern Div.	—	—		Chuck Knox
1979	7	9	0	.438	268	279	4th/AFC Eastern Div.	—	—		Chuck Knox
1980	11	5	0	.688	320	260	1st/AFC Eastern Div.	0	1	AFC div. playoff game	Chuck Knox
1981	10	6	0	.625	311	276	3rd/AFC Eastern Div.	1	1	AFC div. playoff game	Chuck Knox
1982	4	5	0	.444	150	154	T8th/AFC	—	—		Chuck Knox
1983	8	8	0	.500	283	351	T2nd/AFC Eastern Div.	—	—		Kay Stephenson
1984	2	14	0	.125	250	454	5th/AFC Eastern Div.	—	—		Kay Stephenson
1985	2	14	0	.125	200	381	5th/AFC Eastern Div.	—	—		Hank Bullough
1986	4	12	0	.250	287	348	4th/AFC Eastern Div.	—	—		H. Bullough, M. Levy
1987	7	8	0	.467	270	305	4th/AFC Eastern Div.	—	—		Marv Levy
1988	12	4	0	.750	329	237	1st/AFC Eastern Div.	1	1	AFC championship game	Marv Levy
1989	9	7	0	.563	409	317	1st/AFC Eastern Div.	0	1	AFC div. playoff game	Marv Levy
1990	13	3	0	.813	428	263	1st/AFC Eastern Div.	2	1	Super Bowl	Marv Levy
1991	13	3	0	.813	458	318	1st/AFC Eastern Div.	2	1	Super Bowl	Marv Levy
1992	11	5	0	.688	381	283	2nd/AFC Eastern Div.	3	1	Super Bowl	Marv Levy
1993	12	4	0	.750	329	242	1st/AFC Eastern Div.	2	1	Super Bowl	Marv Levy
1994	7	9	0	.438	340	356	4th/AFC Eastern Div.	—	—		Marv Levy
1995	10	6	0	.625	350	335	1st/AFC Eastern Div.	1	1	AFC div. playoff game	Marv Levy
1996	10	6	0	.625	319	266	2nd/AFC Eastern Div.	0	1	AFC wild-card game	Marv Levy
1997	6	10	0	.375	255	367	4th/AFC Eastern Div.	—	—		Marv Levy
1998	10	6	0	.625	400	333	T2nd/AFC Eastern Div.	0	1	AFC wild-card game	Wade Phillips
1999	11	5	0	.688	320	229	2nd/AFC Eastern Div.	0	1	AFC wild-card game	Wade Phillips

*American Football League.

FIRST-ROUND DRAFT PICKS

1960—Richie Lucas, QB, Penn State
1961—Ken Rice, T, Auburn* (AFL)
1962—Ernie Davis, RB, Syracuse
1963—Dave Behrman, C, Michigan State
1964—Carl Eller, DE, Minnesota
1965—Jim Davidson, T, Ohio State
1966—Mike Dennis, RB, Mississippi
1967—John Pitts, DB, Arizona State
1968—Haven Moses, WR, San Diego St.
1969—O.J. Simpson, RB, Southern California*
1970—Al Cowlings, DE, Southern California
1971—J.D. Hill, WR, Arizona State
1972—Walt Patulski, DE, Notre Dame*
1973—Paul Seymour, T, Michigan
      Joe DeLamielleure, G, Michigan State
1974—Reuben Gant, TE, Oklahoma State
1975—Tom Ruud, LB, Nebraska
1976—Mario Clark, DB, Oregon
1977—Phil Dokes, DT, Oklahoma State
1978—Terry Miller, RB, Oklahoma State
1979—Tom Cousineau, LB, Ohio State*
      Jerry Butler, WR, Clemson
1980—Jim Ritcher, C, North Carolina State
1981—Booker Moore, RB, Penn State
1982—Perry Tuttle, WR, Clemson
1983—Tony Hunter, TE, Notre Dame
      Jim Kelly, QB, Miami (Fla.)
1984—Greg Bell, RB, Notre Dame
1985—Bruce Smith, DT, Virginia Tech*
      Derrick Burroughs, DB, Memphis State
1986—Ronnie Harmon, RB, Iowa
      Will Wolford, T, Vanderbilt
1987—Shane Conlan, LB, Penn State
1988—None
1989—None
1990—James Williams, DB, Fresno State
1991—Henry Jones, S, Illinois
1992—John Fina, T, Arizona
1993—Thomas Smith, DB, North Carolina
1994—Jeff Burris, DB, Notre Dame
1995—Ruben Brown, G, Pittsburgh
1996—Eric Moulds, WR, Mississippi State
1997—Antowain Smith, RB, Houston
1998—None
1999—Antoine Winfield, DB, Ohio State
2000—Erik Flowers, DE, Arizona State
*First player chosen in draft.

FRANCHISE RECORDS

Most rushing yards, career
11,938—Thurman Thomas
Most rushing yards, season
2,003—O.J. Simpson, 1973
Most rushing yards, game
273—O.J. Simpson at Det., Nov. 25, 1976

Most rushing touchdowns, season
16—O.J. Simpson, 1975
Most passing attempts, season
508—Joe Ferguson, 1983
Most passing attempts, game
55—Joe Ferguson at Mia., Oct. 9, 1983

Most passes completed, season
304—Jim Kelly, 1991
Most passes completed, game
38—Joe Ferguson at Mia., Oct. 9, 1983
Most passing yards, career
35,467—Jim Kelly

Most passing yards, season
3,844—Jim Kelly, 1991
Most passing yards, game
419—Joe Ferguson at Mia., Oct. 9, 1983
Most touchdown passes, season
33—Jim Kelly, 1991
Most pass receptions, career
941—Andre Reed
Most pass receptions, season
90—Andre Reed, 1994
Most pass receptions, game
15—Andre Reed vs. G.B., Nov. 20, 1994

Most receiving yards, career
13,095—Andre Reed
Most receiving yards, season
1,368—Eric Moulds, 1998
Most receiving yards, game
255—Jerry Butler vs. NYJ, Sept. 23, 1979
Most receiving touchdowns, season
11—Bill Brooks, 1995
Most touchdowns, career
87—Andre Reed
Thurman Thomas
Most field goals, season
33—Steve Christie, 1998

Longest field goal
59 yards—Steve Christie vs. Mia., Sept. 26, 1993
Most interceptions, career
40—George Byrd
Most interceptions, season
10—Billy Atkins, 1961
Tom Janik, 1967
Most sacks, career
171—Bruce Smith
Most sacks, season
19—Bruce Smith, 1990

SERIES RECORDS

Buffalo vs.: Arizona 4-3; Atlanta 4-3; Baltimore 1-0; Carolina 2-0; Chicago 2-5; Cincinnati 9-10; Cleveland 4-7; Dallas 3-3; Denver 17-12-1; Detroit 2-3-1; Green Bay 5-2; Indianapolis 34-24-1; Jacksonville 1-1; Kansas City 17-14-1; Miami 25-42-1; Minnesota 2-6; New England 38-41-1; New Orleans 4-2; N.Y. Giants 5-3; N.Y. Jets 45-34; Oakland 15-16; Philadelphia 5-4; Pittsburgh 8-8; St. Louis 4-4; San Diego 7-17-2; San Francisco 4-3; Seattle 2-5; Tampa Bay 2-4; Tennessee 13-22; Washington 5-4.

COACHING RECORDS

Hank Bullough, 4-17-0; Joe Collier, 13-16-1 (0-1); Harvey Johnson, 2-23-1; Chuck Knox, 37-36-0 (1-2); Marv Levy, 112-70-0 (11-8); Wade Phillips, 21-11-0 (0-2); Buster Ramsey, 11-16-1; John Rauch, 7-20-1; Jim Ringo, 3-20-0; Lou Saban, 68-45-4 (2-2); Kay Stephenson, 10-26-0.
NOTE: Playoff games in parentheses.

RETIRED UNIFORM NUMBERS

No.	Player
	None

CAROLINA PANTHERS
YEAR-BY-YEAR RECORDS

	REGULAR SEASON						PLAYOFFS			
Year	W	L	T	Pct.	PF	PA	Finish	W	L	Highest round	Coach
1995	7	9	0	.438	289	325	T3rd/NFC Western Div.	—	—		Dom Capers
1996	12	4	0	.750	367	218	1st/NFC Western Div.	1	1	NFC championship game	Dom Capers
1997	7	9	0	.438	265	314	T2nd/NFC Western Div.	—	—		Dom Capers
1998	4	12	0	.250	336	413	T4th/NFC Western Div.	—	—		Dom Capers
1999	8	8	0	.500	421	381	2nd/NFC Western Div.	—	—		George Seifert

FIRST-ROUND DRAFT PICKS

1995—Kerry Collins, QB, Penn State
Tyrone Poole, DB, Fort Valley (Ga.) St.
Blake Brockermeyer, T, Texas
1996—Tim Biakabutuka, RB, Michigan

1997—Rae Carruth, WR, Colorado
1998—Jason Peter, DT, Nebraska
1999—None
2000—Rashard Anderson, DB, Jackson State

FRANCHISE RECORDS

Most rushing yards, career
2,001—Fred Lane
Most rushing yards, season
1,120—Anthony Johnson, 1996
Most rushing yards, game
147—Fred Lane vs. Oak., Nov. 2, 1997
Most rushing touchdowns, season
7—Fred Lane, 1997
Most passing attempts, season
571—Steve Beuerlein, 1999
Most passing attempts, game
53—Kerry Collins vs. G.B., Sept. 27, 1998
Most passes completed, season
343—Steve Beuerlein, 1999
Most passes completed, game
29—Steve Beuerlein at Green Bay, Dec. 12, 1999

Most passing yards, career
8,960—Steve Beuerlein
Most passing yards, season
4,436—Steve Beuerlein, 1999
Most passing yards, game
373—Steve Beuerlein at Green Bay, Dec. 12, 1999
Most touchdown passes, season
36—Steve Beuerlein, 1999
Most pass receptions, career
231—Wesley Walls
Most pass receptions, season
96—Muhsin Muhammad, 1999
Most pass receptions, game
11—Muhsin Muhammad vs. S.F., Dec. 18, 1999

Most receiving yards, career
2,787—Wesley Walls
Most receiving yards, season
1,253—Muhsin Muhammad, 1999
Most receiving yards, game
192—Muhsin Muhammad at N.O., Sept. 13, 1998
Most receiving touchdowns, season
12—Patrick Jeffers, 1999
Most touchdowns, career
33—Wesley Walls
Most field goals, season
37—John Kasay, 1996
Longest field goal
56 yards—John Kasay vs. G.B., Sept. 27, 1998

– 365 –

Most interceptions, career
20—Eric Davis
Most interceptions, season
6—Brett Maxie, 1995

Most sacks, career
41.5—Kevin Greene

Most sacks, season
15—Kevin Greene, 1998

SERIES RECORDS

Carolina vs.: Arizona 1-0; Atlanta 5-5; Buffalo 0-2; Baltimore 1-0; Chicago 0-1; Cincinnati 1-0; Cleveland 1-0; Dallas 1-1; Denver 0-1; Detroit 0-1; Green Bay 1-2; Indianapolis 2-0; Jacksonville 0-2; Kansas City 0-1; Miami 0-1; Minnesota 0-2; New England 1-0; New Orleans 6-4; N.Y. Giants 1-0; N.Y. Jets 1-1; Oakland 1-0; Philadelphia 1-1; Pittsburgh 1-1; St. Louis 5-5; San Diego 1-0; San Francisco 5-5; Seattle 0-0; Tampa Bay 1-2; Tennessee 1-0; Washington 0-4.

COACHING RECORDS

Dom Capers, 30-34-0 (1-1); George Seifert, 8-8-0.
NOTE: Playoff games in parentheses.

RETIRED UNIFORM NUMBERS

No.   Player
None

CHICAGO BEARS
YEAR-BY-YEAR RECORDS

	REGULAR SEASON						PLAYOFFS			
Year	W	L	T	Pct.	PF	PA	Finish	W	L	Highest round	Coach
1920*	10	1	2	.909	...	...	2nd				George Halas
1921†	9	1	1	.900	...	...	1st				George Halas
1922	9	3	0	.750	...	...	2nd				George Halas
1923	9	2	1	.818	...	...	2nd				George Halas
1924	6	1	4	.857	...	...	2nd				George Halas
1925	9	5	3	.643	...	...	7th				George Halas
1926	12	1	3	.923	...	...	2nd				George Halas
1927	9	3	2	.750	...	...	3rd				George Halas
1928	7	5	1	.583	...	...	5th				George Halas
1929	4	9	2	.308	...	...	9th				George Halas
1930	9	4	1	.692	...	...	3rd				Ralph Jones
1931	8	5	0	.615	...	...	3rd				Ralph Jones
1932	7	1	6	.875	...	...	1st				Ralph Jones
1933	10	2	1	.833	133	82	1st/Western Div.	1	0	NFL champ	George Halas
1934	13	0	0	1.000	286	86	1st/Western Div.	0	1	NFL championship game	George Halas
1935	6	4	2	.600	192	106	T3rd/Western Div.	—	—		George Halas
1936	9	3	0	.750	222	94	2nd/Western Div.	—	—		George Halas
1937	9	1	1	.900	201	100	1st/Western Div.	0	1	NFL championship game	George Halas
1938	6	5	0	.545	194	148	3rd/Western Div.	—	—		George Halas
1939	8	3	0	.727	298	157	2nd/Western Div.	—	—		George Halas
1940	8	3	0	.727	238	152	1st/Western Div.	1	0	NFL champ	George Halas
1941	10	1	0	.909	396	147	1st/Western Div.	2	0	NFL champ	George Halas
1942	11	0	0	1.000	376	84	1st/Western Div.	0	1	NFL championship game	George Halas, Hunk Anderson-Luke Johnsos
1943	8	1	1	.889	303	157	1st/Western Div.	1	0	NFL champ	H. Anderson-L. Johnsos
1944	6	3	1	.667	258	172	T2nd/Western Div.	—	—		H. Anderson-L. Johnsos
1945	3	7	0	.300	192	235	4th/Western Div.	—	—		H. Anderson-L. Johnsos
1946	8	2	1	.800	289	193	1st/Western Div.	1	0	NFL champ	George Halas
1947	8	4	0	.667	363	241	2nd/Western Div.	—	—		George Halas
1948	10	2	0	.833	375	151	2nd/Western Div.	—	—		George Halas
1949	9	3	0	.750	332	218	2nd/Western Div.	—	—		George Halas
1950	9	3	0	.750	279	207	2nd/National Conf.	0	1	Nat. Conf. champ. game	George Halas
1951	7	5	0	.583	286	282	4th/National Conf.	—	—		George Halas
1952	5	7	0	.417	245	326	5th/National Conf.	—	—		George Halas
1953	3	8	1	.273	218	262	T4th/Western Conf.	—	—		George Halas
1954	8	4	0	.667	301	279	2nd/Western Conf.	—	—		George Halas
1955	8	4	0	.667	294	251	2nd/Western Conf.	—	—		George Halas
1956	9	2	1	.818	363	246	1st/Western Conf.	0	1	NFL championship game	Paddy Driscoll
1957	5	7	0	.417	203	211	5th/Western Conf.	—	—		Paddy Driscoll
1958	8	4	0	.667	298	230	T2nd/Western Conf.	—	—		George Halas
1959	8	4	0	.667	252	196	2nd/Western Conf.	—	—		George Halas
1960	5	6	1	.455	194	299	5th/Western Conf.	—	—		George Halas
1961	8	6	0	.571	326	302	T3rd/Western Conf.	—	—		George Halas
1962	9	5	0	.643	321	287	3rd/Western Conf.	—	—		George Halas
1963	11	1	2	.917	301	144	1st/Western Conf.	1	0	NFL champ	George Halas
1964	5	9	0	.357	260	379	6th/Western Conf.	—	—		George Halas
1965	9	5	0	.643	409	275	3rd/Western Conf.	—	—		George Halas
1966	5	7	2	.417	234	272	5th/Western Conf.	—	—		George Halas
1967	7	6	1	.538	239	218	2nd/Central Div.	—	—		George Halas

HISTORY — Team by team

REGULAR SEASON / PLAYOFFS

Year	W	L	T	Pct.	PF	PA	Finish	W	L	Highest round	Coach
1968	7	7	0	.500	250	333	2nd/Central Div.	—	—		Jim Dooley
1969	1	13	0	.071	210	339	4th/Central Div.	—	—		Jim Dooley
1970	6	8	0	.429	256	261	T3rd/NFC Central Div.	—	—		Jim Dooley
1971	6	8	0	.429	185	276	3rd/NFC Central Div.	—	—		Jim Dooley
1972	4	9	1	.321	225	275	4th/NFC Central Div.	—	—		Abe Gibron
1973	3	11	0	.214	195	334	4th/NFC Central Div.	—	—		Abe Gibron
1974	4	10	0	.286	152	279	4th/NFC Central Div.	—	—		Abe Gibron
1975	4	10	0	.286	191	379	T3rd/NFC Central Div.	—	—		Jack Pardee
1976	7	7	0	.500	253	216	2nd/NFC Central Div.	—	—		Jack Pardee
1977	9	5	0	.643	255	253	2nd/NFC Central Div.	0	1	NFC div. playoff game	Jack Pardee
1978	7	9	0	.438	253	274	T3rd/NFC Central Div.	—	—		Neill Armstrong
1979	10	6	0	.625	306	249	2nd/NFC Central Div.	0	1	NFC wild-card game	Neill Armstrong
1980	7	9	0	.438	304	264	3rd/NFC Central Div.	—	—		Neill Armstrong
1981	6	10	0	.375	253	324	5th/NFC Central Div.	—	—		Neill Armstrong
1982	3	6	0	.333	141	174	T11th/NFC	—	—		Mike Ditka
1983	8	8	0	.500	311	301	T2nd/NFC Central Div.	—	—		Mike Ditka
1984	10	6	0	.625	325	248	1st/NFC Central Div.	1	1	NFC championship game	Mike Ditka
1985	15	1	0	.938	456	198	1st/NFC Central Div.	3	0	Super Bowl champ	Mike Ditka
1986	14	2	0	.875	352	187	1st/NFC Central Div.	0	1	NFC div. playoff game	Mike Ditka
1987	11	4	0	.733	356	282	1st/NFC Central Div.	0	1	NFC div. playoff game	Mike Ditka
1988	12	4	0	.750	312	215	1st/NFC Central Div.	1	1	NFC championship game	Mike Ditka
1989	6	10	0	.375	358	377	4th/NFC Central Div.	—	—		Mike Ditka
1990	11	5	0	.688	348	280	1st/NFC Central Div.	1	1	NFC div. playoff game	Mike Ditka
1991	11	5	0	.688	299	269	2nd/NFC Central Div.	0	1	NFC wild-card game	Mike Ditka
1992	5	11	0	.313	295	361	T3rd/NFC Central Div.	—	—		Mike Ditka
1993	7	9	0	.438	234	230	4th/NFC Central Div.	—	—		Dave Wannstedt
1994	9	7	0	.563	271	307	T2nd/NFC Central Div.	1	1	NFC div. playoff game	Dave Wannstedt
1995	9	7	0	.563	392	360	3rd/NFC Central Div.	—	—		Dave Wannstedt
1996	7	9	0	.438	283	305	3rd/NFC Central Div.	—	—		Dave Wannstedt
1997	4	12	0	.250	263	421	5th/NFC Central Div.	—	—		Dave Wannstedt
1998	4	12	0	.250	276	368	5th/NFC Central Div.	—	—		Dave Wannstedt
1999	6	10	0	.375	272	341	5th NFC Central Div.	—	—		Dick Jauron

*Decatur Staleys.
†Chicago Staleys.

FIRST-ROUND DRAFT PICKS

1936—Joe Stydahar, T, West Virginia
1937—Les McDonald, E, Nebraska
1938—Joe Gray, B, Oregon State
1939—Sid Luckman, B, Columbia
     Bill Osmanski, B, Holy Cross
1940—C. Turner, C, Hardin-Simmons
1941—Tom Harmon, B, Michigan*
     Norm Standlee, B, Stanford
     Don Scott, B, Ohio State
1942—Frankie Albert, B, Stanford
1943—Bob Steuber, B, Missouri
1944—Ray Evans, B, Kansas
1945—Don Lund, B, Michigan
1946—Johnny Lujack, QB, Notre Dame
1947—Bob Fenimore, B, Oklahoma A&M*
1948—Bobby Layne, QB, Texas
     Max Baumgardner, E, Texas
1949—Dick Harris, C, Texas
1950—Chuck Hunsinger, B, Florida
1951—Bob Williams, B, Notre Dame
     Billy Stone, B, Bradley
     Gene Schroeder, E, Virginia
1952—Jim Dooley, B, Miami
1953—Billy Anderson, B, Compton (Ca.) J.C.
1954—Stan Wallace, B, Illinois
1955—Ron Drzewiecki, B, Marquette
1956—Menan (Tex) Schriewer, E, Texas
1957—Earl Leggett, DT, Louisiana State
1958—Chuck Howley, LB, West Virginia
1959—Don Clark, B, Ohio State
1960—Roger Davis, G, Syracuse
1961—Mike Ditka, E, Pittsburgh

1962—Ron Bull, RB, Baylor
1963—Dave Behrman, C, Michigan State
1964—Dick Evey, DT, Tennessee
1965—Dick Butkus, LB, Illinois
     Gale Sayers, RB, Kansas
     Steve DeLong, DE, Tennessee
1966—George Rice, DT, Louisiana State
1967—Loyd Phillips, DE, Arkansas
1968—Mike Hull, RB, Southern California
1969—Rufus Mayes, T, Ohio State
1970—None
1971—Joe Moore, RB, Missouri
1972—Lionel Antoine, T, Southern Illinois
     Craig Clemons, DB, Iowa
1973—Wally Chambers, DE, Eastern Kentucky
1974—Waymond Bryant, LB, Tennessee State
     Dave Gallagher, DE, Michigan
1975—Walter Payton, RB, Jackson State
1976—Dennis Lick, T, Wisconsin
1977—Ted Albrecht, T, California
1978—None
1979—Dan Hampton, DT, Arkansas
     Al Harris, DE, Arizona State
1980—Otis Wilson, LB, Louisville
1981—Keith Van Horne, T, Southern California
1982—Jim McMahon, QB, Brigham Young
1983—Jimbo Covert, T, Pittsburgh
     Willie Gault, WR, Tennessee
1984—Wilber Marshall, LB, Florida
1985—William Perry, DT, Clemson
1986—Neal Anderson, RB, Florida
1987—Jim Harbaugh, QB, Michigan

1988—Brad Muster, RB, Stanford
Wendell Davis, WR, Louisiana State
1989—Donnell Woolford, DB, Clemson
Trace Armstrong, DE, Florida
1990—Mark Carrier, DB, Southern California
1991—Stan Thomas, T, Texas
1992—Alonzo Spellman, DE, Ohio State
1993—Curtis Conway, WR, Southern California
1994—John Thierry, LB, Alcorn State
1995—Rashaan Salaam, RB, Colorado
1996—Walt Harris, DB, Mississippi State
1997—None
1998—Curtis Enis, RB, Penn State
1999—Cade McNown, QB, UCLA
2000—Brian Urlacher, LB, New Mexico
*First player chosen in draft.

FRANCHISE RECORDS

Most rushing yards, career
16,726—Walter Payton
Most rushing yards, season
1,852—Walter Payton, 1977
Most rushing yards, game
275—Walter Payton vs. Min., Nov. 20, 1977
Most rushing touchdowns, season
14—Gale Sayers, 1965
Walter Payton, 1977
Walter Payton, 1979
Most passing attempts, season
522—Erik Kramer, 1995
Most passing attempts, game
60—Erik Kramer vs. NYJ, Nov. 16, 1997
Most passes completed, season
315—Erik Kramer, 1995
Most passes completed, game
34—Jim Miller vs. Min., Nov. 14, 1999 (OT)
33—Bill Wade at Was., Oct. 25, 1964

Most passing yards, career
14,686—Sid Luckman
Most passing yards, season
3,838—Erik Kramer, 1995
Most passing yards, game
468—Johnny Lujack vs. Chi. Cards, Dec. 11, 1949
Most touchdown passes, season
29—Erik Kramer, 1995
Most pass receptions, career
492—Walter Payton
Most pass receptions, season
93—Johnny Morris, 1964
Most pass receptions, game
14—Jim Keane at NYG, Oct. 23, 1949
Most receiving yards, career
5,059—Johnny Morris
Most receiving yards, season
1,400—Marcus Robinson, 1999
Most receiving yards, game
214—Harlon Hill at S.F., Oct. 31, 1954

Most receiving touchdowns, season
13—Ken Kavanaugh, 1947
Dick Gordon, 1970
Most touchdowns, career
125—Walter Payton
Most field goals, season
31—Kevin Butler, 1985
Longest field goal
55 yards—Bob Thomas at L.A. Rams, Nov. 23, 1975
Kevin Butler vs. Min., Oct. 25, 1993
Kevin Butler at T.B., Dec. 12, 1993
Most interceptions, career
38—Gary Fencik
Most interceptions, season
10—Mark Carrier, 1990
Most sacks, career
124.5—Richard Dent
Most sacks, season
17.5—Richard Dent, 1984

SERIES RECORDS

Chicago vs.: Arizona 54-26-6; Atlanta 9-10; Baltimore 1-0; Buffalo 5-2; Carolina 1-0; Cincinnati 2-4; Cleveland 3-8; Dallas 8-9; Denver 5-6; Detroit 73-55-3; Green Bay 83-70-6; Indianapolis 16-21; Jacksonville 1-1; Kansas City 5-3; Miami 3-5; Minnesota 33-42-2; New England 2-5; New Orleans 11-7; N.Y. Giants 25-16-2; N.Y. Jets 4-2; Oakland 4-6; Philadelphia 25-5-1; Pittsburgh 19-6-1; St. Louis 36-27-3; San Diego 4-4; San Francisco 25-25-1; Seattle 2-5; Tampa Bay 30-14; Tennessee 4-4; Washington 14-14.
NOTE: Includes records as Decatur Staleys in 1920 and Chicago Staleys in 1921.

COACHING RECORDS

Hunk Anderson-Luke Johnsos*, 23-11-2 (1-1); Neill Armstrong, 30-34-0 (0-1); Mike Ditka, 106-62-0 (6-6); Jim Dooley, 20-36-0; Paddy Driscoll, 14-9-1 (0-1); Abe Gibron, 11-30-1; George Halas, 318-148-31 (6-3); Dick Jauron, 6-10-0; Ralph Jones, 24-10-7; Jack Pardee, 20-22-0 (0-1); Dave Wannstedt, 40-56-0 (1-1).
NOTE: Playoff games in parentheses.
*Co-coaches.

RETIRED UNIFORM NUMBERS

No.	Player
3	Bronko Nagurski
5	George McAfee
7	George Halas
28	Willie Galimore
34	Walter Payton
40	Gale Sayers
41	Brian Piccolo
42	Sid Luckman
51	Dick Butkus
56	Bill Hewitt
61	Bill George
66	Bulldog Turner
77	Red Grange

CINCINNATI BENGALS
YEAR-BY-YEAR RECORDS

		REGULAR SEASON					PLAYOFFS			
Year	W	L	T	Pct.	PF	PA	Finish	W	L	Highest round	Coach
1968*	3	11	0	.214	215	329	5th/Western Div.	—	—		Paul Brown
1969*	4	9	1	.308	280	367	5th/Western Div.	—	—		Paul Brown
1970	8	6	0	.571	312	255	1st/AFC Central Div.	0	1	AFC div. playoff game	Paul Brown
1971	4	10	0	.286	284	265	4th/AFC Central Div.	—	—		Paul Brown
1972	8	6	0	.571	299	229	3rd/AFC Central Div.	—	—		Paul Brown
1973	10	4	0	.714	286	231	1st/AFC Central Div.	0	1	AFC div. playoff game	Paul Brown

HISTORY Team by team

Year	W	L	T	Pct.	PF	PA	Finish	W	L	Highest round	Coach
1974	7	7	0	.500	283	259	T2nd/AFC Central Div.	—	—		Paul Brown
1975	11	3	0	.786	340	246	2nd/AFC Central Div.	0	1	AFC div. playoff game	Paul Brown
1976	10	4	0	.714	335	210	2nd/AFC Central Div.	—	—		Bill Johnson
1977	8	6	0	.571	238	235	T2nd/AFC Central Div.	—	—		Bill Johnson
1978	4	12	0	.250	252	284	4th/AFC Central Div.	—	—		B. Johnson, H. Rice
1979	4	12	0	.250	337	421	4th/AFC Central Div.	—	—		Homer Rice
1980	6	10	0	.375	244	312	4th/AFC Central Div.	—	—		Forrest Gregg
1981	12	4	0	.750	421	304	1st/AFC Central Div.	2	1	Super Bowl	Forrest Gregg
1982	7	2	0	.778	232	177	T2nd/AFC	0	1	AFC first-round pl. game	Forrest Gregg
1983	7	9	0	.438	346	302	3rd/AFC Central Div.	—	—		Forrest Gregg
1984	8	8	0	.500	339	339	2nd/AFC Central Div.	—	—		Sam Wyche
1985	7	9	0	.438	441	437	T2nd/AFC Central Div.	—	—		Sam Wyche
1986	10	6	0	.625	409	394	2nd/AFC Central Div.	—	—		Sam Wyche
1987	4	11	0	.267	285	370	4th/AFC Central Div.	—	—		Sam Wyche
1988	12	4	0	.750	448	329	1st/AFC Central Div.	2	1	Super Bowl	Sam Wyche
1989	8	8	0	.500	404	285	4th/AFC Central Div.	—	—		Sam Wyche
1990	9	7	0	.563	360	352	1st/AFC Central Div.	1	1	AFC div. playoff game	Sam Wyche
1991	3	13	0	.188	263	435	4th/AFC Central Div.	—	—		Sam Wyche
1992	5	11	0	.313	274	364	4th/AFC Central Div.	—	—		David Shula
1993	3	13	0	.188	187	319	4th/AFC Central Div.	—	—		David Shula
1994	3	13	0	.188	276	406	3rd/AFC Central Div.	—	—		David Shula
1995	7	9	0	.438	349	374	T2nd/AFC Central Div.	—	—		David Shula
1996	8	8	0	.500	372	369	T3rd/AFC Central Div.	—	—		D. Shula, B. Coslet
1997	7	9	0	.438	355	405	4th/AFC Central Div.	—	—		Bruce Coslet
1998	3	13	0	.188	268	452	5th/AFC Central Div.	—	—		Bruce Coslet
1999	4	12	0	.250	283	460	5th/AFC Central Div.	—	—		Bruce Coslet

*American Football League.

FIRST-ROUND DRAFT PICKS

1968—Bob Johnson, C, Tennessee
1969—Greg Cook, QB, Cincinnati
1970—Mike Reid, DT, Penn State
1971—Vernon Holland, T, Tennessee State
1972—Sherman White, DE, California
1973—Issac Curtis, WR, San Diego State
1974—Bill Kollar, DT, Montana State
1975—Glenn Cameron, LB, Florida
1976—Billy Brooks, WR, Oklahoma
    Archie Griffin, RB, Ohio State
1977—Eddie Edwards, DT, Miami (Fla.)
    Wilson Whitley, DT, Houston
    Mike Cobb, TE, Michigan State
1978—Ross Browner, DE, Notre Dame
    Blair Bush, C, Washington
1979—Jack Thompson, QB, Washington State
    Charles Alexander, RB, Louisiana State
1980—Anthony Munoz, T, Southern California
1981—David Verser, WR, Kansas
1982—Glen Collins, DE, Mississippi State
1983—Dave Rimington, C, Nebraska
1984—Ricky Hunley, LB, Arizona
    Pete Koch, DE, Maryland
    Brian Blados, T, North Carolina
1985—Eddie Brown, WR, Miami (Fla.)
    Emanuel King, LB, Alabama
1986—Joe Kelly, LB, Washington
    Tim McGee, WR, Tennessee
1987—Jason Buck, DT, Brigham Young
1988—Rickey Dixon, S, Oklahoma
1989—None
1990—James Francis, LB, Baylor
1991—Alfred Williams, LB, Colorado
1992—David Klingler, QB, Houston
    Darryl Williams, DB, Miami (Fla.)
1993—John Copeland, DE, Alabama
1994—Dan Wilkinson, DT, Ohio State*
1995—Ki-Jana Carter, RB, Penn State*
1996—Willie Anderson, T, Auburn
1997—Reinard Wilson, LB, Florida State
1998—Takeo Spikes, LB, Auburn
    Brian Simmons, LB, North Carolina
1999—Akili Smith, QB, Oregon
2000—Peter Warrick, WR, Florida State
*First player chosen in draft.

FRANCHISE RECORDS

Most rushing yards, career
6,447—James Brooks
Most rushing yards, season
1,239—James Brooks, 1989
Most rushing yards, game
246—Corey Dillon vs. Ten., Dec. 4, 1997
Most rushing touchdowns, season
15—Ickey Woods, 1988
Most passing attempts, season
567—Jeff Blake, 1995
Most passing attempts, game
56—Ken Anderson at S.D., Dec. 20, 1982

Most passes completed, season
326—Jeff Blake, 1995
Most passes completed, game
40—Ken Anderson at S.D., Dec. 20, 1982
Most passing yards, career
32,838—Ken Anderson
Most passing yards, season
3,959—Boomer Esiason, 1986
Most passing yards, game
490—Boomer Esiason at L.A. Rams, Oct. 7, 1990

Most touchdown passes, season
29—Ken Anderson, 1981
Most pass receptions, career
473—Carl Pickens
Most pass receptions, season
100—Carl Pickens, 1996
Most pass receptions, game
13—Carl Pickens vs. Pit., Oct. 11, 1998
Most receiving yards, career
7,101—Isaac Curtis
Most receiving yards, season
1,273—Eddie Brown, 1988

Most receiving yards, game
216—Eddie Brown vs. Pit., Nov. 16, 1988
Most receiving touchdowns, season
17—Carl Pickens, 1995
Most touchdowns, career
70—Pete Johnson
Most field goals, season
29—Doug Pelfrey, 1995

Longest field goal
55 yards—Chris Bahr vs. Hou., Sept. 23, 1979
Most interceptions, career
65—Ken Riley
Most interceptions, season
9—Ken Riley, 1976

Most sacks, career
83.5—Eddie Edwards
Most sacks, season
21.5—Coy Bacon, 1976

SERIES RECORDS

Cincinnati vs.: Arizona 4-2; Atlanta 7-2; Baltimore 3-5; Buffalo 10-9; Carolina 0-1; Chicago 4-2; Cleveland 26-27; Dallas 3-4; Denver 6-14; Detroit 4-3; Green Bay 4-5; Indianapolis 8-12; Jacksonville 4-6; Kansas City 9-11; Miami 3-12; Minnesota 4-5; New England 7-9; New Orleans 4-5; N.Y. Giants 4-2; N.Y. Jets 6-10; Oakland 7-16; Philadelphia 6-2; Pittsburgh 26-33; St. Louis 5-4; San Diego 9-15; San Francisco 2-7; Seattle 7-8; Tampa Bay 3-3; Tennessee 28-33-1; Washington 2-4.

COACHING RECORDS

Paul Brown, 55-56-1 (0-3); Bruce Coslet, 21-36-0; Forrest Gregg, 32-25-0 (2-2); Bill Johnson, 18-15-0; Homer Rice, 8-19-0; Dave Shula, 19-52-0; Sam Wyche, 61-66-0 (3-2). NOTE: Playoff games in parentheses.

RETIRED UNIFORM NUMBERS

No.	Player
54	Bob Johnson

CLEVELAND BROWNS
YEAR-BY-YEAR RECORDS

	REGULAR SEASON						PLAYOFFS			
Year	W	L	T	Pct.	PF	PA	Finish	W	L	Highest round	Coach
1946*	12	2	0	.857	423	137	1st/Western Div.	—	—		Paul Brown
1947*	12	1	1	.923	410	185	1st/Western Div.	—	—		Paul Brown
1948*	14	0	0	1.000	389	190	1st/Western Div.	—	—		Paul Brown
1949*	9	1	2	.900	339	171	1st	—	—		Paul Brown
1950	10	2	0	.833	310	144	1st/American Conf.	2	0	NFL champ	Paul Brown
1951	11	1	0	.917	331	152	1st/American Conf.	0	1	NFL championship game	Paul Brown
1952	8	4	0	.667	310	213	1st/American Conf.	0	1	NFL championship game	Paul Brown
1953	11	1	0	.917	348	162	1st/Eastern Conf.	0	1	NFL championship game	Paul Brown
1954	9	3	0	.750	336	162	1st/Eastern Conf.	1	0	NFL champ	Paul Brown
1955	9	2	1	.818	349	218	1st/Eastern Conf.	1	0	NFL champ	Paul Brown
1956	5	7	0	.417	167	177	4th/Eastern Conf.	—	—		Paul Brown
1957	9	2	1	.818	269	172	1st/Eastern Conf.	0	1	NFL championship game	Paul Brown
1958	9	3	0	.750	302	217	2nd/Eastern Conf.	0	1	E. Conf. championship game	Paul Brown
1959	7	5	0	.583	270	214	T2nd/Eastern Conf.	—	—		Paul Brown
1960	8	3	1	.727	362	217	2nd/Eastern Conf.	—	—		Paul Brown
1961	8	5	1	.615	319	270	3rd/Eastern Conf.	—	—		Paul Brown
1962	7	6	1	.538	291	257	3rd/Eastern Conf.	—	—		Paul Brown
1963	10	4	0	.714	343	262	2nd/Eastern Conf.	—	—		Blanton Collier
1964	10	3	1	.769	415	293	1st/Eastern Conf.	1	0	NFL champ	Blanton Collier
1965	11	3	0	.786	363	325	1st/Eastern Conf.	0	1	NFL championship game	Blanton Collier
1966	9	5	0	.643	403	259	T2nd/Eastern Conf.	—	—		Blanton Collier
1967	9	5	0	.643	334	297	1st/Century Div.	0	1	E. Conf. championship game	Blanton Collier
1968	10	4	0	.714	394	273	1st/Century Div.	1	1	NFL championship game	Blanton Collier
1969	10	3	1	.769	351	300	1st/Century Div.	1	1	NFL championship game	Blanton Collier
1970	7	7	0	.500	286	265	2nd/AFC Central Div.	—	—		Blanton Collier
1971	9	5	0	.643	285	273	1st/AFC Central Div.	0	1	AFC div. playoff game	Nick Skorich
1972	10	4	0	.714	268	249	2nd/AFC Central Div.	0	1	AFC div. playoff game	Nick Skorich
1973	7	5	2	.571	234	255	3rd/AFC Central Div.	—	—		Nick Skorich
1974	4	10	0	.286	251	344	4th/AFC Central Div.	—	—		Nick Skorich
1975	3	11	0	.214	218	372	4th/AFC Central Div.	—	—		Forrest Gregg
1976	9	5	0	.643	267	287	3rd/AFC Central Div.	—	—		Forrest Gregg
1977	6	8	0	.429	269	267	4th/AFC Central Div.	—	—		F. Gregg, Dick Modzelewski
1978	8	8	0	.500	334	356	3rd/AFC Central Div.	—	—		Sam Rutigliano
1979	9	7	0	.563	359	352	3rd/AFC Central Div.	—	—		Sam Rutigliano
1980	11	5	0	.688	357	310	1st/AFC Central Div.	0	1	AFC div. playoff game	Sam Rutigliano
1981	5	11	0	.313	276	375	4th/AFC Central Div.	—	—		Sam Rutigliano
1982	4	5	0	.444	140	182	T8th/AFC	0	1	AFC first-round pl. game	Sam Rutigliano
1983	9	7	0	.563	356	342	2nd/AFC Central Div.	—	—		Sam Rutigliano
1984	5	11	0	.313	250	297	3rd/AFC Central Div.	—	—		Rutigliano, Schottenheimer
1985	8	8	0	.500	287	294	1st/AFC Central Div.	0	1	AFC div. playoff game	Marty Schottenheimer
1986	12	4	0	.750	391	310	1st/AFC Central Div.	1	1	AFC championship game	Marty Schottenheimer
1987	10	5	0	.667	390	239	1st/AFC Central Div.	1	1	AFC championship game	Marty Schottenheimer
1988	10	6	0	.625	304	288	T2nd/AFC Central Div.	0	1	AFC wild-card game	Marty Schottenheimer

Year	W	L	T	Pct.	PF	PA	Finish	W	L	Highest round	Coach
1989	9	6	1	.594	334	254	1st/AFC Central Div.	1	1	AFC championship game	Bud Carson
1990	3	13	0	.188	228	462	4th/AFC Central Div.	—	—		Bud Carson, Jim Shofner
1991	6	10	0	.375	293	298	3rd/AFC Central Div.	—	—		Bill Belichick
1992	7	9	0	.438	272	275	3rd/AFC Central Div.	—	—		Bill Belichick
1993	7	9	0	.438	304	307	3rd/AFC Central Div.	—	—		Bill Belichick
1994	11	5	0	.688	340	204	2nd/AFC Central Div.	1	1	AFC div. playoff game	Bill Belichick
1995	5	11	0	.313	289	356	4th/AFC Central Div.	—	—		Bill Belichick
1999	2	14	0	.125	217	437	6th/AFC Central Div.	—	—		Chris Palmer

*All-America Football Conference.

FIRST-ROUND DRAFT PICKS

1950—Ken Carpenter, B, Oregon State
1951—Ken Konz, B, Louisiana State
1952—Bert Rechichar, DB, Tennessee
   Harry Agganis, QB, Boston University
1953—Doug Atkins, DT, Tennessee
1954—Bobby Garrett, QB, Stanford*
   John Bauer, G, Illinois
1955—Kent Burris, C, Oklahoma
1956—Preston Carpenter, B, Arkansas
1957—Jim Brown, B, Syracuse
1958—Jim Shofner, DB, Texas Christian
1959—Rich Kreitling, DE, Illinois
1960—Jim Houston, DE, Ohio State
1961—None
1962—Gary Collins, WR, Maryland
   Leroy Jackson, B, Western Illinois
1963—Tom Hutchinson, TE, Kentucky
1964—Paul Warfield, WR, Ohio State
1965—None
1966—Milt Morin, TE, Massachusetts
1967—Bob Matheson, LB, Duke
1968—M. Upshaw, DE, Trinity (Tex.)
1969—Ron Johnson, RB, Michigan
1970—Mike Phipps, QB, Purdue
   Bob McKay, T, Texas
1971—Clarence Scott, DB, Kansas State
1972—Thom Darden, DB, Michigan
1973—Steve Holden, WR, Arizona State
   Pete Adams, G, Southern California

1974—None
1975—Mack Mitchell, DE, Houston
1976—Mike Pruitt, RB, Purdue
1977—Robert Jackson, LB, Texas A&M
1978—Clay Matthews, LB, Southern California
   Ozzie Newsome, WR, Alabama
1979—Willis Adams, WR, Houston
1980—Charles White, RB, Southern California
1981—Hanford Dixon, CB, Southern Mississippi
1982—Chip Banks, LB, Southern California
1983—None
1984—Don Rogers, DB, UCLA
1985—None
1986—None
1987—Mike Junkin, LB, Duke
1988—Clifford Charlton, LB, Florida
1989—Eric Metcalf, RB, Texas
1990—None
1991—Eric Turner, S, UCLA
1992—Tommy Vardell, FB, Stanford
1993—Steve Everitt, C, Michigan
1994—Antonio Langham, DB, Alabama
   Derrick Alexander, WR, Michigan
1995—Craig Powell, LB, Ohio State
1999—Tim Couch, QB, Kentucky*
2000—Courtney Brown, DE, Penn State*
*First player chosen in draft.

FRANCHISE RECORDS

Most rushing yards, career
12,312—Jim Brown
Most rushing yards, season
1,863—Jim Brown, 1963
Most rushing yards, game
237—Jim Brown vs. L.A., Nov. 24, 1957
   Jim Brown vs. Phi., Nov. 19, 1961
Most rushing touchdowns, season
17— Jim Brown, 1958
   Jim Brown, 1965
Most passing attempts, season
567—Brian Sipe, 1981
Most passing attempts, game
57—Brian Sipe vs. S.D., Sept. 7, 1981
Most passes completed, season
337—Brian Sipe, 1980
Most passes completed, game
33—Brian Sipe vs. S.D., Dec. 5, 1982
Most passing yards, career
23,713—Brian Sipe

Most passing yards, season
4,132—Brian Sipe, 1980
Most passing yards, game
444—Brian Sipe vs. Bal., Oct. 25, 1981
Most touchdown passes, season
30—Brian Sipe, 1980
Most pass receptions, career
662—Ozzie Newsome
Most pass receptions, season
89—Ozzie Newsome, 1983
   Ozzie Newsome, 1984
Most pass receptions, game
14—Ozzie Newsome vs. NYJ, Oct. 14, 1984
Most receiving yards, career
7,980—Ozzie Newsome
Most receiving yards, season
1,236—Webster Slaughter, 1989
Most receiving yards, game
191—Ozzie Newsome vs. NYJ, Oct. 14, 1984

Most receiving touchdowns, season
13—Gary Collins, 1963
Most touchdowns, career
126—Jim Brown
Most field goals, season
29—Matt Stover, 1995
Longest field goal
60 yards—Steve Cox at Cin., Oct. 21, 1984
Most interceptions, career
45—Thom Darden
Most interceptions, season
10—Thom Darden, 1978
Most sacks, career
63.5—Clay Matthews
Most sacks, season
14.5—Bill Glass, 1965

SERIES RECORDS

Cleveland vs.: Arizona 32-10-3; Atlanta 8-2; Baltimore 0-2; Buffalo 7-4; Carolina 0-1; Chicago 8-3; Cincinnati 27-26; Dallas 15-9; Denver 5-13; Detroit 3-12; Green Bay 6-8; Indianapolis 13-8; Jacksonville 0-4; Kansas City 8-7-2; Miami 4-6; Minnesota 3-8; New England 10-5; New Orleans 10-3; N.Y. Giants 25-17-2; N.Y. Jets 9-6; Oakland 3-9; Philadelphia 31-12-1; Pittsburgh 53-41; St. Louis 8-8; San Diego 6-10-1; San Francisco 9-6; Seattle 4-9; Tampa Bay 5-0; Tennessee 30-23; Washington 32-9-1.

COACHING RECORDS

Bill Belichick, 36-44 (1-1); Paul Brown, 158-48-8 (4-5); Bud Carson, 11-12-1 (1-1); Blanton Collier, 76-34-2 (3-4); Forrest Gregg (18-23); Dick Modzelewski, 0-1; Chris Palmer, 2-14-0; Sam Rutigliano, 47-50 (0-2); Marty Schottenheimer, 44-27 (2-4); Jim Shofner, 1-7; Nick Skorich, 30-24-2 (0-2).
NOTE: Playoff games in parentheses.

RETIRED UNIFORM NUMBERS

No.	Player
14	Otto Graham
32	Jim Brown
45	Ernie Davis
46	Don Fleming
76	Lou Groza

DALLAS COWBOYS
YEAR-BY-YEAR RECORDS

Year	W	L	T	Pct.	PF	PA	Finish	W	L	Highest round	Coach
1960	0	11	1	.000	177	369	7th/Western Conf.	—	—		Tom Landry
1961	4	9	1	.308	236	380	6th/Eastern Conf.	—	—		Tom Landry
1962	5	8	1	.385	398	402	5th/Eastern Conf.	—	—		Tom Landry
1963	4	10	0	.286	305	378	5th/Eastern Conf.	—	—		Tom Landry
1964	5	8	1	.385	250	289	5th/Eastern Conf.	—	—		Tom Landry
1965	7	7	0	.500	325	280	T2nd/Eastern Conf.	—	—		Tom Landry
1966	10	3	1	.769	445	239	1st/Eastern Conf.	0	1	NFL championship game	Tom Landry
1967	9	5	0	.643	342	268	1st/Capitol Div.	1	1	NFL championship game	Tom Landry
1968	12	2	0	.857	431	186	1st/Capitol Div.	0	1	E. Conf. championship game	Tom Landry
1969	11	2	1	.846	369	223	1st/Capitol Div.	0	1	E. Conf. championship game	Tom Landry
1970	10	4	0	.714	299	221	1st/NFC Eastern Div.	2	1	Super Bowl	Tom Landry
1971	11	3	0	.786	406	222	1st/NFC Eastern Div.	3	0	Super Bowl champ	Tom Landry
1972	10	4	0	.714	319	240	2nd/NFC Eastern Div.	1	1	NFC championship game	Tom Landry
1973	10	4	0	.714	382	203	1st/NFC Eastern Div.	1	1	NFC championship game	Tom Landry
1974	8	6	0	.571	297	235	3rd/NFC Eastern Div.	—	—		Tom Landry
1975	10	4	0	.714	350	268	2nd/NFC Eastern Div.	2	1	Super Bowl	Tom Landry
1976	11	3	0	.786	296	194	1st/NFC Eastern Div.	0	1	NFC div. playoff game	Tom Landry
1977	12	2	0	.857	345	212	1st/NFC Eastern Div.	3	0	Super Bowl champ	Tom Landry
1978	12	4	0	.750	384	208	1st/NFC Eastern Div.	2	1	Super Bowl	Tom Landry
1979	11	5	0	.688	371	313	1st/NFC Eastern Div.	0	1	NFC div. playoff game	Tom Landry
1980	12	4	0	.750	454	311	2nd/NFC Eastern Div.	2	1	NFC championship game	Tom Landry
1981	12	4	0	.750	367	277	1st/NFC Eastern Div.	1	1	NFC championship game	Tom Landry
1982	6	3	0	.667	226	145	2nd/NFC	2	1	NFC championship game	Tom Landry
1983	12	4	0	.750	479	360	2nd/NFC Eastern Div.	0	1	NFC wild-card game	Tom Landry
1984	9	7	0	.563	308	308	T3rd/NFC Eastern Div.	—	—		Tom Landry
1985	10	6	0	.625	357	333	1st/NFC Eastern Div.	0	1	NFC div. playoff game	Tom Landry
1986	7	9	0	.438	346	337	3rd/NFC Eastern Div.	—	—		Tom Landry
1987	7	8	0	.467	340	348	T2nd/NFC Eastern Div.	—	—		Tom Landry
1988	3	13	0	.188	265	381	5th/NFC Eastern Div.	—	—		Tom Landry
1989	1	15	0	.063	204	393	5th/NFC Eastern Div.	—	—		Jimmy Johnson
1990	7	9	0	.438	244	308	4th/NFC Eastern Div.	—	—		Jimmy Johnson
1991	11	5	0	.688	342	310	2nd/NFC Eastern Div.	1	1	NFC div. playoff game	Jimmy Johnson
1992	13	3	0	.813	409	243	1st/NFC Eastern Div.	3	0	Super Bowl champ	Jimmy Johnson
1993	12	4	0	.750	376	229	1st/NFC Eastern Div.	3	0	Super Bowl champ	Jimmy Johnson
1994	12	4	0	.750	414	248	1st/NFC Eastern Div.	1	1	NFC championship game	Barry Switzer
1995	12	4	0	.750	435	291	1st/NFC Eastern Div.	3	0	Super Bowl champ	Barry Switzer
1996	10	6	0	.625	286	250	1st/NFC Eastern Div.	1	1	NFC div. playoff game	Barry Switzer
1997	6	10	0	.375	304	314	4th/NFC Eastern Div.	—	—		Barry Switzer
1998	10	6	0	.625	381	275	1st/NFC Eastern Div.	0	1	NFC wild-card game	Chan Gailey
1999	8	8	0	.500	352	276	2nd/NFC Eastern Div.	0	1	NFC wild-card game	Chan Gailey

FIRST-ROUND DRAFT PICKS

1961—Bob Lilly, DT, Texas Christian
1962—None
1963—Lee Roy Jordan, LB, Alabama
1964—Scott Appleton, DT, Texas
1965—Craig Morton, QB, California
1966—John Niland, G, Iowa
1967—None
1968—Dennis Homan, WR, Alabama
1969—Calvin Hill, RB, Yale
1970—Duane Thomas, RB, West Texas State
1971—Tody Smith, DE, Southern California
1972—Bill Thomas, RB, Boston College
1973—Billy Joe DuPree, TE, Michigan State
1974—Ed Jones, DE, Tennessee State*

Charles Young, RB, North Carolina State
1975—Randy White, LB, Maryland
Thomas Henderson, LB, Langston
1976—Aaron Kyle, DB, Wyoming
1977—Tony Dorsett, RB, Pittsburgh
1978—Larry Bethea, DE, Michigan State
1979—Robert Shaw, C, Tennessee
1980—None
1981—Howard Richards, T, Missouri
1982—Rod Hill, DB, Kentucky State
1983—Jim Jeffcoat, DE, Arizona State
1984—Billy Cannon Jr., LB, Texas A&M
1985—Kevin Brooks, DE, Michigan
1986—Mike Sherrard, WR, UCLA
1987—Danny Noonan, DT, Nebraska
1988—Michael Irvin, WR, Miami (Fla.)
1989—Troy Aikman, QB, UCLA*
1990—Emmitt Smith, RB, Florida
1991—Russell Maryland, DL, Miami (Fla.)*
Alvin Harper, WR, Tennessee
Kelvin Pritchett, DT, Mississippi
1992—Kevin Smith, DB, Texas A&M
Robert Jones, LB, East Carolina
1993—None
1994—Shante Carver, DE, Arizona State
1995—None
1996—None
1997—David LaFleur, TE, Louisiana State
1998—Greg Ellis, DE, North Carolina
1999—Ebenezer Ekuban, DE, North Carolina
2000—None

*First player chosen in draft.

FRANCHISE RECORDS

Most rushing yards, career
13,963—Emmitt Smith
Most rushing yards, season
1,773—Emmitt Smith, 1995
Most rushing yards, game
237—Emmitt Smith at Phi., Oct. 31, 1993
Most rushing touchdowns, season
25—Emmitt Smith, 1995
Most passing attempts, season
533—Danny White, 1983
Most passing attempts, game
57—Troy Aikman vs. Min., Nov. 26, 1998
Most passes completed, season
334—Danny White, 1983
Most passes completed, game
34—Troy Aikman at NYG, Oct. 5, 1997
Troy Aikman vs. Min., Nov. 26, 1998
Most passing yards, career
31,310—Troy Aikman

Most passing yards, season
3,980—Danny White, 1983
Most passing yards, game
460—Don Meredith at S.F., Nov. 10, 1963
Most touchdown passes, season
29—Danny White, 1983
Most pass receptions, career
750—Michael Irvin
Most pass receptions, season
111—Michael Irvin, 1995
Most pass receptions, game
13—Lance Rentzel vs. Was., Nov. 19, 1967
Most receiving yards, career
11,904—Michael Irvin
Most receiving yards, season
1,603—Michael Irvin, 1995
Most receiving yards, game
246—Bob Hayes at Was., Nov. 13, 1966
Most receiving touchdowns, season
14—Frank Clarke, 1962

Most touchdowns, career
147—Emmitt Smith
Most field goals, season
34—Richie Cunningham, 1997
Longest field goal
54 yards—Toni Fritsch at NYG,
Sept. 24, 1972
Ken Willis at Cle., Sept. 1, 1991
Richie Cunningham at Den., Sept. 13, 1998
Most interceptions, career
52—Mel Renfro
Most interceptions, season
11—Everson Walls, 1981
Most sacks, career
114—Harvey Martin
Most sacks, season
20—Harvey Martin, 1977

SERIES RECORDS

Dallas vs.: Arizona 50-24-1; Atlanta 12-6; Buffalo 3-3; Carolina 1-1; Chicago 9-8; Cincinnati 4-3; Cleveland 9-15; Denver 4-3; Detroit 7-6; Green Bay 9-10; Indianapolis 7-4; Jacksonville 1-0; Kansas City 4-3; Miami 3-6; Minnesota 9-8; New England 7-1; New Orleans 14-5; N.Y. Giants 47-26-2; N.Y. Jets 5-2; Oakland 3-4; Philadelphia 48-30; Pittsburgh 14-11; St. Louis 8-9; San Diego 5-1; San Francisco 7-12-1; Seattle 5-1; Tampa Bay 6-0; Tennessee 5-4; Washington 45-31-2.

COACHING RECORDS

Chan Gailey, 18-14-0 (0-2); Jimmy Johnson, 44-36-0 (7-1); Tom Landry, 250-162-6 (20-16); Barry Switzer, 40-24-0 (5-2).
NOTE: Playoff games in parentheses.

RETIRED UNIFORM NUMBERS

No. Player
None

DENVER BRONCOS
YEAR-BY-YEAR RECORDS

		REGULAR SEASON					PLAYOFFS			
Year	W	L	T	Pct.	PF	PA	Finish	W	L	Highest round	Coach
1960*	4	9	1	.308	309	393	4th/Western Div.	—	—		Frank Filchock
1961*	3	11	0	.214	251	432	3rd/Western Div.	—	—		Frank Filchock
1962*	7	7	0	.500	353	334	2nd/Western Div.	—	—		Jack Faulkner
1963*	2	11	1	.154	301	473	4th/Western Div.	—	—		Jack Faulkner
1964*	2	11	1	.154	240	438	4th/Western Div.	—	—		J. Faulkner, M. Speedie
1965*	4	10	0	.286	303	392	4th/Western Div.	—	—		Mac Speedie
1966*	4	10	0	.286	196	381	4th/Western Div.	—	—		M. Speedie, Ray Malavasi
1967*	3	11	0	.214	256	409	4th/Western Div.	—	—		Lou Saban
1968*	5	9	0	.357	255	404	4th/Western Div.	—	—		Lou Saban

HISTORY — Team by team

Year	W	L	T	Pct.	PF	PA	Finish	W	L	Highest round	Coach
1969*	5	8	1	.385	297	344	4th/Western Div.	—	—		Lou Saban
1970	5	8	1	.385	253	264	4th/AFC Western Div.	—	—		Lou Saban
1971	4	9	1	.308	203	275	4th/AFC Western Div.	—	—		Lou Saban, Jerry Smith
1972	5	9	0	.357	325	350	3rd/AFC Western Div.	—	—		John Ralston
1973	7	5	2	.571	354	296	T2nd/AFC Western Div.	—	—		John Ralston
1974	7	6	1	.536	302	294	2nd/AFC Western Div.	—	—		John Ralston
1975	6	8	0	.429	254	307	2nd/AFC Western Div.	—	—		John Ralston
1976	9	5	0	.643	315	206	2nd/AFC Western Div.	—	—		John Ralston
1977	12	2	0	.857	274	148	1st/AFC Western Div.	2	1	Super Bowl	Red Miller
1978	10	6	0	.625	282	198	1st/AFC Western Div.	0	1	AFC div. playoff game	Red Miller
1979	10	6	0	.625	289	262	2nd/AFC Western Div.	0	1	AFC wild-card game	Red Miller
1980	8	8	0	.500	310	323	T3rd/AFC Western Div.	—	—		Red Miller
1981	10	6	0	.625	321	289	2nd/AFC Western Div.	—	—		Dan Reeves
1982	2	7	0	.222	148	226	12th/AFC	—	—		Dan Reeves
1983	9	7	0	.563	302	327	T2nd/AFC Western Div.	0	1	AFC wild-card game	Dan Reeves
1984	13	3	0	.813	353	241	1st/AFC Western Div.	0	1	AFC div. playoff game	Dan Reeves
1985	11	5	0	.688	380	329	2nd/AFC Western Div.	—	—		Dan Reeves
1986	11	5	0	.688	378	327	1st/AFC Western Div.	2	1	Super Bowl	Dan Reeves
1987	10	4	1	.700	379	288	1st/AFC Western Div.	2	1	Super Bowl	Dan Reeves
1988	8	8	0	.500	327	352	2nd/AFC Western Div.	—	—		Dan Reeves
1989	11	5	0	.688	362	226	1st/AFC Western Div.	2	1	Super Bowl	Dan Reeves
1990	5	11	0	.313	331	374	5th/AFC Western Div.	—	—		Dan Reeves
1991	12	4	0	.750	304	235	1st/AFC Western Div.	1	1	AFC championship game	Dan Reeves
1992	8	8	0	.500	262	329	3rd/AFC Western Div.	—	—		Dan Reeves
1993	9	7	0	.563	373	284	1st/AFC Western Div.	0	1	AFC wild-card game	Wade Phillips
1994	7	9	0	.438	347	396	4th/AFC Western Div.	—	—		Wade Phillips
1995	8	8	0	.500	388	345	T3rd/AFC Western Div.	—	—		Mike Shanahan
1996	13	3	0	.813	391	275	1st/AFC Western Div.	0	1	AFC div. playoff game	Mike Shanahan
1997	12	4	0	.750	472	287	2nd/AFC Western Div.	4	0	Super Bowl champ	Mike Shanahan
1998	14	2	0	.875	501	309	1st/AFC Western Div.	3	0	Super Bowl champ	Mike Shanahan
1999	6	10	0	.375	314	318	5th/AFC Western Div.	—	—		Mike Shanahan

*American Football League.

FIRST-ROUND DRAFT PICKS

1960—Roger Leclerc, C, Trinity (Conn.)
1961—Bob Gaiters, RB, New Mexico State
1962—Merlin Olsen, DT, Utah State
1963—Kermit Alexander, DB, UCLA
1964—Bob Brown, T, Nebraska
1965—None
1966—Jerry Shay, DT, Purdue
1967—Floyd Little, RB, Syracuse
1968—None
1969—None
1970—Bob Anderson, RB, Colorado
1971—Marv Montgomery, T, Southern California
1972—Riley Odoms, TE, Houston
1973—Otis Armstrong, RB, Purdue
1974—Randy Gradishar, LB, Ohio State
1975—Louis Wright, DB, San Jose State
1976—Tom Glassic, G, Virginia
1977—Steve Schindler, G, Boston College
1978—Don Latimer, DT, Miami (Fla.)
1979—Kevin Clark, T, Nebraska
1980—None
1981—Dennis Smith, DB, Southern California
1982—Gerald Willhite, RB, San Jose State
1983—Chris Hinton, G, Northwestern
1984—None
1985—Steve Sewell, RB, Oklahoma
1986—None
1987—Ricky Nattiel, WR, Florida
1988—Ted Gregory, DT, Syracuse
1989—Steve Atwater, DB, Arkansas
1990—None
1991—Mike Croel, LB, Nebraska
1992—Tommy Maddox, QB, UCLA
1993—Dan Williams, DE, Toledo
1994—None
1995—None
1996—John Mobley, LB, Kutztown (Pa.)
1997—Trevor Pryce, DT, Clemson
1998—Marcus Nash, WR, Tennessee
1999—Al Wilson, LB, Tennessee
2000—Deltha O'Neal, DB, California

FRANCHISE RECORDS

Most rushing yards, career
6,624—Terrell Davis
Most rushing yards, season
2,008—Terrell Davis, 1998
Most rushing yards, game
215—Terrell Davis vs. Cin., Sept. 21, 1997
Most rushing touchdowns, season
21—Terrell Davis, 1998

Most passing attempts, season
605—John Elway, 1985
Most passing attempts, game
59—John Elway at G.B., Oct. 10, 1993
Most passes completed, season
348—John Elway, 1993
Most passes completed, game
36—John Elway vs. S.D., Sept. 4, 1994

Most passing yards, career
51,475—John Elway
Most passing yards, season
4,030—John Elway, 1993
Most passing yards, game
447—Frank Tripucka at Buf., Sept. 15, 1962
Most touchdown passes, season
27—John Elway, 1997

Most pass receptions, career
543—Lionel Taylor
Most pass receptions, season
100—Lionel Taylor, 1961
Most pass receptions, game
13—Lionel Taylor vs. Oak., Nov. 29, 1964
Robert Anderson vs. Chi., Sept. 30, 1973
Shannon Sharpe vs. S.D., Oct. 6, 1996
Most receiving yards, career
6,983—Shannon Sharpe

Most receiving yards, season
1,244—Steve Watson, 1981
Most receiving yards, game
199—Lionel Taylor vs. Buf., Nov. 27, 1960
Most receiving touchdowns, season
13—Steve Watson, 1981
Most touchdowns, career
63—Terrell Davis
Most field goals, season
31—Jason Elam, 1995

Longest field goal
63 yards—Jason Elam vs. Jac., Oct. 25, 1998
Most interceptions, career
44—Steve Foley
Most interceptions, season
11—Goose Gonsoulin, 1960
Most sacks, career
97.5—Simon Fletcher
Most sacks, season
16—Simon Fletcher, 1992

SERIES RECORDS

Denver vs.: Arizona 4-0-1; Atlanta 6-3; Baltimore 1-0; Buffalo 12-17-1; Carolina 1-0; Chicago 6-5; Cincinnati 14-6; Cleveland 13-5; Dallas 3-4; Detroit 5-3; Green Bay 5-3-1; Indianapolis 9-2; Jacksonville 2-1; Kansas City 34-45; Miami 2-7-1; Minnesota 4-6; New England 20-13; New Orleans 4-2; N.Y. Giants 3-4; N.Y. Jets 13-13-1; Oakland 28-49-2; Philadelphia 3-6; Pittsburgh 10-6-1; San Diego 43-36-1; St. Louis 4-4; San Francisco 4-4; Seattle 29-16; Tampa Bay 3-2; Tennessee 11-20-1; Washington 5-3.

COACHING RECORDS

Jack Faulkner, 9-22-1; Frank Filchock, 7-20-1; Ray Malavasi, 4-8-0; Red Miller, 40-22 (2-3); Wade Phillips, 16-16-0 (0-1); John Ralston, 34-33-3; Dan Reeves, 110-73-1 (7-6); Lou Saban, 20-42-3; Mike Shanahan, 53-27-0 (7-1); Jerry Smith, 2-3; Mac Speedie, 6-19-1.
NOTE: Playoff games in parentheses.

RETIRED UNIFORM NUMBERS

No.	Player
7	John Elway
18	Frank Tripucka
44	Floyd Little

DETROIT LIONS
YEAR-BY-YEAR RECORDS

	REGULAR SEASON						PLAYOFFS			
Year	W	L	T	Pct.	PF	PA	Finish	W	L	Highest round	Coach
1930*	5	6	3	.455	...	...	T7th	—	—		Tubby Griffen
1931*	11	3	0	.786	...	...	2nd	—	—		Potsy Clark
1932*	6	2	4	.750	...	...	3rd	—	—		Potsy Clark
1933*	6	5	0	.545	128	87	2nd/Western Div.	—	—		Potsy Clark
1934	10	3	0	.769	238	59	2nd/Western Div.	—	—		Potsy Clark
1935	7	3	2	.700	191	111	1st/Western Div.	1	0	NFL champ	Potsy Clark
1936	8	4	0	.667	235	102	3rd/Western Div.	—	—		Potsy Clark
1937	7	4	0	.636	180	105	T2nd/Western Div.	—	—		Dutch Clark
1938	7	4	0	.636	119	108	2nd/Western Div.	—	—		Dutch Clark
1939	6	5	0	.545	145	150	3rd/Western Div.	—	—		Gus Henderson
1940	5	5	1	.500	138	153	3rd/Western Div.	—	—		Potsy Clark
1941	4	6	1	.400	121	195	3rd/Western Div.	—	—		Bill Edwards
1942	0	11	0	.000	38	263	5th/Western Div.	—	—		B. Edwards, John Karcis
1943	3	6	1	.333	178	218	3rd/Western Div.	—	—		Gus Dorais
1944	6	3	1	.667	216	151	T2nd/Western Div.	—	—		Gus Dorais
1945	7	3	0	.700	195	194	2nd/Western Div.	—	—		Gus Dorais
1946	1	10	0	.091	142	310	2nd/Western Div.	— —			Gus Dorais
1947	3	9	0	.250	231	305	5th/Western Div.	— —			Gus Dorais
1948	2	10	0	.167	200	407	5th/Western Div.	— —			Bo McMillin
1949	4	8	0	.333	237	259	4th/Western Div.	— —			Bo McMillin
1950	6	6	0	.500	321	285	4th/National Conf.	— —			Bo McMillin
1951	7	4	1	.636	336	259	T2nd/National Conf.	— —			Buddy Parker
1952	9	3	0	.750	344	192	1st/National Conf.	2	0	NFL champ	Buddy Parker
1953	10	2	0	.833	271	205	1st/Western Conf.	1	0	NFL champ	Buddy Parker
1954	9	2	1	.818	337	189	1st/Western Conf.	0	1	NFL championship game	Buddy Parker
1955	3	9	0	.250	230	275	6th/Western Conf.	— —			Buddy Parker
1956	9	3	0	.750	300	188	2nd/Western Conf.	— —			Buddy Parker
1957	8	4	0	.667	251	231	1st/Western Conf.	2	0	NFL champ	George Wilson
1958	4	7	1	.364	261	276	5th/Western Conf.	— —			George Wilson
1959	3	8	1	.273	203	275	5th/Western Conf.	— —			George Wilson
1960	7	5	0	.583	239	212	T2nd/Western Conf.	— —			George Wilson
1961	8	5	1	.615	270	258	2nd/Western Conf.	— —			George Wilson
1962	11	3	0	.786	315	177	2nd/Western Conf.	— —			George Wilson
1963	5	8	1	.385	326	265	T4th/Western Conf.	— —			George Wilson
1964	7	5	2	.583	280	260	4th/Western Conf.	— —			George Wilson
1965	6	7	1	.462	257	295	6th/Western Conf.	— —			Harry Gilmer
1966	4	9	1	.308	206	317	T6th/Western Conf.	— —			Harry Gilmer
1967	5	7	2	.417	260	259	3rd/Central Div.	— —			Joe Schmidt

REGULAR SEASON / PLAYOFFS

Year	W	L	T	Pct.	PF	PA	Finish	W	L	Highest round	Coach
1968	4	8	2	.333	207	241	4th/Central Div.	—	—		Joe Schmidt
1969	9	4	1	.692	259	188	2nd/Central Div.	—	—		Joe Schmidt
1970	10	4	0	.714	347	202	2nd/NFC Central Div.	0	1	NFC div. playoff game	Joe Schmidt
1971	7	6	1	.538	341	286	2nd/NFC Central Div.	—	—		Joe Schmidt
1972	8	5	1	.607	339	290	2nd/NFC Central Div.	—	—		Joe Schmidt
1973	6	7	1	.464	271	247	2nd/NFC Central Div.	—	—		Don McCafferty
1974	7	7	0	.500	256	270	2nd/NFC Central Div.	—	—		Rick Forzano
1975	7	7	0	.500	245	262	2nd/NFC Central Div.	—	—		Rick Forzano
1976	6	8	0	.429	262	220	3rd/NFC Central Div.	—	—		R. Forzano, T. Hudspeth
1977	6	8	0	.429	183	252	3rd/NFC Central Div.	—	—		Tommy Hudspeth
1978	7	9	0	.438	290	300	T3rd/NFC Central Div.	—	—		Monte Clark
1979	2	14	0	.125	219	365	5th/NFC Central Div.	—	—		Monte Clark
1980	9	7	0	.563	334	272	2nd/NFC Central Div.	—	—		Monte Clark
1981	8	8	0	.500	397	322	2nd/NFC Central Div.	—	—		Monte Clark
1982	4	5	0	.444	181	176	T8th/NFC	0	1	NFC first-round pl. game	Monte Clark
1983	9	7	0	.563	347	286	1st/NFC Central Div.	0	1	NFC div. playoff game	Monte Clark
1984	4	11	1	.281	283	408	4th/NFC Central Div.	—	—		Monte Clark
1985	7	9	0	.438	307	366	T3rd/NFC Central Div.	—	—		Darryl Rogers
1986	5	11	0	.313	277	326	3rd/NFC Central Div.	—	—		Darryl Rogers
1987	4	11	0	.267	269	384	T4th/NFC Central Div.	—	—		Darryl Rogers
1988	4	12	0	.250	220	313	T4th/NFC Central Div.	—	—		Darryl Rogers
1989	7	9	0	.438	312	364	3rd/NFC Central Div.	—	—		Wayne Fontes
1990	6	10	0	.375	373	413	T2nd/NFC Central Div.	—	—		Wayne Fontes
1991	12	4	0	.750	339	295	1st/NFC Central Div.	1	1	NFC championship game	Wayne Fontes
1992	5	11	0	.313	273	332	T3rd/NFC Central Div.	—	—		Wayne Fontes
1993	10	6	0	.625	298	292	1st/NFC Central Div.	0	1	NFC wild-card game	Wayne Fontes
1994	9	7	0	.563	357	342	T2nd/NFC Central Div.	0	1	NFC wild-card game	Wayne Fontes
1995	10	6	0	.625	436	336	2nd/NFC Central Div.	0	1	NFC wild-card game	Wayne Fontes
1996	5	11	0	.313	302	368	5th/NFC Central Div.	—	—		Wayne Fontes
1997	9	7	0	.563	379	306	T3rd/NFC Central Div.	0	1	NFC wild-card game	Bobby Ross
1998	5	11	0	.313	306	378	4th/NFC Central Div.	—	—		Bobby Ross
1999	8	8	0	.500	322	323	3rd/NFC Central Div.	0	1	NFC wild-card game	Bobby Ross

*Portsmouth Spartans.

FIRST-ROUND DRAFT PICKS

1936—Sid Wagner, G, Michigan State
1937—Lloyd Cardwell, B, Nebraska
1938—Alex Wojciechowicz, C, Fordham
1939—John Pingel, B, Michigan State
1940—Doyle Nave, B, Southern California
1941—Jim Thomason, B, Texas A&M
1942—Bob Westfall, B, Michigan
1943—Frank Sinkwich, B, Georgia*
1944—Otto Graham, B, Northwestern
1945—Frank Szymanski, B, Notre Dame
1946—Bill Dellastatious, B, Missouri
1947—Glenn Davis, B, Army
1948—Y.A. Tittle, B, Louisiana State
1949—John Rauch, B, Georgia
1950—Leon Hart, E, Notre Dame*
      Joe Watson, C, Rice
1951—None
1952—None
1953—Harley Sewell, G, Texas
1954—Dick Chapman, T, Rice
1955—Dave Middleton, B, Auburn
1956—Howard Cassidy, B, Ohio State
1957—Bill Glass, G, Baylor
1958—Alex Karras, DT, Iowa
1959—Nick Pietrosante, B, Notre Dame
1960—John Robinson, DB, Louisiana State
1961—None
1962—John Hadl, QB, Kansas
1963—Daryl Sanders, T, Ohio State
1964—Pete Beathard, QB, Southern California
1965—Tom Nowatzke, RB, Indiana
1966—None
1967—Mel Farr, RB, UCLA
1968—Greg Landry, QB, Massachusetts
      Earl McCullouch, E, Southern California
1969—None
1970—Steve Owens, RB, Oklahoma
1971—Bob Bell, DT, Cincinnati
1972—Herb Orvis, DE, Colorado
1973—Ernie Price, DE, Texas A&I
1974—Ed O'Neil, LB, Penn State
1975—Lynn Boden, G, South Dakota State
1976—James Hunter, DB, Grambling State
      Lawrence Gaines, FB, Wyoming
1977—None
1978—Luther Bradley, DB, Notre Dame
1979—Keith Dorney, T, Penn State
1980—Billy Sims, RB, Oklahoma*
1981—Mark Nichols, WR, San Jose State
1982—Jimmy Williams, LB, Nebraska
1983—James Jones, RB, Florida
1984—David Lewis, TE, California
1985—Lomas Brown, T, Florida
1986—Chuck Long, QB, Iowa
1987—Reggie Rogers, DE, Washington
1988—Bennie Blades, S, Miami (Fla.)
1989—Barry Sanders, RB, Oklahoma State
1990—Andre Ware, QB, Houston
1991—Herman Moore, WR, Virginia
1992—Robert Porcher, DE, South Carolina State
1993—None
1994—Johnnie Morton, WR, Southern California
1995—Luther Elliss, DT, Utah
1996—Reggie Brown, LB, Texas A&M
      Jeff Hartings, G, Penn State
1997—Bryant Westbrook, DB, Texas
1998—Terry Fair, DB, Tennessee
1999—Chris Claiborne, LB, Southern California
      Aaron Gibson, T, Wisconsin
2000—Stockar McDougle, T, Oklahoma
    *First player chosen in draft.

FRANCHISE RECORDS

Most rushing yards, career
15,269—Barry Sanders
Most rushing yards, season
2,053—Barry Sanders, 1997
Most rushing yards, game
237—Barry Sanders vs. T.B., Nov. 13, 1994
Most rushing touchdowns, season
16—Barry Sanders, 1991
Most passing attempts, season
583—Scott Mitchell, 1995
Most passing attempts, game
50—Eric Hipple at L.A. Rams, Oct. 19, 1986
   Scott Mitchell at Was., Oct. 22, 1995
   Scott Mitchell at Atl., Nov. 5, 1995
   Scott Mitchell at Oak., Oct. 13, 1996
   Scott Mitchell vs. T.B., Sept. 7, 1997
Most passes completed, season
346—Scott Mitchell, 1995
Most passes completed, game
33—Eric Hipple at Cle., Sept. 28, 1986
   Chuck Long vs. G.B., Oct. 25, 1987

Most passing yards, career
15,710—Bobby Layne
Most passing yards, season
4,338—Scott Mitchell, 1995
Most passing yards, game
410—Scott Mitchell vs. Min., Nov. 23, 1995
Most touchdown passes, season
32—Scott Mitchell, 1995
Most pass receptions, career
626—Herman Moore
Most pass receptions, season
123—Herman Moore, 1995
Most pass receptions, game
14—Herman Moore vs. Chi., Dec. 5, 1995
Most receiving yards, career
8,664—Herman Moore
Most receiving yards, season
1,686—Herman Moore, 1995
Most receiving yards, game
302—Cloyce Box vs. Bal., Dec. 3, 1950

Most receiving touchdowns, season
15—Cloyce Box, 1952
Most touchdowns, career
109—Barry Sanders
Most field goals, season
34—Jason Hanson, 1993
Longest field goal
56 yards—Jason Hanson vs. Cle., Oct. 8, 1995
Most interceptions, career
62—Dick LeBeau
Most interceptions, season
12—Don Doll, 1950
   Jack Christiansen, 1953
Most sacks, season
23—Al Baker, 1978

SERIES RECORDS

Detroit vs.: Arizona 28-17-3; Atlanta 20-7; Baltimore 0-1; Buffalo 3-2-1; Carolina 1-0; Chicago 55-73-3; Cincinnati 3-4; Cleveland 12-3; Dallas 6-7; Denver 3-5; Green Bay 59-68-6; Indianapolis 19-17-2; Jacksonville 1-1; Kansas City 3-6; Miami 2-4; Minnesota 28-47-2; New England 3-3; New Orleans 6-8-1; N.Y. Giants 14-14-1; N.Y. Jets 5-3; Oakland 2-6; Philadelphia 11-11-2; Pittsburgh 14-12-1; St. Louis 28-32-1; San Diego 3-4; San Francisco 26-29-1; Seattle 4-4; Tampa Bay 25-19; Tennessee 3-4; Washington 4-24.
NOTE: Includes records only from 1934 to present.

COACHING RECORDS

Dutch Clark, 14-8-0; Monte Clark, 43-61-1 (0-2); Potsy Clark, 53-25-7 (1-0); Gus Dorais, 20-31-2; Bill Edwards, 4-9-1; Wayne Fontes, 66-67-0 (1-4); Rick Forzano, 15-17-0; Harry Gilmer, 10-16-2; Hal Griffen, 5-6-3; Elmer Henderson, 6-5-0; Tommy Hudspeth, 11-13-0; John Karcis, 0-8-0; Don McCafferty, 6-7-1; Alvin McMillin, 12-24-0; Buddy Parker, 47-23-2 (3-1); Darryl Rogers, 18-40-0; Bobby Ross, 22-26-0 (0-2); Joe Schmidt, 43-34-7 (0-1); George Wilson, 53-45-6 (2-0).
NOTE: Playoff games in parentheses.

RETIRED UNIFORM NUMBERS

No.	Player
7	Dutch Clark
22	Bobby Layne
37	Doak Walker
56	Joe Schmidt
85	Chuck Hughes
88	Charlie Sanders

GREEN BAY PACKERS
YEAR-BY-YEAR RECORDS

		REGULAR SEASON						PLAYOFFS			
Year	W	L	T	Pct.	PF	PA	Finish	W	L	Highest round	Coach
1921	3	2	1	.600	...	...	T6th				Curly Lambeau
1922	4	3	3	.571	...	...	T7th				Curly Lambeau
1923	7	2	1	.778	...	...	3rd				Curly Lambeau
1924	7	4	0	.636	...	...	6th				Curly Lambeau
1925	8	5	0	.615	...	...	9th				Curly Lambeau
1926	7	3	3	.700	...	...	5th				Curly Lambeau
1927	7	2	1	.778	...	...	2nd				Curly Lambeau
1928	6	4	3	.600	...	...	4th				Curly Lambeau
1929	12	0	1	1.000	...	...	1st				Curly Lambeau
1930	10	3	1	.769	...	...	1st				Curly Lambeau
1931	12	2	0	.857	...	...	1st				Curly Lambeau
1932	10	3	1	.769	...	...	2nd				Curly Lambeau
1933	5	7	1	.417	170	107	3rd/Western Div.	—	—		Curly Lambeau
1934	7	6	0	.538	156	112	3rd/Western Div.	—	—		Curly Lambeau
1935	8	4	0	.667	181	96	2nd/Western Div.	—	—		Curly Lambeau
1936	10	1	1	.909	248	118	1st/Western Div.	1	0	NFL champ	Curly Lambeau
1937	7	4	0	.636	220	122	T2nd/Western Div.	—	—		Curly Lambeau
1938	8	3	0	.727	223	118	1st/Western Div.	0	1	NFL championship game	Curly Lambeau
1939	9	2	0	.818	233	153	1st/Western Div.	1	0	NFL champ	Curly Lambeau
1940	6	4	1	.600	238	155	2nd/Western Div.	—	—		Curly Lambeau

HISTORY — Team by team

Year	W	L	T	Pct.	PF	PA	Finish	W	L	Highest round	Coach
1941	10	1	0	.909	258	120	2nd/Western Div.	0	1	W. Div. championship game	Curly Lambeau
1942	8	2	1	.800	300	215	2nd/Western Div.	—	—		Curly Lambeau
1943	7	2	1	.778	264	172	2nd/Western Div.	—	—		Curly Lambeau
1944	8	2	0	.800	238	141	1st/Western Div.	1	0	NFL champ	Curly Lambeau
1945	6	4	0	.600	258	173	3rd/Western Div.	—	—		Curly Lambeau
1946	6	5	0	.545	148	158	T3rd/Western Div.	—	—		Curly Lambeau
1947	6	5	1	.545	274	210	3rd/Western Div.	—	—		Curly Lambeau
1948	3	9	0	.250	154	290	4th/Western Div.	—	—		Curly Lambeau
1949	2	10	0	.167	114	329	5th/Western Div.	—	—		Curly Lambeau
1950	3	9	0	.250	244	406	T5th/National Conf.	—	—		Gene Ronzani
1951	3	9	0	.250	254	375	5th/National Conf.	—	—		Gene Ronzani
1952	6	6	0	.500	295	312	4th/National Conf.	—	—		Gene Ronzani
1953	2	9	1	.182	200	338	6th/Western Conf.	—	—		Gene Ronzani, Hugh Devore-S. McLean
1954	4	8	0	.333	234	251	5th/Western Conf.	—	—		Lisle Blackbourn
1955	6	6	0	.500	258	276	3rd/Western Conf.	—	—		Lisle Blackbourn
1956	4	8	0	.333	264	342	5th/Western Conf.	—	—		Lisle Blackbourn
1957	3	9	0	.250	218	311	6th/Western Conf.	—	—		Lisle Blackbourn
1958	1	10	1	.091	193	382	6th/Western Conf.	—	—		Scooter McLean
1959	7	5	0	.583	248	246	T3rd/Western Conf.	—	—		Vince Lombardi
1960	8	4	0	.667	332	209	1st/Western Conf.	0	1	NFL championship game	Vince Lombardi
1961	11	3	0	.786	391	223	1st/Western Conf.	1	0	NFL champ	Vince Lombardi
1962	13	1	0	.929	415	148	1st/Western Conf.	1	0	NFL champ	Vince Lombardi
1963	11	2	1	.846	369	206	2nd/Western Conf.	—	—		Vince Lombardi
1964	8	5	1	.615	342	245	T2nd/Western Conf.	—	—		Vince Lombardi
1965	10	3	1	.769	316	224	1st/Western Conf.	2	0	NFL champ	Vince Lombardi
1966	12	2	0	.857	335	163	1st/Western Conf.	2	0	Super Bowl champ	Vince Lombardi
1967	9	4	1	.692	332	209	1st/Central Div.	3	0	Super Bowl champ	Vince Lombardi
1968	6	7	1	.462	281	227	3rd/Central Div.	—	—		Phil Bengtson
1969	8	6	0	.571	269	221	3rd/Central Div.	—	—		Phil Bengtson
1970	6	8	0	.429	196	293	T3rd/NFC Central Div.	—	—		Phil Bengtson
1971	4	8	2	.333	274	298	4th/NFC Central Div.	—	—		Dan Devine
1972	10	4	0	.714	304	226	1st/NFC Central Div.	0	1	NFC div. playoff game	Dan Devine
1973	5	7	2	.429	202	259	3rd/NFC Central Div.	—	—		Dan Devine
1974	6	8	0	.429	210	206	3rd/NFC Central Div.	—	—		Dan Devine
1975	4	10	0	.286	226	285	T3rd/NFC Central Div.	—	—		Bart Starr
1976	5	9	0	.357	218	299	4th/NFC Central Div.	—	—		Bart Starr
1977	4	10	0	.286	134	219	4th/NFC Central Div.	—	—		Bart Starr
1978	8	7	1	.531	249	269	2nd/NFC Central Div.	—	—		Bart Starr
1979	5	11	0	.313	246	316	4th/NFC Central Div.	—	—		Bart Starr
1980	5	10	1	.344	231	371	T4th/NFC Central Div.	—	—		Bart Starr
1981	8	8	0	.500	324	361	3rd/NFC Central Div.	—	—		Bart Starr
1982	5	3	1	.611	226	169	3rd/NFC	1	1	NFC second-round pl. game	Bart Starr
1983	8	8	0	.500	429	439	T2nd/NFC Central Div.	—	—		Bart Starr
1984	8	8	0	.500	390	309	2nd/NFC Central Div.	—	—		Forrest Gregg
1985	8	8	0	.500	337	355	2nd/NFC Central Div.	—	—		Forrest Gregg
1986	4	12	0	.250	254	418	4th/NFC Central Div.	—	—		Forrest Gregg
1987	5	9	1	.367	255	300	3rd/NFC Central Div.	—	—		Forrest Gregg
1988	4	12	0	.250	240	315	T4th/NFC Central Div.	—	—		Lindy Infante
1989	10	6	0	.625	362	356	2nd/NFC Central Div.	—	—		Lindy Infante
1990	6	10	0	.375	271	347	T2nd/NFC Central Div.	—	—		Lindy Infante
1991	4	12	0	.250	273	313	4th/NFC Central Div.	—	—		Lindy Infante
1992	9	7	0	.563	276	296	2nd/NFC Central Div.	—	—		Mike Holmgren
1993	9	7	0	.563	340	282	T2nd/NFC Central Div.	1	1	NFC div. playoff game	Mike Holmgren
1994	9	7	0	.563	382	287	T2nd/NFC Central Div.	1	1	NFC div. playoff game	Mike Holmgren
1995	11	5	0	.689	404	314	1st/NFC Central Div.	2	1	NFC championship game	Mike Holmgren
1996	13	3	0	.813	456	210	1st/NFC Central Div.	3	0	Super Bowl champ	Mike Holmgren
1997	13	3	0	.813	422	282	1st/NFC Central Div.	2	1	Super Bowl	Mike Holmgren
1998	11	5	0	.688	408	319	2nd/NFC Central Div.	0	1	NFC wild-card game	Mike Holmgren
1999	8	8	0	.500	357	341	4th/NFC Central Div.	—	—		Ray Rhodes

FIRST-ROUND DRAFT PICKS

1936—Russ Letlow, G, San Francisco
1937—Ed Jankowski, B, Wisconsin
1938—Cecil Isbell, B, Purdue
1939—Larry Buhler, B, Minnesota
1940—Hal Van Every, B, Marquette
1941—George Paskvan, B, Wisconsin
1942—Urban Odson, T, Minnesota
1943—Dick Wildung, T, Minnesota
1944—Merv Pregulman, G, Michigan
1945—Walt Schlinkman, G, Texas Tech
1946—Johnny Strzykalski, B, Marquette
1947—Ernie Case, B, UCLA
1948—Earl Girard, B, Wisconsin
1949—Stan Heath, B, Nevada
1950—Clayton Tonnemaker, G, Minnesota
1951—Bob Gain, T, Kentucky

1952—Babe Parilli, QB, Kentucky
1953—Al Carmichael, B, Southern California
1954—Art Hunter, T, Notre Dame
   Veryl Switzer, B, Kansas State
1955—Tom Bettis, G, Purdue
1956—Jack Losch, B, Miami
1957—Paul Hornung, B, Notre Dame*
   Ron Kramer, E, Michigan
1958—Dan Currie, C, Michigan State
1959—Randy Duncan, B, Iowa*
1960—Tom Moore, RB, Vanderbilt
1961—Herb Adderley, DB, Michigan State
1962—Earl Gros, RB, Louisiana State
1963—Dave Robinson, LB, Penn State
1964—Lloyd Voss, DT, Nebraska
1965—Donny Anderson, RB, Texas Tech
   Larry Elkins, E, Baylor
1966—Jim Grabowski, RB, Illinois
   Gale Gillingham, G, Minnesota
1967—Bob Hyland, C, Boston College
   Don Horn, QB, San Diego State
1968—Fred Carr, LB, Texas-El Paso
   Bill Lueck, G, Arizona
1969—Rich Moore, DT, Villanova
1970—Mike McCoy, DT, Notre Dame
   Rich McGeorge, TE, Elon
1971—John Brockington, RB, Ohio State
1972—Willie Buchanon, DB, San Diego State
   Jerry Tagge, QB, Nebraska
1973—Barry Smith, WR, Florida State
1974—Barty Smith, RB, Richmond
1975—None
1976—Mark Koncar, T, Colorado
1977—Mike Butler, DE, Kansas
   Ezra Johnson, DE, Morris Brown
1978—James Lofton, WR, Stanford
   John Anderson, LB, Michigan
1979—Eddie Lee Ivery, RB, Georgia Tech
1980—Bruce Clark, DT, Penn State
   George Cumby, LB, Oklahoma
1981—Rich Campbell, QB, California
1982—Ron Hallstrom, G, Iowa
1983—Tim Lewis, DB, Pittsburgh
1984—Alphonso Carreker, DT, Florida State
1985—Ken Ruettgers, T, Southern California
1986—None
1987—Brent Fullwood, RB, Auburn
1988—Sterling Sharpe, WR, South Carolina
1989—Tony Mandarich, T, Michigan State
1990—Tony Bennett, LB, Mississippi
   Darrell Thompson, RB, Minnesota
1991—Vincent Clark, DB, Ohio State
1992—Terrell Buckley, DB, Florida State
1993—Wayne Simmons, LB, Clemson
   George Teague, DB, Alabama
1994—Aaron Taylor, T, Notre Dame
1995—Craig Newsome, DB, Arizona State
1996—John Michaels, T, Southern California
1997—Ross Verba, T, Iowa
1998—Vonnie Holliday, DT, North Carolina
1999—Antuan Edwards, DB, Clemson
2000—Bubba Franks, TE, Miami (Fla.)
   *First player chosen in draft.

FRANCHISE RECORDS

Most rushing yards, career
8,207—Jim Taylor
Most rushing yards, season
1,474—Jim Taylor, 1962
Most rushing yards, game
190—Dorsey Levens vs. Dal., Nov. 23, 1997
Most rushing touchdowns, season
19—Jim Taylor, 1962
Most passing attempts, season
599—Don Majkowski, 1989
Most passing attempts, game
61—Brett Favre vs. S.F., Oct. 14, 1996 (OT)
59—Don Majkowski at Det., Nov. 12, 1989
Most passes completed, season
363—Brett Favre, 1994
Most passes completed, game
36—Brett Favre at Chi., Dec. 5, 1993
Most passing yards, career
30,894—Brett Favre

Most passing yards, season
4,458—Lynn Dickey, 1983
Most passing yards, game
418—Lynn Dickey at T.B., Oct. 12, 1980
Most touchdown passes, season
39—Brett Favre, 1996
Most pass receptions, career
595—Sterling Sharpe
Most pass receptions, season
112—Sterling Sharpe, 1993
Most pass receptions, game
14—Don Hutson at NYG, Nov. 22, 1942
Most receiving yards, career
9,656—James Lofton
Most receiving yards, season
1,497—Robert Brooks, 1995
Most receiving yards, game
257—Bill Howton vs. L.A. Rams, Oct. 21, 1956

Most receiving touchdowns, season
18—Sterling Sharpe, 1994
Most touchdowns, career
105—Don Hutson
Most field goals, season
33—Chester Marcol, 1972
Longest field goal
54 yards—Chris Jacke at Det., Jan. 2, 1994
Most interceptions, career
52—Bobby Dillon
Most interceptions, season
10—Irv Comp, 1943
Most sacks, career
84—Ezra Johnson
Most sacks, season
20.5—Ezra Johnson, 1978

SERIES RECORDS

Green Bay vs.: Arizona 42-21-4; Atlanta 10-9; Baltimore 1-0; Buffalo 2-5; Carolina 2-1; Chicago 70-83-6; Cincinnati 5-4; Cleveland 8-6; Dallas 10-9; Denver 3-5-1; Detroit 68-59-6; Indianapolis 18-19-1; Jacksonville 1-0; Kansas City 1-5-1; Miami 1-8; Minnesota 37-39-1; New England 3-3; New Orleans 13-4; N.Y. Giants 23-20-2; N.Y. Jets 2-5; Oakland 3-5; Philadelphia 21-9; Pittsburgh 21-12; St. Louis 27-40-1; San Diego 6-1; San Francisco 24-25-1; Seattle 4-4; Tampa Bay 26-15-1; Tennessee 4-3; Washington 9-11.

COACHING RECORDS

Phil Bengtson, 20-21-1; Lisle Blackbourn, 17-31-0; Dan Devine, 25-27-4 (0-1); Hugh Devore-Ray (Scooter) McLean, 0-2-0; Forrest Gregg, 25-37-1; Mike Holmgren, 75-37-0 (9-5); Lindy Infante, 24-40-0; Curly Lambeau, 209-104-21 (3-2); Vince Lombardi, 89-29-4 (9-1); Ray (Scooter) McLean, 1-10-1; Ray Rhodes, 8-8-0; Gene Ronzani, 14-31-1; Bart Starr, 52-76-3 (1-1).
NOTE: Playoff games in parentheses.

RETIRED UNIFORM NUMBERS

No.	Player
3	Tony Canadeo
14	Don Hutson
15	Bart Starr
66	Ray Nitschke

INDIANAPOLIS COLTS
YEAR-BY-YEAR RECORDS

HISTORY *Team by team*

		REGULAR SEASON					PLAYOFFS			
Year	W	L	T	Pct.	PF	PA	Finish	W	L	Highest round	Coach
1953*	3	9	0	.250	182	350	5th/Western Conf.	—	—		Keith Molesworth
1954*	3	9	0	.250	131	279	6th/Western Conf.	—	—		Weeb Ewbank
1955*	5	6	1	.455	214	239	4th/Western Conf.	—	—		Weeb Ewbank
1956*	5	7	0	.417	270	322	4th/Western Conf.	—	—		Weeb Ewbank
1957*	7	5	0	.583	303	235	3rd/Western Conf.	—	—		Weeb Ewbank
1958*	9	3	0	.750	381	203	1st/Western Conf.	1	0	NFL champ	Weeb Ewbank
1959*	9	3	0	.750	374	251	1st/Western Conf.	1	0	NFL champ	Weeb Ewbank
1960*	6	6	0	.500	288	234	4th/Western Conf.	—	—		Weeb Ewbank
1961*	8	6	0	.571	302	307	T3rd/Western Conf.	—	—		Weeb Ewbank
1962*	7	7	0	.500	293	288	4th/Western Conf.	—	—		Weeb Ewbank
1963*	8	6	0	.571	316	285	3rd/Western Conf.	—	—		Don Shula
1964*	12	2	0	.857	428	225	1st/Western Conf.	0	1	NFL championship game	Don Shula
1965*	10	3	1	.769	389	284	2nd/Western Conf.	0	1	W. Conf. champ. game	Don Shula
1966*	9	5	0	.643	314	226	2nd/Western Conf.	—	—		Don Shula
1967*	11	1	2	.917	394	198	2nd/Coastal Div.	—	—		Don Shula
1968*	13	1	0	.929	402	144	1st/Coastal Div.	2	1	Super Bowl	Don Shula
1969*	8	5	1	.615	279	268	2nd/Coastal Div.	—	—		Don Shula
1970*	11	2	1	.846	321	234	1st/AFC Eastern Div.	3	0	Super Bowl champ	Don McCafferty
1971*	10	4	0	.714	313	140	2nd/AFC Eastern Div.	1	1	AFC championship game	Don McCafferty
1972*	5	9	0	.357	235	252	3rd/AFC Eastern Div.	—	—		McCafferty, John Sandusky
1973*	4	10	0	.286	226	341	T4th/AFC Eastern Div.	—	—		Howard Schnellenberger
1974*	2	12	0	.143	190	329	5th/AFC Eastern Div.	—	—		H. Schnellenberger, Joe Thomas
1975*	10	4	0	.714	395	269	1st/AFC Eastern Div.	0	1	AFC div. playoff game	Ted Marchibroda
1976*	11	3	0	.786	417	246	1st/AFC Eastern Div.	0	1	AFC div. playoff game	Ted Marchibroda
1977*	10	4	0	.714	295	221	1st/AFC Eastern Div.	0	1	AFC div. playoff game	Ted Marchibroda
1978*	5	11	0	.313	239	421	T4th/AFC Eastern Div.	—	—		Ted Marchibroda
1979*	5	11	0	.313	271	351	5th/AFC Eastern Div.	—	—		Ted Marchibroda
1980*	7	9	0	.438	355	387	4th/AFC Eastern Div.	—	—		Mike McCormack
1981*	2	14	0	.125	259	533	T4th/AFC Eastern Div.	—	—		Mike McCormack
1982*	0	8	1	.056	113	236	14th/AFC	—	—		Frank Kush
1983*	7	9	0	.438	264	354	T4th/AFC Eastern Div.	—	—		Frank Kush
1984	4	12	0	.250	239	414	4th/AFC Eastern Div.	—	—		Frank Kush, Hal Hunter
1985	5	11	0	.313	320	386	4th/AFC Eastern Div.	—	—		Rod Dowhower
1986	3	13	0	.188	229	400	5th/AFC Eastern Div.	—	—		Rod Dowhower, Ron Meyer
1987	9	6	0	.600	300	238	1st/AFC Eastern Div.	0	1	AFC div. playoff game	Ron Meyer
1988	9	7	0	.563	354	315	T2nd/AFC Eastern Div.	—	—		Ron Meyer
1989	8	8	0	.500	298	301	T2nd/AFC Eastern Div.	—	—		Ron Meyer
1990	7	9	0	.438	281	353	3rd/AFC Eastern Div.	—	—		Ron Meyer
1991	1	15	0	.063	143	381	5th/AFC Eastern Div.	—	—		Ron Meyer, Rick Venturi
1992	9	7	0	.563	216	302	3rd/AFC Eastern Div.	—	—		Ted Marchibroda
1993	4	12	0	.250	189	378	5th/AFC Eastern Div.	—	—		Ted Marchibroda
1994	8	8	0	.500	307	320	3rd/AFC Eastern Div.	—	—		Ted Marchibroda
1995	9	7	0	.563	331	316	T2nd/AFC Eastern Div.	2	1	AFC championship game	Ted Marchibroda
1996	9	7	0	.563	317	334	3rd/AFC Eastern Div.	0	1	AFC wild-card game	Lindy Infante
1997	3	13	0	.188	313	401	5th/AFC Eastern Div.	—	—		Lindy Infante
1998	3	13	0	.188	310	444	5th/AFC Eastern Div.	—	—		Jim Mora
1999	13	3	0	.813	423	333	1st/AFC Eastern Div.	0	1	AFC div. playoff game	Jim Mora

*Baltimore Colts.

FIRST-ROUND DRAFT PICKS

1953—Billy Vessels, B, Oklahoma
1954—Cotton Davidson, B, Baylor
1955—George Shaw, B, Oregon*
Alan Ameche, B, Wisconsin
1956—Lenny Moore, B, Penn State
1957—Jim Parker, T, Ohio State
1958—Lenny Lyles, B, Louisville
1959—Jackie Burkett, C, Auburn
1960—Ron Mix, T, Southern California
1961—Tom Matte, RB, Ohio State
1962—Wendell Harris, DB, Louisiana State
1963—Bob Vogel, T, Ohio State
1964—Marv Woodson, DB, Indiana
1965—Mike Curtis, LB, Duke
1966—Sam Ball, T, Kentucky

1967—Bubba Smith, DT, Michigan State*
Jim Detwiler, RB, Michigan
1968—John Williams, G, Minnesota
1969—Eddie Hinton, WR, Oklahoma
1970—Norm Bulaich, RB, Texas Christian
1971—Don McCauley, RB, North Carolina
Leonard Dunlap, DB, North Texas State
1972—Tom Drougas, T, Oregon
1973—Bert Jones, QB, Louisiana State
Joe Ehrmann, DT, Syracuse
1974—John Dutton, DE, Nebraska
Roger Carr, WR, Louisiana Tech
1975—Ken Huff, G, North Carolina
1976—Ken Novak, DT, Purdue
1977—Randy Burke, WR, Kentucky

– 380 –

1978—Reese McCall, TE, Auburn
1979—Barry Krauss, LB, Alabama
1980—Curtis Dickey, RB, Texas A&M
   Derrick Hatchett, DB, Texas
1981—Randy McMillan, RB, Pittsburgh
   Donnell Thompson, DT, North Carolina
1982—Johnie Cooks, LB, Mississippi State
   Art Schlichter, QB, Ohio State
1983—John Elway, QB, Stanford*
1984—L. Coleman, DB, Vanderbilt
   Ron Solt, G, Maryland
1985—Duane Bickett, LB, Southern California
1986—Jon Hand, DT, Alabama
1987—Cornelius Bennett, LB, Alabama
1988—None
1989—Andre Rison, WR, Michigan State
1990—Jeff George, QB, Illinois*
1991—None
1992—Steve Emtman, DE, Washington*
   Quentin Coryatt, LB, Texas A&M
1993—Sean Dawkins, WR, California
1994—Marshall Faulk, RB, San Diego State
   Trev Alberts, LB, Nebraska
1995—Ellis Johnson, DT, Florida
1996—Marvin Harrison, WR, Syracuse
1997—Tarik Glenn, T, California
1998—Peyton Manning, QB, Tennessee*
1999—Edgerrin James, RB, Miami (Fla.)
2000—Rob Morris, LB, Brigham Young
*First player chosen in draft.

FRANCHISE RECORDS

Most rushing yards, career
5,487—Lydell Mitchell
Most rushing yards, season
1,659—Eric Dickerson, 1988
Most rushing yards, game
198—Norm Bulaich vs. NYJ, Sept. 19, 1971
Most rushing touchdowns, season
16—Lenny Moore, 1964
Most passing attempts, season
575—Peyton Manning, 1998
Most passing attempts, game
59—Jeff George at Was., Nov. 7, 1993
Most passes completed, season
331—Peyton Manning, 1999
Most passes completed, game
37—Jeff George at Was., Nov. 7, 1993
Most passing yards, career
39,768—Johnny Unitas
Most passing yards, season
4,135—Peyton Manning, 1999

Most passing yards, game
404—Peyton Manning at S.D., Sept. 26, 1999
Most touchdown passes, season
32—Johnny Unitas, 1959
Most pass receptions, career
631—Raymond Berry
Most pass receptions, season
115—Marvin Harrison, 1999
Most pass receptions, game
13—Lydell Mitchell vs. NYJ, Dec. 15, 1974
   Joe Washington at K.C., Sept. 2, 1979
   Marvin Harrison at S.D., Sept. 26, 1999
Most receiving yards, career
9,275—Raymond Berry
Most receiving yards, season
1,663—Marvin Harrison, 1999
Most receiving yards, game
224—Raymond Berry at Was., Nov. 10, 1957

Most receiving touchdowns, season
14—Raymond Berry, 1959
Most touchdowns, career
113—Lenny Moore
Most field goals, season
36—Cary Blanchard, 1996
Longest field goal
58 yards—Dan Miller at S.D., Dec. 26, 1982
Most interceptions, career
57—Bob Boyd
Most interceptions, season
11—Tom Keane, 1953
Most sacks, career
56.5—Fred Cook
Most sacks, season
17—John Dutton, 1975

SERIES RECORDS

Indianapolis vs.: Arizona 6-6; Atlanta 10-1; Baltimore 0-1; Buffalo 24-34-1; Carolina 0-2; Chicago 21-16; Cincinnati 12-8; Cleveland 8-13; Dallas 4-7; Denver 2-9; Detroit 17-19-2; Green Bay 19-18-1; Jacksonville 1-0; Kansas City 6-6; Miami 20-40; Minnesota 11-7-1; New England 23-36; New Orleans 3-4; N.Y. Giants 6-5; N.Y. Jets 36-23; Oakland 2-5; Philadelphia 8-6; Pittsburgh 4-13; St. Louis 21-17-2; San Diego 8-11; San Francisco 22-17; Seattle 4-3; Tampa Bay 5-4; Tennessee 7-7; Washington 17-9.
NOTE: Includes records as Baltimore Colts from 1953 through 1983.

COACHING RECORDS

Rod Dowhower, 5-24-0; Weeb Ewbank, 59-52-1 (2-0); Hal Hunter, 0-1-0; Lindy Infante, 12-19-0 (0-1); Frank Kush, 11-28-1; Ted Marchibroda, 71-67-0 (2-4); Don McCafferty, 22-10-1 (4-1); Mike McCormack, 9-23-0; Ron Meyer, 36-35-0 (0-1); Keith Molesworth, 3-9-0; Jim Mora, 16-16-0 (0-1); John Sandusky, 4-5-0; Howard Schnellenberger, 4-13-0; Don Shula, 71-23-4 (2-3); Joe Thomas, 2-9-0; Rick Venturi, 1-10.
NOTE: Playoff games in parentheses.

RETIRED UNIFORM NUMBERS

No.	Player
19	Johnny Unitas
22	Buddy Young
24	Lenny Moore
70	Art Donovan
77	Jim Parker
82	Raymond Berry
89	Gino Marchetti

JACKSONVILLE JAGUARS
YEAR-BY-YEAR RECORDS

		REGULAR SEASON					PLAYOFFS			
Year	W	L	T	Pct.	PF	PA	Finish	W	L	Highest round	Coach
1995	4	12	0	.250	275	404	5th/AFC Central Div.	—	—		Tom Coughlin
1996	9	7	0	.563	325	335	2nd/AFC Central Div.	2	1	AFC championship game	Tom Coughlin
1997	11	5	0	.688	394	318	2nd/AFC Central Div.	0	1	AFC wild-card game	Tom Coughlin
1998	11	5	0	.688	392	338	1st/AFC Central Div.	1	1	AFC div. playoff game	Tom Coughlin
1999	14	2	0	.875	396	217	1st/AFC Central Div.	1	1	AFC championship game	Tom Coughlin

FIRST-ROUND DRAFT PICKS

1995—Tony Boselli, T, Southern California
James Stewart, RB, Tennessee
1996—Kevin Hardy, LB, Illinois
1997—Renaldo Wynn, DT, Notre Dame
1998—Fred Taylor, RB, Florida
Donovin Darius, DB, Syracuse
1999—Fernando Bryant, DB, Alabama
2000—R. Jay Soward, WR, Southern California

FRANCHISE RECORDS

Most rushing yards, career
2,951—James Stewart
Most rushing yards, season
1,223—Fred Taylor, 1998
Most rushing yards, game
183—Fred Taylor vs. Det., Dec. 6, 1998
Most rushing touchdowns, season
14—Fred Taylor, 1998
Most passing attempts, season
557—Mark Brunell, 1996
Most passing attempts, game
52—Mark Brunell at St.L., Oct. 20, 1996
Most passes completed, season
353—Mark Brunell, 1996
Most passes completed, game
37—Mark Brunell at St.L., Oct. 20, 1996
Most passing yards, career
15,477—Mark Brunell

Most passing yards, season
4,367—Mark Brunell, 1996
Most passing yards, game
432—Mark Brunell at N.E., Sept. 22, 1996
Most touchdown passes, season
20—Mark Brunell, 1998
Most pass receptions, career
381—Jimmy Smith
Most pass receptions, season
116—Jimmy Smith, 1999
Most pass receptions, game
16—Keenan McCardell at St.L., Oct. 20, 1996
Most receiving yards, career
5,674—Jimmy Smith
Most receiving yards, season
1,636—Jimmy Smith, 1999
Most receiving yards, game
232—Keenan McCardell at St.L., Oct. 20, 1996

Most receiving touchdowns, season
8—Jimmy Smith, 1998
Most touchdowns, career
38—James Stewart
Most field goals, season
31—Mike Hollis, 1997, 1999
Longest field goal
53 yards—Mike Hollis vs. Pit., Oct. 8, 1995
Mike Hollis vs. Car., Sept. 29, 1996
Most interceptions, career
11—Aaron Beasley
Most interceptions, season
6—Aaron Beasley
Most sacks, career
29.5—Tony Brackens
Most sacks, season
12.0—Tony Brackens, 1999

SERIES RECORDS

Jacksonville vs.: Arizona 0-0; Atlanta 2-0; Baltimore 8-0; Buffalo 1-1; Carolina 2-0; Chicago 1-1; Cincinnati 6-4; Cleveland 4-0; Dallas 0-1; Denver 1-2; Detroit 1-1; Green Bay 0-1; Indianapolis 0-1; Kansas City 2-0; Miami 1-0; Minnesota 0-1; New England 0-2; New Orleans 1-1; N.Y. Giants 1-0; N.Y. Jets 2-1; Oakland 1-1; Philadelphia 1-0; Pittsburgh 6-4; St. Louis 0-1; San Diego 0-0; San Francisco 1-0; Seattle 1-1; Tampa Bay 1-1; Tennessee 4-6; Washington 0-1.

COACHING RECORDS

Tom Coughlin, 49-31-0 (4-4).
NOTE: Playoff games in parentheses.

RETIRED UNIFORM NUMBERS

No.	Player
None	

KANSAS CITY CHIEFS
YEAR-BY-YEAR RECORDS

Year	W	L	T	Pct.	PF	PA	Finish	W	L	Highest round	Coach
1960*†	8	6	0	.571	362	253	2nd/Western Div.	—	—		Hank Stram
1961*†	6	8	0	.429	334	343	2nd/Western Div.	—	—		Hank Stram
1962*†	11	3	0	.786	389	233	1st/Western Div.	1	0	AFL champ	Hank Stram
1963*	5	7	2	.417	347	263	3rd/Western Div.	—	—		Hank Stram
1964*	7	7	0	.500	366	306	2nd/Western Div.	—	—		Hank Stram
1965*	7	5	2	.583	322	285	3rd/Western Div.	—	—		Hank Stram
1966*	11	2	1	.846	448	276	1st/Western Div.	1	1	Super Bowl	Hank Stram
1967*	9	5	0	.643	408	254	2nd/Western Div.	—	—		Hank Stram
1968*	12	2	0	.857	371	170	2nd/Western Div.	0	1	W. Div. champ. game	Hank Stram
1969*	11	3	0	.786	359	177	2nd/Western Div.	3	0	Super Bowl champ	Hank Stram
1970	7	5	2	.583	272	244	2nd/AFC Western Div.	—	—		Hank Stram
1971	10	3	1	.769	302	208	1st/AFC Western Div.	0	1	AFC div. playoff game	Hank Stram
1972	8	6	0	.571	287	254	2nd/AFC Western Div.	—	—		Hank Stram
1973	7	5	2	.571	231	192	T2nd/AFC Western Div.	—	—		Hank Stram
1974	5	9	0	.357	233	293	T3rd/AFC Western Div.	—	—		Hank Stram
1975	5	9	0	.357	282	341	3rd/AFC Western Div.	—	—		Paul Wiggin
1976	5	9	0	.357	290	376	4th/AFC Western Div.	—	—		Paul Wiggin
1977	2	12	0	.143	225	349	5th/AFC Western Div.	—	—		Paul Wiggin, Tom Bettis
1978	4	12	0	.250	243	327	5th/AFC Western Div.	—	—		Marv Levy
1979	7	9	0	.438	238	262	5th/AFC Western Div.	—	—		Marv Levy
1980	8	8	0	.500	319	336	T3rd/AFC Western Div.	—	—		Marv Levy

			REGULAR SEASON						PLAYOFFS		
Year	W	L	T	Pct.	PF	PA	Finish	W	L	Highest round	Coach
1981	9	7	0	.563	343	290	3rd/AFC Western Div.	—	—		Marv Levy
1982	3	6	0	.333	176	184	11th/AFC	—	—		Marv Levy
1983	6	10	0	.375	386	367	T4th/AFC Western Div.	—	—		John Mackovic
1984	8	8	0	.500	314	324	4th/AFC Western Div.	—	—		John Mackovic
1985	6	10	0	.375	317	360	5th/AFC Western Div.	—	—		John Mackovic
1986	10	6	0	.625	358	326	2nd/AFC Western Div.	0	1	AFC wild-card game	John Mackovic
1987	4	11	0	.267	273	388	5th/AFC Western Div.	—	—		Frank Gansz
1988	4	11	1	.281	254	320	5th/AFC Western Div.	—	—		Frank Gansz
1989	8	7	1	.531	318	286	2nd/AFC Western Div.	—	—		Marty Schottenheimer
1990	11	5	0	.688	369	257	2nd/AFC Western Div.	0	1	AFC wild-card game	Marty Schottenheimer
1991	10	6	0	.625	322	252	2nd/AFC Western Div.	1	1	AFC div. playoff game	Marty Schottenheimer
1992	10	6	0	.625	348	282	2nd/AFC Western Div.	0	1	AFC wild-card game	Marty Schottenheimer
1993	11	5	0	.688	328	291	1st/AFC Western Div.	2	1	AFC championship game	Marty Schottenheimer
1994	9	7	0	.563	319	298	2nd/AFC Western Div.	0	1	AFC wild-card game	Marty Schottenheimer
1995	13	3	0	.813	358	241	1st/AFC Western Div.	0	1	AFC div. playoff game	Marty Schottenheimer
1996	9	7	0	.563	297	300	2nd/AFC Western Div.	—	—		Marty Schottenheimer
1997	13	3	0	.813	375	232	1st/AFC Western Div.	0	1	AFC div. playoff game	Marty Schottenheimer
1998	7	9	0	.438	327	363	4th/AFC Western Div.	—	—		Marty Schottenheimer
1999	9	7	0	.563	390	322	2nd/AFC Western Div.	—	—		Gunther Cunningham

*American Football League.
†Dallas Texans.

FIRST-ROUND DRAFT PICKS

1960—Don Meredith, QB, Southern Methodist
1961—E.J. Holub, C, Texas Tech
1962—Ronnie Bull, RB, Baylor
1963—Buck Buchanan, DT, Grambling* (AFL)
    Ed Budde, G, Michigan State
1964—Pete Beathard, QB, Southern California
1965—Gale Sayers, RB, Kansas
1966—Aaron Brown, DE, Minnesota
1967—Gene Trosch, DE, Miami
1968—Mo Moorman, G, Texas A&M
    George Daney, G, Texas-El Paso
1969—Jim Marsalis, DB, Tennessee State
1970—Sid Smith, T, Southern California
1971—Elmo Wright, WR, Houston
1972—Jeff Kinney, RB, Nebraska
1973—None
1974—Woody Green, RB, Arizona State
1975—None
1976—Rod Walters, G, Iowa
1977—Gary Green, DB, Baylor
1978—Art Still, DE, Kentucky
1979—Mike Bell, DE, Colorado State
    Steve Fuller, QB, Clemson
1980—Brad Budde, G, Southern California
1981—Willie Scott, TE, South Carolina
1982—Anthony Hancock, WR, Tennessee
1983—Todd Blackledge, QB, Penn State
1984—Bill Maas, DT, Pittsburgh
    John Alt, T, Iowa
1985—Ethan Horton, RB, North Carolina
1986—Brian Jozwiak, T, West Virginia
1987—Paul Palmer, RB, Temple
1988—Neil Smith, DE, Nebraska
1989—Derrick Thomas, LB, Alabama
1990—Percy Snow, LB, Michigan State
1991—Harvey Williams, RB, Louisiana State
1992—Dale Carter, DB, Tennessee
1993—None
1994—Greg Hill, RB, Texas A&M
1995—Trezelle Jenkins, T, Michigan
1996—Jerome Woods, DB, Memphis
1997—Tony Gonzalez, TE, California
1998—Victor Riley, T, Auburn
1999—John Tait, T, Brigham Young
2000—Sylvester Morris, WR, Jackson State
*First player chosen in draft.

FRANCHISE RECORDS

Most rushing yards, career
4,897—Christian Okoye
Most rushing yards, season
1,480—Christian Okoye, 1989
Most rushing yards, game
200—Barry Word vs. Det., Oct. 14, 1990
Most rushing touchdowns, season
13—Abner Haynes, 1962
Most passing attempts, season
603—Bill Kenney, 1983
Most passing attempts, game
55—Joe Montana at S.D., Oct. 9, 1994
    Steve Bono at Mia., Dec. 12, 1994
Most passes completed, season
346—Bill Kenney, 1983
Most passes completed, game
37—Joe Montana at S.D., Oct. 9, 1994
Most passing yards, career
28,507—Len Dawson

Most passing yards, season
4,348—Bill Kenney, 1983
Most passing yards, game
435—Len Dawson vs. Den., Nov. 1, 1964
Most touchdown passes, season
30—Len Dawson, 1964
Most pass receptions, career
416—Henry Marshall
Most pass receptions, season
80—Carlos Carson, 1983
Most pass receptions, game
12—Ed Podolak vs. Den., Oct. 7, 1973
Most receiving yards, career
7,306—Otis Taylor
Most receiving yards, season
1,351—Carlos Carson, 1983
Most receiving yards, game
309—Stephone Paige vs. S.D., Dec. 22, 1985

Most receiving touchdowns, season
12—Chris Burford, 1962
Most touchdowns, career
60—Otis Taylor
Most field goals, season
34—Nick Lowery, 1990
Longest field goals
58 yards—Nick Lowery at Was., Sept. 18, 1983
    Nick Lowery vs. L.A. Raiders, Sept. 12, 1985
Most interceptions, career
58—Emmitt Thomas
Most interceptions, season
12—Emmitt Thomas, 1974
Most sacks, career
126.5—Derrick Thomas
Most sacks, season
20—Derrick Thomas, 1990

SERIES RECORDS

Kansas City vs.: Arizona 5-1-1; Atlanta 4-0; Baltimore 1-0; Buffalo 14-17-1; Carolina 1-0; Chicago 3-5; Cincinnati 11-9; Cleveland 7-8-2; Dallas 3-4; Denver 45-34; Detroit 6-3; Green Bay 5-1-1; Indianapolis 6-6; Jacksonville 0-2; Miami 10-10; Minnesota 4-3; New England 15-8-3; New Orleans 4-3; N.Y. Giants 3-7; N.Y. Jets 14-13-1; Oakland 40-37-2; Philadelphia 2-1; Pittsburgh 7-15; St. Louis 2-4; San Diego 41-37-1; San Francisco 3-4; Seattle 27-15; Tampa Bay 5-3; Tennessee 24-17; Washington 4-1.
NOTE: Includes records as Dallas Texans from 1960 through 1962.

COACHING RECORDS

Tom Bettis, 1-6-0; Gunther Cunningham, 9-7-0; Frank Gansz, 8-22-1; Marv Levy, 31-42-0; John Mackovic, 30-34-0 (0-1); Marty Schottenheimer, 101-58-1 (3-7); Hank Stram, 124-76-10 (5-3); Paul Wiggin, 11-24-0.
NOTE: Playoff games in parentheses.

RETIRED UNIFORM NUMBERS

No.	Player
3	Jan Stenerud
16	Len Dawson
28	Abner Haynes
33	Stone Johnson
36	Mack Lee Hill
63	Willie Lanier
78	Bobby Bell
86	Buck Buchanan

MIAMI DOLPHINS
YEAR-BY-YEAR RECORDS

Year	W	L	T	Pct.	PF	PA	Finish	W	L	Highest round	Coach
1966*	3	11	0	.214	213	362	T4th/Eastern Div.	—	—		George Wilson
1967*	4	10	0	.286	219	407	T3rd/Eastern Div.	—	—		George Wilson
1968*	5	8	1	.385	276	355	3rd/Eastern Div.	—	—		George Wilson
1969*	3	10	1	.231	233	332	5th/Eastern Div.	—	—		George Wilson
1970	10	4	0	.714	297	228	2nd/AFC Eastern Div.	0	1	AFC div. playoff game	Don Shula
1971	10	3	1	.769	315	174	1st/AFC Eastern Div.	2	1	Super Bowl	Don Shula
1972	14	0	0	1.000	385	171	1st/AFC Eastern Div.	3	0	Super Bowl champ	Don Shula
1973	12	2	0	.857	343	150	1st/AFC Eastern Div.	3	0	Super Bowl champ	Don Shula
1974	11	3	0	.786	327	216	1st/AFC Eastern Div.	0	1	AFC div. playoff game	Don Shula
1975	10	4	0	.714	357	222	2nd/AFC Eastern Div.	—	—		Don Shula
1976	6	8	0	.429	263	264	3rd/AFC Eastern Div.	—	—		Don Shula
1977	10	4	0	.714	313	197	2nd/AFC Eastern Div.	—	—		Don Shula
1978	11	5	0	.688	372	254	2nd/AFC Eastern Div.	0	1	AFC wild-card game	Don Shula
1979	10	6	0	.625	341	257	1st/AFC Eastern Div.	0	1	AFC div. playoff game	Don Shula
1980	8	8	0	.500	266	305	3rd/AFC Eastern Div.	—	—		Don Shula
1981	11	4	1	.719	345	275	1st/AFC Eastern Div.	0	1	AFC div. playoff game	Don Shula
1982	7	2	0	.778	198	131	T2nd/AFC	3	1	Super Bowl	Don Shula
1983	12	4	0	.750	389	250	1st/AFC Eastern Div.	0	1	AFC div. playoff game	Don Shula
1984	14	2	0	.875	513	298	1st/AFC Eastern Div.	2	1	Super Bowl	Don Shula
1985	12	4	0	.750	428	320	1st/AFC Eastern Div.	1	1	AFC championship game	Don Shula
1986	8	8	0	.500	430	405	3rd/AFC Eastern Div.	—	—		Don Shula
1987	8	7	0	.533	362	335	T2nd/AFC Eastern Div.	—	—		Don Shula
1988	6	10	0	.375	319	380	5th/AFC Eastern Div.	—	—		Don Shula
1989	8	8	0	.500	331	379	T2nd/AFC Eastern Div.	—	—		Don Shula
1990	12	4	0	.750	336	242	2nd/AFC Eastern Div.	1	1	AFC div. playoff game	Don Shula
1991	8	8	0	.500	343	349	3rd/AFC Eastern Div.	—	—		Don Shula
1992	11	5	0	.688	340	281	1st/AFC Eastern Div.	1	1	AFC championship game	Don Shula
1993	9	7	0	.563	349	351	2nd/AFC Eastern Div.	—	—		Don Shula
1994	10	6	0	.625	389	327	1st/AFC Eastern Div.	1	1	AFC div. playoff game	Don Shula
1995	9	7	0	.563	398	332	T2nd/AFC Eastern Div.	0	1	AFC wild-card game	Don Shula
1996	8	8	0	.500	279	454	4th/AFC Eastern Div.	—	—		Jimmy Johnson
1997	9	7	0	.563	339	327	T2nd/AFC Eastern Div.	0	1	AFC wild-card game	Jimmy Johnson
1998	10	6	0	.625	321	265	T2nd/AFC Eastern Div.	1	1	AFC div. playoff game	Jimmy Johnson
1999	9	7	0	.563	326	336	3rd/AFC Eastern Div.	1	1	AFC div. playoff game	Jimmy Johnson

*American Football League.

FIRST-ROUND DRAFT PICKS

1966—Jim Grabowski, RB, Illinois*
    Rick Norton, QB, Kentucky
1967—Bob Griese, QB, Purdue
1968—Larry Csonka, RB, Syracuse
    Doug Crusan, T, Indiana
1969—Bill Stanfill, DE, Georgia
1970—None
1971—None
1972—Mike Kadish, DT, Notre Dame

1973—None
1974—Don Reese, DE, Jackson State
1975—Darryl Carlton, T, Tampa
1976—Larry Gordon, LB, Arizona State
    Kim Bokamper, LB, San Jose State
1977—A.J. Duhe, DE, Louisiana State
1978—None
1979—Jon Giesler, T, Michigan
1980—Don McNeal, DB, Alabama

1981—David Overstreet, RB, Oklahoma
1982—Roy Foster, G, Southern California
1983—Dan Marino, QB, Pittsburgh
1984—Jackie Shipp, LB, Oklahoma
1985—Lorenzo Hampton, RB, Florida
1986—None
1987—John Bosa, DE, Boston College
1988—Eric Kumerow, DE, Ohio State
1989—Sammie Smith, RB, Florida State
   Louis Oliver, DB, Florida
1990—Richmond Webb, T, Texas A&M
1991—Randal Hill, WR, Miami (Fla.)
1992—Troy Vincent, DB, Wisconsin
   Marco Coleman, LB, Georgia Tech
1993—O.J. McDuffie, WR, Penn State
1994—Tim Bowens, DT, Mississippi
1995—Billy Milner, T, Houston
1996—Daryl Gardener, DT, Baylor
1997—Yatil Green, WR, Miami (Fla.)
1998—John Avery, RB, Mississippi
1999—None
2000—None
   *First player chosen in draft.

FRANCHISE RECORDS

Most rushing yards, career
6,737—Larry Csonka
Most rushing yards, season
1,258—Delvin Williams, 1978
Most rushing yards, game
197—Mercury Morris vs. N.E., Sept. 30, 1973
Most rushing touchdowns, season
15—Karim Abdul-Jabbar, 1997
Most passing attempts, season
623—Dan Marino, 1986
Most passing attempts, game
60—Dan Marino vs. NYJ, Oct. 23, 1988
   Dan Marino at N.E., Nov. 23, 1997
Most passes completed, season
385—Dan Marino, 1994
Most passes completed, game
39—Dan Marino at Buf., Nov. 16, 1986
Most passing yards, career
58,913—Dan Marino

Most passing yards, season
5,084—Dan Marino, 1984
Most passing yards, game
521—Dan Marino vs. NYJ, Oct. 23, 1988
Most touchdown passes, season
48—Dan Marino, 1984
Most pass receptions, career
550—Mark Clayton
Most pass receptions, season
90—O.J. McDuffie, 1998
Most pass receptions, game
12—Jim Jensen at N.E., Nov. 6, 1988
Most receiving yards, career
8,869—Mark Duper
Most receiving yards, season
1,389—Mark Clayton, 1984
Most receiving yards, game
217—Mark Duper vs. NYJ, Nov. 10, 1985
Most receiving touchdowns, season
18—Mark Clayton, 1984

Most touchdowns, career
82—Mark Clayton
Most field goals, season
39—Olindo Mare, 1999
Longest field goal
59 yards—Pete Stoyanovich at NYJ, Nov. 12, 1989
Most interceptions, career
35—Jake Scott
Most interceptions, season
10—Dick Westmoreland, 1967
Most sacks, career
67.5—Bill Stanfill
Most sacks, season
18.5—Bill Stanfill, 1973

SERIES RECORDS

Miami vs.: Arizona 8-0; Atlanta 6-2; Baltimore, 1-0; Buffalo 42-25-1; Carolina 1-0; Chicago 5-3; Cincinnati 12-3; Cleveland 6-4; Dallas 6-3; Denver 7-2-1; Detroit 4-2; Green Bay 8-1; Indianapolis 40-20; Jacksonville 0-1; Kansas City 10-10; Minnesota 4-2; New England 40-27; New Orleans 6-4; N.Y. Giants 1-3; N.Y. Jets 33-32-1; Oakland 8-15-1; Philadelphia 7-3; Pittsburgh 9-7; St. Louis 7-1; San Diego 7-10; San Francisco 4-3; Seattle 4-2; Tampa Bay 4-2; Tennessee 14-11; Washington 5-3.

COACHING RECORDS

Jimmy Johnson, 36-28-0 (2-3); Don Shula, 257-133-2 (17-14); George Wilson, 15-39-2.
NOTE: Playoff games in parentheses.

RETIRED UNIFORM NUMBERS

No.	Player
12	Bob Griese
13	Dan Marino

MINNESOTA VIKINGS
YEAR-BY-YEAR RECORDS

		REGULAR SEASON						PLAYOFFS		
Year	W	L	T	Pct.	PF	PA	Finish	W	L	Highest round	Coach
1961	3	11	0	.214	285	407	7th/Western Conf.	—	—		Norm Van Brocklin
1962	2	11	1	.154	254	410	6th/Western Conf.	—	—		Norm Van Brocklin
1963	5	8	1	.385	309	390	T4th/Western Conf.	—	—		Norm Van Brocklin
1964	8	5	1	.615	355	296	T2nd/Western Conf.	—	—		Norm Van Brocklin
1965	7	7	0	.500	383	403	5th/Western Conf.	—	—		Norm Van Brocklin
1966	4	9	1	.308	292	304	T6th/Western Conf.	—	—		Norm Van Brocklin
1967	3	8	3	.273	233	294	4th/Central Div.	—	—		Bud Grant
1968	8	6	0	.571	282	242	1st/Central Div.	0	1	W. Conf. champ. game	Bud Grant
1969	12	2	0	.857	379	133	1st/Central Div.	2	1	Super Bowl	Bud Grant
1970	12	2	0	.857	335	143	1st/NFC Central Div.	0	1	NFC div. playoff game	Bud Grant
1971	11	3	0	.786	245	139	1st/NFC Central Div.	0	1	NFC div. playoff game	Bud Grant
1972	7	7	0	.500	301	252	3rd/NFC Central Div.	—	—		Bud Grant
1973	12	2	0	.857	296	168	1st/NFC Central Div.	2	1	Super Bowl	Bud Grant
1974	10	4	0	.714	310	195	1st/NFC Central Div.	2	1	Super Bowl	Bud Grant
1975	12	2	0	.857	377	180	1st/NFC Central Div.	0	1	NFC div. playoff game	Bud Grant

HISTORY — Team by team

Year	W	L	T	Pct.	PF	PA	Finish	W	L	Highest round	Coach
1976	11	2	1	.821	305	176	1st/NFC Central Div.	2	1	Super Bowl	Bud Grant
1977	9	5	0	.643	231	227	1st/NFC Central Div.	1	1	NFC championship game	Bud Grant
1978	8	7	1	.531	294	306	1st/NFC Central Div.	0	1	NFC div. playoff game	Bud Grant
1979	7	9	0	.438	259	337	3rd/NFC Central Div.	—	—		Bud Grant
1980	9	7	0	.563	317	308	1st/NFC Central Div.	0	1	NFC div. playoff game	Bud Grant
1981	7	9	0	.438	325	369	4th/NFC Central Div.	—	—		Bud Grant
1982	5	4	0	.556	187	198	T4th/NFC	1	1	NFC second-round pl. game	Bud Grant
1983	8	8	0	.500	316	348	T2nd/NFC Central Div.	—	—		Bud Grant
1984	3	13	0	.188	276	484	5th/NFC Central Div.	—	—		Les Steckel
1985	7	9	0	.438	346	359	T3rd/NFC Central Div.	—	—		Bud Grant
1986	9	7	0	.563	398	273	2nd/NFC Central Div.	—	—		Jerry Burns
1987	8	7	0	.533	336	335	2nd/NFC Central Div.	2	1	NFC championship game	Jerry Burns
1988	11	5	0	.688	406	233	2nd/NFC Central Div.	1	1	NFC div. playoff game	Jerry Burns
1989	10	6	0	.625	351	275	1st/NFC Central Div.	0	1	NFC div. playoff game	Jerry Burns
1990	6	10	0	.375	351	326	T2nd/NFC Central Div.	—	—		Jerry Burns
1991	8	8	0	.500	301	306	3rd/NFC Central Div.	—	—		Jerry Burns
1992	11	5	0	.688	374	249	1st/NFC Central Div.	0	1	NFC wild-card game	Dennis Green
1993	9	7	0	.563	277	290	T2nd/NFC Central Div.	0	1	NFC wild-card game	Dennis Green
1994	10	6	0	.625	356	314	1st/NFC Central Div.	0	1	NFC wild-card game	Dennis Green
1995	8	8	0	.500	412	385	4th/NFC Central Div.	—	—		Dennis Green
1996	9	7	0	.563	298	315	2nd/NFC Central Div.	0	1	NFC wild-card game	Dennis Green
1997	9	7	0	.563	354	359	T3rd/NFC Central Div.	1	1	NFC div. playoff game	Dennis Green
1998	15	1	0	.938	556	296	1st/NFC Central Div.	1	1	NFC championship game	Dennis Green
1999	10	6	0	.625	399	335	2nd/NFC Central Div.	1	1	NFC div. playoff game	Dennis Green

FIRST-ROUND DRAFT PICKS

1961—Tommy Mason, RB, Tulane*
1962—None
1963—Jim Dunaway, T, Mississippi
1964—Carl Eller, DE, Minnesota
1965—Jack Snow, WR, Notre Dame
1966—Jerry Shay, DT, Purdue
1967—Clint Jones, RB, Michigan State
   Gene Washington, WR, Michigan State
   Alan Page, DT, Notre Dame
1968—Ron Yary, T, Southern California*
1969—None
1970—John Ward, DT, Oklahoma State
1971—Leo Hayden, RB, Ohio State
1972—Jeff Siemon, LB, Stanford
1973—Chuck Foreman, RB, Miami (Fla.)
1974—Fred McNeill, LB, UCLA
   Steve Riley, T, Southern California
1975—Mark Mullaney, DE, Colorado State
1976—James White, DT, Oklahoma State
1977—Tommy Kramer, QB, Rice
1978—Randy Holloway, DE, Pittsburgh
1979—Ted Brown, RB, North Carolina State
1980—Doug Martin, DT, Washington
1981—None
1982—Darrin Nelson, RB, Stanford
1983—Joey Browner, DB, Southern California
1984—Keith Millard, DE, Washington State
1985—Chris Doleman, LB, Pittsburgh
1986—Gerald Robinson, DE, Auburn
1987—D.J. Dozier, RB, Penn State
1988—Randall McDaniel, G, Arizona State
1989—None
1990—None
1991—None
1992—None
1993—Robert Smith, RB, Ohio State
1994—DeWayne Washington, CB, North Carolina State
   Todd Steussie, T, California
1995—Derrick Alexander, DE, Florida State
   Korey Stringer, T, Ohio State
1996—Duane Clemons, DE, California
1997—Dwayne Rudd, LB, Alabama
1998—Randy Moss, WR, Marshall
1999—Daunte Culpepper, QB, Central Florida
   Dimitrius Underwood, DE, Michigan State
2000—Chris Hovan, DT, Boston College
   *First player chosen in draft.

FRANCHISE RECORDS

Most rushing yards, career
5,879—Chuck Foreman
Most rushing yards, season
1,266—Terry Allen, 1997
Most rushing yards, game
200—Chuck Foreman at Phi., Oct. 24, 1976
Most rushing touchdowns, season
13—Chuck Foreman, 1975
   Chuck Foreman, 1976
   Terry Allen, 1992
Most passing attempts, season
606—Warren Moon, 1995
Most passing attempts, game
63—Rich Gannon at N.E., Oct. 20, 1991

Most passes completed, season
377—Warren Moon, 1995
Most passes completed, game
38—Tommy Kramer vs. Cle., Dec. 14, 1980
   Tommy Kramer vs. G.B., Nov. 29, 1981
Most passing yards, career
33,098—Fran Tarkenton
Most passing yards, season
4,264—Warren Moon, 1994
Most passing yards, game
490—Tommy Kramer at Was., Nov. 2, 1986
Most touchdown passes, season
34—Randall Cunningham, 1998

Most pass receptions, career
835—Cris Carter
Most pass receptions, season
122—Cris Carter, 1994, 1995
Most pass receptions, game
15—Rickey Young at N.E., Dec. 16, 1979
Most receiving yards, career
10,238—Cris Carter
Most receiving yards, season
1,413—Randy Moss, 1999
Most receiving yards, game
210—Sammy White vs. Det., Nov. 7, 1976

Most receiving touchdowns, season
17—Cris Carter, 1995
Randy Moss, 1998
Most touchdowns, career
95—Cris Carter
Most field goals, season
46—Fred Cox, 1970

Longest field goal
54 yards—Jan Stenerud vs. Atl., Sept. 16, 1984
Most interceptions, career
53—Paul Krause
Most interceptions, season
10—Paul Krause, 1975

Most sacks, career
130—Carl Eller
Most sacks, season
21—Chris Doleman, 1989

SERIES RECORDS

Minnesota vs.: Arizona 7-8; Atlanta 14-6; Baltimore 1-0; Buffalo 6-2; Carolina 2-0; Chicago 42-33-2; Cincinnati 5-4; Cleveland 8-3; Dallas 8-9; Denver 6-4; Detroit 47-28-2; Green Bay 39-37-1; Indianapolis 7-11-1; Jacksonville 1-0; Kansas City 3-4; Miami 2-4; New England 3-4; New Orleans 14-6; N.Y. Giants 8-5; N.Y. Jets 1-5; Oakland 3-7; Philadelphia 11-6; Pittsburgh 8-4; St. Louis 16-11-2; San Diego 4-4; San Francisco 17-17-1; Seattle 2-4; Tampa Bay 29-15; Tennessee 5-3; Washington 5-6.

COACHING RECORDS

Jerry Burns, 52-43-0 (3-3); Bud Grant, 158-96-5 (10-12); Dennis Green, 81-47-0 (3-7); Les Steckel, 3-13-0; Norm Van Brocklin, 29-51-4.
NOTE: Playoff games in parentheses.

RETIRED UNIFORM NUMBERS

No.	Player
10	Fran Tarkenton
22	Paul Krause
88	Alan Page

NEW ENGLAND PATRIOTS
YEAR-BY-YEAR RECORDS

		REGULAR SEASON							PLAYOFFS		
Year	W	L	T	Pct.	PF	PA	Finish	W	L	Highest round	Coach
1960*†	5	9	0	.357	286	349	4th/Eastern Div.	—	—		Lou Saban
1961*†	9	4	1	.692	413	313	2nd/Eastern Div.	—	—		Lou Saban, Mike Holovak
1962*†	9	4	1	.692	346	295	2nd/Eastern Div.	—	—		Mike Holovak
1963*†	7	6	1	.538	327	257	1st/Eastern Div.	1	1	AFL championship game	Mike Holovak
1964*†	10	3	1	.769	365	297	2nd/Eastern Div.	—	—		Mike Holovak
1965*†	4	8	2	.333	244	302	3rd/Eastern Div.	—	—		Mike Holovak
1966*†	8	4	2	.667	315	283	2nd/Eastern Div.	—	—		Mike Holovak
1967*†	3	10	1	.231	280	389	5th/Eastern Div.	—	—		Mike Holovak
1968*†	4	10	0	.286	229	406	4th/Eastern Div.	—	—		Mike Holovak
1969*†	4	10	0	.286	266	316	T3rd/Eastern Div.	—	—		Clive Rush
1970†	2	12	0	.143	149	361	5th/AFC Eastern Div.	—	—		Clive Rush, John Mazur
1971	6	8	0	.429	238	325	T3rd/AFC Eastern Div.	—	—		John Mazur
1972	3	11	0	.214	192	446	5th/AFC Eastern Div.	—	—		J. Mazur, Phil Bengtson
1973	5	9	0	.357	258	300	3rd/AFC Eastern Div.	—	—		Chuck Fairbanks
1974	7	7	0	.500	348	289	T3rd/AFC Eastern Div.	—	—		Chuck Fairbanks
1975	3	11	0	.214	258	358	T4th/AFC Eastern Div.	—	—		Chuck Fairbanks
1976	11	3	0	.786	376	236	2nd/Eastern Div.	0	1	AFC div. playoff game	Chuck Fairbanks
1977	9	5	0	.643	278	217	3rd/AFC Eastern Div.	—	—		Chuck Fairbanks
1978	11	5	0	.688	358	286	1st/AFC Eastern Div.	0	1	AFC div. playoff game	Chuck Fairbanks, Hank Bullough-R. Erhardt
1979	9	7	0	.563	411	326	2nd/AFC Eastern Div.	—	—		Ron Erhardt
1980	10	6	0	.625	441	325	2nd/AFC Eastern Div.	—	—		Ron Erhardt
1981	2	14	0	.125	322	370	T4th/AFC Eastern Div.	—	—		Ron Erhardt
1982	5	4	0	.556	143	157	7th/AFC	0	1	AFC first-round pl. game	Ron Meyer
1983	8	8	0	.500	274	289	T2nd/AFC Eastern Div.	—	—		Ron Meyer
1984	9	7	0	.563	362	352	2nd/AFC Eastern Div.	—	—		R. Meyer, R. Berry
1985	11	5	0	.688	362	290	T2nd/AFC Eastern Div.	3	1	Super Bowl	Raymond Berry
1986	11	5	0	.688	412	307	1st/AFC Eastern Div.	0	1	AFC div. playoff game	Raymond Berry
1987	8	7	0	.533	320	293	T2nd/AFC Eastern Div.	—	—		Raymond Berry
1988	9	7	0	.563	250	284	T2nd/AFC Eastern Div.	—	—		Raymond Berry
1989	5	11	0	.313	297	391	4th/AFC Eastern Div.	—	—		Raymond Berry
1990	1	15	0	.063	181	446	5th/AFC Eastern Div.	—	—		Rod Rust
1991	6	10	0	.375	211	305	4th/AFC Eastern Div.	—	—		Dick MacPherson
1992	2	14	0	.125	205	363	5th/AFC Eastern Div.	—	—		Dick MacPherson
1993	5	11	0	.313	238	286	4th/AFC Eastern Div.	—	—		Bill Parcells
1994	10	6	0	.625	351	312	2nd/AFC Eastern Div.	0	1	AFC wild-card game	Bill Parcells
1995	6	10	0	.375	294	377	4th/AFC Eastern Div.	—	—		Bill Parcells
1996	11	5	0	.687	418	313	1st/AFC Eastern Div.	2	1	Super Bowl	Bill Parcells
1997	10	6	0	.625	369	289	1st/AFC Eastern Div.	1	1	AFC div. playoff game	Pete Carroll
1998	9	7	0	.563	337	329	4th/AFC Eastern Div.	0	1	AFC wild-card game	Pete Carroll
1999	8	8	0	.500	299	284	5th/AFC Eastern Div.	—	—		Pete Carroll

*American Football League.
†Boston Patriots.

HISTORY — Team by team

FIRST-ROUND DRAFT PICKS

1960—Ron Burton, RB, Northwestern
1961—Tommy Mason, RB, Tulane
1962—Gary Collins, WR, Maryland
1963—Art Graham, E, Boston College
1964—Jack Concannon, QB, Boston College* (AFL)
1965—Jerry Rush, DE, Michigan State
       Dave McCormick, T, Louisiana State
1966—Karl Singer, T, Purdue
       Willie Townes, T, Tulsa
1967—John Charles, DB, Purdue
1968—Dennis Byrd, DE, North Carolina State
1969—Ron Sellers, WR, Florida State
1970—Phil Olsen, DT, Utah State
1971—Jim Plunkett, QB, Stanford*
1972—None
1973—John Hannah, G, Alabama
       Sam Cunningham, RB, Southern California
       Darryl Stingley, WR, Purdue
1974—None
1975—Russ Francis, TE, Oregon
1976—Mike Haynes, DB, Arizona State
       Pete Brock, C, Colorado
       Tim Fox, DB, Ohio State
1977—Raymond Clayborn, DB, Texas
       Stanley Morgan, WR, Tennessee
1978—Bob Cryder, G, Alabama
1979—Rick Sanford, DB, South Carolina
1980—Roland James, DB, Tennessee
       Vagas Ferguson, RB, Notre Dame
1981—Brian Holloway, T, Stanford
1982—Kenneth Sims, DT, Texas*
       Lester Williams, DT, Nebraska
1983—Tony Eason, QB, Illinois
1984—Irving Fryar, WR, Nebraska*
1985—Trevor Matich, C, Brigham Young
1986—Reggie Dupard, RB, Southern Methodist
1987—Bruce Armstrong, G, Louisville
1988—J. Stephens, RB, Northwestern Louisiana State
1989—Hart Lee Dykes, WR, Oklahoma State
1990—Chris Singleton, LB, Arizona
       Ray Agnew, DL, North Carolina State
1991—Pat Harlow, T, Southern California
       Leonard Russell, RB, Arizona State
1992—Eugene Chung, T, Virginia Tech
1993—Drew Bledsoe, QB, Washington State*
1994—Willie McGinest, DE, Southern California
1995—Ty Law, DB, Michigan
1996—Terry Glenn, WR, Ohio State
1997—Chris Canty, DB, Kansas State
1998—Robert Edwards, RB, Georgia
       Tebucky Jones, DB, Syracuse
1999—Damien Woody, C, Boston College
       Andy Katzenmoyer, LB, Ohio State
2000—None
*First player chosen in draft.

FRANCHISE RECORDS

Most rushing yards, career
5,453—Sam Cunningham
Most rushing yards, season
1,487—Curtis Martin, 1995
Most rushing yards, game
212—Tony Collins vs. NYJ, Sept. 18, 1983
Most rushing touchdowns, season
14—Curtis Martin, 1995, 1996
Most passing attempts, season
691—Drew Bledsoe, 1994
Most passing attempts, game
70—Drew Bledsoe vs. Min., Nov. 13, 1994 (OT)
60—Drew Bledsoe at Pit., Dec. 16, 1995
Most passes completed, season
400—Drew Bledsoe, 1994
Most passes completed, game
45—Drew Bledsoe vs. Min., Nov. 13, 1994 (OT)
39—Drew Bledsoe at Pit., Dec. 16, 1995
Most passing yards, career
26,886—Steve Grogan

Most passing yards, season
4,555—Drew Bledsoe, 1994
Most passing yards, game
426—Drew Bledsoe vs. Min., Nov. 13, 1994 (OT)
423—Drew Bledsoe vs. Mia., Nov. 23, 1998
Most touchdown passes, season
31—Babe Parilli, 1964
Most pass receptions, career
534—Stanley Morgan
Most pass receptions, season
96—Ben Coates, 1994
Most pass receptions, game
13—Terry Glenn at Cle., Oct. 3, 1999
Most receiving yards, career
10,352—Stanley Morgan
Most receiving yards, season
1,491—Stanley Morgan, 1986
Most receiving yards, game
214—Terry Glenn at Cle., Oct. 3, 1999

Most receiving touchdowns, season
12—Stanley Morgan, 1979
Most touchdowns, career
68—Stanley Morgan
Most field goals, season
32—Tony Franklin, 1986
Longest field goal
55 yards—Matt Bahr at Mia., Nov. 12, 1995
       Adam Vinatieri at St.L., Dec. 13, 1998
Most interceptions, career
36—Raymond Clayborn
Most interceptions, season
11—Ron Hall, 1964
Most sacks, career
100—Andre Tippett
Most sacks, season
18.5—Andre Tippett, 1984

SERIES RECORDS

New England vs.: Arizona 4-6; Atlanta 3-6; Baltimore 2-0; Buffalo 41-38-1; Carolina 0-1; Chicago 5-2; Cincinnati 9-7; Cleveland 5-10; Dallas 1-7; Denver 13-20; Detroit 3-3; Green Bay 3-3; Indianapolis 36-23; Jacksonville 2-0; Kansas City 8-15-3; Miami 27-40; Minnesota 4-3; New Orleans 6-3; N.Y. Giants 3-3; N.Y. Jets 35-43-1; Oakland 12-13-1; Philadelphia 2-6; Pittsburgh 4-11; St. Louis 3-4; San Diego 16-11-2; San Francisco 2-7; Seattle 6-7; Tampa Bay 3-1; Tennessee 18-14-1; Washington 1-5.
NOTE: Includes records as Boston Patriots from 1960 through 1970.

COACHING RECORDS

Phil Bengtson, 1-4-0; Raymond Berry, 48-39-0 (3-2); Hank Bullough, 0-1-0; Pete Carroll, 27-21-0 (1-2); Ron Erhardt, 21-27-0; Chuck Fairbanks, 46-39-0 (0-2); Mike Holovak, 52-46-9 (1-1); Dick MacPherson, 8-24-0; John Mazur, 9-21-0; Ron Meyer, 18-15-0 (0-1); Bill Parcells, 32-32-0 (2-2); Clive Rush, 5-16-0; Rod Rust, 1-15-0; Lou Saban, 7-12-0. NOTE: Playoff games in parentheses.

RETIRED UNIFORM NUMBERS

No.	Player
20	Gino Cappelletti
40	Mike Haynes
57	Steve Nelson
73	John Hannah
79	Jim Hunt
89	Bob Dee

NEW ORLEANS SAINTS
YEAR-BY-YEAR RECORDS

Year	W	L	T	Pct.	PF	PA	Finish	W	L	Highest round	Coach
1967	3	11	0	.214	233	379	4th/Capitol Div.	—	—		Tom Fears
1968	4	9	1	.308	246	327	3rd/Century Div.	—	—		Tom Fears
1969	5	9	0	.357	311	393	3rd/Capitol Div.	—	—		Tom Fears
1970	2	11	1	.154	172	347	4th/NFC Western Div.	—	—		Tom Fears, J.D. Roberts
1971	4	8	2	.333	266	347	4th/NFC Western Div.	—	—		J.D. Roberts
1972	2	11	1	.179	215	361	4th/NFC Western Div.	—	—		J.D. Roberts
1973	5	9	0	.357	163	312	T3rd/NFC Western Div.	—	—		John North
1974	5	9	0	.357	166	263	3rd/NFC Western Div.	—	—		John North
1975	2	12	0	.143	165	360	4th/NFC Western Div.	—	—		J. North, Ernie Hefferle
1976	4	10	0	.286	253	346	T3rd/NFC Western Div.	—	—		Hank Stram
1977	3	11	0	.214	232	336	4th/NFC Western Div.	—	—		Hank Stram
1978	7	9	0	.438	281	298	3rd/NFC Western Div.	—	—		Dick Nolan
1979	8	8	0	.500	370	360	2nd/NFC Western Div.	—	—		Dick Nolan
1980	1	15	0	.063	291	487	4th/NFC Western Div.	—	—		Dick Nolan, Dick Stanfel
1981	4	12	0	.250	207	378	4th/NFC Western Div.	—	—		Bum Phillips
1982	4	5	0	.444	129	160	T8th/NFC	—	—		Bum Phillips
1983	8	8	0	.500	319	337	3rd/NFC Western Div.	—	—		Bum Phillips
1984	7	9	0	.438	298	361	3rd/NFC Western Div.	—	—		Bum Phillips
1985	5	11	0	.313	294	401	3rd/NFC Western Div.	—	—		B. Phillips, Wade Phillips
1986	7	9	0	.438	288	287	4th/NFC Western Div.	—	—		Jim Mora
1987	12	3	0	.800	422	283	2nd/NFC Western Div.	0	1	NFC wild-card game	Jim Mora
1988	10	6	0	.625	312	283	3rd/NFC Western Div.	—	—		Jim Mora
1989	9	7	0	.563	386	301	3rd/NFC Western Div.	—	—		Jim Mora
1990	8	8	0	.500	274	275	2nd/NFC Western Div.	0	1	NFC wild-card game	Jim Mora
1991	11	5	0	.688	341	211	1st/NFC Western Div.	0	1	NFC wild-card game	Jim Mora
1992	12	4	0	.750	330	202	2nd/NFC Western Div.	0	1	NFC wild-card game	Jim Mora
1993	8	8	0	.500	317	343	3rd/NFC Western Div.	—	—		Jim Mora
1994	7	9	0	.438	348	407	T2nd/NFC Western Div.	—	—		Jim Mora
1995	7	9	0	.438	319	348	T3rd/NFC Western Div.	—	—		Jim Mora
1996	3	13	0	.188	229	339	T4th/NFC Western Div.	—	—		Jim Mora, Rick Venturi
1997	6	10	0	.375	237	327	4th/NFC Western Div.	—	—		Mike Ditka
1998	6	10	0	.375	305	359	3rd/NFC Western Div.	—	—		Mike Ditka
1999	3	13	0	.188	260	434	5th/NFC Western Div.	—	—		Mike Ditka

FIRST-ROUND DRAFT PICKS

1967—Les Kelley, RB, Alabama
1968—Kevin Hardy, DE, Notre Dame
1969—John Shinners, G, Xavier (Ohio)
1970—Ken Burrough, WR, Texas Southern
1971—Archie Manning, QB, Mississippi
1972—Royce Smith, G, Georgia
1973—None
1974—Rick Middleton, LB, Ohio State
1975—Larry Burton, WR, Purdue
　　　 Kurt Schumacher, G, Ohio State
1976—Chuck Muncie, RB, California
1977—Joe Campbell, DE, Maryland
1978—Wes Chandler, WR, Florida
1979—Russell Erxleben, P, Texas
1980—Stan Brock, T, Colorado
1981—George Rogers, RB, South Carolina*
1982—Lindsay Scott, WR, Georgia
1983—None
1984—None

1985—Alvin Toles, LB, Tennessee
1986—Jim Dombrowski, T, Virginia
1987—Shawn Knight, DE, Brigham Young
1988—Craig Heyward, RB, Pittsburgh
1989—Wayne Martin, DE, Arkansas
1990—Renaldo Turnbull, DE, West Virginia
1991—None
1992—Vaughn Dunbar, RB, Indiana
1993—Willie Roaf, T, Louisiana Tech
　　　 Irv Smith, TE, Notre Dame
1994—Joe Johnson, DE, Louisville
1995—Mark Fields, LB, Washington State
1996—Alex Molden, DB, Oregon
1997—Chris Naeole, G, Colorado
1998—Kyle Turley, T, San Diego State
1999—Ricky Williams, RB, Texas
2000—None
　　*First player chosen in draft.

– 389 –

HISTORY *Team by team*

FRANCHISE RECORDS

Most rushing yards, career
4,267—George Rogers
Most rushing yards, season
1,674—George Rogers, 1981
Most rushing yards, game
206—George Rogers vs. St.L., Sept. 4, 1983
Most rushing touchdowns, season
13—George Rogers, 1981
    Dalton Hilliard, 1989
Most passing attempts, season
567—Jim Everett, 1995
Most passing attempts, game
55—Jim Everett at S.F., Sept. 25, 1994
Most passes completed, season
346—Jim Everett, 1994
Most passes completed, game
33—Archie Manning at G.B., Sept. 10, 1978
Most passing yards, career
21,734—Archie Manning

Most passing yards, season
3,970—Jim Everett, 1995
Most passing yards, game
377—Archie Manning at S.F., Dec. 7, 1980
Most touchdown passes, season
26—Jim Everett, 1995
Most pass receptions, career
532—Eric Martin
Most pass receptions, season
85—Eric Martin, 1988
Most pass receptions, game
14—Tony Galbreath at G.B., Sept. 10, 1978
Most receiving yards, career
7,844—Eric Martin
Most receiving yards, season
1,090—Eric Martin, 1989
Most receiving yards, game
205—Wes Chandler vs. Atl., Sept. 2, 1979
Most receiving touchdowns, season
9—Henry Childs, 1977

Most touchdowns, career
53—Dalton Hilliard
Most field goals, season
31—Morten Andersen, 1985
Longest field goal
63 yards—Tom Dempsey vs. Det., Nov. 8, 1970
Most interceptions, career
37—Dave Waymer
Most interceptions, season
10—Dave Whitsell, 1967
Most sacks, career
115—Rickey Jackson
Most sacks, season
17—Pat Swilling, 1991

SERIES RECORDS

New Orleans vs.: Arizona 10-12; Atlanta 24-37; Baltimore 0-2; Buffalo 2-4; Carolina 4-6; Chicago 7-11; Cincinnati 5-4; Cleveland 3-10; Dallas 5-14; Denver 2-4; Detroit 8-6-1; Green Bay 4-13; Indianapolis 4-3; Jacksonville 1-1; Kansas City 3-4; Miami 4-6; Minnesota 6-14; New England 3-6; N.Y. Giants 8-12; N.Y. Jets 4-4; Philadelphia 8-12; Oakland 3-4-1; Pittsburgh 5-6; St. Louis 25-33; San Diego 1-6; San Francisco 16-43-2; Seattle 4-2; Tampa Bay 13-6; Tennessee 4-5-1; Washington 5-12.

COACHING RECORDS

Mike Ditka, 15-33-0; Tom Fears, 13-34-2; Ernie Hefferle, 1-7-0; Jim Mora, 93-74-0 (0-4); Dick Nolan, 15-29-0; John North, 11-23-0; Bum Phillips, 27-42-0; Wade Phillips, 1-3-0; J.D. Roberts, 7-25-3; Dick Stanfel, 1-3-0; Hank Stram, 7-21-0; Rick Venturi, 1-7-0.
NOTE: Playoff games in parentheses.

RETIRED UNIFORM NUMBERS

No.	Player
31	Jim Taylor
81	Doug Atkins

NEW YORK GIANTS
YEAR-BY-YEAR RECORDS

	REGULAR SEASON						PLAYOFFS			
Year	W	L	T	Pct.	PF	PA	Finish	W	L	Highest round	Coach
1925	8	4	0	.667	122	67	T4th				Bob Folwell
1926	8	4	1	.667	147	51	T6th				Joe Alexander
1927	11	1	1	.917	197	20	1st				Earl Potteiger
1928	4	7	2	.364	79	136	6th				Earl Potteiger
1929	13	1	1	.929	312	86	2nd				LeRoy Andrews
1930	13	4	0	.765	308	98	2nd				L. Andrews, Benny Friedman-Steve Owen
1931	7	6	1	.538	154	100	5th				Steve Owen
1932	4	6	2	.400	93	113	5th				Steve Owen
1933	11	3	0	.786	244	101	1st/Eastern Div.	0	1	NFL championship game	Steve Owen
1934	8	5	0	.615	147	107	1st/Eastern Div.	1	0	NFL champ	Steve Owen
1935	9	3	0	.750	180	96	1st/Eastern Div.	0	1	NFL championship game	Steve Owen
1936	5	6	1	.455	115	163	3rd/Eastern Div.	—	—		Steve Owen
1937	6	3	2	.667	128	109	2nd/Eastern Div.	—	—		Steve Owen
1938	8	2	1	.800	194	79	1st/Eastern Div.	1	0	NFL champ	Steve Owen
1939	9	1	1	.900	168	85	1st/Eastern Div.	0	1	NFL championship game	Steve Owen
1940	6	4	1	.600	131	133	3rd/Eastern Div.	—	—		Steve Owen
1941	8	3	0	.727	238	114	1st/Eastern Div.	0	1	NFL championship game	Steve Owen
1942	5	5	1	.500	155	139	3rd/Eastern Div.	—	—		Steve Owen
1943	6	3	1	.667	197	170	2nd/Eastern Div.	0	1	E. Div. champ. game	Steve Owen
1944	8	1	1	.889	206	75	1st/Eastern Div.	0	1	NFL championship game	Steve Owen
1945	3	6	1	.333	179	198	T3rd/Eastern Div.	—	—		Steve Owen
1946	7	3	1	.700	236	162	1st/Eastern Div.	0	1	NFL championship game	Steve Owen
1947	2	8	2	.200	190	309	5th/Eastern Div.	—	—		Steve Owen
1948	4	8	0	.333	297	388	T3rd/Eastern Div.	—	—		Steve Owen
1949	6	6	0	.500	287	298	3rd/Eastern Div.	—	—		Steve Owen

HISTORY Team by team

Year	W	L	T	Pct.	PF	PA	Finish	W	L	Highest round	Coach
				REGULAR SEASON						PLAYOFFS	
1950	10	2	0	.833	268	150	2nd/American Conf.	0	1	Am. Conf. champ. game	Steve Owen
1951	9	2	1	.818	254	161	2nd/American Conf.	—	—		Steve Owen
1952	7	5	0	.583	234	231	T2nd/American Conf.	—	—		Steve Owen
1953	3	9	0	.250	179	277	5th/Eastern Conf.	—	—		Steve Owen
1954	7	5	0	.583	293	184	3rd/Eastern Conf.	—	—		Jim Lee Howell
1955	6	5	1	.545	267	223	3rd/Eastern Conf.	—	—		Jim Lee Howell
1956	8	3	1	.727	264	197	1st/Eastern Conf.	1	0	NFL champ	Jim Lee Howell
1957	7	5	0	.583	254	211	2nd/Eastern Conf.	—	—		Jim Lee Howell
1958	9	3	0	.750	246	183	1st/Eastern Conf.	1	1	NFL championship game	Jim Lee Howell
1959	10	2	0	.833	284	170	1st/Eastern Conf.	0	1	NFL championship game	Jim Lee Howell
1960	6	4	2	.600	271	261	3rd/Eastern Conf.	—	—		Jim Lee Howell
1961	10	3	1	.769	368	220	1st/Eastern Conf.	0	1	NFL championship game	Allie Sherman
1962	12	2	0	.857	398	283	1st/Eastern Conf.	0	1	NFL championship game	Allie Sherman
1963	11	3	0	.786	448	280	1st/Eastern Conf.	0	1	NFL championship game	Allie Sherman
1964	2	10	2	.167	241	399	7th/Eastern Conf.	—	—		Allie Sherman
1965	7	7	0	.500	270	338	T2nd/Eastern Conf.	—	—		Allie Sherman
1966	1	12	1	.077	263	501	8th/Eastern Conf.	—	—		Allie Sherman
1967	7	7	0	.500	369	379	2nd/Century Div.	—	—		Allie Sherman
1968	7	7	0	.500	294	325	2nd/Capitol Div.	—	—		Allie Sherman
1969	6	8	0	.429	264	298	2nd/Century Div.	—	—		Alex Webster
1970	9	5	0	.643	301	270	2nd/NFC Eastern Div.	—	—		Alex Webster
1971	4	10	0	.286	228	362	5th/NFC Eastern Div.	—	—		Alex Webster
1972	8	6	0	.571	331	247	3rd/NFC Eastern Div.	—	—		Alex Webster
1973	2	11	1	.179	226	362	5th/NFC Eastern Div.	—	—		Alex Webster
1974	2	12	0	.143	195	299	5th/NFC Eastern Div.	—	—		Bill Arnsparger
1975	5	9	0	.357	216	306	4th/NFC Eastern Div.	—	—		Bill Arnsparger
1976	3	11	0	.214	170	250	5th/NFC Eastern Div.	—	—		B. Arnsparger, J. McVay
1977	5	9	0	.357	181	265	T4th/NFC Eastern Div.	—	—		John McVay
1978	6	10	0	.375	264	298	T4th/NFC Eastern Div.	—	—		John McVay
1979	6	10	0	.375	237	323	4th/NFC Eastern Div.	—	—		Ray Perkins
1980	4	12	0	.250	249	425	5th/NFC Eastern Div.	—	—		Ray Perkins
1981	9	7	0	.563	295	257	3rd/NFC Eastern Div.	1	1	NFC div. playoff game	Ray Perkins
1982	4	5	0	.444	164	160	T8th/NFC	—	—		Ray Perkins
1983	3	12	1	.219	267	347	5th/NFC Eastern Div.	—	—		Bill Parcells
1984	9	7	0	.563	299	301	2nd/NFC Eastern Div.	1	1	NFC div. playoff game	Bill Parcells
1985	10	6	0	.625	399	283	2nd/NFC Eastern Div.	1	1	NFC div. playoff game	Bill Parcells
1986	14	2	0	.875	371	236	1st/NFC Eastern Div.	3	0	Super Bowl champ	Bill Parcells
1987	6	9	0	.400	280	312	5th/NFC Eastern Div.	—	—		Bill Parcells
1988	10	6	0	.625	359	304	2nd/NFC Eastern Div.	—	—		Bill Parcells
1989	12	4	0	.750	348	252	1st/NFC Eastern Div.	0	1	NFC div. playoff game	Bill Parcells
1990	13	3	0	.813	335	211	1st/NFC Eastern Div.	3	0	Super Bowl champ	Bill Parcells
1991	8	8	0	.500	281	297	4th/NFC Eastern Div.	—	—		Ray Handley
1992	6	10	0	.375	306	367	4th/NFC Eastern Div.	—	—		Ray Handley
1993	11	5	0	.688	288	205	2nd/NFC Eastern Div.	1	1	NFC div. playoff game	Dan Reeves
1994	9	7	0	.563	279	305	2nd/NFC Eastern Div.	—	—		Dan Reeves
1995	5	11	0	.313	290	340	4th/NFC Eastern Div.	—	—		Dan Reeves
1996	6	10	0	.375	242	297	5th/NFC Eastern Div.	—	—		Dan Reeves
1997	10	5	1	.656	307	265	1st/NFC Eastern Div.	0	1	NFC wild-card game	Jim Fassel
1998	8	8	0	.500	287	309	3rd/NFC Eastern Div.	—	—		Jim Fassel
1999	7	9	0	.438	299	358	3rd/NFC Eastern Div.	—	—		Jim Fassel

FIRST-ROUND DRAFT PICKS

1936—Art Lewis, T, Ohio
1937—Ed Widseth, T, Minnesota
1938—George Karamatic, B, Gonzaga
1939—Walt Nielson, B, Arizona
1940—Grenville Lansdell, B, Southern California
1941—George Franck, B, Minnesota
1942—Merle Hapes, B, Mississippi
1943—Steve Filipowicz, B, Fordham
1944—Billy Hillenbrand, B, Indiana
1945—Elmer Barbour, B, Wake Forest
1946—George Connor, T, Notre Dame
1947—Vic Schwall, B, Northwestern
1948—Tony Minisi, B, Pennsylvania
1949—Paul Page, B, Southern Methodist
1950—Travis Tidwell, B, Auburn
1951—Kyle Rote, B, Southern Methodist*
    Kim Spavital, B, Oklahoma A&M

1952—Frank Gifford, B, Southern California
1953—Bobby Marlow, B, Alabama
1954—None
1955—Joe Heap, B, Notre Dame
1956—Henry Moore, B, Arkansas
1957—None
1958—Phil King, B, Vanderbilt
1959—Lee Grosscup, B, Utah
1960—Lou Cordileone, G, Clemson
1961—None
1962—Jerry Hillebrand, LB, Colorado
1963—None
1964—Joe Don Looney, RB, Oklahoma
1965—T. Frederickson, RB, Auburn*
1966—Francis Peay, T, Missouri
1967—None
1968—None

– 391 –

HISTORY Team by team

1969—Fred Dryer, DE, San Diego State
1970—Jim Files, LB, Oklahoma
1971—Rocky Thompson, RB, West Texas State
1972—Eldridge Small, DB, Texas A&I
　　　Larry Jacobson, DT, Nebraska
1973—None
1974—John Hicks, G, Ohio State
1975—None
1976—Troy Archer, DE, Colorado
1977—Gary Jeter, DT, Southern Cal
1978—Gordon King, T, Stanford
1979—Phil Simms, QB, Morehead State
1980—Mark Haynes, DB, Colorado
1981—Lawrence Taylor, LB, North Carolina
1982—Butch Woolfolk, RB, Michigan
1983—Terry Kinard, DB, Clemson
1984—Carl Banks, LB, Michigan State
　　　Bill Roberts, T, Ohio State
1985—George Adams, RB, Kentucky
1986—Eric Dorsey, DT, Notre Dame
1987—Mark Ingram, WR, Michigan State
1988—Eric Moore, T, Indiana
1989—Brian Williams, G, Minnesota
1990—Rodney Hampton, RB, Georgia
1991—Jarrod Bunch, FB, Michigan
1992—Derek Brown, TE, Notre Dame
1993—None
1994—Thomas Lewis, WR, Indiana
1995—Tyrone Wheatley, RB, Michigan
1996—Cedric Jones, DE, Oklahoma
1997—Ike Hilliard, WR, Florida
1998—Shaun Williams, DB, UCLA
1999—Luke Petitgout, T, Notre Dame
2000—Ron Dayne, RB, Wisconsin
*First player chosen in draft.

FRANCHISE RECORDS

Most rushing yards, career
6,897—Rodney Hampton
Most rushing yards, season
1,516—Joe Morris, 1986
Most rushing yards, game
218—Gene Roberts vs. Chi. Cardinals, Nov. 12, 1950
Most rushing touchdowns, season
21—Joe Morris, 1985
Most passing attempts, season
533—Phil Simms, 1984
Most passing attempts, game
62—Phil Simms at Cin., Oct. 13, 1985
Most passes completed, season
286—Phil Simms, 1984
Most passes completed, game
40—Phil Simms at Cin., Oct. 13, 1985
Most passing yards, career
33,462—Phil Simms

Most passing yards, season
4,044—Phil Simms, 1984
Most passing yards, game
513—Phil Simms at Cin., Oct. 13, 1985
Most touchdown passes, season
36—Y.A. Tittle, 1963
Most pass receptions, career
395—Joe Morrison
Most pass receptions, season
79—Amani Toomer, 1999
Most pass receptions, game
12—Mark Bavaro at Cin., Oct. 13, 1985
Most receiving yards, career
5,434—Frank Gifford
Most receiving yards, season
1,209—Homer Jones
Most receiving yards, game
269—Del Shofner vs. Was., Oct. 28, 1962

Most receiving touchdowns, season
13—Homer Jones, 1967
Most touchdowns, career
78—Frank Gifford
Most field goals, season
35—Ali Haji-Sheikh, 1983
Longest field goal
56 yards—Ali Haji-Sheikh at Det., Nov. 7, 1983
Most interceptions, career
74—Emlen Tunnell
Most interceptions, season
11—Otto Schellbacher, 1951
　　Jimmy Patton, 1958
Most sacks, career
132.5—Lawrence Taylor
Most sacks, season
20.5—Lawrence Taylor, 1986

SERIES RECORDS

N.Y. Giants vs.: Arizona 74-39-2; Atlanta 6-7; Baltimore, 0-1; Buffalo 3-5; Carolina 0-1; Chicago 16-25-2; Cincinnati 2-4; Cleveland 17-25-2; Dallas 26-47-2; Denver 4-3; Detroit 14-14-1; Green Bay 20-23-2; Indianapolis 5-6; Jacksonville 0-1; Kansas City 7-3; Miami 3-1; Minnesota 5-8; New England 3-3; New Orleans 12-8; N.Y. Jets 5-4; Oakland 2-6; Philadelphia 69-59-2; Pittsburgh 44-28-3; St. Louis 7-21; San Diego 5-3; San Francisco 11-12; Seattle 5-3; Tampa Bay 9-5; Tennessee 5-1; Washington 68-53-3.

COACHING RECORDS

Joe Alexander, 8-4-1; LeRoy Andrews, 24-5-1; Bill Arnsparger, 7-28-0; Jim Fassel, 25-22-1 (0-1); Bob Folwell, 8-4-0; Benny Friedman, 2-0-0; Ray Handley, 14-18-0; Jim Lee Howell, 53-27-4 (2-2); John McVay, 14-23-0; Steve Owen, 153-100-17 (2-8); Bill Parcells, 77-49-1 (8-3); Ray Perkins, 23-34-0 (1-1); Earl Potteiger, 15-8-3; Dan Reeves, 31-33-0 (1-1); Allie Sherman, 57-51-4 (0-3); Alex Webster, 29-40-1.
NOTE: Playoff games in parentheses.

RETIRED UNIFORM NUMBERS

No.	Player
1	Ray Flaherty
4	Tuffy Leemans
7	Mel Hein
11	Phil Simms
14	Y.A. Tittle
32	Al Blozis
40	Joe Morrison
42	Charlie Conerly
50	Ken Strong
56	Lawrence Taylor

NEW YORK JETS
YEAR-BY-YEAR RECORDS

		REGULAR SEASON					PLAYOFFS		
Year	W	L	T	Pct.	PF	PA	Finish	W	L	Highest round	Coach
1960*†	7	7	0	.500	382	399	2nd/Eastern Div.	—	—		Sammy Baugh
1961*†	7	7	0	.500	301	390	3rd/Eastern Div.	—	—		Sammy Baugh

HISTORY Team by team

Year	W	L	T	Pct.	PF	PA	Finish	W	L	Highest round	Coach
1962*†	5	9	0	.357	278	423	4th/Eastern Div.	—	—		Bulldog Turner
1963*	5	8	1	.385	249	399	4th/Eastern Div.	—	—		Weeb Ewbank
1964*	5	8	1	.385	278	315	3rd/Eastern Div.	—	—		Weeb Ewbank
1965*	5	8	1	.385	285	303	2nd/Eastern Div.	—	—		Weeb Ewbank
1966*	6	6	2	.500	322	312	3rd/Eastern Div.	—	—		Weeb Ewbank
1967*	8	5	1	.615	371	329	2nd/Eastern Div.	—	—		Weeb Ewbank
1968*	11	3	0	.786	419	280	1st/Eastern Div.	2	0	Super Bowl champ	Weeb Ewbank
1969*	10	4	0	.714	353	269	1st/Eastern Div.	0	1	Div. playoff game	Weeb Ewbank
1970	4	10	0	.286	255	286	3rd/AFC Eastern Div.	—	—		Weeb Ewbank
1971	6	8	0	.429	212	299	T3rd/AFC Eastern Div.	—	—		Weeb Ewbank
1972	7	7	0	.500	367	324	2nd/AFC Eastern Div.	—	—		Weeb Ewbank
1973	4	10	0	.286	240	306	T4th/AFC Eastern Div.	—	—		Weeb Ewbank
1974	7	7	0	.500	279	300	T3rd/AFC Eastern Div.	—	—		Charley Winner
1975	3	11	0	.214	258	433	T4th/AFC Eastern Div.	—	—		C. Winner, Ken Shipp
1976	3	11	0	.214	169	383	4th/AFC Eastern Div.	—	—		Lou Holtz, Mike Holovak
1977	3	11	0	.214	191	300	T4th/AFC Eastern Div.	—	—		Walt Michaels
1978	8	8	0	.500	359	364	3rd/AFC Eastern Div.	—	—		Walt Michaels
1979	8	8	0	.500	337	383	3rd/AFC Eastern Div.	—	—		Walt Michaels
1980	4	12	0	.250	302	395	5th/AFC Eastern Div.	—	—		Walt Michaels
1981	10	5	1	.656	355	287	2nd/AFC Eastern Div.	0	1	AFC wild-card game	Walt Michaels
1982	6	3	0	.667	245	166	T4th/AFC	2	1	AFC championship game	Walt Michaels
1983	7	9	0	.438	313	331	T4th/AFC Eastern Div.	—	—		Joe Walton
1984	7	9	0	.438	332	364	3rd/AFC Eastern Div.	—	—		Joe Walton
1985	11	5	0	.688	393	264	T2nd/AFC Eastern Div.	0	1	AFC wild-card game	Joe Walton
1986	10	6	0	.625	364	386	2nd/AFC Eastern Div.	1	1	AFC div. playoff game	Joe Walton
1987	6	9	0	.400	334	360	5th/AFC Eastern Div.	—	—		Joe Walton
1988	8	7	1	.531	372	354	4th/AFC Eastern Div.	—	—		Joe Walton
1989	4	12	0	.250	253	411	5th/AFC Eastern Div.	—	—		Joe Walton
1990	6	10	0	.375	295	345	4th/AFC Eastern Div.	—	—		Bruce Coslet
1991	8	8	0	.500	314	293	2nd/AFC Eastern Div.	0	1	AFC wild-card game	Bruce Coslet
1992	4	12	0	.250	220	315	4th/AFC Eastern Div.	—	—		Bruce Coslet
1993	8	8	0	.500	270	247	3rd/AFC Eastern Div.	—	—		Bruce Coslet
1994	6	10	0	.375	264	320	5th/AFC Eastern Div.	—	—		Pete Carroll
1995	3	13	0	.188	233	384	5th/AFC Eastern Div.	—	—		Rich Kotite
1996	1	15	0	.063	279	454	5th/AFC Eastern Div.	—	—		Rich Kotite
1997	9	7	0	.563	348	287	T2nd/AFC Eastern Div.	—	—		Bill Parcells
1998	12	4	0	.750	416	266	1st/AFC Eastern Div.	1	1	AFC championship game	Bill Parcells
1999	8	8	0	.500	308	309	4th/AFC Eastern Div.	—	—		Bill Parcells

*American Football League.
†New York Titans.

FIRST-ROUND DRAFT PICKS

1960—George Izo, QB, Notre Dame
1961—Tom Brown, G, Minnesota
1962—Sandy Stephens, QB, Minnesota
1963—Jerry Stovall, RB, Louisiana State
1964—Matt Snell, RB, Ohio State
1965—Joe Namath, QB, Alabama
        Tom Nowatzke, RB, Indiana
1966—Bill Yearby, DT, Michigan
1967—Paul Seiler, G, Notre Dame
1968—Lee White, RB, Weber State
1969—Dave Foley, T, Ohio State
1970—Steve Tannen, DB, Florida
1971—John Riggins, RB, Kansas
1972—Jerome Barkum, WR, Jackson State
1972—Mike Taylor, LB, Michigan
1973—Burgess Owens, DB, Miami
1974—Carl Barzilauskas, DT, Indiana
1975—None
1976—Richard Todd, QB, Alabama
1977—Marvin Powell, T, Southern California
1978—Chris Ward, T, Ohio State
1979—Marty Lyons, DT, Alabama
1980—Lam Jones, WR, Texas
1981—Freeman McNeil, RB, UCLA
1982—Bob Crable, LB, Notre Dame
1983—Ken O'Brien, QB, California-Davis
1984—Russell Carter, DB, Southern Methodist
        Ron Faurot, DE, Arkansas
1985—Al Toon, WR, Wisconsin
1986—Mike Haight, T, Iowa
1987—Roger Vick, FB, Texas A&M
1988—Dave Cadigan, T, Southern California
1989—Jeff Lageman, LB, Virginia
1990—Blair Thomas, RB, Penn State
1991—None
1992—Johnny Mitchell, TE, Nebraska
1993—Marvin Jones, LB, Florida State
1994—Aaron Glenn, DB, Texas A&M
1995—Kyle Brady, TE, Penn State
        Hugh Douglas, DE, Central State (O.)
1996—Keyshawn Johnson, WR, Southern California*
1997—James Farrior, LB, Virginia
1998—None
1999—None
2000—Shaun Ellis, DE, Tennessee
        John Abraham, LB, South Carolina
        Chad Pennington, QB, Marshall
        Anthony Becht, TE, West Virginia
*First player chosen in draft.

HISTORY — Team by team

FRANCHISE RECORDS

Most rushing yards, career
8,074—Freeman McNeil
Most rushing yards, season
1,464—Curtis Martin, 1999
Most rushing yards, game
199—Adrian Murrell at Ariz., Oct. 27, 1996
Most rushing touchdowns, season
11—Emerson Boozer, 1972
  Johnny Hector, 1987
  Brad Baxter, 1991
Most passing attempts, season
518—Richard Todd, 1983
Most passing attempts, game
62—Joe Namath vs. Bal., Oct. 18, 1970
Most passes completed, season
308—Richard Todd, 1983
Most passes completed, game
42—Richard Todd vs. S.F., Sept. 21, 1980
Most passing yards, career
27,057—Joe Namath

Most passing yards, season
4,007—Joe Namath, 1967
Most passing yards, game
496—Joe Namath at Bal., Sept. 24, 1972
Most touchdown passes, season
29—Vinny Testaverde, 1998
Most pass receptions, career
627—Don Maynard
Most pass receptions, season
93—Al Toon, 1988
Most pass receptions, game
17—Clark Gaines vs. S.F., Sept. 21, 1980
Most receiving yards, career
11,732—Don Maynard
Most receiving yards, season
1,434—Don Maynard, 1967
Most receiving yards, game
228—Don Maynard at Oak., Nov. 17, 1968
Most receiving touchdowns, season
14—Art Powell, 1960
  Don Maynard, 1965

Most touchdowns, career
88—Don Maynard
Most field goals, season
34—Jim Turner, 1968
Longest field goal
55 yards—Pat Leahy vs. Chi., Dec. 14, 1985
  John Hall at Sea., Aug. 31, 1997
Most interceptions, career
34—Bill Baird
Most interceptions, season
12—Dainard Paulson, 1964
Most sacks, career
107.5—Mark Gastineau
Most sacks, season
22—Mark Gastineau, 1984

SERIES RECORDS

N.Y. Jets vs.: Arizona 3-2; Atlanta 4-4; Baltimore, 1-1; Buffalo 34-45; Carolina 1-1; Chicago 2-4; Cincinnati 10-6; Cleveland 6-9; Dallas 2-5; Denver 13-13-1; Detroit 3-5; Green Bay 5-2; Indianapolis 23-36; Jacksonville 1-2; Kansas City 13-14-1; Miami 32-33-1; Minnesota 5-1; New England 43-35-1; New Orleans 4-4; N.Y. Giants 4-5; Oakland 10-17-2; Philadelphia 0-6; Pittsburgh 1-12; St. Louis 2-7; San Diego 9-17-1; San Francisco 1-7; Seattle 7-8; Tampa Bay 6-1; Tennessee 13-20-1; Washington 1-6.
NOTE: Includes records as New York Titans from 1960 through 1962.

COACHING RECORDS

Sammy Baugh, 14-14-0; Pete Carroll, 6-10-0; Bruce Coslet, 26-38-0 (0-1); Weeb Ewbank, 71-77-6 (2-1); Mike Holovak, 0-1-0; Lou Holtz, 3-10-0; Rich Kotite, 4-28-0; Walt Michaels, 39-47-1 (2-2); Bill Parcells, 29-19-0 (1-1); Ken Shipp, 1-4-0; Clyde Turner, 5-9-0; Joe Walton, 53-57-1 (1-2); Charley Winner, 9-14-0.
NOTE: Playoff games in parentheses.

RETIRED UNIFORM NUMBERS

No.	Player
12	Joe Namath
13	Don Maynard

OAKLAND RAIDERS
YEAR-BY-YEAR RECORDS

Year	W	L	T	Pct.	PF	PA	Finish	W	L	Highest round	Coach
1960*	6	8	0	.429	319	388	3rd/Western Div.	—	—		Eddie Erdelatz
1961*	2	12	0	.143	237	458	4th/Western Div.	—	—		E. Erdelatz, Marty Feldman
1962*	1	13	0	.071	213	370	4th/Western Div.	—	—		M. Feldman, Red Conkright
1963*	10	4	0	.714	363	288	2nd/Western Div.	—	—		Al Davis
1964*	5	7	2	.417	303	350	3rd/Western Div.	—	—		Al Davis
1965*	8	5	1	.615	298	239	2nd/Western Div.	—	—		Al Davis
1966*	8	5	1	.615	315	288	2nd/Western Div.	—	—		John Rauch
1967*	13	1	0	.929	468	233	1st/Western Div.	1	1	Super Bowl	John Rauch
1968*	12	2	0	.857	453	233	1st/Western Div.	1	1	AFL championship game	John Rauch
1969*	12	1	1	.923	377	242	1st/Western Div.	1	1	AFL championship game	John Madden
1970	8	4	2	.667	300	293	1st/AFC Western Div.	1	1	AFC championship game	John Madden
1971	8	4	2	.667	344	278	2nd/AFC Western Div.	—	—		John Madden
1972	10	3	1	.750	365	248	1st/AFC Western Div.	0	1	AFC div. playoff game	John Madden
1973	9	4	1	.679	292	175	1st/AFC Western Div.	1	1	AFC championship game	John Madden
1974	12	2	0	.857	355	228	1st/AFC Western Div.	1	1	AFC championship game	John Madden
1975	11	3	0	.786	375	255	1st/AFC Western Div.	1	1	AFC championship game	John Madden
1976	13	1	0	.929	350	237	1st/AFC Western Div.	3	0	Super Bowl champ	John Madden
1977	11	3	0	.786	351	230	2nd/AFC Western Div.	1	1	AFC championship game	John Madden
1978	9	7	0	.563	311	283	T2nd/AFC Western Div.	—	—		John Madden
1979	9	7	0	.563	365	337	T3rd/AFC Western Div.	—	—		Tom Flores
1980	11	5	0	.688	364	306	2nd/AFC Western Div.	4	0	Super Bowl champ	Tom Flores
1981	7	9	0	.438	273	343	4th/AFC Western Div.	—	—		Tom Flores
1982†	8	1	0	.889	260	200	1st/AFC	1	1	AFC second-round pl. game	Tom Flores

– 394 –

HISTORY — Team by team

REGULAR SEASON / PLAYOFFS

Year	W	L	T	Pct.	PF	PA	Finish	W	L	Highest round	Coach
1983†	12	4	0	.750	442	338	1st/AFC Western Div.	3	0	Super Bowl champ	Tom Flores
1984†	11	5	0	.688	368	278	3rd/AFC Western Div.	0	1	AFC wild-card game	Tom Flores
1985†	12	4	0	.750	354	308	1st/AFC Western Div.	0	1	AFC div. playoff game	Tom Flores
1986†	8	8	0	.500	323	346	4th/AFC Western Div.	—	—		Tom Flores
1987†	5	10	0	.333	301	289	4th/AFC Western Div.	—	—		Tom Flores
1988†	7	9	0	.438	325	369	3rd/AFC Western Div.	—	—		Mike Shanahan
1989†	8	8	0	.500	315	297	3rd/AFC Western Div.	—	—		Mike Shanahan, Art Shell
1990†	12	4	0	.750	337	268	1st/AFC Western Div.	1	1	AFC championship game	Art Shell
1991†	9	7	0	.563	298	297	3rd/AFC Western Div.	0	1	AFC wild-card game	Art Shell
1992†	7	9	0	.438	249	281	4th/AFC Western Div.	—	—		Art Shell
1993†	10	6	0	.625	306	326	2nd/AFC Western Div.	1	1	AFC div. playoff game	Art Shell
1994†	9	7	0	.563	303	327	2nd/AFC Western Div.	—	—		Art Shell
1995	8	8	0	.500	348	332	T3rd/AFC Western Div.	—	—		Mike White
1996	7	9	0	.438	340	293	T4th/AFC Western Div.	—	—		Mike White
1997	4	12	0	.250	324	419	T4th/AFC Western Div.	—	—		Joe Bugel
1998	8	8	0	.500	288	356	2nd/AFC Western Div.	—	—		Jon Gruden
1999	8	8	0	.500	390	329	4th/AFC Western Div.	—	—		Jon Gruden

*American Football League.
†Los Angeles Raiders.

FIRST-ROUND DRAFT PICKS

1960—Dale Hackbart, DB, Wisconsin
1961—Joe Rutgens, DT, Illinois
1962—Roman Gabriel, QB, North Carolina State* (AFL)
1963—None
1964—Tony Lorick, RB, Arizona State
1965—Harry Schuh, T, Memphis State
1966—Rodger Bird, DB, Kentucky
1967—Gene Upshaw, G, Texas A&I
1968—Eldridge Dickey, QB, Tenn. State
1969—Art Thoms, DT, Syracuse
1970—Raymond Chester, TE, Morgan State
1971—Jack Tatum, DB, Ohio State
1972—Mike Siani, WR, Villanova
1973—Ray Guy, P, So. Mississippi
1974—Henry Lawrence, T, Florida A&M
1975—Neal Colzie, DB, Ohio State
1976—None
1977—None
1978—None
1979—None
1980—Marc Wilson, QB, Brigham Young
1981—Ted Watts, DB, Texas Tech
    Curt Marsh, G, Washington
1982—Marcus Allen, RB, Southern California
1983—Don Mosebar, T, Southern California
1984—None
1985—Jessie Hester, WR, Florida State
1986—Bob Buczkowski, DT, Pittsburgh
1987—John Clay, T, Missouri
1988—Tim Brown, WR, Notre Dame
    Terry McDaniel, CB, Tennessee
    Scott Davis, DE, Illinois
1989—None
1990—Anthony Smith, DE, Arizona
1991—Todd Marinovich, QB, Southern California
1992—Chester McGlockton, DT, Clemson
1993—Patrick Bates, DB, Texas A&M
1994—Rob Fredrickson, LB, Michigan State
1995—Napoleon Kaufman, RB, Washington
1996—Rickey Dudley, TE, Ohio State
1997—Darrell Russell, DT, Southern California
1998—Charles Woodson, DB, Michigan
    Mo Collins, T, Florida
1999—Matt Stinchcomb, T, Georgia
2000—Sebastian Janikowski, PK, Florida State
*First player chosen in draft.

FRANCHISE RECORDS

Most rushing yards, career
8,545—Marcus Allen
Most rushing yards, season
1,759—Marcus Allen, 1985
Most rushing yards, game
221—Bo Jackson at Sea., Nov. 30, 1987
Most rushing touchdowns, season
16—Pete Banaszak, 1975
Most passing attempts, season
521—Jeff George, 1997
Most passing attempts, game
59—Todd Marinovich vs. Cle., Sept. 20, 1992
Most passes completed, season
304—Ken Stabler, 1979
    Rich Gannon, 1999
Most passes completed, game
34—Jim Plunkett at K.C., Sept. 12, 1985
Most passing yards, career
19,078—Ken Stabler

Most passing yards, season
3,917—Jeff George, 1997
Most passing yards, game
424—Jeff Hostetler vs. S.D., Oct. 18, 1993
Most touchdown passes, season
34—Daryle Lamonica, 1969
Most pass receptions, career
770—Tim Brown
Most pass receptions, season
104—Tim Brown, 1997
Most pass receptions, game
14—Tim Brown vs. Jac., Dec. 21, 1997
Most receiving yards, career
10,944—Tim Brown
Most receiving yards, season
1,408—Tim Brown, 1997
Most receiving yards, game
247—Art Powell vs. Hou., Dec. 22, 1963

Most receiving touchdowns, season
16—Art Powell, 1964
Most touchdowns, career
98—Marcus Allen
Most field goals, season
35—Jeff Jaeger, 1993
Longest field goal
54 yards—George Fleming vs. Den., Oct. 2, 1961
Most interceptions, career
39—Willie Brown
    Lester Hayes
Most interceptions, season
13—Lester Hayes, 1980
Most sacks, career
107.5—Greg Townsend
Most sacks, season
17.5—Tony Cline, 1970

SERIES RECORDS

Oakland vs.: Arizona 3-1; Atlanta 6-3; Baltimore 0-2; Buffalo 16-15; Carolina 0-1; Chicago 6-4; Cincinnati 16-7; Cleveland 9-3; Dallas 4-3; Denver 49-28-2; Detroit 6-2; Green Bay 5-3; Indianapolis 5-2; Jacksonville 1-1; Kansas City 37-40-2; Miami 15-8-1; Minnesota 7-3; New England 13-12-1; New Orleans 4-3-1; N.Y. Giants 6-2; N.Y. Jets 17-10-2; Philadelphia 3-4; Pittsburgh 7-5; St. Louis 7-2; San Diego 48-30-2; San Francisco 5-3; Seattle 24-20; Tampa Bay 4-1; Tennessee 20-15; Washington 6-3.
NOTE: Includes records as Los Angeles Raiders from 1982 through 1994.

COACHING RECORDS

Joe Bugel, 4-12-0; Red Conkright, 1-8-0; Al Davis, 23-16-3; Eddie Erdelatz, 6-10-0; Marty Feldman, 2-15-0; Tom Flores, 83-53-0 (8-3); Jon Gruden, 16-16-0; John Madden, 103-32-7 (9-7); John Rauch, 33-8-1 (2-2); Mike Shanahan, 8-12-0; Art Shell, 54-38-0 (2-3); Mike White, 15-17-0.
NOTE: Playoff games in parentheses.

RETIRED UNIFORM NUMBERS

No.	Player
	None

PHILADELPHIA EAGLES
YEAR-BY-YEAR RECORDS

		REGULAR SEASON					PLAYOFFS		
Year	W	L	T	Pct.	PF	PA	Finish	W	L	Highest round	Coach
1933	3	5	1	.375	77	158	4th/Eastern Div.	—	—		Lud Wray
1934	4	7	0	.364	127	85	T3rd/Eastern Div.	—	—		Lud Wray
1935	2	9	0	.182	60	179	5th/Eastern Div.	—	—		Lud Wray
1936	1	11	0	.083	51	206	5th/Eastern Div.	—	—		Bert Bell
1937	2	8	1	.200	86	177	5th/Eastern Div.	—	—		Bert Bell
1938	5	6	0	.455	154	164	4th/Eastern Div.	—	—		Bert Bell
1939	1	9	1	.100	105	200	T4th/Eastern Div.	—	—		Bert Bell
1940	1	10	0	.091	111	211	5th/Eastern Div.	—	—		Bert Bell
1941	2	8	1	.200	119	218	4th/Eastern Div.	—	—		Greasy Neale
1942	2	9	0	.182	134	239	5th/Eastern Div.	—	—		Greasy Neale
1943*	5	4	1	.556	225	230	3rd/Eastern Div.	—	—		G. Neale-Walt Kiesling
1944	7	1	2	.875	267	131	2nd/Eastern Div.	—	—		Greasy Neale
1945	7	3	0	.700	272	133	2nd/Eastern Div.	—	—		Greasy Neale
1946	6	5	0	.545	231	220	2nd/Eastern Div.	—	—		Greasy Neale
1947	8	4	0	.667	308	242	1st/Eastern Div.	1	1	NFL championship game	Greasy Neale
1948	9	2	1	.818	376	156	1st/Eastern Div.	1	0	NFL champ	Greasy Neale
1949	11	1	0	.917	364	134	1st/Eastern Div.	1	0	NFL champ	Greasy Neale
1950	6	6	0	.500	254	141	T3rd/American Conf.	—	—		Greasy Neale
1951	4	8	0	.333	234	264	5th/American Conf.	—	—		Bo McMillin, Wayne Millner
1952	7	5	0	.583	252	271	T2nd/American Conf.	—	—		Jim Trimble
1953	7	4	1	.636	352	215	2nd/Eastern Conf.	—	—		Jim Trimble
1954	7	4	1	.636	284	230	2nd/Eastern Conf.	—	—		Jim Trimble
1955	4	7	1	.364	248	231	T4th/Eastern Conf.	—	—		Jim Trimble
1956	3	8	1	.273	143	215	6th/Eastern Conf.	—	—		Hugh Devore
1957	4	8	0	.333	173	230	5th/Eastern Conf.	—	—		Hugh Devore
1958	2	9	1	.182	235	306	T5th/Eastern Conf.	—	—		Buck Shaw
1959	7	5	0	.583	268	278	T2nd/Eastern Conf.	—	—		Buck Shaw
1960	10	2	0	.833	321	246	1st/Eastern Conf.	1	0	NFL champ	Buck Shaw
1961	10	4	0	.714	361	297	2nd/Eastern Conf.	—	—		Nick Skorich
1962	3	10	1	.231	282	356	7th/Eastern Conf.	—	—		Nick Skorich
1963	2	10	2	.167	242	381	7th/Western Conf.	—	—		Nick Skorich
1964	6	8	0	.429	312	313	T3rd/Eastern Conf.	—	—		Joe Kuharich
1965	5	9	0	.357	363	359	T5th/Eastern Conf.	—	—		Joe Kuharich
1966	9	5	0	.643	326	340	T2nd/Eastern Conf.	—	—		Joe Kuharich
1967	6	7	1	.462	351	409	2nd/Capitol Div.	—	—		Joe Kuharich
1968	2	12	0	.143	202	351	4th/Capitol Div.	—	—		Joe Kuharich
1969	4	9	1	.308	279	377	4th/Capitol Div.	—	—		Jerry Williams
1970	3	10	1	.231	241	332	5th/NFC Eastern Div.	—	—		Jerry Williams
1971	6	7	1	.462	221	302	3rd/NFC Eastern Div.	—	—		J. Williams, Ed Khayat
1972	2	11	1	.179	145	352	5th/NFC Eastern Div.	—	—		Ed Khayat
1973	5	8	1	.393	310	393	3rd/NFC Eastern Div.	—	—		Mike McCormack
1974	7	7	0	.500	242	217	4th/NFC Eastern Div.	—	—		Mike McCormack
1975	4	10	0	.286	225	302	5th/NFC Eastern Div.	—	—		Mike McCormack
1976	4	10	0	.286	165	286	4th/NFC Eastern Div.	—	—		Dick Vermeil
1977	5	9	0	.357	220	207	T4th/NFC Eastern Div.	—	—		Dick Vermeil
1978	9	7	0	.563	270	250	2nd/NFC Eastern Div.	0	1	NFC wild-card game	Dick Vermeil
1979	11	5	0	.688	339	282	2nd/NFC Eastern Div.	1	1	NFC div. playoff game	Dick Vermeil
1980	12	4	0	.750	384	222	1st/NFC Eastern Div.	2	1	Super Bowl	Dick Vermeil
1981	10	6	0	.625	368	221	2nd/NFC Eastern Div.	0	1	NFC wild-card game	Dick Vermeil
1982	3	6	0	.333	191	195	T11th/NFC	—	—		Dick Vermeil

HISTORY — Team by team

Year	W	L	T	Pct.	PF	PA	Finish	W	L	Highest round	Coach
1983	5	11	0	.313	233	322	4th/NFC Eastern Div.	—	—		Marion Campbell
1984	6	9	1	.406	278	320	5th/NFC Eastern Div.	—	—		Marion Campbell
1985	7	9	0	.438	286	310	4th/NFC Eastern Div.	—	—		M. Campbell, Fred Bruney
1986	5	10	1	.344	256	312	4th/NFC Eastern Div.	—	—		Buddy Ryan
1987	7	8	0	.467	337	380	T2nd/NFC Eastern Div.	—	—		Buddy Ryan
1988	10	6	0	.625	379	319	1st/NFC Eastern Div.	0	1	NFC div. playoff game	Buddy Ryan
1989	11	5	0	.688	342	274	2nd/NFC Eastern Div.	0	1	NFC wild-card game	Buddy Ryan
1990	10	6	0	.625	396	299	T2nd/NFC Eastern Div.	0	1	NFC wild-card game	Buddy Ryan
1991	10	6	0	.625	285	244	3rd/NFC Eastern Div.	—	—		Rich Kotite
1992	11	5	0	.688	354	245	2nd/NFC Eastern Div.	1	1	NFC div. playoff game	Rich Kotite
1993	8	8	0	.500	293	315	3rd/NFC Eastern Div.	—	—		Rich Kotite
1994	7	9	0	.438	308	308	4th/NFC Eastern Div.	—	—		Rich Kotite
1995	10	6	0	.625	318	338	2nd/NFC Eastern Div.	1	1	NFC div. playoff game	Ray Rhodes
1996	10	6	0	.625	363	341	2nd/NFC Eastern Div.	0	1	NFC wild-card game	Ray Rhodes
1997	6	9	1	.406	317	372	3rd/NFC Eastern Div.	—	—		Ray Rhodes
1998	3	13	0	.188	161	344	5th/NFC Eastern Div.	—	—		Ray Rhodes
1999	5	11	0	.313	272	357	5th/NFC Eastern Div.	—	—		Andy Reid

*Phil-Pitt "Steagles," a combined squad of Philadelphia Eagles and Pittsburgh Steelers.

FIRST-ROUND DRAFT PICKS

1936—Jay Berwanger, B, Chicago*
1937—Sam Francis, B, Nebraska*
1938—John McDonald, B, Nebraska
1939—Davey O'Brien, QB, Texas Christian
1940—Wes McAfee, B, Duke
1941—None
1942—Pete Kmetovic, B, Stanford
1943—Joe Muha, B, Virginia Military
1944—Steve Van Buren, B, Louisiana State
1945—John Yonaker, E, Notre Dame
1946—Leo Riggs, B, Southern California
1947—Neil Armstrong, E, Oklahoma A&M
1948—Clyde Scott, B, Arkansas
1949—Chuck Bednarik, C, Pennsylvania*
      Frank Tripucka, QB, Notre Dame
1950—Bud Grant, E, Minnesota
1951—Ebert Van Buren, B, Louisiana State
      Chet Mutryn, B, Xavier
1952—John Bright, B, Drake
1953—None
1954—Neil Worden, B, Notre Dame
1955—Dick Bielski, B, Maryland
1956—Bob Pellegrini, C, Maryland
1957—Clarence Peaks, B, Michigan State
1958—Walter Kowalczyk, B, Michigan State
1959—None
1960—Ron Burton, B, Northwestern
1961—Art Baker, B, Syracuse
1962—None
1963—Ed Budde, T, Michigan State
1964—Bob Brown, T, Nebraska
1965—None
1966—Randy Beisler, T, Indiana
1967—Harry Jones, RB, Arkansas
1968—Tim Rossovich, DE, Southern California

1969—Leroy Keyes, RB, Purdue
1970—Steve Zabel, E, Oklahoma
1971—Richard Harris, DE, Grambling State
1972—John Reaves, QB, Florida
1973—Jerry Sisemore, T, Texas
      Charle Young, TE, Southern California
1974—None
1975—None
1976—None
1977—None
1978—None
1979—Jerry Robinson, LB, UCLA
1980—Roynell Young, DB, Alcorn State
1981—Leonard Mitchell, DE, Houston
1982—Mike Quick, WR, North Carolina State
1983—Michael Haddix, RB, Mississippi State
1984—Kenny Jackson, WR, Penn State
1985—Kevin Allen, T, Indiana
1986—Keith Byars, RB, Ohio State
1987—Jerome Brown, DT, Miami (Fla.)
1988—Keith Jackson, TE, Oklahoma
1989—None
1990—Ben Smith, DB, Georgia
1991—Antone Davis, T, Tennessee
1992—None
1993—Lester Holmes, T, Jackson State
      Leonard Renfro, DT, Colorado
1994—Bernard Williams, T, Georgia
1995—Mike Mamula, DE, Boston College
1996—Jermane Mayberry, T, Texas A&M-Kingsville
1997—Jon Harris, DE, Virginia
1998—Tra Thomas, T, Florida State
1999—Donovan McNabb, QB, Syracuse
2000—Corey Simon, DT, Florida State
    *First player chosen in draft.

FRANCHISE RECORDS

Most rushing yards, career
6,538—Wilbert Montgomery
Most rushing yards, season
1,512—Wilbert Montgomery, 1979
Most rushing yards, game
205—Steve Van Buren vs. Pit., Nov. 27, 1949
Most rushing touchdowns, season
15—Steve Van Buren, 1945

Most passing attempts, season
560—Randall Cunningham, 1988
Most passing attempts, game
62—Randall Cunningham at Chi., Oct. 2, 1989
Most passes completed, season
301—Randall Cunningham, 1988
Most passes completed, game
34—Randall Cunningham at Was., Sept. 17, 1989

Most passing yards, career
26,963—Ron Jaworski
Most passing yards, season
3,808—Randall Cunningham, 1988
Most passing yards, game
447—Randall Cunningham at Was., Sept. 17, 1989
Most touchdown passes, season
32—Sonny Jurgensen, 1961

HISTORY Team by team

Most pass receptions, career
589—Harold Carmichael
Most pass receptions, season
88—Irving Fryar, 1996
Most pass receptions, game
14—Don Looney at Was., Dec. 1, 1940
Most receiving yards, career
8,978—Harold Carmichael
Most receiving yards, season
1,409—Mike Quick, 1983
Most receiving yards, game
237—Tommy McDonald vs. NYG, Dec. 10, 1961

Most receiving touchdowns, season
13—Tommy McDonald, 1960
Tommy McDonald, 1961
Mike Quick, 1983
Most touchdowns, career
79—Harold Carmichael
Most field goals, season
30—Paul McFadden, 1984
Longest field goal
59 yards—Tony Franklin at Dal., Nov. 12, 1979
Most interceptions, career
34—Eric Allen
Bill Bradley

Most interceptions, season
11—Bill Bradley, 1971
Most sacks, career
124—Reggie White
Most sacks, season
21—Reggie White, 1987

SERIES RECORDS

Philadelphia vs.: Arizona 49-51-5; Atlanta 9-9-1; Baltimore, 0-0-1; Buffalo 4-5; Carolina 1-1; Chicago 5-25-1; Cincinnati 2-6; Cleveland 12-31-1; Dallas 30-48; Denver 6-3; Detroit 11-11-2; Green Bay 9-21; Indianapolis 6-8; Jacksonville 0-1; Kansas City 1-2; Miami 3-7; Minnesota 6-11; New England 6-2; New Orleans 12-8; N.Y. Giants 59-69-2; N.Y. Jets 6-0; Oakland 4-3; Pittsburgh 44-26-3; St. Louis 14-14-1; San Diego 2-5; San Francisco 6-14-1; Seattle 4-3; Tampa Bay 3-3; Tennessee 6-0; Washington 56-66-6.
NOTE: Includes records when team combined with Pittsburgh squad and was known as Phil-Pitt in 1943.

COACHING RECORDS

Bert Bell, 10-44-2; Fred Bruney, 1-0-0; Marion Campbell, 17-29-1; Hugh Devore, 7-16-1; Ed Khayat, 8-15-2; Rich Kotite, 36-28-0 (1-1); Joe Kuharich, 28-41-1; Mike McCormack, 16-25-1; Alvin McMillin, 2-0-0; Wayne Millner, 2-8-0; Earle (Greasy) Neale, 63-43-5 (3-1); Andy Reid, 5-11-0; Ray Rhodes, 29-34-1 (1-2); Buddy Ryan, 43-35-1 (0-3); Buck Shaw, 19-16-1 (1-0); Nick Skorich, 15-24-3; Jim Trimble, 25-20-3; Dick Vermeil, 54-47-0 (3-4); Jerry Williams, 7-22-2; Lud Wray, 9-21-1.
NOTE: Playoff games in parentheses.

RETIRED UNIFORM NUMBERS

No.	Player
15	Steve Van Buren
40	Tom Brookshier
44	Pete Retzlaff
60	Chuck Bednarik
70	Al Wistert
99	Jerome Brown

PITTSBURGH STEELERS
YEAR-BY-YEAR RECORDS

		REGULAR SEASON					PLAYOFFS			
Year	W	L	T	Pct.	PF	PA	Finish	W	L	Highest round	Coach
1933*	3	6	2	.333	67	208	5th/Eastern Div.	—	—		Jap Douds
1934*	2	10	0	.167	51	206	5th/Eastern Div.	—	—		Luby DiMello
1935*	4	8	0	.333	100	209	3rd/Eastern Div.	—	—		Joe Bach
1936*	6	6	0	.500	98	187	2nd/Eastern Div.	—	—		Joe Bach
1937*	4	7	0	.364	122	145	3rd/Eastern Div.	—	—		Johnny Blood
1938*	2	9	0	.182	79	169	5th/Eastern Div.	—	—		Johnny Blood
1939*	1	9	1	.100	114	216	T4th/Eastern Div.	—	—		J. Blood-W. Kiesling
1940*	2	7	2	.222	60	178	4th/Eastern Div.	—	—		Walt Kiesling
1941	1	9	1	.100	103	276	5th/Eastern Div.	—	—		Bert Bell-Buff Donelli-Walt Kiesling
1942	7	4	0	.636	167	119	2nd/Eastern Div.	—	—		Walt Kiesling
1943†	5	4	1	.556	225	230	3rd/Eastern Div.	—	—		W. Kiesling-Greasy Neale
1944‡	0	10	0	.000	108	328	5th/Western Div.	—	—		W. Kiesling-Phil Handler
1945	2	8	0	.200	79	220	5th/Eastern Div.	—	—		Jim Leonard
1946	5	5	1	.500	136	117	T3rd/Eastern Div.	—	—		Jock Sutherland
1947	8	4	0	.667	240	259	2nd/Eastern Div.	0	1	E. Div. champ. game	Jock Sutherland
1948	4	8	0	.333	200	243	T3rd/Eastern Div.	—	—		John Michelosen
1949	6	5	1	.545	224	214	2nd/Eastern Div.	—	—		John Michelosen
1950	6	6	0	.500	180	195	T3rd/American Conf.	—	—		John Michelosen
1951	4	7	1	.364	183	235	4th/American Conf.	—	—		John Michelosen
1952	5	7	0	.417	300	273	3rd/American Conf.	—	—		Joe Bach
1953	6	6	0	.500	211	263	4th/Eastern Conf.	—	—		Joe Bach
1954	5	7	0	.417	219	263	4th/Eastern Conf.	—	—		Walt Kiesling
1955	4	8	0	.333	195	285	6th/Eastern Conf.	—	—		Walt Kiesling
1956	5	7	0	.417	217	250	5th/Eastern Conf.	—	—		Walt Kiesling
1957	6	6	0	.500	161	178	3rd/Eastern Conf.	—	—		Buddy Parker
1958	7	4	1	.636	261	230	3rd/Eastern Conf.	—	—		Buddy Parker
1959	6	5	1	.545	257	216	4th/Eastern Conf.	—	—		Buddy Parker
1960	5	6	1	.455	240	275	5th/Eastern Conf.	—	—		Buddy Parker
1961	6	8	0	.429	295	287	5th/Eastern Conf.	—	—		Buddy Parker
1962	9	5	0	.643	312	363	2nd/Eastern Conf.	—	—		Buddy Parker

— 398 —

HISTORY Team by team

Year	W	L	T	Pct.	PF	PA	Finish	W	L	Highest round	Coach
1963	7	4	3	.636	321	295	4th/Eastern Conf.	—	—		Buddy Parker
1964	5	9	0	.357	253	315	6th/Eastern Conf.	—	—		Buddy Parker
1965	2	12	0	.143	202	397	7th/Eastern Conf.	—	—		Mike Nixon
1966	5	8	1	.385	316	347	6th/Eastern Conf.	—	—		Bill Austin
1967	4	9	1	.308	281	320	4th/Century Div.	—	—		Bill Austin
1968	2	11	1	.154	244	397	4th/Century Div.	—	—		Bill Austin
1969	1	13	0	.071	218	404	4th/Century Div.	—	—		Chuck Noll
1970	5	9	0	.357	210	272	3rd/AFC Central Div.	—	—		Chuck Noll
1971	6	8	0	.429	246	292	2nd/AFC Central Div.	—	—		Chuck Noll
1972	11	3	0	.786	343	175	1st/AFC Central Div.	1	1	AFC championship game	Chuck Noll
1973	10	4	0	.714	347	210	2nd/AFC Central Div.	0	1	AFC div. playoff game	Chuck Noll
1974	10	3	1	.750	305	189	1st/AFC Central Div.	3	0	Super Bowl champ	Chuck Noll
1975	12	2	0	.857	373	162	1st/AFC Central Div.	3	0	Super Bowl champ	Chuck Noll
1976	10	4	0	.714	342	138	1st/AFC Central Div.	1	1	AFC championship game	Chuck Noll
1977	9	5	0	.643	283	243	1st/AFC Central Div.	0	1	AFC div. playoff game	Chuck Noll
1978	14	2	0	.875	356	195	1st/AFC Central Div.	3	0	Super Bowl champ	Chuck Noll
1979	12	4	0	.750	416	262	1st/AFC Central Div.	3	0	Super Bowl champ	Chuck Noll
1980	9	7	0	.563	352	313	3rd/AFC Central Div.	—	—		Chuck Noll
1981	8	8	0	.500	356	297	2nd/AFC Central Div.	—	—		Chuck Noll
1982	6	3	0	.667	204	146	T4th/AFC	0	1	AFC first-round pl. game	Chuck Noll
1983	10	6	0	.625	355	303	1st/AFC Central Div.	0	1	AFC div. playoff game	Chuck Noll
1984	9	7	0	.563	387	310	1st/AFC Central Div.	1	1	AFC championship game	Chuck Noll
1985	7	9	0	.438	379	355	T2nd/AFC Central Div.	—	—		Chuck Noll
1986	6	10	0	.375	307	336	3rd/AFC Central Div.	—	—		Chuck Noll
1987	8	7	0	.533	285	299	3rd/AFC Central Div.	—	—		Chuck Noll
1988	5	11	0	.313	336	421	4th/AFC Central Div.	—	—		Chuck Noll
1989	9	7	0	.563	265	326	T2nd/AFC Central Div.	1	1	AFC div. playoff game	Chuck Noll
1990	9	7	0	.563	292	240	3rd/AFC Central Div.	—	—		Chuck Noll
1991	7	9	0	.438	292	344	2nd/AFC Central Div.	—	—		Chuck Noll
1992	11	5	0	.688	299	225	1st/AFC Central Div.	0	1	AFC div. playoff game	Bill Cowher
1993	9	7	0	.563	308	281	2nd/AFC Central Div.	0	1	AFC wild-card game	Bill Cowher
1994	12	4	0	.750	316	234	1st/AFC Central Div.	1	1	AFC championship game	Bill Cowher
1995	11	5	0	.689	407	327	1st/AFC Central Div.	2	1	Super Bowl	Bill Cowher
1996	10	6	0	.625	344	257	1st/AFC Central Div.	1	1	AFC div. playoff game	Bill Cowher
1997	11	5	0	.688	372	307	1st/AFC Central Div.	1	1	AFC championship game	Bill Cowher
1998	7	9	0	.438	263	303	3rd/AFC Central Div.	—	—		Bill Cowher
1999	6	10	0	.375	317	320	4th/AFC Central Div.	—	—		Bill Cowher

*Pittsburgh Pirates.
†Phil-Pitt "Steagles," a combined squad of Philadelphia Eagles and Pittsburgh Steelers.
‡Card-Pitt, a combined squad of Chicago Cardinals and Pittsburgh Steelers.

FIRST-ROUND DRAFT PICKS

1936—Bill Shakespeare, B, Notre Dame
1937—Mike Basrak, C, Duquesne
1938—Byron White, B, Colorado
       Frank Filchock, B, Indiana
1939—None
1940—Kay Eakin, B, Arkansas
1941—Chet Gladchuk, C, Boston College
1942—Bill Dudley, B, Virginia*
1943—Bill Daley, B, Minnesota
1944—Johnny Podesto, B, St. Mary's (Calif.)
1945—Paul Duhart, B, Florida
1946—Doc Blanchard, B, Army
1947—Hub Bechtol, E, Texas
1948—Dan Edwards, E, Georgia
1949—Bobby Gage, B, Clemson
1950—Lynn Chandnois, B, Michigan State
1951—Clarence Avinger, B, Alabama
1952—Ed Modzelewski, B, Maryland
1953—Ted Marchibroda, QB, St. Bonaventure
1954—John Lattner, B, Notre Dame
1955—Frank Varrichione, T, Notre Dame
1956—Gary Glick, B, Colorado State*
       Art Davis, B, Mississippi State
1957—Len Dawson, QB, Purdue
1958—None
1959—None
1960—Jack Spikes, B, Texas Christian
1961—None
1962—Bob Ferguson, RB, Ohio State
1963—None
1964—Paul Martha, RB, Pittsburgh
1965—None
1966—Dick Leftridge, RB, West Virginia
1967—None
1968—Mike Taylor, T, Southern California
1969—Joe Greene, DT, North Texas State
1970—Terry Bradshaw, QB, Louisiana Tech*
1971—Frank Lewis, WR, Grambling State
1972—Franco Harris, RB, Penn State
1973—James Thomas, DB, Florida State
1974—Lynn Swann, WR, Southern California
1975—Dave Brown, DB, Michigan
1976—Bennie Cunningham, TE, Clemson
1977—Robin Cole, LB, New Mexico
1978—Ron Johnson, DB, Eastern Michigan
1979—Greg Hawthorne, RB, Baylor
1980—Mark Malone, QB, Arizona State
1981—Keith Gary, DE, Oklahoma
1982—Walter Abercrombie, RB, Baylor
1983—Gabriel Rivera, DT, Texas Tech
1984—Louis Lipps, WR, Southern Mississippi
1985—Darryl Sims, DT, Wisconsin
1986—John Rienstra, G, Temple
1987—Rod Woodson, DB, Purdue
1988—Aaron Jones, DE, Eastern Kentucky
1989—Tim Worley, RB, Georgia

– 399 –

Tom Ricketts, T, Pittsburgh
1990—Eric Green, TE, Liberty (Va.)
1991—Huey Richardson, LB, Florida
1992—Leon Searcy, T, Miami (Fla.)
1993—Deon Figures, DB, Colorado
1994—Charles Johnson, WR, Colorado
1995—Mark Bruener, TE, Washington
1996—Jermain Stephens, T, North Carolina A&T
1997—Chad Scott, DB, Maryland
1998—Alan Faneca, G, Louisiana State
1999—Troy Edwards, WR, Louisiana Tech
2000—Plaxico Burress, WR, Michigan State
*First player chosen in draft.

FRANCHISE RECORDS

Most rushing yards, career
11,950—Franco Harris
Most rushing yards, season
1,690—Barry Foster, 1992
Most rushing yards, game
218—John Fuqua at Phi., Dec. 20, 1970
Most rushing touchdowns, season
14—Franco Harris, 1976
Most passing attempts, season
486—Neil O'Donnell, 1993
Most passing attempts, game
55—Neil O'Donnell vs. G.B., Dec. 24, 1995
Most passes completed, season
270—Neil O'Donnell, 1993
Most passes completed, game
34—Neil O'Donnell at Chi., Nov. 5, 1995 (OT)
31—Joe Gilliam at Den., Sept. 22, 1974 (OT)
30—Terry Bradshaw vs. Cle., Nov. 25, 1979 (OT)
29—Terry Bradshaw vs. Cin., Sept. 19, 1982 (OT)
28—Kent Nix vs. Dal., Oct. 22, 1967

Most passing yards, career
27,989—Terry Bradshaw
Most passing yards, season
3,724—Terry Bradshaw, 1979
Most passing yards, game
409—Bobby Layne vs. Chi. Cardinals, Dec. 13, 1958
Most touchdown passes, season
28—Terry Bradshaw, 1978
Most pass receptions, career
537—John Stallworth
Most pass receptions, season
85—Yancey Thigpen, 1995
Most pass receptions, game
14—Courtney Hawkins vs. Ten., Nov. 1, 1998
Most receiving yards, career
8,723—John Stallworth
Most receiving yards, season
1,398—Yancey Thigpen, 1997
Most receiving yards, game
235—Buddy Dial vs. Cle., Oct. 22, 1961

Most receiving touchdowns, season
12—Buddy Dial, 1961
Louis Lipps, 1985
Most touchdowns, career
100—Franco Harris
Most field goals, season
34—Norm Johnson, 1995
Longest field goal
55 yards—Gary Anderson vs. S.D., Nov. 25, 1984
Most interceptions, career
57—Mel Blount
Most interceptions, season
11—Mel Blount, 1975
Most sacks, career
73.5—L.C. Greenwood
Most sacks, season
15—Mike Merriweather, 1984

SERIES RECORDS

Pittsburgh vs.: Arizona 30-21-3; Atlanta 11-1; Baltimore 6-2; Buffalo 8-8; Carolina 1-1; Chicago 6-19-1; Cincinnati 33-26; Cleveland 41-53; Dallas 11-14; Denver 6-10-1; Detroit 12-14-1; Green Bay 12-21; Indianapolis 13-4; Jacksonville 4-6; Kansas City 15-7; Miami 6-9; Minnesota 4-8; New England 11-4; New Orleans 6-5; N.Y. Giants 28-44-3; N.Y. Jets 13-1; Oakland 5-7; Philadelphia 26-44-3; St. Louis 6-17-2; San Diego 16-5; San Francisco 8-9; Seattle 6-7; Tampa Bay 4-1; Tennessee 35-24; Washington 25-39-4.
NOTE: Includes records as Pittsburgh Pirates from 1933 through 1940; also includes records when team combined with Philadelphia squad and was known as Phil-Pitt in 1943 and when team combined with Chicago Cardinals squad and was known as Card-Pitt in 1944.

COACHING RECORDS

Bill Austin, 11-28-3; Joe Bach, 21-27-0; Bert Bell, 0-2-0; Bill Cowher, 77-51-0 (5-6); Luby DiMelio, 2-10-0; Aldo Donelli, 0-5-0; Forrest Douds, 3-6-2; Walt Kiesling, 30-55-5; Jim Leonard, 2-8-0; Johnny (Blood) McNally, 6-19-0; Johnny Michelosen, 20-26-2; Mike Nixon, 2-12-0; Chuck Noll, 193-148-1 (16-8); Buddy Parker, 51-47-6 (0-1); Jock Sutherland, 13-9-1 (0-1).
NOTE: Playoff games in parentheses.

RETIRED UNIFORM NUMBERS

No.	Player
	None

ST. LOUIS RAMS
YEAR-BY-YEAR RECORDS

	REGULAR SEASON						PLAYOFFS			
Year	W	L	T	Pct.	PF	PA	Finish	W	L	Highest round	Coach
1937*	1	10	0	.091	75	207	5th/Western Div.	—	—		Hugo Bezdek
1938*	4	7	0	.364	131	215	4th/Western Div.	—	—		Hugo Bezdek, Art Lewis
1939*	5	5	1	.500	195	164	4th/Western Div.	—	—		Dutch Clark
1940*	4	6	1	.400	171	191	4th/Western Div.	—	—		Dutch Clark
1941*	2	9	0	.182	116	244	5th/Western Div.	—	—		Dutch Clark
1942*	5	6	0	.455	150	207	3rd/Western Div.	—	—		Dutch Clark
1943*	Rams did not play in 1943.										
1944*	4	6	0	.400	188	224	4th/Western Div.	—	—		Buff Donelli
1945*	9	1	0	.900	244	136	1st/Western Div.	1	0	NFL champ	Adam Walsh
1946†	6	4	1	.600	277	257	2nd/Western Div.	—	—		Adam Walsh

– 400 –

HISTORY Team by team

REGULAR SEASON / PLAYOFFS

Year	W	L	T	Pct.	PF	PA	Finish	W	L	Highest round	Coach
1947†	6	6	0	.500	259	214	4th/Western Div.	—	—		Bob Snyder
1948†	6	5	1	.545	327	269	3rd/Western Div.	—	—		Clark Shaughnessy
1949†	8	2	2	.800	360	239	1st/Western Div.	0	1	NFL championship game	Clark Shaughnessy
1950†	9	3	0	.750	466	309	1st/National Conf.	1	1	NFL championship game	Joe Stydahar
1951†	8	4	0	.667	392	261	1st/National Conf.	1	0	NFL champ	Joe Stydahar
1952†	9	3	0	.750	349	234	2nd/National Conf.	0	1	Nat. Conf. champ. game	J. Stydahar, Hamp Pool
1953†	8	3	1	.727	366	236	3rd/Western Conf.	—	—		Hamp Pool
1954†	6	5	1	.545	314	285	4th/Western Conf.	—	—		Hamp Pool
1955†	8	3	1	.727	260	231	1st/Western Conf.	0	1	NFL championship game	Sid Gillman
1956†	4	8	0	.333	291	307	6th/Western Conf.	—	—		Sid Gillman
1957†	6	6	0	.500	307	278	4th/Western Conf.	—	—		Sid Gillman
1958†	8	4	0	.667	344	278	T2nd/Western Conf.	—	—		Sid Gillman
1959†	2	10	0	.167	242	315	6th/Western Conf.	—	—		Sid Gillman
1960†	4	7	1	.364	265	297	6th/Western Conf.	—	—		Bob Waterfield
1961†	4	10	0	.286	263	333	6th/Western Conf.	—	—		Bob Waterfield
1962†	1	12	1	.077	220	334	7th/Western Conf.	—	—		B. Waterfield, H. Svare
1963†	5	9	0	.357	210	350	6th/Western Conf.	—	—		Harland Svare
1964†	5	7	2	.417	283	339	5th/Western Conf.	—	—		Harland Svare
1965†	4	10	0	.286	269	328	7th/Western Conf.	—	—		Harland Svare
1966†	8	6	0	.571	289	212	3rd/Western Conf.	—	—		George Allen
1967†	11	1	2	.917	398	196	1st/Coastal Div.	0	1	W. Conf. champ. game	George Allen
1968†	10	3	1	.769	312	200	2nd/Coastal Div.	—	—		George Allen
1969†	11	3	0	.786	320	243	1st/Coastal Div.	0	1	W. Conf. champ. game	George Allen
1970†	9	4	1	.692	325	202	2nd/NFC Western Div.	—	—		George Allen
1971†	8	5	1	.615	313	260	2nd/NFC Western Div.	—	—		Tommy Prothro
1972†	6	7	1	.464	291	286	3rd/NFC Western Div.	—	—		Tommy Prothro
1973†	12	2	0	.857	388	178	1st/NFC Western Div.	0	1	NFC div. playoff game	Chuck Knox
1974†	10	4	0	.714	263	181	1st/NFC Western Div.	1	1	NFC championship game	Chuck Knox
1975†	12	2	0	.857	312	135	1st/NFC Western Div.	1	1	NFC championship game	Chuck Knox
1976†	10	3	1	.750	351	190	1st/NFC Western Div.	1	1	NFC championship game	Chuck Knox
1977†	10	4	0	.714	302	146	1st/NFC Western Div.	0	1	NFC div. playoff game	Chuck Knox
1978†	12	4	0	.750	316	245	1st/NFC Western Div.	1	1	NFC championship game	Ray Malavasi
1979†	9	7	0	.563	323	309	1st/NFC Western Div.	2	1	Super Bowl	Ray Malavasi
1980†	11	5	0	.688	424	289	2nd/NFC Western Div.	0	1	NFC wild-card game	Ray Malavasi
1981†	6	10	0	.375	303	351	3rd/NFC Western Div.	—	—		Ray Malavasi
1982†	2	7	0	.222	200	250	14th/NFC	—	—		Ray Malavasi
1983†	9	7	0	.563	361	344	2nd/NFC Western Div.	1	1	NFC div. playoff game	John Robinson
1984†	10	6	0	.625	346	316	2nd/NFC Western Div.	0	1	NFC wild-card game	John Robinson
1985†	11	5	0	.688	340	277	1st/NFC Western Div.	1	1	NFC championship game	John Robinson
1986†	10	6	0	.625	309	267	2nd/NFC Western Div.	0	1	NFC wild-card game	John Robinson
1987†	6	9	0	.400	317	361	3rd/NFC Western Div.	—	—		John Robinson
1988†	10	6	0	.625	407	293	2nd/NFC Western Div.	0	1	NFC wild-card game	John Robinson
1989†	11	5	0	.688	426	344	2nd/NFC Western Div.	2	1	NFC championship game	John Robinson
1990†	5	11	0	.313	345	412	T3rd/NFC Western Div.	—	—		John Robinson
1991†	3	13	0	.188	234	390	4th/NFC Western Div.	—	—		John Robinson
1992†	6	10	0	.375	313	383	T3rd/NFC Western Div.	—	—		Chuck Knox
1993†	5	11	0	.313	221	367	4th/NFC Western Div.	—	—		Chuck Knox
1994†	4	12	0	.250	286	365	4th/NFC Western Div.	—	—		Chuck Knox
1995	7	9	0	.438	309	418	T3rd/NFC Western Div.	—	—		Rich Brooks
1996	6	10	0	.375	303	409	3rd/NFC Western Div.	—	—		Rich Brooks
1997	5	11	0	.313	299	359	5th/NFC Western Div.	—	—		Dick Vermeil
1998	4	12	0	.250	285	378	5th/NFC Western Div.	—	—		Dick Vermeil
1999	13	3	0	.813	526	242	1st/NFC Western Div.	3	0	Super Bowl champ	Dick Vermeil

*Cleveland Rams.
†Los Angeles Rams.

FIRST-ROUND DRAFT PICKS

1937—Johnny Drake, B, Purdue
1938—Corbett Davis, B, Indiana*
1939—Parker Hall, B, Mississippi
1940—Ollie Cordill, B, Rice
1941—Rudy Mucha, C, Washington
1942—Jack Wilson, B, Baylor
1943—Mike Holovak, B, Boston College
1944—Tony Butkovich, B, Illinois
1945—Elroy Hirsch, B, Wisconsin
1946—Emil Sitko, B, Notre Dame
1947—Herman Wedemeyer, B, St. Mary's (Cal.)
1948—None
1949—Bobby Thomason, B, Virginia Military

1950—Ralph Pasquariello, B, Villanova
       Stan West, G, Oklahoma
1951—Bud McFadin, G, Texas
1952—Bill Wade, B, Vanderbilt*
       Bob Carey, E, Michigan State
1953—Donn Moomaw, C, UCLA
       Ed Barker, E, Washington State
1954—Ed Beatty, C, Cincinnati
1955—Larry Morris, C, Georgia Tech
1956—Joe Marconi, B, West Virginia
       Charlie Horton, B, Vanderbilt
1957—Jon Arnett, B, Southern California
       Del Shofner, B, Baylor

HISTORY — Team by team

1958—Lou Michaels, T, Kentucky
Jim Phillips, E, Auburn
1959—Dick Bass, B, Pacific
Paul Dickson, G, Baylor
1960—Billy Cannon, RB, Louisiana State*
1961—Marlin McKeever, LB, Southern California
1962—Roman Gabriel, QB, North Carolina State
Merlin Olsen, DT, Utah State
1963—Terry Baker, QB, Oregon State*
Rufus Guthrie, G, Georgia Tech
1964—Bill Munson, QB, Utah State
1965—Clancy Williams, DB, Washington State
1966—Tom Mack, G, Michigan
1967—None
1968—None
1969—Larry Smith, RB, Florida
Jim Seymour, E, Notre Dame
Bob Klein, TE, Southern California
1970—Jack Reynolds, LB, Tennessee
1971—Isiah Robertson, LB, Southern
Jack Youngblood, DE, Florida
1972—None
1973—None
1974—John Cappelletti, RB, Penn State
1975—Mike Fanning, DT, Notre Dame
Dennis Harrah, G, Miami (Fla.)
Doug France, T, Ohio State
1976—Kevin McLain, LB, Colorado State
1977—Bob Brudzinski, LB, Ohio State
1978—Elvis Peacock, RB, Oklahoma
1979—George Andrews, LB, Nebraska
Kent Hill, G, Georgia Tech
1980—Johnnie Johnson, DB, Texas
1981—Mel Owens, LB, Michigan
1982—Barry Redden, RB, Richmond
1983—Eric Dickerson, RB, Southern Methodist
1984—None
1985—Jerry Gray, DB, Texas
1986—Mike Schad, T, Queens College (Ont.)
1987—None
1988—Gaston Green, RB, UCLA
Aaron Cox, WR, Arizona State
1989—Bill Hawkins, DE, Miami (Fla.)
Cleveland Gary, RB, Miami (Fla.)
1990—Bern Brostek, C, Washington
1991—Todd Lyght, CB, Notre Dame
1992—Sean Gilbert, DE, Pittsburgh
1993—Jerome Bettis, RB, Notre Dame
1994—Wayne Gandy, T, Auburn
1995—Kevin Carter, DE, Florida
1996—Lawrence Phillips, RB, Nebraska
Eddie Kennison, WR, Louisiana State
1997—Orlando Pace, T, Ohio State*
1998—Grant Wistrom, DE, Nebraska
1999—Torry Holt, WR, North Carolina State
2000—Trung Canidate, RB, Arizona
*First player chosen in draft.

FRANCHISE RECORDS

Most rushing yards, career
7,245—Eric Dickerson
Most rushing yards, season
2,105—Eric Dickerson, 1984
Most rushing yards, game
247—Willie Ellison vs. N.O., Dec. 5, 1971
Most rushing touchdowns, season
18—Eric Dickerson, 1983
Most passing attempts, season
554—Jim Everett, 1990
Most passing attempts, game
55—Mark Rypien vs. Buf., Dec. 10, 1995
Most passes completed, season
325—Kurt Warner, 1999
Most passes completed, game
35—Dieter Brock vs. S.F., Oct. 27, 1985
Most passing yards, career
23,758—Jim Everett
Most passing yards, season
4,353—Kurt Warner, 1999

Most passing yards, game
554—Norm Van Brocklin at N.Y. Yanks, Sept. 28, 1951
Most touchdown passes, season
41—Kurt Warner, 1999
Most pass receptions, career
593—Henry Ellard
Most pass receptions, season
119—Isaac Bruce, 1995
Most pass receptions, game
18—Tom Fears vs. G.B., Dec. 3, 1950
Most receiving yards, career
9,761—Henry Ellard
Most receiving yards, season
1,781—Isaac Bruce, 1995
Most receiving yards, game
336—Willie Anderson at N.O., Nov. 26, 1989
Most receiving touchdowns, season
17—Elroy Hirsch, 1951

Most touchdowns, career
58—Eric Dickerson
Most field goals, season
30—David Ray, 1973
Longest field goal
57 yards—Jeff Wilkins vs. Ari., Sept. 27, 1998
Most interceptions, career
46—Ed Meador
Most interceptions, season
14—Night Train Lane, 1952
Most sacks, career
151.5—Deacon Jones
Most sacks, season
22—Deacon Jones, 1964
Deacon Jones, 1968

SERIES RECORDS

St. Louis vs.: Arizona 16-14-2; Atlanta 41-23-2; Baltimore 1-1; Buffalo 4-4; Carolina 5-5; Chicago 27-36-3; Cincinnati 4-5; Cleveland 8-8; Dallas 9-8; Denver 4-4; Detroit 32-28-1; Green Bay 40-27-1; Indianapolis 17-21-2; Jacksonville 1-0; Kansas City 4-2; Miami 1-7; Minnesota 11-16-2; New England 4-3; New Orleans 33-25; N.Y. Giants 21-7; N.Y. Jets 7-2; Oakland 2-7; Philadelphia 14-14-1; Pittsburgh 17-6-2; San Diego 3-3; San Francisco 49-47-2; Seattle 4-2; Tampa Bay 8-3; Tennessee 5-3; Washington 7-16-1.
NOTE: Includes records as Los Angeles Rams from 1946 through 1994.

COACHING RECORDS

George Allen, 47-17-4 (2-2); Hugo Bezdek, 1-13-0; Rich Brooks, 13-19-0; Dutch Clark, 16-26-2; Aldo Donelli, 4-6-0; Sid Gillman, 28-31-1 (0-1); Chuck Knox, 69-48-1 (3-5); Art Lewis, 4-4-0; Ray Malavasi, 40-33-0 (3-3); Hamp Pool, 23-10-2 (0-1); Tommy Prothro, 14-12-2; John Robinson, 75-68-0 (4-6); Clark Shaughnessy, 14-7-3 (0-1); Bob Snyder, 6-6-0; Joe Stydahar, 17-8-0 (2-1); Harland Svare, 14-31-3; Dick Vermeil, 22-26-0 (3-0); Adam Walsh, 15-5-1 (1-0); Bob Waterfield, 9-24-1.
NOTE: Playoff games in parentheses.

RETIRED UNIFORM NUMBERS

No.	Player
7	Bob Waterfield
74	Merlin Olsen
78	Jackie Slater

SAN DIEGO CHARGERS
YEAR-BY-YEAR RECORDS

		REGULAR SEASON					PLAYOFFS			
Year	W	L	T	Pct.	PF	PA	Finish	W	L	Highest round	Coach
1960*†	10	4	0	.714	373	336	1st/Western Div.	0	1	AFL championship game	Sid Gillman
1961*	12	2	0	.857	396	219	1st/Western Div.	0	1	AFL championship game	Sid Gillman
1962*	4	10	0	.286	314	392	3rd/Western Div.	—	—		Sid Gillman
1963*	11	3	0	.786	399	256	1st/Western Div.	1	0	AFL champ	Sid Gillman
1964*	8	5	1	.615	341	300	1st/Western Div.	0	1	AFL championship game	Sid Gillman
1965*	9	2	3	.818	340	227	1st/Western Div.	0	1	AFL championship game	Sid Gillman
1966*	7	6	1	.538	335	284	3rd/Western Div.	—	—		Sid Gillman
1967*	8	5	1	.615	360	352	3rd/Western Div.	—	—		Sid Gillman
1968*	9	5	0	.643	382	310	3rd/Western Div.	—	—		Sid Gillman
1969*	8	6	0	.571	288	276	3rd/Western Div.	—	—		S. Gillman, C. Waller
1970	5	6	3	.455	282	278	3rd/AFC Western Div.	—	—		Charlie Waller
1971	6	8	0	.429	311	341	3rd/AFC Western Div.	—	—		Harland Svare
1972	4	9	1	.308	264	344	4th/AFC Western Div.	—	—		Harland Svare
1973	2	11	1	.179	188	386	4th/AFC Western Div.	—	—		H. Svare, Ron Waller
1974	5	9	0	.357	212	285	T3rd/AFC Western Div.	—	—		Tommy Prothro
1975	2	12	0	.143	189	345	4th/AFC Western Div.	—	—		Tommy Prothro
1976	6	8	0	.429	248	285	3rd/AFC Western Div.	—	—		Tommy Prothro
1977	7	7	0	.500	222	205	3rd/AFC Western Div.	—	—		Tommy Prothro
1978	9	7	0	.563	355	309	T2nd/AFC Western Div.	—	—		T. Prothro, Don Coryell
1979	12	4	0	.750	411	246	1st/AFC Western Div.	0	1	AFC div. playoff game	Don Coryell
1980	11	5	0	.688	418	327	1st/AFC Western Div.	1	1	AFC championship game	Don Coryell
1981	10	6	0	.625	478	390	1st/AFC Western Div.	1	1	AFC championship game	Don Coryell
1982	6	3	0	.667	288	221	T4th/AFC	1	1	AFC second-round pl. game	Don Coryell
1983	6	10	0	.375	358	462	T4th/AFC Western Div.	—	—		Don Coryell
1984	7	9	0	.438	394	413	5th/AFC Western Div.	—	—		Don Coryell
1985	8	8	0	.500	467	435	T3rd/AFC Western Div.	—	—		Don Coryell
1986	4	12	0	.250	335	396	5th/AFC Western Div.	—	—		D. Coryell, Al Saunders
1987	8	7	0	.533	253	317	3rd/AFC Western Div.	—	—		Al Saunders
1988	6	10	0	.375	231	332	4th/AFC Western Div.	—	—		Al Saunders
1989	6	10	0	.375	266	290	5th/AFC Western Div.	—	—		Dan Henning
1990	6	10	0	.375	315	281	4th/AFC Western Div.	—	—		Dan Henning
1991	4	12	0	.250	274	342	5th/AFC Western Div.	—	—		Dan Henning
1992	11	5	0	.688	335	241	1st/AFC Western Div.	1	1	AFC div. playoff game	Bobby Ross
1993	8	8	0	.500	322	290	4th/AFC Western Div.	—	—		Bobby Ross
1994	11	5	0	.688	381	306	1st/AFC Western Div.	2	1	Super Bowl	Bobby Ross
1995	9	7	0	.563	321	323	2nd/AFC Western Div.	0	1	AFC wild-card game	Bobby Ross
1996	8	8	0	.500	310	376	3rd/AFC Western Div.	—	—		Bobby Ross
1997	4	12	0	.250	266	425	T4th/AFC Western Div.	—	—		Kevin Gilbride
1998	5	11	0	.313	241	342	5th/AFC Western Div.	—	—		K. Gilbride, June Jones
1999	8	8	0	.500	269	316	3rd/AFC Western Div.	—	—		Mike Riley

*American Football League.
†Los Angeles Chargers.

FIRST-ROUND DRAFT PICKS

1960—Monty Stickles, E, Notre Dame
1961—Earl Faison, E, Indiana
1962—Bob Ferguson, RB, Ohio State
1963—Walt Sweeney, E, Syracuse
1964—Ted Davis, E, Georgia Tech
1965—Steve DeLong, DE, Tennessee
1966—Don Davis, T, Los Angeles State
1967—Ron Billingsley, DT, Wyoming
1968—Russ Washington, T, Missouri
       Jim Hill, DB, Texas A&I
1969—Marty Domres, QB, Columbia
       Bob Babich, LB, Miami of Ohio
1970—Walker Gillette, WR, Richmond
1971—Leon Burns, RB, Long Beach State
1972—None
1973—Johnny Rodgers, WR, Nebraska
1974—Bo Matthews, RB, Colorado
       Don Goode, LB, Kansas
1975—Gary Johnson, DT, Grambling State
       Mike Williams, DB, Louisiana State
1976—Joe Washington, RB, Oklahoma

1977—Bob Rush, C, Memphis State
1978—John Jefferson, WR, Arizona State
1979—Kellen Winslow, TE, Missouri
1980—None
1981—James Brooks, RB, Auburn
1982—None
1983—Billy Ray Smith, LB, Arkansas
       Gary Anderson, WR, Arkansas
       Gill Byrd, DB, San Jose State
1984—Mossy Cade, DB, Texas
1985—Jim Lachey, G, Ohio State
1986—Leslie O'Neal, DE, Oklahoma State
       Jim FitzPatrick, T, Southern California
1987—Rod Bernstine, TE, Texas A&M
1988—Anthony Miller, WR, Tennessee
1989—Burt Grossman, DE, Pittsburgh
1990—Junior Seau, LB, Southern California
1991—Stanley Richard, CB, Texas
1992—Chris Mims, DT, Tennessee
1993—Darrien Gordon, DB, Stanford
1994—None

1995—None
1996—None
1997—None
1998—Ryan Leaf, QB, Washington State
1999—None
2000—None

FRANCHISE RECORDS

Most rushing yards, career
4,963—Paul Lowe
Most rushing yards, season
1,350—Natrone Means, 1994
Most rushing yards, game
217—Gary Anderson vs. K.C., Dec. 18, 1988
Most rushing touchdowns, season
19—Chuck Muncie, 1981
Most passing attempts, season
609—Dan Fouts, 1981
Most passing attempts, game
58—Mark Herrmann at K.C., Dec. 22, 1985
Most passes completed, season
360—Dan Fouts, 1981
Most passes completed, game
37—Dan Fouts vs. Mia., Nov. 18, 1984 (OT)
Mark Herrmann at K.C., Dec. 22, 1985
Most passing yards, career
43,040—Dan Fouts

Most passing yards, season
4,802—Dan Fouts, 1981
Most passing yards, game
444—Dan Fouts vs. NYG, Oct. 19, 1980
Dan Fouts at S.F., Dec. 11, 1982
Most touchdown passes, season
33—Dan Fouts, 1981
Most pass receptions, career
586—Charlie Joiner
Most pass receptions, season
90—Tony Martin, 1995
Most pass receptions, game
15—Kellen Winslow at G.B., Oct. 7, 1984
Most receiving yards, career
9,585—Lance Alworth
Most receiving yards, season
1,602—Lance Alworth, 1965
Most receiving yards, game
260—Wes Chandler vs. Cin., Dec. 20, 1982

Most receiving touchdowns, season
14—Lance Alworth, 1965
Tony Martin, 1996
Most touchdowns, career
83—Lance Alworth
Most field goals, season
34—John Carney, 1994
Longest field goal
54 yards—John Carney vs. Sea., Nov. 10, 1991
John Carney vs. Buf., Sept. 6, 1998
Most interceptions, career
42—Gill Byrd
Most interceptions, season
9—Charlie McNeil, 1961
Most sacks, career
105.5—Leslie O'Neal
Most sacks, season
17.5—Gary Johnson, 1980

SERIES RECORDS

San Diego vs.: Arizona 6-2; Atlanta 1-5; Baltimore, 2-0; Buffalo 17-7-2; Carolina 0-1; Chicago 4-4; Cincinnati 15-9; Cleveland 10-6-1; Dallas 1-5; Denver 36-43-1; Detroit 4-3; Green Bay 1-6; Indianapolis 11-8; Jacksonville 0-0; Kansas City 37-41-1; Miami 10-7; Minnesota 4-4; New England 11-16-2; New Orleans 6-1; N.Y. Giants 3-5; N.Y. Jets 17-9-1; Oakland 30-48-2; Philadelphia 5-2; Pittsburgh 5-16; St. Louis 3-3; San Francisco 3-5; Seattle 22-20; Tampa Bay 6-1; Tennessee 19-13-1; Washington 0-6.
NOTE: Includes records as Los Angeles Chargers in 1960.

COACHING RECORDS

Don Coryell, 69-56-0 (3-4); Kevin Gilbride, 6-16-0; Sid Gillman, 86-53-6 (1-4); Dan Henning, 16-32-0; June Jones, 3-7-0; Tommy Prothro, 21-39-0; Mike Riley, 8-8-0; Bobby Ross, 47-33-0 (3-3); Al Saunders, 17-22-0; Harland Svare, 7-17-2; Charlie Waller, 9-7-3; Ron Waller, 1-5-0.
NOTE: Playoff games in parentheses.

RETIRED UNIFORM NUMBERS

No.	Player
14	Dan Fouts

SAN FRANCISCO 49ERS
YEAR-BY-YEAR RECORDS

Year	W	L	T	Pct.	PF	PA	Finish	W	L	Highest round	Coach
1946*	9	5	0	.643	307	189	2nd/Western Div.	—	—		Buck Shaw
1947*	8	4	2	.667	327	264	2nd/Western Div.	—	—		Buck Shaw
1948*	12	2	0	.857	495	248	2nd/Western Div.	—	—		Buck Shaw
1949*	9	3	0	.750	416	227	2nd	—	—		Buck Shaw
1950	3	9	0	.250	213	300	T5th/National Conf.	—	—		Buck Shaw
1951	7	4	1	.636	255	205	T2nd/National Conf.	—	—		Buck Shaw
1952	7	5	0	.583	285	221	3rd/National Conf.	—	—		Buck Shaw
1953	9	3	0	.750	372	237	2nd/Western Conf.	—	—		Buck Shaw
1954	7	4	1	.636	313	251	3rd/Western Conf.	—	—		Buck Shaw
1955	4	8	0	.333	216	298	5th/Western Conf.	—	—		Red Strader
1956	5	6	1	.455	233	284	3rd/Western Conf.	—	—		Frankie Albert
1957	8	4	0	.667	260	264	2nd/Western Conf.	0	1	W. Conf. champ. game	Frankie Albert
1958	6	6	0	.500	257	324	4th/Western Conf.	—	—		Frankie Albert
1959	7	5	0	.583	255	237	T3rd/Western Conf.	—	—		Red Hickey
1960	7	5	0	.583	208	205	T2nd/Western Conf.	—	—		Red Hickey
1961	7	6	1	.538	346	272	5th/Western Conf.	—	—		Red Hickey
1962	6	8	0	.429	282	331	5th/Western Conf.	—	—		Red Hickey
1963	2	12	0	.143	198	391	7th/Western Conf.	—	—		R. Hickey, J. Christiansen
1964	4	10	0	.286	236	330	7th/Western Conf.	—	—		Jack Christiansen
1965	7	6	1	.538	421	402	4th/Western Conf.	—	—		Jack Christiansen
1966	6	6	2	.500	320	325	4th/Western Conf.	—	—		Jack Christiansen

HISTORY Team by team

Year	W	L	T	Pct.	PF	PA	Finish	W	L	Highest round	Coach
1967	7	7	0	.500	273	337	3rd/Coastal Div.	—	—		Jack Christiansen
1968	7	6	1	.538	303	310	3rd/Coastal Div.	—	—		Dick Nolan
1969	4	8	2	.333	277	319	4th/Coastal Div.	—	—		Dick Nolan
1970	10	3	1	.769	352	267	1st/NFC Western Div.	1	1	NFC championship game	Dick Nolan
1971	9	5	0	.643	300	216	1st/NFC Western Div.	1	1	NFC championship game	Dick Nolan
1972	8	5	1	.607	353	249	1st/NFC Western Div.	0	1	NFC div. playoff game	Dick Nolan
1973	5	9	0	.357	262	319	T3rd/NFC Western Div.				Dick Nolan
1974	6	8	0	.429	226	236	2nd/NFC Western Div.	—	—		Dick Nolan
1975	5	9	0	.357	255	286	2nd/NFC Western Div.	—	—		Dick Nolan
1976	8	6	0	.571	270	190	2nd/NFC Western Div.	—	—		Monte Clark
1977	5	9	0	.357	220	260	3rd/NFC Western Div.	—	—		Ken Meyer
1978	2	14	0	.125	219	350	4th/NFC Western Div.	—	—		Pete McCulley, Fred O'Connor
1979	2	14	0	.125	308	416	4th/NFC Western Div.	—	—		Bill Walsh
1980	6	10	0	.375	320	415	3rd/NFC Western Div.	—	—		Bill Walsh
1981	13	3	0	.813	357	250	1st/NFC Western Div.	3	0	Super Bowl champ	Bill Walsh
1982	3	6	0	.333	209	206	T11th/NFC	—	—		Bill Walsh
1983	10	6	0	.625	432	293	1st/NFC Western Div.	1	1	NFC championship game	Bill Walsh
1984	15	1	0	.938	475	227	1st/NFC Western Div.	3	0	Super Bowl champ	Bill Walsh
1985	10	6	0	.625	411	263	2nd/NFC Western Div.	0	1	NFC wild-card game	Bill Walsh
1986	10	5	1	.656	374	247	1st/NFC Western Div.	0	1	NFC div. playoff game	Bill Walsh
1987	13	2	0	.867	459	253	1st/NFC Western Div.	0	1	NFC div. playoff game	Bill Walsh
1988	10	6	0	.625	369	294	1st/NFC Western Div.	3	0	Super Bowl champ	Bill Walsh
1989	14	2	0	.875	442	253	1st/NFC Western Div.	3	0	Super Bowl champ	George Seifert
1990	14	2	0	.875	353	239	1st/NFC Western Div.	1	1	NFC championship game	George Seifert
1991	10	6	0	.625	393	239	3rd/NFC Western Div.	—	—		George Seifert
1992	14	2	0	.875	431	236	1st/NFC Western Div.	1	1	NFC championship game	George Seifert
1993	10	6	0	.625	473	295	1st/NFC Western Div.	1	1	NFC championship game	George Seifert
1994	13	3	0	.813	505	296	1st/NFC Western Div.	3	0	Super Bowl champ	George Seifert
1995	11	5	0	.688	457	258	1st/NFC Western Div.	0	1	NFC div. playoff game	George Seifert
1996	12	4	0	.750	398	257	2nd/NFC Western Div.	1	1	NFC div. playoff game	George Seifert
1997	13	3	0	.813	375	265	1st/NFC Western Div.	1	1	NFC championship game	Steve Mariucci
1998	12	4	0	.750	479	328	2nd/NFC Western Div.	1	1	NFC div. playoff game	Steve Mariucci
1999	4	12	0	.250	295	453	4th/NFC Western Div.	—	—		Steve Mariucci

*All-America Football Conference.

FIRST-ROUND DRAFT PICKS

1950—Leo Nomellini, T, Minnesota
1951—Y.A. Tittle, QB, Louisiana State
1952—Hugh McElhenny, RB, Washington
1953—Harry Babcock, E, Georgia*
       Tom Stolhandske, E, Texas
1954—Bernie Faloney, QB, Maryland
1955—Dick Moegel, HB, Rice
1956—Earl Morrall QB, Michigan State
1957—John Brodie, QB, Stanford
1958—Jim Pace, RB, Michigan
       Charles Krueger, T, Texas A&M
1959—Dave Baker, RB, Oklahoma
       Dan James, C, Ohio State
1960—Monty Stickles, E, Notre Dame
1961—Jim Johnson, RB, UCLA
       Bernie Casey, RB, Bowling Green State
       Billy Kilmer, QB, UCLA
1962—Lance Alworth, RB, Arkansas
1963—Kermit Alexander, RB, UCLA
1964—Dave Parks, E, Texas Tech*
1965—Ken Willard, RB, North Carolina
       George Donnelly, DB, Illinois
1966—Stan Hindman, DE, Mississippi
1967—Steve Spurrier, QB, Florida
       Cas Banaszek, LB, Northwestern
1968—Forrest Blue, C, Auburn
1969—Ted Kwalick, TE, Penn State
       Gene Washington, WR, Stanford
1970—Cedrick Hardman, DE, North Texas State
       Bruce Taylor, DB, Boston University
1971—Tim Anderson, RB, Ohio State
1972—Terry Beasley, WR, Auburn
1973—Mike Holmes, DB, Tex. Southern
1974—Wilbur Jackson, RB, Alabama
       Bill Sandifer, DT, UCLA
1975—Jimmy Webb, DT, Mississippi State
1976—None
1977—None
1978—Ken McAfee, TE, Notre Dame
       Dan Bunz, LB, Long Beach State
1979—None
1980—Earl Cooper, RB, Rice
       Jim Stuckey, DE, Clemson
1981—Ronnie Lott, DB, Southern California
1982—None
1983—None
1984—Todd Shell, LB, Brigham Young
1985—Jerry Rice, WR, Mississippi Valley State
1986—None
1987—Harris Barton, T, North Carolina
       Terrence Flager, RB, Clemson
1988—None
1989—Keith DeLong, LB, Tennessee
1990—Dexter Carter, RB, Florida State
1991—Ted Washington, DL, Louisville
1992—Dana Hall, DB, Washington
1993—Dana Stubblefield, DT, Kansas
       Todd Kelly, DE, Tennessee
1994—Bryant Young, DT, Notre Dame
       William Floyd, RB, Florida State
1995—J.J. Stokes, WR, UCLA
1996—None
1997—Jim Druckenmiller, QB, Virginia Tech
1998—R.W. McQuarters, DB, Oklahoma State
1999—Reggie McGrew, DT, Florida
2000—Julian Peterson, LB, Michigan State
       Ahmed Plummer, DB, Ohio State
*First player chosen in draft.

HISTORY *Team by team*

FRANCHISE RECORDS

Most rushing yards, career
7,344—Joe Perry
Most rushing yards, season
1,570—Garrison Hearst, 1998
Most rushing yards, game
198—Garrison Hearst vs. Det., Dec. 14, 1998
Most rushing touchdowns, season
10—Joe Perry, 1953
J.D. Smith, 1959
Billy Kilmer, 1961
Ricky Watters, 1993
Derek Loville, 1995
Most passing attempts, season
578—Steve DeBerg, 1979
Most passing attempts, game
60—Joe Montana at Was., Nov. 17, 1986
Most passes completed, season
347—Steve DeBerg, 1979
Most passes completed, game
37—Joe Montana at Atl., Nov. 6, 1985

Most passing yards, career
35,142—Joe Montana
Most passing yards, season
4,170—Steve Young, 1998
Most passing yards, game
476—Joe Montana at Atl., Oct. 14, 1990
Most touchdown passes, season
36—Steve Young, 1998
Most pass receptions, career
1,206—Jerry Rice
Most pass receptions, season
122—Jerry Rice, 1995
Most pass receptions, game
16—Jerry Rice at L.A. Rams, Nov. 20, 1994
Most receiving yards, career
18,442—Jerry Rice
Most receiving yards, season
1,848—Jerry Rice, 1995

Most receiving yards, game
289—Jerry Rice vs. Min., Dec. 18, 1995
Most receiving touchdowns, season
22—Jerry Rice, 1987
Most touchdowns, career
180—Jerry Rice
Most field goals, season
30—Jeff Wilkins, 1996
Longest field goal
56 yards—Mike Cofer at Atl., Oct. 14, 1990
Most interceptions, career
51—Ronnie Lott
Most interceptions, season
10—Dave Baker, 1960
Ronnie Lott, 1986
Most sacks, career
112.5—Cedrick Hardman
Most sacks, season
18—Cedrick Hardman

SERIES RECORDS

San Francisco vs.: Arizona 11-9; Atlanta 41-24-1; Baltimore 1-0; Buffalo 3-4; Carolina 5-5; Chicago 25-25-1; Cincinnati 7-2; Cleveland 6-9; Dallas 12-7-1; Denver 4-4; Detroit 29-26-1; Green Bay 25-24-1; Indianapolis 17-22; Jacksonville 0-1; Kansas City 4-3; Miami 3-4; Minnesota 17-17-1; New England 7-2; New Orleans 43-16-2; N.Y. Giants 12-11; N.Y. Jets 7-1; Oakland 3-5; Philadelphia 14-6-1; Pittsburgh 9-8; St. Louis 47-49-2; San Diego 5-3; Seattle 4-2; Tampa Bay 12-2; Tennessee 7-3; Washington 12-7-1.
NOTE: Includes records only from 1950 to present.

COACHING RECORDS

Frankie Albert, 19-16-1 (0-1); Jack Christiansen, 26-38-3; Monte Clark, 8-6-0; Red Hickey, 27-27-1; Steve Mariucci, 29-19-0 (2-2); Pete McCulley, 1-8-0; Ken Meyer, 5-9-0; Dick Nolan, 54-53-5 (2-3); Fred O'Connor, 1-6-0; George Seifert, 98-30-0 (10-5); Buck Shaw, 33-25-2; Red Strader, 4-8-0; Bill Walsh, 92-59-1 (10-4).
NOTE: Playoff games in parentheses.

RETIRED UNIFORM NUMBERS

No.	Player
12	John Brodie
16	Joe Montana
34	Joe Perry
37	Jimmy Johnson
39	Hugh McElhenny
70	Charlie Krueger
73	Leo Nomellini
87	Dwight Clark

SEATTLE SEAHAWKS
YEAR-BY-YEAR RECORDS

		REGULAR SEASON						PLAYOFFS			
Year	W	L	T	Pct.	PF	PA	Finish	W	L	Highest round	Coach
1976	2	12	0	.143	229	429	5th/NFC Western Div.	—	—		Jack Patera
1977	5	9	0	.357	282	373	4th/AFC Western Div.	—	—		Jack Patera
1978	9	7	0	.563	345	358	T2nd/AFC Western Div.	—	—		Jack Patera
1979	9	7	0	.563	378	372	T3rd	—	—		Jack Patera
1980	4	12	0	.250	291	408	5th/AFC Western Div.	—	—		Jack Patera
1981	6	10	0	.375	322	388	5th/AFC Western Div.	—	—		Jack Patera
1982	4	5	0	.444	127	147	T8th/AFC	—	—		J. Patera, Mike McCormack
1983	9	7	0	.562	403	397	T2nd/AFC Western Div.	2	1	AFC championship game	Chuck Knox
1984	12	4	0	.750	418	282	2nd/AFC Western Div.	1	1	AFC div. playoff game	Chuck Knox
1985	8	8	0	.500	349	303	T3rd/AFC Western Div.	—	—		Chuck Knox
1986	10	6	0	.625	366	293	T2nd/AFC Western Div.	—	—		Chuck Knox
1987	9	6	0	.600	371	314	2nd/AFC Western Div.	0	1	AFC wild-card game	Chuck Knox
1988	9	7	0	.563	339	329	1st/AFC Western Div.	0	1	AFC div. playoff game	Chuck Knox
1989	7	9	0	.438	241	327	4th/AFC Western Div.	—	—		Chuck Knox
1990	9	7	0	.563	306	286	3rd/AFC Western Div.	—	—		Chuck Knox
1991	7	9	0	.438	276	261	4th/AFC Western Div.	—	—		Chuck Knox
1992	2	14	0	.125	140	312	5th/AFC Western Div.	—	—		Tom Flores
1993	6	10	0	.375	280	314	5th/AFC Western Div.	—	—		Tom Flores
1994	6	10	0	.375	287	323	5th/AFC Western Div.	—	—		Tom Flores
1995	8	8	0	.500	363	366	T3rd/AFC Western Div.	—	—		Dennis Erickson

REGULAR SEASON | PLAYOFFS

Year	W	L	T	Pct.	PF	PA	Finish	W	L	Highest round	Coach
1996	7	9	0	.438	317	376	T4th/AFC Western Div.	—	—		Dennis Erickson
1997	8	8	0	.500	365	362	3rd/AFC Western Div.	—	—		Dennis Erickson
1998	8	8	0	.500	372	310	3rd/AFC Western Div.	—	—		Dennis Erickson
1999	9	7	0	.563	338	298	1st/AFC Western Div.	0	1	AFC wild-card game	Mike Holmgren

FIRST-ROUND DRAFT PICKS

1976—Steve Niehaus, DT, Notre Dame
1977—Steve August, G, Tulsa
1978—Keith Simpson, DB, Memphis State
1979—Manu Tuiasosopo, DT, UCLA
1980—Jacob Green, DE, Texas A&M
1981—Kenny Easley, DB, UCLA
1982—Jeff Bryant, DE, Clemson
1983—Curt Warner, RB, Penn State
1984—Terry Taylor, DB, Southern Illinois
1985—None
1986—John L. Williams, RB, Florida
1987—Tony Woods, LB, Pittsburgh
1988—None
1989—Andy Heck, T, Notre Dame
1990—Cortez Kennedy, DT, Miami (Fla.)
1991—Dan McGwire, QB, San Diego State
1992—Ray Roberts, T, Virginia
1993—Rick Mirer, QB, Notre Dame
1994—Sam Adams, DE, Texas A&M
1995—Joey Galloway, WR, Ohio State
1996—Pete Kendall, T, Boston College
1997—Shawn Springs, CB, Ohio State
       Walter Jones, T, Florida State
1998—Anthony Simmons, LB, Clemson
1999—Lamar King, DE, Saginaw Valley State
2000—Shaun Alexander, RB, Alabama
       Chris McIntosh, T, Wisconsin

FRANCHISE RECORDS

Most rushing yards, career
6,706—Chris Warren

Most rushing yards, season
1,545—Chris Warren, 1994

Most rushing yards, game
207—Curt Warner vs. K.C., Nov. 27, 1983 (OT)
192—Curt Warner vs. Den., Dec. 20, 1986

Most rushing touchdowns, season
15—Chris Warren, 1995

Most passing attempts, season
532—Dave Krieg, 1985

Most passing attempts, game
51—Dave Krieg vs. Atl., Oct. 13, 1985

Most passes completed, season
313—Warren Moon, 1997

Most passes completed, game
33—Dave Krieg vs. Atl., Oct. 13, 1985

Most passing yards, career
26,132—Dave Krieg

Most passing yards, season
3,678—Warren Moon, 1997

Most passing yards, game
418—Dave Krieg vs. Den., Nov. 20, 1983

Most touchdown passes, season
32—Dave Krieg, 1984

Most pass receptions, career
819—Steve Largent

Most pass receptions, season
81—Brian Blades, 1994

Most pass receptions, game
15—Steve Largent vs. Det., Oct. 18, 1987

Most receiving yards, career
13,089—Steve Largent

Most receiving yards, season
1,287—Steve Largent, 1985

Most receiving yards, game
261—Steve Largent vs. Det., Oct. 18, 1987

Most receiving touchdowns, season
13—Daryl Turner, 1985

Most touchdowns, career
101—Steve Largent

Most field goals, season
34—Todd Peterson, 1999

Longest field goal
55 yards—John Kasay vs. K.C., Jan. 2, 1994

Most interceptions, career
50—Dave Brown

Most interceptions, season
10—John Harris, 1981
     Kenny Easley, 1984

Most sacks, career
116.0—Jacob Green

Most sacks, season
16.5—Michael Sinclair, 1998

SERIES RECORDS

Seattle vs.: Arizona 1-5; Atlanta 5-2; Baltimore, 0-1; Buffalo 4-2; Carolina 0-0; Chicago 5-2; Cincinnati 8-7; Cleveland 9-4; Dallas 1-5; Denver 16-29; Detroit 4-4; Green Bay 4-4; Indianapolis 3-4; Jacksonville 1-1; Kansas City 15-27; Miami 2-4; Minnesota 4-2; New England 7-6; New Orleans 2-4; N.Y. Giants 3-5; N.Y. Jets 8-7; Oakland 20-24; Philadelphia 3-4; Pittsburgh 7-6; St. Louis 2-4; San Diego 20-22; San Francisco 2-4; Tampa Bay 4-1; Tennessee 7-4; Washington 4-5.

COACHING RECORDS

Dennis Erickson, 31-33-0; Tom Flores, 14-34-0; Mike Holmgren, 9-7-0 (0-1); Chuck Knox, 80-63-0 (3-4); Mike McCormack, 4-3-0; Jack Patera, 35-59-0.
NOTE: Playoff games in parentheses.

RETIRED UNIFORM NUMBERS

No.	Player
80	Steve Largent

TAMPA BAY BUCCANEERS
YEAR-BY-YEAR RECORDS

REGULAR SEASON | PLAYOFFS

Year	W	L	T	Pct.	PF	PA	Finish	W	L	Highest round	Coach
1976	0	14	0	.000	125	412	5th/AFC Western Div.	—	—		John McKay
1977	2	12	0	.143	103	223	5th/NFC Central Div.	—	—		John McKay
1978	5	11	0	.313	241	259	5th/NFC Central Div.	—	—		John McKay
1979	10	6	0	.625	273	237	1st/NFC Central Div.	1	1	NFC championship game	John McKay

– 407 –

HISTORY — Team by team

REGULAR SEASON / PLAYOFFS

Year	W	L	T	Pct.	PF	PA	Finish	W	L	Highest round	Coach
1980	5	10	1	.344	271	341	T4th/NFC Central Div.	—	—		John McKay
1981	9	7	0	.563	315	268	1st/NFC Central Div.	0	1	NFC div. playoff game	John McKay
1982	5	4	0	.556	158	178	4th/NFC	0	1	NFC first-round pl. game	John McKay
1983	2	14	0	.125	241	380	5th/NFC Central Div.	—	—		John McKay
1984	6	10	0	.375	335	380	3rd/NFC Central Div.	—	—		John McKay
1985	2	14	0	.125	294	448	5th/NFC Central Div.	—	—		Leeman Bennett
1986	2	14	0	.125	239	473	5th/NFC Central Div.	—	—		Leeman Bennett
1987	4	11	0	.267	286	360	T4th/NFC Central Div.	—	—		Ray Perkins
1988	5	11	0	.313	261	350	3rd/NFC Central Div.	—	—		Ray Perkins
1989	5	11	0	.313	320	419	5th/NFC Central Div.	—	—		Ray Perkins
1990	6	10	0	.375	264	367	T2nd/NFC Central Div.	—	—		R. Perkins, R. Williamson
1991	3	13	0	.188	199	365	5th/NFC Central Div.	—	—		Richard Williamson
1992	5	11	0	.313	267	365	T3rd/NFC Central Div.	—	—		Sam Wyche
1993	5	11	0	.313	237	376	5th/NFC Central Div.	—	—		Sam Wyche
1994	6	10	0	.375	251	351	5th/NFC Central Div.	—	—		Sam Wyche
1995	7	9	0	.438	238	335	5th/NFC Central Div.	—	—		Sam Wyche
1996	6	10	0	.375	221	293	4th/NFC Central Div.	—	—		Tony Dungy
1997	10	6	0	.625	299	263	3rd/AFC Western Div.	1	1	NFC div. playoff game	Tony Dungy
1998	8	8	0	.500	314	295	3rd/AFC Western Div.	—	—		Tony Dungy
1999	11	5	0	.688	270	235	1st/NFC Central Div.	1	1	NFC championship game	Tony Dungy

FIRST-ROUND DRAFT PICKS

1976—Lee Roy Selmon, DE, Oklahoma*
1977—Ricky Bell, RB, Southern California*
1978—Doug Williams, QB, Grambling State
1979—None
1980—Ray Snell, T, Wisconsin
1981—Hugh Green, LB, Pittsburgh
1982—Sean Farrell, G, Penn State
1983—None
1984—None
1985—Ron Holmes, DE, Washington
1986—Bo Jackson, RB, Auburn*
     Rod Jones, DB, Southern Methodist
1987—Vinny Testaverde, QB, Miami (Fla.)*
1988—Paul Gruber, T, Wisconsin
1989—Broderick Thomas, LB, Nebraska
1990—Keith McCants, LB, Alabama
1991—Charles McRae, T, Tennessee
1992—None
1993—Eric Curry, DE, Alabama
1994—Trent Dilfer, QB, Fresno State
1995—Warren Sapp, DT, Miami (Fla.)
     Derrick Brooks, LB, Florida State
1996—Regan Upshaw, DE, California
     Marcus Jones, DT, North Carolina
1997—Warrick Dunn, RB, Florida State
     Reidel Anthony, WR, Florida
1998—None
1999—Anthony McFarland, DT, Louisiana State
2000—None
*First player chosen in draft.

FRANCHISE RECORDS

Most rushing yards, career
5,957—James Wilder
Most rushing yards, season
1,544—James Wilder, 1984
Most rushing yards, game
219—James Wilder at Min., Nov. 6, 1983
Most rushing touchdowns, season
13—James Wilder, 1984
Most passing attempts, season
521—Doug Williams, 1980
Most passing attempts, game
56—Doug Williams vs. Cle., Sept. 28, 1980
Most passes completed, season
308—Steve DeBerg, 1984
Most passes completed, game
31—Vinny Testaverde at Hou., Dec. 10, 1989
Most passing yards, career
14,820—Vinny Testaverde

Most passing yards, season
3,563—Doug Williams, 1981
Most passing yards, game
486—Doug Williams at Min., Nov. 16, 1980
Most touchdown passes, season
21—Trent Dilfer, 1997, 1998
Most pass receptions, career
430—James Wilder
Most pass receptions, season
86—Mark Carrier, 1989
Most pass receptions, game
13—James Wilder vs. Min., Sept. 15, 1985
Most receiving yards, career
5,018—Mark Carrier
Most receiving yards, season
1,422—Mark Carrier, 1989
Most receiving yards, game
212—Mark Carrier at N.O., Dec. 6, 1987

Most receiving touchdowns, season
9—Kevin House, 1981
   Bruce Hill, 1988
   Mark Carrier, 1989
Most touchdowns, career
46—James Wilder
Most field goals, season
27—Martin Gramatica, 1999
Longest field goal
57 yards—Michael Husted at L.A. Raiders, Dec. 19, 1993
Most interceptions, career
29—Cedric Brown
Most interceptions, season
9—Cedric Brown, 1981
Most sacks, career
78.5—Lee Roy Selmon
Most sacks, season
13—Lee Roy Selmon, 1977

SERIES RECORDS

Tampa Bay vs.: Arizona 7-7; Atlanta 8-8; Buffalo 4-2; Carolina 2-1; Chicago 14-30; Cincinnati 3-3; Cleveland 0-5; Dallas 0-6; Denver 2-3; Detroit 19-25; Green Bay 15-26-1; Indianapolis 4-5; Jacksonville 1-1; Kansas City 3-5; Miami 2-4; Minnesota 15-29; New England 1-3; New Orleans 6-13; N.Y. Giants 5-9; N.Y. Jets 1-6; Oakland 1-4; Philadelphia 3-3; Pittsburgh 1-4; St. Louis 3-8; San Diego 1-6; San Francisco 2-12; Seattle 1-4; Tennessee 1-5; Washington 4-5.

COACHING RECORDS

Leeman Bennett, 4-28-0; Tony Dungy, 35-29-0 (2-2); John McKay, 44-88-1 (1-3); Ray Perkins, 19-41-0; Richard Williamson, 4-15-0; Sam Wyche, 23-41-0.
NOTE: Playoff games in parentheses.

RETIRED UNIFORM NUMBERS

No.	Player
63	Lee Roy Selmon

TENNESSEE TITANS
YEAR-BY-YEAR RECORDS

		REGULAR SEASON						PLAYOFFS		
Year	W	L	T	Pct.	PF	PA	Finish	W	L	Highest round	Coach
1960*†	10	4	0	.714	379	285	1st/Eastern Div.	1	0	AFL champ	Lou Rymkus
1961*†	10	3	1	.769	513	242	1st/Eastern Div.	1	0	AFL champ	L. Rymkus, Wally Lemm
1962*†	11	3	0	.786	387	270	1st/Eastern Div.	0	1	AFL championship game	Pop Ivy
1963*†	6	8	0	.429	302	372	3rd/Eastern Div.	—	—		Pop Ivy
1964*†	4	10	0	.286	310	355	4th/Eastern Div.	—	—		Sammy Baugh
1965*†	4	10	0	.286	298	429	4th/Eastern Div.	—	—		Hugh Taylor
1966*†	3	11	0	.214	335	396	T4th/Eastern Div.	—	—		Wally Lemm
1967*†	9	4	1	.692	258	199	1st/Eastern Div.	0	1	AFL championship game	Wally Lemm
1968*†	7	7	0	.500	303	248	2nd/Eastern Div.	—	—		Wally Lemm
1969*†	6	6	2	.500	278	279	2nd/Eastern Div.	0	1	Div. playoff game	Wally Lemm
1970†	3	10	1	.231	217	352	4th/AFC Central Div.	—	—		Wally Lemm
1971†	4	9	1	.308	251	330	3rd/AFC Central Div.	—	—		Ed Hughes
1972†	1	13	0	.071	164	380	4th/AFC Central Div.	—	—		Bill Peterson
1973†	1	13	0	.071	199	447	4th/AFC Central Div.	—	—		B. Peterson, S. Gillman
1974†	7	7	0	.500	236	282	T2nd/AFC Central Div.	—	—		Sid Gillman
1975†	10	4	0	.714	293	226	3rd/AFC Central Div.	—	—		Bum Phillips
1976†	5	9	0	.357	222	273	4th/AFC Central Div.	—	—		Bum Phillips
1977†	8	6	0	.571	299	230	T2nd/AFC Central Div.	—	—		Bum Phillips
1978†	10	6	0	.625	283	298	2nd/AFC Central Div.	2	1	AFC championship game	Bum Phillips
1979†	11	5	0	.688	362	331	2nd/AFC Central Div.	2	1	AFC championship game	Bum Phillips
1980†	11	5	0	.688	295	251	2nd/AFC Central Div.	0	1	AFC wild-card game	Bum Phillips
1981†	7	9	0	.438	281	355	3rd/AFC Central Div.	—	—		Ed Biles
1982†	1	8	0	.111	136	245	13th/AFC	—	—		Ed Biles
1983†	2	14	0	.125	288	460	4th/AFC Central Div.	—	—		Ed Biles, Chuck Studley
1984†	3	13	0	.188	240	437	4th/AFC Central Div.	—	—		Hugh Campbell
1985†	5	11	0	.313	284	412	4th/AFC Central Div.	—	—		H. Campbell, J. Glanville
1986†	5	11	0	.313	274	329	4th/AFC Central Div.	—	—		Jerry Glanville
1987†	9	6	0	.600	345	349	2nd/AFC Central Div.	1	1	AFC div. playoff game	Jerry Glanville
1988†	10	6	0	.625	424	365	T2nd/AFC Central Div.	1	1	AFC div. playoff game	Jerry Glanville
1989†	9	7	0	.563	365	412	T2nd/AFC Central Div.	0	1	AFC wild-card game	Jerry Glanville
1990†	9	7	0	.563	405	307	2nd/AFC Central Div.	0	1	AFC wild-card game	Jack Pardee
1991†	11	5	0	.688	386	251	1st/AFC Central Div.	1	1	AFC div. playoff game	Jack Pardee
1992†	10	6	0	.625	352	258	2nd/AFC Central Div.	0	1	AFC wild-card game	Jack Pardee
1993†	12	4	0	.750	368	238	1st/AFC Central Div.	0	1	AFC div. playoff game	Jack Pardee
1994†	2	14	0	.125	226	352	4th/AFC Central Div.	—	—		Jack Pardee, Jeff Fisher
1995†	7	9	0	.438	348	324	T2nd/AFC Central Div.	—	—		Jeff Fisher
1996†	8	8	0	.500	345	319	T3rd/AFC Central Div.	—	—		Jeff Fisher
1997‡	8	8	0	.500	333	310	3rd/AFC Central Div.	—	—		Jeff Fisher
1998‡	8	8	0	.500	330	320	2nd/AFC Central Div.	—	—		Jeff Fisher
1999	13	3	0	.813	392	324	2nd/AFC Central Div.	3	1	Super Bowl	Jeff Fisher

*American Football League.
†Houston Oilers.
‡Tennessee Oilers.

FIRST-ROUND DRAFT PICKS

1960—Billy Cannon, RB, Louisiana State
1961—Mike Ditka, E, Pittsburgh
1962—Ray Jacobs, DT, Howard Payne
1963—Danny Brabham, LB, Arkansas
1964—Scott Appleton, DT, Texas
1965—Lawrence Elkins, WR, Baylor* (AFL)
1966—Tommy Nobis, LB, Texas
1967—George Webster, LB, Michigan State
    Tom Regner, G, Notre Dame
1968—None
1969—Ron Pritchard, LB, Arizona State
1970—Doug Wilkerson, G, North Carolina Central
1971—Dan Pastorini, QB, Santa Clara
1972—Greg Sampson, DE, Stanford
1973—John Matuszak, DE, Tampa*
    George Amundson, RB, Iowa State
1974—None
1975—Robert Brazile, LB, Jackson State
    Don Hardeman, RB, Texas A&I
1976—None
1977—Morris Towns, T, Missouri
1978—Earl Campbell, RB, Texas*
1979—None
1980—None
1981—None
1982—Mike Munchak, G, Penn State
1983—Bruce Matthews, G, Southern California
1984—Dean Steinkuhler, G, Nebraska

– 409 –

1985—Ray Childress, DE, Texas A&M
Richard Johnson, DB, Wisconsin
1986—Jim Everett, QB, Purdue
1987—Alonzo Highsmith, FB, Miami (Fla.)
Haywood Jeffires, WR, North Carolina State
1988—Lorenzo White, RB, Michigan State
1989—David Williams, T, Florida
1990—Lamar Lathon, LB, Houston
1991—None
1992—None
1993—Brad Hopkins, G, Illinois
1994—Henry Ford, DE, Arkansas
1995—Steve McNair, QB, Alcorn State
1996—Eddie George, RB, Ohio State
1997—Kenny Holmes, DE, Miami (Fla.)
1998—Kevin Dyson, WR, Utah
1999—Jevon Kearse, LB, Florida
2000—Keith Bulluck, LB, Syracuse
*First player chosen in draft.

FRANCHISE RECORDS

Most rushing yards, career
8,574—Earl Campbell
Most rushing yards, season
1,934—Earl Campbell, 1980
Most rushing yards, game
216—Billy Cannon at N.Y. Titans, Dec. 10, 1961
Eddie George vs. Oak., Aug. 31, 1997 (OT)
Most rushing touchdowns, season
19—Earl Campbell, 1979
Most passing attempts, season
655—Warren Moon, 1991
Most passing attempts, game
68—George Blanda at Buf., Nov. 1, 1964
Most passes completed, season
404—Warren Moon, 1991
Most passes completed, game
41—Warren Moon vs. Dal., Nov. 10, 1991

Most passing yards, career
33,685—Warren Moon
Most passing yards, season
4,690—Warren Moon, 1991
Most passing yards, game
527—Warren Moon at K.C., Dec. 16, 1990
Most touchdown passes, season
36—George Blanda, 1961
Most pass receptions, career
542—Ernest Givins
Most pass receptions, season
101—Charlie Hennigan, 1964
Most pass receptions, game
13—Charlie Hennigan at Boston, Oct. 13, 1961
Haywood Jeffires at NYJ, Oct. 13, 1991
Most receiving yards, career
7,935—Ernest Givins
Most receiving yards, season
1,746—Charlie Hennigan, 1961

Most receiving yards, game
272—Charlie Hennigan at Boston, Oct. 13, 1961
Most receiving touchdowns, season
17—Bill Groman, 1961
Most touchdowns, career
73—Earl Campbell
Most field goals, season
36—Al Del Greco, 1998
Longest field goal
56 yards—Al Del Greco vs. S.F., Oct. 27, 1996
Most interceptions, career
45—Jim Norton
Most interceptions, season
12—Freddy Glick, 1963
Mike Reinfeldt, 1979
Most sacks, season
15.5—Jesse Baker, 1979

SERIES RECORDS

Tennessee vs.: Arizona 3-4; Atlanta 5-5; Baltimore 5-3; Buffalo 22-13; Carolina 0-1; Chicago 4-4; Cincinnati 33-28-1; Cleveland 23-30; Dallas 4-5; Denver 20-11-1; Detroit 4-3; Green Bay 3-4; Indianapolis 7-7; Jacksonville 6-4; Kansas City 17-24; Miami 11-14; Minnesota 3-5; New England 14-18-1; New Orleans 5-4-1; N.Y. Giants 1-5; N.Y. Jets 20-13-1; Oakland 15-20; Philadelphia 0-6; Pittsburgh 24-35; St. Louis 3-5; San Diego 13-19-1; San Francisco 3-7; Seattle 4-7; Tampa Bay 5-1; Washington 4-3.
NOTE: Includes records as Houston Oilers from 1960 through 1996.

COACHING RECORDS

Sammy Baugh, 4-10-0; Ed Biles, 8-23-0; Hugh Campbell, 8-22-0; Jeff Fisher, 45-41-0 (3-1); Sid Gillman, 8-15-0; Jerry Glanville, 33-32-0 (2-3); Ed Hughes, 4-9-1; Frank Ivy, 17-11-0 (0-1); Wally Lemm, 37-38-4 (1-2); Jack Pardee, 43-31-0 (1-4); Bill Peterson, 1-18-0; Bum Phillips, 55-35-0 (4-3); Lou Rymkus, 11-7-1 (1-0); Chuck Studley, 2-8-0; Hugh Taylor, 4-10-0.
NOTE: Playoff games in parentheses.

RETIRED UNIFORM NUMBERS

No.	Player
34	Earl Campbell
43	Jim Norton
63	Mike Munchak
65	Elvin Bethea

WASHINGTON REDSKINS
YEAR-BY-YEAR RECORDS

Year	W	L	T	Pct.	PF	PA	Finish	W	L	Highest round	Coach
1932*	4	4	2	.500	55	79	4th	—	—		Lud Wray
1933†	5	5	2	.500	103	97	3rd/Eastern Div.	—	—		Lone Star Dietz
1934†	6	6	0	.500	107	94	2nd/Eastern Div.	—	—		Lone Star Dietz
1935†	2	8	1	.200	65	123	4th/Eastern Div.	—	—		Eddie Casey
1936†	7	5	0	.583	149	110	1st/Eastern Div.	0	1	NFL championship game	Ray Flaherty
1937	8	3	0	.727	195	120	1st/Eastern Div.	1	0	NFL champ	Ray Flaherty
1938	6	3	2	.667	148	154	2nd/Eastern Div.	—	—		Ray Flaherty
1939	8	2	1	.800	242	94	2nd/Eastern Div.	—	—		Ray Flaherty
1940	9	2	0	.818	245	142	1st/Eastern Div.	0	1	NFL championship game	Ray Flaherty
1941	6	5	0	.545	176	174	3rd/Eastern Div.	—	—		Ray Flaherty
1942	10	1	0	.909	227	102	1st/Eastern Div.	1	0	NFL champ	Ray Flaherty
1943	6	3	1	.667	229	137	1st/Eastern Div.	1	1	NFL championship game	Dutch Bergman
1944	6	3	1	.667	169	180	3rd/Eastern Div.	—	—		Dudley DeGroot

HISTORY — Team by team

Year	W	L	T	Pct.	PF	PA	Finish	W	L	Highest round	Coach
1945	8	2	0	.800	209	121	1st/Eastern Div.	0	1	NFL championship game	Dudley DeGroot
1946	5	5	1	.500	171	191	T3rd/Eastern Div.	—	—		Turk Edwards
1947	4	8	0	.333	295	367	4th/Eastern Div.	—	—		Turk Edwards
1948	7	5	0	.583	291	287	2nd/Eastern Div.	—	—		Turk Edwards
1949	4	7	1	.364	268	339	4th/Eastern Div.	—	—		John Whelchel, H. Ball
1950	3	9	0	.250	232	326	6th/American Conf.	—	—		Herman Ball
1951	5	7	0	.417	183	296	3rd/American Conf.	—	—		Herman Ball, Dick Todd
1952	4	8	0	.333	240	287	T5th/American Conf.	—	—		Curly Lambeau
1953	6	5	1	.545	208	215	3rd/Eastern Conf.	—	—		Curly Lambeau
1954	3	9	0	.250	207	432	5th/Eastern Conf.	—	—		Joe Kuharich
1955	8	4	0	.667	246	222	2nd/Eastern Conf.	—	—		Joe Kuharich
1956	6	6	0	.500	183	225	3rd/Eastern Conf.	—	—		Joe Kuharich
1957	5	6	1	.455	251	230	4th/Eastern Conf.	—	—		Joe Kuharich
1958	4	7	1	.364	214	268	4th/Eastern Conf.	—	—		Joe Kuharich
1959	3	9	0	.250	185	350	5th/Eastern Conf.	—	—		Mike Nixon
1960	1	9	2	.100	178	309	6th/Eastern Conf.	—	—		Mike Nixon
1961	1	12	1	.077	174	392	7th/Eastern Conf.	—	—		Bill McPeak
1962	5	7	2	.417	305	376	4th/Eastern Conf.	—	—		Bill McPeak
1963	3	11	0	.214	279	398	6th/Eastern Conf.	—	—		Bill McPeak
1964	6	8	0	.429	307	305	T3rd/Eastern Conf.	—	—		Bill McPeak
1965	6	8	0	.429	257	301	4th/Eastern Conf.	—	—		Bill McPeak
1966	7	7	0	.500	351	355	5th/Eastern Conf.	—	—		Otto Graham
1967	5	6	3	.455	347	353	3rd/Capitol Div.	—	—		Otto Graham
1968	5	9	0	.357	249	358	3rd/Capitol Div.	—	—		Otto Graham
1969	7	5	2	.583	307	319	2nd/Capitol Div.	—	—		Vince Lombardi
1970	6	8	0	.429	297	314	4th/NFC Eastern Div.	—	—		Bill Austin
1971	9	4	1	.692	276	190	2nd/NFC Eastern Div.	0	1	NFC div. playoff game	George Allen
1972	11	3	0	.786	336	218	1st/NFC Eastern Div.	2	1	Super Bowl	George Allen
1973	10	4	0	.714	325	198	2nd/NFC Eastern Div.	0	1	NFC div. playoff game	George Allen
1974	10	4	0	.714	320	196	2nd/NFC Eastern Div.	0	1	NFC div. playoff game	George Allen
1975	8	6	0	.571	325	276	3rd/NFC Eastern Div.	—	—		George Allen
1976	10	4	0	.714	291	217	2nd/NFC Eastern Div.	0	1	NFC div. playoff game	George Allen
1977	9	5	0	.643	196	189	2nd/NFC Eastern Div.	—	—		George Allen
1978	8	8	0	.500	273	283	3rd/NFC Eastern Div.	—	—		Jack Pardee
1979	10	6	0	.625	348	295	3rd/NFC Eastern Div.	—	—		Jack Pardee
1980	6	10	0	.375	261	293	4th/NFC Eastern Div.	—	—		Jack Pardee
1981	8	8	0	.500	347	349	4th/NFC Eastern Div.	—	—		Joe Gibbs
1982	8	1	0	.889	190	128	1st/NFC	4	0	Super Bowl champ	Joe Gibbs
1983	14	2	0	.875	541	332	1st/NFC Eastern Div.	2	1	Super Bowl	Joe Gibbs
1984	11	5	0	.688	426	310	1st/NFC Eastern Div.	0	1	NFC div. playoff game	Joe Gibbs
1985	10	6	0	.625	297	312	3rd/NFC Eastern Div.	—	—		Joe Gibbs
1986	12	4	0	.750	368	296	2nd/NFC Eastern Div.	2	1	NFC championship game	Joe Gibbs
1987	11	4	0	.733	379	285	1st/NFC Eastern Div.	3	0	Super Bowl champ	Joe Gibbs
1988	7	9	0	.438	345	387	T3rd/NFC Eastern Div.	—	—		Joe Gibbs
1989	10	6	0	.625	386	308	3rd/NFC Eastern Div.	—	—		Joe Gibbs
1990	10	6	0	.625	381	301	T2nd/NFC Eastern Div.	1	1	NFC div. playoff game	Joe Gibbs
1991	14	2	0	.875	485	224	1st/NFC Eastern Div.	3	0	Super Bowl champ	Joe Gibbs
1992	9	7	0	.563	300	255	3rd/NFC Eastern Div.	1	1	NFC div. playoff game	Joe Gibbs
1993	4	12	0	.250	230	345	5th/NFC Eastern Div.	—	—		Richie Petitbon
1994	3	13	0	.188	320	412	5th/NFC Eastern Div.	—	—		Norv Turner
1995	6	10	0	.375	326	359	3rd/NFC Eastern Div.	—	—		Norv Turner
1996	9	7	0	.563	364	312	3rd/NFC Eastern Div.	—	—		Norv Turner
1997	8	7	1	.533	327	289	3rd/NFC Eastern Div.	—	—		Norv Turner
1998	6	10	0	.375	319	421	4th/NFC Eastern Div.	—	—		Norv Turner
1999	10	6	0	.625	443	377	1st/NFC Eastern Div.	1	1	NFC div. playoff game	Norv Turner

*Boston Braves.
†Boston Redskins.

FIRST-ROUND DRAFT PICKS

1936—Riley Smith, QB, Alabama
1937—Sammy Baugh, QB, Texas Christian
1938—Andy Farkas, B, Detroit
1939—I.B. Hale, T, Texas Christian
1940—Ed Boell, B, New York University
1941—Forrest Evashevski, B, Michigan
1942—Orban Sanders, B, Texas
1943—Jack Jenkins, B, Missouri
1944—Mike Micka, B, Colgate
1945—Jim Hardy, B, Southern California
1946—Cal Rossi, B, UCLA
1947—Cal Rossi, B, UCLA
1948—Harry Gilmer, QB, Alabama*
1949—Rob Goode, RB, Texas A&M
1950—George Thomas, RB, Oklahoma
1951—Leon Heath, RB, Oklahoma
1952—Larry Isbell, QB, Baylor
1953—Jack Scarbath, QB, Maryland
1954—Steve Meilinger, TE, Kentucky
1955—Ralph Guglielmi, QB, Notre Dame
1956—Ed Vereb, RB, Maryland
1957—Don Bosseler, RB, Miami (Fla.)

— 411 —

HISTORY — Team by team

1958—None
1959—Don Allard, QB, Boston College
1960—Richie Lucas, QB, Penn State
1961—Joe Rutgens, T, Illinois
     Norm Snead, QB, Wake Forest
1962—Ernie Davis, RB, Syracuse*
     Leroy Jackson, RB, Illinois Central
1963—Pat Richter, TE, Wisconsin
1964—Charley Taylor, RB, Arizona State
1965—None
1966—Charlie Gogolak, K, Princeton
1967—Ray McDonald, RB, Idaho
1968—Jim Smith, DB, Oregon
1969—None
1970—None
1971—None
1972—None
1973—None
1974—None
1975—None
1976—None
1977—None
1978—None
1979—None
1980—Art Monk, WR, Syracuse
1981—Mark May, T, Pittsburgh
1982—None
1983—Darrell Green, DB, Texas A&I
1984—None
1985—None
1986—None
1987—None
1988—None
1989—None
1990—None
1991—Bobby Wilson, DT, Michigan State
1992—Desmond Howard, WR, Michigan
1993—Tom Carter, DB, Notre Dame
1994—Heath Shuler, QB, Tennessee
1995—Michael Westbrook, WR, Colorado
1996—Andre Johnson, T, Penn State
1997—Kenard Lang, DE, Miami (Fla.)
1998—None
1999—Champ Bailey, DB, Georgia
2000—LaVar Arrington, LB, Penn State
     Chris Samuels, T, Alabama
*First player chosen in draft.

FRANCHISE RECORDS

Most rushing yards, career
7,472—John Riggins
Most rushing yards, season
1,405—Stephen Davis, 1999
Most rushing yards, game
221—Gerald Riggs vs. Phi., Sept. 17, 1989
Most rushing touchdowns, season
24—John Riggins, 1983
Most passing attempts, season
541—Jay Schroeder, 1986
Most passing attempts, game
58—Jay Schroeder vs. S.F., Dec. 1, 1985
Most passes completed, season
316—Brad Johnson, 1999
Most passes completed, game
32—Sonny Jurgensen at Cle., Nov. 26, 1967
    John Friesz at NYG, Sept. 18, 1994
    Brad Johnson at S.F., Dec. 26, 1999 (OT)
Most passing yards, career
25,206—Joe Theismann

Most passing yards, season
4,109—Jay Schroeder, 1986
Most passing yards, game
471—Brad Johnson at S.F. Dec. 26, 1999 (OT)
446—Sammy Baugh vs. N.Y. Yanks, Oct. 31, 1948
Most touchdown passes, season
31—Sonny Jurgensen, 1967
Most pass receptions, career
888—Art Monk
Most pass receptions, season
106—Art Monk, 1984
Most pass receptions, game
13—Art Monk vs. Cin., Dec. 15, 1985
    Kelvin Bryant vs. NYG, Dec. 7, 1986
    Art Monk at Det., Nov. 4, 1990
Most receiving yards, career
12,026—Art Monk
Most receiving yards, season
1,436—Bobby Mitchell, 1963

Most receiving yards, game
255—Anthony Allen vs. St.L., Oct. 4, 1987
Most receiving touchdowns, season
12—Hugh Taylor, 1952
    Charley Taylor, 1966
    Jerry Smith, 1967
    Ricky Sanders, 1988
Most touchdowns, career
90—Charley Taylor
Most field goals, season
33—Mark Moseley, 1983
Longest field goal
57 yards—Steve Cox vs. Sea., Sept. 28, 1986
Most interceptions, career
47—Darrell Green
Most interceptions, season
13—Dan Sandifer, 1948
Most sacks, career
97.5—Dexter Manley
Most sacks, season
18.0—Dexter Manley, 1986

SERIES RECORDS

Washington vs.: Arizona 63-41-1; Atlanta 13-4-1; Baltimore, 0-1; Buffalo 4-5; Carolina 4-0; Chicago 14-14; Cincinnati 4-2; Cleveland 9-32-1; Dallas 31-45-2; Denver 3-5; Detroit 24-4; Green Bay 11-9; Indianapolis 9-17; Jacksonville 1-0; Kansas City 1-4; Miami 3-5; Minnesota 6-5; New England 5-1; New Orleans 12-5; N.Y. Giants 53-68-3; N.Y. Jets 6-1; Oakland 3-6; Philadelphia 66-56-6; Pittsburgh 39-25-4; St. Louis 16-7-1; San Diego 6-0; San Francisco 7-12-1; Seattle 5-4; Tampa Bay 5-4; Tennessee 3-4.
NOTE: Includes records only from 1937 to present.

COACHING RECORDS

George Allen, 67-30-1 (2-5); Bill Austin, 6-8-0; Herman Bell, 4-16-0; Dutch Bergman, 6-3-1 (1-1); Eddie Casey, 2-8-1; Dudley DeGroot, 14-5-1 (0-1); William Dietz, 11-11-2; Turk Edwards, 16-18-1; Ray Flaherty, 54-21-3 (2-2); Joe Gibbs, 124-60-0 (16-5); Otto Graham, 17-22-3; Joe Kuharich, 26-32-2; Curly Lambeau, 10-13-1; Vince Lombardi, 7-5-2; Bill McPeak, 21-46-3; Mike Nixon, 4-18-2; Jack Pardee, 24-24-0; Richie Petitbon, 4-12-0; Dick Todd, 5-4-0; Norv Turner, 42-53-1 (1-1); John Whelchel, 3-3-1; Lud Wray, 4-4-2.
NOTE: Playoff games in parentheses.

RETIRED UNIFORM NUMBERS

No.	Player
33	Sammy Baugh

– 412 –

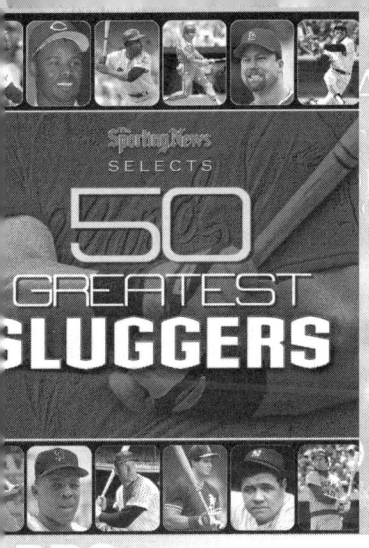

The Sporting News

Add to your sports library with the New 2000 Editions!

Turn the page for special savings!

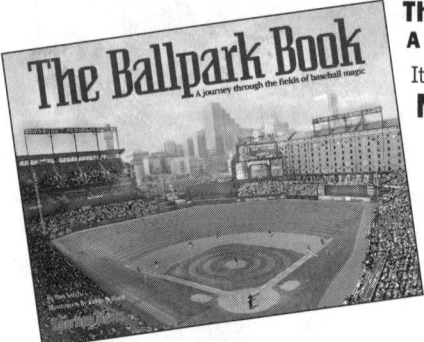

The Ballpark Book
A Journey Through the Fields of Baseball Magic
Item #633 Regularly $39.95
Now only $24.95

The Sporting News Selects 50 Greatest Sluggers
Item #632
Regularly $29.95
Now only $19.95

Complete Baseball Record Book 2000 Edition
Item #627
Regularly $15.95
Now only $12.95

Baseball Register 2000 Edition
Item #629
Regularly $15.95
Now only $12.95
Save $3.00!

Baseball Guide 2000 Edition
#628
Regularly $15.95
Now only $12.95
Save $3.00!

Official Major League Baseball® Fact Book 2000 Edition
Item #630
Regularly $15.95
Now only $12.95
Save $3.00!

Official Baseball Rules 2000 Edition
Item # 631
Regularly $6.95
Now only $5.95
Save $1.00!

Major League Baseball trademarks and copyrights are used with permission of Major League Baseball Properties, Inc. Be sure to visit MLB's Official Web Site, MLB@BAT
www.majorleaguebaseball.com

2000 Pro Football Guide
Item #635
Regularly $15.95
Now only $12.95
Save $3.00!

2000 Pro Football Register
Item #636
Regularly $15.95
Now only $12.95
Save $3.00!

2000-2001 Official NBA Register
Item #640
Regularly $15.95
Now only $12.95
Save $3.00!

2000-2001 Official NBA Guide
Item #639
Regularly $15.95
Now only $12.95
Save $3.00!

2000-2001 Hockey Register
Item #638
Regularly $15.95
Now only $12.95
Save $3.00!

2000-2001 Official NBA Rules
Item #641
Regularly $6.95
Now only $5.95
Save $1.00!

2000-2001 Hockey Guide
Item #637
Regularly $15.95
Now only $12.95
Save $3.00!

For Fastest Service Call Toll Free
1-800-825-8508
Dept. 00FBGD

Or, fax your order to
1-515-699-3738 Dept. 00FBGD
Credit cards only for phone or fax orders.

If you prefer, mail your order along with payment to:

The Sporting News
Attn: Book Dept. 00FBGD
P. O. Box 11229
Des Moines, IA 50340

Shipping and Handling: All U.S. and Canadian orders shipped via UPS. No P.O. Boxes, please. Charges: For U.S. orders, $3.75 for the first book, $1.50 each additional book. For Canadian orders, $6.75 for the first book, $1.50 each additional book. International rates available upon request.

NO RISK GUARANTEE

You can examine any of the books you buy for 15 days without obligation to keep them. Simply return any books that do not meet your needs within 15 days for a full refund.